Encyclopedia
of Sociology

Encyclopedia of Sociology

VOLUME 4

Edgar F. Borgatta
Editor-in-Chief
University of Washington, Seattle

Marie L. Borgatta
Managing Editor
University of Washington, Seattle

MACMILLAN PUBLISHING COMPANY
New York

MAXWELL MACMILLAN CANADA
Toronto

MAXWELL MACMILLAN INTERNATIONAL
New York · Oxford · Singapore · Sydney

Macmillan Publishing Company
866 Third Avenue, New York, NY 10022

Maxwell Macmillan Canada, Inc.
1200 Eglinton Avenue East, Suite 200
Don Mills, Ontario M3C 3N1

Printed in the United States of America

Library of Congress Catalog Card No.: 91-37827

printing number
3   4   5   6   7   8   9   10

Macmillan, Inc., is part of the Maxwell Communication
Group of Companies.

Library of Congress Catalog in Publication Data
Encyclopedia of sociology / Edgar F. Borgatta, editor-in-chief, Marie
    L. Borgatta, managing editor.
        p.   cm.
    Includes bibliographical references and index.
    ISBN 0-02-897051-9 (set).—ISBN 0-02-897052-7 (v. 1) : $90.00
    1. Sociology—Encyclopedias.   I. Borgatta, Marie L.
HM17.E5   1991
301'.03—dc20   91-37827
                                                                CIP

EDITORIAL AND PRODUCTION STAFF

Philip Friedman, *Publisher*

Elly Dickason, *Editor in Chief*

Martha Goldstein, *Senior Project Editor*

Lynn Constantinou, *Production Manager*

Karin K. Vanderveer, *Assistant Editor*

The paper used in this publication meets the minimum requirements
of American National Standard for Information Sciences—Permanence of
Paper for Printed Library Materials. ANSI Z39.48–1984.

Encyclopedia
of Sociology

S

SAMPLING PROCEDURES The analysis of data from samples constitutes a major portion of contemporary research in sociology and the social sciences. Such research depends heavily on a formal logic that enables researchers to use information from samples to make inferences about population characteristics. For example, researchers use sample data from the U.S. population to determine, with specified confidence and precision, such things as the average household size, the proportion of Americans unemployed during a given month, and the correlation between educational attainment and annual salaries for members of the labor force. Characteristics of samples, such as the proportion in a sample who are unemployed, are called *sample statistics,* while the corresponding population values are called *population parameters.* The purpose of sampling is to obtain information about unknown population parameters more cheaply, quickly, and, sometimes, more accurately than would be possible by means of a complete enumeration of the population. Knowledge of the basic principles of sampling is important for both those who draw samples and anyone who uses data from samples.

Statistical theory is the basis for using sample statistics to make inferences about population parameters. It shows that one can, under specified conditions, use data from a single sample to determine how much a sample statistic would vary across many samples drawn from the same population. Knowing a sample statistic's variability (in statistical parlance, its *sampling variance*) in turn makes it possible to draw conclusions about its corresponding population parameter. The key prerequisite for using statistical theory in this way is that the data must come from a *probability sample,* a sample in which each case in the population (cases may be individuals, households, cities, days, etc.) has a known and nonzero probability of being selected into the sample.

Sampling theory, a branch of statistical theory, covers a variety of procedures for drawing probability samples. Many considerations can influence one's choice of a sampling procedure for a given project, including feasibility, time constraints, characteristics of the population to be studied, desired accuracy, and cost. Simple sampling procedures are often sufficient for studying small and relatively homogeneous populations, but, to study large and heterogeneous populations, researchers typically must use more complicated procedures and usually should consult a sampling specialist at a survey organization (each year the fall issue of the quarterly *Survey Research* lists academic survey organizations throughout the world).

Unless cost and time constraints are severe, researchers seeking to estimate population parameters nearly always use sampling procedures that yield probability samples. Nonprobability sampling procedures, such as convenience sampling, purposive sampling, quota sampling, and many forms of snowball sampling, do not insure that a formally random process determines which cases are selected into a sample (Kalton 1983, pp. 90–93). As a result, one can neither be confident that these procedures are unbiased nor make statistical inferences from the samples they yield. However, researchers engaged in nonquantitative or exploratory work frequently use nonprobability sampling profitably.

One should distinguish between the representativeness of a given sample and whether it was drawn according to probability sampling procedures. Although probability samples have a decidedly better track record for representativeness, not all probability samples are representative and not all nonprobability samples are unrepresentative. Political polls based on quota samples, for example, often produce results very close to the subsequent vote. However, there is no reason to believe that a nonprobability sampling procedure that has been successful in the past will continue to yield representative results. In contrast, probability sampling procedures are likely to produce representative samples in the future because they are based on a formally random selection procedure.

Any study seeking to draw a probability sample must begin by defining the population of interest, called the *target population*. The purpose of the study restricts the definition of the target population but rarely specifies it completely. For example, a study of characteristics of U.S. families would obviously define the population as consisting of families, but it would be necessary to define precisely what counts as a family, as well as to decide how to treat various cases from which it may be difficult to collect data (such as the families of U.S. citizens who live overseas). Sudman (1976, pp. 11–14) discusses general issues involved in defining target populations.

The next step in probability sampling is to obtain a means of identifying and locating the cases in the target population so that they can be sampled. The means of doing this, called the *sampling frame*, structures the selection of cases into a sample. The most obvious type of sampling frame is a list of the cases in the target population. Unfortunately, such lists are often unavailable, and researchers must usually construct an alternative. For example, to draw a sample of U.S. public high schools, a researcher might begin with a list of U.S. census tracts, select a sample of those tracts, and then consult maps indicating the locations of public high schools in the selected tracts. In this case, the sampling frame would consist of the list of census tracts and their corresponding maps. A good sampling frame should include all of the cases in the target population, no inappropriate cases, and no duplications. Kish gives a helpful classification of sampling-frame problems and some possible solutions (1965, pp. 53–59, 384–439).

BASIC SAMPLING PROCEDURES

Simple Random Sampling. The most elementary probability sampling procedure is simple random sampling (SRS) and, although used infrequently, it serves as a benchmark for the evaluation of other procedures. To use SRS one's sampling frame must be a list of the cases in the population. Usually the researcher assigns a unique identification number to each entry in the list and then generates random numbers using a random-number table or a computer program that generates random numbers. If a random number matches one of the identification numbers in the list, the researcher adds the indicated case to the sample (unless it has already been selected). This procedure is followed until it produces a desired sample size. It is important that only the randomly generated numbers determine the sample's composition; this condition insures that the sampling procedure will be unbiased and that the chosen cases will be a probability sample.

With SRS, each case in the sampling frame has an equal chance of being selected into the sample. In addition, for a sample of size n, all possible combinations of n different cases in the sampling frame have an equal chance of comprising the sample. The formulas for statistics and their standard errors given in nearly all statistics textbooks assume that SRS generated the sample data, and statistical programs for computers also employ these formulas. Most studies of human populations use sampling procedures that are less efficient than SRS, however, and using SRS formulas in these instances underestimates the sampling variances of statistics. As a consequence, researchers frequently reject null hypotheses when they should fail to do so and construct misleadingly small confidence intervals.

Systematic Simple Random Sampling. When a sampling frame contains many cases or the prospective sample's size is large, researchers often decide to save time and effort by setting a sampling interval and, after a random start, using the interval to choose the cases for the sample. For example, suppose a researcher wanted to select a sample of n cases from a population of size N, and $n/N = 1/25$. To use systematic simple random sampling (SSRS) the researcher would draw a random number between one and twenty-five, r, and, starting with the rth case, select every twenty-fifth case in the sampling frame (for more complicated examples, see Kalton 1983, p. 17). This procedure gives all cases in the frame an equal probability of being chosen for the sample but, unlike SRS, does not give all combinations of cases equal probabilities of selection. In the example just mentioned there are only twenty-five possible combinations of cases that could constitute the resulting sample (for example, cases 105 and 106 could never be in the same sample).

When the order of the cases in the sampling frame is essentially random with respect to the variables of interest in a study, this property of SSRS is inconsequential, but when the frame is ordered, SSRS can differ significantly from SRS. For example, suppose one wished to sample starting players on college basketball teams to determine their average height and had a sampling frame ordered by team and, within each team, by position. Since there are five starting players on each team, a sampling interval of any multiple of five would yield a sample composed of players who all play the same position. There would be a one in five chance that these players would all be centers (usually the tallest players), and a two in five chance that they would all be guards (usually the shortest). Thus, in this instance the sampling variation of the players' mean height would be substantially greater than that produced by SRS. However, there are also situations where SSRS is equivalent to StRS (see later) and yields samples that have smaller sampling variances than SRS (Kish 1965, pp. 113–123). In practice, most sampling frames for human populations have orderings, often alphabetical, that are essentially random with respect to the purposes of a study, and frames with potential problems are usually obvious or are quickly recognized. Thus, in most applications SSRS is essentially equivalent to SRS (Sudman 1976, pp. 56–57).

Stratified Random Sampling. When a sampling frame consists of a list of all the cases in a population and also contains additional information about each case, researchers may use stratified random sampling (StRS). For example, a list of people might also indicate the sex of each person. A researcher can take advantage of this additional information by grouping individuals of each sex into a sublist (called a stratum) and then sampling from each stratum, using SRS or SSRS. One can use either the same sampling fraction for each stratum, in which case the procedure is *proportionate* StRS, or different fractions for different strata (*disproportionate* StRS). In either case one usually aims to use the additional information contained in the sampling frame to produce a sample that will be more efficient than those of other sampling procedures (i.e., will need fewer cases to produce a sample with a given sampling variance).

Efficiency is commonly measured by a sampling procedure's *design effect*: the ratio of the sampling variance of a statistic based on that procedure to the sampling variance of the same statistic derived from an SRS with the same number of cases (Kalton 1983, pp. 21–24). The efficiency of proportionate StRS is directly related to the correlation between the variable used to stratify the sampling frame and the variable(s) being studied. Thus, if one wished to determine the mean individual income of a population of Americans, proportionate StRS based on sex would produce a more efficient sample than SRS and would have a design effect smaller than unity, because sex is correlated with income. In the limiting case where the stratifying variable is perfectly correlated with the variable(s) being studied, for example, if each woman earned $15,000 per annum and each man $25,000, proportionate SrRS would always yield a sample mean exactly equal to the population mean. In contrast, if sex were completely uncorrelated with income, proportionate StRS would be no more efficient than SRS, and StRS's design effect would equal unity. In practice it is usually difficult to obtain sampling frames that contain information about potential stratifying variables that are substantially correlated with variables being studied, especially when the cases are individuals. As a result, the gains in efficiency produced by proportionate StRS are often quite modest.

Proportionate StRS often yields small sample sizes for strata that comprise small proportions of a population. Thus, when researchers want to estimate parameters for each stratum in a population, they sometimes employ disproportionate StRS to insure that there are enough cases from each stratum to support a statistical analysis. A second motive for using disproportionate StRS is to design an optimal sample, one that produces the most precise estimates for a given cost. Optimal samples are feasible when there are differences between the strata in (a) cost of sampling and obtaining data, (b) variability of the variables under study, or (c) prior knowledge about the variables under study. Sudman (1976, pp. 107–130) discusses and gives examples of each of these situations. The benefits of disproportionate StRS may be hard to attain when one wants to draw a multipurpose sample with observations of many variables, because optimal procedures for the different variables may conflict. In addition, although proportionate StRS cannot have a design effect greater than unity, design effects for disproportionate StRS can be larger than unity, meaning that disproportionate StRS can produce samples

that are less efficient than SRS (Kalton 1983, pp. 20–26).

Cluster Sampling. All of the sampling procedures discussed require that the researcher have a sampling frame listing the cases in the target population. Unfortunately, such sampling frames frequently do not exist, especially for human populations defined by area of residence. One can still draw a probability sample, however, if the population can be organized in terms of a grouping principle and each case assigned to one of the groups (called *clusters*). For example, dwellings in cities are located in blocks defined by streets. Even if a list of the dwellings does not exist, it is possible to draw a probability sample by constructing a sampling frame consisting of a listing of the blocks, drawing a random sample of the blocks, and collecting data on the dwellings in the chosen blocks.

This procedure, called *cluster sampling* (CS), is also advantageous when one wishes to use face-to-face interviewing to survey geographically dispersed populations. In this case CS saves on traveling costs because it enables the survey to concentrate interviewers in a small number of locations. However, cluster samples usually have larger sampling variances than SRS. The efficiency of CS is inversely related to (1) the extent to which clusters are internally homogeneous but differ from each other, and (2) the number of cases sampled from each cluster. Cluster sampling is maximally efficient when a population can be divided into clusters that are identical, because each cluster is then a microcosm of the population as a whole. When clusters are internally homogeneous and differ sharply from each other, as is almost always the case for human populations clustered by area of residence, CS is considerably less efficient than SRS (Kalton 1983, pp. 30–33). In this situation, researchers usually attempt a sample of only a few cases from each of many clusters, but this strategy undermines the cost advantages of CS.

Multistage Sampling. Researchers desiring to collect data via face-to-face interviews with a probability sample of people living in a certain area, such as the United States, a state, or even a city, usually combine elements of the previously discussed procedures in a multistage sampling procedure. For example, to draw a probability sample of U.S. adults, one might begin by obtaining a list of counties and parishes in the United States and collecting data on several characteristics of these units (region, average household income, etc.). These variables can be used to group the units, called *primary sampling units,* into strata so one can use StRS. In addition, one would obtain estimates of the number of residents in each unit so that they can be sampled with probabilities proportional to their estimated population sizes (Sudman 1976, pp. 134–150).

After selecting a sample of counties in this fashion, the researcher might proceed to draw a series of nested cluster samples. For example, one could divide each selected county into subareas (perhaps townships or some other area-based governmental divisions) and then select a cluster sample from these units, with probabilities proportional to estimated population size. Next the researcher might divide each of the selected units into subareas (perhaps on the order of the U.S. Census Bureau's blocks) and draw a cluster sample of them. For each chosen block, the researcher might obtain a listing of dwelling units and draw another cluster sample. Finally, from each chosen dwelling unit the researcher would choose, according to a specified procedure (Kish 1965, pp. 396–404), an individual to be interviewed. The selections at each stage of the sampling process *must* be based on a formal random selection procedure. For more detailed discussions and examples of selecting multistage sampling procedures, see Kish (1965, pp. 301–383), Moser and Kalton (1972, pp. 188–210), and Sudman (1976, pp. 131–170). Multistage sampling usually requires considerable resources and expertise, and those wishing to draw such samples should contact a survey organization. Studies of the design effects of multistage samples, such as those carried out by the University of Michigan's Survey Research Center, show that they vary from 1.0 to 2.0, with values around 1.5 being common (Kish 1965, p. 581). Unfortunately, estimating sampling variances for a multistage sample is usually a complicated task, and this complexity, combined with the fact that popular statistics programs for computers use only SRS formulas, has led most researchers to ignore the problem, thereby producing many spurious "statistically significant" findings.

RECENT ADVANCES

Sampling practitioners have made considerable progress recently in developing techniques for drawing probability samples of rare or elusive populations for which there are no lists and for which conventional multistage sampling procedures would produce sufficient cases only at exorbitant cost. Sudman, Sirken, and Cowan (1988) review procedures for screening clusters to determine those containing concentrations of a rare population's members and also discuss how network sampling procedures and capture–recapture methods can be applied to the problem. Researchers can also use network sampling of individuals to draw probability samples of businesses and other social organizations to which individuals belong (Sudman, Sirken, and Cowan 1988, p. 240).

Recent developments in statistical theory and computer software promise to make the determination of standard errors for statistics based on multistage samples much easier than in the past. One approach to overcoming these difficulties is to use a computer program to draw many subsamples from an existing sample and to derive an overall estimate of a standard error from the many estimates given by the subsamples. There are several versions of this general approach, including *bootstrapping, jackknife replication,* and *cross-validation* (Hinkley 1983). A second approach is to develop computer statistical packages that incorporate information about a study's sampling design (Wolter 1985, pp. 393–412, contains a list of such programs). The increased availability of these programs should produce greater recognition of the necessity of taking a study's sampling procedure into account while analyzing the data it yielded.

(SEE ALSO: *Probability Theory; Survey Research*)

REFERENCES

Hinkley, David 1983 "Jackknife Methods." In Samuel Kotz and Norman L. Johnson, eds., *Encyclopedia of Statistical Sciences*, Vol. 4. New York: Wiley.

Kalton, Graham 1983 *Introduction to Survey Sampling.* Newbury Park, Calif.: Sage.

Kish, Leslie 1965 *Survey Sampling.* New York: Wiley.

Moser, C. A., and G. Kalton 1972 *Survey Methods in Social Investigation,* 2nd ed. New York: Basic.

Sudman, Seymour 1976 *Applied Sampling.* New York: Academic Press.

———, Monroe G. Sirken, and Charles D. Cowan 1988 "Sampling Rare and Elusive Populations." *Science* 240:991–996.

Wolter, Kirk M. 1985 *Introduction to Variance Estimation.* New York: Springer-Verlag.

LOWELL L. HARGENS

SCALES AND SCORES   *See* Factor Analysis; Measurement.

SCANDINAVIAN SOCIOLOGY   Scandinavian sociology emerged in its present form as an academic discipline just after World War II, though its roots went back considerably further. In Helsinki, sociologist, ethnologist, and philosopher Edvard A. Westermarck (1862–1939) lectured on sociology from 1890; and in Göteborg Gustaf Fredrik Steffen (1864–1929) became a professor of economics and sociology in 1903.

As early as 1850, the Norwegian clergyman Eilert Sundt (1817–1875) published his study of Norwegian tramps and the lowest layer of the rural population. Between 1850 and 1869 (when he became a vicar) he received state support for his demographic and sociological studies of Norwegian manners and customs, poverty and living conditions. In demography he is still remembered for "Sundt's law," which states that irregularities in the age distribution at a given time generate similar irregularities in the next generation.

Westermarck held chairs in applied philosophy until 1930, and between 1907 and 1930 he also had a sociology chair in London. He belonged to the small group of leading European sociologists and philosophers active in the early part of the century. His best-known works are studies of the history of marriage (first volume published in 1891) and of the origin and development of moral ideas (1906 and 1908; 1932).

Between 1907 and 1913 the statistician A. Gustav Sundbärg (1857–1914) directed "Emigrationsutredningen," an official investigation of Swedish emigration, considered one of the great problems of Swedish society at the time. The final report was given in 1913, and between 1908 and 1912 twenty appendices by Sundbärg himself, Nils R. Wohlin (1881–1948; secretary of the investigation), and others were published. The investigation as a whole contains a wealth of statistical information of great interest even today.

EARLY SOCIOLOGY

In Scandinavia in the 1940s sociology met an established discipline of demography, a reliable and accessible population registration system, a positivistic philosophy, and a reformistic policy in need of empirical studies of societal problems. From then until the late 1960s, Scandinavian sociologists engaged in empirical, mostly quantitative studies of social inequality, social mobility and the educational system, work conditions, physical planning, social epidemiology, alcohol problems, and delinquency. There was a strong American influence from Scandinavians who had studied at American universities, from journals and textbooks, and from several visiting Americans (Norway in particular received a series of Fulbright scholars). Scandinavian sociology became strongly empirical and technical, heavily sociopsychological, and survey oriented. There was less interest in functionalism, Talcott Parsons, and the classics than in survey analysis and social exchange theory.

In the late 1960s and early 1970s, new sociological voices were heard in Scandinavia as elsewhere. The new orientations can summarily be described as aggressively political, antipositivistic, antifunctionalistic, antiquantitative, and strongly Marxist. In general, the new sociology was more theoretical and sociophilosophical and less empirical than the earlier versions. Conflict theories, critical theory, symbolic interactionism, and the labeling perspective came to the fore, as did socioanthropological and hermeneutical methods. One of the main targets for the attacks of Sociology's New Left was the Old Left's reformist welfare-society approach.

INSTITUTIONAL STRUCTURE

In Denmark, the German refugee Theodor Geiger (1891–1952) was appointed a professor of sociology at Aarhus University in 1938. In 1955 Kaare Svalastoga, a Norwegian historian with a sociological education from the University of Washington, became professor of sociology at Copenhagen, where a graduate program in sociology was started in 1958. In the 1960s and 1970s additional chairs were created at Copenhagen and Aalborg and in sociological subdisciplines at universities in Copenhagen, Aarhus, Aalborg, and Roskilde, as well as at the Handelshöjskolen (School of Economics and Business Administration) in Copenhagen. Mostly due to problems at the Copenhagen Sociological Institute from the early 1970s, Danish sociology found itself in a state of crisis and possible reorganization in the late 1980s. With the assistance of a committee of Scandinavian sociologists, the Copenhagen sociology department is now being rebuilt and will probably have three or four chairs. Suggestions for reorganization call for a basic three-year program, plus a further two-year program of mostly sociology leading to a "cand.scient.soc." degree or a four-year Ph.D. program. The institute most important to sociology outside the universities is the Socialforskningsinstitutet (Institute for Social Research). With Henning Friis as director from its start in 1958 until 1979, the institute has carried out a large number of social investigations using its own field organization (e.g., the 1976 and 1986 Danish Welfare Surveys).

In Finland, two of Westermarck's ethnosociological students held chairs in sociology in Helsinki and Turku as early as the 1920s. In the mid-1940s modern-type sociologists got chairs, such as the criminologist Veli Verkko (1893–1955) in 1946 in Helsinki. At present there are sociology chairs at eight Finnish universities; they were first established at Helsinki, Turku, Åbo Academy, and Tampere, and later at Jyväskylä, Oulu, Rovaniemi, and Joensuu. In the eight universities there are about twenty tenured professors and associate professors of sociology. In addition, there are four associate professors of sociology at two other universities and two schools of economics, as well as nine chairs in sociological subdisciplines. There also are some important research institutes outside the universities, such as the Alcohol Research Institute and the National Statistical Center. The *kandidat* (undergraduate) degree takes five years; about half the time is devoted to sociology, after an introductory course common to all social science studies, and the rest of the time is usually divided among two other disciplines.

In Norway, Sverre Holm filled the first sociology chair in 1949 in Oslo, and in the 1960s chairs were added in Bergen, Trondheim, and Tromsø. There are about fifteen professors of sociology altogether at these universities. A basic sociology degree is assumed to take six years, divided in two three-year sections, the first including a general college course and a course in a second social science. Several institutes are important for sociological research and education: Institutt for Samfunnforskning (ISF; Institute for Social Research, from 1950), Institutt for Anvendt Sosialforskning (INAS; Institute for Applied Social Research, from 1968), and Statisisk Sentralbyrå (Statistical Central Bureau), as well as the regional colleges in Rogaland and Nordland and an institute for industrial environmental research in Trondheim (from 1958).

In Sweden, the educator and sociologist E. H. Thörnberg (1873–1961) never held a university position. Gunnar Myrdal had a claim to be the first modern sociologist, but Torgny Segerstedt became the first professor of sociology by converting his chair in applied philosophy to sociology at Uppsala in 1947. Sociology is now taught at the six universities of Uppsala, Stockholm, Lund, Göteborg, Umeå, and (under somewhat different conditions) at Linköping, as well as in several colleges. There are about eighteen sociology professors at these universities. The Arbetslivscentrum, a center in Stockholm for labor-market studies, which may soon be reconstructed, has two chairs for its sociological fields. The undergraduate study of sociology qualifying for graduate studies is scheduled for six or seven twenty-week semesters, of which at least three are devoted to sociology. Doctoral studies take four years in theory but considerably more time in practice. Outside the universities, the private opinion poll institute Svenska institutet för opinionsundersökningar (SIFO), run from 1966 to 1986 by Hans L. Zetterberg, and Statistics Sweden are important for Swedish sociology.

There is considerable interaction among the sociological communities in the Scandinavian countries: professors holding chairs in neighboring countries, such as the leading Finnish alcohol researcher Kettil Bruun (1924–1985) holding a chair in Stockholm from 1982 to 1984 and Swedish sociologists from Lund moving over the Sound to Copenhagen; comparative studies of the Scandinavian countries (Allardt 1975); and cooperation on comparative projects (Allardt and Rokkan 1970, and Erikson et al. 1987, with one editor from each of four countries).

The Scandinavian Sociological Association has some 2,000 members. Since 1955 it has published the *Acta Sociologica,* a refereed quarterly journal. Editorship rotates among the countries: after three years at Copenhagen University it will move to Stockholm University for 1991–1993 with Peter Hedström as editor. Each of the Scandinavian countries has a national sociological association, the Finnish Westermarck Society, founded in 1940, being the oldest. Approximate memberships in 1985 were 350 in Denmark, 30 in Iceland, 600 in Finland, 450 in Norway, and 475 in Sweden. There are also national journals, such as the Finnish Sosiologia (from 1962), the Norwegian Tidskrift for samfunnsforskning (from 1960), and the Swedish Sociologisk forskning (from 1964).

Outside Scandinavia, most contacts are still with the United States, although interaction with European, especially British, French, and German, sociologists tends to be more frequent now than in the early stages. Polish, Hungarian, and Estonian contacts also are important to Finnish sociology. Several Scandinavian sociologists have had most or parts of their careers abroad, especially in the United States, for example, Denmark's Aage Bøttger Sørensen, the Norwegian Stein Rokkan, and the Swedes Bo Anderson and Hans L. Zetterberg.

PRESENT SOCIOLOGY

Even after the wave of left-wing sociology subsided toward the end of the 1970s, Scandinavian sociology remained more diversified than before, with a continued interest in Marxism and the classics, as well as in social exchange theory and in a broad spectrum of data analysis. The statistical analytical orientation has held its own, no doubt at least partly due to developments in computer programs.

In Norway, Vilhelm Aubert (1922–1988) provided an exemplar of a discussion based on soft data (Aubert 1965), Dag Østerberg (1986, 1988) writes in the hermeneutic and humanistic essay tradition, and Jon Elster (1985) is a well-known theoretician and Marxist. In Sweden the social psychologist Johan Asplund (e.g., 1983) has a position in some ways similar to the one held by Dag Østerberg in Norwegian sociology. As to Marxism, Jon Elster's Swedish counterpart would be the internationally known Marxist Göran Therborn (1980, 1986).

A cluster of overlapping core areas concerning forms of inequality has become central to Scandinavian sociology. Studies concern gender inequality, as well as inequality among social classes and other groupings, as to political, economic, educational, and social resources, which can be seen as constituting inequality of welfare in a broad sense, with indicators of various welfare dimensions. In 1968, the reports of an official Swedish investigation focused on low-income categories created considerable political commotion. One of the tasks of the Swedish Institute for Social Research (SOFI) has been to continue this study as a panel with new surveys in 1974, 1981, and 1991. A volume edited by Robert Erikson and Rune Åberg (1987) provides a partial summary. Comprehensive welfare studies (level-of-living studies) were carried out in Denmark, Finland, and Norway between 1972 and 1974 (Allardt 1975; Hernes and Matinussen 1980; Erikson et al. 1987). Statistics Sweden has made annual level-of-living surveys since 1974 (Vogel 1988). Studies by Gudmund Hernes in Norway have been influential both politically and sociologically. He was the leading researcher in the first Norwegian level-of-living survey and also in an official Norwegian 1972–1979 project on power in society (Hernes 1975; 1978, also a contribution to exchange theory). The task force gave its final report in 1982. The official Swedish study of societal power, ordered after the success of the Norwegian study, was run mainly by political scientists and historians, although Rune Åberg (1990) was asked to repeat in modern form a community study from the 1950s (Segerstedt and Lundquist 1952, 1955).

In political sociology Stein Rokkan's (1921–1979) far-reaching project (Rokkan and Lipset 1967; Allardt and Rokkan 1970; Rokkan et al. 1970; Rokkan 1987) was left unfinished. Other important works in this field are Allardt (1965), Korpi (1983, 1989), Therborn (1986), Martinussen (1988), and Alapuro (1988).

Gender studies are an exceptionally strong sociological field in Norway. In the late 1960s Harriet Holter (1970) analyzed sex roles and their impact on work life, political behavior, education, and so forth. Kvinners levekår og livsløp (Women's level of living and life course) is a series of Norwegian gender studies with contributions by Helga Hernes (1982) and Kari Waerness (1982) among others. For a Finnish study in the area, see Haavio-Mannila (1971).

Social stratification and social mobility have long been an area of strong interest in Scandinavian sociology (Carlsson 1958; Svalastoga 1959, 1965). More recent works in this field include those of Gudmund Hernes and Knud Knudsen (1976), Natalie R. Ramsøy (1977), Matti Alestalo (1986), Robert Erikson (1987), Erikson and John Goldthorpe (1987), and Knud Knudsen (1988).

Ever since the Finnish State Alcohol Monopoly established its research institute in 1950, alcohol studies have been a Finnish specialty. Among the publications by its longtime director Kettil Bruun and his successor, Klaus Mäkelä, are Bruun 1959 and 1973, Mäkelä 1981, and Bruun 1985 (from his tenure in Stockholm).

The Finnish demographer Tapani Valkonen is known for his skillful context analyses and epidemiological studies (1969). To revitalize Swedish demography, which had come almost to a standstill in the 1970s, the Norwegian demometrician Jan M. Hoem was called in from Copenhagen in 1983 (Hoem and Hoem 1989).

Within the subfields of sociology of literature and mass media and language sociology, respectively, Karl-Erik Rosengren (1983) and Karmela Liebkind (1984) should be mentioned.

Since the mid-1970s, Swedish, and to some extent Norwegian, statistically oriented behavioral researchers have had problems with privacy-protecting data legislation. The Swedish Data Act of 1973 refers only to computer-run data on identified persons. To handle such data sets, the researcher needs a permit from the Data Inspection Board, which in principle expanded the informed-consent requirement to the use of governmental micro data. Although this principle was waived in many cases, it led to frequent and well-publicized conflicts between the board and the researchers, with the media usually solidly behind the board. In fact, in Sweden the media came to debate privacy issues mostly in connection with statistical data sets, whereas administrative files largely went unnoticed. Still, the rich governmental micro files, including the censuses, remain assets to Scandinavian sociology.

REFERENCES

Alapuro, Risto 1988 *State and Revolution in Finland.* Berkeley: University of California Press.

Alestalo, Matti 1986 *Structural Change, Classes, and the State.* Helsinki: Research Group for Comparative Sociology.

Åberg, Rune (ed.) 1990 *Industrisamhälle i omvandling.* (Industrial Community in Transition). Stockholm: Carlssons.

Allardt, Erik 1965 *Samhällsstruktur och sociala spän-*

ningar (Societal Structure and Social Tension). Tampere: Söderströms. Also in Finnish.

———1975 *Att ha, att älska, att vara.* (To Have, to Love, to Be). Lund: Argos. Also in Finnish.

———1979 *Implications of the Ethnic Revival in Modern Industrialized Society.* Helsinki: Societas Scientiarum Fennica.

———1981 *Språkgränser och samhällsstruktur.* (Language Borders and Social Structure). Stockholm: AWE/Gebers. Also in Finnish, partly also in English, in Allardt 1979.

———1989 "Recent Developments in Scandinavian Sociology." In W. Richard Scott and Judith Blake, eds., *Annual Review of Sociology,* vol. 15. Palo Alto, Calif.: Annual Reviews.

Allardt, Erik, Sverre Lysgaard, and Aage Bøttger Sørensen 1988 *Sociologin i Sverige.* (Sociology in Sweden). Stockholm: HSFR.

Allardt, Erik, and Stein Rokkan (eds.) 1970 *Mass Politics: Studies in Political Sociology.* New York: Free Press.

Allardt, Erik, Aage Bøttger Sørensen, and Walter Korpi 1987 *Forslag till ny uddannelse i sociologi.* (Recommendation for a New Educational Program in Sociology). Copenhagen: Undervisningsministeriet.

Asplund, Johan 1983 *Om undran inför samhället.* (On Wondering at Society). Lund: Argos.

Aubert, Vilhelm 1965 *The Hidden Society.* Totowa, N.J.: Bedminster.

Bruun, Kettil 1959 *Drinking Behavior in Small Groups.* Helsinki: Finnish Foundation for Alcohol Studies.

———1973 Alkohol i Norden. (Alcohol in Scandinavia). Stockholm: Aldus.

Bruun, Kettil, and Per Frånberg (eds.) 1985 *Den svenska supen.* (The Swedish Snaps). Stockholm: Prisma.

Carlsson, Gösta 1958 *Social Mobility and Class Structure.* Lund: Gleerups.

Elster, Jon 1985 *Making Sense of Marx.* Cambridge: Cambridge University Press.

Erikson, Robert 1987 "The Long Arm of the Origin." In Ulla Bergryd and Carl-Gunnar Janson, eds., *Sociological Miscellany.* Stockholm: Department of Sociology, University of Stockholm.

———n.d. "Norsk sociologi—sedd från Sverige." (Norwegian Sociology—Viewed from Sweden). Unpublished.

———, and John Goldthorpe 1987 "Commonality and Variation in Social Fluidity in Industrial Nations, parts I and II." *European Sociological Review* 3:54–77, 145–166.

———, and Rune Åberg (eds.), 1987 *Welfare in Transition.* Oxford: Clarendon Press.

———, Erik Jørgen Hansen, Stein Ringen, and Hannu Uusitalo, eds., 1987 *The Scandinavian Model: Welfare State and Welfare Research.* Armonk, N.Y. and London: M.E. Sharpe.

Haavio-Mannila, Elina 1971 "Convergences Between East and West: Tradition and Modernity of Sex Roles in Sweden, Finland, and the Soviet Union." *Acta Sociologica* 14:114–125.

Hernes, Germund (1975) 1978 *Makt og avmakt.* (Power and Powerlessness). Bergen, Norway: Universitetsforlaget.

———1978 Forhandlingsøkonomi og blandingsadministration. (Transaction Economy and Mixed Administration). Bergen, Norway: Universitetsforlaget.

———, and Knud Knudsen 1976 *Utdanning og ulikhet.* (Education and Inequality). Oslo: NOU 1976:46.

———, and Willy Martinussen 1980 *Demokrati og politiske resurser.* (Democracy and Political Resources). Oslo: NOU 1980:7.

Hernes, Helga 1982 *Welfare State and Woman Power.* Oslo: Norwegian University Press.

Hoem, Jan M., and Brita Hoem 1989 "The Impact of Women's Employment on Second and Third Births in Modern Sweden." *Population Studies* 43:47–67.

Holter, Harriet 1970 *Sex Roles and Social Structure.* Oslo: Norwegian University Press.

Knudsen, Knud 1988 "Class Identification in Norway." *Acta Sociologica* 31:69–79.

Korpi, Walter 1983 *The Democratic Class Struggle.* London: Routledge and Kegan Paul.

———1989 "Power, Politics, and State Autonomy in the Development of Social Citizenship." *American Sociological Review* 54:309–328.

Liebkind, Karmela 1984 *Minority Identity and Identification Processes.* Helsinki: Societas Scientiarum Fennica.

Martinussen, Willy 1988 *Solidaritetens grenser.* (Limits of Solidarity). Oslo: Universitetsforlaget.

Mäkelä, Klaus 1981 *Alcohol, Society, and the State.* Toronto: Addiction Research Foundation.

Østerberg, Dag 1986 *Fortolkende sosiologi.* (Interpretive Sociology). Oslo: Universitetsforlag.

———1988 Metasociology. Oslo: Norwegian University Press.

Ramsøy, Natalie R. 1977 *Sosial mobilitet i Norge.* (Social Mobility in Norway). Oslo: Tiden Norsk Forlag.

Rokkan, Stein 1987 *Stat, nasjon, klasse.* (State, Nation, Class), ed. B. Hagtvet. Oslo: Universitetsforlaget.

————, and S. M. Lipset 1967 (eds.) *Party Systems and Voter Alignments*. New York: Free Press.

————, Angus Campbell, Per Torsvik, and Henry Valen 1970 *Citizens, Elections, Parties*. Oslo: Norwegian University Press.

Rosengren, Karl-Erik 1983 *The Climate of Literature*. Lund: Studentlitteratur.

Segerstedt, Torgny, and Agne Lundquist 1952 *Människan i industrisamhället. Del I.* (Man in Industrial Society, Part I). Stockholm: SNS.

————1955 *Människan i industrisamhället. Del II.* (Man in Industrial Society, Part II). Stockholm: SNS.

Sundbärg, A. Gustav 1913 *Emigrationsutredningen* (Investigation on Emigration). Stockholm: Offentligt betänkande. Twenty appendices 1908–1912.

Svalastoga, Kaare 1959 *Prestige, Class, and Mobility*. Copenhagen: Gyldendal.

————1965 *Social Differentiation*. New York: David McKay.

Therborn, Göran 1980 *What Does the Ruling Class Do When It Rules?* London: Verso.

————1986 *Why Are Some People More Unemployed Than Others?* London: Verso.

Valkonen, Tapani 1969 "Individual and Structural Effects in Ecological Research." In Mattei Dogan and Stein Rokkan, eds., *Quantitative Ecological Analysis in the Social Sciences*. Cambridge, Mass.: MIT Press.

Vogel, Joachim 1988 *Inequality in Sweden*. Stockholm: SCB.

Waerness, Kari 1982 *Kvinneperspektiv på sosialpolitikken*. (Female Perspective on Social Policy). Oslo: Universitetsforlag.

Westermarck, Edvard A. (1891) 1921 *History of Human Marriage*, 3 vols. London: Macmillan.

————1906–1908 *The Origin and Development of Moral Ideas*. London: Macmillan.

————1932 *Ethical Relativity*. New York: Harcourt; paperback ed. 1960 by Littlefield.

CARL-GUNNAR JANSON

SCIENCE Sociologists of science study the social organization of science, the relations between science and other social institutions, social influences on the content of scientific knowledge, and public policy about science. The definition of *science* is problematic. It can refer to a changing body of certified knowledge about nature or to the methods used to obtain that knowledge. As such, science has existed for millenia. Sociologists are more likely to define science in institutional terms, and most research in the area studies those who work in differentiated social institutions.

Unless the production of knowledge about the empirical world is delegated to relatively autonomous specialists, knowledge accumulates at a slow pace. There have been communities of such specialists in several great civilizations, but most failed to produce stable institutions. Modern science dates from seventeenth-century Europe. The Europeans believed in a deity giving laws to nature as well as people and could expect to discover those laws. Seventeenth-century Europeans could build on the basis of a science produced by the medieval schoolmen. With the rise of capitalism, intellectual elites developed strong interests in using new knowledge to improve material conditions and to enrich themselves. Merton ([1938] 1970), the leading founder of the sociology of science, argued that, in addition to these conditions, Puritanism contributed to the scientific ethos with its emphasis on work in the everyday world, its rationalism and empiricism, its openness to free inquiry, and its desire to glorify God by describing creation. (This still controversial thesis is reviewed in a symposium in *Isis*, 1988.)

A distinctive normative ethos was institutionalized in modern science. Merton (1973, chap. 13) identified four salient norms: (1) The norm of "universalism" requires that scientific contributions be evaluated according to general impersonal criteria without regard to such "irrelevant" characteristics of the contributors as their race, religion, or nationality. It also requires that scientists be rewarded according to their scientific contributions without regard for such irrelevant criteria. (2) The norm of "communism" requires that knowledge must be shared and not kept secret. Thus, the only way a scientist can claim a discovery as "his" or "her" discovery is to make it known to others. In this regard, modern scientists differ from Renaissance mathematicians and magicians, who were often quite secretive. (3) "Disinterestedness" refers to the injunction that the procedures and products of science not be appropriated for private gain. It need not imply altruism, although scientists are often driven to discover as an end in itself; but in addition, situations are usually structured so that it is in the scientist's career interests to act in a disinterested manner. (4) Finally, "organized skepticism" permits and encourages challenges to knowledge claims. Science tends to be unlike many other areas of social life, where conformity in matters of belief is demanded as a sign of loyalty.

Merton's essay on the normative ethos of science, first published in 1942, has drawn fruitful criticism. While Merton argued that the ethos was functional for the advancement of knowledge, Mitroff (1974) argued that scientists could invoke "counternorms"—for example, could fail to be skeptical about their own theories—that could be equally functional in some situations. Mulkay (1980, p. 112) invoked ethnomethodological ideas to make an argument of general significance: "We should not assume that any norm can have a single literal meaning independent of the contexts in which it is applied." Scientists must engage in inferential and interpretive work on norms. They are likely to do this after their actions, in order to construct acceptable accounts of their behavior. The norms do not determine behavior. And it remains an empirical matter to determine the extent of commitment and conformity to the normative ethos described by Merton. While deviant behavior is relatively rare in science, it exists; evidence and theories about such deviance is summarized in Zuckerman (1988).

Scientists in the seventeenth and eighteenth centuries were usually amateurs, like Robert Boyle or Benjamin Franklin, or the intellectual servants of such amateurs. In the later eighteenth and nineteenth centuries, science became professionalized. Scientists experienced formal education in modern universities, found full-time employment, often in the universities, formed self-governing associations, and developed the modern scientific journal and other means of communication. The process is described by Joseph Ben-David (1984), who noted the importance of national differences in the organization of science. Science may be

more or less centralized, or organizations may be more or less competitive. Ben-David showed that there was more competition among universities in Germany and the United States in the late nineteenth and twentieth centuries than in Britain or France, and he claimed that this partly accounted for the greater productivity of science in the first two countries. There are also national differences in the autonomy of science. Lack of autonomy in totalitarian regimes has sometimes distorted and retarded the development of science.

SOCIAL STRATIFICATION IN SCIENCE

Competition remains intense among organizations engaged in basic research in the United States, particularly universities. Organizational prestige is central; as is usually true when it is difficult to measure organizational outputs directly, social comparisons become more important. Periodic surveys of faculty have been used to rate the prestige of research departments. While outputs are difficult to measure, it is true that departments of high prestige are more successful in obtaining research resources and have higher rates of research productivity.

Competition is also intense among individual scientists. They compete for the recognition from their peers for being the first to make valued discoveries (Merton 1973, chaps. 14–15; Hagstrom 1965, 1974). Competition may lead to secretive behavior and premature publication; it may also have the effect of encouraging scientists to move into new areas where there is less competition. A common consequence of competition is simultaneous, or multiply independent, discovery (see Zuckerman 1988 and the references cited there). The frequency of such events is testimony to the extent to which science is a social product. When apparently simultaneous discoveries occur, those involved often engage in priority disputes; they are often ambivalent in such disputes, torn between a desire for the recognition due originality and the demand for humility, the recognition of their dependence on the work of others.

There is very large inequality in the research

productivity of scientists. The chances that a scientist will publish as many as n papers is $1/n^2$; in other words, about 6 percent of all scientists produce 50 percent of all published papers (Price [1963] 1986). Inequality is even greater if one looks at the distribution of citations to the work of scientists. With some reservations, the number of citations can be taken as a measure of the quality of the work; highly cited papers are usually those that other scientists have found useful in their own research. If c is the number of citations, the chances that the work of a scientist will have c citations is proportional to $1/c^3$—or about 3 percent of all scientists receive 50 percent of all the citations to scientific papers.

Inequality of productivity increases over the careers of scientists (Allison, Long, and Krauze 1982). The initially more productive scientists obtain more and better resources for research, their work is more visible to others, and they are more likely to interact with other highly productive scientists. There is considerable mobility of scientists among organizations (more in the United States than in most other countries), and increased research productivity predicts mobility to institutions of higher prestige and to higher rank in institutions. That is, organizations tend to conform to universalistic norms in making appointments and promotions (Cole and Cole 1973). There is an apparent exception to this in the early phases of careers, when productivity is difficult to assess; the prestige of a scientist's Ph.D. department is strongly correlated with the prestige of the initial employer. Being employed in a high prestige organization in turn tends to be a cause of higher later productivity (Allison and Long 1990).

WORK GROUPS, SPECIALTIES, AND DISCIPLINES

Scientific research is a nonroutine activity; outcomes and problems cannot be predicted, and it is difficult to plan research. As organization theories lead one to expect in such situations, work tends to be done in small groups with few hierarchical levels and a small span of control for supervisors (Hagstrom 1976). Most basic research in universities is done by groups of four to nine graduate students and technicians led by one to a few professors. Over the course of time, faculty have found it increasingly desirable to collaborate with their faculty peers, and most publications are multiply authored. Some aspects of research can be routinized, and the extent to which this can be done varies among disciplines; for example, work is routinized in chemistry more readily than in mathematics (Hargens 1975). As one would expect, work groups are smaller in mathematics than in chemistry. Chemists can delegate tasks to assistants, mathematicians cannot; while the number of assistants does not explain much of the variation in the productivity of mathematicians, it does so for the productivity of chemists. In other areas of science, major changes in research methods have led to what is called "big science." Big science is epitomized by high energy physics. Despite the use of labor-saving devices, the work groups at high energy particle laboratories can be very large, with well over 150 personnel. Such groups have a greater division of labor, a broader span of supervisory control, and greater centralization of decision making.

These work groups are ordinarily embedded in larger organizations such as universities and governmental or industrial establishments. They are also likely to be linked informally with other groups working on the same or related research problems in other establishments. These loosely linked and loosely bounded sets of work groups can be called "specialties" or more evocatively "invisible colleges" (Price [1963] 1986). Groups in a specialty simultaneously compete with one another and make contributions to one another's research. The number of groups in a specialty in the entire world (there is a great deal of international collaboration) is ordinarily small, perhaps fifty on the average, seldom over 100, although specialties of over 500 groups have existed. Scientists spend much of their time communicating with one another—writing papers, reviewing papers by others, and meeting at scientific societies or informally (Nelson and Pollock 1970).

Specialties usually exist within disciplines represented by their own university departments and scientific societies. However, interdisciplinary research is common. The growth of an interdisciplinary area can lead to the differentiation of disciplines, so that the number of scientific disciplines has continually grown (Hagstrom 1965). The different scientific disciplines differ greatly in the degree of consensus about theories and methods; one indicator of this is variation in the rejection rates of manuscripts submitted to scientific journals, which is high in such fields as sociology, low in such fields as physics (Hargens 1975; 1988). Variations in consensus can affect the careers of scientists by affecting consensus on the merits of the work of individuals; it is easier to achieve early success in disciplines with high consensus. Disciplines also vary in the typical degree to which the work of different scientists depends on and contributes to the work of others in their disciplines. This interdependence is related to Durkheim's concept of "organic solidarity." It is lower in mathematics than in the empirical sciences, as indicated by fewer references in and citations to papers written by mathematicians, and it can be experienced as a problem by mathematicians (Hagstrom 1965).

SOCIOLOGY OF SCIENTIFIC KNOWLEDGE

The Structure of Scientific Revolutions by the historian Thomas S. Kuhn (1970), first published in 1962, strongly influenced the sociology of science. Kuhn made a distinction between normal and revolutionary science. Normal science is a puzzle-solving activity governed by paradigms. A paradigm consists of shared commitments by a group of scientists to a set of values, presuppositions about nature, methods of research, symbolic generalizations such as Newton's laws, and especially exemplars, such as particular exemplary experiments. In normal science researchers force nature into agreement with the paradigm; apparently disconfirming evidence does not weaken commitments to the paradigm. Normally scientists are successful in explaining away apparently disconfirming evidence, but persistent critical

anomalies can trigger a scientific revolution. In a successful revolution one paradigm is succeeded by another with quite different presuppositions and exemplars. Kuhn argued that the contending paradigms in revolutionary situations are "incommensurable"; the choice between them is not and cannot be determined by evidence and formal decision rules alone. Kuhn illustrated his argument with evidence from major revolutions, from the Copernican Revolution of the sixteenth century to the revolutions that overthrew Newtonian physics in the twentieth, as well as with smaller revolutions affecting the work of smaller sets of scientists.

Those sociologists who developed the sociology of scientific knowledge, initially largely British, advanced radical arguments far beyond those of Kuhn. Not only are paradigms, or theories, "underdetermined" by data, theories are largely or entirely socially constructed. In Harry Collins' words, "the natural world has a small or nonexistent role in the construction of scientific knowledge. . . . Nothing outside the courses of linguistics, conceptual and social behaviour can affect the outcome of these arguments" (quoted in Gieryn 1982, p. 287). The constructivists have done a number of detailed case studies of changes in the content of science to support their claims. The early work is summarized in Collins (1983). Collins showed how "data" was insufficient for resolving conflicts about an allegedly new type of laser. Others have studied such cases as disputes about gravity waves, the construction of quarks, and the history of statistics and genetics in the early twentieth century. In an exemplary ethnographic study of a laboratory studying neurohormones, Latour and Woolgar (1979) described how facts were socially constructed. For example, initial claims comprise conjectures, and lower order factual statements are qualified by the names of those making the claims; but when successfully constructed these qualifications are dropped and the facts are simply taken for granted, perhaps embedded in laboratory equipment or algorithms. Related work by other sociologists involved detailed analyses of scientific discourse. Gilbert and Mulkay (1984) studied biochemists who did research on the process of oxidative phosphorylation. They showed that the sober prose of the scientific papers, where evidence and argument lead to conclusions, was contradicted by the informal discourse of the same scientists, who were partly aware that evidence and argument would be insufficient to persuade their opponents.

The constructivist position naturally leads to a relativist position: If theories are social constructs, they could as well be otherwise. From his detailed study of the ways in which physicists constructed quarks in the period 1964 to 1974, Pickering (1984, p. 413) concluded that "there is no obligation upon anyone framing a view of the world to take account of what twentieth-century physics has to say. The particle physicists of the late nineteen-seventies were themselves quite happy to abandon most of the phenomenal world and much of the explanatory framework which they had constructed in the previous decade. There is no reason for outsiders to show the *present* HEP world-view any more respect." This relativism leads the constructivists to challenge the conventional demarcation between science and nonscience or pseudoscience. Thus, an article reporting a study of parapsychologists is titled "The Construction of the Paranormal: Nothing Unscientific Is Happening."

These extreme claims have elicited lively and continuing controversy. Representative criticisms can be found in Gieryn (1982) and Amsterdamska (1990). Nevertheless, persuasive evidence has been produced about the importance of social factors in changing scientific knowledge. Stewart (1990) studied the recent revolution most widely known to the general public, plate tectonics in the 1950s and 1960s. He found strong resistance to the revolution. Earth scientists who had invested heavily in earlier perspectives were most likely to resist plate tectonics. Conversion to the new paradigm was usually gradual, sealed when the scientists saw the relevance of the paradigm for their own research, but Stewart found some whose acceptance of plate tectonics came as the kind of "gestalt switch" described by Kuhn. In the conflicts accompanying the revolution, scientists on both sides deviated from conventional norms and

used coercive methods to advance their own positions and resist their opponents. Such intense conflict does not always accompany revolutions; in the one in physics that produced quarks, there was little acrimony or duress (Pickering 1984).

APPLIED RESEARCH AND DEVELOPMENT

The preceding discussion has concerned mostly basic research, oriented primarily to the advancement of knowledge. Most research is done to advance other goals—corporate profits, weaponry, health, and other aspects of human welfare. Of the 2 to 4 percent of their gross national products that advanced industrial countries devote to research and development, less than 10 percent is devoted to basic research (National Science Foundation 1985). Of the remainder, much is devoted to defense, particularly in the United States, where a substantial majority of federal R&D expenditures are devoted to it.

Independent inventors are still an important source of innovations, but most applied scientists and engineers are salaried employees of corporations and mission-oriented government agencies. Such employees lack most of the autonomy of basic scientists. University trained scientists are likely to chafe under this loss of autonomy, but successful applied research organizations have developed procedures for accommodating their scientists' desires for autonomy with the organizations' desires for useful knowledge (Kornhauser 1962). Engineers are important in transforming knowledge into products and processes. Engineers are more pragmatic than scientists, less committed to paradigms and more to physical objects (when a scientist moves, he or she is likely to pack journals first; when an engineer moves, he or she packs catalogs). While scientists tend to seek autonomy in organizations, engineers tend to seek power; it is usually necessary to control organizational resources to do successful engineering work.

One of the conflicts that can occur between scientists and their industrial employers concerns communications. Scientists want to communicate their discoveries to their colleagues to gain recognition; their employers want to profit from the discoveries, and that may require keeping them secret. The patent system can provide an accommodative mechanism; discoveries are made public, but those who wish to use the discoveries for practical purposes must pay royalties to the patent holder. The patent system represents one aspect of the commodification of knowledge. Marxist theories imply that in capitalist social formations goods and services are increasingly produced for sale as commodities on markets, not for use, and this is increasingly the case for scientific knowledge. Kloppenburg (1988) has applied Marxist thought effectively in his history of plant breeding. There were and are inherent problems in making seeds into a commodity, since seeds tend to reproduce themselves; they can be both objects of consumption and part of the means of production. Until recently seeds were seldom produced as commodities; new varieties were exchanged among farmers or distributed to them by government agencies at little cost, and the farmers would then grow their own seeds. This changed first with the development of hybrid corn, which required that farmers could not use the corn they produced as seed and had to buy new seed from the seed companies each season. This has since been extended to other crops. In addition, consistent with Marxist thought, the industry has become increasingly centralized and concentrated, with fewer and larger firms dominating the industry. Those firms also expand into world markets, acquiring germ plasm in third world countries and selling seeds as commodities in such countries. The development of biotechnology has increasingly taken the commodity form. Rapid developments in the area blur the distinction between basic and applied research. The emerging pattern seems to be one in which research that cannot be used for profit is done in universities and governmental agencies, usually at public expense, while research that can be used for profit is done in corporations.

Modern science has led to massive changes in the lives of people in all countries, and it has the potential for further massive changes. Not all the changes are beneficial, and not all of the benefi-

cial changes are equitably allocated. Some have voiced concern that science and technology are out of control, but individuals and collectivities do make choices. Students of public policy are concerned with public choices that influence resource inputs into science and technology, the organization of science, and the utilization of scientific knowledge. (See the essays in Spiegel-Rosing and Price 1977.) Knowledge about the organization of science and its relations with other institutions is important for making effective and equitable public policy about science.

(SEE ALSO: *Inventions; Professions; Scientific Explanation*)

REFERENCES

Allison, Paul D., and J. Scott Long 1990 "Departmental Effects on Scientific Productivity." *American Sociological Review* 55:469–478.

Allison, Paul D., J. Scott Long, and Tad K. Krauze 1982 "Cumulative Advantage and Inequality in Science." *American Sociological Review* 47:615–625.

Amsterdamska, Olga 1990 Review of *Science in Action* by Bruno Latour. *Science, Technology, and Human Values* 15:495–504.

Ben-David, Joseph 1984 *The Scientist's Role in Society*. Chicago: University of Chicago Press.

Cole, Jonathan R., and Stephen Cole 1973 *Social Stratification in Science*. Chicago: University of Chicago Press.

Collins, Harry M. 1983 "The Sociology of Scientific Knowledge: Studies of Contemporary Science." In R. H. Turner and J. F. Short, Jr., ed., *Annual Review of Sociology*, vol. 9. Palo Alto, Calif.: Annual Reviews.

Gieryn, Thomas F. 1982 "Relativist/Constructivist Programmes in the Sociology of Science: Redundance and Retreat." *Social Studies of Science* 12:279–297.

Gilbert, G. Nigel, and Michael Mulkay 1984 *Opening Pandora's Box: A Sociological Analysis of Scientists' Discourse*. Cambridge: Cambridge University Press.

Hagstrom, Warren O. 1965 *The Scientific Community*. New York: Basic Books.

——1974 "Competition in Science." *American Sociological Review* 39:1–18.

——1976 "The Production of Culture in Science." *American Behavioral Scientist* 19:753–768.

Hargens, Lowell L. 1975 *Patterns of Scientific Research: A Comparative Analysis of Research in Three Scientific Fields*. Washington, D.C.: American Sociological Association.

———1988 "Scholarly Consensus and Journal Rejection Rates." *American Sociological Review* 53:139–151.

Isis 1988 Special symposium issue of *Isis* 79:571–605.

Kloppenburg, Jack R., Jr. 1988 *First the Seed: The Political Economy of Plant Biotechnology 1492–2000*. New York: Cambridge University Press.

Kornhauser, William 1962. *Scientists in Industry: Conflict and Accommodation*. Berkeley: University of California Press.

Kuhn, Thomas S. 1970 *The Structure of Scientific Revolutions*. Chicago: University of Chicago Press.

Latour, Bruno, and Steve Woolgar 1979 *Laboratory Life: The Social Construction of Scientific Facts*. Beverly Hills, Calif.: Sage.

Merton, Robert K. [1938] 1970 *Science, Technology, and Society in Seventeenth-Century England*. New York: Howard Fertig.

———1973 *The Sociology of Science*. Chicago: University of Chicago Press.

Mitroff, Ian 1974 "Norms and Counternorms in a Select Group of Scientists: A Case Study in the Ambivalence of Scientists." *American Sociological Review* 39:579–595.

Mulkay, Michael J. 1980 "Interpretation and the Use of Rules: The Case of the Norms of Science." In T. F. Gieryn, ed., *Science and Social Structure: A Festschrift for Robert K. Merton*. New York: New York Academy of Sciences.

National Science Foundation 1985 *Science Indicators 1984*. Washington, D.C.: National Science Foundation.

Nelson, Carnot E., and Donald K. Pollock (eds.) 1970 *Communication among Scientists and Engineers*. Lexingon, Mass.: D. C. Heath.

Pickering, Andrew 1984 *Constructing Quarks: A Sociological History of Particle Physics*. Chicago: University of Chicago Press.

Price, Derek J. de S. (1963) 1986 *Little Science, Big Science . . . and Beyond*. New York: Columbia University Press.

Spiegel-Rosing, Ina, and Derek J. de Solla Price (eds.) 1977 *Science, Technology, and Society: A Cross-Disciplinary Perspective*. Beverly Hills, Calif.: Sage.

Stewart, John A. 1990 *Drifting Continents and Colliding Paradigms: Perspectives on the Geoscience Revolution*. Bloomington: Indiana University Press.

Zuckerman, Harriet 1988 "The Sociology of Science." In Neil J. Smelser, ed., *Handbook of Sociology*. Newbury Park, Calif.: Sage.

WARREN O. HAGSTROM

SCIENTIFIC EXPLANATION Science and scientific knowledge have achieved high status in twentieth-century Western societies, yet there continues to be disagreement among scientists and those who study science (historians, philosophers, and sociologists of science) as to the meaning of *scientific explanation*. Indeed, the use of the word *explanation* itself has been the subject of many heated debates (Keat and Urry 1982).

One way of making sense of science is to "reconstruct" the logic that scientists use to produce scientific knowledge. The reconstructed logic of science differs from what scientists actually do when they are doing research. The research process is seldom as clear, logical, and straightforward as the reconstructed logic presented here makes it appear. For a long time the most popular reconstruction of the logic of the scientific process was the "hypothetico-deductive" model. In this model "the scientist, by a combination of careful observation, shrewd guesses, and scientific intuition arrives at a set of postulates governing the phenomena in which he is interested; from these he deduces observable consequences; he then tests these consequences by experiment, and so confirms or disconfirms the postulates, replacing them, where necessary, by others, and so continuing" (Kaplan 1964, pp. 9–10; see also Braithwaite 1968; Nagel 1961). The description of scientific explanation presented below is broadly consistent with this model as used in the social sciences.

Scientific explanations can be contrasted to other, nonscientific types of explanation (Babbie 1989; Kerlinger 1973; Cohen and Nagel 1934). Some explanations obtain their validity because they are offered by someone in authority, for example, a police officer, the President, or parents. Validity may also rest on tradition. For instance, the correct way to do a folk dance is the way it has always been danced, handed down over the generations. This knowledge is not obtained by going through textbooks or conducting experiments but is stored in the memories and beliefs of individuals.

Another way of knowing is called a priori, or intuitive knowledge. This is based on things that "stand to reason," or seem to be obvious, but are not necessarily based on experience. People tend to cling strongly to intuitive knowledge even if the "facts" do not match their experience. The situation that contrasts with beliefs is explained away as a unique occurrence that will not happen again. For example, it "stands to reason" that if you are nice to other people, they will in turn be nice to you.

The scientific method is a way of obtaining information, or knowledge, about the real world. The same knowledge will be obtained by everybody who asks the same question and uses the same investigative method. Scientific explanation uses theories, deductive and inductive logic, and empirical observation to determine what is true and what is false. Unlike authoritarian, traditional, or intuitive explanations, scientific knowledge is always supposed to be open to challenge and continual correction.

One of the goals of science is to develop and test theories, although some scientists believe science proceeds purely by collecting facts. A theory is a hypothetical explanation for either a question or an observation such as "Why is the sky blue?" or "Why do victims of child abuse often grow up to be perpetrators?" Scientists develop and test theories using deductive logic, trying to show that empirical observations are instances of more general laws.

Scientific theories are hypothetical explanations that state the possible relationships among scientific concepts. Theories consist of "a set of interrelated constructs (concepts), definitions, and propositions that present a systematic view of phenomena by specifying relations among variables, with the purpose of explaining and predicting the phenomena" (Kerlinger 1973, p. 9). Theories are also "the device for interpreting, criticizing, and unifying established laws, modify-ing them to fit data unanticipated in their formulation, and guiding the enterprise of discovering new and more powerful generalizations" (Kaplan 1964, p. 295).

Scientific theories generally take the form of "If 'X' happens, then 'Y' will happen." For instance, Karl Marx's theory of surplus value suggested that as the level of surplus value in a capitalist society increased, so would inequality.

Science uses nomothetic methods to establish universal laws, laws that are applicable for all times and places for similar types of events. Scientific theories try to generalize, or predict, beyond the specific data that support them to other similar circumstances. Idiographic methods used in fields such as history seek to establish knowledge of individual, particular events. For example, both social scientists and historians investigate wars. The social scientist seeks to explain what is common to all wars, to develop a general theory of intersocietal conflict. In contrast, the historian studies individual wars and tries to chronicle the events that resulted in that specific war.

Scientific laws fall broadly into two types: deterministic laws and stochastic (or probabilistic) laws. For deterministic laws, if the scientist knows the initial conditions and the forces acting on a system, and these do not change, the state of the system can be determined for all times and places. Deterministic laws are the ideal of the Newtonian, or mechanistic, model of science. In this model of science, it is assumed that causes precede effects and that changes come only from the immediately preceding or present state, never from future states. It is assumed that if two systems are identical and subject to the same initial conditions and forces, the two systems will reach the same endpoint in the same way. Deterministic laws assume that it is possible to make a complete separation between the system and the environment and that the properties of the system arise from its smallest parts. The "smallest" parts of a system are those for which nothing can be said except their location and direction. There is nothing in the parts themselves that influences the system, and all changes in the state of the system come from the forces acting on it. Deterministic laws are based on the assumption that the universe is regular and connections between events are independent of time and space. All other things being equal (*ceteris paribus*), identical circumstances will lead to identical results.

Stochastic laws are expressed in terms of probability. For large or complex systems it is not possible to identify precisely what state the system will be in at any given time but only to assess the probability of its being in a certain state. Quantum physics, chemistry, card games, and lotteries utilize stochastic laws. Stochastic laws are stated in terms of probability over time and apply to classes of events rather than to specific instances. Most relationships in the social sciences are stated in stochastic terms because individual behavior is very difficult to predict. The use of probability does not mean that events are viewed as "random," or "uncaused," but simply that the behavior of individual elements of a system cannot be predicted perfectly accurately.

Scientific theories are systematically linked to existing knowledge that is derived from other generally accepted theories. Each scientist builds on the work of other scientists, using tested theories to develop new theories. The scientific method is dedicated to changing theories, and scientific knowledge progresses through the challenge and revision of theories.

Often a new theory is preferred not because it is based on facts (or data) that are different from those on which the old theory was based but because it is a more comprehensive explanation of existing data. For example, Newton's theory of the solar system superseded Kepler's explanation of planetary motion because Newton's theory included the theory of gravity (which predicted a gravitational attraction between every physical body in the universe) as well as his laws of motion. The two theories together provided many circumstances that could "test" the theory because they predicted not only where planets should be in relation to each other at given times but also the phenomena such as falling apples and swinging pendulums. Newton's theory was more comprehensive and more economical, and although it provided more opportunities for falsification than

Kepler's (which made it more vulnerable), it also resisted falsification better and became the accepted scientific explanation (Chalmers 1982).

The premises, or propositions, in a scientific theory must lead logically to the conclusions. Scientific explanations show that the facts, or data, can be deduced from the general theory. Theories are tested by comparing what deduction says "should" hold if the theory is true, with the state of affairs in the world (observations). In turn, the purpose of a theory is to describe, explain, and predict observations.

The classic example of deductive logic is the familiar syllogism: "All men are mortal; Socrates is a man; therefore Socrates is mortal." Deductive conclusions include only the information included in the propositions. Thus, deductive reasoning can be logically correct but empirically incorrect. If the theory is based on empirically false premises, it will probably result in empirically false conclusions. A scientific test of the truth of the conclusions requires a comparison of the statements in the conclusion with actual states of affairs in the "real" world.

Scientific explanations and theories are usually quite complex, and thus they often require more information than can be included in a deductively valid argument. Sometimes it is necessary to know that a conclusion is probably true, or at least justified, even if it does not follow logically from a set of premises and arguments (Giere 1984). Thus the need for inductive logic, which is based on particular instances (facts or observations) and moves to general theories (laws).

Many sociologists and other scientists believe that scientific knowledge is produced mainly by induction (Glaser and Strauss 1967). For example, after observing many politicians, a theory might postulate that "most politicians are crooked." Although this theory is based on many observations, its proof, or verification, would require observing every politician, past, present, and future. To falsify the theory would require finding a substantial number of politicians who were not crooked. The absolute and final verification of scientific theories is not possible. However, it should be possible to "falsify" any given scientific theory by finding events, or classes of events, that do not support the theory (Stinchcombe 1987; Popper 1959).

Because inductive arguments are always subject to falsification, they are stated in terms of probabilities. Good inductive arguments are those that have a high probability associated with their being true. This high probability comes from a large number of similar observations over time and in different circumstances. For example, although it is not absolutely certain that if someone in North America becomes a medical doctor he or she will earn a high income, the evidence provided by observing doctors in many places and many times means that a high probability can be assigned to the assertion that medical doctors will earn high incomes.

Inductive arguments are not truth preserving. Even with true premises, an inductive argument can have a false conclusion because the conclusions of inductive arguments generally contain more information or make wider generalizations than the premises (Giere 1984). Science requires both deductive and inductive methods to progress. This progress is circular: Theories are developed and tested, new data gives rise to new theories, which are then in turn tested (Wallace 1971).

There are several steps involved in testing scientific theories. Theories must first be expressed in both abstract, verbal terms as well as in concrete, operationalized terms. Concepts and constructs are both rich, complex, abstract descriptions of the entity to be measured or studied. Concepts have nominal definitions (they are defined by other words) and are specifically developed for scientific purposes. A variable is operationally defined to allow the measurement of one specific aspect of a concept. Operationalization is a set of instructions for how the researcher is going to measure the concepts and test the theory. These instructions should allow events and individuals to be unambiguously classified and should be precise enough so that the same results will be achieved by any one who uses them (Blalock 1979).

For example, one theory posits that the relationship between "anxiety" and test performance is curvilinear. This theory predicts that very little anxiety leads to poor performance on tests (as measured by grades), a medium amount of anxiety increases test performance, and very high anxiety again causes poor test performance. If drawn on a graph this curve would be an upside down U. To test this theory, both anxiety and test performance must be measured as variables expressed in empirical terms. For an observation to be empirical means that it is, or hypothetically could be, experienced or observed in a way that can be measured in the same way by others in the same circumstances.

As a concept, anxiety encompasses many different things. The measurement theory must specify whether anxiety will be measured as feelings, such as being tense, worried, or "uptight," or as physical reactions, such as shortness of breath, heart palpitations, or sweaty palms. The researcher may decide to measure anxiety by asking subjects how worried or tense they felt prior to an exam. Racing hearts, sweating palms, and upset stomachs are still part of the concept, but they are excluded from the operationalization. The researcher must decide whether this is or is not a valid (measures what it purports to measure) and reliable (accurate) measure of anxiety, in part by comparing the results of the research to other research on anxiety and test performance. It is also necessary to strike a balance between the scope of the concept (different things it refers to) and precision. The wider the scope of a concept, the more it can be generalized to other conditions, and the fewer are required to construct a theory, making it more parsimonious. However, if the scope of a concept is too wide it loses precision and becomes meaningless.

Scientific explanation involves the accurate and precise measurement of phenomena. Measurement is the assignment of symbols, usually numbers, to the properties of objects or events (Stevens 1951). The need for precise measurement has led to an emphasis on quantification. Some sociologists feel that some qualities and events that humans beings experience defy quantification, arguing that numbers can never express the meaning that people's behavior holds for them.

However, mathematics is only a language, based on deductive logic, that expresses relationships symbolically. Assigning numbers to human experiences forces the researcher to be precise, even when the concepts, such as "anxiety" or "job satisfaction," are quite fuzzy.

Another important aspect of scientific explanations is that they attempt to be "objective." In science this term has two broad meanings. First, *objective* means that observers agree on what they have observed. For example, a group of scientists observing the behavior of objects when they are dropped would agree that they saw the objects "fall" to the ground. For this observation to be objective (1) there must be an agreed-upon method for producing it (dropping an object); (2) the observation must be replicable (more than one object is released and they all "fall"; and (3) the same results must occur regardless of who performs the operation and where they perform it (objects must behave the same way for all observers, anywhere in the world). Scientific operations must be expressed clearly enough that other people can repeat the procedures. Only when all these conditions are met is it possible to say that an observation is objective. This form of objectivity is called "intersubjectivity" and is crucial to scientific explanations.

The second use of the word *objective* in science means that scientific explanations are not based on the values, opinions, attitudes, or beliefs of the researcher. In other words, scientific explanations are "value-free." A researcher's values and interests may influence what kinds of things she or he chooses to study (i.e., why one person becomes a nuclear physicist and another person becomes a sociologist), but once the problem for study is chosen, the scientist's personal values and opinions do not influence the type of knowledge produced. The "value-free" nature of science is the goal of making scientific explanations free from the influence of any individual or group's particular biases and opinions.

The relationships in a theory state how abstract constructs are to be linked so that antecedent properties or conditions can be used to explain consequent ones. An antecedent condition may be seen as either necessary or sufficient to cause or produce a consequent condition. For example, higher social status may be seen as *sufficient* to increase the probability that farmers will adopt new farming techniques (innovation). It could also be argued that awareness and resources are *necessary* conditions for innovation. Without both, innovation is unlikely (Gartrell and Gartrell 1979).

Relationships may be asymmetric (the antecedent produces the effect) or symmetric (both cause each other). Frustration may cause aggression, and aggression may cause frustration. Relationships may be direct, or positive, (an increase in knowledge causes an increase in innovation), or negative (an increase in stress leads to a decrease in psychological well-being). They may be described as monotonic, linear, or curvilinear. Sociologists often assume relationships are linear, partly because this is the simplest form of the relationship.

Relationships between variables are expressed using a wide variety of mathematical theories, each of which have their own "language." Algebra and calculus use the concepts of "greater than," "less than," and "equal to." Set theory talks about things being "included in," and graph theory uses "connectedness" or "adjacency between." Markov chains attempt to identify a connectedness in time or a transition between states, and symbolic logic uses "union" and "intersection" to talk about relationships.

Scientific explanation is also very explicit about the units to which relationships between propositions refer. Sociologists refer to a host of collectivities (cultures, social systems, organizations, communities), relationships (world systems, families), and parts of collectivities (social positions, roles). There is strength in this diversity of subject matter but also potential weakness in failing explicitly to define the unit of analysis. Some properties cannot be attributed to all units of analysis. For example, "income" is a concept that can apply to an individual or a group (as "average" income), but "inequality" is always a property of an aggregate. The "ecological fallacy" (Hannan 1970) involves the incorrect attribution of properties of aggregates to individuals. Aggregation is not simple addition, and some of the relationships between subunits (homogeneity, complexity, inequality) have complicated aggregation algorithms. Care must be taken when switching units of reference from social collectivities to individuals. For example, it may be true that communities with high divorce rates also have high homicide rates, but this does not necessarily imply that divorced couples kill one another or are more likely to be homicide victims or perpetrators.

To test theories, the relationships among concepts are stated as hypotheses, linking variables in operationalized form. Since the existence of a relationship cannot be proven conclusively, the scientist instead tries to show that there is no relationship between the variables by testing hypotheses that are stated in "null" form. In the test performance and anxiety example, a null hypothesis would state that "there is no curvilinear relationship between the number of correct responses on tests and the reported level of worry and tension." If this hypothesis was rejected, that is, found to be highly unlikely, the researcher would have evidence to support the alternative hypothesis suggested by the theory—that there is a curvilinear relationship between the variables.

Social scientists use a variety of methods to study human behavior, including experiments, surveys, participant observation, and unobtrusive methods. In essence, experiments try to identify causal sequences by determining the effect of an independent variable (the stimulus) on a dependent variable. Experiments require stringent conditions that are often difficult to fulfill with human beings, sometimes for ethical reasons, but more often because there is a wide variation in individual responses to the same stimulus (Babbie 1989; Kerlinger 1973; Cook and Campbell 1979).

Social scientists have developed other research methods such as surveys and field research, which allow them to produce scientific knowledge without the need for experimental manipulation. Statistical analysis of survey data allows social scientists to examine complex problems in large populations by statistically controlling several variables representing competing explanations (Blalock 1964). The distinctive characteristic of survey research is that the subjects of the study tell the scientist about themselves.

Social scientists also use qualitative methods, such as participant observation, to conduct research in the "field" where the phenomena actually occur. Field research focuses on the empirical richness and complexity of the whole subject in order to understand what is subjectively meaningful. Participant observation proceeds inductively rather than deductively. The researcher observes and participates to understand (subjectively) and then attempts to externalize the observations by constructing categories of responses, or theory. In contrast to other research designs, participant observation deliberately does not attempt to control conditions; the researcher strives to obtain an unbiased picture of how the subjects see things in their natural setting (Whyte 1961). The emphasis is on the richness in subjects' understanding of events and on subjectivity rather than objectivity. Theory developed from this type of research is called grounded theory (Glaser and Strauss 1967). Unobtrusive methods, such as content analysis, focus on the study of artifacts (newspapers, homes), partly in order to overcome reactivity by subjects and biases on the part of the researcher.

CRITIQUES OF THE
HYPOTHETICO-DEDUCTIVE MODEL
OF SCIENCE

During the 1930s and 1940s, the dominant view of science was "radical positivism," which viewed science as a process based only on inductive generalizations and empirical verification. Abstract theoretical concepts that could not be observed were quite literally meaningless. The revision of positivism in the 1950s (logical empiricism) recognized the importance of abstract concepts and theories, but it continued to insist that all scientific statements be subject to empirical falsification. In short, the empiricists persisted in their belief that "facts" were purely objective entities and that what was viewed as a fact did not depend on theory or theoretical concepts. However, theories play as big a role in scientific change and knowledge production as do empirical observations. In part, this internal confusion laid the ground for a wide range of critiques of both positivism and empiricism (Alexander 1982; Bernstein 1976).

Reconstructed logic suggests that scientific knowledge can be accounted for by following formal rules of logic. The progress of knowledge is such that unscientific or prescientific explanations for phenomena are successively replaced by scientific explanations, which are ever closer approximations to the "truth." It stresses that the knowledge produced by the scientific method is objective and value-free, reflecting the "facts" of matters as they really are, not as seen by a particular group of people in a particular social and historical location.

However, the "facts" upon which scientific explanations are based are not independent of "point of view" (Polanyi 1958). All scientific data are theoretically informed. What is "fact" and what is "theory" are what is convenient to the focus of scientific attention at a particular time. Because science is a social and cultural activity, it is grounded in an everyday, taken-for-granted reality. Scientists can perceive "facts" only in a particular social and cultural context. Observations take place within a cultural milieu that literally affects what the observer perceives, not just how it is interpreted. The totally objective, theory-free observation aspired to in science is not possible; to "see" something is always to see it "as" something. For example, to observe the medical "facts" in an x-ray, a physician must first learn what parts of the picture to ignore. The "fact" that objects "fall" to the ground is a fact only in a social context where gravity is an accepted explanation for the behavior of falling objects. Scientific facts are constructed and developed, they do not have an independent, objective existence of their own (Fleck 1979).

Science can be seen as primarily a social activity, an interplay between empirical observations and broad theoretical "paradigms" (Kuhn 1970; Fleck 1979). Paradigms dictate the valid questions for research as well as the range of possible answers and can be so powerful that contradictory data (anomalies) are simply explained away under the assumption that they can be brought within the theory at a later time. Confronted by contradictory empirical evidence that cannot be ignored, adherents to a particular theory often develop ad hoc hypotheses and residual categories to account for anomalies. Thus, they encompass or explain observations that contradict their theories and cling to their theories in an often dogmatic fashion. The reconstructed logic of science leads us to believe that theories would be rejected under these conditions. Part of the problem is that the decision of whether certain experiments or observations are critical to the proof or falsification of a given theory is possible only after the fact, not before, and the possibility always exists that an experiment failed because it was not competently performed.

It is difficult to establish the criteria for determining whether an experiment has been successful. To know whether the experimental apparatus, the theory, and the competence of the researcher have combined to produce a successful experiment, it is necessary to know beforehand what the correct outcome is. However, the definition of a competently performed experiment is having a successful outcome, leading to the "experimenter's regress" (Collins 1985).

The replication of results is an essential criterion for the stability of scientific knowledge, but scientific inquiry requires a high degree of tacit or personal knowledge (Polanyi 1958). This knowledge is by its very nature invisible, but its importance is also strongly denied by a scientific community that bases its validity claims on the potential for replication. Scientific developments often cannot be replicated unless there is direct, personal contact between the original researcher and the people attempting to do the replication. Few replications are possible using published results and procedures, and successful replication often rests on the tacit knowledge of the original researcher, knowledge that is not easily transferable (Collins 1985). To complicate matters, science reserves its highest rewards for original research rather than replication. In consequence, there is little glory and less funding for replication, and the "replicability" requirement is reduced to demonstrating the possibility of replication.

The value-free nature of scientific knowledge has also been challenged by historians and sociologists of science. The reconstructed logic suggests that "the data" decide between competing scientific theories. However, sometimes a theory wins out over its competitors because its survival is in the best interests of a group or researcher (Woolgar 1981; Shapin 1979). For example, when high-energy particle physicists were searching for the subatomic particles now known as quarks, two competing explanations were advanced: the "charm" and "color" theories. Both models were consistent with the data. The ultimate success of the charm model occurred because more people had an interest in seeing it succeed. Charm theorists were more successful at relating their theory to an existing body of practice and interests. The color theory was never empirically refuted but eventually "died" because its proponents were reduced to talking to themselves (Pickering 1982).

Feminists have also added their voice to the critiques of science and the scientific method. The most successful feminist critiques of science are those identified as "feminist empiricist," which attempt to restructure "bad science" and provide a more objective, gender-free knowledge (Harding 1986). Feminists have pointed out some androcentric (male-centered) categories in science and have identified the patriarchal social organization of science as an institution. "Power" based on gender has become a permanent category of analysis in feminist approaches (Smith 1987; Connel 1983).

By differentiating between "good science" and "bad science," feminist empiricists strive to separate the wheat from the chaff by eradicating gender biases in the scientific process. The ultimate goal is to provide a more objective, value-free knowledge (Harding 1987). This perspective has had some success in the social sciences, perhaps because its revisions provide results that are intuitively appealing. By including categories that are often ignored, oppressed, and invisible to traditional sociology, feminist research gives a voice to what were previously "nonquestions"

under a strictly male-stream model of science (Vickers 1982). For example, feminist research suggests that many women do not make a "yes" or "no" decision about having children but instead leave it to luck or time to decide. This type of decision-making behavior has implications for fertility and deserves the same theoretical status as the "yes" and "no" categories. However, a male-stream model of science that assumed that fertility decisions were the outcome of a series of rational, cost-benefit analyses was blind to this conceptualization (Currie 1988).

The irony is that while feminist empiricist criticisms of "bad" science aspire to strengthen science, in fact they ultimately subvert the understandings of science they attempt to reinforce. "If the concepts of nature, of dispassionate, value-free, objective inquiry, and of transcendental knowledge are androcentric, white, bourgeois, and Western, then no amount of more rigorous adherence to scientific method will eliminate such bias, for the methods themselves reproduce the perspectives generated by these hierarchies and thus distort our understandings" (Harding 1987, p. 291).

Another critique of science comes from the hermeneutic, or interpretive, perspective, which takes issue with the positivist assumption that the concepts, categories, and methods used to describe the physical world are also applicable to human behavior. Human studies proponents insist that the universal categories and objective arguments required for prediction and explanation in the natural sciences cannot be achieved in the social sciences. The proper subject matter of the social sciences are the internal, or subjective, meanings of human behavior that guide human action. Because these meanings are nonempirical, subjective rather than objective, they cannot meet the requirements for scientific explanations. Therefore, the goal of the social sciences is to understand rather than predict and explain human behavior (Hughes 1961; Habermas 1971; Gadamer 1976). Validation of interpretations is one of the biggest problems with the hermeneutic position because no firm ground exists from which to judge the validity of different interpretations of meaning and behavior. Hermeneutic explanations are ultimately subjective and in their extreme form focus solely on the explanation of individual, unique events (Alexander 1982).

The value-free nature of scientific knowledge has also been challenged by critical theory, which suggests that scientific knowledge is knowledge that is one-sided and specifically oriented to the domination and control of nature. This "interest" in domination and control lies not in the application of scientific knowledge but is intrinsic to the knowledge itself. In contrast, communicative knowledge is knowledge that is oriented to reaching understanding and human emancipation (Habermas 1971).

CONCLUSION

Although scientific explanation has been the subject of many critiques, it is still the most methodical, reliable form of knowledge we have. It is somewhat ironic that while the natural sciences are becoming less positivistic and beginning to recognize nonempirical, subjective, and cultural influences on scientific knowledge, the social sciences continue to emphasize the refinement of methodology and measurement, trying to become more positivistic (Alexander 1982). The result is that within sociology, theoretical inquiry is increasingly divorced from empirical research. Paradoxically, this schism may be a source of strength if the two sides can learn to communicate. Sociology may be in a unique position to integrate critiques of the scientific model with ongoing empirical research, perhaps producing a hybrid that is neither relativistic nor positivistic.

(SEE ALSO: *Causal Inference Models; Epistemology; Experiments; Measurement; Metatheory; Positivism; Quasi-Experimental Research Designs; Reliability; Validity; Statistical Inference*)

REFERENCES

Alexander, Jeffrey C. 1982 *Positivism, Presuppositions, and Current Controversies.* Berkeley: University of California Press.

Babbie, Earl 1989 *The Practice of Social Research,* 5th ed. Belmont, Calif.: Wadsworth.

Bernstein, Richard J. 1976 *The Restructuring of Political and Social Theory.* Philadelphia: University of Pennsylvania Press.

Blalock, Hubert M. 1964 *Causal Inferences in Non-Experimental Research.* Chapel Hill: University of North Carolina Press.

———1979 *Social Statistics,* rev. 2nd ed. New York: McGraw-Hill.

Braithwaite, Richard Bevan 1968 *Scientific Explanation.* London: Cambridge University Press.

Chalmers, A. F. 1982 *What Is This Thing Called Science?* Milton Keynes, England: Open University Press.

Cohen, M., and E. Nagel 1934 *An Introduction to Logic and Scientific Method.* New York: Harcourt.

Collins, H. M. 1985 *Changing Order. Replication and Induction in Scientific Practice.* Beverly Hills, Calif.: Sage Publications.

Connell, R. W. 1983 *Which Way Is Up?* Boston: Allen and Unwin.

Cook, Thomas D., and Donald T. Campbell 1979 *Quasi-Experimentation: Design and Analysis Issues for Field Settings.* Chicago: Rand McNally.

Currie, Dawn 1988 "Re-Thinking What We Do and How We Do It: A Study of Reproductive Decisions." *Canadian Review of Sociology and Anthropology* 25:231–253.

Fleck, Ludwik 1979 *Genesis and Development of a Scientific Fact.* Chicago: University of Chicago Press. (Originally published in German in 1935.)

Gadamer, Hans-Georg 1976 *Philosophical Hermeneutics.* Berkeley: University of California Press.

Gartrell, John W., and C. David Gartrell 1979 "Status, Knowledge, and Innovation: Risk and Uncertainty in Agrarian India." *Rural Sociology* 44:73–94.

Giere, Ronald N. 1984 *Understanding Scientific Reasoning,* 2nd ed. New York: Holt, Rinehart and Winston.

Glaser, Barney G., and Anselm L. Strauss 1967 *The Discovery of Grounded Theory.* Chicago: Aldine.

Habermas, Jurgen 1971 *Knowledge and Human Interests.* Boston: Beacon Press.

———1984 *The Theory of Communicative Action.* Boston: Beacon Press.

Hannan, Michael T. 1970 *Problems of Aggregation and Disaggregation in Sociological Research.* Chapel Hill: University of North Carolina Press.

Harding, Sandra 1986 *The Science Question in Feminism.* Ithaca, N.Y.: Cornell University Press.

———1987 "The Instability of the Analytical Categories of Feminist Theory." In Sandra Harding and

Jean F. O'Barr, eds., *Sex and Scientific Inquiry.* Chicago: University of Chicago Press.

Hughes, Stuart 1961 *Consciousness and Society.* New York: Vintage.

Kaplan, Abraham 1964 *The Conduct of Inquiry: Methodology for Behavioral Science.* San Francisco: Chandler.

Keat, R., and J. Urry 1982 *Social Theory as Science.* London: Routledge and Kegan Paul.

Kerlinger, Fred N. 1973 *Foundations of Behavioral Research,* 2nd ed. New York: Holt, Rinehart and Winston.

———1979 *Behavioral Research: A Conceptual Approach.* New York: Holt, Rinehart and Winston.

Kuhn, Thomas 1970 *The Structure of Scientific Revolutions,* 2nd ed. Chicago: University of Chicago Press.

Nagel, Ernest 1961 *The Structure of Science: Problems in the Logic of Scientific Explanation.* New York: Harcourt, Brace and World.

Pfeffer, Jeffrey 1985 "Organizations and Organization Theory." In G. Linzey and F. Aronson, eds., *The Handbook of Social Psychology,* 3rd ed. Reading, Mass.: Addison-Wesley.

Pickering, Andrew 1982 "Interests and Analogies." In B. Barnes and D. Edge, eds., *Science in Context.* Milton Keynes, England: Open University Press.

Polanyi, Michael 1958 *Personal Knowledge.* Chicago: University of Chicago Press.

Popper, Karl R. 1959 *The Logic of Scientific Discovery.* London: Hutchinson.

Shapin, Steven 1979 "The Politics of Observation: Cerebral Anatomy and Social Interests in the Edinburgh Phrenology Disputes." In Roy Wallis, ed., *On the Margins of Science: The Social Construction of Rejected Knowledge.* Monograph 27, *1979 Sociological Review.*

Smith, Dorothy 1987 *The Everyday World as Problematic.* Boston: Northeastern University Press.

Stevens, S. S. 1951 "Mathematics, Measurement, and Psychophysics." In S. S. Stevens, ed., *Handbook of Experimental Psychology.* New York: Wiley.

Stinchcombe, Arthur L. 1987 *Constructing Social Theories.* Chicago: University of Chicago Press.

Vickers, Jill 1982 "Memoirs of an Ontological Exile: The Methodological Rebellions of Feminist Research." In Angela Miles and Geraldine Finn, eds., *Feminism in Canada: From Pressure to Politics.* Montreal: Black Rose.

Wallace, Walter L. 1971 *The Logic of Science in Sociology.* Chicago: Aldine.

Whyte, William Foote 1961 *Street Corner Society: The Social Structure of an Italian Slum,* 2nd ed. Chicago: University of Chicago Press.

Woolgar, Steve 1981 "Interests and Explanation in the Social Study of Science." *Social Studies of Science* 11:365–394.

LINDA DERKSEN
JOHN GARTRELL

SCIENTIFIC METHOD   *See* Epistemology; Positivism; Scientific Explanation.

SECONDARY DATA ANALYSIS AND DATA ARCHIVES

The creation and explosive growth of publicly accessible data archives (or data banks) have revolutionized the way sociologists conduct research. These resources have made possible a variety of secondary analyses, often utilizing the data in ways never anticipated by their creators. Traditionally, secondary data analysis implies the use of an available data resource by researchers to study a problem different from the focus of the original analysis. For example, a researcher might have conducted a survey of workers' reactions to technological change and analyzed those data to evaluate whether workers welcomed or resisted such change in the workplace. As a matter of secondary interest, she collects data on workers' perceptions of the internal labor-market structures of their firms. She then lends these data to a colleague who studies the determinants of (workers' perceptions of) job-ladder length and complexity in order to understand their views on prospects for upward mobility in their places of employment. This latter investigation is the secondary analysis.

More recently, however, the definition of secondary analysis has expanded as more data sets are explicitly constructed with multiple purposes and multiple users in mind. The creators, or principal investigators, exercise control over data set content but are responsive to a variety of constituencies likely to use the resource. The creators may undertake analyses of the data, addressing questions of intellectual interest to themselves while simultaneously releasing the data to the public or depositing the data resource in a data archive. Data archives are depositories where data produced by a number of investigators are available to members for secondary analyses. The data bank generally takes responsibility for providing documentation on the data sets and other information necessary to their use. Data archives can also refer more generally to any source of data already produced that an investigator may uncover in the course of an investigation, such as government or business records housed in libraries. For example, the U.S. government archives thousands of government documents yearly in libraries around the world. The data in these documents cover a wide variety of topics and are often of use in sociological investigations. It remains the responsibility of the analyst to configure those data in a way useful to his or her investigation.

This entry will illustrate these expanded opportunities by describing one key data archive and by indicating the extent and breadth of data resources that this and other archives include. It will then describe the nature of conducting secondary analyses from resources such as these.

DATA ARCHIVES

One of the most important data archives for social scientists is the Interuniversity Consortium for Political and Social Research (ICPSR) located at the University of Michigan, Ann Arbor. It publishes an annual *Guide to Resources and Services* (much of this description of ICPSR was taken from the 1990–1991 volume). The consortium was founded in 1962 as a partnership between the Survey Research Center at the University of Michigan and twenty-one universities in the United States. In 1990 their holdings included over 2,000 titles, some of them capturing several panels of data on the same respondents or several waves of data tapping comparable information. These titles are available to researchers at member institutions. The consortium charges fees on a sliding scale to academic institutions for membership privileges; researchers whose institutions are not

members of ICPSR can still obtain data for a fee. In 1990, over 340 institutions in the United States, Canada, and fourteen countries throughout the world were ICPSR members. While ICPSR originated as a service to political analysts, it currently serves a broad spectrum of the social sciences including economics, sociology, geography, psychology, and history as well, and its data resources have also been used by those in education, social work, foreign policy, criminal justice, and urban affairs.

Although ICPSR provides training in research and statistical methods, and provides members with help in effective use of computing resources, its central function is the archiving, processing, and distribution of machine-readable data of interest to social scientists. Although attitudes tapping elements of the U.S. political process are well represented in the holdings, data are available on consumer attitudes, educational processes and attainment, health-care utilization, social indicators tapping the quality of American life, employment conditions, workers' views on technology, and criminal behavior. The data come from over 130 countries, include both contemporary and historical censuses, and are not confined to the individual level but rather also tap characteristics of nations and organizational attributes. ICPSR actively seeks out quality data sets, and they use their user fees to finance additional data acquisition. They also encourage investigators to deposit their data holdings in the archives to make them available to researchers for secondary analyses. Researchers whose data production efforts are funded by federal agencies such as the National Science Foundation now are required to make their data publicly available after their grants have expired, and ICPSR is a logical depository for many such data sets produced in the social sciences.

ICPSR maintains over fifty serial data holdings, including the National Longitudinal Surveys of Labor Market Experience (or NLS, discussed below), the Survey of Income and Program Participation, the General Social Surveys, National Crime Surveys, the Panel Study of Income Dynamics, the Detroit Area Studies, the U.S. Census of Population and Housing, and the American National Elections Studies. These serial holdings include longitudinal surveys (meaning the same respondents are interviewed repeatedly over time), such as the NLS and the Panel Study of Income Dynamics. These resources are particularly useful for determining the impact of earlier life events on later life outcomes, since the causal orders of all events measured on the data sets are clearly indicated. The holdings also include sets of cross-sectional studies conducted at regular intervals, for example, the Detroit Area Studies and the General Social Surveys (GSS). These studies contain different cross sections from the same populations over time and are useful in charting trends in attitudes of the respective populations over time, assuming that the same questions are repeated. Sources such as the GSS that do ask the same questions over several years allow the researcher to pool samples across those years to obtain larger numbers of cases useful in multivariate analyses.

To illustrate one data set contained in the ICPSR archives, consider the National Longitudinal Surveys of Labor Market Experience. These surveys are produced by the Center for Human Resource Research (CHRR) at Ohio State University. The CHRR produces a yearly *NLS Handbook,* and much of the following information regarding the NLS was taken from the 1990 *NLS Handbook.* These surveys began in 1966 with a study of older men ages forty-five to fifty-nine and a survey of young men ages fourteen to twenty-four, continued in 1967 with a survey of mature women ages thirty to forty-four, and followed up with a survey of young women ages fourteen to twenty-four in 1968. In 1979, CHRR began a new survey of youth ages fourteen to twenty-one, known as the NLSY. The five major surveys contain a wealth of data on labor-force experience (e.g., labor-force and employment status, work history, earnings) as well as investments in education and training, marital status, household composition and fertility, background material on respondents' parents, work-related attitudes, health, alcohol and drug use, and region of residence.

Each of these cohorts has been followed at varying intervals since the surveys' inceptions. For example, the young men have been surveyed every year, as have the youth, while the older men were surveyed every year until 1983, and they (or their widows) were resurveyed in 1990. In 1986 and 1988 the NLS added a survey of the children of the NLSY cohort's women; this survey tapped the social, cognitive, and physiological development of these children and, given the longitudinal nature of the data on the mothers, allows explanation of these child outcomes in terms of maternal background and current maternal characteristics. In 1990 the children of the NLSY women were surveyed again; this accumulated longitudinal data base on child outcomes will allow important inferences regarding the process of child development, with numbers of children surveyed far exceeding most other available sources. This additional resource expands the NLSY's usefulness to other disciplines, including psychology and to other researchers interested in child development.

The NLS data sets are produced with the cooperation of CHRR, NORC (formerly the National Opinion Research Center) at the University of Chicago, and the U.S. Bureau of the Census. For example, for the NLSY, the CHRR takes responsibility for questionnaire construction, documentation, and data dissemination, while NORC has handled sample design, fieldwork, and data reduction. The Census Bureau has handled sample] design, fieldwork, and data reduction for the four original cohorts. All data are available on magnetic tape from the CHRR (as well as from ICPSR, as noted above); in addition, the NLSY data from 1979 to 1988 are available on CD-ROM.

Social scientists from several disciplines, including sociology, economics, and industrial relations, have found the NLS to be a critical resource for the study of earnings and income attainment, human capital investments, job search, fertility, race and sex discrimination, and the determinants of labor supply. Inferences from these studies have been useful to theory as well as to policy formation. Other topics that the data resource can usefully inform include family structure and processes, child outcomes, and aging processes. The CHRR estimates that by 1990 over 2,500 articles, books, working papers, and dissertations had been produced using the NLS data. The 1990 *NLS Handbook* provides a wealth of detail regarding the designs of the respective surveys, survey procedures, variables, and tape/CD availability. It also describes the extensive documentation available on the NLS data sets and lists publications resulting from the data sets. This resource would be indispensable for any researcher considering a secondary analysis using NLS data. The CHRR at Ohio State University disseminates the data and provides documentation and assistance to users who have questions about using the data sets; some of these functions are also provided by ICPSR.

Because of the increased resources devoted to survey research in sociology and related social sciences, the ICPSR holdings containing surveys of individuals have grown rapidly. However, ICPSR also archives data produced at varying levels of aggregation, thus facilitating secondary analyses where the theoretically appropriate units of analysis are countries or organizations. For example, ICPSR archives the World Tables of Economic and Social Indicators, 1950–1987; these data were provided by the World Bank. These data contain economic and social indicators from 136 countries, where the indicators include such measures as gross national product, value of imports and exports, gross national savings, value added across major industrial categories, net direct foreign investment, public long-term debt, international reserves excluding gold, and gold holdings at London market price. Demographic and social variables include population, total fertility rate, crude birthrate, percent of the labor force in agriculture, percent of the labor force that is female, and primary and secondary school enrollment rates. An older data set, also from the World Bank, contains similar measures from 1950 to 1981 as well as some additional indicators not included in the data set covering the 1950–1987 period. Because these are also longitudinal data sets, there is the potential for pooling across time variation in these measures across the 136 coun-

tries so that cross-sectional and longitudinal variation can be studied simultaneously.

ICPSR also maintains a small number of holdings useful to studying organizational processes. For example, a 1972 study of industrial location decisions, obtained from the Economic Behavior Program, Survey Research Center at the University of Michigan, surveyed 173 industrial plants in Detroit, Chicago, and Atlanta. Interviewees were organizational informants such as president, vice president, general manager, or public relations director. Items included reasons for the location of the plant as well as the advantages and disadvantages for the location; other constructs measured included duration of plant operations, levels of sales and production, production problems, and plans for future expansion.

Recent arguments, however, have suggested that although sociology has invested considerably in surveys of individuals, it has insufficiently invested in surveys of organizations (Freeman 1986). The National Science Foundation has sponsored conferences to grapple with theoretical and design issues relevant to producing a data base on a national sample of organizations. They have also funded a number of pilot projects to investigate alternative methods of sampling organizations for such a data base (Parcel, Kaufman, and Jolly 1991) and to study the problems of measuring common constructs within the context of a survey studying diverse organizations. One possibility would be to produce a longitudinal organizational data base, the explicit purpose of which would be to provide increased opportunities for secondary data analyses of organizations analogous to those described above at the individual level. Clearly, our capacity to conduct secondary analyses at the organizational level is in its infancy relative to the potential for such studies of individual level processes and phenomena.

Finally, ICPSR also archives a variety of data sets that make possible historical analyses of social, economic, and political processes. For example, they archive the Annual Time Series Statistics for the United States, 1929–1968, which includes 280 variables for most of the period, although only 127 variables between 1947 and 1968. Available data include population characteristics, measures of political characteristics of the U.S. Congress, business and consumer expenditures, and expenditures by various federal government departments. They also archive Political Systems Performance Data for France, Sweden, and the United States, 1950–1965, in which central constructs measured include size of public debt, GNP, energy consumption, income tax rates, birth and death rates, labor force and unemployment, voting behavior, urbanization, and agricultural growth. Each of these historical data sources makes possible time series analyses of the macrolevel phenomena they measure.

Additional major archives include the Roper Center for Public Opinion Research at the University of Connecticut and the Lewis Harris Data Center at the University of North Carolina at Chapel Hill (see Kiecolt and Nathan 1985 for additional information regarding major archives). Stewart (1984) outlines the extensive holdings in U.S. Government Document Depositories, especially the products of the Bureau of the Census. Other important archives include several in Europe with which ICPSR maintains relationships, for example, the Norwegian Social Science Data Services, the Australian Social Science Data Archives, and the Zentralarchiv für empirische Sozialforschung (ZA), Universität zu Köln. There is the potential for member institutions to obtain from ICPSR data contained in those local archives as well. The International Social Survey Program (ISSP) has worked toward coordinating survey research internationally by deciding to ask common questions cross-nationally in given years, thus facilitating cross-cultural analyses of social phenomena (*GSS News* September 1990). For example, in 1990 social surveys in Austria, West Germany, Great Britain, Hungary, Ireland, Israel, Italy, the Netherlands, and Norway all included questions on work, including consequences of unemployment, union activities, working conditions, and preferred job characteristics. A comparable module in 1987 focused on social inequality in Australia, Austria, West Germany, Great Britain, Hungary, Italy, and the United States. Data from the ISSP are available from ICPSR.

THE NATURE OF SECONDARY DATA ANALYSIS

The key advantage of secondary data analysis also contains the seeds of its key disadvantage: The researcher gains access to a wealth of information, usually far in excess of what he or she could have produced with individual resources, but in exchange must accept the myriad of operational decisions that the investigator(s) producing the data have made. On the positive side, the researcher frequently is able to take advantage of a national sample of respondents, or data produced on national populations, when individual resources might only have supported local primary data production. The numbers of cases available in secondary resources often far outstrip the sample sizes that individual investigators could have afforded to produce; these large sample sizes enhance the precision of parameter estimates and render possible forms of multivariate analyses that smaller sample sizes preclude. The secondary analyst can also take full advantage of the significant expertise concentrated in the large survey organizations that produce data sets available for secondary analysis. This collective expertise may exceed that of any single investigator. Despite these advantages, the researcher must carefully match the requirements of the research project to the characteristics of the data set. When the match is close, use of secondary data will enhance the research effort by making use of existing resources and by taking advantage of the time, money, and expertise of others devoted to data production. If the match is poor, the research project will fail since the data will be inadequate to address the questions posed.

Because many secondary analyses are conducted on survey data, effective use of secondary survey sources will frequently depend on knowledge of sample design, question wording, questionnaire construction, and measurement. Ideally, the researcher should conceptualize precisely what he or she wishes to do with the data in analysis, since analytic requirements must be met by existing data. If the research questions posed are longitudinal in nature, the researcher must be sure that the respective survey questions are measured at time points that mirror the researcher's assumptions of causal order.

The researcher must also be certain that the survey samples all respondents relevant to the problem. For example, analyses of racial differences in socioeconomic outcomes must use data sets where racial minorities are oversampled to ensure adequate numbers of cases for analyses. The researcher must also be certain that the data set contains sufficient cases for the analysis she intends to perform. Kiecolt and Nathan (1985) stress the challenges for trend or cross-cultural studies due to changes in sampling procedures over time. For example, suppose a researcher wants to ascertain whether more people support a voucher system for public education in 1990 as compared with 1980. It may be that changes in the sampling frame over the decade will introduce variations into survey responses that would not otherwise exist. These variations can be in either direction, and hypotheses regarding their direction are a function of the nature of sample changes. For example, Gallup surveys have increased their coverage of noninstitutionalized civilian adult populations over time, with the result that there is an artifactual decrease in the levels of education they report (Kiecolt and Nathan 1985, pp. 62–63), since the later surveys progressively included groups with lower levels of schooling. Sampling changes can also occur over time because of changes in geographic boundaries. Cities change boundaries owing to annexation of areas, and new Metropolitan Statistical Areas or MSAs (formerly Standard Metropolitan Statistical Areas or SMSAs) are created over time as increased numbers of counties meet the population and economic criteria for defining MSAs.

The most common problem in conducting secondary analyses, however, is likely in the questionnaire coverage of items needed to construct appropriate measures. It is likely that the original survey was constructed with one purpose in mind, and asked adequate numbers and forms of questions regarding the constructs central to that problem but gave only cursory attention to other items. The secondary researcher must carefully evaluate whether the questions included that tap his or her area of central interest are adequate for measurement and for analytic tasks. The biggest fear of the secondary researcher is that some variables needed for proper model specification are omitted. Omitted variables pose potentially severe problems of misspecification in estimating the parameters of variables that *are* included in the models. In these cases, the researcher must decide whether an adequate proxy (or substitute) variable exists on the data set, whether the research problem can be reformulated in such a way that omission of that construct is less critical, or whether the initially chosen data set is unsuitable and another must be sought. Researchers can also purchase time on major social surveys, such as the General Social Survey (GSS) administered by NORC. For example, plans for the 1991 GSS topical module called for questions on job activities, job evaluations, and labor–management relations to be included (*GSS News* September 1990). This strategy enables those researchers with financial resources to be certain that questions needed to investigate the issues of interest to them will be included in a national survey. This strategy mixes primary data production with secondary analysis of a multipurpose data set. The entire data resource then becomes available to other secondary analysts.

Other challenges for secondary analysts occur as a function of the particular form of secondary analysis used. For example, Kiecolt and Nathan (1985) note that survey researchers producing the series of cross sections of data useful in studying trends may "improve" the wording of questions over time. Again, considering the problem of voucher systems in public education, the researcher may observe increased percentages of survey respondents favoring this option over the period covered by the surveys but still may have difficulty in eliminating the possibility that question wording in the later survey(s) may be encouraging a more positive response. Such changes can also occur if the wording of the question remains the same over time but the nature of the response categories changes. Secondary analysts who conduct cross-cultural comparisons must be sensitive to the fact that the "same" question can mean different things in different cultures, thus interfering with the ability to compare the same social phenomenon cross-culturally.

Dale, Arber, and Proctor (1988) note that in-depth studies of specific populations may be most realistic with national samples that provide sufficient cases for analyses of the subgroups while still allowing the researcher to place those data within a broader empirical context. It is also possible that surveys produced by different survey organizations may produce different results, even when question wording, response categories, and sampling procedures remain the same (Kiecolt and Nathan 1985, p. 67). The secondary analyst must also be certain that the survey organization or individual responsible for producing the data set has exercised appropriate care in constructing the data resource. As noted above, detailed familiarity with the documentation describing the data set production procedures is essential, as is a codebook indicating frequencies on categorical variables, appropriate ranges for continuous variables, and codes for missing data.

In reality, there is often an interactive nature to the process of conducting a secondary data analysis. While the researcher's theoretical interests may be reasonably well formulated when she identifies a useful data set, it is likely that the variables present in the data resource will suggest additional empirical opportunities of theoretical interest that she had not previously devised. It is also likely that familiarity with data resources can facilitate formulation of empirical investigations that might otherwise not be initiated. Once a researcher has familiarity with the features of a particular secondary source, accessing additional variables for analysis of a related problem may require less investment than accessing a new data resource. However, there is general agreement that data availability should never dictate the nature of the research question. Although it is legitimate for a researcher to use his or her awareness of data resources to recognize that analyses of problems of long-standing interest are now empirically tractable, "data dredging" has a

deservedly negative connotation and will not result in the advancement of social science. Hyman's (1972) classic treatment of secondary analyses of survey data richly chronicles the experiences of a number of sociologists as they interactively considered the matching of theoretical interests and data availability in formulating and conducting secondary analyses. He also describes a number of ways in which secondary analysts can configure existing data to test hypotheses.

Within the respective multipurpose data sets, research traditions often arise from the sometimes unique suitability of certain resources for addressing given problems. For example, the NLSY with Mother and Child Supplements is virtually unique in its combination of a large sample size, longitudinal data on maternal familial and work histories, observed child outcomes, and oversamplings of racial minorities. Problems tracing the impact of maternal events on child outcomes are addressable with this data resource in a way that they would not be with other resources. Investigators having an interest in these issues will use the data and exchange information regarding strategies for measuring constructs and data analysis, and they will exchange findings. Over time, bodies of findings emerge from common data sources where the findings are contributed by a number of secondary investigators, although the particular problems, theoretical frameworks, and empirical strategies represented in each may differ markedly. As suggested above, multipurpose data sets frequently allow secondary analyses by researchers from several disciplines. Products from these investigations bear the stamps of their respective disciplines.

Another model for conducting secondary research is suggested by those researchers who use census data produced by the U.S. Department of Commerce. Census holdings cover not only information on the general U.S. population but also businesses, housing units, governments, and agricultural enterprises. Researchers using these sources either singly or in combination must be familiar with the questionnaires used to produce the data and with relevant features of sample coverage. While some census data are available on machine-readable tape, other data exist only in printed form. In these cases, the researcher must configure the needed data into a form suitable for analyses—in many cases a rectangular file where cases form row entries and variables form vertical entries. Data produced on cities from the County and City Data Books, for example, allow a variety of analyses tapping the relationships among urban social and economic characteristics. In these analyses, the unit of analysis is likely an aggregate unit such as the county or cities, thus illustrating the applicability of secondary analysis to problems conceptualized at a level of aggregation higher than that of the individual.

Another advantage of secondary analyses is the potential for those most interested in a particular set of findings to replicate them using the same data and to introduce additional variables or alternative operationalizations as a method for evaluating the robustness of the first secondary investigator's findings. A well-known example is Beck, Horan, and Tolbert's (1978) investigation of differences in earnings attainment processes by economic sector. Hauser's (1980) reanalysis of those data suggested that most of the sectoral earnings differences reported in the original study were a function of coding decisions for low-earnings respondents, since the differences disappeared when low earnings was coded slightly differently. It is interesting to note that despite this criticism, the impact of the original investigation has been enormous, with many additional investigators exploring the structure and implications of economic sectors. The point, of course, is that such debate is more likely when researchers have access to common data sets, although gracious investigators often lend their data resources to interested critics. Hauser (1980) acknowledges that Beck, Horan, and Tolbert shared their original data, even though he could have obtained the original data set from ICPSR.

Secondary data sets can be augmented with additional data to enrich the data resource and allow derivation of additional theoretical and empirical insights. Contextual analysis, or the investi-

gation of whether social context influences social outcomes, is a key example. Parcel and Mueller (1983) use the 1975 and 1976 panels from the Michigan Panel Study of Income Dynamics (PSID) to study race and sex differences in earnings attainment. In order to evaluate the impact of occupational, industrial, and local labor-market conditions on workers' earnings, they augmented the PSID data with archival data from U.S. Census and Dictionary of Occupational Titles sources based on the occupations, industries, and local markets of respective PSID respondents. Illustrative contextual indicators included occupational complexity, industrial profitability, and local-market manufacturing-sector productivity. Analyses then suggested how these contextual, as well as individual level, indicators affected workers' earnings differently depending on ascriptive statuses.

It is probably true that the potential for many sociologists to use secondary analysis to conduct studies of theoretical and practical importance has contributed to a change in productivity standards in sociology, particularly in certain subfields. The fact that certain issues can be addressed using existing data can result in enormous savings in time, relative to what would be required if primary data had to be produced. Research-oriented departments either implicitly or explicitly take this into account in assigning rewards such as salaries, tenure, and promotion. Potential for secondary analyses thus may create pressures toward increased scientific productivity; whether these pressures work generally for the good of social science or against it may be a matter of some debate.

It is undeniably true that progress in addressing some of the most important problems in social science has been greatly facilitated by the existence of multipurpose data sets and secondary resources generally. It is also true that the resources needed to produce and disseminate these data are considerable and that the existence and continuation of these resources are vulnerable to changes in political climate and priorities when these priorities influence resource allocation. It is critical that such resource allocation decisions, particularly those made at the level of the federal government, recognize the important role that secondary resources have played in furthering both basic social science and applications informing social policy.

(SEE ALSO: *Census; Social Indicators; Survey Research*)

REFERENCES

Beck, E. M., Patrick Horan, and Charles W. Tolbert II 1978 "Stratification in a Dual Economy: A Sectoral Model of Earnings Determination." *American Sociological Review* 43:704–720.

Dale, Angela, Sara Arber, and Michael Proctor 1988 *Doing Secondary Analysis.* London: Unwin Hyman.

Freeman, John 1986 "Data Quality and the Development of Organizational Social Science: An Editorial Essay." *Administrative Science Quarterly* 31:298–303.

GSS News September 1990 Chicago: NORC.

Guide to Resources and Services, 1990–1991. Ann Arbor, Mich.: Interuniversity Consortium for Political and Social Research, the University of Michigan.

Hauser, Robert 1980 "Comment on 'Stratification in a Dual Economy.'" *American Sociological Review* 45:702–712.

Hyman, Herbert H. 1972 *Secondary Analysis of Sample Surveys: Principles, Procedures, and Potentialities.* New York: Wiley.

Kiecolt, K. Jill, and Laura E. Nathan 1985 *Secondary Analysis of Survey Data.* Sage University Paper Series on Quantitative Applications in the Social Sciences, series no. 07-053. Beverly Hills, Calif.: Sage Publications.

NLS Handbook 1990 Columbus, Ohio: Center for Human Resource Research, Ohio State University.

Parcel, Toby L., and Charles W. Mueller 1983 *Ascription and Labor Markets: Race and Sex Differences in Earnings.* New York: Academic Press.

———, Robert L. Kaufman, and Leeann Jolly 1991 "Going Up the Ladder: Multiplicity Sampling to Create Linked Macro–Micro Organizational Samples." *Sociological Methodology* 21:43–80.

Stewart, David W. 1984 *Secondary Research: Information Sources and Methods.* Beverly Hills, Calif.: Sage Publications.

U.S. Department of Commerce [various years] *County and City Data Book.* Washington, D.C.: U.S. Government Printing Office.

TOBY L. PARCEL

SECULARIZATION *See* Convergence Theories.

SEGREGATION AND DESEGREGATION In the early years of the American colonies and the new republic of the United States, segregation was not only impractical but undesirable. To benefit from slavery, slave masters had to manage and control slaves. They therefore had to work with them. Not all slaves were field hands or agricultural workers; some were domestic servants, which meant that the slave master and mistress had to share their private quarters with slaves. Thus, many white Americans, especially Southerners in the pre–Civil War South, accepted daily, intimate, personal, primary face-to-face contact with slaves as a necessity. They insisted, however, that all such contacts reflect proper social distance: Slaves were always to be subservient; behavioral assimilation was allowed only to a point; slaves were supposed to know dominant-group culture, use it when and where appropriate, yet always recognize that they were not the equals of their masters. Although structural assimilation was occurring at a primary level, it was not among equals.

With the Emancipation Proclamation of 1863 and the ratification of the Thirteenth Amendment in 1865, some Americans seriously considered the idea of separating blacks and whites. As some blacks emigrated to poor urban areas in the South, and as their numbers increased, some whites recognized that blacks were becoming a threat to the hard-won victories of higher priced white labor (Bonacich 1972). They recognized that the former mechanisms of deference and social distance would no longer allow whites to maintain the subordination of black men and women. And so they insisted on a system of separation. It was not enough to separate residentially; it was necessary to establish a caste system that would deny blacks access to most jobs, social and governmental services, schools and colleges, public accommodations, and the right to vote.

In both the South and the North, segregation was practiced long before it became embodied in law. It was a Supreme Court decision, however, that in 1896 established segregation as the law of the land. It was through the medium of statutes, therefore, that domination was ultimately exercised. In other words, it was the polity, not the economy, that suppressed the competition of black urban laborers and that established this shift from paternalistic to competitive race relations (Scott 1977; van den Berghe 1967).

Segregationist laws were passed as early as 1875 in Tennessee; they rapidly advanced throughout the South and by the 1880s blacks were separated on all modes of transportation (Franklin 1947). Very soon, however, the Civil Rights Act of 1875, which guaranteed black Americans all the privileges and rights of citizenship, became an impediment to the policy of segregation. But the impediment was removed in 1883 when the Supreme Court declared the Civil Rights Act of 1875 unconstitutional. Soon after the High Court's decision, black Americans were banned in certain Southern venues, from hotels and other places of public accommodation—restaurants, theaters, and places of public amusement. As the process continued, by 1885 most Southern states had enacted laws requiring separate schools for blacks and for whites. Finally, on May 18, 1896, the Supreme Court in its infamous *Plessy* v. *Ferguson* decision made segregation the law of the land (Kromkowski 1991). Both the North and the South were elated, but the implication of the decision and the way it was to be implemented would be considerably different in these two regions. As a result, the consequences and effects of segregation in the South would be different from those in the North.

If segregation had not legitimated the rights of Southern whites to degrade and control blacks, blacks might have seen opportunities for independent growth in segregation. Segregation in the South meant biracialism, and biracialism meant the creation of black institutions, institutions that were to some extent administered and controlled by blacks. Although most blacks in the South worked for whites, they did not have to depend on them for all their basic services. They had separate schools, hospitals, and churches. Most blacks in the South became sharecroppers, working rented land. The land meant debt to the sharecropper on one hand, but it also meant a certain amount of daily independence, on the other. It is conceivable, therefore, that under a more positive set of circumstances blacks could have focused on the "equal requirement" of the *Plessy* "separate but equal" decision. But because segregation became the detested symbol of injustice, Southern blacks insisted on destroying it.

As blacks struggled against segregation they were beaten and murdered. Law enforcement participated in these affronts either by refusing to protect black people or by becoming the perpetrators of violence. Such actions reinforced the view in the minds of Southern blacks that segregation was the symbol of black inferiority. As blacks struggled to defend themselves they learned that sheriffs and law enforcement officials, mayors, governors, the FBI, the federal government, the Attorney General of the United States, and even the president participated in one way or another in the maintenance of a system of segregation that declared black people inferior.

Although Southern blacks were eventually successful in destroying the system of segregation in the South, blacks in the North, where the *Plessy* decision had been implemented differently, often failed. Because the major problem in the North was not segregation, the strategies of Southern blacks were inappropriate for the problems of Northern blacks and those who moved north. Desegregationist strategies were designed for problems like residential segregation but not for problems like poverty and differential access to occupational opportunities. This is why the Southern Christian Leadership Conference left the urban slums of Chicago, where the real problems were, and attacked the issue of segregated housing in Cicero, Illinois, which for blacks during this period of their history was irrelevant and insignificant.

Although Southern whites insisted on black inferiority, one should not assume that they therefore wanted to dispose of blacks. They needed blacks for at least two reasons: first, to establish their alleged superiority and, second, to exploit black labor. Blacks had been their slaves, had worked their fields, had stablized and maintained their households, and had been a source of wealth and sometimes even pleasure. Many Southern whites had even developed a degree of affection for blacks.

Northern whites were quite different in this regard. Some knew the value of black Americans, but their major goal was to make certain that blacks and whites remained apart. A biracial system was not required because occupational and economic discrimination kept blacks and whites apart. And, when and where necessary, whites would use restrictive real estate clauses to keep the races separate. Whites in the North wanted blacks to stay completely to themselves unless there was some need for their labor. With the exception of hiring black women, whites did not really want to make much competitive use of black labor. It seems that Northern whites wanted blacks to disappear, and so they pretended they did not exist.

In the South, segregationist policies eventually led to a biracial system that produced unanticipated consequences. It actually laid the groundwork for the development of a black middle class composed of clergy, college administrators and professors, medical doctors, journalists, school teachers, artisans, and skilled craftspeople, all of whom had learned to be independent in their respective institutional settings. They were the decision makers and leaders of their people. They would train the new teachers, the new professionals, even a new business elite. Their protégés would become the new entrepreneurs and open businesses of various kinds—barbershops, beauty shops, grocery stores, restaurants, and nightclubs. They would establish black banks, publish black newspapers, and establish professional societies. Many of the college graduates would become ministers and establish their own churches. In time all of these professionals would combine their resources and expertise and, using their two institutional bases, the school and the church, would lead a struggle against the very system that made their existence possible, the system of segregation. In the South segregation did not mean separation only. It meant the right of whites to degrade blacks, to treat blacks unjustly, and mostly to keep blacks in an inferior condition.

Eventually the black church, a product of segregation and discrimination, would become the institutional base for the fight against segregation and discrimination. Not only did the black church provide the leadership, it also provided the following. However, since black churches had existed for decades, and their congregations were ready for change for decades, why did the "movement" take until 1955 to start? A critical component is the size of the black middle and skilled-worker classes. In the mid-to-late 1950s these two classes constituted approximately 39 percent of the black community, a larger percentage than before. World War II had been a major period of opportunity for these people, and as a result they garnered more resources and began to expect more from the system. In short, they experienced a revolution of rising expectations. They had become intolerant of abuse and of insults to their dignity. They were in need of a social movement.

DESEGREGATION: THE CIVIL-RIGHTS MOVEMENT

The impetus for the civil-rights movement, the movement to desegregate the South, actually began before Mrs. Rosa Parks's heroic refusal in 1955 to give up her bus seat to a white person. The initial stimulus was the May 17, 1954, decision of the Supreme Court, in *Brown* v. *Board of Education* (1954), that the 1896 *Plessy* decision was unconstitutional. Black soldiers returning from World War II and the burgeoning black middle class heralded the decision and proclaimed that the *Brown* decision must usher in "a new order of things."

No sooner had the decision been made, however, than the nation was shocked by the grizzly murder of a young teenager, Emmett Till, in Sumner, Mississippi. The murder dramatized the fact that no change in the law would change the customs of Southern whites, and the case demonstrated how circumstances of blacks in the South were radically different from those in the North. According to Emmett Till's uncle, Emmett had been bragging to some black youngsters outside a rural store. He claimed to have white friends, even white girlfriends, in Chicago and showed photographs of his friends. Emmett had just arrived in Sumner, and was trying to impress these young boys, to gain their friendships. One of the boys apparently said to Emmett, "I bet you won't go into that store and say something to that white lady." Till accepted the challenge, went in, purchased some candy, and in leaving said "'bye, baby." Late the same night two or more white men knocked at the door of Emmett's grandfather, Mose Wright, and took the boy away in a car. When Emmett Till was found, he had been mutilated and beaten beyond recognition, with a bullet hole through his temple. The picture of Emmett Till's disfigured body was published in *Jet* magazine by Johnson Publications, a black publishing firm. Black people throughout the nation saw the picture. Till's mother insisted on an open casket. Two men were charged with the murder, but both were found not guilty. Passionately, black people recognized that a change in the law was not enough. More had to be done.

Emmett Till was a Northern urban kid who had grown up and apparently gone to school with some liberal whites, and although the commingling of whites and blacks in the North could lead to violence, in some circles it was tolerated. Because the issue in the North was residential separation, it was easy for a black person to find himself in a predominantly black school, though generally there were at least a few white students. More important, however, was the fact that the overwhelming majority of the teachers were white (Jones 1985, p. 180). These teachers and other professionals usually lived outside the school district in which they taught. Although they insisted that black schoolchildren should obey them, they did not insist that blacks should act subservient and inferior. As teachers they were proud of their successful black students. Northern blacks thus developed self-esteem, a sense of "somebodyness," a belief that they were the equals of others. This attitude was reinforced in black urban enclaves. In the South, however, every contact a black person had with a white person required a demonstration of black inferiority, even fear. The idea of being equal to whites was generally unthinkable, that is, if the idea was to be put into action. Northern blacks were always warned by their relatives when they went to the South that the rules were quite different there—that not obeying them could place everybody in jeopardy and could even lead to the loss of life.

Emmett Till was a tough urban kid, not unlike many of the gang members of the 1990s, and the fact that he was not afraid of his captors and refused to stop fighting back made them angrier. He obviously did not know that what he did in the North could get him killed in the South. He either had not been warned, or he did not heed the warning.

Emmett Till's murder and the injustice of the final verdict produced mounting frustration. Thus, on December 1, 1955, Mrs. Rosa Parks told a bus driver who asked her to give her seat to a white person, which was the law, that she would not. This galvanized the entire black population of Montgomery, Alabama. The black community organized a bus boycott, and soon the buses were empty. The leadership was surprised (Raines 1977). Black people were fed up. They had always been angered by such demands and customs, but as Christians they had been taught to accept them and hope for change. By now, however, former soldiers and their families who had been patriotic and who had sacrificed during World War II had become intolerant. Segregation did not mean biracialism to them. Instead it meant abuse and insult. A social movement had started.

Soon a brilliant young black Baptist minister would join the movement, and even though only twenty-six years of age he would become the leader. That leader, Martin Luther King, Jr., defined the enemy as segregation. Segregation, King insisted, "scars the soul of the segregated. . . . It not only harms one physically, but injures one spiritually." It is a system, asserted King, that "forever stares the segregated in the face saying you are less than, you are not equal to." Segregation denies a human being the right to express his or her true essence; therefore, it must be destroyed. King declared that nonviolence would be the movement's strategy and philosophy. Nevertheless, violence erupted immediately. Whites were resisting, but the Montgomery Improvement Association won its victory when the Supreme Court declared segregated busing unconstitutional. King and his leadership cadre immediately set about the task of desegregating other public facilities in Montgomery. The movement had begun, and from this point on other struggles would erupt spontaneously across the South. All of them devoted themselves to desegregation.

As black college students observed the activities of Dr. King and his organization, the Southern Christian Leadership Conference (SCLC), they decided to continue the process of desegregation. Dr. King was desegregating downtown department stores in Montgomery; they would desegregate lunch counters. It was the custom in the South not to serve blacks at lunch counters in the various dime stores, especially the Woolworth's chain. So on November 1, 1960, four students from the local black college took seats at the lunch counter in Greensboro, North Carolina. They asked to be served, and when the management refused they resolved to stay. After a day or two violence began. A group of young white toughs and some older adults began to pull them out of their seats and beat them. The police were called in but refused to arrest the perpetrators of the violence. Instead they arrested the victims, those who were involved peacefully in what became known as the sit-ins. As a result of the police actions, Southern blacks noted again that not only were the citizens of the South opposed to their rights, but so were the public officials. Segregation had to be destroyed "lock, stock, and barrel, top to bottom, left to right" (Carmichael 1971), because it even corrupted public officials and offi-

cers of the law, whose sworn duty it was to protect the citizenry. From this point on segregation was the enemy, and going to jail to end it became a badge of honor.

The issue of segregation on buses involving interstate travel remained a problem even after the Montgomery victory. Therefore it was not long before groups of Freedom Riders were mobilized to test the Supreme Court decision's relevance to interstate travel. The Freedom Riders included blacks and whites, a fact that should not be forgotten. In some instances whites actually outnumbered blacks. The Freedom Rides began in May 1961 and were immediately confronted with violence. Buses were bombed. Freedom Riders were beaten unmercifully at most destinations. Some were permanently disabled. The perpetrators were indiscriminate: They beat blacks and whites. In fact, their hatred seemed greater for whites—"Nigger lovers," they were called—than for blacks. The Freedom Riders expected to be protected by the FBI, but J. Edgar Hoover, the director, made it clear that his agency had no intention of protecting these agitators. The failure of the federal government to uphold the law, in this instance, finally communicated to black people and some whites that the existence of segregation had corrupted not just local public officials but even officials of the federal government. The fight had to begin at the top.

The next major chapter in the effort to desegregate the South took place in Albany, Georgia, in 1961. Failing in their desegregation efforts there, King and the SCLC launched a new project to protest segregated lunch counters in downtown Birmingham, Alabama. King was jailed. While in jail, he wrote his philosophically brilliant "Letter from a Birmingham Jail." Although Birmingham's white business leaders agreed on a desegregation plan, King's motel was still bombed. Medgar Evers was shot to death in neighboring Jackson, Mississippi, and four young children were murdered in the bombing of the Sixteenth Street Baptist Church in Birmingham. Blacks learned that even if they could get local public officials and businessmen to change segregationist policies, some Southern whites, perhaps even the majority, would not accept change. They also learned that among the majority there were those that were willing to use violence. Blacks had to have protection from some other source.

In 1964 the Student Nonviolent Coordinating Committee (SNCC) began its Freedom Summers Project in Mississippi. Mississippi was considered by blacks to be the most dangerous state in the South, and it lived up to its reputation. On Sunday, August 4, 1964, Mississippi claimed three lives, those of James Chaney, Michael Swerner, and Andrew Goodman—the two latter were white. All three were members of SNCC's Freedom Summer Project. Their only offense was that they had volunteered to teach black youth, work with the rural poor, and register blacks to vote. If it was not apparent during the Freedom Rides, it was now apparent that Southern whites would kill anybody, whites included, who opposed their way of life. Blacks now had a growing collection of concerned Northern whites. Swerner's wife commented that it was unfortunate, but apparently whites had to die before other, complacent whites would listen. The parents of the two young white students, Swerner and Goodman, talked about the martyrdom of their children. They were proud but grief-stricken. They insisted that the monstrous evil of segregation must be destroyed. Black members of the Congress on Racial Equality (CORE) and SNCC were furious. Some of them had been personal friends of James Chaney, who was black. They passionately blamed the governor of the state and the federal government for what happened in Philadelphia, Mississippi, during the summer of 1964. As a result of these murders by law enforcement authorities, SNCC and the SCLC decided to march from Selma to Montgomery. Near the end of their march, however, as they approached the Edmond Pettus Bridge, they were attacked by mounted sheriff's officers wielding clubs. They were beaten indiscriminately, men and women, young adults and children.

In sum, the central focus of black struggle in the South from 1955 to 1965 was desegregation. Blacks insisted on desegregating public transportation facilities, public eating establishments, public water fountains, public bathrooms, and public

institutions of higher education. As a result of their sacrifices during this decade black Southerners had learned that desegregation required changes in the law at the national level. A civil-rights bill was therefore required. It also required a willingness on the part of government officials to protect and defend the rights of black Americans.

It was not long after Selma that Watts, an urban ethnic enclave near Los Angeles, blew up in the race riots of 1965. Stores were torched and looted. Surveying the destruction in Watts, Dr. King and the SCLC decided that it was time to take their movement to the North. What they were not aware of was that their desegregation strategies would not solve the problems of Northern blacks, because the central problem for this group was *not* segregation. To understand this we need to contrast the evolution of the black middle class in the South with that in the North.

DESEGREGATION VERSUS INTEGRATION

A biracial system similar to the South never surfaced in the American North. As a result blacks there depended almost completely on whites for employment. Northern whites, furthermore, had not come to depend on black labor, with the possible exception of domestic labor. Domestic labor, however, did not produce wealth; it was a symbol of surplus wealth. In addition, Northern whites wanted to remain physically (residentially) separated from blacks and whites did not feel any need to employ them. With the influx of European immigrants, Northern whites preferred to hire the sons and daughters of Europe rather than the emancipated slaves of the South (Blauner 1972; Jones 1985). In fact, from the turn of the century to the beginning of World War II, Northern blacks never established a foothold in the manufacturing industries of the North (Jones 1985). Indeed, according to Blauner, in those ancillary industries such as meat packing where blacks gained a foothold, they were actually displaced by European immigrants.

Given this background, the black middle class developed differently in the North than in the

South. At first the Northern middle class was a status category more than a class and was composed primarily of the biracial offspring of blacks and whites (then called mulattoes). Generally, they had disdain for the new black immigrants, who were darker, usually rural, and less "cultured" (i.e., less civilized). As a "class" the mulattoes tended to have reasonably good relationships with upper middle class whites. Often, they had white clients, lived in white neighborhoods, and attended white schools and churches (Landry 1987). They did not serve the black community. By 1915 they would be replaced by a new and different Northern black middle class. And as the black population increased, this new black middle class began to serve the black community. They opened their own businesses: Beauty parlors, grocery stores, barbershops, cleaners, funeral parlors, and restaurants proliferated. With the exception of the black church, none of these businesses was associated with a large institutional base like the black schools in the South. The majority of teachers who taught black students in the North were white, whether the schools were in adjacent white or black communities (Jones 1985, p. 180).

In this context it is surprising that the issue of desegregating Northern schools came up. If black students were not learning in schools and were not learning from white teachers, then it seems reasonable to ask whether the white teachers should have been viewed as the problem. But, instead, it was the fact that black students were not learning in an environment with other blacks that was defined as the problem. This meant that integrationists believed that black pupils could learn only when they were in a setting where there were white pupils, and that blacks do not develop adequately and perform productively when they are in predominantly black settings.

In the North, the issue was to integrate everything, but especially the schools. Perhaps this whole issue turns on the matter of law. *Plessy* v. *Ferguson* was a constitutional and therefore a national issue, but it had to be implemented by a proliferation of local statutes. This had occurred in the South but not generally in the North. In the North, therefore, it was assumed necessary only to change customs and normative patterns of behavior, and the way to do this was thought to be by integration. Even though black businesses proliferated from 1915 to 1945 in Northern black communities, black people remained dependent on white businesses for both services and jobs, just as they were dependent on white teachers for their education (Landry 1987). The problem for the black middle class in the North, then, was different from that for the black middle class in the South. And the leadership of the civil-rights movement knew it. At one point Dr. King said that "the struggles of the past decade were not national in scope; they were Southern; they were specifically designed to change life in the South" (1968, p. 70).

Northern blacks had only been segregated (*de facto*) residentially. Otherwise they could ride public transportation and eat at many of the major restaurants, although it was understood that some owners would discourage blacks from coming by being discourteous. The major concern of Northern middle class blacks, therefore, was not formal desegregation but rather discrimination and unequal access. They insisted that they should get the same quality of goods or service for their money. They also insisted on greater job opportunities. They rejected the idea of caste barriers in employment. They insisted on fair evaluation for good performance. And they insisted that promotions be tied fairly to evaluation, irrespective of race. They rejected job ceilings and the idea of determining job status on the basis of race. These kinds of problems could not be solved by civil rights marches. They could not be solved simply by changing the law. Such changes would help, perhaps, but what was required was to get the federal government to establish civil-rights policies that would declare such acts as violations of the law and then, and even more important, connect these policies to some kind of enforcement device so that private corporations and governmental agencies would comply with the law. This is exactly what the Civil Rights Act of 1964 did.

THE FAILURE OF INTEGRATION:
THE URBAN POOR

Soon after the Civil Rights Act was passed by Congress and signed by President Lyndon B. Johnson, Executive Orders 11246 and 11375 were issued. These executive orders led to the policy of affirmative action (Black 1981). Affirmative action policies essentially required that all city, state, or federal agencies, as well as any private corporation that contracted with the federal government, make every reasonable attempt to increase the proportion of minority workers in their work force. Affirmative action was to be a device to address the effects of past discrimination. It did not take long to realize, however, that mostly middle class blacks were benefiting from affirmative-action policies (Wilson 1987). The reason for this was twofold. First, middle class blacks were the only ones who had competitive resources (such as skills they had acquired from higher education), who owned businesses, or who had parents who as a result of their professional status (i.e., doctors, dentists, ministers, etc.) were able to provide a competitive advantage for their children. Second, the American economy underwent structural changes that created more opportunities for professional, technical, human service, and clerical staff. As these opportunities increased, affirmative-action policies increased the likelihood that some of these jobs would go to black Americans. It was not long, however, before it also became apparent that neither affirmative-action policies nor the structural shift in the economy would aid black Americans who were poor and unskilled. In fact, as the economy shifted from a majority of manufacturing industries to a majority of service industries, a segmented labor market developed. A segmented labor market is one that provides differential rates of mobility for differing class segments of the same group (Wilson 1978; 1981; 1987).

It is not surprising then that when Mayor Richard Daly of Chicago and Martin Luther King, Jr., met early in 1966, and King complained about the slum housing of poor blacks in that city, Daly responded, "How do you expect me to solve the problems of poverty and joblessness overnight?" King had no answer. He would quickly leave Chicago and the North after unsuccessful attempts both to help the impoverished and to desegregate Cicero, Illinois. It is to Dr. King's credit, however, that he recognized that the problems of the poor had not been solved and that a Poor People's Campaign was required.

Oblivious to the needs of the poor in the black community, Northern blacks who had turned a desegregationist movement into an integrationist movement (those that Sowell [1984] incorrectly labels as people with a civil-rights vision) pursued integration with a vengeance. When the Civil Rights Act of 1964 became the law of the land, affirmative action was to be its guiding policy and equal opportunity and equal access the measure of fairness. It was not long, however, before civil-rights advocates recognized that something was amiss, not only for the Northern black poor but also for the middle class. For example, although data from the 1970 census show that black male college graduates in 1969 received a slightly higher average income than comparable whites, other data demonstrate that the majority of black college students do not graduate from college. In fact, when Fleming (1985) researched this issue and compared the performance of black colleges with limited resources to predominantly white urban universities with considerably more resources that attract black students with higher SAT scores, she found that the black colleges produced more intellectual and psychosocial development among black students than did the white colleges. Further, she found that typically white colleges produced "academic deterioration" among black students and concluded that better facilities and more institutional resources do not necessarily translate into a higher quality college or university education (Fleming 1985, p. 186). She added that similar findings have been reported in desegregated or so-called integrated public schools (Knowles 1962).

The fact is that, whether or not schools are integrated, the situation confronting black children in most Northern and Southern public schools is catastrophic. Indeed, for the most part integration has failed black children. Once they enter school they fall quickly behind their white counterparts on most measures of intelligence and scholastic achievement (Coleman 1966; Denton 1981). In fact, the longer black children remain in school the further they fall behind. Denton (1981) reports that, compared to white children, black children are three times as likely to be labeled mentally retarded, twice as likely to be suspended for discipline and attendance problems, and twice as likely to drop out of high school (White 1984, pp. 102–103). Black students who remain in school on average are two to three years below grade level in all of the basics—reading, writing, and arithmetic. These kinds of problems compound in later life such that black students have only "half as much of a chance as a white child of finishing college and becoming a professional person," twice as much chance of being unemployed, a one in ten chance of getting in trouble with the law, (and, if these students are young males, they have a one in four chance of involvement with the criminal justice system); finally, as they age, black students have a life expectancy that is five years shorter than white adults (White 1984, p. 103). Integration in this context has led to less growth and, even worse, the actual deterioration of the academic potential of black students in institutions of higher education. In those situations where deterioration does not actually occur, stagnation does (Black 1981). Wilson (1981, 1987) examined the combined indicators of unemployment rates, labor-force participation rates, employment–population ratios, and work experience and concluded that not only do these indicators reveal a disturbing picture of joblessness, but they also indicate that a growing percentage of young black males are not marriageable, that is, they cannot contribute to the support of a family. Examining rates of teenage pregnancy, crime and violence, especially homicide, and increases in substance abuse, Wilson argues that many of these young men are more likely to become predators than responsible workers.

Further, according to Wilson, poverty has compounded in black urban ethnic enclaves. He demonstrated that there had been a significant increase in what he called extreme poverty areas (i.e., areas with a poverty rate of at least 40 percent) in the black urban ethnic enclave. Wilson contrasted the growth of these areas with low poverty areas (census tracts with a poverty rate of at least 20 percent) and high poverty areas (with a poverty rate of at least 30 percent). The number of extreme poverty areas, he emphasized, increased by a staggering 161 percent.

Wilson also demonstrated that the black community is losing its vertical class integration. Middle-class and stable working-class black families are choosing to live in the suburbs, and as they do the institutions they used to support and nourish decline in importance and eventually pass away.

The eventual demise of urban ethnic enclaves has been experienced by all ethnic groups in America; for Europeans the process has taken from four to six generations. For blacks the process began in the late 1960s and for many the early 1970s. Of course resistance existed for residential integration, as mirrored in the hostility that exploded in Cicero, Illinois, in the 1960s. Nor is resistance to residential integration infrequent in the 1990s. If it was not a significant issue for most Northern blacks in the 1960s, it is one now in the 1990s. Although blacks residing in white suburbs are often racially harassed, residential integration is gaining momentum, according to Wilson, even as some whites move out of suburbia to exurbia or back to the city.

It should be noted, however, that the process of ethnic enclave decline for blacks is fundamentally different from that for European ethnics. Europeans settled in urban areas at a time when urban job opportunities were increasing. Most of the jobs were in manufacturing and did not require skilled labor. And since Europeans were preferred over blacks the sheer numbers of jobs allowed them to lift a whole mass of people out of squalor. As economic stability increased, European ethnics began the process of preparing themselves for increased mobility within the American occupational structure. To do this, education was critical —educational institutions are essentially preparatory institutions. In sum, occupational and economic success for European ethnics required a stable economic base first, education second, and occupational success third (Greeley 1976). The circumstances for black Americans (a sizable segment of whom were denied stable employment opportunities in the North) were totally different. For those who were already in the North when European ethnics were reaping the benefits of full employment, the denial of job opportunities undermined their ability to establish a stable economic base. And for those who would come later, when manufacturing jobs were actually diminishing rather than increasing, there would be nothing but long-term unemployment. These groups would eventually form the black underclass as one generation of unemployed workers would quickly give rise to another. European ethnics were described by the sociologists of the 1920s and 1930s as socially disorganized (Thomas and Zananiecki 1927). Their communities were plagued by crime, delinquency, gangs, prostitution, and filth, but the availability of employment opportunities allowed many to "lift themselves up by their own bootstraps."

The jobs that are available to blacks now because of the growth in the service sector of the American economy are jobs that require considerable education and training, and so black urban ethnic enclaves are likely to undergo a different kind of transformation than the European ethnic enclaves of the early 1900s. The middle class will be increasingly siphoned off from such enclaves, leaving behind a large residue of the most despondent and dependent, the most impoverished, the most violent, and the most criminal elements. Without new institutions to play the role of surrogate parents, without some kind of mandatory civilian social service corps, blacks in these communities may become a permanent underclass. A residue was also left behind by European ethnics, but it was much smaller and therefore much less problematic. As the black middle class leaves, it leaves its ethnic community devoid of the leadership or resources needed to regain its health. And as the numbers of female-headed families increase, the middle class will eventually have left

the majority of black people behind. Integration, then, has undermined the health and the integrity of the black community.

Surprisingly, given this set of circumstances, Wilson's proposed solution jettisons race as a pivotal factor. The solution, he proposed, requires jobs, training programs, residential relocation, a child-care strategy, a child-support assurance program, a family-allowance program, a tight labor market, fiscal and monetary policies to stimulate noninflationary growth, and an increase in the competitiveness of American goods on both the domestic and international markets. Race-specific strategies, he has warned, will not solve the problems. They also run the risk of losing the support of political officials and the American public. But much of what Wilson has suggested would increase the rate of integration in America and would therefore undermine black ethnic enclaves even more.

The counterposition is now being proffered by many people, organizations, and school systems throughout the United States. This can be seen in the proliferation of segregated black programs where black youngsters are being taught only by black teachers. In this context, race clearly is the critical issue. Gender, however, has also become an issue. In many of these schools black males insist that only they can do the job. Since black women have had to bear the burden of rearing the children alone for so long, there is no doubt but that they can use some help. One critical problem remains for people of this persuasion, however, and that is the continuing trend of black middle-class and stable working-class flight. Can the black community stem the tide? It is not suggested here that the black middle class can solve the problem alone but rather that they must provide the leadership, as they have in the segregated black institutions of the South, and that government must pay for it. Can the exodus be diminished? Only time will tell. If the history of European ethnic enclaves is at all indicative, it would appear that as those who are able to compete are accepted in the broader society, ethnicity for some blacks then may become like ethnicity for most European ethnics, symbolic (Gans 1979). If this occurs, then the problems of the truly disadvantaged will not be solved by the black middle class, and therefore Wilson's proposed nonracial solution may indeed be the only answer.

(SEE ALSO: *Apartheid; Discrimination; Equality of Opportunity; Ethnicity; Prejudice; Race; Segregation and Desegregation; Slavery and Involuntary Servitude*)

REFERENCES

Adam, Herbert 1971 *Modernizing Racial Domination: The Dynamics of South African Politics.* Berkeley: University of California Press.

Black, Albert N., Jr. 1977 "Racism Has Not Declined, It Has Just Changed Form." *Umojo* 1, no. 3 (fall).

———1981 "Affirmative Action and the Black Academic Situation." *Western Journal of Black Studies* 5:87–94.

Blauner, Robert 1972 *Racial Oppression in America.* New York: Harper and Row.

Blumer, Herbert 1965 "Industrialization and Race Relations." In G. Hunter, ed., *Industrialization and Race Relations: A Symposium.* New York: Oxford University Press.

Bonacich, Edna 1972 "A Theory of Ethnic Antagonism: The Split Labor Market." *American Sociological Review* 37 (October): 547–559.

Coleman, James S. 1966 *Equality of Educational Opportunity.* Washington, D.C.: U.S. Government Printing Office.

Denton, Herbert 1981 "Future Still Bleak for Black Children, Lobbying Group's Statistics Show." *Los Angeles Times,* January 14(1A):4.

Exum, William H. 1983 "Climbing the Crystal Stair: Values, Affirmative Action, and Minority Faculty." *Social Problems* 30:383–399.

Fleming, Jacqueline 1985 *Blacks in College.* San Francisco: Jossey-Bass.

Franklin, John Hope 1947 *From Slavery to Freedom: A History of Negro Americans,* 4th ed. New York: Alfred A. Knopf.

Gans, Herbert 1979 "Symbolic Ethnicity: The Future of Ethnic Groups and Culture in America." *Ethnic and Racial Studies* 2, no. 1.

Gordon, Milton M. 1961 "Assimilation in America: Theory and Reality." *Daedalus* 90, no. 2: 263–285.

Greeley, Andrew M. 1976 "The Ethnic Miracle." *The Public Interest* 45 (fall): 20–36.

Gutman, H. G. 1976 *The Black Family in Slavery and Freedom, 1750–1925.* New York: Pantheon.

Jones, Jacqueline 1985 *Labor of Love, Labor of Sorrow: Black Women, Work and the Family, From Slavery to the Present.* New York: Vintage.

King, Martin Luther, Jr. 1968 *Where Do We Go From Here: Chaos or Community?* Boston: Beacon Press.

Knowles, L. W. 1962 "Part 1, Kentucky." In United States Commission on Civil Rights, *Civil Rights USA: Public Schools, Southern States.* Washington, D.C.: U.S. Government Printing Office.

Krombowski, John A. (ed.) 1991 *Annual Edition: Race and Ethnic Relations, 91 to 92.* Guilford, Conn.: Dushkin.

Landry, Bart 1987 *The New Black Middle Class.* Berkeley: University of California Press.

Raines, Howell 1977 *My Soul Is Rested.* New York: Penguin.

Scott, Joseph W. 1977 "Afro-Americans as a Political Class: Towards Conceptual Clarity." *Sociological Focus* 10, no. 4:383–395.

Sowell, Thomas 1984 *Civil Rights: Rhetoric or Reality?* New York: Morrow.

Thomas, William I., and Florian Zananiecki 1927 *The Polish Peasant in Europe and America.* New York: Alfred A. Knopf.

van den Berghe, Pierre L. 1967 *Race and Racism: A Comparative Perspective.* New York: Wiley.

White, Joseph 1984 *The Psychology of Blacks: An Afro-American Perspective* Englewood Cliffs, N.J.: Prentice-Hall.

Wilson, William J. 1978 "The Declining Significance of Race: Revisited but Not Revised." *Society,* vol. 15.

———1981 "The Black Community in the 1980s: Questions of Race, Class, and Public Policy." *Annals of the American Academy of Political and Social Science,* vol. 454.

———1987 *The Truly Disadvantaged: The Inner City, Underclass, and Public Policy.* Chicago: University of Chicago Press.

ALBERT N. BLACK, JR.

SEGREGATION INDICES Residential segregation has been a prominent topic in sociology since Ernest Burgess (1928) first published his landmark study on the subject more than sixty years ago; and for almost as long, sociologists have argued about how to measure it. The debate has ebbed and flowed, and for a time the issue seemed settled. In 1955, Otis Dudley Duncan and Beverly Duncan published a landmark article demonstrating that there was little information contained in any of the prevailing indices that was not already captured by the index of dissimilarity. For twenty years thereafter, this measure was employed as the standard index of residential segregation.

This *Pax Duncanae* came to an abrupt end in 1976, with the publication of a critique of the dissimilarity index by Charles Cortese and his colleagues, ushering in another period of debate that still has not ended. Since 1976 a variety of old indices has been reintroduced and new ones have been invented, yielding a multiplicity of potential segregation measures.

In an effort to bring some order to this methodological disarray, Douglas Massey and Nancy Denton in 1988 undertook a systematic analysis of twenty segregation indices they identified from a review of the literature. They argued that segregation is not a unidimensional construct but encompasses five distinct dimensions of spatial variation. No single dimension is intrinsically more "correct" than any other; each reflects a different facet of the spatial distribution of social groups. The five dimensions they identified are the following: evenness, exposure, clustering, concentration, and centralization.

To verify this conceptualization, Massey and Denton carried out a factor analysis. Their results showed that each index correlated with one of five factors corresponding to the dimensions they postulated. On theoretical, empirical, and practical grounds, they selected a single "best" indicator for each dimension of segregation. These indices are described in the ensuing paragraphs. Other researchers have surveyed the literature and reached different conclusions; contrasting views are noted and discussed when appropriate.

The first dimension of segregation is evenness; it refers to the unequal distribution of social groups across areal units of a city. A minority group is segregated if it is unevenly spread across neighborhoods. Evenness is not measured in an absolute sense, but is scaled relative to another

group. It is maximized when all areal units have the same relative number of minority and majority members as the city as a whole, and is minimized when minority and majority members share no areas in common.

The index of dissimilarity quantifies the degree of departure from an even residential distribution. It computes the number of minority members who would have to change neighborhoods to achieve an even distribution and expresses this quantity as a proportion of the number who would have to change ares under conditions of maximum unevenness. The index varies between 0 and 1, and for any two groups X and Y is computed as:

$$D = .5 \sum_{i=1}^{n} \left| \frac{x_i}{X} - \frac{y_i}{Y} \right|, \qquad (1)$$

where x_i and y_i are the number of X and Y members in areal unit i, and X and Y are the number of X and Y members in the city as a whole, which is subdivided into n areal units.

Among its properties, the index is inflated by random factors when the number of minority members is small relative to the number of areal units (Cortese et al. 1976). It is also insensitive to the redistribution of minority members among areal units with minority proportions above or below the city's minority proportion (James and Taeuber 1985; White 1986). Only transfers of minority members from areas where they are overrepresented (above the city's minority proportion) to areas where they are underrepresented (below the minority proportion) affect the value of the index.

The latter property means that the dissimilarity index fails the "transfers principle," which requires that segregation be lowered whenever minority members move to areas where they are a smaller proportion of the population. This and other problems led David James and Karl Taeuber (1985) to recommend using another measure of evenness, the Atkinson index (Atkinson 1970). Massey and Denton, however, point out that the Atkinson and dissimilarity indices are highly correlated and generally yield the same substantive conclusions. Moreover, the Atkinson index is actually a family of indices, each of which gives a slightly different result, thereby creating problems of comparability. Given that D has been the standard index for more than thirty years, that a large body of findings has accumulated using it, and that the index is easy to compute and interpret, Massey and Denton recommend using it to measure evenness in most cases.

Michael White (1986) points out, however, that another index may be preferred when measuring segregation among multiple groups, since the dissimilarity index is cumbersome to compute and interpret when the number of groups exceeds two. Thus, if one wants to generate an overall measure of segregation among ten ethnic groups, separate dissimilarity indices would have to be computed among all possible pairs of groups and averaged to get a single measure. An alternative index, however, is Theil's (1972) entropy index, which yields a single comprehensive measure of ethnic segregation. The entropy index can also be expanded to measure segregation across two or more variables simultaneously (e.g., ethnicity and occupation), and can be decomposed into portions attributable to each variable and their interaction (see White 1986).

The second dimension of segregation is exposure, which refers to the degree of potential contact between groups within neighborhoods of a city. Exposure indices measure the extent to which groups must physically confront one another by virtue of sharing a common residential area. For any city, the degree of minority exposure to the majority is defined as the likelihood of sharing a neighborhood in common. Rather than measuring segregation as a departure from some abstract ideal of "evenness," however, exposure indices get at the *experience* of segregation from the viewpoint of the average person.

Although indices of exposure and evenness are correlated empirically, they are conceptually distinct because the former depend on the relative size of the groups being compared, while the latter do not. Minority members can be evenly distributed among residential areas of a city, but at the same time experience little exposure to majority members if they comprise a relatively large share of the city. Conversely, if they are a small proportion of the city, minority members tend to experience high levels of exposure to the majority no matter what the level of evenness. Exposure indices take explicit account of such compositional effects in determining the degree of segregation between groups.

The importance of exposure was noted early by Bell (1954), who introduced several indices. However, with the establishment of the *Pax Duncanae* in 1955, sentiment coalesced around the dissimilarity index, and exposure was largely forgotten until Stanley Lieberson reintroduced the P* index in the early 1980s. This index has two basic variants. The interaction index ($_xP^*_y$) measures the probability that members of group X share a neighborhood with members of group Y, and the isolation index ($_xP^*_x$) measures the probability that group X members share an area with each other.

The interaction index is computed as the minority-weighted average of each neighborhood's majority proportion:

$$_xP^*_y = \sum_{i=1}^{n} [\frac{x_i}{X}][\frac{y_i}{t_i}],\qquad(2)$$

where x_i, y_i, and t_i are the numbers of X members, Y members, and the total population of unit i, respectively, and X represents the number of X members citywide. The isolation index is computed as the minority-weighted average of each neighborhood's minority proportion:

$$_xP^*_x = \sum_{i=1}^{n} [\frac{x_i}{X}][\frac{x_i}{t_i}].\qquad(3)$$

Both indices vary between 0 and 1 and give the probability that a randomly drawn X member shares a neighborhood with a member of group Y (in the case of $_xP^*_y$) or with another X member (in the case of $_xP^*_x$). Values of $_yP^*_x$ and $_yP^*_y$ can be computed analogously from equations (2) and (3) simply by switching the x and y subscripts. When there are only two groups, the isolation and interaction indices sum to 1, so that $_xP^*_y + _xP^*_x = 1.0$ and $_yP^*_x + _yP^*_y = 1.0$. The interaction indices are also asymmetrical; only when X and Y comprise the same proportion of the population does $_xP^*_y$ equal $_yP^*_x$.

P* indices can be standardized to control for population composition and eliminate the asymmetry (Bell 1954; White 1986). Standardizing the isolation index yields the well-known correlation ratio, or Eta^2 (White 1986). Linda Stearns and John Logan (1986) argue that Eta^2 constitutes an independent dimension of segregation, but Massey and Denton hold that it straddles two dimensions. Being derived from P*, Eta^2 displays some properties associated with an exposure measure; but standardization also gives it the qualities of an evenness index. Massey and Denton demonstrate this duality empirically and argue that it is better to use D and P* as separate measures of evenness and exposure rather than employing an index that confounds the two.

A third dimension of segregation is clustering, or the extent to which areas inhabited by minority members adjoin one another in space. A high degree of clustering implies a residential structure where minority areas are arranged contiguously, creating one large enclave, whereas a low level of clustering means that minority areas are widely scattered around the urban environment, like a checkerboard.

The index of clustering recommended by Massey and Denton is White's (1983) index of spatial proximity, SP. It is constructed by calculating the average distance between members of the same group and the average distance between members of different groups, and then computing a weighted average of these quantities. The average distance, or proximity, between group X members is:

$$P_{xx} = \sum_{i=1}^{n} \sum_{j=1}^{n} \frac{x_i \, x_j \, c_{ij}}{X^2};$$ (4)

and the average proximity between members of X and Y is:

$$P_{xy} = \sum_{i=1}^{n} \sum_{j=1}^{n} \frac{x_i \, y_j \, c_{ij}}{XY},$$ (5)

where Y is the number of Y members citywide; x_i and y_j are the numbers of X and Y members in units i and j; and c_{ij} is a distance function between these two areas, defined here as a negative exponential: $c_{ij} = \exp(-d_{ij})$. The term d_{ij} represents the linear distance between the centroids of units i and j, and d_{ii} is estimated as $(.6a_i) \cdot 5$, where a_i is the area of the spatial unit. Use of the negative exponential implicitly assumes that the likelihood of interaction declines rapidly as the distance between people increases.

Average proximities may also be calculated among Y members (P_{yy}) and among all members of the population (P_{tt}) by analogy with equation (4). White's SP index represents the average of intragroup proximities, P_{xx}/P_{tt} and P_{yy}/P_{tt}, weighted by the fraction of each group in the population:

$$SP = \frac{X \, P_{xx} + Y \, P_{yy}}{T \, P_{tt}}.$$ (6)

SP equals 1 when there is no differential clustering between X and Y, and is greater than 1 when X members live nearer to each other than to Y members. In practice, SP can be converted to a 0–1 scale by taking the quantity SP-1 (Massey and Denton 1988). White (1984) has also proposed a more complex standardization by taking $f(d_{ij}) = d_{ij}^2$, which yields a statistic equivalent to the proportion of spatial variance explained.

Jakubs (1981) and Morgan (1983a, 1983b) have proposed that D and P* be adjusted to incorporate the effects of clustering. Massey and Denton argue against this procedure because it confounds two different dimensions of segregation. They maintain it is better to measure clustering directly as a separate dimension rather than trying to adjust other measures to reflect it.

The fourth dimension of segregation is centralization, or the degree to which a group is located near the center of an urban area. In the postwar period, African-Americans became increasingly isolated in older central cities as whites gravitated to suburbs. Centralization is measured by an index that reflects the degree to which a group is spatially distributed close to, or far away from, the central business district (CBD). It compares a group's distribution around the CBD to the distribution of land area around the CBD using a formula adapted from Duncan (1957):

$$CE = (\sum_{i=1}^{n} X_{i-1} A_i) - (\sum_{i=1}^{n} X_i A_{i-1}),$$ (7)

where the n areal units are ordered by increasing distance from the CBD, and X_i and A_i are the respective cumulative proportions of X members and land area in unit i.

The centralization index varies between $+1$ and -1, with positive values indicating a tendency for group X members to reside close to the city center, and negative values indicating a tendency for them to live in outlying areas. A score of 0 means that the group has a uniform distribution throughout the metropolitan area. The index states the proportion of X members who would have to change their area of residence to achieve a uniform distribution around the central business district.

The last dimension of segregation is concentration, or the relative amount of physical space occupied by a minority group in the urban environment. Concentration is a relevant dimension of segregation because discrimination restricts minorities to a small set of neighborhoods that together comprise a small share of the urban environment. The index of concentration takes the average amount of physical space occupied by group X relative to group Y, and compares this quantity to the ratio that would obtain if group X were maximally concentrated and group Y were maximally dispersed:

$$CO = \frac{\sum\limits_{i=1}^{n}\frac{x_i a_i}{X} \sum\limits_{i=1}^{n}\frac{y_i a_i}{Y} - 1}{\sum\limits_{i=1}^{n_1}\frac{t_i a_i}{T_1} \sum\limits_{i=n_2}^{n}\frac{t_i a_i}{T_2} - 1}, \quad (8)$$

where areal units are ordered by geographic size from smallest to largest, a_i is the land area of unit i, and the two numbers n_1 and n_2 refer to different points in the rank ordering of areal units from smallest to largest: n_1 is rank of the unit where the cumulative total population of units equals the total minority population of the city, summing from the smallest unit up; and n_2 is the rank of the areal unit where the cumulative total population of units equals the minority population totaling from the largest unit down. T_1 equals the total population of areal units from 1 to n_1, and T_2

equals the total population of areal units from n_2 to n. As before, t_i refers to the total population of unit i, and X is the number of group X members in the city. The resulting index varies from -1 to $+1$; a score of 0 means that the two groups are equally concentrated in urban space, and a score of -1 means that Y's concentration exceeds X's to the maximum extent possible; a score of $+1$ means the converse.

Which of these five indices of segregation is chosen for a particular application depends on the purpose of the study. All are valid measures, and arguments about which one is "correct" or "best" are meaningless. They measure different facets of segregation. D provides an overall measure of evenness that is highly comparable with prior work, widely understood, readily interpretable, and independent of population composition. P* captures the degree of inter- and intragroup contact likely to be experienced by members of different groups, and it directly incorporates the effect of population composition.

Neither D nor P* is inherently spatial, however, and each may be applied to study nongeographic forms of segregation, such as the segregation between men and women across occupations (see Jacobs 1989). The remaining three dimensions are relevant whenever it is important to know about the physical location of a group in space. If the extent to which group members cluster is important, then SP should be computed; if it is important to know how close to the city center a group has settled, then CE may be calculated; and if the sheer amount of physical space occupied by a group is relevant, then CO is the appropriate index.

The most comprehensive understanding of residential segregation is achieved, however, when all five indices are examined simultaneously. Such a multidimensional approach yields a fuller picture of segregation than can be achieved by using any single index alone. Thus, Massey and Denton (1989) found that blacks in certain U.S. cities were highly segregated on all five dimensions simultaneously, a pattern they called "hypersegregation." By relying primarily on the index of dissimilarity, prior work overlooked this unique aspect of black urban life and understated the severity of black segregation in U.S. cities.

(SEE ALSO: *Cities; Demographic Methods; Segregation Indices*)

REFERENCES

Atkinson, A. B. 1970 "On the Measurement of Inequality." *Journal of Economic Theory* 2:244–263.

Bell, Wendell 1954 "A Probability Model for the Measurement of Ecological Segregation." *Social Forces* 32:357–364.

Burgess, Ernest W. 1928 "Residential Segregation in American Cities." *Annals of the American Academy of Political and Social Science* 14:105–115.

Cortese, Charles F., R. Frank Falk, and Jack C. Cohen 1976 "Further Considerations on the Methodological Analysis of Segregation Indices." *American Sociological Review* 41:630–637.

Duncan, Otis Dudley 1957 "The Measurement of Population Distribution." *Population Studies* 11:27–45.

———, and Beverly Duncan 1955 "A Methodological Analysis of Segregation Indices." *American Sociological Review* 20:210–217.

Jacobs, Jerry A. 1989 *Revolving Doors: Sex Segregation and Women's Careers* Stanford, Calif.: Stanford University Press.

Jakubs, John F. 1981 "A Distance-Based Segregation Index." *Journal of Socio-Economic Planning Sciences* 15:129–136.

James, David R., and Karl E. Taeuber 1985 "Measures of Segregation." In Nancy B. Tuma, ed., *Sociological Methodology 1985*. San Francisco: Jossey-Bass.

Lieberson, Stanley 1980 *A Piece of the Pie: Blacks and White Immigrants Since 1880*. Berkeley: University of California Press.

———1981 "An Asymmetrical Approach to Segregation." In Ceri Peach, Vaughn Robinson, and Susan Smith, eds., *Ethnic Segregation in Cities*. London: Croom Helm.

Massey, Douglas S., and Nancy A. Denton 1988 "The Dimensions of Residential Segregation." *Social Forces* 67:281–315.

———1989 "Hypersegregation in U.S. Metropolitan Areas: Black and Hispanic Segregation Along Five Dimensions." *Demography* 26:373–393.

Morgan, Barrie S. 1983a "An Alternate Approach to the Development of a Distance-Based Measure of Racial Segregation." *American Journal of Sociology* 88:1237–1249.

———1983b "A Distance-Decay Interaction Index to Measure Residential Segregation." *Area* 15:211–216.

Stearns, Linda B., and John R. Logan 1986 "Measuring Segregation: Three Dimensions, Three Measures." *Urban Affairs Quarterly* 22:124–150.

Theil, Henri 1972 *Statistical Decomposition Analysis*. Amsterdam: North-Holland.

White, Michael J. 1983 "The Measurement of Spatial Segregation." *American Journal of Sociology* 88:1008–1019.

———1984 "Reply to Mitra." *American Journal of Sociology* 90:189–191.

———1986 "Segregation and Diversity: Measures in Population Distribution." *Population Index* 52:198–221.

DOUGLAS S. MASSEY

SELF-CONCEPT The self is the central concept representing individuals in sociological social psychology. The importance of the self in part reflects the influence of symbolic interactionism in sociology. More recently, social psychologists trained in psychology have also developed a strong interest in the self as their emphasis has shifted from behavioristic to cognitive theories.

STABLE SELF-CONCEPTS

Some sociologists, particularly those with a more philosophical and qualitative bent, view the self as a process involving the internal conversations people have with themselves. On the other hand, those with a more positivistic and quantitative orientation emphasize more stable aspects of the self. From their point of view, the self refers to all those ways in which people describe themselves. Thus, *self-concept* refers to the way people think they are, not their actual personality characteristics. This conception is based on the idea that people are reflexive, responding to themselves just as they respond to other "objects." Further, since reflexive thinking requires language, it is assumed that infants and nonhuman animals lack self-concepts. However, there is some evidence that chimpanzees are aware of what they look like since they notice markings on their faces (Gallup 1977). This self-recognition suggests that some animals and prelinguistic humans have a rudimentary self but that it lacks meaning or content.

Since people describe themselves in many different ways, it is said that the self is multidimensional. One way to find out what these dimensions are is to ask people to respond to the question "Who am I?" Responses to this question reveal that people often think of themselves in terms of their roles (or role identities). For example, people may describe themselves on the basis of their sex, age, race, or occupation. Stryker (1968) suggests that these and other roles are organized in a hierarchy according to their salience for the person. The salience of a role is based in part on the extent to which adequate performance of that role affects relationships with "significant others." Salience is also a function of how distinctive a role is (McGuire and Padawer-Singer 1976). For example, a female is more likely to mention her sex in describing herself if she is the only female in a group of males.

People also describe themselves in terms of personal attributes such as "lazy," "smart," or "attractive." In contrast to roles—which tend to be nouns—these attributes are more likely to be adjectives. They often reflect individuals' conceptions of their ability or performance in different roles. For example, on a questionnaire children can be asked, "How smart in school do you think you are? Among the smartest, above average, average, or below average?" Respondents sometimes try to be objective in answering this type of question and to place themselves according to the criteria they think the researcher is using. They can also report more subjective feelings about where they stand by using their own standards. Other personal attributes involve self-attributed traits such as "aggressive" or "nice." Included also are the ways people characterize their own beliefs and attitudes. For example, people may conceive of themselves as prejudiced or not, independently of whether they are by some objective standard.

While individuals think of themselves in terms of specific roles and specific evaluations of their personal attributes, they also have a more general opinion of themselves. This global evaluation is called *self-esteem* and is measured by such statements as "I feel I do not have much to be proud of" and "At times I think I am no good at all" (Rosenberg 1965). The global nature of self-esteem is indicated by the tendency of individuals to describe themselves consistently positive or negative on different personal attributes. However, self-esteem also has different dimensions such as self-efficacy and self-worth (Gecas 1982). Self-esteem, like depression and anxiety, is usually considered an aspect of mental health. Research using longitudinal data has shown that self-esteem affects and is affected by depression among adolescents (Rosenberg et al. 1989).

There is considerable evidence that people are motivated to have high self-esteem. For example, respondents tend to give inflated evaluations of themselves on anonymous questionnaires. In addition, subjects in experiments are more likely to explain their successes in terms of internal attributes such as effort and ability, while they tend to attribute their failures to external factors such as task difficulty (Bradley 1978).

SITUATIONAL SELF-IMAGES

Some self-statements are more temporary than those described above. They can refer to the roles or personal attributes people use to describe themselves in particular situations. For example, individuals may think of themselves as "teachers" when they are talking to students and as "foolish" when they have made a mistake. If repeated these situational images can become stable as people come to believe in them. Emotions can also be considered temporary self-concepts, if one considers them as statements about how people say they feel rather than as some physiological process (see Gordon 1981 for a review). Thinking about emotions in this way leads to the examination of how emotions are affected by social processes.

Some scholars focus on the presentation of situational self-images to others (e.g., Goffman

1959). Borrowing language from the theater, this approach views behavior as a performance displayed in front of an audience. Behavior involves self-presentation or impression management, and interaction involves a negotiation of situational identities or self-images. This approach presents a challenge to those who seek to measure self-concepts because it suggests that responses on guestionnaires may reflect self-presentation rather than privately held beliefs. Researchers attempt to minimize this problem by the use of carefully worded questions and the guarantee of anonymity.

Situational self-images are often studied in laboratory experiments (see Schlenker 1980 for a review). For example, subjects may be asked to respond after receiving false feedback about themselves. To determine whether or not a self-description involves impression management, the privacy of subjects' responses may be manipulated. When behavior in front of an audience is different from behavior performed in private, it suggests that the behavior reflects impression management rather than privately held beliefs. This type of research can also tell us something about how behavior is affected by subjects knowing that they are being studied. Some behaviors in experimental settings have been shown to result from subjects doing what they think is expected of them (Orne 1962).

DEVELOPMENT OF SELF-APPRAISALS

Three processes have been used to explain why people have favorable or unfavorable opinions about themselves: (1) attribution, (2) social comparison, and (3) reflected appraisal. The first two processes have been emphasized more by the psychological social psychologists while the third has been the focus of sociological social psychologists, particularly those sympathetic with symbolic interactionism.

According to attribution theory, we learn about ourselves and others in similar ways. We make judgments about ourselves based on observations of our own behavior just as we make judgments about others based on our observations of their behavior (Bem 1972). These judgments are socially influenced because beliefs about the association of behaviors and personal attributes are learned from others. For example, in judging our abilities we rely in part on observations of our performances on tasks that we believe reflect these abilities. Thus, children who get high grades tend to attribute more ability to themselves. We are likely to attribute a high level of ability to ourselves when there is a consistent pattern of success (Kelley 1967).

When we view our behavior as externally caused, we treat it as uninformative about ourselves. However, when we view our behavior as internally caused, there is likely to be some change in our self-appraisals. For example, research shows that external rewards can sometimes reduce the motivation of children to do things they have enjoyed in the past, such as playing with magic markers (Deci and Ryan 1980). If they are rewarded for playing with magic markers, they tend to lose interest when they are no longer rewarded because they attribute their behavior to the reward rather than to their own intrinsic motivation. The external reward can decrease their interest in the behavior because it affects their judgments about why they were doing it. More generally, there is evidence that behaviors can affect attitudes, just as attitudes can affect behavior (Liska, Felson, Chamlin, and Baccaglini 1984).

People use different standards in judging their behavior. For example, a "B" can be a good or a poor grade, depending on the standard used. Standards are a function of two types of comparison. Temporal comparison refers to comparison of present performance with past performance. People are likely to judge their performance more harshly if they have been successful in the past. Social comparison refers to comparison of one's own behavior to the behavior of others. The more successful these others, the higher the standard, and the more negative the self-appraisal. Thus, subjects are more negative in describing themselves when there is another person with very positive qualities present than when that person has negative qualities (Gergen and Wishnov 1965). This implies that self-appraisals tend to be more favorable if one is a "big fish in a small pond." For example, research shows that high school students tend to have more negative self-appraisals of academic ability if their schoolmates are bright (Felson and Reed 1986). On the other hand, people can also "borrow status" from successful others with whom they are associated and "bask in reflected glory" (Cialdini et al. 1976).

Festinger (1954) suggested that social comparison processes are the result of the desire to gain accurate appraisals of our ability and to find out whether our opinions are correct. When objective information is not available, we compare ourselves to others. Further, he suggested that we usually choose similar others for comparison because their behavior provides the most information. Current research is examining Goethals and Darley's (1977) hypothesis that people evaluate their abilities by comparing themselves to others who are similar to themselves on attributes other than ability that are related to performance. For example, comparisons with people who have engaged in similar effort will be most informative. Similarly, if a boy believes that gender is related to athletic performance, then he will compare himself to other boys in order to decide how much athletic ability he has.

According to the reflected appraisal process, we come to see ourselves as others see us or at least as we think others see us. This is the notion of the "looking glass self," which focuses on how we think we appear to others (Cooley 1902). According to Mead (1934) it helps explain the initial formation of a self in young children. He suggested that when children role play, they respond to themselves when they play the role of others. This role-taking process leads them to see themselves as objects. Later the appraisals of significant others shape the specific content of our self-concepts. The appraisals of these others are accurately perceived and then incorporated into the self-concept. Significant others may have special expertise or they may be parents or close friends, but those who influence one aspect of a person's self do not necessarily influence another aspect.

Experimental research suggests that subjects' self-appraisals are affected by the false feedback they receive from others. Survey research—which examines correlations between self-appraisals, the appraisals of significant others, and the person's perception of those appraisals—suggests that the appraisals of significant others are not very accurately perceived (Schrauger and Schoeneman 1979). Apparently, conversational rules limit the amount of open communication—particularly criticism—making it difficult for people to find out what others think of them (Felson 1980). When feedback is given it tends to involve specific comments about behavior rather than global evaluations. When praise is given, it is often disbelieved. As a result, we usually have only vague, general impressions of what others think of us, and self-appraisals tend to be idiosyncratic and idealized (Felson 1989). While others are in some agreement about us, we do not share in that consensus. And the ambiguous feedback allows us to think more favorably about ourselves and thereby protect our self-esteem.

This discussion also applies to global self-esteem. Educators and parents may overemphasize the importance of praise in the development of self-esteem in children. While there is evidence that parents' praise and other supportive behavior affects the self-esteem of children (Felson and Zielinski 1989), successful performance at activities that children value may be more important.

There are other processes that increase the correspondence between our appraisals of ourselves and the appraisals of others. First, in some instances, we have access to the same information as others have. For example, children's self-appraisals of their ability and their friends' appraisals of them correspond because they are both affected by the children's grades. Second, other people can influence self-concepts if they have control over formal evaluations. For example, teachers influence self-concepts because they assign grades, but that is usually the extent of their influence on self-appraisals.

The discussion above focuses on the interpersonal environment. Social-demographic characteristics also affect self-appraisals. Social class, for example, has been shown to affect the self-esteem of adults but not children (Rosenberg and Pearlin

1978). Blacks and whites, on the other hand, have similar levels of self-esteem (Wylie 1979). A key element here appears to be whether people associate with others like themselves or not. The self-esteem of minorities is likely to be lower in more heterogeneous settings where invidious comparisons are made and where members of higher status groups act in prejudicial ways.

CONSEQUENCES OF SELF-CONCEPT

The way we think of ourselves has an important impact on how we behave. Thus, people who think of themselves in terms of particular role identities tend to act in ways that are consistent with those identities. For example, a man who identifies himself as a father will engage in those behaviors he associates with being a father. These roles provide links between the individual and society. Individuals are plugged into the social structure through the roles that are mapped onto selves. In other words, role performance reflects the way we think about ourselves. Of course, people vary in the importance they attach to different roles. When people must decide between roles, they tend to choose the role more salient to them (Stryker 1968). For example, the choice between doing work or playing with children on a Sunday afternoon may reflect the relative salience of family and occupational roles.

Success and failure are frequently attributed to variations in self-confidence. Self-appraisals and performance are certainly correlated, but this does not necessarily mean that the former causes the latter. Thus, longitudinal studies, which attempt to disentangle these causal relationships, suggest that a students' global self-esteem does not affect academic performance. On the other hand, there is evidence that specific self-appraisals of ability affect performance. Longitudinal analyses of high school students suggest that self-appraisals of academic ability affect grades (Felson 1984). Self-appraisals of ability affect performance through two processes: effort and test anxiety. Those who are self-confident about their ability are likely to work harder because they think effort will bring success. In addition, they are less

anxious when they are tested, so nervousness does not interfere with their performance. However, the effect of self-appraisals on performance is probably not as strong as people think. The effect of grades on self-appraisals is much stronger, suggesting that success is more likely to lead to self-confidence than self-confidence is to lead to success.

Causal interpretation has been problematic in the study of the effects of self-concepts on other behaviors as well. While self-esteem and various self-appraisals have been shown to correlate with behavior, it is difficult to show that the self-concepts cause the behaviors. Relatively few studies have attempted to sort out these relationships. Exceptions include longitudinal studies that show that self-esteem affects delinquency among adolescents (e.g., Kaplan 1980; Rosenberg et al. 1989).

An interesting experimental method for examining the effects of self-concepts has been suggested by Duval and Wicklund (1972). They suggest that since much human behavior is automatic or habitual, people do not always think about themselves before they engage in a behavior. They argue that self-concepts affect behavior when attention is directed toward the self rather than toward the environment, a condition they call "objective self-awareness." Objective self-awareness is likely to occur when people are in unfamiliar surroundings, when there are disruptions in social interaction, and when they find themselves in a minority. In addition, there are individual differences: Some people are more chronically focused on themselves as objects. The behavior of such people is more likely to be consistent with their self-appraisals and their internalized standards. Mirrors are commonly used in experiments to create objective self-awareness. These studies show that subjects are more likely to engage in behavior that is consistent with their self-standards when they are facing a mirror (e.g., Beaman et al. 1979).

A number of researchers have examined the role of self-concepts in resisting change. For example, research suggests that people are motivated to reaffirm self-concepts when they are challenged (Swann 1984). Markus (1977) describes the generalizations we make about ourselves as "self-schemas" that can affect the way we process information. Self-schemas usually refer to traits, such as "independent" and "generous," and are inferred on the basis of past actions. Once formed, they affect what information we attend to and remember and how quickly we process it. For example, we are more likely to learn and recall information that is associated with our self-schemas. In other words, self-schemas act like filters, guiding the processing of incoming information. Thus, self-schemas have a conservative function because they lead us to focus on information that is consistent with our views of ourselves.

The discussion above focuses on the effects of more stable self-concepts. However, earlier it was suggested that self-presentation processes are also important in predicting behavior. Self-presentation behavior is particularly likely when we have done something that may elicit disapproval from an audience. When we find ourselves in these predicaments, we are embarrassed and attempt various forms of "facework" to avoid a negative identity. Frequently, we give excuses and justifications in an attempt to explain our behavior and avoid social punishment. This topic has received considerable attention in experimental research. This research shows that subjects are more likely to use self-presentation tactics when they depend on the audience for rewards. The important role of self-presentation in conformity, altruism, aggression, and other behaviors has also been demonstrated (Schlenker 1980).

SUMMARY

The determinants and consequences of the self have become central concerns for both sociologically and psychologically trained social psychologists. Our self-concepts depend on the way we think we are viewed by others, on our observations of our behavior, and on the standards we use to judge that behavior. These judgments in turn depend on the performance of others (for comparison) and on the appraisals of others. Self-

concepts have consequences in that they affect which roles are performed and how successfully they are performed. They also affect conformity and deviance and the management of impressions. Finally, they are important in their own right as indicators of mental health.

(SEE ALSO: *Identity Theory; Role Theory; Symbolic Interaction Theory*)

REFERENCES

Beaman, A. L., B. Klentz, E. Diener, and S. Svanum 1979 "Objective Self-Awareness and Transgression in Children: A Field Study." *Journal of Personality and Social Psychology* 37:1835–1846.

Bem, Daryl 1972 "Self-Perception Theory." In L. Berkowitz, ed., *Advances in Experimental Social Psychology*. New York: Academic Press.

Bradley, G. W. 1978 "Self-Serving Biases in the Attribution Process: A Reexamination of the Fact or Fiction Question." *Journal of Personality and Social Psychology* 36:56–71.

Cialdini, R. B., R. J. Borden, A. Thorne, M. R. Walker, S. Freeman, and L. R. Sloan 1976 "Basking in Reflected Glory: Three (Football) Field Studies." *Journal of Personality and Social Psychology* 34:366–374.

Cooley, Charles H. 1902 *Human Nature and the Social Order.* New York: Scribner's.

Deci, E. L. and R. M. Ryan 1980 "The Empirical Exploration of Intrinsic Motivational Processes." In L. Berkowitz, ed., *Advances in Experimental Social Psychology*. New York: Academic Press.

Duval, S., and R. A. Wicklund 1972 *A Theory of Objective Self-Awareness*. New York: Academic Press.

Felson, Richard B. 1980 "Communication Barriers and the Reflected Appraisal Process." *Social Psychology Quarterly* 43:223–233.

——1984 "The Effects of Self-Appraisals of Ability on Academic Performance." *Journal of Personality and Social Psychology* 47:944–952.

——1989 "Parents and the Reflected Appraisal Process: A Longitudinal Analysis." *Journal of Personality and Social Psychology* 56:965–971.

——, and Mark Reed 1986 "The Effect of Parents on the Self-Appraisals of Children." *Social Psychology Quarterly,* 49:302–308.

——, and Mary Zielinski 1989 "Children's Self-

Esteem and Parental Support." *Journal of Marriage and the Family* 51:727–735.

Festinger, Leon 1954 "A Theory of Social Comparison Processes." *Human Relations* 7:117–140.

Gallup, G. G., Jr. 1977 "Self-Recognition in Primates: A Comparative Approach to the Bidirectional Properties of Consciousness." *American Psychologist* 32:329–338.

Gecas, Viktor 1982 "The Self-Concept." *Annual Review of Sociology* 8:1–33.

Gergen, K. J., and B. Wishnov 1965 "Others' Self-Evaluation and Interaction Anticipation as Determinants of Self-Presentation." *Journal of Personality and Social Psychology* 2:348–358.

Goethals, G. and J. Darley 1977 "Social Comparison Theory: An Attributional Approach. In J. M. Suls and R. L. Miller, eds., *Social Comparison Processes: Theoretical and Empirical Perspectives*. Washington, D.C.: Halsted-Wiley.

Goffman, Erving 1959 *The Presentation of Self in Everyday Life*. Garden City, NY: Doubleday/Anchor.

Gordon, Steven L. 1981 "The Sociology of Sentiments and Emotion." In Morris Rosenberg and Ralph H. Turner, eds., *Social Psychology: Sociological Perspectives*. New York: Basic Books.

Kaplan, Howard B. 1980 *Deviant Behavior in Defense of Self*. New York: Academic Press.

Kelley, H. H. 1967 "Attribution Theory in Social Psychology." In D. Levine, ed., *Nebraska Symposium on Motivation*. Lincoln: University of Nebraska Press.

Liska, A., R. Felson, M. Chamlin, and W. Baccaglini 1984 "Estimating Attitude-Behavior Relations within a Theoretical Specification." *Social Psychology Quarterly* 47:15–23.

McGuire, William J., and A. Padawer-Singer 1976 "Trait Salience in the Spontaneous Self-concept." *Journal of Personality and Social Psychology* 33:743–754.

Markus, H. 1977 "Self-Schemata and Processing Information about the Self." *Journal of Personality and Social Psychology* 35:63–78.

Mead, G. H. 1934 *Mind, Self, and Society*. Chicago: University of Chicago Press.

Orne, Martin T. 1962 "On the Social Psychology of the Psychological Experiment: With Particular Reference to Demand Characteristics and Their Implications." *American Psychologist* 17:776–783.

Rosenberg, Morris 1965 *Society and the Adolescent Self-Image*. Princeton: Princeton University Press.

Rosenberg, Morris, and Leonard Pearlin 1978 "Social Class and Self-Esteem among Children and Adults." *American Journal of Sociology* 84:53–87.

Rosenberg, Morris, Carmi Schooler, and Carrie Schoenback 1989 "Self-Esteem and Adolescent Problems." *American Sociological Review* 54:1,004–1,018.

Schlenker, B. R. 1980 *Impression Management: The Self-Concept, Social Identity, and Interpersonal Relations*. Monterey, Calif.: Brooks/Cole.

Schrauger, J. S., and T. J. Schoeneman 1979 "Symbolic Interactionist View of Self: Through the Looking Glass Darkly." *Psychological Bulletin* 86:549–573.

Stryker, Sheldon 1968 "Identity Salience and Role Performance: The Relevance of Symbolic Interaction Theory for Family Research." *Journal of Marriage and the Family* 30:558–564.

Swann, W. B. 1984 "Self-Verification: Bringing Social Reality into Harmony with the Self." In J. Suls and A. G. Greenwald, eds., *Psychological Perspective on the Self*. Hillsdale, N.J.: Erlbaum.

Wylie, Ruth 1979 *The Self-Concept*. Rev. ed. Vol. 2, *Theory and Research on Selected Topics*. Lincoln: University of Nebraska Press.

RICHARD B. FELSON

SEX DIFFERENCES "Sex differences" is the traditional rubric for considering variations between women and men. The use of the term *sex* reflects the basis of selection, dividing women and men into two groups on the basis of their unique biological features. The term *differences* derives from the tradition of differential psychology, in which distinct groups of people (defined by either natural categories such as sex or constructed categories such as socioeconomic class) are compared in terms of some outcome.

Both terms have been criticized. To many people, references to sex differences imply a biological determinism that ignores the role of socialization and context. The more contemporary usage of "gender" directs attention to the social meanings assigned to the categories of male and female. In neither case, however, is it necessary to assume a particular causal factor for an observed pattern of differences. The term "differences" raises questions as well. An emphasis on the term "differences" can suggest that differences are the norm and similarities the exception. More appropriately, one makes comparisons to see if there are similarities or differences.

Comparisons between women and men, whatever the rubric used to characterize the investigation, pervade the social science literature. Literally thousands of studies exist, analyzing sex-related patterns in physical performance, cognitive abilities, personality traits, moral reasoning, social interaction, occupational choice, sexual behavior, and almost any other domain of human activity that one can imagine. To learn how these behaviors emerge, developmental psychologists explore the ways in which specific socialization practices contribute to observed differences in girls and boys and, by extension, women and men. Sociologists direct their attention to structural features that shape the roles of women and men in organizational settings, family units, and labor markets. All of these analyses contribute to our understanding of gender.

Not all of these topics can be discussed here. Nor will this discussion deal with sexual behavior or the biological differences related to sexuality. Here the focus is on sex differences in two general domains: cognitive abilities and social behaviors. Within those domains, the most well documented areas take precedence. In most cases this means that a large set of studies have been analyzed using meta-analysis, a statistical technique that enables researchers to combine results across studies. Chance findings are discarded through this procedure, and a more accurate picture of the stability and reliability of a particular sex difference emerges (cf. Ashmore, 1990; Hyde & Linn 1986).

SEX DIFFERENCES IN COGNITIVE ABILITIES

The question of who is smarter has fascinated social scientists for decades. In the late nineteenth century, many psychologists and physiologists devoted themselves to measuring the size of male and female brains. Their biases often intruded, and conclusions about sex differences were fre-

quently in error (Shields 1975; Rosenberg 1982). In the early twentieth century, pencil-and-paper intelligence tests replaced tape measures and scales as a way of assessing mental capacity. In developing these intelligence tests, investigators concluded that there were no significant differences between males and females in intellectual ability. Thus the Stanford-Binet IQ test, for example, shows no systematic sex differences. More specific cognitive abilities, however, continued to intrigue researchers interested in possible sex differences. Three specific areas of investigation are mathematical abilities, spatial skills, and verbal abilities.

Males and females differ in their performance on tests of mathematical skill. The difference is small, however, accounting for only 1 percent of the variance in scores across assorted tasks and age groups (Hyde 1981). Furthermore, the difference is smaller now than it was some years ago (Rosenthal and Rubin 1982). Sex differences are greater among selected samples of mathematically talented youth tested on the mathematics section of the Scholastic Aptitude Test (Benbow 1988; Benbow and Stanley 1980). Overall, the average scores of 12- and 13-year-old boys are higher than those of girls in these samples; the variability in the boys' scores is also greater. As a result, in the upper 3 percent of the distribution defined as mathematically precocious, boys outnumber girls in ratios that sometimes are quite dramatic. Yet it must be remembered that these are very specifically selected groups, of a particular age performing a particular task. They are not a random sample of the general population.

Spatial ability is another type of cognitive skill. One reason for an interest in this skill is its possible link to mathematical aptitude and scientific achievement (which is not at all certain, however). Investigators studying spatial skill discovered that there are several kinds of spatial skills, not necessarily related very closely to another. Three specific categories are mental rotation, spatial perception, and spatial visualization (Linn and Petersen 1985, 1986). Sex differences favoring men are largest in the first of these categories, which refers to people's ability to visualize the rotation of a three-dimensional object. Spatial perception, which for example, involves determining the true vertical plane when one is seated in a tilted chair, shows a smaller but still significant male advantage. The third category, exemplified by the Embedded Figures Task, which requires people to find a simple shape embedded in a complex pattern of shapes, yields no sex differences. Thus, sex differences in this domain are quite task-specific.

Many people think that women excel in verbal abilities. In fact, there are no substantial differences between women and men (Hyde and Linn 1988). They are equivalent on verbal ability in general and in most more specific types of verbal ability such as vocabulary, verbal analogies, and reading comprehension. The one possible exception is speech production, as indexed by the quality of speech, where women show a slight superiority. Age has no effect on these patterns. More interesting is the influence of time. As in the case of mathematical ability, recent studies are much less likely to find a sex difference than are earlier studies.

It is one thing to find a difference between males and females in some area of cognitive performance. More difficult is the task of explaining why observed differences occur. Investigators invoke both biological and experiential factors and debate which cause is most likely. At the same time, many reported sex differences change significantly over relatively short periods of time. Thus, whatever their origin, most of these abilities are rather easily modified by experience. Experience with spatial activities plays a demonstrable role in one's level of spatial skills, for example. Similarly, specific training programs designed to improve spatial skills are equally effective for women and men (Baenninger and Newcombe 1989). Goals, values, and the expectations of others also affect a person's performance in cognitive domains. Gender-stereotyped beliefs of parents, for example, predict students' performance in mathematics courses. Parents who believe that girls are inferior in mathematical ability are more likely to have daughters who do poorly in mathematics. The value that students themselves place on the particular cognitive ability also influences their performance (Eccles 1985).

How general are any of these cognitive skills? Within a general domain, such as spatial ability, quite different patterns sometimes emerge. Changing the content of the question, from mechanics to health care, for example, can alter the performance of women and men. Thus, although many of these tests show sex differences, generalizations should be made very cautiously. Publicity about sex differences often obscures these distinctions.

SEX DIFFERENCES IN SOCIAL BEHAVIORS

Conclusions regarding sex differences in cognitive abilities are not simple. Yet the picture for social behaviors is even more complex. The presence or absence of a sex difference in social behavior depends heavily on the situation, and the parameters of social situations are far more numerous and less easily catalogued than task characteristics. Thus, simple "more or less" statements almost always require qualification.

Aggression is an area in which simple statements are often made. It is true that men are more aggressive than women. However, the difference is only moderate in size, amounting to half of a standard deviation or less (Eagly 1987; Hyde 1986). Sex differences are larger for physical aggression than for psychological or verbal aggression. Differences are also more pronounced for younger children than for adults, suggesting that societal norms and socialization pressures play a large role in aggression.

Some other areas for male–female comparisons include nonverbal communication, social influence, group interaction, and leadership behaviors. Extensive observations suggest that women are more skilled and more involved in interpersonal communication than are men. The difference is particularly strong in nonverbal forms of communication. In transmitting messages nonverbally, women do a better job than men do. They code their intended messages more efficiently and they transmit them to partners more effectively. They also smile significantly more when talking to others, and they spend more time gazing at their conversational partners (Hall and Halberstadt 1986). Yet, even though sex differences are stronger in this area than elsewhere, many modifying conditions exist. Differences are larger in laboratory studies than in natural settings, for example, and are greater when the context is social than impersonal.

Social influence is a general term referring to reactions such as conforming to the pressures of group opinion or responding favorably to persuasive messages. Overall, women are more easily influenced than men. This difference is most evident in a group setting in which there are pressures to go along with other group members, and it is much less evident when people are responding to a written message or a persuasive television commercial. Differences between women and men are more pronounced when other people are present, suggesting the influence of gender-linked social norms. Outside of the research laboratory, power differences in role relationships, for example between a male supervisor and a female secretary, undoubtedly exacerbate these sex differences in social influence (Eagly 1987).

Group interactions also foster sex differences on some occasions. Men tend to focus more on the goal-directed, task features of a situation, whereas women contribute to the socioemotional climate. This pattern is particularly likely when the topic of discussion is a neutral one. When women and men have different amounts of knowledge or experience in a topic area, task-related behaviors are more likely to come from whichever sex is more familiar with the topic of discussion. Sex differences in group interaction are most likely when it is unclear how competent other group members are. In such circumstances, gender acts as an implied status characteristic, and men are assumed to have greater competence than women. Specific information about the competence of

members counteracts these stereotypes and, in turn, eliminates sex differences in group interaction. For similar reasons, men are more likely to emerge as leaders in initially leaderless groups. Men are most likely to be chosen as leaders when the group is focused on a specific task and when social interaction needs are minimal (Eagly and Karau forthcoming). Again, we see how the assumptions about gender can create sex differences in behavior.

How large are any of these sex differences? If one uses occupational segregation or division of labor as the reference point, the differences in cognitive abilities and social behaviors are really quite small. By themselves, they can hardly explain the occupational and economic disparities between women and men (cf., Hess and Ferree 1987). Some differences are larger than others, of course. Performance on mental rotation tasks, for example, shows a relatively large sex difference. Differences in aggression, gazing behaviors, and some mathematics skills are somewhat smaller. For smiling, social influence, and leadership emergence, the differences are smaller still. In many other areas of social and cognitive behavior, men and women do not differ at all. Questions of sex differences, as suggested earlier, sometimes mask sex similarities.

CONTEXTUAL INFLUENCES ON SEX-RELATED PATTERNS

Summarizing the differences between women and men is not an easy task, once one leaves the obvious biological domains. Both task characteristics and social context are influential, creating sex differences or making them disappear. As Deaux and Major (1987) suggest, the basic repertoires of women and men are quite similar, particularly when it comes to social behaviors. Both women and men know how to be aggressive, how to be helpful, how to smile, and how to be rude. What they actually do is determined less by differential abilities than by the context in which they are acting. Attitudes and actions of others affect what people do. Societal norms and expectations are also influential. So, too, do people alter their own behavior from one situation to another, depending on their goals and objectives.

Comparisons of women and men cannot be analyzed in a vacuum, independent of their social context. Even in the area of cognitive abilities, the differences between women and men have shifted over time. Now there are fewer differences than there were twenty years ago. In considering context, it is also important to recognize that most research has been done in the United States. Sex differences observed here may not be true in other countries or even in less frequently studied subcultures within the United States.

No doubt people will continue to ask how men and women differ. But the answers will never be simple ones. Nor can observed differences between the sexes be used as a simple explanation for the broader gender roles of women and men. Indeed, the causal direction may be just the reverse: Accepted roles may channel men and women into different patterns of behavior. Whatever the patterns observed, most sex differences will continue to reflect a gendered environment and be subject to further change.

(SEE ALSO: *Gender; Intelligence; Socialization*)

REFERENCES

Ashmore, R. D. 1990 "Sex, Gender, and the Individual." In L. A. Pervin, ed., *Handbook of Personality Theory and Research*. New York: Guilford Press.

Baenninger, M., and N. Newcombe 1989 "The Role of Experience in Spatial Test Performance: A Meta-analysis." *Sex Roles* 20:327–344.

Benbow, C. P. 1988 "Sex Differences in Mathematical Reasoning Ability in Intellectually Talented Preadolescents: Their Nature, Effects, and Possible Causes." *Behavioral and Brain Sciences* 11:169–232.

———, and J. C. Stanley 1980 "Sex Differences in Mathematics Ability: Fact or Artifact?" *Science* 210:1,262–1,264.

Deaux, K., and B. Major 1987 "Putting Gender into Context: An Interactive Model of Gender-Related Behavior." *Psychological Review* 94:369–389.

Eagly, A. E. 1987 *Sex Differences in Social Behavior: A Social Role Interpretation*. Hillsdale, N.J.: Erlbaum.

———, and S. J. Karau (Forthcoming). "Gender and the Emergence of Leaders: A Meta-analysis." *Journal of Personality and Social Psychology*.

Eccles, J. E. 1985 "Sex Differences in Achievement Patterns." In T. B. Sonderegger, ed., *Psychology and Gender. Nebraska Symposium on Motivation, 1984*. Lincoln, Nebr.: University of Nebraska Press.

Hall, J. A., and A. G. Halberstadt 1986 "Smiling and Gazing." In J. S. Hyde and M. C. Linn, eds., *The Psychology of Gender: Advances through Meta-Analysis*, pp. 136–158. Baltimore: Johns Hopkins University Press.

Hess, B., and M. Ferree eds. 1987 *Analyzing Gender: A Handbook of Social Science Research*. Newbury Park, Calif.: Sage.

Hyde, J. S. 1981 "How Large Are Cognitive Gender Differences? A Meta-analysis Using ω^2 and d." *American Psychologist* 36:892–901.

———1986 "Gender Differences in Aggression." In J. S. Hyde and M. C. Linn, eds., *The Psychology of Gender: Advances through Meta-Analysis*, pp. 51–66. Baltimore: Johns Hopkins University Press.

———, and M. C. Linn (eds.) 1986 *The Psychology of Gender: Advances through Meta-Analysis*. Baltimore: Johns Hopkins University Press.

———1988 "Gender Differences in Verbal Ability: A Meta-analysis." *Psychological Bulletin* 10:53–69.

Linn, M. C., and A. C. Petersen 1985 "Emergence and Characterization of Sex Differences in Spatial Ability: A Meta-analysis." *Child Development* 56:1,479–1,498.

———1986 "A Meta-analysis of Gender Differences in Spatial Ability: Implications for Mathematics and Science Achievement." In J. S. Hyde and M. C. Linn, eds., *The Psychology of Gender: Advances through Meta-Analysis*. Baltimore: Johns Hopkins University Press.

Rosenberg, R. 1982 *Beyond Separate Spheres: Intellectual Roots of Modern Feminism*. New Haven, Conn.: Yale University Press.

Rosenthal, R., and D. B. Rubin 1982 "Further Meta-analytic Procedures for Assessing Cognitive Gender Differences." *Journal of Educational Psychology* 74:708–712.

Shields, S. A. 1975 "Functionalism, Darwinism, and the Psychology of Women: A Study in Social Myth." *American Psychologist* 30:739–754.

KAY DEAUX

SEXISM *See* Feminist Theory; Gender.

SEX-ROLE MODELS *See* Gender; Role Models.

SEXUAL BEHAVIOR AND MARRIAGE

A particular view of sexuality, derived from a synthesis of Freudian and functionalist elements, has dominated sociology for most of its history. Sex was said to be a powerful biological drive, exceedingly difficult to harness, and capable of being extraordinarily disruptive for society. The family was said to function as the major social control mechanism of sexuality, both in terms of adult needs and in terms of the production and care of the outcomes of sex, namely children (Davis 1976). From a theoretical standpoint, the family has been viewed as the more general and more significant phenomenon, subsuming beneath it numerous issues, including sexuality. Given the decline of functionalism in mainstream sociology, alternative models have appeared describing the connections between sex and society in dialectic terms (Scanzoni et al. 1989; Stein, 1989). Our purpose here is to focus on the literature describing the socially legitimate and nonlegitimate connections between sex and marriage and to do so in the context of these two competing theoretical paradigms.

In 1964 Ehrmann observed that family sociologists had relegated the study of sex to a status peripheral to their major concern with "marital adjustment, happiness," and the like. Sexual satisfaction was conceptualized as one of the several correlates of "adjustment." If we use Booth's (1990) review of 1980s family sociology as an indicator, it appears that in thirty years the study of sexuality has not advanced beyond its peripheral status. In spite of significant societal changes in sexual phenomena, no review essay systematically addressed connections between those phenomena and changes in families.

Why the peripheral status of sexuality? Max Weber (Collins 1986) and Murdock (1949) both argued that marriage rests on twin interdependencies: economic and sexual. With the movement of women into paid labor, economic interdependence has gotten attention, although prior to this movement economics was also relatively peripheral. Most U.S. sociologists avoided the issue of how persons and groups (re)create marriage. Instead, working from organicist assumptions, they assumed marriage to be a "natural given" requisite for the survival of society. The organicism that has pervaded family sociology for a century led researchers to ignore the issue of "marriage construction" and to focus instead on how marriages could thrive and thus benefit society. They argued that a major function of marriage for society was to control both sexuality and childbearing (Davis 1976). To achieve control, dominant norms prescribed chastity prior to the wedding and fidelity afterwards. Children presumably learned these norms and later conformed accordingly.

Prior to the 1960s researchers paid scant attention to violations of the chastity norm and even less to deviance from the fidelity norm, although Kinsey (a zoologist) et al. (1948, 1953) had documented a surprising amount of nonconformity on both counts. Assuming conformity to be the predominant pattern, most sociologists continued to describe how sexual satisfaction contributed to marital quality. Nevertheless, evidence of increasing deviance from the chastity norm forced researchers to take notice, although, as Ehrmann (1964) observed, their major concern was the potential dysfunctions of premarital sex for marriage and society. Davis (1976), for example, used terms such as *anomie* and *disorganization* to describe "contemporary sexual behavior" in the forms of "illicit pregnancy . . . abortions . . . venereal disease." Ironically, since the incidence of nonmarital sex has increased substantially without accompanying chaos, some analysts now allege that they have discovered the *positive* functions of nonmarital sex. Having sex before marriage, they say, enables persons to sort out sexual "incompatibles," thus increasing the likelihood of stability. Hence, even though one might wonder whether nonmarital sex is getting out of control, we are assured such worry is groundless because sex is "subordinate to the family" (Davis 1976, p. 226).

Davis asserts (and Sprey 1986 concurs) that societies allow sex to interfere with the engendering and enhancement of children *only to a limited degree.* By making marital sex "normatively superior" to all forms of nonmarital sex, these forms are structurally constrained in their potential threats to marriage. Hence, in functionalist thought, sex is secondary because it is analyzed in terms of its functions and dysfunctions for the larger whole of marriage—the whole being much more significant than any of its parts.

This reasoning is particularly pertinent to extramarital sex relations because Davis (1976, p. 242), following Malinowski (1930), argues that most civilizations and tribes have been much more rigid in their proscriptions of extra- than of premarital sex, especially for women. Although some explicit arguments have been made asserting the functions of extramarital coitus (EMC) for (open) marriage (Smith and Smith 1974), most sociologists accept tacitly the functionalist reasoning that EMC violations ultimately reinforce the "normative superiority" of marriage. Davis (1976, p. 243) maintains that media-reported EMC violations "arouse sensational attention . . . for they represent both a suspension of the rule and provision of opportunities." In that regard, Sponaugle (1989) documents recent instances of public figures whose professional lives have been severely discredited because of media reports of their EMC violations (Gary Hart, Ted Kennedy, Wilbur Mills, Robert Baumann, Jimmy Baker, Jimmy Swaggart, and so on). Furthermore, observes Sponaugle, EMC is "one of the most common themes" in both literary fiction and nonfiction—the latter including accounts of the EMC behaviors of figures such as Franklin Roosevelt and John Kennedy. Finally, newspapers, magazines, drama, cinema, TV, music, and humorists also make EMC "a mainstay topic."

Although in 1976 Davis (p. 243) contended that media attention to EMC extended "far beyond . . . [its] numerical significance" in the population, by 1989 Sponaugle asserted that millions of persons engage in EMC at some point in their lives and that millions more are indirectly affected by those EMC behaviors. Using conservative estimates from the literature that 50 percent of ever-married males and 30 percent of ever-married females have engaged in EMC, and using as a base 1986 census figures for the ever- or currently married, Sponaugle calculates that "at least 52,000,000 Americans eighteen and older have been engaged in . . . [EMC] at least once while married." Second, to that number Sponaugle adds the so-far undocumented (but "substantial") numbers of never-married persons who have had coitus with married persons (Richardson 1986). Finally, he says that if we add to that figure persons *indirectly* affected by EMC ("spouses, children, parents, siblings, other relatives, friends, and colleagues"), the sum represents a majority of citizens (Sponaugle 1989, p. 189). Moreover, in European societies such as the Netherlands, EMC violations are apparently even more common than they are in the United States, and attitudes toward it are more tolerant (Buunk 1983, p. 314). In addition, countries having the strictest proscriptions and most severe penalties against EMC (e.g., Islamic and Roman Catholic) are known for widespread EMC deviation by males (W. J. Goode 1963). Finally, in view of increases in heterosexual cohabitators (characterized by similar monogamy norms) throughout Western societies, and in view of evidence (Blumstein and Schwartz 1983) that they are no more monogamous than marrieds, we may expand significantly the proportion of the population affected by violations of exclusivity norms.

How is it that such a ubiquitous rule coexists alongside such widespread deviation? How valid is functionalist reasoning that, by tacitly allowing elasticity in the rule, societies actually reinforce the uniqueness of marriage? Is Davis correct in asserting that EMC violations occur because of the "very intensity" of the rule (rules are made to be broken, and the more powerful the rule the greater the challenge to break it)? Although Sponaugle does not address these conceptual issues, he does review the empirical literature on *attitudes* toward EMC in the United States. He reports that although EMC attitudes have been investigated since the 1920s, the research has been of "poor quality" (p. 192). Most of the research is devoted to accounting for variation in indicators such as the following: "What is your opinion about a *married* person having sexual relations with someone *other* than the marriage partner? Is it always wrong, almost always wrong, wrong only sometimes, or not wrong at all?" In 1985, the percentages of a national sample of Americans choosing these four categories were 73.7, 13.4, 8.4, and 2.8, respectively (National Opinion Research Center 1986). (The remainder said "don't know" or did not answer.) This type of item is said to measure the respondent's belief in the appropriateness of EMC in terms of *general* societal norms. Separate "self-focused" indicators measure how appropriate the respondent perceives EMC is for himself or herself.

Sponaugle (1989, p. 205) summarizes eighteen "independent variables" shown by the literature to be related to the *approval* of EMC. These include approval of premarital coitus, lower marital satisfaction, years of schooling, less religiosity, larger community size, perceived opportunity for EMC, diffuse intimacy conception ("defined as the degree to which an individual focuses his or her satisfaction of intimacy needs on more than just his or her mate," Sponaugle, p. 197), male gender, premarital sexual activity, endorsement of gender equality, sociopolitical liberalism, younger age, being unmarried, being child free, less satisfaction with marital sex, autonomy of heterosexual interaction, marital power, and sexual pleasure emphasis.

What has been the underlying theoretical rationale for this type of research? From a functionalist perspective, variation in EMC attitudes is an indicator of the degree of social control of sexuality. Discovering the conditions under which persons approve or disapprove of EMC indicates the extent to which persons subjectively conform to dominant norms. As long as functionalist thought pervaded studies of marriage, it made sense to concentrate on EMC attitudes.

However, Stein (1989, p. 11) reports that recent theory on sexuality has moved beyond functionalist notions of " 'social control' to . . . [focus on] 'social change'. Individuals came to be seen as playing a greater part in shaping sexual behavior through social learning and daily situational interaction." Importantly, Stein indicates that "the theory of sexuality implicit in this latter paradigm differed from . . . [functionalism because] there is no natural sexual impulse which must be repressed in order for society to function smoothly." Her critique (1989, p. 12) of the functionalist alignment between marriage and sex is a modern statement of the question posed above by Weber and by Murdock: How do persons and groups struggle at both the micro and macro levels in order to create arrangements that facilitate their goals regarding sex? That these goals are as much *political* as they are personal is witnessed by ongoing struggles between New Right and progressive interest groups.

This fresh theory of sexuality turns the century-old functionalist alignment between marriage and sex on its head. Instead of marriage being viewed as conceptually more significant than sex, sexual interdependence occupies a conceptually prior position. Contemporary analysts no longer view "the sex drive as an object of regulation" (Davis 1976, p. 223) in the interests of social equilibrium. Stein argues instead that goals regarding sexuality are socially constructed. Consequently, rather than focusing either on the functions of sex for marital quality or on social control in the form of variation in EMC attitudes, the research emphasis shifts to (among other issues) the dialectics involved in creating and maintaining varied social expressions of sexual interdependencies. These expressions—whether marriage, cohabitation, or partners living in separate households—are subsumed by what Scanzoni et al. (1989) describe as the "sexually bonded primary relationship" (SBPR). Since SBPR partners are engaged in ongoing dialectics regarding a wide range of issues, their relationship is in continual development (Scanzoni and Marsiglio [a, b]).

One of the implications of this approach is that coitus with someone other than one's legal (or nonlegal) partner is no longer explored from a functionalist perspective. A more conceptually fruitful approach would, for instance, be to examine conditions and consequences of persons in

SBPRs having multiple sexual relationships in which marital status is, to be sure, a crucial variable. Underlying that issue is the social organization of the SBPR: What is it about the SBPR that makes multiple relationships a scientific issue as well as a trigger for media sensationalism? Some clues emerge from the recently developing "sociology of emotions" literature. Several analysts, including Collins (1981), argue that in addition to the cognitive and normative dimensions that preoccupied functionalists, emotions play an important part in shaping and in changing social organization at all levels of society. Thoits (1989, p. 318) defines emotions as "culturally delineated *types* of feelings or affects. . . . Emotions involve: (a) appraisals of a situational stimulus or context, (b) changes in physiological or bodily sensations, (c) the free or inhibited display of expressive gestures, and (d) a cultural label applied to specific constellations of one or more of the first three components."

In a recent anthology exploring love, no essay systematically examined the love–marriage connection, although all contributors acknowledged that, among other things, love is a powerful emotion (Sternberg and Barnes 1988). Likewise, in family sociology, little attention was paid to the theoretical connections between love and marriage. The most systematic treatment was W. J. Goode's (1959) functionalist argument that love, like sex, requires social control lest it disrupt social order. Peele (1988) and Berscheid (1988) contend that love tends to be correlated with another variable that is, among other things, also a powerful emotion—jealousy for one's sexual "property." Jealousy has received even less attention than love in the marriage literature (White and Mullen 1989). But if we draw on Thoits's definition of emotions, we can conceptualize jealousy as an "independent" variable that is at least as powerful as normative elements in circumscribing the SBPR as well as in accounting for persons' strong reactions to multiple sexual partnerships (MSP).

Besides love and jealousy, Katz (1988) identifies a third pertinent emotional dimension. In his review of Katz, E. Goode (1990) suggests that

deviance in general (including "adultery," p. 8), "is the existential pursuit of passion, a 'lucid' enterprise . . . a fevered out-of-one's head experience, a world of beauty all its own, accessible only to the . . . daring members of a soulful elite" (p. 7). If for want of a better label we call this the "heady experience" dimension, we may ask how all three emotions, alongside cognitive elements, help us grasp the complex intertwinings of sex and social relationships.

Cognitive elements circumscribing the SBPR include the all-important *definition of the situation*—a person perceives that she or he is or is not sexually interdependent with another—and these elements include norms prescribing meanings and degrees of sexual exclusivity. Simultaneously, *emotional* elements include the degree of jealousy felt for that sexual interdependence. Scanzoni et al. (1989) suggest that the SBPR, like all forms of social organization, passes through at least three phases of structuring or development—formation, maintenance and change (MC), and dissolution. Persons A and B may experience coitus but feel no jealousy (or love), nor define themselves as being sexually interdependent. If A and B subsequently define themselves as sexually interdependent, then they can be said to have entered an MC phase; moreover, there is very likely a high correlation between that definition and the rapid emergence of feelings of jealousy. Simultaneously, A or B may also be in a previously existing SBPR that may or may not include marriage, and that person may or may not reveal this to the other.

The 1980s saw several authors analyze multiple sexual relationships from a "woman's" or "feminist" perspective. (No comparable work examined them from a male perspective.) Among these, Lawson (1989) approached "adultery" from an essentially functionalist position, whereas Atwater (1982) approached the "extramarital connection" in terms of what Stein identified as choice and personal control. During 1974 and 1975, Atwater interviewed fifty self-selected women who had recently been or were then in an SBPR with one person while married to another person. Atwater begins her report by describing the several steps in the process of "getting involved." Step one is *preinvolvement.* Its first aspect is degree of premarital sexual activity. Atwater states that her respondents' premarital sexual behavior was high (80 percent) for that era. This indicates, she says, that her respondents had been actively engaging in sexual choices for a large portion of their lives. She calls the second aspect of preinvolvement "first opportunities." She reports that although all her respondents chose to "resume sexual monogamy at marriage," most women, regardless of marital status, receive subtle sexual invitations and sometimes outright propositions from men. Atwater indicates that her respondents "felt they did not suggest or invite" male overtures and were ill-prepared for this type of struggle. However, that kind of dialectic had an effect on the women's own development: They first had to come to terms with the unexpected reality that, contrary to folklore, being married does not (as Farber noted in 1964) exclude one from the "market." Second, they had to cultivate (or revive) skills necessary to resist unwanted overtures. Atwater identifies the existence of a role model (friend or kin who had "done it") as the third aspect. A fourth aspect (often overlapping with the third) is discussing MSP with a friend; and fifth is a period of serious reflection regarding potential sexual involvement. According to Atwater, these women did not merely "drift into 'affairs'" or become "spontaneously" swept away.

Atwater's step two, or *involvement,* describes the processes of entry into formation of an SBPR alongside marriage (p. 40). First she identifies situations such as work that supply the context for "repeated exposure" to another, and this repeated exposure "introduces a note of 'gradualism' which serves to ease the transition to extramarital involvement." Second, Atwater addresses the issue of emotions and concludes that women in her sample did not feel "in love" prior to first coitus, nor did they consider love a requisite for it. They did, however, report that the other person was a friend or that they "liked" him. Nonetheless, many women (and men) in an SBPR have experienced the phenomena described so far but chose not to have coitus with the other person. Hence,

to account for choice, Atwater reports that, in line with the literature, she found that the third and crucial element precipitating coitus subsumes a complex combination of current marital dissatisfaction and "personal needs for growth, knowledge, and sex" (p. 43). In some cases, there was very little dissatisfaction but extremely high personal needs.

Step three is *extramarital sex* or entry into a phase of maintenance/change. Atwater (p. 35) notes that the question of precisely when this occurs rests with a person's own definition—especially in light of evidence since Kinsey that a certain proportion of married women, in addition to those acknowledging coitus, admit extramarital "petting." Nevertheless, for Atwater's respondents, "genital intercourse" (p. 35) appeared to be the Rubicon. Previously, they had been "just friends" with the other person (even if they had petted); now they became lovers as well. In interpreting their pleasurable reactions to what for most of her respondents was their first extramarital coitus, Atwater asserts that her evidence "contradicts traditional myths that women can achieve sexual satisfaction only in marriage, and that guilt will ruin any sex that violates the marriage bed. . . . The extra sex is often equally as good or better than marital sex." In addition, Atwater identifies a second reaction: "a sense of learning, self-recognition, and self-discovery" (p. 47).

Step four is *afterwards* and explores women's emotions about being in a second SBPR. Atwater reports (p. 51) that although guilt did not undermine pleasure, nevertheless many of her respondents felt it very keenly. Richardson's (1986, 1988) studies of single women's relationships with married men suggest that secrecy is a major guilt-precipitating element in any covert multiple partner situation, and Atwater (p. 79) reports a similar finding. Although guilt among Atwater's respondents was assuaged by the presence of a "'peculiarly modern type of justification, namely, *self-fulfillment*'" (p. 51), they were well aware that their choices to exercise personal control are labeled as deviant. Their choices clash with the efforts of others (their husbands in particular) to exercise control over them via negative sanctions. Secrecy is a means to avoid those sanctions and the overt clashes that accompany them. Secrecy also postpones facing the *currently* unwanted choice between husband and lover (pp. 79–80).

It was beyond the scope of Atwater's investigation to detail the conditions under which women in her sample might move from either formation or maintenance/change into a dissolution phase of their nonlegal SBPR. Similarly, her main task was not to focus on the conditions under which some of the women separated from or remained with their husbands, nor to investigate whether a woman eventually did or did not marry a man with whom she had been covertly sexual. Nor did she explicitly address feelings of jealousy among her respondents. Nevertheless, her data and their interpretation are a prime example of the dialectic approach to sexuality described by Stein. Women *and* men are viewed as struggling for a wide range of personal (and political) goals. Dominant norms structuring marriage have limited women's goal attainment, most fundamentally in terms of their self-fulfillment *and not merely via the economic marketplace.* Waller (1938) was among the first to argue that the double standard allows men to enhance self-fulfillment through deviant sexual adventures.

Atwater (pp. 57ff) argues that a vital component of self-fulfillment among her respondents was the quest for *emotional intimacy,* defined by one as "the closeness and the ability to communicate with a male." Lacking intimacy with their husbands, respondents were seeking it with other men. At the same time, Atwater suggests a second component in the quest for fulfillment, namely, Katz's "heady experience" described above. The descriptions of their deviance provided by several of Atwater's respondents (pp. 60–63) are strongly analogous to experiential descriptions supplied by Katz's respondents of their deviance: "It was an ego trip"; "It was fun. . . . There's something very therapeutic about spending a couple of hours in a hotel room in the middle of business day"; "I get a kick out of the relationship. It's a thrill for me . . . the thrill of being with a man who wants

me as a woman, in a sexy way." This latter respondent connects her heady experience with intimacy: "If I hadn't gotten involved with him, I wouldn't have known him as well."

Modell (1989) describes younger persons over the past fifty years as "innovators" because they have created whole new sets of norms and behaviors regarding nonmarital sex. Atwater's argument is that younger married women (and men) are also creating new sets of norms and behaviors regarding sex and social relationships (SBPRs) *including marriage.* Her pivotal point is that as women are increasingly freed from economic dependence on men, women as well as men become freer to seek higher levels of emotional intimacy and "heady experience." She emphasizes that these goals "contrast with the traditional male emphasis on physical satisfaction" and conquest (Atwater 1982, p. 191). She implies that with persons seeking intimacy and experience, the norm is being created that if multiple sexual relationships enhance those goals, then persons may justify those relationships. Consequently, says Atwater (p. 204), we may expect that the incidence of multiple sexual relationships is likely to increase in the future.

RESEARCH DIRECTIONS

Lawson (1989, p. 309) predicts the future very differently: "There will . . . be less rather than more adultery . . . because . . . people will not stay married long enough to see it increase." Testing these alternative predictions involves a host of complex issues. For example, if and when a person is becoming preinvolved or involved she or he must face the issues of secrecy and guilt. It is those issues that most complicate Atwater's notion of emerging patterns. Formerly, secrecy was synonomous with "cheating." During the past two decades, proponents of "swinging" and other forms of "open" sexual patterns argued that openness eliminates cheating. However, observers such as Weis (1983) find no evidence to support either widespread creation of norms supporting openness or reduced inclinations toward sexual jealousy. To test Atwater, one must examine the degree to which persons now relabel secrecy to be what Becker (1960) called a "hedge" on their prior relationship. To what extent is the hedge justified in terms of intimacy and heady experience, thus muting the cheating label and minimizing guilt? Moreover, what part do a person's perceptions of another's jealousy play in researching the conditions under which secrecy is or is not being widely redefined as a mechanism to prolong one person's prior relationship until hard choices must be made?

These kinds of questions require a research design in which couples are followed over time and that describes the gradual development of persons and the structuring of their relationships.

First, among those already in an SBPR (whether legal or not), what are the conditions under which a person might enter a formation phase with a particular "prospect," i.e., someone with whom a person feels she or he might potentially establish an additional SBPR? What are the conditions under which the prospect becomes a sexual partner, that is, the person actually crosses into a maintenance/change phase of an additional SBPR? For instance, was the person in a dissolution phase of the relationship with his or her prior partner? Once SBPR multiplicity occurs, what are the consequences for the person's relationship with the prior partner? What are the conditions under which the person continues it, or else terminates sexual interdependence with the prior partner? If the person is residing with and/or is married to the prior partner, how are those two variables connected with the person's choices? These choices began with the allowance of a prospect and later a partner and thus multiplicity; and now entail wrestling with whether or not to continue that multiplicity.

Second, if relationship phases are so crucial, how may we describe them and account for movement across them? We might say that a formation phase is characterized by a person's discovery of high levels of intimacy and heady experience with another. An MC phase is characterized by the hope that these exchanges will continue and perhaps increase. A dissolution phase is characterized by the dimunition of these exchanges and uncertainty that they can or will expand. Third, Atwater (p. 193) argues that negotiation dynamics and their outcomes are strongly associated with intimacy, heady experience, and thus relationship phase. Once in an ongoing MC phase, the dialectics that the couple experience pertaining to day-to-day as well as to long-range matters keenly influence both kinds of benefits (Scanzoni et al. 1989) and thus through them affect the probability of seeking those benefits elsewhere.

In sum, sociologists are beginning to appreciate the complexities inherent in multiple sexual relationships—complexities that writers have wrestled with since the Old Testament (Heller 1984). A simple dichotomy between marital and extramarital sex reveals little about the emerging world scene in which women's historic economic dependence on men is being eroded at the same time that both genders are enlarging their mutual expectations for intimacy and experience. Added to those divergent trajectories are the constants of jealousy, distaste for secrecy, and the importance of hedging one's bets. The resulting sum of empirical complexities challenge sociologists to devise conceptual models in which "control of sex" is replaced by the "dialectics of sex."

(SEE ALSO: *Alternative Life-Styles; Heterosexual Behavior Patterns*)

REFERENCES

Atwater, Lynn 1982 *The Extramarital Connection.* New York: Irvington.

Becker, Howard S. 1960 "Notes on the Concept of Commitment." *American Journal of Sociology* 66:32–40.

Berscheid, Ellen 1988 "Some Comments on Love's Anatomy: Or, Whatever Happened to Old-Fashioned Lust?" In Robert J. Sternberg and Michael L. Barnes, eds., *The Psychology of Love.* New Haven: Yale University Press.

Blumstein, Philip, and Pepper Schwartz 1983 *American Couples: Money, Work, and Sex.* New York: Morrow.

Booth, Alan, ed. 1990 "Decade Review of the 1980s." *Journal of Marriage and Family* 52.

Buunk, Bram 1983 "Alternative Lifestyles from an

International Perspective: A Trans-Atlantic Comparison." In Eleanor D. Macklin and Roger H. Rubin, eds., *Contemporary Families and Alternative Lifestyles.* Beverly Hills, Calif.: Sage.

Collins, Randall 1981 "On the Microfoundations of Macrosociology." *American Journal of Sociology* 86: 984–1,014.

——1986 *Weberian Sociologial Theory.* New York: Cambridge University Press.

Davis, Kingsley 1976 "Sexual Behavior." In Robert Merton and Robert Nisbet, eds., *Contemporary Social Problems.* New York: Harcourt Brace Jovanovich.

Ehrman, Winston 1964 "Marital and Nonmarital Sexual Behavior." In Harold T. Christensen, ed., *Handbook of Marriage and Family.* Chicago: Rand McNally.

Farber, Bernard 1964 *Family Organization and Interaction.* San Francisco: Chandler.

Goode, Erich 1990 "Crime Can Be Fun: The Deviant Experience." *Contemporary Sociology* 19:5–12.

Goode, William J. 1959 "The Theoretical Importance of Love." *American Sociological Review* 24:38–47.

——1963 *World Revolution and Family Patterns.* New York: Free Press.

Heller, Joseph. 1984. *God Knows.* New York: Knopf.

Katz, Jack 1988 *Seductions of Crime: Moral and Sensual Attractions of Doing Evil.* New York: Basic Books.

Kinsey, Alfred C., Wardell Pomeroy, and Clyde Martin 1948 *Sexual Behavior in the Human Male.* Philadelphia: Saunders.

——1953 *Sexual Behavior in the Human Female.* Philadelphia: Saunders.

Lawson, Annette 1989 *Adultery: An Analysis of Love and Betrayal.* New York: Basic Books.

Malinowski, Bronislaw 1930 "Parenthood: The Basis of Social Structure." In V. F. Calverton and S. D. Schmalhausen, eds., *The New Generation.* New York: McCauley.

Modell, John 1989 *Into One's Own: From Youth to Adulthood in the United States, 1920–1975.* Berkeley: University of California Press.

Murdock, George P. 1949 *Social Structure.* New York: Macmillan.

National Opinion Research Center 1986 *General Social Surveys, 1972–1986; Cumulative Codebooks.* Chicago: University of Chicago, NORC.

Peele, Stanton 1988 "Fools for Love: The Romantic Ideal, Psychological Theory, and Addictive Love." In Robert J. Sternberg and Michael L. Barnes, eds., *The Psychology of Love.* New Haven, Conn.: Yale University Press.

Richardson, Laurel 1986 *The New Other Woman: Contemporary Single Women in Affairs with Married Men.* New York: Free Press.

——1988 "Secrecy and Status: The Social Construction of Forbidden Relationships." *American Sociological Review* 53:209–219.

Scanzoni, John, Karen Polonko, Jay Teachman, Linda Thompson 1989 *The Sexual Bond: Rethinking Families and Close Relationships.* Newbury Park, Calif.: Sage.

Scanzoni, John, and William Marsiglio (Forthcoming) (a) "Marriage and Sex as Social Constructs: Conceptual Issues and Research Questions." *Marriage and Family Review.*

——(Forthcoming) (b) "The Social Organization of Primary Relations: Toward a Recasting of the Institution of Families."

Smith, James R., and Lynn G. Smith, eds. 1974 *Beyond Monogamy: Recent Studies of Sexual Alternatives in Marriage.* Baltimore: Johns Hopkins University Press.

Sponaugle, George C. 1989 "Attitudes toward Extramarital Relations." In Kathleen McKinney and Susan Sprecher, eds., *Human Sexuality: The Societal and Interpersonal Context.* Norwood, N.J.: Ablex.

Sprey, Jetse 1986 "A Reply to Kersti Yllo." *Journal of Marriage and Family* 48:887.

Stein, Arlene 1989 "Three Models of Sexuality: Drives, Identities, and Practices." *Sociological Theory* 7:1–13.

Sternberg, Robert J., and Michael L. Barnes, eds. 1988 *The Psychology of Love.* New Haven, Conn.: Yale University Press.

Thoits, Peggy A. 1989 "The Sociology of Emotions." In Richard Scott and Judith Blake, eds., *Annual Review of Sociology,* Vol. 15. Palo Alto: Annual Reviews, Inc.

Waller, Willard 1938 *The Family: A Dynamic Interpretation.* New York: Dryden.

Weis, David L. 1983 " 'Open' Marriage and Multilateral Relationships: The Emergence of Nonexclusive Models of the Marriage Relationship." In Eleanor D. Macklin and Roger H. Rubin, eds., *Contemporary Families and Alternative Lifestyles.* Newbury Park, Calif.: Sage.

White, Gregory L., and Paul E. Mullen 1989 *Jealousy: Theory, Research, and Clinical Strategies.* New York: Guilford.

JOHN SCANZONI
WILLIAM MARSIGLIO

SEXUALLY TRANSMITTED DISEASES

Until the 1980s, social science research on sexually transmitted diseases (STDs) has been focused primarily on the history of various pestilences, the epidemiology of these diseases, and the description of mass disaster (Brandt 1985; Aral and Holmes 1989). The topic commonly considered was syphillis, long the most identified and feared of the STDs. Historians and anthropologists have written numerous treatises on its origin and the social consequences of its introduction into isolated, tribal, or Third World societies (Wood 1978; Crosby 1969; Hart 1978). More recently, the consequences of other STDs have been studied, especially as a sequela of prostitution (Kalm 1985; Porde 1981; Poherat, Rothenberg, and Bross 1981).

When awareness of the "sexual revolution" finally sank in enough to get social scientists and epidemiologists thinking about the effects of STDs on less traditionally sexually active parties than prostitutes and their clients, the literature turned to the newly sexually active and therefore newly vulnerable teenagers (Washington, Sweet, and Shafer 1985; Zelnik and Kanter 1980) and to other young people involved in premarital sex (McCormack et al. 1985; O'Reilly and Aral 1985). The intensification of discussion and research on STDs, however, came only with the medical community's horrified acknowledgment that the newest STD to become epidemiologically important was also the deadliest, and that *social*, not just biological, information was essential in order to combat it.

When AIDS (acquired immune deficiency syndrome) first began to be discussed in the late 1970s—long before it was given its current appellation—the medical community was already alarmed at its mystery and virulence (Aral and Holmes 1989). But unhappily it took years before extraordinary measures, such as institutes devoted to AIDS research, were hurried into being. Journalists like Randy Shilts persuasively argue that the lack of a three-alarm reaction right from the start was due to the fact that the early victims were homosexual men and not Legionnaires or Girl Scouts (Shilts 1987). While at least the basic facts

of AIDS—for example, that in the United States homosexual men are disproportionately infected, along with people who mix blood during exchange of hypodermic needles—are inescapable in today's media, the sharing of information in the early 1980s was abysmally inadequate, and myth and rumor educated more people than did either social or medical research.

With the fine accuracy of hindsight, it is clear that sociologists should have immediately looked at the sociocultural histories of recent sexual behavior in sectors of homosexual and heterosexual life and used this information to help study disease transmission—indeed, even to predict the eventual holocaust. But no one was proactive, and it took years for a pertinent literature to emerge. The exceptions to this rule were a small group of social researchers at the Centers for Disease Control, whose work was restricted to STD-related topics, and a few epidemiologists studying the social location of this disease in the gay male world (Aral and Holmes 1990) and in Africa. Otherwise, the analysis of AIDS remained mostly ghettoized in medical literatures until the mid-1980s.

Finally, the combination of organized gay activism and public alarm made more research money available and launched a flood of AIDS research. Indeed, interest in sex research in general, previously an area treated like a poor and unwelcome relative, received more credibility and funding—though not enough to allow a national probability study on sex behaviors to get funded. A large, approved study to be funded by the National Institutes of Health was stopped in 1990 after Senator Jesse Helms convinced the U.S. Senate that Americans should not be exposed to "dirty" questions. Nonetheless, research on sexuality, especially on STDs and on sexuality and STDs among gay men, found funds—and larger, more diverse, professional audiences. Before AIDS prevalence among gay men was well understood or publicized, research was describing how great numbers of anonymous sexual contacts in gay bars, baths, and parks happened and how such activity set the stage for infection (Darrow 1979; Ross 1984; Klovdahl 1985). By the mid-1980s research attention had become racheted on how gay and other sexual cultures exposed people to AIDS.

As AIDS gained its terrible momentum, a smaller preceding and parallel literature on herpes, mostly focused on the stigma of having the disease and/or its impact on subsequent behavior, paled in importance. Still, this research provides for interesting comparisons between herpes sufferers and HIV-positive persons. For example, a study of 1,016 college students found that 2.6 percent of them had had herpes; 89 percent of these students informed partners, and 65 percent looked for similarly infected partners; most did not opt for sexual abstinence (Mirotznik et al. 1987). These responses can be compared with those given when the stakes became deadlier.

Current AIDS literature centers on two main questions: (1) who is at risk and why; and (2) risk-reduction factors, including education.

WHO IS AT RISK AND WHY

While more heterosexual men and women have contracted the disease in Africa and worldwide and the World Health Organization projects that by the year 2000, up to 90 percent of all HIV infections in the world will be transmitted heterosexually, most of the AIDS literature in the United States is primarily on homosexual men and secondarily on intravenous-drug users (Aral and Holmes 1991). Research established that transmission of body fluids, semen and especially blood, made infection possible, though not 100 percent predictable (Aral and Holmes 1990; Winkelstein et al. 1987). Many researchers are interested in rates and ratios of both heterosexual and homosexual anal sex, since it is believed that the abrasion of skin during anal intercourse creates an opportunity of infection from HIV-laced blood or semen (Voeller 1989; Sion et al. 1988). The interaction of co-factors in transmission is, however, still far from an uncontroversial topic (Peterman and Curran 1986), especially since researchers disagree or demur as to what is risk-related.

Most researchers include in their lists of risk factors number of partners, sex of partners, IV-drug use or IV-drug-using partners (Anderson and Johnson 1990), frequency of intercourse (Aral and Cates 1989), use of condoms (Aral and Cates 1989; Stall 1988), contact with prostitutes (Reinish, Sanders, and Zeimba-Davis 1988), and sex with bisexual men (Reinish, Sanders, and Tremla-Davis 1989). This last factor has been of increasing interest, since there seems to be more bisexuality than mainstream research acknowledged previously, and because this is an obvious bridge between high- and low-HIV-rate populations, information about bisexuality has become critical. A study of lesbian women, a group usually thought of as low-risk, showed that not only had 81 percent of these women had sex with men, but at least one-third of their male partners had had sex with another man. Women with bisexual male partners were also more likely to have had anal sex (Padian et al. 1987). Bisexual men constitute a particularly great risk factor if they make regular forays into the gay-male world unbeknownst to their female partner. This proves likely to be the situation, especially among married couples or in a minority community where the behavior itself may necessitate utmost secrecy and may even be defined by the participant as "not homosexual" and therefore not risky (Carrier 1985; Blumstein, and Schwartz 1977).

Other, less obvious risks include the general possibility of deviousness and lies from a partner. In a poll conducted by Cochran and Mays (1990), 196 men and 226 women aged eighteen to twenty-five completed an anonymous eight-page questionnaire on sexual strategies. The findings indicated that a significant number of both men and women told a lie in order to have sex. Men lied more frequently than women, but both sexes were actively and passively willing to deceive a date.

Age itself has been studied as a high-risk factor. Teenagers have been shown to have irregular sexual contact and therefore less risk of STDs (Reinish, Sanders, and Zeimba-Davis 1988); age also correlates with significant levels of unprotected sex, including anal intercourse and multiple partners who are acquaintances or strangers (Reinish et al. 1990). College students studied by Reinish et al. (1990) were particularly casual about condom use: Less than two-thirds had used a condom in the previous year, less than one-third had used a condom the last time they had vaginal or anal intercourse, and only half had ever used contraceptive methods that protected against STD transmission. Of the respondents, those in exclusive sexual relationships reported the highest levels of intercourse. This finding prompted the researchers' concern that while it might seem that a committed sexual relationship lowered the overall risk of HIV infection by reducing the number of partners, risk might be increased because of *frequency* of relations, unless partners used condoms and knew enough *true* information about their partners' social and drug history. A recent set of qualitative research notes indicates that condom use may decrease, even among populations that most need to use them, for socioemotional reasons. Kane's population of women with HIV-probable partners in the drug culture refused, as an act of solidarity, to use condoms. These women felt that using a condom would indicate their awareness and condemnation of their partner's addiction, thereby alienating him and harming the relationship (Kane 1990).

The most voluminous risk research concerns drug users themselves. The use of alcohol and various other drugs has been shown to correlate strongly with unsafe health and sex practices (Stall et al. 1988; Stall 1988; Siegel et al. 1989). Researchers have gone on to specify when drugs are used, by whom, and so forth. For example, Leigh (1990) found that heterosexual and homosexual patterns of drug use differ: Gay men were less affected by drinking and did more risk taking when using cocaine, whereas heterosexual risk taking was predicted largely by total frequency of sex, with only a small amount of the variance explained by having partners who used drugs or alcohol. Fullilove and Fullilove (1989) found that 62 percent of the 222 black inner-city teenagers they studied used crack, and 51 percent of the users said they combined crack use with sex. Forty-one percent of the teenagers had had at least one STD; those who used crack with sex had a significantly higher rate of STD infection. The correlation between crack use, sex, and STD

transmission has been found by many other investigators (Goldsmith 1988).

Researchers' concern with drug use covers not only the loss of judgment, the sale of sex for drugs, and the limited use of safe-sex practices; it has increasingly become concentrated on infection by exchange of blood by mutual use of the same needles during intravenous-drug use. In a paper by Freeman et al. (1987), a comparison of gay male and IV-drug users showed that peer support helped create safer sexual practices for gays while lack of social organization reduced IV-drug users' chances of self-protection. Of the drug users, 93 percent were well aware of their exposure, and 68 percent knew that needle sharing could transmit AIDS. Some individual attempts at decreasing the use of potentially contaminated needles had been made, but the authors felt the only way to help reduce risk in this population was to create organizations for needle dispensation, which could eventually create a culture of mutual protection. Opinion has changed from considering IV-drug users uneducable to recognizing substantial successes in changing their drug regime to include more self-protective habits (Hopkins 1988). Still, ethnography shows that needle sharing between addicted partners is seen as an intimate and bonding behavior, and this makes change more difficult.

Perhaps the newest risk group to receive research attention is women. Since AIDS surfaced in this country among gay males, the lack of attention to women might seem reasonable—until one remembers that, as partners of bisexual men, as drug users, or as inhabitants of lands where AIDS is not a "gay disease," they would always have been at risk.

At present, the majority of women with AIDS are intravenous-drug users. The next most beset population—and one that has grown steadily—is women with a partner who is at risk for AIDS. As of November 1986, women in this latter category constituted only 7 percent of all AIDS sufferers (Guman and Hardy 1987); but by January 1989 the figure had increased to 9 percent (Campbell 1990). Most of the women in Campbell's study are in their childbearing years; 79 percent are between the ages of thirteen and thirty-nine. Slightly more than half are black; about one-fifth are Hispanic. At present, AIDS cases occur fourteen times more frequently among black women and nine times more frequently among Hispanic women than among white women.

A good deal of concern today focuses on perinatal transmission of AIDS. Children of infected mothers have about a 50 percent chance of being born with the disease (Aral and Holmes 1990), and many women, even with knowledge of this risk, choose not to abort (*Proceedings NIMH/ NIDA Conference on Women and AIDS* 1989). AIDS concerns attend other reproductive issues as well, such as the safety of artificial insemination. While the American Fertility Association has guidelines that exclude high-risk men from donating sperm, methods for testing for HIV seem to be inconsistent—and private physicians may not test at all (Campbell 1990).

Tackling the problem of women and STDs on an international level presents special problems. In Asia and the Middle East, where women's sexual activity outside marriage at best damages their chance for marriage and at worst is a death sentence, getting knowledge and contraception to them is a herculean job (Leslie-Harwit and Meheus 1989). Data indicate that these women are increasingly at risk. In Taiwan, for example, nearly 50 percent of married women aged twenty to twenty-four reported having experienced premarital intercourse, compared with 14 percent of married women aged thirty-five to thirty-nine (Cernada et al. 1986). In Thailand, women are essentially sexually ignorant, yet there are approximately 700,000 prostitutes there, most between the ages of fifteen and twenty-four and with a history of STDs. There as in other such countries, contrary to supposition, prostitutes are well utilized by indigenous men, not just by tourists and military, so STDs are regularly brought home to wives and girlfriends (Harwit-Leslie et al. 1989; Aral and Holmes 1991). In Kenya, the same study showed the incidence of general STDs for women under twenty to be 57 percent. Even more than a decade ago, similar statistics existed for Nigeria (Sogbetun et al. 1977). Miscarriages and infertility

are extremely common, but unfortunately that is secondary compared with the high percentages of seropositivity for HIV now surfacing throughout Africa (Quinn et al. 1986). Besides inadequate clinical help and information, cultural norms impede self-protection.

RISK REDUCTION AND EDUCATION

It is difficult to discuss risk without touching on risk reduction. Nonetheless, there is a literature that investigates specific risk-reduction strategies, curricula, and behavior modification, and that targets specific populations—such as gay men, minorities, teenagers, mothers, or drug users—with what is hoped to be a useful approach.

The most encouraging findings indicate that for at least one targeted group, gay men, changing risky sexual behavior is possible. This is a significant discovery, since such personal habits as drinking and overeating have been notoriously resistant to sustained modification (Research and Decisions Corporation 1984). Researchers in San Francisco, however, have found that gay men there have reduced numbers of partners and frequency of sex and increased safe-sex practices (McKeisick, Horstman, and Coates 1985; McKeisick, Wiley et al. 1985). But since much of this change is attributed to the extraordinary social power of organized homosexual groups in the city, the question arose as to whether such extraordinary change could occur among gay men operating with less daily construction and maintenance of safe-sex norms (Fisher 1988). However, change *has* happened across the United States, indicating both the strength of educational and social-control efforts among gay activists—and, perhaps, the great motivation for change when suffering and death are not only possible but probable (Feldman 1986; Martin 1987; Siegel and Glassman 1989).

If this conclusion seems self-evident, it is not, because change in gay-male circles is *not* 100 percent—or even close to it. Changes in behavior are associated with proximity to especially plagued populations; the more distance, the less change in behavior (Fox et al. 1987). Furthermore, even in densely infected areas, a full 25 percent of HIV-negative men seem to continue risky sexual practices (Willoughby et al. 1987). There is even evidence that for some men, fear wears off and unprotected sex practices increase (Martin 1987).

Naturally, a great deal of pressure is on researchers to find out what helps all kinds of people protect themselves from AIDS. Depressingly but predictably, research finds that education alone is inadequate for behavioral change. For example, Calabrese, Harris, and Easly (1987) found that for gay men outside big cities, attendance at a safe-sex lecture, reading a safe-sex brochure, HIV-antibody testing, advice from a physician, and counseling were all inadequate. Other sex-education efforts have found limited effect and often for a limited period of time. For example, researchers assessed the impact of a ten-week university course on human sexuality and AIDS-related behavior. While students who had taken the course possessed more information about actual risk, worried about AIDS more, and asked sexual partners more questions relating to AIDS than did a control group, they did *not* increase their use of condoms or other contraceptives, decrease their number of sexual partners, or spend a longer time getting to know a prospective sexual partner (Baldwin, Whitely, and Baldwin 1990).

The disappointing results of sex education have caused researchers to look for other hooks. Because self-esteem and confidence give ego strength, and presumably the ability to protect oneself from others'—as well as one's own—desires, a number of researchers have pursued this avenue for AIDS prevention (Becher 1988). Role playing, assertiveness skills, and so forth are seen as having long-term payoff (Strecher et al. 1986). Some researchers reasonably argue that people have to learn the same approach to *many* risky behaviors and that consistent attitudes will help them in their sexual life as well as when they face such temptations as drugs and alcohol (Boyer 1989).

No one pretends that any one approach is appropriate for all audiences. Increasingly, this literature studies separate strategies for different groups. Students of race, ethnicity, and gender understand not only that these groups interpret language through their own matrix, but also that reality is filtered through culture. Finally, this basic sociological truism has benefited research and education among at-risk populations. An example is gender differences; Campbell (1990) noted the limitations of education programs aimed at women, especially non-IV-drug users, who resist feeling at risk. She finds partners of IV-drug users unlikely to be assertive and unable to insist on safe sex. Most of these women are already in subordinate, if not abusive, situations, and their vulnerability and passivity have to be addressed before any other kind of progress can be made. She adds that there are special issues about condom use among minority women, since minority males reject them more resolutely than do Caucasian men. Campbell also reminds the reader that educating prostitutes, both for their own safety and for that of others, needs to take in the dual issues of their gender and their profession. She also makes a good point about overreliance on women as the safety net in sexual relations.

Among working-class and lower-income black women, gender issues often make safe-sex guidelines seem impossibly theoretical. Unemployment has set black men in more transient relations to these black women, and partners are unlikely to be engaged in the kind of cooperative communication many of the safe-sex guidelines assume (Fullilove et al. 1989). Fullilove and Fullilove also highlight black women's and teenagers' increased vulnerability to disease because of relatively high rates of nonmonogamy among potential partners. The authors feel that individual strategies are unlikely to be as powerful as a "reknitting of community connections" for the evolution of protective norms. Social disorganization further complicates things by giving less, and less accurate, information to black and Hispanic populations.

But even designing messages directly for minorities or finding community outlets for dissemination doesn't begin to handle the delicacy of reaching and influencing at-risk persons. Target audiences for the researcher are not necessarily so self-identified. For example, lesbian women who have occasional intercourse with bisexual partners may not consider themselves at risk (Reinish et al. 1990). Hispanic men irregularly visiting gay bars and having unprotected anal intercourse may not use condoms with their wives in part because, as the "activo," they do not see themselves as homosexual or having participated in a homosexual act and therefore do not perceive themselves as being at risk. Issues about identification, culture, and gender relations constantly bedevil both researcher and health worker (Magana 1990).

The emergence of AIDS as a social issue has not only revitalized interest in the social context and consequences of sexually transmitted diseases; it has finally caused medical research to understand more fully how disease can never be effectively studied outside of social conditions or without adequate information about relevant social actors. Still just in its infancy is a fuller consideration of institutional and public responses to STDs, for example, how public policy gets made and by whom (Volinn 1989), or why some communities respond with compassion, others with fear, and others not at all. The social construction of disease, and of STDs in particular, is an intriguing area of social science research.

(SEE ALSO: *Alternative Life-Styles; Drug Abuse; Heterosexual Behavior Patterns; Sexual Behavior and Marriage; Sexual Orientation*)

REFERENCES

Anderson, R. M., and A. M. Johnson 1990 "Rates of Sexual Partner Change in Heterosexual and Homosexual Populations in the United Kingdom." In B. Voeller, J. M. Reinisk, and M. Gottlieb, eds., *AIDS and Sex: An Integrated Biomedical and Behavioral Approach.* New York: Oxford University Press.

Aral, S., and W. Cates 1989 "The Multiple Dimensions of Sexual Behavior as Risk Factors for Sexually Transmitted Disease: The Sexually Experienced Are Not Necessarily Active." *Sexually Transmitted Diseases* 16:173–177.

Aral, S., and K. Holmes 1990 "Epidemiology of Sexually Transmitted Diseases." In K. Holmes, P. A. Mardh, P. F. Sparling, and P. J. Wiesner, eds., *Sexually Transmitted Diseases.* New York: McGraw-Hill.

———1991 "Sexually Transmitted Diseases in the AIDS Era." *Scientific American* 264 (February):62–69.

Baldwin, J. I., S. Whitely, and J. D. Baldwin 1990 "Changing AIDS and Fertility Related Behavior: The Effectiveness of Sexual Education." *Journal of Sex Research* 27:245–262.

Becher, M. H. 1988 "AIDS and Behavior Change." *Public Health Review* 16:1–11.

Boyer, R. 1989 *Private Acts, Social Consequences.* New York: Free Press.

Blumstein, P., and Pepper Schwartz 1977 "Male Bisexuality." *Urban Life.*

Brandt, A. M. 1985 *No Magic Bullet.* New York: Oxford University Press.

Calabrese, L. H., B. Harris, and K. Easly 1987 "Analysis of Variables Impacting on Safe Sexual Behavior among Homosexual Men in an Area of Low Incidence for AIDS." Paper presented at the Third International Conference on AIDS, Washington, D.C.

Campbell, Carol A. 1990 "Women and AIDS." *Social Science and Medicine* 30:407–415.

Carrier, J. M. 1985 "Mexican Male Bisexuality." *Journal of Homosexuality* 1:75–85.

Cernada, G. P., M. Chang, H. Lin, T. Sun, and C. Cernada 1986 "Implications for Adolescent Sex Education in Taiwan." *Studies in Family Planning* 17:181–187.

Cochran, S. D., and V. M. Mays 1990 "Sex, Lies and HIV." *New England Journal of Medicine* 322:774–775.

Crosby, A. W. 1969 "The Early History of Syphillis: A Reappraisal." *American Anthropologist* 71:218–227.

Darrow, William 1979 "Sexually Transmitted Diseases in Gay Men: An Insider's View." *Sexually Transmitted Diseases* 6:278–280.

Feldman, D. A. 1986 "AIDS Health Promotion and Clinically Applied Anthropology." In D. A. Feldman and T. K. Jolinson, eds., *Method and Theory.* New York: Praeger.

Fisher, J. D. 1988 "Possible Effects of Reference Group Based Social Influence on AIDS-risk Behavior and AIDS Prevention." *American Psychologist* 43:914–920.

Fox, R., D. Ostrow, R. Valdiserri, B. Van Rader, and B. F. Pall 1987 "Changes in Sexual Activities among Participants in the Multi Center AIDS Cohort

Study." Paper presented at the Third International Conference on AIDS, Washington, D.C.

Freeman, S. R., D. C. Des Jarlais, J. L. Sotheran, J. Garber, H. Cohen, and D. Smith 1987 "AIDS and Self-Organization among Intravenous Drug Users." *International Journal of Addictions* 23:201–219.

Fullilove, M. T., and R. E. Fullilove 1989 "Intersecting Epidemics: Black Teen Crack Use and Sexually Transmitted Disease." *Journal of American Medical Women's Association* 44:146–153.

Fullilove, M. T., R. E. Fullilove, K. Hayes, and S. Gross 1990 "Black Women and AIDS Prevention: A View Towards Understanding the Gender Rules," *Journal of Sex Research,* 27(1), p. 47–64.

Goldsmith, M. F. 1988 "Sex Tied to Drugs = STD Spread." *Journal of the American Medical Association* 260:2009.

Guman, M. E., and A. Hardy 1987 "Epidemiology of AIDS in Women in the United States 1981 through 1986." *Journal of American Medical Association* 257:2039–2042.

Hart, G. 1978 "Social and Psychological Aspects of Venereal Disease in Papua New Guinea." *British Journal of Venereal Disease* 54:215–217.

Hopkins, William 1988 "Needle Sharing and Street Behavior in Response to AIDS in New York City." In National Institute on Drug Abuse Research Monograph Series, Mono 80–40–58 (HV 5825 n.38a no.80).

Kalm, F. 1985 "The Two Faces of Antillean Prostitution." *Archives of Sexual Behavior* 203–217. Vol 14. No 3 June, 1985.

Kane, S. 1990 "AIDS, Addiction and Condom Use: Sources of Sexual Risk for Heterosexual Women." *Journal of Sex Research* 27:427–444.

Klovdahl, Alden S. 1985 "Social Networks and the Spread of Infectious Diseases: The AIDS Example." *Social Science Medicine* 21:1203–1216.

Leigh, B. C. 1990 "Sex and Drugs." *Journal of Sex Research* 27:199–213.

Leslie-Harwit, M., and A. Meheus 1989 "Sexually Transmitted Disease in Young People: The Importance of Health Education." *Sexually Transmitted Diseases.*

Magana, Raul 1990 "Bisexuality Among Hispanics." Paper Presented at *CDC Workshop on Bisexuality and AIDS, American Institutes for Research.*

Martin, J. L. 1987 "The Impact of AIDS on Gay Male Sexual Behavioral Patterns in New York City." *American Journal of Public Health* 77:578–584.

McCormack, W. M., B. Rosner, D. E. McComb et al. 1985 "Infection with Chlamydia Trachimates in Women College Students." *American Journal of Epidemiology* 121:107–115.

McKeisick, L., W. Horstman, and T. J. Coates 1985 "AIDS and Sexual Behavior Reported by Gay Men in San Francisco." *American Journal of Public Health* 75:493–496.

McKeisick, L., J. A. Wiley, T. J. Coates, R. Stall, G. Sarka, S. Morin, K. Charles, W. Horstman, and M. A. Conant 1985 "Recent Reported Changes in Sexual Behavior of Men at Risk for AIDS in San Francisco 1982–1984. The AIDS Behavioral Research Project." *Public Health Report* 100:622–629.

Mirotznik, J., R. D. Shapiro, O. E. Steinhart, and O. Gillespie 1987 "Genital Herpes: An Investigation into Its Attitudinal and Behavioral Correlates." *Journal of Sex Research* 23:266–272.

O'Reilly, K. R., and S. O. Aral 1985 "Adolescence and Sexual Behavior: Trends and Implications for STDs." *Journal of Adolescent Health Care* 6:262–270.

Padian, N., L. Marquis, D. P. Francis, R. E. Anderson, G. W. Rutherford, P. M. O'Malley, and W. Winkelstein 1987 "Male to Female Transmission of Human Immunodeficiency Virus." *Journal of the American Medical Association* 258:788–790.

Peterman, T. A., and J. W. Curran 1986 "Sexual Transmission of Human Immunovirus." *Journal of American Medical Association* 256:2222–2226.

Poherat, J. J., R. Rothenberg, and D. C. Bross 1981 "Gonorrhea in Street Prostitutes: Epidemiology and Legal Implications." *Sexually Transmitted Diseases* 8:241–244.

Porde, S. 1987 "Sexually Transmitted Disease in Ethiopia: Social Factors Contributing to Their Speed and Implications for Developing Countries." *British Journal of Venereal Disease* 557:357–362.

Quinn, T. C., J. M. Mann, J. W. Curran, and P. Piot. "AIDS in Africa." *Science* 234:955–963.

Proceedings NIMH/NIDA Conference on Women and AIDS: Promoting Health Behavior 1989 Washington, D.C.: American Psychiatric Press.

Reinish, J. M., C. A. Hill, S. A. Sanders, and M. Ziemba-Davis 1990 "Sexual Behavior among Heterosexual College Students." *Focus 5:3.*

Reinish, J. M., S. A. Sanders, and M. Ziemba-Davis 1989 "Self-labeled orientation, sexual behavior and knowledge about AIDS; Implications for biomedical research and education programs." In S. J. Blumenthal, A. Eichler, and G. Weissman, eds., *Proceedings of NIMH/NIDA Workshop on Women and AIDS: Pro-*

moting Health Behavior. Washington, D.C.: American Psychiatric Press.

Reinish, J., S. Sanders, and Mary Zeimba-Davis 1988 "The Study of Sexual Behavior in Relation to the Transmission of Human Immunovirus." *American Psychologist* 43:11,921–927.

Research and Decisions Corporation 1984 "Designing an Effective AIDS Prevention Campaign Strategy for San Francisco: Results from the First Probability Study of an Urban Gay Male Community." San Francisco AIDS Foundation. Also see Second Probability Study, 1985.

Ross, M. W. 1984 "Sexually Transmitted Diseases in Homosexual Men: A Study of Four Societies." *British Journal of Venereal Disease* 60:52–66.

Shilts, Randy 1987 *And the Band Played On.* New York: St. Martin's.

Siegel, K., F. P. Mesagno, J. Y. Chen, and G. Christ 1989 "Factors Distinguishing Risky and Safer Sex." *Social Science and Medicine* 28:561–569.

Siegel, Karolyn, and Marc Glassman 1989 "Individual and Aggregate Level Change in Sexual Behavior among Gay Men at Risk for AIDS." *Archives of Sexual Behavior* 18:335–348.

Sion, F. S., C. A. Morais De Sa, M. C. Rachid DeLacerda, E. P. Quinhoes, M. S. Pereira, B. Galvao, and E. A. Casrilno 1988 "The Importance of Anal Intercourse in Transmission to Women." Paper presented at the Fourth Annual International Conference on AIDS, Stockholm Abstract 4007.

Sogebetun, A. O., K. O. Alausa, and A. O. Osaba. "Sexually Transmitted Diseases in Ibadan, Nigeria." *British Journal of Venereal Disease* 53:155–160.

Stall, R. 1988 "The Prevention of HIV Infection Associated with Drug and Alcohol Use During Sexual Activity." *Advances in Alcohol and Substance Abuse* 7:73–88.

———, S. McKeisick, J. A. Wiley, T. J. Coates, and S. Ostrow 1988 "Alcohol and Drug Use During Sexual Activity and Compliance with Safe Sex Guidelines for AIDS: The AIDS Behavioral Research Project." *Health Education Quarterly* 13:359–371.

Strecher, V. J., B. M. DeVellis, M. H. Becher, and I. M. Resenstock 1986 "The Role of Self Efficacy in Achieving Health Behavior Change." *Health Education Quarterly* 13:73–92.

Voeller, B. 1989 "Heterosexual Anal Intercourse." Mariposa Occasional Paper 1B. New York: Mariposa Education and Research Foundation.

Volinn, Isle 1989 "Issues of Definitions and Their Implication: AIDS and Leprosy." *Social Science and Medicine* 20:1157–1162.

Washington, A. E., R. L. Sweet, and M. A. B. Shafer 1985 "Pelvic Inflammatory Disease and Its Sequellae in Adolescents." *Journal of Adolescent Health Care* 6:298–310.

Willoughby, B., M. T. Scheiter, W. J. Boyko, K. J. P. Craib, M. S. Weaver, and B. Douglas 1987 "Sexual Practices and Condom Use in a Cohort of Homosexual Men: Evidence of Differential Modification Behavior Between Seropositive and Seronegative Men." Paper presented at the Third International Conference on AIDS, Washington, D.C.

Winkelstein, W., D. H. Lyman, N. Padian, R. Grant, M. Samuel, J. A. Wilay, R. W. Anderson, W. Lang, J. Riggs, and J. A. Levy 1987 "Sexual Practices and Risk of Infection by the Human Immunodeficiency Virus." *Journal of the American Medical Association* 16:321–325.

Wood, C. S. 1978 "Syphillis in Anthropological Perspective." *Social Science Medicine* 12:47–55.

Zelnik, M., and M. Kanter 1980 "Sexual Activity, Contraceptive Use and Pregnancy among Metropolitan Area Teenagers 1971–1979." *Family Planning Perspectives* 12:230–237.

Zelnik, M. and M. Kanter, 1977 "Contraceptive Experience of Young Unmarried Women in the United States 1976–71." *Family Planning Perspectives* 9:55–71.

SEXUAL ORIENTATION As Nietzsche observed, "[O]nly that which has no history is definable" (1968, p. 516). By these terms the concept of *sexual orientation* may be difficult to define with any assurance of general agreement. It is mired in conflicting interpretations of the history of the behaviors presumed to be the expression of specific orientations and, perhaps more important, mired in an unresolved history of attempts to define the very meaning of the concept. The question of sexual orientation currently is something of a conceptual battleground where some of the most critical issues regarding the nature of human sexuality, if not the human condition itself, are being debated.

Sexual orientation generally can be described as the integration of the ways individuals experience the intersection of sexual desires and available sexual social roles. For some, this is experienced happily, as an unproblematic confluence; for others, it is experienced as a persistent conflict; and for still others, as an occasion for experimentation, compromise, and, sometimes, change, both in how they see themselves and in how they present themselves to others.

Sexual orientation is also part of the conceptual apparatus of contemporary scientific and popular discourse; it becomes a way in which we recognize and "explain" sexual behavior. It is as if, to establish an individual's sexual orientation, however inaccurately, is enough to explain most of what need be known about that individual's sexuality.

SEXUAL ORIENTATION AND GENDER

Following Freud's 1905 distinction between the "object" (the "who") and the "aim" (the "what") of sexual desire (1953), current conceptions of sexual orientation can be said to focus primarily upon the nature of the object defined in narrow terms. This almost exclusive distinction derives from the dimorphic nature of the human species, that is, two genders giving rise to three possible categories: homosexual, heterosexual, and bisexual, although within each of these categories there is a wide range of variations in both sexual and nonsexual attributes of individuals and many aspects of sexual preference that are shared across these categories. Among such aspects of desire would be the other's age, race, social class, or ethnic status; the nature of the emotional bond; and the conventions of physical beauty.

Important differences regarding sexual aims, such as sadomasochism, pedophilia, and transvestism, are most often subsumed within each of these gender-based categories. Most often, they become adjectives modifying the label *homosexual* or *heterosexual*.

The significance of gender may reflect the fact that, within modern Western societies, gender is possibly the last fully pervasive aspect of identity, serving to provide cohesion to our increasingly complex components of identity. Such distinctions establish the *sexual identity* of others and ourselves. The gender of the object of our desires has come to dominate the meaning of sexual

orientation to the exclusion of almost all the other attributes of potential partners that contribute to, or preclude, sexual interest or excitement.

This emphasis upon the gender of the desired object may be a culturally specific development. Some, for example, have argued that, in other cultural or historical contexts, gender may be less significant in defining categories of legitimate sexual access than other social distinctions. Thus, the acceptability of same-gender sexual contacts among males in ancient Greece was contingent upon differences in age (adult versus youth) or social status (free citizen versus slave) and required that there be no direct reciprocity, that the "active" role (the seeking of sexual pleasure) and the "passive" role (the providing of sexual pleasure) remain respectful of social status (Halperin 1989). Men engaging in such behavior were viewed as conventional so long as these rules were maintained.

Such examples remind us that not all persons engaging in sexual acts experience their participation as erotic, experience such activities in the context of what might be termed *sexual excitement*. And, by the same token, they also remind us that not all motives for engaging in specific sexual acts derive from intrinsically sexual motives.

Through much of the twentieth century the question of sexual orientation would not have appeared problematic. In a range of theoretical positions, from Freud's 1905 assumption of an inherent bisexuality (1953) to those postulating an exclusive heterosexuality, sexual orientation was taken as being so firmly rooted in the "natural" processes of human psychosexual development that it was treated as a transcultural phenomenon (Simon 1989). This was true for heterosexuality, which often was, and for many still is, viewed as being phylogenetically programmed as a requirement of species survival (Symons 1979). Homosexuality and bisexuality were viewed either as a disturbance of "normal" development (Freud 1953), an inherited decadence (Ellis 1937), a gender-discordant development (Krafft-Ebing [1896] 1965) or, more recently, a normal, but minor, genetic variant (Kinsey, Pomeroy, and Martin 1948).

Explanations of sexual orientation currently might be described as a continuum anchored at one polar position by the assumption of an entirely biological or phylogenetic source (essentialism) and at the other pole by sources reflecting the adaptation of specific individuals within given sociocultural settings (constructionism).

Essentialist Perspectives The commitment of the extreme essentialist position leads to a view of sexual orientation (as gender preference) potentially present in all human populations, varying only in its manifest expression as a result of differing qualities of encouragement or repression (Gladue 1987; Boswell 1983; Whitam 1983). Other biologically oriented explanations are those linking biological developments with experiential adaptations. Typically, such approaches link variations in such phenomena as prenatal hormonal chemistry with critical, but often unpredictable, postnatal experiences in the shaping of sexual orientation (Money 1988).

The essentialistic end of the conceptual continuum shares the assumption that, at some basic level of character or personality, there are objective, constitutional sources of sexual orientation (Green 1988). It is almost as if such approaches viewed different categories of sexual orientation as different species or subspecies, as if all included within a specific category of sexual interactions shared some common origin. A commitment to such permanent distinctions is often evident in the use of a concept like *latent homosexuality,* which implies that, even where such differences fail to be manifested or are manifested late in life, this orientation is viewed as the ''real'' one.

Constructionist Perspectives At the other end of this continuum are constructionists, who view sexual orientation as the product of specific historical contingencies, as something to be acquired or perhaps even ''an accomplishment'' (Stoller 1985a). Most of those holding this position reject the idea of a sexual drive or, at best, see such a drive as an unformed potential largely dependent upon experience to give it power and directionality. ''Every culture has a distinctive cultural configuration with its own 'anthropological' assumptions in the sexual area. The empirical relativity of these configurations, their immense variety, and luxurious inventiveness, indicate that they are products of man's own socio-cultural formations rather than a biologically fixed human nature'' (Berger and Luckman 1966, p. 49).

For most constructionists, sexual orientation is a reflection of the more general practices of a time and place, and it is expressive of social power (Foucault 1976; Weeks 1985; Padgug 1979; Greenberg 1988; Halperin 1989). Others would add concern for the specific contexts of interaction and the management of identities and social roles (Simon and Gagnon 1967; McIntosh 1976; Plummer 1975; Ponse 1968; Weinberg 1983) and still others would add concern for the experiences that constitute primary socialization (Gagnon and Simon 1973; Stoller 1985b; Simon and Gagnon 1986; Mitchell 1988).

From a constructionist perspective, the concept of sexual orientation itself is viewed as an aspect of the very cultural practices that sustain the differential evaluations of the sexual behaviors the concept purports to explain. The focusing of attention on something that can be called sexual orientation is seen as signifying an importance to be assigned to the sexual that may not be intrinsic to it but that may derive from the evolved meanings and uses that constitute the sexual.

Where essentialists tend to view the sexual as a biological constant that presses upon evolving social conventions, constructionists view the sexual as the product of the individual's contingent response to the experiencing of such social conventions. For the former, the sexual might be said to develop from the inside out, whereas, for the latter, the sexual, like most other social practices, is learned from the outside in. A middle ground is taken by many that view sexual behavior as the outcome of a dialectical relationship between biology and culture (Erikson 1950).

CURRENT CONCEPTS

If only in recognition of the enormous diversity of sexual practices in different cultural and historical settings, despite the relative stability of human physiology, almost all who have approached the study of human sexuality admit the need for some degree of sociological explanation of specific patterns of sexual interaction and the significance accorded them (Gregersen 1983). The question of homosexuality was the dominant issue in most discussions of sexual orientation. Heterosexuality, insofar as it was viewed as doing what came naturally, seemingly required no "explanation," unless it was expressed in unconventional ways. Rather, it was homosexuality that was viewed as problematic, if not pathological, and whose explanation was more urgent. The medicalization of same-gender sexual preference, which preceded the initial public uses of such terms as homosexuality and heterosexuality in 1880 (Herzer 1985), involved the "disease" model of seeking a specific cause, as well as a mode of prevention and possible cure. This implicitly homophobic commitment continues to persist in some parts of the scientific community's considerations of homosexuality (Irving 1990).

The increasing acceptance of homosexuality as an alternative life-style, however, did not necessarily require abandonment of concern for explaining its appearance; it merely made it more obvious that heterosexuality could not be taken for granted, that it also might require explanation (Katz 1990). One characteristic of the modern Western condition is that it has made sexual orientation and the closely related issue of sexual identity problematic. The question, What will I be when I grow up? is asked of an ever-growing number of dimensions of life, including the sexual, and asked with an increasing uncertainty regarding possible answers.

Heterosexuality Heterosexuality, defined as *cross-gender sexual intercourse,* has been a preference in all societies, though not necessarily an exclusive preference in all societies. Nor does the universality of this preference limit definitions of with whom, when, where, or in what manner it should occur. Thus, outside of incest taboos involving immediate family members and a variable list of other close relatives, varied cultures and periods of history have defined legitimate and illegitimate sexual contacts in dramatically contrasting ways (Bullough [1978] 1980). These differences involve not only what might be called the

mechanics of sexual acts, that is, matters of relationship, time, place, costume, sequence of gestures, and positions but also the determinants of their relative significance.

The potential reproductive consequences of heterosexual, genital intercourse inevitably led to linking the desire for sex with some conscious or unconscious desire for reproduction. This view has been criticized as resting upon the questionable assumption of a biologically rooted commitment to species survival (Beach 1956). Valid or not, such views constitute a cultural legacy that gives credence to many current norms regarding sexual acts, norms that enhance the social regulation of reproduction in the name of some assumed natural mandate.

More specifically, expectations regarding gender and family, influenced by many aspects of social life, have generally shaped the social meaning of sexual acts. Our current language for describing cross-gender sexual contacts explicitly assumes a relationship to the family—marital sex, premarital sex, postmarital sex, and extramarital sex—and implicitly evaluates behaviors in terms of their "distance" from location within the family.

Similarly, genital intercourse is still commonly viewed as the ultimate form of sexual exchange, as the "fulfillment of nature's intent." As a result, it continues to serve as the measure of the "normality" of alternative forms of sexual contact. This was reflected in the historic, but declining, practice of criminalizing not only sexual acts occurring outside of marriage but also those involving oral or anal contact or viewing masturbation as pathogenic when practiced by the young and symptomatic when practiced by adults.

Many of the conventions surrounding gender expectations also directly reinforced the "scripting," or construction, of heterosexuality. This involves presenting images of the sexual that both naturalize and normalize evolved Western heterosexual practices, making them appear unquestionably proper. The terms *active* and *passive,* terms that had application in many domains of social life, virtually became synonymous with *masculine* and *feminine,* respectively. Even physical position

—"Who is on top?"—often has had to pay honor to prevailing patterns of social domination.

The nineteenth century witnessed the elaboration of images of the female as fragile, domestic, nurturant, receptive, and either only minimally sexual or capable of insatiable lusts. These images of femininity were complemented by images of the male as strong, given to exploratory curiosity, possessively protective, and aggressively lustful. Though applied diffusely, these implicit norms were not always applied equally. The restraint and fragility of the female found more common application in the parlors and bedrooms of the urban middle class and rural gentry and far less in the fields, factories, servants' quarters, and brothels of the day.

While the images of heterosexuality reinforced patterns of family life and gender differentiation, it is equally appropriate to speak of the ways in which patterns of family life and gender differentiation reinforced prevailing concepts of heterosexuality. This same gender-based division of labor within the family was taken for granted by mid-twentieth-century sociological theorists (Parsons and Bales 1955), as it was inscribed in the most widely held views regarding "normal" human development (Erikson 1950).

From the late nineteenth century on concepts of the family became substantially more voluntary and egalitarian. However, such modifications served to further empower the heterosexual scenario, which now serves an even more important role in the creation of marital bonding and the preservation of the nuclear family. Heterosexuality simultaneously became a near-constant threat and vital aspect of family life.

This greater emphasis placed upon the heterosexual scenario led, in turn, to greater emphasis upon the subjective aspects of one's sexual orientation. Faith in the mute logic of "nature's" intent gave way to concerns for the fashioning and maintenance of individual desire. Women were increasingly expected not only to be receptive but to desire and be desirable, as men were increasingly expected to use the sexual to affirm their masculinity not only by their ability to find sexual pleasure, but also by their ability to provide pleasure to their partners. Heterosexual preference continued to be taken for granted while heterosexual competence was being placed on the agenda in new and unanticipated ways.

In recent years, evident trends call into question many of these practices, challenging many of the previous basic expectations regarding family and gender. The conjugal family is no longer the exclusive social address for heterosexuality. Premarital sex has become statistically normal at all social levels, and it approaches becoming attitudinally normative. Moreover, the age at which sexual intercourse first occurs has declined, particularly for females (by age eighteen over half are no longer virgins, which is more than double the proportion of nonvirgins reported a generation ago), which suggests that most of what occurs can be described as prepremarital, as much of this early sexual behavior occurs outside of the context of family-forming courtship, where much of the premarital experiences of older generation took place.

Similarly, at both the stages of premarital and postmarital, there has been increasing acceptance of nonmarital cohabitation, in the sense that it tends to be more openly acknowledged, with little anticipation of social rejection or stigmatization. And, while the number of middle- to upper-middle-class females who have deliberately borne children without marriage or an acknowledged male partner is not great, that this practice has achieved considerable legitimacy is itself significant.

Reflecting the diffusion of feminist values, support for women, with regard to sexual interest, sexual activity, and, especially, sexual competence, the latter as measured by capacities for achieving orgasm, has visibly increased (Ehrenreich, Hess, and Jacobs 1986). As a result, gender stereotypes with regard to sexual behavior have also experienced changes; changes that, for the most part, served to blur many of the gender distinctions that previously appeared to give heterosexuality its distinctive complementarity.

Specific behaviors, such as oral sex, that once were associated with devalued sexual actors, homosexuals and prostitutes, in recent years have become a conventional part of the heterosexual script. This is particularly true at higher social class levels, where it tends to occur regularly, often substituting for genital intercourse (Gagnon and Simon 1987; Blumstein and Schwartz 1983).

Heterosexuality remains the dominant erotic imagery of Western societies. However, changing concerns for reproduction, continuing changes in the organization of family life, and the constraints describing gender presentations would indicate that present trends toward a pluralization of the ways in which heterosexuality is experienced and in the contexts within which it is expressed will continue into the imaginable future.

Homosexuality Same-gender sexual interactions have been reported in a sufficient number of social settings to suggest that they fall within the normal range of human behaviors (Ford and Beach 1951; Gregersen 1983). As Alfred Kinsey (Kinsey, Pomeroy, and Martin 1948) observed, "The homosexual has been a significant part of human sexual activity ever since the dawn of history, primarily because it is an expression of capacities that are basic in the human animal" (p. 666). This essentialist view implies that predispositions to same-gender sexual acts are immutable facts of nature, like gender and race and, as such, are totally independent of personal preferences and societal values (Green 1988).

At the same time, the facts that same-gender sexual involvements fail to be reported or to occur as atypical behaviors in sufficient numbers suggests that there is little about them upon which to predicate some universal or singular explanation. The specific forms of homosexual behavior, kinds of sexual acts and the relationships within which they occur, like those of most aspects of heterosexuality, vary so much that understanding must be sought in terms of the contingent features of specific social contexts. In other words, apparent uniformity of acts, such as members of the same gender engaging in sexual acts, allows us to assume very little, if any, uniformity of actors, of their development, of their motives, or of the social and personal meanings of the behavior.

When constructionists assert that the homosexual is an invention of the modern world, they are not suggesting that same-gender sexual contacts were unknown in earlier periods of Western history or in other cultural settings. What they do suggest is that the processes that constitute the behavior, that give it meaning, that transform otherwise identical forms of "behavior" into different forms of evaluated "conduct" may be of a fundamentally different character.

The variety of meanings given to same-gender "sexual" contacts is as wide as that given to cross-gender contacts. ("Sexual" is placed in quotation marks as a reminder that, while genital contact and orgasm may be present, in many instances the behavior is not necessarily experienced as sexual in the contemporary Western sense of that word.) Such same-gender, genital contacts range from those that are incidental to religious rites or rites of puberty, to those that are specific to certain statuses that may be temporary and that are not, in themselves, significant aspects of the individual's social identity, to those in which such same-gender contacts are defined as permanent features of the individual's character.

An example of the age-specific, same-gender, sexual contact can be found among the Sambians of New Guinea. Male children at about age six are removed to the men's hut, where they ingest semen, viewed as necessary for full masculine development, by engaging in fellation with older, unmarried, fellow villagers. At puberty, such males enter the role of semen donor by making their penises available to their younger fellow villagers. During early adulthood, they enter arranged marriages and are expected to exclusively practice heterosexual sex for the remainder of their lives. Observers report a near universal absence of fixation with regard to the activities of earlier stages or a reversal of age roles (Herdt 1981; Stoller 1985a).

This, of course, stands in dramatic contrast with the modern Western experience, in which the imagery of the behavior is associated with powerful meanings such that their very invocation is often capable of exciting intense emotional responses of all kinds. Thus, negative images promote strong feelings of homophobia and, at times, cause "homosexual panic." At the same time, the possibility of same-gender sexual contacts often generates responses sufficiently strong to allow many individuals to experience and accept themselves as being homosexual despite the antihomosexual character of their social settings (Bell and Weinberg 1979; Weinberg 1983).

In the examples of both the Sambians and the contemporary Western experience the biological processes associated with arousal and orgasm are undoubtedly the same. What differs are the meanings and their representation that occasion arousal. As Beach noted, "Human sexual arousal is subject to extensive modification as a result of experience. Sexual values may become attached to a wide variety of biologically inappropriate stimulus objects or partners" (1956, p. 27).

Patterns of homosexual behavior, like those of heterosexual behavior, have manifested persistent change. While same-gender sexual contact was known in premodern Europe and severely sanctioned, often treated as a capital offense, it was not viewed as being the behavior of a different kind of person but as moral failing, a sin, to which all might be vulnerable (Bray 1982). Some have argued that a conception of homosexuality as a sexual orientation involving a distinct kind of person was a correlate of many of the changing patterns and values associated with the emergence of urban, industrial capitalism (Adam 1878; Hocquenghem 1978).

Within the category of male homosexuality, different styles of homosexual activity predominated in different periods of history and in different social settings. If the concept of homosexuality is to have any meaning, such variations suggest that modern forms of homosexuality reflect an eroticization of gender and not a fixation upon a specific form of sexual activity. In other words, it is the gender of the participants that generates and sustains sexual interest and only secondarily the specific form of sexual activity (Gagnon 1990; Simon, Kraft, and Kaplan forthcoming).

The significance of gender in considerations of homosexuality has marked much of its recent history. Initial nineteenth-century views defined, and implicitly explained, homosexuality as an inversion of gender. Lesbians were often viewed as "men trapped in women's bodies" and gay men the reverse. Consistent with this, a common designation was "invert." Despite this early view, more recent research indicates that in many regards lesbians and gay men tend in their sexual development and subsequent behavior to approximate their gender. This suggests that sexual development tends to follow gender socialization: Gender roles influence sexuality more often than sexuality prompts changes in gender identity (Gagnon and Simon 1973; Blumstein and Schwartz 1983).

Change in sexual patterns has been a critical aspect of recent social history. Whereas heterosexual practice might be described as being increasingly privatized and disassociated from the major institutions of society, homosexual practice has moved from the margins of society to sharing the central stage. Whereas the family becomes less and less the exclusive legitimate context for heterosexual activities, the appearance and survival of bonded relationships among homosexuals, particularly gay men, has visibly increased. Whereas the larger community appears increasingly anomic, gay communities (which once were limited to bars, discreet networks of friends, and, for gay men, locations for anonymous sexual contacts) now rival even the most solidary of ethnic groups. There is a flowering of recreational, religious, welfare, political, and other affinity groups and organizations, as well as of areas of residential dominance (Epstein 1987; Escoffier 1985; Levine 1986).

Homosexuality remains negatively valued, remains stigmatized. Discrimination in employment and housing, instances of "gay bashing," and criminalization of same-gender sexual activity in some jurisdictions speaks directly to continued homophobic practices and fears. However, on the whole, the 1960s, 1970s, and 1980s witnessed increasing acceptance of both homosexuality and the homosexual. Even the identification of gay men with the transmission of the HIV virus, which initially was associated with an incipient moral panic and occasioned expressions of antihomosexual attitudes, became an occasion for sympathetic representation in the major public media and broadened understanding of gay men, of their life-styles, and of the many roles they play in, and contributions they make to, the larger society.

Two kinds of questions have persisted, those of cause and of numbers. Many explanations for the development of either a homoerotic preference or a homoerotic capacity have been offered. None of these has found general support, from the psychoanalytic emphasis upon internal family dynamics to the emphasis on genetic predispositions (Bell, Weinberg, and Hammersmith 1981). What is clear is that there may be many more reasons for developing a homosexual orientation than there are ways of giving it expression. What once was viewed as a single phenomenon is now more generally seen as pluralized. It now encompasses different developmental histories, affording different ways of incorporating a homoerotic commitment within a specific life history. The same, it might be said, is true for the development of a heterosexual orientation (Murray 1984; Stoller 1985a).

Aspects of development such as variations in the development of a gender identity may be significant in the development of homosexual orientations for some individuals (Harry 1982; Green 1987), but these may have to be reconsidered as society modifies its more general beliefs and practices regarding gender identity. For example, the question must be asked, On what basis should "effeminacy" in male children be treated as symptomatic of some pathology, any more than comparable displays of "effeminacy" in female children? Or the reverse, regarding what is commonly referred to as *tomboyishness* among young females? Similarly we might ask, What basis exists for looking at heterosexual preferences as more desirable outcomes of the child-rearing process than homosexual preferences? This is not to suggest that gender stereotyping and a societal preference for heterosexual outcomes are about to disappear but that the very meaning of all sexual orientations may be in the process of change.

While individuals with a marked homosexual preference appear in virtually all social contexts —within different types of community settings; at different class levels; in all racial, ethnic and religious categories; and from all manner of fami-

ly background (Gebhard and Johnson 1979; Bell, Weinberg, and Hammersmith 1981)—absence of unbiased and comprehensive data makes it difficult to determine with any confidence whether there are significant effects associated with possible differentials. An equal sense of uncertainty surrounds the question of numbers. Answers depend upon definitions of what constitutes homosexuality or homosexuals. All existing estimates are based upon data that are limited in their ability to provide reliable population projections. However, for what they are worth, these suggest that exclusive homosexual behavior describes about 3 percent to 5 percent of men, with about 10 percent to 12 percent having had a more than casual or experimental period of homosexual activity. Estimates for lesbian experience tend to be somewhat less than these percentages. There is reason to suspect that such statistics can provide only an approximation of current populations and a very poor guide to future developments, developments that depend more on society's conceptions and uses of sex and gender, which appear to be in continuing transition.

Bisexuality Bisexuality is a complex concept; it can refer to behavior (those who have had both homosexual and heterosexual experience), to psychic response (those capable of being erotically aroused by both homosexual and heterosexual imagery), and to either social or self-labeling. Substantial numbers have had, if only incidentally, both homosexual and heterosexual experiences while retaining a firm self-identity as being one or the other. Still larger numbers have or can be assumed to have experienced sexual arousal in association with both heteroerotic and homoerotic imagery (Kinsey, Wardell, and Clyde 1948; Kinsey et al. 1952; Bell and Weinberg 1978; Bell, Weinberg, and Hammersmith 1981). Few, however, would conceive of themselves as bisexual or would be labeled as such, particularly if the concept were defined as an attraction to both genders and an attraction for the sexual behaviors commonly attributed to both genders. That is, the mere experience of having sex with members of both genders may not be sufficient to justify the application of the term *bisexual*. Thus, situational, same-gender, sexual contacts, as occur in single-sex penal institutions, may represent little more than conventionally styled heterosexual orientations expressed in restrictive circumstances (Gagnon and Simon 1973).

Many whose sexual histories involve interactions with both genders still see themselves as being either homosexual or heterosexual in orientation. This may be a reflection of the fact that outside of relatively few "bisexual support groups," neither heterosexual nor homosexual social worlds appear to accept or validate such an identity. Though a large number of the psychotherapeutic communities accept bisexuality as a distinct type of psychosexual development (Hill 1989), even among those who identify themselves as bisexual are some who tend to have patterns of sexual behavior that are "amazingly diverse and that [their] day to day life styles are greatly different from one another . . . [and] it is clear that the people come to bisexuality in an incredibly diverse number of ways" (Blumstein and Schwartz 1976, p. 180).

Until recently the very concept of bisexuality, when used to refer to a specific type of person, was viewed with skepticism (Tripp 1987). Most commonly, having bisexual interests was viewed as a mask or apology for an underlying homosexual orientation. Undoubtedly, for some the bisexual label served as a transitional phase in the often complicated task of identity transformation.

Bisexuality, as denoting a special orientation, tends to be a recent conceptualization, one that reflects increased consideration of gender as crystallizations of erotic responses that are not necessarily constrained by the logic of an excluding complementarity. Prior images of bisexuality reflected the assumed differences of masculinity and femininity such as the persistently masculinized dominant sexual actor or the individual who could switch between stereotypical presentations of gender. Increased recognition of a bisexual possibility follows the recognition of the possible absence of complementarity, that is, each participant providing what is absent in and desired by the other, within many heterosexual and homosexual relationships and a calling into question of an implicit complementarity within existing conceptions of gender.

Transvestism and Transsexuality These two concepts do not represent discrete categories so much as a continuum describing the degree to which an individual biologically of one gender desires and enacts the role or aspects of the role of the other (Feinbloom 1976). For an unknown number this is limited to using the clothing of the other gender to illicit sexual excitement, with little more involved. For most, however, more is involved; for most it involves adopting and enacting, if only for an audience of oneself, aspects of the identity and selected roles of the other gender, not merely cross-dressing but cross-gendering. However, for transvestites, cross-dressing is temporary, and they do not abandon their primary gender identity; they play at being the other (Newton 1979).

At the other end of the continuum is the transsexual who ideally seeks to adopt permanently the gender, costumes, and roles of the other gender (Green 1974). And, while an absolute realization of this aspiration is impossible, combined modern surgical and pharmacological techniques and permissive bureaucracies (the former cosmetically "redesigning" the body, while the latter allows for a redesigning of one's identifying credentials) have brought us to the possibility of coming close to allowing some to more fully realize their aspiration to live their lives, as fully as possible, in the costumes and roles of the other gender (Bolin 1988; Lothstein 1983).

The desirability of supporting transsexuality remains a matter of continuing contention involving issues of mental health and gender. Several medical centers that once maintained programs of "surgical gender reassignment" have suspended such programs, reporting results that were too mixed to justify their continuation. Additionally, feminists have criticized such programs as catering to the desire to enact some of the most extreme forms of gender stereotypes (Irving 1990).

Midway between these extremes, between the erotic fetishizing of the clothing of the opposite gender and the desire to become the opposite gender, are those who prefer the costumes and behavior styles of the opposite gender without wanting to or needing to abandon their own initial gender. This ranges from those who deliberately blur costumes and the coding or semiotic of gestures to obscure distinctions—women who have masculinized or men who have feminized their presentation of self—to those who experience a continuing conflict between a "masculine self" and a "feminine self," feeling that each of these components of a divided self requires its own costumes, vocabulary of gestures, and social space.

Again, as is true for most forms of stigmatized behavior, estimates of how many individuals are involved in such practices are virtually impossible to determine with any accuracy. Across this continuum of cross-gendering, both males and females can be observed. Most researchers speculate that more males than females are involved, if only generalizing the apparent tendency for significantly more males than females to be involved in various kinds of sexual deviance.

This speculation is made additionally plausible by the manifest tendency for violations of gender expectations by men to generate more nervousness and be more heavily sanctioned against than might comparable violations by females. It is possible for many females to mask their transvestic desires by the broader range of fashion available to women. By way of example, female cross-dressing in film and literature often involves the beginnings of romantic involvement, while male cross-dressing is almost entirely restricted to the comic mode.

These two concepts, transvestism and transsexuality, perhaps more than any other, speak to the powers of gender and its multiple correlates. They speak, as well, to the complex relationship between gender and sexuality. For relatively few are gender presentations altered to facilitate some specific sexual aim; more often the sexual is organized to facilitate desired gender effects. Little that is manifestly sexual appears in the cross-gendering of some, as would be true of many male heterosexual transvestites. In the case of the transsexual, surgical procedures often diminish orgas-mic capacity. However, confirmation of gender is often one of the major motives for engaging in sexual behavior and a major source of its capacity to gratify.

CONCLUSIONS

Sexual orientation is a complex construct, rather than a simple thing. While it tends to identify individuals in terms of commitment to similar sexual preferences, it also has the capacity to mask differences among those who appear to otherwise share identical orientations. This is not surprising. Sexual behaviors, like other aspects of the human that are rooted in biology, are also historical and given to change and, as such, reflect the very connections of the sexual ultimately to the total fabric of social life.

At the same time, concepts of sexual orientation are aspects of the cultural apparatus of a time and place and are used to explain the behavior of others, as well as our own. As such they have the capacity to influence the very behaviors that they appear merely to describe. Thus, to view the sexual in isolation from the continuing dynamic of social life, which until recently has largely been its fate, is to run the risk of transforming the science of social life into an unselfconscious instrument of social life.

(SEE ALSO: *Alternative Life-Styles; Heterosexual Behavior Patterns; Sexual Behavior and Marriage*)

REFERENCES

Adam, Barry 1978 "Capitalism, the Family, and Gay People." *Sociologists Gay Caucus Working Papers 1.*

Beach, Frank A. 1956 "Characteristics of Masculine 'Sex Drive.'" In Marshall R. Jones, ed., *Nebraska Symposium on Motivation.* Lincoln: University of Nebraska Press.

Bell, Allen C., and Martin S. Weinberg 1978 *Homosexualities: A Study of Diversity Among Men and Women.* New York: Simon and Schuster.

Bell, Allen C., Martin S. Weinberg, and Susan Hammersmith 1981 *Sexual Preference.* Bloomington: Indiana University Press.

Berger, Peter, and Thomas Luckman 1966 *The Social Construction of Reality.* Garden City, N.Y.: Doubleday.

Blumstein, Phillip W., and Pepper Schwartz 1976 "Bisexuality in Women." *Archives of Sexual Behavior* 5(2):171–181.

———1983 *The American Couple.* New York: Morrow.

Bolin, Anne 1988 *In Search of Eve: Transsexual Rites of Passage.* South Hadley, Mass.: Bergin and Garvey.

Boswell, John 1983 "Revolutions, Universals, and Sexual Categories." *Salmagundi* 58–59:89–113.

Bray, Alan 1982 *Homosexuality in Renaissance England.* London: Gay Men's Press.

Bullough, Vern L. (1978) 1980 *Sexual Variance in Society and History.* Chicago: University of Chicago Press.

DuBay, William H. 1987 *Gay Identity: The Self Under Ban.* Jefferson, N.C.: McFarland.

Ehrenreich, Barbara, Elizabeth Hess, and Gloria Jacobs 1986 *Remaking Love: The Feminization of Sex.* New York: Doubleday, Anchor.

Ellis, Havelock 1937 *Studies in the Psychology of Sex,* Vol. 2. New York: Random House.

Epstein, Steven 1987 "Gay Politics, Gay Identity: The Limits of Social Construction." *Socialist Review* 93/94:9–53.

Erikson, Erik H. 1950 *Childhood and Society.* New York: Norton.

Escoffier, Jeffery 1985 "Sexual Revolution and the Politics of Gay Identity." *Socialist Review* 82/83: 119–153.

Feinbloom, Deborah 1976 *Transvestites and Transsexuals: Mixed Views.* New York: Delacorte.

Ford, Clellan, and Frank A. Beach 1951 *Patterns of Sexual Behavior.* New York: Harper.

Foucault, Michel 1978 *The History of Sexuality.* Vol. I: *An Introduction.* New York: Pantheon.

Freud, Sigmund (1905) 1953 "Three Essays on the Theory of Sexuality." *Collected Works,* Vol. 7, pp. 125–243. London: Hogarth.

Gagnon, John H. 1990 "Gender Preferences in Erotic Relations, the Kinsey Scale, and Sexual Scripts." In David McWhorter, Stefanie Sanders, and June Reinisch, eds., *Heterosexuality, Homosexuality, and the Kinsey Scale.* New York: Oxford University Press.

———, and William Simon 1973 *Sexual Conduct: The Social Sources of Human Sexuality.* Chicago: Aldine.

———1987 "The Sexual Scripting of Oral Genital Contacts." *Archives of Sexual Behavior* 16(1): 1–25.

Gebhard, Paul H., and Alan B. Johnson 1979 *The Kinsey Data: Marginal Tabulations of the 1938–1963 Interviews Conducted by the Institute for Sex Research.* Philadelphia: Saunders.

Gladue, Brian A. 1987 "Psychobiological Contributions." In Louis Diamant, ed., *Male and Female Homosexuality: Psychological Approaches,* pp. 129–154. New York: Hemisphere.

Green, Richard 1974 *Sexual Identity Conflict in Children and Adults.* New York: Basic.

———1987 *The "Sissy Boy Syndrome" and the Development of Homosexuality.* New Haven, Conn.: Yale University Press.

———1988 "The Immutability of (Homo)Sexual Orientation: Behavioral Science Implications for a Constitutional (Legal) Analysis." *Journal of Psychiatry and Law* Winter: 537–557.

Greenberg, David F. 1988 *The Construction of Homosexuality.* Chicago: University of Chicago Press.

Gregersen, Edgar 1983 *Sexual Practices: The Story of Human Sexuality.* New York: Franklin Watts.

Halperin, David M. 1989 *One Hundred Years of Homosexuality: And Other Essays on Greek Love.* New York: Routledge, Chapman, and Hall.

Harry, Joseph 1982 *Gay Children Grow Up.* New York: Praeger.

Herdt, Gilbert H. 1981 *Guardians of the Flute: Idioms of Masculinity.* New York: McGraw-Hill.

Herzer, Manfred 1985 "Kertbeny and the Nameless Love." *Journal of Homosexuality* 12(1):1–23.

Hill, Ivan (ed.) 1989 *The Bisexual Spouse: Different Dimensions in Human Sexuality.* New York: Harper, Perennial.

Hocquenghem, Guy 1978 *Homosexual Desire,* trans. Danniella Dangoor. London: Allison and Busby.

Irvine, Janice M. 1990 *Disorders of Desire: Sex and Gender in Modern American Sexology.* Philadelphia: Temple University Press.

Katz, Jonathan H. 1990 "The Invention of Heterosexuality." *Socialist Reivew* 90/91:7–34.

Kinsey, Alfred C., Wardell B. Pomeroy, and Clyde E. Martin 1948 *Sexual Behavior in the Human Male.* Philadelphia: Saunders.

Kinsey, Alfred C., Wardell B. Pomeroy, Clyde E. Martin, and Paul H. Gebhard 1953 *Sexual Behavior in the Human Female.* Philadelphia: Saunders.

Krafft-Ebing, Richard von (1886) 1965 *Psychopathia Sexualis,* trans. Harry E. Wedeck. New York: Putnam's.

Levine, Martin P. 1986 *The Gay Clone.* Ph.D. diss., New York University.

Lothstein, Leslie 1983 *Female to Male Transsexualism: Historical, Clinical, and Theoretical Issues.* Boston: Routledge and Kegan Paul.

Mitchell, Stephan A. 1988 *Relational Concepts in Psychoanalysis.* Cambridge, Mass.: Harvard University Press.

McIntosh, Mary 1976 "The Homosexual Role." *Social Problems* 16(2):182–192.

Money, John 1988 *Gay, Straight, and In-Between: The Sexology of Erotic Orientations.* New York: Oxford University Press.

Murray, Stephen 1984 *Social Theory, Homosexual Reality.* New York: Gay Academic Union.

Nietzsche, Frederic (1887) 1968 *On the Genealogy of Morals.* In Walter Kaufmann trans., *The Basic Writings of Nietzsche.* New York: Modern Library.

Newton, Esther 1979 *Mother Camp: Female Impersonators in America.* Chicago: University of Chicago Press.

Padgug, Robert A. 1979 "Sexual Matters: On Conceptualizing Sexuality in History." *Radical History Review* 20:3–33.

Parsons, Talcott, and Robert F. Bales 1955 *Family Socialization and Interaction Process.* New York: Free Press.

Plummer, Kenneth 1975 *Sexual Stigma: An Interactionist Approach.* London: Routledge and Kegan Paul.

Ponse, Barbara 1978 *Identity in the Lesbian World.* Westport, Conn.: Greenwood.

Simon, William 1989 "The Postmodernization of Sex." *Journal of Psychology and Human Sexuality* 2(1):9–37.

———, and John H. Gagnon 1967 "Homosexuality: The Formulation of a Sociological Perspective." *Journal of Health and Human Behavior* 8(1):77–85.

———1986 "Sexual Scripts: Permanence and Change." *Archives of Sexual Behavior* 15(2):97–120.

Simon, William, Diane Kraft, and Howard Kaplan forthcoming "Oral Sex: A Critical Overview." In J. Reinisch, B. Vollmer, and R. Goldstein, eds., *AIDS and Sex: A Biomedical and Behavioral Approach.* New York: Oxford University Press.

Stoller, Robert J. 1985a *Observing the Erotic Imagination.* New Haven, Conn.: Yale University Press.

———1985b *Presentations of Gender.* New Haven, Conn.: Yale University Press.

Symons, Donald 1979 *The Evolution of Human Sexuality.* New York: Oxford University Press.

Tripp, Clarence A. 1987 *The Homosexual Matrix,* 2nd ed. New York: New American Library.

Weeks, Jeffrey 1985 *Sexuality and Its Discontents: Meanings, Myths, and Modern Sexualities.* London: Routledge and Kegan Paul.

Weinberg, Thomas S. 1983 *Gay Men, Gay Selves.* New York: Irvington.

Whitam Frederic L. 1983 "Culturally Invariable Properties of Male Homosexuals." *Archives of Sexual Behavior* 12:207–222.

WILLIAM SIMON

SEXUAL VIOLENCE AND ABUSE

Sexual violence and abuse are social problems that remained relatively invisible as research topics until the late 1960s. For purposes of this presentation the focus is primarily on rape, various types of child abuse, and related issues.

THE PROBLEM OF RAPE

Rape was not conceptualized as a major problem in the United States until the late 1960s, an awareness that came with the resurrected women's movement and the establishment of the National Center for the Prevention and Control of Rape. After this awakening, enough information was generated to document the fact that there were more than biological and psychological explanations for rape. Society, its institutions, laws, and attitudes were seen as greatly contributing to the problem. During the 1970s rape became clearly defined as a social problem.

The definition of rape that served as the basis for most rape laws is grounded in English common law: "the unlawful carnal knowledge of a woman by force and against her will" (Green 1988, p. 6). At the national level the definition has not changed, although clinical definitions are less restrictive. During the 1970s many states redefined rape laws to more comprehensively describe those behaviors that constituted rape and age of consent. The concept of spousal immunity was challenged, and some states rewrote their laws so that women could bring marital rape charges. By the end of the decade, forty-one states had also passed some form of rape shield laws that limited admissibility of victims' prior sexual conduct with persons other than the offender (Green 1988, pp. 16–40).

Considered the second most serious crime indexed in the Uniform Crime Reports, in 1988 there were officially 92,486 reported rapes in the United States (U.S. Department of Justice 1989, p. 16), a 2-percent increase over 1987. According to a recent ABC news report by Carole Simpson (ABC American Agenda News Report, January 7, 1991), rape is currently the fastest growing crime in the United States. In some major cities, rape increased by 50 percent in 1990. Increases across the United States are attributed not only to increased reporting but also to increases in incidents. Some estimate that, for every rape reported, three to ten are not. And, while trend research has shown a general escalation, with the most dramatic increases occurring before 1981 (Russell 1984, p. 29), the 1990s appear to be ushering in a significant upward swing.

Victimization studies such as the National Crime Survey (NCS) and other research projects were initiated to get better estimates of rape. These studies show that the amount of rape is greatly underestimated, although prevalence rates vary from study to study and are hard to reconcile, due to variations in research designs, samples, and geographic locations.

Rape is described in a number of ways. Sometimes it is discussed in terms of the number of offenders per victim: the single-offender; two-offender; or multiple, group, or gang rape. Victimization statistics for these are respectively, 81 percent, 10 percent, and 8 percent (Koss and Harvey 1987, p. 10). Rape is also classified as stranger rape, when the victim and offender have no relationship to one another, or acquaintance rape, which includes date rape and rape between individuals who knew each other prior to the assault. NCS's rape statistics indicate that 60 percent to 75 percent of rapes that happen to women aged 16–24 are stranger rapes and that 27 percent of rapes involve multiple offenders. War-

shaw (1988, chap. 1) citing statistics from the *MS. Magazine* Project on Campus Assault, reports fewer stranger (16 percent) and group rapes (15 percent), however, with the vast majority of incidents being individual assaults (95 percent) that involve acquaintances or dates (84 percent). A third type of rape, marital rape, occurs when the victim and offender are spouses or living in a spouselike arrangement. Although this was thought to be rare, Russell (1984, p. 59) found that 8 percent of ever-married women in her study reported being raped by their husbands.

Rape is sometimes defined in terms of motivation. While earlier researchers viewed rape as sexually motivated, more recent ones refer to it as power- or anger-motivated rape. Power rapes are motivated by a need to dominate the victim, whereas anger rapes are driven by a hatred of the victim or hatred of women in general (Groth, 1979). Further, most rapes, particularly group rapes, are planned, not impulsive, acts (Warshaw, 1988). Some rapes do appear to happen, however, simply because opportunities arise.

Researchers generally agree that the social characteristics of rapists and their victims are similar for most types of rape. While exact age ranges vary among studies, both rapists and their victims appear to be young (less than twenty-five), nonwhite (overrepresentation of Afro-Americans), and from the lower socioeconomic classes. Victims tend to be single, with more variations in marital status occurring among offenders. Rural/urban and regional rates vary and appear to be somewhat related to population density.

EXPLANATIONS FOR RAPE

Explanations for rape come from a variety of disciplines, although most explanations have been dominated by the psychiatric perspective and the medical model (Koss and Leonard 1984, pp. 213–232). The basic assumption underlying this thinking is that rapists are psychologically sick and that rape is sexually motivated. Hence, many explanations focus on developing profiles of rapists (e.g., Groth, Burgess, and Holmstrom 1977), a body of research whose validity is questioned because it is based primarily on non-representative clinical or prison populations (Schwendinger and Schwendinger 1983; Russell 1984, chap. 4).

Cross-cultural support for the biological explanation of rape is provided by Levine (1977), although his work also supports a sociocultural explanation, because the Gussi in Kenya are characterized by male dominance, low female status, and high rates of crime and violence.

Sociological explanations of rape focus on the social dynamics of society that promote, treat, or proscribe such behaviors and include sociocultural, sociohistorical, and sociopsychological analyses. While these types of explanations lagged behind those of psychology and biology, they offer an alternative to the individual-based theories.

Sociocultural explanations of rape are supported by large cross-cultural studies of tribal societies (Sanday 1981) and by large studies of nonindustrialized nations (Reiss 1986). All studies draw similar research conclusions. Rape-prone societies endorse the macho personality and fundamental belief in the inferiority of females, a belief system that incorporates an acceptance of physical aggression, a high amount of risk taking, and a casual attitude toward sex. Schwendinger and Schwendinger (1983) note that rape is also related to a culture's socioeconomic structure.

Among industrialized societies, the United States has substantially higher rape rates. In 1984, the Bureau of Justice reported a rape rate of 35.4 per 100,000 population for the United States, compared with a 5.4 average for European nations (Abramson and Hayashi 1984). Some researchers argue that the higher incidence of rape in the United States indicates that it has cultural and societal supports, one of which increasingly appears to be college campuses (Martin and Hummer 1989).

Baron and Straus's (1989, p. 180) state-level analyses show that rape rates vary by region and state within the United States and that rates are positively related to the amount of social disorganization, sex magazine circulation (pornography), and gender inequality in the state or region. This adds weight to earlier research that ties rape-specific myths and attitudes to a larger attitudinal construct supportive of sex-role stereotyping, violence against women, and adversarial sexual beliefs.

The sociocultural and sociopsychological explanations of rape support the sociohistorical analysis of feminist writer Susan Brownmiller (1975). While Brownmiller has been criticized for exaggerating the notion of male intimidation, sociological and anthropological research does indicate that rape is a socially created phenomenon that is much more likely to happen in cultures that support patriarchy and violence. Sociocultural explanations may also explain why the majority of offenders are male, irrespective of whether the victims are male or female, adult or child (Finkelhor and Russell 1984, chap. 11). Further, these explanations, combined with the legal definition of rape, might explain the lack of research on male victims.

Regardless of the varied theoretical perspectives, most researchers agree that multifactor (psychological and sociological factors), as compared with single-factor, explanations are better predictors of rape. Russell (1984, p. 111) notes that most rape theories could fit into Finkelhor's (1984) four-factor explanation of child sexual abuse discussed below.

THE PROBLEM OF CHILD SEXUAL ABUSE

Since the mid-1970s there has been increased interest in understanding child sexual abuse. This concern has led to the founding of the National Center on Child Abuse and Neglect and the passage of the 1977 Protection of Children Against Sexual Exploitation Act. A review of the child sex abuse research (Finkelhor et al. 1986) demonstrates many similarities with what we know about rape. Paralleling Brownmiller's (1975) historical analysis of rape, for example, is Florence Rush's (1980) analysis of child sexual abuse. Like Brownmiller, Rush elevates child sexual abuse to the level of a social problem by tracing its roots to patriarchal societies and their social institutions, belief systems, and myths. It should be noted, however, that there are groups that do not view child–adult sex as a problem (e.g., North American Man Boy Love Association). In fact, they advocate it.

In contrast to the concept of rape, researchers have not reached a consensus on what to call sexual relations between adults and children. Those who study victims tend to refer to the behavior as child sexual abuse, assault, maltreatment, or exploitation, whereas offender researchers call it child molestation or pedophilia. As with the definitional problems associated with rape, researchers likewise place varying limits on the ages of victims and offenders, the acts that are considered abuse, and the relationship of the victim and offender (Araji and Finkelhor 1986, pp. 89–91; Russell 1984, p. 177; Bolten, Morris, and MacEachron 1989, pp. 31–35).

While all states consider child sexual abuse a crime, definitions vary from state to state, and some even leave the interpretation to the courts. As an ever-increasing number of child sexual abuse cases move into the court systems, particularly in cases involving divorce and custody, concern for balancing the needs of the legal system against those of children has arisen (Bolten, Morris, and MacEachron, 1989, chap. 10). Placing children in the courtroom subjects them to many of the same problems faced by rape victims: victim blaming and other courtroom-produced traumas. Although still in the early stage, reforms are being suggested and implemented (Bolten and Bolten 1987, chap. 10; Bulkley and Davidson 1981), with one of the largest areas of legislative reform having focused on increasing convictions and penalties of offenders.

As interest in understanding child sexual abuse grew, so did incidence and prevalence studies. Statistics provided by the American Humane Association (1981) and the 1981 national incidence study (National Center on Child Abuse and Neglect 1981) were used to arrive at national preva-

lence estimates. Today there is little agreement among social scientists as to the true extent of child sexual abuse (Peters, Wyatt, and Finkelhor 1986, p. 16), but all concede that the number of reported cases is increasing significantly and that the actual numbers are underestimated, particularly for males (Bolten, Morris, and MacEachron 1989, chap. 2). A comparison of national findings with less comprehensive research studies reveals conflicting estimates of the incidence of child sexual abuse. Still, commonly cited estimates suggest that one in four girls and one in nine boys will be sexually abused by the time they reach eighteen (Peters, Wyatt, and Finkelhor 1986, chap. 1).

At present, it is too early to make accurate cross-national comparisons of the extent of child sexual abuse. Some research has been conducted in several European countries, and recent reports from Great Britain (Glaser and Frosh 1988) and Sweden (Finkelhor et al. 1986, pp. 5–6) suggest that, as in the United States, the problem is widespread.

In contrast with rape, studies do not support a general, social-characteristics profile of victims or offenders of child sexual abuse, although females tend to be at greater victimization risk than males and males are overwhelmingly the offenders. The ages of greatest risk for victimization appear to be between eight and twelve (Finkelhor et al. 1986, pp. 61–66). Against the tide of current myths, most offenders are either known by or related to their victims and are not old. The largest groups are teenagers and young adults (Finkelhor 1979, pp. 73–74). In a review of studies, Finkelhor et al. (1986, pp. 67–71) found no consistent link between social class and sexual abuse, although the lower socioeconomic class is most likely overrepresented. He also found no consistent significant differences between racial groups.

EXPLANATIONS OF CHILD SEXUAL ABUSE

The development of child sexual abuse explanations is similar to that of rape, as most early studies focused on offenders' psychopathological or biological motivations, or attempted to develop profiles of child molesters, victims, and families, or both. As with rape, most explanations offered only single-factor explanations, an approach criticized by Finkelhor et al. (1986, chap. 4). As an alternative, he proposed a four-factor explanation of child sexual abuse that includes the categories of emotional congruence, sexual arousal, blockage, and disinhibition. Respectively, these factors incorporate explanations of why an adult would have an emotional need to relate to a child, could be sexually aroused by a child, would not have alternative sources of gratification, and would not be deterred from such an interest by normal prohibitions (Araji and Finkelhor 1986, p. 117). The model includes both individual (e.g., arrested emotional development) and sociocultural (pornography) factors. As previously noted, Russell (1984, p. 111) believes that this model could be adapted to explain rape.

INCEST

Most researchers and practitioners consider incest different from child sexual abuse, with incest viewed as *intrafamilial* and child sexual abuse as *extrafamilial* sexual relations. While some argue that the two types of abuse have much in common, one of the most significant differences between child sexual abuse and incest is that the victims of incest are always betrayed by someone who has been charged with loving and protecting them. Such experiences can have extremely destructive results.

The most common type of incest researched and written about is between father and daughter (Herman and Hirschman 1981), although the most common type may be brother–sister (Finkelhor 1979, p. 89). An emerging concern as more stepfamilies are formed is the probability of increased incestuous relationships involving stepfathers.

Incest has been viewed as a threat to societies and, as such, called the "ultimate taboo." This, combined with other reasons suggested by Rush (1980, chap. 7) and Finkelhor (1979, pp. 9, 11),

may have led to a covering up of the prevalence of this act. Rates recently coming to light show estimates ranging from a high of 38 percent of females in Russell's 1983 study to about 25 percent in several other survey studies (e.g., Finkelhor 1979).

The same research problems surrounding rape and child sexual abuse extend to the incest literature: underestimating the extent of the crime, not accurately defining it, facing theory and sample problems.

TREATMENT AND PREVENTION

A considerable body of literature on prevention and treatment of sexual violence and abuse has emerged from applied disciplines such as social work and clinical psychology, as well as from various community and feminist organizations. An extensive discussion is beyond the scope of this entry, so only a few generalizations are noted.

First, as treatment programs follow from the variety of theories of sexual abuse and violence previously discussed, it is not surprising that an array of treatment programs exist (Bolten, Morris, and MacEachron 1989, chap. 5, 6). With respect to offenders, most programs focus on punishment and/or rehabilitation (Groth 1979; Conte and Berliner 1981), and many are based on the psychiatric or medical model. In cases of child sexual abuse and incest, programs typically focus on helping the victims and their families through the crisis (Giaretto 1981). In the area of rape, programs have been primarily aimed at treating victims and families for the *rape trauma syndrome*. Treatment programs have also been developed to deal with the short- and long-term effects of victims' abuse (Brown and Finkelhor 1986) and can be either clinically or community based (Koss and Harvey 1987). Some are also beginning to focus on sex and ethnic differences. At present, however, there remain debates among professionals and practitioners as to what the appropriate treatments are, which ones work, and how well.

Stemming from myths and callous societal attitudes toward sexual aggression and the extensive involvement of feminists, prevention programs have followed a *victim advocacy* model (Araji 1989, chap. 17). Under this concept, potential victims are taught, in various ways, how to protect themselves from becoming victims. Some newer programs are aimed at males and promote the development of a nurturant, rather than macho, male image.

PORNOGRAPHY, SEXUAL VIOLENCE, AND ABUSE

A discussion of sexual assault would not be complete without some mention of pornography, a concept that challenges definition and remains a source of confusion and controversy. With respect to the rape–pornography connection, many feminists believe that pornography causes rape (Russell 1988); a scientific link, however, has yet to be established. With regard to social policy, some feminists advocate censorship of such materials while researchers Baron and Straus (1989, pp. 188–191) argue against this position.

Beginning in 1977 as a moral crusade, the child pornography movement led to the 1978 signing of Public Law 95–225, an amendment to the United States code concerning use of children in obscene materials. In spite of this, pornography continues to increase at alarming rates, and, as a research topic, the issue of pornography shares many of the previously noted problems associated with studying rape and child sexual abuse.

OTHER AREAS OF SEXUAL ABUSE

Several other areas of sexual abuse that are gaining increasing attention are pre-adolescent and adolescent sexual abuse, abuse of very young children, and sexual harassment. One of the reasons that researchers and practitioners are becoming interested in the first two issues is the realization of how prominently youth figure as both victims and offenders in sexual assault statistics (Becker 1988; Herman 1989) and how very young some of the offenders and victims are. There is also an increasing interest in the belief that offenders against young children may actually begin before or at the time they enter adolescence (Knopp 1982). Sexual harassment is generating increased interest because it is viewed as one more form of violence against women and those in less powerful positions.

SUMMARY AND CONCLUSIONS

Extensive public and professional attention to sexual violence and abuse has come about only since 1960 and has been primarily a grass-roots movement. As a result, a large body of cross-discipline literature has developed, and various reforms have taken place, with more planned. While no consensus exists as to the scope of the problems, rates at which they are increasing, definitions, explanations, social policies, and solutions, sociologists, particularly feminists, conclude that sexual violence and abuse will never be reduced or eliminated until societies stop supporting and/or promoting aggression, violence, and inequality.

(SEE ALSO: *Family Violence; Incest*)

REFERENCES

Abramson, P., and H. Hayashi 1984 "Pornography in Japan." In N. Malamuth and E. Donnerstein, eds., *Pornography and Sexual Aggression.* New York: Academic Press.

American Humane Association 1981 *National Study on Child Neglect and Abuse Reporting.* Denver, Colo.: AHA.

Araji, S. 1989 "The Effects of Advocates on Prevention." In N. C. Barker, ed., *Child Abuse and Neglect: An Interdisciplinary Method of Treatment.* Dubuque, Iowa: Kendall/Hunt.

———, and D. Finkelhor 1986 "Abusers: A Review of the Research." In D. Finkelhor, S. Araji, L. Baron, A. Brown, S. Doyle Peters, and G. E. Wyatt, eds., *A Sourcebook on Child Sexual Abuse.* Beverly Hills: Sage Publications.

Baron, L., and M. Straus 1989 *Four Theories of Rape in American Society.* New Haven, Conn.: Yale University Press.

Becker, J. V. 1988 "The Effects of Sexual Abuse on Adolescent Sexual Offenders." In G. W. Wyatt and G. J. Powell, eds., *Lasting Effects of Child Sexual Abuse.* Beverly Hills, Calif.: Sage.

Bolton, F. G., and S. R. Bolton 1987 *Working with Violent Families.* Beverly Hills, Calif.: Sage.

Bolton, F. G., Jr., L. A. Morris, and A. E. MacEachron 1989 *Males at Risk: The Other Side of Child Sexual Abuse.* Beverly Hills, Calif.: Sage.

Brown, A., and D. Finkelhor 1986 "Impact of Child Sexual Abuse: A Review of the Research." *Psychological Bulletin* 99:16–77.

Brownmiller, S. 1975 *Against Our Will: Men, Women, and Rape.* New York: Simon and Schuster.

Bulkley, J., and H. Davidson 1981 *Child Sexual Abuse: Legal Issues and Approaches.* Washington, D.C.: American Bar Association, National Resource Center for Child Advocacy and Protection.

Conte, J. R., and L. Berliner 1981 "Prosecution of the Offender in Cases of Sexual Assault against Children." *Victimology* 6:102–109.

Finkelhor, D. 1979 *Sexually Victimized Children.* New York: Free Press.

———1984 *Child Sexual Abuse: New Theory and Research.* New York: Free Press.

———, S. Araji, L. Baron, A. Brown, S. Doyle Peters, and G. E. Wyatt 1986 *A Sourcebook on Child Sexual Abuse.* Beverly Hills, Calif.: Sage.

———, and D. Russell 1984 "Women as Perpetrators: Review of the Evidence." In David Finkelhor, ed. *Child Sexual Abuse: New Theory and Research.* New York: Free Press.

Giaretto, H., 1981. "A Comprehensive Child Sexual Abuse Treatment Program." *Child Abuse and Neglect* 6:263–278.

Glaser, D., and S. Frosh 1988 *Child Sexual Abuse.* Chicago: Dorsey Press.

Green, W. M. 1988 *Rape.* Lexington, Mass.: Lexington Books.

Groth, A. N. 1979 *Men Who Rape.* New York: Plenum.

———, A. W. Burgess, and H. Holmstrom 1977 "Rape: Power, Anger and Sexuality." *American Journal of Psychiatry* 134:1239–1243.

Herman, D. F. 1989 "The Rape Culture." In J. Freeman, ed., *Women: A Feminist Perspective.* Mountain View, Calif.: Mayfield.

Herman, J. L., and L. Hirschman 1981 *Father–Daughter Incest.* Cambridge, Mass.: Harvard University Press.

Knopp, F. H. 1982 *Remedial Intervention in Adolescent Sex Offenders: Nine Program Descriptions.* New York: Safer Society Press.

Koss, M., and M. Harvey 1987 *The Rape Victim: Clinical and Community Approaches to Treatment.* Lexington, Mass.: Stephan Green Press.

Koss, M. P., and K. E. Leonard 1984 "Sexually Aggressive Men: A Review of Empirical Findings." In N. Malamuth and E. Donnerstein, eds., *Pornography and Sexual Aggression.* New York: Academic Press.

Levine, R. A. 1977 "Gussi Sex Offenses: A Study in Social Control." In D. Chappell, R. Geis, and G. Geis, eds., *Forcible Rape: The Crime, the Victim, and the Offender.* New York: Columbia University Press.

Martin, P. Y., and R. A. Hummer 1989 "Fraternities and Rape on Campuses." *Gender and Society* 3:457–473.

National Center on Child Abuse and Neglect 1981 *Study Findings: National Study of Incidence and Severity of Child Abuse and Neglect.* Washington, D.C.: Department of Health, Education and Welfare.

Peters, S. D., G. E. Wyatt, and D. Finkelhor 1986 "Prevalence." In D. Finkelhor, S. Araji, L. Baron, A. Browne, S. Doyle Peters, and G. E. Wyatt, eds., *A Sourcebook on Child Sexual Abuse.* Beverly Hills, Calif.: Sage.

Reiss, I. L. 1986 *Journey into Sexuality: An Exploratory Voyage.* Englewood Cliffs, N.J.: Prentice-Hall.

Rush, F. 1980 *The Best Kept Secret: Sexual Abuse of Children.* New York: McGraw-Hill.

Russell, D. 1983 "Incidence and Prevalence of Intrafamilial and Extrafamilial Sexual Abuse of Female Children." *Child Abuse and Neglect* 7:133–146.

———1984. *Sexual Exploitation, Rape, Child Sexual Abuse, and Workplace Harassment.* Beverly Hills, Calif.: Sage.

———1988 "Pornography and Rape: A Causal Model." *Political Psychology* 9:41–73.

Sanday, P. R. 1981 "The Socio-cultural Context of Rape: A Cross-cultural Study." *Journal of Social Issues* 37:5–27.

Schwendinger, J. R., and H. Schwendinger 1983 *Rape and Inequality.* Beverly Hills, Calif.: Sage.

U. S. Department of Justice, Federal Bureau of Investigation 1989 *Crime in the United States: Uniform Crime Reports, 1988.* Washington, D.C.: U.S. Government Printing Office.

Warshaw, R. 1988 *I Never Called It Rape.* New York: Harper & Row.

SHARON K. ARAJI

PEPPER SCHWARTZ

SLAVERY AND INVOLUNTARY SERVITUDE

Although many observers view slavery and freedom as polar opposites, both slave and free wage labor systems rely upon compulsion. Slave systems depended ultimately upon physical coercion to force slaves to work for masters although cultural, ideological, and economic pressures typically augmented the effectiveness of force. Wage labor systems, by contrast, depend upon workers being free "in the double sense" (Marx 1967, pp. 168-169). Not only must they be free, non-slave workers, who can seek employment from others as they wish, but they must be free of all other means of subsistence that would permit voluntary withdrawal from the labor market. In the absence of subsistence alternatives, economic necessity compels "free" workers to exchange labor services for wages. Nevertheless, cultural expectations, ideological appeals, and physical coercion have often been used to reinforce market mechanisms, especially during periods of declining profits. Thus, large-scale labor systems are typically maintained by a mixture of physical and economic coercion that varies with the availability of subsistence alternatives.

How the actual constellation of physical and economic coercion and subsistence alternatives is determined by the power of contending groups as well as by historically specific cultural and ideological factors has been of great interest to social scientists. Perhaps the simplest and most durable statement of the causes of slavery is a classic conjecture known as the Nieboer-Domar hypothesis (Nieboer 1900; Domar 1970; Engerman 1986a; see Patterson 1977b for a critique), which links slavery to an abundance of arable land combined with a shortage of labor. After distinguishing slavery from other forms of involuntary servitude, this hypothesis is amended below to provide a provisional explanation for the worldwide trend from slavery toward freedom in large-scale labor systems during the past several hundred years.

SLAVERY AND OTHER FORMS OF INVOLUNTARY SERVITUDE

Patterson (1982, p. 13) argues that slavery is defined by three conditions. First, slaves suffer perpetual domination that is ultimately enforced by violence. The permanent subjugation of slaves is predicated upon the capacity of masters to coerce them physically. Second, slaves suffer natal alienation, which is the severance of all family ties and the nullification of all claims of birth. They inherit no protection or privilege from ancestors, nor can they convey protection or privilege to their descendents. Finally, slaves are denied honor whereas masters are socially exalted. This last condition appears to be derivative, rather than definitive, of slavery because all hierarchical social systems develop legitimating ideologies that elevate elites and denigrate those at lower levels. The first two conditions, which distinguish slavery from other forms of involuntary servitude, constitute the working definition used here.

In chattel slave systems, slaves are movable property owned by masters and exchanged through market processes. Because some societies constructed elaborate slave systems without well-developed notions of property and property rights, property relationships cannot be an essential defining element of slavery (Patterson 1982; Patterson 1977a). Nevertheless, property relations and economic processes had important effects on slavery and other forms of unfree labor in the Americas, Europe, and Africa from the fifteenth century on, which is the major focus of this analysis.

No unfree laborer can voluntarily terminate service to a master once the servile relationship is established. Slavery maximizes the subordination of servant to master. Other servile workers, such as indentured and contract laborers, debt servants, peons, and pawns are less dominated than slaves and they do not suffer natal alienation. Pawns, for example, were offered by their families in return for loans. Pawns maintained kinship ties to their original families, which provided them some protection, and were freed once the loans were repaid. Indentured servants were bound to a master for a specific term, such as seven years, to which they agreed in exchange for passage to America, for example (Morris 1946; Smith 1947; Morgan 1975). Contract laborers were also bound for specified terms but could not be sold against their will to other masters, as was the case with indentureds. Debt servitude consists of labor service obligations that are not reduced by the amount of work performed (Morris 1946; Sawyer 1986). Peons are tied to land as debt servants and owe labor services to a landlord. Serfs are not debt servants, but they are tied to land and perform labor services on their lords' estates. The right to labor services enjoyed by European feudal lords was vested in their political authority rather than land ownership, although serfs were reduced to slaves in all but name in some instances (e.g., Russia in the nineteenth century, Kolchin 1987).

Indentured servants and contract laborers may agree to the initial terms of their servitude, but they cannot willingly end it during its term once it begins. Usually some form of coercion, such as poverty, debt, or impending imprisonment, was necessary to force people to agree to terms of contractual servitude or pawnship. By contrast, the status of slave, serf, peon, and debt servant was typically inherited or imposed on workers against their will.

SLAVERY, THE LAND/LABOR RATIO, AND THE STATE

In its simplest form, the Nieboer-Domar hypothesis states that abundant free land makes it impossible for free workers and nonworking landowners to coexist. If free land is available and laborers can desert landowners whenever they choose, landlords will be unable to keep enough workers to maintain their status as nonworkers. If landlords can compel workers to perform labor services despite the availability of free land, then landlords become labor lords, and workers are not free. On the other hand, scarce land combined with an abundant labor supply drives wages down making wage laborers less expensive than slaves or other servile workers.

The model appears deficient in at least four ways. First, as Domar recognized, political factors determine the degree of freedom enjoyed by workers. Chief among these is the extent to which the state protects the interests of landowners when they conflict with those of laborers. Large-scale slave labor systems cannot exist in the absence of states that defend the power of slave masters to control and utilize the labor of slaves. A powerful state is essential for protecting slave masters against slave rebellions, capturing runaways, and enforcing slave discipline. State power is required for the enslavement of new supplies of slaves. If the state is responsive to the demands of workers, or if workers can voluntarily withdraw labor services as they choose, unfree labor systems cannot be maintained.

Second, the model presumes that slave masters exploit slaves in response to economic incentives. But slaves and other unfree laborers often performed military, administrative, domestic, and sexual services that were largely unrelated to economic activities (Roberts and Miers 1988; Patterson 1982). The Nieboer-Domar hypothesis therefore does not apply to societies that employ slaves and other servile workers in noncommercial or minor economic roles (Lovejoy 1983; Finley 1968). Nor does it apply to states that use race, religion, gender, or other status criteria to restrict the freedom of workers for reasons other than economic ones (James 1988).

Third, the key issue from an employer's perspective is not simply the ratio of land to labor but the relative costs and benefits of different forms of labor that can be profitably employed using existing capital (including land). A more general version of the Nieboer-Domar model compares the stock of available capital to the availability of different forms of labor at prevailing prices. Thus, labor scarcity means the scarcity of labor at prices that can be profitably employed.

Finally, the simple version of the Nieboer-Domar hypothesis ignores the organizational capacities of workers and capitalists' capacities to adopt labor-saving innovations. If workers demand concessions that threaten profits or engage in strikes and other production disruptions, capitalists experience "labor shortages" that stem not from insufficient numbers but from the organized resistance of workers who are present (Miles 1987). Faced with such disruptions, capitalists with sufficient capital may adopt labor-saving innovations if they are available. When capitalists are unable to adopt labor-saving innovations, they often resort to labor coercive strategies to curb workers' market-based demands (Paige 1975). This case contradicts the Nieboer-Domar hypothesis, which assumes that high labor to capital (or land) ratios make coercive labor control strategies unnecessary.

UNFREE LABOR IN THE AMERICAS

From the fifteenth through the nineteenth centuries, Europe, Africa, and the Americas became closely linked by flows of people and commodities (Lovejoy 1983; Eltis 1987). The colonization of the Americas by strong European states provided vast, lightly populated lands for commercial exploitation. Expanding commodity markets in Europe for sugar, cotton, tobacco, coffee, and other products stimulated the demand for greater supplies of servile labor to work the plantations and mines of the Americas. Weak states throughout large areas of sub-Saharan Africa left large populations vulnerable to the armed predations of stronger states that supplied the expanding markets for slaves.

Estimates of the numbers of bondsmen and slaves transported to the Americas are subject to sizable errors, given the paucity and unreliability of existing records, but relative magnitudes are thought to be reasonable (see Table 1). Differences in the sources of servile labor produced different racial compositions across American regions. Slaves from Africa outnumbered arrivals from Europe nearly four to one before 1820, and most were bound for sugar cane plantations in Brazil and the West Indies. British North America was atypical because its early immigrants were predominantly white indentured servants from

Britain, Ireland, and Germany; perhaps two-thirds of the white immigrants who arrived before the American Revolution were bonded servants (Smith 1947, p. 336). Before being displaced by African slaves, white bondsmen were the principal source of labor in the plantation regions of all British colonies, including those in the Caribbean (Engerman 1986a; Galenson 1981).

Indentured servitude was the principal method of defraying the costs of supplying the colonies with workers. British laws and customs regulating master-servant relationships were modified significantly to adapt them to American circumstances (Galenson 1981). Because of the high cost of transatlantic passage, longer periods of service were required, typically four to seven years rather than the one year or less in England. English servants could not be sold against their will to another master, but the practice was sanctioned in colonial laws and customs because European servants could not negotiate terms with prospective masters before passage to America. Finally, opportunities for escape were much greater in America. Consequently, elaborate state enforcement mechanisms were implemented to discourage runaways and to catch, punish, and return those who did. Most indentured servants were transported to plantation regions because plantation labor produced greater returns than any other economic activity in the Americas (Galenson 1981). Employers in areas such as New England could afford few or no servants because they specialized in trades with lower labor productivities and lower profit margins.

White servile labor was replaced by black slavery throughout the Americas between 1600 and 1800, and although racial prejudice encouraged the shift, it probably was not decisive (Morgan 1975). First, the limited supply of indentured servants could not satisfy the demand for servile labor, whereas the supply of African slaves was almost completely elastic. Improving economic conditions in Britain and state restrictions on the emigration of British servants reduced the numbers seeking passage to America, causing the price of servants to increase. As the price of servants exceeded the price of slaves, first for unskilled and

TABLE 1
Immigration to and Populations of Regions in the Americas (in thousands)

	Total Immigration to the Americas up to circa 1820			
	African	*European*	*Total*	*% African*
United States	550	651	1,201	46
Continental Spanish America	1,072	750	1,822	59
Brazil and the West Indies	6,777	964	7,741	88
Total	8,399	2,365	10,764	78

	Total population circa 1650			
	Native Americans & Mestizos	*Europeans*	*Blacks & Mulattos*	*Total*
North America	860 (86%)	120 (12%)	22 (2%)	1,002 (100%)
Continental Spanish America (excluding Peru)	8,773 (90%)	575 (6%)	437 (4%)	9,785 (100%)
Brazil, the West Indies, and the Guyanas	843 (51%)	154 (9%)	667 (40%)	1,664 (100%)
	10,476 (84%)	849 (7%)	1,126 (9%)	12,451 (100%)

	Total Population circa 1825			
	Native Americans & Mestizos	*Europeans*	*Blacks & Mulattos*	*Total*
North America	423 (4%)	9,126 (80%)	1,920 (17%)	11,469 (100%)
Continental Spanish America (excluding Peru)	12,660 (79%)	2,937 (18%)	387 (2%)	15,984 (100%)
Brazil, the West Indies, and the Guyanas	381 (5%)	1,412 (20%)	5,247 (75%)	7,040 (100%)
	13,464 (39%)	13,475 (39%)	7,554 (22%)	34,493 (100%)

SOURCES: Immigration rates are adapted from Eltis (1983, p. 278). Population figures are adapted from Slicher Van Bath (1986, p. 21), in which the West Indies include the Spanish Islands but exclude the Bahamas.

later for skilled workers, slaves were preferred to bonded servants (Galenson 1981). Second, Africans were better acclimated to the diseases of the tropics, where the most important export crops were grown (Eltis 1983).

Third, slaves could be compelled to comply with the labor-intensive plantation work regime that developed (Fogel 1989). Slaves were more efficient and profitable than free or indentured workers in sugar, cotton, coffee, rice, and tobacco because the work required by these crops could be efficiently performed by slave work gangs. Work gangs were organized according to specialized tasks, and slaves were assigned to particular gangs according to their skills and capacities. The work was performed under close supervision to maintain work intensity and quality. Slave masters often used brutal violence to enforce slave discipline, but naked force may have been used less than was previously thought. Slave masters experimented with different mixtures of positive and negative incentives in order to encourage slaves to maximize output (Fogel 1989). Thus, slave plantations prefigured the discipline of workers in the great factories of industrial capitalism, in which assembly lines regulate the rhythms and intensity of work.

Forced migration from Africa greatly exceeded all migration from Europe as sugar production became the greatest consumer of servile labor in the Americas. High death rates and a preference for male slaves in the sugar producing regions led to net population declines among blacks and mulattoes (compare immigration numbers to population sizes in Table 1). Nevertheless, the proportion of blacks in the British West Indies increased from 25 to 91 percent between 1650 and 1770 (Fogel 1989, p. 30). By the 1820s, the proportion of blacks and mulattoes in Brazil, the Guyanas, and the West Indies together reached 75 percent.

British North America was an exception to this pattern as both black and white populations had high rates of natural increase. Almost all major slave societies were unable to maintain the size of slave populations without continuous replenishment from outside sources. By contrast, the United States slave population multiplied because of unusually high fertility rates and lower mortality rates than elsewhere (see Table 1 and Fogel 1989).

Political factors also encouraged the transition from white servitude to black slavery (Engerman 1986b; Galenson 1981). As British citizens, indentured servants retained state protected natal rights, which their masters were obliged to respect. For example, masters could beat servants and slaves to enforce work discipline, but colonial courts protected servants against unfair punishment (Smith 1947). Importantly, Europeans could choose the place of their servitude and most refused transportation to the plantation regions from the eighteenth century on. African slaves could not avoid the plantation regions and were citizens of no state in Africa or America that would defend their interests.

Because Spain conquered the continental regions with the largest Native American populations (Table 1), it had less need of African slaves to satisfy labor shortages there. Instead, Spanish colonists installed a coercive labor system patterned on Spanish feudalism that forced natives to work part-time on colonial estates although slavery was still preferred in the mines (Slicher Van Bath 1986; Kloosterboer 1960). Unfree labor markets and compulsory labor endured for 400 years, eventually evolving into debt servitude by the nineteenth century. Consequently, Native Americans and mestizos composed nearly 80 percent of the population of continental Spanish America by 1825 but were almost annihilated in the West Indies (Table 1).

Nowhere in the Americas was slavery in danger of withering away economically at the time that it was abolished (Eltis 1987). Strong states with dynamic economies based upon free wage labor where abolitionist ideologies flourished imposed abolition on weaker states. A principal exception was Haiti where slave owners were deposed by a slave revolt in 1804. Although Britain controlled one-half of the world's exports in sugar and coffee and one-half of the transatlantic commerce in slaves by the early nineteenth century (Eltis 1987), it played the dominant role in abolishing the transatlantic slave trade and, finally, in the worldwide abolition of slavery. Britain outlawed the slave trade in 1808 and freed the slaves in its West Indian colonies in 1833 over the strenuous objections of slave owners. The United States prohibited the importation of slaves after 1808 and Civil War led to abolition in 1865. By the 1870s, all of the major European and American maritime and commercial powers had acquiesced to British pressure and outlawed the slave trade. Brazil became the last state in the Americas to abolish slavery in 1888.

The land/labor ratio strongly affected planters' responses to abolition. Where ex-slaves could find no alternative to plantation work, such as on Barbados and Antigua, the transition to free labor was rapid, and plantation production did not decline appreciably (Boogaart and Emmer 1986). Where land or alternative employment was available as in Jamaica and Trinidad, the ex-slaves abandoned the plantations, and plantation productivity declined (Engerman 1985). In response, planters implemented a variety of servile labor systems with mixed results. A second wave of indentured servants was imported chiefly from Asia, especially China and India, which more than compensated for the labor shortages induced by abolition in some cases such as Mauritius and British Guiana (Engerman 1985, 1986b). China and colonial India eventually banned servant recruitments because of objections to employers' poor treatment of servants, and Brazil was never able to negotiate access to Asian indentured laborers (Boogaart and Emmer 1986).

Where planters retained a degree of political power, as in the West Indies and Brazil, vagrancy statues and other compulsory labor schemes were used to force workers to accept wages below free market levels (Kloosterboer 1960; Huggins 1985). Indentured labor and other forms of involuntary servitude were banned in the United States by the Thirteenth Amendment (1865) to the U.S. Constitution, but planters regained substantial influence over black workers through their control of racially discriminatory state and local governmental institutions (James 1988). Blacks were disfranchised by 1900, which made them especially vulnerable to racial segregation, physical coercion, and economic discrimination. The extent to which racial discrimination interfered with free labor markets in the South is controversial (e.g., Wright 1986). Nevertheless, the most determined resistance to the civil rights movement of the 1960s was located in the plantation regions (James 1988).

UNFREE LABOR IN AFRICA AND ASIA

Slavery was an indigenous institution in Africa and Arabia for centuries before Europeans entered the African slave trade. While approximately 9.9 million Africans were transported to the Americas before the Atlantic slave trade was suppressed (Fogel 1989), an additional 5.2 million African slaves were transported across the Sahara, Red Sea, and Indian Ocean into the Islamic world between 1500 and 1900. Moreover, perhaps 6.4 million more were exported to Islamic societies between A.D. 650 and 1500 ("a rough approximation," Lovejoy 1983, p. 24). Millions more were enslaved in African societies.

Whereas chattel slavery in the Americas was predicated upon profit making, African slavery typically had no such narrow economic basis. African slaves were menial servants and field workers, but they might also have been concubines, surrogate kin, soldiers, commercial agents, and candidates for human sacrifice (Roberts and Miers 1988, p. 5). Female slaves were especially valued because women performed most agricultural and domestic work. African societies were based upon kinship relations in which all individuals were linked in a complex network of dependency. Because power in kinship systems depends on the size of social groups, slave masters could increase their power by obtaining more slaves. Furthermore, slaves were immune to the appeals of their master's rivals within kin groups because they had no kinship ties that mediated their subordination to their masters.

Islamic slavery also differed from chattel slavery in important ways. Islamic law prohibited the enslavement of Muslims but permitted the enslavement of persons born to slave parents or captured for the purpose of conversion to Islam (Gordon 1989). Concubines could not be sold if they bore a child to their master and the child could not be enslaved. Allowing slaves to purchase their freedom brought honor to former masters. Manumitting slaves was also meritorious and could atone for certain sins and public offenses.

Islamic slaves were typically employed as household servants, domestic workers, concubines, and, to a lesser extent, soldiers. Female slaves typically brought higher prices than males because the heads of patriarchal Muslim families prized female slaves for assignment to sexual and domestic roles in their households. Slave eunuchs performed special tasks in large households and usually brought higher prices than female slaves. Consequently, pre-twentieth-century slave traders castrated large numbers of African slave boys in crude operations, which killed perhaps 90 percent of them (Gordon 1989, pp. 91-97). But Islamic slave masters also responded to economic incentives, as did their American counterparts, when market opportunities arose. During the nineteenth century, over 750,000 slaves were transported to the clove plantations on Zanzibar and other locations on the east coast of Africa, for example (Cooper 1977; Lovejoy 1983, p. 151).

British diplomatic and military pressure finally led to the suppression of the Islamic and African slave trades as it did with the transatlantic traffic. In 1890, all of the European powers agreed to suppress slavetrading and slaveraiding and to assist ex-slaves, a commitment that legitimated the conquest of Africa in the eyes of European citizens. But European colonial administrators were reluctant abolitionists (Roberts and Miers 1988). Inadequate military and administrative power, fear of economic and political disruptions, and unfamiliarity with African customs delayed the process.

Colonial governments essentially ended slavery in sub-Saharan Africa by the 1930s, but involuntary servitude persisted. Roberts and Miers (1989, pp. 42-47) identify three factors that retarded the emergence of free labor markets in Africa. The first two were responses to abundant land and scarce labor, at least in part. First, colonial states conscripted natives, imposed labor levies that local chiefs had to fill, and implemented other compulsory labor mechanisms to maintain a supply of cheap labor for European employers and administrators. Second, many Africans had access to land or livestock and were unwilling to work for wages. Colonial states tried to reduce the attractiveness of nonwage occupations by, for example, raising taxes above what peasant agriculturalists and pastoralists could pay, and prohibiting Africans from growing lucrative cash crops. In settler colonies such as South Africa, Africans were pushed off the land and confined to strictly regulated labor markets by pass laws. Third, Africans resorted widely to pawnship after abolition.

The reluctance of colonial administrators and the power of postcolonial states allowed slavery to survive in some Islamic nations of North Africa and the Arabian Peninsula well into the twentieth century. Pressure from the United Nations and world opinion finally led to formal abolition in the remaining slave states: Ethiopia in 1942; Saudi Arabia in 1962; Muscat and Oman in 1970;

Mauritania for the third time in 1980. Nevertheless, reports of slavery persist. Saudi Arabia allegedly failed to free some 250,000 slaves in the late 1960s; an estimated 100,000 chattel slaves existed in Saharan regions of Mauritania in 1980, but most, if not all, were freed by 1984; nomadic tribesmen allegedly held 250,000 slaves in the Sahelian districts of Mali in 1984 (Gordon 1989, pp. 232-234; United Nations 1984, pp. 18-19; United Nations 1988, p. 197; Sawyer 1986, p. 14).

Other forms of servitude persist, although they are illegal in most nations. For example, India outlawed bondage in 1976, but a survey found more than 2.5 million bonded workers in 1978; only 163,000 had been freed by 1985 (Sawyer 1986, pp. 124-134). Debt servitude was reported since 1970 among landless peasants in India and Nepal and Native American rubber collectors in the Peruvian Amazon. As late as 1986, the Dominican Republic used the army to round up Haitian immigrants and forced them to work on sugar plantations during the harvest season (Plant 1987).

CURRENT PATTERNS OF SLAVERY AND UNFREE LABOR

States have shaped the persistence and patterns of slavery and other forms of unfree labor since the fifteenth century. For most of this period, states defended the interests of slave masters, slave raiders, slave traders, merchants, landlords, planters, capitalists, state officials, and others who benefited from the services of unfree workers. The Nieboer-Domar hypothesis, suitably modified, provides a preliminary explanation for the persistence of slavery and unfree labor in the Americas and some parts of Africa during this period (see Patterson 1977b for an opposing view) but cannot account for the patterns of nonchattel slavery in Africa and Asia, where political and cultural factors were key.

The expansion of capitalism and increasing world population displaced large numbers from subsistence agriculture and other means of support in many regions. Great disparities between rich and poor nations drive many people across state boundaries in search of jobs and improved living conditions. State power still plays a crucial role in shaping migration and in molding the relationship between capital and labor, but states with expanding economies now prevent the entrance of many willing workers rather than compel the entrance of the unwilling. The whip of unemployment and poverty replaces the slave master's lash as free labor replaces slavery.

All nations regulate the passage of individuals across their boundaries and universally assign superior rights and privileges to citizens as compared to noncitizens. In the advanced capitalist democracies with ostensibly free labor markets, the state enforced distinction between citizen and noncitizen is a key mechanism in maintaining dual labor markets that disproportionately relegate noncitizens to the lowest paying jobs (e.g., Thomas 1985; Miles 1987; Cohen 1987). Typically, noncitizen "guest workers" are less likely to enjoy state protection and are more vulnerable to discrimination. Any reemergence of large-scale, state-enforced slave systems in countries with expanding economies will probably be for political or cultural rather than economic reasons. Because the demand for cheap labor can be satisfied largely by choosing among citizens and noncitizens who have no other labor market alternatives, democratic states can regulate noncitizens' access to domestic labor markets rather than forcibly import unfree workers from foreign lands.

But many modern states are not liberal democracies. Thousands were confined for political reasons in forced labor camps during the Stalin era in the USSR. Nazi Germany forced Jews and other minorities into slavery where they were to be "worked to death" (Sawyer 1986). Blacks were disfranchised and rigidly segregated in the southern United States for much of the twentieth century, making them vulnerable to coercive labor practices. The Republic of South Africa's policy of apartheid denies citizenship status to native blacks, who compose 70 percent of the population and are an essential component of the work force.

Claiming the right to regulate immigration as all nations do, South Africa uses citizenship status to create unfree labor markets that benefit white employers and impose severe burdens on disfavored racial and ethnic groups.

Slavery has been formally abolished everywhere, but many states do not provide equal protection of the law to all groups. Race and ethnic violence is severe in many places (e.g., Senegal, Mauritania, Sri Lanka, Somalia, India), which creates great pressure for states to enforce racial or ethnic bias. Nevertheless, state-enforced racial and ethnic distinctions are almost universally condemned by international organizations. Many nations enforce sanctions against South Africa because of its blatant racial bias, for example, but discrimination against disfavored ethnic groups persists in a number of other countries (U.S. Department of State 1990). For example, ethnic Albanians cannot buy real property in the Yugoslavian province of Serbia. Ethnic hiring quotas for government positions are observed in Nigeria. State-enforced race or ethnic discrimination was also reported in China, the USSR, Romania, Rwanda, Burundi, Mauritania, Senegal, Sudan, and India (U.S. Department of State 1990).

State-enforced religious bias appears to be more widespread than race discrimination. Most Islamic nations impose restrictions on non-Muslims, but Saudi Arabia and Iran are especially harsh. For example, all citizens of Saudi Arabia must be Muslims and conversion to a different religion is punishable by death (U.S. Department of State 1990). Saudi Arabia also prohibits the public or private practice of non-Muslim religions and restricts economic opportunities for non-Muslims and Shi'a Muslims. Iran imposes barriers to education, jobs, and public accommodations for Christians, Jews, Zoroastrians, and Bahais. Although religious discrimination is officially prohibited in India, China, the USSR, and Israel, religious minorities in these nations continue to complain of state-enforced biases.

Discrimination against women is more widespread and pernicious than other forms of state-enforced status bias, and even extreme cases seldom provoke criticism from other nations (U.S. Department of State 1990). Sex discrimination in varying degree is characteristic of Islamic nations. Saudi Arabian women have few political rights: they cannot travel abroad without permission from their nearest male relative, cannot operate automobiles or travel alone, must keep their faces covered in public, and inherit smaller amounts than their brothers. In Pakistan, press reports suggest an increase in the number of newlywed wives who are thought to have been murdered, often by burning, by husbands who were dissatisfied with the size of their wives' dowries. Violence against women is seldom investigated or punished (Muslim advice columns in Saudi Arabia and Pakistan advocate wife beating as an appropriate form of discipline).

Most Islamic states discriminate against women in the inheritance and ownership of property and in family and marriage issues, but similar biases exist in African and Asian non-Muslim nations, where traditional courts or Muslim minorities are allowed to adjudicate these issues as in Sudan, South Africa, Mauritania, Senegal, Chad, Nigeria, Rwanda, and India, for example (U.S. Department of State 1990). South African women of all races can be legally dismissed from their jobs if they become pregnant. Dowry deaths seldom result in convictions in India.

Most of the remaining countries officially condemn discrimination against women, but state-enforced bias persists (U.S. Department of State 1990). For example, women in the Philippines have restricted rights to buy and sell property. China enforces sex differences in access to jobs and education, and a number of nations in the Americas enforce some form of sex bias.

The historic decline in the land/labor ratio did not produce the abolition of slavery and involuntary servitude as the simple version of the Nieboer-Domar hypothesis suggests. Many states still enforce race, religious, sex, and other status and class distinctions among citizens that discriminate against unfavored groups or make them vulnerable to coercive labor relations and slavery-like practices. The exercise of political power, the pressure of economic necessity, and cultural practices are inextricably linked.

(SEE ALSO: *African-American Studies; African Studies; Apartheid; Prejudice; Segregation and Desegregation; Social Inequality; Social Stratification*)

REFERENCES

Boogaart, Ernst van den, and P.C. Emmer 1986 "Colonialism and Migration: An Overview." In P.C. Emmer, ed., *Colonialism and Migration.* Dordrecht, The Netherlands: Martinus Nijhoff.

Cohen, Robin 1987 *The New Helots.* Brookfield, Vt.: Gower Publishing.

Cooper, Frederick 1977 *Plantation Slavery on the East Coast of Africa.* New Haven, Conn.: Yale University Press.

Domar, Evesy D. 1970 "The Causes of Slavery or Serfdom: A Hypothesis." *Journal of Economic History* 30:18–31.

Eltis, David 1983 "Free and Coerced Transatlantic Migrations: Some Comparisons." *American Historical Review* 88:251–280.

———1987 *Economic Growth and the Ending of the Transatlantic Slave Trade.* New York: Oxford University Press.

Engerman, Stanley L. 1985 "Economic Change and Contract Labour in the British Caribbean." In D. Richardson, ed., *Abolition and Its Aftermath.* London: Frank Cass.

———1986a "Slavery and Emancipation in Comparative Perspective: A Look at Some Recent Debates." *Journal of Economic History* 46:317–339.

———1986b "Servants to Slaves to Servants: Contract Labour and European Expansion." In P. C. Emmer, ed., *Colonialism and Migration,* Dordrecht, The Netherlands: Martinus Nijhoff.

Finley, M. I. 1968 "Slavery." *International Encyclopedia of the Social Sciences,* Vol. 14, pp. 307–313. New York: Macmillan and Free Press.

Fogel, Robert W. 1989 *Without Consent or Contract.* New York: Norton.

Galenson, David W. 1981 *White Servitude in Colonial America.* New York: Cambridge University Press.

Gordon, Murray 1989 *Slavery in the Arab World.* New York: New Amsterdam Books.

Huggins, Martha K. 1985 *From Slavery to Vagrancy in*

Brazil. New Brunswick, N.J.: Rutgers University Press.

James, David R. 1988 "The Transformation of the Southern Racial State: Class and Race Determinants of Local-State Structures." *American Sociological Review* 53:191–208.

Kloosterboer, W. 1960 *Involuntary Labour Since the Abolition of Slavery.* Leiden: E. J. Brill.

Kolchin, Peter 1987 *Unfree Labor: American Slavery and Russian Serfdom.* Cambridge: Harvard University Press.

Lovejoy, Paul E. 1983 *Transformations in Slavery.* Cambridge: Cambridge University Press.

Marx, Karl (1867) 1967 *Capital,* Vol. 1. New York: International Publishers.

Miles, Robert 1987 *Capitalism and Unfree Labour.* London: Tavistock.

Morgan, Edmund S. 1975 *American Slavery, American Freedom.* New York: Norton.

Morris, Richard B. 1946 *Government and Labor in Early America.* New York: Columbia University Press.

Nieboer, Herman J. 1900 *Slavery as an Industrial System.* The Hague: Martinus Nijhoff.

Paige, Jeffery 1975 *Agrarian Revolution.* New York: Free Press.

Patterson, Orlando 1977a "Slavery." *Annual Review of Sociology* 3:407–449.

———1977b "The Structural Origins of Slavery: A Critique of the Nieboer Domar Hypothesis." *Annuals New York Academy of Sciences* 292:12–34.

———1982 *Slavery and Social Death.* Cambridge, Mass.: Harvard University Press.

Plant, Roger 1987 *Sugar and Modern Slavery.* London: Zed.

Roberts, Richard, and Suzanne Miers 1988 "The End of Slavery in Africa." In S. Miers and R. Roberts, eds., *The End of Slavery in Africa.* Madison: University of Wisconsin Press.

Sawyer, Roger 1986 *Slavery in the Twentieth Century.* London: Routledge and Kegan Paul.

Slicher Van Bath, B. H. 1986 "The Absence of White Contract Labour in Spanish America During the Colonial Period." In P.C. Emmer, ed., *Colonialism and Migration.* Dordrecht, The Netherlands: Martinus Nijhoff.

Smith, Abbot Emerson 1947 *Colonists in Bondage.* Chapel Hill: University of North Carolina Press.

Thomas, Robert J. 1985 *Citizenship, Gender, and Work.* Berkeley: University of California Press.

United Nations 1984 "Slavery: Report Prepared by B. Whitaker, Special Rapporteur of the Sub-Commission on Prevention of Discrimination and Protection of Minorities." New York: United Nations.

———1988 "United Nations Action in the Field of Human Rights." New York: United Nations.

United States Department of State 1990 *Country Reports on Human Rights Practices for 1989.* Washington, D.C.: U.S. Government Printing Office.

Wright, Gavin 1986 *Old South, New South.* New York: Basic Books.

DAVID R. JAMES

SMALL GROUPS In sociology, the concept "group" implies more than simply an aggregate of persons. Additional elements involved are (1) structure—interaction patterned in terms of statuses and roles; (2) history—some regularity or frequency of interaction over time; (3) interdependence—some degree of members' mutual reliance on each other for needed or valued material and nonmaterial resources; and (4) common identity—grounded in shared meanings, values, experiences, and goals. Frequently there is some group product, not necessarily of a material nature, that is the outcome or consequence of collective effort and interaction.

These elements are dimensional in that groups possess and manifest them to greater or lesser degrees. At one extreme, family groups typically have well-established and enduring structures, share extensive histories, encompass a wide range of activities, exert a broad scope of influence, and provide the basis of individual identity. At the other extreme, ad hoc work groups may be assembled to perform specific tasks of very limited duration, with virtually no relevance for or influence on the members outside a clearly defined situation and range of activity. McGrath (1984) has developed a comprehensive typology of groups in terms of origin, scope of activity, task, duration, and interaction.

Groups are regarded as "small" if meaningful and direct face-to-face interaction can take place among all members. The number of members is usually thought of as ranging from two to twenty, with three to seven common in many laboratory studies of groups.

Cooley (1909) identified a fundamental type of small group, which he regarded as the basic building block of society. It is characterized by intimate face-to-face association and cooperation. Cooley called groups of this sort "primary groups" and held them to be forms of association found everywhere, which work on the individual to develop the social nature of the person. "This nature consists of certain primary social sentiments and attitudes, such as consciousness of one's self in relation to others, love of approbation, resentment of censure, emulation, and a sense of social right and wrong formed by the standards of a group" (1909, p. 32).

Membership and participation in primary groups are valued and rewarding for their own sake. The groups typically are long-lasting. Members interact as "whole persons" rather than merely in terms of specialized, partial roles. Such groups are basic sources of socioemotional support and gratification, and participation in them is considered essential for a person's psychological and emotional well-being. Some (the family, the neighborhood peer group) are also primary in the sense that they are settings for early childhood socialization and personality development.

In contrast are groups formed and maintained to accomplish some task and to which people belong for extrinsic purposes (because they are paid, or to gain some external goal). These "secondary groups" are characterized by limited, instrumental relationships. They may be relatively short-term, and their range of activity is restricted. Affective ties and other "irrational" personal influences are intended to be minimized or eliminated.

It is widely observed, however, that primary relationships develop pervasively within secondary groups and organizations. In a synthesis of observations and research findings, Homans (1950) attempted to identify universal variables of group behavior. He sought to develop a general theoretical scheme that would permit understanding of groups as diverse as an industrial work unit, a street-corner gang, and a Polynesian family. Homans approached the small group as a system in which activity, interaction, and sentiment are in-

terrelated. He concluded that interaction among group members increases their liking for each other and that they tend to express their friendship in an increasing scope of activities and to interact more frequently. Affective elements emerge in virtually all ongoing groups, and may function to facilitate or interfere with the purposes for which the group was established. Soldiers are motivated to fight, and workers to increase or restrict work output, by loyalty to their friends and the norms of the immediate group.

BASES AND DEVELOPMENT OF SMALL GROUP RESEARCH

Sociological interest in small groups has a number of bases, including (1) the perception of small groups as fundamental, universal social units upon which all larger structures of organization depend; (2) a concern with description and understanding of particular small groups both for their own sake and as a source of observations from which hypotheses and general theories can be developed; and (3) the usefulness of the laboratory group as a research context in which to study characteristics of the group as the unit of interest and as a setting for study of influences on individual cognitions and behavior.

Foundations for small group research may be seen in nineteenth-century sociological thought, such as Emile Durkheim's analyses of development of social structures, specialization and task differentiation, and the bases of social cohesion, and Georg Simmel's work on the importance of group size and coalition formation. Early in the present century Charles H. Cooley and George Herbert Mead stressed the origins of the self as socially constructed through interaction within immediate group settings.

In the 1930s and 1940s Jacob L. Moreno developed a systematic approach to the understanding and charting of group structure, and Muzafer Sherif conducted key studies of group influence and conformity. Kurt Lewin's work of that period provided influence and inspiration for the postwar generation of social psychologists (Borgatta 1981). Lewin combined principles of

Gestalt psychology and concepts from the physical sciences to develop field theory in social psychology as a basis for the study of group dynamics. He was interested in both theoretical and applied aspects of group interaction; the widely utilized sensitivity-training group technique originated serendipitously in sessions organized by Lewin in 1946.

The era from the end of World War II to the early 1960s produced burgeoning activity in small-group research. In addition to the pervasive effect of Lewin's ideas, substantial work reflected concerns with functional needs that groups must meet to survive, and with the relationship of these functions to dimensions of interpersonal behavior (Hare 1976). Influences from anthropology, economics, and behavioral psychology were melded in a view of social interaction as an exchange of resources, a perspective applied to the analysis of interdependence, cooperation and competition, and personal relationships. And during those years small-group research shared the methodological advances occurring throughout social science, developing an increasing sophistication in issues of research design, measurement, and analysis.

Small-group research since the 1960s does not appear as prominent or compelling as it was during the postwar period, when social psychology was virtually dominated by the small groups "movement" (Borgatta 1981). Studies are being produced at a pace that is steady though moderate compared to the peak period (Steiner 1983). Significant attempts are being made to organize and conceptually integrate the diverse body of work and theory that has accumulated (Hare 1982; McGrath 1984).

APPROACHES TO SMALL-GROUP RESEARCH

Small-group studies are diverse, characterized by a wide variety of research techniques and theoretical and practical concerns. Research methods vary in regard to the types of groups and circumstances studied—whether these are "natural" or contrived for research purposes—and in the intrusiveness of the research procedures. Some investigators are concerned with properties of the group itself as the unit of interest, while others use the small group setting as a context for exploration of individual behavior. While laboratory studies predominate, techniques employed include direct observation of group interaction in natural as well as controlled settings; the use of formal systems for coding communication or other aspects of behavior; the use of questionnaires or interviews to elicit ratings, choices, opinions, or attitudes from group members; and field experimentation.

Laboratory studies have marked advantages in the control and manipulation of variables and in precision of observation and measurement. The procedures normally permit replication of observation under controlled conditions. The experimental method is held to be superior to others for rigorously testing causal hypotheses. Fundamental issues are whether relevant variables can be brought into laboratory situations and whether a meaningful range of variation can be achieved.

Criticisms of laboratory research center on the artificiality of the setting and the usually short-term nature of the studies. The representativeness of subject groups, and hence the generalization of findings, are also questioned. Concerns for protecting the rights and well-being of human subjects have led to procedural safeguards that now inhibit or prevent practices typical of some well-known earlier studies.

The technical advantages of laboratory procedures, the desire to emulate the natural sciences in developing theory based on experimental evidence, and the compatibility of laboratory research with the academic context in which most researchers have worked all have contributed to the proliferation of laboratory studies that make up the largest part of small group research.

Direct observation of group behavior under basically uncontrolled conditions may be coupled with the investigator's more or less active participation in the affairs of the group. Such research can employ structured systems for coding behavior and interaction patterns, to be used by uninvolved "objective" observers, as when a children's play group is studied by adults. A more informal ethnographic approach was employed by Erving Goffman (1959) in collecting the information that illustrated his characterization of human interaction as an elaborate sequence of symbolic presentations of self, and groups as collaborating teams of performers.

Participant observation is a procedure in which the researcher acts as part of a (usually natural) group to understand a situation from within, as members of the group define and experience it. Group members may know the observer is an outsider, there for his or her own purposes, or may be led or allowed to believe the observer is simply another "genuine" group member. In either case the observer's status influences and constrains both the kinds and amount of information available and the opportunities for recording information. The observer also has some influence on the situations and processes being studied, thus producing research results different from those that would occur in the absence of observation. The use of multiple observers provides increased opportunities for observation while also increasing the probable effect of the research on the group's behavior (Festinger, Riecken, and Schachter 1964). For these reasons, reliability and validity are particularly problematic issues in using this technique.

Participant observation is regarded as primarily useful for descriptive and exploratory research and for generating or illustrating (as opposed to testing) theory. The approach is favored by those resolved to understand the meanings of actions and situations generated and maintained by groups in their natural, everyday environments.

An important naturalistic study was conducted in the late 1930s by William Foote Whyte (1955), who studied a street-corner gang as a participant observer over a period of three and a half years. (The appendix to his monograph provides an informative discussion of practical and ethical issues in participant observation.) Whyte gained access to the gang through association with its leader, and his view is from the top of the social structure. He described the structure of social relationships among members, group values and

codes of behavior, the existence of implicit exchange relationships, territorial behavior, and the nature and functions of gang leadership. Whyte's work effectively contradicted the prevailing view that city slum districts were devoid of social organization.

Whyte's observations of the ways in which members' social rankings in the group affected their performance in athletic competition suggested a program of experimental studies of diffuse status characteristics—an exploration of the manner in which "logically" irrelevant social rank affects the amount of influence an individual has on others in activities ranging from pedestrian behavior to making perceptual judgments.

Sociometry, a technique for eliciting and representing the patterns and structure of choices and liking among group members, was developed by Jacob L. Moreno (1953). While the most common procedure is for researchers to ask group members who they like, dislike, would prefer to work with, or would like to "be like," ratings can also be based on direct observation of members' behavior. The information can be represented as a sociogram, showing individuals as circles and choices as arrows between the circles: The diagram depicts group structure in terms of affective relations. Indices of liking or disliking can be computed for each member, and ratings can be organized in matrix format. The density and patterning of the network of choices may be taken as indicators of group cohesiveness. In practical applications the sociometric data are used to restructure the group based on mutual choices.

INTERACTION PROCESS RESEARCH

A prominent research concern has been the description and analysis of group interaction processes, focusing primarily on communication. The approaches employed have ranged from purely formal examination of the amount of communication sent and received by each member of the group, to extremely detailed analyses of linguistic and paralinguistic material, including posture, gestures, and inflection.

The widely used system for Interaction Process

Analysis developed by Bales (1950) involves a set of twelve categories for coding units (acts) of communication. The categories reflect Bales's conclusion that all groups confront two domains of concerns: instrumental concerns related to whatever task the group must accomplish, and expressive concerns associated with the socioemotional needs and interrelationships of the group members. Both sets of concerns operate continually and must be dealt with if a group is to succeed and survive, and there is a virtually constant conflict between them. The system of categories is used by observers to code types of active and passive task-related acts, and positive and negative socioemotional acts, as they are generated by group members in the course of interaction.

Numerous studies using the IPA system have sought to document the patterns or "phase movements" of instrumental and expressive communication as groups attempt to establish the equilibrium necessary to operate. Attention has also been paid to the roles of particular group members in exercising task leadership or socioemotional leadership. The division of group leadership into instrumental and expressive functions proved compatible with accepted notions of "typical" male and female personal attributes, and with a conceptualization of the family (at least in the Western world) as a small group having the father as task leader and the mother as socioemotional specialist. Recent research comparing "natural" families with ad hoc laboratory groups indicates that the instrumental versus expressive specialization found in the laboratory does not hold for groups in natural settings. There is greater diversity of behavior and less gender-linked stereotypical conduct in longer-lasting groups covering a greater scope of activities (McGrath 1984).

The IPA system has been criticized on both theoretical and operational grounds, and numerous alternatives have been suggested. Bales and his colleagues have developed a new observation system, SYMLOG (Bales and Cohen 1979), which models personal space in three dimensions: dominant-submissive, friendly-unfriendly, and instrumentally controlled-emotionally expressive.

Group interaction is observed and members' behaviors are coded on each dimension by outside observers or by group members themselves. Based on combinations of multiple observations, each individual is located within the three-dimensional space, and the positions of all group members are charted. The resulting diagram, and indices based on the scores, indicate the degree to which members are perceived as interacting in a similar fashion. Interest in the SYMLOG technique is substantial, and it is utilized in many studies of group structure and performance.

GROUP COHESION

The understanding of what holds a social unit together, a central issue in sociology, has also been central in small-group analysis. Cohesion, the sum of the forces that bind members to the group, was viewed by Lewin and other Gestaltists as a property or characteristic of the group itself, a sort of force field analogous to a magnetic or gravitational field. However, the assessment of cohesion depends on observations of attitudes and behaviors of the individual members: their self-reported attraction to the group, their feelings of being accepted by the group, similarity in expressions of sentiment, how regularly they attend group meetings, how prompt or tardy they are, or how responsible they are in performing actions that benefit the group. Steiner suggests that "A true test of a group's cohesion would entail observation of its members' reactions to disruptive influences," but rejects such a procedure on technical and ethical grounds (1972, p. 161).

The bases of cohesion include (1) rewards available within and through the group; (2) the congruence between individual and group goals; (3) the attraction/liking of members for each other; (4) the importance of the group as source or ground of an individual's identity and self-perception and his or her internalization of group culture and values; and (5) in psychoanalytic group theory, the members' identification with and attraction to the group leader and "the alignment between particular individual superego formation and its corresponding punitive group structure" (Kellerman 1981, p. 11).

While high cohesiveness is often taken as indicating a "healthy" group, its effect is to heighten members' susceptibility to influences in the group. Thus group productivity, for example, may be increased or decreased depending on the nature of the predominant influences.

A major emphasis in analysis of cohesiveness has been placed on interpersonal attraction and interdependence, emphasizing the exchange of emotional and affective resources. Work by Tajfel (1981) and Turner (1987) supports, alternatively, an emphasis on self-categorization. A concept of cohesion based on individual attraction unmediated by shared group membership is held to be inadequate (Hogg 1987).

Interdependence in a most elemental form has been realized in experiments with the "minimal social situation" (Sidowski 1957). Two subjects, each of whom controls resources that may reward or punish the other and each of whom depends primarily on the other's behavior as a source of reward or punishment, learn to exchange rewards despite being completely unaware of the nature of the situation. Self-categorization in a most elemental form is demonstrated in "minimal group" experiments (Tajfel 1981). Subjects are divided into two groups, sometimes presumably on the basis of some arbitrary and unimportant criterion and sometimes in an obviously random manner. The participants do not interact within or between groups during the experiment. Given the task of dividing a sum of money between two other persons about whom they know nothing except their group membership, subjects show a marked bias favoring members of their own group.

Thibaut and Kelley (1959) identified two criteria used in evaluating the rewards available within a particular situation: a usual, expected level of reward to which the person feels entitled, called the "comparison level"; and the person's perceived best level of reward available outside of the situation, called the "comparison level for alternatives." A member's satisfaction with his or her group membership and participation depends on the relation of rewards available within the group to his or her comparison level, while the likelihood that one will stay in or leave a group depends on the comparison level for alternatives.

Although the value and availability of rewards are usually emphasized in assessing the attractiveness of a group, Leon Festinger has pointed out the interesting persistence of loyalty to lost causes and the effect that insufficient reward, or even aversive experiences, can have in strengthening members' positive attitudes. One experiment (Aronson and Mills 1959) showed that potential group members who were subjected to a severe initiation expressed greater liking for the group than those who had a mild initiation. And while an equitable and balanced exchange of rewarding outcomes is considered important in sustaining interpersonal relationships and participants' satisfaction with them, Kelley and Thibaut (1978) noted that problematic situations provide particular opportunities. Attributions about a partner's personality and motivations, and self-presentations that encode messages of commitment and concern for the other person, are facilitated when behavior cannot be explained simply in terms of "rational" self-interest. Such attributions and encodings strengthen affective ties and promote interdependence of characteristics and attitudes displayed in the relationship.

GROUP INFLUENCE

Social Facilitation and Inhibition. In a study credited to be the first social psychological experiment (1897), Triplett measured the average time his subjects took to wind 150 turns on a fishing reel, working alone and in competition with each other. Subjects working in competition wound the reels faster than those working alone. Numerous subsequent experiments (including some with nonhuman subjects) have supported and modified these findings. It was found that the mere presence of other persons (as observers or coactors, whether or not they were competitors) facilitated the emission of well-learned responses, but that the presence of others interfered with the acquisition of new responses. This "audience effect," in brief, facilitates performance but inhibits learning. Various explanations of social facilitation and inhibition have been proposed, generally incorporating the idea that the presence of others produces increased motivational arousal. Such arousal is a basic feature of the group environment.

Conformity. Similarities of values, attitudes, beliefs, perceptions, and behavior are a ubiquitous (virtually defining) feature of group existence. Such similarities can facilitate coordination of goal-directed activity, motivate members, provide sources of psychological security and emotional reward, reinforce members' identification with the group, and increase cohesiveness. They also may prevent reasoned consideration of alternatives to group decisions and potential consequences of group actions, reduce flexibility in adapting to new circumstances, and inhibit change in general. Closed circles of conformity in groups isolated from dissenting viewpoints have been implicated in producing Fascist atrocities, government scandals, and space shuttle disasters. Conformity (to modeled indifference or uncertainty) is a factor in the failure of bystanders to help others in emergencies.

The amount of conformity in a group may be seen as a characteristic of the collectivity. Experimental studies, however, usually have been concerned with effects on the individual. Considered from this standpoint, conformity is defined as a change in an individual's attitude, belief, or behavior in the direction of a group norm. It is an example of social control resulting from peer influence (as distinct from, e.g., obedience to some constituted authority). Two types of conformity are identified: belief (or informational) conformity and behavioral (or normative) conformity.

Belief conformity involves an internalized and lasting change grounded in an individual's dependence on social sources of information and guidance. Once internalized, the group's standards and perceptions are constantly carried with the individual and constitute an ongoing element of social control.

Muzafer Sherif (1935) asked individual subjects to judge the apparent movement of a pinpoint of light in an otherwise totally dark room. Under these conditions the light, which in fact was stationary, appeared to most people to move. Different individuals perceived different amounts of movement. Assembled in small groups viewing the light together, the subjects began to agree on the amount of movement perceived: A group norm emerged in the ambiguous situation. Following the group interaction, subjects were asked to view the light again, in isolation. They continued to see the amount of movement agreed on by the group, rather than the amount they originally perceived individually. The group's perceptions apparently had been internalized.

The strength of belief conformity varies according to the ambiguity and unfamiliarity of the situation, the individual's trust in the credibility of group, the individual's attraction to and identification with the group, and the individual's prior experience and confidence or lack of these.

Behavioral conformity is grounded in the potential rewards and punishments disbursed by the group and in the individual's previous experience with the consequences of conformity and nonconformity. The consequences of agreeing with others' judgments and opinions, emulating others' behaviors, and following the customs of a group are usually pleasant, while disagreement and deviancy generally lead to unpleasant effects. Group members holding deviant positions typically receive, at first, greater than normal amounts of communication in an attempt to influence them to conform. If these efforts fail they are likely to be isolated or rejected, depending on the severity of the deviance. Monitoring of behavior is necessary if reward or punishment is to depend on its occurrence; thus this type of influence is effective only if and when an individual's actions are known to the group.

Experiments conducted by Asch (1951) demonstrated behavioral conformity. Subjects engaged in a perceptual estimation task that required them to pick out lines of the same length on boards presented side by side. Boards were presented in pairs, and the judgment of each pair comprised one experimental trial. In a typical experiment there was only one real subject; the other participants were employed by Asch, and their judgments were prearranged. After a number of trials in which correct judgments were given, the confederate "subjects" began stating unanimous wrong judgments. The real subjects conformed to a substantial extent by expressing judgments that agreed with the group. When removed from the group (or allowed to make judgments in private), the real subjects did not persist in the errors. Their conformity occurred only when it was witnessed by the other group members.

The strength of behavioral conformity varies according to the size and unanimity of the group, the importance of the group to the individual, and the disclosure of relevant judgments or behaviors to the group.

Belief and behavioral conformity can be distinguished analytically (and empirically under some laboratory conditions), but in natural situations they operate in conjunction. The group member not only is rewarded for conforming but also depends on others as models for behavior and as guides for judgments and opinions. And while it is common to think of beliefs and attitudes as existing prior to the behaviors that reflect them, a large body of research indicates that people come to believe the opinions they express: "Mere" behavioral conformity can lead to internalization.

Conformity effects are usually thought to reflect the majority influence in a group, but evidence shows that a determined minority can prevail. Minority influence seems especially relevent for internalization (Moscovici 1980).

Group Polarization. Early theories of "group contagion" and the madness of crowds notwithstanding, a general assumption has been that conformity processes within a group operate to bring extreme opinions and judgments in toward the center of the range of such opinions and judgments. However, a body of research contradicts the notion that group actions are more moderate than those of individuals.

The experimental procedure called for individual subjects to evaluate each of twelve "choice dilemmas"—situations in which a person was to choose between a highly desirable, risky alternative and a less desirable but certain alternative. Subjects were instructed to indicate, for each dilemma, the lowest probability of success they would accept in recommending that the desirable risky alternative be chosen. Probabilities were averaged for each subject over all dilemmas to generate a "riskiness" score for that person. Small groups of subjects were then formed and instructed to discuss each situation, reach a group decision, and indicate the group riskiness score for the dilemma. A group's scores were averaged over the twelve situations, and that value was compared to the mean of the individual scores of the members.

Initial research using the choice dilemmas procedure found a significant "risky shift" in the group decisions, compared to the mean of the individual scores. Numerous experiments and further analyses followed that extended and qualified these findings. Certain kinds of choice dilemma scenarios produced risky shifts, while others produced conservative shifts or no significant difference. Shifts tended to move in the direction of initial group inclinations: The interaction resulted in a collective outcome more extreme than might be predicted on the basis of individual positions, but the individual positions forecast the nature of the shift.

Group polarization, as the effect is now called, has been theoretically interpreted in terms of risk as a cultural value, the persuasive influence of "risky" individuals, and the diffusion of responsibility in group action. However, the effect is well explained as due to the normative and informational influences involved in conformity processes (McGrath 1984).

GROUP INTERACTION AND PERFORMANCE

Group performance in terms of productivity or effectiveness is a subject of both practical and theoretical concern. The establishment of an appropriate basis of evaluation is often problematical, and expected outcomes depend heavily on the type of task undertaken. Steiner (1972) has distinguished between tasks that require a coordinated division of effort, labeled divisible, and those with a single outcome or product, called unitary. Disjunctive unitary tasks are those that can be successfully performed by one individual alone. In such cases the group should be as "good" as the best member. Conjunctive unitary tasks require all members to contribute satisfactorily; in these, the group can only be as good as the worst member. Tasks in which members' contributions are simply summed to produce the group outcome are called additive, and group performance should depend on the "average" member.

Many studies have been aimed at evaluating the effects of different patterns of interaction on performance. Typically, groups of three to five persons were required to combine information distributed across the individual members, communicating only through channels provided by the experimenters. Various networks of communication channels have been investigated to see how they affect the group's efficiency and members' satisfaction. The networks differ in terms of how centralized or open they are. The most centralized network compels all messages to flow through one position, while the most open permits direct communication among all members.

Conclusions from this research are that centralized networks are most efficient in dealing with simple tasks but that group members tend to be dissatisfied except for the person occupying the central position. In more complex tasks the advantages of centralization are lost. Burgess (1969) suggested that the network experiments had been basically flawed in failing to provide meaningful consequences for group performance and in studying groups only for brief time periods, while they were learning to use the networks. Burgess had groups work with different networks over ten one-hour work sessions, and provided incentives for productivity. He found that when subjects had adequate time to learn to use the channels provided and received rewards based on performance, there were no differences between the networks. Given time and motivation, efficient adaptation overcame the structural constraints.

Problems of motivation often cause group performance to fall short of what it "should be."

Motivation is affected by the degree to which elements of the task can be identified, the extent to which the quantity and quality of members' performance can be evaluated, and the manner in which reward contingencies are linked to task performance. Motivation is reduced when members can gain rewards despite poor performance or when good work is not rewarded. These possibilities are evident when the consequences of task success or failure apply mutually to all group members.

Processes of influence and conformity may degrade performance quality. Majorities generate social pressure whether or not they are competent. Techniques have been devised to control these effects by regulating the kind of interaction that can take place. Such procedures often require the accomplishment of task elements in specified sequences or impose particular structures of communication in decision-making processes (McGrath 1984).

Frequently, the degree of influence exerted by group members and the impact of their contributions to the group's effort are not highly correlated with their task-related competence and abilities. Inequalities in participation, in evaluation of performance outputs, and in influence over the group's decisions reflect inequalities in status characteristics that members bring to the group. These tend to be maintained within the group whether or not they are task-relevant. Evaluations of performance output depend on previous evaluations, and expectations that arise out of task-related interaction influence subsequent interaction so as to produce their own confirmation (Berger, Rosenholtz, and Zelditch 1980).

COOPERATION AND COMPETITION IN GROUPS

Two different orientations are evident within the research on cooperation and competition within groups. One approach has treated cooperation and competition as imposed external conditions that influence task performance and the quality of group interaction. Alternatively, cooperation and competition have been studied as dependent behaviors, affected by reward and risk contingencies, the availability of communication, and other situational factors.

Numerous studies have compared the productivity and efficiency of groups working under cooperative conditions (defined as working for group goals) and competitive conditions (defined as working for individual goals). The concept of cooperation in early research usually specified only mutual dependency of outcomes, with little attention to the interdependency of members' task activities. The findings indicated that efficiency of work under competition was greater than that under cooperation for tasks not requiring coordination of effort. Some research indicated that cooperative groups worked together more frequently and were more highly coordinated.

Analysis of research focusing on the nature of tasks used as criteria in comparing cooperative and competitive reward structures points to the importance of "means interdependence"—the degree to which group members are reliant on one another (Schmitt 1981). When tasks are simple, requiring no division of labor or sharing of information or resources, the advantage of competitive contingencies seems to hold. However, cooperative contingencies are typically superior for tasks high in means interdependence involving distribution of effort, coordination of responses, or information-sharing. In a number of cases an additional element of competition between groups has been found to increase the productivity of internally cooperative groups.

Research treating cooperation as a dependent effect has focused on the participants' choice of cooperative rather than competitive behaviors and the distribution and coordination of responses. The effects of threat and communication were studied in a well-known experiment in which two subjects could cooperate by alternately using a "short route" to reach a destination (Deutsch and Krauss 1962). Cooperation was reduced when one subject could block the route with a gate ("unilateral threat") and extremely rare when both had gates ("bilateral threat"). Communication between subjects did not increase cooperation under the threat conditions.

Communication has sometimes been found to increase cooperation in studies using the "Prisoner's Dilemma." The situation provides that participants benefit moderately if both choose to cooperate and loose substantially if both "defect." If either chooses to cooperate while the other defects, the cooperator suffers a very large loss and the defector's outcome is highly favorable. Thus cooperation involves risk, while defection implies motives of self-protection, exploitation, or both. The structure of outcomes is paradoxical: The rational choices of each individual lead to poor collective consequences. Rates of cooperation have usually been low.

Inequity of outcomes and the presence of risk have been found to reduce cooperation across a range of experimental research (Marwell and Schmitt 1975). Beneficial effects of communication were dependent on the timing of its availability and the pattern of behavior that had occurred before communication took place.

Studies of cooperation and competition have addressed problems of motivation and coordination, issues of equity, the effects of short-term and long-term consequences, and the relationship of individual to collective outcomes. The ongoing analysis of these topics is a notable feature of current small-group research.

(SEE ALSO: *Compliance and Conformity; Group Problem Solving; Group Size Effects; Observation Systems; Social Psychology*)

REFERENCES

Aronson, Elliot, and Judson Mills 1959 "The Effect of Severity of Initiation on Liking for a Group." *Journal of Abnormal and Social Psychology* 59:177–181.

Asch, Solomon E. 1951 "Effects of Group Pressure upon the Modification and Distortion of Judgments." In H. Guetzkow, ed., *Groups, Leadership, and Men*. Pittsburgh, Pa.: Carnegie Press.

Bales, Robert F. 1950 *Interaction Process Analysis: A Method for the Study of Small Groups*. Cambridge, Mass.: Addison-Wesley.

———, and Stephen P. Cohen 1979 *SYMLOG: A System for the Multiple-Level Observation of Groups*. New York: Free Press.

Berger, Joseph, Susan J. Rosenholtz, and Morris Zelditch, Jr. 1980 "Status Organizing Processes." *Annual Review of Sociology* 6:479–508.

Borgatta, Edgar F. 1962 "A Systematic Study of Interaction Process Scores, Peer and Self-Assessments, Personality and Other Variables." *Genetic Psychology Monographs* 65:269–290.

————1981 "The Small Groups Movement: Historical Notes." *American Behavioral Scientist* 24:607–618.

Burgess, Robert L. 1969 "Communication Networks: An Experimental Evaluation." In R. L. Burgess and D. Bushell, Jr., eds., *Behavioral Sociology: The Experimental Analysis of Social Process.* New York: Columbia University Press.

Cartwright, Dorwin 1973 "Determinants of Scientific Progress: The Case of Research on the Risky Shift." *American Psychologist* 28:222–231.

————, and Alvin Zander (eds.) 1968 *Group Dynamics: Research and Theory*, 3rd ed. New York: Harper and Row.

Cooley, Charles H. 1909 *Social Organization*. New York: Scribners.

Deutsch, Morton, and Robert M. Krauss 1962 "Studies of Interpersonal Bargaining." *Journal of Conflict Resolution* 6:52–76.

Festinger, Leon, Henry W. Riecken, and Stanley Schachter 1964 *When Prophecy Fails.* New York: Harper and Row.

Goffman, Erving 1959 *The Presentation of Self in Everyday Life.* Garden City, NY: Doubleday.

Hare, A. Paul 1976 *Handbook of Small Group Research*, 2nd ed. New York: The Free Press.

————1982 *Creativity in Small Groups.* Beverly Hills, Calif.: Sage Publications.

————, Edgar F. Borgatta, and Robert F. Bales, eds. 1965 *Small Groups: Studies in Social Interaction*, rev. ed. New York: Alfred A. Knopf.

Hogg, Michael 1987 "Social Identity and Group Cohesiveness." In J. C. Turner, ed., *Rediscovering the Social Group: A Self-Categorization Theory.* Oxford: Basil Blackwell.

Homans, George C. 1950. *The Human Group.* New York: Harcourt, Brace.

————1974 *Social Behavior: Its Elementary Forms,* rev. ed. New York: Harcourt Brace Jovanovich.

Kellerman, Henry 1981 "The Deep Structures of Group Cohesion." In H. Kellerman, 2 ed., *Group Cohesion: Theoretical and Clinical Perspectives.* New York: Grune and Stratton.

Kelley, Harold H., and John W. Thibaut 1978 *Interpersonal Relations: A Theory of Interdependence.* New York: Wiley.

McGrath, Joseph E. 1984 *Groups: Interaction and Performance.* Englewood Cliffs, N.J.: Prentice-Hall.

Marwell, Gerald, and David R. Schmitt 1975 *Cooperation: An Experimental Analysis.* New York: Academic Press.

Milgram, Stanley 1974 *Obedience to Authority.* New York: Harper and Row.

Miller, L. Keith, and Robert L. Hamblin 1963 "Interdependence, Differential Rewarding, and Productivity." *American Sociological Review* 28:768–778.

Moreno, Jacob L. 1953 *Who Shall Survive?*, rev. ed. Beacon, N.Y.: Beacon House.

Moscovici, Serge 1980 "Toward a Theory of Conversion Behavior." In L. Berkowitz, ed., *Advances in Experimental Social Psychology,* vol. 13. New York: Academic Press.

Ofshe, Richard A. (ed.) 1973 *Interpersonal Behavior in Small Groups.* Englewood Cliffs, N.J.: Prentice-Hall.

Olmstead, Michael, and A. Paul Hare 1978 *The Small Group,* 2nd ed. New York: Random House.

Schmitt, David R. 1981 "Performance Under Cooperation or Competition." *American Behavioral Scientist* 24:649–679.

Sherif, Muzafer 1935 "A Study of Some Social Factors in Perception." *Archives of Psychology* 27, No. 187.

Sidowski, Joseph B. 1957 "Reward and Punishment in a Minimal Social Situation." *Journal of Experimental Psychology* 54:318–326.

Steiner, Ivan D. 1972 *Group Process and Productivity.* New York: Academic Press.

————1983 "Whatever Happened to the Touted Revival of the Group?" In H. H. Blumberg, A. P. Hare, V. Kent, and M. Davies, eds., *Small Groups and Social Interaction,* vol. 2. Chichester, Eng.: Wiley.

Tajfel, Henri 1981 *Human Groups and Social Categories.* Cambridge: Cambridge University Press.

Thibaut, John W., and Harold H. Kelley 1959 *The Social Psychology of Groups.* New York: Wiley.

Triplett, N. 1897 "The Dynamogenic Factors in Pacemaking and Competition." *American Journal of Psychology* 9:507–533.

Turner, John C. 1987 *Rediscovering the Social Group: A Self-Categorization Theory.* Oxford: Basil Blackwell.

Whyte, William Foote 1955 *Street Corner Society: The Social Structure of an Italian Slum,* 2nd ed. Chicago: University of Chicago Press.

Zajonc, Robert B. 1966 *Social Psychology: An Experimental Approach.* Belmont, Calif.: Brooks/Cole.

ROBERT W. SHOTOLA

SOCIAL-AREA ANALYSIS *See* Cities.

SOCIAL CHANGE Social change is ubiquitous. Although earlier sociologists often treated stability as normal and significant social change as an exceptional process deserving special explanation, scholars now expect to see some continuous level of change in all social organizations. Sharp, discontinuous changes are of course rarer but still a normal part of social life. As Bourdieu (1990) and Giddens (1986) suggest, we need to see human social life as always structured but incompletely so. "Structuration" is as much a process of change as a reflection of stability. Indeed, the existence of stable social patterns over long periods of time requires at least as much explanation as does social change.

Cumulative social change must be distinguished from the universal, processual aspect of all social life. Sociologists do study the latter, for example by focusing attention on those dynamic processes through which particular characteristics of social life may change, even though overall patterns remain relatively constant. Marriages and divorces are thus major changes in particular social relationships, but a society may have a roughly constant marriage or divorce rate for long periods of time. Likewise, markets involve a continuous flow of changes in who holds money or goods, who stands in the position of creditor or debtor, who is employed or unemployed, and so forth. These specific changes, however, generally do not alter the nature of the markets themselves. Sociologists both study the form of particular transactions and develop models to describe the dynamics of large-scale statistical aggregations of such processes (see "Social Dynamics").

Sometimes, specific processes of social life undergo long-term transformations. These transformations in the nature, organization, or outcomes of the processes themselves are what is usually studied under the label "social change." Social life always depends, for example, on the processes of birth and death, which reproduce populations through generations. These rates (adjusted for the age of populations) may be in equilibrium for long periods of time, resulting in little change in the overall size of populations. Or birthrates may exceed death rates most of the time, resulting in gradual population growth, but periodic disasters like war, famine, and pestilence may cut the population back. In the latter case, the population may show little or no cumulative growth but rather a dynamic equilibrium in which every period of increase is offset by a rapid decline. Approximations to these two patterns characterize a great deal of world history. Population growth has generally been quite slow—though in fact periodic declines have not offset all increases. In the last 300 years, however, a new phenomenon has been noted. As societies industrialize and generally grow richer and change the daily lives of their members, they undergo a "demographic transition." First, death rates are apt to drop rapidly as a result of better nutrition, sanitation, and health care. This results in rapid population growth. Eventually, fertility rates (birthrates standardized by the number of women of childbearing age) tend also to drop, and a new equilibrium may be reached; population growth will slow or stop. This is a cumulative transition because after it the typical rates of both birth and death are much lower, though the total population may be much larger. A variety of other changes may be related to this. For example, family life may change with declining numbers of children; parents' (especially women's) lives are apt to change as fewer of their years are devoted to bearing and raising children; childhood deaths will become rarities rather than common experiences.

Human social history is given its shape by cumulative social changes. Many of these are quite basic, like the demographic transition or the creation of the modern state; others are more minor, like the invention of the handshake as a form of greeting; most, like the development of team sports, fast-food restaurants, and international academic conferences lie in the broad area in between. Thus, cumulative social changes may take place on a variety of different scales, from the patterns of small group life through institutions like the business corporation or church to overall societal arrangements. Significant changes tend to have widespread repercussions, however, and so it is rare that one part of social life changes dramatically without changes occurring in others. While some important changes are basically linear—like increasing population—others are discontinuous. There are two senses of discontinuity. The first is abruptness, like the dramatic shrinkage of the European population in the wake of the plague and other calamities of the fourteenth century, or the occurrence of the Russian Revolution after centuries of Czarist rule and failed revolts. Second, some social changes alter not just the values of variables but their relationship to each other. Thus, for much of history the power (and wealth) of a ruler was directly related to the number of subjects; growing populations meant an increasing total population from which to extract tribute, taxes, or military service. With the transformation first of agriculture and then of industrial production in the early capitalist era (or just before it), this relationship was in many cases upset. From the sixteenth through the eighteenth centuries, for example, the heads of Scottish clans increasingly found that a small population raising sheep could produce more wealth than a large one farming; their attempt to maximize this advantage helped to cause the migration of Scots to Ireland and America. This process was of course linked also to growing demand for wool and the development of industrial production of textiles. These in turn involved new divisions of social labor and increased long-distance trade. At the same time, the development of industrial production and related weapons technologies reduced the military advantages of large population size, in contrast to epochs when wars were generally won by the largest armies; indeed, population may even come to be inversely related to power if it impedes industrialization.

Sociologists have generally taken three approaches to studying cumulative social changes. The first is to look for generalizable patterns in how all sorts of changes occur. Sociologists may thus look for characteristic phases through which any social innovation must pass—for example, skepticism, experimentation, early diffusion among leaders, and later general acceptance. Og-

burn (1950) was a pioneer in this sort of research, examining topics like the characteristic "lag" between cultural innovations and widespread adjustments to them or exploitation of their potentials. For example, when improved health care and nutrition make it possible for nearly all children to survive to adulthood, it takes a generation or two before parents stop having extremely large families as "insurance policies" to provide for their support in old age. Earlier researchers often hoped to find general laws explaining the duration of such lags and accounting for other features of all processes of social change. Contemporary sociologists tend to place much more emphasis on differences among various kinds of social changes and their settings. Their generalizations are accordingly more specific. Researchers may limit their studies to the patterns of innovation among business organizations, for example, recognizing that these may act quite differently from others; or they may ask questions such as why do innovations gain acceptance more rapidly in formal organizations (like businesses) than in informal, primary groups (like families), or what sorts of organizations are more likely to innovate? The changes may be very specific—like the introduction of new technologies of production—or very general, like the Industrial Revolution as a whole (e.g., Smelser 1958). The key distinguishing feature of all these sorts of studies is that they regard changes as individual units of roughly similar sorts and aim at generalizations about them.

The second major sociological approach to cumulative change has been to seek an explanation for the whole pattern of cumulation. The most important such efforts are based on evolutionary theories. The most prominent contemporary social evolutionist, Gerhard Lenski, has thus argued that increases in technological capacity (including information processing as well as material production, distribution, etc.) account for most of the major changes in human social organization. In his synthesis (Lenski, Lenski, and Nolan 1990) he arranges the major forms of human societies in a hierarchy based on their technological capacity and shows how other features such as their typical patterns of religion, law, government, class inequality, or relations between the sexes are rooted in these technological differences. In support of the notion that there is an overall evolutionary pattern, sociologists like Lenski point to the tendency of social change to move only in one direction. Thus, there are many cases of agricultural states being transformed into industrial societies but very few (if any) of the reverse. Moreover, states with more-advanced technology tend to dominate regional or even broader social processes. Of course, Lenski acknowledges that human evolution is not completely irreversible; he notes, however, not only that cases of reversal are relatively few but that they commonly result from some external cataclysm. Similarly, Lenski indicates that the direction of human social evolution is not strictly dictated from the start but channeled in certain directions only. There is room for human ingenuity to determine the shape of the future through a wide range of potential differences in invention and innovation.

There are a number of other important versions of the evolutionary approach to cumulative social change. Some stress different material factors such as human adaptation to ecological constraints (Harris 1979; White 1949); others stress culture and other patterns of thought more than material conditions (Parsons 1968; Habermas 1978). Some versions of Marxism have attempted a similar explanation of all historical social change in terms of a few key factors—notably improvement in the means of production and class struggle (e.g., Engels 1972). Other readings of Marx suggest that his mature theory is better understood as specific to capitalism (Postone forthcoming).

Adherents to the third major approach to cumulative social change argue that there can be no single evolutionary explanation for all the important transitions in human history. They also stress differences among the particular instances of specific sorts of changes. These historical sociologists place their emphasis on the importance of dealing adequately with particular changes by locating them in their historical and cultural context (Abrams 1982; Calhoun 1991). Weber was an especially important pioneer of this approach

(though as noted Marx can be interpreted as also offering an argument for historical specificity of explanatory categories). Historical sociologists have argued that a particular sort of transformation—like the development of a capacity for industrial production—may result from different causes and hold different implications on different occasions. The Industrial Revolution in eighteenth- and nineteenth-century Britain thus developed with no advance model and without competition from any established industrial powers. Countries industrializing today are influenced by both models and competition from existing industrial countries (not to mention influences from multinational corporations). The development of the modern world system has thus fundamentally altered the conditions of future social changes, making it misleading to lump together cases of early and late industrialization for generalization (Wallerstein 1974–88).

The development of the modern world system, however, may not have been the result of a process of evolution either. Rather, accident and disorder may have played a crucial role (Simmel 1977; Boudon 1984). Thus, Wallerstein shows the centrality of historical conjunctures and contingencies—the partially fortuitous relationships between different sorts of events. For example, the outcomes of military battles between Spain (an old-fashioned empire) and Britain (the key industrial-capitalist pioneer) were not foregone conclusions. There was room for bravery, weather, strategy, and a variety of other factors to play a role. But certain key British victories (notably in the sixteenth century) helped to make not only British history but world history different by creating the conditions for the modern world system to take the shape it did. The importance of contingency and conjunctures are not the only arguments historical sociologists pose against evolutionary explanation. A crucial one is that different factors explain different transformations. Thus, no amount of study of the factors that brought about the rise of capitalism and industrial production would provide the necessary insight into the decline of the Roman Empire and the eventual development of feudalism in Europe, or into the consolidation of China's very different regions into the world's most enduring empire and most populous state. These different kinds of events have their own, different sorts of causes.

Predictably, some sociologists seek ways to combine some of the benefits of each sort of approach to explaining cumulative social change. Historical sociologists who emphasize the singularity of specific transformations can nonetheless learn from comparisons among such changes and can achieve at least partial generalizations about them. Thus, different factors are involved in every social revolution, yet certain key elements seem also to be present, like crises (often financial) in the existing government's capacity to rule. Recognizing this (following Skocpol 1979) helps to avoid placing exclusive stress on the revolutionaries and their ideologies and actions, as some previous histories had done, and focuses attention on structural factors that may help to create potentially revolutionary situations. Similarly, even though there may be a variety of specific factors determining the transition to capitalism or industrial society in every instance, some version of a demographic transition does seem to play a role in nearly all cases. Even evolutionary explanation, which is widely dismissed by historical sociologists, might be of more use. In fact, many historical sociologists who do not fully adhere to evolutionary explanations nonetheless look to them for suggestions as to what factors might be important. Thus, Lenski's emphasis on technology or Marx's on the relations of production and class struggle can provide foci for research, and that research can help to determine whether these factors are equally important in all societal transformations and whether they work the same way in each. More radically, evolutionary sociology might follow biology in focusing less on the selection of whole populations (societies) for success or failure and look instead at the selection of specific social practices (e.g., the bearing of large numbers of children) for reproduction or disappearance. Such an evolutionary theory might provide a great deal of insight into how practices become more or less common, following biology in looking for something like mechanisms of reproduction and

inheritance, the initiation of new practices (mutation), the clustering of practices in interacting groups (speciation), as well as selection. It would, however, necessarily give up the capacity to offer a single explanation for all the major transitions in human social history, which is one of the attractions of evolutionary theory to its adherents.

Certain basic challenges are particularly important to the study of cumulative social change today. In addition to working out a satisfactory relationship among the three main approaches, perhaps the most important challenge is to distinguish those social changes that are basic from those that are more ephemeral or less momentous. Sociologists, like historians and other scholars, need to be able to characterize broad patterns of social arrangements. This is what we do when we speak of "modernity" or "industrial society." Such characterizations involve at least implicit theoretical claims as to what are the crucial factors distinguishing these eras or forms. In the case of complex, large-scale societal processes, these are hard to pin down. How much industrial capacity does a society need to have before we call it industrial; how small must employment in its increasingly automated industries become before we call it postindustrial? Is current social and economic "globalization" the continuation of a long-standing trend or part of a fundamental transformation? Though settling such questions is hard, debating them is crucial, for we are unable to get an adequate grasp on the historical contexts of the pheomena we study if we try to limit ourselves only to studying particulars or seeking generalizations from them without seeking to understand the differences among historical epochs (however hard to define sharply) and cultures (however much these may shade into each other with contact). Particularly because of the many current contentions that we stand on the edge of a new age—postmodern, postindustiral, or something else—sociologists need to take on the challenge of developing theories capable of giving strong answers to the question of what it means to claim that one epoch ends and another begins.

Many of the most prominent social theorists have treated all of modernity as a continuous era and stressed its distinction from previous (or anticipated future) forms of social organization. Durkheim (1893) argued that a new, more complex division of labor was central to a dichotomous distinction of modern (organically solidary) from premodern (mechanically solidary) society. Weber (1922) saw Western rationalization of action and relationships as basic and as continuing without rupture through the whole modern era. Marx (1867) saw the transition from feudalism to capitalism as basic but held that no change in modernity would be fundamental unless it overthrew the processes of private capital accumulation and the commodification of labor. Recent Marxists thus argue that the social changes of the last 300 to 500 years are phases within capitalism, not breaks with it (Mandel 1974; Wallerstein 1974–88; Harvey 1989). Many sociologists would add a claim about the centrality of increasing state power as a basic, continuous process of modernity (e.g., Tilly 1990 emphasizes the distinctive form of the nation-state). More generally, Habermas (1984–88) has stressed the split between a lifeworld in which everyday interactions are organized on the basis of mutual agreement, and an increasingly prominent systemic integration through the impersonal relationships of money and power outside the reach of linguistically mediated cooperative understanding. Common to all these positions is the notion that there is a general process (not just a static set of attributes) common to all modernity. Some would also claim to discern a causal explanation; others only point to the trends, suggesting these may have several causes but no single "prime mover" to explain an overall pattern of evolution. All would agree that no basic social change can be said to have occurred until the fundamental processes they identify have been ended or reversed. Obviously, a great deal depends on what processes are taken to be fundamental.

Rather than stressing the common processes organizing all modernity, some other scholars have pointed to the disjunctures between relatively stable periods. Foucault (1973), for example, has emphasized basic transformations in the way knowledge was constituted and an order ascribed to the world of things, people, and ideas. Renais-sance culture was characterized by an emphasis on resemblances among the manifold different elements of God's single, unified creation. Knowledge of fields as diverse (to our eyes) as biology, aesthetics, theology, and astronomy was thought to be unified by the matching of similar characteristics, with those in each field serving as visible signs of counterparts in the others. The "classical" modernity of the seventeenth and early eighteenth centuries marked a radical break by treating the sign as fundamentally distinct from the thing it signified—noting, for example, that words have only arbitrary relationships to the objects they name. The study of representation thus replaced that of resemblances. In the late eighteenth and early nineteenth centuries, still another rupture came with the development of the modern ideas of classification according to hidden, underlying causes (rather than superficial resemblances) and an examination of human beings as the basic source of systems of representation. Only this last period could give rise to the "human sciences"—psychology, sociology, and so forth—as we know them. Where most theories of social change emphasize processes, Foucault's "archaeology of knowledge" emphasizes the internal coherence of relatively stable cultural configurations and the ruptures between them.

Foucault's work has recently been taken as support for the claim (which he never endorsed) that the modern era has ended. Theories of "postmodernity" (reviewed well in Harvey 1989; see also Lash 1990) argue that at some point the modern era gave way to a successor. Generally, they hold that where modernity was rigid, linear, and focused on universality, postmodernity is flexible, fluidly multidirectional, and focused on difference. Some postmodernist theories emphasize the impact of new production technologies (especially computer-assisted flexible automation), while others are more exclusively cultural. The label *postmodernity* has often been applied rather casually to point to interesting features of the present period without clearly indicating why they should be taken as revealing a basic discontinuous shift between eras.

At stake in debates over the periodization of

social change is not just the labeling of eras but the analysis of what factors are most fundamentally constitutive of social organization. Should ecology and politics be seen as determinative over, equal to, or derivative of the economy? Is either demography or technological capacity prior to the other? What gives capitalism, feudalism, a kinship system, or any other social order its temporary and relative stability? Such questions must be approached not just in terms of manifest influence at any one point in time or during specific events but also in terms of the way particular factors figure in long-term processes of cumulative social change.

(SEE ALSO: *Convergence Theories; Evolution: Biological, Social, Cultural; Marxist Sociology; Modernization Theory; Social Dynamics; Technology and Society*)

REFERENCES

Abrams, P. 1982 *Historical Sociology.* Ithaca, N.Y.: Cornell University Press.

Boudon, R. 1986 *Theories of Social Change.* Cambridge: Polity Press.

Bourdieu, P. 1990 *The Logic of Practice.* Stanford, Calif.: Stanford University Press (orig. 1980, trans. by R. Nice. Paris: Editions de Minuit).

Calhoun, C. 1991 "Culture, History, and the Problem of Specificity in Social Theory." In S. Seidman and D. Wagner, eds., *Postmodernism and General Social Theory.* New York and Oxford: Basil Blackwell.

Durkheim, Emile 1893 *The Division of Labor in Society.* New York: Free Press.

Engels, Friedrich 1972 *The Origin of the Family, Private Property, and the State.* London: Lawrence and Wishart.

Foucault, M. 1973 *The Order of Things: An Archaeology of the Human Sciences.* New York: Random House.

Giddens, A. 1986 *The Constitution of Society.* Berkeley: University of California Press.

Habermas, J. 1978 *Communication and the Evolution of Society.* Boston: Beacon Press.

———1984–88 *The Theory of Communicative Action,* 2 vols. Boston: Beacon Press.

Harris, Marvin 1979 *Cultural Materialism.* New York: Vintage.

Harvey, D. 1989 *The Postmodern Condition.* Oxford: Basil Blackwell.

Lash, S. 1990 *Postmodern Sociology.* London: Routledge.

Lenski, G., J. Lenski, and P. Nolan 1990 *Human Societies.* New York: McGraw-Hill.

Mandel, E. 1974 *Late Capitalism.* London: New Left Books.

Marx, Karl 1867 *Capital (Das Kapital),* vol. 1. London: Lawrence and Wishart.

Ogburn, W. F. 1950 *Social Change with Respect to Culture and Original Nature.* New York: Viking.

Parsons, Talcott 1968 *The Evolution of Societies.* New York: Free Press.

Postone, M. Forthcoming *The Present as Necessity: The Marxian Critique of Labor and Time.* New York: Cambridge University Press.

Simmel, Georg 1977 *The Problem of the Philosophy of History.* New York: Free Press.

Skocpol, T. 1979 *States and Social Revolutions.* New York: Cambridge University Press.

Smelser, N. J. 1958 *Social Change in the Industrial Revolution.* London: Routledge and Kegan Paul.

Tilly, C. 1990 *Coercion, Capital, and European States, AD 990–1990.* Oxford: Basil Blackwell.

Wallerstein, I. 1974–88 *The Modern World System,* 3 vols. San Diego: Academic Press.

Weber, Max 1922 *Economy and Society.* Berkeley: University of California Press.

White, Leslie A. 1949 *The Science of Culture.* New York: Grove Press.

CRAIG CALHOUN

SOCIAL COMPARISON THEORY

How do people come to understand themselves? A response to this age-old question involves what has been labeled everyone's "second favorite theory" (see Goethals 1986): social comparison. The original formulation of social comparison theory (Festinger 1954) demonstrated how, in the absence of objective standards, individuals use other people to fulfill their informational needs to evaluate their own opinions and abilities. The process of social comparison underlies social evaluation (Pettigrew 1967) and relates to reference group processes (e.g., Hyman and Singer 1968), which in turn are critical to the understanding of a diverse set of sociological issues pertaining, for example, to identity development, justice, intergroup relationships, and group decision making. Thus, the "second favorite" status of social comparison theory reflects the preference of researchers for particular theories about each of these topics, which nonetheless promote the centrality and breadth of social comparison processes to sociological pursuits.

To understand the multifaceted role of social comparisons, emphasis here first rests upon the theory and its elaborations. Emphasis then shifts to an exploration of a sampling of the extensive applications of the theory.

HISTORY AND THEORY

For nearly forty years, social comparison theory has teetered between the categories of "lost and found" (Goethals 1986): The theory flourishes for awhile and then lies dormant. Suls (1977) outlines the first twenty years of social comparison research, beginning with its inception in 1954 by the psychologist Leon Festinger, its theoretical decline while applications to affiliation (Schachter 1959), emotions (Schachter and Singer 1962), and justice (Adams 1965) emerged, its momentary revival in a 1966 supplement to the *Journal of Experimental Social Psychology,* and its second, more enduring revival in 1977 with a landmark volume of collected essays (Suls and Miller 1977). In its fourth decade, the resurgence of social comparisons research (Wood 1989) anchors it firmly in the "found" category.

Festinger (1954) incorporates his observations regarding research on aspiration levels and social pressures in the premises of his formal theory of social comparison. First, individuals are driven to evaluate their abilities and opinions. This drive to evaluate increases with the importance of the ability or opinion, its relevance to immediate behavior, the relevance of the group to the ability or opinion, or the individual's attraction to the group. These factors also increase the pressure toward uniformity with relevant others. Second, people first attempt to make these evaluations through objective, nonsocial means, but if these are unavailable, people are likely to compare themselves to others. And, third, individuals are likely to choose as their comparison someone

close to their opinion or ability (the "similarity hypothesis"). Festinger further notes that social comparisons may be based on the similarity of attributes related to the dimension under evaluation (the "related attributes hypothesis"). As rationale for the preference for similar others, Festinger argues that comparisons with divergent others produce imprecise and unstable evaluations. Comparisons with moderately different others (those within tolerable limits of discrepancy), however, produce changes in individuals' evaluations of their own or the other's abilities or opinions. These changes ensure uniformity in the group and reinforce stable and precise evaluations.

Although Festinger treats abilities and opinions similarly in most respects, he notes a major distinction that may influence comparison consequences. In the case of abilities, the cultural value of doing "better and better" encourages individuals to make upward comparisons. Typically, because of the pressure toward uniformity, the upward drive is limited to comparisons with those slightly better. This unidirectional drive upward, however, inspires competition among group members that may inhibit the emergence of social uniformity. In contrast, no such upward drive characterizes comparisons of opinions. Given pressure toward uniformity, the absence of such a drive coupled with the greater flexibility of opinions (compared to the nonsocial constraints on changes in abilities) suggest that a state of social quiescence is more likely to emerge in the evaluation of opinions.

Despite the greater likelihood of opinion uniformity, Festinger notes that if potential comparison others hold highly discrepant opinions, the cessation of the comparison process may result in hostility toward or derogation of discrepant others. These negative reactions stem from the belief that opinion discrepancy suggests that an individual's opinions are incorrect. In contrast, no such negative implications characterize discrepant abilities, which are more independent from relative value orientations indicating different forms of "correctness."

As suggested by his emphasis on group uniformity, one of Festinger's major concerns was the role of social comparison processes for group formation and maintenance as well as for social structure. Presumably, people possessing similar abilities and opinions group together; as a result of distinguishing themselves from others, segments form in society. These two implications of social comparison processes are represented in research on group decision making and intergroup relations, discussed further below. Although Festinger's perspective suggests a wide range of implications, the theory is hardly definitive. In fact, Arrowood (1986) has labeled the 1954 version a "masterpiece of ambiguity."

Points of ambiguity revolve around theoretical issues regarding the nature of social comparison per se, the motivations underlying comparison choice, and choice of comparison other (especially the meaning of similarity). Elaborations of social comparison theory, which partly address some ambiguities, focus on the role of attributions in assessing similarity, the relationship between the individual and the group, and the extension of social comparison processes to network relationship.

In Festinger's formulation, the nature of the social comparison is rather oblique, referring only to nonobjective information regarding abilities and opinions. Others have extended the domain of social comparisons to include emotions (Schachter and Singer 1962), outcomes (Adams 1965), and traits (Thorton and Arrowood 1966). Suls (1986), however, questions the inclusion of traits as points of social comparison, arguing that traits, unlike abilities and opinions, are defined in absolute not relative terms. He further suggests that if individuals use recall of past experiences to generate a "consensus estimate" of how others rate on a dimension, this projection suffices as comparison information, and the pursuit of active comparisons ceases. When people are unable to project a consensus estimate, the type of nonobjective information available to them may vary in ways that affect comparison consequences.

Nonobjective information may include personal comparisons (see Masters and Keil 1987). Such comparisons involve information about the self and draw attention to time as an important factor characterizing the nature of comparisons. Temporal comparisons (Albert 1977) involve a "now versus then" dimension, meaning that a person compares pieces of information about an ability or opinion at different points in time.

Arrowood (1986) describes several forms of nonobjective (ability) information operationalized in a variety of social comparison studies: for example, presentation of two ratings (the evaluator's and an unidentified other), display of a distribution of ratings including the evalutor's, or presentation of the evaluator's rating plus identifying characteristics of potential comparison others and their ratings. The latter two allow development of a consensus estimate, with the last one also allowing assessment of similarity. While all forms of information presentation may stimulate the comparison process, their effects may depend upon the self-relevance of the information. Concern with self-relevance raises the issue of motivations underlying comparison choice.

The most explicit, but general, motivation represented in Festinger's perspective is that people need information. Fazio (1979) specifies two types of information motivations underlying self-evaluations. The "construction" motivation refers to a person's desire to obtain information that he or she lacks, whereas the "validation" motivation represents the use of information to determine the valid source (e.g., the person or the entity) of a person's judgment about an entity. Typically, individuals appear motivated by construction when they lack information; when they hold sufficient information, they are more likely to attempt to validate their opinions (Fazio 1979). Validation, however, is somewhat distinct from a third motivation: self- (or ego) enhancement. Although Festinger's emphasis on evaluation assumes that individuals are rational and accurate in their information processing, there is growing evidence that people are not unbiased evaluators of information about themselves and potential comparison others (Wood 1989). Festinger hinted at the possibility of self-enhancement when he posited that, in evaluations of abilities, individuals are likely to make upward comparisons; by noting "how close" one is to a superior performer, the individual enhances the evaluation of his or her own ability. Underlying comparison motivations (or goals) are critical in determining choice of comparison others.

In his extensive review of choice of comparison others, Gruder (1977) examines the conflict between evaluation and enhancement motivations. He concludes that the evaluation motivation is important in new situations and, under such conditions, individuals are likely to choose others who are similar in terms of the ability or opinion at issue. Enhancement motivations arise when enhancement is feasible and under conditions that threaten an individual's self-esteem. Situational conditions structure the comparisons that fulfill enhancement motivations. For example, in the absence of self-esteem threats, individuals are likely to make upward, self-enhancing comparisons if possible; in contrast, when self-esteem is threatened, people are more likely to make downward (defensive) comparisons (e.g., Hakmiller 1966; Taylor and Lobel 1989). In effect, to protect one's self-esteem, individuals choose dissimilar others (i.e., more inferior performers) for their comparisons. But, whether individuals choose similar or dissimilar others for their comparison depends in part on the nature of the dimension under scrutiny, the context (including characteristics of potential comparison others), and the importance of the enhancement goal (Wood 1989).

Questions about the choice of comparison others typically raise the issue of the meaning of similarity. Festinger offers different yet potentially complementary definitions of similarity: closeness of ratings on abilities or opinions and attributes related to the evaluation dimension. Goethals and Darley (1977) note that similarity in the first sense is paradoxical; ". . . presumably the comparison is made in order to find out what the other's opinion or score is, yet prior knowledge of the similarity of his score or opinion is assumed as the basis for comparison" (p. 265). They advocate the interpretation of similarity based on "related attributes."

People are likely to choose others for comparison who *should be* close to one's own ability or opinion by virtue of their standing on characteristics related to the evaluative dimension. Wheeler, Koestner, and Driver (1982) review the extensive support for the related attributes hypothesis. But other evidence indicates that people choose comparisons with those with similar characteristics, regardless of whether the attribute relates to the dimension under scrutiny (Wood 1989); for example, people of the same sex are more likely to compare themselves to each other, even if sex is unrelated to the ability.

Concern with related attributes similarity and its evaluative consequences provides the basis for the most pivotal elaboration of social comparison theory since 1970: Goethals and Darley's (1977) attributional approach. Their approach applies Kelley's attributional concepts of discounting and augmentation to assess the certainty of one's standing on an ability or opinion.

With regard to abilities, attribution logic focuses on the configuration of possible comparison others and of one's own ability level. For example, individuals can compare themselves to others whose related attributes suggest advantaged, equal, or disadvantaged performances, while considering that their own performance is better than, the same as, or worse than the others'. A person who compares to an advantaged other would expect his or her performance to be worse. If so, the implications for an ability evaluation are ambiguous; his or her ability may indeed be low, but other plausible causes (the superior related attributes) allow discounting of the conclusion. In contrast, if the individual performed equally as well or better than the advantaged other, then he or she overcame inhibitory causes (the inferior related attributes), which augment a claim to higher ability. In general, conclusive ability evaluations are most likely when a person compares to others of similar attributes.

The role of attributions in evaluating opinions is more complicated. With regard to beliefs, the unexpected cases (disagreement with similar others and agreement with dissimilar others) result in more useful information than expected cases. The former validate the evaluator's opinion, whereas the latter provide redundant information. But with regard to values, it seems that comparisons with similar others—even if they disagree—provide information validating the evaluator's values. Despite the complexities, researchers are now investigating other cognitive processes (e.g., the use of heuristics, memory) to understand social comparisons better (see Masters and Keil 1987).

Complementing the micro focus of psychologists on individuals' perceptions of social comparison information are the more macro developments of sociologists who extend social comparison theory from the intra- and interpersonal levels to intergroup relations. Tajfel and Turner (1979) build upon Festinger's assumption that a major consequence of social comparisons (requiring assessments of similarity) is the development of groups or, in their terms, social categories. They argue that social comparisons between categories, complemented by individuals' needs for a positive group identity (i.e., the self-enhancement motive), are likely to stimulate ingroup bias; people tend to emphasize the positive characteristics of their group while derogating those of other groups. Evidence of such bias is particularly strong in competitive situations. Intergroup discrimination and conflict are potential consequences of these intergroup comparisons.

Gartrell (1987) also emphasizes the connection between the individual and the group. Rather than relying upon motives for a positive social identity, his analysis concentrates on networks—that is, the relations among concrete entities. Network analysis highlights an often overlooked aspect of comparison choice: the social context in which individuals make comparisons. Examination of a person's social network relations is a means to understanding more clearly not only the selection of relevant comparisons but also whether people seek comparisons actively or passively accept those readily present in the network. In addition, network analyses may inform how comparison choices affect the network and how they influence the ties among a person's multiple networks.

SOCIAL COMPARISON AND SOCIAL BEHAVIOR: APPLICATIONS OF THE THEORY

The foregoing review of developments in social comparison theory raises issues at the individual, group, and intergroup levels. Similarly, the extensive applications of the theory crosscut levels of analysis.

Festinger's assumption that individuals are driven to evaluate themselves implies a concern with self-knowledge that underlies self-concept and identity formation as well as self-esteem. A number of studies examine the role of social comparisons in shaping individual identity across the life course. For example, Chafel (1988) concludes that during childhood, achievement identities first reflect autonomous, self-generated norms, then social comparison norms, and finally an integration of the two. Another study (Young and Ferguson 1979) demonstrates how comparison choices vary by children's ages (in grades 5, 7, 9, and 12) as well as by the nature of the evaluative dimension. Findings show that across all grade levels, parents are the comparison choice for the evaluation of moral items, whereas peers typically serve as a reference point for social issues, especially among older students. With regard to informational issues, however, there is a shift in comparison choices from parents to other adults as children age. Despite the prevalence of social comparisons early in life, Suls and Mullen (1983–1984) demonstrate that the elderly are more likely to evaluate their abilities in terms of temporal comparisons.

Just as choice of comparison other provides the basis for self-knowledge, comparisons of opinions within a group affect group dynamics. A large body of research examines choice shift or group polarization, in which the group voices a more extreme opinion than would be expected on the basis of initial individual opinions. The social comparison explanation of polarization is that people want their own opinions to remain somewhat distinct from others; as individuals learn what others think, they shift their own stances to remain unique; as a result the subsequent group opinion is more extreme. The social comparison explanation appears to be most appropriate when group members have access to other's opinions without group discussion (Cotton and Baron 1980).

Concerns with justice potentially stimulate social comparisons at all levels. To assess justice, people evaluate how their outcomes stack up against what they have earned in the past (internal comparison), what another individual like them earns (local or egoistic comparison), what members of their group typically earn (the referential comparison), and what their group earns compared to another group (intergroup or fraternalistic comparison). The type of comparison and the specific person or group chosen defines whether an individual is likely to perceive him- or herself or the group as unfairly treated. Justice obtains when outcomes (or the ratio of outcomes to inputs) are equal across the comparison. Equity theory (Adams 1965) focuses on local comparisons as the basis for individual reactions to an imbalance in outcome/input ratios, while relative deprivation theory (focusing on outcomes only) attempts to explain when an individual or group will feel deprived and opts for collective action to redress the deprivation (see Masters and Smith 1987; Olson, Herman, and Zanna 1986).

These applications attest to the pivotal role of social comparisons in explaining diverse phenomena. They also reiterate concern with theoretical issues regarding the nature of comparisons and comparison choices. Specific theories about identity formation, group decision making, or justice may be "favorites," but their explanatory success depends upon everyone's second favorite theory: social comparison.

(SEE ALSO: *Attribution Theory; Equity Theory; Reference Group Theory; Self-Concept; Social Perception; Social Psychology*)

REFERENCES

Adams, J. Stacy 1965 "Inequity in Social Exchange." *Advances in Experimental Social Psychology* 2: 267–299.

Albert, S. 1977 "Temporal Comparison Theory." *Psychological Review* 84:485–503.

Arrowood, A. John 1986 "Comments on 'Social Comparison Theory: Psychology from the Lost and Found'." *Personality and Social Psychology Bulletin* 12:279–281.

Chafel, Judith A. 1988 "Social Comparisons by Children: Analysis of Research on Sex Differences." *Sex Roles* 18:461–487.

Cotton, John L., and Robert S. Baron 1980 "Anonymity, Persuasive Arguments, and Choice Shifts." *Social Psychology Quarterly* 43:391–404.

Fazio, Russel H. 1979 "Motives for Social Comparison: The Construction–Validation Destination." *Journal of Personality and Social Psychology* 37:1,683–1,698.

Festinger, Leon 1954 "A Theory of Social Comparison." *Human Relations* 14:48–64.

Gartrell, C. David 1987 "Network Approaches to Social Evaluations." *Annual Review of Sociology* 13:49–66.

Goethals, George R. 1986 "Social Comparison Theory: Psychology from the Lost and Found." *Personality and Social Psychology Bulletin* 12:261–278.

———, and John M. Darley 1977 "Social Comparison Theory: An Attributional Approach." In J. Suls and R. L. Miller, eds., *Social Comparison Processes: Theoretical and Empirical Perspectives*. Washington, D.C.: Hemisphere.

Gruder, Charles L. 1977 "Choice of Comparison Persons in Evaluations of Oneself." In J. Suls and R. L. Miller, eds., *Social Comparison Processes: Theoretical and Empirical Perspectives*. Washington, D.C.: Hemisphere.

Hakmiller, K. 1966 "Threat as a Determinant of Downward Comparison." *Journal of Experimental Social Psychology* 2 (supplement 1):32–39.

Hyman, Herbert H., and Eleanor Singer 1968 *Readings in Reference Group Theory and Research*. New York: Free Press.

Masters, John C., and Linda J. Keil 1987 "Generic Comparison Processes in Human Judgment and Behavior." In J. C. Masters and W. P. Smith, eds., *Social Comparison, Social Justice, and Relative Deprivation*. Hillsdale, N.J.: L. Erlbaum.

Masters, John C., and William P. Smith (eds.) 1987 *Social Comparison, Social Justice, and Relative Deprivation*. Hillsdale, N.J.: L. Erlbaum.

Olson, James M., C. Peter Herman, and Mark P. Zanna, (eds.) 1986 *Relative Deprivation and Social Comparison*. The Ontario Symposium, vol. 4. Hillsdale, N.J.: L. Erlbaum.

Pettigrew, Thomas F. 1967 "Social Evaluation Theory." In D. Levine, ed., *Nebraska Symposium on Motivation*. Lincoln: University of Nebraska Press.

Schachter, Stanley 1959 *The Psychology of Affiliation*. Stanford, Calif.: Stanford University Press.

———, and Jerome E. Singer 1962 "Cognitive, Social, and Physiological Determinants of Emotional State." *Psychological Review* 69:379–399.

Suls, Jerry M. 1977 "Social Comparison Theory and Research: An Overview from 1954." In J. Suls and R. L. Miller, eds., *Social Comparison Processes: Theoretical and Empirical Perspectives*. Washington, D.C.: Hemisphere.

———1986 "Notes on the Occasion of Social Comparison Theory's Thirtieth Birthday." *Personality and Social Psychology Bulletin* 12:289–296.

———, and Richard L. Miller, eds. 1977 *Social Comparison Processes: Theoretical and Empirical Perspectives*. Washington, D.C.: Hemisphere.

———, and Brian Mullen 1983–84. "Social and Temporal Bases of Self-Evaluation in the Elderly: Theory and Evidence." *International Journal of Aging and Human Development* 18:111–120.

Tajfel, Henri, and John C. Turner 1979 "An Integrative Theory of Intergroup Conflict." In W. G. Austin and S. Worchel, eds., *The Social Psychology of Intergroup Relations*. Monterey, Calif.: Brooks/Cole.

Taylor, Shelley E., and Marci Lobel 1989 "Social Comparison Activity Under Threat: Downward Evaluation and Upward Contacts." *Psychological Review* 96:569–575.

Thorton, D., and A. John Arrowood 1966 "Self-Evaluation, Self-Enhancement, and the Locus of Social Comparison." *Journal of Experimental Social Psychology* 2 (supplement 1):40–48.

Wheeler, L., R. Koestner, and R. E. Driver 1982 "Related Attributes in the Choice of Comparison Other: It's There, But It Isn't All There Is." *Journal of Experimental Social Psychology* 18:489–500.

Wood, Joanne 1989 "Theory and Research Concerning Social Comparisons of Personal Attributes." *Psychological Bulletin* 106:231–248.

Young, James W., and Lucy Rau Ferguson 1979 "Developmental Changes Through Adolescence in the Spontaneous Nomination of Reference Groups as a Function of Decision Content." *Journal of Youth and Adolescence* 8:239–252.

KAREN A. HEGTVEDT

SOCIAL CONTROL The study of social control has been an integral part of sociology since its inception. Originally, the concept was defined as any structure, process, relationship, or act that contributes to the social order. Indeed, to some extent, the study of social order and social control were indistinguishable. This conceptual problem was particularly evident in the early Chicago perspective in which the concepts *social disorganization*, *social control*, and *deviance* were not distinguished. Deviance was thought to be the consequence of lack of social control and was often used to measure the presence of social control. Within the structural functionalism of the late 1940s and 1960s, the study of social control was allocated to the sidelines. It dealt with residual problems of deviance in a social system assumed to be generally integrated and well functioning. By the early 1960s society was, again, assumed to be considerably less orderly and integrated and, again, the concept of social control rose to the forefront. Studies examined both the causes and the consequences of social control. Thus, by the mid-1960s the intellectual ground had been laid for renewed scholarly interest in the study of social control. This chapter reviews the study of social control from that time through the 1970s and 1980s.

A consensus is now emerging that distinguishes social control from the social order it is meant to explain and that distinguishes among social-control processes. One basic distinction is among processes of internal control and external control. The former refers to a process whereby people adhere to social norms because they believe in them, feeling good, self-righteous, and proud when they do and feeling bad, self-critical, and guilty when they do not. This process has recently been termed *socialization*. External control refers to a social process whereby people conform to norms or rules because they are rewarded with status, prestige, money, and freedom when they do and are punished with the loss of them when they do not. This process has sometimes been termed *coercive, external,* or just *social* control.

Reflecting contemporary usage, this chapter

emphasizes social control as external or coercive control. Research is organized, first, and foremost by whether social control is studied as an independent or dependent variable and, second, by whether it is studied at the micro level (the study of individuals) or the macro level (the study of cities, states, regions, and countries).

SOCIAL CONTROL AS AN INDEPENDENT VARIABLE

Social-control theories assume that norm violations can frequently be so pleasurable and profitable that many, if not most, people are motivated to violate them. Thus, it is not necessary to study deviant motives; rather it is necessary to study what constrains or controls most people from acting on their deviance motives most of the time. Studies of social control as an independent variable focus on the relative effectiveness of social relationships and arrangements in constraining behavior to social norms and laws. Three general areas have developed. One examines the effectiveness of social ties (bonds, relationships, attachments) to conventional institutions in constraining people from acting on deviant motives. The second examines the effectiveness of macro structures and processes in providing the foundation for these ties. The third examines the effectiveness of the criminal justice system in constraining people from violating the law.

Drawing on a long tradition of work, Hirschi (1969) published an influential formulation of micro social-control theory. He states that the relationship between people and conventional society consists of four bonds: belief, attachment, commitment, and involvement. *Belief* refers to the extent to which conventional norms are internalized (another term for internal control). *Commitment* refers to the extent to which people's social rewards are tied to conformity; the more people have to lose upon being socially identified as norm violators, the lower their likelihood of violating the social norms. *Attachment* refers to people's sensitivity to the opinions of others; the more people are concerned with the respect and status

afforded them by others, the more they are subject to social control. *Involvement* refers to the amount of time people spend on conventional activities; the more people are involved in conventional activities, the less time they have left for deviant activities.

This theory has inspired considerable research on juvenile delinquency. Studies from the 1960s to the 1980s (e.g., Kornhauser 1978; and Matsueda 1982) show that, as attachment to parents and school increase, delinquency decreases. These studies, however, do not show the casual order underlying the relationship between social attachment and delinquency. The theory assumes that low attachment leads to high delinquency; yet high delinquency could very well lead to low attachment. Trying to unravel these causal processes, Liska and Reed (1985) show that low parent attachment leads to high delinquency and that high delinquency leads to low school attachment.

From the 1920s onward, sociologists at the University of Chicago have been interested in the ecological distribution of deviance. Their studies of delinquency, mental illness, and suicide, for example, show that deviance tends to center in cities, particularly in the area where residential and business activity intermesh. They argued that the ecological conditions that disrupt traditional social-control processes are accentuated in these areas, and, when social-control processes weaken, deviance occurs. Industrialization creates a need for the concentration of labor, thereby increasing population size and density through migration and immigration. Both industrialization and urbanization lead to value and norm conflicts, social mobility, cultural change, and weak primary ties. These social conditions, in turn, disrupt internal and external processes of social control. The internal process is weakened because people are unlikely to accept normative standards as right and proper when they experience value and norm conflicts and social change. The external process is weakened because people are unlikely to constrain their behavior to conventional norms when social support for unconventional behavior is readily visible and primary ties to family and conventional friends are weak. In small towns, for example, people may conform even though they may not accept the moral standard because their deviance is easily visible to family and conventional friends.

Perhaps the major problem with this line of research was the failure to measure the disruptive processes directly and the tendency to infer them from either remote causes such as industrialization and urbanization or more immediate causes such as the social, racial, and class composition of areas. Unable to solve this problem, the theory withered from the 1950s through the 1970s.

During the 1980s a group of young sociologists reexamined the theory to understand the renewed disorder of cities. Directly addressing the problem of measuring the processes that disrupt social control, Sampson and Groves (1989) show how community structural characteristics (such as racial, class, and ethnic composition; residential mobility; and divorce rate) affect crime by weakening ties to conventional institutions. Contrary to the early Chicagoans, Bursik (1986) shows that the ecological distribution of crime is no longer stable over time, that crime rates actually influence community characteristics, and that changes in these structures influence social deviance.

A third body of research examines the effectiveness of the criminal justice system in controlling crime. The underlying theory (deterrence) ignores inner controls and emphasizes punishment as the means of social control, particularly state-administered punishment. It assumes that people are rational and that crime is the result of calculating the costs and benefits of law violations; therefore, it assumes that, the higher the costs of crime, the lower the level of crime. As state-administered punishment is a significant cost of crime, it follows that the higher the level of such punishment, the lower the level of crime.

Two types of deterrence processes have been studied: general and specific. *General* refers to a process by which the punishment of some law violators provides information about the costs of crime to those unpunished (the general public), thereby reducing their law violations. *Specific* refers to a process by which punishment reduces the future law violations of those punished. Research focuses on three dimensions of punishment: severity, certainty, and celerity. *Severity* refers to the harshness of punishment, such as the length of incarceration; *certainty* refers to the probability of punishment, such as the likelihood of being arrested; and *celerity* refers to the swiftness of punishment. In sum, deterrence theory predicts that crime is lowest when punishment is severe, certain, and swift.

The political climate of the 1980s stimulated considerable interest in this theory, leading to hundreds of studies (Cook 1980). Yet, after all this research, it is still difficult to find any firm evidence for either specific or general deterrence. Regarding general deterrence, which has generated the bulk of the research, there is little consistent evidence of a severity effect. There is somewhat more evidence for a certainty effect, although its strength and duration remain unclear. For example, some studies suggest that, as certainty of punishment increases, crime rates decrease but that the decrease does not occur until certainty reaches about 30 percent, which is infrequently reached (Tittle and Rowe 1974). Some studies suggest that the certainty effect only occurs for crimes about which people have the opportunity to think and calculate, like property crimes, but not for violent crimes. And some studies of drunken driving suggest that the certainty effect occurs only if high certainty is well publicized, and even this effect is short lived (Ross 1984).

In sum, assuming that people are generally motivated to deviate, researchers have tried to understand how people are constrained from acting on their motives. Contemporary studies of social control focus on three areas: the interpersonal relationships that constrain people from acting on their motives, the macro structures and processes that provide the social foundation for these relationships, and the criminal justice system as a source of legal constraints.

SOCIAL CONTROL AS A DEPENDENT VARIABLE

During the 1960s sociologists began to question the assumption of normative consensus and stability and, thus, by implication the viability of the theories built on them. Without clear and stable references points from which to judge behavior, deviance is difficult to define. Many sociologists came to define it in terms of visible social efforts to control it. Deviance is thus defined as that behavior that society controls, and deviants are defined as those people whom society controls. Research shifts from studying social control as a cause of deviance to studying the causes of social control.

Micro-level studies examine the social processes by which acts and people are defined, labeled, and treated as deviants by family, friends, the public, and formal agencies of social control such as the criminal justice and mental health systems. Drawing on labeling and conflict theories, many sociologists argue that social control is directed against those who are least able to resist (the disadvantaged and the unfortunate) and that social-control agencies are used by the powerful to control the behavior of others.

During the 1960s, research reported that resources and power (as indicated by class, ethnicity, and race) significantly affect defining, treating, and controlling people as criminals (Black and Reiss 1970), such as arresting, prosecuting, and sentencing them. Unfortunately, these studies do not adjust for the effects of legal considerations, such as seriousness and frequency of offense, which are related to social resources. Without examining the effects of both legal and social resource variables in the same analysis it is difficult to isolate the effects of one from those of the other.

During the 1970s studies addressed this issue. The results are inconsistent, some studies showing race and class effects and some showing no such effects (Cohen and Kleugel 1978).

During the 1980s research tried to resolve these inconsistencies. One group of researchers tried to show that the effect of resources depends on the stage of the criminal justice process (e.g., arrest, prosecution) and the characteristics of the local community. Some stages may be more sensitive to social status and social power than are others, and some communities may be more sensitive to status and power than are others. Dannefer and Schutt (1982) report more racial discrimination at the arrest stage than at other stages, arguing that police have more discretion than do other decision makers, and they report more racial discrimination when the percentage of nonwhites is high, arguing that a high percentage of nonwhites is threatening to authorities.

Macro studies of social control examine the level and the form of social control across such units as cities, states, regions, and countries. They study why one form of control (physical pain) occurs at one time and place and another form (incarceration) occurs at another time and place.

Since the 1970s, conflict theory has provided the major stimulus for this research. It assumes that social control is more likely when the ruling class or the authorities perceive their interests to be threatened. Threat is thought to be associated with the presence of disruptive acts (crime, civil disorders, social movements) and problematic people (the unemployed, minorities, the urban lower class). The theory assumes that, as disruptive acts and problematic people increase, authorities expand the capacity for social-control bureaucracies and pressure existing bureaucracies to expand the level of control.

Research has focused on the expansion and contraction of three such bureaucracies: the criminal justice system, the mental health system, and the welfare system. It generally suggests that the expansion of the criminal justice system is not necessarily a response to crime, that the expansion of the mental health system is not necessarily a response to mental health, and that the expansion of the welfare system is not necessarily a response to economic need. Rather the expansion and contraction of all three are responses by authorities to the acts and people deemed threatening to their interests.

Studies of the criminal justice system have examined the expansion of the police force in the late 1960s and 1970s, as an indicator of the potential for social control, and the expansion of the prison population in the 1980s, as an indicator of the actual level of control. Liska, Lawrence, and Benson (1981) report that, while the size of the police force is sensitive to the crime rate, it may be even more sensitive to the level of civil disorders, the relative size and segregation of the minority population, and the level of economic inequality. Studies of the prison population and admission rates show that, while these rates, too, are sensitive to the crime rate, they are equally sensitive to the size of problematic or threatening populations such as the unemployed. Studies in England, Canada, and the United States show a substantial relationship between the prison admission rate and the unemployment rate, adjusting for the crime rate (Berk et al. 1981; Inverarity and McCarthy 1988).

Some historical studies (Foucault 1965) assert that mental asylums emerged in the seventeenth century as another social mechanism for controlling the poor urban masses. During the twentieth century the population of mental asylums in the United States continually increased, reaching about 550,000 by the mid-1950s, while the prison population, in comparison, was less than 200,000 at the time. The mental health system seemed to be taking over the role of the criminal justice system in controlling problematic populations. However, since that time the trends for both bureaucracies have reversed. The mental asylum population has decreased from 500,000 to 150,000 and the prison population has increased from 200,000 to 300,000. These trend reversals have stimulated research to examine the extent to which the two bureaucracies are functional alternatives for controlling threatening or problematic populations and acts. Some research (Steadman 1979) studies how various threatening populations that in the past might have been admitted directly into asylums are now first processed in the criminal justice system. Then some of them remain in local jails and others, through various mechanisms such as pleas of *Incompetent to Stand Trial* and *Not Guilty by Reason of Insanity* are channeled into asylums.

Welfare is frequently conceptualized as a form of social control. Piven and Cloward (1971) have stimulated considerable controversy by arguing that the welfare expansion in the United States during the mid- and late 1960s was a response to the urban riots of that period, an attempt to control an economically deprived and threatening population. Various studies provide some support for this thesis. Schram and Turbett (1983) report that the riots affected welfare in two stages. Riots during the mid-1960s prodded the federal government to liberalize welfare policies generally; these policies were then more likely to be implemented in the late 1960s by those states experiencing the most rioting.

In sum, the 1970s and 1980s evidenced a research effort to explain the expansion and contraction of bureaucracies of social control, not so much as responses to crime, mental illness, or economic need, but as responses by authorities to control acts and populations deemed threatening to their interests.

The study of social control has come a long way since its inception at the birth of sociology, at which time it was vaguely defined and not distinguishable from the concept *social order*. Contemporary usage distinguishes the sources of social order from the order itself. The concept *socialization* has come to refer to internal sources of control, and the concept *social control* has come to refer to external sources of control, the processes whereby people conform to social norms because they are rewarded when they do and punished when they do not. Studying social control as an independent variable, a body of research examines the relative effects of interpersonal relations, social institutions, and formal agencies in constraining social behavior. Studying social control as a dependent variable, another body of research examines how social resources influence social control and how the aggregate amount and form of control varies over time and place.

(SEE ALSO: *Crime Theories of; Criminal Sanctions; Criminology; Deviance Theories; Juvenile Delinquency, Theories of: Law and Society; Sociology of Law*)

REFERENCES

Berk, Richard A., David Rauma, Sheldon L. Messinger, and Thomas F. Cooley 1981 "A Test of the Stability of the Punishment Hypothesis: The Case of California, 1851–1970." *American Sociological Review* 46:805–829.

Black, Donald J., and Albert J. Reiss 1970 "Police Control of Juveniles." *American Sociological Review* 35:63–77.

Bursik, Robert Jr., 1986 "Ecological Stability and the Dynamics of Delinquency." In Albert J. Reiss and Michael Tonry, eds., *Communities and Crime*, pp. 35–66. Chicago: University of Chicago Press.

Cohen, Lawrence E., and James R. Kluegel 1978 "Determinants of Juvenile Court Dispositions." *American Sociological Review* 43:162–177.

Cook, Philip J. 1980 "Research in Criminal Deterrence: Laying the Groundwork for the Second Decade." In Norval Morris and Michael Tonry, eds., *Crime and Justice: An Annual Review of Research*, pp. 211–268. Chicago: University of Chicago Press.

Dannefer, Dale, and Russell K. Schutt 1982 "Race and Juvenile Justice Processing in Court and Police Agencies." *American Journal of Sociology* 87:1113–1132.

Foucault, M. 1965 *Madness and Civilization*. New York: Vintage.

Hirschi, Travis 1969 *Causes of Delinquency*. Berkeley: University of California Press.

Inverarity, James, and Daniel McCarthy 1988 "Punishment and Social Structure Revisited: Unemployment and Imprisonment in the United States, 1948–1984." *Sociological Quarterly* 29:263–279.

Kornhauser, Ruth 1978 *Social Sources of Delinquency*. Chicago: University of Chicago Press.

Liska, Allen E., Joseph J. Lawrence, and Michael Benson 1981 "Perspectives on the Legal Order: The Capacity for Social Control." *American Journal of Sociology* 87:412–426.

Liska, Allen E., and Mark Reed 1985 "Ties to Conventional Institutions and Delinquency: Estimating Reciprocal Effects." *American Sociological Review* 50:547–560.

Matsueda, Ross L. 1982 "Testing Control Theory and Differential Association: A Causal Modeling Approach." *American Sociological Review* 47:489–504.

Ross, H. Lawrence 1984 "Social Control through Deterrence: Drinking and Driving Laws." In Ralph H. Turner and James F. Short, Jr., eds., *Annual Review of Sociology*, Palo Alto, Calif.: Annual Reviews.

Piven, Frances Fox, and Richard A. Cloward 1971 *Regulating the Poor: The Functions of Public Welfare*. New York: Vintage.

Sampson, Robert J., and W. B. Groves 1989 "Community Structure and Crime: Testing Social Disorganization Theory." *American Journal of Sociology* 94:774–802.

Schram, Stanford F., and J. Patrick Turbett 1983 "Civil Disorder and the Welfare Expansion: A Two-Step Process." *American Sociological Review* 48:408–414.

Steadman, Hank J. 1979 *Beating a Rap*. Chicago: University of Chicago Press.

Tittle, Charles R., and Allan R. Rowe 1974 "Certainty of Arrest and Crime Rates: A Further Test of the Deterrence Hypothesis." *Social Forces* 52:455–562.

ALLEN E. LISKA

SOCIAL DYNAMICS The term *social dynamics* is used in a wide variety of contexts that vary in level from the societal to the individual, and in approach from qualitative (verbal) to quantitative (mathematical). For example, on the societal level one can point on the one hand to Pitirim Sorokin's qualitative approach in his disquisition *Social and Cultural Dynamics* (1957), and on the other extreme to Jay Forrester's mathematical, computer-oriented approach in *World Dynamics* (1971). On the individual level, work ranges from qualitative approaches such as Glen Elder's *Children of the Great Depression* (1974) to mathematical approaches like Harrison White's *Chains of Opportunity* (1970). Because of the tremendous diversity in substance and approach, one cannot identify a single line of cumulative research on social dynamics. Rather, there are distinct, loosely related developments arising in several contexts.

This article has five main sections. The first describes the three main sociological contexts for studies of social dynamics and summarizes their contributions to cumulative sociological research.

Since the term *social dynamics* invariably implies a focus on change over time in some social entity, it is closely related to the term *social change*. Some of the key differences between these two similar terms are discussed in the second section. The third summarizes reasons for studies of social dynamics in general and for formulation of dynamic models in particular. The fourth section explains fundamental differences between dynamic models and other types of models. The fifth section reviews the main variations in the types of dynamic models that sociologists have used.

MAIN CONTEXTS

In one context social scientists refer to the *dynamics of* a phenomenon, meaning that they focus on how it changes over time. In this, the most traditional usage, the emphasis is primarily on the substantive social phenomenon, and research progress depends on acquiring a deeper theoretical understanding and on expanding empirical knowledge of that particular phenomenon. Topics vary, for example, from "group dynamics" (meaning social interactions of members of a small group over time) to the "dynamics of development" (meaning change from a traditional rural society to a modern urban industrial society). It is hard to find substantive commonalities across disparate topic areas except ones of the most abstract sort: for example, that social change is universal but varies in speed. Despite the limited number of substantive generalizations about social dynamics, the study of social dynamics is theoretically and methodologically helpful for reasons summarized in the third section.

In a second context, more typical in recent work, researchers refer to a *dynamic model* of a social phenomenon, meaning that their goal is to formulate, test, or explore the consequences of a set of mathematical assumptions or of a computer algorithm thought to behave in a way analogous to the given phenomenon. For example, they may treat a model of population growth and decline in a society; a model of foundings, reorganizations, divestments, mergers, and failures of businesses or other organizations; or a model of diffusion of an innovation through a population (e.g., adoption of a new social policy by governments or of a new contraceptive by women). Despite the substantive diversity, formal properties of dynamic models of different phenomena are often similar. This similarity has fostered cumulative progress in studies of social dynamics, since a model developed for one topic may be transferable to another topic with only minor modifications of its formal properties. For example, the notion that growth rates are density dependent (vary with population size) arose first in dynamic models of population growth, the main rationale being that a growing population depletes environmental resources, which eventually leads to a lower rate of growth. Later this notion was applied to explorations of density dependence in dynamic models of formation and survival of unions, businesses, and other kinds of organizations (see, e.g., Hannan and Freeman 1989).

In a third context, authors discuss *dynamic analysis* of data on a phenomenon, meaning some form of temporal (longitudinal) analysis of data pertaining to different points in time. Since dynamic analyses are based on dynamic models, work done in the second and third contexts has close parallels. Typically, however, a focus on dynamic models implies a greater emphasis on the model itself, whereas a focus on dynamic analyses indicates a greater stress on problems of estimating and testing the model, as well as on the resulting substantive empirical findings. Advances made in methods for dynamic analysis of one social phenomenon can often be used in dynamic analyses of other phenomena. This fact has also facilitated cumulative progress in research on social dynamics. For example, the proposal of Tuma et al. (1979) for dynamic analysis of event history data, originally applied to data on marriage formation and dissolution, has subsequently been applied to dynamic analysis of data on occupational and geographic mobility, organizational mergers and failures, changes in political regimes, adoption of governmental policies, and many other social phenomena.

SOCIAL DYNAMICS VERSUS SOCIAL CHANGE

Although the terms *social dynamics* and *social change* both indicate a focus on change over time, they are used in rather different circumstances. Of the two, *social dynamics* has a more precise meaning.

First, social dynamics usually presumes change within a social system. The system may consist of similar entities (e.g., members of a family, families in a neighborhood, nations in the world) or disparate entities (e.g., different types of actors in a political or economic system), or various attributes of a single social entity (e.g., an individual's education, occupational prestige, and income; a business firm's age, size, and structure). The system is usually regarded as bounded, allowing the rest of the world to be ignored for purposes of explanation.

Whether the system consists of actors or variables, the term *system* presumes interdependence and typically involves feedback. Thus, action of one entity in the system leads to counteraction by another entity; for example, managers of a firm may counter a workers' strike by acquiescing to workers' demands, by outwaiting them, by hiring nonunion laborers, and so on. Alternatively, change in one variable in the system leads to an opposing or reinforcing change in one or more other variables; for example, an increase in education level is followed by an increase in prestige and then by an increase in income. Changes resulting from interdependent forces and feedback effects within the system are called endogenous changes.

There may also be exogenous changes, that is, there may be unexplained (perhaps random) changes that influence change within the system but whose causes originate outside the system. For example, in studies of interaction between a husband and a wife, changes in the economy and society in which the couple lives are likely to be treated as exogenous changes that affect the couple's behavior but are not themselves explained.

Because of the interdependent forces and feedback effects, as well as possible exogenous chang-

es, social dynamics typically implies a concern with complex changes. Simple linear changes or straightforward extrapolation of previous trends is rarely of primary interest.

Second, social dynamics connotes social changes that have a regular pattern. The pattern may be one of growth (e.g., economic growth), decline (e.g., rural depopulation, extinction of a cultural trait), cyclical change (e.g., boom and bust of [the business cycle), a distinctive but nonetheless recurring transition (e.g., ethnic succession in neighborhoods, societal modernization, the demographic transition from high mortality and fertility to low mortality and fertility), or simply a drift in a particular direction (e.g., the slow spread of a social belief or practice through a population).

Third, social dynamics usually implies some degree of predictability: that social change not only can be comprehended in terms of post hoc reasons but also can be explicitly modeled. The model, whether it consists of verbal statements or mathematical equations or computer instructions, involves a set of assumptions or propositions that permit fundamental patterns of change to be deduced. In contrast, though a unique historical event may foster social change, its uniqueness foils successful prediction. One challenge in studies of social dynamics is, therefore, to convert phenomena that are unique on one level to phenomena that are representative, and therefore predictable, on another level. Thus, what some regard as a unique historical event (e.g., the Russian Revolution of 1917), others see as an example of a regular pattern of change (e.g., they may regard the Russian Revolution of 1917 as exemplifying a response to changes in underlying social conditions). For example, while recognizing many distinctive factors, Theda Skocpol (1979) argued that some similar patterns of causes underlie the dramatic political and social transformations that historians call the French, Russian, and Chinese revolutions.

Fourth, the term *social dynamics* is more commonly used than the term *social change* when regularity in patterns of change is associated with some kind of equilibrium (steady state or homeostasis)—that is, when feedback effects are such that small deviations from equilibrium lead to compensating effects that cause equilibrium to be restored. For example, in the United States the distribution of family income (the share of total income going to different families) has been remarkably stable throughout the twentieth century, despite tremendous growth in population and in economic output, and despite social upheavals including the civil rights and women's liberation movements. This stability suggests that the process governing the allocation of family income is nearly in equilibrium. The term *social change,* especially *change* seen as part of a unique historical process, is usually associated with change from one distinctive situation to another, very different situation; it implies the antithesis of social equilibrium. The way that the social status of women and minorities has changed during the twentieth century exemplifies social disequilibrium.

It is important to emphasize that studies of social dynamics do not necessarily assume the existence of an equilibrium. This point is made clear by the many studies of the dynamics of economic growth, which often envision a process of never-ending expansion and improvement. Similarly, some dynamic processes imply not a steady-state condition but, rather, continual oscillation between conditions. A classic sociological example is Vilfredo Pareto's (1935) argument about the circulation of elites.

Fifth, the term *social dynamics* is almost always used in situations in which there is an interest in the process of change: the step-by-step sequence of causes and effects, and the way intermediate changes unfold. It is rarely used when only a simple before/after comparison of the condition of the system is the object of interest. Rather, when authors use the term *social dynamics,* there is usually a sense that the details and sequencing of changes are important because changes are contingent: If the sequence is interrupted or altered at an intermediate point, the final outcome may be different. For example, models of social protest often recognize that the state's response to protests may range from peaceful conciliation to violent suppression. The nature of the state's response is an important contingency because it affects the likelihood, timing, and character of future protests.

Sometimes the sequence of changes occurs on the level of the system as a whole rather than on the level of its individual members. For example, in a simple model of population growth, individual-level changes are very elementary: birth followed by death, with the timing of the two the only question. On the population level the addition and loss of individuals over time represents a sequence of changes, even though on the individual level there may be few (if any) intermediate changes, and hence little sense of a sequence of causes and effects.

REASONS FOR STUDYING SOCIAL DYNAMICS

What motivates sociological interest in social dynamics in general and in dynamic models in particular? The most potent reason is the long-standing interest of sociologists in social change, coupled with an increasing recognition that tremendous scientific leverage can be gained from identifying regularities in patterns of change and then formulating sociological theories that explain these regularities—that is, from studying social dynamics and not just unique historical events. Leverage comes not only from the increased theoretical richness of theories of social dynamics but also from greater methodological power in discriminating among competing explanations.

Not surprisingly, as observers of the great social transformations of the nineteenth century, the founders of modern sociology (e.g., Karl Marx, Herbert Spencer, Max Weber) were keenly interested in social change. However, during the middle of the twentieth century, when structural-functionalism and Parsonian thought were dominant, social change was regarded as a minor subfield of sociology. Interest in social change was renewed following a reawakened recognition of social conflict and the concomitant criticism of the assumption of social equilibrium in structural-functional theories.

An accelerating pace of global change may have added to this interest. Rapid growth of the world's population, high levels of migration between and within nations, the transformation of agricultural societies into industrial and postindustrial societies, social upheavals ranging from strikes to social protests to wars, creation of new organizational forms (e.g., holding companies, multinational corporations, international organizations), major transformations of political regimes (including the failure of communist experiments), steady increases in the number and volume of new technological innovations, depletion of natural resources, extinction of plant and animal species, and apparently human-induced changes in climate make it virtually impossible for sociologists studying large-scale social systems to be disinterested in social change.

Though some scholars view many of these changes as historically unique, the concrete social and economic problems that result from them motivate attempts to find regular patterns and to predict future changes—in short, to develop dynamic models of societal and global changes. Consider, for example, the massive changes in Eastern European nations initiated in the late 1980s. Many people think that the failure of command-type socialist economies and totalitarian polities (the condition in these nations from the late 1940s to the late 1980s) will eventually lead to new market-type capitalist economies and democratic polities. The intellectual challenge (as well as the main political problem) is to develop a theory of the transition from one to the other— that is, a theory of the dynamics of the social change that is expected to occur. That no satisfactory theory existed when the transition began was acutely apparent to the general public as well as to social scientists, and indicates the practical as well as scholarly value of studying social dynamics.

Sociologists studying micro-level phenomena (individuals and families) are equally unable to ignore social change. The life course of individu-als in modern societies has a typical sequence of activities associated with aging (e.g., birth, day care, school, work, marriage, child rearing, retirement, death) that commands considerable attention from sociologists. Historical changes in family patterns (e.g., increases in premarital cohabitation, delays in marriage, changes in husband-wife roles, increases in divorce, babybooms and babybusts, increasing institutionalization of the elderly) put social change at the forefront of the attention of sociologists studying the family. These subjects are perhaps more easily viewed in terms of social dynamics than are ones pertaining to global and societal changes because similar patterns across individuals and families are more readily apparent.

Sociologists studying behavior in small groups (group dynamics) were among the earliest sociologists to express an interest in social dynamics. This interest received a major boost from Robert Bales's *Interaction Process Analysis* (1950). Game theorists, who seek to explain moves and countermoves of actors in highly structured situations, also exhibit a concern with social dynamics in small groups, though they, much more than Bales and his intellectual progeny, concentrate on formal models and deemphasize hypothesis testing and empirical results.

There are also metatheoretical and methodological reasons for studying social dynamics, even when the primary intellectual concern is with statics, that is, with relationships among actors or variables at a point in time. First, studies of relationships at a point in time implicitly assume a steady state or equilibrium. Otherwise, relationships at a given point in time must be transitory and in the process of changing, which degrades their potential contribution to enduring sociological knowledge. A steady state may or may not exist. If it does not exist, one needs to study social dynamics to understand relationships at a point in time. If a steady state does exist, much can be learned by studying social dynamics that cannot easily be learned by studying relationships at a point in time. For one thing, two theories may imply the same relationship among variables at a given point in time but imply different time paths of change. In that case a study of social dynamics can differentiate between them, whereas a study of the steady state cannot. For another thing, a theory of relationships at a point in time is invariably the special case of one or more theories of change over time, and the latter almost always have a richer set of implications than the former. This means that in general there are more ways to test theories of social dynamics than theories of social statics.

THE NATURE OF DYNAMIC MODELS

Developments in dynamic models (and derivative developments in methods of dynamic analysis) are the major commonality in sociological studies of social dynamics. In order to understand the main features of dynamic models, it is important first to differentiate them from other types of models.

The most basic distinction is between static and dynamic models. Static models describe relationships among social actors in a system or among attributes of a social entity at a given point in time. They implicitly assume a steady state or equilibrium, a phenomenon that is probably about as common in nature as a vacuum. In contrast, dynamic models describe the process or sequence of changes among actors in a social system or among attributes of some social system.

Dynamic models can also be contrasted with comparative static models, which are especially common in economic analyses and in analyses of social experiments. Although both are about change over time, they differ in an important way. The process of change leading from conditions at the earlier time point to conditions at the later time point is fundamental to a dynamic model. In contrast, the change process is ignored in a comparative static model; it resembles a black box that relates conditions at one point in time to conditions at a later time.

To illustrate this distinction, consider alternative ways of explaining a son's occupational prestige. In a comparative static model the son's prestige might be related to his father's socioeco-nomic status and his own education without any attention to the mechanisms and processes that lead from these background conditions to the son's condition as an adult. In a dynamic model the father's socioeconomic status and the son's education might be seen as giving access to certain entry-level jobs, which in turn provide opportunities for further career mobility, leading to jobs with varying levels of prestige. In the latter type of model, the timing and sequence of job shifts, rather than just the son's initial condition (his father's social status and his own education), are of concern. In sum, dynamic models are used to explain not only why the later condition of some phenomenon differs from its earlier condition, but also how a sequence of changes leads from one condition to the other.

TYPES OF DYNAMIC MODELS

Different types of dynamic models are distinguished on the basis of a variety of formal properties. One basic distinction might seem to be whether the components of the system are social actors or attributes of a social entity. In the former, dynamic models of the behavior of social actors are developed: Actor A does X, in response Actor B does Y, then Actor A does Z, and so on. Though game theory is not ordinarily regarded as concerned with dynamic models, it formulates precisely such kinds of models. In the latter, values of variables describing the social entity are related to one another. Ecological theories of organizational survival utilize such models, for example, relating the degree of environmental variability and the degree of specialization of various types of social organizations in the environment to the survival of these types. The distinction between systems of actors and systems of variables is not as important as it may seem at first because behaviors of actors can usually be translated into variables.

A more basic and important distinction is whether time is discrete or continuous. Most empirical phenomena can change at any moment, which would lead one to expect that time would be treated as continuous in most dynamic models. In fact, time is probably more often treated as discrete, for two main reasons. First, empirical data used to test a dynamic model usually measure time at only a few discrete points. Researchers then often find it convenient to build a dynamic model of the data rather than to model the underlying social process. Second, some researchers consider discrete-time models to be simpler and believe that little information is lost from approximating truly continuous-time processes by discrete-time models. If the discrete time points in the data are sufficiently numerous and close enough together, the approximation is almost always satisfactory. If they are not, then important intermediate steps in the process are likely to be ignored, which may result in misleading conclusions. Whether discrete-time models are simpler than continuous-time models is less clear; to some extent it is a matter of a researcher's taste and training.

Another key distinction concerns whether the variables describing the social system are discrete, metric, or some mixture of the two. Discrete variables are ones that have a finite set of values; for example, political regimes may be categorized into a small number of basic types. Metric variables have a continuum of values; for example, a person's income and occupational prestige are usually treated as continuous variables. In fact, in both instances the number of values is finite but so large that treating them as continuous may be convenient and is often fairly realistic. Age is a continuous variable, but measurements of it are always discrete (e.g., to the nearest year, month, and day).

A distinction may also be made in the way variables in the system change over time. By their very nature discrete variables can change only in jumps; for example, there may be a sudden change from a military political regime to a multiparty government. Metric variables are often regarded as changing gradually; for example, a firm's profits may be treated as shifting upward or downward by small increments. In fact, metric variables may also change in jumps; for example, income may fall from a high value to nearly zero when a family's main breadwinners lose their jobs.

Yet another important distinction is whether the change process is treated as deterministic or as stochastic (as having a random component). There is a broad consensus that stochastic models are almost always more realistic. Few social changes occur in a strictly determined fashion, and those that do change in this fashion are rarely sociologically interesting. Nevertheless, deterministic models can be useful when solution of realistic stochastic models presents severe technical problems. Such formidable problems tend to occur when there is a high degree of interdependence within the social system (e.g., in models of diffusion of an innovation) and when both time and outcomes are treated as continuous. Thus, continuous-time models of changes in metric variables are typically deterministic. In contrast, models of changes in discrete variables, whether time is treated as discrete or continuous, are invariably stochastic because the fact that change occurs in jumps almost always dictates treatment in terms of probabilities.

Formal dynamic models are of two main types. In one the model consists of a set of mathematical equations relating some elements of the system to other elements. In the other the model consists of a set of computer instructions relating inputs of various variables and/or actors at one time to outputs at a later time. The set of computer instructions represents, in fact, mathematical equations that are so complex they cannot be solved in practice without the aid of a computer. Still, it is convenient to think of computer models merely as very complicated mathematical models.

An exceptionally clear introduction to both discrete-time and continuous-time deterministic models of metric variables can be found in William Baumol's classic *Economic Dynamics* (1951). Baumol's book also introduces several economic theories of potential interest to sociologists, including theories of wages and profits in firms and of economic growth. For a discussion of deterministic models of change in metric variables, see Doreian and Hummon (1976).

Two of the earlier classic discussions of stochastic models of change in discrete variables are James S. Coleman's *Introduction to Mathematical Sociology* (1964) and David J. Bartholomew's *Stochastic Models for Social Processes* (1973). Finally,

Tuma and Hannan's *Social Dynamics* (1984) discusses both deterministic and stochastic models of change in metric variables in continuous time as well as continuous-time stochastic models of change in discrete variables. This work also discusses metatheoretical and methodological reasons for studying social dynamics, applies dynamic models to a variety of different sociological problems, and provides an extensive bibliography pertaining to models and methods used in studying social dynamics.

CONCLUSION

Sociologists, whether studying whole societies or small groups, have had a long-standing and far-reaching interest in social change. Traditional approaches focused on specific substantive phenomena and, especially in macrolevel studies, often stressed unique historical occurrences rather than common dimensions underlying patterns of change. Recent studies of social dynamics usually shift their focus to what is regular and predictable about social change and to a concern with the social mechanisms generating a sequence of contingent changes. Often they embed ideas about change in dynamic models and test them in dynamic analyses of over-time data. This approach has been especially valuable in fostering cumulative research.

(SEE ALSO: *Longitudinal Research; Paradigms and Models; Social Change; Systems Theory*)

REFERENCES

Bales, Robert F. 1950 *Interaction Process Analysis: A Method for the Study of Small Groups*. Cambridge, Mass.: Addison-Wesley.

Bartholomew, David J. 1973 *Stochastic Models for Social Processes*. New York: Wiley.

Baumol, William J. 1951 *Economic Dynamics: An Introduction*. New York: Macmillan.

Coleman, James S. 1964 *Introduction to Mathematical Sociology*. New York: Free Press.

Doreian, Patrick, and Norman P. Hummon 1976 *Modeling Social Processes*. Amsterdam: Elsevier.

Elder, Glen H. 1974 *Children of the Great Depression: Social Change in Life Experience*. Chicago: University of Chicago Press.

Forrester, Jay W. 1971 *World Dynamics*. Cambridge, Mass.: Wright-Allen.

Hannan, Michael T., and John Freeman 1989 *Organizational Ecology*. Cambridge, Mass.: Harvard University Press.

Pareto, Vilfredo 1935 *The Mind and Society*, vol. 3. Arthur Livingston, ed.; Andrew Bongiorno and Arthur Livingston, trans. New York: Harcourt, Brace.

Skocpol, Theda 1979 *States and Social Revolutions in France, Russia, and China*. Cambridge: Cambridge University Press.

Sorokin, Pitirim A. (1937–1941) 1957 *Social and Cultural Dynamics: A Study of Change in Major Systems of Art, Truth, Ethics, Law and Social Relationships*, rev. and abr. 4 vol. Boston: Porter Sargent.

Tuma, Nancy Brandon, and Michael T. Hannan 1984 *Social Dynamics: Models and Methods*. Orlando, Fla.: Academic Press.

———, and Lyle P. Groeneveld 1979 "Dynamic Analysis of Event Histories." *American Journal of Sociology* 84:820–854.

White, Harrison C. 1970 *Chains of Opportunity: Systems Models of Mobility in Organizations*. Cambridge, Mass.: Harvard University Press.

NANCY BRANDON TUMA

SOCIAL FORECASTING Forecasting has been important in sociological thought. Early European sociologists presented theories arguing that societies progress through inevitable historical stages; these theories helped sociologists predict all societies' futures. Early American sociologists adopted the pragmatists' hypothesis that a science proved it "worked" by making predictions of future events (Schuessler 1971). Sociologists, however, have only recently adopted methods appropriate for these early goals. A review of this delayed development of social forecasting will include (1) three sociologists' conceptual uses of forecasting and some reasons their suggestions were not followed; (2) qualitative and quantitative methods of forecasting; (3) recent indications of increased interest in forecasting.

FORECASTING TRADITIONS

Sociologists have contributed several social forecasting concepts that were historically significant enough to have become traditional orientations in the analysis of the future. William F. Ogburn "held that in the modern world technological inventions commonly come first and social effects later. By reason of this lag, it is possible, he argued, to anticipate the future and plan for its eventualities" (Schuessler 1971, p. 309). For example, new possibilities came into conflict with family values because the invention of effective birth control gave women new choices. Ogburn's contribution was to suggest that cultural lags were inevitable but that their period of disruption could be shortened (Reiss 1986).

Merton (1949) challenged Ogburn's idea that inventions' effects could be easily anticipated. Each invention has an apparent goal, or manifest function, that it is hoped it will perform in society. Each change, however, also contains the possibility of performing a number of *latent functions.* These are unanticipated side effects, often not desired and sometimes dangerous. The institutions of society are closely intertwined, and an invention in one area can cause shocks throughout the system. The automobile is an example. Its manifest function of changing transportation has been fulfilled, but at the cost of serious ecological and sociological changes.

Merton's (1949) second warning was that social forecasting is unique because it tries to predict the behavior of humans, who change their minds. The *self-fulfilling prophecy* is a forecast that makes people aware of real or imagined new opportunities or dangers to be avoided. Merton demonstrated that false forecasts can have powerful effects if they gain public acceptance. A sound bank can be destroyed by a run on its funds caused by a prediction of failure. Henshel's more inclusive concept, the self-altering prediction, shows that forecasts can be self-defeating as well as self-fulfilling. W. I. Thomas's theorem, "If men define situations as real, they are real in their consequences," applies particularly to the definitions

societies make of the future (Henshel 1978, p. 100).

Moore challenged sociologists to go beyond safe prophecy based on orderly trends and to attack the difficult problem of "how to handle sharp changes in the magnitude of change, and sharp (or at least clear) changes in direction" (Moore 1964, p. 332). There are four types of *discontinuous societal change:* (1) Some societies are drastically changed by an *exogeneous variable,* an idea or value from another society. Modern Japan is an example. (2) A society's rate of development can spontaneously increase, creating an abundance of new ideas. This is an exponential acceleration, a *change in the rate of change.* (3) Moore attributes *changes in direction of change* to the existence of a dialectic of values within each society's apparent trend. For example, a society may appear to be profit-oriented and ecologically exploitative, but there also exists a counterset of values that stress harmony with each other and nature. If a shift in such basic value emphases could be predicted, many other associated forecasts could be made. (4) Finally, Moore recognizes that there are *pure emergents,* inventions such as money or writing that cannot be thought of as parts of trends.

Moore drew a methodological moral from these complexities: "One must somehow move from discrete necessary conditions to cumulative and sufficient ones" (Moore 1964, p. 334). That is, the search for the one trend or causal variable that drives societal change should be abandoned. Events are created by the summation, and particularly the interaction, of many component developments.

In 1966 Moore asked sociologists to put aside value-free scientific rules and attempt to construct *preferable futures* that might assist in helping "mankind survive for the next twenty years" (Moore 1966, p. 270). Moore was confronting what he felt to be the main reason that forecasting was done so infrequently. It is professionally permissible for sociologists to examine social change both currently and retrospectively, but making a forecast invites being labeled a utopian (Winthrop 1968, p.

136). Utopian thinking is in disrepute because past advocates have allowed their values to cloud their constructions. On the other hand, images of the future provide goals and determine how we plan and therefore how we behave in the present. Moore sought utopias that performed a necessary social planning function by constructing alternative directions for human purpose.

WHY SOCIAL FORECASTING HAS DEVELOPED SLOWLY

Sociologists' basic methodological orientations preclude an interest in forecasting. Sociologists analyze society's static interconnections and concentrate on the social structures that persist. They have not yet developed skill in isolating the sequences of dynamic social behavior (Moore 1966). They are better at categorizing and typing people than predicting how individuals might change from one type to another.

Many sociologists feel that not enough is known to predict future events. They point to economists and demographers and ask, If they are failing with their more quantifiable data, then how can complex social changes be anticipated? One substantial school of thought sees sociology as a qualitative art form that will never be a statistically modeled science. The critical sociologists object on moral grounds. They feel that society requires essential restructuring before positive change can be effected. Since most forecasting is based on models of the current structure, they feel it merely gives credence to unjust social arrangements (Henshel 1982).

JUDGMENTAL AND QUALITATIVE FORECASTING METHODS

The futurists see "the challenge being not just to forecast what the future will be, but to make it what it ought to be" (Enzer 1984, p. 202). The pace of change is considered too rapid to be captured by traditional methods' reliance on careful quantitative reconstruction of the past. This justifies the use of experts' opinions, and futurist's

methods are ways of systematizing these judgments (Allen 1978, p. 79).

A discontinuous social change is usually preceded by a "substantial restructuring of basic tenets and beliefs" (Holroyd 1978, p. 37). Such paradigm shifts are revolutionary, such as the rejection of the earth as the center of the universe. They appear within fields of knowledge in which one system of thought seems to be in control but is unable to solve important problems. Holroyd, for example, predicts a paradigm shift in economics because the current theories are unable to deal with essential problems such as ecological scarcity. Futurists anticipate shifts by compiling lists of crucial issues in the institutions of society. When the gap between current and desired conditions is large, that area is monitored closely for discontinuous change (Holroyd 1978, p. 38).

Cross-impact matrices are constructed by listing all possible future events in the problem area under study (Allen 1978, pp. 132–145). Each event is then recorded as a row and a column of a square matrix. This allows the explicit examination of every intersection of events by asking: "What is the probability that the first will occur if it has been preceded by the other?" The probabilities of occurrence can be derived from available data but are often judgments. Cross-impact analysis is a systematic way of heeding Merton's warning about not overlooking possibly damaging latent consequences. It is a tool for spotting crucial turning points or originating novel viewpoints by examining the intersections of change at which experts' judgments conflict.

Delphi surveys are an ingenious method for allowing the interaction of expert judgments while avoiding the contamination of social status or damage to reputations because of radical or mistaken pronouncements (Henshel 1982). In a series of survey rounds, everyone sees the distribution of the others' responses without knowing their identities. A composite forecast emerges as anonymous modifications are made at each round.

After a review of forecasting methods Ascher (1978) chose *scenarios* as one of only two methods he could recommend. A scenario is "a hypothetical sequence of events constructed for the purpose of focusing attention on causal processes and decision points" (Herman Kahn, quoted in Wilson 1978, p. 225). It is a story, but a complex one based on all available data, and usually constructed after a cross-impact analysis has isolated possible turning points. Usually, two or three related scenarios are constructed to illustrate alternate futures that could be determined by particular decisions.

It is not surprising that an expert's decision process can be made explicit. What is surprising is that in many studies the systematic model of the expert often forecasts better than the person (Armstrong 1978). In *bootstrapping* the forecaster's own individualized decision procedures become the "bootstraps" by which a systematized procedure is "lifted" into an orderly routine. Such a model can be made deductively through interviews that isolate and formalize the decision rules or inductively by starting with a series of past forecasts and attempting to infer the rules that accounted for differences between them.

SOCIAL DEMOGRAPHY

Demography is the most established form of social forecasting and its methods and record can be found elsewhere (Henshel 1982). This article will discuss only two elements from its continuing development: a method that has had wide influence and the instructiveness of its frequent failures to predict future population sizes.

A cohort is an aggregate of individuals of similar age who therefore experience events during the same time period (Reiss 1986, p. 47). *Cohort analysis* was first used by Norman Ryder to study the changing fertility behaviors of women born during the same five-year periods. Cohorts have since been used in the study of many areas of social change to differentiate the changes that are the result of individuals maturing through the stages of life from those due to powerful societal events or value shifts.

Demographers failed to anticipate the postwar baby boom and the onset of its decline. These errors were due to *assumption drag*, "the continued use of assumptions long after their validity has been contradicted by the data" (Ascher 1978, p. 53). Henshel (1982) says that demographers probably ignored these turning points because they simply talked to each other too much. They reassured each other that their assumptions, and their extrapolations from past trends, would soon reassert themselves in the data. Recognition of this error of developing an isolated club of forecasters has helped economists and will help sociologists avoid a similar regimentation of estimates.

The mix of assumptions and actual data varies widely in *simulation models*. The most useful models test a set of explicit assumptions in order that no interactions between variables are overlooked. Models have contributed the idea of the feedback loop as an important caution against unidirectional thinking. This common system characteristic occurs when an effect reaches a sensitive level and begins a reaction that modifies its own cause (Simmons 1973, p. 195). Often, however, the mix of assumptions and facts in simulations leans too heavily toward judgments. So-called black-box modeling (McLean 1978), in which equations are hidden, can produce output that is plausible and provocative but also unrealistic. The creator of the *Limits to Growth* study admitted that "in *World Dynamics* . . . there is no attempt to incorporate formal data. . . . All relationships are intuitive" (Simmons 1973, p. 208). That study extrapolated assumptions of geometric growth, unchecked by social adaptation. Its dramatic predictions of imminent shortages had a wide but unwarranted impact (Cole et al. 1973).

PRAGMATIC STATISTICAL ANALYSIS OF TIME SERIES

Attention has recently shifted to techniques that are less concerned with demonstrating the effects of assumed patterns. Time series are records of observations through time. They are being explored from the viewpoint that a variable may be uniquely complex and subject to sudden change.

Time series regressions uncover structural relationships involved in the history of two or more variables. Before the relationship can be assessed, sources of error must be isolated and controlled. The most important of these are (1) the overall trend of change that would obscure any specific interrelationship, and (2) the autocorrelation effect of internal dependence of an observation on previous observations. If a relationship seems to explain the data series's movements, it is tested with ex-post forecasts that can be verified within the range of available data. If these succeed, then "ex-ante-forecasts can be used to provide educated guesses about the path of the variables into the blind future" (Ostrom 1990, p. 77).

Autoregressive moving average (ARIMA) models predict one variable's current status using a combination of its previous observations and mathematically approximated random shocks. The goal is to find a pattern that fits the immediate data, not to understand relationships. ARIMA models are useful in *interrupted time series analysis,* in which the impact of a policy or other intervention can be examined by seeing how different the variable's patterns are before and after the intervention (McDowall et al. 1980). Autoregressive models have a limitation important for social forecasting, in which historical data is relatively scarce. "Because ARIMA models must be identified from the data to be modeled, relatively long time series are required" (McCleary and Hay 1980, p. 20). Fifty observations are recommended.

Exponential smoothing is widely used and is as reliable as more complicated methods (Gardner 1985). In its simplest form the next period's forecast is based on the current forecast plus a portion of the error it made. That is, the difference between the current time period's forecast and the actual value is weighted and used to adjust the next period's expected value. The higher the value of the weight used, the more the error adjustment contributes and the quicker the model will respond to changes. Exponential smoothing is used in early detection of curvilinear changes, when the rate of change speeds up or slows down (Gardner 1987).

FUTURE TRENDS IN SOCIAL FORECASTING

Forecasting is being done. It is central in business and government planning. Even though many of these forecasts' essential variables are social or found in social contexts (such as family decisions to move, build, and purchase or the development of social problems), economists have become society's designated forecasters (Henshel 1982; Stimson and Stimson 1976). Sociologists will not change this imbalance easily, but there are some indications that forecasting may finally become part of everyday sociological work.

Assumptions that a particular cycle or curve is the natural or underlying process of change have been abandoned, and pragmatic methods are now widespread. It is also accepted that a forecast is developed only to be monitored for possible discontinuities. Trend extrapolations are rarely done without accompanying methods for describing the expected deviations.

Society has recognized the wisdom of the early concern about anticipating the latent effects of social and technological inventions. Progress no longer seems inevitable. The popular question now is "Can someone assure us that a new element will not be as destructive as past introductions?"

Two forecasting methods are particularly promising because they allow sociologists to build on traditional skills. Componential or segmentation forecasting (Armstrong 1978) recognizes that an aggregate forecast can be improved by combining forecasts made on the component groups. Sociologists are best able to distinguish the groups that should be treated separately. Pooled time series analysis (Sayrs 1989) combines cross-sectional descriptions such as one-time surveys. Sociologists are expert at describing the interconnections in the structures of organizations or societies, and now they have the opportunity to study these social arrangements over time.

(SEE ALSO: *Human Ecology and the Environment; Population; Scientific Explanation; Social Dynamics; Social Indicators*)

REFERENCES

Allen, T. Harrell 1978 *New Methods in Social Science Research: Policy Sciences and Futures Research.* New York: Praeger.

Armstrong, J. Scott 1978 *Long-Range Forecasting: From Crystal Ball to Computer.* New York: Wiley.

Ascher, William 1978 *Forecasting: An Appraisal for Policymakers and Planners.* Baltimore: Johns Hopkins University Press.

Cole, H. S. D., Christopher Freeman, Marie Jahoda, and K. L. R. Pavitt (eds.) 1973 *Models of Doom: A Critique of the Limits to Growth.* New York: Universe Books.

Enzer, Selwyn 1984 "Anticipating the Unpredictable." *Technological Forecasting and Social Change* 26:201–204.

Gardner, Everette S., Jr. 1985 "Exponential Smoothing: The State of the Art." *Journal of Forecasting* 4:1–28.

——1987 "Short-Range Forecasting." *LOTUS* 3 (Feb.):54–58.

Henshel, Richard L. 1978 "Self-Altering Predictions." In Jib Fowles, ed., *Handbook of Futures Research.* Westport, Conn.: Greenwood Press.

——1982 "Sociology and Social Forecasting." In Ralph H. Turner and James F. Short, eds., *Annual Review of Sociology.* Vol. 8. Palo Alto, Calif.: Annual Reviews.

Holroyd, P. 1978 "Change and Discontinuity: Forecasting for the 1980s." *Futures* 10 (Feb.):31–43.

McLean, J. Michael 1978 "Simulation Modeling." In Jib Fowles, ed., *Handbook of Futures Research.* Westport, Conn.: Greenwood Press.

McCleary, Richard, and Richard A. Hay, Jr. 1980 *Applied Time Series Analysis for the Social Sciences.* Beverly Hills, Calif.: Sage.

McDowall, David, Richard McCleary, Errol E. Meidinger, and Richard A. Hay, Jr. 1980 *Interrupted Time Series.* Newbury Park, Calif.: Sage.

Merton, Robert K. 1949 *Social Theory and Social Structure.* Rev. ed. Glencoe, Ill.: Free Press.

Moore, Wilbert E. 1964 "Predicting Discontinuities in Social Change." *American Sociological Review* 29:331–338.

——1966 "The Utility of Utopias." *American Sociological Review* 31:756–772.

Ostrom, Charles W., Jr. 1990 *Time Series Analysis: Regression Techniques.* 2nd ed. Newbury Park, Calif.: Sage.

Reiss, Albert J., Jr. 1986 "Measuring Social Change." In Neil J. Smelser and Dean R. Gerstein, eds., *Behavioral and Social Science: Fifty Years of Discovery.* Washington, D.C.: National Academy Press.

Sayrs, Lois W. 1989 *Pooled Time Series Analysis.* Beverly Hills, Calif.: Sage.

Schuessler, Karl 1971 "Continuities in Social Prediction." In H. L. Costner, ed., *Sociological Methodology, 1971.* San Francisco: Jossey-Bass.

Simmons, Harvey 1973 "System Dynamics and Technocracy." In H.S.D. Cole et al., eds. *Models of Doom: A Critique of the Limits to Growth.* New York: Universe Books.

Stimson, John, and Ardyth Stimson 1976 "Sociologists Should Be Put to Work as Forecasters." *American Sociologist* 11:49–56.

Wilson, Ian H. 1978 "Scenarios." In J. B. Fowles, ed. *Handbook of Futures Research.* Westport, Conn.: Greenwood Press.

Winthrop, Henry 1968 "The Sociologist and the Study of the Future." *American Sociologist* 3:136–145.

JOHN STIMSON

SOCIAL GERONTOLOGY Social gerontology, or the sociology of aging, has two primary foci: (a) social factors during later life and (b) social antecedents and consequences of the aging process. Thus, social gerontology includes examination of both the status of being old and the process of becoming old. This is a vast arena, and the substance of social gerontology is appropriately informed by the theories and methods of many sociological subspecialties ranging from macro historical comparative and demographic perspectives to the micro orientations of social psychology and ethnomethodology.

Historically, social gerontology emerged from a social-problems orientation and focused on the deprivations and losses that were expected to characterize late life (Maddox and Campbell 1985). Early research in social gerontology focused on issues such as poverty during later life; old age as a marginal status, reflecting problems of social integration; adjustment to losses of old age; negative effects of institutionalization and poor quality of long-term care; and ageism and age discrimination. A significant proportion of recent research also focuses on the deprivations of old age. Investigators remain concerned about social integration and adjustment to loss. The majority of funding for gerontological research is provided by the National Institute on Aging, which is mandated to support health-related research. Consequently, much of social gerontology focuses on illness and the health care delivery system. The dramatic aging of populations in industrialized societies (Myers 1990) leads to questions about the capacities of social institutions and public policies to meet the needs of an unprecedented number and proportion of older adults. Scholars using the perspectives of political economy focus on the ways in which societies respond to the dependency needs of older adults and the social implications of those responses (Quadagno 1988).

Although much gerontological research remains focused on the problems of later life, sociologists now recognize the broader importance and implications of old age and aging. Two factors appear to account for this broader and more complex view. First, despite the social-problem orientation of earlier research, empirical data failed to confirm a bleak picture of old age. For example, in spite of higher rates of illness and disability, the vast majority of older adults are competent and able to live independent, autonomous lives (U.S. Public Health Service 1987). Similarly, rather than representing involuntary loss of a treasured role, retirement is actively sought by the majority of older workers and seldom poses adaptive problems (Palmore et al. 1985). In addition, some of the problems observed in early studies have been remedied by the increased resources that recent cohorts have brought to late life and by effective public policies (Crystal 1982). Thus, although health care costs remain a burden for many older adults, Medicare and Medicaid substantially reduced barriers to health care among older people. Similarly, as a result of improvements in Social Security benefits and increased participation in private pensions, older Americans now are no more likely to live in poverty than younger adults and, indeed, are less likely to live in poverty than children. Such findings pushed social gerontology toward more complex and empirically defensible perspectives on old age and aging.

Second, sociologists now recognize that age plays a fundamental role in social structure and social organization. Age is a major factor in the organization of society, affecting the allocation of social resources and social roles. Along with sex and race, age is an ascribed status, in that it is immutable and cannot be voluntarily chosen. But age also is unique among ascribed statuses in that it changes over time, and movement across age categories results in changing expectations for behavior, changing access to social resources, and changing personal and social responsibilities. Because of the fundamental role of age in social structure and personal biography, sociologists are committed to better understanding age groups and the aging process.

Isolating the effects of age and characterizing the aging process are difficult tasks, and available research represents only beginning efforts toward those goals. Because many factors affect social structure and individual behavior, it is always difficult to isolate the effects of one particular factor. But this task is even more difficult with regard to age, because it is inherently confounded with the effects of two other factors: cohort and time of measurement (Rodgers 1982). *Age*, of course, refers to time since birth, and *age effects* refers to patterns resulting from the passage of time or sheer length of life. *Cohorts* refer to persons born at the same or approximately the same time (e.g., the 1920 cohort, the 1940–1944 cohort). There are two primary kinds of *cohort effects*. One type results from historical factors. For example, cohorts that lived through the Great Depression or World War II had different life experiences than cohorts that were not exposed to these historical events (Elder 1974). Those life experiences may have implications for late life. The second type of cohort effect reflects compositional characteristics. Thus, large cohorts (such as the Baby Boomers) may face greater competition for social resources than smaller cohorts (such as those born during the Great Depression, when fertility rates were low), and differential access to social resources may affect status and well-being in old age (Easterlin 1980). *Period effects* (also called *time of measurement effects*) result from events or situations that happen at a particular time. For example, faith in government decreased among all Americans (regardless of age or cohort) at the time of the Watergate scandal.

Age, cohort, and period effects are intertwined. If one knows when an individual was born and also knows the time of measurement, simple subtraction provides accurate information about the individual's age. Similarly, if one knows an individual's age and time of measurement, one can easily calculate date of birth or birth cohort. There are no easy methods for disentangling age, period, and cohort effects. In general, however, the most compelling research results are those that are based on examination of multiple cohorts measured at different times (Rodgers 1982). If the same age patterns are observed across different cohorts measured at different times, those patterns are likely to reflect age effects. If patterns are not similar across cohorts and times of measurement, however, they are unlikely to reflect age effects.

Age, cohort, and period effects are all important in gerontological research. Age effects provide information about human development as it unfolds in social context. Cohort effects permit us to observe the social implications of shared history and cohort composition. Period effects provide information about the effects of contemporaneous events and situations on social structure and individual behavior. Although social factors are relevant to age, cohort, and period effects, distinguishing among them has important implications for generalization of research results. Age effects are the same or highly similar across time and

place; thus, they are generalizable. In contrast, cohort and period effects are, by definition, variable across time. Consequently, generalization is limited.

Examination of age, period, and cohort effects requires large data bases in which multiple cohorts are observed on multiple occasions, often over long periods of time. Because of these stringent requirements, few studies in social gerontology focus specifically upon disentangling these confounded factors. But recognition of these sources of confounding appropriately tempers investigators' generalizations. In addition, this issue has sensitized investigators to the need to examine change over time, with the result that longitudinal studies, in which individuals are observed at multiple points in time, have become the dominant research design in efforts to characterize the aging process.

Not all studies in social gerontology focus on isolating the effects of age or characterizing the aging process. Another major focus of social gerontology is examining the heterogeneity, or variability, among older persons. The older population is highly heterogeneous, and there is evidence that variability is greater among older than younger adults. It is important to understand the sources and consequences of this diversity. In addition, recognition of this variability helps to avoid narrow, sterotypic images of old age. For example, some investigators are interested in identifying the social factors associated with different levels of financial resources during later life. Similarly, some researchers study the implications of varying levels of social integration on perceptions of well-being among older adults. Cross-sectional research designs, in which study participants are observed at a single time, are sometimes appropriate for such studies, although longitudinal research is also valuable for understanding the antecedents and consequences of heterogeneity in the older population. Also, even when the research focus is variability among older adults, investigators need to recognize that their findings may not generalize to other cohorts or times of measurement.

No single theme nor easily summarized list of topics does justice to the scope and diversity of research in social gerontology. Nonetheless, brief review of several major research areas can provide a general sense of the important themes in social gerontology.

AGE STRATIFICATION

Stratification refers to the ranking of categories or classes in a hierarchical system. Because of their hierarchical form, stratification systems involve inequality; that is, some classes or categories are more highly valued and receive more social resources than others. *Age stratification* refers to the division of society into meaningful age groups that differ in social value and allocation of social resources (e.g., Riley 1985). The concept of age stratification has proven to be useful in a variety of ways. At the broadest level, it reminds us that age is a fundamental parameter of social organization and social structure. Age stratification has proven particularly useful in helping to account for age-related roles and norms. Reminders to "act our age" testify to the presence of age-related norms, and society allocates substantial numbers of roles on the basis of age, ranging from the right to vote and drive a car to eligibility for Social Security and Medicare. Age stratification has a social psychological parameter also: age consciousness or awareness of and identification with members of one's age group. Evidence indicates that most older adults are reluctant to label themselves as such, probably because of ageism and negative attitudes toward aging and old age (George 1985).

STATUS OF OLD AGE

Two research traditions inform us about the status of old age. The first focuses on the emergence of late life as a distinctive and socially recognized segment of the life course. Old age did not emerge as a socially meaningful concept until social, health, and environmental conditions reached a level that resulted in significant proportions of persons living to advanced age (Clausen 1986). Thus, industrialization, public health measures, and technological development played criti-

cal roles in leading to the distinction between middle and old age. Life expectancy and preservation of health and autonomy in late life continue to increase, leading some observers to hypothesize that the distinction between "young-old" and "old-old" is increasingly salient (Neugarten and Neugarten 1986). The second research tradition focuses on the social value placed upon old age and the extent to which older persons receive inferior, equal, or superior treatment, compared to other age groups. Early research suggested that old age was valued less in modern, industrialized societies than in less-developed societies. More recent research, however, indicates that this conclusion is oversimplified (Keith, Fry, and Ikels 1990). The status of old age depends on a broad mix of social factors including cultural and religious traditions, family structure, and the social organization of the means of production. Although it is not possible to make broad statements about the relationship between modernization and the status of the elderly, negative stereotypes of older people and age discrimination are common in American society.

OLD AGE AS THE CULMINATION OF LIFE-COURSE EXPERIENCES

Congruent with sociologists' increasing attention to the life course as a whole, gerontological research reveals that the past is indeed prologue to the future. Thus, status and personal well-being in late life depend in large part on events and achievements experienced earlier in the life course. Research on socioeconomic status (SES) in later life provides an excellent illustration of this research tradition (O'Rand 1990). There is compelling evidence that the economic resources available to older people are a function of educational, occupational, and economic decisions made in early and middle adulthood. In the occupational arena, factors such as occupational sector, length and continuity of job history, and pension coverage are important predictors of SES in old age. Personal decisions about savings and home ownership also affect financial resources in later life. The increased poverty of older women and older minority groups reflects the culmination of life-course experiences. Compared to white men, women and members of minority groups have shorter, more discontinuous job histories, are employed in occupations with lower pay and less opportunity for advancement, and are less likely to have private pensions. Marriage and fertility patterns in early and middle adulthood also have important implications for later life (Hagestad 1988). Financial resources, health, and perceptions of well-being during late life are enhanced by stable marriages. The age difference between spouses is significantly associated with the timing and length of widowhood. Children and grandchildren typically enhance well-being in later life and provide important sources of assistance for frail or dependent older adults.

PERCEPTIONS OF WELL-BEING IN LATER LIFE

Study of life satisfaction, or perceptions of well-being, has been the dominant theme in social gerontology since the late 1950s. The gerontological research community has been particularly intrigued by the degree to which and the ways in which older people sustain a sense of well-being despite age-related losses of social and personal resources and increased proximity to death. Research strongly indicates that the vast majority of older people experience high life satisfaction and a sense of well-being (George 1990). Indeed, levels of life satisfaction are at least as high among older adults as among middle-aged and younger adults, and may be somewhat higher. For older adults, as for the population generally, perceived well-being is strongly related to the availability of social resources and meaningful ties to social structure. Thus, the determinants of life satisfaction in later life (and during adulthood generally) include financial resources, meaningful relationships with family and friends, and a sense that the physical and social environments are secure and supportive. Despite similarities in the predictors of life satisfaction, there are two ways in which perceived well-being differs for older and younger adults. First, there is clear evidence that older adults

express high levels of life satisfaction in the presence of less attractive objective conditions than is true for younger and middle-aged adults. For example, older people are satisfied with far fewer financial resources and lower levels of health than their younger peers. Second, the processes or mechanisms by which objective life conditions affect perceptions of life quality appear to differ for older and younger adults. It appears that these two differences are related such that younger persons evaluate their life quality on the basis of comparisons of desired and actual levels of resources, whereas older adults evaluate their life quality on the basis of perceptions of equity (Carp and Carp 1982). Thus, young and middle-aged adults are satisfied with their lives when their achievements match their aspirations; older adults are satisfied with life when they perceive their life conditions to be fair and just. It remains unclear whether these age differences reflect age changes in perceptions of well-being or whether they are cohort effects.

ENVIRONMENT AND AGING

A major tenet of sociology is that the physical and social environments, or, as more recently termed, *social context,* are important for understanding individual attitudes and behavior. Despite the importance of this proposition in social science theory, it is difficult to measure environments and document their effects. One contribution of gerontological research is its support of the importance of environment. Many older persons live in restricted or bounded environments such as nursing homes and retirement communities. Measuring environmental dimensions and observing their effects is considerably easier in restricted environments than in broader, more complex, social settings. In addition, there is evidence that, because of increased illness and frailty, older adults are often more sensitive to environmental demands than are younger adults (Lawton 1974). Thus, even rather small differences in environments can have substantial impact on older persons' attitudes and behaviors. Research on environments and aging documents the importance of environment, or context, for behavior during later life. Among the consistent findings are (a) that physical environments can be manipulated to facilitate or impede social interaction and the development of social bonds, (b) that objective environmental parameters are strongly associated with the perceived stressfulness of specific environments, and (c) that environments that foster a sense of personal control are associated with better health and functioning, as well as with higher levels of perceived well-being (George and Maddox 1989). These findings are of practical and theoretical value; dimensions of the physical and social environment can be purposely manipulated to generate favorable outcomes.

Social gerontology is an important field. It provides us with information about what it means to be "old," about the antecedents and consequences of stability and change during later life, and about the ways that older adults negotiate the development of meaningful life-styles. Social gerontology is especially important in that it focuses sociologists' attention on the dynamics of process and change and on the intersections of social structure, social change, and personal biography. At its best, social gerontology effectively links processes and dynamics at the macro historical and societal levels with individual attitudes and behaviors. In addition, later life provides an excellent context for testing and, indeed, challenging some commonly held assumptions and hypotheses about the dynamics of social influence. In this way, it offers valuable insights and information to the larger sociological enterprise.

(SEE ALSO: *Cohort Analysis; Cohort Perspectives; Death and Dying; Filial Responsibility; Intergenerational Relations; Intergenerational Resource Transfers; Long-Term Care; Longitudinal Research; Nursing Homes; Retirement; Widowhood*)

REFERENCES

Carp, Frances M., and Abraham Carp 1982 "Test of a Model of Domain Satisfactions and Well-being: Equity Considerations." *Research on Aging* 4:503–522.

Clausen, John A. 1986 *The Life Course*. Englewood Cliffs, N.J.: Prentice-Hall.

Crystal, Stephen 1982 *America's Old Age Crisis: Public Policy and the Two Worlds of Aging*. New York: Basic Books.

Easterlin, Richard A. 1980 *Birth and Fortune: The Impact of Numbers on Personal Welfare*. New York: Basic Books.

Elder, Glen H., Jr. 1974 *Children of the Great Depression*. Chicago: University of Chicago Press.

George, Linda K. 1985 "Socialization to Old Age: A Path Analytic Model." In E. Palmore, J. Nowlin, E. W. Busse, I. C. Siegler, and G. L. Maddox, eds., *Normal Aging III*. Durham, N.C.: Duke University Press.

—— 1990 "Social Structure, Social Processes, and Social–Psychological States." In R. H. Binstock and L. K. George, eds., *Handbook of Aging and the Social Sciences*, 3rd ed. New York: Academic Press.

——, and George L. Maddox 1989 "Social and Behavioral Aspects of Institutional Care." In M. G. Ory and K. Bond, eds., *Aging and Health Care: Social Science and Policy Perspectives*, London: Tavistock.

Hagestad, Gunhild O. 1988 "Demographic Change and the Life Course: Some Emerging Trends in the Family Realm." *Family Relations* 37:405–410.

Keith, Jennie, Christine L. Fry, and Charlotte Ikels 1990 "Community as Context for Successful Aging." In J. Sokolovsky, ed., *The Cultural Context of Aging: Worldwide Perspectives*. New York: Greenwood Press.

Lawton, M. Powell 1974 "Social Ecology and the Health of Older People." *American Journal of Public Health* 64:257–260.

Maddox, George L., and Richard T. Campbell 1985 "Scope, Concepts, and Methods in the Study of Aging." In R. H. Binstock and E. Shanas, eds., *Handbook of Aging and the Social Sciences*, 2nd ed., New York: Van Nostrand Reinhold.

Myers, George C. 1990 "Demography of Aging." In R. H. Binstock and L. K. George, eds., *Handbook of Aging and the Social Sciences*, 3rd ed. New York: Academic Press.

Neugarten, Bernice L., and Dale A. Neugarten 1986 "Age in the Aging Society." *Daedalus* 115:31–49.

O'Rand, Angela M. 1990 "Stratification and the Life Course." In R. H. Binstock and L. K. George, eds., *Handbook of Aging and the Social Sciences*, 3rd ed. New York: Academic Press.

Palmore, Erdman, Bruce M. Burchett, Gerda G. Fillenbaum, Linda K. George, and Laurence Wallman

1985 *Retirement: Causes and Consequences.* New York: Springer.

Quadagno, Jill 1988 *The Transformation of Old Age Security.* Chicago: University of Chicago Press.

Riley, Matilda White 1985 "Age Strata in Social Systems." In R. H. Binstock and E. Shanas, eds., *Handbook of Aging and the Social Sciences,* 2nd ed. New York: Van Nostrand Reinhold.

Rodgers, Willard L. (1982) "Estimable Functions of Age, Period, and Cohort Effects." *American Sociological Review* 47:774–787.

U.S. Public Health Service 1987 *Current Estimates from the National Health Interview Survey, United States, 1986* (DHHS Pub. No. PHS 87-1592). Washington, D.C.: U.S. Government Printing Office.

LINDA K. GEORGE

SOCIAL HONOR Social honor refers to the esteem given individuals, social positions, or groups judged superior according to some valued criteria. Evaluations of worth and attributions of prestige are both central to the concept of social honor. At all levels of the social order, evaluations and attributions of social honor are made. At the global level, core nations in the world system enjoy respect, deference, and influence as compared to their dependent and less developed counterparts. Organizations such as sociology departments are assigned more or less prestige. Families enjoy social standing on the basis of the ascribed and achieved characteristics of household members (Nock and Rossi 1978). Some social roles or positions, notably professional, technical, and managerial occupations, are highly regarded, and their incumbents have high social standing. Exceptional performance, even in humble capacities, may earn a certain respect.

Characteristics of groups and individuals generate status outcomes. Within groups, some members are accorded more esteem than others. Whether an individual enjoys the group's esteem depends not only on his or her qualities and performance but also on how large, selective, or exacting the group. College students, for example, evaluate their academic competence on the basis of both their grades and the selectivity of their institution (Bassis 1977). Belonging to a prestigious group confers social honor on individuals; physicists doing high quality work in a top department are more visible to other scientists than those producing high quality research in a less prestigious setting (Cole and Cole 1973). Of course, individuals who enjoy high esteem boost the honor of organizations with which they are associated. Thus, institutions often scramble to establish some connection to a Nobel Prize winner (Zuckerman 1970).

According to Weber (1946), "status" or social honor is seen in the very life-style expected of those who belong to a particular status group. Status coexists with economic class and political power as critical dimensions in Weber's theory of social stratification. Although class, status, and power typically go together, theoretical perspectives differ on the exact relation of social honor to other aspects of social hierarchy (Hatch 1989). The material perspective argues that prestige is accorded those who have what is universally desired—wealth and power. Thus, systems of social honor are subordinate to political and economic systems that allocate the material rewards. The alternative theoretical approach stresses the importance of nonmaterial motivations—the pursuit of social honor in its own right. This perspective accounts for systems of social honor based on nonmaterial values (e.g., religious purity or contributions to scientific knowledge) as well as for honor-sensitive societies preoccupied with guarding personal integrity from slights, betrayals, and attacks (Campbell 1964).

If honor is a social reward desired by most, if not all, people, it is surely central to processes of social control that constrain individual action toward social ends (Goode 1978). Pursuit of honor encourages individuals to conform in ways calculated to gain the approval of others. What is honored by one group or society, however, may be viewed with indifference or even disapproval by another. What is esteemed may also change with time as evidenced by the long-term decline in the standing of clerks and rise in the prestige of physicians.

Shils (1970) emphasized the expression of social honor in terms of interpersonal deference behavior—interactions of appreciation or degradation based on evaluations of the perceived deference-entitling characteristics of self and other. However, many interesting institutional mechanisms also exist to create, acquire, allocate, and protect social honor (Goode 1978). Awards, prizes, honorary titles, and memberships in highly selective groups illustrate formal honors bestowed. Formal recognitions may serve to celebrate group values, to identify and publicize individual accomplishment, and to motivate effort, particularly in areas where success may not be accompanied by monetary rewards.

(SEE ALSO: *Occupational Prestige*)

REFERENCES

Bassis, Michael S. 1977 "The Campus as a Frog Pond: A Theoretical and Empirical Reassessment." *American Journal of Sociology* 83:1318–1326.

Campbell, J. K. 1964 *Honor, Family, and Patronage: Institutions and Moral Values in a Greek Mountain Community.* New York: Oxford University Press.

Cole, Jonathan R. and Stephen Cole 1973 *Social Stratification in Science.* Chicago: University of Chicago Press.

Goode, William J. 1978 *The Celebration of Heroes: Prestige as a Social Control System.* Berkeley: University of California Press.

Hatch, Elvin 1989 "Theories of Social Honor." *American Anthropologist* 91:341–353.

Nock, Steven L. and Peter M. Rossi 1978 "Ascription Versus Achievement in the Attribution of Family Social Status." *American Journal of Sociology* 84: 565–590.

Shils, Edward A. 1970 "Deference." In Edward O. Laumann, Paul M. Siegel, and Robert W. Hodge, eds., *The Logic of Social Hierarchies.* Chicago: Markham Publishing Co.

Weber, Max 1946 "Class, Status, Party." In H. H. Gerth and C. Wright Mills, eds. and trans. *From Max Weber: Essays in Sociology.* Oxford: Oxford University Press.

Zuckerman, Harriet A. 1970 "Stratification in American Science." *Sociological Inquiry* 40:235–257.

JUDITH TREAS

SOCIAL IMITATION Social imitation is a process by which the behavior of one individual becomes similar in form to that of another. The concept of social imitation is akin to that of conformity in that both refer to overt similarities in behavior among two or more persons. Conformity, however, has generally been explained in terms of social pressures and rationalistic processes. Social imitation, on the other hand, has a longer and distinct history and has been explained primarily in instinctivist, associationist, and learning theory principles.

INSTINCTIVIST THEORIES

Interest in the phenomenon of social imitation can be traced back to Aristotle. It was not until the late nineteenth century, however, in an emerging French school of social thought, that social imitation achieved importance as a scientific concept. Two prominent theorists in this movement were Gustave LeBon and Gabriel Tarde. Both LeBon and Tarde were greatly influenced by Charcot's study of hypnosis, and they drew heavily on Charcot's "principle of suggestion" to explain social imitation.

LeBon (1896) believed that man has an inherent predisposition toward suggestion and posited the existence of a "group mind" that transformed the thinking and behavior of individuals who are in a crowd from the way they would normally think and behave when alone. Imitation was viewed simply as a manifestation of heightened suggestibility. Along with suggestion went the notion of contagion. Trained as a physician and noting the involuntary manner in which one person contracts a disease from another, LeBon applied the same mechanism to imitation. The actions and feelings of one person in a crowd were seen to spread to others like an infectious disease until the state of persons within the crowd became identical. For Tarde (1903), social imitation had a somewhat different function. It was the primary vehicle for the spread of new ideas and for the transmission of culture from one generation to the next.

Edward Ross (1908), in one of the first textbooks on social psychology, also paid particular attention to the phenomena of suggestion and social imitation. Like LeBon, Ross considered imitation to be the consequence of suggestion and posited an instinctive basis for it. He also believed that suggestibility varied according to species, race, age, sex, and mental condition. Unlike Le-Bon, however, Ross did not view physical proximity as a prerequisite for mass suggestion. Instead, he thought that with the use of developing technology such as the telegraph in facilitating mass communication, remote individuals could, in a sense, be brought into one another's presence. Through such processes a "mob mind" could be created. Crazes and fads were viewed as manifestations of "that irrational unanimity of interest, feeling, opinion, or deed in a body of communicating individuals, which results from suggestion and imitation" (1908, p. 65).

During this same period, C. Lloyd Morgan (1896) sought to make a distinction between instinctive and voluntary forms of imitation. Instinctive imitation can be illustrated by the flight impulse among animals in a herd or flock. In contrast, voluntary imitation was viewed as "intelligent" behavior, such as an attempt by a child to reproduce a sound. Although Morgan postulated an innate proclivity to imitate, he attributed voluntary imitation to the consequent satisfaction that was derived from the act. As such, his approach was a precursor to operant learning approaches.

The instinctivist approaches rapidly fell out of favor as learning theory gained in popularity during the early twentieth century. These approaches were important, however, in that they established social imitation as an important social scientific phenomenon for study. Unfortunately, the instinctivist theories were all primarily descriptive in nature and did little to elucidate the mechanism underlying the behavior.

ASSOCIATIONIST THEORIES

As the instinctivist doctrine gradually fell into disrepute, theorists attempted to account for social imitation using classical conditioning models.

The work of George Humphrey (1921) illustrates this orientation. He argued that the fundamental characteristic of an imitative response is that it is similar to the stimulus that produced it. For example, in a stampeding herd, each animal will, as it runs, see others running. Over time, the sight of a herd member running will come to serve as the conditioned stimulus for the response of running.

OPERANT AND SOCIAL LEARNING THEORIES

Neal Miller and John Dollard (1941) provided an extensive, Hullian-based theory of social imitation where (1) the behavior of another serves as a cue; (2) this cue leads to an internal response; (3) this internal response produces a drive to imitate; (4) this drive activates imitative responding; and (5) the imitative responding leads to a reward that reduces the drive and serves to increase the probability that imitation will occur on subsequent occasions. Miller and Dollard contended that this general model was sufficient to account for all cases of imitative behavior. Within this framework they defined three types of social imitation: (1) same behavior, (2) matched-dependent behavior, and (3) copying.

B. F. Skinner (1953) also believed that imitation could be explained using a learning framework. Unlike Miller and Dollard, however, he did not deem it necessary to posit any internal, mediating response. Instead, he viewed imitation as a straightforward matter of discriminative learning.

The major critic of the Skinnerian position has been Albert Bandura (1969), who proposed a social learning approach. Bandura contended that a person can acquire an observed behavior without performing the behavior overtly and being reinforced for it. The behavior must only occur in some cognitive representational form. Bandura described three subprocesses that mediate the extent of any imitative or observational learning; these are attentional, retention, and motor reproduction processes.

Historically, attempts to explain social imitation have been, in large part, reflections of the theories of human behavior popular at the time. As a result, no "general theory" of social imitation can be said to have emerged apart from these broader theories, nor, arguably, has one been needed.

(SEE ALSO: *Behaviorism; Social Psychology*)

REFERENCES

Bandura, Albert 1969 *Principles of Behavior Modification*. New York: Holt, Rinehart and Winston.

Humphrey, George 1921 "Imitation and the Conditioned Reflex." *Pedagogical Seminary* 28:1–21.

LeBon, Gustave 1896 *The Crowd*. Dunwoody, Ga: Norman S. Berg.

Miller, Neal, and John Dollard 1941 *Social Learning and Imitation*. New Haven, Conn.: Yale University Press.

Morgan, C. Lloyd 1896 *Habit and Instinct*. London: E. Arnold.

Ross, Edward 1908 *Social Psychology*. New York: Macmillan.

Skinner, B. F. 1953 *Science and Human Behavior*. New York: Macmillan.

Tarde, Gabriel 1903 *The Laws of Imitation*. New York: Henry Holt.

KARL KOSLOSKI

SOCIAL INDICATORS

Social indicators are statistical time series ". . . used to monitor the social system, helping to identify changes and to guide intervention to alter the course of social change" (Ferriss 1988, p. 601). Examples are unemployment rates, crime rates, estimates of life expectancy, health status indices such as the incidence of acute conditions per hundred persons or the percent of the population that does not smoke cigarettes, school enrollment rates, average achievement scores on standardized tests, rates of voting in elections, and measures of subjective well-being such as satisfaction with life as a whole.

HISTORICAL DEVELOPMENTS

Social Indicators in the 1960s. The term *social indicators* was born and given its initial meaning in an attempt, undertaken by the American Academy of Arts and Sciences for the National Aeronautics and Space Administration, to detect and anticipate the nature and magnitude of the second-order consequences of the space program for American society (Land 1983, p. 2). Frustrated by the lack of sufficient data to detect such effects and the absence of a systematic conceptual framework and methodology for analysis, some of those involved in the Academy project attempted to develop a system of social indicators —statistics, statistical series, and other forms of evidence—with which to detect and anticipate social change as well as to evaluate specific programs and determine their impact. The results of this part of the Academy project were published in a volume (Bauer 1966) bearing the name *Social Indicators*.

The appearance of this volume was not an isolated event. Several other influential publications commented on the lack of a system for charting social changes and advocated that the U.S. government establish a "system of social accounts" that would facilitate a cost-benefit analysis of more than the market-related aspects of society already indexed by the National Income and Product Accounts (see, e.g., National Commission on Technology, Automation and Economic Progress 1966; Sheldon and Moore 1968). The need for social indicators also was emphasized by the publication of the 101-page *Toward a Social Report* on the last day of the Johnson administration in 1969. Conceived of as a prototypical counterpart to the annual economic reports of the president, each of its seven chapters addressed major issues in an important area of social concern (health and illness; social mobility; the physical environment; income and poverty; public order and safety; learning, science, and art; and participation and alienation) and provided its readers with an assessment of prevalent conditions. In addition, the document firmly established the link of social indicators to the idea of systematic reporting on social issues for the purpose of public enlightenment.

Generally speaking, this sharp impulse of interest in social indicators in the 1960s grew out of the movement toward collection and organization of national social, economic, and demographic data that began in Western societies during the seventeenth and eighteenth centuries and accelerated in the twentieth century (Gross 1966; Carley 1981, pp. 14–15). The work of William F. Ogburn and his collaborators at the University of Chicago in the 1930s and 1940s on the theory and measurement of social change is more proximate and sociologically germane (Land 1975). As chairman of President Herbert Hoover's Research Committee on Social Trends, Ogburn supervised production of the two-volume *Recent Social Trends* (1933), a path-breaking contribution to social reporting. Ogburn's ideas about the measurement of social change influenced several of his students —notably Albert D. Biderman, Otis Dudley Duncan, Albert J. Reiss, Jr., and Eleanor Bernert Sheldon—who played major roles in the emergence and development of the field of social indicators in the 1960s and 1970s.

Social Indicators in the 1970s and 1980s. At the end of the 1960s, the enthusiasm for social indicators was sufficiently strong and broad-based for Duncan (1969, p. 1) to write of the existence of a social indicators movement. In the early 1970s, this led to numerous developments, including the establishment in 1972, with National Science Foundation support, of the Social Science Research Council Center for Coordination of Research on Social Indicators in Washington, D.C.; the publication of several major efforts to define and develop a methodology for the measurement of indicators of subjective well-being (Campbell and Converse 1972; Andrews and Withey 1976; Campbell, Converse, and Rodgers 1976); the commencement of a series of comprehensive social indicators books of charts, tables, and limited analyses (U.S. Department of Commerce 1974, 1978, 1980); the initiation of several continuing data series based on periodic sample surveys of the national population (such as the annual National Opinion Research Center's General Social Survey or the Bureau of Justice Statistics' annual National Crime Survey); the publication in 1974 of the first volume of the international journal *Social Indicators Research;* and the spread of the ideas of social indicators/social reporting to numerous other nations and interna-

tional agencies, such as the United Nations and the Organization for Economic Cooperation and Development.

In contrast to the 1970s, social indicators activities slowed in the 1980s, as funding cuts or nonrenewals led to the closing of the Center for Coordination of Research on Social Indicators; the discontinuation of related work at several international agencies; the termination of government-sponsored social indicators reports in some countries, including the United States; and the reduction of statistical efforts to monitor various aspects of society. Several explanations have been cited for this turnabout (Andrews 1989; Bulmer 1989; Innes 1989; Johnston 1989; Rockwell 1987). Certainly, politics and the state of national economies in the early 1980s are among the most identifiable proximate causes. Administrations that came to power in the United States and elsewhere based decisions more on a "conservative ideology" and less on current social data than had been the case earlier. And faltering economies producing large government budget deficits provided the incentive to make funding cuts. In addition to these immediate factors, however, there was a perceived lack of demonstrated usefulness of social indicators in public policymaking. This was due, in part, to an overly simplistic view of how and under what conditions knowledge influences policy, a topic discussed more fully below in discussions of current uses of social indicators. Before that, a more detailed discussion of types of indicators and their measurement and organization into accounting systems is necessary.

THREE TYPES OF SOCIAL INDICATORS

Criterion Indicators. Based on the premise that social indicators should relate directly to social policymaking considerations, an early definition by Mancur Olson, the principal author of *Toward a Social Report,* characterized a social indicator as a ". . . statistic of direct normative interest which facilitates concise, comprehensive and balanced judgments about the condition of major aspects of a society" (U.S. Department of

Health, Education, and Welfare 1969, p. 97). Olson went on to state that such an indicator is, in all cases, a direct measure of welfare and is subject to the interpretation that if it changes in the "right" direction, while other things remain equal, things have gotten better, or people are better off. Accordingly, by this definition statistics on the number of doctors or policemen could not be social indicators, whereas figures on health or crime rates could be.

In the language of policy analysis (Fox 1974, pp. 120–123), social indicators are "target" or "output" or "end-value" variables, toward changes in which some public policy (program, project) is directed. Such a use of social indicators requires (Land 1983, p. 4) that (a) society agree about what needs improving; (b) it be possible to decide unambiguously what "getting better" means; and (c) it be meaningful to aggregate the indicators to the level of aggregation at which the policy is defined.

In recognition of the fact that various other meanings have been attached to the term *social indicators,* the tendency among recent authors is to use a somewhat different terminology for the class of indicators identified by Olson. For instance, Land (1983, p. 4) termed this the class of *normative welfare indicators.* Building on the Olson approach, MacRae (1985, p. 5) defined *policy indicators* as "measures of those variables that are to be included in a broadly policy-relevant system of public statistics." With a meaning similar to that of MacRae, Ferriss (1989, p. 416) used the felicitous term *criterion indicators.*

Satisfaction Indicators. Another class of social indicators has its roots in the work of Angus Campbell and Philip E. Converse in the early 1970s. In *The Human Meaning of Social Change* (1972), they argued that the direct monitoring of key social-psychological states (attitudes, expectations, feelings, aspirations, and values) in the population is necessary for an understanding of social change and the quality of life. In this approach, social indicators seek to measure psychological satisfaction, happiness, and life fulfillment by using survey research instruments that ascertain the subjective reality in which people

live. The result may aptly be termed *satisfaction, subjective well-being,* or *perceptual indicators.*

The Campbell-Converse approach led to two major methodological studies (Andrews and Withey 1976; Campbell, Converse, and Rodgers 1976) and an edited volume (Andrews 1986) exploring the utility of various survey and analytic techniques for mapping individuals' feelings of satisfaction with numerous aspects ("domains") of their experiences. These studies examine domains ranging from the highly specific (house, family, etc.) to the global (life as a whole). Numerous other applications of these concepts and techniques have appeared over the past two decades; one or more studies of subjective well-being indicators can be found in almost any issue of the journal *Social Indicators Research.* Research on the related concept of happiness as an index of well-being was surveyed by Veenhoven (1984). The principle that the link between changes in objective conditions and psychological states is both indeterminate and sometimes paradoxical and therefore that subjective as well as objective states should be monitored is well established in the social indicators literature.

Descriptive Social Indicators. Building on the Ogburn legacy of research on social trends, a third approach to social indicators focuses on social measurements and analyses designed to improve our understanding of what the main features of society are, how they interrelate, and how these features and their relationships change (Sheldon and Parke 1975, p. 696). This produces *descriptive social indicators*—indexes of the state of society and changes taking place therein. Although descriptive social indicators may be more or less directly related to the well-being goals of public policies or programs and thus include policy or criterion indicators, they are not limited to such uses. For instance, in the area of health, descriptive indicators might include preventive indicators such as the percent of the population that does not smoke cigarettes, as well as criterion indicators such as the incidence of acute conditions per hundred persons or an index of self-reported satisfaction with health. Ferriss (1990) gives a recent compilation of descriptive indicators for the United States; national social indicator compilations for other nations similarly contain numerous examples.

The various statistical forms that descriptive social indicators can take are described by Land (1983, p. 6). These can be ordered by degree of abstraction from those that require only one or two data series and little processing (e.g., an age-specific death rate) to those that involve more complicated processing of several data series into a single summary index (e.g., a life-expectancy index). Descriptive social indicators can be formulated at any of these levels of abstraction. Moreover, as described in Juster and Land (1981), these indicators can, at least in principle, be organized into demographic- or time-budget-based systems of social accounts. Experience with aggregation in social accounting systems over the past two decades suggests, however, that some early visions of global aggregation of indicators into the system wide "social" analogue of the Gross National Product (e.g., Gross 1966) were impossibly ambitious. Nonetheless, the organization of indicators into, say, demographic accounts for specific subsystems such as education, health, crime, or housing has proven quite feasible and useful (see, e.g., the various chapters in Juster and Land 1981).

THE ENLIGHTENMENT FUNCTION: MONITORING, SOCIAL REPORTING, AND FORECASTING

The Social Indicators Movement was motivated by the principle that it is important to *monitor changes over time* in a broad range of social phenomena that extend beyond the traditional economic indicators and that include indicators of "life quality" (Andrews 1989, p. 401). Many organized actors in contemporary society—including government agencies, organizations and activists interested in social change programs, scholars, and marketing researchers interested in market development and product innovations—monitor indicators in which they have a vested interest and want to see increase or decline (Ferriss 1988, p. 603).

A second principle that has been part of the Social Indicators Movement from the outset (e.g., Biderman 1970) is that a critically important role of social indicators in contemporary democratic societies is *public enlightenment through social reporting*. Recently, Theodore D. Woolsey stated this principle very directly:

How else does the ordinary citizen assess the problems of society and the success or failure of his, or her, government in dealing with those problems? The citizen reads or hears about the rate of inflation; the rate of unemployment; changes in the cost of living; the growth and movement of the population estimates, however poor, or illegal immigration; crime rates; the degree of success we are having in education of our children; the rate of divorce; the increasing numbers of single-parent families; the spread of AIDS; the number of teenagers killed in auto accidents or committing suicide; and hundreds of other descriptors of today's life. These social indicators . . . absolutely must be made available to any interested citizen with a minimum of expense and difficulty because an informed electorate is an absolute requirement of a working democracy. (1986; as quoted in Ferriss 1988)

In brief, modern democracies require social reporting to describe social trends, explain why an indicator series behaves as it does and how this knowledge affects interpretation, and highlight important relationships among series (Parke and Seidman 1978, p. 15).

It also is important to suggest the consequences that are reasonably attributable to changes in a series. This includes the systematic use of social indicators to *forecast trends in social conditions and/or turning points therein* (Land 1983, p. 21). To be sure, the art of projection or forecasting is filled with uncertainties. Techniques range from the naive extrapolation of recent trends to futuristic scenario construction to complicated model-building with regression, time series, or stochastic process techniques. Moreover, there appear to be intrinsic limits to the accuracy of forecasts in large-scale natural and social systems (Land and Schneider 1987). But demands for the anticipation of the future (at a minimum, for the description of "what will happen if present trends continue"), for foresight and forward thinking in the public and private sectors, and for the assessment of critical trends (Gore 1990) appear to be an intrinsic part of contemporary postindustrial societies. Thus, it is prudent to expect that the "anticipation" task will become an increasingly important part of the enlightenment function of social indicators.

Social Reporting in the 1990s. As the decade of the 1990s unfolds, the model of a comprehensive national social report in the tradition pioneered by Ogburn and Olson has faltered in the United States, at least in the sense of federal government sponsorship and/or production. But the key ideas of monitoring, reporting, and forecasting are evident to greater or lesser extents in the production of continuing, periodic subject–matter–specific publications by various federal agencies, including *Science Indicators* (published by the National Science Foundation), *Health United States* (published by the Department of Health and Human Services), *The Condition of Education* (published by the Department of Education), *Indicators of Housing and Neighborhood Quality* (published by the Department of Housing and Urban Development), the *Report to the Nation on Crime and Justice* (published by the Department of Justice), and numerous Bureau of the Census publications. In addition, various scholars and private research organizations continue to produce reports, monographs, and books interpreting social trends and developments in various areas of social concern.

In contrast to the situation in the United States, comprehensive social reports/social indicators compendiums continue to be published periodically in several other countries. Examples are the *Social Trends* series published annually since 1970 by the United Kingdom's Central Statistical Office and the *Datenreport* series published biennially since 1983 by the Federal Republic of Germany. Citations and summary reports on these and other social indicators/social reports publications can be found in the quarterly newsletter publication *SINET: Social Indicators Network News.*

The difference in the organization of social indicators/reporting work in the United States as compared to that in other countries is in part attributable to the lack of a central statistical office responsible for the coordination of all government statistical activities in the former. More generally, it is indicative of the fact that, despite the invention of the ideas of social indicators and comprehensive social reporting in the United States, the nation has lagged in their institutionalization (Johnston 1989). Whether a new round of legislative effort (e.g., Senator Albert Gore, Jr.'s proposed Critical Trends Assessment Act [Gore 1990]) will eventually create the necessary institutional base remains to be seen. Perhaps marking a turning point and indicative of things to come is Public Law 100–297, enacted April 28, 1988, which requires an annual education indicators report to the president and Congress.

THE POLICY ANALYSIS FUNCTION: POLICY GUIDANCE AND DIRECTED SOCIAL CHANGE

Policy analysts distinguish various ways of guiding or affecting public policy, including *problem definition, policy choice and evaluation of alternatives,* and *program monitoring* (MacRae 1985, pp. 20–29). The social reporting/public enlightenment approach to social indicators centers around the first of these, namely the use of social indicators in problem definition and the framing of the terms of policy discourse. Indeed, studies of the actual use of social indicators suggests that this is precisely the manner in which they have affected public action (Innes 1989).

But policy analysts from Olson to MacRae always have hoped for more from social indicators —namely, the shaping of public policy and planning through the policy choice process. At a minimum this requires the identification of key variables that determine criterion indicators and changes therein (i.e., causal knowledge). More generally, it requires the construction of elaborate causal models and forecasting equations (often in the form of a "computer model") that can be used to simulate "what would happen if" under a variety of scenarios about policies and actions. An example of this is the development of the National Cancer Institute model for the control and reduction of the incidence of cancer in the United States to the year 2000 (Greenwald and Sondik 1986). Various policy and action scenarios involving prevention, education, screening, treatment, etc., and their implications for cancer mortality were simulated and estimated with this computer model. These simulations led to a decision to allocate funds to a prevention program rather than to additional clinical treatment.

It can be anticipated that many more applications of social indicators to policy choice and evaluation will appear in the future. In particular, such applications probably will occur in three areas. The first is the additional development of well-grounded, theoretically informed, and policy-relevant indicators and models for national- and/or regional-level analyses within particular fields, such as health, education, crime, and science (Bulmer 1989). In such applications, the phenomena to be included are definable and delimited, and the limitations of the data on which the indicators are based are known. The second is the use of social indicators in the field of social impact assessment (Finsterbusch 1980; Land 1982), which has arisen as part of environmental impact assessment legislation and attempts to anticipate the social effects of large-scale public projects (e.g., dams, highways, nuclear waste disposal facilities) as well as to assess the damage of both natural and human-made disasters (e.g., earthquakes, oil spills, nuclear plant accidents). This application of social indicators in impact assessments brings the field back full circle to its point of origination in the American Academy effort of the 1960s. Finally, and not of least importance, the many time series of indicators now available will increasingly be used by sociologists to assess theories, hypotheses, and models of social change, thus bringing social indicators data to bear on core issues in sociology.

(SEE ALSO: *Attitudes; Longitudinal Research; Public Opinion; Quality of Life; Social Change; Social Forecasting*)

REFERENCES

Andrews, Frank M. (ed.) 1986 *Research on the Quality of Life.* Ann Arbor, Mich.: Institute for Social Research.

———1989 "The Evolution of a Movement." *Journal of Public Policy* 9:401–405.

———, and Stephen B. Withey 1976 *Social Indicators of Well-Being: Americans' Perceptions of Life Quality.* New York: Plenum.

Bauer, Raymond A. (ed.) 1966 *Social Indicators.* Cambridge, Mass.: MIT Press.

Biderman, Albert D. 1970 "Information, Intelligence, Enlightened Public Policy: Functions and Organization of Societal Feedback." *Policy Sciences* 1: 217–230.

Bulmer, Martin 1989 "Problems of Theory and Measurement." *Journal of Public Policy* 9:407–412.

Campbell, Angus, and Philip E. Converse 1972 *The Human Meaning of Social Change.* New York: Russell Sage Foundation.

Campbell, Angus, Philip E. Converse, and Willard L. Rodgers 1976 *The Quality of American Life: Perceptions, Evaluations, and Satisfactions.* New York: Russell Sage Foundation.

Carley, Michael 1981 *Social Measurement and Social Indicators: Issues of Policy and Theory.* London: George Allen and Unwin.

Duncan, Otis Dudley 1969 *Toward Social Reporting: Next Steps.* New York: Russell Sage Foundation.

Ferriss, Abbott L. 1988 "The Uses of Social Indicators." *Social Forces* 66:601–617.

———1989 "Whatever Happened, Indeed!" *Journal of Public Policy* 9:413–417.

———1990 "The Quality of Life in the United States." *SINET: Social Indicators Network News* 21:1–8.

Finsterbusch, Kurt 1980 *Understanding Social Impacts: Assessing the Effects of Public Projects.* Beverly Hills, Calif.: Sage.

Fox, Karl A. 1974 *Social Indicators and Social Theory: Elements of an Operational System.* New York: Wiley-Interscience.

Gore, Albert, Jr. 1990 "The Critical Trends Assessment Act: Futurizing the United States Government." *The Futurist* 24:22–28.

Greenwald, Peter, and Edward J. Sondik (eds.) 1986 *Cancer Control Objectives for the Nation: 1985–2000.* NCI Monographs 2. Washington, D.C.: U.S. Government Printing Office.

Gross, Bertram A. 1966 "The State of the Nation: Social Systems Accounting." In Raymond A. Bauer, ed., *Social Indicators*. Cambridge, Mass.: MIT Press.

Innes, Judith Eleanor 1989 "Disappointment and Legacies of Social Indicators." *Journal of Public Policy* 9:429–432.

Johnston, Denis F. 1989 "Some Reflections on the United States." *Journal of Public Policy* 9:433–436.

Juster, F. Thomas, and Kenneth C. Land 1981 *Social Accounting Systems: Essays on the State of the Art*. New York: Academic Press.

Land, Kenneth C. 1975 "Theories, Models and Indicators of Social Change." *International Social Science Journal* 27:7–37.

————1982 "Ex Ante and Ex Post Assessment of the Social Consequences of Public Projects and Policies." *Contemporary Sociology* 11:512–514.

————1983 "Social Indicators." *Annual Review of Sociology* 9:1–26.

————, and Stephen H. Schneider 1987 "Forecasting in the Social and Natural Sciences: An Overview and Statement of Isomorphisms." In K. C. Land and S. H. Schneider, eds., *Forecasting in the Social and Natural Sciences*. Boston: D. Reidel.

MacRae, Duncan, Jr., 1985 *Policy Indicators: Links Between Social Science and Public Policy*. Chapel Hill: University of North Carolina Press.

National Commission on Technology, Automation and Economic Progress 1966 *Technology and the American Economy*, vol. 1. Washington, D.C.: U.S. Government Printing Office.

Parke, Robert, and David Seidman 1978 "Social Indicators and Social Reporting." *Annals of the American Academy of Political and Social Science* 435:1–22.

President's Research Committee on Social Trends 1933 *Recent Trends in the United States*. New York: McGraw-Hill.

Rockwell, Richard C. 1987 "Prospects for Social Reporting in the United States: A Receding Horizon." In Jesse R. Pitts and Henri Mendras, eds., *The Tocqueville Review*, vol. 8. Charlottesville: University Press of Virginia.

Sheldon, Eleanor B., and Wilbert E. Moore (eds.) 1968 *Indicators of Social Change: Concepts and Measurements*. New York: Russell Sage Foundation.

Sheldon, Eleanor B., and Robert Parke 1975 "Social Indicators." *Science* 188:693–699.

U.S. Department of Commerce 1974 *Social Indicators, 1973*. Washington, D.C.: U.S. Government Printing Office.

————1978 *Social Indicators, 1977*. Washington, D.C.: U.S. Government Printing Office.

————1980 *Social Indicators, III*. Washington, D.C.: U.S. Government Printing Office.

U.S. Department of Health, Education, and Welfare 1969 *Toward a Social Report*. Washington, D.C.: U.S. Government Printing Office.

Veenhoven, Ruut 1984 *Conditions of Happiness*. Boston: D. Reidel.

Woolsey, Theodore D. 1986 "Retiring Chair Shares Thoughts with Council." *News from COPAFS* 51:3.

KENNETH C. LAND

SOCIAL INEQUALITY

SOCIAL INEQUALITY Social inequality refers to the graduated dimensions (Blau 1977), vertical classifications (Ossowski 1963; Schwartz 1981), or hierarchical relations (Burt 1982) by which human populations at varying levels of aggregation are differentiated. As such, this concept is among the oldest and most diversely defined in sociology, extending back at least as far as Plato's conception of the Republic and developed subsequently in the social theories of Marx (1859), Mosca (1939), Weber (1947), Simmel (1896), Sorokin (1941), Eisenstadt (1971), Merton (1968), and others. The construct is often used interchangeably with such related (though relatively more specific) concepts as social class, social stratification, socioeconomic status, power, privilege, accumulative advantage, dependence, and dominance. And it is relevant for the study of social systems that range in size from the dyad (Simmel 1896) to the modern world-system (Wallerstein 1974).

SOCIAL INEQUALITY AS A GRADUATED DIMENSION

When social inequality is conceptualized as a graduated dimension, it is treated as a distributional phenomenon. Here the approach is to define inequality in terms of the distribution of socially valued attributes, such as education, income, information, health, and influence, in a population. However, distributional phenomena can be examined from one of two very different assumptions. The first views inequality as an outcome of, or generated by, the underlying distribution(s) of valued traits among individuals. In this sense, it refers to "regular differences in power, goods, services, and privileges among defined sets" of actors (Granovetter and Tilly 1988). The second assumption views inequality strictly as a system-level property with individual-level differences defined as derivative rather than generative (Blau 1977). Distributions such as the size of the system and its total volume of resources are examined as higher levels of aggregation, with the goal of determining the overall level of inequality (oligarchy) across systems and without reference to individual differences (e.g., Lenski 1966; Mayhew 1973; Mayhew and Schollaert 1980).

Both approaches parameterize populations along criteria usually measurable at the level of individual actors (persons, races, gender categories, organizations, nation-states) in a system. Early applications of the first assumption can be found in Pareto's ([1897] 1980) examinations of income distributions and of the circulation of elites. He proposed that economic and political inequality emerged from the distribution and redistribution of "congenital abilities" valued within social systems. Sorokin (1941) proposed similar arguments to explain social and cultural processes of mobility and inequality.

Among the most influential and controversial conceptualizations of inequality as a graduated dimension emerging from individual differences was Davis and Moore's (1945) functionalist statement of the principles of stratification. They argued that social inequality results from the differential distribution of societal rewards to individuals based on their relative achievement of ranked social positions. This achievement process, with its implications for social mobility, was formally specified by Blau and Duncan (1967), who established that educational attainment mediated the process of intergenerational social mobility among men. They defined social inequality as socioeconomic status based on the economic and prestige rewards accorded achieved occupational positions in American society. The strong parallel between this model of inequality and the neoclassical model of human capital and economic inequality (see Becker 1964) is well established (Wright 1978).

The most prominent distributional theories of inequality, however, are founded on macrosocial views regarding the division of labor, the rationalization of authority, and the distribution of social and economic rewards in industrial societies. Weber's (1947) theory of economic organization proposed that capitalist systems of property, power, and prestige developed out of the conjunction of changing systems of economic exchange (money economies) and accounting (double-entry bookkeeping) with rationalized systems of social control (rational-legal authority). Thus, social inequality in industrial society developed along economic and political dimensions to produce the multidimensional bases of inequality: class, status, and party. Lenski's (1966) comparative study of the evolution of inequality attempted a direct test of Weber's rationalization thesis that inequality evolves necessarily (functionally) with increasing differentiation in the direction of systems of privilege based on rational authority and away from socially illegitimate systems of force or economic dominance.

Accordingly, distributional inequality can be concerned with more than the single dimension of individual socioeconomic outcomes. It also addresses macrosocial patterns of inequality (Eisenstadt 1971). The parameters of social structure, according to Blau (1977), include inequality and heterogeneity—or graduated and nominal dimensions, respectively—which intersect to constrain and differentiate individuals' opportunities, as well as their motivations and outcomes. The intersection of graduated and nominal parameters creates diverse systems or populations with differing distributional properties that cannot be reduced to an original individual source. Blau's distributional theory is "macrosocial in the sense that the 'cases' are populations or communities and the 'variables' measure some aspect (a rate or a distributional property) of these populations"

(Skvoretz and Fararo 1986, p. 30). Following this approach, indicators of inequality can be defined in such terms as Lorenz curves (e.g., Gini indices), social welfare functions, or similar distributional properties (see Allison 1978).

Thus, economic inequality may intersect with the nominal category of race, for example, and produce more diverse outcomes than traditional functional or neoclassical economic theories would predict. Examinations of patterns of inter-racial/interethnic marriage, for example, indicate that the association between occupational achievement and race is mediated by the extent of interracial/interethnic marriage in a community (see Blum 1984; Blau, Blum, and Schwartz 1982). This treatment of inequality, based on notions of dispersion and association, departs from the simple reduction of unequal outcomes to individual attributes and embeds the process in extended distributional contexts.

Other distributional approaches introduce mesoscopic constructs to explain inequality at levels above individual attributes, although individuals usually remain the units of analysis. Spatial and temporal contexts, for example, define and constrain distributions of individual outcomes. The examination of occupational mobility within organizational or labor-market contexts attempts to nest the process of inequality in the workplace within organizational and occupational boundaries. The availability of occupational positions within a system is independent of the motivations and other attributes of workers. White's (1970) influential notion of "vacancy chains" exemplifies this approach with its argument that job vacancies produce opportunity structures for individual mobility and define the mobility chances, and distributional outcomes, of individuals. Vacancy-chain models have been particularly useful for examining closed opportunity systems, such as internal labor markets (Sorensen 1977).

Distributions of individuals in systems of inequality are also influenced by temporal factors. Merton's (1968) provocative discussion of the "Matthew Effect" in scientific career systems argues that, over time, initial inequalities in a system bias distributional outcomes in favor of initial advantage. Formal extensions and applications of Merton's notion of accumulative advantage have been applied across contexts (Cole and Cole 1973; Allison and Stewart 1974) to establish patterns of temporal regulation of distributional outcomes over and above the attributes of individuals over time.

SOCIAL INEQUALITY AS A VERTICAL CLASSIFICATION

When social inequality is conceptualized as a vertical classification system, it is treated as an oppositional phenomenon. Here the approach is to define inequality in terms of "the relative position in a matrix of oppositions" (Schwartz 1981, p. 94) of social categories that determine relations of dominance, such as class, race, and gender. Vertical classifications grow out of antagonistic and contradictory interests in the relations of "objective" positions in the social division of labor, not out of the dispersed motivations and interests of individuals. Dominance and subordination emerge from the objective opposition of social categories. Dichotomous, binary, and polar conceptions of inequality (e.g., ruler–ruled, rich–poor, white–black, masculine–feminine) generally subscribe to an oppositional framework. Some have argued that this approach to inequality may be the most ancient in human social consciousness (Ossowski 1963; Schwartz 1981).

Class theories following Marxian frameworks dominate this approach (Braverman 1974; Wright 1985). Marx's theory of class proposes that class relations in capitalist systems are inevitably in conflict. Since all value is ultimately produced by labor, all (capitalist) profit must be at the expense of labor. The objective positions of owning class (bourgeoisie) and laboring class (proletariat), therefore, are necessarily antagonistic. Advanced capitalist systems sustain the exploitation of labor through rationalized job-definition systems and the degradation of work (Braverman 1974). Wright (1978) has argued, furthermore, that in advanced capitalist societies the elaborate differentiation of functions originally embodied in entrepreneurial capitalism into many different categories has not overcome the fundamental oppositional inequality of its origins; contradictory class positions continue to exist as a result of the underlying structure of capitalist relations.

Oppositional frameworks lend themselves to the examination of such classlike relations as those observable in race- and gender-centered systems of inequality. Oppositional approaches to the examination of race inequality can be traced to Myrdal's (1944) pioneering analysis of racial exploitation in the U.S. context. These approaches argue that race is an invariant principle of vertical classification masked by ideologies of economic progress and attainment (Pinkney 1984). Debates regarding the inevitability of racial opposition as the basis of inequality center on the substitutability of race and class as categories in the recent history of U.S. inequality. Wilson (1980) has proposed the controversial argument that class inequality has superseded race inequality as the basis of cross-race differences in economic and social outcomes.

Theories of gender inequality extend back to Mill's 1859 libertarian essay on the subjection of women and to Engels's Marxian analysis, written two decades later, of the relationship between private property and the stratification of family (gender) roles. But contemporary feminist theories provide the strongest argument for gender inequality as an oppositional, vertical classification system. The sex/gender system, it is argued, subordinates women in patriarchal relations that exist over and above class relations (Jaggar 1984), since male dominance over women's productive and reproductive roles predates the emergence of capitalism (Harding 1983). This system of inequality leads inevitably to a conflict of interests and to the emergence of competing ideologies.

Since the notion of dominance is central to vertical-classification approaches to inequality, these are also readily applied to the analysis of large-scale systems of inequality, such as the state (Skocpol 1979) and the modern world-system (Wallerstein 1974). Mechanisms of domination

extend beyond class (or classlike) interests alone and are observable in the historical relations of nation-states (Reddy 1987) and multistate sectors of the modern world-system (Wallerstein 1974). Asymmetrical relations of exchange and dependence between states and geopolitical state sectors create relations of dominance, which define global inequalities. Such inequalities can be formulated as distributional phenomena following a functional framework; however, the historical analysis of dominance systems lends itself more readily to oppositional analysis. The classification of the world-system into core and periphery sectors that resulted from historically contingent factors introduces notions of centrality and dominance that suggest more than an underlying distribution of resources (Wallerstein 1974).

SOCIAL INEQUALITY AS HIERARCHICAL RELATIONS

When social inequality is conceptualized as hierarchical relations, it is treated as a system of interactions or interdependencies characterized by relative symmetry (equality) and asymmetry (inequality) among relations. Here the approach is usually to define the form of social relations rather than the attributes of individuals in these relations and to account for patterns of unequal relations without necessary reference to oppositions. Inequality or dominance stems from positions in hierarchical relations, not from the a priori possession or control of resources or power by individuals, groups, or categories (Marsden 1983). This relational approach to inequality can be traced to Simmel (1896), whose studies of the structures of superordination–subordination by persons, groups, and principles continue to inform research on hierarchical relations and social networks in modern life (Coleman 1982).

Because social relationships have such formal properties as connectedness, transitivity, reciprocity, and multiplexity, they are measurable units of analysis for the study of social inequality within populations at all levels, from siblings to communities to transnational trading systems (Lin and Marsden 1982). These social units make up complex configurations of social relations within which distinctive positions of relative equivalence or centrality can be revealed (Burt 1982). Thus, in their study of coalitions and elite structures in a German community named Altneustadt, Laumann and Pappi (1976) determined the relational bases of influence between natives and newcomers using network techniques emphasizing associational patterns over personal attributes. Patterns of social distance and connectedness among corporate actors, not the preexisting distribution of resources, defined the influence process in this community.

A provocative study by Granovetter (1974) of the job-search process clearly demonstrates the relative utility of relational over distributional approaches to inequality. Granovetter demonstrates that weak ties, rather than strong ties, in a community prevail in the successful job search. The "strength of weak ties" hypothesis (related to Simmel's *tertius gaudens,* or the third who enjoys) provides the counterintuitive argument that weaker (secondary) social contacts increase individuals' access to jobs more than stronger (primary) ties. These ties operate independently of the attributes of individual job seekers.

The "strength of weak ties" phenomenon can be extended beyond the job-search process to examine structures of relational inequality in different contexts. Studies of interlocking directorates and informational brokerage systems, for example, demonstrate that loosely coupled relational systems of different forms produce different systems of social inequality (Burt 1982). The network of ties constitutes a social-constraint context within which actors are "captured." Burt's (1983) study of corporate philanthropy as a cooptive relation is a specific example of the relational bases of inequality in a market context. Using Internal Revenue Service data on firm expenditures on advertising and philanthropy, Burt demonstrates that firm philanthropy coopts the household sector by legitimizing the firm to the public as a protector and by improving the ability of specific classes to purchase the firm's products (Burt 1983, p. 424). The strength of this approach

is that advertising, which is more blatantly cooptive, does not escape public suspicion where philanthropy does more easily. Firms in an economic sector perform unequally as a result of their relative cooptive relations with the public; and the public exists in a cooptive relationship as consumers in this context.

Finally, it should be mentioned that, despite the rationale provided above for the bulk of sociological research on relational inequality, the relational approach has been used to examine the importance of individual resources for social inequality. Indeed, early experimental efforts to study small-group processes of inequality demonstrated that both individual resources and social relations can create systems of inequality, whether measured as leadership processes or communication networks (Thibaut and Kelley 1959). And, more recently, studies of what Burt (1982) has termed "ego-centered" networks examine network position itself as an individual resource with implications for social inequality.

APPROACHES TO SOCIAL INEQUALITY

The three major approaches to the study of social inequality outlined above have different implications for theory as well as for method. The distributional approach that examines social inequality as a graduated dimension depends primarily upon sample data and can be directed toward individual as well as structural explanations of inequality. The oppositional approach to vertical classifications may use sample data but has tended to adopt historical and qualitative approaches to study the institutionalization of dominance in various forms, that is, as class, race, or gender or as other forms of subordination. Finally, the relational approach, which provides a direct method for examining the social context of inequality, may use sample or case data to map the configurations of the relations of inequality with implications for explanation at both the individual and structural levels.

(SEE ALSO: *Equality of Opportunity; Equity Theory; Social Stratification*)

REFERENCES

Allison, Paul D. 1978 "Measures of Inequality." *American Sociological Review* 43:865–880.

———, and John A. Stewart 1974 "Productivity Differences among Scientists: Evidence for Accumulative Advantage." *American Sociological Review* 39:596–606.

Becker, Gary S. 1964 *Human Capital*. Chicago: University of Chicago Press.

Blau, Peter M. 1977 *Inequality and Heterogeneity*. New York: Free Press.

———, Terry C. Blum, and Joseph E. Schwartz 1982 "Heterogeneity and Intermarriage." *American Sociological Review* 47:45–62.

———, and Otis Dudley Duncan 1967 *The American Occupational Structure*. New York: John Wiley.

Blum, Terry C. 1984 "Racial Inequality and Salience: An Examination of Blau's Theory of Social Structure." *Social Forces* 62:607–617.

Braverman, Harry 1974 "Labor and Monopoly Capital: The Degradation of Work in the Twentieth Century." *Monthly Review* 26:1–134.

Burt, Ronald S. 1982 *Toward a Structural Theory of Action: Network Models of Social Structure, Perception, and Action*. New York: Academic Press.

———1983 "Corporate Philanthropy as a Cooptive Relation." *Social Forces* 62:419–449.

Cole, Jonathan R., and Stephen Cole 1973 *Social Stratification in Science*. Chicago: University of Chicago Press.

Coleman, James S. 1982 *The Asymmetric Society*. Syracuse, N.Y.: Syracuse University Press.

Davis, Kingsley, and Wilbert E. Moore 1945 "Some Principles of Stratification." *American Sociological Review* 10:242–249.

Eisenstadt, S. M. 1971 *Social Differentiation and Stratification*. Glencoe, Ill.: Scott Foresman.

Engels, Frederick (1884) 1942 *The Origin of the Family, Private Property and the State*. New York: International Publishers.

Granovetter, Mark 1974 *Getting a Job*. Cambridge: Harvard University.

———, and Charles Tilly 1988 "Inequality and Labor Processes." In Neil J. Smelser, ed., *Handbook of Sociology*. Beverly Hills, Calif.: Sage.

Harding, Sandra G. 1983 *Discovering Reality: Feminist Perspectives on Epistemology, Metaphysics, Methodology, and Philosophy of Science*. Dordrecht, Holland: D. Reidel.

Jaggar, Alison M. 1984 *Feminist Frameworks: Alternative Theoretical Accounts of the Relations Between Men and Women*, 2nd ed. New York: McGraw-Hill.

Laumann, Edward O., and Franz U. Pappi 1976 *Networks of Collective Action: A Perspective on Community Influence Systems*. New York: Academic Press.

Lenski, Gerhard E. 1966 *Power and Privilege*. New York: McGraw-Hill.

Lin, Nan, and Peter V. Marsden (eds.) 1982 *Social Structure and Network Analysis*. Beverly Hills, Calif.: Sage.

Marsden, Peter V. 1983 "Restricted Access in Networks and Models of Power." *American Journal of Sociology* 88:686–717.

Marx, Karl (1859) 1976–1978 *Capital: A Critique of Political Economy*. Harmondsworth, England: Penguin Books.

Mayhew, Bruce H. 1973 "System Size and Ruling Elites." *American Sociological Review* 38:468–475.

———, and Paul T. Schollaert 1980 "The Concentration of Wealth: A Sociological Model." *Sociological Focus* 13:1–35.

Merton, Robert K. 1968 "The Matthew Effect in Science." *Science* 159:56–63.

Mill, John Stuart (1859) 1970 *The Subjection of Women*. New York: Source Book Press.

Mosca, G. 1939 *The Ruling Class*. New York: McGraw-Hill.

Myrdal, Gunnar 1944 *An American Dilemma: The Negro Problem and Modern Democracy*. New York: Harper and Brothers.

Ossowski, Stanislav 1963 *Class Structure in the Social Consciousness*. New York: Free Press.

Pareto, Vilfredo (1897) 1980 *Compendium of General Sociology*. Minneapolis: University of Minnesota Press.

Pinkney, Alphonso 1984 *The Myth of Black Progress*. New York: Cambridge University Press.

Reddy, William 1987 *Money and Liberty in Modern Europe*. Cambridge: Cambridge University Press.

Schwartz, Barry 1981 *Vertical Classification*. Chicago: University of Chicago Press.

Simmel, Georg 1896 "Superiority and Subordination as Subject Matters of Sociology," trans. A. Small. *American Journal of Sociology* 2:167–189, 392–415.

Skocpol, Theda 1979 *States and Social Revolutions*. New York: Cambridge University Press.

Skvoretz, John, and Thomas J. Fararo 1986 "Inequality and Association: A Biased Net Theory." *Current Perspectives in Social Theory* 7:29–50.

Sorensen, Aage 1977 "The Structure of Inequality and

the Process of Attainment." *American Sociological Review* 42:965–978.

Sorokin, Pitirim A. 1941 *Social and Cultural Dynamics.* New York: Bedminster.

Thibaut, John W., and Harold H. Kelley 1959 *The Social Psychology of Groups.* New York: Wiley.

Wallerstein, Immanuel Maurice 1974 *The Modern World System.* New York: Academic Press.

Weber, Max (1947) 1978 *Economy and Society,* Vols. I and II. Berkeley: University of California Press.

White, Harrison C. 1970 *Chains of Opportunity.* Cambridge, Mass.: Harvard University Press.

Wilson, William J. 1980 *The Declining Significance of Race: Blacks and Changing American Institutions.* Chicago: University of Chicago Press.

Wright, Erik Olin 1978 *Class, Crisis, and the State.* London: NLB.

———1985 *Classes.* London: Verso.

ANGELA M. O'RAND

SOCIALISM The origins of socialism are obscure. Intellectual historians have traced its beginnings, variously, to the religious utopias of the Old Testament (Laidler 1968), the principles of Mosaic law (Gray 1963), the anti-individualism of radical sects that emerged from the French Revolution (Lichtheim 1969), and the publication of the *Communist Manifesto* (Sweezy 1983). As far as can be determined, the word made its first appearance in print in Italian, in 1803, although its meaning at that time appeared to differ somewhat from current interpretations (Cole 1959). For this reason, the origin of the term is usually attributed to a later publication, in English: The word *socialist* was used in 1827 in the *London Co-Operative Magazine* to designate followers of Robert Owen (Nuti 1981). The first French usage followed shortly thereafter: In 1832 a French periodical, *Le Globe,* used it to characterize the writings of Saint-Simon (Bell 1968; Kolakowski 1978).

Despite such murky beginnings, by 1840 the concept was commonly used across Europe and was making its way across the Atlantic to the United States. By the early 1920s, one country (the Soviet Union) had already claimed "socialism" as its overall organizing principle; ironically, at that time over 260 definitions of this term were available in the social-scientific literature (Griffiths 1924), thereby rendering its meaning somewhat ambiguous. Since then, further graftings of the concept have appeared; for instance, we now differentiate among Chinese socialism, corporatist socialism, democratic socialism, radical socialism, and Russian socialism.

What constitutes the common core of socialist ideas is hard to define. To be sure, all socialists were critical of the competitive and unequal nature of capitalist society and, without fail, they championed a more egalitarian and just future. At the same time, their visions regarding the organization of a socialist future were sufficiently diverse to render a single definition of the term practically impossible. It is frequently assumed, for example, that all socialists wanted to establish communal ownership; yet, many were content with the centralization of resources in the hands of the state (e.g., Bernstein 1961), and others actually protested the abolition of private property (e.g., Saint-Simon 1964). Disagreements were also waged over the role of the state: some believed that centrally managed administrative organs would become superfluous under a socialist regime (Proudhon 1966), while others regarded these organs as essential for the management of community affairs (e.g., Cabet 1975). Many argued that the freedom of the individual must be guaranteed at all costs even under socialism (e.g., Fourier 1971), while others were willing to impose limitations on such freedom in the name of equality and efficient production (Mao 1971). Some believed that socialism could be realized by gradual reforms (Bernstein 1961), while others thought that it was possible only through a major revolution (Lenin 1971).

Given the nontrivial nature of these differences, a single definition of socialism is likely to conceal more than it might illuminate. For this reason, it is more productive to highlight features of the concept by examining separately some of the best-known schools of socialist thought.

THE IDEA OF SOCIALISM

It is useful to begin this discussion by considering briefly the ideas of utopian socialists. It is no exaggeration to say that they considered socialism to be little more than a pleasant dream, a romantic vision whose purpose was not necessarily to be realized but was to serve as an ideal against which the evils of capitalism could be compared. The specific content of this vision, of course, varied from author to author. Two central themes, however, united them all.

The first of them is the idea of community. From Fourier to Cabet, through Owen and Saint-Simon, all utopian theorists championed a new social order, organized around small communities. In most sketches of socialism this vision was realized in an agrarian setting (e.g., Cabet 1975), although some required advanced industrial development (e.g., Saint-Simon 1964). In either case, however, it was assumed that these communities would be based on fellowship, harmony, and altruism—virtues that utopian theorists favored, on moral grounds, over bourgeois individualism.

Nostalgia for the past is the second common theme in utopian socialist thought. It frequently appeared in utopian novels and usually assumed one of two forms. In some versions the main characters are returned to the gaiety of their childhood times, while in others they reside in the Middle Ages or tell their stories against the backdrop of a less distant past (e.g., Morris 1970). In spite of such variation in the settings of these novels, the message that they hoped to convey was more or less the same: In the transition to industrial capitalism, we have abandoned the "golden age" of social harmony and replaced it with a fragmented and competitive social order that is unable to provide for the full satisfaction of our human needs.

In the hands of scientific socialists, the idea of socialism represented more than just an attractive dream (Marx and Engels 1968). Karl Marx, for example, considered it to be a historically possible future to capitalism. He believed, in fact, that the internal contradictions within capitalism will create some of the preconditions for socialism. According to his theory of historical materialism, the demands made by capitalist development will create increasingly grave crises for the ruling class. He maintained that with the mechanization of production and the concentration of capital in the hands of a few, there will be greater polarization in class inequalities and an increase in the degree of exploitation of the working class. As capitalism enters its advanced stage, the conditions of the working class will deteriorate and the struggle over the quality of their existence will intensify. At first the war between the "two hostile camps" of capitalist society (the bourgeoisie and the proletariat) will be waged within the boundaries of particular nation-states. However, as capitalism expands into new markets on the international scene, workers across the world will be forced to unite in their effort to overthrow capitalist society. Socialism, according to Marx, will emerge out of this final instance of class struggle.

It is ironic that the "father of socialism" never provided us with a detailed blueprint for his model of the future. It is evident from a number of passages in Marx, however, that he envisioned two stages in the evolution of socialism. In the lower stage (which he referred to as *socialism*, or the "dictatorship of the proletariat") he foreshadowed major improvements in the human condition. He predicted, for example, that private property would be abolished, the forces of production would be nationalized in the hands of the state, rights of inheritance would be eliminated, universal suffrage would be introduced, state representatives would be elected from among the working people, and education would become accessible to all. At the same time, because Marx expected this to be a transitional stage, he believed that some elements of capitalist society would continue to prevail. Specifically, he mentioned that income inequalities would continue to exist in the lower stage because workers would still be paid according to the amount of work that they contributed to the social good.

At some point, according to Marx, this transitional phase in the development of human history would evolve into the higher stage of socialism, a stage that he often referred to as *communism,* or the "realm of freedom." Under communism, work would no longer be an obligation but a free and creative activity, alienation would be transcended, the production process would be under the direct control of the producers, and the distribution of rewards would be changed from "to each according to his ability" to "to each according to his needs."

Principles of scientific socialism gained considerable popularity among French, German, and British socialists during the nineteenth century. Many agreed with Marx's assessment of bourgeois society and were attracted to his vision of the future. As the century progressed, however, and the Marxist scenario still appeared to be far away, some began to raise questions about the continued relevance of scientific socialism in the modern age. The main protagonist in this debate was Eduard Bernstein, a leading advocate of democratic socialism.

Bernstein and his followers called into question various elements of scientific socialism, but they were especially concerned about Marx's predictions concerning the development of industrial capitalism. On the basis of new empirical evidence, Bernstein (1961) noted that the standard of living at the turn of the century was improving rather than deteriorating; class inequalities were far from polarized; and the ownership of capital, rather than being concentrated in the hands of a few, was in fact becoming diversified. In addition, he observed that general strikes were becoming less frequent and socialist parties were gaining considerable strength in the political organization of the state. In light of these findings, Bernstein called for a revision of the Marxist program and offered a new interpretation of socialism.

According to Bernstein, democracy was the most important feature of socialist society. He discouraged his confederates from describing socialism as a "dictatorship of the proletariat" and recommended that they acknowledge its fundamentally pluralist character. Of course, for Bernstein the significance of democracy was not simply that it guaranteed the representation of minority rights under socialism; it was also that it assured a peaceful transition from capitalism through a series of parliamentary reforms. For many later socialists this accent on reform came to represent the essence of democratic socialism; it was this idea, in fact, that earned the "revisionist" label for this school of socialist thought.

Needless to say, Eduard Bernstein was not the only theorist to revise Marx's ideas on socialism. During the early part of the twentieth century, V.I. Lenin (1971) also amended the concept by adding to it several new notions—some of which were derived from his experiences with political organization in tsarist Russia. Taken together, these propositions comprise Russian socialism, also known as Bolshevik theory.

The best-known contribution of this school of thought to socialist theory is the idea of the "vanguard party." According to Lenin, Marx was unduly optimistic in his belief that the proletariat could develop the necessary class consciousness to overthrow capitalism. If left to their own devices, he claimed, workers would defend only their immediate (economic or trade union) interests and would not know how to translate these into revolutionary action. To assist them in this task, Lenin suggested that a vanguard party of intellectuals must be formed, the task of which would be to develop a revolutionary theory, to "go among the classes," and to politically educate the proletariat. It follows, then, for Lenin, that the success of the socialist revolution depends not on the political maturity of the working class but on the strength of the vanguard party.

A second feature of Russian socialism that sets it apart from the Marxist scheme is grounded in its claim that prospects of a proletarian revolution can arise not only in advanced industrial societies but also in precapitalist economic formations. Given the importance of the vanguard party in Lenin's rendition of socialism, this idea makes perfect sense: as long as a country is equipped with a group of willing, dedicated, and professional revolutionaries, it should be able to make the transition to socialism without the benefits of advanced technology and without having passed through the capitalist stage.

Last, but not least, it is important to mention that Lenin took from Marx the idea that socialism will come in two stages. In terms of his scheme, however, the lower stage (the "dictatorship of the proletariat") would not be a brief transitional period but would require a whole epoch in human history. During this time the bourgeois state would be "smashed," the class rule of the proletariat would be institutionalized, and opponents of the socialist regime would be suppressed by the "special coercive force" of the proletarian state. The higher stage of socialism ("communism") would be realized once the socialist state had "withered away" and democracy had become a "force of habit."

Russian socialism constitutes one of many indigenous graftings of the socialist vision. Another well-known attempt in this direction was made by Mao Zedong (1971), who accommodated the idea of socialism to the conditions of a peasant country. These revisions led to the emergence of what we now know as Chinese socialism, or Maoism.

Unlike most interpretations of socialism, Mao's is famous for its glorification of the peasantry. Earlier socialists, among them Marx and Lenin, were skeptical about the revolutionary potential of agricultural laborers. For the most part they regarded them as inherently petty bourgeoisie and, consequently, as unlikely allies of the proletariat. Mao argued, however, that in a peasant country, like China, traditionally conceived paths to socialism are not viable because they require the mass mobilization of something that his country did not have—an industrial proletariat. He insisted, therefore, that the socialist revolution in China was a peasant revolution and had no reservations about organizing agricultural workers into a revolutionary force on his side.

Another trademark of Chinese socialism that deserves attention is its lack of confidence in the guaranteed future of socialism. According to Mao's writings, socialist victories are not everlasting; even as the dust from the revolution begins to settle, old inequalities can resurface and new ones may emerge. For this reason, the work of the revolutionaries is never completed—they must be constantly on guard against opposition

and they must be prepared to wage a permanent revolution.

THE REALITY OF SOCIALISM

During the nineteenth century a number of communities were established to attempt the realization of the socialist vision. These included Étienne Cabet's Icaria in Illinois, Charles Fourier's Brook Farm in Massachusetts, William Lane's New Australia in Paraguay, and Robert Owen's New Harmony in Indiana. In nearly all of these cases, an attempt was made to isolate a small group of dedicated socialists from the rest of society and to create a model environment for efficient production and egalitarian social exchange. The documented history of these communities suggests that they experienced varying amounts of success (Ross 1935). Some attracted a large number of followers (e.g., Icaria) and prospered for more than a decade (e.g., Brook Farm). Others were fraught with hardships from the beginning (e.g., New Australia) and some collapsed within a few years (e.g., New Harmony). In the end, however, all the utopian experiments failed: they suffered from lack of preparation and meager financial support, harsh living environments and a dearth of agricultural skills, heterogeneous membership and a lack of long-term commitment to the socialist vision. The individuals who flocked to these communities were sufficiently adventuresome to embark on a project to build a new world, but they were not prepared for the trials of pioneer life.

Experiments with socialism during the twentieth century were more successful and somewhat longer-lasting than their utopian counterparts. After the Russian Revolution, 1917–1923, the Soviet Union was the first country to call itself socialist. By the middle of the century, however, there were regimes in Europe, Asia, Latin America, Africa, and the Near East modeling themselves on the Soviet scheme. At the risk of oversimplifying, the following may be identified as the most important features of those "actually existing" (Bahro 1978) socialist societies: (a) there is common ownership of the means of production and distribution; (b) economic activities are centrally planned by the state, and market forces play little or no role in the allocation of resources; (c) one party rules political life and legitimates itself by reference to some version of Marxism and Leninism; (d) this party dominates political culture with a unitary ideology and directs all executive, legislative, and judiciary powers.

In their purest form, Soviet-type societies have secured a number of major achievements. Within decades of the revolution they industrialized their outmoded economies (Berend and Ránki 1974); guaranteed full employment and attained price stability (Nove 1989); incorporated women into their labor force and expanded child-care services (Rueschemeyer and Szelényi 1989); developed their natural resources and fared well in the advancement of science and technology (Nuti 1981); strengthened their military power (Starr 1988); and improved their educational, health care, and welfare systems (Ferge 1979). Along with these changes, socialist societies made strong commitments to reducing income, educational, and occupational differentials following World War II. Empirically, a number of studies have shown that these formally egalitarian policies have had impressive results—in nearly all these countries, inequalities in income have decreased (Matthews 1972; Walder 1989), educational opportunities have expanded (Lane 1976), and distinctions of prestige between manual and nonmanual occupations have narrowed (Parkin 1971; Giddens 1973). Policies were also implemented by socialist states to reduce the intergenerational transmission of social inequalities—inheritance of wealth was eliminated and quotas were imposed on educational and occupational recruitment to favor children from the working class and from peasant families (Simkus and Andorka 1982).

Perhaps in part as a result of these changes, socialist societies carved out for themselves a position of considerable importance in the world system during the twentieth century. During the 1960s, for example, the Soviet Union competed directly with the United States in space exploration, the race for military power, and the development of science, technology, athletics, and the arts.

The economic and social miracles obtained by these countries in the years following World War II could not be long sustained. By the early 1970s, in fact, centrally managed economies began to exhibit multiple signs of internal strain. Bureaucratic blunders on the part of state officials resulted in poor investment decisions (Nove 1983b), frequent bottlenecks created breakdowns in production (Bauer 1978), chronic shortages of consumer items provoked anger and dissatisfaction among citizens (Kornai 1986), and curious managerial techniques (in the form of bribing, hoarding, and informal networking) had to be developed to mitigate the ineffective relationship between economic units and the state (Stark 1986).

Problems with central management, of course, were not restricted to the economic sphere. With a growing number of empirical studies during the 1970s (see Hollander 1983), the social and political consequences of Soviet-type planning became evident, although most scholars continued to be impressed by the initially positive outcome of egalitarian state policies in socialist societies. At the same time, they soon began to realize that the quotas introduced after World War II were often inconsistently applied and, in almost all circumstances, disturbingly short-lived. It is clear from these studies that the initial attempts made by socialist states to "build socialism" were soon overturned by a "second stage" in socialist development (Kelley and Klein 1986), which was marked by the crystallization of inequalities and the emergence of new privileges (Ossowski 1963; Nove 1983a). By the 1970s many of these societies began to demonstrate substantial inequalities in their prestige hierarchy (Inkeles 1966), patterns of social mobility (Connor 1979), opportunities for educational attainment (Simkus and Andorka 1982), and distributions of nonmonetary rewards (I. Szelényi 1976; Walder 1986).

Political inequalities in Soviet-type societies are well documented. Many studies have shown, for example, that Communist Party functionaries enjoy definite social, political, and economic advantages: they attend Party schools, shop at special stores, vacation at the most desirable holiday resorts, and have better access to decision-making posts (see S. Szelényi 1987). Party members are also more likely to receive state-subsidized housing, purchase a car or vacation home, eat meat several times a week, and frequently participate in cultural activities. Such differences in the allocation of resources have led many to conclude that the political sphere is central to the stratification system of socialist societies (Goldthorpe 1966; Bauman 1974). Others have gone so far as to suggest that the political elite constitutes the New (dominant) Class in socialist regimes (Djilas 1957; Konrád and Szelényi 1979).

In light of these problems, as well as of the apparent failure of the egalitarian experiment, socialist states made a number of attempts to reform their economies that became ailing. Yugoslavia was the first to begin this trend by introducing a new economic program that combined free-market principles with workers' self-management; in 1949 Yugoslav leaders abandoned central planning, tied wages to the financial success of firms, and liberalized foreign trade (Sirc 1979). Hungary followed suit in 1968 by introducing its version of market socialism (Hare, Radice, and Swain 1981); and China joined this trend in the late 1970s with similar economic reforms (Nee 1989).

Partial reprivatization, however, was not the only way for centrally managed economies to embark on the road to recovery. East Germany, for example, refused to combine planning with market reforms and chose to strengthen the operations of its central management (I. Szelényi 1989). In an effort to "scienticize" economic planning, East German leaders purchased state-of-the-art computers and sophisticated econometric programs to model the behavior of thousands of firms and anticipate the needs of millions of consumers. Cuba also refrained from market reforms during the late 1960s (Leogrande 1981). Hoping to prevent the restoration of capitalism in his country, Fidel Castro argued against the implementation of profit incentives to motivate

workers. Instead, he introduced a rigorous political education program, the main purpose of which was to convince workers that they needed to expend maximum effort at work, not for financial benefit but out of moral commitment to socialism.

In spite of these efforts to revitalize their economies, socialist societies were unable to recover from their experiences with overcentralization. Paradoxically, perhaps, reform plans were inconsistently applied, market rules were not rigorously followed, and the state continued its paternalistic practice of bailing out unsuccessful firms. Meanwhile, political opposition to these regimes began to grow—peasants were asking for further market reforms (Lewis 1979); workers demanded a hand in management (Pravda 1979); and intellectuals called for political democracy and a protection of their civil rights (Harman 1983).

In the spring of 1989, many of these conflicts came to a head as a "gentle revolution" began to unfold within these countries. With a few exceptions, Soviet-type societies formally accepted the principles of multiparty democracy and announced their intention to move in the direction of a market economy. The source of these changes is still unclear, as is the nature of postcommunism. One thing is certain, however: the transitions that are under way in these countries have brought a controversial chapter in the history of the socialist idea to an abrupt close.

(SEE ALSO: *Marxist Sociology; Soviet Sociology; Utopian Analysis and Design*)

REFERENCES

Bahro, Rudolf 1978 *The Alternative in Eastern Europe.* London: New Left Books.

Bauer, T. 1978 "Investment Cycles in Planned Economies." *Acta Oeconomica* 21, no. 3:243–260.

Bauman, Zygmunt 1974 "Officialdom and Class: Basis of Inequality in Socialist Society." In Frank Parkin, ed., *The Social Analysis of Class Structure.* London: Tavistock.

Bell, Daniel 1968 "Socialism." In David L. Sills, ed.,

International Encyclopedia of the Social Sciences, vol. 14. New York: Macmillan and Free Press.

Berend, Iván T., and György Ránki 1974 *Economic Development in East-Central Europe in the 19th and 20th Centuries.* New York: Columbia University Press.

Bernstein, Eduard 1961 *Evolutionary Socialism,* Edith C. Harvey, trans. New York: Schocken Books.

Cabet, Etienne 1975 *History and Constitution of the Icarian Community,* Thomas Teakle, trans. New York: AMS Press.

Cole, George D. H. 1959. *A History of Socialist Thought,* 5 vols. London: Macmillan.

Connor, Walter D. 1979 *Socialism, Politics, and Equality.* New York: Columbia University Press.

Djilas, Milovan 1957 *The New Class: An Analysis of the Communist System.* New York: Harcourt Brace Jovanovich.

Ferge, Zsuzsa 1979 *A Society in the Making.* New York: M. E. Sharpe.

Fourier, Charles 1971 *Harmonian Man: Selected Writings of Charles Fourier,* Mark Poster, ed.; Susan Hanson, trans. Garden City, N.Y.: Doubleday.

Giddens, Anthony 1973 *The Class Structure of the Advanced Societies.* London: Hutchinson.

Goldthorpe, John H. 1966 "Social Stratification in Industrial Society." In Reinhard Bendix and Seymour Martin Lipset, eds., *Class, Status, and Power.* New York: Free Press.

Gray, Alexander 1963 *The Socialist Tradition: Moses to Lenin.* London: Longmans.

Griffiths, D. F. 1924 *What Is Socialism? A Symposium.* London: Richards.

Hare, P., H. Radice, and Nigel Swain 1981 *Hungary: A Decade of Economic Reform.* London: Allen and Unwin.

Harman, Chris 1983 *Class Struggles in Eastern Europe, 1945–1983.* London: Pluto Press.

Hollander, Paul 1983 *The Many Faces of Socialism.* New Brunswick, N.J.: Transaction Books.

Inkeles, Alex 1966 "Social Stratification and Mobility in the Soviet Union." In Reinhard Bendix and Seymour Martin Lipset, eds., *Class, Status, and Power.* New York: Free Press.

Kelley, Jonathan, and Herbert S. Klein 1986 "Revolution and the Rebirth of Inequality: Stratification in Post-Revolutionary Society." In Jack A. Goldstone, ed., *Revolutions.* San Diego: Harcourt Brace Jovanovich.

Kolakowski, Leszek 1978 *Main Currents of Marxism,* 3 vols., P. S. Falla, trans. Oxford: Oxford University Press.

Konrád, György, and Iván Szelényi 1979 *The Intellectuals on the Road to Class Power,* Andrew Arato and Richard E. Allen, trans. New York: Harcourt Brace Jovanovich.

Kornai, János 1986 *Contradictions and Dilemmas: Studies on the Socialist Economy and Society,* I. Lukacs, J. Parti, B. McLean, and G. Hajdú, trans. Cambridge, Mass.: MIT Press.

Laidler, Harry W. 1968 *History of Socialism.* New York: Crowell.

Lane, David 1976 *The Socialist Industrial State: Towards a Political Sociology of State Socialism.* London: Allen and Unwin.

Lenin, V. I. 1971 *Selected Works.* New York: International Publishers.

Leogrande, William 1981 "Republic of Cuba." In Bogdan Szajkowski, ed., *Marxist Governments,* vol. 2. New York: St. Martin's.

Lewis, Paul G. 1979 "Potential Sources of Opposition in the East European Peasantry." In Rudolf L. Tökés, ed., *Opposition in Eastern Europe.* Baltimore: Johns Hopkins University Press.

Lichtheim, George 1969 *The Origins of Socialism.* New York: Praeger.

Mao Zedong 1971 *Selected Readings from the Works of Mao Tsetung.* Peking: Foreign Languages Press.

Marx, Karl, and Frederick Engels 1968 *Selected Works.* Moscow: Progress Publishers.

Matthews, Mervyn 1972 *Class and Society in Soviet Russia.* New York: Walker.

Morris, William 1970 *News from Nowhere.* London: Routledge and Kegan Paul.

Nee, Victor 1989 "A Theory of Market Transition: From Redistribution to Markets in State Socialism." *American Sociological Review* 54:663–681.

Nove, Alec 1983a "The Class Nature of the Soviet Union Revisited." *Soviet Studies* 3:298–312.

———— 1983b *The Economics of Feasible Socialism.* London: Allen and Unwin.

———— 1989 *An Economic History of the USSR,* 2nd ed. Harmondsworth, England: Penguin.

Nuti, Domenico Mario 1981 "Socialism on Earth." *Cambridge Journal of Economics* 5 (December):391–403.

Ossowski, Stanislaw 1963 *Class Structure in the Social Consciousness.* London: Routledge and Kegan Paul.

Parkin, Frank 1971 *Class Inequality and Political Order.* New York: Praeger.

Pravda, Alex 1979 "Industrial Workers: Patterns of Dissent, Opposition, and Accommodation." In Rudolf L. Tökés, ed., *Opposition in Eastern Europe*. Baltimore: Johns Hopkins University Press.

Proudhon, Pierre Joseph 1966 *What Is Property? An Inquiry into the Principle of Right and of Government*, B.R. Tucker, trans. New York: H. Fertig.

Ross, Lloyd 1935 *William Lane and the Australian Labor Movement*. Sydney: The Forward Press.

Rueschemeyer, Marilyn, and Szonja Szelényi 1989 "Socialist Transformation and Gender Inequality: Women in the GDR and Hungary." In David Childs, Thomas A. Baylis, and Marilyn Rueschemeyer, eds., *East Germany in Comparative Perspective*. London: Routledge.

Saint-Simon, Claude H. 1964 *Social Organization, The Science of Man, and Other Writings*, Felix M. H. Markham, ed. and trans. London: Harper and Row.

Simkus, Albert A., and Rudolf Andorka 1982 "Inequalities in Educational Attainment in Hungary, 1923–1973." *American Sociological Review* 47:740–751.

Sirc, Ljubo 1979 *The Yugoslav Economy Under Self-Management*. London: Macmillan.

Stark, David 1986 "Rethinking Internal Labor Markets: New Insights from a Comparative Perspective." *American Sociological Review* 51:492–504.

Starr, Richard F. 1988 *Communist Regimes in Eastern Europe*, 5th ed. Stanford, Calif.: Hoover Institution.

Sweezy, Paul M. 1983 "Socialism." In Tom Bottomore, ed., *A Dictionary of Marxist Thought*. Cambridge, Mass.: Harvard University Press.

Szelényi, Iván 1976 "The Housing System and Social Structure in Hungary." In Bernard Lewis Faber, ed., *The Social Structure of Eastern Europe*. New York: Praeger.

—— 1989 "Eastern Europe in an Epoch of Transition: Toward a Socialist Mixed Economy?" In Victor Nee and David Stark, eds., *Remaking the Economic Institutions of Socialism*. Stanford, Calif.: Stanford University Press.

Szelényi, Szonja 1987 "Social Inequality and Party Membership: Patterns of Recruitment into the Hungarian Socialist Workers' Party." *American Sociological Review* 52 (October):559–573.

Walder, Andrew G. 1986 *Communist Neo-Traditionalism: Work and Authority in Chinese Industry*. Berkeley: University of California Press.

—— 1989 "Social Change in Post-Revolutionary China." *American Review of Sociology* 15:405–424.

SZONJA SZELÉNYI

SOCIALIZATION Socialization has had a diversity of meanings in the social sciences, partly because a number of disciplines claim it as a central process. In its most common and general usage, socialization refers to the process of interaction through which an individual (a novice) acquires the norms, values, beliefs, attitudes, and language characteristics of his or her group. In the course of acquiring these cultural elements, the individual self and personality are created and shaped. Socialization, therefore, addresses two important problems in social life: the problem of societal continuity from one generation to the next, and the problem of human development.

Different disciplines, however, have emphasized different aspects of this process. Anthropologists tend to view socialization primarily as cultural transmission from one generation to the next, sometimes substituting the term "enculturation" for socialization (Herskovits 1948). Anthropological interest in socialization or "enculturation" coincides with the emergence of the "culture and personality" orientation in the late 1920s and 1930s. During this period, the works of Margaret Mead (1928), Ruth Benedict (1934), and Bronislaw Malinowski (1927) focused on cultural practices affecting child rearing, value transmission, and personality development and helped shape the anthropological approach to socialization. Much of the work in the culture and personality field was influenced by psychoanalytic theory.

Psychologists have been less likely to emphasize the transmission of culture and more likely to emphasize various aspects of the individual's development (see Goslin 1969). There is considerable diversity within psychology regarding the aspect of socialization studied. For developmental psychologists, particularly those influenced by Piaget (1926), socialization is largely a matter of cognitive development, which is typically viewed as a combination of social influence and maturation. For behavioral psychologists, socialization is synonymous with learning patterns of behavior. For clinical psychologists and personality theorists, socialization is viewed as the establishment of character traits usually within the context of early childhood experiences. The subfield of child development is most closely associated with the topic of socialization within psychology, where socialization is largely equated with child rearing (see Clausen 1968 for a historical overview of socialization in these disciplines).

Political science has also shown some interest in socialization, but in a much more limited sense. Its interests have not gone much beyond political socialization—that is, the process by which political attitudes and orientations are formed. However, a different and more esoteric usage of the term occasionally appears in this literature: socialization as "collectivization," that is, the transformation of capitalism to socialism and/or communism.

Within sociology there have been two main orientations to socialization. One views socialization primarily as the learning of social roles. From this perspective, individuals become integrated members of society by learning and internalizing the relevant roles and statuses of the groups to which they belong (Brim 1966). This view has been present in some form from the beginnings of sociology as a discipline but has been most closely associated with structural-functionalist perspectives (Clausen 1968).

The other, and more prevalent, sociological orientation views socialization mainly as self-concept formation. The development of self and identity in the context of intimate and reciprocal interaction is considered to be the core of socialization. This view of socialization is closely associated with the symbolic interactionist perspective—a synthesis of various strands of pragmatism, behaviorism, and idealism that emerged in the 1920s and 1930s in the writings of a number of scholars at the University of Chicago, especially George H. Mead (1934). In Mead's writings, the self is a reflexive, thoroughly social phenomenon that develops through language or symbolic interaction. Through role-taking the individual is able to view himself or herself from the perspective of another. This becomes the basis for selfhood and also for the interpenetration of self and society. Mead and other symbolic interactionists have argued that self and society are two sides of the same coin. The basis for this assertion is that the contents of self-conceptions (e.g., identities) reflect those aspects of the social process with which the individual is involved, through the internalization of role identities, values, and meanings. This internalization, in turn, reproduces society. From the interactionist perspective, both self and society depend on the same process of social interaction whereby "realities" are created and constantly negotiated (Gecas 1982, 1986).

For contemporary interactionists as well, socialization is distinguished from other types of learning and other forms of social influence by its relevance for self-conceptions—that is, for our thoughts and feelings about ourselves. As such, socialization is not merely the process of learning rules or norms or behavior patterns. It is learning these things only to the extent that they become part of the way in which we think of ourselves. The mark of successful socialization is the transformation of social control into self-control. This is largely accomplished through the development of identities, the various labels and characteristics attributed to the self. Commitment to identities (such as son, mother, professor, honest person) is a source of motivation for individuals to act in accordance with the values and norms implied by these identities (Foote 1951; Stryker 1980; Gecas 1986). The focus on identity also emphasizes the membership component of socialization: To be socialized is to belong, via idealification with one's group.

Socialization as identity formation occurs through a number of more specific processes associated with self-concept development: reflected appraisals, social comparisons, self-attributions, and identification (see Gecas 1982, 1986 and Rosenberg 1979 for discussions of these processes). Reflected appraisals, based on Cooley's (1902) "looking-glass self" metaphor, refers to our perceptions of how others see us and evaluate us. To some extent we come to see ourselves as we think others (particularly significant others) see us (see Shrauger and Schoeneman [1979] for a review and assessment of the research on this proposition). We also develop conceptions of ourselves with regard to specific attributes by comparing ourselves to others (social comparisons) and by making self-inferences from observing our own actions and their consequences (self-attributions). Particularly important to socialization as identity formation is the process of identification. Initially used by Sigmund Freud, it refers to the child's emotional attachment to the parent and desire to be like the parent, as a consequence of which the child internalizes and adopts the parent's values, beliefs, and other characteristics. Among other things, through identification with the parent the child becomes more receptive to parental influence.

Identification is also used to refer to the imputation or ascription of identities. Here the focus is on the establishment of identities in social interaction and is an important aspect of defining situations and constructing realities. This also has important socializing consequences, as much of the literature on labeling, stereotyping and expectancy effects attests (see Jones 1977).

CONTENT AND CONTEXTS OF SOCIALIZATION

Much of the research on socialization has been concerned with identifying what aspects of the socializee's development are affected by which agents and contexts of socialization and through what processes. Most of the focus has been on the family context, where the initial or *primary* socialization of the individual takes place. Studies of childrearing in "normal" as well as "abnormal" situations (e.g., institutionalized children, "closet children," "feral children") have identified a number of conditions that must be present for primary socialization to take place—that is, for the child to become a person. These include the use of symbolic interaction (language) in the context of an intimate, nurturant relationship between an adult and a child. These conditions are necessary for the initial sense of self to emerge and for normal cognitive development and even physical development to take place. The claim that the family (in some form) is a universal feature of human societies is based in large part on this important socialization function (Weigert and Thomas 1971).

Parental support continues to be important in the socialization of offspring through childhood, adolescence, and beyond. It is one of the most robust variables in the literature on child rearing. Parental support has been found to be positively related to the child's cognitive development, moral behavior, conformity to adult standards, self-esteem, academic achievement, and social competence (see Rollins and Thomas 1979; Peterson and Rollins 1987; and Thomas et al. 1974 for reviews). Conversely, lack of parental support is associated with negative socialization outcomes for children and adolescents: low self-esteem, delinquency, deviance, drug use, and various other problem behaviors.

Parental control is almost as important as support in the socialization literature. "Control" refers to the degree and manner in which parents attempt to place constraints on the child's behavior. Other terms used for this dimension of parenting are punishment, discipline, restrictiveness, permissiveness, protectiveness, supervision, strictness, and monitoring. Parental control is a more complicated variable than is parental support. It is necessary to distinguish different types or styles of control because they frequently have opposite socialization consequences. An important distinction is between "authoritarian" and "authoritative" control (Baumrind 1978) or "coercion" and "induction" (Rollins and Thomas 1979). Authoritarian or coercive control (i.e., control based on force, threat, or physical punishment) is associated with negative or unfavorable socialization outcomes, whereas authoritative or inductive control (i.e., control based on reason and explanation) has positive outcomes.

The most powerful models of parental influence in the socialization of children are those that combine the dimensions of support and control.

Parents are most effective as agents of socialization when they express a high level of support and exercise inductive control. Under these conditions, children are most likely to identify with their parents, internalize parental values and expectations, use parents as their models, and become receptive to parental influence attempts. Conversely, low parental support combined with reliance on coercive control are associated with unfavorable socialization outcomes (for reviews of this literature see Peterson and Rollins 1987; Maccoby and Martin 1983; Rollins and Thomas 1979).

Parental support and control cover much of the ground in the literature on child rearing, but not all of it. Other important socialization variables are extent of parental involvement with the child (e.g., time spent); extent to which political or religious beliefs and value systems are taught to the child by the parent; and various characteristics of the parent, such as patience, tolerance, honesty, integrity, competence, and age, as well as the sex of the parent and of the child. Many factors affect the process and outcomes within family socialization.

Much of the socialization that takes place in the family involves learning appropriate role behavior associated with the various family positions. For the child, the most significant of these are sex and age roles. Through processes of reinforcement from parents and others, through identification with various role models, and through parental admonitions and instructions, the child is socialized into the behavioral expectations associated with these roles. Of the two, sex roles have received most of the research attention on role-learning in the family (see Maccoby and Jacklin 1974 and Block 1983 for reviews). This research suggests that sex-role socialization is extensive (usually starting at birth with differential treatment of male and female infants), pervasive (by various agents and contexts of socialization), and consequential for a wide range of other individual and social outcomes. A prominent theme in much of the contemporary research on sex-role socialization is that the differential treatment of boys and girls that emphasizes "masculine" characteristics for boys and "feminine" characteristics for girls is detrimental to the development of both girls and boys and to the relationship between the sexes (see Bem 1974 on the virtues of androgyny). This research reflects the ethos of equality between the sexes evident in most modern societies.

Most studies of socialization within the family assume a unidirectional influence, from parent to child. Parents are typically viewed as agents of socialization (part of the job description of "parent") and children as objects of socialization, and given the disparities in power, status, and competence between parent and child, it is justifiably assumed that the direction of influence is mainly from parent to child. However, it is also increasingly evident that socialization is a reciprocal process of influence, with children influencing parents as well as the reverse. Over the past few decades, the thinking with regard to socialization processes has shifted from unidirectional to bidirectional and reciprocal models (Peterson and Rollins 1987; Gecas 1981). For example, in considering the association between parental punishment and a child's deviant behavior, it can be argued that the child's behavior is both a consequence and a cause of the parental behavior. Socialization is increasingly viewed as reciprocal, even though the degree of influence is typically not equal.

Besides parents and other adult kin, siblings serve as agents of socialization within the family context. For that matter, as family size increases, more of the socialization of the younger children is taken on by their older siblings, either by default or because parents delegate this responsibility to the older children. Some have argued that this puts younger children in large families at a disadvantage (with regard to cognitive development), since they have relatively less contact with the most competent and committed family members, the parents (Zajonc 1976). However, these findings, based mostly on cross-sectional data, have not gone unchallenged (Galbraith 1982).

An increasingly pervasive agent of socialization within contemporary families is television. Children spend more time watching television than at any other activity except school and sleep (Bronfenbrenner 1970). The purpose of most television programs that children watch is typically not to socialize or educate children, but to entertain and to sell products. However, a good deal of unintended socialization is likely to occur, from shaping conceptions of reality (e.g., sex roles) to styles of behavior and tastes. In general, television is perceived as having a negative influence on children (with the exception of a few educational programs on public television). Much of the concern has focused on the extensive violence and aggression in television programs. Bandura et al.'s (1963) work on modeling has persuasively shown that exposure to aggressive behavior tends to increase aggression in the viewer. Along with the undesirable consequences for child socialization of the content of television programs, Bronfenbrenner (1970) observes that television is detrimental to child development with regard to the behavior it prevents—that is, the human interaction forgone in the course of being a passive viewer. The role of television as an agent of socialization in families seems to be increasing by default, as the amount of contact between parents and their children decreases. Various social forces (especially proportion of working mothers, dual-career families, and professionalization of child care) have operated to decrease the amount of parent/child interaction and hence the parent's role as a socializing agent. This vacuum, Bronfenbrenner (1970) argues, has been increasingly filled by the child's involvement with television and with peers. For children in American society, television, peer group, and school are increasingly important agents of socialization.

Like the family, the school is an institution whose mandate is to socialize children. The school's mission, however, is more narrowly defined than is that of the family and is primarily concerned with the formal instruction of children and the development of their cognitive skills. In this sense, the school context is less involved in *primary* socialization (i.e., the development of basic values, beliefs, motivations, and conceptions of self) and more involved in *secondary* socialization (i.e., the development of knowledge and skills). This is not a very precise distinction,

however. In the course of the socialization experienced in the school, things other than skills and knowledge are also learned, such as norms, values, and attitudes, and various aspects of the child's personality and self-concept are affected. Much more is typically learned in school than what is explicitly taught.

Many of the activities associated with the school (specifically within the classroom) have implications for the child's self-concept. For example, one of the most important activities involves evaluation of the student's performance by the teacher. Success in various evaluated activities, based on one's own efforts, is good for self-esteem and builds confidence in one's abilities. But failure is not, and *public* failure is worse. The school provides numerous opportunities to the child for public failure as well as for public success. One of the consequences of performance evaluations may be the categorization or "labeling" of students, by teachers as well as others, as "smart," "dumb," "slow learner," "underachiever," etc. Negative as well as positive labels affect the way in which others respond to the person, and through their responses reinforce and shape the person in the labeled direction. This process is called "expectancy effects" (Jones 1977) or "self-fulfilling prophecy" (Merton 1957). Rosenthal and Jacobson (1968) found that teachers' expectations of students, even when based on erroneous information, had a significant effect on how these students developed over the course of the school year: When the teacher was led to believe that a student in her class would be a "slow learner," the student was more likely to do poorly in class. Labeling and expectancy effects occur in most socialization contexts and have important consequences for self-concept development.

But students, like other socializees, are not passive recipients of the pressures they experience. Covington and Beery (1976) propose that two fundamentally different motivation patterns emerge in schools as a result of these pressures: one is oriented toward striving for success; the other is oriented toward avoiding failure. Failure-avoiding strategies (such as nonparticipation, withdrawal, procrastination, and putting off work assignments until too late) are attempts to disassociate one's performance from one's ability and worth. Failure, then, can be attributed to lack of effort or to various external circumstances (less damaging attributions for self) and not to one's lack of ability (a more damaging attribution). This is a form of role-distancing, the separation of self from the behavior required of a role occupant. It is also an obstacle to school achievement. As Covington and Beery (1976) point out, failure-avoiding strategies are self-defeating: In their attempts to avoid the feelings of failure, these students increase the probability of actual failure. For some students this is one of the unintended and undesirable consequences of classroom socialization. In the process of socializing students toward achievement and mastery (desirable socialization outcomes), pressures are generated that may result in undesirable adaptations.

The third most important context for the socialization of children, especially adolescents, is the peer group. In terms of structure and function, the peer group is a very different context of socialization from family and school. Unlike the previous two contexts, it is not the "job" of peers to socialize each other, even though a great deal of childhood socialization occurs in this context— some of it in reaction against the socialization experienced in family and school.

There are several important features of the peer group as a context of socialization. Most important, it is a *voluntary* association. For most children, it is their first. This permits greater freedom of choice regarding associations in the group. A second important feature is that association is between status equals. Consequently, interaction is more likely to be based on egalitarian norms. Status distinctions do emerge, of course, but are more likely to be based on achievement and negotiation. But the basic relationship within peer groups is not hierarchical; rather it is a friendship bond based on equality, mutual tolerance, and concern. Third, the peer group is an arena for the exercise of independence from adult control. As such, it is often the context for the development of values, norms, and behavior in opposition to those of adults (such as the subcul-

tures described by Coleman 1961 and in much of the literature on juvenile delinquency). Fourth, children's peer groups (in contemporary American society at least) are typically segregated by sex. An important socialization consequence of intensive association with same-sex peers and involvement in sex-typed activities is that it strongly reinforces identification and belongingness with members of the same sex. Not only sex-role identity but also much of the sexual socialization during childhood occurs in the context of peer rather than parent-child associations (Fine 1987). Peers provide an alternate reference group for children as well as an alternate source of self-esteem and identity. For these reasons, attachment to peers may be even stronger than attachment to family, especially for adolescents.

The socialization experienced by adults generally falls in the category of secondary socialization, building on the socialization experiences of childhood. Much of this is role-specific (Brim 1968)—that is, learning the knowledge and skills required for the performance of specific adult roles (e.g., occupation, marriage, parenthood). As individuals become committed to the roles they play, they come to identify themselves and think of themselves in terms of these role identities (Stryker 1980).

Since work is a dominant activity and setting for most adult men and women in our society, much of adult socialization involves either preparation for an occupation or career (which usually takes place within specialized schools or training programs—e.g., law school, medical school, college), or on-the-job training. The work setting itself can have a substantial socializing effect on workers, affecting more than just their knowledge and skills. Kohn and Schooler (1983) have shown how certain occupational conditions affect the development of the worker's values and personality. Specifically, they found that work that is routine, closely supervised, and relatively uncomplicated gives rise to values of conformity in workers, whereas work that is complex and encourages self-direction increases the value workers place on independence and autonomy. Kanter (1977) also found that the nature of work relations, particularly the structure of opportunity on the job, affects workers' attitudes and behaviors as a consequence of their adaptations to the work situation. Workers' adaptations to their work situations do not necessarily imply commitment to the job or self-investment in terms of the occupational role. On the contrary, a prevalent theme in much of the sociological literature on work and workers (especially from a Marxist perspective) deals with the alienating consequences of work in capitalist societies.

Many other contexts have socializing consequences for adults: family, political and religious organizations, recreational settings, and various voluntary associations. The socialization that takes place within these contexts can be considered "developmental" (Wheeler 1966) because it builds on previous socialization and is a continuation and expansion of past socialization experiences. *Resocialization,* however, refers to socialization experiences representing a more radical change in the person. Resocialization contexts (e.g., mental hospitals, some prisons, reform schools, therapy groups, political indoctrination camps, religious conversion settings) have as their explicit goal the transformation of the individual. An important feature of resocialization is the replacement of one's previous set of beliefs, values, and (especially) conceptions of self with a new set grounded in the new group's ideology or worldview. This has been described as a process of death and rebirth of the self (Lifton 1963). Typically this is accomplished through intense small-group interaction, in which the physical and symbolic environments are highly controlled by the agents of socialization. It is an experience that usually involves considerable stress for the socializee (see Gecas 1981 for an analysis and comparison of contexts of socialization).

SOCIALIZATION OVER THE LIFE COURSE

Socialization is a lifelong process of change. Even though the socialization experienced in the family is in some ways the most consequential, there are important socializing experiences that individuals typically have throughout their lives. A central theme in the life course literature is the degree of continuity and consistency in personality as the individual moves through the life course (Mortimer and Simmons 1978). Positions on this issue range from the claim that personality is largely shaped during early childhood (most likely held by those with a psychoanalytic orientation) to the position that people are thoroughly malleable, changing across situations and throughout their lives (characteristic of situational orientations to personality and behavior). The majority appear to argue for an intermediate position, maintaining that the "core" personality or self-conception develops in early socialization experiences, while various other characteristics are added to self through the acquisition of new roles, identities, and socializing experiences (Brim 1966, 1968; Clausen 1986). The previous discussion suggests how contexts of socialization, which are typically age-graded, can contribute to the development of different aspects of individuals associated with different ages and stages of life.

Some of the important socializing experiences and changes individuals undergo are keyed to developmental or maturational considerations: The concerns and capabilities of children tend to be different from those of adolescents; young adults from those in middle age and from those in old age. Erikson's (1959) developmental scheme, building on the Freudian theory of psychosexual development in childhood, has emphasized the different developmental tasks associated with different stages of life. The challenges or developmental tasks proposed by Erikson are: (1) trust vs. mistrust; (2) autonomy vs. shame; (3) initiative vs. guilt; (4) industry vs. inferiority; (5) identity vs. identity confusion; (6) intimacy vs. isolation; (7) generativity vs. self-absorption; and (8) integrity vs. despair. Most of the socialization research guided by Erikson's formulations has focused on stage 5, adolescence, and the developmental task highlighting identity concerns. Adolescence, in our society, has long been considered a time when self-concept concerns increase in prominence. Physiological changes and changes in social circumstances (e.g., high school, dating, career considerations) contribute to an increase in self-awareness and concern about how one is viewed by others. Research by developmental psychologists has generally found that good family relations (i.e., those high in parental support, communication, involvement, and inductive control) facilitate the development of ego identity in adolescence (see Gecas and Seff 1990, for a review). By adolescence, however, the influence of parents is substantially less than it was during childhood. Increasingly other agents and contexts of socialization become important to the adolescent: peers, school, friends, coaches, etc. The adolescent's struggles with identity need to be worked out in a number of competing arenas.

Identity concerns are not limited to adolescence, of course. If we consider socialization to be a process of self-concept formation and a lifelong process, then matters of identity are important at various stages of the individual's development. Identity concerns are most likely to be accentuated during periods of transition, particularly those involving entrance into or exit from social statuses and roles. Some of these role transitions are institutionalized and highly ritualized. The rites of passage in various cultures marking the transition from childhood to adulthood can be quite elaborate and dramatic. Sometimes this involves acquiring a new name as well as a new status (as in many of the Plains Indian cultures). In contemporary Western societies, these status passages may be less dramatic but still quite consequential for the person: getting a driver's license; high-school graduation; marriage; divorce; first full-time job; retirement; widowhood. In general, each major transition initiates a new socializing experience or situation, having implications for the individual's self-concept.

Some stage theorists have focused on transitions in adulthood (Levinson 1978) and examined the circumstances that can lead to a "midlife crisis," an acute reexamination of self. But the middle years of life are still relatively neglected by life-course scholars, compared to studies of childhood, adolescence, and (increasingly) old age.

In considering socialization over the life cycle,

we need to take history and culture into account. Not just the content of socialization during various "stages" of life, but also the stages themselves vary by culture and historical context. For example, adolescence as an identifiable stage of life is a relatively recent historical emergent in Western societies, closely associated with the extension of formal education to high school (Gecas and Seff 1990). Even childhood, as Aries (1960) amply documents, is not universally considered as a distinct stage of life. The modern conception of childhood as an identifiably distinct stage emerged during the European Renaissance, partly as a consequence of the emergence of parochial schools. More recently, Elder (1974) has shown a historical consciousness in his life-course analyses, by examining how specific historical events (e.g., the Great Depression, World War II) differentially affected two cohorts of children and their families. Whether there are eight stages of life, or four stages, or seven stages (as Shakespeare observed) depends on the society and on one's analytical purposes.

CONTEMPORARY ISSUES AND THEMES IN SOCIALIZATION RESEARCH

In the past, the concept of socialization has been heavily imbued with the notion of adaptation and conformity of the individual to societal expectations (Zigler and Seitz 1978). The past few decades, however, have seen a marked shift to a more active view of the self, to an emphasis on self-socialization. Renewed interest in the self-concept as a source of motivation (Gecas 1986) and as an agent in its environment has contributed to this shift, as has the increased interest in adult socialization (Mortimer and Simmons 1978; Bush and Simmons 1981). But even in studies of parent-child interaction, the child (even the infant) is increasingly viewed as an active partner in his or her socialization (Rheingold 1969). In short, the outcomes of socialization (whether these are conceptualized as values, self-conceptions, behavior patterns, or beliefs) are increasingly viewed as the products of reciprocal interactions between agent and socializee (itself a somewhat arbitrary distinction).

A concern with social structure and its effects on the process and outcomes of socialization is still the hallmark of the sociological orientation to socialization, from social class influences (see Gecas 1979) to the effects of family structure. Changes in family structure over the past few decades have increased interest in the effects of single-parent families, reconstituted families, and day care for child socialization. Rarely are these changes viewed as favorable for child socialization (Bronfenbrenner 1979). But the evidence is inconclusive on just how negative their consequences may be for child socialization. Given the increasing rate of social and cultural change in contemporary societies, it is clear that socialization of children and adults is becoming increasingly problematic.

(SEE ALSO: *Adulthood; Behaviorism; Gender; Moral Development; Parental Roles; Role Models; Sex Differences; Social Psychology*)

REFERENCES

Aries, Phillip 1960 *Centuries of Childhood: A Social History of Family Life.* New York: Random House.

Bandura, Albert, Dorothea Ross, and Sheila A. Ross 1963 "Imitation of Film-Mediated Aggressive Models." *Journal of Abnormal and Social Psychology* 66:3–11.

Baumrind, Diana 1978 "Parental Disciplinary Patterns and Social Competence in Children." *Youth and Society* 9:239–276.

Bem, Sandra L. 1974 "The Measurement of Psychological Androgyny." *Journal of Consulting and Clinical Psychology* 42:155–162.

Benedict, Ruth 1934 *Patterns of Culture.* Boston: Houghton Mifflin.

Block, Jean H. 1983 "Differential Premises Arising from Differential Socialization of the Sexes: Some Conjectures." *Child Development* 54:1335–1354.

Brim, Orville G., Jr. 1966 "Socialization Through the Life Cycle." In O. G. Brim, Jr., and S. Wheeler, eds., *Socialization After Childhood: Two Essays.* New York: Wiley.

——— 1968 "Adult Socialization." In J. A. Clausen, ed., *Socialization and Society.* Boston: Little, Brown.

Bronfenbrenner, Urie 1970 *Two Worlds of Childhood: U.S. and U.S.S.R.* New York: Russell Sage Foundation.

——— 1979 *The Ecology of Human Development: Experiments by Nature and Design.* Cambridge, Mass.: Harvard University Press.

Bush, Diane M., and Roberta G. Simmons 1981 "Socialization Processes over the Life Course." In M. Rosenberg and R. H. Turner, eds., *Social Psychology: Sociological Perspectives.* New York: Basic Books.

Clausen, John A. 1968. "A Historical and Comparative View of Socialization Theory and Research." In J. A. Clausen, ed., *Socialization and Society.* Boston: Little, Brown.

——— 1986 *The Life Course: A Sociological Perspective.* Englewood Cliffs, N.J.: Prentice-Hall.

Coleman, James S. 1961 *The Adolescent Society.* New York: Free Press.

Cooley, Charles H. (1902) 1964 *Human Nature and the Social Order.* New York: Scribners.

Covington, Martin V., and Richard G. Beery 1976 *Self-Worth and School Learning.* New York: Holt, Rinehart, and Winston.

Elder, Glen H., Jr. 1974 *Children of the Great Depression.* Chicago: University of Chicago Press.

Erikson, Erik H. 1959 *Identity and the Life Cycle.* New York: International Universities Press.

Fine, Gary A. 1987 *With the Boys: Little League Baseball and Preadolescent Culture.* Chicago: University of Chicago Press.

Foote, Nelson N. 1951 "Identification as the Basis for a Theory of Motivation." *American Sociological Review* 16:14–21.

Galbraith, Robert C. 1982 "Sibling Spacing and Intellectual Development: A Closer Look at the Confluence Models." *Development Psychology* 18:151–173.

Gecas, Viktor 1979 "The influence of social class on socialization." In W. R. Burr, R. Hill, F. I. Nye, and I. L. Reiss, eds., *Contemporary Theories About the Family*, Vol. 1. New York: Free Press.

——— 1981 "Contexts of Socialization." In M. Rosenberg and R. H. Turner, eds., *Social Psychology: Sociological Perspectives.* New York: Basic Books.

——— 1982 "The Self-Concept." In R. H. Turner and J. F. Short, Jr., eds., *Annual Review of Sociology*, Vol. 8. Palo Alto, Calif.: Annual Reviews.

——— 1986 "The Motivational Significance of Self-Concept for Socialization Theory." In E. J. Lawler, ed., *Advances in Group Processes,* vol. 3. Greenwich, CT: JAI Press.

———, and Monica Seff 1990 "Families and adolescents: 1980s Decade Review." *Journal of Marriage and the Family* 52:941–958.

Goslin, David A. 1969 *Handbook of Socialization Theory and Research.* Chicago: Rand McNally.

Herskovits, Melville J. 1948 *Man and His Works: The Science of Cultural Anthropology.* New York: Alfred A. Knopf.

Jones, R. A. 1977 *Self-Fulfilling Prophecies: Social Psychological and Physiological Effects of Expectancies.* New York: Wiley.

Kanter, Rosabeth M. 1977 *Men and Women of the Corporation.* New York: Basic Books.

Kohn, Melvin L., and Carmi Schooler 1983 *Work and Personality: An Inquiry into the Impact of Social Stratification.* Norwood, N.J.: Ablex.

Levinson, Daniel J. 1978 *The Seasons of a Man's Life.* New York: Alfred A. Knopf.

Lifton, Robert J. 1963 *Thought Reform and the Psychology of Totalism: A Study of "Brainwashing" in China.* New York: W. W. Norton.

Maccoby, Eleanor E., and Carol N. Jacklin 1974 *The Psychology of Sex Differences.* Stanford, Calif.: Stanford University Press.

Maccoby, Eleanor E., and John A. Martin 1983 "Socialization in the Context of the family: Parent-Child Interaction." In P. H. Mussen, ed., *Handbook of Child Psychology,* vol. 4. New York: Wiley.

Malinowski, Bronislaw (1927) 1953 *Sex and Repression in Savage Society.* London: Routledge.

Mead, George H. 1934 *Mind, Self, and Society.* Chicago: University of Chicago Press.

Mead, Margaret 1928 *Coming of Age in Samoa.* New York: William Morrow.

Merton, Robert K. 1957 *Social Theory and Social Structure.* New York: Free Press.

Mortimer, Jeylan T., and Roberta G. Simmons 1978 "Adult Socialization." In R. H. Turner, J. Coleman, and R. C. Fox, eds., *Annual Review of Sociology,* vol. 4. Palo Alto, Calif.: Annual Reviews.

Peterson, Gary W., and Boyd C. Rollins 1987 "Parent-Child Socialization: A Review of Research and Applications of Symbolic Interaction Concepts." In M. B. Sussman and S. K. Steinmetz, eds., *Handbook of Marriage and the Family.* New York: Plenum Press.

Piaget, Jean 1926 *The Language and Thought of the Child.* London: Kegan Paul.

Rheingold, Harriet L. 1969 "The Social and Socializing Infant." In D. A. Goslin, ed., *Handbook of Socialization Theory and Research.* Chicago: Rand McNally.

Rollins, Boyd C., and Darwin L. Thomas 1979 "Parental Support, Power, and Control Techniques in the Socialization of Children." In W. R. Burr, R. Hill, F. I. Nye, and I. L. Reiss, eds., *Contemporary Theories About the Family,* vol. 1. New York: Free Press.

Rosenberg, Morris 1979 *Conceiving the Self.* New York: Basic Books.

Rosenthal, Robert, and L. Jacobson 1968 *Pygmalion in the Classroom.* New York: Holt, Rinehart, and Winston.

Shrauger, J. S., and T. J. Schoeneman 1979 "Symbolic Interactionist View of Self-Concept: Through the Looking-glass Darkly." *Psychological Bulletin* 86: 549–573.

Stryker, Sheldon 1980 *Symbolic Interactionism: A Social Structural Version.* Menlo Park, Calif.: Benjamin/Cummings.

Thomas, Darwin L., Viktor Gecas, Andrew Weigert, and Elizabeth Rooney 1974 *Family Socialization and the Adolescent.* Lexington, Mass.: D. C. Heath.

Weigert, Andrew J., and Darwin L. Thomas 1971 "Family as a Conditional Universal." *Journal of Marriage and the Family* 33:188–196.

Wheeler, Stanton 1966 "The Structure of Formally Organized Socialization Settings." In O. G. Brim, Jr., and S. Wheeler, eds., *Socialization After Childhood: Two Essays.* New York: Wiley.

Zajonc, Robert B. 1976 "Family Configuration and Intelligence." *Science* 192:227–236.

Zigler, Edward, and Victoria Seitz 1978 "Changing Trends in Socialization Theory and Research." *American Behavioral Scientist* 21:731–756.

VIKTOR GECAS

SOCIAL MOBILITY Social mobility has been defined as movement through "social space" from one status category (the origin) to another status category (the destination). In general, *vertical mobility* refers to individual or group movement upward or downward in the social hierarchy, but the possibility of downward mobility is seldom considered. *Horizontal mobility* involves moving from one social status to another of about equal rank. Other nonvertical forms of mobility have been discussed, most often in terms of movement across social categories not typically defined as hierarchical, such as religion, political party affiliation, age, citizenship, and so forth (Schnore 1961; Sorokin 1927).

Social mobility, then, is reflected as changes in relative social standing or status. Social status has been defined as one's community standing (e.g., one's position of power or influence), organizational membership, kinship relations, property ownership, education, and wealth or income, among other criteria. Yet empirical studies of social mobility have focused almost entirely on occupational positions as the sole indicator of social status. And while occupations differ in terms of prestige, income, influence, access to valued resources, and relationship to the mode of production, studies have overwhelmingly relied on occupational prestige scores to measure occupational achievement. Supporters of this method argue that in an industrial-urban society, occupational prestige is the best singular indicator of social status. It is a particularly useful measure in that it is linked to economic status and educational background and is, therefore, correlated with the "pattern of living" of an individual. In addition, several studies have shown a stable relationship between occupation and prestige that is attached to the position but is occupied by the individual (Treiman 1977). Occupations have also been shown to be strongly related to a class concept (Wright et al. 1982).

Those who argue against such a unidimensional perspective of social status point out that respondents asked to rate occupations consider a variety of factors, such as the level of information, or lack thereof, concerning the occupation, the occupation's relation to their own position (Goldthorpe and Hope 1974), the income of the occupation, and the typical sex of the occupation's incumbents (Bose 1973).

Most research on mobility has focused on *intergenerational mobility,* which refers to a change of social status from one generation to the next. The change is typically measured by comparing the son's occupation to his father's. *Intragenerational mobility,* on the other hand, typically refers to the vertical mobility experienced by an individual within his or her own lifetime, as through job promotions and other career advancements.

Although most work in the field has taken place in the post-World War II era, social mobility has been seen since Plato's time as providing efficiency and stability in state formation and maintenance. In his *Republic* (c. 380 B.C.) Plato described individuals as being of gold, silver, or bronze thread. While heredity of social status was expected, Plato argued that gold children of bronze parents should be promoted to their rightful place of leadership. Likewise, gold parents of bronze children need to recognize their children's limitations, for the ruin of the state was prophesied if it came to be led by men of bronze. In addition, Plato's student Aristotle, (c. 384–322 B.C.) discussed class formation and the logic of state rule by the middle class. Citizens among the "mean" were thought to counter the political ambitions of the two extremes.

Even Marx recognized the stabilizing effects of upward mobility for the ruling class. He believed that the high rates of mobility that characterize the United States were partly responsible for the lack of organized labor. A class that is self-recruiting will more readily develop class consciousness. On the other hand, high rates of upward mobility between classes acts as a safety valve, keeping down the pressure of the discontented lower class (Marx 1958).

LANDMARKS

Sorokin's classic work, *Social Mobility* (1927), is often considered the first modern treatise in the field. The basic outline of Sorokin's argument is that there are certain permanent and universal bases of occupational inequality: "At least two conditions seem to have been fundamental. . . . First, the importance of an occupation for the survival and existence of a group as a whole; second, the degree of intelligence necessary for a successful performance of an occupation" (pp. 100–101).

Social mobility is necessary to secure the allocation of talents to occupations. Without the lure of the power and privilege associated with social mobility, incompetent people are found in positions of importance, resulting in inefficiency and possible disruption. Like the sentiments voiced by Marx, Sorokin believed that social mobility provided motivation to members of the lower class and thus, "instead of becoming leaders of a revolution, they are turned into protectors of social order" (p. 533). Although Sorokin argued for the inevitability of social mobility, one of the underlying themes of his work is the lack of a linear progression. He saw no definite perpetual trend toward either an increase or a decrease of the intensity and generality of mobility.

In the early post–World War II period, a major concern of mobility studies was the determination of the rate of mobility of a society, community, or population. This concern stemmed from interest in the degree of "openness" referring to the fluidity of movement among social strata in societies, which was thought to be a measure of inequality. A society is characterized as open, fair, or equitable depending on how advantages are passed from one generation to the next. Early comparative research within this theme was supported and encouraged by the International Sociological Association, which sought comparative studies in Britain, Scandinavia, and the United States.

Since Sorokin's work, little theoretical advancement has been made to accompany the major breakthroughs in data collection and analysis. The first general population study concerning intergenerational social mobility was carried out by David Glass in 1949 (*Social Mobility in Britain*). Glass began a new trend in social mobility studies: a focus on social inequalities rather than on societal stability, as was seen in Plato, Marx, and Sorokin. The main findings from the analysis of movement from father's occupation to son's occupation was that Great Britain "exhibited a considerable amount of relatively short-range mobility coupled with a higher degree of rigidity and self-recruitment at the extremes, and in particular at the upper levels of the social structure where

there was the strongest tendency for sons to follow in their father's footsteps and enter broadly comparable occupations" (Heath 1981, p. 31). The line between manual and nonmanual labor has been seen as a barrier to long-range movement on the order of rags to riches or vice versa (see Westergaard and Resler 1975).

Only a decade after Glass's study in Great Britain, Lipset and Bendix (1959) set out to better understand mobility patterns in industrial societies through a secondary analysis of data available from nine industrialized societies: Denmark, France, Germany, Great Britain, Italy, Japan, Sweden, Switzerland, and the United States. By reassigning respondents to either manual or nonmanual occupational positions, they examined upward and downward mobility as a measure of the total vertical mobility between middle and working classes. Contrary to their expectations, Lipset and Bendix found no evidence that the United States was more open than the traditional societies of Europe. What they did find was that virtually all the nine countries exhibited similar, high rates of total vertical mobility.

The consequences that social mobility held for the individual and society became the theme that dominated this analysis. Additional work by Lipset (1960) was primarily concerned with the stability of American society. While he acknowledged the perspective of prior theorists who viewed social mobility as contributing to stability, Lipset placed most of his emphasis on the *destabilizing* processes of too much mobility. The source of this destabilizing effect is the problem of "status inconsistency." Lipset viewed stratification as a multidimensional system containing a number of different hierarchies based on status, class, and authority. From this perspective, one individual may be mobile on one dimension but not on another. For example, a person may acquire a high occupational position but encounter social ostracism because of his or her low social origins. On the other hand, an upper-class family may become economically impoverished but retain its high social position. Lipset saw this type of disjunction or inconsistency as a possible source of frustration; such frustration may predispose individuals to accept extremist politics.

A stimulating conclusion in terms of inspiring additional research was the "industrialization hypothesis" developed by Lipset and Zetterberg (1956). These researchers observed that during the nineteenth century, the proportion of the labor force in urban occupations increased while the proportion in agriculture decreased. This observation led to the hypothesis that the overall pattern of social mobility appears to be much the same in industrialized societies of various Western countries. Additionally, they felt that a threshold effect was operating; social mobility would become high once the level of industrialization and economic expansion reached a certain level. Lipset and Zetterberg predict that as societies industrialize, they require a set of standardized features from social institutions: smaller, nuclear, and socially mobile families, mass education, a pluralistic political structure, and social mobility based on meritocratic lines (Heath 1981). Many critics argue that the authors were providing support for the functional perspective of the American stratification system. Tests and elaborations of this hypothesis are further addressed below.

Perhaps the most influential and important work in the 1960s is Blau and Duncan's *The American Occupational Structure* (1967). In the tradition of Glass's *Social Mobility in Britain,* this work focused on the issue of status attainment and inequality. Blau and Duncan recognized the basis of the American stratification system as determined by the individual's position in the occupational structure. This structure is also seen as the connecting link between different social institutions and spheres of social life. The processes of intra- and intergenerational occupational mobility are reflected in the dynamics of the occupational structure. Blau and Duncan attempted to analyze social mobility by investigating the patterns of movement between occupations, the conditions that affect those movements, and their consequences. Focusing on allocation factors, such as education, they examined what influence different factors had on occupational achievement and how

these factors modify the effects of social origins on achievement. The basic question they addressed was how the status that individuals "achieve" is affected by the statuses "ascribed" to them earlier in life.

Expanding earlier work that focused on a simple dichotomy of manual and nonmanual workers, Blau and Duncan used seventeen occupational categories in examining movement from father's occupation to son's. The results of this analysis found that upward mobility was primarily the result of an expansion of opportunity in occupational categories of higher status and a contraction of opportunity in lower-level categories. In addition, fertility rates in occupations at the top of the hierarchy were lower than those at the bottom, creating occupational openings. The combination of these factors created a chain-reaction "pull" from the top and "push" from the bottom, which has been termed *structural mobility*. Structural mobility is due to structural changes in the economic sphere that "force" sons into alternative occupational categories from those of their fathers. The most commonly cited explanation of structural mobility is the shift from farm labor to urban labor resulting from an increase in industrialization (Lipset and Zetterberg 1956), technological progress, immigration, and differential fertility (Sibley 1942).

An important contribution made by this work was in the application of new statistical techniques. Blau and Duncan have been credited with providing the first major empirical application of path analysis to sociological data. The basic model involves five variables: father's education, father's occupation, respondent's education, respondent's first job, and respondent's occupation in 1962. This model is then elaborated in various ways to take into account additional ascribed statuses. Similar to Glass's findings, Blau and Duncan found most occupational movement within short ranges. Contrary to Glass, however, they found the American stratification system to be divided into three social categories, white collar, blue collar, and farm, with semipermeable class boundaries prohibiting long-range movement.

INTERNATIONAL COMPARISONS

Several problems arise in attempts to compare social mobility across different societies; of these, finding an appropriate measure is foremost. Two primary problems in measuring social mobility have been discussed (Raftery 1985). First, studies of social mobility most often use mobility tables that are a cross-classification of occupational categories for sons and fathers; change in occupational category from his father's represents mobility for the son. Because of the inconsistency in data collection across countries, crude dichotomies or trichotomies are used in an effort to obtain the data in parallel form. The problem lies in what to do with the farm category. For example, the son of a large farm owner is forced into manual labor because of the loss of jobs in agriculture resulting from economic or technological shifts. This move would likely be classified as upward mobility, yet the impact for the individual is downward (from a self-employed farm owner to a manual laborer). In addition, much apparent mobility is primarily due to shifts in occupational categories or "shifts in the marginals." The problem in using two or three occupational categories to examine social mobility is that much short-range mobility is missed. It also gives equal weight to movements across the manual nonmanual boundary, be they short-range or long-range.

A second problem in measuring mobility involves the variability among countries as to the structure of their stratification systems (Tyree, Semyonov, and Hodge 1979). Some countries have obvious delineations between social strata, while others possess systems that form a continuum of occupational categories without obvious breaks. This second group of societies, and the inherent problems of investigating social mobility within them, was first discussed by Tyree et al., who referred to them as "glissandos," as opposed to the first group, which contained "gaps" between occupational categories or groupings. If social stratification is of the "glissando" type, the crude categories used to create mobility tables will hide much mobility. For example, the respondents lying on the diagonal (the immobiles) may in fact have experienced mobility that would be revealed if the categories were smaller or otherwise differently defined.

The total amount of social mobility found can be decomposed into circulation mobility and structural mobility (sometimes also called "net" and "exchange" mobility). *Circulation mobility* is defined as the residue remaining after structural mobility has been accounted for. It, therefore, is the difference between total and structural mobility. "Circulatory mobility can be viewed as a zero-sum game. Net of movement forced by changes in the occupational structure over time and differential fertility, one's move up implies another's move down" (Tyree, Semyonov, and Hodge 1979, p. 413).

Given these conceptual and methodological difficulties, comparative studies must be reviewed with caution. Several recent international comparisons find that total mobility seems to have increased in most Western countries. This increase is primarily due to increasing structural mobility and, especially, increasing nonmanual employment and diminishing agricultural employment. The trends in circulation mobility are much less clear (Matras 1980). Overall, comparative studies have found that the United States and Great Britain appear to have consistently high levels of intergenerational mobility, Spain and the Philippines have consistently low levels, and Denmark, Sweden, and Belgium have consistently intermediate levels.

The industrialization thesis, as previously discussed, has been specified more precisely by Treiman (1970), who held that total and circulation mobility increase with increasing industrialization. This hypothesis has not received convincing support in the more extensive comparative studies (Hazelrigg and Garnier 1976; Tyree, Semyonov, and Hodge 1979), but it has received some support from studies that examined trends over time in conjunction with studies of changing occupational composition (Rogoff-Ramsoy 1977; Hauser and Featherman 1977; Goldthorpe, Payne, and Llewellyn 1978).

Additional work by Featherman, Jones, and Hauser (1975) suggests an alternative hypothesis (referred to as the FJH hypothesis) that variations in intergenerational mobility emerge from historical or cultural differences in occupational structure, but not from differences in exchanges between occupations. It is predicted, therefore, that "mobility chances are invariant once variations in origin and destination distributions have been controlled" (Grusky and Hauser 1984, p. 19).

Questioning the process by which economic development would decrease inequality (an assumed result of increased social mobility), Rubinson (1976) developed an alternative model that views cross-national differences in inequality as the result of differing relations of the states to the world-economy. This model is based on two assumptions: The first is that countries are not autonomous units of production but share in a world economic system of production, which contains multiple political units. Second, the model assumes that the social control and organization of production determines the distribution of income. Rubinson hypothesizes that the "greater the economic dominance and influence that states . . . have in the world-economy, the more equal the distribution of power within states, and consequently, the more equal the distribution of rewards" (p. 640).

SOCIAL MOBILITY OF BLACKS AND WOMEN

The majority of social mobility studies have focused on the dominant male population. In Western Europe and the United States, this means there are extensive data and analyses of the mobility patterns of white males but very little information on the mobility patterns of blacks and women. Part of this problem lies in the focus on occupations as the measure of achieved status, since nonmajority groups may focus their energies on other forms of achievement, such as family formation. In addition, special consideration needs to be given to the history of discrimination, which has traditionally disadvantaged minority members and may act as a barrier to their chances for mobility.

In order to compensate for some of these problems, many researchers have directed their research on changes over time. Farley (1984) operationalizes inequality as differences in level of education, occupational prestige, and income. He shows that income disparities between blacks and whites in the United States have narrowed between 1960 and 1980, that there has been a trend toward equity in educational attainment between blacks and whites, and that race differences in occupations have declined. Featherman and Hauser (1978) examine class inheritance and find that the profiles of black and white men are growing more similar. In fact, blacks gained more than whites in socioeconomic status between 1962 and 1973 although in 1973 they still lagged behind the occupational status of 1962 white men (a sure indication that they had a lot of catching up to do). The researchers also found that the effect of first job on occupational status in 1973 was similar for blacks and whites. These changes appear to be most evident with younger men, indicating positive trends for the future.

Examining mobility between 1962 and 1973, Hout (1984) shows that intergenerational mobility patterns were appreciably different for blacks and whites in those years, and that there was an increase in net upward mobility for black men. Regarding intragenerational mobility of blacks, he argues that class effects were more important than race effects. Hout cautions that, although his finding is positive in terms of blacks' occupational standing, they still receive lower returns for schooling than do whites. His research supports the notion that as the American population becomes more educated (particularly college educated), there appears to be more universalism and increasing social mobility (Hout 1988).

Rosenberg (1980), examining a dual labor market model, compared black and white mobility from their first job to their job in 1970. Rosenberg found that white men were more likely to move upward than blacks, though the differentials were modest. Examining upward mobility from a set of low-paying occupations to a mainstream stratum consisting of all occupations that pay at least moderately well, Pomer (1984, 1985) found marked black white differentials for the period 1965 to 1970. Using the 1973 Occupational Change in a Generation (OCG) data, he found that one's position in a segmented labor market is important in accounting for differential mobility patterns for blacks and whites (Pomer 1986). Mobility is less extensive for blacks than for whites, and more restricted to short-range mobility.

The strategy most often used by status attainment and mobility researchers to cope with issues of inequality between men and women is to absorb sex as a variable into existing models. Methods and measures previously developed to study men have been applied to women. In spite of some differences in labor market experiences between men and women the most consistent and surprising findings are that the occupational and marital mobility patterns of women are not much different from those of men (Tyree and Treas 1974; Dunton and Featherman 1983). In addition, females' occupational prestige scores are either equal to or higher than men's (Featherman and Hauser 1976; Farmer et al. 1990). Yet these findings should not be taken as evidence of gender equality. The finding of equal occupational prestige is an artifact of the truncated/clustered distribution of female prestige scores (Bose 1973). Hauser and Featherman (1977), examining social mobility for men and women, find that the destinations for women are very different from those of men.

ADDITIONAL CONSIDERATIONS

A serious question remains concerning just what is being measured and described by the overall level of mobility. In the traditional measures of total or circulation mobility, the concept refers to an actual or adjusted percentage of respondents who report occupations different (or in a different category) from those of their fathers; in the more recent log linear measures it refers to the size (smallness) of statistical interactions between occupations of respondents and those of

their father's in the various time periods, cohorts, or societies. One occupational category may be relatively open while another is relatively closed—a fact that is obscured in "overall" measures. Within countries or societies the rules for classifying occupations and for determining sameness or difference in occupational category are often the same across cohorts or time periods, but this is not often the case for cross-national comparisons. "But even when we assume that the classifications and rules are uniform across countries, generations, cohorts, time periods, etc., the meaning of the mobility rate of a country, or of the differences between the mobility rates of two or more countries, is still in question" (Matras 1980, p. 413).

It was noted above that social mobility was defined as movement through social space. While this movement has been described as both vertical and horizontal, few researchers have systematically evaluated nonvertical forms of social mobility (see Sorokin 1927 for one example). In fact, the primary has been on vertical occupational changes from one generation to the next. While a small number studies have recognized the influence on differential stratification structures and the influence of economic systems, few if any have acknowledged differential bases of stratification other than occupational or economic. There is a vast array of ways in which people organize and categorize themselves, from membership by virtue of birth (ascribed) to voluntary membership (achieved). Within these social categories, divisions and hierarchies emerge based on a variety of criteria. For example, societies have based their stratification regime on kinship structures, such as through rules of membership, including patrilineal, matrilineal, and bilineal systems. Other stratification regimes are based on religion, as is found in the Indian caste system. Here, social mobility theoretically occurs with reincarnation or, in rare cases, when an individual can "pass" as a member of a higher strata. Occupational position is ascribed by religious doctrine, and typical social mobility studies would not tap into issues of inequality as culturally defined by these societies. Other societies stratified on the bases of race, ethnicity, gender, age, and so forth demand different questions and measures.

(SEE ALSO: *Education and Mobility; Occupational and Career Mobility; Social Inequality; Social Stratification; Societal Stratification; Status Attainment*)

REFERENCES

Aristotle (384–322 B.C.) 1943 *Politics,* trans. Benjamin Jawett. New York: Modern Library.

Blau, Peter M., and Otis Dudley Duncan 1967 *The American Occupational Structure.* New York: Wiley.

Bose, Christine E. 1973 *Jobs and Gender: Sex and Occupational Prestige,* Baltimore: Johns Hopkins University, Center of Metropolitan Planning and Research.

Dunton, Nancy, and David L. Featherman 1983 "Social Mobility Through Marriage and Careers." In Janet T. Spence, ed., *Achievement and Achievement Motives.* San Francisco: Freeman.

Farley, Reynolds 1984 *Blacks and Whites: Closing the Gap?* Cambridge, Mass.: Harvard University Press.

Farmer, Yvette, Lynn M. Ries, David G. Nickinovich, Yoshinori Kamo, and Edgar F. Borgatta 1990 "The Status Attainment Model and Income." *Research on Aging* 12:113–132.

Featherman, David, and Robert Hauser 1976a, "Sexual Inequalities and Socioeconomic Achievement in the U.S., 1962–1973." *American Sociological Review* 41:462–483.

—— 1976b "Changes in the Socioeconomic Stratification of the Races, 1962–1973." *American Journal of Sociology* 82:621–651.

——, F. L. Jones and, R. M. Hauser 1975 "Assumptions of Social Mobility Research in the U.S.: The Case of Occupational Status." *Social Science Review* 4:329–360.

Glass, David, ed. 1949 *Social Mobility in Britain.* London: Routledge and Kegan Paul.

Goldthorpe, J. H., and K. Hope 1974 *The Social Grading of Occupations: A New Approach and Scale.* New York: Oxford Books.

Goldthorpe, J. H., C. Payne, and C. Llewellyn 1978 "Trends in Class Mobility." *Sociology* 12:441–468.

Grusky, David and Robert Hauser 1984 "Comparative Social Mobility Revisited: Models of Convergence and Divergence in 16 Countries." *American Sociological Review* 49:19–38.

Hauser, Robert M., and D. L. Featherman 1977 "The Measurement of Occupation in Social Surveys." In Robert M. Hauser and David L. Featherman, eds., *The Process of Stratification: Trends and Analyses.* New York: Academic Press.

Hauser, Robert M., and David B. Grusky 1988 "Cross-National Variation in Occupational Distributions, Relative Mobility Chances, and Intergenerational Shifts in Occupational Distributions." *American Sociological Review* 53:723–741.

Hazelrigg, L. E., and M. A. Garnier 1976 "Occupational Mobility in Industrial Societies: A Comparative Analysis of Differential Access to Occupational Ranks in Seventeen Countries." *American Sociological Review* 41:498–511.

Heath, Anthony 1981 *Social Mobility.* Glasgow: Fontana.

Horan, Patrick 1978 "Is Status Attainment Research Atheoretical?" *American Sociological Review* 43:534–541.

Hout, Michael 1984a "Occupational Mobility of Black Men: 1962 to 1973." *American Sociological Review* 49:308–322.

—— 1984b "Status, Autonomy, and Training in Occupational Mobility." *American Sociological Review* 2:114–137.

—— 1988 "More Universalism, Less Structural Mobility: The American Occupational Structure in the 1980s." *American Journal of Sociology* 93:1358–1400.

Lipset, Seymour M. 1960 *Political Man: The Social Bases of Politics.* New York: Doubleday.

——, and R. Bendix 1959 *Social Mobility in Industrial Society.* Berkeley: University of California Press.

——, and H. Zetterberg 1956 "A Theory of Social Mobility." *Transactions of the Third World Congress for Sociology* 66:16–22.

Marx, Karl 1958 *Selected Works.* Moscow: Foreign Language Publishing House.

Matras, Judah 1980 "Comparative Social Mobility." *Annual Review of Sociology* 6:401–431.

Plato (c. 380 B.C.) 1955 *The Republic,* trans. H. D. P. Lee. Harmondsworth, England: Penguin.

Pomer, Marshall I. 1984 "Upward Mobility of Low-Paid Workers: A Multivariate Model for Occupational Changers." *Sociological Perspectives* 27:427–442.

—— 1985 "The Immobility of Low-Paid Workers." *Journal of Sociology and Social Welfare* 12:287–310.

—— 1986 "Labor Market Structure, Intragenerational Mobility, and Discrimination: Black Male Advancement out of Low-Paying Occupations, 1962–1973." *American Sociological Review* 51:650–659.

Raftery, Adrian 1985 "Social Mobility Measures for

Cross-National Comparisons." *Quality and Quantity* 19:167–182.

Rogoff-Ramsoy, Natalie 1977 "Social Mobility and Changes in the Economy." Paper presented at ISA Research Committee on Social Stratification meeting, Dublin, April 5–7.

Rosenberg, Sam 1980 "Male Occupational Standing and the Dual Labor Market." *Industrial Relations* 19:34–49.

Rubinson, Richard 1976 "The World Economy and the Distribution of Income Within States: A Cross-National Study." *American Sociological Review* 41:638–659.

Schnore, Leo 1961 "Social Mobility in Demographic Perspective." *American Sociological Review* 26:407–423.

Sibley, Elbridge 1942 "Some Demographic Clues to Stratification." *American Sociological Review* 7:322–330.

Sorokin, P. A. 1927 *Social Mobility*. New York: Harper.

Treiman, Donald J. 1970 "Industrialization and Social Stratification." In Edward O. Laumann, ed., *Social Stratification: Research and Theory for the 1970s*. Indianapolis: Bobbs-Merrill.

——— 1977 *Occupational Prestige in Comparative Perspective*. New York: Academic Press.

Tyree, A., M. Semyonov, and R. W. Hodge 1979 "Gaps and Glissandos: Inequality, Economic Development, and Social Mobility in 24 Countries." *American Sociological Review* 44:410–424.

Tyree, Andrea, and Judith Treas 1974 "The Occupational and Marital Mobility of Women." *American Sociological Review* 39:293–302.

Westergaard, J., and H. Resler 1975 *Class in a Capitalist Society: A Study of Contemporary Britain*. London: Heinemann.

Wright, Erik O., C. Costello, D. Hachen, and J. Sprague 1982 "The American Class Structure." *American Sociological Review* 42:709–726.

Lynn M. Ries

SOCIAL MOVEMENTS Social movements are described most simply as collective attempts to promote or resist change in a society or a group. The degree of change advocated and the level at which changes are pursued vary across all types of social movements, be they religious, political, or student. Some movements clamor for sweeping, revolutionary transformations, whereas others pursue specific, moderate reforms. The level at which changes are sought varies from global and national alterations of social structures to attitudinal, spiritual, or life-style changes.

TYPES OF MOVEMENTS

Revolutionary movements, like the Bolshevik, Palestinian, Islamic jihad, and Irish Republican movements, seek fundamental structural changes. Such movements pursue radical changes in a society's basic institutions or, in some cases, major changes in the world order. Because they challenge the legitimacy of extant authorities, powerful elites typically use every available means, including violence, to repress revolutionary movements.

Reform movements, on the other hand, seek to modify structural relations without seriously threatening existing institutions. Consequently, while some elites oppose any reforms, they are usually more tolerant of reform movements than they are of revolutionary ones. Some reform movements, such as the peace, women's, and environmental movements, are general in scope (Blumer 1946). They often blend a plethora of political and life-style objectives (Turner and Killian 1987, p. 221). Peace movements, for example, not only pursue a variety of political objectives (e.g., preventing and stopping wars, opposing specific weapons, promoting disarmament, seeking foreign policy changes, establishing conflict resolution institutions), they also strive to convince individuals to change their attitudes and live more peaceful everyday lives.

Other reform movements, such as the anti-abortion, women's temperance, and the anti-drunken-driving movements, focus on quite specific issues. Although specific reform movements are considerably narrower in scope than general reform movements, they too sometimes organize around both political and life-style objectives (Staggenborg 1987).

Still other reform movements, such as various self-help, human potential, and "New Age" movements (e.g., EST, rebirthing, transcendental meditation), focus almost exclusively on life-style issues. In contrast to other movements, these tend to disregard social structural issues. Instead, they concentrate on changing individuals.

Finally, social movements frequently generate organized opposition in the form of countermovements. Countermovements seek to prevent revolutionary or reform movements from securing the changes they promote. Given their counter-reformist tendencies, most countermovements (e.g., anti-busing, McCarthyist, stop-ERA, and moral majority movements) are conservative (Lo 1982). That is, they seek to preserve extant institutions and life-styles.

Regardless of the particular type of social movement and the scope and level of change it advocates or opposes, all movements share some common characteristics of interest to social scientists. First, all movements emerge under a specific, complex set of historical, cultural, and structural conditions. Second, as a movement emerges, a variety of participation issues arise, including recruiting new members, building commitment, and sustaining participation. Third, every movement is organized to some degree. The most visible manifestations of movements are their social movement organizations and their strategies and tactics. Last, by virtue of their existence, every social movement has some consequences, however minimal they might be. Though researchers are frequently concerned with the extent to which movements affect social change, definitive answers to this question have proved illusory.

MOVEMENT EMERGENCE

Social scientists have devoted considerable attention to the factors associated with the emergence of social movements. Early theory and research asserted that movements arise when societies undergo structural strain, as during times of rapid social change (Smelser 1962). These "breakdown theories" posited that "large structural rearrangements in societies—such as urbanization and industrialization"—lead to dissolution of social controls and heighten "the impulse toward antisocial behavior" (Tilly, Tilly, and Tilly 1975,

p. 4). Hence, these systemic "breakdowns" were said to cause an increase in strikes, violent collective action, and social movements.

Contemporary movement scholars criticized breakdown theories on empirical and theoretical grounds. Rather than viewing movement emergence and participation as aberrations, scholars now view them as "simply politics by other means,' often the *only* means open to relatively powerless challenging groups" (McAdam 1988, pp. 127–128). To understand the conditions that affect the likelihood that such challenging groups will mobilize, researchers turned to the structural factors conducive to movement emergence.

One macro structural factor concerns the "structure of political opportunities" (Eisinger 1973). This refers to "the receptivity or vulnerability of the political system to organized protest" by a social movement (McAdam, McCarthy, and Zald 1988, p. 699). Research on the civil rights movement, for example, indicates that the movement's emergence was facilitated by a series of interrelated changes in the structure of political opportunities. These included the decline of cotton markets, black migration to the North, the expansion of the black vote, and the electoral shift to the Democratic party (McAdam 1982).

Another macro factor researchers have identified is the absence of repression. Social movements are sometimes spared a violent or otherwise repressive response from authorities, not only during times of breakdown or regime crisis (Skocpol 1979), but also during periods of expanding political opportunities. Continuing with the example of the civil rights movement, Doug McAdam (1982) documents how black lynchings declined as blacks' political opportunities increased from 1930 to 1955.

Research suggests that the relationship between collective action and repression is bell-shaped (Tilly 1978). Authorities' initial attempts to repress movements often fan the flames of discontent and fuel further protest activities. However, if authorities respond by increasing the severity of the repression, as when Chinese authorities ordered tanks and troops into Tiananmen Square to fire on student demonstrators, the costs of collective action usually become too high for movements to continue their challenges.

Indigenous organization constitutes a third major structural factor associated with movement emergence (Morris 1984). Pre-existing organizations serve as communication networks for discontented members of a population (Freeman 1973). They also provide a base for mobilizing the resources needed to sustain a movement. Various churches, for example, were important indigenous organizations that contributed to the emergence of the contemporary peace, civil rights, and Moral Majority movements.

Finally, several European scholars contend that state intervention into private domains of life have generated "new social movements." According to this perspective, various structural changes in Western industrialized societies, especially changes in the system of production, led the state to seek control over previously private domains. Consequently, private domains such as sexual relations, biological identity, birth and death, illness and aging, and one's relationship to nature "have entered the realm of 'public' conflict" (Melluci 1980, p. 219). New social movements (e.g., women's, gay rights, euthanasia, environmental) emerged to reclaim those areas from the state.

The foregoing indicates that numerous structural factors are crucial to the emergence of social movements. Yet structural factors alone cannot account for the rise of a particular movement. Why is it that when the structural conditions appear to be ripe for the emergence of a particular movement, frequently no movement appears? To address this question, some researchers have begun to investigate the micro interactional factors associated with social-movement emergence.

The bulk of this research focuses on grievance interpretation processes. These refer to the means by which people collectively arrive at similar definitions of the situation or "interpretive frames" regarding social changes they support or oppose (Snow et al. 1986). Before an aggrieved, but previously unmobilized, category of people are likely to engage in sustained protest activity, they must revise the manner in which they look at some problematic condition or aspect of life. Social arrangements that were ordinarily considered "just and immutable" must come to be seen as "unjust and mutable" (Piven and Cloward 1977, p. 12). This "cognitive liberation" process typically involves an attributional shift from blaming oneself to blaming the system for particular problems (McAdam 1982). In sum, social movements are most likely to emerge when the structural conditions for mobilization are ripe and when the collective interpretation of grievances produces cognitive liberation.

MOVEMENT PARTICIPATION

Closely related to the issue of movement emergence are questions regarding movement participation. Who joins and why? What conditions affect the likelihood of participating? How do movements build membership commitment and sustain participation? Initial attempts to address questions concerning movement participation were also influenced by breakdown theories. Movement participation was viewed as an irrational response to social-structural strains. The factors regarded as key determinants of movement participation ranged from alienation and social isolation to status strains and relative deprivation (for reviews, see Gurney and Tierney 1982; Zurcher and Snow 1981). Each of these approaches suggested that some sort of psychological malaise or personality defect predisposed some individuals to react to structural strains by participating in social movements.

The outburst of collective action and the proliferation of social movements in the 1960s led many social scientists to reconsider breakdown-theory assumptions (Jenkins 1983). Some theorists redefined movement participation as a rational choice (Oberschall 1973). According to this perspective, potential participants take part in social movement activities only when they perceive that the anticipated benefits outweigh the expected costs of participation (Klandermans 1984). An avalanche of research on the conditions affecting cost-benefit participation decisions (e.g., Oliver 1984) indicates that it is a complex process involving numerous structural and social-psychological factors.

Social networks are another crucial factor that affect differential recruitment to social movements. Movements tend to recruit the majority of their new members from the networks of existing members (Snow, Zurcher, and Ekland-Olson 1980). A person typically decides to attend their first movement function because a friend, coworker, or relative invited them. Those outside such networks are less likely to be aware of the existence of specific movement groups. Moreover, they are less likely to attend a movement function if they are not sure there would be others present whom they know.

While having social ties to people who are movement participants increases the likelihood of movement participation, other social ties can diminish that probability. Social ties in the form of family and career attachments can constrain movement participation in a number of ways. For one, these competing commitments may result in role conflict. The demands of being a movement participant and the demands of being a parent or employee may at times be incompatible. Married persons who have parental responsibilities as well as full-time jobs may not have sufficient discretionary time to participate in social movements (McCarthy and Zald 1973). Furthermore, spouses and employers can be displeased by a person's movement participation.

To justify their movement participation to themselves and others, participants develop vocabularies of motives (Snow and Benford 1988). These are rationales that offer compelling reasons for their participation, particularly when their actions are called into question by employers, family members, or friends. Research suggests that movement participants socially construct these vocabularies of motive as they interact with one another (Benford 1988). Activists, in turn, employ these rationales as motivational prods to encourage sympathizers and adherents to take action on behalf of movement goals.

Vocabularies of motive not only facilitate recruitment to movements, but also serve as commitment-building mechanisms. They help partici-

pants justify to themselves making sacrifices on behalf of a cause. The more sacrifices they make, the more costly leaving the movement seems to be. As they relinquish old attachments in favor of new ones, their commitment grows deeper (Kanter 1968). Research indicates that such conversion and commitment-building processes are, contrary to popular myths regarding participation in new religious movements and cults, typically voluntary (Snow and Machalek 1984).

Taken together, research on social movements reveals that participation motives and experiences are quite diverse. No single explanation suffices to account for movement participation. Rather, a confluence of factors affect the decision to participate. Likewise, there are a variety of ways individuals may participate, ranging from those that require little commitment of time, such as signing a petition or writing a letter to a political official, to those requiring extensive commitment, such as coordinating national campaigns or committing acts of civil disobedience.

MOVEMENT ORGANIZATIONS

The activities of movements and their participants are coordinated by social movement organizations (SMOs) (Zald and Ash 1966). Most general reform movements spawn numerous SMOs. For example, by 1984, the U.S. nuclear-disarmament movement included some 3,000 independent SMOs as well as another 1,000 local chapters of national organizations. Specific reform movements, by contrast, tend to generate fewer SMOs. Regardless, SMOs are formal movement groups that can be thought of as "the command posts of movements" (McAdam, McCarthy, and Zald 1988). They acquire and deploy resources, mobilize adherents, and plot movement strategy.

Resource mobilization theorists were among the first to emphasize the importance of SMOs in performing these functions. In particular, they point out that in the absence of an organization it is difficult for movements to acquire the resources needed to sustain their challenges (Tilly 1978). Contemporary movements require money for advertising, printing, postage, lobbying, staff, and the like.

Other resource-mobilization theorists have suggested that studying SMOs reveals how the macro and micro levels are reciprocally linked (McAdam, McCarthy, and Zald 1988). For example, the resource level of a society affects the resources available to SMOs, which in turn affect recruitment efforts (McCarthy and Zald 1977). During times of economic prosperity, as in the 1960s, the entire social-movement sector expands. There are simply more discretionary resources available for movements during these periods. In this illustration, the macro level (a society's surplus resources), mediated by SMOs, affects the micro level (individual participation).

Yet many movements also seek to affect the macro level from below. Again, SMOs play a mediating role. Individuals with similar grievances get together in an informal, small group setting, what McAdam (1988) refers to as a "micromobilization context." Sometimes participants at these ad hoc meetings decide to establish a more formal, enduring organization to act on the participants' collective grievances (i.e., an SMO). The SMO in turn devises a strategy aimed at changing the system in some way. Occasionally, SMOs succeed in bringing about macro-level changes.

The tactics and strategies a movement employs in pursuit of its objectives are typically selected or devised by SMOs. A movement strategy refers to the "broad organizing plans" for the acquisition and use of resources toward achieving movement goals (Turner and Killian 1987, p. 286). For example, as previously suggested, movements may pursue social change by devising strategies aimed at changing structural arrangements or at changing people or both. Similarly, movements may choose between legal and illegal strategies, and between violent and nonviolent strategies.

Tactics refer to the specific techniques movements employ to carry out their strategies. Teach-ins, sit-ins, marches, rallies, strikes, and mass mailings are but a few of the tactics contemporary reform movements typically utilize. There appears to be considerable tactical borrowing across the political spectrum. Conservative movements of the 1980s and 1990s, such as the Moral Majority and the anti-abortion movements, for example, used many of the tactics of the civil rights and New Left movements of the 1960s.

Charles Tilly made a similar observation regarding the eighteenth-century American revolutionary-movement tactics he studied. He accounted for tactical similiarities across movements and SMOs by noting that every place and time has limited "repertoires of collective action" that are well defined but limited compared to the various tactical options theoretically available. These "standard forms are learned, limited in scope, slowly changing, and peculiarly adapted to their settings" (Tilly 1979, p. 131).

While tactical diffusion across movements and SMOs occurs, a division of tactical labor also commonly arises within movements (Benford and Zurcher 1990). Each SMO tends to develop its own specific tactical preferences and expertise. These specializations arise as a consequence of cooperation and competition among the various SMOs that comprise a movement (Zald and McCarthy 1980). By refining and employing specialized tactics, an SMO is able to carve out a niche within the movement that distinguishes it from other SMOs.

Once an SMO establishes an organizational identity, it is in a position to build a stable resource base. Indeed, some SMOs have been so successful in that regard that they survive the decline of a movement. Recent research on the women's movement indicates that such "abeyance organizations" provide continuity from one cycle of movement activity to the next (Taylor 1989). They do so by sustaining activist interaction and commitment during periods when the opportunity structures are unfavorable to mass mobilization. In sum, SMOs contribute at least some temporary stability to what is otherwise a fluid, emergent phenomenon.

MOVEMENT OUTCOMES

What effects, if any, do social movements actually have on social change? This obviously crucial question is not as easy to answer as might be assumed. Because of the difficulties associated with studying a large sample of movements, most researchers choose to study movements one at a time. Whereas these case studies provide researchers with rich, detailed data on a specific movement, they are not very helpful in making generalizations. But even with case studies, the question of the effects of a particular movement is difficult to answer. First, the logic employed is counterfactual (Moore 1978). That is, in evaluating the effects of a particular movement, researchers are in a position of having to speculate on what the outcome would have been had the movement *not* existed. Second, the effects of movements are not always immediate and apparent. Some movements, like the civil rights and women's movements, produce rippling effects that gradually engulf society's institutions, at times generating effects several decades after the movement's most intense period of agitation has ceased.

In general, movements seem to be more effective in producing cultural rather than structural changes. The enduring legacy of the movements of the 1960s, for example, appears to be cultural. These cultural changes are reflected in attitudinal shifts regarding women and minorities (liberalized), fashion trends (relaxed), life-styles (hedonistic), and the like. Nevertheless, the movements of the sixties had a rather negligible impact on structural changes. While it is true that civil rights legislation helped dismantle caste restrictions and nearly equalized voting rights in the South, blacks continued to suffer "grinding poverty" and "persistent institutional discrimination in jobs, housing, and education" (McAdam 1982, p. 234). Women realized even fewer structural gains than blacks. Despite popular myths to the contrary, they still suffer gross inequities in the workplace and at home. Finally, the sweeping changes in the economic, political, and educational institutions advocated by student activists never came to pass.

That does not mean that movements always fail to achieve their structural objectives. In the late 1980s and early 1990s, grass-roots movements radically transformed the totalitarian political structures of a number of Eastern European countries into more democratic states. The mid-

nineteenth-century abolitionist movement succeeded in abolishing slavery. Similarly, today's global movement against apartheid has produced a number of reforms in the treatment of blacks in South Africa. In short, although movements do occasionally achieve such dramatic outcomes, social structures initially tend to be more resistant than cultures to the revolutionary or reform efforts of social movements.

William Gamson (1990) is one of the few researchers who has attempted to identify systematically the conditions under which social movements are likely to achieve their objectives. He traced the activities of a representative sample of fifty-three "challenging groups," SMOs that emerged in the United States between 1800 and 1945. Gamson measured the relative success or failure of the SMOs in terms of whether or not they (1) gained new advantages and/or (2) gained acceptance from their antagonists. He found that thirty-one (58 percent) of the SMOs either gained new advantages or acceptance; twenty (38 percent) gained both.

One of Gamson's strongest findings pertained to the degree of change advocated. Movement groups that sought to displace extant elites rarely succeeded. Gamson reported that the SMOs most likely to succeed exhibited the following additional characteristics: selective incentives for participants (some form of inducement, including rewards or punishment, to participate); unruly tactics (e.g., strikes, violence), especially when the target was relatively weak; bureaucratic, centralized organizational structures; and the absence of factional splits within the group. Although Gamson's research has been criticized as simplistic, it does identify several factors that affect the outcomes of social movements.

Frequently, before social movements are able to change social structures, they must change the way at least some people view or "frame" a social issue or domain of life. Movement activists devote considerable time to the task of transforming people's interpretive frames (Snow et al. 1986). If the movement's framing efforts are successful, a general shift in public opinion can occur, as has been the case for the movement against drunk driving (Gusfield 1981). Those who were once thought of as foolish or careless have been redefined as "killer drunks." Subsequently, the movement has found it relatively easy to secure legislation raising minimum drinking ages and increasing the penalties for driving under the influence of alcohol. Although favorable public opinion is not a sufficient condition for social change to occur, it can lead to advantageous changes in the opportunity structure as well as the availability of resources.

Social movements may not always succeed in achieving their goals. Movements have, however, played a significant role in most societal reforms, revolutions, and changes in the world order.

(SEE ALSO: *Collective Behavior; Feminist Theory; Labor Movements and Unions; Protest Movements; Religious Movements; Revolutions; Segregation and Indices; Social Change; Student Movement*)

REFERENCES

Benford, Robert D. 1988 "Motivational Framing: The Social Construction of Motives within the Nuclear Disarmament Movement." Paper presented at the Annual Meetings of the Midwest Sociological Society, Minneapolis, Minn., April.

———, and Louis A. Zurcher 1990 "Instrumental and Symbolic Competition among Peace Movement Organizations." In Sam Marullo and John Lofland, eds., *Peace Action in the Eighties*. New Brunswick, N.J.: Rutgers University Press.

Blumer, Herbert 1946 "Collective Behavior." In A. M. Lee, ed., *A New Outline of the Principles of Sociology*. New York: Barnes and Noble.

Eisinger, Peter K. 1973 "The Conditions of Protest Behavior in American Cities." *American Political Science Review* 67:11–28.

Freeman, Jo 1973 "The Origin of the Women's Liberation Movement." *American Journal of Sociology* 78:792–811.

Gamson, William A. 1990 *The Strategy of Social Protest*, 2nd ed. Belmont, Calif.: Wadsworth.

Gurney, Joan Neff, and Kathleen J. Tierney 1982 "Relative Deprivation and Social Movements: A Critical Look at Twenty Years of Theory and Research." *Sociological Quarterly* 23:33–47.

Gusfield, Joseph R. 1981 *The Culture of Public Problems: Drinking-Driving and the Symbolic Order*. Chicago: University of Chicago Press.

Jenkins, J. Craig 1983 "Resource Mobilization Theory and the Study of Social Movements." *Annual Review of Sociology* 9:527–553.

Kanter, Rosabeth M. 1968 "Commitment and Social Organization: A Study of Commitment Mechanisms in Utopian Communities." *American Sociological Review* 33:499–517.

Klandermans, Bert 1984 "Mobilization and Participation: Social-Psychological Expansions of Resource Mobilization Theory." *American Sociological Review* 49:583–600.

Lo, Clarence Y. 1982 "Countermovements and Conservative Movements in the Contemporary U.S." *Annual Review of Sociology* 8:107–134.

McAdam, Doug 1982 *Political Process and the Development of Black Insurgency, 1930–1970*. Chicago: University of Chicago Press.

——— 1988 "Micromobilization Contexts and Recruitment to Activism." *International Social Movement Research* 1:125–154.

———, John D. McCarthy, and Mayer N. Zald 1988 "Social Movements." In N. Smelser, ed., *Handbook of Sociology*. Newbury Park, Calif.: Sage Publications.

McCarthy, John D. 1977 "Resource Mobilization and Social Movements: A Partial Theory." *American Journal of Sociology* 82:1212–1241.

———, and Mayer N. Zald 1973 *The Trend of Social Movements in America: Professionalization and Resource Mobilization*. Morristown, N.J.: General Learning Press.

Melluci, Alberto 1980 "The New Social Movements: A Theoretical Approach." *Social Science Information*. 19:199–226.

Moore, Barrington, Jr. 1978 *Injustice: The Social Bases of Obedience and Revolt*. White Plains, N.Y.: M. E. Sharpe.

Morris, Aldon D. 1984 *The Origins of the Civil Rights Movement: Black Communities Organizing for Change*. New York: Free Press.

Oberschall, Anthony 1973 *Social Conflict and Social Movements*. Englewood Cliffs, N.J.: Prentice-Hall.

Oliver, Pamela 1984 "'If You Don't Do It, Nobody Else Will': Active and Token Contributors to Collective Action." *American Sociological Review* 49:601–610.

Piven, Frances Fox, and Richard A. Cloward 1977 *Poor*

Peoples' Movements: Why They Succeed, How They Fail. New York: Vintage.

Skocpol, Theda 1979 *States and Social Revolutions.* New York: Cambridge University Press.

Smelser, Neil J. 1962 *Theory of Collective Behavior.* New York: Free Press.

Snow, David A., and Robert D. Benford 1988 "Ideology, Frame Resonance, and Participant Mobilization." *International Social Movement Research* 1: 197–217.

Snow, David A., and Richard Machalek 1984 "The Sociology of Conversion." *Annual Review of Sociology* 10:167–180.

Snow, David A., E. Burke Rochford, Jr., Steven K. Worden, and Robert D. Benford 1986 "Frame Alignment Processes, Micromobilization, and Movement Participation." *American Sociological Review* 51:464–481.

Snow, David A., Louis A. Zurcher, Jr., and Sheldon Ekland-Olson 1980 "Social Networks and Social Movements: A Microstructural Approach to Differential Recruitment." *American Sociological Review* 45:787–801.

Staggenborg, Suzanne 1987 "Life-style Preferences and Social Movement Recruitment: Illustrations from the Abortion Conflict." *Social Science Quarterly* 68:779–797.

Taylor, Verta 1989 "Social Movement Continuity: The Women's Movement in Abeyance." *American Sociological Review* 54:761–775.

Tilly, Charles 1978 *From Mobilization to Revolution.* Reading, Mass.: Addison-Wesley.

——— 1979 "Repertoires of Contention in America and Britain, 1750–1830." In M. N. Zald and J. D. McCarthy, eds., *The Dynamics of Social Movements.* Cambridge, Mass.: Winthrop.

———, Louise Tilly, and Richard Tilly 1975 *The Rebellious Century: 1830–1930.* Cambridge: Harvard University Press.

Turner, Ralph H., and Lewis M. Killian 1987 *Collective Behavior*, 3rd ed. Englewood Cliffs, N.J.: Prentice-Hall.

Zald, Mayer N., and Roberta Ash 1966 "Social Movement Organizations: Growth, Decay and Decline." *Social Forces* 44:327–341.

Zald, Mayer N., and John D. McCarthy 1980 "Social Movement Industries: Competition and Cooperation among Movement Organizations." In L. Kriesberg, ed., *Research in Social Movements, Conflict and Change.* Greenwich, Conn.: JAI Press.

Zurcher, Louis A., and David A. Snow 1981 "Collective Behavior: Social Movements." In M. Rosenberg and R. H. Turner, eds., *Social Psychology: Sociological Perspectives.* New York: Basic Books.

ROBERT D. BENFORD

SOCIAL NETWORK THEORY   To those who regard sociology as the study of social relations, social networks are fundamental. A social network orientation conceptualizes social phenomena as patterned arrays of relationships that join social actors. As such, it is attractive to sociologists concerned with bridging micro and macro levels of analysis. The approach suggests that the structures of social institutions such as families and formal organizations should be depicted as distinct configurations of links joining persons or social positions. Applied at higher levels of analysis, it views organizational fields, communities, or systems of international relations as complexes of ties among establishments, firms, cities, industries, or nation-states. Among its general postulates is that features such as an individual's education or a nation's level of development are often better interpreted as correlates of the social networks to which actors have access than as essential characteristics of individual units.

Moreover, a social network perspective claims that individual action is embedded in, and therefore continually affected by, social ties joining specific actors (Granovetter 1985). This leads to two distinct theoretical views of the way that networks mold action. One theoretical view treats individuals as largely passive recipients of environmental pressure; in this structural emphasis, social networks constitute *constraints* that limit discretion. A second views networks as *social resources;* this orientation treats individuals as actors in a context of constrained voluntarism and assumes that individuals are proactive, self-interested agents who use their social networks to manipulate outcomes to their advantage (Haines 1988; Coleman 1990).

Emphasis on social networks in general, and

informal social networks in particular, arose in conjunction with important substantive observations about contemporary society. Large-scale transformations associated with industrialization, especially urbanization, bureaucratization, and the development of mass media, were thought by many early twentieth-century observers to have led to a "mass society" of atomized individuals in which formal, special-purpose ties were substituted for diffuse interpersonal relations. Several lines of research, however, pointed to the continuing vitality of social ties. Industrial sociologists found that the informal structures of organizations were crucial to their day-to-day functioning. Indeed, workplace social networks came to be seen as one solution to bureaucratic inflexibility and overformalization and as important incentives for, or impediments to, individual employees. Urban sociologists found that friendship, neighboring, and informal assistance remained prominent in large cities, though developments in transportation and communication meant that these social ties were less constrained by spatial factors. Rural–urban migrants were not rootless citizens in a normless society but instead tended to settle in urban districts populated by persons drawn from their homelands. Similarly, social movement researchers found that protesters and activists were drawn from among those persons best integrated into communities, in contrast to the expectations of strain and mass society theories.

While social scientists have used the term *social network* in a metaphorical way for some time, scholars in the 1970s and 1980s devoted a great deal of effort to the analytical development of the social network approach, establishing it as a distinct specialty. Much of this work was of a methodological character and stressed development of concepts and techniques for studying relations between interdependent social units—as distinct from typical analytic methods used to study relations between variables within presumably autonomous units. It would be a mistake to dismiss this work as atheoretical because much of it is guided by carefully constructed models. At the same time, the theoretical presumptions of these models are sometimes implicit (Granovetter 1979), and a distinct "network theory" has not been developed. Instead, contemporary studies draw on diverse sociological and social psychological theories in formulating models and interpreting analyses of network data.

PRECURSORS

Some foundations of a methodology for studying networks of social relations were laid in J. L. Moreno's *Who Shall Survive?* (1934). Moreno coined the term *sociometry* to refer to methods for describing group structures and individual positions within them. His work focused on the affinities and disaffinities of individuals for one another, and his "sociometric test" accordingly stressed affective choices and rejections. These network data were mapped in sociometric diagrams and used as the basis for classifying individuals as attractive, isolated, rejected, and so forth. Collaborating with Moreno in developing sociometric methods was Helen Hall Jennings; her own (1943) work reported on studies of attractiveness and emotional expansiveness. Sociometry as practiced by Moreno and Jennings had a notable applied component: They sought to use sociometric measurements as a basis for rearranging groups in order to enhance both group functioning and individual creativity.

Social anthropologists engaged in fieldwork in complex societies also made important contributions to the development of network studies. They observed that categorical concepts of a structural-functional approach were insufficient for the study of societies in which not all behavior was regulated by "corporate groups"—institutions of kinship, community, or work. J. A. Barnes (1954) is generally credited with the first use of the term *social network* to refer to a set of actually existing social relationships as distinct from cultural prescriptions about the construction of such ties. Initial formulations of the concept tended to use it to refer to extrainstitutional links, but it was soon noted that formalized relations and groups too could be analyzed as networks of interactions.

Studies in this tradition display the same variability in theoretical orientations seen in present-day work: Elizabeth Bott (1957) treated social networks as sources of norms prescribing an appropriate allocation of tasks between spouses, while Jeremy Boissevain (1974) stressed instead the potential use of networks by maneuvering, self-interested entrepreneurs.

THE STRUCTURING OF NETWORKS

Several generalizations about the micro-level patterning of social ties have been reasonably well established by network research. Many social relationships tend to exhibit *reciprocity*. This sometimes involves *symmetry*—a "mechanical" pairing of ties with common content such as positive affect. A more "organic" reciprocity is an *exchange,* in which a flow of one type in one direction is accompanied by a complementary one in the reverse direction. Networks are often *multiplex:* One type of tie tends to appear together with a second. Social ties, especially those involving positive sentiment, tend to form *transitive* configurations: If two actors are mutually joined to a third, they tend to be linked to one another as well. Finally, many social relations display *homophily:* They tend to join actors having similar attributes or statuses. There are various theoretical accounts for these findings, and the generalizations themselves have important implications for more macro aspects of network structures. Likewise, exceptions to these generalizations are not to be seen as errors but instead have notable consequences.

Rational choice explanations for the formation of network ties are based on exchange theory; by this logic, social relations form when actors depend on one another for resources. Related behaviorist accounts stress a reinforcement history. A common exemplar is Blau's (1955) description of the exchange of advice for expressions of deference among coworkers in a bureaucracy. The terms of exchange, and in turn the relative power of the actors involved, depend on the number of alternative actors holding control over different resources, on the extent of unity among those in possession of a given resource, and on the parties' relative interests in outcomes controlled by others (Cook 1982; Burt 1980).

Exchange-theoretic reasoning provides a basis for some observed micro-level network patternings. To maintain autonomy and avoid power disadvantages, actors should avoid asymmetric relations. Similarly, multiplex ties in which ties of solidarity overlay instrumental exchange relations can serve as a guard against exploitation by an actor in a position of power. These ideas have played an important part in resource dependence theories of interorganizational relations. These theories suggest, for example, that interdependent organizations will tend to form ties such as long-term contracts, joint ventures, interlocking directors, and mergers (Pfeffer 1987).

There have been some attempts to explain tendencies toward homophily. Preference-driven accounts reason that people actively seek out similar associates; among the arguments are that communication tends to be easier if people share implicit premises regarding interaction and that trustworthiness in the face of uncertainty is enhanced if partners can assume that they have shared interests.

Another line of theorizing, developed furthest by Peter Blau and supported by empirical research (Blau and Schwartz 1984), views variations in homophily as the result of differing distributions of opportunities for association. Blau shows, without requiring any assumptions about preferences, that intergroup relations—the converse of homophilous ones—are more likely for small than for large groups; more likely when there is great inequality or heterogeneity in a population; and more likely when different characteristics (e.g., socioeconomic status, race, ethnicity) that structure the formation of social ties are intersecting (or uncorrelated) rather than consolidated. His work further demonstrates that implications of these distributional factors for intergroup relations are conditional on the degree to which they penetrate into substructures such as families, work groups, and voluntary associations. These substructures provide the opportunity sets of accessible partners within which many social ties form, and distributional effects on intergroup association are strongest when heterogeneity, inequality, and intersection lie within rather than between substructures.

Symmetry, multiplexity, and homophily are all dyadic properties, but a very important theme in network analysis is that events in different dyads are not independent of one another. Transitive patterns in triads are the smallest-scale illustration of this principle; if one actor is linked to a second, and the second is tied to a third, then the first will also tend to be related to the third. Transitivity has been most intensively studied for sociometric relations of positive sentiment; there the theoretical case for it rests on balance theories positing pressures toward cognitive consistency (Davis and Leinhardt 1972). Transitivity in dominance relations has been predicted on the basis of expectation states theory (Fararo and Skvoretz 1986).

Transitivity is of special importance because it leads to a rich set of observations about macro-level structures. A pure transitivity principle leads to hierarchy in a group. In combination with tendencies toward symmetry and homophily, transitivity tends to create densely interconnected subgroups of homogeneous actors, often called *clusters* or *cliques;* such interconnectedness is thought to be an essential precondition for coalitions or collective action. The conjoint presence of symmetry and transitivity (clustering and hierarchy) implies a macro-level structure of stratified cliques (Davis and Leinhardt 1972).

Intransitivities are theoretically important as well. Mark Granovetter's (1973) influential discussion of "weak ties" defines tie strength in terms of intimacy, intensity, exchange of services, and time commitments. The "strength of weak ties," however, lies in their lack of transitivity rather than their dyadic content. Weak ties, Granovetter argues, are least subject to the pressures that induce transitivity and are hence those most likely to serve as bridges joining distinct clustered subgroups. They therefore serve as channels for integration and diffusion, countering the tendency of transitive strong ties to create fragmentation.

This property of weak ties was integrated into biased network models to demonstrate that transitivity inhibits diffusion (Fararo and Skvoretz 1987).

Network analysts have given a great deal of attention to developing procedures for representing group structures by using relational data (Marsden and Laumann 1984). One line of work has stressed methods for isolating the clusters or cohesive subgroups mentioned above. A second perspective (Laumann and Pappi 1976) is that social differentiation creates systematic biases toward formation or avoidance of relationships, that is, social distances. This approach places emphasis on discovering distance-generating mechanisms that tend to array actors close to or far from one another along continuous dimensions.

Blockmodel analysis and related methods are a distinct and important approach to studying network structure (White, Boorman, and Breiger 1976; Burt 1982). In place of the criterion of dense interconnectedness, which defines a cohesive subgroup, this approach relies on the notion of *structural equivalence* as a basis for a social position. Structurally equivalent actors are, from an observer's standpoint, substitutable: They are tied to other actors in identical ways.

Actors in a clique are structurally equivalent, but not all equivalent actors need be in cliques. Relaxing the requirement of cohesion in favor of equivalence yields considerable flexibility. New types of social positions can be identified, including "hangers-on" or "sycophants," socially defined by their common ties to outsiders, isolated individuals lacking any social relations, and brokers mediating relations between others. Moreover, nothing in the logic of structural equivalence requires that it be confined to a single type of tie. Thus, the blockmodel approach defines positions on the basis of patterns in multistranded relations rather than by extracting a single type of tie from its context for this purpose. It is possible in studies of networks of international trade relations, for example, to look for patterns of asymmetric exchange of raw materials and processed goods.

Structural analysis based on the concept of structural equivalence has stimulated a great deal of theoretical, methodological, and substantive work. Among the more provocative theoretical ideas are more abstract conceptions of equivalence that define actors as substitutable when they display identical patterns of network ties to similar, rather than identical, others (Reitz and White 1989). Extensions beyond blockmodels use these representations to identify lawful patterns of interlock among different types of social relations (Boorman and White 1976). Transitivity, in which the presence of two ties implies a third, is an elementary example, as are compound kinship ties. Study of the interpenetration of multiple types of ties permits comparison of the relational logics for disjoint sets of actors.

NETWORKS AND OUTCOMES

Since a network perspective postulates that group-level structures are composed of actors and the relationships among them, it lends itself to the construction of theories at multiple levels. Group-level theorizing about effects of properties of total networks is not especially well developed; as James Coleman (1990) stresses, such theorizing is a rather demanding enterprise. More common are contextual theories specifying effects of an actor's position in a network on well-being and other outcomes. Power, social support, diffusion and influence, and network entrepreneurship are among the most prominent themes developed in such approaches.

Substantial attention has been given to the connection between network *centrality* and power or influence. Linton Freeman (1979) reviewed the conceptual foundations of common network measures of positional centrality in communication networks. He distinguished those that focus on activity (the number of contacts), those that focus on the capacity to control others, and those that focus on the capacity to avoid the controlling actions of others. The capacity to control others rests on betweenness, which in turn is defined in terms of intransitivity: To the extent that actors serve as the sole links between others, they are brokers in a position to facilitate or interrupt communication or exchange. A capacity to avoid

the control of others means independence from brokers, the absence of a need for intermediaries; actors in such a position are relatively close to others. Exchange-theoretic approaches to centrality focus on networks of dependency relations; powerful actors are those having predominantly favorable exchange ratios with others (Cook 1982).

Empirical studies, both experimental and non-experimental, document an association between centrality and manifestations of power. No universal principle leads to such a connection, however. Exchange theorists argue that it depends upon a particular form of exchange. For Cook (1982) this is "positively connected" or "productive" exchange, in which actors must combine diverse resources in order to be successful; hence the use of one exchange relation tends to encourage the use of others, and advantages emerge for those in intermediary positions. For Coleman (1990), the requisite conditions include resource transferability or fungibility: For systems of social exchange to develop fully, actors must be able to transfer not only control over resources but also the right to further transfer such control.

Other conditions of exchange lead to different consequences of network positions for power. The most studied of these is what Cook (1982) calls "negatively connected" exchange networks, in which the use of one relation rules out (or makes less likely) the use of others. Matching systems such as marriage or dating markets exemplify negatively connected networks. Among their key properties is that resources exchanged do not flow beyond the dyad. Under these conditions no special advantages accrue to an actor in a position between others; instead, more powerful actors are those capable of excluding others from exchanges (Markovsky, Willer, and Patton 1988). An actor's capacity to exclude others can depend quite subtly on distal aspects of a network's structure. This often induces a curvilinear association between centrality and power and can also lead to centrifugal tendencies that cause a network to decompose into small substructures as some potential exchange relations fall into disuse.

A large research literature on the sociology of

health and illness draws a connection between social networks, the availability of social support, and well-being (Cohen and Syme 1985). A "direct effect" view of social support states that it enhances well-being under all conditions, while the "buffering hypothesis" suggests instead a conditional effect: Those with supportive networks will have less severe responses to stressful life events.

The way in which aspects of social networks are thought to translate into support is not always made precise, and perhaps for that reason empirical studies have produced uneven results. Arguments stressing the sheer availability of support resources imply an association between the size of an individual's personal network and measures of physical or psychological health. Other versions have a more Durkheimian emphasis. They suggest that people integrated into *dense networks*—that is, strongly tied to a number of partners who themselves are strongly tied to each other—will have better-defined social identities, stronger senses of internal control, and more positive self-evaluations. Randall Collins (1988) suggests that network density indicates that the individual is integrated into "interaction rituals" of a solidary group, which in turn produces moral sentiments and energies that enhance well-being.

Some work on networks of influence and diffusion echoes these themes. This work rests on theories of social comparisons and reference groups (Erickson 1988). Under conditions of uncertainty, people are thought to look to their close associates for guidance toward appropriate attitudes, conduct, or both. Network closure is viewed as a source of locally defined norms: Persons in dense networks are exposed to consistent influences from their strong ties and are under strong social pressures toward conformity.

An important alternative contagion process is suggested by Ronald Burt (1987). He contends that actors look for normative direction to a reference group composed not of their contacts but of their competitors. Here, norms are less imposed by those in the social environment than they are actively sought out by the actor. Burt's claim is that actors regard those structurally equivalent to them as competitors and hence that

attitudes and behaviors diffuse most rapidly between structurally equivalent actors.

The purposive use of networks as "social capital" is a prominent theme in much writing about network effects. One perspective draws on the ideas about centrality, brokerage, and power discussed above, suggesting that incumbency in interstitial positions is advantageous because it allows one to serve as an entrepreneur and avoid excessive dependence and constraint (Burt 1980). A second argument, stressing informational advantages, emanates from Granovetter's (1973) discussion of weak ties; it suggests that actors with many weak ties—or wide-ranging networks—will be positioned so as to receive earlier and better information. Because weak ties are more likely than strong ones to connect an actor to diverse information sources, information acquired through them will tend to be novel, creating further advantages. In addition to the form of such networks, the content flowing through them is relevant; in a hierarchically organized system, it is expected that superior social resources will be obtained from highly ranked actors, irrespective of whether one is joined to them through strong or weak ties (Lin 1982).

The "social support" and "social capital" strands in network theory make conflicting observations about network density. If density integrates an actor into a subculture and provides a well-defined social identity, it simultaneously reduces integration into a wider network and subjects the actor to conformity pressures. Whether this is a genuine tradeoff or whether wide-ranging networks with dense cores might provide both sets of advantages is not yet known; it is notable, however, that both the "support" and "capital" perspectives suggest that large social networks may be to an actor's advantage.

As noted, rigorous theories about network effects on properties of aggregates are at best partially formulated. Much of what there is deals with social movements and political conflict. A general theme concerns networks and collective action: Social density is thought by many to be part of an infrastructure that permits latent "interest groups" to overcome social dilemmas (Marwell, Oliver, and Prahl 1988). Granovetter's (1973) argument warns against excessive closure, however: Once formed, a coalition or "collective actor" may lack social connections required for ultimate political success.

Coleman (1990) suggests that closed social networks can create and enforce strong norms that facilitate collective action. In densely interconnected systems, actors can expect to encounter one another frequently in the future, and a reputation for trustworthiness therefore becomes valuable. Moreover, frequent communication among densely linked actors means that information about a failure to honor obligations diffuses quickly and that sanctions in response to it can be applied rapidly. Strong norms of trust are essential to the creation of "social credit"—exchanges in which actions are contributed at one time for compensation deferred to the future.

Propositions advanced by Edward Laumann and his colleagues (Laumann and Pappi 1976; Laumann and Knoke 1987) suggest numerous ways that the social networks linking policy actors can shape the outcomes of decision-making processes. These specify, for example, that "policy domains" with centralized structures will winnow options and reach authoritative decisions more rapidly than decentralized domains, while domain polarization will have the opposite effect.

FURTHER LITERATURE

A number of review articles and collections treat network analysis in greater depth than possible here. Mitchell (1974) gives a useful review of the anthropological approach. Wellman (1983) reviews basic principles from a sociological perspective. Two collections illustrating substantive applications are Marsden and Lin (1982) and Wellman and Berkowitz (1988). There is a voluminous methodological literature, much of which appears in the journal *Social Networks* (1978–present), edited by Linton Freeman. Marsden (1990) surveys literature on measurement; Marsden and Laumann (1984) discuss models for representing structure and their mathematical foundations; collections edited by Burt and Minor

(1983) and Freeman, White, and Romney (1989) include strategies for data analysis.

(SEE ALSO: *Exchange Theory; Social Dynamics; Social Support*)

REFERENCES

Barnes, J. A. 1954 "Class and Committees in a Norwegian Island Parish." *Human Relations* 7:39–58.

Blau, Peter M. 1955 *The Dynamics of Bureaucracy*. Chicago: University of Chicago Press.

Blau, Peter M., and Joseph E. Schwartz 1984 *Crosscutting Social Circles*. New York: Academic Press.

Boissevain, Jeremy 1974 *Friends of Friends*. New York: St. Martin's.

Boorman, Scott A., and Harrison C. White 1976 "Social Structure from Multiple Networks II: Role Structures." *American Journal of Sociology* 81:1,384–1,446.

Bott, Elizabeth 1957 *Family and Social Network*. London: Tavistock.

Burt, Ronald S. 1980 "Autonomy in a Social Topology." *American Journal of Sociology* 85:892–925.

——— 1982 *Toward a Structural Theory of Action*. New York: Academic Press.

——— 1987 "Social Contagion and Innovation: Cohesion versus Structural Equivalence." *American Journal of Sociology* 92:1,287–1,335.

———, and Michael J. Minor (eds.) 1983 *Applied Network Analysis*. Beverly Hills, Calif.: Sage.

Cohen, Sheldon, and S. Leonard Syme, eds. 1985 *Social Support and Health*. New York: Academic Press.

Coleman, James S. 1990 *Foundations of Social Theory*. Cambridge, Mass.: Harvard University Press.

Collins, Randall 1988 *Theoretical Sociology*. New York: Harcourt Brace Jovanovich.

Cook, Karen S. 1982 "Network Structures from an Exchange Perspective." In Peter V. Marsden and Nan Lin, eds., *Social Structure and Network Analysis*. Beverly Hills, Calif.: Sage.

Davis, James A., and Samuel Leinhardt 1972 "The Structure of Positive Interpersonal Relations in Small Groups." In Joseph Berger, Morris Zelditch, Jr., and Bo Anderson, eds., *Sociological Theories in Progress*. Boston: Houghton Mifflin.

Erickson, Bonnie H. 1988 "The Relational Basis of Attitudes." In Barry Wellman and S. D. Berkowitz, eds., *Social Structures*. New York: Cambridge University Press.

Fararo, Thomas J., and John Skvoretz 1986 "E-State Structuralism: A Theoretical Method." *American Sociological Review* 51:591–602.

——— 1987 "Unification Research Programs: Integrating Two Structural Theories." *American Journal of Sociology* 92:1,183–1,209.

Freeman, Linton C. 1979 "Centrality in Social Networks I: Conceptual Clarification." *Social Networks* 1:215–239.

———, Douglas R. White, and A. Kimball Romney, eds. 1989 *Research Methods in Social Network Analysis.* Fairfax, Va.: George Mason University Press.

Granovetter, Mark S. 1973 "The Strength of Weak Ties." *American Journal of Sociology* 78:1360–1380.

——— 1979 "The Theory-Gap in Social Network Analysis." In Paul W. Holland and Samuel Leinhardt, eds., *Perspectives on Social Network Research.* New York: Academic Press.

——— 1985. "Economic Action and Social Structure: The Problem of Embeddedness." *American Journal of Sociology* 91:481–510.

Haines, Valerie A. 1988 "Social Network Analysis, Structuration Theory and the Holism-Individualism Debate." *Social Networks* 10:157–182.

Jennings, Helen Hall 1943 *Leadership and Isolation.* New York: Longmans, Green.

Laumann, Edward O., and David Knoke 1987 *The Organizational State.* Madison: University of Wisconsin Press.

Laumann, Edward O., and Franz U. Pappi 1976 *Networks of Collective Action.* New York: Academic Press.

Lin, Nan 1982 "Social Resources and Instrumental Action." In Peter V. Marsden and Nan Lin, eds., *Social Structure and Network Analysis.* Beverly Hills, Calif.: Sage.

Markovsky, Barry, David Willer, and Travis Patton 1988 "Power Relations in Exchange Networks." *American Sociological Review* 53:220–236.

Marsden, Peter V. 1990 "Network Data and Measurement." *Annual Review of Sociology* 16:435–463.

———, and Edward O. Laumann 1984 "Mathematical Ideas in Social Structural Analysis." *Journal of Mathematical Sociology* 10:271–294.

———, and Nan Lin (eds.) 1982 *Social Structure and Network Analysis.* Beverly Hills, Calif.: Sage.

Marwell, Gerald, Pamela E. Oliver, and Ralph Prahl 1988 "Social Networks and Collective Action: A Theory of the Critical Mass III." *American Journal of Sociology* 94:502–534.

Mitchell, J. Clyde 1974 "Social Networks." *Annual Review of Anthropology* 3:279–299.

Moreno, J. L. 1934 *Who Shall Survive?* Washington, D.C.: Nervous and Mental Disease Publishing Co.

Pfeffer, Jeffrey 1987 "A Resource Dependence Perspective on Intercorporate Relations." In Mark S. Mizruchi and Michael Schwartz, eds., *Intercorporate Relations.* New York: Cambridge University Press.

Reitz, Karl P., and Douglas R. White 1989 "Rethinking the Role Concept: Homomorphisms on Social Networks." In Linton C. Freeman, Douglas R. White, and A. Kimball Romney, eds., *Research Methods in Social Network Analysis.* Fairfax, Va.: George Mason University Press.

Wellman, Barry 1983 "Network Analysis: Some Basic Principles." *Sociological Theory* 1:155–199.

———, and S. D. Berkowitz, eds. 1988 *Social Structures.* New York: Cambridge University Press.

White, Harrison C., Scott A. Boorman, and Ronald L. Breiger 1976. "Social Structure from Multiple Networks I: Blockmodels of Roles and Positions." *American Journal of Sociology* 81:730–780.

PETER V. MARSDEN

SOCIAL ORGANIZATION It is necessary to highlight this central area selectively, considering the breadth and variety in its specification, and to emphasize current concerns, relying on past overviews to detail their origins (e.g., by Znaniecki 1945; Gerth and Mills 1953; Faris 1964; Eisenstadt 1968; Parsons 1968; Udy 1968; Smelser 1988).

Social organization is nonrandom *pattern* within human populations that comprise society by sharing the main aspects of a common existence over time as well as nonrandom *patterning*, the human and interhuman activities through which patterns are formed, retained, altered, or replaced. These twin aspects of social organization had been considered *structure*, relatively stable patterns of interrelations among persons or other social units, and *process*, the manner in which the patterns are produced, reproduced, or transformed (see, e.g., Faris 1964). The distinction is blurred to the extent that interrelations vary in *degrees* of regularity, uniformity, and permanence in the rhythms of coexistence, contact, or avoidance of which they consist (Williams 1976). In short, structure can also be viewed as patterned process among human agents (e.g., Blumer 1969, pp. 78–89; Giddens 1979, pp. 49–95; Coleman 1990, esp. pp. 1–44).

At issue is not what is patterned or how, but simply the extent to which there is any pattern or patterning at all. The antithesis of social organization is not opposition or discord. Conflict and other aspects of tension or unrest can, for example, exhibit regularity and uniformity as readily as can union, harmony, and tranquillity. Rather it is randomness, consisting of chaos, formlessness, and idiosyncratic human behavior (Blau 1975) and is called social *dis*organization. Yet patterned *occurrence* of disorganization is no contradiction.

Social organization is characterized by *interdependence*—that is, what occurs among certain components has, to varying degree, consequences for some or all of the other components and their relations with one another. These consequences can range from loss, even annihilation, to survival and other types of gain. Subsumed are regulation and stability as well as replacement and transformation.

The socially organized units or sets of units are generally activities or actors, individual or plural, that affect one another more immediately—even if simply by coexisting or by their sheer numbers —than do other activities or actors. The former are therefore distinguished (to varying extents) from an environment that might include those other units.

The units considered vary in their distinguishability, modifiability, and permanence. For some purposes they have been defined as concrete entities, such as persons or countries, or as activities by these entities, such as acts of persuasion or conquest. For other purposes the units have been defined abstractly as only certain aspects of concrete entities or of their activities, called roles or functions (e.g., Hawley 1986, pp. 31–32), that signify position or participation in a particular aspect of collective living, or as complexes of these entities or activities. Examples are worker, labor, industry in production; official or bureau, directive, central administration in governance; judge

or court, adjudication, court system in jurisprudence; supplicant or temple, prayer, denomination in religion; friend or friendship group, attachment, solidary web in emotional bonding; and lecturer or college, teaching, school system in social learning. It will be noted from these examples that units can be sets or combinations of other units. They are called substructures when they constitute broad components of social organization not detailed as to their composition. Examples of *societal* substructures are political state, economy, or moral community.

Structure subsumes both form and content: form generally in the senses of numbers, sizes, shapes, assemblage, connections among units, and directions of flow (say, of resources or persuasion); content in the sense of type of unit, substructure, relationship, or process. Clearly this distinction, though convenient for exposition, is not absolute. Units have been assigned to types on the basis of their forms. And there is form when the same everyday dramas can be "performed" in virtually any setting, whether work or nonwork (Goffman 1959).

FORM

In conventional usage, form implies arrangement in space (not necessarily physical space) and in time. It also implies relationships among elements, in this case the units, against a background —the environment—which is conceived as external to structure (Hawley 1986, pp. 10–44; Smelser 1988). The environment may contain units with which concrete portions of the structure have relationships. Thus environment's separation from structure is often abstract, especially where environment's nonphysical attributes are concerned.

Form can be classified by the processes that occur among the units. Among pure types that are widely investigated are markets, characterized by competition and exchange; arenas, characterized by interunit struggle and alliance; collectivities, characterized by cooperation in joint activity— that is, acting in concert (Parsons and Smelser [1956] 1965, p. 15), even if coerced; and aggregates, characterized by the absence of relations between the units.

These forms occur with a variety of contents. For example, markets not only process goods, services, and labor; they can also process social resources, such as information, intimacy, commitment, information, influence, and prestige. Arenas need not only be political; they can also exist within, say, the family. Collectivities may be found in any or all aspects of human living. And labor forces, electorates, viewerships, school enrollments, and populations of organizations (Aldrich and Marsden 1988) may all be conceived to constitute aggregates. Crosscutting the degrees to which these pure types are approximated are the variables of segmentation, stratification, specialization, scale, and endurance.

Segmentation. Segmentation is division into or banding together of like units (Parsons and Smelser [1956] 1965, p. 256; Parsons [1966] 1977, p. 25; Luhmann [1977] 1982, pp. 231–235, 242–245; Wallace 1988). Tribal societies, for example, can, in their inception, be considered markets constituted by exchange of spouses among relatively small family groups—the segments—that avoid internal marriages (Habermas [1981] 1987, pp. 161–162). In the case of collectivities, segmentation—called categoric organization (Hawley 1986, pp. 70–73)—enables each to accomplish more than could be accomplished separately, as, say, in the union of family groups in hunting and gathering societies (Duncan 1964; Lenski 1975; Hawley 1986, pp. 34–35), in a union of persons pursuing the same occupation, or in the replacement of one national corporation with several regional units. Categoric organization can also replace, at least in part, what would otherwise be mutually destructive competition or conflict or can otherwise create a more predictable environment for the participating unit. Examples are umbrella units that form among populations of special collectivities facing unpredictability in "turbulent environments" (cited by Scott 1987, pp. 122–123), even if they serve as no more than clearinghouses for information. All things being equal, ethnic pluralism—that is, subdivision into collectivities having different his-

tories and life-styles—is another illustration of segmentation.

Stratification. For present purposes, stratification means the ranking of units or sets of units in their capacities to affect the existence and activity of other units or sets by controlling resources. This occurs through manipulation or struggle, as a result of competition or exchange, or voluntarily. Stratification and segmentation can co-occur. Where agriculture is the main economic activity, for example, it has been observed that rank tends to be associated primarily with size of landholding, if any; and where land ownership is also associated with other ranking criteria, as in earlier India, it is likely to serve as a basis either for strata (layers) or for collectivities of same-rank kinship units (Landecker 1981, pp. 33–34, 97). More complex social organization can consist of stratification among units that are themselves stratified. For example, it has been shown that the nations of the world are both internally stratified and stratified vis-à-vis one another (Wallerstein 1979), although effects of the one structure on the other are variable (see, e.g., Evans and Stephens 1988).

Specialization. In its pure sense, specialization refers to composition of unlike units that only taken together can accomplish all that is deemed significant. As a division of labor (Smith [1789] 1976; Durkheim [1902] 1964; Rueschemeyer 1986), specialization is characterized by greater interdependence—facilitative *or* inhibitory—than in the cases of simple segmentation or stratification. Segments can be added or lost with little effect; specialties cannot. Specialization ranges from little more than by age and sex in hunting and gathering societies, possibly with part-time political and religious leadership, to thousands of occupational specialties and nonoccupational roles in industrial and postindustrial societies (Lenski 1975, 1979; Hawley 1986, pp. 31–37, 64–67).

Generally also stratified, this form of social organization has been called corporate in distinction to categoric (Hawley 1986, pp. 68–69). The specialized units can be individuals or certain of their roles, as in a family, a small commune, or a small business enterprise; or they can themselves be segmented, stratified, or specialized internally.

Scale. Frequently associated with other aspects of social organization is its scale, variously specified as, for example, the number of units encompassed; the number of levels at which units are nested into progressively more comprehensive units; or lengths of chains in the modification and flow of materials and services, information, influence, or command.

Contrasted with today's enormous urban settlements and nation-states are the unspecialized and unnested bands of twenty-five to forty or so hunters and gatherers (Lenski 1979). Specific examples of nesting—often accompanying or accompanied by stratification and one type of chain—are world system, country, province, and locality; Catholic Church, archdiocese, diocese, parish, and priest or parishioner; corporation, division, department, and job. Nesting is bypassed when, for example, transnational corporations become disassociated from local, provincial, or national jurisdictions; when religious ties crosscut nation-states; or when staff activities or occupational associations occur irrespective of level (Turk 1977, pp. 223–224; Tilly 1984, p. 136; Hawley 1986, p. 104).

The more activities become organized into large, specialized, but unnested units at higher levels of social organization, according to one body of theory, the less likely are the constituent units to be interconnected (references cited by Turk 1977, p. 65; McAdam et al. 1988). Each of the aggregates that result, sometimes the set of all such aggregates, is called a mass. An example is loss of relationships based on common residence to the extent that the local community is penetrated by specialized large-scale nonlocal collectivities called organizations (e.g., Turk 1977, pp. 65–66, 208–209).

Endurance. An important basis of classifying structure—or, for that matter, any complex unit or relationship that comprises structure—is by the extent to which it predates and outlives, or is otherwise independent of, specific units. Factory workers and managers are relatively replaceable, but a marriage does not substitute a new spouse

for one that has been lost without becoming a different marriage. A market can be independent of particular producers and consumers, but a partnership or international bloc is not. Moreover, general features of factory, family, market, partnership, or bloc—or the means of generating these—tend to predate and survive as prototypes any of their specific instances (see, e.g., Jackson 1990).

Combinations. Hybrid forms, some of them complex, occur when segmentation, stratification, specialization, and nesting are considered with respect to one another or with respect to markets, arenas, collectivities, and aggregates. Further, units can themselves be composed of other units in ways other than by nesting, or they can themselves be patterned. A few illustrations follow.

Organizations are specialized collectivities. Defined as complexes of more or less cooperative relations directed toward more or less specific objectives, these units have been said to occur in every known society as "the major vehicle through which concentrated goal-directed effort takes place" (Udy 1979). They, the aggregates they comprise, and relations among them—including organizations of organizations—are considered to be primary units of social organization, at least in industrial and postindustrial communities and nations (see, e.g., Turk 1977, 1985; Skocpol 1979; Perrow 1986; Evans and Stephens 1988; Perrucci and Potter 1989; Coleman 1990).

Markets and arenas generally affect and are affected by collectivities—including ones that they nest or in which they are nested, that they constrain or by which they are constrained—shaping units so they can compete, exchange, struggle, or ally themselves with one another (see, e.g., Stinchcombe 1986; Coleman 1990, esp. pp. 266–321, 371–396, 689). Indeed, organizations and other kinds of collectivities can affect the conditions under which other organizations are formed in substitution for markets (Williamson 1990). Clearly, positions within the organizational substitutes may be filled in turn by labor markets (Stinchcombe 1986; Granovetter and Tilly 1988).

Sizes of aggregates can affect social organization (see citations by Eisenstadt 1968). Sheer numbers make it impossible for each unit to have relations with each other one. This affects the probabilities of positions, networks, or organizations that channel and mediate social relationships (research stimulated by Simmel 1908, pp. 55–56). More recent work shows how specific interconnections, such as marriage or crowd behavior under conditions of threat, can be affected by aggregates, by their relative sizes and other properties, and by relations among these properties (e.g., Blau 1987, Coleman 1990).

Network analysis has added precision to the measurement of form—say, of stratification or of degrees of interconnectedness—by detailing the connections (links) among units and the patterns that these provide (see, e.g., Cook 1977; Leinhardt 1977; Burt 1982; Turner 1986, pp. 287–305). Its techniques are uniquely suited to the chains, clusters, and sequences of exchange, cooperation, alliance, or command over which goods, services, money, information, or influence flow. Associated with scale, for example, can be the number of points between origin of flow and its completion. Network formulations have also proven especially useful in identifying relations among organizations that affect concerted action locally (Turk 1977; Galaskiewicz 1989) and ones that affect it nationally (Laumann and Knoke 1989).

Complexity. The very complexity of social organization—the number and variety of units, levels, and interconnections—is itself an aspect of form. Though admittedly crude (Luhmann [1977] 1982, pp. 232–233; Tilly 1984, pp. 48–50; Rueschemeyer 1986, p. 168), this variable can be used to account for other aspects of social organization (e.g., Lenski 1975, 1979; Turk 1977; Habermas [1981] 1987, pp. 153–197; Luhmann [1977] 1982, pp. 229–254; Rueschemeyer 1986).

CONTENT

Classification of units—including complex units—is necessary for similarity, stratification, or specialization to signify more than simply differences in form. Among many, two bases of classification stand out. Sometimes applied jointly, the one emphasizes objective consequences—positive, negative, or neutral, and varying from 0 in degree—the other communicated, remembered, or recorded meanings and rules. Examples of the two bases follow.

Consequences. Substructure has been classified according to its consequences for stability and change in overall structure (e.g., Marx and Engels [1846] 1970; Marx [1859] 1971; Parsons [1966, 1971] 1977; Luhmann [1977] 1982; Habermas [1981] 1987; Hawley 1986). Among these, adaptation to the environment and of units to one another have been stressed (see, e.g., Duncan 1964; Lenski 1975, 1979; Parsons [1966, 1971] 1977; Habermas [1981] 1987; Luhmann [1974–1977] 1982; Hawley 1986), quite likely because socially organized life has been observed to be the major adaptive means available to primates (e.g., by Lenski 1975).

Thus, the distinction is often made between (1) economic substructure affecting environmental adaptation for the generation and distribution of general resources (e.g., gross national product, homelessness) and (2) political substructure affecting the generation and distribution of general capacity to mobilize resources for concerted action, including action by opposing collectivities (e.g., national efforts, party campaigns, uprisings). Further distinction involves (3) substructure affecting the generation and distribution of general bonds or schisms that provide harmony or discord among units (e.g., community cohesion, solidary antagonism; see Parsons and Smelser [1956] 1965, pp. 48–49; Parsons [1966] 1977, pp. 135–140; Hawley 1986, p. 66; Coleman 1990, pp. 91–116, 175–196, 517–527) and (4) substructure affecting the generation, distribution, and maintenance of participation in structure: recruitment of units (including but not limited to procreation) and their training, allocation, motivation, and retention—in short, the populating and regulating of social structure.

Meanings and Rules. The classification of content can also rest on disputed or common meanings, understandings, purposes, or binding rules (including law) that are communicated about environment and structure. Communication can involve all kinds of participants or only certain ones and can be modified depending on the context (Goffman 1959). The products of communication vary in their permanence through repetition, recording, or recall; in their breadth of dissemination and acceptance; and in their association with sanction—that is, support by enforcement or other incentives to comply. They can, but often do not, coincide with the structure's objective consequences (Habermas [1981] 1987, esp. pp. 153–197) but can affect it.

Most theories of social organization allow for the effects on stability and change of sanctioned agreement, or of oppositions among sanctioned agreements, calling the product institutional or cultural. They differ in terms of the importance the institutional component is said to have for structure.

Near the one extreme, institutional rules are viewed as "higher level" determinants of social organization (Parsons [1971] 1977, pp. 234–236), not only of relations among units but also of the units themselves (Meyer et al. 1987; Coleman 1990, pp. 43–44, 325–70). Here the rules governing specific structure are considered to be products of more inclusive structure, such as political state or church (Znaniecki 1945; Turk 1977, pp. 210, 215–221), or to be elements of a world "culture pool" (Moore 1988; Meyer et al. 1987). Near the other extreme, meanings ("ideas") are viewed primarily as by-products of the material relations of production (Marx and Engels [1846] 1970, pp. 57–60) or in terms of their significance for organized adaptive processes vis-à-vis the environment (e.g., Duncan 1964; Lenski 1975). Meaning, if the concept is employed at all, is restricted to the acting unit's purposive rationality: its adoption, within the limits of error and imperfect knowledge or skill, of means that are appropriate to specified outcomes (see, e.g., Hawley 1986, pp. 6–7).

A second source of variability is the degree to which the institutional can be seen as analytically distinct from structure. Some consider the institutional to be an aspect of the environments of substructures and other units (Parsons 1968; Meyer and Rowan 1978; Hawley 1986, p. 79; Meyer et al. 1987; Coleman 1990, pp. 43–44).

Others see it as relatively inextricable from structure (e.g., Giddens 1979, pp. 49–85), specifically where structure is viewed as formed and modified through interpretive interaction between persons or groups, in which interpretations are frequently but not always shared (Blumer 1969, pp. 86–88).

The third issue regards the degree to which structure is "spelled out" by the institutional. There can be precise rules that govern even the minutiae, as on an assembly line or in religious ritual. There are also general principles that reduce the number of structural alternatives without determining structure precisely (Parsons [1971] 1977, pp. 193–194), as in such ideals as freedom, rationality, retribution, obedience, protest, solidarity, revolution, contract, and property. Relatedly, there can be shared common-sense reasoning (Collins 1988, pp. 273–291 on Garfinkel) on the basis of which "sense" is made of structure. Or there can be broad myths that serve to provide accounts of social organization (Meyer and Rowan 1978, Goffman 1959) on the basis of which, rather than on the basis of performance, structure is justified.

Agency, as do most theories incorporating meaning, rests on the general idea of interest—variously called purpose, intention, motive, or goal and variably emerging during a course of action—and on the availability of action alternatives (e.g., Giddens 1979, pp. 55–56). Agency is the extent to which purposive action by and interaction among the units affect social organization. There is little need to consider what individual units contribute to organization or why (Hawley 1986, pp. 6–7). When structure, environment, or rule are viewed as an absolute constraint or as providing only limited choice (see, e.g., Blau 1987), or where social organization results from natural selection (Lenski 1975, 1979).

This is not the case where structure and culture simply set loose conditions for action and interaction. Important here for structural and cultural stability and change are the processes (1) by which interests are pursued under the influence and constraint of other actors (Homans 1975); (2) by which the conditions of action are interpreted through social interaction (Blumer 1969); (3) by which the acting unit monitors and adjusts the components of action, even intention, throughout (Giddens 1979, pp. 53–59); and (4) by which individual and collective actors choose means of implementing their interests (Coleman 1990). These processes are significant both to the reproduction and to the transformation of structure and institutional rule.

Classifications of meaning are numerous. Yet they frequently rest on one or more of the following variables (polar approximations in parentheses): (1) specificity: the scope of the relationship, from specific to diffuse content (e.g., organizations or special markets vs. unspecialized collectivities or conflict arenas); (2) universalism: the extent to which relationships hold for all units belonging to a category or only for particular ones from that category (e.g., upholding sovereignty of any nation or opposition toward all governments vs. a treaty or a declaration of war); (3) neutrality: the extent to which relationships are means to ends vs. ends in themselves (e.g., banking transactions or job competition vs. flag-raising or flag-burning ceremonies); and (4) performance: the extent to which relationships are based on what units do rather than on what they are (e.g., production relations or industrial conflict vs. aristocracy or racial conflict).

Concrete as well as abstract structures have been classified according to various combinations of values of these variables, leading to widely used typologies. More generally, any variables used to define content and form serve the analysis of overall structure by describing its various aspects or its different parts.

FORM AND CONTENT

Structure can vary in the extent to which substructures—such as the four whose consequences were noted—are abstractions, involving the same concrete units rather than different ones. At the low end of this continuum, the units comprise a single unstratified and unspecialized collectivity, approximated by a tribal society or a commune, in which each act affirms the totality (Durkheim [1902] 1964; Luhmann [1974] 1982,

1987, pp. 153–197), having every kind of consequence for it. In it myth tends to blur distinctions among the objective, social, and subjective worlds and between society and its natural surroundings (Habermas [1981] 1987, pp. 158–159), and there is comprehensive and detailed regulation of activity. The units not only resemble one another but also tend not to have separate identities. In short, relations tend to be particular to the given collectivity, not universal; affective, not neutral; ascriptive, not performance-based; and diffuse, not specific.

In examples of this noncomplex instance, economic and political organization tend to be extensions of family, extended family, religious group, and common territory, which overlap to considerable degrees. Commitment to any one aspect of social life tends to be supported and sanctioned within all of the others (Habermas [1981] 1987, pp. 156–157), and there are relatively few conflicting constraints, structural or cultural (Blumer 1969, pp. 87–88).

Compliance to one cluster of rules and understandings is approximated, with utility, sanction, attachment, and/or commitment as its basis or bases. Here change has been attributed, in the main, to changes in the environment or in ways of coping with it (e.g., Hawley 1986, pp. 15–18) or to ubiquitous "tension" between rules of action and the situation of the acting unit (e.g., Parsons and Smelser [1956] 1965, esp. pp. 50–51). There is little institutional provision for change.

With greater complexity, however, activities can be removed from these primordial units and assumed by large-scale economic, political, and other kinds of organizations (e.g., Lenski 1979; Coleman 1990, pp. 584–585). Varied organizational purpose as well as interaction among organizations can constitute bases of change that are themselves institutionalized.

Domination. Stratification implies domination—that is, setting the conditions of existence by certain units for other units through disposition over key resources; over the generation and selection of often self-serving meanings and rules (see, e.g., Landecker 1981); and over the means of securing compliance. Such disproportion is one of the most widely considered sources of strain, hence of change through conflict (see, e.g., the modifications of Marxian theory by Dahrendorf 1959 and Skocpol 1979).

Considered under various names (see, e.g., Marx and Engels [1846] 1970; Parsons and Smelser [1956] 1965; Dahrendorf 1959; Duncan 1964; Hawley 1986; Giddens 1985), domination includes disposition over means of coercion, material inducement, social support, or rules of command (adapted from Weber [1920] 1978, pp. 53–54; Hawley 1986, pp. 33–37). Domination reflects power, the capacity to affect action and its outcomes (Giddens 1979, pp. 88–94). Suggested by Weber ([1920] 1978, p. 53) as the probability that the acting unit can carry out its will despite resistance, power has also been defined as the structure's capacity to mobilize resources in effecting outcomes through concerted action, such as the production of sustenance (or other ways of supporting units) and environmental control (Parsons and Smelser [1956] 1965, p. 48; Hawley 1986, pp. 36–37). This capacity is conceived to be distributed in different ways, depending on the structure under consideration (Hawley 1986, pp. 74–77), serving political relations as money serves economic relations (Parsons 1975).

Domination can effect both form and content. For example, domination can cause segmentation to give way to stratification, frequently as a result of conquest, as when multicommunal societies become kingdoms or empires (Lenski 1979) or numerous petty sovereignties are gathered under nation-states (Tilly 1984, p. 48). By setting the conditions for competition and exchange or more directly by affecting concerted action that favors certain specialties or even by imposition, domination can also make specialization possible or influence its nature and degree (Habermas [1981] 1987, pp. 161–163; Hawley 1986, pp. 64–67, 91–95; Rueschemeyer 1986).

The resources on which domination is based need not only be material. They can be social— for example, active support, institutionalization by organizations and movements that generate and implement ideology or legality, and the absence of opposition. Generalized control over all manner

of resources has been called hegemony, and political processes have been characterized as struggles for hegemony (Wallerstein 1979, 1984; Tuchman 1988). Domination has been conceived, in its extreme form, as rendering certain alternatives invisible (Giddens 1985, pp. 8–10) through taken-for-granted opposition by powerful units (Polsby 1980, pp. 189–218), lack of relevant language (Parsons 1975), absence of relevant substructures, agendas set by the mass media of communication (Tuchman 1988), and uncontested legitimacy— that is, common understandings as to what is valid or binding. The elementary stratified society is, by definition, hegemonic, since it is unspecialized in terms of the control of various types of resources.

Domination can be by one or more substructures over the others. History shows, for example, cases of kinship-based, religious, military, economic, and political domination (e.g., Tilly 1984; Evans and Stephens 1988). The hypothesis has been suggested that the greater the specialization, the less stable is domination through fusion of, say, political with economic activities (Parsons and Smelser [1956] 1965, p. 83). The expected trend is for substructures to become concretely separate. For example, underground markets arise as responses to shortages and bottlenecks in socialist societies, which are characterized by political domination of economic activity, or by the "informally" organized demands of their workers (Jones 1984).

Pluralism and Plasticity. The degree to which meanings are single or plural can be affected by segmentation or specialization. Different collectivities, constituted, say, on the basis of different fundamental beliefs, different descent, or different economic circumstances (Landecker 1981), coexist segmentally either by loose agreement or by coercive regulation, each with separate rules and understandings (Tenbruck 1989), or struggle with one another over which ones shall prevail (e.g., Landecker 1981, pp. 136–169; Wallace 1988).

The greater the specialization among units, all things being equal, the greater also is the plurality of interests, according to some models. A recurrent theme is that this form of pluralism affects the probabilities of different degrees of involvement by given units and of different alignments among units from one issue to the next. Such differential participation can have a negative effect on the probability of broad or intense conflict (Dahrendorf 1959, pp. 215–231; Polsby 1980, pp. 84–97, 122–138; Turk 1977, pp. 97–103, 1985; McAdam et al. 1988).

Specialized forms, including organizations, are by definition relatively indifferent to the activities or aspirations of supporting, component, or utilizing units in other social settings (Luhmann [1975] 1982, pp. 78–79; Labovitz and Hagedorn 1977, pp. 12–15). Entire areas of indifference are seen to result, for example, from "gaps" left between interests served by organizations (Luhmann [1975] 1982, pp. 79–80, 87, [1977] 1982, p. 237). The intrusion of, say, race and gender in contemporary labor markets suggests, however, that organizational indifference is a matter of degree (see, e.g., Stinchcombe 1986; Granovetter and Tilly 1988).

Accompanying segmentation or specialization, according to several theories, is plasticity: the probability of loose and variable connections among segments or among organizations subsumed by substructures like the four singled out. Here overall organization is limited to compatibility, falling short of the pursuit of unified or concerted outcomes across substructures (see, e.g., Luhmann [1975] 1982, pp. 78–79). Change is endemic in the absence of overall structure, save for markets and conflict arenas and rules that govern these (Luhmann [1977] 1982, pp. 238–242). It tends to occur as accommodation (1) through exchange, say, between segments or between political and economic substructures (Parsons and Smelser [1956] 1965), or (2) through new forms and modification of older ones in responses to changes elsewhere, as in the case of the family's loss of economic activity in the United States but its growing importance in providing incentive for such activity (Schumpeter, cited by Suttles and Janowitz 1979).

The greater the segmentation or specialization, the more general the accommodative meanings and rules that encompass social organization over-

all—for example, the idea of tolerance and its enforcement, or of universal civility (Parsons [1971] 1977, pp. 182–193; Hawley 1986, p. 66). Another example is the idea of freedom in classic liberal society, implemented as economic laissez faire, religious autonomy, voluntary rather than arranged marriage, political competition for electoral support, and stratum membership on the basis of achievement rather than family (Gerth and Mills 1964, pp. 354–357).

There is disagreement about the extent of hegemony under conditions of specialization, even where, say, political or economic organizations overshadow other organizations in control over resources. At the one extreme incumbents of dominant positions within the various specialized organizations have been conceived as constituting a single elite capable of joint domination (e.g., Mills 1956) or as being generally dominant to the extent that they hold positions in multiple organizations (Perrucci and Pilisuk 1970). Relatedly, large organizations have been observed to divorce themselves from the interests they were established to represent—as, say, those of capital and labor—and strike bargains with one another (Evans and Stephens 1988). These conceptions of unified domination have partly been verified and partly refuted (e.g., by Lieberson 1971; Mizruchi 1982; Johnsen and Mintz 1989).

Specialized as they are, according to another partly verified view, the same set of organizations can facilitate one another in certain respects and be in mutual struggle in others, therefore resisting direct domination by any one or a few of their number (citations in Turk 1985). Under these conditions policy that is the basis for binding domination is formed through action by those masses or by those nonpermanent coalitions of public agencies and private organizations that are concerned with any particular matter (Turk 1977, pp. 136–205; Galaskiewicz 1989; Laumann and Knoke 1989).

Crosscutting the issue is the question of whether, given specialization, either an organized elite or an interorganizational coalition has the capacity for concerted action that transcends the substructures. Specialization can mean that, at the most, even the most powerful organization is dominant only with respect to one or two issue areas (Luhmann [1975] 1982, pp. 76–89; Polsby 1980, pp. 122–128). However, even within organizations the normal decision process has been defined as organized anarchy by certain investigators (e.g., citations by Scott 1987, pp. 277–282; Meyer and Rowan 1978). Carried to an extreme, the question is one of the extent to which coordination by domination is haphazard, whether actual coordination might not result from the "invisible hand" of a market (Smith [1789] 1976, Vol. 1, pp. 477–478) or of an arena of conflict.

Standardization. Mitigating the diversifying possibilities of segmentation and specialization that have been noted are tendencies for units to become alike in certain aspects of form and content—that is, isomorphic (Hawley 1986, pp. 66–70; Udy 1979; Kerr 1983, pp. 85–89). This can be because units require similar internal arrangements for purposes of connection with one another (Hawley 1986, p. 70), or model themselves after other units in the preservation of competitive effectiveness (suggested by Aldrich and Marsden 1988, citing DiMaggio and Powell). It can also be through institutionalization by drawing upon a common "culture pool" available, say, to the countries of the world (Moore 1988) or through, say, political or religious imposition within a given society (Znaniecki 1945; Landecker 1981, p. 136) or by either (Hawley 1986, p. 66; Meyer et al. 1987).

Not only can there be standardization of form, there can also be standardization of process. For reasons of predictability and economy of effort, among others, the joint reproduction of habitual patterns has been considered to lie at the heart of social life (e.g., Berger and Luckmann 1966). This not only accounts in part for compliance with meanings and rules that standardize feeling, thinking, and acting in such relatively unspecialized settings as tribal societies, it also accounts for standardized, partly area-specific media and codes that symbolize and routinize all manner of activities and products where there is more specialization. Examples are language (Habermas [1981] 1987, pp. 56–57), money, property, prestige,

influence, power, legality, administrative principles, criteria of truth (Parsons 1975, Habermas [1981] 1987, pp. 153–197, 367–373; Luhmann [1974] 1982, pp. 168–170), and credentialed expertise (Collins 1988, pp. 174–184; Luhmann [1976] 1982, pp. 303–331; Bauman 1989). These standardize and objecify aspects of markets, conflict arenas, collectivities, or aggregates. Unless it fails noticeably, it is believed, routine tends not to be questioned, especially where relevant knowledge is not widely pursued and alternatives are not at hand.

Collective Agency. Mainly based on exchange, conquest, or revolution, change is seldom institutionalized in segmental or stratified society. Pluralism generally includes provisions for categoric organization in the form of mass action, say through referenda, or in the form of movement and interest organizations, which not only participate in the coalitions that seek to dominate given matters but also define matters for action by the mass. These institutionalized means of structural and cultural change through collective agency are thought to occur where pluralism means lack of overall institutional detail (e.g., Gusfield 1979). Recent investigations have not only examined their causes and effects but also their forms and ways of acting (Zurcher and Snow 1981; McAdam et al. 1988). Their efforts can be toward increasing the material and social resources controlled by given categories of units, as in the case of gay rights, or they can be directed toward broad structural changes or changes in meaning that occur for their participants and for nonparticipants alike, as in the case of civil liberties (Gusfield 1979). Like revolutions, movements have been considered to be processes that can begin by effecting transitional social organization and end with new institutionalized structure (Alberoni [1981] 1984).

Commitment and Trust. Commitment of units to one another and to their common structure is a widely recognized influence. The "we" that characterizes collectivities (Cooley 1902, 1916) or the "consciousness" that causes support of existing social organization or generates struggle within it (Marx and Engels [1846] 1970;

Durkheim [1902] 1964) is seen as having either of two effects. It can be direct, producing commitment to the given structure, or indirect by habitualizing the commitment and trust that serves participation in a variety of settings, even ones that are specific and neutral (also see Coleman 1990, p. 297).

Increasing specialization and other forms of organizational complexity and increasing scale have been viewed as negative influences on commitment, even on commitment to disputing factions or to revolutionary movements seeking structural change. Commitment to large-scale organizations comprising specialized substructure is generally considered less than to other kinds of collectivities because of anonymity among the constituent units, which are likely to have the characteristics of a mass, and because only part of the constituent is involved.

With complexity and scale, participation in one substructure is less contingent on participation in others, incurring separate, possibly conflicting obligations; indeed, everyday interactions that produce common meaning have been considered divorced from structure and rules (Luhmann [1974–1977] 1982, 1987; Habermas [1981] 1987, pp. 117, 153–197), and even everyday life is penetrated by the actions and generalized media controlled by organizations (e.g., legal and monetary), reducing its potential for social integration (Habermas [1981] 1987, pp. 267, 330–331, 367–373). Under these conditions the influence of trust on social organization is less likely (Coleman 1990, pp. 300–321), and benefits are more likely sought without corresponding contributions (Coleman 1990, pp. 650–655).

The greater the specialization and accompanying standardization, it has been observed, the more of the population can be included in whatever substructures comprise various areas of social life (Parsons [1966] 1977)—that is, the more universalistic, for example, are criteria for suffrage and military service, access to public facilities, mass education, and employment opportunity. One reason follows. The more social structure consists of aggregates of organizations whose concerted activities are narrowly focused on special-

ized consequences—meaning specific and neutral orientation toward performance—that tend to be unranked, the less relevant these aggregates are to one another as criteria of exclusion (Luhmann [1977] 1982, pp. 236–238). Examples can be found in references to "customer," "patient," "student," or "defendant," independently of the beneficiary's other social attributes. At its extreme it can even lead to "the gall bladder in bed 27." Aided by standardized media such as money, the result of inclusion can be the diminution of commitment and trust through the transformation of agents into commodities for exchange (e.g., Marx [1859] 1971, pp. 78–84), or their more general removal from meaningful communicative interaction (Habermas [1981] 1987, e.g., p. 343).

The other side of inclusion is regulation. The more central that large, specialized organizations are to social structure, it has also been claimed, the less social organization depends on commitment and the greater is the shift from mutual trust to trust in expertise. The state, for example, is said to require less legitimacy as its expert-driven political technology provides, say, surveillance, "correction," welfare supervision, "medicalization," or "psychiatrization" (Bauman 1989). Indeed, the electorate's growing cynicism about government (e.g., Institute for Social Research 1979) has had little apparent effect on political structure in the United States.

(SEE ALSO: *Organizational Structure; Social Dynamics; Social Network Theory; Social Structure*)

REFERENCES

Alberoni, Francesco (1981) 1984 *Movement and Institution,* trans. P.C.A. Delmoro. New York: Columbia University Press.

Aldrich, Howard E., and Peter V. Marsden 1988 "Environments and Organizations." In N. J. Smelser, ed., *Handbook of Sociology.* Beverly Hills, Calif.: Sage.

Bauman, Zygmunt 1989 "Legislators and Interpretors: Culture as Ideology of Intellectuals." In H. Haferkamp, ed., *Social Structure and Culture.* New York: Walter de Gruyter.

Berger, Peter L., and Thomas Luckmann 1966 *The*

Social Construction of Reality: A Treatise in the Sociology of Knowledge. Garden City, N.Y.: Doubleday.

Blau, Peter M. 1975 "Introduction: Parallels and Contrasts in Structural Inquiries." In P. M. Blau, ed., *Approaches to the Study of Social Structure.* New York: Free Press.

——— 1987 "Contrasting Theoretical Perspectives." In J. C. Alexander, B. Giesen, R. Münch, and N. J. Smelser, eds., *The Micro-Macro Link.* Berkeley: University of California Press.

Blumer, Herbert 1969 *Symbolic Interactionism: Perspective and Method.* Englewood Cliffs, N.J.: Prentice-Hall.

Burt, Ronald S. 1982 *Toward a Structural Theory of Action: Network Models of Social Structure, Perception, and Action.* New York: Academic Press.

Coleman, James S. 1990 *Foundations of Social Theory.* Cambridge, Mass.: Harvard University Press.

Collins, Randall 1988 *Theoretical Sociology.* New York: Harcourt Brace Jovanovich.

Cook, Karen S. 1977 "Exchange and Power in Networks of Interorganizational Relations." *Sociological Quarterly* 18:62–82.

Cooley, Charles Horton 1902 *Human Nature and the Social Order.* New York: Scribners.

——— 1916 *Social Organization: A Study of the Larger Mind.* New York: Scribners.

Dahrendorf, Ralf 1959 *Class and Class Conflict in Industrial Society.* Stanford, Calif.: Stanford University Press.

Duncan, Otis Dudley 1964 "Social Organization and the Ecosystem." In R. E. L. Faris, ed., *Handbook of Sociology.* Chicago: Rand McNally.

Durkheim, Emile (1902) 1964 *The Division of Labor in Society,* trans. George Simpson. New York: Free Press.

Eisenstadt, Shmuel N. 1968 "Social Institutions, I: The Concept." In D. L. Sills, ed., *International Encyclopedia of the Social Sciences.* New York: Macmillan.

Evans, Peter B., and John D. Stephens 1988 "Development and the World Economy." In N. J. Smelser, ed., *Handbook of Sociology.* Beverly Hills, Calif.: Sage.

Faris, Robert E. L. 1964 "Social Organization (Sociology)." In J. Gold and W. L. Kolb, eds., *A Dictionary of the Social Sciences.* New York: Free Press.

Galaskiewicz, Joseph 1989 "Interorganizational Networks Mobilizing Action at the Metropolitan Level." In R. Perrucci and H. R. Potter, eds., *Networks of Power: Organizational Actors at the National, Corporate, and Community Levels.* New York: Aldine de Gruyter.

Gerth, Hans, and C. Wright Mills (1953) 1964 *Character and Social Structure: The Psychology of Social Institutions.* New York: Harcourt, Brace and World.

Giddens, Anthony 1979 *Central Problems in Social Theory: Action, Structure and Contradiction in Social Analysis.* Berkeley: University of California Press.

——— 1985 *The Nation-State and Violence.* Berkeley: University of California Press.

Goffman, Erving 1959 *The Presentation of Self in Everyday Life.* Garden City, N.Y.: Doubleday.

Granovetter, Mark, and Charles Tilly 1988 "Inequality and Labor Processes." In N. J. Smelser, ed., *Handbook of Sociology.* Beverly Hills, Calif.: Sage.

Gusfield, Joseph 1979 "The Modernity of Social Movements: Public Roles and Private Parts." In A. H. Hawley, ed., *Societal Growth: Processes and Implications.* New York: Free Press.

Habermas, Jurgen (1981) 1987 *The Theory of Communicative Action.* Vol. 2: *Lifeworld and System: A Critique of Functionalist Reason,* trans. Thomas McCarthy. Boston: Beacon Press.

Hawley, Amos H. 1986 *Human Ecology: A Theoretical Essay.* Chicago: University of Chicago Press.

Homans, George C. 1975 "What Do We Mean by Social 'Structure'?" In P. M. Blau, ed., *Approaches to the Study of Social Structure.* New York: Free Press.

Institute for Social Research 1979 "Deepening Distrust of Political Leaders Is Jarring Public's Faith in Institutions." *ISR Newsletter* 7:4–5.

Jackson, John E. 1990 "Institutions in American Society: An Overview." In J. E. Jackson, ed., *Institutions in American Society: Essays in Market, Political, and Social Organizations.* Ann Arbor: University of Michigan Press.

Johnsen, Eugene, and Beth Mintz 1989 "Organizational versus Class Components of Director Networks." In R. Perrucci and H. R. Potter, eds., *Networks of Power: Organizational Actors at the National, Corporate, and Community Levels.* New York: Aldine de Gruyter.

Jones, A. Anthony 1984 "Models of Socialist Development." In Lenski, Gerhard, ed., *Current Issues and Research in Macrosociology.* Leiden, Neth.: E. J. Brill.

Kerr, Clark 1983 *The Future of Industrial Societies: Convergence or Continuing Diversity?* Cambridge, Mass.: Harvard University Press.

Labovitz, Sanford, and Robert Hagedorn 1977 "Social Norms." In Sanford Labovitz, *An Introduction to Sociological Concepts.* New York: Wiley.

Landecker, Werner S. 1981 *Class Crystallization.* New Brunswick, N.J.: Rutgers University Press.

Laumann, Edward O., and David Knoke 1989 "Policy Networks of the Organizational State: Collective

Action in the National Energy and Health Domains." In R. Perrucci and H. R. Potter, eds., *Networks of Power: Organizational Actors at the National, Corporate, and Community Levels.* New York: Aldine de Gruyter.

Leinhardt, Samuel (ed.) 1977 *Social Networks: A Developing Paradigm.* New York: Academic Press.

Lenski, Gerhard E. 1975 "Social Structure in Evolutionary Perspective." In P. M. Blau, ed., *Approaches to the Study of Social Structure.* New York: Free Press.

——— 1979 "Directions and Continuities in Societal Growth." In A. H. Hawley, ed., *Societal Growth: Processes and Implications.* New York: Free Press.

Lieberson, Stanley 1971 "An Empirical Study of Military-Industrial Linkages." *American Sociological Review* 76:562–585.

Luhmann, Niklas (1974–1977) 1982 *The Differentiation of Society,* parts trans. S. Holmes and C. Larmore. New York: Columbia University Press.

——— 1987 "The Evolutionary Differentiation Between Society and Interaction." In J. C. Alexander, B. Giesen, R. Münch, and N. J. Smelser, eds., *The Micro-Macro Link.* Berkeley: University of California Press.

Marx, Karl (1859) 1971 *The Grundrisse,* D. McLellan, ed. and trans. New York: Harper and Row.

Marx, Karl, and Frederick [sic] Engels (1846) 1970 *The German Ideology,* ed. C. J. Arthur, trans. W. Lough, C. Dutt, and C. P. Magill. New York: International Publishers.

McAdam, Doug, John D. McCarthy, and Mayer N. Zald 1988 "Social Movements." In N. J. Smelser, ed., *Handbook of Sociology.* Beverly Hills, Calif.: Sage.

Meyer, John W., John Boli, and George M. Thomas 1987 "Ontology and Rationalization in the Western Cultural Account." In G. M. Thomas, J. W. Meyer, F. O. Ramirez, and J. Bali, eds., *Institutional Structure: Constituting State, Society, and the Individual.* Beverly Hills, Calif.: Sage.

Meyer, John W., and Brian Rowan 1978 "The Structure of Educational Organizations." In M. Meyer and associates. *Environments and Organizations.* San Francisco: Jossey-Bass.

Mills, C. Wright 1956 *The Power Elite.* New York: Oxford University Press.

Mizruchi, Mark S. 1982 *The American Corporate Network, 1904–1974.* Beverly Hills, Calif.: Sage.

Moore, Wilbert E. 1988 "Social Change." In E. F. Borgatta and K. S. Cook, eds., *The Future of Sociology.* Beverly Hills, Calif.: Sage.

Parsons, Talcott 1968 "Social Systems." In D. L. Sills, ed., *International Encyclopedia of the Social Sciences.* New York: Macmillan.

——— 1975 "The Present Status of 'Structural-Functional' Theory in Sociology." In L. A. Coser, ed., *The Idea of Social Structure: Papers in Honor of Robert K. Merton.* New York: Harcourt Brace Jovanovich.

——— (1966, 1971) 1977 *The Evolution of Societies,* ed. Jackson Toby. Englewood Cliffs, N.J.: Prentice-Hall.

Parsons, Talcott, and Neil J. Smelser (1956) 1965 *Economy and Society: A Study in the Integration of Economic and Social Theory.* New York: Free Press.

Perrow, Charles 1986 *Complex Organizations: A Critical Essay,* 3rd ed. New York: Random House.

Perrucci, Robert, and Marc Pilisuk 1970 "Leaders and Ruling Elites: The Interorganizational Bases of Community Power." *American Sociological Review* 35:1040–1057.

Perrucci, Robert, and Harry R. Potter 1989 "The Collective Actor in Organizational Analysis." In R. Perrucci and H. R. Potter, eds., *Networks of Power: Organizational Actors at the National, Corporate, and Community Levels.* New York: Aldine de Gruyter.

Polsby, Nelson W. 1980 *Community Power and Political Theory: A Further Look at Problems of Evidence and Inference,* 2nd ed. New Haven, Conn.: Yale University Press.

Rueschemeyer, Dietrich 1986 *Power and the Division of Labor.* Stanford, Calif.: Stanford University Press.

Scott, W. Richard 1987 *Organizations: Rational, Natural, and Open Systems,* 2nd ed. Englewood Cliffs, N.J.: Prentice-Hall.

Simmel, Georg 1908 *Soziologie: Untersuchungen über die Formen der Vergesellschaftung.* Leipzig: Duncker und Humblot.

Skocpol, Theda 1979 *States and Social Revolutions: A Comparative Analysis of France, Russia, and China.* New York: Cambridge University Press.

Smelser, Neil J. 1988 "Social Structure." In N. J. Smelser, ed., *Handbook of Sociology.* Beverly Hills, Calif.: Sage.

Smith, Adam [1789] 1976 *The Wealth of Nations.* Chicago: University of Chicago Press.

Stinchcombe, Arthur L. 1986 "Economic Sociology: Rationality and Subjectivity." In U. Himmelstrand, ed., *Sociology: From Crisis to Science?,* vol. 1, *The Sociology of Structure and Action.* Beverly Hills, Calif.: Sage.

Suttles, Gerald, and Morris Janowitz 1979 "Metropolitan Growth and Democratic Participation." In A. H.

Hawley, ed., *Societal Growth: Processes and Implications.* New York: Free Press.

Tenbruck, Friedrich H. 1989 "The Cultural Foundations of Society." In H. Haferkamp, ed., *Social Structure and Culture.* New York: Walter de Gruyter.

Tilly, Charles 1984 *Big Structures, Large Processes, Huge Comparisons.* New York: Russell Sage Foundation.

Tuchman, Gaye 1988 "Mass Media Institutions." In N. J. Smelser, ed., *Handbook of Sociology.* Beverly Hills, Calif.: Sage.

Turk, Herman 1977 *Organizations in Modern Life: Cities and Other Large Networks.* San Francisco: Jossey-Bass.

—— 1985 "Macrosociology and Interorganizational Relations: Theory, Strategies, and Bibliography." *Sociology and Social Research* 69:487–500. (Reprint with corrected typography is available.)

Turner, Jonathan H. 1986 *The Structure of Sociological Theory,* 4th ed. Chicago: Dorsey Press.

Udy, Stanley, H., Jr. 1968 "Social Structure: Social Structural Analysis." In D. L. Sills, ed., *International Encyclopedia of the Social Sciences.* New York: Macmillan.

—— 1979 "Societal Growth and Organizational Complexity." In A. H. Hawley, ed., *Societal Growth: Processes and Implications.* New York: Free Press.

Wallace, Walter L. 1988 "Toward a Disciplinary Matrix in Sociology." In N. J. Smelser, ed., *Handbook of Sociology.* Beverly Hills, Calif.: Sage.

Wallerstein, Immanuel 1979 "World Networks and the Politics of the World Economy." In A. H. Hawley, ed., *Societal Growth: Processes and Implications.* New York: Free Press.

—— 1984 "The Three Instances of Hegemony in the History of the Capitalist World Economy." In G. Lenski, ed., *Current Issues and Research in Macrosociology.* Leiden, Neth.: E. J. Brill.

Weber, Max (1920) 1978 *Economy and Society: An Outline of Interpretive Sociology,* G. Roth and C. Wittich, eds.; E. Fischoff, H. Gerth, A. M. Henderson, C. W. Mills, T. Parsons, M. Rheinstein, G. Roth, and C. Wittich, trans. Berkeley: University of California Press.

Williams, Raymond 1976 *Keywords: A Vocabulary of Culture and Society.* New York: Oxford University Press.

Williamson, Oliver E. 1990 "Chester Barnard and the Incipient Science of Organization." In O. E. Williamson, ed., *Organization Theory: From Chester Barnard to the Present and Beyond.* New York: Oxford University Press.

Znaniecki, Florian 1945 "Social Organization and Institutions." In G. Gurvitch and W. E. Moore, eds., *Twentieth Century Sociology.* New York: Philosophical Library.

Zurcher, Louis A., and David A. Snow 1981 "Collective Behavior: Social Movements." In M. Rosenberg and R. H. Turner, eds., *Social Psychology: Sociological Perspectives.* New York: Basic Books.

HERMAN TURK

SOCIAL PERCEPTION As the label implies, social perception theories and research are concerned with the nature, causes, and consequences of perceptions of social entities. Closely related work has developed under a variety of headings: social cognition, person perception, social representation, impression formation, attribution, social judgment. *Social perception* is best viewed as an umbrella term that covers numerous loosely related and, for the most part, loosely formulated theoretical conjectures and associated research. Only a fraction of this work can be discussed here. The rest, however, is easily accessed. In books, chapters, and articles under the various headings, reference lists tend to intersect rather than to parallel, and virtually all of the work can be found cataloged under the "social perception" heading.

Following a brief introduction to perception in general, three subsequent sections will address the major areas of social perception research: self-perception, person perception, and group perception.

PERCEPTION

Each of the senses acts as a transducer, encoding particular forms of energy into signals that are meaningful to the brain. In the brain these complex patterns of bioelectrical impulses are transformed into neural representations virtually as they arrive. Conditional upon neural structure, prior experiences, and the pattern of the impulses, these representations may or may not reach conscious awareness in the form of a perception. When sensations do surpass sensory thresholds, survive filtering by the brain, and manage to break through into conscious awareness, experiences of these sensations tend to exhibit three qualities: structure, stability, and meaning (Schneider, Hastorf, and Ellsworth 1979). As a consequence, perceptual experiences are forged in ways that often bias one's impressions of the stimuli that produced them.

Structure. Humans experience the world as structured in the sense that they expect and observe that its elements correspond to one another in patterned ways. At times, one person's perceptions may be very different from those of others because of differences in how his or her expectations have structured his or her perceptions. Each person may impose a different subjective structure on the same objective reality. Every sports fan *knows,* for example, that his or her favorite player or team is consistently the victim of more "bad calls" by the officials than the opponent. Of course, supporters of the opponent generally disagree. What fans actually "see" are slices of reality chosen to conform to their beliefs and expectations.

Stability. Different sports fans may see different things, but they invariably agree on much more than they realize: players do not dematerialize here and rematerialize there, and the ball does not literally grow and shrink as it moves nearer to and farther from the fan/observer. In general, of the myriad sensations to which one might attend in a given situation, attention is biased toward those which engender a sense of stability—a sense of the temporal endurance of these patterned sensations.

Meaning. If structure and stability were the only properties of experience, then the world would appear merely as successions of discrete objects and events with no particular import. In contrast, most perceptions *seem* meaningful, that is, they fit into still larger patterns and have significance, purpose, causes, and consequences beyond their own existence. Along with human cognitive development comes the ability to recognize and select impressions and events that are significant in terms of the information they con-

vey. As will be discussed later, meaningfulness and significance do not imply accuracy or correctness. Perceptions—especially *social* perceptions—are imperfect representations and often highly misleading.

SELF-PERCEPTION

Self-perception is social perception with the self as the object. Through introspection and information from others, people develop beliefs about their many qualities—personality, physical appearance, behavioral proclivities, moral stature, athletic prowess, and so on. *Self-concept* is the general term for the system of beliefs about the self. Although introspection is a source of self-knowledge (e.g., Andersen and Williams 1985), mounting evidence suggests that it is not the predominant source that people generally have believed it to be, and that it is frequently biased and inaccurate (e.g., Nisbett and Wilson 1977; Wilson, Hull, and Johnson 1981). One major branch of self-perception research focuses on inaccuracies in self-knowledge, a second on how information from others shapes the self-concept. An excellent example of work in the first branch is a review by Greenwald (1980) of evidence of three types of self-conceptual biases. These include (1) *egocentricity:* the anchoring of judgments, recollections, thought experiments, and attributions about others with reference to the self; (2) *beneffectance:* the tendency to perceive the self as generally efficacious; and (3) *cognitive conservatism:* a resistance to cognitive change. Bem's influential self-perception theory (1972) goes so far as to assert that under conditions of uncertainty, people use their own behavior as a guide to inferences about their inner selves. Recent approaches to the self-concept focus on structures such as category systems, conceptual networks, and complex schemata that are capable of representing explicit connections and nonconnections among elements of the self-concept (see Greenwald and Pratkanis 1984).

The early insights of Cooley (1964) and Mead (1934) still guide contemporary sociological theory and research on social origins of the self-concept, the second branch mentioned above. Cooley described the "looking-glass self" as the use of others' appraisals as mirrors of the "true" self. Mead noted that the images people form of themselves are greatly affected by how they *imagine* significant others would respond to and evaluate them. Social comparison theory (Festinger 1954; Suls and Miller 1977) deals with, among other issues, the question of to whom one refers when seeking comparative self-knowledge, as well as the effects on one's self-concept and behavior of the various social referents that are available.

Under the rubric *self-perception* are such topics as *self-efficacy, self-evaluation, self-esteem,* and *self-identity.* Self-efficacy is the perception of one's competence with respect to specific tasks (Bandura 1986; Cervone and Peake 1986). Self-esteem is the extent to which one thinks positively about himself or herself (Rosenberg 1979). The concept of self-evaluation, when distinguished from efficacy and esteem, has been used in theory and research on how characteristics of evaluators affect self-evaluations in specific, collective task situations (Webster and Sobieszek 1974). Self-identity approaches emphasize ways that self-categorizations hinge upon salient properties of the groups with which individuals align themselves (Brown 1988; Hogg and Abrams 1988). Choe (1991) provides a typology that identifies commonalities and differences among the various approaches to aspects of self-perception. Dimensions include (1) scope (specific-global): the comprehensiveness of self-perception; (2) time frame (short-long): the period over which the perception develops; and (3) perspective (own-other): the degree to which the self-perceiver believes the perception is introspectively derived as opposed to reflecting the opinions of others.

PERSON PERCEPTION

The lion's share of social perception theory and research deals with how people formulate impressions about the inner qualities and outward behaviors of others. The focal points for this work include properties of the people perceived and of the situations in which the perception is developed, the logic by which basic sensations are integrated to form complex social perceptions, and when perceptions, once formed, are or are not affected by new information.

Attribution theories are concerned with how people form inferences about the causes of others' behaviors. The basic question of these approaches concerns the conditions under which another's behavior is attributed to an internal disposition or to aspects of the situation in which it occurred (see Ross and Fletcher 1985). The so-called *fundamental attribution error* is the pervasive tendency for observers to underestimate the impact of situational factors on others' behavior (Ross 1977). In fact, people tend to make personal attributions for others' behavior and situational attributions for their own (e.g., Jones and Nisbett 1972). Gilbert (1989) has modified the question in a potentially fruitful way by asserting that personal attributions occur automatically. Situational attributions, then, occur only as the possible result of an effortful search for additional information (Gilbert, Pelham, and Krull 1988).

Other approaches to person perception focus on the integration of pieces of information associated with particular others. Information integration theory (Anderson 1981) provides rigorous mathematical models of how an observer employs weighted combinations of another's traits to form an overall impression. Social psychophysics (Stevens 1975; Lodge 1981) applies a magnitude scaling technology first developed for expressing judgments of physical properties (e.g., weight, brightness, numerosity, loudness, saltiness) to the quantification and validation of judgments of personal or social properties (e.g., competence, fairness, attractiveness, etc.). Status characteristics theory (e.g., Berger, Fisek, Norman, and Zelditch 1985) explains the emergence of status and influence hierarchies in collective, task-performing groups on the basis of individuals' relative standings on combinations of salient characteristics— characteristics that can order interaction whether or not they are explicitly relevant to the task.

Attributional and social perceptual biases comprise a vast field of inquiry in their own right. In recent years a number of universal human perceptual inclinations have been cataloged, all of which are capable of generating perceptual biases. Many perceptions depend on the ability to gauge one's own relevant behaviors and characteristics, yet people often have difficulty assessing their own qualities and properties in any absolute way (e.g., Bem 1972). Preconceived notions have a powerful influence on subsequent perceptions by inducing selective perceptions. Once an idea is accepted, falsifying information is discounted and verifying information is accepted uncritically. Not only are people subject to such errors of perception, but they also underestimate the degree to which this is so. They are overconfident in their judgments; employ useless, distracting, and unrepresentative information contained in anecdotes; and infer illusory covariations among social characteristics. In recent years cognitive and social psychologists have begun to identify and systematically examine these and other types of social perceptual biases. (For some excellent examples see Taylor and Fiske 1978; Taylor, Fiske, Etcoff, and Ruderman 1978; Nisbett and Ross 1980; Kahneman, Slovic, and Tversky 1982.)

GROUP PERCEPTION

Two approaches to group perception predominate—those concerned with reference group choices and effects, and those addressing social categorization processes. Research on reference group phenomena represents one of the first and longest-lived attempts in sociology and social psychology to understand how individuals orient themselves to groups, which groups they choose, and the consequences of their choices. (See Newcomb 1943; Merton and Rossi 1968; Singer 1981.) Such factors as attitude similarity, structural inducements, and normative prescriptions have been shown to affect referent choices in both natural and experimental settings. Consequences of referential comparisons that have received study include the treatment of social deviants and emergence of negative social evaluations, changes in self-esteem, and feelings of relative deprivation, gratification, or inequity. Although a good deal of interesting research and theoretical conjectures

has been associated with this area of inquiry, as Singer (1981) noted, there is no reference group theory and the explanatory promise of this area remains unfulfilled. However, many of the research lines originally spawned by interests in reference groups remain active.

The reference group literature takes as given the existence of groups and the issue of who are and are not members. Social categorization approaches (Tajfel 1981; Wilder 1986) are closely related to the social identity literature noted earlier and view the perception of membership versus nonmembership as problematic. In general, people say that they detest being categorized and that they avoid categorizing others. However, social categorization is a manifestation of a perceptual process that is fundamental to survival. Everyone does it, consciously or not. By learning to recognize and categorize elements of the environment, the human animal is able to distinguish nutriment from poison, and ally from adversary.

Despite its indispensability, however, the categorization process has side effects in the social realm. The most important and robust of these effects is the tendency for people to overestimate the differences between groups and to underestimate the differences among group members. "They" appear uniform, but "we" are individuals (Quattrone 1986). This phenomenon is at the heart of stereotyping. Stereotypes, once formed, are readily maintained by virtue of the types of perceptual biases previously noted, such as forming illusory correlations and relying on anecdotes. A now classic finding in research on social identity theory (Tajfel 1982; Turner 1987) demonstrated that arbitrary we/they distinctions created by random assignments to groups in a laboratory setting were sufficient to produce in-group favoritism and a variety of negative attributions regarding the out-group.

Discrimination—the differential treatment of others based solely upon their group memberships—and prejudice—negative attitudes toward certain groups and their members—are the too-frequent behavioral manifestations of perceptual stereotyping. In American society, and in the social and behavioral sciences, gender- and race-based forms of discrimination and prejudice have received the most attention (e.g., Eagly 1987; Dovidio and Gaertner 1986, respectively), although the list of actual bases for discrimination is probably as long as the list of conceivable social characteristics.

CONCLUSIONS

Social perception theory and research embrace the analytic levels of cognitive processing, individual and interpersonal behavior, perceptions of groups, and group behavior. The social perception theories that may hold the greatest promise for the future are those amenable to integrating explicit formulations developed within these different levels of analysis.

What may be the most promising approach yet to emerge is not even generally recognized as falling within the social perception literature. Burt's (1982) approach integrates a psychophysical model of human perception with explicit models of social network structure. The result is a conceptualization of social groupings at any scale in which network members (1) receive information on certain properties of others (e.g., resource holdings, attitudes), (2) take into account structural information on those others (e.g., the patterns of their social relations, and of their relations' relations, and so on), (3) evaluate and combine the information received, and (4) make self-referential comparisons involving the information obtained from the network (e.g., relative resource holdings). Even more impressive, however, is the ability of Burt's rigorous models to show precisely how structural configurations of social relationships, in combination with individually based social perception and comparison processes, can theoretically account for a far broader class of phenomena than either individual-level theories that do not consider structures, or structural theories that do not consider individuals.

There is no lack of good ideas in the social perception field, and there is every chance that this area will play a central role in future attempts to integrate micro sociology and macro sociology. Most lacking, however, are concerted, program-matic efforts to develop and test explicit and rigorous social perception theories. Some exceptions were noted above. For the most part, however, the absence of explicitness and rigor has resulted in a minimal level of competition among different approaches, virtually no critical testing between formulations, and few time-tested conceptual and methodological refinements. At the same time, this area remains attractive to a relatively large number of psychologists and sociologists, in part because of its many unanswered questions, and of the ubiquity of its phenomena.

(SEE ALSO: *Attribution Theory; Reference Group Theory; Self-Concept; Social Comparison Theory; Social Psychology*)

REFERENCES

Andersen, Susan M., and Marirosa Williams, 1985 "Cognitive/Affective Reactions in the Improvement of Self-Esteem: When Thoughts and Feelings Make a Difference." *Journal of Personality and Social Psychology* 49:1086–1097.

Anderson, Norman H. 1981 *Foundations of Information Integration Theory.* New York: Academic Press.

Bandura, Albert 1986 *Social Foundations of Thought and Action.* Englewood Cliffs, N.J.: Prentice-Hall.

Bem, Daryl 1972 "Self-Perception Theory." In Leonard Berkowitz, ed., *Advances in Experimental Social Psychology,* vol. 6. New York: Academic Press.

Berger, Joseph, M. Hamit Fisek, Robert Z. Norman, and Morris Zelditch, Jr. 1985 "Expectation-States Theory." In Joseph Berger and Morris Zelditch, Jr., eds., *Status, Rewards, and Influence.* San Francisco: Jossey-Bass.

Brown, Rupert 1988 *Group Processes: Dynamics Within and Between Groups.* Oxford: Basil Blackwell.

Burt, Ronald S. 1982 *Toward a Structural Theory of Action.* New York: Academic Press.

Cervone, Daniel, and Philip K. Peake 1986 "Anchoring, Efficacy, and Action: The Influence of Judgmental Heuristics on Self-Efficacy Judgments and Behavior." *Journal of Personality and Social Psychology* 50:492–501.

Choe, Joon-Young 1991 "Self-Evaluations and the Sense of Injustice." Ph. D. diss. Department of Sociology, University of Iowa.

Cooley, Charles Horton (1902) 1964 *Human Nature and the Social Order.* New York: Schocken.

Dovidio, John F., and Samuel L. Gaertner (eds.) 1986 *Prejudice, Discrimination, and Racism: Theory and Research.* Orlando, Fla.: Academic Press.

Eagly, Alice H. 1987 *Sex Differences in Social Behavior: A Social-Role Interpretation.* Hillsdale, N.J.: Erlbaum.

Festinger, Leon 1954 "A Theory of Social Comparison Processes." *Human Relations* 7:117–140.

Gilbert, Daniel T. 1989 "Thinking Lightly About Others: Automatic Components of the Social Inference Process." In James S. Uleman and John A. Bargh, eds., *Unintended Thought: Limits of Awareness, Intention, and Control.* New York: Guilford.

——— Brett W. Pelham, and Douglas S. Krull 1988 "On Cognitive Busyness: When Person Perceivers Meet Persons Perceived." *Journal of Personality and Social Psychology* 54:733–740.

Greenwald, Anthony G. 1980 "The Totalitarian Ego: Fabrication and Revision of Personal History." *American Psychologist* 35:603–618.

———, and Anthony R. Pratkanis 1984 "The Self." In Robert S. Wyer, Jr., and Thomas K. Srull, eds., *Handbook of Social Cognition,* vol. 3. Hillsdale, N.J.: Erlbaum.

Hogg, Michael A., and Dominic Abrams 1988 *Social Identifications.* London: Routledge.

Jones, Edward E., and Richard E. Nisbett 1972 "The Actor and the Observer: Divergent Perceptions of Causality." In Edward E. Jones et al., eds., *Attribution: Perceiving the Causes of Behavior.* Morristown, N.J.: General Learning Press.

Kahneman, Daniel, Paul Slovic, and Amos Tversky (eds.) 1982 *Judgment Under Uncertainty: Heuristics and Biases.* New York: Cambridge University Press.

Lodge, Milton 1981 *Magnitude Scaling.* Beverly Hills, Calif.: Sage.

Mead, George Herbert 1934 *Mind, Self, and Society.* Chicago: University of Chicago Press.

Merton, Robert K., and Alice S. Rossi 1968 "Contributions to the Theory of Reference Group Behavior." In Robert K. Merton, ed., *Social Theory and Social Structure,* New York: Free Press.

Newcomb, Theodore M. 1943 *Personality and Social Change.* New York: Dryden.

Nisbett, Richard E., and Lee Ross 1980 *Human Inference: Strategies and Shortcomings of Social Judgment.* Englewood Cliffs, N.J.: Prentice-Hall.

Nisbett, Lee, and Timothy DeCamp Wilson 1977. "Telling More Than We Can Know: Verbal Reports on Mental Processes." *Psychologial Review* 84:231–259.

Quattrone, George A. 1986 "On the Perception of a Group's Variability." In Stephen Worchel and William G. Austin, eds., *Psychology of Intergroup Relations,* 2nd ed. Chicago: Nelson-Hall.

Rosenberg, Morris 1979 *Conceiving of the Self.* New York: Basic Books.

Ross, Lee 1977 "The Intuitive Psychologist and His Shortcomings: Distortions in the Attribution Process." In Leonard Berkowitz, ed., *Advances in Experimental Social Psychology,* vol. 10. New York: Academic Press.

Ross, Michael, and Garth J. O. Fletcher 1985 "Attribution and Social Perception." In Gardner Lindzey and Elliot Aronson, eds., *The Handbook of Social Psychology,* vol. 2, 3rd ed. New York: Random House.

Schneider, David J., Albert H. Hastorf, and Phoebe C. Ellsworth 1979 *Person Perception,* 2nd ed. Reading, Mass.: Addison-Wesley.

Singer, Eleanor 1981 "Reference Groups and Social Evaluations." In Morris Rosenberg and Ralph H. Turner, eds., *Social Psychology: Sociological Perspectives.* New York: Basic Books.

Stevens, S. S. 1975 *Psychophysics: Introduction to Its Perceptual, Neural, and Social Prospects.* Beverly Hills, Calif.: Sage.

Suls, Jerry M., and Richard L. Miller (eds.) 1977 *Social Comparison Processes.* Washington, D.C.: Halsted-Wiley.

Tajfel, Henri 1981 *Human Groups and Social Categories.* Cambridge: Cambridge University Press.

——— 1982 *Social Identity and Intergroup Relations.* London: Cambridge University Press.

Taylor, Shelley E., and Susan T. Fiske, 1978 "Salience, Attention, and Attribution: Top of the Head Phenomena." In Leonard Berkowitz, ed., *Advances in Experimental Social Psychology,* vol. 11. New York: Academic Press.

Taylor, Shelley E., Susan T. Fiske, Nancy L. Etcoff, and Audrey J. Ruderman 1978 "The Categorical and Contextual Bases of Person Memory and Stereotyping." *Journal of Personality and Social Psychology* 36:778–793.

Turner, John C. 1987 *Rediscovering the Social Group: A Self-Categorization Theory.* Oxford: Basil Blackwell.

Webster, Murray, and Barbara Sobieszek 1974 *Sources of Self Evaluation.* New York: Wiley.

Wilder, David A. 1986 "Social Categorization: Implications for Creation and Reduction of Intergroup

Bias." In Leonard Berkowitz, ed., *Advances in Experimental Social Psychology,* vol. 19. New York: Academic Press.

Wilson, Timothy D., Jay G. Hull, and Jim Johnson 1981 "Awareness and Self-Perception: Verbal Reports on Internal States." *Journal of Personality and Social Psychology* 40:53–71.

BARRY MARKOVSKY

SOCIAL PHILOSOPHY American sociology, with the significant exception of symbolic interactionism, has generally turned to Europe for its philosophical grounding. The years after World War II, when Talcott Parsons at Harvard and Paul Lazarsfeld and Robert Merton at Columbia dominated the field, were no exception. Parsons had studied in Germany and had translated Weber. Lazarsfeld was European-born and brought to the United States an Austrian philosophical heritage. Merton was a specialist in the philosophy and sociology of science. Under the influence of these three men, American sociology was strongly influenced by the philosophy of the Vienna Circle, especially Carnap and Popper, and, to a lesser degree, by British logical positivism.

The common ingredient that tied this philosophical heritage together was the notion that there were few obstacles to the creation of a science of human behavior modeled on the natural sciences. A great deal of attention was paid to hypothesis testing, criteria of evidence, and the nature of statistical proof. Most important, this way of thinking assumed that there was a social reality in the world that would prove to be of the same nature as physical reality. A predictive science of human behavior was possible because the social world was presumed to work in lawlike ways. The problems of the social sciences lay in discovering reality, not in the nature of reality itself.

This presumption would come to be disturbed from two different directions. On the one hand, sociologists would, in many cases, lose their faith in the natural science model as the most appropriate way to think about society. In part due to the political upheavals of the 1960s, adherence to the

patient accumulation of facts so as to verify what Merton called "middle level" theories about the world was difficult to maintain. On the other hand, philosophers themselves increasingly came to question the epistemology associated with the natural science model. Thomas Kuhn's thesis that scientific insight occurred as the result of a new paradigm had a stunning effect on social science, while Michael Polanyi argued for a more "artistic" and "sociological" conception of scientific inquiry (Kuhn 1970; Polanyi 1968). If epistemological skepticism began to invade the natural sciences, its implications for the social sciences would be even more serious.

One of the first consequences of this increasing skepticism was the discovery in America that the European philosophical heritage was far broader than it had at first appeared. Weber, for example, had been influenced strongly by Nietzsche, yet Parsons's interpretation of Weber downplayed the significance of heroism, irrationality, and cultural pessimism and turned Weber into an American pluralist. The two philosophers who had perhaps the greatest influence in Europe in the years during and after Parsons's visits to Germany were Heidegger and Husserl, and neither played any significant role in Parsons's outlook. The late Wittgenstein was discovered to be quite different from the earlier one, who had been convinced that pure logic would make philosophy unnecessary. French existentialism would become famous in the 1960s, yet this fame would not last, and existentialism's influence on American sociology was minimal. What had been a selective and partial reading of European philosophy by American sociology could no longer last.

Even during the years when Parsons was the leading American sociologist, alternatives had existed. Husserl's phenomenology was one such alternative. As brought to the United States and applied to sociology in the work of Alfred Schutz (1967), phenomenology argued for the importance of the "life-world," the everyday events out of which our understanding of the world around us becomes possible. Schutz was unable to convince Parsons of the importance of phenomenology (see Schutz 1978), but he did influence one of Parsons's most brilliant students, Harold Garfinkel (1967). Ethnomethodology became the single most important alternative to structural functionalism in the 1960s and 1970s. The legacy of phenomenology could also be seen in the work of others such as Berger and Luckman (1967). Other alternative traditions such as the influence of Wittgenstein also existed during this period, especially in Great Britain. Finally, among Marxists, the traditions of the Frankfurt School and the legacy of Lukacs constituted an important strain for social science theorizing (Arato and Gebhart 1977).

As the wide variety of ideas associated with European philosophy became increasingly known to sociologists, the earlier confidence in the natural sciences as a model for the social sciences gave way to far more nuanced approaches. No theorist in contemporary sociology was more aware than Jurgen Habermas (1987) of the necessity of incorporating insights from a wide variety of philosophical traditions. Not only did Habermas bring to the task of sociological theorizing his own background in Frankfurt School Marxism, plus a far more realistic reading of Weber than the one offered by Parsons, he also grounded his work in British linguistic philosophy, the Schutzian lifeworld, and American pragmatism. To read Habermas was to learn about those whom Habermas had read, thereby bringing wide swaths of European philosophy to the attention of many, especially American, readers.

Habermas argued for the importance of modernity, for the possibility of protecting rationality as a standard by which communicative utterances could be judged, thereby making possible a social order held together by norms that lay outside the purely subjective preferences of those who constituted that social order. It was precisely this belief in reason that would lead others to criticize him as excessively rationalistic and therefore too close to the assumptions of a nonproblematic reality that had guided Parsons (Lyotard 1984). Postmodernism would become the most radical challenge imaginable to the earlier Parsons's faith in a scientific model for the social sciences.

With postmodernism, the very philosophers once ignored by American social science became the most important philosophers to read. Michel Foucault (1971), under the spell of Nietzsche, argued that knowledge is the product of a general *episteme,* which itself is not a reflection of a reality in the world but is the product of a particular historical period and its self-understanding. Jean-François Lyotard (1984), borrowing from Wittgenstein, viewed science as a "language game," preoccupied with strategy and tactics, anything but a dispassionate and objective search after truth. Jacques Derrida (1978), under the influence of Heidegger, argued for the indeterminacy of such concepts as truth, justice, and morality. Philosophers could not seek fixed universals; they were instead engaged in the practice of rhetoric, defending or attacking contingent, local, and socially constructed practices that attempted to define truth, justice, or morality in the interests of certain groups and against the interests of others.

Postmodernism has not had the impact in sociology that it has had in other fields, especially literary criticism, history, and law. (For an exception with respect to sociology, see Lamont 1987.) Numerous sociologists continue to study the empirical world by testing various hypotheses on the basis of evidence collected through surveys, demographic data, or other essentially quantitative methods. Yet the postmodern challenge to normal science will likely prove to be a significant one. Postmodernism is the culmination of all the challenges to the Parsonian consensus that once existed in the field; it represents what seems to be an endpoint to the process of questioning the existence of a nonproblematic social reality that can be understood by an observer standing outside that reality.

The question raised by the varieties of epistemological skepticism currently popular in the humanities is whether any science, let alone any social science, is possible. Just as some scientific fields seek to reduce the laws of one field, such as biology, to those of another, say biochemistry, postmodernism argues that all fields of inquiry can be reduced to the study of rhetoric. In a perhaps unintended fashion, the implication of this argument is an imperialist one: The rhetorical methods associated with literary criticism will become the model for all inquiry, just as science was once understood to be a model for all inquiry.

There are obviously rhetorical issues involved in social science theorizing, ones that have been analyzed, for economics, by McCloskey (1985). In addition, some recent work in the sociology of science has made it clear that scientists have strategies by which they present themselves to the world and hope to gain acceptance. (For one example, see Latour 1987.) But does it follow that there is no grounding whatever for social science, no Durkheimian facts in the world to which we can appeal in order to resolve disputes about knowledge? There is, of course, no way to answer such a large question satisfactorily in the course of this brief review, but it is possible to offer the hope that both science and rhetoric have a role to play in the sociological enterprise.

Sociology itself began, as Lepenies (1988) has recently argued, "between science and literature." Its most important theorists were attracted to positivistic understandings of knowledge, but they were also essayists dealing with some of the most significant issues in moral philosophy of their time. One could argue that this "ambivalence" between fields has consistently characterized sociology at its best (Merton 1976). Merton, for example, though engaged in what he called the "systematics" of theory, was also a historian of science, wrote with reference to the entire Western tradition of philosophy and literature, and was very much part of the milieu of the New York intellectuals of his day (see Merton 1967, pp. 1–37).

The fate of the sociologist may thus lie in finding a balance between a scientific grounding in fact and an appreciation of how rhetorical strategies play a role in the ways in which scholars argue about facts. Unlike the sociologists of an earlier period, we can no longer be confident that there will exist a one-to-one relationship between social reality and its representations; we ought always be skeptical that the indicators we use actually measure the real world per se. But this does not necessarily mean that we ought to give up

collecting evidence, testing hypotheses, or trying to establish fact. It means only that the truths we uncover by these methods are not universals that exist for all time but are contingent on historical periodization and location.

From this perspective, the question then becomes how long are the historical periods and how wide are the locations by which we can judge the truths we discover. If we can determine that it is possible to discover regularities in, for example, the way liberal democracies have organized themselves over the past 200 years, that would be a significant and important accomplishment. It would not mean that we had discovered an unchanging reality, nor would it mean that our discoveries are simply part of a rhetorical strategy. A sociology that modeled itself neither on physics nor on literary readings, but combined elements of both, would be a sociology that is more chastened than Parsonianism but also more hopeful than postmodernism.

(SEE ALSO: *Epistemology; Human Nature; Marxist Sociology; Postmodernism; Pragmatism*)

REFERENCES

Arato, Andrew, and Eike Gerhardt (eds.) 1977 *The Frankfurt School Reader.* New York: Urizen Books.

Berger, Peter, and Thomas Luckmann 1967 *The Social Construction of Reality: A Treatise in the Sociology of Knowledge.* Garden City, N.Y.: Doubleday.

Derrida, Jacques 1978 *Writing and Difference.* Alan Bass, trans. Chicago: University of Chicago Press.

Foucault, Michel 1971 *The Order of Things: An Archeology of the Human Sciences.* New York: Pantheon.

Garfinkel, Harold 1967 *Studies in Ethnomethodology.* Englewood Cliffs, N.J.: Prentice Hall.

Habermas, Jurgen 1987 *Lifeworld and System: A Critique of Functionalist Reason,* vol. 2 of *The Theory of Communicative Action.* Thomas McCarthy, trans. Boston: Beacon Press.

Kuhn, Thomas S. 1970 *The Structure of Scientific Revolutions.* Chicago: University of Chicago Press.

Lamont, Michele 1987 "How to Become a Dominant French Philosopher: The Case of Jacques Derrida." *American Journal of Sociology* 93:584–622.

Latour, Bruno 1987 *Science in Action: How to Follow*

Scientists and Engineers through Society. Cambridge, Mass.: Harvard University Press.

Lepenies, Wolf 1988 *Between Literature and Science: The Rise of Sociology.* R. J. Hollingdale, trans. Cambridge: Cambridge University Press.

Lyotard, Jean-François 1984 *The Post-Modern Condition: A Report on Knowledge.* Geoff Bennington and Brian Massumi, trans. Minneapolis: University of Minnesota Press.

McCloskey, Donald 1985 *The Rhetoric of Economics.* Madison: University of Wisconsin Press.

Merton, Robert K. 1967 *On Theoretical Sociology: Five Essays, Old and New.* New York: Free Press.

——— 1976 *Sociological Ambivalence and Other Essays.* New York: Free Press.

Polanyi, Michael 1968 *Personal Knowledge: Towards a Post-Critical Philosophy.* Chicago: University of Chicago Press.

Schutz, Alfred 1967 *The Phenomenology of the Social World.* George Walsh and Frederick Lehnert, trans. Evanston, Ill.: Northwestern University Press.

——— 1978 *The Theory of Social Action: The Correspondence of Alfred Schutz and Talcott Parsons.* Richard Grathoff, ed. Bloomington: Indiana University Press.

ALAN WOLFE

SOCIAL-POLICY ANALYSIS *See* Public Policy Analysis.

SOCIAL PRESTIGE *See* Occupational Prestige; Social Honor; Social Mobility.

SOCIAL PROBLEMS The discipline of sociology was born during a century of rapid social change attributable in large part to the Industrial Revolution. Social theorists in nineteenth-century Europe devoted much of their attention to analyzing the institutional consequences of the erosion of the old social structure. American sociologists in the late nineteenth and early twentieth centuries, especially at the University of Chicago, added an intellectual orientation derived from the political idealism and meliorist pragmatism then fashionable in this country. "So-cial problems" were generally understood to be those conditions that disrupted peaceful social life (e.g., crime) or that produced obvious human misery (e.g., poverty) and that could be eliminated or alleviated by enlightened social policy. Nearly all the conditions so defined were associated with the burgeoning cities of the time and the dispossessed immigrants (foreign and domestic) that they attracted. Few scholars doubted that these social problems could be objectively diagnosed and treated, much like a malady in the human body.

By midcentury, however, American sociology was increasingly influenced by the functionalism and positivism of some of the earlier European masters, whose major works had only recently been translated into English. Under this influence, sociologists assumed a somewhat more detached and value-neutral posture toward traditional social problems. While still acknowledging certain social conditions as problematic, most sociologists considered their responsibilities to be limited to scientific analysis of problems and their causes, with meliorist activism left up to politicians, social workers, and various interest-group partisans. A split within the American Sociological Association between the more detached and the more activist visions of the discipline led to the formation in 1952 of the Society for the Study of Social Problems, which publishes the quarterly *Social Problems* and generally promotes a more actively meliorist role for sociology.

THE TRADITIONAL PARADIGM

Whether activist or not, the reigning paradigm in the sociology of social problems has properly been called an *objectivist* one. Most textbooks define social problems as conditions that are in some sense undesirable to any trained and objective observer. Interest-group differences are acknowledged in how the problems should be defined and corrected, but it is taken for granted that the problems themselves exist as objective realities. In most literature on social problems (including textbooks), one sees an implicit analogy to medical diagnosis; that is, a social problem is to the society as a disease is to the body, an objective reality quite apart from popular opinion. Often even conventional medical terms are used such as *pathology* (or *social pathology*), *epidemiology,* and *etiology,* not only for social problems that might be quasi-medical in nature (like alcoholism), but even for those that are entirely societal (like poverty or juvenile delinquency). All require the investigation of diagnostic experts, meaning social scientists.

The diagnostic experts, as it turns out, also come from different schools of thought, as is often the case in other disciplines. Two theoretical orientations have tended to dominate the diagnosis and analysis of social problems by sociologists. The first is functionalism in one version or another. From this perspective, the society in general is a more or less organic entity of interdependent parts (institutions), in which breakdowns may occasionally occur but which generally succeeds in maintaining its natural state of equilibrium. These breakdowns (also called *dysfunctions* or *social disorganization*) are the social problems, and, once they are fixed, the social system can return to normal. This perspective has been criticized by activists as carrying the conservative assumption that the existing social system is generally all right as it is, with only meliorative adjustments needed to deal with the occasional breakdowns.

Generally preferred by activists in the discipline is the more radical theoretical perspective sometimes called *critical theory,* derived mainly from the Marxist heritage. From this perspective, social problems are the inevitable and endemic characteristics of a capitalist system. Efforts to deal with social problems in such a system can never produce more than temporary palliatives, or, worse still, produce simply the co-optation of discontent and protest in the class interests of the dominant and oppressive establishment. Only the drastic overhaul or total overthrow of the capitalist system will produce a society that can be freed from social problems. Note that this radical perspective, however, shares with its more conservative functionalist counterpart the premise that social problems can, in principle, be objectively identified, diagnosed, analyzed, and corrected.

This same premise, of course, has traditionally informed public policy at local, state, and federal levels of government in the United States and elsewhere. Accordingly, public funding for research and amelioration of various conditions officially designated as social problems has helped greatly to promote the objectivist paradigm in the discipline of sociology. Whether in the War on Poverty of the 1960s or in the War on Drugs of the 1990s, billions of dollars in government support have gone into research on the prevention and/or correction of those social problems deemed most serious in a given era. Both the objectivist paradigm itself and the professional careers of its proponents have been strengthened in the process.

THE EMERGENT PARADIGM

While the overwhelming majority of social-problems textbooks continue to embody one or another version of the traditional objectivist paradigm, the more professional literature of sociology has in recent decades promoted a robust alternative theoretical paradigm. Generally called *subjectivist,* in contrast with its traditional counterpart, this paradigm derives from different epistemological premises. Its roots are found in phenomenology and in symbolic interactionism, rather than in the positivism of the objectivist paradigm. It is thus akin to what is sometimes called the *labeling* perspective in the study of crime and deviance. Intimations of this subjectivist paradigm can be found in some of the nineteenth-century European theoretical literature and even in the work of some American sociologists earlier in the twentieth century (e.g., Fuller 1937; Fuller and Myers 1941a, 1941b; Mills 1943; Waller 1936). The emergence of the paradigm into the mainstream of the discipline, however, has occurred mainly since 1960 in the work of Howard S. Becker (1966), Herbert Blumer (1971), and the team of John Kitsuse and Malcolm Spector (Kitsuse and Spector 1973; Spector and Kitsuse 1973, 1977).

In the simplest terms, the subjectivist paradigm holds that a social problem is in the eye of the beholder, not in objective reality. To be sure, certain social *conditions* may be real (e.g., deviance, inequality), but to term them *problems* requires an evaluative judgment not inherent in the condition itself. That judgment comes out of the political, economic, cultural, moral, religious, or other interests of the persons alleging the existence of a given problem. Thus, the subjectivist paradigm denies the analogue to medical diagnosis on the grounds that there are no generally accepted scientific standards in sociology, as there are in medicine, for judging what is "pathological." For example, there is in the study of societies no counterpart for the medical standard that "normal" human body temperature is 98.6 degrees fahrenheit (and that significant departures from that figure are symptomatic of pathology). Instead, the judgment that a given social condition is undesirable or problematic in any sense is entirely relative to culture (or subculture), generation, and many other social variables.

As evidence of the relativity and variability in the definition of *social problems*, subjectivists make at least two historical observations. First, social conditions once regarded as serious "problems" in the United States are no longer so regarded, whether or not they are still extant. One example would be witchcraft, which would not now be considered ever to have existed at all "in reality" but which nevertheless was a major social problem in seventeenth-century Massachusetts and elsewhere. Other, more recent examples, would include miscegenation, which gave rise to a powerful eugenics movement early in the twentieth century; prostitution, which is now legal in some jurisdictions, illegal in others, but nowhere regarded as the national social problem that it was at one time; and homosexuality, which once rated attention, along with prostitution, in most social-problems textbooks and even a listing as a disorder in the official diagnostic manual of psychiatry, but which now is protected by civil rights legislation. Note that in none of these examples has there been any evidence of reduction in the *actual incidence* of the condition, so the erosion in their status as "real" social problems can be attributed only to changes in public *perception*.

The second observation, related to the first, is that no consistent relationship is apparent between the waxing and waning of given social *conditions,* on the one hand, and the official or public designation of those conditions as "problems," on the other hand. Thus, the official and professional recognition of racial discrimination as a social problem in the United States came, not while the Jim Crow regime was at its worst (prior to World War II), but only after the lot of African-Americans had already begun to improve significantly. The War on Poverty of the 1960s was effectively bumped from the national agenda of social problems with no change in the actual incidence of poverty, however measured. The national War on Drugs was officially declared after more than a decade of *decline* in the incidence of alcohol and drug use by both adults and youth in the United States.

This common and paradoxical lack of correspondence between the *objective* social *conditions* and the ebb and flow of social *problems* means that the two phenomena can vary quite independently. From the subjectivist viewpoint, then, the traditional objectivist focus has made the mistake of studying, not social problems, but only certain social conditions. In evaluating these conditions as problems, the objectivists have not been assuming the positivist, value-neutral stance of science, as they have supposed; rather, they have willy-nilly accepted the transitory evaluative definitions of interest groups, of government funding agencies, and of a fickle public. If the objectivists, then, have been studying the wrong thing, what *should* the focus be for sociologists of social problems?

From the subjectivist viewpoint, the sociological study of social problems, properly understood, is the study of the process by which putative social conditions come to be defined as social problems by governments and by publics (Spector and Kitsuse 1977). The study of the social conditions themselves can be left to sociologists with other specialties: Criminologists can and should study crime; family sociologists should study divorce, spousal conflict, and child-rearing stresses; specialists in stratification should study inequality, and so on. None of this other work, however important, constitutes the sociology of *social problems*, for social problems do not originate in the conditions themselves. They originate in the *claims-making activities* of interest groups and partisans who undertake to gain political acceptance for their definitions of certain conditions as "problems". It is those claims-making activities, then, that should comprise the focus of study of the sociology of social problems. Put another way, the study of social problems is a study in the social construction of reality (Berger and Luckmann 1966). Thus, subjectivists who study social problems in this way are also called *social constructionists* (or simply *constructionists*).

As understood by Kitsuse, Spector, and their disciples, claims-making activities consist of the usual tactics of interest groups in asserting claims and grievances, including boycotts, demonstrations, and lawsuits, as well as in the strategic uses of terms, labels, semantics, and other rhetorical devices, all aimed at winning over political support and public opinion for their definitions of certain putative social conditions as problems (Spector and Kitsuse 1977, pp. 9–21, 72–79; Schneider 1985, pp. 213–218; 224). The particular arena within which claims-making activities may occur can be as large as American society or as small as a college campus, a corporation, or even a professional society. Whatever the arena, though, it is those claims-making activities or "social-problems work" that constitute the appropriate focus of research in what we call *social problems* (Miller and Holstein 1989).

While the subjectivist or social constructionist paradigm is relatively recent as a theoretical alternative to the positivist or objectivist tradition in the study of social problems per se, it is actually cognate to several other well-established lines of inquiry in sociology. One of these is *cultural analysis*, represented especially in the work of Mary Douglas (Douglas 1966; Douglas and Wildavsky 1982). Broadly defined, cultural analysis is the study of the production and distribution of culture (including popular culture). As applied to social problems, cultural analysis includes the assessment of risk as a cultural product, much like a religious ideology (see Stallings 1990). Miller

and Holstein (1989) see a parallel here to the early Durkheimian concept of *collective representations,* which they understand as a cultural product of social problems work (see also Gusfield 1981).

A second theoretical linkage can be made between the social constructionist approach to social problems and *conflict theory* (see Pong 1989). Inspired partly by Marxism, conflict theory, like its cousin critical theory, rejects the functionalist assumption that the natural condition of society is a state of equilibrium among interdependent parts (institutions). Instead, conflict theory emphasizes the naturally conflicting tendencies in society among the various economic, political, religious, and other interest groups (e.g., Eitzen and Zinn 1988; Skolnick and Currie 1985). While the objectivist tendency in the way conflict theory *defines* social problems would not accord well with the social constructionist paradigm, nevertheless the claims-making activities so important in that paradigm are classical examples of the political struggle and agitation that constitute the typical focus of conflict theorists.

The social constructionist perspective converges perhaps even more closely with a third important preoccupation of sociology, namely *social movement theory.* The claims-making activities that comprise the principal focus of the constructionist approach are also the classical tactics and strategies of social movement activists. This would include both rhetorical products, like ideology and propaganda, and mobilizing activities, like demonstrations, agitation, and political organization (see Hilgartner and Bosk 1988). The "resource mobilization" approach to social movements that has gained currency in recent years seems especially close to the "claims-making" focus of the subjectivist or constructionist perspective on social problems (see Zald and McCarthy 1987; Turner 1981).

Two of the most recent annual conferences of the Society for the Study of Social Problems (1985 and 1989) have actually featured the theme of social problems as social movements, but proponents of the subjectivist perspective are not entirely agreed on whether the study of social problems should be subsumed by social movement theory, as advocated by Mauss (Mauss and Associates 1975; Mauss 1989), or should be approached as a theoretically distinct field of study (see Spector and Kitsuse 1977; Schneider 1985; Troyer 1989).

THE CURRENT INTELLECTUAL STATE OF AFFAIRS

In effect, two paradigms for understanding and explaining social problems are in contention for hegemony in the discipline of sociology. The traditional objectivist paradigm evaluates certain social conditions as problems by definition. In this conceptualization, there is an implicit analogy to a cancer or other disease in the human body. That is, a social problem is understood as an objectively real and undesirable condition in society that should be diagnosed and treated by experts (especially sociologists). The emergent subjectivist paradigm, in contrast, denies that any particular social condition can be defined objectively as a social problem, for such a definition depends upon the evaluation and claims-making activities of interest groups. These groups organize and mobilize social movements in an attempt to gain general political acceptance for certain "undesirable" conditions as "social problems." Indeed, from this perspective, a social problem might be essentially the same thing as a social movement.

The objectivist paradigm is likely to remain dominant in the foreseeable future, at least in the textbooks on social problems. One reason for this dominance is the objectivist bias in the political culture of North America, in which public opinion has traditionally taken for granted the amenability of social ills to objective diagnosis and the responsibility of the political system to ameliorate those ills. Another reason is the lack of intellectual sophistication typically found at the freshman and sophomore levels of college education, where most courses in social problems are taught. The phenomenological epistemology of the subjectivist paradigm is simply too abstract for most college students. The emergent subjectivist paradigm is likely, however, to provide the basis for the most novel and creative scholarly and professional literature on social problems in the coming decades. This is precisely because its epistemology and methodology still leave so much room for development, in comparison with objectivism and positivism.

Some attempts have been made to reconcile these two paradigms, usually in textbooks, which are notorious for their sacrifice of theoretical focus in favor of eclecticism. Ultimately, however, the two probably cannot be reconciled, since they proceed from different epistemologies and study different topics. Objectivism focuses on certain social conditions, such as inequality or deviant behavior, taking for granted the evaluation of those conditions as problems. Subjectivism focuses on the *political players and processes* by which those conditions come to be defined as problems.

(SEE ALSO: *Alcohol; Criminal and Delinquent Subcultures; Deviance; Drug Abuse; Homelessness; Illegitimacy; Juvenile Deliquency and Juvenile Crime; Poverty; Prejudice; Sexual Violence and Abuse; Sexually Transmitted Diseases; Violent Crime*)

REFERENCES

Becker, Howard S. 1966 *Social Problems: A Modern Approach.* New York: Wiley.

Berger, Peter L., and Thomas Luckmann 1966 *The Social Construction of Reality.* New York: Doubleday.

Blumer, Herbert 1971 "Social Problems as Collective Behavior." *Social Problems* 18:298–306.

Douglas, Mary L. 1966 *Purity and Danger: An Analysis of Concepts of Pollution and Taboo.* New York: Praeger.

———, and Aaron Wildavsky 1982 *Risk and Culture* Berkeley, Calif.: University of California Press.

Eitzen, D. Stanley, and Maxine B. Zinn 1988 *Social Problems,* 4th ed. Boston: Allyn and Bacon.

Fuller, Richard C. 1937 "Sociological Theory and Social Problems." *Social Forces* 4:496–502.

Fuller, Richard C., and Richard R. Myers 1941a. "Some Aspects of a Theory of Social Problems." *American Sociological Review* 6:24–32.

——— 1941b. "The Natural History of a Social Problem." *American Sociological Review* 6:320–328.

Gusfield, Joseph R. 1981 *The Culture of Public Problems:*

Drinking-Driving and the Symbolic Order. Chicago: University of Chicago Press.

Hilgartner, Stephen, and Charles L. Bosk 1988 "The Rise and Fall of Social Problems: A Public Arenas Model." *American Journal of Sociology* 94(1):53–78.

Kitsuse, John I., and Malcolm Spector 1973 "Toward a Sociology of Social Problems: Social Conditions, Value Judgments, and Social Problems." *Social Problems* 20:407–419.

Mauss, Armand L. 1989 "Beyond the Illusion of Social Problems Theory." In James A. Holstein and Gale Miller, eds., *Perspectives on Social Problems,* Vol. 1. Greenwich, Conn.: JAI Press.

———, and Associates 1975 *Social Problems as Social Movements.* Philadelphia: Lippincott.

Miller, Gale, and James A. Holstein 1989 "On the Sociology of Social Problems." In James A. Holstein and Gale Miller, eds., *Perspectives on Social Problems,* Vol. 1. Greenwich, Conn.: JAI Press.

Mills, C. Wright 1943 "The Professional Ideology of Social Pathologists." *American Journal of Sociology* 49:165–180.

Pong, Raymond W. 1989 "Social Problems as a Conflict Process." In James A. Holstein and Gale Miller, eds., *Perspectives on Social Problems,* Vol. 1. Greenwich, Conn.: JAI Press.

Schneider, John W. 1985 "Social Problems Theory: The Constructionist View." *Annual Review of Sociology* 11:209–229.

Skolnick, Jerome H., and Elliott Currie (eds.) 1985 *Crisis in American Institutions,* 6th ed. Boston: Little, Brown.

Spector, Malcolm, and John I. Kitsuse 1973 "Social Problems: A Reformulation." *Social Problems* 21:145–159.

——— 1977. *Constructing Social Problems.* Menlo Park, Calif.: Cummings.

Stallings, Robert A. 1990 "Media Discourse and the Social Construction of Risk." *Social Problems* 37:80–95.

Troyer, Ronald J. 1989 "Are Social Problems and Social Movements the Same Thing?" In James A. Holstein and Gale Miller, eds., *Perspectives on Social Problems,* Vol 1. Greenwich, Conn.: JAI Press.

Turner, Ralph H. 1981 "Collective Behavior and Resource Mobilization as Approaches to Social Movements: Issues and Continuities." In Louis Kriesberg, ed., *Research in Social Movements Conflicts, and Change,* Vol. 4. Greenwich, Conn.: JAI Press.

Waller, Willard 1936 "Social Problems and the Mores." *American Sociological Review* 1:922–933.

Zald, Mayer N., and John D. McCarthy 1987 *Social Movements in an Organizational Society: Collected Essays.* New Brunswick, N.J.: Transaction Books.

ARMAND L. MAUSS

SOCIAL PSYCHOLOGY Social psychology is the study of individual behavior and psychological structures and processes as outcomes of and influences upon interpersonal relationships, the functioning of groups and other collective forms, and culturally defined macrosocial structures and processes. Social psychologists vary in the theoretical orientations and methods they use, the conceptual discriminations they draw, and the specific substantive causal linkages with which they are concerned. Much of the variability in these regards is accounted for by the academic tradition in which the social psychologist was trained.

Contemporary social psychology has intellectual roots in both psychology and sociology. Psychological social psychologists are guided by social learning theory, as well as by other orientations such as exchange and role theories. For the most part, their methods are laboratory and field experiments, and data analysis is accomplished through quantitative techniques. They discriminate between individual behavior and psychological structures and processes and interpersonal settings. The primary interest of psychological social psychology is the influence of the perceived social environment on individual cognitive, affective, and behavioral responses.

Contemporary sociological social psychology encompasses two major perspectives: symbolic interactionist, and personality and social structure. Within the symbolic interactionist school, other distinctions are drawn according to the degree to which the proponents emphasize consistencies in human behavior, as opposed to creative and emergent aspects of behavior, the influence of social structure in placing constraints upon social interaction through which concepts of the self and others are formed, and the relative merits of qualitative and quantitative research methods. Considering the various perspectives together, sociological social psychologists are influenced most frequently by symbolic interactionism, role theory, and exchange theory. They employ a range of research methods, including social surveys, unstructured interviews, observational techniques, and archival research methods; however, laboratory and field experiments are also used on occasion. Data analysis is accomplished by both qualitative and quantitative techniques. Distinctions are drawn between individual behaviors, psychological structures, groups and other interpersonal systems, and culturally defined macrosocial structures and processes. Sociological social psychologists focus upon the reciprocal causal influences either between individual psychological structures and macrosocial structures and processes or between psychological processes and ongoing interpersonal systems (Blumer 1969; Cartwright 1979; House 1977; Kohn 1989; Michener, DeLamater, and Schwartz 1990; Rosenberg and Turner 1981; Stryker 1980; Turner 1988).

The current state of social psychology is best understood by describing the range of theoretical orientations and research methods used, the conceptual discriminations that are drawn, and the causal linkages that are investigated by representatives of the two social psychological traditions.

THEORY AND METHOD

A broad range of theoretical perspectives and research methods are used by social psychologists to study the reciprocal causal linkages between individual-level and social-level variables.

Theoretical Perspectives. Among the more frequently used theoretical perspectives are symbolic interactionism, role theory, exchange theory, and social learning theory.

Symbolic interactionism. From this perspective, human beings are perceived as acting toward others depending upon the meaning that those others and their behaviors have for the actors. The meanings are derived and modified in the course

of social interaction in which people communicate with one another through the use of shared symbols. Symbolic interactionism encompasses the notion that people's ability to respond to themselves as objects permits them to communicate to themselves, by the use of symbols, the meanings that are given to people and objects by the persons perceiving them. Thus, people interpret the world to themselves and respond according to that interpretation. The interpretation of the situation occurs in the course of ongoing social interaction. In short, persons become objects to themselves, interact with themselves, and interpret to themselves the ongoing events and objects in the environment.

Proponents of symbolic interactionism vary in the extent to which they focus on the influence of a stable social structure on these processes. Those who deny the significance of a social structure focus solely on the process of cognitive interpretation and the creative construction of behavior that grows out of the person's interpretation of the ongoing interactive situation. Appropriate to this emphasis, empirical investigations employ observation and in-depth interviewing to the exclusion of experimental and quantitative, nonexperimental methods (the Chicago School). Derivatives of this approach to symbolic interactionism are the dramaturgical school, in which the metaphor of the theater is used to study how people create impressions of themselves in the course of face-to-face interaction; and ethnomethodology, from which perspective students study the implicit rules governing interaction in any particular situation in order to understand how people construct reality through social interaction.

For those who focus on the significance of social structures to symbolic interaction, the meanings of the behaviors in social interaction depend on the relevance of the behaviors for social-identity-related standards by which people evaluate themselves. Individuals interact within a framework defining the social identities of the interacting parties and the normative expectations that are applicable to each identity as it relates to the other identities in the situation. Those behaviors have the most meaning that are relevant for highly placed standards in the person's hierarchy of values. The more a behavior of the person or the others with whom he is interacting validates or contradicts the social identity (male, father) that is important to him, the more meaningful the behavior will be to him. To the extent that the behaviors of others toward the person signify evaluatively significant aspects of the self, it becomes important to anticipate the responses from others. Those others whose responses are more likely to signify evaluatively relevant information about the self are significant others (House 1977; Kaplan 1986; Stephan and Stephan 1990; Stryker 1980).

Role theory. From this perspective, human social behavior is viewed in the context of people playing roles (that is, conforming to normative expectations) that apply to people who occupy various social positions and are interacting with people who occupy complementary social positions. As individuals change from one social position to another in the course of a day, they will play different roles (as a father, for example, then as an employer). The roles individuals play will also change as they interact with people in different positions (a professor interacting with a colleague, with the dean, and with a student). As people shift roles, they also change the ways in which they view the world, the attitudes they hold toward different phenomena, and their behaviors. Though people identify more with some roles than others, their ability to play their preferred roles is limited by the contradictory demands made on them by the other roles they are called upon to play (Biddle 1979).

Exchange theory. This perspective is relevant to the question of the conditions under which individuals will enter into and maintain stable relationships. One is most likely to do so when the rewards gained from the relationship are perceived as high, the costs are low, and the reward–cost differential is favorable compared with perceived alternatives. Rewards (power, prestige, material goods) and costs (interpersonal hostility, great expenditures of money, long hours of work)

are defined by personal values. Attraction to relationships is also a function of the extent to which the participants perceive each other as receiving outcomes (rewards) that are appropriate to their inputs (costs). In the absence of such equity, the participants will adjust their behavior or way of thinking in an attempt to restore the fact or appearance of equity in the relationship (Stephan and Stephan 1990; Walster, Walster, and Berscheid 1978).

Social learning theory. This orientation addresses the question of how individuals learn new responses that are appropriate in various social situations. The primary processes through which social learning occurs are conditioning, whereby one acquires new responses through reinforcement (that is, the association of rewards and punishments with particular behaviors); and imitation, whereby one observes the reinforcement elicited by another person's behavior (Bandura 1986).

Methods. Social psychological research employs a variety of methods, including social surveys, naturalistic observation, experiments, and analysis of archival data. Social surveys may be conducted by personal or telephone interview or by self-administered questionnaire. For the most part, naturalistic observation involves observing ongoing activity in everyday settings (that is, field studies); in participant observation, the investigator plays an active role in the interaction rather than merely observing. Experimental research involves the manipulation of independent variables to assess their effects on outcomes. Subjects are assigned at random to the independent conditions. The experiments may be conducted in the laboratory or in natural settings; in the latter, the experimenter has less control over theoretically irrelevant variables, but the experimental conditions are more realistic for the subjects. Archival research involves the use of already existing data to test hypotheses. In some instances the data can be used exactly as they appear, as with some statistical data. In other instances, such as newspaper stories, the data must be converted into another form—as, for example, for use in content analysis, which involves categorizing and counting particular occurrences.

CONCEPTUAL DISCRIMINATIONS

The pursuit of the goals of social psychology by scientists from psychological and sociological traditions has entailed the differentiation between concepts at both the individual and the social level.

Individual-Level Concepts. Social psychologists have variously focused on dynamic psychological structures, intrapsychic response, and individual behaviors as outcomes of or influences on social structures and processes.

Psychological structures. At the individual level, psychological structures have been represented as dynamic organizations of dispositions to respond at the intrapsychic or behavioral level. More inclusive concepts, such as the personality, have reflected the organization of psychological dispositions in terms of a structure of relatively stable cognitive, evaluative, affective, and behavioral tendencies. The concept of the person has been understood in terms of a structure of predispositions to respond at the intrapsychic or behavioral level that are organized around a hierarchically related system of social identities. The self has been treated as an inclusive structure of dispositions to respond reflexively at the cognitive, evaluative, affective, and behavioral levels. Less inclusive structures refer to organizations of particular psychological dispositions, such as personal value systems, treated as the hierarchy of situationally applicable criteria for self-evaluation, the structure of attitudes or generalized evaluative responses, or the system of concepts and schemas (structures of related concepts) that the person uses to order stimuli.

These structures are treated as components related to one another in stable dynamic equilibrium, and at the same time as having the potential to change. The structures of predispositions, when stimulated by internal or external cues, respond at the intrapsychic or behavioral level. The predispositions are inferred from the observed behaviors and self-reports of intrapsychic

responses to recurrent situationally nested stimuli.

Intrapsychic responses. These are cognitive (including awareness and conceptual structuring), evaluative, and affective (or emotional) responses to contemporary stimuli, including one's own or others' behaviors in particular situational contexts. The current situation may stimulate one to attend to particular aspects of oneself, to classify others in terms of group-membership concepts, to attribute others' failures to external rather than internal causes, to evaluate oneself as a failure, or to experience attraction to other people. Intrapsychic responses are inferred from one's perceptible behaviors or self-reports of percepts, beliefs, attitudes, and feelings relating to the current situation.

Behavior. Individual behavior refers to that class of responses that are perceptible to others as well as oneself. Behavior is distinguished from intrapsychic responses and/or the stable organization of dispositions to respond (person or personality) that are perceptible only to the self. Behavior includes purposive or unintended communications about oneself or others, helping and hurtful responses, affiliation and disaffiliation with other individuals or groups, conformity to or deviation from one's own or others' expectations, cooperation and competition, positive and negative sanctioning of one's own or others' behaviors, and the myriad other perceptible responses one may make to oneself, others, or other aspects of one's environment (Kaplan 1986; Michener, De-Lamater, and Schwartz 1990; Stephan and Stephan 1990). Behavior is conceptualized as the outcome of socially influenced psychological structures and intrapsychic processes, and as influencing social-level variables.

Social-Level Concepts. These include interpersonal systems and culturally defined macrosocial structures.

Interpersonal systems. Interpersonal systems are defined as two or more individuals interacting with each other or otherwise influencing each other over a brief or extended period of time. The interaction or mutual influence is governed by shared normative expectations that define appropriate behavior for the individuals who occupy complementary or common social positions in the course of the interaction or mutual influence. The shared expectations may exist before participation in the interpersonal system and reflect the common culturally defined macrosocial structure, or may be refined or emerge in the course of the ongoing social interaction or mutual influence in response to the unique characteristics of the interacting individuals or other situational demands. The social positions that a person occupies and the interpersonal systems in which he or she participates as a consequence may be given at birth or may be adopted later in life according to stage in the life cycle and current situational demands. Interpersonal systems include interpersonal relationships, groups, and collective forms.

Interpersonal relationships consist of two individuals in ongoing interaction that is governed by their shared normative expectations. These expectations are derived from social definitions that define appropriate behavior for people occupying the social positions that characterize the individuals and emerge in the course of the ongoing social interaction. For example, a married couple's shared expectations depend upon common understandings of the obligations and rights of a husband and a wife in relationship to each other, and the same is true of friends; in addition, in the course of social interaction, specific evaluative expectations regarding what each person in the relationship will and should do in various circumstances will develop. Individuals may interact with one another in the capacity of having the same status (such as group member or friend) or complementary statuses (such as husband and wife), or in the capacity of representing different conflicting or cooperating groups. Relationships develop through predictable stages. Intimate relationships develop from awareness of available partners, to contact with those who are thought to be desirable, to various stages of emotional involvement. Accompanying increases in emotional involvement are increases in self-disclosure, trust, and mutual dependence (Huston 1974; Michener, DeLamater, and Schwartz 1990).

A group consists of a number of individuals in ongoing interaction who share a set of normative expectations governing the behavior of the group members in relationship to one another. Normative expectations may refer uniformly to all group members as they interact with one another and with nongroup members, or to different individuals in their various social relational contexts. Individuals share an identity as members of the group, as well as common goals; these may include the personal satisfaction gained from the intrinsically or instrumentally satisfying intragroup relationship or from a group identity that evokes favorable responses from extragroup systems. Group members may share norms from the outset and refine or change expectations over time, or the norms may emerge in the course of member interaction. Groups include friendship networks, work groups, schools, families, voluntary associations, and other naturally occurring or purposively formed ad hoc associations. Groups vary in size, stability, degree to which interaction among members is regulated by preexisting role definitions, and complexity of role differentiation, as well as in the extent to which the group is embedded in more-inclusive group settings. Groups vary also according to whether the gratifications achieved from participation in the group are intrinsic to the social relationships and are diffuse, as opposed to instrumental to the achievement of other ends and delimited.

Over the course of time, groups develop structures characterized by status hierarchies and functional role differentiation, or these structures are predefined for new group members. Status hierarchies reflect the values placed by group members on positions within the group. Individuals who occupy those positions are more or less esteemed depending upon the valuation (status) of the position. Individuals who have higher status positions and are consequently more highly esteemed ordinarily receive greater rewards (as these are defined by group members) and exercise greater influence over group decisions. In formal groups functional differentiation is indicated by the formal role definitions associated with the various social positions making up the group. In informal groups, over time some individuals come to be expected to perform certain functions, such as leading the group toward solving a problem (the task leader) or accepting responsibility for relieving tensions and maintaining group solidarity (the social-emotional leader) (Cartwright and Zander 1968; Hare 1976; Myers 1982).

Collective forms include publics, audiences, crowds, and social movements. Collective forms are characterized by the mutual influence of individuals to respond cognitively, affectively, and behaviorally to a common focus. Individuals are undifferentiated according to social position. They share the social position defined by their common attention to some idea, person, object, or behavior. The common stimulus, previously learned dispositions to respond to the stimulus, and mutual influences by processes of social contagion, social observation, and emergent norms that govern mood, action, and imagery, lead to collective behaviors. Collective behaviors by large numbers of individuals not physically proximate in response to mass media and interpersonal stimulation include mass expressions of attitudes (public opinions), attraction (fads, fashions, crazes), and anxiety (panics). Crowd behaviors are collective responses by large numbers of physically proximate individuals who are influenced by social contagion, observation, and resultant emergent norms. Social movements are expressions of dispositions to behave with regard to some social issue (McCarthy and Zald 1977; Smelser 1963; Turner and Killian 1957).

Culturally defined macrosocial structures. The inclusive sociocultural structure provides shared meanings and defines relationships among individuals depending upon their social positions or identities in the situation. The social structure is made up of the stable relationships between social positions or identities that are culturally defined in terms of the rights and obligations people occupying one position have in interacting with people occupying another. In the course of the socialization process individuals learn the rights and obligations that apply to those who occupy the various social positions, and these rights and obligations constitute the role that defines the social position. The inclusive social structure is a system consisting of components that are related to one another in a relatively stable dynamic equilibrium but may change over time as changes in structural positions and their role definitions become prevalent in interpersonal settings throughout the society. The culturally defined inclusive macrosocial structure encompasses systems of stratification, social differentiation according to race or ethnicity, and major social institutions, as well as other consensually defined social structures (House 1977).

CAUSAL RELATIONSHIPS

Within a social psychological framework, a person's psychological structure, intrapsychic responses, and behaviors are viewed in terms of the profound influence exerted upon him by his past and continuing participation in interpersonal and social systems. In turn, he behaves in ways that have consequences for the interpersonal systems and social structures in which he participates. Implicit in this framework is a general causal model. Social structural arrangements define systems of shared meanings that, in turn, define the role expectations governing behavior in interpersonal systems. The person is born into functioning interpersonal systems and throughout the life cycle comes to participate in other interpersonal systems that together reflect culturally defined macrosocial structures and processes. In the course of the person's life in the context of dynamically evolving interlocking interpersonal systems, biogenetically given capabilities are actualized; he learns to view the world through a system of concepts, internalizes needs, symbolizes the needs as values, accepts social identities, and develops emotional cognitive and behavioral dispositions to respond. These relatively stable psychological structures are stimulated by contemporary social situations that have symbolic significance for the individual and, as such, evoke predictable personal responses. Over time, the same social situations stimulate personal change.

The development of language skills, along with the person's experiences as the object of others' responses to him in the course of the socialization process, influences the development of his tendencies to become aware of, conceive of, evaluate, and have feelings about himself, as well as dispositions to behave in ways that are motivated by the need to protect or enhance the self. The nature of his responses to himself are influenced by past and present social experiences. These responses, in turn, influence the relationships and groups in which he participates, and indirectly influence the more inclusive social system, and so intervene between social influences on him and his influence on interpersonal systems and the culturally defined social structure (Featherman and Lerner 1988; Kaplan 1986; Rosenberg 1979; Stryker 1989; Wegner and Vallacher 1980).

The substantive concerns of social psychological theory and research reflect detailed consideration of these general processes. These concerns address (1) the influence of culturally defined macrosocial structures and processes or interpersonal systems on psychological structures, intrapsychic responses, and individual behaviors; or (2) the influence of psychological structures, intrapsychic responses, and individual behaviors on interpersonal systems and culturally defined macrosocial structures and processes.

Social Influences on Psychological Structures. Substantive concerns with social influences on individual psychological structures, intrapsychic responses, and behaviors have variously focused on long-term social structural influences via socialization processes and contemporary interpersonal influences in interpersonal settings.

Social structural effects. Social structural arrangements define the content, effectiveness, and style of the socialization experience and thereby influence the person's psychological structures. Individuals occupy social positions by being born into them or by achieving them later in life. Each social position is defined in terms of role expectations that specify appropriate behavior for people occupying the position in the context of particular relationships. As a result of occupying positions, people become part of interpersonal systems consisting of themselves and those who occupy complementary positions. In these relationships and groups people become socialized. Socialization is

the lifelong process through which the individual learns, and becomes motivated to conform to, the norms defining the social roles that are played or might be played in the future by her or him and those with whom she or he interacts. Socialization occurs in a variety of social contexts, including the family, school, play group, and work groups, through processes of the experiences of rewards and punishment consequent to performing behaviors, observation of the consequences of behaviors for others, direct and intended instruction by others, and self-reinforcement. The acquisition of language skills permits one to be rewarded and punished through the use of symbolic responses, to communicate with others about the appropriateness of various responses, and to reinforce responses through the process of becoming an object to oneself and disapproving or approving of one's past or anticipated behaviors. The cognitive structures used in coding and processing information about one's own behavior (Markus 1977) and the hierarchy of self-evaluative criteria (Kaplan 1986) also are learned in the course of socialization experiences.

The content of the role definitions and the centrality of particular roles for the person's identity structure depend on stage in the life cycle, role definitions associated with other social positions, and historical era. Those roles that are most central to the person's identity and that contribute most to self-esteem depend upon his or her position in the social structure, including their age and gender. During a particular historical period, for example, men may base their self-esteem more on success in the occupational sphere, whereas women in the same stage of life may base theirs on adequate performance of family roles.

The effectiveness of the socialization process is influenced by more or less invariant developmental stages of cognitive and emotional development in interaction with the varying demands made upon the individual at various stages in the life cycle (Bronfenbrenner 1970; Bush and Simmons 1981; Denzin 1977; Goslin 1969), as well as by discrepancies between the demands made upon the person and the available resources that would permit her or him to meet the demands (Baltes and Brim 1980; Elder 1975; Kaplan 1983; Riley 1987).

The social structure affects the style of the socialization process as well. Higher-socioeconomic-status parents are more likely than lower-class parents to base rewards and punishment on the child's intentions than on actual behavior, and to rely on reasoning and the induction of shame and guilt rather than physical punishment. As the family size becomes larger, parents are more likely to exercise autocratic parenting styles, while children elicit less attention from parents and develop more independence (Michener, DeLamater, and Schwartz 1990).

The end result of the social-structure-influenced socialization process is the development of psychological structures that variously are stimulated by social-identity-related situations or are more generally evoked in the course of social interaction. Depending on whether persons are born to male or female social positions, they will develop different achievement orientations and evaluate themselves according to the success they have in approximating whatever standards of achievement they set for themselves. Individuals in higher socioeconomic classes tend to value a sense of accomplishment and family security more highly than those of lower socioeconomic status, who tend to put more emphasis on a comfortable life and salvation. More specifically, individuals who are born into a higher social class are more likely to be socialized to value educational achievement and aspire to higher levels of education. Those who achieve at higher levels in school will be more likely to interact with others who respond to them in ways that reinforce academically orientated self-images and values that reflect achievement orientations. Individuals whose occupational status involves self-direction tend to develop higher valuation of responsibility, curiosity, and good sense, while occupational positions characterized by close supervision, routine activities, and low levels of complexity in work tasks tend to develop high valuation of conformity (Heiss 1981; House 1981; Kohn et al. 1983; Rokeach 1973; Sewell and Hauser 1980).

In general, in the course of socialization people become disposed to identify others in their environment, to anticipate their responses, to imagine aspects of themselves as eliciting those responses, to behave in ways calculated to elicit those responses, and to value the responses of others and the aspects of self that elicit those responses. Radical resocialization, whereby an individual unlearns lifelong patterns and learns new attitudes, values, and behaviors, may occur in circumstances in which the agents of socialization have uniform and total control over the individual's outcomes, as in the cases of some psychiatric hospitals, penal institutes, traditional military academies, and prisoner-of-war camps (Goffman 1961).

Interpersonal effects. The contemporary interpersonal context stimulates self-conceptions and self-evaluative, affective, and behavioral responses. Each social situation provides participants with physical cues that allow them to make inferences about the social identities of the other participants, the role expectations that each person holds of the others, and the perceived causes of the behaviors of the interacting parties. These conceptions regarding the situated identities are in part responses to the demand characteristics of the situation, and in part the outcomes of the need of one party to project a particular social identity on the other person in order that the former can play a desired complementary role (Alexander and Wiley 1981). The situational context provides symbolic cues that specify the relevance of particular traits, behaviors, or experience for one's current situation; it also provides a basis for comparing one's own characteristics with those of other people.

The current social situation defines the relevance of some self-evaluative standards rather than others. The presence of other people, cameras, or mirrors makes people more self-aware and so stimulates their disposition to evaluate themselves. Certain responses of others (sanctions), in addition to constituting intrinsically value-relevant responses, communicate to persons the degree to which they have approximated self-evaluative standards. In the early stages of development of the group, individuals may be assigned higher status positions on the basis of status characteristics (such as those relating to age, sex, ethnicity, and physical attractiveness) that have evaluative significance in the more inclusive society. Although these characteristics may not be relevant to the ability to perform the functions for which the group exists, the high evaluation of the status characteristics may lead to the assignment of the individual to high status positions within the group through a process of status generalization (Berger, Zelditch, and Anderson 1989). As a consequence of culturally defined preconceptions regarding the merits of various status characteristics, persons with these characteristics are expected to perform better on a group task.

With regard to affective responses, social stimuli evoke physiological reactions that are labeled as specific emotional states, depending upon the cues provided by social circumstances (Kelley and Michela 1980). In turn, individuals who label their experience as a particular emotional state will selectively perceive bodily sensations as cues that validate the experience (Leventhal 1980; Pennebaker 1980). Social stimuli that evoke psychological distress include contexts in which the person is unable to fulfill role requirements due to the absence of personal and interpersonal resources or the presence of situational barriers to fulfilling the obligations associated with the social positions the person occupies. Other such stimuli are represented by intrinsically distressing aspects of social positions. People may be distressed, not only because of being unable to do their jobs well, but also because of the absence of meaning that the job has for them and because of other noxious circumstances correlated with the position (time pressures, noise, lack of autonomy, conflicting expectations).

Situational contexts define expectations regarding appropriate and otherwise attractive behavior and so stimulate behavior that anticipates fulfillment of the expectations and achievement of the goals (including avoidance of noxious states). In collective forms of interpersonal systems, emergent norms govern actions as well as moods and imagery for publics and crowds, and so lead to such mass behaviors as crazes and panics, and such crowd behavior as rioting (Turner and Killi-

am 1957). The motivation for participation in social movements is influenced by expectations regarding the value and likelihood of success of the movement (McCarthy and Zald 1977).

In interpersonal relationships as well, shared expectations govern attraction to others, helping behavior, and aggressive behavior. An individual will tend to be attracted to those with whom interaction is facilitated, those who are characterized by socially appropriate and desirable traits (including physical attributes), those who share tastes with and are otherwise like the individual, those who manifest liking for him or her, and, in general, those who may be expected to occasion rewarding outcomes (Huston 1974). Helping behavior is evoked by situational demand characteristics, such as role definitions that define helping behavior as appropriate for people who occupy particular social positions in the situation, or by interpersonal expectations that helping behavior by the other should be reciprocated. The likelihood of conforming to these situational demand characteristics is increased when the person perceives that rewards for doing so will be forthcoming (including personal satisfaction in helping others, a sense of fulfillment in doing what one is called upon to do, approval by others) and that failure to do so will bring negative sanctions (social disapproval, a self-evaluation of having failed to do the right thing). Conformity to demand characteristics that require helping behavior may be impeded if the person perceives that it would involve costs, such as hindering the achievement of other goals. The awareness of potential rewards or costs for engaging or failing to engage in helping behavior is facilitated by situational characteristics, such as the presence of observers and circumstances that produce self-awareness. The need to help others is increased by experiences that evoke negative self-evaluations. Resulting negative self-feelings motivate helping behavior as a way of increasing positive self-evaluation (Bar-Tal 1976; Cunningham, Steinberg, and Grev 1980; Macaulay and Berkowitz 1970; Phelps 1975; Schwartz and Howard 1981).

Aggressive behavior may arise in response to situational demand characteristics, such as perceiving oneself as playing a role that requires aggressive behavior, either as a response to intentional aggressive behavior directed toward one by others or simply as a communication of an aggressive stance. Reinforcement by rewards increases the frequency or continuity of aggressive patterns. Rewarding outcomes of aggression include the related rewards of social approval, position in the prestige hierarchy of the group, self-approval, and material gain. Individuals are inhibited from engaging in aggressive behavior when they perceive the act as contrary to normatively proscribed roles or otherwise anticipate adverse consequences of the behavior. Such inhibiting effects may be obviated by reduced self-awareness that results from being part of a crowd, for example, or from the administration of psychotropic drugs (Bandura 1973; Baron 1977; Kaplan 1972; Singer 1971).

In group contexts, role definitions and influences upon self-awareness affect individual behavior. The assignment of individuals to higher status positions in the group and concomitant expectations of higher levels of performance or of the adoption of particular functional roles frequently motivate people to conform to those expectations or lead to the provision of resources that permits them to do so (Berger, Zelditch, and Anderson 1989). Where socially induced self-awareness causes people to attend to public aspects of themselves, they tend to be responsive to group influences. Where self-awareness causes them to attend to their personal standards, they tend to guide their behavior in conformity with these values even where they conflict with group standards. Thus, exposure to cameras induces public self-awareness and increases social conformity, while exposure to mirrors evokes private self-awareness and an increase in self-direction (Scheier and Carver 1983).

The effects of social stimuli on deviant, as opposed to conforming, behavior have been addressed from a variety of theoretical frameworks, including structured strain theory, differential association and deviant subculture theories, control theory, self-theory, and the labeling perspective. Attempts to integrate or elaborate any one of these approaches encompass the following ideas

(Gibbs 1981; Hollander 1975; Kaplan 1984; Messner, Krohn, and Liska 1989; Moscovici 1985). First, individuals who experience rejection and failure in conventional social groups will lose motivation to conform to conventional norms and will be motivated to deviate from those norms. At the same time, the individuals will be disposed to seek alternative deviant patterns in order to attain or restore feelings of self-worth. Second, individuals who participate in groups that endorse behaviors that happen to be defined as deviant in other groups (whether because of seeking alternative deviant patterns through which they can improve self-worth, or because of long-term identification with deviant subculture) positively value the "deviant" patterns and are provided with opportunities and the necessary resources to engage in the deviant behavior. Third, individuals with the motivation and the opportunity to engage in deviant behavior will be deterred by anticipated negative responses from groups that define the behavior as deviant and to which the person remains emotionally bonded. Individuals will tend to conform to the normative expectations of a group to the extent that they are made aware of the deviant nature of their behavior or attributes, they are attracted to the group and therefore are highly vulnerable to the sanctions that the group might administer for deviant behavior, they are prevented from leaving the group and so freeing themselves from vulnerability to the group's negative sanctions, they identify with the group and so adopt the normative standards of that group, and they internalize the normative standards and regard conformity as intrinsically valuable. Fourth, individuals who evoke negative social sanctions in response to initial deviance will continue or increase the level of deviant behavior as a result of the effects of the negative social sanctions on increased alienation from the conventional group, increased association with deviant peers, and increased motivation to justify the initial deviance by increasing positive evaluation of the deviant acts. Continuity or escalation of deviant behavior is also likely to occur if motives that ordinarily inhibit the performance of deviant acts are weakened and if the person perceives an association between the deviant behavior and satisfaction of preexisting needs (including the need to enhance self-esteem).

Psychological Influences on Social Systems. The consequences of socially influenced psychological processes may be observed at the interpersonal level and at the more inclusive, culturally defined macrosocial-structure level.

Interpersonal systems. Intrapsychic responses and behaviors influence interpersonal systems in a wide variety of ways. Among the more salient consequences are those relating to the stability and functioning of groups, intragroup influences, group membership, and intergroup relationships.

Individuals affect both the *stability and functioning* of their groups by their behavior. Stability of a group is enhanced to the extent that individuals conform to the expectations that other people have of them and thereby validate the expectations. An individual contributes to group functioning by playing the roles that other people expect her or him to play in the group, thereby permitting others to play their complementary roles. Conformity is influenced by the need for self-approval and approval of others where the criteria for approval are the group standards. If personal and group standards reflect the value of scholarship, individuals may study hard; if approximation to the standards of a particular social identity (such as male) is a salient basis for self-evaluation, people will strive to conform to what they perceive as the role expectations associated with that position. More generally, the persons may evaluate themselves in terms of conforming to others' expectations. A salient value may be to evoke approving responses from others. To that end the person may behave in any number of ways, including conforming to others' expectations or presenting oneself to others in ways calculated to evoke approving responses. However, she or he will strive to conform to group standards in order to approximate self-values only to the extent that success or failure is attributed to the degree of personal effort rather than to circumstances. Conformity is also an outcome of the need for others' approval. In groups in which the members are highly attracted to the group, conformity to group norms, including those related to productivity, is high. In such cohesive groups, members have greater power over one another than in groups where the individuals are less attracted to and dependent upon the group (Cartwright and Zander 1968; Hare 1976). The need for others' approval is reflected in the use of disclaimers and excuses to mitigate others' responses to personal behaviors (Hewitt and Stokes 1975; Karp and Yoels 1986; Spencer 1987). A perceived threat to the group increases members' attraction to the group and conformity to shared norms while decreasing tolerance of deviance.

Interpersonal influence occurs through the use of both overt and covert behaviors. Overt methods of persuasion include the use of information or arguments, the offering of rewards, or the threat of punishment. Covert attempts to influence others are reflected in self-presentation in order to create the impression of ourselves as likable or otherwise to manipulate the impression others have of us. Attempts at persuasion will be more or less effective depending on the characteristics of the source of the communication, the message itself, and the target of the communication. For example, communications will be more persuasive if they come from a number of independent sources, each of which is perceived to be expert, trustworthy, or otherwise attractive to the target of the communication, than in mutually exclusive circumstances. The effectiveness of threats and promises in influencing others depends upon the magnitude and certainty of the proffered rewards and punishments. Where the parties involved in the influence process all have the capacity to reward or punish one another, change in opinions or behaviors will be influenced by bargaining and negotiation processes. Among the possible outcomes, depending upon a number of circumstances, are mutual influence, escalation of conflict, accommodation of one person to the demands of the other, or, simply, failure of the parties to agree (Michener, DeLamater, and Schwartz 1990). In the course of group interaction, individuals develop more extreme attitudes than they held as individuals. This may be due to the pooling of arguments, which adds new reasons for the initially held attitude, or to the social support provided by other group members, which permits the person to be more extreme in his opinions with less fear of group rejection (Brandstatter, Davis, and Stocker-Kreichgauer 1982).

Persons are motivated to present themselves in ways that evoke desired responses from others. This is accomplished through a variety of tactics. A significant feature of self-presentation is the individual's social identity in the situation. By projecting a particular identity, he effectively imposes complementary identities on others; if the other people perform the roles associated with those identities, they in effect endorse the identity that he wishes to project. Such imposition of social identities on others (altercasting) has the desirable effect of affirming the social identity he wishes to project. For example, by complying with his demands or following his lead, the others affirm the person's position of authority or leadership. In addition, people's favorable responses are intrinsically valued, other rewarding outcomes are contingent upon them, and they indicate to the person that his public image reflects his personal ideals. Self-presentation may be used to create false as well as true images of ourselves. Creation of false images (impression management) is also used to evoke responses from others that will serve our personal needs. Tactics involving the false presentation of self include pretenses that we admire the other individuals or share their opinions, or presenting ourselves as if we have admirable qualities that we do not in fact possess (Baumeister 1982; Tedeschi 1981).

The attraction and maintenance of group membership is a function of the perception by members that group participation is intrinsically desirable or instrumental to the achievement of shared or individually defined goals (Evans and Jarvis 1980). Relationships, as well as larger groups, grow and become resistant to dissolution as the partners become increasingly dependent upon each other for need satisfaction, which may lie in the relationship itself or in the role the partner plays in facilitating the satisfaction of other needs outside the relationship (that is, by providing social support). Primary relationships will dissolve to the extent that the costs come to exceed the rewards—whether in absolute terms or relative to the cost–benefit ratio that may be obtained from alternative relationships—and to the extent that the costs of remaining in the relationship outweigh the costs (including social disapproval) associated with terminating the relationship (Kelley and Thibaut 1978; Kerckhoff 1974). Among the costs are perceptions of inequity. Group members tend to compare the relationship between their own contributions to the group and the rewards they receive with other members' contributions and rewards. Judgments of inequity are made when members perceive rewards to be out of proportion to contributions. Judgments that inequitable states exist stimulate responses to reduce the inequity or, at least, the perception of the inequity. The inability to redress or tolerate inequitable relationships may lead to eschewing membership in the group (Walster, Walster, and Berscheid 1978). In general, people select group memberships, where they have a choice, and maintain group memberships according to their value in facilitating self-approving responses. People maintain relationships by whose standards they may evaluate themselves positively and tend not to associate with groups by whose standards they would be considered failures (Kaplan 1986).

The nature of the *responses that groups evoke from nonmembers* is influenced by the nonmembers' perceptions, evaluations, and feelings directed toward themselves and others. Negative emotions, such as anger, and consequent aggressive behavior may be directed toward groups when individuals' interests cannot be served except at the cost of frustration of the objectives of another group, or when the individuals associate the other group with past experiences of failure. Among the benefits that persons may experience at the cost of the other group's outcomes is increased self-esteem. Aggressive behavior directed toward others deflects anger that might have been directed toward oneself. When the basis of one's feelings of accomplishment are judged relative to the achievements of the other group, aggressive behaviors that lead to the failure or destruction of the other group enhance feelings of pride in one's own group.

Stronger levels of identification with one's group or social category will increase the need to enhance one's group identity at the cost of adverse outcomes for other groups (Bobo 1983; LeVine and Campbell 1972; Worchel and Austin 1986; Zillman 1979). The tendency to devalue others as they deviate from one's own group's standards increases the justification for negative attitudes and hostile actions toward the other group. The need to justify aggressive attitudes toward another group also frequently leads to biased perceptions that reinforce or validate the preexisting attitudes toward the other group. Reversal of the process is impeded by the decreases in communication that accompany negative attitudes toward the group. Frequent experiences of observing aggressive responses desensitize the person to the effects of these responses and establish normative judgment that they are within the expected range of responses.

Other individuals or groups may be the objects of helping behavior, depending upon the actor's intrapsychic responses. Negative affect (particularly negative self-feelings) decreases helping behavior by focusing attention inward and away from the plight of other individuals. Thus, individuals are less likely to empathize with or even be aware of others' needs. At the same time, distressful self-feelings motivate the individual to behave in ways that will earn self-approval. Helping behavior may serve this function by fulfilling others' expectation that helping behavior be offered, by conforming to role definitions of helping behavior as appropriate for particular social identities, and by conforming to self-values regarding altruistic behavior and thereby compensating for feelings of rejection and failure (Dovidio 1984).

Macrosocial structures. Psychological structures, intrapsychic responses, and behaviors influence the substance of the social structure at any given time, and social change over time. Dimensions of personality reflecting evaluative standards affect the positions an individual has in the social structure. High value placed upon educational attainment and achievement orientation leads ultimately to educational achievement and high occupational status. Similarly, studies of the relationship between the occupational structure and personality suggest that workers may be selected into jobs because of the fit between their personality characteristics and the requirements of the work situation (Kerckhoff 1989). Individuals who value self-direction select occupations that permit the exercise of self-direction, that is, ones that involve less routine, more complex tasks, and low levels of supervision. Persons who place a high value on conformity tend to opt for occupations that are closely supervised, routine, and noncomplex.

The effects of persons—as products of past socialization experiences and as stimulated by contemporary social situations—upon interpersonal social systems and the more inclusive social structure are mediated by the responses of those persons to themselves. The individual influences current and future functioning of interpersonal systems by first becoming self-aware and conceiving of the self in particular ways; by evaluating the self as more or less closely approximating personal standards; and by experiencing self-feelings that stimulate self-protective and self-enhancing responses, some of which directly and indirectly affect the functioning of the interpersonal or social systems in which the individual participates.

If the person fails to behave in ways that meet self-imposed demands, he or she will experience negative self-feelings that motivate him or her to behave in ways that will reduce the self-rejecting feelings. If the person identifies the self-rejecting experiences with particular social identities, he may reject his group and define it as a negative-reference group, overidentify with the group and reevaluate formerly denigrated attributes as desirable ones, or project undesirable characteristics onto other groups or social categories and act with hostility toward them. Negative self-feelings may also lead to reduced levels of socioeconomic aspirations, occupational change, withdrawal from political participation or association with political activism, and changes in patterns of religious affiliation and participation (Kaplan 1986; Rosenberg and Kaplan 1982). If the circumstances hindering the person from behaving in ways that earn self-approval and the self-protective responses they stimulate are widespread, the inclusive social structure will be affected. The person's responses directly affect interpersonal systems, that is, individuals who interact in the context of social relationships or groups that are governed by shared situation-specific, identity-specific, or person-specific expectations. If the individual is motivated to withdraw from or otherwise disrupt the functioning of the interpersonal systems in which she or he participates, the functioning of the other individuals will be similarly disrupted, since others' performance is contingent upon her or his conformity to their expectations. However, the functioning of the interpersonal system will be facilitated if the individual is motivated to conform to the normative expectations that the participants in the interaction situation view as applicable to the person in that particular situational context. If the disposition to deviate from normative expectations is prevalent, then disruptions of social relationships will be widespread and the social structure will be less resistant to changes in patterns of response over time. While widespread conformity to shared expectations in particular social contexts will have stabilizing influences on the broader social structure, widespread innovation or deviation from them will influence the development of new social structural arrangements and definitions.

(SEE ALSO: *Affect Control Theory and Impression Formation; Aggression; Attitudes; Attribution Theory; Behaviorism; Coercive Persuasion and Attitude Change; Cognitive Consistency Theories; Collective Behavior; Decision-Making Theory and Research; Equity Theory; Exchange Theory; Field Theory; Game Theory and Strategic Interaction; Identity Theory; Intelligence; Interpersonal Attraction; Personality and Social Structure; Personality Theories; Persuasion; Prejudice; Reference Group Theory; Role Models; Role Theory; Social Perception; Self-Concept; Small Groups; Socialization; Symbolic Interaction Theory*)

REFERENCES

Alexander, C. Norman, Jr., and Mary Glenn Wiley 1981 "Situated Activity and Identity Formation." In M. Rosenberg and R. H. Turner, eds., *Social Psychology: Sociological Perspectives.* New York: Basic Books.

Baltes, Paul B., and Orville G. Brim, Jr. (eds.) 1980 *Life-Span Development and Behavior,* Vol. 3. New York: Academic Press.

Bandura, Albert 1973 *Aggression: A Social Learning Analysis.* Englewood Cliffs, N.J.: Prentice-Hall.

———1986 *The Social Foundations of Thought and Action.* Englewood Cliffs, N.J.: Prentice-Hall.

Baron, Robert A. 1977 *Human Aggression.* New York: Plenum.

Bar-Tal, Daniel 1976 *Prosocial Behavior: Theory and Research.* New York: Halsted.

Baumeister, Roy F. 1982 "A Self-Presentational View of Social Phenomena." *Psychological Bulletin* 91:3–26.

Berger, Joseph, Morris Zelditch, Jr., and Bo Anderson, eds. 1989 *Sociological Theories in Progress.* Newbury Park, Calif.: Sage.

Biddle, Bruce J. 1979 *Role Theory: Expectations, Identities, and Behaviors.* New York: Academic Press.

Blumer, Herbert 1969 *Symbolic Interactionism: Perspective and Method.* Englewood Cliffs, N.J.: Prentice-Hall.

Bobo, Lawrence 1983 "Whites' Opposition to Busing: Symbolic Racism or Realistic Group Conflict?" *Journal of Personality and Social Psychology* 45:1196–1210.

Brandstatter, Hermann, James H. Davis, and Gisela Stocker-Kreichgauer, eds. 1982 *Group Decision Making.* New York: Academic Press.

Bronfenbrenner, Urie 1970 *Two Worlds of Childhood.* New York: Russell Sage Foundation.

Bush, Diane M., and Roberta G. Simmons 1981 "Socialization Processes over the Life Course." In M. Rosenberg and R. H. Turner, eds., *Social Psychology: Sociological Perspectives.* New York: Basic Books.

Cartwright, Dorwin 1979 "Contemporary Social Psychology in Historical Perspective." *Social Psychology Quarterly* 42:82–93.

———, and Alvin Zander 1968 *Group Dynamics.* New York: Harper & Row.

Cunningham, M. R., J. Steinberg, and R. Grev 1980 "Wanting to and Having to Help: Separate Motivations for Positive Mood and Guilt-induced Helping." *Journal of Personality and Social Psychology* 38:181–192.

Denzin, Norman K. 1977 *Childhood Socialization.* San Francisco: Jossey-Bass.

Dovidio, J. H. 1984 "Helping Behavior and Altruism: An Empirical and Conceptual Overview." In L. Berkowitz, ed., *Advances in Experimental Social Psychology,* Vol. 17. New York: Academic Press.

Elder, Glen H., Jr. 1975 "Age Differentiation and the

Life Course." In A. Inkeles, J. Coleman, and N. Smelser, eds., *Annual Review of Sociology,* Vol. 1. Palo Alto, Calif.: Annual Reviews, Inc.

Evans, N. J., and Patricia A. Jarvis 1980 "Group Cohesion, a Review and Reevaluation." *Small Group Behavior* 11:359–370.

Featherman, David L., and Richard M. Lerner (eds.) 1988 *Life Span Development and Behavior.* New York: Academic Press.

Gibbs, Jack P. 1981 *Norms, Deviance, and Social Control.* New York: Elsevier.

Goffman, Erving 1961 *Asylums.* Garden City, N.Y.: Anchor.

Goslin, David A. (ed.) 1969 *Handbook of Socialization Theory and Research.* Chicago: Rand McNally.

Hare, A. Paul 1976 *Handbook of Small Group Research.* New York: Free Press.

Heiss, Jerold 1981 "Social Roles." In M. Rosenberg and R. H. Turner , eds., *Social Psychology: Sociological Perspectives.* New York: Basic Books.

Hewitt, John P., and R. Stokes 1975 "Disclaimers." *American Sociological Review* 40:1–11.

Hollander, Edwin P. 1975 "Independence, Conformity and Civil Liberties: Some Implications from Social Psychological Research." *Journal of Social Issues* 31:55–67.

House, James S. 1977 "The Three Faces of Social Psychology." *Sociometry* 40:161–177.

—— 1981 "Social Structure and Personality." In M. Rosenberg and R. Turner, eds., *Social Psychology: Sociological Perspectives.* New York: Basic Books.

Huston, Ted L. (ed.) 1974 *Foundations of Interpersonal Attraction.* New York: Academic Press.

Kaplan, Howard B. 1972 "Toward a General Theory of Psychosocial Deviance: The Case of Aggressive Behavior." *Social Science and Medicine* 6:593–617.

—— 1984 *Patterns of Juvenile Delinquency.* Beverly Hills, Calif.: Sage.

—— 1986 *Social Psychology of Self-Referent Behavior.* New York: Plenum Press.

—— (ed.) 1983 *Psychosocial Stress: Trends in Theory and Research.* New York: Academic Press.

Karp, David Allen, and William C. Yoels 1986 *Sociology and Everyday Life.* Itasca, Ill.: Peacock Publishing.

Kelley, Harold H., and J. Michela 1980 "Attribution Theory and Research." *Annual Review of Psychology* 31:457–501.

Kelley, Harold H., and John W. Thibaut 1978 *Interpersonal Relations: A Theory of Interdependence.* New York: Wiley.

Kerckhoff, Alan C. 1974 "The Social Context of Inter-

personal Attraction." In T. Huston, ed., *Foundations of Interpersonal Attraction.* New York: Academic Press.

—— 1989 "On the Social Psychology of Social Mobility Processes." *Social Forces* 68:17–25.

Kohn, Melvin L. 1989 "Social Structure and Personality: A Quintessentially Sociological Approach to Social Psychology." *Social Forces* 68:26–33.

——, and Carmi Schooler, with the collaboration of Joanne Miller, K. Miller, S. Schoenbach, and R. Schoenberg 1983 *Work and Personality: An Inquiry into the Impact of Social Stratification.* Norwood, N.J.: Ablex Publishing.

Leventhal, Howard 1980 "Toward a Comprehensive Theory of Emotion." In L. Berkowitz, ed., *Advances in Experimental Social Psychology,* Vol. 13. New York: Academic Press.

LeVine, Robert A., and Donald T. Campbell 1972 *Ethnocentrism: Theories of Conflict, Ethnic Attitudes and Group Behavior.* New York: Wiley.

Macaulay, Jacqueline R., and Leonard Berkowitz (eds.) 1970 *Altruism and Helping Behavior.* New York: Academic Press.

Markus, Hazel 1977 "Self-Schemata and Processing Information about the Self." *Journal of Personality and Social Psychology* 35:63–78.

McCarthy, John D., and Mayer N. Zald 1977 "Resource Mobilization and Social Movements: A Partial Theory." *American Journal of Sociology* 82:1212–1241.

Messner, Steven F., Marvin D. Krohn, and Allen E. Liska 1989 *Theoretical Integration in the Study of Deviance and Crime: Problems and Prospects.* Albany: State University of New York Press.

Michener, H. Andrew, John D. DeLamater, and Shalom H. Schwartz 1990 *Social Psychology,* 2nd ed. New York: Harcourt Brace Jovanovich.

Moscovici, Serge 1985 "Social Influence and Conformity." In G. Lindzey and E. Aronson, eds., *Handbook of Social Psychology,* Vol. 2, 3rd ed. Reading, Mass.: Addison-Wesley.

Myers, D. G. 1982 "Polarizing Effects of Social Interaction." In H. Brandstatter, J. H. Davis, and G. Stocker-Kreichgauer, eds., *Group Decision Making.* New York: Academic Press.

Pennebaker, James W. 1980 "Self-Perception of Emotion and Internal Sensation." In D. W. Wegner and R. R. Vallacher, eds., *The Self in Social Psychology.* New York: Oxford University Press.

Phelps, Edmund S. 1975 *Altruism, Morality and Economic Theory.* Chicago: Russell Sage Foundation.

Riley, Matilda W. 1987 "On the Significance of Age in Sociology." *American Sociology Review* 52:1–14.

Rokeach, Milton 1973 *The Nature of Human Values*. New York: Free Press.

Rosenberg, Morris 1979 *Conceiving the Self*. New York: Basic Books.

————, and Howard B. Kaplan (eds.) 1982 *The Social Psychology of the Self-Concept*. Arlington Heights, Ill.: Harlan Davidson.

———— and Ralph H. Turner (eds.) 1981 *Social Psychology: Sociological Perspectives*. New York: Basic Books.

Scheier, Michael F., and Charles Carver 1983 "Two Sides of the Self: One for You and One for Me." In J. Suls and A. G. Greenwald, eds., *Psychological Perspectives on the Self*, Vol. 2. Hillsdale, N.J.: L. Erlbaum.

Schwartz, Shalom H., and Judith A. Howard 1981 "A Normative Decision-Making Model of Altruism." In J. P. Rushton and R. M. Sorrentino, eds., *Altruism and Helping Behavior*. Hillsdale, N.J.: Erlbaum.

Sewell, William H., and Robert M. Hauser 1980 "The Wisconsin Longitudinal Study of Social and Psychological Factors in Aspirations and Achievements." *Research in Sociology of Education and Socialization* 1:59–99.

Singer, Jerome L. (ed.) 1971 *The Control of Aggression and Violence: Cognitive and Physiological Factors*. New York: Academic Press.

Smelser, Neil J. 1963 *Theory of Collective Behavior*. New York: Free Press.

Spencer, J. William 1987 "Self-Work in Social Interaction: Negotiating Role-Identities." *Social Psychology Quarterly* 50:131–142.

Stephan, Cookie White, and Walter G. Stephan 1990 *Two Social Psychologies*, 2nd ed. Belmont, Calif.: Wadsworth.

Stryker, Sheldon 1980 *Symbolic Interactionism: A Social Structural Version*. Menlo Park, Calif.: Benjamin/ Cummings.

———— 1989 "The Two Psychologies: Additional Thoughts." *Social Forces* 68:45–54.

Tedeschi, James T. (ed.) 1981 *Impression Management Theory and Social Psychological Research*. New York: Academic Press.

Turner, Ralph H. 1988 "Personality in Society: Social Psychology's Contribution to Sociology." *Social Psychology Quarterly* 51:1–10.

————, and L. M. Killian 1957 *Collective Behavior*. Englewood Cliffs, N.J.: Prentice-Hall.

Walster (Hatfield), Elaine, William Walster, and Ellen Berscheid, eds. 1978 *Equity: Theory and Research*. Boston: Allyn and Bacon.

Wegner, Daniel M., and Robin R. Vallacher (eds.) 1980 *The Self in Social Psychology*. New York: Oxford University Press.

Worchel, Stephen, and William G. Austin (eds.) 1986 *The Social Psychology of Intergroup Relations*. Monterey, Calif.: Brooks/Cole.

Zillman, Dolf 1979 *Hostility and Aggression*. Hillsdale, N.J.: Erlbaum.

Zurcher, Louis A., and David A. Snow 1981 "The Sociology of Deviance and Social Control." In M. Rosenberg and R. H. Turner, eds., *Social Psychology: Sociological Perspectives*. New York: Basic Books.

HOWARD B. KAPLAN

SOCIAL RESOURCES THEORY This article introduces the theory of social resources (Lin 1982, 1983). It describes the fundamental propositions of the theory and reviews empirical research programs and results pertaining to the theory. It concludes with a discussion of some issues regarding extensions and modifications of the theory.

Resources are goods, material as well as symbolic, that can be accessed and used in social actions. Of particular interest are the valued resources—resources consensually considered as important for maintaining and improving individuals' chances of survival as they interact with the external environment. In general, valued resources are identified with indicators of class, status, and power in most societies. In the following discussion, resources refer to valued resources.

Resources can be classified in two categories: personal resources and social resources. *Personal resources* are resources belonging to an individual; they include such ascribed and achieved characteristics as gender, race, age, religion, education, occupation, and income as well as familial resources. These resources are in the possession of the individual and at the disposal of the individual. *Social resources*, on the other hand, are resources embedded in one's social network and social ties. These are the resources in the possession of the other individuals to whom ego has either direct or indirect ties. A friend's car, for example, may be ego's social resources. Ego may borrow it for use and return it to the friend. Ego does not possess the car, and accesses and uses it only if the friend is willing to lend it. The friend retains the ownership. Similarly, a friend's social, economic, or political position may be seen as ego's social resources. Ego may seek the friend's help in exercising that resource in order for ego to obtain or achieve a specific goal.

Much of sociological research focuses on personal resources. While social network analysis has been a long-standing research tradition in sociology and psychology, attention had been given to the structure and patterns of ties and relations. Only recently, in the past two decades, sociologists and anthropologists have explored the theoretical significance of the resources brought to bear in the context of social networks and social ties. The theory of social resources makes explicit the assumption that resources embedded in social connections play important roles in the interaction between social structure and individuals. More specifically, the theory explores how individuals access and use social resources to maintain or promote self-interests in a social structure that consists of social positions hierarchically related and organized in terms of valued resources. It has been argued that social resources are accessed and mobilized in a variety of actions by an individual to achieve instrumental and/or expressive goals.

Two terms need some clarifications here. I assume that a social structure consists of different levels, each of which can include a set of structurally equivalent positions. They are equivalent primarily on the basis of levels of similar valued resources, and secondarily, similar life-styles, attitudes, and other cultural and psychological factors. For the purposes here, the terms, "levels" and "positions," are used interchangeably. Also, status attainment is assumed to refer to the voluntary aspect of social mobility. Involuntary social mobility, due to job dissatisfaction, lack of alternatives, or other "pushing" or forced factors, is excluded from consideration. As Granovetter (1986) pointed out, voluntary social mobility generally results in wage growth. Likewise, it is argued

that voluntary social mobility accounts for the majority of occurrences in status attainment.

THEORY OF SOCIAL RESOURCES AND SOCIAL ACTIONS

Attention in this article will be given to the theory of social resources as it is applied to the context of instrumental actions. Instrumental actions are a class of actions motivated by the intent to gain valued resources (e.g., seeking a better occupational position). In contrast, expressive actions are a class of actions motivated by the intent to maintain valued resources (e.g., seeking to maintain a marital relationship). Social resources have broad implications for both types of social actions (Lin 1986). However, for the present discussion, social resources will be considered in the perspective of instrumental actions only. To carry the discussion at a more concrete level, attention will be given to the status attainment process, which can be seen as a typical process focusing on an instrumental goal. In the following material, the propositions of the theory of social resources will be presented in the specific framework of the status attainment process, to illuminate clearly and concretely the theoretical implications in a specific research tradition.

I have specified three hypotheses (Lin 1982): the social resources hypothesis, the strength-of-position hypothesis, and the strength-of-ties hypothesis. The *social resources hypothesis*, the primary proposition of the theory, states that *access to and use of better social resources leads to more successful instrumental action.* In the case of status attainment, it predicts that job-seekers are more likely to find a better job (in terms of prestige, power, and/or income) when they are able to contact a source with better resources (in terms of occupation, industry, income, etc.).

The other two hypotheses identify factors that determine the likelihood of access to and use of better social resources. The *strength-of-position hypothesis* stipulates that *the level of original position* is positively *associated with access to and use of social resources.* For the process of status attainment, it suggests that the original social position of a job-seeker is positively related to the likelihood of contacting a source of better resources. Position of origin can be represented by characteristics of ego's parents or previous jobs.

The *strength-of-ties hypothesis* proposes that *use of weaker ties is positively related to access to and use of social resources*. For status attainment, it states that there is a positive relationship between the use of weaker ties and the likelihood of contacting a source of better resources. For the formulation of the strength of weak ties argument, see Granovetter (1973, 1974).

Thus, the theory contains one proposition postulating the effect of social resources and two propositions postulating causes of social resources. The strength-of-position hypothesis implies an inheritance effect. A given position of origin in the hierarchical structure in part decides how well one may get access to better social resources embedded in the social structure. It is a *structural* factor and independent of individuals in the structure, although individuals may benefit. On the other hand, the strength-of-ties hypothesis suggests the need for *individual action*. Normal interactions are dictated by the homophily principle, the tendency to engage in interaction with others of similar characteristics and life-styles. Going beyond the routine set of frequent interactants and seeking out weaker ties represent action choices beyond most of the normative expectations of the macrostructure (see Granovetter 1973, 1974).

It is true that the beginning of a job search often is unplanned. Many job leads become available through casual occasions (e.g., parties) and through interactions with casual acquaintances. It is not necessarily the case that a job search always begins with the individual actively seeking out contacts for this purpose. However, this does not negate the basic premise that individuals are situated at different levels of positions in the structure and have, therefore, access to "casual" occasions involving participants of certain types and amounts of resources, including social resources. In fact, it has been empirically demonstrated (Campbell, Marsden, and Hulbert 1986; Lin and Dumin 1986) that higher-level positions have greater access to more diverse and heterogenous levels of positions in the hierarchical structure than lower-level positions, therefore having greater command of social resources. Thus, it can be expected that "casual" occasions for the higher-level positions are structurally richer in job and other types of information and influence. Such structural advantage, deducible from the pyramidal assumption of the theory, has distinct effect when a job search is eventually launched by the individual. *In relative terms, the strength of position should have stronger effects on social resources than the strength of ties.* This statement recognizes the significance of structural constraints everywhere in the social structure. In empirical systems, both factors are expected to operate, even though their relative effects may vary.

EMPIRICAL RESEARCH AND THEORETICAL EXTENSIONS

Research programs examining the theory of social resources in the context of socioeconomic attainment have been carried out in North America (Ensel 1979; Lin, Ensel, and Vaughn 1981; Lin, Vaughn, and Ensel 1981; Marsden and Hulbert 1988), in West Germany and the Netherlands (Flap and De Graaf 1988; De Graaf and Flap 1988; Sprengers, Tazelaar and Flap 1988; Boxman, Flap, and De Graaf 1989; Wegener 1991), in Taiwan (Sun and Hsiong 1988), and in China (Lin and Bian 1990). Thus far, evidence strongly supports two of the three hypotheses: the social-resource hypothesis and the strength-of-positions hypothesis. Those with better origins tend to find sources for better resources in job-seeking, while contacting a source of better resources increases the likelihood of finding a better job. These relations hold even after the usual status attainment variables (e.g., education and first-job status) are taken into account. These results, as Marsden and Hulbert showed, are not biased by the fact that only those contacting interpersonal sources in job-seeking are selected for study.

However, evidence is equivocal on the strength-of-(weak) ties hypothesis. For example, Lin and associates have found evidence that weaker ties linked job-seekers to contacts with better resources, whereas Marsden and Hulbert (1988) did not. The different findings may be due to the interaction between the two exogenous variables: the strength of position and the strength of ties. Lin and others have found that the advantage of using weaker ties over the use of stronger ties decreases as the position of origin approaches the top of the levels. Lin, Ensel, and Vaughn (1981) hypothesized a ceiling effect for weak ties. At the top of the hierarchical structure there is no advantage to using weak ties, since such ties are likely to lead to inferior positions and therefore inferior resources. They did not anticipate similar ineffectiveness of weaker ties toward the bottom of the structure. Marsden and Hulbert (1988), however, also found that those with the lowest origins did not benefit more from contacts with weaker ties in gaining access to better resources than from contacts with stronger ties. One speculation is that those at the lower positions have more restricted range of contacts (Campbell, Marsden and Hulbert 1986; Lin and Dumin 1986), rendering the weaker ties accessible less effective. Thus, a nonlinear relationship (interaction) between strength of ties and social resources may be involved (Wegener 1991).

Another elaboration concerns the distinction between two types of social resources: network resources and contact resources. Network resources refer to resources embedded in one's ongoing social networks and ties. In this conceptualization, the researcher is interested in identifying the ongoing social ties, and from these identified ties, exploring resources they have. These resources are seen as social resources to ego (Campbell, Marsden, and Hulbert 1986; Lin and Dumin 1986; Boxman and Flap 1990). Contact resources, on the other hand, refer to resources associated specifically with a tie or ties accessed and mobilized in a particular action. For example, the researcher is interested in identifying the contact ego used in a particular job-seeking situation and specifying the social resources in terms of what resources the contact possessed (Lin, Ensel, and Vaughn 1981; Marsden and Hulbert 1988; Sun and Hsiong 1988; Lin and Bian 1990). Recent

research (Lai, Leung, and Lin 1990) shows that network resources and contact resources are two conceptually distinctive and causally related components of social resources. Network resources, reflecting resources in ego's social network, contribute to the access of contact resources in the context of a particular action (e.g., seeking a job). Each in turn contributes to the ultimate success of the action (e.g., getting a high-status occupation).

FURTHER RESEARCH ISSUE

Some theoretical and methodological issues remain in the extension and application of the social resources theory.

One issue concerns the cost of social resources. Unlike personal resources, which ego may use and dispose of relatively free of constraints, social resources are "borrowed" from one's social ties. Thus, there should be a cost attached to such access. In most cases there is an implied obligation of reciprocity—that is, ego is committed to offer his or her resources as social resources to the alter from whom resources have been borrowed. The problem arises when ego and the alter do not occupy similar social positions, thus possessing dissimilar resources. In the case of ego seeking help from the alter, in fact, the better the social position the alter occupies, the more effective it provides social resources to ego. It is conceivable that ego possesses other resources, which may provide to be useful to the alter in the reciprocity process. For example, a banker (ego) may seek political influence from a politician (the alter), who in turn may secure financial benefit with ego's help. Fair exchange of different valued resources occurs. There will also be situations where ego with inferior resources gains as a result of help from an alter with superior resources (e.g., a graduate student getting a desirable job with the help of a professor), the reciprocity becomes more intricate. One way of reciprocity requires quantity in compensation of quality (e.g., willingness to put more effort into a research or writing collaboration). Another form of reciprocity requires efforts to increase the value of the alter's resources (e.g., citations to the professor's work in one's publications). Variations in such reciprocal uses of social resources and, therefore, in cost deserve further conceptualization and research.

Another area worthy of research attention is the use of social resources for expressive actions. It has been hypothesized that, in contrast to instrumental actions, expressive actions would be more effective if ego and the alter share similar traits and experiences. The argument is that homophily (sharing similar characteristics and life-styles) increases the likelihood of the alter understanding the emotional stress experienced by ego (Lin 1986). Thus, the expectation is that strong ties, rather than weak ties, may provide the more desirable social resources for expressive actions. However, reality is much less tidy than this conceptualization. In some expressive actions (e.g., seeking support in time of a divorce), both emotional and instrumental support are needed. Further complicating the situation is that often the strong ties (e.g., spouse) are the sources of stress, and expressive actions must by definition be provided by either weaker ties or surrogate strong ties (e.g., relatives or a friend or professional helper) (Lin and Westcott forthcoming). Much more conceptual and empirical work is needed to tease out these issues.

Finally, there is the intriguing question of whether the theory of social resources can help conceptualizing the interplays between social structure and social action. I argue that the theory of social resources makes two kinds of contributions toward an understanding of social structure and social action (Lin 1990a, 1990b). First, research on social resources has offered the plausibility that under structural constraints, individual choices (in terms of social ties and social contacts) may yield different and meaningful consequences. It has been shown that given two individuals with similar personal resources (including original social positions), they might experience different outcomes in instrumental actions, depending on social resources they access and use. To an extent such different access is dictated by structural constraints. As mentioned earlier, original position affects the range of social ties in the social hierarchy and therefore the likelihood of access-

ing better social resources. However, after such structural constraints have been taken into account, there is evidence that some flexibility remains in the choice of social ties and use of social resources, and such choice and use yield meaningful and different results.

Second, much of past research on social structure as well as social resources has assumed that social structure has a priori existence and imposes constraints within which individuals conduct meaningful actions. The theoretical possibility that individual actions and choices may constitute fundamental driving forces in the formation and functioning of social structures has gained currency in sociology (Coleman 1986, 1988, 1990). Social resources, it is argued, may also contribute to this theoretical formulation.

One may assume that individuals strive to gain resources for the promotion and maintenance of one's survival and well-being. Personal resources may be preferred to social resources in this striving, since the former incur less cost and are more manipulatable. However, the speed of cumulation may differ for the two types of resources. Acquisition and cumulation of personal resources may be additive. On the other hand, acquisition and cumulation of social resources may be exponential, in that once a social tie is established, not only the tie's personal resources become social resources to ego, but the tie's social resources (through its ties) also become social resources. Thus, social ties, through their networking patterns and dynamics, accelerate one's social resources. While social resources come at a cost, as discussed earlier, it is to the benefit of ego to acquire as much social resources as possible. Thus, social resources constitute the fundamental motivation to networking in the promotion and maintenance of one's self-interest and well-being. Such networking constitutes the elementary blocks in the emergence of social structure. Subsequently, the management and manipulation of the constructed and extended network that contains increasingly heterogeneous participants with varying demands for secondary resources (e.g., quality of life considerations) dictate the development of hierarchical positions and role expectations, which in turn reduce the range of possible individual action choices. Further theoretical work along these lines promises to contribute to the current interest and debate in the interrelationships between social actions and social structure.

(SEE ALSO: *Exchange Theory; Social Network Theory; Social Support*)

REFERENCES

Boxman, E. A. W., Hendrik D. Flap, and P. M. De Graaf 1989 "Social Capital, Human Capital, and Income Attainment: the Impact of Social Capital and Human Capital on the Income Attainment of Dutch Managers in 1986." Paper presented at the European Conference on Social Network Analysis, June, Groningen, Netherlands.

Boxman, E. A. W., and Hendrik D. Flap 1990 "Social Capital and Occupational Chances." Paper presented at the International Sociological Association, XIIth World Congress of Sociology, July, Madrid.

Campbell, Karen E., Peter V. Marsden and Jeanne S. Hulbert, 1986 "Social Resources and Socioeconomic Status," *Social Networks,* 8(1):97–116.

Coleman, James S 1986 *Individual Interests and Collective Action.* Cambridge: Cambridge University Press.

——— 1988. "Social Capital in the Creation of Human Capital," *American Journal of Sociology* 94(Supplement):S95–S120.

——— 1990. *Foundations of Social Theory.* Cambridge, Mass.: Harvard University Press.

De Graaf, Nan Dirk, and Hendrik Derk Flap 1988 "With a Little Help from My Friends," *Social Forces* 67-2:452–472.

Ensel, Walter M 1979 "Sex, Social Ties, and Status Attainment." Ph.D. diss., Department of Sociology, State University of New York at Albany.

Flap, Hendrik D. and Nan Dirk DeGraaf 1988 "Social Capital and Attained Occupational Status," *Netherlands Journal of Sociology.*

Granovetter, Mark 1973 "The Strength of Weak Ties." *American Journal of Sociology* 78:1360–1380.

——— 1974 *Getting a Job.* Cambridge, Mass.: Harvard University Press.

——— 1982 "The Strength of Weak Ties: A Network Theory Revisited." In Peter V. Marsden and Nan Lin, eds., *Social Structure and Network Analysis.* Beverly Hills: Sage.

Lai, Gina Wan-foon, Shu-yin Leung, and Nan Lin 1990 "Network Resources, Contact Resources, and Status Attainment: Structural and Action Effects of Social Resources." Paper presented at the annual meeting of the American Sociological Association, August, Washington, D.C.

Lin, Nan 1982 "Social Resources and Instrumental Action." In Peter V. Marsden and Nan Lin, eds., *Social Structure and Network Analysis.* Beverly Hills: Sage.

——— 1983 "Social Resources and Social Actions: A Progress Report." *Connections* 6:10–16.

——— 1986 "Conceptualizing Social Support." In Nan Lin, Alfred Dean, and Walter M. Ensel, eds., *Social Support, Life Events, and Depression.* Orlando, Fla.: Academic Press.

——— 1990a "Social Resources and Social Mobility: A Structural Theory of Status Attainment," In Ronald Breiger, ed., *Social Mobility and Social Structure.* New York: Cambridge University Press.

——— 1990b "Social Resources and the Emergence of Social Structure," Paper presented at the XII World Congress of Sociology, July, Madrid.

———, and Yan-jie Bian 1990 "Getting Ahead in Urban China: Differential Effects of Social Connections (Guanxi)." Paper presented at the Sunbelt Network Conference, February, San Diego.

———, and Mary Dumin 1986 "Access to Occupations through Social Ties." *Social Networks* 8:365–385.

———, Walter M. Ensel, and John C. Vaughn 1981 "Social Resources and Strength of Ties: Structural Factors in Occupational Status Attainment." *American Sociological Review* 46:393–405.

———, John C. Vaughn, and Walter Ensel 1981 "Social Resources and Occupational Status Attainment." *Social Forces* 59:1163–1181.

———, and Jeanne Westcott (Forthcoming) "Marital Engagement/Disengagement, Social Networks, and Mental Health." In John Eckenrode, ed., *The Social Context of Stress and Coping.* New York: Plenum.

Marsden, Peter, and Jeanne Hulbert 1988 "Social Resources and Mobility Outcomes: A Replication and Extension," *Social Forces* 66(4):1038–1059.

Sprengers, Maarten, Frits Tazelaar, and Hendrik D. Flap 1988 "Social Resources, Situational Constraints, and Reemployment." *Netherlands Journal of Sociology* 24.

Sun, Chingshan, and Ruimei Hsiong 1988 *Social Resources and Social Mobility.* Taiwan: Tunghai University.

Wegener, Bernd 1991 "Job Mobility and Social Ties: Social Resources, Prior Job and Status Attainment." *American Sociological Review* 56(February)1–12.

NAN LIN

SOCIAL SCIENCE RESEARCH COUNCIL

The Social Science Research Council (SSRC) is an autonomous, nongovernmental, not-for-profit, international association of over 300 social scientists devoted to the advancement of interdisciplinary research. It accomplishes this through a wide variety of workshops and conferences, research consortia, fellowships and grants, summer training institutes, scholarly exchanges, and publications.

HISTORY AND GOVERNANCE

The SSRC is the product of a remarkable five-year period in the history of American social science. For example, in 1919 representatives of a number of humanistic and social science organizations established the American Council of Learned Societies (ACLS); the New School for Social Research was founded that year in New York; and in 1923 planning began for the *Encyclopaedia of the Social Sciences,* a landmark project of collaborative scholarship. During the 1920s the social sciences were becoming fully professionalized and compartmentalized. Separate university departments, distinct disciplinary literatures, and diverse national associations proliferated. Many social scientists recognized that these trends of specialization and professionalization, while facilitating the codification of knowledge, also tended to fragment and balkanize scholarship; they also threatened to undermine comprehensive and integrative understandings that are born of inter-disciplinary discourse and inquiry. SSRC was founded in 1923 to transcend disciplinary and institutional separatism within the social and behavioral sciences and to devote itself exclusively to the advancement of the frontiers of research.

Through the initiative of the American Political Science Association's committee on research, headed by Charles E. Merriam of the University of Chicago, SSRC was created by representatives of the American Economics Association, the American Sociological Association, and the American Statistical Association. By the time of its legal incorporation in 1924, SSRC's founders included national associations in anthropology, history, and psychology. Ever since, the membership of the SSRC's Board of Directors has reflected this history by consisting of directors elected or nominated by the seven founding associations. However, the board consists of an additional and numerically larger segment of "at-large" directors who have no representational role, either nominal or historic, for any disciplinary association; at-large directors, from diverse fields and disciplines and from several continents, ensure that the voices of governance at the SSRC echo a rich spectrum of methodological and theoretical approaches within the international social science community. Thus, at its roots and in its governance, the SSRC is an interdisciplinary and international organization. However, SSRC's agenda is not controlled by professional associations, the founding disciplines, or the SSRC's funding sponsors.

The social science research community sets SSRC's mandate through the Board of Directors and a Committee on Problems and Policy, which regularly review and approve SSRC's scientific and intellectual program. The board elects the president, who serves no statutory term of office. Practically speaking, however, the operational arm of SSRC is a rotating set of over 300 social scientists who, together with a salaried professional staff of about fifteen program officers, create and discharge the council's program. This program is vested in some thirty different committees, working groups, and research consortia that are devoted to research planning and grants sponsorship, doctoral and postdoctoral fellowship administration, and advanced training for the evolving scientific and intellectual frontiers of interdisciplinary research. During the 1980s, between 2,000 and 3,000 researchers and graduate students participated each year in SSRC-sponsored activities around the globe, and more than 300 received significant grant or fellowship support in any year.

PROGRAMMATIC BREADTH

Throughout its history, the SSRC has worked in most areas that have been of scientific interest, many of which have also been of pressing public and national concern. Despite the breadth of its activities, the SSRC has maintained its underlying goal of advancing research frontiers and of developing the human and material resources for social science. Many of the committees have been concerned with developing and improving new methodologies and techniques for research. For example, in 1931, when social science methods in the United States were in their infancy, one committee published a collection of exemplary case approaches, *Methods in Social Science: A Case Book,* edited by Stuart A. Rice. In the 1950s, attention to upgrading the mathematical competence of social scientists led to various summer workshops and textbooks, including the 1956 classic by John G. Kemeny and others, *Introduction to Finite Mathematics.* Qualitative and historical approaches, bridging the social sciences and humanities, were advanced (*The Social Sciences in Historical Study,* 1954; *Generalization in the Writing of History,* 1963, edited by Louis Gottschalk). In 1973, in a period of greater quantitative sophistication, another publication expanded expertise in statistical modeling and the inference of causality (*Structural Equation Models in the Social Sciences,* edited by Arthur S. Goldberger and Otis Dudley Duncan). And in 1974 another publication introduced experimental approaches to "natural experiments" and to the assessment of governmental and other programs of intervention (*Social Experimentation: A Method for Planning and Evaluating Social Intervention,* edited by Henry W. Riecken and Robert F. Boruch).

Topically focused committees have probed many areas, for example, the interaction of heredity and environment (e.g., Genetics and Behavior; Biosocial Bases of Parenting); the nexus of personality, life-span development, and culture (e.g., Socialization and Social Structure; Life-Span Development and Aging); various intellective processes (e.g., Linguistics and Psychology; Cognition and Survey Research); the behavioral study of

politics (e.g., Measurement of Attitudes and Public Opinion; Political Behavior); social and economic welfare in the United States (e.g., Economic Growth and Change; Social Indicators; Urban Underclass); international economies (e.g., Project LINK); population studies (e.g., Social Aspects of the Great Depression; Migration; Contemporary Hispanic Issues; Census Monograph Series, 1980 and 1990 censuses); technological change (e.g., Social Aspects of Atomic Energy; Computers and Society); human agency in environmental change (e.g., Global Environmental Change); and international relations (e.g., Foreign Policy; International Peace and Security). In considering the establishment of such topical committees, whose lifetimes typically run three to five years, the SSRC's board and Committee on Problems and Policy give priority to those scholarly and public policy questions that involve potential contributions from several disciplines, show promise of responding to collaborative effort and discussion, and might profit from international scholarly collaboration or comparative research.

Since the 1940s, the SSRC also has commissioned committees to examine this country's needs and requirements for advanced scholarship about foreign cultures, societies, and world regions. These committees, administered jointly by SSRC and the ACLS and composed of both social scientists and humanists, are charged to develop basic knowledge about language, culture, history, and current events in these world areas. They accomplish this task by holding conferences and workshops, commissioning review papers and pilot research projects, and training graduate students. The joint foreign area committees also identify the needs for teaching and research personnel required to build and maintain national scholarly competence about these regions, and they select predoctoral and postdoctoral fellows to study and conduct research abroad. Often in full partnership with foreign scholars, joint committees also plan and design collaborative research that synthesizes area scholarship with the theory-building objectives of discipline-based and interdisciplinary research. The latter projects often emerge from collaboration between area and thematic committees (e.g., a project on environment-based risks to national security in the Soviet Union and Central Europe, involving the collaboration of committees on International Peace and Security, Global Environmental Change, and Soviet Studies). This research, which frequently links a region comparatively to others, lends itself to the evolution of international scholarship that is more transnational in character and less oriented to the theoretical paradigms of particular disciplines or area specialists or to any idiosyncratic cultural orientation of North American scholarship.

Indeed, the SSRC is a major node in the infrastructure of international social science. In addition to their joint administration of the foreign area committees, the SSRC and ACLS are the founders and sponsors of the International Research and Exchange Board (IREX). SSRC assisted in founding the Consortium of Social Science Associations (COSSA). Together with the National Academy of Sciences/National Research Council (NAS/NRC) and the American Council of Education, the SSRC and the ACLS constitute the Conference Board of Associated Research Councils. The same organizations were the progenitors of the Council of International Exchange of Scholars (CIES), which selects the senior Fulbright scholars. SSRC occupies an official seat as observer on the Standing Committee for the Social Sciences of the European Science Foundation. It cooperates on special projects with the Center for Advanced Study in the Behavioral Sciences, the Council of Professional Associations on Federal Statistics, the Commission on Behavioral and Social Sciences and Education (CBASSE of the NAS/NRC), the Inter-University Program for Latino Research, and the International Social Science Council.

FOUNDATION SUPPORT

Over SSRC's nearly seventy-year history, financial support has come mainly from private philanthropic foundations. For example, the Laura Spelman Rockefeller Memorial Fund and then the Rockefeller Foundation and the General Educa-

tion Board were the largest early funders. Since the 1950s, the Ford Foundation's support of the joint area committees and the overall international program has constituted the largest single sponsor. Some of the other nearly thirty private contributors each year have included the Carnegie Corporation of New York, the Russell Sage Foundation, the John D. and Catherine T. MacArthur Foundation, the Andrew W. Mellon Foundation, the Grant Foundation, the Spencer Foundation, the John and Mary R. Markle Foundation, and the Twentieth Century Fund. Federal grants and contracts from the National Endowment for the Humanities, the National Science Foundation, the National Institute of Mental Health, the Federal Reserve System, and the U.S. Department of State constitute a small fraction of the annual portfolio of support.

The SSRC's budget has recently been about $9 million per year, of which it expends about $1.5 million for general administration and as seed money for new projects. The balance of $7.5 million supports the activities of the committees that the SSRC itself administers, including $4 million for awards and $3.5 million for research planning. Grants and contracts to the council—both considered restricted funds—fund these activities. Assets total over $28 million, most of which is endowment restricted to the support of particular programs and is raised from private foundations and governmental agencies. Thus, the SSRC is a direct source of funding only on the small scale made possible by investment income; it is not an operating foundation, like the Russell Sage Foundation.

SSRC historically has played a role as a partner with private foundations that have sought to promote the development and application of the social sciences through general or core support to the council. Recently, it also has functioned as an extramural agent for the foundations by recruiting top scholars and focusing the expertise of social scientists on pressing issues that have become current priorities for foundations' boards and for which the foundations' internal staff are insufficient or lack appropriate background. Increasingly, many private foundations are acquiring resident professional staff in the social sciences; these operating foundations call on the partnership of the SSRC as an adjunct to their own expertise and priorities in directing the course of social science research through funding initiatives. Thus, the SSRC continues to expand its collaborative efforts in the accomplishment of its broad mission.

REFERENCE

Sibley, Elbridge 1974 *Social Science Research Council: The First Fifty Years.* New York: Social Science Research Council.

DAVID L. FEATHERMAN
RICHARD C. ROCKWELL

SOCIAL SECURITY SYSTEMS
In the United States, Social Security refers to a set of programs, including old-age, survivors, and disability insurance, directed toward the elderly and their dependents. This particular usage of the term *social security* relates as much to the special and delimited character of the welfare state in the United States as it does to the generally accepted meaning of the term. For organizations such as the International Labour Office and the International Social Security Association, and for scholars concerned with comparative studies, social security refers to a wider variety of programs than those aimed at the elderly. For instance, in its volume *Social Security throughout the World,* the Social Security Administration states

> The term "social security" in the context of this report refers to programs established by government statutes which insure individuals against interruption or loss of earning power, and for certain special expenditures arising from marriage, birth, or death. (1985, p. ix)

The concept of social protection underlying this definition includes unemployment programs to cover involuntary, temporary loss of work, sickness programs to cover loss of income from sickness and the cost of medical care, disability or occupational injury programs to cover physical limitations to work, family allowances to cover loss of economic status from addition of members to the family, and social assistance to cover other circumstances such as family disruption causing income to fall below specified levels. Protection of earning power from loss of work or from health conditions associated with old age also remains crucial. Still, many of the other programs, more common among advanced welfare systems of Western European nations than in the United States, must still be considered part of social security systems.

The relative size of programs devoted to the elderly perhaps warrants the special attention to old age in social security systems. Of all expenditures for education and social security programs, those for old-age pensions represent the largest component, averaging 36 percent across high income nations in 1985 (Organization for Economic Development and Cooperation 1988, Tables 1 and 3). The next largest component, 22 percent, is devoted to health care, which also disproportionately benefits the elderly. Furthermore, the growth rate of programs for the aged has exceeded those for other programs, and in the future expenditures for such programs will consume an even greater proportion of the total. Spending for unemployment, family allowances, and social assistance represents a relatively small part of social security programs. As Myles (1984) notes, the welfare state is primarily a welfare state for the elderly.

The need for collective protection—for the aged or otherwise—stems from the existence of economic insecurity. Loss of earning power from poor health, old age, or unemployment remains a possibility for nearly all participants in a market economy but at the same time is uncertain enough to make it difficult to predict loss of income or future savings potential. Traditional protection against such risk in preindustrial societies developed informally through the family. Children and relatives, under ideal circumstances, could support parents unable to provide for themselves or desiring to step down from their economic role of provider. Social security thus took the form of an intergenerational contract, based on norms of filial piety and parental control over wealth, between children or other relatives and parents (Simmons 1960). Never a guaranteed source of protection, however, other family members became an even less reliable source of support with the decrease in family size, increase in mobility, and industrialization of labor that accompanied the demographic and industrial transitions. With the development of large-scale corporate capitalism in the late nineteenth and early twentieth centuries, the risks of forced retirement and unemployment also grew. Systems of social security collectivized and formalized the relationship between young workers and elderly, unemployed, or disabled nonworkers. Workers would contribute support to certain categories of nonworkers in return for the expectation they would be covered should they be unable to work.

The state has always played a crucial role in the collectivized contract by making participation in the system compulsory for most workers. Voluntary programs of saving for unexpected contingencies are insufficient because many people are not rational in saving for events that may not occur or may occur only in the far future. Private compulsory systems within industries, unions, or businesses likewise face problems of incomplete coverage, financial insolvency, and job movement. In contrast, collectivizing social security provides for reliable funding, and it is easier to predict events for a group than for individuals.

Most nations provide for more than social security alone. The broader welfare state in capitalist societies also supports education, retraining, full employment, business regulation, price supports, infrastructure, and legal rights. In socialist societies, social security systems exist but involve broader social protection through guaranteed employment, subsidized food, housing, and energy prices, and the reduced importance of market performance as the primary criterion for economic support. Still, market-oriented reforms in Eastern Europe may yet expand the emphasis on social security systems as typically and more narrowly defined in capitalist societies.

If motives of social protection are common to social security systems, the coverage of the population and the distribution of benefits show wide variation. Benefits may be distributed on the basis of at least four criteria, each of which may be emphasized or deemphasized in particular systems. First, citizenship entitlement provides basic benefits—usually in the form of flat-rate cash payments—to individuals or families as a right of citizenship, regardless of work history, contributions, or income. Second, employment-related criteria base eligibility on wage or payroll contributions made before the contingency causing earnings to cease. As a form of public or social insurance, these benefits reinforce market criteria of income determination. Third, need-based criteria provide benefits by comparing resources against a standard typically based on subsistence needs. Means-tested or social assistance programs target benefits at the most needy, usually those otherwise not covered by citizenship or insurance programs. Fourth, entitlement is sometimes granted on the basis of marital or family status, usually to women and homemakers, or to families with young children.

To a large extent, nations mix their degree of reliance on the different criteria. Nations that began with universal systems added earnings-based supplements (e.g., Sweden), and those originally enacting earnings-based benefits have added universal benefits (e.g., Great Britain) or some form of minimum benefit (e.g., the United States). Similar claims have been made about the mix of public and private systems. Nations that have traditionally relied on private systems (e.g., the United States) have, to limit inequality, increasingly expanded public system benefits, while nations relying traditionally on public system benefits (e.g., West Germany) have increasingly expanded private benefits for high-income workers wanting more return on their contributions.

Some argue that social citizenship remains the most important component of social protection because security is not complete until the state grants alternative means to economic welfare to the market (Esping-Andersen 1989; Korpi 1989). Because meager means-tested benefits are structured to avert work disincentive effects, they fail to emancipate individuals from market dependence. Because social insurance benefits stem from labor-based contributions—that is, qualification based on previous contributions defines the right to benefits—they maintain links to the market. And because family benefits depend on qualification of others by virtue of need or contribution, they likewise fail to detach distribution from the market mechanism. A definition of social security would thus require decommodifying labor or insulating workers from dependence on the market for economic support. According to Esping-Anderson, in decommodifying welfare states

citizens can freely, and without potential losses of job, income or general welfare, opt out of work under conditions when they themselves consider it necessary for reasons of health, family, age or even educational self-improvement; when, in short, they deem it necessary for participating in the social community. (1989, p. 22)

Few if any nations meet the high standards defined by citizenship rights or decommodification. Nearly all nations rely at least partially on earnings-related benefits to supplement universal benefits; flat-rate benefits available to all are too expensive to provide generously for all elderly persons. Still, the trend is toward expanded social rights. Recent efforts to gain the right to protection from economic insecurity follow efforts in previous centuries to gain civil rights such as freedom of speech and equality before the courts and political rights for universal voting (Marshall 1964). This highlights the dynamic meaning of social security and the continuing evolution of its definition.

Political debate over how far governments should go in extending definitions of social security to include citizenship rights reflects larger tensions between the relative roles in the market and the state in public policy (Myles 1984). On one hand, inequality in earnings and contributions during work life means the market remains a strong influence on social security benefits and on the financial circumstances of nonworkers. On the other hand, equality of participation in the democratic political system provides impetus for equality in benefits unrelated to the market. The underlying dynamics of market and democracy—

differentiation versus equality—both show in varying degrees in the benefit structures of different systems and in debates over the appropriate definition of what social security should provide.

HISTORICAL BACKGROUND

A formal social security system was slow to come to the United States. The first public social security system (albeit one limited in coverage and generosity) emerged in Bismarckian Germany in 1889 and was followed within the next several decades by systems in Denmark in 1891, New Zealand in 1898, Austria in 1906, and Australia and Great Britain in 1908 (Social Security Administration 1985). Yet legislation was not passed at the national level in the United States until 1935, and the first old-age pension was not paid until 1940. In part, the expansion of disability benefits to Civil War veterans (even if they had not been injured or seen combat) in 1890 provided a de facto pension system for northern whites but did not promote implementation of a more general national pension system for nonveterans as well (Orloff and Skocpol 1984).

The reasons Civil War pensions did not lead to a more comprehensive social security system have been examined extensively. A historical persistence of individualist, laissez-faire values obstructed public support for public programs (Rimlinger 1971). Big business preferred private negotiation with labor, and small business wanted to avoid altogether the cost of social security provisions. Relative to a powerful business community, weak, decentralized labor unions in the United States were unable to agree on a common approach or push redistributive public programs as they did in several European nations (Stephens 1979). Relatedly, the United States did not have a socialist or social democratic party closely committed to labor goals, as regional, ethnic, and racial divisions split clearly defined class interests in support of social legislation. Southern congressional representatives, who desired to maintain cheap agricultural (particularly black) labor in their region, used their power in a committee-dominated federal legislature to block legislation (Quadagno

1988). Finally, the lack of a professional civil-service bureaucracy to administer the program, and the existence of often corrupt patronage politics at the local level, may have limited public support for a large public social security system (Skocpol and Ikenberry 1983). All of these forces had some role in blocking attempts during the first several decades of the twentieth century to expand protection beyond the veteran's pension and partial state-based programs for mothers' pensions or industrial accidents.

The impetus for passage of old-age and unemployment social security came from the Great Depression. Rapidly expanding costs of private pensions and a crisis of capitalist growth lessened opposition of big business to federal pension legislation and a more general role of the government in the capitalist economy (Jenkins and Brents 1989). Southern congressmen were persuaded to support legislation by excluding agricultural and domestic workers and by insisting that means-tested levels for old-age assistance be set at the state level. Both would limit disruption of the low-wage southern economy. Popular demands during the early 1930s of several hundred thousand supporters of the Townsend movement for a federal government pension to each citizen over sixty may have hastened enactment (Williamson, Evans, and Powell 1982). Ultimately, the goal of reducing unemployment by removing older workers from the labor force and of supporting at least temporarily those who were unemployed proved crucial in passing the initial legislation in 1935 (Schulz 1988; Graebner 1980).

The original 1935 Social Security Act mandated only limited coverage and benefit levels for old-age retirement. Only 60 percent of the work force was covered: agricultural, domestic, and self-employed workers, military personnel, federal, state, and local employees, and employees of nonprofit, tax-exempt organizations were all excluded. Moreover, benefit levels were quite low: policy makers intended not to replace work income fully or assure maintenance of the workers' preretirement standard of living but to supplement private sources of retirement income with minimal public benefits (Achenbaum 1986).

Social Security benefits would alone hardly meet what at the time would be considered poverty levels in many states (Quadagno 1984).

The initial structure of the social security system, along with incremental changes made in the following decades, was for the most part market-conforming. Early debates over the degree to which the program should redistribute income across classes were settled in favor of those who desired to maintain the connection between contributions and benefits (Cates 1983). Funding from general revenues was rejected in favor of contribution-based financing, which reinforced the view of the system as an insurance system. Flat-rate benefits were rejected as unsuitable for a nation of such regional and social heterogeneity; benefits were instead to reflect preretirement income levels. A cap placed on taxable wages, which ostensibly concentrated both contributions and benefits for ordinary, middle-income wage workers, introduced some regressiveness into the formula. The major exception to this strategy was that benefits for low-wage workers were higher, relative to contributions, than those for high-wage workers (Myers 1981). Also, provisions for unemployment, aid to dependent children, and relief for the blind targeted modest benefits for needy groups (Achenbaum 1989). The system thus began and remains as a mixture of social insurance based on contributions and social adequacy based on social need (Munnell 1977).

Expansion of the system began before the first benefits were ever paid out and continued on for several more decades. In 1939, dependents and survivors were made eligible for benefits. Coverage was extended in the 1950s to include most self-employed, domestic, and agricultural workers, and participation of state and local employees was made elective (federal employees kept their own system until 1984). In 1956, actuarially reduced benefits were made available at ages sixty-two to sixty-four for women, and in 1961 the same option for early retirement was made available to men—an option now exercised by a majority of new beneficiaries. Also in the 1950s, benefits equal to those for retirees were added for disabled persons ages fifty to sixty-four and still later for disabled workers of all ages. In 1965, Medicare for the elderly and Medicaid for the poor were added to provide protection from the high costs of medical care. Benefit and contribution levels also rose with extensions of coverage and disability. Ad hoc adjustments to benefit levels, which well exceeded inflation (Tomasson 1984), were common until 1972 when benefits were linked to yearly increases in the consumer price index. Payroll taxes and the maximum taxable wage also increased.

Growth of benefits and coverage nonetheless proceeded more quickly than contributions, and by the late 1970s this situation resulted in funding problems. The concept of accumulation of a reserve was replaced very quickly by a pay-as-you-go system in which current workers paid for current retirees (with surplus enough to cover year-to-year fluctuations). In the early years of the system, the ratio of one retiree to 120 workers made such funding workable. By the 1970s, the ratio of retirees to workers was one to five. Combined with increasingly high benefit levels, the growing dependency ratio resulted in payments that exceeded contributions. Amendments in 1977 "deliberalized" benefits for the first time by, among other things, freezing minimum benefits and making the earnings test more stringent (Tomasson 1984). Far from sufficient to deal with the implications of higher benefits and an older age structure, the changes only delayed more serious restructuring. A $17 billion deficit in 1983 required further deliberalization. In 1981, a Reagan administration proposal to lower benefits, change the retirement age, delay cost-of-living increases, and reduce family benefits for dependents and survivors was met with near universal opposition. To move negotiation out of the public eye, where painful and politically unpopular choices could be agreed upon, a bipartisan commission was appointed to develop proposals to deal with both short-term and long-term funding problems (Light 1985). The commission offered a compromise plan that was quickly passed by Congress and signed by President Reagan.

To summarize a complex 1983 amendment, a number of major changes were made in the direction the system was to take compared to previous decades. For the first time, Social Security benefits above specified levels were to be taxed. The age of eligibility for full retirement benefits was to be extended gradually to age sixty-seven beginning in 1999. And payroll taxes were to be increased along with the maximum taxable wage base. All these changes have had the desired effect: Contributions now exceed benefits paid. The long-run projection is that the surplus accrued during the next thirty years will likely balance the expected deficit when large, baby-boom cohorts reach retirement age (Social Security Administration 1989). The surplus, however, is by law used to purchase Treasury bonds, which fund deficits in general revenue spending. Since the bonds will need to be paid off by the taxpayers through general income taxes later on, funding problems will not disappear.

The cumulative changes in the system now result in coverage of over 90 percent of the workers, who qualify for benefits by satisfying forty quarters or ten years of covered employment. Besides the basic benefit, a minimum benefit is available for those with long-term covered employment at low wages, a dependent's benefit at 50 percent of spouses' benefits is available to spouses, and a survivor's benefit is available at 100 percent of the deceased spouse's benefits. Supplemental Security Income (SSI) provides cash assistance—unrelated to contributions and funded from general revenues—for needy aged, disabled, and blind persons who meet the means test. Among the elderly, 38 percent of all income comes from Social Security and a majority of the elderly depend on Social Security income for more than half of their income (Sherman 1987).

The position of the U.S. Social Security system relative to other nations depends on how generosity is measured. As a percent of gross domestic product (GDP), the United States ranks quite low. Considering pensions alone, however, a measure of the benefit of a new retiree as a percent of the wage of the average manufacturing worker ranks the United States higher. It falls slightly below average for single workers and slightly above average for married workers (Aldrich 1982). Part of the discrepancy stems from the concentration of public spending on pensions in the United States to the neglect of other programs. Family allowance spending and free health care for the nonaged common in other advanced industrial democracies are absent altogether in the United States (except for need-based public assistance such as Aid to Families with Dependent Children and Medicaid). The United States provides well for those whose contributions during their work lives are high—the average retiree in other words—but spends less in the aggregate for those who are not covered. Finally, the low percentage aged in the United States relative to other advanced industrial nations makes it possible to replace an above-average proportion of preretirement wages while spending a below-average fraction of GDP.

COMPARATIVE PERSPECTIVES

Many developing nations have begun to implement more formal social security systems, primarily for the benefit of urban workers and civil servants, but seldom have the economic resources to provide more than minimal coverage or protection from economic contingencies (Midgley 1984). Comparative studies have instead concentrated on the historical emergence and current policies of mature welfare states in advanced industrial nations.

Among the high-income democracies, substantial variation exists in spending levels and the structure of benefit distribution. Including pensions, health care, occupational injury, unemployment, family allowances, public assistance, and related programs for civil servants and veterans, mean spending as a percent of GDP in 1980 is 19 percent (International Labour Organization 1985). Nations spending the most include Sweden (31.2 percent), the Netherlands (27.6 percent), Denmark (26.2 percent), and France (25.5 percent), and nations spending the least are Japan (9.8 percent), Italy (11.3 percent), Australia (11.6 percent), and the United States (12.2 percent). As discussed earlier, nations also vary in the extent to which they rely on universal benefits relative to

insurance or need-based benefits. According to Esping-Andersen (1989), Sweden and Norway, in particular, have the most equalizing social security programs; Finland, Denmark, Belgium, and the Netherlands also structure benefits on the basis of citizenship rights. English-speaking nations and Switzerland tend to base their systems most on market-related criteria.

Comparison of maximum and minimum benefit levels of pensions further illustrates important country differences. In the United States, the difference between the maximum and minimum benefit in dollars is $9,900; in West Germany it is $11,000 (Social Security Administration 1985). These figures contrast with those for nations with primarily flat-rate systems such as Canada ($500), Denmark ($1,300), or the Netherlands ($0). Nations differ as well on the frequency of adjustment for the cost of living, the ages of eligibility for early or normal retirement, the degree of retirement required for receipt of benefits upon reaching retirement age (i.e., the existence of a retirement test), and the wage ceiling for social security taxation. Scales summarizing national differences on all these dimensions provide an overview of the divergence in pensions (Day 1978; Myles 1984).

Scholars during the 1950s and 1960s predicted convergence in social security systems as advanced industrial technology spread. The standardizing effects of technology would reduce preexisting cultural and political differences among the economically developed nations. The need for a recently trained, highly educated, and geographically mobile labor force in industrial economies made older workers superfluous to the production process. Without means of employment, the elderly depended on government programs for economic support. In this functionalist framework, the state meets the needs of business for a differentiated labor force while simultaneously meeting the financial needs of surplus labor unable to find employment (Wilensky 1975). Hence, retirement and social security grew rapidly among all developed nations, especially during the decades after World War II.

Similar convergence in social security systems is

predicted by neo-Marxist theories of monopoly capitalism. Here the focus is on the requirements of the capitalist mode of production and on the power of the capitalist elite. State-sponsored insurance subsidizes the costs of production of capital, and state-sponsored social assistance helps maintain legitimacy of the political-economic system in the face of discontent among the superfluous population (O'Connor 1973). The standardizing force is therefore the needs of increasingly monopolized capital to maintain high profit and investment, but the consequence is still the expansion of the state in similar forms among advanced industrial nations. Partisan democratic politics play little role in either the industrialist or capitalist logic.

The fact that, in contrast to predictions of convergence theories, expenditure levels have continued to diverge across nations over the last several decades has led more recently to a number of political explanations of variation in social security. The most common explanations focus on the differential political power of labor unions across the advanced industrial democracies. Where labor is centralized and has high membership, it gains power in negotiation with capital but can also contribute to the election of socialist, social democratic, or labor parties that best represent their interests. As a result, social legislation decreasing the scope of the market and emphasizing distribution based on political power emerges where labor is strong and where leftist parties have ruled for significant periods. Where labor is weaker and more fragmented, rightist parties are more powerful, and market-reinforcing programs with low benefits are common. Relatedly, the emergence of corporatist bargaining structures in which officially designated representatives of labor and capital negotiate economic policy with state managers has emerged in some nations—usually small nations with strong political representation of labor. The corporatist bargain has been for labor to hold down wage demands in return for full employment and generous, redistributive welfare spending (Goldthorpe 1984).

Other theories agree with the importance of political forces in generating divergence but focus on the political activity of the aged and other ascriptive groups as well as on classes (Pampel and Williamson 1989). Even among the advanced industrial nations, substantial differences in the percent aged exist and appear related to welfare spending through both demographic and political channels. Given the same benefit level in 1980 as in 1960, aging of the population can account for only some of the observed increase in pension spending. However, the size of benefit increases over time correlates closely with the size of the elderly population. Beyond just demographic effects, then, the elderly would appear in at least some countries to be an influential political interest group in support of higher pension and health care spending.

Still others have emphasized the role of the state in divergent social security policies. Beginning with the assumption that public policies cannot be reduced to the demands and preferences of any social group, state-based theories have examined how the structure of relatively autonomous state agencies and the interests of state managers can shape the way demands are expressed and translated into legislation. Qualitative studies have identified, within specific historical and national contexts, the state characteristics important for the particular policy outcomes. The quantitative literature, however, has had less success relating state characteristics such as size or centralization to measures of social security spending or citizenship rights.

Any resolution to the theoretical debates and mixed empirical results will come from synthetic efforts at theory building and statistical analysis. Class, status-demographic, political, productive, and state factors may all prove important for understanding social security system development once theories and models more clearly specify how one set of factors varies by the level of the others. Efforts to estimate nonlinear, interactive models are already under way and should prove crucial for future research (Hicks, Swank, and Ambuhl 1989; Pampel, Williamson, and Stryker 1990).

CONSEQUENCES

A huge literature on the consequences of social security spending for social equality and social behavior can only be given the broadest overview. Controversy exists not so much on whether spending has any effect but on what kinds of social phenomena it most affects.

One view is that social security spending directly reduces economic inequality without substantially changing social behavior such as labor force participation, living arrangements, or savings. The major evidence in favor of the redistributive consequences comes from studies that subtract transfers from total income and compare inequality with and without the transfers included (Smeeding, Torrey, and Rein 1988). In the United States and a number of European nations, pretransfer inequality and poverty are higher than for posttransfer income distribution. Particularly egalitarian, according to the results of this methodology, are expenditures for pensions. However, advocates of this view have been less willing to accept the claim that transfers promote inequality by providing incentives to leave the labor force—in other words, by inducing behavior that indirectly contributes to higher poverty and inequality. Implicitly, unemployment and low income are seen as the result of discrimination and lack of opportunities—situations that do not change with the receipt of benefits.

Other views weigh the behavioral responses to transfers as important relative to the redistributive consequences. If transfers themselves induce labor force and living arrangement changes that make pretransfer income distribution less egalitarian than it would otherwise be if transfers were not present, the evidence of redistribution cited above would be flawed (Danziger, Haverman, and Plotnick 1981). For instance, pensions have the largest effect in reducing pretransfer inequality but also induce voluntary retirement that lowers earnings relative to what they would be without pensions or retirement. Similarly, transfers increase an individual's ability to afford independent living arrangements, which makes pretransfer income figures misleading.

Trends in poverty and inequality do not provide unambiguous evidence for either view. Certainly the absolute income of the elderly in the United States has risen with the growth of Social Security benefits. As Social Security benefits rose dramatically during the last several decades, poverty among the aged declined from a level of 35 percent (compared to 22 percent for the population) in 1960 to a level of 12 percent (compared to 13 percent for the population) by 1987 (U.S. Bureau of the Census 1989). However, the improved economic position of the elderly also stems from the fact that recent cohorts entering old age have been better off financially than previous cohorts and more likely to have accumulated private pensions and savings to support them. For overall income inequality, the trend shows little change (at least until 1980) despite the massive growth of transfers (Levy 1987). Either transfers were not redistributive or pretransfer inequality increased. Perhaps household changes, in part an indirect response to transfers, balanced the direct effects of transfers on inequality (Treas 1983). After 1980 inequality grew, but, again, separating the effects of changes in the occupation structure from changes in real Social Security benefits for the poor and unemployed is difficult.

Comparative evidence on the relationship between social security spending and inequality across advanced industrial nations is also mixed (compare Pampel and Williamson 1989 with Esping-Andersen 1985). Nations with high spending levels and benefit structures based on citizenship rights such as in Scandinavia have always had lower levels of income inequality among both the aged and the general population. Yet, establishing a causal association between those levels and social security benefits across nations that differ in so many other social and economic characteristics is difficult.

Given the mixed empirical evidence, views on the redistributive consequences of the welfare state reflect theoretical assumptions about the determinants of social security spending levels and structure. Neo-Marxist theories of monopoly capitalism, assuming high inequality is an inherent and necessary feature of advanced capitalism, argue social security systems help maintain that structure rather than change it. Interest-group or neopluralist theories see middle-class, politically powerful groups as the primary recipients of most spending, which limits the extent of redistribution to the poor. Other theories claim just the opposite. For industrialism theories, spending is directed at surplus workers most in need. For social democratic theories, spending is directed to the working class and poor represented by leftist parties and unions. Still others would claim that the state and institutional context shapes the ability of spending to reduce inequality. As in the study of the determinants of spending, interactive or contextual studies will likely be needed to make sense of the comparative experience.

ISSUES

A number of issues or problems face policymakers dealing with social security systems. A few of these can be reviewed briefly. Some apply especially or primarily to the United States, while others apply to all advanced industrial nations or to third-world nations.

First, concern has been expressed over the inequitable treatment of women in earnings-related social security systems. When receipt of benefits for women in old age depends on the benefits of spouses, high rates of marital breakup and widowhood make reliance on this source of financial security risky. When receipt of benefits of women in old age depend on wage contributions, the discontinuous labor force participation during years of childbearing penalizes women. Universal benefits provide some support for older women, but other policy options are emerging to deal more directly with the gender-based problems. Some nations give social security contribution credits to women out of the labor force to raise children or split earned credits of a couple equally between the spouses.

Second, the improved economic position of the elderly, declining poverty rates, and higher public benefits during the 1970s and the 1980s contrast with the declining real level of benefits and increasing poverty among children in the United States. The improved position of the elderly relative to children may stem from the increasing size (and political power) of elderly cohorts compared to the smaller-sized cohorts of children (Preston 1984). That benefits for children take the form of means-tested social assistance—a type of program that receives weak public support relative to pensions because it is not shared by large parts of the population—also contributes to the inequality. Other nations that have family allowance systems to provide cash benefits to all or nearly all parents have experienced little in the way of concern over generational equity.

Third, after decades of expansion, policymakers must face problems of balancing continued demands for more spending with limits on taxation. On one hand, given problems of support that still exist among certain vulnerable groups such as the oldest old, minorities, and widowed women, more spending is needed. Increasingly expensive health and long-term care for the elderly and disabled add particularly to the cost of social security systems. Despite the cost, support for pension and health care continues strong (Coughlin 1980). On the other hand, critics have argued that the rising costs of social security contribute to economic problems of inflation and unemployment by reducing savings and productivity. Others who are more sociologically oriented suggest that high expenditures tend to weaken community and family bonds, which ultimately are the source of protection for those in need (Glazer 1988). Certainly concern with high tax levels has led politicians to attempt to control spending and reduce taxes in nearly all advanced industrial democracies. Balancing these goals without deficit spending will remain the task of governments in the decades to come.

Fourth, concern over population aging relates to debates over controlling costs of social security. Whatever the difficulties in meeting funding demands, they are likely to worsen in the next century with the entrance of large baby-boom cohorts into old age. In part, the problem is one of declining fertility, which reduces the size of younger, working cohorts relative to older, retired cohorts. In the recent past, when the relative sizes of working and elderly cohorts were reversed, social security recipients were treated generously: They received benefits worth five to six times their contributions and interest (Wolff 1987). Future retiring cohorts are not likely to experience such high returns on their contributions (and are sometimes skeptical of receiving any at all). Still, funding problems for aging populations are not insurmountable. Many European nations, whose fertility levels fell faster than those in the United States, already have aged populations as large as 17 percent of the total—levels not to be reached for thirty years in the United States. Through appropriate political and economic policy, the United States can meet the needs of its elderly population (Aaron, Bosworth, and Burtless 1989).

Finally, these same issues are emerging as important in third-world nations. Though the percentage aged in these nations is small, and social security remains primarily a family rather than a state responsibility, the situation can change quickly. Rapid declines in fertility sharply increase the percent aged, make family care for the elderly difficult, and generate demands for public support. With scare resources, the state may risk being overwhelmed by the demands. Our understanding of the process of building social security systems for these nations remains meager.

(SEE ALSO: *Government Regulation; Public Policy Analysis; Retirement; Social Gerontology*)

REFERENCES

Aaron, Henry J., Barry P. Bosworth, and Gary Burtless 1989 *Can America Afford to Grow Old? Paying for Social Security*. Washington D.C.: Brookings Institution.

Achenbaum, W. Andrew 1986 *Social Security: Visions and Revisions*. Cambridge: Cambridge University Press.

——— 1989 "Public Pensions as Intergenerational Transfers in the United States." In Paul Johnson, Christoph Conrad, and David Thomson, eds., *Workers Versus Pensioners: Intergenerational Justice in an Aging World*. Manchester: Manchester University Press.

Aldrich, Jonathan 1982 "The Earnings Replacement Rate of Old-Age Benefits in Twelve Countries, 1969–80." *Social Security Bulletin* 445(12): 3–11.

Cates, Jerry R. 1983 *Insuring Inequality: Administrative Leadership in Social Security, 1935–53*. Ann Arbor: University of Michigan Press.

Coughlin, Richard M. 1980 *Ideology, Public Opinion, and Welfare Policy*. Berkeley: Institute of International Studies, University of California.

Danziger, Sheldon, Robert H. Haverman, and Robert Plotnick 1981 "How Income Transfer Programs Affect Work, Savings, and the Income Distribution: A Critical Review." *Journal of Economic Literature* 19:975–1,028.

Day, Lincoln 1978 "Government Pensions for the Aged in Nineteen Industrialized Countries." *Comparative Studies in Sociology* 1:217–234.

Esping-Andersen, Gosta 1985 "Power and Distributional Regimes." *Politics and Society* 14:222–255.

——— 1989 "The Three Political Economies of the Welfare State." *Canadian Review of Sociology and Anthropology* 26:10–35.

Glazer, Nathan 1988 *The Limits of Social Policy*. Cambridge, Mass.: Harvard University Press.

Goldthorpe, John H. 1984 "The End of Convergence: Corporatist and Dualist Tendencies in Modern Western Societies." In John H. Goldthorpe, ed., *Order and Conflict in Contemporary Capitalism*. Oxford: Clarendon.

Graebner, William 1980 *A History of Retirement*. New Haven: Yale University Press.

Hicks, Alexander, Duane Swank, and Martin Ambuhl 1989 "Welfare Expansion Revisited: Policy Routines and Their Mediation by Party, Class, and Crisis, 1959–1982." *European Journal of Political Research* 4:401–430.

International Labour Organization 1985 *The Cost of Social Security*. Geneva: International Labour Organization.

Jenkins, J. Craig, and Barbara G. Brents 1989 "Social Protest, Hegemonic Competition, and Social Reform: A Political Struggle Interpretation of the Origins of the American Welfare State." *American Sociological Review* 54:891–909.

Korpi, Walter 1989 "Power, Politics, and State Autonomy in the Development of Social Citizenship: Social Rights during Sickness in Eighteen Countries since 1930." *American Sociological Review* 54:309–328.

Levy, Frank 1987 *Dollars and Dreams: The Changing American Income Distribution*. New York: Russell Sage.

Light, Paul 1985 *Artful Work: The Politics of Social Security Reform*. New York: Random House.

Marshall, T. H. 1964 *Class, Citizenship, and Social Development*. Chicago: University of Chicago Press.

Midgley, James 1984 *Social Security, Inequality, and the Third World*. New York: Wiley.

Munnell, Alice H. 1977 *The Future of Social Security*. Washington D.C.: Brookings Institution.

Myers, Robert J. 1981 *Social Security*. Rev. ed. Homewood, Ill.: Irwin.

Myles, John 1984 *Old Age in the Welfare State: The Political Economy of Public Pensions*. Boston: Little, Brown.

O'Connor, James 1973 *The Fiscal Crisis of State*. New York: St. Martin's.

Organization for Economic Cooperation and Development 1988 *The Future of Social Protection*. OECD Social Policy Studies No. 6. Paris: Organization for Economic Cooperation and Development.

Orloff, Ann Shola, and Theda Skocpol 1984 "Why Not Equal Protection? Explaining the Politics of Public Social Spending in Britain, 1900–1911, and the United States, 1880–1920s." *American Sociological Review* 49:725–750.

Pampel, Fred C., and John B. Williamson 1989 *Age, Class, Politics, and the Welfare State*. Cambridge: Cambridge University Press.

Pampel, Fred C., John B. Williamson, and Robin Stryker 1990 "Class Context and Pension Response to Demographic Structure." *Social Problems* 37:535–550.

Preston, Samuel H. 1984 "Children and the Elderly: Divergent Paths for America's Dependents." *Demography* 21:435–457.

Quadagno, Jill S. 1984 "Welfare Capitalism and the Social Security Act of 1935." *American Sociological Review* 49:632–647.

——— 1988 *The Transformation of Old Age Security: Class and Politics in the American Welfare State*. Chicago: University of Chicago Press.

Rimlinger, Gaston 1971 *Welfare Policy and Industrialization in Europe, America, and Russia*. Toronto: John Wiley.

Schulz, James 1988 *The Economics of Aging*. Dover, Mass.: Auburn House.

Sherman, Sally R. 1987 "Fast Facts and Figures about Social Security." *Social Security Bulletin* 50(5): 5–25.

Simmons, Leo 1960 "Aging in Preindustrial Societies." In Clark Tibbits, ed., *Handbook of Social Gerontology*. Chicago: University of Chicago Press.

Skocpol, Theda, and John Ikenberry 1983 "The Political Formation of the American Welfare State in Historical and Comparative Perspective." *Comparative Social Research* 6:87–148.

Social Security Administration 1985 *Social Security throughout the World*. Washington D.C.: U.S. Government Printing Office.

——— 1989 "Actuarial Status of the OASI and DI Trust Funds." *Social Security Bulletin* 52(6): 2–7.

Smeeding, Timothy, Barbara Boyle Torrey, and Martin Rein 1988 "Patterns of Income and Poverty: The Economic Status of Children and the Elderly in Eight Countries." In John L. Palmer, Timothy Smeeding, and Barbara Boyle Torrey, eds., *The Vulnerable*. Washington D.C.: Brookings Institution.

Stephens, John D. 1979 *The Transformation from Capitalism to Socialism*. London: Macmillan.

Tomasson, Richard F. 1984 "Government Old Age Pensions under Affluence and Austerity: West Germany, Sweden, the Netherlands, and the United States." *Research in Social Problems and Public Policy* 3:217–272.

Treas, Judith 1983 "Trickle-Down or Transfers? Postwar Determinants of Family Income Inequality." *American Sociological Review* 48:546–559.

U.S. Bureau of the Census 1989 *Statistical Abstract*. Washington D.C.: U.S. Government Printing Office.

Wilensky, Harold 1975 *The Welfare State and Equality*. Berkeley: University of California Press.

Williamson, John B., Linda Evans, and Lawrence Powell 1982 *The Politics of Aging*. Springfield, Ill.: Charles C. Thomas.

Wolff, Nancy 1987 *Income Redistribution and the Social Security Program*. Ann Arbor: University of Michigan Press.

FRED C. PAMPEL

SOCIAL STRATIFICATION In all complex societies, the total stock of valued resources is distributed unequally, with the most privileged individuals or families enjoying a disproportionate share of property, power, or prestige. Although it might be possible to construct an exhaustive rank-ordering of individuals based on their control over these resources, most scholars attempt to identify a set of classes or strata that reflect the major cleavages in the population. The task of stratification research is to describe the structure of these social groupings and to specify the processes by which they are generated and maintained. The following types of questions are central to the field:

1. What are the major forms of stratification in human history? Is stratification an inevitable feature of human life?
2. Are there well-defined classes or status groupings in advanced industrial societies? If so, what are the principal features of these groupings?
3. What types of social processes and institutions serve to maintain or alter ascriptive forms of stratification (e.g., racial stratification, gender stratification)? Are these ascriptive processes weakening with the transition to advanced industrialism?
4. How frequently do individuals move across class, status, or occupational boundaries? Is the process of occupational attainment governed by ascriptive traits (e.g., family background) or by achieved characteristics (e.g., education)?

There is a long tradition of commentary on questions of this kind. For the greater part of history, the stratification regime was regarded as an immutable feature of society, and the implicit objective of commentators was to explain or justify the existing order in terms of religious or quasi-religious doctrines (see Bottomore 1965). It was only with the Enlightenment that a "rhetoric of equality" emerged in opposition to the legal and political advantages accorded to privileged status groupings. After the latter privileges were weakened in the nineteenth century, this egalitarian ideal was redirected against emerging forms of economic stratification; the result was the rise of socialist and Marxist interpretations of human history. It is out of this conflict between egalitarian values and the brute facts of economic inequality that modern theories of stratification emerged.

This is not to imply that the field of stratification has been dominated by a simple Marxist model. It would be no exaggeration, in fact, to say that much of modern stratification theory has been formulated in *reaction* to Marxist and neo-Marxist theories. Indeed, the term *stratification* is often seen as anti-Marxist, since it places emphasis on the purely hierarchical ranking of classes rather than the exploitative relations between them. Moreover, modern scholars have typically attempted to adopt a value-free orientation, with their research focusing on description and analysis rather than "praxis" in its purest form.

FORMS OF STRATIFICATION

The starting point for any theory of stratification is the purely descriptive task of classification. It is conventional among contemporary theorists to distinguish between modern *class systems* and the *estates* or *castes* found in advanced agrarian societies (e.g., Mayer and Buckley 1970). As shown in table 1, this conventional typology can be elaborated by introducing additional categories for tribal systems (panel A), slave systems (panel B), and state socialist societies (panel C). It should be kept in mind that these various forms of stratification are best seen as ideal types rather than descriptions of existing societies. Indeed, the stratification systems of advanced societies are complex and multidimensional, if only because their past institutional forms tend to persist despite the emergence of new forms. It follows that most systems of stratification are a complex mixture of elements from several of the ideal-typical forms specified in Table 1 (for related topologies, see Wright 1985; Runciman 1974).

The first panel in this table lists some of the basic principles underlying tribal systems of stratification (see line A1). It should be emphasized that the most extreme forms of inequality were eliminated from these societies through gift exchanges and other redistributive practices (Lenski 1966, pp. 102–112). In fact, some of the early students of tribal societies spoke of a "primitive communism," since the means of production (i.e., land) were communally owned, and other forms of property were distributed evenly among tribal members. This is not to say, of course, that a *perfect* equality prevailed. After all, some of the more powerful medicine men ("shamans") lived off the surplus production of others, and the tribal chief often exerted considerable influence on the political decisions of the day. The impor-

TABLE 1
The Principal Assets, Major Strata, and Justifying Ideologies for Six Forms of Social Stratification

System	Principal Assets	Major Strata	Justifying Ideology
A. *Hunting and Gathering Society*			
1. Tribal System	Hunting Skills and Magic	Chiefs, Shamans, and Followers	Meritocratic Selection
B. *Horticultural and Agrarian Society*			
2. Feudal System	Land and Labor Power	Kings, Lords, and Serfs	Tradition and Religious Doctrine
3. Slave System	Human Property	Owners and Slaves	Natural and Social Inferiority
4. Caste System	Ethnic Purity	Castes	Tradition and Religious Doctrine
C. *Industrial Society*			
5. Class System	Means of Production	Capitalists and Workers	Classical Liberalism
6. State Socialism	Organizational and Party Assets	Managers and Managed	Marxism and Leninism

tant point, however, is that these residual forms of power and privilege could not be inherited; it was only by demonstrating superior abilities in hunting, magic, or leadership that tribal members could secure political office or acquire prestige. It might be said, then, that tribal systems rested on meritocratic principles of a most basic kind.

With the emergence of agrarian forms of production, the economic surplus became large enough to support more complex systems of stratification. The Indian caste system, for example, is based on an elaborate and intricate classification of hereditary groupings. As indicated in Table 1, these groupings can be ranked on a continuum of ethnic purity, with the highest positions in the system reserved for castes that prohibit activities or behaviors that are seen as "polluting" (e.g., eating meat, scavenging). Although a caste system of this kind is often taken to be the limiting case of stratification, it should be noted that feudal systems were also based on a rigid system of quasi-hereditary groups. The distinctive feature of feudalism was the institution of personal bondage; that is, medieval serfs were obliged to live on a manor and pay rents of various kinds (e.g., "corvée labor"), since the feudal lord held the legal rights to their labor power (see line B3). If a serf fled to the city, this was considered a form of theft; the serf was stealing that portion of his labor power owned by his lord (Wright 1985, p. 78). It must be stressed, however, that the serfs of feudal society typically retained some degree of control over their labor power. If this control is completely stripped away, then workers become nothing more than *human* property, and the distinction between feudalism and slavery disappears (see line B4).

The most striking development of the modern era has been the rise of egalitarian ideologies. This can be seen, for example, in the revolutions of the eighteenth and nineteenth centuries, where the ideals of the Enlightenment were directed against the privileges of rank and the political power of the aristocracy. In the end, these struggles eliminated the last residues of feudal privilege, but they also made possible the emergence of new forms of inequality and stratification. It is usually argued that a *class system* developed in the early-industrial period, with the major inequalities in this system defined in economic terms and legitimated as the natural outcome of individual competition (i.e., "classical liberalism"). There is, however, considerable controversy over the contours and boundaries of these economic classes. As indicated in line C5, a simple Marxist model might focus on the cleavage between capitalists and workers, whereas other models represent the class structure as a continuous graduation of "monetary wealth and income" (Mayer and Buckley 1970, p. 15).

Whatever the relative merits of these models might be, the Marxist one became the ideology for the socialist revolutions of the nineteenth and twentieth centuries. The intellectual heritage of these revolutions can again be traced to the Enlightenment; however, a new "rhetoric of equality" was fashioned for the times, with the attack now focusing on the economic power of the capitalist class rather than the privileges of the aristocracy. The available evidence from Eastern Europe and elsewhere suggests that this egalitarian rhetoric was only partially realized (see, e.g., Lenski 1992). To be sure, private property was largely eliminated in socialist societies, yet various commentators have suggested that new lines of stratification crystallized in the "secondary stage" of socialist development (Kelley 1981; Giddens

1973). It is often claimed, for instance, that an intellectual or bureaucratic elite emerged under state socialism to take the place of the old capitalist class (see, e.g., Gouldner 1979; Djilas 1965). Of course, this elite cannot formally own the means of production, yet it does control the production of goods and the allocation of valued resources. There is an emerging consensus, moreover, that the power of intellectuals has been *further* strengthened with the recent antisocialist revolutions in Eastern Europe (e.g., Szelényi 1992). The obvious irony of this development is that the intellectual elite may ultimately be sowing the seeds of its own demise by reconstituting the old capitalist class.

SOURCES OF STRATIFICATION

The foregoing sketch makes it clear that a wide range of stratification systems has emerged over the course of human history. The question that naturally arises, then, is whether some form of stratification is an inevitable feature of human societies. In addressing this question, it is useful to begin with the functionalist approach (Davis and Moore 1945), since this is the best-known attempt to understand "the universal necessity which calls forth stratification in any system" (p. 242; also, see Davis 1953; Moore 1963a; 1963b). The starting point for Davis and Moore (1945) is the premise that all societies must devise some means to motivate the best workers to fill the most important and difficult occupations. This "motivational problem" might be addressed in a variety of ways, but perhaps the simplest solution is to construct a hierarchy of rewards (e.g., prestige, property, power) that privileges the incumbents of functionally significant positions. As noted by Davis and Moore (1945, p. 243), this amounts to setting up a system of institutionalized inequality (i.e., a "stratification system"), with the occupational structure serving as a conduit through which unequal rewards and perquisites are disbursed. The stratification system may be seen, therefore, as an "unconsciously evolved device by which societies insure that the important positions are conscientiously filled by the most qualified persons" (Davis and Moore 1945, p. 243). Under the Davis-Moore formulation, the only empirical claim is that *some form* of inequality is needed to allocate labor efficiently; the authors are silent, however, when it comes to specifying *how much* inequality is sufficient for this purpose. It is well to bear in mind that the extreme forms of stratification found in existing societies may exceed the "minimum . . . necessary to maintain a complex division of labor" (Wrong 1959, p. 774).

The Davis-Moore hypothesis has come under considerable criticism from several quarters (see Huaco 1966 for an early review). The prevailing view, at least among the postwar commentators, is that the original hypothesis cannot adequately account for inequalities in "stabilized societies where statuses are ascribed" (Wesolowski 1962, p. 31; Tumin 1953). Indeed, whenever the vacancies in the occupational structure are allocated on purely hereditary grounds, the stratification system is no longer ensuring that the most important positions are "conscientiously filled by the most qualified persons" (Davis and Moore 1945, p. 243). What must be recognized, however, is that a *purely* hereditary system is rarely achieved in practice; in fact, even in the most rigid caste societies, the most talented and qualified individuals may have some opportunities for upward mobility. Under the Davis-Moore formulation (1945), this slow trickle of mobility is regarded as essential to the functioning of the social system, so much so that elaborate systems of inequality have been devised to ensure that the trickle continues (see Davis 1948, pp. 369–370, for additional and related comments). This suggests, then, that the Davis-Moore hypothesis might be used to explain inequalities in societies with relatively rigid mobility regimes. However, when opportunities for mobility are completely closed off, most commentators would concede that the original hypothesis becomes somewhat less credible.

Whereas the early debates addressed conceptual issues of this kind, the focus ultimately shifted to constructing "critical tests" of the Davis-Moore hypothesis. This research effort continued apace throughout the 1970s, with some commentators reporting evidence consistent with functionalist theory (e.g., Cullen and Novick 1979), and others being somewhat less sympathetic in their assessments (e.g., Broom and Cushing 1977). Although the following decade was a period of relative quiescence, the debate over functionalism resurfaced when Lenski (1992) suggested that "many of the internal, systemic problems of Marxist societies were the result of inadequate motivational arrangements" (p. 6). This analysis focused on the unintended consequences of the socialist "experiments in destratification" (Lenski 1978); that is, Lenski argued that the socialist commitment to wage leveling made it difficult to recruit and motivate highly skilled workers, while the "visible hand" of the socialist economy could never be calibrated to mimic the natural incentive of capitalist profit-taking. These results led Lenski to conclude that "successful incentive systems involve . . . motivating the best qualified people to seek the most important positions" (p. 11). It remains to be seen whether this interpretation will generate a new round of functionalist theorizing and debate.

THE STRUCTURE OF MODERN STRATIFICATION

The recent history of stratification theory is in large part a history of debates about the contours of class, status, and prestige hierarchies in advanced industrial societies. These debates have been waged on a wide variety of fronts; however, for the present essay, it will suffice to focus on three distinct schools of thought (see Wright 1979, pp. 3–18, for a comprehensive review). The various debates within these schools might appear to be nothing more than academic infighting, but in fact they have been regarded by many postwar European intellectuals as a "necessary prelude to the conduct of political strategy" (Parkin 1979, p. 16). This form of political strategizing plays an especially prominent role within Marxist and neo-Marxist circles; for instance, a good deal of energy has been devoted to drawing the correct dividing line between the working class and the bourgeoisie, since the task of identifying the oppressed class is seen as a prerequisite to devising a political strategy that might appeal to it. It goes without saying that political and scholarly goals are often conflated in such mapmaking efforts; and, consequently, the assorted debates in this subfield are infused with more than the usual amount of normative excitement.

Marxists and Neo-Marxists. The debates within the Marxist and neo-Marxist camps have been especially contentious, not only because of the foregoing political motivations, but also because the discussion of class within *Capital* (Marx [1894] 1972) is too fragmentary and unsystematic to adjudicate between various competing interpretations. At the end of the third volume of *Capital,* we find the now-famous fragment on "the classes" (Marx [1894] 1972, pp. 862–863), but this discussion breaks off at just that point where Marx appeared ready to advance a formal definition of the term. It is clear, nonetheless, that his abstract model of capitalism was resolutely dichotomous, with the conflict between capitalists and workers constituting the driving force behind further social development. This simple two-class model should be viewed as an ideal type designed to capture the "developmental tendencies" of capitalism; indeed, whenever Marx carried out concrete analyses of *existing* capitalist systems, he acknowledged that the class structure was complicated by the persistence of transitional classes (i.e., landowners), quasi-class groupings (e.g., peasants), and class fragments (e.g., the lumpen-proletariat). It was only with the progressive maturation of capitalism that Marx expected these complications to disappear as the "centrifugal forces of class struggle and crisis flung all *dritte Personen* to one camp or the other" (Parkin 1979, p. 16).

The recent history of modern capitalism suggests that the class structure has not evolved in such a precise and tidy fashion. To be sure, the available evidence makes it clear that the old middle class of artisans and shopkeepers has declined in relative size (Gagliani 1981; cf. Steinmetz and Wright 1989), yet a "new middle class" of managers, professionals, and nonmanual workers has expanded to occupy the newly vacated space. The last fifty years of neo-Marxist theorizing might be seen as an "intellectual fallout" from this development, with some commentators seeking to minimize its implications, and others putting forward a revised mapping of the class structure that accommodates the new middle class in explicit terms. Within the former camp, the principal tendency is to claim that the lower sectors of the new middle class are in the process of being proletarianized, since "capital subjects [nonmanual labor] . . . to the forms of rationalization characteristic of the capitalist mode of production" (Braverman 1974, p. 408). This line of reasoning suggests that the working class may gradually expand in relative size and thereby regain its earlier power.

At the other end of the continuum, Poulantzas (1974) has argued that most members of the new intermediate stratum fall *outside* the working class proper, since they are engaged in "unproductive labor" of various kinds. This approach may have the merit of keeping the working class conceptually pure, but some commentators have noted that it also reduces the size of this class to trivial proportions. The latter result has motivated contemporary scholars to develop class models that fall somewhere between the extremes advocated by Braverman (1974) and Poulantzas (1974). For example, the neo-Marxist model proposed by Wright (1978) generates an American working class that is acceptably large (i.e., approximately 46 percent of the labor force), yet the class mappings in this model still pay tribute to the various cleavages and divisions among workers who sell their labor power (also, see Wright et al. 1982). In fact, the model places professionals in a *distinct* "semi-autonomous class" by virtue of their control over the work process, while upper-level supervisors are located in a "managerial class" by virtue of their authority over workers (Wright 1978; also, see Wright 1985; Westergaard and Resler 1975). It should be noted that the dividing lines proposed in these neo-Marxist class models often rest on concepts (e.g., authority relations) that were once purely the province of "bourgeois sociology." This development led Parkin (1979) to conclude that "inside every neo-Marxist there seems to be a Weberian struggling to get out" (p. 25).

Weberians and Neo-Weberians: The rise of the "new middle class" is less problematic for scholars working within a Weberian framework. Indeed, the class model advanced by Weber suggests a *multiplicity* of class cleavages, because it equates the economic class of workers with their "market situation" (Weber [1922] 1968, pp. 926–940). This model implies that wealthy property-owners are in a privileged class; after all, members of this class can outbid workers for valued goods in the commodity market, and they can also convert their wealth to capital and thereby monopolize entrepreneurial opportunities. However, Weber emphasized that skilled workers are also privileged under modern capitalism, since their services are in high demand on the labor market. The end result, then, is a new middle class of skilled workers that intervenes between the "positively privileged" capitalist class and the "negatively privileged" mass of unskilled laborers (Weber [1922] 1968, pp. 927–928). At the same time, the stratification system is further complicated by the existence of *status groupings,* which Weber saw as forms of social affiliation that often competed with class-based forms of organization. Although an economic class is merely an aggregate of individuals in a similar market situation, a status grouping is defined as a community of individuals who share a "style of life" and interact as status equals (e.g., the nobility, an ethnic caste, etc.). Under some circumstances, the boundaries of a status grouping are determined by purely economic criteria, yet Weber notes that "status honor need not necessarily be linked with a class situation" (Weber [1922] 1968, p. 932). The *nouveaux riches,* for instance, are never immediately accepted into "high society," even when their wealth clearly places them in the uppermost economic class (Weber [1922] 1968, pp. 936–937).

The Weberian approach has been elaborated and extended by sociologists seeking to understand the "American form" of stratification. During the decades following World War II, American sociologists typically dismissed the Marxist model of class as overly simplistic and one-dimensional, whereas they celebrated the Weberian model as properly distinguishing between the numerous variables that Marx had conflated in his definition of class (see, e.g., Barber 1968). In the most extreme versions of this approach, the dimensions identified by Weber were disaggregated into a multiplicity of stratification variables (e.g., income, education, ethnicity), and the correlations between these variables were then shown to be weak enough to generate various forms of "status inconsistency" (e.g., a poorly educated millionaire). The resulting picture suggested a "pluralistic model" of stratification; that is, the class system was represented as intrinsically multidimensional, with a host of crosscutting affiliations producing a complex patchwork of internal class cleavages. Although one well-known critic has remarked that the multidimensionalists provided a "sociological portrait of America as drawn by Norman Rockwell" (Parkin 1979, p. 604), it must be kept in mind that some of these theorists also emphasized the seamy side of pluralism. In fact, Lenski (1954) and others (e.g., Lipset 1959) have argued that the modern stratification system might be seen as a breeding ground for personal stress and political radicalism, since individuals with contradictory statuses may feel relatively deprived and thus support "movements designed to alter the political *status quo*" (Lenski 1966, p. 88). This interest in the consequences of status inconsistency died out in the early 1970s under the force of negative and inconclusive findings (e.g., Jackson and Curtis 1972). However, among recent researchers and commentators, there appears to be a resurgence of interest in issues of status disparity and relative deprivation. It is notable that American scholars have *not* been the driving force behind this "second wave" of multidimensional theorizing; to be sure, some Americans have participated in the revival (e.g., Baron 1992), but most of the new theorizing is European in origin (e.g., Beck 1987) and focuses on the generic properties of all "post-modern" stratification systems.

It would be a mistake, of course, to regard these multidimensionalists as the *only* intellectual descendants of Weber. In fact, some neo-Weberians contend that identifiable classes can develop under modern capitalism, despite the fragmenting effects of crosscutting affiliations and cleavages (e.g., Goldthorpe 1980). The prevailing view within this revisionist camp is that various forms of *social closure* and *exclusion* play an important role in generating social classes with a shared culture and style of life (e.g., Giddens 1973; Breiger 1981). In modern industrial societies, there are no legal sanctions that prevent labor from freely flowing across class boundaries, but there are various social, cultural, and institutional mechanisms that effectively "channel" children into occupations that are similar to those of their parents. These exclusionary mechanisms produce a class structure with a relatively stable and permanent membership; as a result, a set of distinctive class cultures may emerge, and this in turn may generate a minimal level of class awareness and identification. In most countries, one would expect to see a fundamental "class divide" between manual and nonmanual labor, since the strongest barriers to mobility are found precisely at this boundary. Although barriers of this kind are not the only source of class structuration (e.g., see Giddens 1973, pp. 107–112), they may well contribute to the formation of identifiable "collar classes" under modern industrialism.

Gradational Models. The distinction between categorical and gradational models of stratification has long been important in American sociology. Whereas neo-Marxists seek to describe the stratification system with a small number of discrete categories (i.e., "classes"), gradational theorists map the contours of modern stratification in terms of *ordered levels* (see Ossowski 1963). This distinction played an especially prominent role in the community studies completed after World War II; for instance, Lenski (1952) emphasized that the residents of a New England mill town were stratified into "graded prestige levels" rather than "discrete social classes," while Landecker (1960) attempted to locate the "natural breaks" and cleavages within the status hierarchy of Detroit. As the discipline matured, the focus shifted away from critical tests of this kind, and the two approaches developed into distinct research traditions with their own methods of inquiry. It is commonly argued that American sociologists have an "elective affinity" for gradational models; in fact, when Ossowski (1963) surveyed the history of stratification research, he concluded that the "American class structure is [typically] interpreted . . . in terms of a scheme of gradation" (p. 102).

The gradational approach can be operationalized by measuring the income, prestige, or status of individuals. While there is some sociological precedent for treating income as an indicator of class distinctions (e.g., Mayer and Buckley 1970, p. 15), most sociologists seem content with a disciplinary division of labor that leaves the income distribution to economists. This is perhaps unfortunate; after all, if one is indeed intent on assessing the "market situation" of workers, there is much to recommend a direct measurement of their income and wealth. Despite the merits of this method, it never enjoyed much popularity: the preferred approach is to define classes as "groups of persons who are members of effective kinship units which, as units, are approximately equally valued" (Parsons 1954, p. 77). The latter method was operationalized in the postwar community studies (e.g., Warner 1949) by constructing broadly-defined categories of reputational equals (i.e., "upper-upper class," "upper-middle class," etc.). However, when the disciplinary focus shifted to national surveys, the measure of choice soon became interval-level scales constructed from detailed occupational codes (see, e.g., Duncan 1961; Siegel 1971; Treiman 1977). These scales now serve as standard measures of "class background" in sociological research of all kinds.

ASCRIPTIVE FORMS OF STRATIFICATION

The long-standing tendency within both the Marxist and non-Marxist schools has been to treat ethnicity, race, and gender as purely "secondary forces" in history. There was always considerable disagreement within these schools over the appropriate way to define social classes; nevertheless, despite these various conflicts and disputes, the shared presumption was that modern society is essentially a *class system*. In almost all formulations, the nuclear family was seen as the elemental unit of stratification, with the *occupation* or *employment status* of the family head (i.e., the husband) defining the class position of all its members. This approach had the effect of reducing various types of intraclass cleavages (e.g., ethnic cleavages, gender-based cleavages) to the status of "complicating factors" or historically contingent developments (see Parkin 1979, pp. 29–31, for an incisive review). To be sure, it was typically recognized that the competing bonds of race or ethnicity were still salient for some individuals, yet these ties were viewed as vestiges of traditional loyalties that would ultimately wither away under the rationalizing influence of capitalism or industrialism. It was often argued that this decline in purely ascriptive forces proceeded from the functional requirements of modern industrial societies (e.g., Levy 1966).

This so-called "conventional model" of stratification has come under criticism on both empirical and theoretical grounds. The first step in the gradual breakdown of this model was the fashioning of a multidimensional approach to stratification systems (see earlier section on the Structure of Modern Stratification). Whereas the conventional model gave theoretical and conceptual priority to the economic dimension of stratification, the multidimensionalists emphasized that the status of individuals reflected a wider array of ascriptive and achieved outcomes (e.g., race, gender, education, occupation). This approach had the obvious effect, then, of forcing sociologists to attend more closely to ascriptive sources of status and solidarity. The breakdown of the conventional model was further accelerated by the accumulating evidence in the 1970s that racial, ethnic, and gender-based conflicts were emerging in intensified form. Far from withering away under the force of industrialism, the bonds of ethnicity appeared to be alive and well; the consensus view was that "there had been a . . . sudden increase in tendencies by people in many countries and many circumstances to insist on the significance of their group distinctiveness" (Glazer and Moynihan 1975, p. 3). At the same time, the 1970s witnessed a concurrent growth in various types of feminist movements, which had the effect of politicizing the *gender* of individuals. These developments made it manifestly clear that ascriptive forms of solidarity continue to be salient in modern industrial societies.

The radical response to this evidence was to proclaim that the ascriptive factors of race, ethnicity, or gender are the driving forces behind further social development. In their latest formulation, Glazer and Moynihan (1975) conclude that "property relations [formerly] obscured ethnic ones" (p. 16), but now it is "property that begins to seem derivative, and ethnicity that seems to become a more fundamental source of stratification" (p. 17). There is, of course, an analogous position within the field of gender stratification; the "radical wing" within feminist circles has long argued for the "primacy of men's dominance over women as the cornerstone on which all other oppression (class, age, race) rests" (Hartmann 1981, p. 12; Firestone 1972). It should be noted, however, that the latter formulations beg the question of timing; after all, if the forces of ethnicity or gender are truly primordial, it is natural to ask why they only began expressing themselves with relative vigor in recent decades. In addressing this issue, Bell (1975) has suggested that a trade-off exists between class-based and ethnic forms of solidarity, with the latter strengthening as the former weaken. With the institutionalization of industrial conflict in modern societies (i.e., the rise of "trade unionism"), Bell argues that class-based affiliations gradually lost their *moral* or *affective* content; it was ethnic groups, then, that filled the gap by providing individuals with a new sense of identification and commitment (see Olzak 1983 for a comprehensive review of competing theories). It might be added that for some individuals it was gender politics that apparently filled the "moral vacuum" (Parkin 1979, p. 34) brought about by the weakening of class-based ties.

It may be misleading, of course, to treat the competition between ascriptive and class-based forces as a sociological horse race in which one, and only one, of these two principles can ultimately win out. In a pluralist society of the American kind, workers can *choose* an identity appropriate to the situational context; a modern-day individual might behave as "an industrial worker in the morning, a black in the afternoon, and an American in the evening" (Parkin 1979, p. 34). Although this "situational model" of status has not been widely adopted in contemporary research, there is nontheless an emerging tendency among scholars to take into account the multiple affiliations of individuals. The preferred approach, especially among feminist theorists, is to assume that the major status groupings in contemporary societies are defined by the *intersection* of ethnic, gender, or class-based affiliations (e.g., black working-class women, white middle-class men, etc.). The theoretical framework motivating this approach is not always well-articulated, but the implicit claim seems to be that these subgroupings shape the "life chances and experiences" of individuals (Ransford and Miller 1983, p. 46) and define the social settings in which subcultures typically emerge (also, see Gordon 1978; Baltzell 1964). The obvious effect of this approach is to invert the traditional post-Weberian perspective on status groupings; indeed, whereas orthodox multidimensionalists described the stress experienced by individuals in inconsistent statuses (e.g., poorly-educated doctors), these new multidimensionalists emphasize the shared cultures generated within commonly encountered status sets (e.g., black working-class women).

The popularity of this revised form of multidimensionalism reflects, at least in part, a growing dissatisfaction with classical sociological theories that take the nuclear family to be the elementary unit of stratification (e.g., Parsons 1954). As was noted earlier, the "conventional model" of class represents the stratification system as a graded hierarchy of households, with the socioeconomic standing of all household members (e.g., wives) determined by the occupation or employment status of the family head. While most scholars agree that this model has been serviceable in describing past stratification systems, there is some concern that it no longer adequately represents the life chances and class situation of women

in advanced industrial societies. Among the various positions that have emerged in this debate, the following ones have achieved some prominence:

1. According to some scholars, the conventional class system is receding in significance, and the *individual* is emerging as the new "elementary unit" of stratification. This revolution in class structure and identification is typically linked to the breakdown of the nuclear family, the growth of an autonomous female labor force, and the rise of individualist values (e.g., Szelényi 1988; also, see Davis and Robinson 1988).

2. At the other end of the continuum, Britten and Heath (1983) continue to see the nuclear family as the basic unit of stratification, yet they modify the conventional model by taking into account the work situation of *both* husbands and wives. This approach makes it possible to identify and describe various types of "cross-class families" in which the husband and wife work in different class situations.

3. The conventional model has also been defended in its original form (e.g., Goldthorpe 1983). Although this defense has been waged on a variety of fronts, the main point emphasized by Goldthorpe (1983) and others (e.g., Giddens 1973, p. 288) is that the male head still makes the *principal* commitment to paid employment, whereas the female spouse typically enters the labor force in "an intermittent and limited" fashion (Goldthrope 1983, p. 481). The implication, therefore, is that ongoing changes in female labor force participation have not undermined the conventional model to the extent that some critics have supposed.

Within American sociology, the first of these three positions has become the *de facto* standard; it is now common practice to carry out virtually all types of stratification analysis with separate male and female subsamples. The analytic assumptions underlying these analyses are not typically spelled out, but it would be difficult indeed to reconcile this form of subsampling with a conventional class model in its original or modified form.

GENERATING STRATIFICATION

The language of stratification research makes a sharp distinction between the structure of *socioeconomic inequality* (i.e., the "class structure") and the structure of *opportunities* by which individuals are allocated into differential outcomes (i.e., the "opportunity structure"). Whereas most Americans are willing to tolerate sizable inequalities in the distribution of resources, they typically insist that individuals from all backgrounds should have an equal opportunity to secure these resources. It might be said, then, that our primary interest rests in "running the race fairly" rather than equalizing the rewards distributed at the finish line (see, e.g., Hochschild 1981; Kluegel and Smith 1986). Whatever the wisdom of this logic might be, sociologists have long sought to explore its factual underpinnings; there is a substantial body of research that seeks to measure the objective opportunities for mobility against our shared expectations for a "fair race." This research agenda might be operationalized in various ways; the standard starting point, however, is to construct a mobility table that cross-classifies the occupational origins and destinations of individuals. Although most of the current research has focused on parent-child comparisons ("intergenerational mobility"), there is also a parallel tradition of work examining the contours of mobility within the life course of individuals ("intragenerational mobility"). These various types of mobility tables have served as the "anvil for sociological craftwork since the days when blacksmiths outnumbered social scientists" (Breiger 1981, p. 604).

It is no easy task to analyze tables of this kind. As is often the case, substantive issues turn on technical matters; the history of mobility research is marked by methodological signposts as much as substantive ones. The driving force behind these methodological developments has been the long-standing attempt to distinguish between *structural* and *circulation* mobility. This conceptual distinction derives, of course, from the well-known fact that social mobility is generated by structural shifts in the shape of the class structure as well as

underlying patterns of exchange between classes (see Duncan 1966 for details and qualifications). The former component is often regarded as a nuisance factor, whereas the latter pertains to the openness of the mobility regime and the contours of class-based differences in life chances. While the verbal distinction between structural and circulation mobility is easy to maintain, it turns out to be difficult to represent this distinction in formal models of the mobility regime. It was only with the emergence of log-linear modeling in the early 1970s that the fundamental problem of "structurally induced" mobility was finally solved (see, e.g., Goodman 1972; Hauser 1978; Hout 1983; Sobel, Hout, and Duncan 1985).

The descriptive power of this approach is best demonstrated by turning directly to an illustrative analysis based on a major survey of stratification outcomes and processes (see Featherman and Hauser 1978). The densities plotted in Figure 1 (see pp. 1966–1967) refer to patterns of career mobility over the period between the point of first entry into the labor force ("first occupation") and the time when the survey was administered ("current occupation"). As indicated in the stub to this figure, the rows and columns of the matrix index the origin and destination occupations, and the vertical dimension maps the estimated densities of career persistence and mobility for our sample of American males (see Stier and Grusky 1990 for further details). The height of the bars refers to the relative likelihood of persistence or mobility after the structural forces of occupational supply and demand have been purged from the data. The topography of this simple figure suggests the following five conclusions:

1. The towering peaks on the main diagonal testify to the strength of occupational persistence within the life course. The farming peak, for example, indicates that workers originating as farmers are 69.7 times more likely to remain in that occupation than to move to the top of the class structure (Stier and Grusky 1990, p. 747).

2. The clustering on the main diagonal follows a

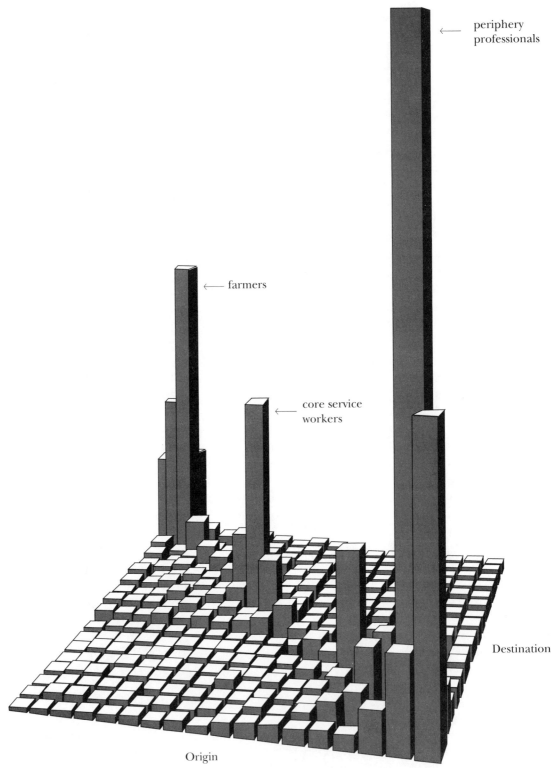

FIGURE 1

Densities of Mobility and Immobility for an 18 × 18 Intragenerational Table.

W-shaped pattern. Although the tallest peaks are found at the two extremes of the hierarchy, a set of secondary peaks emerge in the center of the class structure. This result indicates that *some* sectors of the middle class (i.e., service sectors) are relatively successful in retaining their incumbents.

3. The strength of the manual-nonmanual divide reveals itself in a low-lying ridge marking out the northwest and southeast quadrants. At the top of each ridge, the mobility data form a broad plateau; the height of these plateaus speak to the "holding power" of the manual and nonmanual strata.

4. The distribution of destination points for long-distance movers is surprisingly uniform. The valleys in the northeast and southwest quadrants are flat and uncontoured; there is no evidence, then, of a "distance gradient" that channels long-distance movers into the closest occupations.

5. The design matrix is symmetric around the main diagonal. The implication is that patterns of occupational inflow and outflow are identical once the structural forces of supply and demand are controlled (see Hauser 1981).

Taken as a whole, the figure suggests a broad valley rising into a pair of low-lying plains, with the plains then rising into a jagged mountain ridge that cuts across the valley (see Featherman and Hauser 1978 for a similar description). While this overall picture can be generated under a wide range of log-linear specifications (Stier and Grusky 1990), it is always possible to devise competing models that yield somewhat different interpretations (see, e.g., MacDonald 1981). These differences have generated a continuing debate over the merits or shortcomings of particular types of log-linear models (e.g., Pöntinen 1982; Grusky and Hauser 1984; Kim 1987).

It should be emphasized that the preceding figure can only be used to characterize the structure of male career mobility in the early 1970s. Although the available evidence suggests a "family resemblance" in the basic topology of all mobility regimes, it is clear that systematic variations in the contours of mobility can also be found. The last decade of stratification research has been devoted, in large part, to documenting the structure of these differences across subpopulations defined by nation, region, gender, race, or time (e.g., Hout 1984; Grusky and Hauser 1984). The latter research effort has been complemented by a parallel stream of research focusing on the mediating variables (e.g., education) that account for the origin-by-destination association in a mobility table. It could well be argued that these two subfields are producing new findings "faster and more furiously . . . than any other [subfields] in sociology" (Hout 1984, p. 1379).

(SEE ALSO: *Ethnicity; Income Distribution in the United States; Marxist Sociology; Occupational Prestige; Slavery and Involuntary Servitude; Social Mobility; Socialism; Societal Stratification; Status Attainment*)

REFERENCES

Baltzell, Edward Digby 1964 *The Protestant Establishment.* New York: Random House.

Barber, Bernard 1968 "Social Stratification." In D. L. Sills, ed., *International Encyclopedia of the Social Sciences.* New York: Macmillan and Free Press.

Baron, James N. 1992 "Reflections on Recent Generations of Mobility Research." In David B. Grusky, ed.,

FIGURE NOTE: The origin axis indexes "first occupations" and the destination axis indexes "current occupations." Moving from left to right on the origin axis, the occupational categories are ordered as follows: farm laborers, farmers, periphery laborers, core laborers, periphery operatives, core operatives, periphery service, core service, periphery crafts, core crafts, periphery clerical, core clerical, periphery sales, core sales, periphery managers, core managers, periphery professionals, and core professionals. The ordering is identical for the destination axis (moving from top to bottom). The persistence ratio for periphery professionals has been reduced by one-third for purposes of presentation. See Stier and Grusky (1990) for details.

Social Stratification: Class, Race, and Gender in Sociological Perspective. Boulder, Colo.: Westview.

Beck, Ulrich 1987 "Beyond Status and Class: Will There be an Individualized Class Society?" In Volker Meja, Dieter Misgeld, and Nico Stehr, eds., *Modern German Sociology.* New York: Columbia University Press.

Bell, Daniel 1975. "Ethnicity and Social Change." In Nathan Glazer and Daniel P. Moynihan, eds., *Ethnicity: Theory and Experience.* Cambridge: Harvard University Press.

Bottomore, Thomas B. 1965 *Classes in Modern Society.* London: Allen and Unwin.

Braverman, Harry 1974 *Labor and Monopoly Capital.* New York: Monthly Review Press.

Breiger, Ronald L. 1981 "The Social Class Structure of Occupational Mobility." *American Journal of Sociology* 87:578–611.

Britten, Nicky, and Anthony Heath 1983 "Women, Men and Social Class." In Eva Gamarnikow, David H. J. Morgan, June Purvis, and Daphne E. Taylorson, eds., *Gender, Class and Work.* London: Heinemann.

Broom, Leonard, and Robert G. Cushing 1977 "A Modest Test of an Immodest Theory: The Functional Theory of Stratification." *American Sociological Review* 42 (1):157–169.

Cullen, John B., and Shelley M. Novick 1979 "The Davis-Moore Theory of Stratification: A Further Examination and Extension." *American Journal of Sociology* 84 (6):1424–1437.

Davis, Kingsley 1948 *Human Society.* New York: Macmillan.

——— 1953 "Reply." *American Sociological Review* 18:394–397.

Davis, Kingsley, and Wilbert E. Moore 1945 "Some Principles of Stratification." *American Sociological Review* 10:242–249.

Davis, Nancy J., and Robert V. Robinson. 1988 "Class Identification of Men and Women in the 1970s and 1980s." *American Sociological Review* 53:103–112.

Djilas, Milovan 1965 *The New Class.* New York: Praeger.

Duncan, Otis Dudley 1961 "A Socioeconomic Index for All Occupations." In Albert J. Reiss, Jr., ed., *Occupations and Social Status.* New York: Free Press.

——— 1966 "Methodological Issues in the Analysis of Social Mobility." In Neil J. Smelser and Seymour M. Lipset, eds., *Social Structure and Mobility in Economic Development.* Chicago: Aldine.

Featherman, David L., and Robert M. Hauser 1978 *Opportunity and Change.* New York: Academic.

Firestone, Shulamith 1972 *The Dialectic of Sex.* New York: Bantam.

Gagliani, Giorgio 1981 "How Many Working Classes?" *American Journal of Sociology* 87:259–285.

Giddens, Anthony 1973 *The Class Structure of the Advanced Societies.* London: Hutchinson.

Glazer, Nathan, and Daniel P. Moynihan 1975 "Introduction." In Nathan Glazer and Daniel P. Moynihan, eds., *Ethnicity: Theory and Experience.* Cambridge: Harvard University Press.

Goldthorpe, John H. 1980 *Social Mobility and Class Structure in Modern Britain.* Oxford, England: Clarendon Press.

——— 1983 "Women and Class Analysis: In Defence of the Conventional View." *Sociology* 17: 465–488.

Goodman, Leo A. 1972 "Some Multiplicative Models for the Analysis of Cross-Classified Data." In *Proceedings of the Sixth Berkeley Symposium on Mathematical Statistics and Probability.* Berkeley: University of California Press.

Gordon, Milton M. 1978 *Human Nature, Class, and Ethnicity.* New York: Oxford University Press.

Gouldner, Alvin 1979 *The Future of Intellectuals and the Rise of the New Class.* New York: Seabury.

Grusky, David B., and Robert M. Hauser 1984 "Comparative Social Mobility Revisited: Models of Convergence and Divergence in 16 Countries." *American Sociological Review* 49:19–38.

Hartmann, Heidi 1981 "The Unhappy Marriage of Marxism and Feminism: Towards a More Progressive Union." In Lydia Sargent, ed., *Women and Revolution.* Boston: South End Press.

Hauser, Robert M. 1978 "A Structural Model of the Mobility Table." *Social Forces* 56: 919–953.

——— 1981 "Hope for the Mobility Ratio." *Social Forces* 60:572–584.

Hochschild, Jennifer L. 1981 *What's Fair? American Beliefs about Distributive Justice.* Cambridge: Harvard University Press.

Hout, Michael 1983 *Mobility Tables.* Beverly Hills: Sage.

——— 1984 "Status, Autonomy, and Training in Occupational Mobility." *American Journal of Sociology* 89:1379–1409.

Huaco, George A. 1966. "The Functionalist Theory of Stratification: Two Decades of Controversy." *Inquiry* 9:215–240.

Jackson, Elton F., and Richard F. Curtis 1972 "Effects of Vertical Mobility and Status Inconsistency: A Body of Negative Evidence." *American Sociological Review* 37:701–713.

Kelley, Jonathan 1981 *Revolution and the Rebirth of Inequality.* Berkeley: University of California Press.

Kim, Jae-On 1987 "Social Mobility, Status Inheritance, and Structural Constraints: Conceptual and Methodological Considerations." *Social Forces* 65:783–805.

Kluegel, James R., and Eliot R. Smith 1986 *Beliefs About Inequality: Americans' Views of What Is and What Ought to Be.* New York: Aldine.

Landecker, Werner S. 1960 "Class Boundaries." *American Sociological Review* 25:868–877.

Lenski, Gerhard E. 1952 "American Social Classes: Statistical Strata or Social Group?" *American Journal of Sociology* 58:139–144.

——— 1954 "Status Crystallization: A Non-vertical Dimension of Social Status." *American Sociological Review* 19:405–413.

——— 1966 *Power and Privilege.* New York: McGraw-Hill.

——— 1978 "Marxist Experiments in Destratification: An Appraisal." *Social Forces* 57:364–383.

——— 1992 "New Light on Old Issues: The Relevance of 'Really Existing Socialist Societies' for Stratification Theory." In David B. Grusky, ed., *Social Stratification: Class, Race, and Gender in Sociological Perspective*, Boulder, Colo.: Westview.

Levy, Marion, Jr., 1966 *Modernization and the Structure of Societies.* Princeton, N.J.: Princeton University Press.

Lipset, Seymour Martin 1959 *Political Man: The Social Bases of Politics.* Baltimore, Md.: Johns Hopkins University Press.

MacDonald, K. I. 1981 "On the Formulation of a Structural Model of the Mobility Table." *Social Forces* 60:557–571.

Marx, Karl (1894) 1972 *Capital,* 3 vols. London: Lawrence and Wishart.

Mayer, Kurt B., and Walter Buckley 1970 *Class and Society.* New York: Random House.

Moore, Wilbert E. 1963a "But Some Are More Equal Than Others." *American Sociological Review* 28:13–28.

——— 1963b "Rejoinder." *American Sociological Review* 28:27.

Olzak, Susan 1983 "Contemporary Ethnic Mobilization." *Annual Review of Sociology* 9:355–374.

Ossowski, Stanislaw 1963 *Class Structure in the Social Consciousness.* New York: Free Press.

Parkin, Frank 1979 *Marxism and Class Theory: A Bourgeois Critique.* New York: Columbia University Press.

Parsons, Talcott 1954 *Essays in Sociological Theory.* Glencoe, Ill.: Free Press.

Pöntinen, Seppo 1982 "Models and Social Mobility Research: A Comparison of Some Log-Linear Models of a Social Mobility Matrix." *Quality and Quantity* 16:91–107.

Poulantzas, Nicos 1974 *Classes in Contemporary Capitalism.* London: Verso.

Ransford, H. Edward, and Jon Miller 1983 "Race, Sex and Feminist Outlooks." *American Sociological Review* 48:46–59.

Runciman, Walter G. 1974 "Towards a Theory of Social Stratification." In Frank Parkin, ed., *The Social Analysis of Class Structure.* London: Tavistock.

Siegel, Paul M. 1971 *Prestige in the American Occupational Structure.* Unpublished Ph.D. dissertation, University of Chicago.

Sobel, Michael E., Michael Hout, and Otis D. Duncan 1985 "Exchange, Structure, and Symmetry in Occupational Mobility." *American Journal of Sociology* 91:359–372.

Steinmetz, George, and Erik O. Wright 1989 "The Fall and Rise of the Petty Bourgeoisie: Changing Patterns of Self-Employment in the Postwar United States." *American Journal of Sociology* 94:973–1018.

Stier, Haya, and David B. Grusky 1990 "An Overlapping Persistence Model of Career Mobility." *American Sociological Review* 55:736–756.

Szelényi, Ivan 1992 "Post-industrialism, Post-communism, and the New Class." In David B. Grusky, ed., *Social Stratification: Class, Race, and Gender in Sociological Perspective.* Boulder, Colo.: Westview.

Szelényi, Szonja 1988 "Economic Subsystems and the Occupational Structure," Unpublished paper, Dept. of Sociology, Stanford University.

Treiman, Donald J. 1977 *Occupational Prestige in Comparative Perspective.* New York: Academic.

Tumin, Melvin M. 1953 "Some Principles of Stratification: A Critical Analysis." *American Sociological Review* 18:378–394.

Warner, W. Lloyd 1949 *Social Class in America.* Chicago: Science Research Associates.

Weber, Max (1922) 1968 *Economy and Society.* Berkeley: University of California Press.

Wesolowski, Wlodzimierz 1962 "Some Notes on the Functional Theory of Stratification." *Polish Sociological Bulletin* 3–4:28–38.

Westergaard, John, and Henrietta Resler 1975 *Class in a Capitalist Society: A Study of Contemporary Britain.* London: Heinemann.

Wright, Erik O. 1978 *Class, Crisis, and the State.* London: New Left Books.

——— *Class Structure and Income Determination.* New York: Academic.

——— 1985 *Classes.* London: Verso.

Wright, Erik O., Cynthia Costello, David Hachen, and Joey Sprague 1982. "The American Class Structure." *American Sociological Review* 47:709–726.

Wrong, Dennis H. 1959 "The Functional Theory of Stratification: Some Neglected Considerations." *American Sociological Review* 24:772–782.

DAVID B. GRUSKY
AZUMI ANN TAKATA

SOCIAL STRUCTURE *Social structure* is a general term for any collective social circumstance that is unalterable and given for the individual. Social structure thus provides a context or environment for action. The size of organizations, distribution of activities in space, shared language, and the distribution of wealth might all be regarded as social structural circumstances that set limits on feasible activities for individuals.

Social structure is objective in the sense that it is the same for all and is beyond the capacity for alteration by any individual will. Accordingly, social structure is often spoken of in the singular and as a thing apart, as if there is but one social structure, from whose effects no one can escape. Such usage masks disagreement about the exact extension of the term and reflects the intent of authors to highlight abstract patterns as an inflexible collective circumstance to which individuals must adapt.

Social structure, or the weaker structural regularities, arise because of the prevalence of social routine. Many social patterns change very slowly, either through unmotivated inertia, through willful efforts to renew or reproduce them, or as a collective consequence of individual efforts undertaken for independent reasons. An image or picture, such as a map colored by the linguistic practices of the inhabitants of geographic areas, will lose accuracy slowly but might still be somewhat valid after a century or more. Such substantial durability and accompanying slow, continuous change suggest the possibility that regularities or even scientific laws govern the phenomena underlying the description.

Routines endure, and structural regularities persist, for at least three general reasons. Social life is subject to physical constraints like distance. Thus, most people live close to where they work, if indeed living and working are spatially separated. For related reasons, many persons maintain stable residences. Furthermore, many people need or desire the company or cooperation of representative social types such as those sharing religious convictions or particular work skills. Accordingly, one can associate social attributes with geographical maps. This was a central activity of the Chicago school of sociology (Park and Burgess 1924) and gave rise to the perspective of human ecology (Hawley 1986). The location of particular social types and activities in particular places is subject to powerful incentives that induce continuity in the face of turnover by individuals. For example, ethnic concentrations result in specialized facilities, like food shops, that attract replacements that conserve the ethnic character of a neighborhood. Such patterns often persist beyond the lifetimes of the people that participate in them.

A second source of routine is limited learning capacity or the complexity of many social activities. Linguistic rules, moral codes, and work skills are examples of social capacities whose acquisition requires considerable time and effort. Such socialization often requires extended exposure to others who know the routines well, especially where the delicate skills of interpretation are involved.

The difficulties of acquiring capacity can confound individual wills. Bernstein (1975) described how linguistic conventions, acquired in the home, reflect the conditions of adult work and render individuals unsuited for occupations that are not similar to those of their parents. In the same way, a New Yorker who wished to speak in Latin would first have to make a huge investment in learning a novel linguistic code. But this would not undo the investment in English by other New Yorkers, which makes Latin impractical for directing taxi drivers. Similar reasons impel newcomers to adopt the abrasive social style of New Yorkers. The general principle is that most people must adapt to many surrounding ways of doing because these change so slowly.

A third source of structural regularity is laws governing averages. One example is the suicide rates studied by Durkheim. People commit suicide for a variety of personal motives, and the act is never repeated by anyone. Yet the frequency of the act is fairly stable over time and stably different among different populations. This is because variable causes tend to average into stable totals whenever many instances are drawn from constant underlying conditions. Many of the social rates that result are sufficiently stable to sustain plans and projections, which in turn can be embedded in routines, even though the underlying activity is incredibly complex in its detailed causation.

The several sources of stable routine underlie properties frequently associated with proposed structural regularities. Structural regularities are often seen as abstract, enduring, and operative across a large scale of units because they build on the history of routines that made large scale feasible. For example, Tilly (1975) has shown how the modern European state resulted from similar decisions by state-makers forced by military competition to pursue centralization by reordering established routines of ordinary folk. The history of collective contention (Tilly 1986) can be seen as the efforts of the victims to defend older patterns against intrusions by state agents like tax collectors and against the vast reorganization of work and fortune implicit in the expansion of capitalism.

Mann (1986) has argued that large-scale cooperation rests on enduring patterns of power. For example, shared religious ideology is a form of power since it makes people subject to claims on their activity. Rapid religious change is not infrequently the result of conquest. Once established, religion is often compulsory. Coercion aside, religious conformity can be a safeguard against the risks and pains of social isolation. Other large-scale patterns, like the division of labor, are maintained in the face of considerable shifting by persons among different roles. This is often implemented by powerful actors motivated to induce

(or coerce) approximate substitutes to fill in for those who withdraw (or die). In such terms, abstract stability, large scale, and consequent duration can often be seen to be sustained through underlying causal regularities. In human terms, the reproduction of social structure is a myriad of modest efforts that sum to a stable result.

This interdependence underlies the transcendence of abstract structural regularity over individual will. Generally, one cannot learn more than locally applicable routines and must rely on others for critical needs. Thus, one assumes that the staff of the emergency room will not all take the day off. This frees accountants from the necessity of acquiring medical skill to meet their own needs. As a result, the details of actual routines are only known locally, and the only possible knowledge of the overall pattern is coarse or abstract. Even accountants cannot count up the details they must count on. A further implication is that the alternatives to enacting the routines with which one is familiar are often quite limited. It requires time on a historical scale to construct such a pattern. Once it is in motion, most people would be in a terrible fix if the conditions that made their limited learning practical were suddenly to cease.

A special case of social routines are those worked out with others, who are then more or less hard to replace. Such social relations can be mapped as social networks describing the pattern of links that surround individuals. The analysis of such patterns is not infrequently (or unreasonably) called *structural analysis,* though this restricted sense hardly exhausts the term.

Routines, and especially relations, are subject to pressures to isomorphy, which means common anatomy or structure. One example is the formation of families, which are different in detail but share common features partly in response to common problems to be solved within a shared environment. Goode (1970) analyzed the sources and consequences of such regularities. In modern societies, assumptions about such features are often written into administrative procedures such as tax codes, which provide further impetus for individuals to adopt some variant of the pattern defined as normal. Changing and varied individual desires are often in tension with such pressures to cooperate in the reproduction of the supposed "normal" pattern.

Emergent properties that apply to wholes but not to parts are often attributed to social structure. Some properties, like size distributions or complexity, do not have direct individual analogs. Others arise because the net result of many partially independent actions can be different from the intent of individuals. Thus, markets with many participants can experience crashes in value when many try to sell in anticipation that others are about to do so, producing a result that no one desires. Kindleberger (1980) describes the recurrence of such crises. Routines are executed by people, are only locally adapted, somewhat independent, and imperfectly flexible. Many properties of the resulting averages or combinations do not follow from the components in any simple sense.

One counterpart of emergence is the difficulty of much social engineering. Since the exact nature of local routines is usually unknown, it is no small feat to supply sufficient detail to make alternatives practical. Enforcing the learning and practice of such detail is still another problem. A simple command to meet an abstract goal can then be futile. For example, many people could not obey an order to cease gender discrimination, since they are not necessarily conscious of which elements of their routines contribute to the aggregate result. Many would see the novelty as inconsistent with other objectives, and such judgments leave ample latitude for concealing bad faith. In extreme cases, the only realistic course is replacement of those committed to old routines by persons familiar with newer ones, and this process could require socialization of a whole new generation.

As the preceding suggests, structural visions are quite various. One unifying theme is an appeal to abstract, extraindividual patterns that change slowly or even not at all. A second unifying theme is that such regularities cause or condition many of the choices and much of the behavior of individuals. A final common theme is less unifying than divisive. Some structural visions are accompanied by claims of centrality. A particular array of simple elements is proclaimed, often on metatheoretical or philosophic grounds, to be the central deep structure whose inevitable unfolding underlies an astonishing array of surface appearances. Such comprehensive views have inspired competing, incompatible schools of thought on whose behalf claim is sometimes laid to *the* structural vision of society or of the human condition.

Most of these structural visions are comprehensive world views that require detailed study in their own right. Among the most prominent are those of Marx and Freud, but there have been structuralist movements in nearly every field of social studies. Nearly all proceed from some highly abstract characterization of the human mind, laws of thought, or human condition. All of social or mental life is viewed as a manifestation of the reproduction of such elements, often unfolding dialectically. This is presented as the inevitable underpinnings of individual or collective biographies. Piaget (1970) has provided an unusually concise description of an interdisciplinary structuralism based on mathematical progress; this description parallels his more famous theory of discontinuous advance in human cognitive development. Originators and their descendants often delight in such subtle and insightful reductions of familiar patterns to the chosen central supports.

The term *structure* is most commonly employed in sociology without such comprehensive connotations. In empirical sociology, especially quantitative studies based on random samples of persons, the term is invoked for quite varied efforts to use the larger, often more durable, features of social life as explanatory factors for individual conduct and outcomes. The most common contrast is with individual level causes, including attitudes and aspirations. Sometimes attributes such as race, gender, and class are labeled structural to imply that the underlying mechanism is an external force imposed on individuals independent of their wills.

The reasoning behind this is not always explicit, but the usage is justifiable. Generally speaking, the factors labeled structural are alternatives among a differentiated array of possibilities to which individuals are confined for substantial periods. "Structure" then refers to differentiating average conditions within which people live out their lives. At least implicitly, such differences correspond to differences in the routines employed to adapt to local conditions. Classifying people by indicators of the local conditions that surround them reflects the opportunities that they have for association and hence for processes such as influence, cooperation, and victimization. Some characterizations also correspond to labels, most notably race and gender, and broadly indicate common tendencies in routines by others to which one is likely to be exposed. Such differences are quite stable, impersonal, and unavoidable. Taken together, such differences in conditions contribute to differences in average responses or individual behavior.

Some confusion is evident about the nature of such structural causation. It is often framed as an alternative explanation to individual choice. Persuasive force often comes from stories in which the more common outcome appears inevitable. This is at odds with the normal empirical result of a difference in rates. Rules that hold without exception are rare. This should be expected. Structural abstractions mask much detail that varies. The implicit reference is to averages over multiple executions of complex routines. To take one obvious example, racial discrimination over job applicants is not invariant but occurs often enough to lead to considerable differences.

Structural causes are not literally an antithesis of individual choice. More precisely, they reflect patterns over which individuals have limited control. Yet within those patterns, considerable options remain for individual responses. It is not appropriate to think of structural regularities as eliminating choice but as a narrowing of alternatives that leads to a different range, and average, of responses for people in different average conditions.

Such empirical applications generally draw on fragments of social structure taken as conditioning factors for particular outcomes. The larger challenge is to translate the impersonal, durable complexity of stable differences of condition into

a formal calculus, or theory of social structure. Talcott Parsons's extensive analysis of the logic of social systems was an early and seminal attempt. His student Robert Merton, under the banner of "theories of the middle range," provided a more easily applied set of general tools for structural analysis. Several of Merton's students, including Raymond Boudon, Peter Blau, and James Coleman, have further developed formal calculi that take advantage of mathematical tools.

Parsons's complex system begins with the conditions for stabilizing interaction, or, in present terms, for meshing routines. He characterized the routines governing choice as extended chains of logic linking means to ends. At their most abstract, such chains are anchored in ultimate ends or values. Durable stability comes from consensus on the values that are installed in individuals by more or less extended socialization.

In Parsons's view, the logical chains governing decision making were morally potent norms or rules governing social conduct. The durable web shaping individual choice was therefore the complex of norms animated by the anchoring ultimate values. He imposed on this a logical calculus of the different functions necessary for ensuring that the pattern was resistant to shocks drawing it away from equilibrium. A concomitant of this theme of differentiation was complementary specialization in distinct but interdependent expectations bundled into social roles enacted by different players.

Parsons's calculus of the functional necessities of meshing differentiated normative specifications proved widely compelling but not easy to apply. His presentation is notoriously hard to read. Applications of the scheme usually consisted of classifying normative elements into taxonomies delimiting functional contributions. These qualitative operations were by no means mechanical nor easily communicated as a stable procedure such that different investigators would reach identical results. This rendered moot the possibility of generating conclusions from initial conditions by application of formal tools. In a similar way, while many were inclined to agree that Parsons's system illuminated how a social system governed by logic over normative rules might work, it was less than evident that concrete social systems had such logical coherence.

Merton's (1968) "theories of the middle range" provided a more readily applicable set of tools. Like Parsons, Merton proposed that the enduring regularities making up social structure were normatively defined. But instead of attempting to calculate over extended normative webs, he drew attention to the implications of positions. Thus, he emphasized that roles placed individuals in relations with concrete others or that membership in groups, both present and anticipated, provided reference points for calculating comparisons of expectations and outcomes. Unlike Parsons's more elaborate concerns, Merton's lent themselves to the construction and interpretation of surveys and other manageable research projects.

Merton did not assume, as Parsons did, that norms and roles could be divined from an overarching logic. More frequently, he treated norms as empirical concomitants of lay distinctions among different roles or group memberships. This can be viewed as one central motivation for the common use of structural concepts outlined above. But Merton more often used factual (or readily inferred) norms grounded in different stable positions to highlight dilemmas. Concrete people could be understood as facing practical problems of resolving competing, often contrary, normative standards. This strategy of framing the practical problem as the resolution of contrary expectations frequently leads to insight into choices that at first sight seem senseless or even self-defeating.

Merton's analyses rested on qualitative inferences, often turning on the meaning of norms. One of Merton's students, Boudon (1982), has provided formulations where social structure refers to numerically definite distributions so that the implications of such extraindividual constraints emerge from formal calculations. For example, he posits an array of young persons, committed to personal advance, who undertake investments in education. Yet when all do what is individually sensible, the collective result illustrates Merton's unintended consequences. If there is a fixed and therefore scarce supply of desired positions that will go to those who achieve the most education, many of those who strive to invest will discover that their efforts are frustrated by the simultaneous striving by others. Boudon has provided many illustrations of the perverse effects that can obtain when individual motive operates against a backdrop of a fixed system of positions.

Another of Merton's students, Blau (1977), has presented a deductive structural theory based on the notion that social structure consists of arrays of positions, which he called parameters. He divided differentiation into two types, among unranked or nominal categories, such as religion, and among continuous arrays of ranked positions that differ in amounts of some scarce and valued resource. The distribution of individuals over positions gives rise to numerical properties of whole social structures, including the heterogeneity of nominal differences, the inequality among ranks, and consolidation versus intersection or the degree of correlation versus independence of positions on separate dimensions.

Blau's concept of social structure leads to differences in the sizes of collections of individuals occupying different positions. Size, in turn, strongly conditions the rate of interaction, or social association. More differentiated structures result in higher rates of intergroup association, and Blau argues that this would lead to the successful meshing of routines, or social integration. The intersection of different dimensions, which results in even smaller subgroups defined by multiple positions, would also enhance social integration. Conversely, the consolidation of dimensions, homogeneity rather than heterogeneity, will diminish rates of intergroup contact and hence hinder social integration. Inequality is a special case that illustrates Blau's taste for paradoxical results. Greater inequality leads to smaller strata and fosters intergroup relations, but these often take the form of interpersonal conflict, including crime (Blau and Blau 1982).

Blau's notions are particularly suitable for research application because his notion of structure more or less directly corresponds to widely used operationalizations such as gender, race, ethnicity, religion, occupational rank, and wealth. Of course, these are social constructs and in some final analysis defined by norms and other ideal elements. At the same time, they are for most people most of the time, subject to slow (or even no) change. This sustains the usefulness of a numerical calculus resting on the notion that size is an objective, impersonal, and durable reality.

The most recent effort to specify social structure as a mathematically tractable map of interdependence is by Coleman (1990). He posits actors with rights of control over their own actions and over tangible things desired by others or resources. His actors maximize the achievement of their desires by exchanging their control in return for what others control. The result, in general, is an equilibrium, where initial control in conjunction with the desires of others produces differential power. Within this apparatus, Coleman is able to provide a quite rigorous analysis of the emergence of larger-scale phenomena including groups, norms, and corporate actors.

Though these various accounts lie along a single path of intellectual descent, there is a major divide with respect to the elemental nature of social structure. For Parsons, it was an interdependent complex of norms. Unfortunately, there does not exist at present any way to formalize or calculate the mutual implications in a web of symbolic elements. The later analysts who have gone much farther in rendering complexity calculable have done so from "hard" assumptions that take social structure from the outset as a set of objective positions (with objective properties) so that size, distribution, rates of exchange, and so forth can be treated mathematically.

One noteworthy, shared deficiency is that none of the formal theories illuminates how such "hard" properties come into being. They therefore leave open issues of variability and interpretive options (or meaning) that others see as fundamental. Indeed, some authors believe human judgment is distinctive and that no mechanical analog or simulation of human society (Habermas 1987) or human cognition (Penrose 1989) will ever be possible.

In sum, there is not yet any widely accepted set of notions that capture all of the properties that have been seen as fundamental to the concept of social structure. The huge catalog of demonstrated effects of structural regularities cannot yet be organized in any tidy way. Enthusiasm for the different attempts to represent the concept in compact terms varies widely. Sufficiently close attention to the details of competing claims could convince one that no shared subject is really at issue. Like the analysis of social structure itself, it is necessary carefully to select the right degree of abstraction and appropriate pattern of highlighting to discern any common pattern in the competing pictures, but there is nevertheless pattern there to be found.

(SEE ALSO: *Complex Organizations; Organizational Structure; Social Organization*)

REFERENCES

Bernstein, Basil 1975 *Class, Codes, and Control.* New York: Schocken Books.

Blau, Judith, and Peter Blau 1982 "The Cost of Inequality: Metropolitan Structure and Violent Crime." *American Sociological Review* 47:114–129.

Blau, Peter 1977 *Inequality and Heterogeneity.* New York: Academic Press.

Boudon, Raymond 1982 *The Unintended Consequences of Social Action.* New York: St. Martin's.

Coleman, James S. 1990 *Foundations of Social Theory.* Cambridge, Mass.: Harvard University Press.

Goode, William J. 1970 *World Revolution in Family Patterns.* New York: Free Press.

Habermas, Jurgen 1987 *The Theory of Communicative Action,* vol. 2, *Lifeworld and System: A Critique of Functionalist Reason.* Boston: Beacon Press.

Hawley, Amos 1986 *Human Ecology.* Chicago: University of Chicago Press.

Kindleberger, Charles 1980 *Panics, Manias, and Crashes.* New York: Basic Books.

Mann, Michael 1986 *The Sources of Social Power,* vol. 1, *A History of Social Power from the Beginning to A.D. 1760.* New York: Cambridge University Press.

Merton, Robert 1968 *Social Theory and Social Structure.* New York: Free Press.

Park, Robert, and Ernest Burgess 1924 *Introduction to*

the Science of Sociology. Chicago: University of Chicago Press.

Parsons, Talcott 1951 *The Social System.* New York: Free Press.

Penrose, Roger 1989 *The Emperor's New Mind.* New York: Oxford University Press.

Piaget, Jean 1970 *Structuralism.* New York: Basic Books.

Tilly, Charles 1975 *The Formation of Nation States in Western Europe.* Princeton: Princeton University Press.

———1986 *The Contentious French.* Cambridge, Mass.: Harvard University Press.

STEVEN L. RYTINA

SOCIAL SUPPORT The study of social support attracts multidisciplinary interest, including the fields of sociology, epidemiology, clinical psychology, health-services research, and social work. Social support has been defined in several ways: the individual's perceptions of his/her support network, the effect or outcome of the supportive exchange, and the specific types of support provided to the individual. Generally, however, social support is the provision of resources (emotional, informational, or tangible) by others (the social network) to an individual who is experiencing some level of difficulty. This definition of social support suggests a conceptual distinction between functional (content) dimensions of support and structural dimensions of support. A National Academy of Sciences panel suggests that research on social support usually includes one or more of the following as conceptualizations of social support: emotional support, instrumental support (including material and economic aid), informational support, and social integration (Cohen et al. 1982). Emotional support is behavior of a member of the support network, such as sympathy, love, caring, or trust. Instrumental support is help that is directly rendered to the individual. The helping person intervenes in the situation and provides tangible aid, such as a financial contribution, helping with work or household duties, or some other material aid or direct service. Informational support helps others to help themselves by providing them with information that they may use to resolve a problem situation. Finally, social integration is the extent to which a person is embedded in a social network. This integration provides the individual with a sense of belonging, as well as reciprocal obligations and responsibilities (House 1981). These dimensions of social support are characteristics of the *content,* or functions, of the interaction between an individual and the network.

It is important that a social network be considered the baseline indicator of social support, since social support cannot exist without the presence of others (O'Reilly 1988). Most researchers distinguish between support and network on the basis of physical properties. Network characteristics are usually measured in terms of network size (the number of relationships an individual has), density (the level of interaction between network members other than the central individual), and frequency of interaction with the central individual (Mitchell 1969). These are measures of the *structure* of the relationships within which the interaction occurs.

There is a general belief that social support is beneficial, which is based on the assumption that social isolation is pathologic, or that it leads to pathologic states such as poor physical or mental health. There is a further general belief that for persons who are in poor physical or mental health, social support has beneficial effects that are sufficiently strong to ameliorate the individual's situation. The majority of social support research supports these beliefs. However, recent research on social support shows that support networks may have deleterious effects on an individual if the support is given unwillingly or without regard for the recipient's perceptions. Support may have negative results on people's health by upsetting them, if they feel that the help is given grudgingly, or with nonreciprocal expectations. Negative interactions within a support network have been associated with reduced satisfaction with the support network and increased depression in the central individual of the network (Rook 1984; Pagel, Erdly, and Becker 1987). It is likely that being upset interferes with the effectiveness of the network in promoting the patient's mental health by increasing the stress involved in the support relationship.

Social support has been measured in various ways. Initially, studies that included information on social support were not overly concerned with its accurate measurement, and so analyses could use only ad hoc measures of support. Because of a lack of attention to measurement, and the lack of definitional consensus, measures of social support have ranged from a single item such as marital status to very complex, multidimensional instruments that try to tap into all areas of support (e.g., OARS Multidimensional Functional Assessment Questionnaire [Duke University 1978]; Krause and Markides 1990).

There are two major statistical models that depict the relationship between social support and physical, mental, and social health outcomes: the buffering effects model and the main effects model (Cohen and Wills 1985). The buffering hypothesis states that social support improves an individual's health status by mediating the effects of stress. It posits that when periods of life stress occur, those who have low levels of support will show more symptoms of poor health. The main effects model assumes that support affects the individual regardless of the levels of stress experienced.

There is empirical support for both models (Thoits 1982). In their review of the research in this area, Ronald Kessler and Jane McLeod (1985) found strong evidence for the buffering hypothesis. They also found that those studies that did not find evidence of buffering had significant main effects. They concluded that both models depict the effects of different *types* of support. The buffering effect is generally limited to emotional support and perceived availability of support, and the main effects of social support are primarily a function of the individual's social integration.

One of the strongest criticisms leveled against studies of the relationship between social support and various outcome measures has been the issue of causal inference, specifically (1) spurious relationships of social support with other variables

and (2) reverse causation. A relationship between two variables is considered spurious when it is actually accounted for by the relationship of the two variables to a third variable. For example, a relationship may be observed between the size of a person's social support network and her/his poorer health status. However, a personal attribute, such as age, may account for both the declining social network size and deteriorating health status. Two excellent summaries of the issues involved in understanding the causal relationship between social support and health outcomes are found in Turner (1981) and Dooley (1985).

With regard to reverse causation, effects on mental or physical health that are attributed to the influence of a social network can be causally confounded with the effects that a person's health may have on the network. For instance, a social support network may have significant positive effects on a schizophrenic's condition. However, because of the difficulty of interaction with such a patient, network members may reduce the amount of contact they have with the patient, increase the number of negative interactions they experience with the patient, or simply leave the network. This may decrease the healthful effects of the network on the person's condition, as well as reduce the network size. In this way, the causal direction of the relationship between social support and mental health is reversed; poor mental health causes a decline in the beneficial effects and the size of the social support network.

Support may be defined differently by recipients and providers at different stages of the life cycle (Schulz and Rau 1985; Kasl and Wells 1985). Acts that are considered support by recipients at one time may be deemed interference at others. For example, aid that is rendered to a young couple who are adjusting to the demands of their first child, such as someone bringing in meals or doing laundry, may be welcomed; but an elderly individual may perceive these same actions as a compromise of his/her independence.

Although instrumental aid is a necessary part of social support for frail populations such as the disabled or the elderly, it has proved difficult to measure because it is conceptually confounded with other variables, such as functional status (Minkler 1985). There is a question as to how instrumental support should be used when defining social support in a functionally dependent population. It is not clear whether dependence in activities of daily living (bathing, dressing, toileting, etc.), which are primarily used as measures of functional status, also measures levels of instrumental support.

Studies of social support have been mostly concerned with its relationship to mental health; however, research has begun to focus on the effects of support on physiological measures of health. Social support has been shown to have positive effects on pregnancy, blood pressure, and other physical conditions that involve stress. Researchers have shown a relationship between social support and reduced morbidity and mortality (Blazer 1982). In the future, research on broader measures of symptomatology will include social support measures as predictor variables. Much of the research on social support has had to rely on analyses of cross-sectional data. As more longitudinal data become available, researchers will be able to test hypotheses about the direction and magnitude of the effects of social support on measures of health.

Further comparisons of the buffering hypothesis to the main effects model will do little to enhance our understanding of the relationship between social support and health outcomes (Cohen and Syme 1985, p. 6). Future research should concentrate on more specific hypotheses that explain the mechanisms by which social support affects health. For example, Duck (1990) presents social support as a function of the interpersonal relationships between the central individual and those who comprise her/his network.

Research has begun that explores negative as well as positive effects of social support systems. As more information of this type becomes available, it will serve to fill some large gaps in the social support research.

Finally, other aspects of social support relationships must be more clearly studied. The great majority of caregiving and support is provided by family members, and so social support research has concentrated largely on those who have traditional family support structures where adult children care for elderly parents, or parents and siblings provide care for acutely ill or disabled family members. There has been less emphasis on the characteristics of the support systems of those who do not have available family, such as the elderly who live in retirement communities, those who leave home at an early age, or those who are homeless. In what ways do ethnic and cultural minority group social support systems compare to those in the general U.S. population, and how does the United States compare with other cultures worldwide? Social support is not only interesting from a theoretical standpoint but also has broad implications for future policy decisions (e.g., what is the role of social support in a long-term health care policy?) as well as clinical applications. Social support will continue to be included as an important variable not only in studies of health outcomes, but across a wide range of social and behavioral research.

(SEE ALSO: *Intergenerational Relations; Social Gerontology; Social Network Theory; Social Resources Theory*)

REFERENCES

Blazer, Dan G. 1982 "Social Support and Mortality in an Elderly Community Population." *American Journal of Epidemiology* 115 (5):684–694.

Cohen, F., M. Horowitz, R. Lazarus, R. Moos, L. Robbins, R. Rose, and M. Rutter 1982 "Panel Report on Psychosocial Stress." In G. Elliott and C. Eisdorfer, eds., *Stress and Human Health: Analysis and Implications for Research.* New York: Springer.

Cohen, Sheldon, and S. Leonard Syme 1985 *Social Support and Health.* New York: Academic.

Cohen, Sheldon, and T. A. Wills 1985 "Stress, Social Support, and the Buffering Hypothesis." *Psychological Bulletin* 98 (2):310–357.

Dooley, David 1985 "Causal Inference in the Study of Social Support." In Sheldon Cohen and S. Leonard

Syme, eds., *Social Support and Health.* New York: Academic.

Duck, Steve 1990 *Personal Relationships and Social Support.* Newbury Park, Calif.: Sage.

Duke University Center for the Study of Aging and Human Development 1978 *Multidimensional Functional Assessment: The OARS Methodology,* 2nd ed. Durham, N.C.: Duke University.

House, J.S. 1981 *Work, Stress and Social Support.* Reading, Mass.: Addison-Wesley.

Kasl, Stanislav, and James Wells 1985 "Social Support and Health in the Middle Years: Work and the Family." In Sheldon Cohen and S. Leonard Syme, eds., *Social Support and Health.* New York: Academic.

Kessler, Ronald C., and Jane D. McLeod 1985 "Social Support and Mental Health in Community Samples." In Sheldon Cohen and S. Leonard Syme, eds., *Social Support and Health.* New York: Academic.

Krause, Neal, and Kyriakos Markides 1990 "Measuring Social Support among Older Adults." *International Journal of Aging and Human Development* 30 (1):37–53.

Minkler, Meredith 1985 "Social Support and Health of the Elderly." In Sheldon Cohen and S. Leonard Syme, eds., *Social Support and Health.* New York: Academic.

Mitchell, J.C. 1969 "The Concept and Use of Social Networks." In J.C. Mitchell, ed., *Social Networks in Urban Situations: Analyses of Personal Relationships in Central African Towns.* Manchester: Manchester University Press.

O'Reilly, P. 1988 "Methodological Issues in Social Support and Social Network Research." *Social Science Medicine* 26 (8):863–873.

Pagel, Mark D., William W. Erdly, and Joseph Becker 1987 "Social Networks: We Get by with (and in Spite of) a Little Help from Our Friends." *Journal of Personality and Social Psychology* 53:793–804.

Rook, Karen 1984 "The Negative Side of Social Interaction: Impact on Psychological Well-Being." *Journal of Personality and Social Psychology* 46:1097–1108.

Schulz, Richard, and Marie T. Rau 1985 "Social Support through the Life Course." In Sheldon Cohen and S. Leonard Syme, eds., *Social Support and Health.* New York: Academic.

Thoits, Peggy 1982 "Conceptual, Methodological, and Theoretical Problems in Studying Social Support as a Buffer Against Life Stress." *Journal of Health and Social Behavior* 23 (June):145–159.

Turner, R. J. 1981 "Social Support as a Contingency in Psychological Well-Being." *Journal of Health and Social Behavior* 22:357–367.

J. RANDAL JOHNSON

SOCIAL WORK Professional social work has its roots in the emergence of social welfare as a social institution. Social welfare, as we have come to know it, resulted from society's numerous attempts to accommodate historical changes in economic and social relationships over time. The beginning of institutionalized social welfare is frequently traced to the English Poor Law of 1601. As the most critical part of modern social welfare's foundation, the most salient characteristic of Elizabethan poor laws was the articulation and promulgation of the principle of public responsibility and obligation for the economic well-being of the people. Yet "the Poor Laws in England and in American communities were not primarily concerned with poverty and how to eliminate it. Instead, they were concerned with pauperism and the potential claims on community funds, the danger that paupers might get by without working" (Dolgoff and Feldstein 1984, p. 80). This continuing ambivalance and tension between public obligation and social control is one of several dualities that characterize the context of professional social work practice. Institutionalized social welfare is the environment within which the profession of social work developed.

The history of social welfare is paralleled by and enmeshed with the increasing professionalism of those who administer social welfare programs. Modern professional social work has been defined as

the professional activity of helping individuals, groups, or communities enhance their capacity for social functioning and creating societal conditions favorable of this goal. Social work practice consists of the professional application of social work values, principles, and techniques to one or more of the following ends: helping people obtain tangible services; counseling and psychotherapy with individ-

uals, families, and groups; helping communities or groups provide or improve social and health services; and participating in relevant legislative processes. (National Association of Social Workers 1974, pp. 4–5)

PROFESSIONAL ROOTS

Early social work was characterized by two streams of activity: social reform and direct assistance to individuals and families. The practice of friendly visiting and the development of both the Charity Organizations Societies and settlement houses illustrate both types of effort. Representatives of Charity Organization Societies, the so-called friendly visitors, engaged in social investigation and moral suasion designed to improve the lives of the poor. The thrust of these encounters was to place responsibility on the person or families for their present economic and social status, what we now know as "blaming the victim." The work of Charity Organization Societies formed the origins of the social work method later to be known as social casework.

Residents of settlement houses, Jane Addams included, were friendly visitors who came to stay. A group of middle or upper class individuals moved into a residence in a poor area in an effort to understand neighborhood conditions firsthand and to work with neighborhood residents on solving neighborhood problems. While some settlement house efforts might have attempted to uplift the poor, further program development came to focus on improving conditions in immigrant communities. In cities across the nation, the contribution of settlement houses to the acculturation of large numbers of immigrants in the early part of this century is legend. Settlement house activities emphasized teaching English, health practices, occupational skills, and environmental change through cooperative efforts. Settlement house staff developed social group work, community organization, social action, and environmental change efforts. Furthermore, settlement house workers were also active in the legislative arena, gathering and promulgating facts in order to influence social policy and legislation.

An early and continuing cleavage in the profession has its origins in differing explanations of social dysfunction. Some early social workers espoused the theory of social causation of social problems and sought governmental responsibility for meeting needs and developed coalitions for reform and institutional change. Others emphasized individual causation of social problems. These social workers identified the need to develop psychological theory and subsequently used it, promoting an individually focused therapeutic approach to helping. These two primary orientations would feed the development of professional social work and would provide the basis for considerable conflict within the practice community and in professional social work education.

PROFESSIONALIZATION

An issue throughout the development of professional social work has been the nature of its professional status. In 1915 Abraham Flexner critiqued the professional status of social work at the National Conference of Charities and Corrections. Although Flexner criticized social work as lacking a specific skill for a specific function, he did also recognize its professional spirit. The landmark publication of Mary Richmond's *Social Diagnosis* followed in 1917. This volume organized the contemporary theory and method of social work and formulated a data collection approach designed to be the foundation for diagnosis. Richmond's contribution to the organization of what would eventually become social casework practice is legendary, forming the bedrock of clinical social work.

In the 1920s the practice of social work emerged in so-called fields of practice or settings: family and child welfare and medical, psychiatric, and school social work. Social workers defined their central problem and responsibility as that characteristic of their particular field. Along with the concept of setting, the concept of method emerged during this period. Method developed first around casework and later in relation to both group work and community organization. Methods were based on selected theories of human behavior, drawn from psychology and sociology. Setting referred to the organizational context within which services were delivered.

This combination of method and field of practice or setting served to fragment professional social work, slowing the development of an integrated theoretical base for practice across methods and settings. Social casework theory and method developed to a large extent in isolation from group work and community organization. Curricula for professional social work education followed the same pattern, with separate tracks for each method. It took until the 1970s for the development of a conceptual approach that was based on the essential components within professional practice regardless of where the social worker was employed. Pincus and Minahan (1970) articulated a conceptual framework for generalist practice, for social work service delivery across practice settings. This approach encompassed three major components: the *social systems* in relation to which the social worker carries out his or her role: client, action, and target systems; the stages of *planned change* or problem-solving processes; interactional and analytic *skills* for data collection, analysis, and intervention.

The ideal-type model of a profession has been the conception against which social work has measured itself through much of its history. Greenwood's (1957) analysis examined the extent to which social work possessed five classic traits of the professions: systematic theory, authority, community sanction, ethical codes, and a professional culture. Characterizing social work as a less-developed profession, Greenwood concluded that social work possessed these attributes to a moderate extent. The predominant direction with the field, however, has been to continue its professional development along all five dimensions. Recent emphasis on building the empirical base of practice coupled with increasing licensure requirements by states are indicators of the continued progression of social work toward greater professional status. It would be incorrect to assume, however, that this direction for social work is embraced by the profession as a whole. For those whose dominant professional identification is with social work's social action tradition, increasing professionalization means being co-opted as a result of achieving the public acceptance accorded a profession.

THE BUREAUCRATIC CONTEXT

One characteristic that distinguishes social work is that the majority of its members are employed in public and private social welfare agencies. Although many modern formal organizations may not approach the classic Weberian model of bureaucracy, these enduring organizational characteristics, however manifested, dramatically shape the practice environment for professionally trained social workers. This organizational base, together with expectations for professional autonomy, creates conflict for the professional social worker in the bureaucracy. The image of the autonomous professional, who may be self-employed, is no longer an accurate picture for physicians who are employed by health maintenance organizations or attornies who are members of law firms. Much of our professional workforce has become bureaucratically based. Even so, the process of professional socialization is designed to instill a culture, a set of values and expectations, that can conflict with the work environment.

There are problems with the fit between the professional's culture and the demands of bureaucratic requirements. Professionals' autonomy is seriously circumscribed by organizational commitments, policies, and procedures. Under these circumstances, just whose agent is the professional social worker: the agency's, the client's, the community's, or her or his own as an autonomous professional? Given organizational life, what form can a social worker's social action efforts take? Just how far can an employed social worker go in challenging agency priorities, policies, and procedures before her or his services are no longer desired? How long does it take before the professional social worker starts to identify more as an agency employee and less as an autonomous professional? These realities produce a conservatizing effect on social work, limiting many workers' willingness or ability to take risks as autonomous professionals in the name of social justice and reform. Under these circumstances, it becomes easy to see how theories of individual causation would prevail over explanations that invoke influence of larger social forces. Explanations based in individual causation do not directly challenge the agency, its programs, and its priorities. Taken together, the agency base of the profession and preferential adherence to individual causal explanations of social problems has seriously overshadowed social work's historic commitment to ameliorating the effects of larger social forces. This tension, with its roots in the origins of the profession, continues today as demonstrated by the overwhelming preference of students and professionals for work with individuals and families, mostly in the psychotherapeutic mode.

KNOWLEDGE BASE

The creation of a systematic body of theory has been under development from the early days of the profession. Mary Richmond's *Social Diagnosis* organized and analyzed her naturalistic observations made while working with individuals and families. Her work is the origin of psychosocial history taking and treatment plan development, perhaps the core of social casework practice methods. Richmond's approach, later to be known as empirically based practice, represents one of the two major streams of knowledge and theory development in social work. The other major focus has relied heavily on the application of social science (primarily sociological and psychological) theory to the explanation of social problems and the development of interventions designed to improve or ameliorate those problems.

Over time the link between social work and sociology has been strong, although in recent times increasingly distant. It is not unusual for casual observers who do not understand the distinctions between the two fields to confuse social workers with sociologists. This ambiguity can become even more dense when the notion of "applied sociology" is introduced. While the main

body of sociological thought focuses on exploratory, descriptive, and explanatory theory, modeling, and empirical testing, so-called applied sociology emerged in response to the increasing interest in social program evaluation and to the limited supply of trained methodologists who could design and execute well-formulated evaluative studies. As such, applied sociology also potentially provided an alternative career path for sociologists, one that focused more on public-policy-oriented social research and that led to job opportunities in locations other than universities. It should also be noted that landmark social program evaluation studies were undertaken by sociologists, some of whom were on faculties of schools of social work, in the late 1950s and 1960s (Meyer and Borgatta 1959; Meyer, Borgatta, and Jones 1965).

There can be little doubt, however, regarding the importance of sociological theory and research for the development of the knowledge and theoretical base of social work practice. For example, small group theory, organizational theory, community development and dynamics, family studies, work and professionalization, determinants of juvenile delinquency and adult criminal behavior, and life span theories represent a limited list of areas of sociological theory development and research that have informed and directly influenced both the theory and the practice of social work.

EMPIRICALLY BASED PRACTICE

Sociological theory and research provided significant empirical anchors for the development of social work practice theory. In the early 1970s, however, the course of social work's development took another turn. This direction came to be known as the practice effectiveness movement. As articulated by Joel Fischer, the question became "Is Casework Effective?" (Fischer 1973). This emphasis built on an earlier concern with professional accountability articulated in the late 1960s, when the profession was admonished to develop empirically based justifications for programs, services, and budgets. Program evaluation became the dominant focus of much social work research during this period, and it stressed methodology, design, outcomes, and accountability.

These concerns with the outcomes of social work interventions were coupled with a concept of the social worker as both practitioner and researcher. From this perspective of the practitioner/researcher, social workers are seen as having the opportunity to develop methods and skills from an empirical base, from the experience provided in their own practices to develop, test, and refine practice innovations. Embedded in this tide of social work thought during this period was the notion that evaluation and research were too critical to leave in the hands of a group of research "specialists." Perhaps more fundamental is the belief that social work research is too important to leave in the hands of nonsocial workers. "It is the practicing professional who encounters and struggles with current issues and who is most sensitive to the critical knowledge gaps in the field. Thus social workers are in the best position to formulate and conduct the needed research and evaluation and they must be committed to acquiring the understanding required to direct the helping effort" (Grinnell 1981, p. 5).

These developments coincided with the expansion of doctoral education in social work. While past doctoral preparation often focused on the development of advanced clinical skills, contemporary training at the doctoral level is almost exclusively research based, designed to prepare students with the skills to contribute to the empirically anchored knowledge base of the profession. As a result, a cohort of social work researchers has been trained over the last twenty years, and this group has developed a body of theory and knowledge that has been generated directly as social work research. While there certainly has been interdisciplinary exchange of theories, concepts, methods, and analyses during this time, social work researchers now function far more autonomously than in the past.

The breadth of social work practice (encompassing work with individuals, families, groups,

and communities and including social program administration, public policy development, and social planning) provides a rich and continually changing field for the exploratory, descriptive, and explanatory empirical efforts. Further, since social work as a profession is concerned with social change and the improvement of conditions under which people live, its orientation cannot be value-free or purely theoretical. In a similar vein, social work research and practice continue to reflect early commitments of the profession. In 1936, Helen Hall, a pioneer of the settlement house movement, stated, "in the long run it is both poor case work and poor health work merely to move particular families and do nothing toward changing the conditions out of which you have taken them and into which others will move. . . . Social action for change in advance is inescapable, unless we are willing to drift along eternally patching up the consequences of social neglect and industrial breakdown" (Hall 1936, pp. 235, 237).

(SEE ALSO: *Applied Sociology; Evaluation Research; Public Policy Analysis*)

REFERENCES

Dolgoff, Ralph, and Donald Feldstein 1984 *Understanding Social Welfare,* 2nd ed. New York: Longman.

Fischer, Joel 1973 "Is Casework Effective? A Review." *Social Work* 18:5–20.

Greenwood, Ernest 1957 "Attributes of a Profession." *Social Work* 2:45–55.

Grinnell, Richard 1981 *Social Work Research and Evaluation.* Itasca, Ill.: Peacock.

Hall, Helen 1936 "The Consequences of Social Action for the Group Work Agency." *Proceedings of the National Conference on Social Work.* National Conference on Social Welfare, Columbus, Ohio.

Meyer, Henry, and Edgar Borgatta 1959 *An Experiment in Mental Patient Rehabilitation: Evaluating a Social Agency Program.* New York: Russell Sage Foundation.

Meyer, Henry, Edgar Borgatta, and Wyatt Jones 1965 *Girls at Vocational High: An Experiment in Social Work Intervention.* New York: Russell Sage Foundation.

National Association of Social Workers 1974 *Standards for Social Service Manpower.* Washington, D.C.: National Association of Social Workers.

Newman, Edward, and Jerry Turem 1974 "The Crisis of Accountability." *Social Work* 19:5–16.

Pincus, Allen, and Anne Minahan 1970 "Toward a Model for Teaching a Basic First Year Course in Methods for Social Work Practice." In Lillian Ripple, ed., *Teaching Social Work Practice.* New York: Council on Social Work Education.

Raymond, Frank 1977 "A Changing Focus for the Profession: Product Rather Than Process." *Journal of Social Welfare* 4:9–16.

Richmond, Mary 1917 *Social Diagnosis.* New York: Russell Sage Foundation.

CAROL D. AUSTIN

SOCIETAL STRATIFICATION Societal stratification phenomena are the relatively enduring, rank-ordered relationships among the small units of which society is composed. These units are adults, gainfully employed men and/or women, nuclear families, or, sometimes, extended families or households. They are ordered from highest to lowest in terms of political power, acquisitive power, prestige, and informational standing. Everybody experiences stratification every day, though we often notice it only in the sense that some people seem better off or worse off than we are. Social thinkers, powerful people, and revolutionaries have been especially concerned with stratification from time out of mind.

Secure knowledge of the varying forms stratification structures may take is important because of the effects they have on so many aspects of human experience such as people's dreams of a better life, their efforts to improve their situations, their strivings for success, their fears of failure, their sympathy for the less fortunate, their envy of others' good fortune, even their feelings about revolution.

A complete understanding of stratification requires several kinds of knowledge: first, what stratification structures consist of and how they vary; second, the individual and collective consequences of the different states of such structures; and third, the factors that make stratification structures change. This article provides a view of present thinking regarding the first of these.

HISTORY: CLASSICAL THEORY

There are two different lines of thought behind modern theory of societal stratification. One is classical theory. Concerned with power and privilege, it employs historical evidence. The other is the empirical tradition. It is concerned with systematic data on stratification as it exists contemporarily. Present-day theory of the behavior of stratification phenomena can be traced to Karl Marx's challenge to the manufacturing and financial elites of his day. Behind his concerns, and those of the working class for whom he was Europe's chief spokesman for many years, lay the great economic and political upheavals of the eighteenth and nineteenth centuries.

The American and French revolutions and their aftermath culminated in legislation that made adults in many countries equal before the law. The related wave of emancipation of slaves and serfs that swept over Europe and the Americas was also a part of the intellectual environment of the day. Of more direct relevance to Marx's thinking was the rise of trade and the factory system, along with the growth of cities and the expansion of wealth. Marx saw the urban populations dividing into opposed classes. Basically there was the capitalist class, who employed the workers, owned the workplaces, machines, and tools, and had ready access to large amounts of money for investment; they were opposed by their employees, the working class, who had nothing to offer but their time and energy. These two classes differ in terms of power and privilege: power because capitalists give orders that workers must accept, privilege because capitalists take the surplus, which is whatever is left after paying the cost of production, for themselves and their investments, leaving for workers only the wages that the market for labor forces them to pay. Actually, Marx was interested in how these classes came into being and in the conflicting interests they expressed. He did not write specifically on societal stratification as we understand it today.

Later writers on stratification, inspired to either elucidate or contradict Marx, spelled out more complex sets of stratification dimensions.

Max Weber (1946, 1947) saw power as the factor basic to enduring inequalities. Sometimes, like Marx, he used categories whose underlying dimensions remained to be elucidated. To be specific, class, status groups, and party were his key concepts. When these are dimensionalized, class is seen to express a hierarchical order of economic status. Similarly, he noted that the distinguishing variable immediately underlying status groups was their hierarchical order according to the degree of social honor they claimed and received. When his "party" is dimensionalized, it is seen to be legitimate political influence. In other writings he saw education as a stratification variable. In still others, he often wrote of authority, or legitimate superordinate and subordinate relations of power. One final note: Weber said nothing about how people are distributed in these dimensions, nor, of course, about how and why such distributions vary.

More thoroughly and precisely than Marx or Weber, Pitirim A. Sorokin (1927) crafted the bases of modern theory of societal stratification. He distinguished political stratification, economic stratification, and occupational stratification. The first is a dimension of power and the second of income and wealth. The dimensionality of occupational status he left unclear, sometimes implying that it was authority, sometimes privilege, sometimes intelligence. Much of Sorokin's theory of societal stratification remains intact today. First, he noted that all societies are stratified to one degree or another, a position widely accepted today. Second, empirical researchers continue to be active in refining and elucidating his concepts of occupational status and occupational mobility. Third, in this connection he asked why occupational stratification exists and concluded that organized communal life requires mechanisms and people to coordinate essential activities and that such coordination demands and rewards unusual intelligence. This view, now called *the functionalist hypothesis,* has been elaborated and debated ever since. Fourth, he held that the degree of stratification varies from society to society and over time within any given society: Stratification, he said, is in "ceaseless fluctuation." He specified several

ways stratification structures may vary. The whole structure may rise or fall. The top may rise or fall, changing the degree of inequality. The "profile," or shape of the distribution, may vary. Similarly, the rate of individual upward or downward mobility may vary, and whole strata may rise or fall.

Sorokin thus presented a theory specifying (1) the general dimensions by which people are stratified within a society; (2) some ways by which the distributions of people on these dimensions vary; (3) why stratification exists; (4) a realistic appraisal of the fact of changes in stratification.

The latest work in the classical tradition is that of Gerhardt Lenski (1966). His key dimensions are power, privilege, and prestige, in that order of importance. Beyond this, he offers three main ideas. First, both functional theory and conflict theory, its opposite, are partly right. Society's needs demand coordination, implying the existence of strata based upon power or authority and implying a degree of consent on the part of many of those whose activities are organized by others. But conflict is a consequence of such control: Authority is often misused, and, even when it is not, it may be misunderstood. Second, inequalities are mostly those of power, with inequalities of privilege and prestige following mostly as consequences of these. Third, the degree of inequality, seen as a single phenomenon encompassing the rate of mobility and distance between strata, is said to have increased with the comprehensiveness and complexity of society until the Industrial Revolution, after which it declined. According to Lenski, the main forces driving change in the degree of inequality are the size of the surplus of production and, behind this, the march of technological efficiency.

Lenski is clearly in the classical tradition in his concern with power and privilege and in his dependence upon historical evidence. To some extent, he echoes Sorokin's concern with variations in stratification structures through his emphasis on the degree of inequality. He provides a compelling treatment of the issue of conflict versus societal necessity regarding the existence of stratification. He uses historical evidence effectively and systematically to mark variations of inequality in agrarian and horticultural societies. Yet his emphasis on two main, all-encompassing aspects of stratification, power (his key criterion variable) and inequality (used to denote the way power and its concomitants are apportioned), forces too many separately varying stratification phenomena into too few molds. This problem becomes critical in industrial societies, where stratification dimensions do in fact vary independently of one another.

HISTORY: THE EMPIRICAL TRADITION

As noted, this tradition of stratification research is concerned with the here and now. This is a line of research that developed excellence in the measurement of the status of small units within larger stratification structures. Several more or less independent status-measurement devices were formulated in the 1920s and 1930s. Most were concerned with either the prestige of the breadwinner's occupation or the quality of the home. They tended to share certain assumptions: that stratification consisted of a single hierarchy, in the early days usually called *social class;* that one or two different scales were sufficient to test hypotheses concerning *social class;* that social-class positions could be distinguished by direct observation and/or interviews with someone who knew the status holders; that routines could be devised by which to assign valid and reliable numerical scores to each status holder on each of the scales used to measure social class; that the unit to be scored was the household, which could be one or several persons living in a single home; and that it was the whole unit that was to be scored, whether with data on the home or the head of the household. Many of these devices became obsolete because they had to be recalibrated for each new community or type of community in which they were applied. Those that survived, education and occupational status, did so because they provide comparable scores across large populations such as nations.

Of the two main survivors, educational attainment is quite easy to measure: exact number of school years successfully completed, from none through 16, 17, 18, and on. Occupational status is another matter. There are two systems in current use. One, occupational prestige ratings, assumes that each person in a given occupation shares the prestige most people attribute to that occupation. Occupational prestige scales have been constructed for many countries (Treiman 1977). The other system is that of occupational socioeconomic status indexes (SEI). These scales use education and income to measure the status level of each occupation, then attribute to the person the resulting score of her or his occupation. In the United States, Treiman's prestige scale and the SEI provide highly correlated occupational scores (Featherman and Hauser 1978).

Regardless of the original intent behind such scales—to measure positions in what was once believed to be the only stratification hierarchy—these two variables, educational attainment and occupational status, are also appropriate for use with the classical theorists' multidimensional views of stratification.

A SYNTHESIS

The current synthesis was carried out by stratification theorists who were both sensitive to the concerns of classical theorists with power and privilege and steeped in the empirical tradition. Thus, they brought the classical theorists' concern with power and privilege, social honor (Weber), occupational status (Sorokin), and prestige (Lenski) together with the empiricists' concerns with education and occupational status (overlapping Weber, Sorokin, and Lenski) and with quantitative measurement and analysis.

Kaare Svalastoga's little book *Social Differentiation* (1965) appears to be the first statement of the synthesis. He indicates the centrality of four dimensions of status: political, economic, social (mostly occupational), and informational (mostly educational). He calls attention to structural variations through his "parameters": the degree of inequality, the correlation among dimensions, and the degree of permeability (degree of intergenerational circulation mobility or movement up and down the hierarchies). Otis Dudley Duncan (1968) both accepted and clarified Svalastoga's synthesis. His list of "scales of reward or status" provides a good outline of the rather large number of variables that should be measured in order to have a full-scale determination of people's levels on each status dimension. Also, he divides three of Svalastoga's four dimensions into two categories each. He, like Svalastoga, then lists three ways the structure of any stratification variable may vary. One is the degree of inequality. A second is called "rigidity of inequality" or "status crystallization," the same as Svalastoga's "correlation." The third is "rigidity of stratification," which is Svalastoga's "permeability" turned upside down.

Like Sorokin's and others' positions, Archibald O. Haller's (1970) statement of the synthesis assumes stratification exists in all societies at all times. It concentrates on the ways stratification varies. This form of the synthesis first notes that there are two classes of dimensions of stratification, content dimensions and structural dimensions. His content dimensions echo Weber and Sorokin. He lists legitimate power (including political power); wealth (the same as Sorokin's economic stratification and Weber's "class"); and prestige (of which he views occupational prestige as the key variable). Also, for civilized societies, he accepts education as a stratification variable, thus fitting within Svalastoga's and Duncan's category of informational status. Thus, this synthesis encompasses the content dimensions delineated by Weber, Sorokin, and Lenski, while adding Svalastoga's informational status and leaving room for Duncan's detailed specifics.

The position posits Weber's "class," Sorokin's "economic stratification," Lenski's "privilege," and Svalastoga's economic status as each referring to the same set of hierarchical phenomena: access to goods and services—the *economic* dimension of a stratification structure. It posits legitimate political influence (including authority) as the dimension underlying Weber's "party," Sorokin's "political stratification," Lenski's "power," and Svalastoga's "political status" and sees it as referring to a second homogeneous set of hierarchical phenomena: the capability of one set of units to elicit from others the behaviors the first promotes —the *power* dimension of a stratification structure. From Weber it takes the concept of social honor, from Sorokin and the modern occupational status researchers, the concept of occupational stratification; from Svalastoga, that of social status; from Lenski, the concept of prestige. From the empirical tradition, it takes the measurement of occupational status. All these are seen as referring to a third homogeneous set of hierarchical phenomena: the level of respect or deference attributed to a unit because of the latter's participation in a social category (such as an occupation) that has a specific level of evaluation by a society —the *prestige* dimension of societal stratification. From Svalastoga and Duncan, with much support from the empiricists and a little, too, from Weber, it takes informational status as a content dimension of a stratification structure, with education as its main indicator.

At the general level stated, each content dimension is, of course, presumed to be applicable in one form or another to all human societies as far back in time as human communal life can be traced. It is the exact expression of each and the relationship among them that will vary across time and place. For entire contemporary societies, the main expressions of each would seem to be these: for the power dimension, *political influence,* a variable researchers have not yet learned to measure despite its centrality in classical theory; *income* (occasionally wealth) for the economic dimension, a variable of recent serious concern to those in the empirical tradition; *occupational status* in either of its two main forms of occupational prestige ratings (Treiman 1977) or occupational socioeconomic index scores (Featherman and Hauser 1978) for the *prestige dimension;* and for the informational status dimension, *educational attainment level* in terms of years of formal schooling successfully completed. Thus, in recent years it has become apparent that, for today's societies, the main variables of the empirical tradition have central places among the content dimensions of classical tradition. Income, occupational status, and education are the theoretically defensible variables most readily available to measure three of the four classical content dimensions.

Like Sorokin's, Svalastoga's, and Duncan's, Haller's formulation of the synthesis specifies several structural dimensions, each held to be applicable to every appropriate measure of each content dimension. The three structural dimensions of Svalastoga and Duncan are included: degree of inequality, status crystallization, and the degree of status inheritance. Two others of Sorokin's are included, though they are modified to fit today's understandings. One is the general level or central tendency. The other is a specification of his concept of *profile* into two concepts, mode structure and skewness. Each deserves comment. Though calculated from data on small units, each structural dimension applies to the society as a whole. Though logically they are partly dependent on one another, each makes a unique contribution to understanding stratification. Each appears to be amenable to statistical description. Each is applicable to every indicator of the standing of each small unit (say, family) in the society. Valid measures of each content dimension taken at one point in time on a generalizable sample of the population of small units of that society would provide a complete description of the stratification structure of that society at that time. Successive measures would provide a complete description of the evolution of the society's stratification structure over time, thus providing a general idea of the variations in the degree of stratification of that society. Each applies to comparisons over time or among societies.

General Level. As Sorokin realized, the levels of structural dimensions may rise and fall as wholes. That is, the average economic, political, prestige, and informational standing of the small units changes over time. These rises and falls may be seen in changes in the central tendency—say, the arithmetic mean or the median value—of the standing of the small units. Note that the rises and falls of the central tendency of any one of these dimensions do not necessarily follow the same pattern as those of another. Average economic, prestige, and informational standing might in-

crease, for example, while average political influence fell. This could happen in a society where a development-oriented dictatorship reduces citizen political participation while raising levels of income, raising prestige by upgrading the occupational structure, and increasing access to education. Indeed, the economic, prestige, and educational levels of the populations of the more developed democracies have increased almost consistently since World War II, though the same cannot always be said for dictatorships. Note, too, that raising the level of the occupational structure is exactly what some researchers mean by *upward structural mobility*, the case in which almost everyone is carried upward by changes in the economy that eliminate low-skill jobs while adding specialized jobs.

Degree of Inequality. The distance between the small units may increase or decrease over time. This, so to speak, stretches the positions on the content dimensions apart or squeezes them together. The statistical term for this is the *degree of dispersion*. A number of measures of dispersion exist, such as the standard deviation (or its square, the variance), the range, the semi-interquantile (or quintile, decile, etc.) range, the shares, and the Gini, Theil, and Kuznets coefficients. There are two basic types of inequality, absolute and relative. Absolute conceptions assume that the metric on which the degree of inequality is to be measured is fixed so that as, say, real income per capita grows, the dollar difference between the mean of the top 10 percent and the mean of the bottom 10 percent of the small units may increase while each is rising above its previous level, the slope of the top rising faster than the slope of the bottom. For income, a proper description of these phenomena would be "changes in the *size distribution* of income." Absolute inequality and its changes are sometimes published. Much more often published are the *share distributions* of income. For any society at any time, share distributions take the total amount of, say, income as a constant 100 percent (or 1.00) and determine the degree to which the whole amount, regardless of its absolute size, is evenly or unevenly divided among the population. These include the percentage of all income held by the top X percent and the bottom Y percent of the population. Or, as in the case of the Gini, Theil, and Kuznets coefficients, they take values ranging from 1.0 to zero, in which 1.00 is the maximum degree of inequality and zero is complete equality. Viewed at one point in time within a single society, measures of relative inequality are quite useful. But, for comparison among societies or across time in the same society, they may be misleading. In fact, for many years the share distribution measures of the income and degree of inequality of the American people remained essentially unchanged, while the size distributions increased dramatically (U.S. Department of Commerce 1980). This was because real per capita income was increasing rapidly. The greater the degree of inequality, the greater the degree of stratification.

Crystallization. It has long been recognized that a stratification structure may tend toward or away from monolithicity, in which the different content dimensions merge into a single hierarchy or tend to be separate hierarchies. At one extreme, the position of a small unit on any one of the dimensions can be found by knowing its position on any other. In other words, if the four content dimensions are perfectly correlated, those in lofty positions on one dimension would also be in lofty positions on all the other dimensions, while those in humble positions on one, would similarly be in low positions on any other, and so on. At the opposite extreme, a unit's position on a given content dimension would be irrelevant to its position on any other. In the real world, any two or three might be highly interrelated, all might be moderately intercorrelated, and so forth. For obvious reasons, Svalastoga called this structural dimension "correlation." Others have called it *status crystallization.* Note that crystallization levels and forms may be better summarized by a method called *factor analysis* than by the correlations themselves. Factor analysis can show which sets of content variables tend to vary together in a population and which do not. It can also help determine which are the dominant dimensions and

which are of lesser importance in a given stratification structure. For example, it appears that the Soviet stratification structure has been dominated by the power dimension; the American, by the economic dimension. Factor analysis of the correlations of the content dimensions could tell whether these beliefs are true. The greater the degree of crystallization, the greater the degree of stratification.

Status Inheritance. This is the degree to which people's level on a given content dimension is controlled by that of their parents. It is exactly the obverse of circulation mobility. A high degree of status inheritance implies a low degree of circulation mobility. The basic statistical summary of this phenomenon is either the correlation coefficient (r) or the coefficient of determination (r^2) of the content dimension positions of offspring and their parents. (The r^2 tells how much one variable is determined by the others.) The greater the degree of status inheritance, the greater the degree of stratification.

Sorokin's Profile. Every variable has a so-called distribution, a shape that appears when the number of scores (the *frequency*) is plotted against the values of the scores. Much of today's statistical theory assumes that real-world distributions conform to certain mathematical shapes. The bell-shaped "normal" curve is the one most often assumed. For distribution of income, the "log normal" curve, with which the distribution of the natural logarithm of each score turns out to be a normal curve, is often assumed. Stratification researchers often take for granted that the distributions of content dimensions are either normal or log normal. But there is no sociological reason to expect that this is so. The shape of the distribution of a content dimension is precisely what Sorokin meant by his term *profile.* Lacking the data and concepts to proceed further, he simply called the real-world shapes of these distributions their profiles. Today, we can see that there are two aspects of each profile, mode structure and skewness.

In strikingly underdeveloped societies, almost everyone is concentrated at the very lowest possible values of economic status, political influence, occupational status, and education: extremely poor, utterly uninfluential, of low prestige, and illiterate. Above them, their "betters" are arranged in rank order, with a wide status range on which those few people who are above the bottom dwindle up the line to a handful of individuals of lofty standing. Each such distribution would have a very low mode (or distinct cluster of cases) and median (where half of the cases are higher and half lower) and a higher arithmetic mean, with a sharply skewed tail. In somewhat more developed societies, such distributions, instead of yielding bell-shaped curves, might well show multiple modes, with many people concentrated around a fairly low point, quite a few concentrated around a point a bit higher, a few concentrated near the top, and after that a sharp skewing up to the tiny few at the very top. The consequences of such forms for the lives of the people involved are no doubt great indeed. For example, if, in a certain society, almost everyone is destitute, the few who are more or less well-to-do are highly visible. Even if the latter were really not far above the others, everybody would think of that society as being highly stratified. If, in another society, people are bunched together at several points along a hierarchy, thus forming multiple modes, or discrete classes, those in each mode might come to consider themselves members of a special class in opposition to those concentrated at another mode. Thus, the exact forms of profiles are essential to a description of a society's stratification structure. Theory predicts that these forms will have substantial consequences for many stratification-dependent behaviors.

Profile: Mode Structure. Thus, this structural dimension refers to the number, size, and location of distinct modes on the distribution of each content variable. In polymodal structures, the more pronounced the modes, the greater the degree of stratification.

Profile: Skewness. Several statistical devices exist to mark the degree of skewness. The greater the level of skewness, the greater the degree of stratification.

ILLUSTRATIONS

Consider the following examples. Data by which to measure and compare stratification structures are exceedingly difficult to obtain. Consider for a moment that a complete description requires well-measured, valid indicators of four content dimensions, one or more for each dimension. For each indicator, several measurements must be made: the average level, the degree of absolute and relative inequality, the degree and factor-analytic forms of the crystallization of the whole set of indicators of the content dimension, the degree of status inheritance, and the distribution of all must be plotted so as to indicate the mode structure and to measure the skewness of each. To describe such an overall structure at one time requires the construction of twenty-four or more different indicators of structural dimensions. These have to be based upon representative, societywide samples large enough to permit the recording of small differences, as in the few people at the upper end of a skewed distribution. The resulting scores on the indicator variables must be comparable among the small units whose positions on the variables are to be aggregated into a measure of the structural dimensions. The study of variations in the structure of stratification demands that comparable measurements be taken on the same variable in different times and places. In itself, this latter requirement is extremely severe when making comparisons among societies with different cultures or over long periods of time within the same society.

Exploratory work of this sort has been conducted on data provided by Brazil. The data were collected on a national probability sample of households in 1973 and are available on all employed men and women in the households sampled. These people are the "small units" of the descriptive analysis presented later. Brazil is a particularly good place in which to conduct such exploratory research for two reasons. First, it is a large country whose regions are markedly different from each other in terms of development. Second, it has only one language and culture. The first makes it feasible to test for structural variations of stratification associated with development levels, treating regions as societies. The second eases the problem of comparability.

As indicated earlier, it is not now feasible to obtain measures of the power content dimension, in Brazil or anywhere else. However, there is widespread agreement that income is a proper measure of the economic status dimension, that occupational status instruments based on the average education and income of each occupation are proper measures of the prestige dimension, and that education is a similarly appropriate measure of the informational status dimension. These data are available for some of the parameters that would have to be assessed to obtain a complete description of the regional-development variations of the Brazilian stratification structure in 1973.

Here, indeed, we compare sharply different development regions. The stratification structures of three of Brazil's socioeconomic development (SED) macroregions as of 1970 were delineated by obtaining multiple-item, factor-weighted SED scores on the nation's 360 official continental microregions and plotting their levels on the map of Brazil (Haller 1983). This showed the following five macroregions: the Developed South (median SED = 78, on a scale of zero to 100), the South's Developing Periphery (median SED = 54), the Undeveloped Amazonia (median SED = 32.5), the Unevenly Developed Northeast (median SED = 31), and the Underdeveloped Middle North (median SED = 13).

Obviously, we cannot reproduce here each one of the structural dimensions for each SED macroregion for men and for women. Instead, we shall provide a few key illustrations on three of the regions: the Developed, the Developing, and the Underdeveloped.

Variables routinely used as indicators were formulated to measure three of the four stratification content dimensions: education in years successfully completed, occupational status scores (composed of canonically weighted scores based on the education and income of each occupation), and annual income in U.S. dollars of 1973.

The illustrations are based on regularly employed men and women 15 to 65 years of age. All such persons who lived in the three regions under comparison and who were part of the sample have been included. The numbers of sample members vary sharply by region and by sex. The Developed South is much more populous than the other two regions, and about three times more men than women are employed. The largest of the six subsamples thus consists of men in the South— over 40,000 (see Table 1, p. 1992). The smallest is of women in the South's Developing Periphery— over 2,500.

Let us begin with the profiles (see Figure 1, p. 1993), graphs that have been sketched to show the shape of the stratification structures for men and for women as these appear in the three regions. There are two reasons for paying close attention to these curves. First, they show the status relations among the people. The presence of multiple modes shows the existence of discrete and potentially opposed classes. Both the mode structure and the marked skewing indicate a high degree of stratification for each sample. Second, the fact that these distributions diverge sharply from normal or log normal curves shows that the numbers, that is, the data presented in tables 1 and 2 (Table 2 is on p. 1994), are at best approximate. This is because the shapes of the distributions affect their meaning.

The curves show the following:

1. Multiple modes are exhibited by both men and women in eleven of the twelve graphs pertaining to the developed and the developing regions. The exception is distribution of women's income in the Developing region.

2. For the two most developed regions, comparable curves show just about the same mode structure. In these, education tends to be bi- or tri-modal, occupational status to be at least tri-modal. Among men and among women in the developing region, income also exhibits multiple modes. In the underdeveloped region, the shape of the curves is markedly different from those of the others. The curves in this region show a heavy concentration of

TABLE 1
Illustrative Variations of Brazilian Regional Stratification Structures by Development, Employed Persons Age 15–65, 1973

Stratification Content Variable	Region					
	Men			Women		
	Developed	Developing	Underdeveloped	Developed	Developing	Underdeveloped
Education						
General level (average)	4.9	4.2	1.7	5.3	5.1	1.6
Absolute Inequality (standard dev.)	3.9	3.8	2.3	4.3	4.5	2.7
Occupational Status						
General Level (average)	19.4	16.8	6.7	20.3	21.2	8.6
Absolute Inequality (standard dev.)	18.9	18.0	10.8	19.7	20.4	14.6
Circulation Mobility $(1-r^2)$	0.72	0.79	0.85	0.69	0.75	0.63
Income, Annual						
General Level (average)	1,800	1,423	536	891	610	264
Absolute Inequality (standard dev.)	2,670	2,330	903	1,132	864	400
Number of Persons	41,578	7,686	5,841	15,711	2,581	2,777

NOTE: *Education* is in estimated years. *Occupational status* is in canonical socioeconomic status units (0–100); *Circulation mobility* is intergenerational. *Income* is in U.S. dollars.

both men and women at the bottom of each indicator variable, though some of the region's six graphs show the formation of small second and, sometimes third, modes at high status levels. The apparent conclusion to be drawn is that the underdeveloped area exhibits a relatively high degree of equality at the bottom of the Brazilian stratification structure. This is precisely the opposite of common belief among many observers of Brazil, who believe that inequality is greater in the underdeveloped region than in the more advanced south.

3. Each curve shows a high degree of skewness.

That is, the highest statuses are held by a tiny proportion of the people, and, on the whole, as the tail of the distribution lengthens, the higher the level, the tinier the percentage of the people.

4. In every case, the main modes are the one or two at the bottom, where most people tend to be concentrated.

5. Almost every graph shows a tendency for one or two smaller modes to appear toward the middle of the distribution. For education, this is around grade 12. For occupational status it is about fifty units, or the level of office clerks, primary teachers, and the like. For income, it

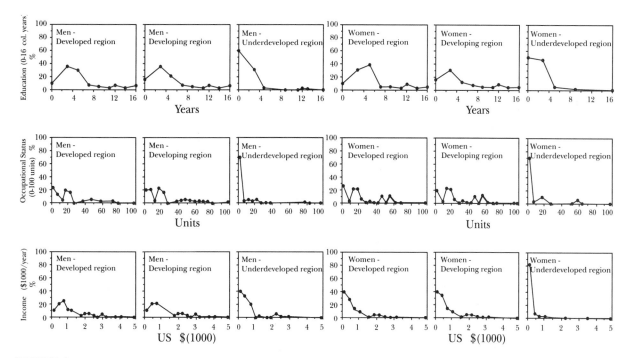

FIGURE 1

Illustrative Variations of Brazilian Regional Stratification Profiles, by Development, Employed Persons Age 15–65, 1973

SOURCE: See Table 1 for definitions and sample sizes.

is about two to three thousand dollars per year, or a monthly wage of between $160 and $250.

6. There may be a tiny mode near the top of the educational and occupational status distribution in the more developed regions.

7. For occupational status and income, women are more concentrated toward the bottom than are men.

8. Clearly, the main regional variations of profile are between the two more developed regions and the underdeveloped region.

9. In terms of mode structure, the more developed areas seem more stratified than the underdeveloped area.

10. In terms of skewness, it would appear that the underdeveloped area is the more highly stratified.

Data on the general levels and absolute inequality levels of the three content dimensions are presented in Table 1. For occupational status, the degree of circulation mobility is also presented. The general level rises with development for all three variables, except for the occupational levels of women in the developing region, whose status is slightly higher than that of women in the developed region. Again, with two exceptions among women in the developing region, the higher the level of development, the greater the degree of absolute inequality. Echoing what was to be gleaned from the graphs, the general level and the absolute inequality levels of the underdeveloped region are markedly lower than those in the other areas. Finally, among men, the higher the level of development, the lower the degree of circulation mobility. Women show no trend in this regard.

Evidence regarding structural crystallization is presented in Table 2. Among men, the higher the level of development, the higher the degree of crystallization. Among women, the same trend may exist, but with one small inconsistency.

TABLE 2
Illustrative Variations in Structural Crystallization Among Brazilian Development Regions, Employed Persons Age 15–65, 1973 (Correlation Coefficients)

Stratification Content Variables	Region					
	Men			Women		
	Developed	Developing	Underdeveloped	Developed	Developing	Underdeveloped
Education by occupational status	.52	.51	.35	.65	.67	.52
Education by income	.27	.18	.16	.23	.20	.20
Occupational status by income	.23	.16	.13	.23	.17	.16

See Table 1 for definitions and sample sizes.

CONCLUSION

This essay attempts to describe the contemporary synthesis of classical and empirical traditions of sociological thought concerning societal stratification, with special emphasis on what may be learned about ways to describe variations in stratification structures. In it, too, are presented some illustrations showing how indicators of some of the structural dimensions vary across development regions among employed men and women of Brazil. In general, they show that the more highly developed the region, the more stratified it is.

Measuring stratification variations among societies is an immense task because of the number of variables that must be studied and because of cultural, language, and social organizational differences among peoples. Still, at both the individual and societal levels, the effects of structural differences of stratification are among the most perplexing of this age, perhaps of all ages. For this reason, understanding how and why stratification structures vary and specifying the consequences of such differences is worth the considerable effort required.

(SEE ALSO: *Marxist Sociology; Occupational Prestige; Social Inequality; Social Stratification*)

REFERENCES

Duncan, Otis Dudley 1968 "Social Stratification and Mobility: Problems in the Measurement of Trend." In Eleanor Bernert Sheldon and Wilbert E. Moore, eds., *Indicators of Social Change: Concepts and Measurements.* New York: Russell Sage Foundation.

Featherman, David L., and Robert M. Hauser 1978 *Opportunity and Change.* New York: Academic Press.

Haller, Archibald O. 1970 "Changes in the Structure of Status Systems." *Rural Sociology* 35:469–487.

———— 1983 *The Socioeconomic Macroregions of Brazil.* Lanham, Md.: Bernam-Unipub.

Lenski, Gerhardt 1966 *Power and Privilege: A Theory of Social Stratification.* New York: McGraw-Hill.

Sorokin, Pitirim A. 1927 *Social Mobility.* New York: Harper.

Svalastoga, Kaare 1965 *Social Differentiation.* New York: David McKay.

Treiman, Donald J. 1977 *Occupational Prestige in Comparative Perspective.* New York: Academic Press.

U.S. Department of Commerce 1980 *Social Indicators II.* Washington, D.C.: U.S. Government Printing Office.

Weber, Max 1946 "Class, Status, and Party." In Hans Gerth and C. Wright Mills, eds., *From Max Weber.* New York: Oxford University Press.

————1947. "Social Stratification and Class Structure." In A. M. Henderson and T. Parsons, eds., *The Theory of Social and Economic Organization.* New York: Free Press.

ARCHIBALD O. HALLER

SOCIOBIOLOGY Sociobiology refers to an alliance of disciplines (e.g., ethology, primatology, molecular biology) that applies the laws of evolutionary biology to the study of animal social behavior. Its emergence is quite recent, but its roots may be traced back to Charles Darwin's ([1859] 1958) theory of evolution by natural selection. For our purposes, this theory may be conveniently stated as follows:

1. The size of populations, if unchecked, increases at a faster rate than the resources needed for their survival.
2. As a consequence, populations suffer from a real or potential scarcity of resources.
3. The scarcity causes competition of various kinds within and between populations—what Darwin termed "the struggle for existence."
4. There are various results of this struggle. The most basic shows that some individuals in any given population are more successful than others in surviving long enough to mate and reproduce.
5. This differential success in reproduction is in the last analysis due to different "variations," what today are called genes, carried by different individuals.
6. That is, some variations are better "adapted" than others to environmental challenges (e.g., acquiring scarce resources). Those variations that are better adapted to environmental challenges are likely to be retained, through offspring, and thus conveyed to future populations; those that are less adapted are also more likely to be wiped out.
7. This differential reproduction, or the preservation of favorable "variations" and the rejection of injurious variations, is referred to as natural selection.
8. Natural selection is considered the basic "mechanism" or driving force of evolution.

This argument contains the basic elements of the theoretical program of sociobiology. Specifically: (1) it establishes a basic mechanism in the evolution of behavior; (2) it underscores competition (the "struggle"), which in sociobiology directs attention to the "selfishness" of behavior;

and (3) it guides inquiry into what scholars in various disciplines have termed a theory of "human nature" (e.g., Darwin 1871; Pareto [1916]1963). Such a theory seeks to answer substantively the following question: In the course of evolutionary time, has natural selection "acted upon" variations to produce *innate* behavioral predispositions (or psychological mechanisms, behavioral adaptations, epigenetic rules) that guide the development of behavior?

For about seventy years, Darwin's theory had little influence on the study of social behavior, especially human. Then around 1930 it united with genetic science to form what has been called the synthetic theory (or modern synthesis) on the general assumption that "all biological organization, down to the level of molecules, has evolved as a result of natural selection acting upon genetic variation" (Dobzhansky et al. 1977, p. 18).

The modern synthesis stimulated various scientific activities, including the evolutionary study of behavior. Scholars in various disciplines (e.g., entomology, primatology, ethology) pursued studies of animal social behavior that revealed many similarities to human behavior (e.g., Altmann 1967; van Lawick-Goodall 1971). On the widespread assumption that animal behavior is largely "instinctive," such studies established a genetic link to animal social behavior. They also raised a compelling question: Does the same link exist in the case of the human animal?

SOCIOBIOLOGY AND HUMAN BEHAVIOR

In 1975 a seminal work was published that proclaimed the advent of a new synthesis. Its synonym is sociobiology (Wilson 1975). The rise of sociobiology is alleged to represent a new stage in the development of the modern synthesis. Specifically, sociobiology seeks to add to the modern synthesis the systematic study of animal social behavior through the application of natural selection theory and laws from genetic science. With respect to human behavior, sociobiology claims the status of synthesis because it also seeks to incorporate into its theoretical program systematic theories of sociocultural behavior. So viewed, it is sometimes referred to as human sociobiology or biocultural science. Human sociobiology hooks up in mutual stimulation with such theoretical orientations as bioethics, biopsychology, bioanthropology, bioeconomics, biopolitics, biosociology, and so forth.

The fountainhead of sociobiology is the revival of the *behavioral* notion on which natural selection was for Darwin himself clearly based, namely, the struggle for existence. The concept of natural selection directs attention to the demographic consequences of behavior—how do the variations of a population evolve in the course of time? The struggle for existence, on the other hand, suggests that individuals compete as such, as members of populations, or as both for the scarce resources available in their environment. But as we have noted, the ultimate consequence of this competition is natural selection, namely, the differential contribution of offspring to future generations. This differential reproduction is a measure of what Darwin, following the sociologist Herbert Spencer, called "fitness." Hence, we may state that in the last analysis individuals (or, simply, organisms) compete with one another for maximal reproductive success or genetic fitness.

This line of reasoning has introduced what is considered the general principle of sociobiology. Sometimes referred to as the maximization principle, it states that organisms tend to behave so as to maximize their inclusive fitness. The use of the adjective *inclusive* is intended to underscore the fact, better understood in the post-Darwin period (Hamilton 1964), that the fitness of organisms is measured in terms of their genetic relationship both to their offspring and to their other blood relatives.

The maximization principle is a crucial lawlike proposition whose function is to guide research toward the wherefores of the emergence and persistence of various kinds of behavior. It is not intended as an all-encompassing, and in itself sufficient, tool of theoretical inquiry. Rather, it must be understood as the fulcrum of an expanding set of laws, theorems, and hypotheses about

social behavior. Together these underscore the fact that human nature consists of a complex, and still largely unspecified and unclassified, set of adaptations (or behavioral predispositions).

The Law of Altruism. The maximization principle manifestly implies a behavioral tendency that may be termed selfish and is metaphorically said to reside in "the selfish gene" (Dawkins 1976). It thus purports to give a scientific answer to the secular question: For whose benefit does the individual behave? Acts that benefit others are commonly observed by sociobiologists as well as their colleagues in the moral and social disciplines. Does it then mean that individuals are altruistic? The sociobiologist's answer is that they are only apparently so, and the natural selection of altruism is, according to Wilson (1975, p. 3), "the central theoretical problem of sociobiology."

The heavy emphasis on the problem of altruism rests on the fact that, from an evolutionary perspective, genuine altruism must be defined as "self-destructive behavior performed for the benefit of others" (Wilson 1975, p. 578). In short, genuine altruism reduces the benefactor's fitness and hence may be expected to be wiped out by natural selection. If, for example, Jane X is driven by her genes to do good for Mary Y at the expense of her own fitness, her altruistic genes will not be represented in the next generation. What then is it that people call altruism? Typically it is either nepotistic favoritism or reciprocal favoritism. Both of these, however beneficial to others, redound to the benefit of the "altruist." The key to the evolution of so-called altruism must apparently be found in "kin selection" (e.g., Hamilton 1964) and "reciprocal altruism" (Trivers 1971).

Kin selection is most dramatically illustrated by the study of eusocial insects, for example, ants. Approximately three-quarters of these animals are female (the "workers"), and only very few reproduce. At one time, this was a Darwinian puzzle. Why should they not reproduce? Are they genuine altruists? As it turns out, they are not. Workers are so named because they are very diligent in catering to the needs of the queen (the reproducing mother or sister) and her usually prodigious brood. Furthermore, given the peculiar reproductive system of such species (haplodiploidy), sisters and aunts are more closely related to the future generations than sisters and aunts in other (the diploid) species (Hamilton 1964). That is, the sacrifice in individual fitness that is potentially incurred because of nonreproduction is small, *and* it is probably compensated for by the special care of the young. In short, eusocial insects have evolved in societies of kin ("sisterhoods"), and it is at this level of organization that natural selection acts favorably or otherwise on their genes.

Among human beings, kin selection is observable in innumerable contexts. For example, we normally favor kin to strangers with our assistance (e.g., Essock-Vitale and McGuire 1985). Perhaps nothing shows the fact better than the history of last wills and testaments.

Reciprocal altruism refers to the prevalent fact that, if and when we engage in actions that benefit others, we do so with the expectation, conscious or otherwise, that they will repay us in kind, especially if they are unrelated to us. The fact is the object of a carefully stated theory by Trivers (1971; for continuing research on this topic, see Taylor and McGuire 1988).

The theory states that the evolution of reciprocal altruism was facilitated by three broad conditions: (1) a high frequency of situations in which the benefit of "altruism" to beneficiaries was, in terms of fitness, greater than the cost incurred by the benefactors; (2) membership in a small and stable social group; (3) equal ability between pairs of individuals to engage in mutual help. These conditions may be elaborated into six socioecological parameters: long life expectancy, low migration rate, high mutual dependence, extended parental care, weak dominance order, and exposure to combat situations. Trivers argues convincingly that these were in place in the evolutionary past of many species, our own included.

The selective retention of reciprocal altruism was, however, threatened by the probability of "cheating," whereby some individuals did not reciprocate according to the benefits they re-

ceived. Indeed, an underlying assumption of the theory is that the real motivation of givers is to receive more than they give. Accordingly, a number of adaptations evolved in the psychological system of individuals to regulate the reciprocally altruistic system. They include such emotions as friendship, sympathy, trust, suspicion, moralistic aggression, and, in view of the inevitability of some cheating, such traits as dishonesty, hypocrisy, and feelings of guilt.

Combining now the logic of kin selection and reciprocal altruism, we may state the law of altruism as follows: In keeping with the maximization principle, socioecological conditions have evolved to predispose individuals to favor others in direct proportion (1) to their degree of genetic relatness and (2) to the extent in which the benefit they derive from doing good to others is, in terms of fitness, greater than their cost.

Within sociology and anthropology, the law is relevant to various phenomena of exchange and reciprocity. It also helps to solve what has long been a puzzling problem. Social scientists have noted that the exchange of gifts is universal in human society (e.g., Mauss [1925] 1954). Associated with this phenomenon, however, is a practice, the potlatch, which, in varying degrees, is "a universal mode of culture" (Lévi-Strauss [1949] 1969). In the potlatch, as was practiced, for example, by the Indians of Vancouver and Alaska, one gives with a view to crushing another and thus gaining "privileges, titles, rank, authority and prestige" (Lévi-Strauss [1949] 1969, chap. 5). Specifically, gifts are often given with the general understanding that the recipients will in the future reciprocate with interest. When such obligations cannot be met, the recipients lose status, titles, prestige, and so forth. Social theory has inexplicably accommodated this sort of behavior under the assumption that exchange is beneficial to all the parties to the exchange, indeed to the group as a whole. The law of altruism predicts conversely that the exchange *may be* beneficial to all *but* that the motivation of givers is selfish and often yields a selfish advantage.

This extreme stress on the selfishness of human

behavior cannot, however, go unchallenged. Consider, for example, Catholic nuns and Buddhist monks. They practice celibacy and typically contribute little or nothing to the fitness-enhancing resources of their blood relations. Thus, genuine or "ascetic altruism" may be rare among humans, but it is a fact (Lopreato 1984, chap. 6).

The Law of Anisogamy. Males and females differ genetically from each other in a most consequential respect (see, e.g., Barash 1982, chap. 10–11). On the average, women produce 350 to 400 relatively large sex cells (eggs, or ova) in the course of a lifetime. The circumstance translates to precious investment in reproduction. By comparison a man can produce more than one billion very tiny sex cells (spermatozoa) in a single day. This difference is referred to as anisogamy. The behavioral consequences of it are numerous and constitute a sizable part of sociobiological research. We shall summarily express them in what may be termed the *law of anisogamy*, as follows: The two sexes are endowed with differing reproductive strategies, and their behaviors reflect that difference in direct proportion to their relevance to it.

This law, too, is subsumable under the theoretical umbrella of the maximization principle. In turn, it is a pivotal point of an increasing number of research hypotheses. The most comprehensive study comprises thirty-seven samples amounting to 10,047 individuals living in thirty-three countries on six continents (Buss 1989). Concentrating on sex differences in mate preferences, the findings suggest that culture has a strong influence on such preferences and that the two sexes are quite agreed on some of the basic requirements of a good mate, for example, dependability. On the other hand, some findings clearly reflect the differing reproductive strategies implicit in anisogamy. For instance, females are significantly more likely than males to value mates with ambition and industriousness—mates, that is, who offer a "good financial prospect." Conversely, males more than females prefer mates who are physically attractive, younger than themselves, and at the peak of their reproductive value.

These facts are predictable from the law of anisogamy. Women, with their limited and precious reproductive capacity, emphasize the resources needed for the good health and survival of their typically few children. Men, with their nearly infinite potential for reproduction, have evolved to value what appear to be the signs of high fertility.

The law of anisogamy implies a number of corollaries, each of which corresponds to one or more adaptations or psychological mechanisms. A particularly productive one is what may be termed the *corollary of sexual selection*. Darwin ([1859] 1958; 1871) distinguished a form of natural selection that he termed *sexual selection*. It refers to the selection that results from competition within each sex for mates. The corollary may be stated to take both sexes into account, or may be divided into two statements, one for each sex. For simplicity's sake, the following states the male case but with a passing reference to females: Given the huge quantity of sex cells produced by males, and in view of the choosiness of females' behavior due to their much more limited reproductive potential, males have been selected to specialize in competitive (agonistic) behavior.

Competitiveness takes many forms. One is reflected in the common practice of polygyny (one husband with multiple wives) found in the history of human society (e.g., Lenski and Lenski 1987). Polygyny is adaptive for the winners, quite maladaptive for the losers. Another form of competition is manifested by violent behavior. Consider the figures on murder. Killing is heavily concentrated among young men, and the victims are typically strangers or mere acquaintances. Very often, homicide is clearly the result of competition for fitness among males of high reproductive potential. Prominent among the motives of homicides are sexual jealousy and rivalry as well as quarrels about dominance in economic and other social contexts (e.g., Daly and Wilson 1988). Little wonder, then, that in countries where the dangers of childbirth have been all but eliminated, women on the average live up to ten years longer than men. Death by trauma (e.g., murder and accidents) accounts for a high percentage of male mortality, and is much more frequent in men than in women (e.g., Verbrugge 1989). Accidents are often the results of agonistic behavior, for example, war and showing-off contests.

In conclusion, it bears noting that, in part because of its recent development, sociobiology is not lacking in controversy. Among social scientists in particular, some scholars have accused others of (1) overstressing the adaptiveness of behavior and (2) using the maximization principle as "a general purpose mechanism" to hide "a large number of mechanisms" (e.g., Tooby and Cosmides 1989; Symons 1989). These criticisms are excessive but not entirely baseless. The introduction of an evolutionary general principle (the maximization principle) into behavioral science has engendered some excessive enthusiasm and some abuse; for some evolutionists, the principle is the first and only scientific law of human behavior. The criticisms are to an extent baseless, however, because all sociobiologists understand the maximization principle as the theoretical anchorage point of a more or less large number of propositions and psychological mechanisms. Together, principle and derivatives will eventually constitute what philosophers and social scientists have long referred to as "the theory of human nature." The principle is thus the theoretical umbrella of this development, much as the law of universal gravitation, for example, is the encompassing principle of celestial mechanics.

This theory constitutes the main sociobiological frontier. Another, closely related, concerns the search for a theory of sociocultural evolution, properly speaking. The latter entails the isolation of a unit of transmission analogous to the gene in biological evolution. Some starts here have been made (e.g., Lumsden and Wilson 1981). But there is no great reason to be optimistic about them (Lopreato 1990). What is more promising is a series of theories, constructed on logico-intuitive grounds, of the evolution and persistence of such phenomena as ethnic conflict (e.g., van den Berghe 1981) and elements of religion (e.g., Lopreato 1984, chap. 6).

(SEE ALSO: *Altruism; Evolution: Biological, Social, Cultural; Sex Differences*)

REFERENCES

Altmann, Stuart A. (ed.) 1967 *Social Communication among Primates.* Chicago: University of Chicago Press.

Barash, David P. 1982 *Sociobiology and Behavior.* New York: Elsevier.

Buss, David M. 1989 "Sex Differences in Human Mate Preferences: Evolutionary Hypotheses Tested in 37 Cultures." *Behavioral and Brain Sciences* 12:1–49.

Daly, Martin, and Margo Wilson 1988 *Homicide.* New York: Aldine.

Darwin, Charles (1859) 1958 *The Origin of Species.* New York: Mentor Books.

——— 1871 *The Descent of Man and Selection in Relation to Sex.* New York: Appleton.

Dawkins, Richard 1976 *The Selfish Gene.* Oxford: Oxford University Press.

Dobzhansky, Theodosius, Francisco J. Ayala, G. Ledyard Stebbins, and James W. Valentine 1977 *Evolution.* San Francisco: W. H. Freeman.

Essock-Vitale, Susan M., and Michael T. McGuire 1985 "Women's Lives Viewed from an Evolutionary Perspective. II. Patterns of Helping." *Ethology and Sociobiology* 6:155–173.

Hamilton, William D. 1964 "The Genetical Theory of Social Behaviour: I and II." *Journal of Theoretical Biology* 7:1–52.

Lenski, Gerhard, and Jean Lenski 1987 *Human Societies.* New York: McGraw-Hill.

Lévi-Strauss, Claude (1949) 1969 *The Elementary Structures of Kinship.* Boston: Beacon Press.

Lopreato, Joseph 1984 *Human Nature and Biocultural Evolution.* Boston: Unwin Hyman.

——— 1990 "From Social Evolutionism to Biocultural Evolutionism." *Sociological Forum* 5:187–212.

Lumsden, Charles J., and Edward O. Wilson 1981 *Genes, Mind, and Culture.* Cambridge, Mass.: Harvard University Press.

Mauss, Marcel (1925) 1954 *The Gift.* London: Cohen and West.

Pareto, Vilfredo (1916) 1963 *A Treatise on General Sociology.* New York: Dover.

Symons, Donald 1989 "A Critique of Darwinian Anthropology." *Ethology and Sociobiology* 10:131–144.

Taylor, Charles E., and Michael T. McGuire (eds.) 1988 *Ethology and Sociobiology* 9:67–257 (special issue on "Reciprocal Altruism").

Tooby, John, and Leda Cosmides 1989 "Evolutionary

Psychology and the Generation of Culture, Part I." *Ethology and Sociobiology* 10:29–49.

Trivers, Robert L. 1971 "The Evolution of Reciprocal Altruism." *Quarterly Review of Biology* 46:35–47.

van den Berghe, Pierre L. 1981 *The Ethnic Phenomenon.* New York: Elsevier.

van Lawick-Goodall, Jane 1971 *In the Shadow of Man.* Boston, Mass.: Houghton Mifflin.

Verbrugge, Lois M. 1989 "The Twain Meet: Empirical Explanations of Sex Differences in Health and Mortality." *Journal of Health and Social Behavior* 30:282–304.

Wilson, Edward O. 1975 *Sociobiology: The New Synthesis.* Cambridge, Mass.: Harvard University Press.

JOSEPH LOPREATO

SOCIOLINGUISTICS When Roger Brown and Albert Gilman published their now classic paper on pronouns of power and solidarity (1960; see also 1989), no one characterized that paper as a major contribution to "sociolinguistics." By the time John Gumperz and Dell Hymes published their *New Directions in Sociolinguistics* (1990; 1972 was based on a 1966 special publication of the American Anthropological Association), they were providing a paradigmatic definition of an already recognizable enterprise; their book included contributions by many of the founders. A two-part survey essay on sociolinguistics written in 1973 (Grimshaw 1973b, 1974a) began with a comment that more had been published on sociolinguistic topics in the early 1970s than in all previous years. The review included comment on about fifty new titles; only a few sociologists (most particularly Basil Bernstein and Joshua Fishman, each with several volumes) were represented. In the nearly two decades since then, interest in language *in use* (what will shortly be characterized as micro sociolinguistics) has continued to grow exponentially; it is probably safe to say that such interest is still not seen as part of mainstream sociology. Interests in more macro dimensions of the sociology of language—for instance, in language conflict, language maintenance, language spread and decline—have also grown, but much more slowly.

SOME ACTIVITIES AND SOME LABELS

There are at least a dozen specialties that investigate some aspect of language: its origins, its structure, its invariant and variant features, its acquisition, its use in social contexts, its change, spread, and death, and so on. Among these there are at least five whose practitioners do not consider themselves sociolinguists or sociologists of language, and whose research is seldom incorporated directly into sociolinguistics/sociology of language (SL/SOL) investigations:

1. Formal linguistics that focuses on language(s) as autonomous system(s) *and how these systems work independently of human/social agency;* this activity is often referred to as "autonomous linguistics" and occasionally as "nonhyphenated linguistics"

2. Anthropological linguistics, the "description" (writing of grammars and dictionaries and audio and phonemic recording of phonological systems) of language(s) in specific, usually nonmodern, societies

3. Psycholinguistics, which covers a wide range of topics including the acoustics of perception, cognitive constraints on the complexity of clausal embedding, theories of innateness and of learning in language acquisition, and the physical location of language functions in the brain

4. Social psychology of language (from *psychological social* psychology), another wide-ranging specialty including research on message characteristics and influence, self-disclosure, relationships between personality and speech, and relationships among body movements, speech, and "meaning."

5. Conversation analysis/ethnomethodology (CA), an approach that views talk in much the same way as formal linguists view language: as a system that is syntactically organized and has a structure that can be discerned independently

of attention to the social attributes of participants in particular talk.

CA *has* identified such devices as "pre-invitations" and "pre-closings," as well as ways of constructing accusations without accusing anyone explicitly (Atkinson and Drew 1979); those in the field are interested in how these devices are used in the course of the immediate talk, not in how they might be directed to more complex goals of conversational participants. Whalen has noted that CA "examines talk as an object in its own right, as a fundamental type of social action, rather than primarily as a resource for documenting other social processes." *None* of the five activities just described is interested in language primarily as social resource.

In contrast, another small handful of specialties focuses on the social dimensions of language/talk: as interactional resource, as a component of individual and group identity, as a social object. The ethnography of speaking and ethnolinguistics, like the anthropological practices from which they have taken their names, focus on the diversity of linguistic resources available and the uses to which those resources are put in individual speech communities and in human society at large, respectively. There is, at least implicitly, a strong comparative dimension to these arenas of investigation.

Sociolinguistics manifests a different kind of comparative orientation. The micro variety of sociolinguistics usually focuses on interactional accomplishment through the medium of *language in use in social contexts:* (a) comparisons of means and ends, including attention both to how individual ends can be accomplished by different means (ways of talking) and to how different outcomes may simultaneously result (intendedly or otherwise) from production of same or very similar bits of talk, and (b) comparisons of the different resources available to different participants in talk. The sociology of language, as the macro variety of sociolinguistics is often called (Grimshaw 1987a), tends to focus on distributional studies of various sorts, such as distribution of

language varieties across individual repertoires, and distribution of repertoires across social aggregates, categories, and groups (nations or classes, genders or age groups, and families or friendship networks, respectively). At the most macro level this implies studies of language maintenance, supersession and change, conflict, and so on.

The *sociological* social psychology of language is, as would be expected, oriented to group effects on individual behaviors, including the acquisition of social-cultural competence through the medium of talk, the role of talk in the acquisition and organization of evaluative orientations, and uses of talk/written language in social control. At some point this last activity seems to shade off into symbolic interactionism; this boundary cannot be explored here. Finally, specialized studies of proxemics (social and interpersonal spacing) and kinesics (body movement, the organization of facial features, gesture, posture) have been done from both sociological and psychological perspectives (see Hall 1966, 1974; Kendon, [1977] 1990).

SOME QUESTIONS OF ORIENTATION

Since the next section includes illustrations of how sociological theory can be enriched by empirical SL/SOL research in specific substantive areas, comments here will be limited to four questions of general orientation in theoretical work in SL/SOL: (1) What are causal and other relations between language/speech and other social behavior(s)? (2) Are grammars of social interaction possible, and is there a universal grammar? (3) What is the relevance of a micro-macro distinction for understanding the importance of language/speech in social life, and how are the two levels articulated in social behavior? (4) Is theoretical advance/understanding best sought through focusing on social processes or on specific substantive arenas of social behavior?

Causal Directionality/Covariation/Cotemporality/Mutuality. As is true of other varieties of social behavior, SL/SOL theory and research must deal with complex problems of cause and effect. There are four principal perspectives on the causal relationship between social structure and language (see Grimshaw 1974b; Hymes 1966):

1. That which sees language as fundamental (or as source, cause, independent variable, or set of independent variables)—a position consonant both with an extreme Whorfian position (that language *determines* how people think) and with the commonsensical observation that we sometimes don't know what is going on until we hear people talking
2. That which sees social structure as a determinant or as an independent variable or set of such variables—a position consonant with our awareness that we ourselves talk differently in different situations, with different interlocutors, and depending on the nature of our interactional goals
3. That which sees neither as prior to the other, both being seen as co-occurring and codetermining, a position that will be briefly explicated below
4. That which sees both as determined by a third factor, whether that third factor be innate features of the human mind—the view of Cartesian linguistics (Chomsky 1966, 1968)— *Weltanschauung,* or the intrinsic demands of an ordered universe.

A majority of SL/SOL correlational studies focus on how location of individuals or groups in the social structure is *reflected* in speech and/or other language behavior, as in the case of regional or class dialects, or *determines* it, as in the case of selection of a language variety in different situations and with different conversational partners (Blom and Gumperz 1972) or of pronominal forms or other names (see, for a review of some of this literature, Grimshaw 1980). A smaller but still large number of correlational studies seek to discover how language use (spoken and written) is associated with interactional outcomes as varied as providing or not providing a requested favor, succeeding or not succeeding in school—or deciding whether to go to war (for a review of some of this literature see Grimshaw 1981. For illustrations of some claims about language use and risks of war see Chilton 1985; Wertsch and Mehan 1988). Although closer scrutiny often reveals that *ways of talking* are themselves resources differentially available to interactants with different social origins, some language resources appear to be available throughout social structures. Ways of talking, in turn, have been shown to have effects independent of structural relations.

Figure 1 is a simplified schematic representation of a mutual-embeddedness perspective—it is simultaneously a schematic of how the process(es)

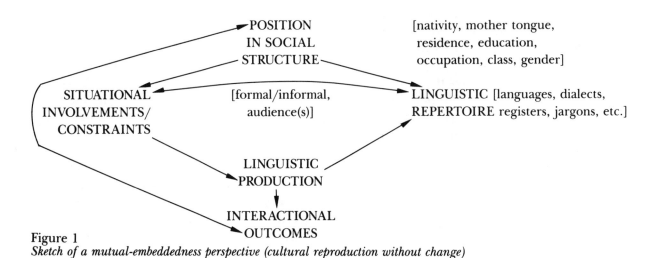

Figure 1
Sketch of a mutual-embeddedness perspective (cultural reproduction without change)

of cultural reproduction would operate in a world without change. Bernstein (1975), Pierre Bourdieu (Bourdieu and Passeron 1977), Aaron Cicourel (1980a, 1980b, 1981), Randall Collins (1981a, 1981b), and Jürgen Habermas (1984–1987) all address the question of cultural reproduction and, in one way or another, questions of change. All take essentially mutuality perspectives. All accord central importance to language in the reproduction process. Collins explicates ways in which he believes language is simultaneously a resource in interaction and a source of change. Only Bernstein and Cicourel actually collect data on language in use, and only Cicourel directly investigates talk. None of these scholars would strongly disagree with this characterization; each would wish to "complete" the chart through incorporation of neglected features (see, e.g., Bernstein's diagram of the process [1975, p. 24], with its foregrounding of different transmission agencies, such as family and education; modes of social control; specific speech varieties; and context-dependent and -independent meanings).

In the mid 1960s John Fischer (1965, 1966) published two papers that may represent a strongest version of the "mutual embeddedness" position and, from the disciplinary perspective of sociology, are perhaps the most esoterically documented. (The papers are extensively reviewed in Grimshaw 1974.) Fischer argued nothing less than that *phonological and syntactic differences between two related but mutually unintelligible* languages (Trukese and Ponapean, separated for about eight centuries) are *isomorphic to differences in the social structures of the two societies:*

As societies become more complex and social roles become more differentiated, the realized meaning of words in particular contexts becomes less important than the common or basic meaning. Speakers are forced to assume a greater cognitive gap between themselves and their listeners. At the same time, the basic meaning of the items of the lexicon tends to become more abstract and attenuated, since speakers have less need for words which can express much meaning in compact form to listeners who are conceived as being much like the self; they have more need, instead, for words which can be used in many different contexts with many different listeners who are conceived of as being very different from the self and from each other (Fischer 1966, p. 178).

The mutuality perspective is a richly suggestive one.

Grammars of Social Interaction/A Grammar of Social Interaction. Linguists write grammars, that is, they describe and write "rules" for phonological and syntactic systems, for individual languages—they are also variously committed to the goal of writing a grammar of language, that is, to identifying in grammars of individual languages features/rules that *hold for all languages:* a universal grammar. They distinguish between absolute and quantitative universals (i.e., between features of all languages that can be explained on theoretical grounds as required constitutents, and features that occur in all or most languages, such as terms for female derived from that for male [this kind of feature is known as marking], but for which no theoretically principled basis can be identified), and between weaker and stronger claims of universality (i.e., between a claim that all languages contain certain elements [nouns, verbs, prepositions] and a claim that those elements appear in the same order in utterances in every language).

An interest in the intrinsic ordering of the universe and a concern to avoid repeating old errors and rediscovering the already known are central among the reasons for linguists' interest in both the regularities within individual languages and universal rules. Sociologists have similar concerns in seeking to discover the rules of interactional grammars for specific societies or groups and in seeking social interactional universals and, for present purposes, the role of language in use in both grammars and *the* grammar. It appears to be the case that although there are greetings in most, if not all, societies (this is more a quantitative than an absolute universal, and there are societies in which greeting is the marked and nongreeting the unmarked case), how they are done, to whom, and to what purpose may vary quite considerably (Firth 1972; Goffman 1971; Ibrahim et al. 1976; Kendon and Ferber 1973).

Similarly, there must be a need for information everywhere—but questions are not the appropriate manner for obtaining information in every society (see E. Goody 1978; sources cited in Grimshaw 1969). Again, it seems likely that interpersonal relations of power and of affect and considerations of valence and of cost are everywhere involved in requesting behavior (Brown and Levinson 1987; Grimshaw 1989); their relative importance and the consequent variety of modes of requesting behaviors vary quite considerably.

Ways of talking are everywhere critical resources in interaction; we know very little, however, about what features of *language in use in social contexts* may be universal. For that matter, we know little about which rules *within* speech communities (or social groups) are variant and which are invariant (Labov 1968, Grimshaw 1973a). Indeed, some sociologists find the notion of rule misleading, on grounds that expectations and behaviors are always under negotiation (Berger and Luckmann 1966). Notions of rule and of exceptions vary across disciplines (Edgerton 1985; Labov 1968; Grimshaw 1973a, 1981).

Micro-Macro, Conversation, and Interaction/ Official Languages and Language Policies, SL/ SOL. These distinctions, along with the familiar polarities of social psychology and social organization—or qualitative and quantitative methods—often appear in discussions of sociological interests in language and language in use. There are really three sorts of questions that can be asked in this arena:

1. What are sociology's interests in what goes on in conversation/interaction, and what does a specific focus on talk teach us that other modes of study do not?
2. What are sociology's interests in looking at language as an individual social attribute that, aggregated, has supraindividual importance in ways similar to ethnic, class, religious, and other categorical attributes? What are sociology's interests in questions about how language is linked to life chances, why and how it becomes a focus of positive and negative atti-

tudes, and how languages spread, change, contract, and die?
3. How do the things that go on in individual conversations on the micro level get articulated with, and aggregated into, processes of change in languages themselves, or in their prestige, or in policies about their use, and so on, on the macro level?

As was suggested above, the micro-macro articulation question is closely related both to those about mutual embeddedness and to those about cultural reproduction. The dimension added by asking the articulation question is that of social change: If socializing/cultural transmission agencies operate so as to *reproduce* values, attitudes, behaviors, and so on in new generations, then how does change occur? A perspective offered by Collins (1981a, 1981b) is that participants in *everyday* conversations bring to those conversations interactional resources that are enhanced or reduced in the course of interaction, and that modest changes in interactional resources ultimately eventuate in changes in institutions and cultural systems—and languages. Related formulations are cited in Grimshaw (1987b). The macro-micro questions constrain us to think deeply both about processes of change and about how we try to get co-conversationalists to agree with us or to do what we want them to.

Substance or Process—"Top-Down" or "Bottom-Up." Two additional questions about the construction and the use of theory have methodological as well as theory-building implications. A first question is whether, when we study uses of language in specific contexts such as educational or military or medical institutions, we are interested primarily in understanding (1) the institutions themselves or (2) social processes such as negotiation or socialization, or, more broadly, conflict or cooperation, or (3) a specific kind of situated interaction, such as an interview, as a representative of a species of situation, or (4) how talk works in interaction. There are, of course, no pure cases.

The second question has been nicely put by Cicourel (1980a) as a distinction between "top-down" and "bottom-up" theorizing. By "top-down" Cicourel means approaching corpora of talk with sets of conceptual notions ranging from the generality of "cultural reproduction" or "role" and/or "conflict" to the specificity of "role-conflict" or different "footings" in talk (Goffman 1981). By "bottom-up" he refers to researchers immersing themselves in their data and identifying regularities, then validating that identification, then discovering regularities in relations between previously observed regularities, and so on. Stated preferences aside, all of the investigators whose work is mentioned in this article—indeed, all sociologists—would like to believe that they let their data guide them to theory construction. Preferences again aside, all of them are to some extent guided in their work by prior theoretical constructions.

DATA, DATA, EVERYWHERE

While sociologists can sometimes be intimidated by the complex structure of formal linguistic theory, they may be equally envious of the easy access of linguists to their data, either in their own intuitions about the language(s) they speak or in the bath of talk and writing in which all of us live (compare the ways of studying phonology in, e.g., Chomsky and Halle 1968; Labov 1980). Students of SL/SOL share the advantage that many of the data in which they may be interested are fairly accessible and, with modern technology, fairly easy to collect (denial of access and questions of ethics aside). They share the disadvantage that many of the sociological questions which they may want to study—matters as various as (1) attitudes about different speech varieties, (2) the impact of stratification on the acquisition of those attitudes, or (3) the ways in which phonological variation *affects* stratification—can be considerably more difficult to identify, conceptualize, and measure. Just as there are fundamental questions about theoretical orientation in SL/SOL, so there are fundamental questions about methods.

There is room in this truncated discussion for brief comment on only a few of these methodological questions: (1) What constitutes optimal data for SL and SOL, or micro and macro, research?

(2) How may such optimal data best be collected? (3) What need is there for modes of work, such as comprehensive discourse analysis (CDA), that differ from more familiar modes of sociological investigation? (4) What are the roles of collaborative and comparative studies in SL/SOL research?

What Constitute Optimal Types of Data for SL/SOL? William Labov (1972a), in one of his many suggestive papers on methodological questions, remarked that linguists work variously in library, bush, closet, laboratory, and street, where they collect/produce data that can be labeled texts, elicitations, intuitions, experimental results, and observations, respectively. Among the many sorts of data that can be useful in investigation of SL/SOL issues, those associated with four "how" questions are arguably more central. The questions, and the optimal data for their study, are as follow:

1. *How* do people actually talk/write? This "how" has two dimensions: (a) What varieties of language (spoken and written will be assumed in all the discussion following) do individual members of speech communities control? (b) How do individuals employ their language resources in social interaction? The optimal data for such studies are extended texts.
2. *How* are language varieties and patterns of use distributed across categories of age, class, gender, occupation, nationality, religious affiliation, residence? The optimal data here are a combination of sampled *texts* and *observations*.
3. *How* do members of social groups learn about language and its appropriate use, and how do they learn second (and higher-order) languages? The optimal data here are *experimental results* and *observations* and, to a somewhat lesser extent, texts.
4. *How* do people feel about language, that is, what are attitudes of individuals and groups toward language varieties, repertoires, language change, literacy? Data that have been employed in addressing these questions have included all five of the varieties listed by Labov; each has proved useful.

What Are Criteria for Optimal Quality Data? There is no such thing as a "verbatim" record without electronic recording, and optimal records of conversation include both high-fidelity audio recording and (possibly) multiple image recordings (for discussions of sound-image recording, including some of the controversies that have characterized the field, see Feld and Williams 1975; Grimshaw 1982, 1989). When working with written texts, optimal data include photographic copies of handwritten originals as well as printed versions. Whatever variety of texts and observations are collected and used as data, however, such materials are valuable only to the extent that contexts of both "situation" and "text" (i.e., embedding talk or written material) are provided (the distinction is Halliday's, following Malinowski); two excellent articulations of the importance of context, suggesting rather different boundaries of what must be taken into account, are those of William Corsaro (1981, 1985) and Cicourel (esp. 1991).

People are often skeptical of claims about what talk is actually like until they see it transcribed; they then are skeptical that the transcription is accurate (I was once told, "Even sociologists don't talk like that!") until they hear electronically recorded audio while reading a transcript. Investigators who work with texts, elicitations, and observations must always take into account the effects of monitoring in the case of most varieties of SL/SOL data; Labov has referred to what he has called the Observer's Paradox, that is, "we want to observe how people talk when they are not being observed" (1972a). We should also keep in mind, however, Sol Worth's observation that *all* behavior, however carefully monitored, is "natural" (personal communication). Labov has developed elicitation techniques that have the advantage of generating different levels of self-consciousness of, and thus monitoring of, talk (see, e.g., 1972b).

Other concerns with data in SL/SOL research are, like those just reviewed, quite similar to those in sociological research in general. Self-report data on language varieties employed by oneself or one's family, or of uses of literacy, are notoriously unreliable; and definitions and measurement(s) of such individual attributes as literacy and bilingual fluency are often inconsistent.

The Need for Methods Specific to SL/SOL. Many of the data employed in SL/SOL research are the same as or very similar to those employed in other arenas of sociology, and the methods employed in analysis are similarly familiar. Such similarity may be least evident in the case of the activities labeled "conversation analysis" (see Whalen 1991) and "comprehensive discourse analysis" (Labov and Fanshel 1977). Labov and Fanshel realize that the goal of comprehensiveness is chimerical; their pioneering study demonstrated the importance of such aspects of talk as prosodic and paralinguistic features. Lexical, syntactic, and even phonological selection are deeply involved in what is "actually said" (i.e., interactionally intended) in talk (for a discussion of the process of "disambiguation" of text, see Grimshaw 1987c). Sociologists have employed CDA and adaptations of it to ask somewhat more specifically sociological questions. Other students have developed similarly fine-grained approaches to written texts (Silverman and Torode 1980). One can hope that sociologists are now aware that questions about language qua language have sociological significance, and that talk and writing are no longer just media that contain answers to other questions.

Collaborative, Comparative, and Corroborative Research on SL/SOL. While SL and SOL research and publications have increased tremendously in the past few decades, their literatures continue to be diffuse. There have been few replications. Most research has been on English, and much of the material on other languages is published *in* English. While much of the early activity in SL was interdisciplinary, there have been few truly interdisciplinary studies (for discussion of problems with such projects, see Grimshaw, Feld, and Jenness 1991) or parallel studies of shared data (see, however, Chafe 1980; Dorval 1990; Grimshaw, Burke, et al. 1991). There have been few explicitly comparative studies in which same or collaborating investigators have simultaneously studied a "same" phenomenon in different speech communities (see, however, Watson-

Gegeo and White 1990) or in different institutional contexts in same societies (see, however, Grimshaw 1990). There is reason to believe that all three of these important kinds of research are on the increase, however, with scholars all over the world trying out SL formulations largely generated in the United States and Europe in their own societies, with more and more work being done on related SL phenomena in societies and speech communities where earlier work followed more traditional courses in linguistics and anthropological linguistics, and with researchers from an increasingly wide range of disciplinary backgrounds finding in SL/SOL data and theory materials to address their own questions.

An Additional, Residual, Neglected Question. Claims about the relative validity, reliability, and general worth of quantitative and qualitative research appear in SL/SOL, as they do in most areas of sociological work. While the modes of work are loosely associated with the micromacro distinction, there are representations of both modes in both arenas. Space limitations make discussion of this important issue impossible —that it exists in SL/SOL work must be reported.

SL/SOL AS A RESOURCE IN SOCIOLOGICAL THEORY BUILDING

Many sociologists are not familiar with SL/SOL and are therefore unaware of both substantive findings and theoretical development that could be helpful to them in their own work. There is no space for an extensive review of the very considerable richness of these resources; it is possible to mention only a few instances of contributions to understanding of (1) substantive areas; (2) social processes; (3) relations among language, literature, identity, and so on.

Suggestive Empirical Findings. Studies of classrooms, courtrooms, and clinics have generated findings that have sometimes resulted in changes in pedagogic, legal, and medical practice as well as contributed to our theoretical understanding of SL/SOL. Studies of a multitude of other settings, ranging from street, to dinner table, to backyard party, to workplace, have also produced important theoretical insights. Two such findings come from Labov's quantitative studies of language use in urban areas of the eastern United States (New York City and Philadelphia); the first has important implications for understanding social stratification, the second for ethnic (and possibly class) relations, and both for processes of social change.

In studies of dialects associated with class, Labov (and others) have repeatedly shown that linguistically insecure informants, who are often women (particularly) with aspirations for upward social mobility (or concerns about slipping), often hypercorrect their phonological production in the direction of what they perceive as prestige variants, thereby producing the prestige variant with higher frequencies than those at social levels above them—and sometimes produce it inappropriately (Labov gives as an example, "Hi, say, that's hawfully good of you"). Awareness of this phenomenon should alert sociologists to look for analogues in other behavioral arenas (there is a family relationship, obviously, to anticipatory socialization; the roots of the labeled behaviors may differ quite considerably); Labov (1972b, 1986) has pointed out its important implications for studies of linguistic (and, we may add, social) change.

Labov's second finding is that the speech of urban blacks who have *any* contact with whites continues to be modified in the direction of the grammar of the dominant group, while blacks in the increasingly segregated inner cities speak increasingly divergent language varieties. This divergence is co-occurring with increasing differentiation in incomes and educational achievement, increasing social distance, and, it would seem likely, increasing intergroup hostility. Labov comments, "The linguistic situation correlates with the formation of what has been called a 'permanent underclass'" (1986, p. 278).

Some Little Concepts and Some Central Processes. Studies of actual talk that occurs in the course of everyday interaction have generated both (1) concepts that allow us to taxonomically identify previously unspecified regularities in that interaction (in a manner similar to Goffman's labeling of, *inter alia,* front and back regions, side involvements, and the more specifically talk-related footing) and (2) new understandings of the working of what might be called "master social processes," such as conflict or socialization. Instances of the former (all from Grimshaw 1989) are identification of hyperinvolvement (a phenomenon in which interactants are so deeply involved in the ongoing that they miss things they are actually monitoring), defects of nerve (a situation in which interactants know a way of doing something but are reluctant to do it because they are concerned that it may generate injury to self or another party), and such phenomena as topic avoidance, topic exploitation, and topic truncation (the last occurring when it becomes obvious to an interactant that interactional goals are not going to be accomplished).

An instance of the latter is Corsaro's (1985) impressive demonstration of the *processes* involved in children's learning how to recognize and to construct the cultures and social structures in which they find themselves. Another is Grimshaw's (1990) distillation of the reported findings of a number of individual studies of conflict talk into propositions about the conflict process.

Language, Writing, Literacy, and Literature. Events of recent years have demonstrated the continuing importance of what Clifford Geertz (1963) labeled "primordial sentiments," and that feelings about language are central among such sentiments. The range of sociological and sociologically relevant ways in which both language in general and writing and literacy in particular permeate/pervade human cultural and social structures and relations, as well as conceptions of identity and of self on the individual level, is too great even to be limned here. People go to court in defense of their mother tongue; people have also fought in the streets and burned themselves alive over language issues. Becoming literate in any language can be primarily an instrumental acquisition; it can in some instances have profound effects on both individual personalities and social organization (see, particularly, J. Goody 1987). The "invention" and development of national languages can have reverberating effects

through previously atomized collectivities (Anderson 1990); when printed material becomes available, it can have critical impacts both on change in general (Eisenstein 1979) and more specifically on the development of national communities and identities (Anderson 1983).

Sociologists of literature have shown how national literatures can reveal cultural and social values (e.g., Moore 1971); sociologists studying both contemporary life and that of past times are becoming increasingly aware of the rich data in personal documents from journals to correspondence. It is even possible to hear the question "Who wants citizens to be literate—and to what ends?" (The implication is that social control may be as much a goal as the enrichment of individual lives [see Kress and Hodge 1979]). Related interests have drawn a number of investigators to the study of *how* written materials affect their readers, a question that has been addressed both by methods which project the "interruption" or "interrogation" of written and/or spoken texts (Silverman and Torode 1980) and by those of psycholinguistics or cognitive science.

APPLIED SOCIOLINGUISTICS, SOCIAL AMELIORATION, AND THEORY BUILDING

The increased interest in SL/SOL has been accompanied by and has been contributed to by a growing public interest in language as a social problem; work on "real" problems in a variety of institutional areas has benefited from a growing body of theory, to which it has in turn contributed. Here again a distinction can be made between micro and macro concerns—micro sociolinguistic research has been done on how communication fails in classrooms, courtrooms, and clinics; macro studies have examined how the speaking of socially disvalued language varieties is associated with educational failure, differential treatment in the judicial system, and unsuccessful interaction with medical services delivery systems. Ameliorative programs have ranged from bilingualism (in various modes) in education to the English-as-official-language movement, from the provision of interpreters in the courtroom to attempts to simplify legal language, from attempts to teach prospective doctors to become better interviewers and listeners to getting doctors to use less technical language. Bitter controversies have raged over how the ways that children talk are related to educational success and failure. Some investigators have argued that there are language varieties which are not suited for abstract, critical, logical, and propositional thought; others, that success and failure of persons who speak in different ways are determined by the *political preferences* about language varieties of gatekeepers such as teachers and employers.

Recent years have seen the development of the role of "language scientist" as expert witness (e.g., Rieber and Stewart 1990); SL considerations are sometimes deeply involved in such testimony. Many of these programs and much of this work initially grew out of concerns with language varieties associated with ethnicity (in the United States, different varieties of Spanish and, particularly, Black Vernacular English [BVE]). There has also been more explicit attention to problems of communication across classes, age groups, and, particularly, gender; Tannen's (1990) popular book on gender differences in talk spent many months on best-seller lists.

On a more explicitly macro level, language planning and language policy have become more visible arenas of government activity in both the rich countries, which must deal with visiting or immigrant workers who speak unfamiliar languages, and the poor countries which must make decisions about which of competing languages are going to receive official status and support—or about which orthography to employ for previously unwritten languages. (The latter is a decision that is likely to have political as well as economic implications.) They must in some cases decide whether high literacy (often seen as an index of modernism) will ultimately contribute to their economies (or other values) as much as or more than would other investments (on outcomes of increases in literacy in industrial[izing] and less developed countries, respectively, see Graff 1979; J. Goody 1987). Both rich and poor countries

must deal with native multilingualism; they have done it with varying success in Belgium, Canada, India, Indonesia, the Soviet Union, Spain, and Switzerland (see McRae 1983, 1986, on Switzerland and Belgium, respectively).

(SEE ALSO: *Conversation Analysis; Ethnomethodology*)

REFERENCES

Anderson, Benedict R. O'G. 1983 *Imagined Communities: Reflections on the Origin and Spread of Nationalism.* London: Verso.

———— 1990 *Language and Power: Exploring Political Cultures in Indonesia.* Ithaca, N.Y.: Cornell University Press.

Atkinson, J. Maxwell, and Paul Drew 1979 *Order in Court: The Organisation of Verbal Interaction in Judicial Settings.* Atlantic Highlands, N.J.: Humanities Press.

Berger, Peter L., and Thomas Luckmann 1966 *The Social Construction of Reality: A Treatise in the Sociology of Knowledge.* Garden City, N.Y.: Doubleday.

Bernstein, Basil 1975 *Class, Codes, and Control.* vol. 3, *Towards a Theory of Educational Transmission.* London: Routledge and Kegan Paul.

Blom, Jan-Petter, and John J. Gumperz 1972 "Social Meaning in Linguistic Structure(s): Code-switching in Norway." In J. J. Gumperz and D. Hymes, eds., *New Directions in Sociolinguistics: The Ethnography of Communication.* New York: Holt, Rinehart and Winston.

Bourdieu, Pierre, and Jean-Claude Passeron 1977 *Reproduction in Education, Society, and Culture,* Richard Nice, trans. London: Sage.

Brown, Penelope, and Steven C. Levinson (1978) 1987 *Politeness: Some Universals in Language Usage.* Cambridge: Cambridge University Press.

Brown, Roger, and Albert Gilman 1960 "The Pronouns of solidarity." In T. A. Sebeok, ed., *Style in Language.* Cambridge, Mass.: MIT Press.

———— 1989 "Politeness Theory and Shakespeare's Four Major Tragedies." *Language in Society* 18:159–212.

Chafe, Wallace (ed.) 1980 *The Pear Stories: Cognitive, Cultural, and Linguistic Aspects of Narrative Production.* Norwood, N.J.: Ablex.

Chilton, Paul (ed.) 1985 *Language and the Nuclear Arms Debate: Newspeak Today.* London: Frances Pinter.

Chomsky, Noam 1966 *Cartesian Linguistics: A Chapter in*

the History of Rationalist Thought. New York: Harper and Row.

——— 1968 *Language and Mind*. New York: Harcourt, Brace and World.

———, and Morris Halle 1968 *The Sound Pattern of English*. New York: Harper and Row.

Cicourel, Aaron V. 1980a "Three Models of Discourse Analysis: The Role of Social Structure." *Discourse Processes* 2:101–131.

——— 1980b "Language and Social Action: Philosophical and Empirical Issues." *Sociological Inquiry* 40:1–30.

——— 1981 "Notes on the Integration of Micro- and Macro-Levels of Analysis." In K. Knorr-Cetina and A. V. Cicourel, eds., *Advances in Social Theory and Methodology: Toward an Integration of Micro- and Macro-Sociologies*. Boston: Routledge and Kegan Paul.

——— 1991 "Theoretical and Methodological Suggestions for Using Discourse to Recreate Aspects of Social Structure." In A. Grimshaw et al., *What's Going on Here: Complementary Studies of Professional Talk*. Norwood, N.J.: Ablex.

Collins, Randall 1981a "On the Microfoundations of Macrosociology." *American Journal of Sociology* 86:984–1014.

——— 1981b "Micro-Translation as a Theory-Building Strategy." In K. Knorr-Cetina and A. V. Cicourel, eds., *Advances in Social Theory and Methodology: Toward an Integration of Micro- and Macro-Sociologies*. Boston: Routledge and Kegan Paul.

Corsaro, William A. 1981 "Communicative Processes in Studies of Social Organization: Sociological Approaches to Discourse Analysis." *Text* 1:5–63.

——— 1985 *Friendship and Peer Culture in the Early Years*. Norwood, N.J.: Ablex.

Dorval, Bruce (ed.) 1990 *Conversational Organization and Its Development*. Norwood, N.J.: Ablex.

Edgerton, Robert B. 1985 *Rules, Exceptions, and Social Order*. Berkeley: University of California Press.

Eisenstein, Elizabeth L. 1979 *The Printing Press as an Agent of Change: Communications and Cultural Transformations in Early Modern Europe*. Cambridge: Cambridge University Press.

Feld, Steven, and Carroll Williams 1975 "Toward a Researchable Film Language." *Studies in the Anthropology of Visual Communication* 2:25–32.

Firth, Raymond 1972 "Verbal and Bodily Rituals of Greeting and Parting." In J. S. La Fontaine, ed., *The Interpretation of Ritual: Essays in Honour of A. I. Richards*. London: Tavistock.

Fischer, John L. 1965 "The Stylistic Significance of Consonantal Sandhi in Trukese and Ponapean." *American Anthropologist* 67:1495–1502.

——— 1966 "Syntax and Social Structure: Truk and Ponape." In W. Bright, ed., *Sociolinguistics: Proceedings of the UCLA Sociolinguistics Conference, 1964*. The Hague: Mouton.

Geertz, Clifford 1963 "The Integrative Revolution: Primordial Sentiments and Civil Politics in the New States." In C. Geertz, ed., *Old Societies and New States: The Quest for Modernity in Asia and Africa*. New York: Free Press.

Goffman, Erving 1971 *Relations in Public: Microstudies of the Public Order*. New York: Basic Books.

——— 1981 *Forms of Talk*. Philadelphia: University of Pennsylvania Press.

Goody, Esther N. 1978 "Towards a Theory of Questions." In E. N. Goody, ed., *Questions and Politeness: Strategies in Social Interaction*. Cambridge: Cambridge University Press.

Goody, Jack 1987 *The Interface Between the Oral and the Written*. Cambridge: Cambridge University Press.

Graff, Harvey J. 1979 *The Literacy Myth: Literacy and Social Structure in the Nineteenth-Century City*. New York: Academic Press.

Grimshaw, Allen D. 1969 "Language as Obstacle and as Data in Sociological Research." *Items* 23:17–21.

——— 1973a "Rules in Linguistic, Social and Sociolinguistic Systems and Possibilities for a Unified Theory." In R. S. Shuy, ed., *Twenty-third Annual Round Table, Monograph Series on Language and Linguistics (1972)*. Washington, D.C.: Georgetown University Press.

——— 1973b "On Language in Society: Part I." *Contemporary Sociology* 2:575–585.

——— 1974a "On Language in Society: Part II." *Contemporary Sociology* 3:3–11.

——— 1974b "Sociolinguistics." In I. de Sola Pool and W. Schramm, eds., *Handbook of Communication*. Chicago: Rand McNally.

——— 1980 "Social Interactional and Sociolinguistic Rules." *Social Forces* 58:789–810.

——— 1981 "Talk and Social Control." In M. Rosenberg et al., eds., *Sociological Perspectives on Social Psychology*. New York: Basic Books.

——— (ed.) 1982 *Sound-Image Records in Social Interaction Research*, a special issue of *Sociological Methods and Research* 11.

——— 1987a "Sociolinguistics Versus Sociology of Language: Tempest in a Teapot or Profound Academic Conundrum." In U. Ammon, N. Dittmar, and K. J. Mattheier, eds., *Sociolinguistics: An International Handbook of the Science of Language and Society,* vol. 1. Berlin: Walter de Gruyter.

———— 1987b "Micro-macrolevels." In U. Ammon, N. Dittmar, and K. J. Mattheier, eds., *Sociolinguistics: An International Handbook of the Science of Language and Society,* vol. 1. Berlin: Walter de Gruyter.

———— 1987c "Disambiguating Discourse: Members' Skill and Analysts' Problem." *Social Psychology Quarterly* 50:186–204.

———— 1989 *Collegial Discourse: Professional Conversation Among Peers.* Norwood, N.J.: Ablex.

———— (ed.) 1990 *Conflict Talk: Sociolinguistic Investigations of Arguments in Conversations.* Cambridge: Cambridge University Press.

————, Peter J. Burke, Aaron V. Cicourel, Jenny Cook-Gumperz, Steven Feld, Charles J. Fillmore, Lily Wong Fillmore, John J. Gumperz, Michael A. K. Halliday, Ruqaiya Hasan, and David Jenness 1991 *What's Going on Here: Complementary Studies of Professional Talk.* Norwood, N.J.: Ablex.

————, Steven Feld, and David Jenness 1991 "The MAP: An Ethnographic History of the Project and a Description of the Data." In A. Grimshaw et al. *What's Going on Here: Complementary Studies of Professional Talk.* Norwood, N.J.: Ablex.

Gumperz, John J., and Dell Hymes (eds.) (1972 [1966]) 1986 *New Directions in Sociolinguistics: The Ethnography of Communication.* Oxford: Basil Blackwell.

Habermas, Jürgen 1981–1984. *The Theory of Communicative Action,* Thomas McCarthy, trans. Boston: Beacon Press.

Hall, Edward T. 1966 *The Hidden Dimension.* Garden City, N.Y.: Doubleday.

———— 1974 *Handbook for Proxemic Research.* Washington, D.C.: Society for the Anthropology of Visual Communication.

Hymes, Dell 1966 "Two Types of Linguistic Relativity (with Examples from Amerindian Ethnography)." In W. Bright, ed., *Sociolinguistics: Proceedings of the UCLA Sociolinguistics Conference, 1964.* The Hague: Mouton.

Ibrahim ag Youssouf, Allen D. Grimshaw, and Charles S. Bird 1976 "Greetings in the Desert." *American Ethnologist* 3:797–824.

Kendon, Adam (1977) 1990 *Conducting Interaction: Patterns of Behavior in Focused Encounters.* Cambridge: Cambridge University Press.

————, and Andrew Ferber 1973 "A Description of Some Human Greetings." In R. P. Michael and J. H. Crooks, eds., *Comparative Ecology and Behavior of Primates.* London: Academic Press.

Kress, Gunther, and Robert Hodge 1979 *Language as Ideology.* London: Routledge and Kegan Paul.

Labov, William 1968 "A Proposed Program for Research and Training in the Study of Language in Its Social and Cultural Settings. New York: Columbia University. (Mimeo.)

———— 1972a "Some Principles of Linguistic Methodology." *Language in Society* 1:97–120.

———— 1972b *Sociolinguistic Patterns.* Philadelphia: University of Pennsylvania Press.

———— (ed.) 1980 *Locating Language in Time and Space.* New York: Academic Press.

———— 1986 "Language Structure and Social Structure." In S. Lindenberg, J. S. Coleman, and S. Nowak, eds., *Approaches to Social Theory.* New York: Russell Sage Foundation.

————, and David Fanshel 1977 *Therapeutic Discourse: Psychotherapy as Conversation.* New York: Academic Press.

McRae, Kenneth D. 1983 *Conflict and Compromise in Multilingual Societies: Switzerland.* Waterloo, Ontario: Wilfred Laurier University Press.

———— 1986 *Conflict and Compromise in Multilingual Societies: Belgium.* Waterloo, Ontario: Wilfred Laurier University Press.

Moore, T. Inglis 1971 *Social Patterns in Australian Literature.* Berkeley: University of California Press.

Rieber, Robert W., and William A. Stewart (eds.) 1990 *The Language Scientist as Expert in the Legal Setting: Issues in Forensic Linguistics,* vol. 606 of *Annals of the New York Academy of Sciences.*

Silverman, David, and Brian Torode 1980 *The Material Word: Some Theories of Language and Its Limits.* London: Routledge and Kegan Paul.

Tannen, Deborah 1990 *You Just Don't Understand: Men and Women in Conversation.* New York: Morrow.

Watson-Gegeo, Karen A., and Geoffrey M. White (eds.) 1990 *Disentangling: Conflict Discourse in Pacific Societies.* Stanford, Calif.: Stanford University Press.

Wertsch, James, and Hugh Mehan, eds. 1988 *Discourse of the Nuclear Arms Debate,* special issue of *Multilingua: Journal of Cross-Cultural and Interlanguage Communication* 7.

Whalen, Jack 1991 "Conversation Analysis." In E. and M. Borgatta, eds., *Encyclopedia of Sociology,* vol. 4. New York: Macmillan.

ALLEN D. GRIMSHAW

SOCIOLOGICAL ORGANIZATIONS

Special interest groups often establish organizations to facilitate communication among members and to advance the purposes of the group. Sociologists have been no different from others in this regard, and over the years they have formed many societies and associations. The first international sociological association was announced by René Worms in the first volume (1893) of the first sociological journal, the *Revue Internationale de Sociologie.* Named to parallel existing institutes of law and of statistics, it was given the name Institut International de Sociologie (IIS).

The organization drew from the distinguished and visible sociologists around the world, although strangely, for an organization with headquarters in France, Émile Durkheim did not participate. Cerase and Varotti (1969) describe the history of the IIS in three periods: from 1893 to 1926, the period associated with René Worms; from 1927 to 1939, the post-Worms period; and from 1950 to 1965, the period associated with Corrado Gini.

In the first period of the IIS, of the twenty-nine presidents, two or more came from France, Great Britain, Belgium, Germany, Austria, Italy, Russia, the United States, and Spain and Portugal, and three more from other European nations. Thus, in the Western world the organization was truly international, and the presidents were among the famous. The official publication of the IIS, *Annales de l'Institut International de Sociologie,* was discontinued in 1931. (After a long lapse the *Annales* was reestablished at the initiative of Paolo Ammassari, president of the IIS, to reflect the theme of the Twenty-ninth International Congress at Rome in 1989, "The Status of Sociology as a Science and Social Policy Formation.")

The bylaws and rules of the IIS, last published in 1968 in the *Revue Internationale de Sociologie* (pp. 2–7), were revised in 1985. The main thrust of revision was to open membership more broadly (e.g., eliminating the initiation fee and restrictions on numbers of members from individual nations), and generally to move the organization from an elite membership to membership of productive and accomplished scholars. The objective of the IIS as stated in the bylaws has been "to bring together sociologists from different countries for the scientific study of sociological questions." The IIS may not affiliate with organizations of a religious or political character; historically it has taken a strong position to support academic freedom and open scholarly exchange at its congresses.

The IIS declined in activity following the Gini period (1950–1965), and revitalization did not occur until support was provided by Vittorio Castellano, at the Twenty-fifth International Congress at Lisbon in 1980, for its restructuring. Since that time the IIS has held congresses in Morelia, Mexico (1982), in Seattle (the first in the United States, 1984), in Albuferia, Portugal (1986), and in Rome (1989). Congresses are scheduled for 1991 in Kobe, for 1993 in Paris (a centennial congress), 1995 in Cracow, and 1997 in Cologne.

As sociology has grown as an academic discipline, sociological organizations have been initiated in nations and international regions. In the United States, where many state and private universities have flourished, organizations have developed associated with regions, states, and even cities. Sociological organizations have developed around special categorical interests, such as religious, ethnic and racial, sex, and sexual orientation. Much of the growth of such organizations occurred during the post-World War II period, when sociology achieved more prominence in universities, especially in the United States, where it became a popular subject. An additional stimulus internationally was the formation of the International Sociological Association.

The International Sociological Association (ISA) was formed in 1949, with the support of UNESCO, and held its first world congress at Zurich in 1950. A brief history of the ISA is reported by Jonassohn (1989). Its membership consisted of organizations, national associations, institutes, and university and other departments. The formation of the ISA was the stimulus for formation of some of the participant organizations, since individual memberships did not exist except under special definitions. The ISA grew quickly, and in 1970 it shifted focus from an organization of organizations to accepting individual memberships. It has grown, in fact, to a size that is seen by many members as too large, apparently in contrast with nostalgic notions of a small group where most people knew each other. However, such size is characteristic of many professional organizations, and the purposes served change with growth. Communication is facilitated through the existence of research committees oriented to particular specialties that not only meet at the world congresses every four years, but also have begun various approaches to further communication, including periodic meetings.

One problem for the ISA as an organization of scholars is that it is not completely free of political involvement. This occurs in two ways:

> *This [ISA] Council was patterned on the model of the United Nations and of UNESCO in that each member country was represented by a delegate. However, there was a fundamental difference in that the delegates that made up the ISA Council did not represent the governments of their countries but rather the sociologists in their countries and their organization(s). In many countries sociological organizations are organs of the government and the delegates from these countries are not necessarily free to ignore their governments' wishes or instructions, even if they would have preferred to do so. In this way it has happened that serious political issues were introduced into the debates within the ISA. The other misunderstanding derived from the ISA's membership in UNESCO, which had on occasion resulted in strong pressure to have the ISA conform to positions voted in UNESCO. (Jonassohn 1989, p. 14)*

An additional type of problem arises from the internal politics, where "the nominations and elections of officers have, on occasion, generated a considerable amount of arm-twisting and block-voting in terms of political considerations rather than professional ones" (Jonassohn 1989, p. 14). In the spirit of scholarly traditions, these kinds of problems presumably will diminish, but trends toward nationalism and ethnocentrism counter the universalistic process. However, the scholarly traditions are fostered by the public forum of the

ISA, including its publications. The ISA now sponsors many publications, including the *ISA Bulletin, Current Sociology, Sage Studies in International Sociology,* and *International Sociology,* plus formal and informal publications sponsored by the research committees. The 1990 world congress was held in Madrid; the location of the next congress is not usually decided until after the congress is concluded.

Sociological organizations are usually encountered by students of sociology as they mature into the professional roles. They are important in providing broader perspectives and countering provincialism, but they also have the liabilities associated with all organizations as they grow, including bureaucratization and reinforcement of dominant ideologies.

(SEE ALSO: *American Sociological Association*)

REFERENCES

Cerase, Francesco P., and Adriano Varotti 1969 "L'Institu International de Sociologie 1893–1969: Fatti e Tendenze." *Revue Internationale di Sociologie* 2nd ser., vol. 5, no. 2:1–18.

Jonassohn, Kurt 1989 "The First Forty Years: A History of the I.S.A." *ISA Bulletin 51* (Autumn 1989):9–17.

EDGAR F. BORGATTA

SOCIOLOGY AND FEDERAL RE-SEARCH SUPPORT From its beginning, American sociology has been propelled by an ambivalent sense of mission. At the first annual meeting of the American Sociological Society in Providence, Rhode Island, Lester F. Ward, on December 27, 1906, concluded his presidential address by asserting "In other words, sociology, established as a pure science, is now entering upon its applied stage, which is the great practical object for which it exists" (1907, p. 587). A generation later, a contrary thrust was voiced at the twenty-fourth annual meeting of the American Sociological Society in Washington, D.C. In his presidential address on December 28, 1929, William F. Ogburn insisted that "sociology as a science is not interested in making the world a better place in which to live, in encouraging beliefs, in spreading information, in dispensing news, in setting forth impressions of life, in leading the multitudes or in guiding the ship of state. Science is interested directly in one thing only, to wit, discovering new knowledge" (1930, p. 9).

How provident were these presidential pronouncements? Ward, of course, was not so much engaged in prophecy as in attempting to prod sociologists to move directly from developing basic knowledge to attacking problems, dispensing treatments, and servicing national needs through ameliorative social intervention. From that time forward many sociologists did respond to the prod, with or without the benefit of a bank of basic knowledge, often to discover only a tenuous linkage of knowledge to policy and practice.

Despite such discovery, sociologists were swept along with the confident positivism that marked mainline social science in the years after World War II. Pitfalls in forecasting outcomes of well-intentioned actions did not dampen the scope of engagement nor discourage the pursuit of resources required to translate promise into knowledge that might nourish practice. However, no matter how persistent, pursuit did not automatically register success or acclaim, particularly in one prominent support domain, the federal government.

Through its vast array of agencies the federal government can extend or withhold support to any field of science in a number of direct and indirect ways: by conferring or restraining eligibility for grants, contracts, fellowships, and employment; by encouraging or inhibiting access to archives, records, and research sites; by using or abusing research findings; and by imposing or relaxing laws and regulations that impinge on scholarly effort, including tax exemptions for institutions.

Out of this array, none stirs a more compelling response than the promise of funds to finance research. Institutions, public and private, profit and nonprofit, scramble to gain government support for individual investigators, teams, or consortia. Through peer review, the standard agency program allocates funds and sometimes extends

support for dissertation work, postdoctoral training, data base maintenance, research workshops, and the like. Federal agencies also support intramural research, and, to serve policy needs, create vast banks of information that can be turned to scientific purposes. The latter is an *inadvertent system* of federal support analyzed by Kenneth Prewitt (1986) to clarify how the expenditure of funds for purposes that themselves were not scientific could serve scientific interests.

To penetrate this dynamic web of possibilities at the most visible level, and to identify its impact on sociology, requires brief reference to the national expenditure for science and to the federal share of this investment. It also requires inspection of federal support of social science, the category in which sociology is embedded as decisions are made on budgets and records are kept on allocations. In other words, when it comes to the funding of research, sociology is a needle in a very large haystack.

SUPPORT FOR SCIENCE

Surveys conducted for the National Science Board (1989) repeatedly show high public acclaim for the contributions of science to society. In both 1957 and 1988, 88 percent of Americans believed that the world was better off because of science. For many years, science has ranked second only to medicine on a list of thirteen institutions in which the public has "a great deal of confidence." (Medicine, science, and the Supreme Court are the top three; the press, television, and organized labor are the bottom three.)

These surveys show that while science yields a positive general reaction, its knowledge does not fully penetrate all areas of understanding. Thus, about three-quarters of the American adult population still believes that antibiotics can kill viruses. About 43 percent doubt that humans are descended from other animal species. Twenty-one percent of Americans believe the sun goes around the earth, and about 6 percent say they act on astrological forecasts.

There is also variation in public expectations about what science can and cannot do. Thus, of special interest to sociologists, the number of people who believed that "science will solve our social problems like crime and mental illness" dropped significantly from 47 percent in 1957 to 23 percent in 1988.

Nonetheless, Americans are generally optimistic about science, and there is strong support for it as a long-range investment. In 1988, 81 percent believed that the government should support scientific research, even when it brings no immediate benefits.

This support underlies the remarkable total national expenditure for research and development (R & D). The United States spends more on R & D than Japan, West Germany, France, and the United Kingdom combined. From 1960 to 1989, U.S. expenditure increased in current dollars from $13.5 billion to $132.4 billion. On a regular annual basis this represents around 2.7 percent of the gross national product (GNP). Also rather consistently, about one-third of this total national investment has been for research, basic and applied, and two-thirds for the development part of R & D. In turn, monies for research also split, with about one-third for basic and two-thirds for applied research.

The federal government is a major agent of this support. Industry, private foundations, universities, and state and local government also contribute to the national investment. In this mix, the role of the federal government has been changing. Since 1980 it has no longer been the foremost supplier of funds for all aspects of research and development. From 1960 to 1989 the percentage of its total contribution dropped from 65 percent to 47 percent; its share of applied research dropped from 56 percent to 40 percent; and its portion of development funds was reduced from 68 percent to 46 percent. However, the government continued to be the dominant source of funds for basic research, as its share increased from 60 percent in 1960 to 65 percent in 1989.

Approximately 10 percent of the national R & D expenditure goes for academic R & D, and for this arena the federal government continues to provide most of the funds. The dependence of university-based disciplines on federal funds is quite varied, as illustrated by obligations in 1987. All sciences combined received 61 percent of their R & D funds from the government; however, by discipline, physics received 80 percent, mathematics got 73 percent, biology took 68 percent, engineering took 59 percent, sociology received 49 percent, economics saw 30 percent, and political science got 29 percent.

In overall terms, federal support of science in the United States does not appear to be a highly partisan political issue. As may be noted in Table 1 (see p. 2016), science has consistently prospered from the Kennedy administration on. Since 1962, the federal research obligations for science have increased in all but two years. In the first fiscal year of the Bush administration, 1990, the federal government obligated just over $21 billion for research in science. This was a sevenfold increase from the $3 billion obligated during the first fiscal year of the Kennedy administration twenty-eight years earlier.

SUPPORT FOR SOCIAL SCIENCE

The relationship between social science and government would appear ripe for mutual advantage. Technological, economic, and social issues are becoming more and more intertwined. This generates knowledge needs and research opportunities. Despite this symbiotic setting, the relationship between government and social science is not without strain. Whereas funding for all of science moved strongly and steadily upward during the 1960s, 1970s, and 1980s, support for social science involves a more perilous journey over a rocky political terrain.

From the social science side comes concern about how dependence on federal subsidies might impede free and critical exploration. Alex Inkeles, even though he doubts any such significant impact in the American case, notes that "prominent among these concerns is the danger of distortion by emphasis on the wrong issues or realms, of distortions due to pressures to reach predetermined, politically preferred conclusions, and of distortions arising from the suppression of unwanted evidence or conclusions" (1986, p. 241).

TABLE 1
Federal Obligations for Research in Science (Current Dollars)

President	FY	All Science (Billions)		Social Science (Millions)		
			% Applied		% of Science	% Applied
Kennedy	1962	3.0	67	62.2	2.1	NA
	1963	3.5	67	79.9	2.3	NA
	1964	3.9	66	102.7	2.6	NA
Johnson	1965	4.2	66	127.4	3.0	NA
	1966	4.7	66	165.6	3.5	NA
	1967	4.6	60	189.1	4.1	75
	1968	4.8	62	195.5	4.1	70
	1969	4.6	58	217.8	4.7	67
Nixon	1970	4.9	61	212.2	4.3	70
	1971	5.1	61	304.0	6.0	77
	1972	5.5	61	306.9	5.6	74
	1973	5.6	60	298.8	5.3	73
	1974	6.2	61	292.2	4.7	74
Ford	1975	6.7	62	301.8	4.5	76
	1976	7.6	64	392.5	5.2	78
	1977	8.5	62	426.1	5.0	77
Carter	1978	9.6	62	489.5	5.1	75
	1979	10.5	60	527.3	5.0	75
	1980	11.6	60	523.8	4.5	71
	1981	12.2	59	497.4	4.1	73
Reagan	1982	13.0	58	385.9	3.0	69
	1983	14.3	56	435.3	3.0	68
	1984	15.0	53	436.3	2.9	69
	1985	16.1	52	460.0	2.8	67
	1986	16.5	51	415.5	2.5	70
	1987	17.9	50	480.0	2.7	73
	1988	18.6	49	485.8	2.6	70
	1989	20.4	49	561.2	2.7	70
Bush	1990	21.1	47	588.6	2.8	66

SOURCE: Compiled from the NSF annual series "Federal Funds for Research and Development, Fiscal Years, Detailed Historical Tables, 1955-1990."
NOTES: Social science includes sociology, anthropology, economics, political science, linguistics, research in education, research in history, socioeconomic geography, and research on the impact of legal systems. Psychology, since 1959, is a separate category.
  NA = Not available.

Government leaders, on the other hand, become uneasy with social science because it often challenges conventional political wisdom. This alone can amplify the disposition to charge social scientists with favoring ideological advocacy over scientific analysis. Because of such arguments the status of social science waxes and wanes in Washington, D.C., as does support for its research.

Nonetheless, over time the language of policymaking has become markedly infused with constructs, inventions, and findings from social science (e.g., GNP, quality control, power, cultural lag, cost-benefit analysis, sample surveys, econometric models, social indicators).

Historically, if social science is defined broadly, the first constitutionally authorized census in

1790 represents an early, if not the first, federal government activity to bolster sociological interests. However, the regular solicitation and use of social science evolved only gradually. Entry was emphasized in times of crises, as in a prominent early instance when William F. Ogburn became Examiner and Head of the Cost of Living Department at the National War Labor Board from 1918 to 1919.

The scope of involvement grew in the 1920s. The Bureau of the Census, the Bureau of Labor Statistics, and the Bureau of Agricultural Economics began analytically oriented activities that went beyond routine data-collecting duties.

The depression era of the 1930s and the war period of the 1940s brought a dramatic rise in the use of social scientists as consultants and in their employment as researchers, agency directors, and policy analysts. There was particular ferment during World War II. Social scientists were mobilized to conduct large-scale research on problems of military recruitment, personnel placement, morale, resource allocation, propaganda analysis, bombing impact, wage and price analysis, and, finally, design of the GI Bill. These research projects provided an important training ground for a number of social scientists who later became distinguished in their disciplines.

Today, the U.S. Office of Personnel Management regularly processes the employment of social scientists through a wide variety of classifications. For example, the Sociology Series GS-184 was updated in December 1988 to emphasize positions utilizing methods to establish, validate, interpret, and apply knowledge about social processes. In 1990, the American Sociological Association, through its Professional Development Program, accelerated efforts to stimulate opportunities for sociologists in government. One bulletin informs government agencies how sociologists could assist in "Maintaining Competence in the Federal Workforce in the 1990s and Beyond." Another bulletin explains "How to Join the Federal Workforce and Advance Your Sociological Career." Similar promotional efforts are made by other social science associations.

Beyond the employment of social scientists lies the funding of their research, a process that has also evolved over time. In the period between World War I and World War II, private foundations were the principal source of direct funding for social science in the United States. Besides supporting the work of individual researchers, these foundations supplied critical support for emerging social science organizations such as the Brookings Institution, the Social Science Research Council, and the National Bureau of Economic Research. It was not the federal government but the Rockefeller Foundation that supplied the funds that produced the landmark two-volume *Recent Social Trends in the United States* in 1933.

In the postwar era the federal government became the dominant source of social science funds for both basic and applied research. Sizable resources were allocated from agencies with wartime roots such as the Office of Naval Research, the Human Resources Research Institute, and the Air Force Office of Scientific Research. Also significant was the strong support for graduate training programs, particularly from agencies such as the National Institute of Mental Health.

A major institutional innovation affecting the linkage of the federal government to science came in 1950 with the creation of the National Science Foundation (Larsen, 1991). Until then, no agency of the government had been engaged in support of any science for the sake of science itself. This idea went far beyond the traditional use of science to serve the practical, operating needs of government. Accordingly, it was not accepted without struggle. A five-year debate preceded the legislative enactment. Social science was one of the sticking points. A compromise permitted the National Science Foundation to support, under close surveillance, some social science types of projects. However, it was not until 1968 that a congressional amendment explicitly included social science in the mandate for the foundation. At the same time, "applied research" became an authorized activity for the NSF.

From this emerged a variety of programs guided by somewhat dubious distinctions between basic and applied research. To meet its national record-keeping obligations, the National Science Foundation classifies all research support as either basic or applied according to the objectives of the sponsoring agency. More is at stake with these categories than record keeping. Implied are differences in how the agenda for research will be set, how legitimacy and status will be accorded, and how resources will be allocated. According to the NSF's ongoing accounts of federal funding, "in basic research the objective of the sponsoring agency is to gain fuller knowledge or understanding of the fundamental aspects of phenomena and of observable facts without specific applications toward processes or products in mind." Further, "in applied research the objective of the sponsoring agency is to gain knowledge or understanding necessary for determining the means by which a recognized and specific need may be met" (National Science Board 1989, p. 89).

When the focus shifts from science to social science, there is a drop in the statistical record from billions to millions of dollars. Furthermore, since 1978 there has been a steady decline in the percentage of federal science funding obligated to applied research. This has ominous implications for social scientists since they continued to be perceived primarily as "applied-siders." The tilt of social science toward applied research is also reflected in the range of government agencies from which social scientists receive support. In 1989, for example, seventy-nine federal agencies supported some applied research, while only thirty-nine obligated funds for basic research. Out of this universe social scientists found funds for applied research in forty-seven agencies and funds for basic research in sixteen agencies.

From agencies at the political apex, the cabinet-level departments, applied research funds were allocated to social science in twelve out of thirteen cases (the Department of Energy did not obligate any funds for either applied or basic research in social science). However, while funds for basic social science research were obligated from seven cabinet departments, none were forthcoming in 1989 from Defense, Commerce, Interior, Energy, Housing and Urban Development, and Transportation.

Support for social science is even more concentrated in the federal bureaucracy than implied earlier. Four agencies accounted for about 90 percent of the monies obligated to social science in 1989, whether for basic or applied research. Two cabinet departments, Health and Human Services, particularly the Alcohol, Drug Abuse and Mental Health Administration; and the Department of Agriculture, particularly the Economic Research Service, were prominent in the support of both basic and applied research in social science. In 1989, the lead agencies for basic research were Health and Human Services, 31.5 percent; National Science Foundation, 27.3 percent; Smithsonian Institution, 20.2 percent; and Department of Agriculture, 13.0 percent. For applied research, the lead agencies were Health and Human Services, 31.0 percent; Department of Education, 23.9 percent; Department of Agriculture, 19.5 percent; and Department of Labor, 15.9 percent.

Overall, social science had more than a ninefold increase in federal research obligations from 1962 to 1990 (from $62 to $589 million). However, there were six serious setbacks over the decades. Furthermore, the social science share of the science budget under the Reagan administration declined back to the level from where it had commenced during the Kennedy years in the early 1960s. Social science reached its peak of nearly 6 percent during the Nixon years, only to begin a steady decline during the Carter administration that continued from 1979 on through the Reagan years, where it grounded at less than 3 percent.

This level of support would seem to be particularly problematic for social scientists, who constitute about one-fifth of the skilled work force presumably best equipped to engage in research. In 1987, there were 209,384 doctoral scientists and engineers employed in the four-year colleges and universities of the United States. In eight scientific fields, social scientists were the least likely to list research as their primary work activity. Only 17 percent of social scientists cited basic or applied research as their focus, whereas 52 percent of life scientists, 44 percent of environmental scientists, 41 percent of physical scientists,

31 percent of engineers, 26 percent of computer scientists, 23 percent of mathematicians, and 19 percent of psychologists listed research as their principal work. On the other hand, social scientists, along with mathematicians, were most likely (67 percent) to designate teaching as their primary activity. These data pose an unanswered chicken-and-egg question: What came first for social science, the heavy commitment to teaching or the relatively low level of federal support for research?

SUPPORT FOR SOCIOLOGY

Like most of their scientific colleagues, sociologists find that the resources required to serve their critical research needs always exceed the funds available. This disposition attests to the robust expectations of a field that in the years 1962–1990 received $1,789,064,000 for research from the federal government (an average of $61.7 million per year). Even though that sum is less than 1 percent of the total federal allocation for research in all science, it is a formidable investment. Furthermore, it is a minimal measure of what sociology has drawn from the federal treasury because sociologists also seek and receive research funds from other areas such as economics and psychology. Here, compared to sociology, the federal government allocated about twice as much for economics ($3.4 billion) and more than three times as much for psychology ($5.5 billion). Together, these three disciplines received 5.3 percent of the total federal obligation to research over the three decades covered.

The pattern of federal support for sociology closely tracks that of social science. Overall, there was a nearly twentyfold increase in obligations for sociology from Kennedy to Bush, or from about $6 million in 1962 to slightly more than $117 million in 1990. But the peaks and valleys for sociology were abrupt and notable. Under Kennedy, the rise was from $6 million to $16 million; under Johnson it rose from $25 million to $50 million first, dropping to $35 million; under Nixon it rose from $38 million to $119 million but ended up at $64 million; with Ford it was steady for 3 years around $54 million; with Carter

it rose from $60 million to $71 million but ended up at $65 million dollars; with Reagan it dropped to $52 million and then fluctuated over the 1980s, to reach $102 million in 1989. This rise in obligations to sociology continued in the first fiscal year of the Bush administration to reach $117 million.

In current dollar terms, the $100-million level of annual support for sociology was reached five times over twenty-nine years encompassing seven administrations. Reagan and Bush each prescribed this pinnacle once, but the most notable period was three years during the Nixon administration in the early 1970s. In 1972, sociology received nearly 40 percent of the total federal social science budget. This was sparked by a spurt of expenditures for special applied research efforts at the National Science Foundation like programs designated as Research Applied to National Needs. But, after the mid-1970s, the climate for social science chilled. The decline in the social science share of the rising science budget was particularly sharp during the Reagan decade. Sociology gained little comfort from the fact that its portion of the shrinking social science allocation actually increased under Reagan and steadied out to a fairly consistent share, around 15 percent.

In the 1980s, sociology, like science in general, but not like social science overall, began markedly to shift emphasis away from applied research. By 1990, basic research received 54 percent of the $117 million federal obligation to sociology, an even greater proportion than noted for all of science. Ogburn might have been pleased with that direction, just as Ward might have applauded the $119 million awarded to sociology in 1972, when 83 percent of the total went to applied research.

In these two premier years for sociology, the obligations came in different degrees from different federal agencies. Thus, monies from the Department of Defense declined from about 4 percent in 1972 to less than 1 percent in 1990, and funds from the NSF increased from 3 percent to 4 percent of the total. But the big increase for sociology came from the various institutes in the Department of Health and Human Services, where the overall change was from 38 percent to 79 percent of the total. Thus, sociology reached its peak level of federal research support in two contrasting years, 1972 with its applied focus and 1990 with its accent on basic research.

These data cannot establish a real change in research behavior. Obviously, political conditions define the level and the direction of research resource use. Sociologists seem to have learned how to thrive, or at least survive, in changing funding milieus. The data even imply that sociologists may be somewhat more perceptive than other social scientists about federal funding dynamics. But all that can be said for certain is that the move back to basic research represents a change in the way in which sociological research projects are being coded in the federal agencies. This, in turn, is part of what marks a fundamental change in American science-funding policy. Congress, long addicted to spending money for readily defined outcomes, now became more understanding of the uncertainties, but long-range possibilities, of investments in basic research. They saw this message in the rationale for the science budgets from both the Reagan and the Bush administrations. For the time being, the political response was positive, more so than in any earlier period. The message also appealed to those agencies engaged in major support of research in universities where basic research is accorded high status. Thus, it was particularly consonant with traditions at the NSF and current definitions in the various institutes associated with medicine, not to mention the influence from the Office of Management and Budget.

SOCIOLOGICAL GRANTSMANSHIP

Part of graduate training in sociology is to learn how to go about getting a research grant. This can be a formidable challenge. The pursuit of federal grants takes one into reams of rules and layers of organization, the latter often marked by acronyms. For instance, a sociologist wishing to pursue some line of demographic research might well be directed to the NICHD (National Institute of Child Health and Human Development). Actu-

ally, that interest will be served in the Demographic and Behavioral Sciences Branch of the Center for Population Research at the NICHD. And so it is for two other agencies of special importance to sociological research: the National Institute of Mental Health (NIMH) and the National Institute on Aging (NIA), both linked to the National Institutes of Health (NIH) in the cabinet Department of Health and Human Services (HHS).

These units are called *mission agencies* because of the substantive focus of their concerns. This accent does not imply that support is limited to applied research. As noted earlier, the Department of Health and Human Services is the largest federal patron of both applied and basic research in the social sciences. But a mission agency necessarily has a special impact on the research agenda, in that it must call for proposals that bear on its mission, such as mental health, aging, and delinquency.

Where, then, does a sociologist turn for support when his or her interests do not coincide with the concerns of a mission agency? If the proposal has the earmarks of basic research, the National Science Foundation is a key place to start. The NSF has the only research-support program in Washington, D.C., labeled "sociology." It relies on investigator-initiated proposals. Currently this program is one of seven in the Division of Social and Economic Science which is part of the Directorate of Biological, Behavioral, and Social Science at the NSF.

To know this location in the NSF's organizational hierarchy is to appreciate the challenge that sociology faces in being heard in the upper reaches of decision making. Clearly, sociology must ally itself with all of the social and behavioral sciences to hold or gain resources. This was particularly important during the early 1980s when the social sciences were under severe attack. When the Office of Management and Budget proposed to reduce funding for the social science programs in the NSF by 75 percent, and to eliminate most social science funding from NIMH, a response was organized, among others, by the Consortium of Social Science Associations to counter the threat. During that period, the social and behavioral sciences at the NSF allocated nearly a million dollars to initiate three studies by the National Research Council of the National Academy of Science. The reports issued in 1982 (Adams, Smelser, and Treiman), 1986 (Smelser and Gerstein), and 1988 (Gerstein, Luce, Smelser, and Sperlich) were valuable instruments in the political struggle for research budgets. Their accounts of achievements, opportunities, and priorities were appreciated by decision makers who not only wanted evidence of scientific credibility but also wanted it to result from a unified deliberative process involving the disparate disciplines that have a history of internal bickering and external misunderstanding.

The ongoing challenge for sociology can be seen in the fact that the capacity of the sociology program at the NSF to support research has not kept pace with the steady rise in NSF's research budget, which grew from $54 million in 1959 to $1.6 billion in 1989. In 1959, sociology's $300,000 represented 0.5 percent of the NSF research resources; in 1969, its $1.7 million was 0.6 percent; in 1979 its $3.7 million equalled 0.5 percent; and by 1989, the $3.9 million obligation for sociology represented only 0.2 percent of the total NSF research budget.

Despite the modest level of these resources, sociology and other social and behavioral science programs at the NSF have national policy significance beyond the number of grants and the magnitude of dollars allocated. The NSF carries the flag for all science. Its structure requires it to explain and defend detailed actions by its programs. In the annual congressional scrutiny of budgets, it is not unusual for the director of the NSF, or the chairman of the National Science Board, both usually physical scientists or engineers, to be called on to explain why the NSF is supporting a given research proposal in sociology. This is particularly true if the proposal has a title that is perceived as being either too explicit (e.g., "sex") or too obscure (i.e., "jargon").

When such concerns are handled adeptly, the NSF can advance the public understanding that sustains federal support for social and behavioral science. The first campaign in this regard, one

that ultimately endowed social science with legitimacy for full entry into the NSF, was managed brilliantly by a sociologist, Harry Alpert, in the early 1950s. Rigorous peer review guides the NSF, the NIMH, the NIA, and other federal agency decisions on research awards to social science. Peer review gives critical control to the scientific community, but it also places strong work demands on the participants. Careful procedures are invoked to ensure independent judgments. Competition for limited dollars is keen. For example, in sociology at the NSF, rarely would more than one-third of the submitted proposals gain grants and usually the money allocated would be about two-thirds of that initially requested. This contrasts with a typical approval rate of over 70 percent for chemistry, physics, and biology. But even nonwinners benefit from a thorough set of critical reviews communicated about their proposals. The scope of such effort for one year is reflected in how four agencies supported sociology. These agencies allocated some 60 percent of all the federal funds for social science in 1989.

The largest effort was made by the National Institute on Aging through its Behavioral and Social Research Program. In 1989, the NIA awarded 188 new and continuing grants allocating $26.9 million. This was followed by the National Institute of Mental Health's awarding of 67 grants to sociologists for $8.2 million. Next was the National Institute of Child Health and Human Development, which, through its Demographic and Behavioral Sciences Branch, made 33 awards in population research, mainly to sociologists, for a total of $4.9 million. Finally, the National Science Foundation, through its program in sociology in the Division of Social and Economic Science, made fifty-eight awards allocating $4.4 million to sociologists.

The titles of the largest grants awarded by each of these programs in 1989 provide additional insight into the direction of support that the federal government extends to sociology. The largest grant from the NSF, $842,976, was awarded to NORC at the University of Chicago for "A National Data Program for the Social Sciences: NORC General Social Survey." From the NICHD, the largest grant, $1,121,187, was awarded to Battele, Seattle, for a study of "Condom Use by Adult Men to Prevent Aids." From the NIMH, the largest grant, $543,032, was awarded to Yale University for research entitled "Pediatric Provision of Mental Health Services." And for the NIA, the largest award, $1,165,232, was made to the University of Michigan for research on "Productivity, Stress and Health in Middle and Later Life."

Competent reviewers believed that support for these projects would yield significant findings. The fruits of the investment will take time to be harvested. From the titles alone it would be difficult to estimate which or how many of the projects would serve basic and which applied interests. Some critical congressman might probe that question at some future hearing of the budget for sociology. Surely there will be questions about knowledge gain and implications for use. Someone will likely challenge the explicitness, as well as the abstractness, of terms. And, inevitably, there will be inquiry about cost and possible duplication of effort. Agency heads, briefed by program officers administering these awards to sociology, will no doubt give good-faith responses, even if it hurts. That is the price the scientific establishment pays to accommodate colleagues in sociology.

(SEE ALSO: *Public Policy Analysis; Science; Social Science Research Council*)

REFERENCES

Adams, Robert McC., Neil J. Smelser, and Donald J. Treiman (eds.) 1982 *Behavioral and Social Science Research: A National Resource.* Washington, D.C.: National Academy Press.

Gerstein, Dean R., R. Duncan Luce, Neil J. Smelser, and Sonja Sperlich (eds.) 1988 *The Behavioral and Social Sciences: Achievements and Opportunities.* Washington, D.C.: National Academy Press.

Inkeles, Alex 1986 "The Intellectual Consequences of Federal Support for the Social Sciences." In S. Klausner and V. Lidz, eds., *The Nationalization of the Social Sciences.* Philadelphia: University of Pennsylvania Press.

Larsen, Otto N. 1991 *Milestones and Millstones for Social Science at the National Science Foundation, 1945–1991.* New Brunswick: Transaction.

National Science Board 1989 *Science & Engineering Indicators—1989.* Washington, D.C.: U.S. Government Printing Office (NSB 89–1).

——— 1989 *Federal Funds for Research and Development: Fiscal Years 1987, 1988, and 1989,* Vol. XXXVII, NSF 89–304. Washington, D.C.: U.S. Government Printing Office.

Ogburn, William F. 1930 "The Folkways of a Scientific Sociology." In *Studies in Quantitative and Cultural Sociology,* Proceedings of the Twenty-fourth Annual Meeting of the American Sociological Society. Chicago: University of Chicago Press.

Prewitt, Kenneth 1986 "Federal Funding for Social Science." In S. Klausner and V. Lidz, eds., *The Nationalization of the Social Sciences.* Philadelphia: University of Pennsylvania Press.

Recent Social Trends in the United States, Vols. 1 and 2. 1933 Report of the President's Research Committee on Social Trends. New York: McGraw-Hill.

Smelser, Neil J., and Dean R. Gerstein (eds.) 1986 *Behavioral and Social Science: Fifty Years of Discovery.* Washington, D.C.: National Academy Press.

Ward, Lester F. 1907 "The Establishment of Sociology." *American Journal of Sociology* 12:579–587.

OTTO N. LARSEN

SOCIOLOGY OF EDUCATION In the broadest light, education involves all efforts to impart knowledge and shape values; hence, it has essentially the same meaning as socialization. Yet, when sociologists speak of education, they generally have a more constricted meaning: the deliberate process, which takes place outside the family, by which societies transmit knowledge, values, and norms, in order to prepare young people for adult roles (and to a lesser extent, adults for new roles). This process acquires institutional status when the related activities make instruction the central, defining purpose; are differentiated from other social realms; and involve defined roles of teacher and learner (Clark 1968). Schools exemplify this institutionalization.

The central insight of the sociology of education is that schools are socially embedded institutions, both crucially shaped by their social environment and crucially shaping it. The field encompasses both micro- and macro-sociological concerns in such diverse subfields as stratification, economic development, socialization and the family, organizations, culture, and the sociology of knowledge. To understand modern society, it is essential to understand the role of education. Not only is education a primary agent of socialization and allocation, but also modern societies have developed formidable ideologies suggesting that education *should* have this defining impact (Meyer 1977).

Durkheim was the intellectual pioneer (especially 1977), historically tracing the connections between the form and content of schools and larger social forces, like the rise of the bourgeoisie and the general trend toward individualism. Although the larger issues raised by the discipline's founding fathers are readily evident in current scholarship, the host of practical, policy-related issues that emerged with the development of a mass education system shaped most research. Essentially, research has focused on whether education has delivered on its promise of creating more rational, culturally adapted, and productive individuals, and, by extension, a "better" society (Meyer 1986).

THEORETICAL DEBATES

Research has been grounded, often implicitly, in more general analytical perspectives about the function of education in modern society. These may be crudely divided into two main orientations, functionalism and conflict theory.

Functionalism. In this view, schools serve the presumed needs of a social order committed to rationality, meritocracy, and democracy: They provide individuals with the necessary cognitive skills and cultural outlooks to be successful workers and citizens (Parsons 1959, Dreeben 1968), and they provide society with an efficient, fair way of sorting and selecting "talents" so that the most capable can assume the most responsible positions (Clark 1962). Complementing this sociological work is human capital theory in economics, which contends that investment in education enhances individual productivity and, relatedly, aggregate economic growth (Schultz 1961). This theoretical orientation undergirds much of the recent criticism that poor schooling has significantly contributed to America's decline in the international economy (Kingston 1986).

Both the increasing prominence of critical political forces and the accumulated weight of considerable research spurred a theoretical challenge in the 1970s. Important parts of functionalism's empirical base were severely questioned: Schools taught productive skills, mass education ushered in a meritocratic social order, and education had furthered social equality (Hurn 1985).

Neo-Marxist Theory. Neo-Marxist scholars have provided the most thorough challenge to the functional position. For all the diversity within this conflict theory, the main point is that the organization of schools largely reflects the dictates of the corporate–capitalist economy. In the most noted formulation, Bowles and Gintis (1976) argue that education must fulfill the needs of capitalism: efficiently allocating differently socialized individuals to appropriate slots in the corporate hierarchy, transferring privilege from generation to generation, and accomplishing both while maintaining a semblance of legitimacy. Thus, the changing demands of capitalist production and the power of capitalist elites determine the nature of the educational system.

Recent neo-Marxist scholarship (Willis 1981) has emphasized that schools are not only agents of social reproduction but also important sites of resistance to the capitalist order. Many neo-Marxists have also emphasized the "relative autonomy" of the state from economic forces and, correspondingly, the partial responsiveness of schools to demands from subordinate groups (Carnoy and Levin 1985).

Status Conflict. Arising out of the Weberian tradition, the status conflict approach emphasizes the attempts of various groups, defined by ethnicity, race, occupational grouping, and class, to use education as a mechanism to win or maintain privilege (Collins 1979). The evolving structure of the educational system reflects the outcomes of these struggles as groups seek to control the system to their benefit. Status groups use education both to build group cohesion and to restrict entry to desired positions to those certified by "their" schools. In this view, then, the educational system itself is not necessarily functional to capitalist interests or other imputed system needs. As lower status groups seek social mobility through acquiring ever more educational credentials, schools may expand beyond what is technically necessary.

Relatedly, a primary effect of schools, especially at the elite level, is to provide *cultural capital,* of which educational credentials are the main markers (Bourdieu and Passeron 1977). This form of capital refers to the personal style, social outlooks and values, and aesthetic tastes that make a person suitable for socially valued positions. (The point of comparison is *human* capital, an individual's productive, technical skills.) In this perspective, education is rewarded because occupational gatekeepers value particular forms of cultural capital.

Although these theoretical perspectives have framed much important empirical research, the interplay between theory and research has not been systematically developed to the point that key theoretical disputes have been resolved.

EMPIRICAL STUDIES

Schooling and Life Chances. As part of the analysis of *status attainment,* researchers have concentrated on measuring the connection between individuals' schooling and their economic position. Building on Blau and Duncan's (1967) pathbreaking work, researchers have repeatedly documented that education (measured in years of schooling and in degree completion) has by far the largest independent impact on adult attainment and that this effect is largely independent of family background measures (Featherman and Hauser 1978, Jencks 1979). To the extent that family background and intellectual ability affect adult attainment, these effects are largely mediated through educational attainment.

The strong connection between schooling and occupational attainment is open to diverse inter-pretations. On the one hand, human capital theory suggests that education enhances productivity, and, because people are paid in accord with their marginal productivity, the well-educated enjoy greater prospects. On the other hand, education is viewed as a sorting device, so that individuals are slotted to particular positions on the basis of academic credentials, with little regard for their individual productive capacities. Both views seem to have some merit.

Family Status and Achievement. Given the centrality of educational achievement in the general attainment process, researchers have turned to explaining the substantial relationship between family status and educational attainment. This association is mostly attributable to the fact that higher-status students achieve better in schools (i.e., have higher grades and test scores). This relationship also reflects higher-status students' receiving greater parental and peer encouragement of educational ambitions.

The indirect effects of school resources and processes appear relatively small or even nonexistent. To note one frequently studied process, researchers have examined the impact of curricular track placement in high school because track placement is related to social status and race, and higher tracks appear to offer better educational experiences. There is little evidence, however, that status considerations *per se* substantially affect this placement. Moreover, controlling for the initial abilities of students, the impact of track placement on academic achievement appears to be modest at best, though placement in the higher tracks seems to increase student aspirations.

Although many have suggested that teachers create self-fulfilling prophecies of lower-class academic failure, there is no rigorous, systematic evidence of this effect. Indeed, the search for systematic, socially discriminatory processes that could explain the link between family status and school achievement has not established that any specific school practices can be held to account.

School Effects. Attempting to identify the characteristics of schools that improved learning, Coleman's (1966) study, largely validated by later researchers, upset conventional wisdom in two respects: (1) The relationship is weak between social status and school quality, as indicated by such measures as per-pupil expenditure, teacher experience, and class size; and (2) these measures of school quality have very little independent effect on school achievement (scores on standardized tests). Later research on so-called compositional effects and the actual educational experiences of students in individual classrooms suggests, however, that schools, not just families, can make a difference. Independent of an individual student's family status, a school's social class and racial composition appear to influence individual achievement. For example, some research indicates that African-American achievement is higher in schools with a majority of white students, especially for African-Americans with white friends.

Although crude measures of school resources like expenditures per pupil appear largely unrelated to school achievement, a burgeoning (though not always rigorous) line of research finds that effective schools can be identified, schools marked by strong leadership committed to order and academically focused goals, high academic demands, and frequent practice of traditional academic skills. This research directs attention to the impact of moral climates and classroom interaction.

Macro-level Effects. If the individual economic benefits of education are clear, the impact of educational expansion on economic growth is less certain. The safest conclusion may be that educational expansion seems, under some circumstances, to modestly stimulate growth, but it provides no certain promise of growth (Walters and Rubinson 1983, Meyer and Hannan 1979). By the same token, although education is associated at the individual level with some democratic values, educational expansion does not appear to contribute to the emergence of democratic regimes or state power.

(SEE ALSO: *Education and Mobility; Educational Organizations; Socialization*)

REFERENCES

Blau, Peter, and Otis D. Duncan 1967 *The American Occupational Structure.* New York: Wiley.

Bourdieu, Pierre, and Jean-Claude Passeron 1977 *Reproduction in Society, Culture, and Education.* Beverly Hills, Calif.: Sage.

Bowles, Samuel, and Herbert Gintis 1976 *Schooling in Capitalist America.* New York: Basic Books.

Carnoy, Martin, and Henry Levin 1985 *Schooling and Work in the Democratic State.* Stanford, Calif.: Stanford University Press.

Clark, Burton 1962 *Educating the Expert Society.* San Francisco: Chandler.

——— 1968 "The Study of Educational Systems." In David L. Sills, ed., *International Encyclopedia of the Social Sciences.* New York: Macmillan and Free Press.

Coleman, James, et al. 1966 *Equality of Educational Opportunity.* Washington, D.C.: U.S. Government Printing Office.

Collins, Randall 1979 *The Credential Society.* New York: Academic Press.

Dreeben, Robert 1968 *On What Is Learned in School.* Reading, Mass.: Addison-Wesley.

Durkheim, Emile 1977 *The Evolution of Educational Thought,* trans. Peter Collins. London: Routledge and Kegan Paul.

Featherman, David, and Robert Hauser 1978 *Opportunity and Change.* New York: Academic Press.

Hurn, Christopher 1985 *The Limits and Possibilities of Schooling.* Boston: Allyn and Bacon.

Jencks, Christopher, et al. 1979 *Who Gets Ahead? The Determinants of Economic Success in America.* New York: Basic Books.

Kingston, Paul 1986 "Theory at Risk: Accounting for the Excellence Movement." *Sociological Forum* 1:632–656.

Meyer, John 1977 "The Effects of Education as an Institution." *American Journal of Sociology* 83:55–77.

——— 1986 "Types of Explanation in the Sociology of Education." In John Richardson, ed., *Handbook of Theory and Research for the Sociology of Education.* Westport, Conn.: Greenwood Press.

———, and Michael Hannan (eds.) 1979 *National and Political Change, 1950–1970.* Chicago: University of Chicago Press.

Parsons, Talcott 1959 "The School Class as a Social System." *Harvard Educational Review* 29:297–308.

Schultz, Theodore 1961 "Investment in Human Capital." *American Economic Review* 51:1–17.

Trow, Martin 1961 "The Second Transformation of American Secondary Education." *International Journal of Comparative Sociology* 2:144–166.

Walters, Pamela, and Richard Rubinson 1983 "Educational Expansion and Economic Output in the United States." *American Sociological Review* 48:480–493.

Willis, Paul 1981 *Learning to Labor.* New York: Columbia University Press.

PAUL W. KINGSTON

SOCIOLOGY OF LAW Law is created, enforced, and utilized in social organizations. For Durkheim, Weber, and other founders of sociology the intersections of law and organization were crucial sites for developing general social theory. Current work in the sociology of law, which dates roughly from the establishment of the Law and Society Association in 1964, has increasingly revived the sensibilities of the classical theorists as a means of focusing and integrating empirical research. The relationship between law and social organization is not the exclusive preserve of this discipline; certain schools of jurisprudence confront them as well, but sociology poses distinctive questions that it seeks to resolve within the limits of its own methods of argument and proof.

SOCIOLOGICAL VERSUS JURISPRUDENTIAL PERSPECTIVES ON THE LAW

As with most institutions, legal practitioners may have few occasions to ponder the social organization matrix that defines and constrains their routine realities. The practitioner's outlook is codified in the theory of *legal formalism*, which envisions law as an autonomous body of abstract concepts and rules requiring primarily powers of inductive logic to reach adequate solutions to concrete issues. Law combines facts with norms to deduce solutions to problems (Dibble 1973; Katz 1987).

Several schools of legal philosophy developed over the past century within U. S. law schools to address the gaps between the actual law in practice and the formal law in legislative statutes and court decisions (*legal realism*). These schools also considered how extralegal factors constrain, if not determine, the decisions in law (*sociological jurisprudence;* for a brief survey of these developments, consult Hunt 1978). Most recently the critical legal studies movement in law schools, begun in 1977, has sought to explore the latent conservative social consequences of liberal legal reforms.

Sociology of law and critical legal studies often address common issues. Both have examined the origins and consequences of the civil rights movements, the commercialization of legal services, and the political consequences of due process. Furthermore, they often draw upon a common body of social theory, most notably that of Marx and Weber. While the nature of their differences has become increasingly debated, one central tendency is the methodological reliance of critical legal scholars on doctrinal analysis, which takes the written decisions of appellate courts as the primary source of information about the legal system (Trubek 1984). This emphasis on textual analysis has more affinity with literary criticism than with sociological methodology, which tends more toward refinements in the arts of drawing inferences from statistical distributions of events. (Differences between these two approaches may concretely compared by contrasting Klare 1978 with Wallace, Rubin, and Smith 1988.)

CRIMINAL VERSUS CIVIL LAW

Accidents of academic history and government funding have made sociology of law preoccupied with criminal rather than civil or administrative law. Oddly, this emphasis is the reverse of that in the law schools. Correcting the imbalance has largely fallen to recent legal scholars investigating the alleged "litigation explosion" and, more broadly, the trends and covariates of the volume of litigation (for overview, see Friedman 1989). In addition, sociological theories have been applied to economic regulation (for summary, see Jones 1982), while empirical studies using innovative methodology have begun to explore determinants of diffusion patterns in worker compensation laws (Pavalko 1989) and wages and hours legislation (Ratner 1980). A relatively neglected (though theoretically critical area of scholarship) is the intersection of civil and criminal law (for a good introduction to these issues, see Abel 1981).

SOCIAL STRATIFICATION AND THE LAW

Stratification is the single aspect of social structure that dominates current sociological investigations of the law. Stratification is of special significance in a legal system based upon the principle of equality. The sociology of law seeks to analyze how the forces of stratification pull the administration of justice away from the norms of legal equality and, conversely, to assess the power of legal norms to alter the inequalities of wealth and power (Baldus and Cole 1980). Apart from being concerned with the discrimination arising from discretionary decision making, researchers have also been concerned with the ways in which a legal system organized on the principle of equality before the law can paradoxically reproduce the existing inequalities of wealth and power. One such formulation is Galanter's (1974) analysis of the advantages that are accumulated by repeat players in such systems. In addition, considerable research has been done on the extent to which the legal profession is stratified and the role that market forces play in differentially allocating access to legal services (Abel and Lewis 1988). Legal action may, under some circumstances, modify the distribution of resources. Of particular concern recently has been assessing the causes and consequences of civil rights statutes and litigation on the economic opportunities for women and racial minorities (e.g., Burstein 1985).

In addition, sociology provides explanations of the emergence of legal equality as a "self-evident truth" among certain types of societies. While the Marxist tradition traces legal equality to demands of the free market in labor power created by the capitalist mode of production, research on the diffusion of legal rights suggests more variegated social bases for legal equality (Therborn 1977).

LEGAL PROCEDURE: SOCIAL CAUSES AND SOCIAL IMPACT

Variations in legal procedure and their social impact were central to the work of Max Weber (see Kronman 1983). Both the Weberian tradition and popular concern have been drawn to three aspects of legal procedure: due process, plea bargaining, and informal justice. The "due process revolution" in U.S. Supreme Court decisions (c. 1953–1969) rationalized criminal procedure by standardizing it among the states. Rather than create new rights, the Warren Court applied the Bill of Rights to those states that applied lower standards of constraint on police powers of government. Although the possible impact of the due process revolution on increasing crime rates became a common theme of law and order political campaigns, no systematic evidence of a noncoincidental relationship has been reported (Horowitz 1977). Changes in due process procedures have, however, had considerable impact on the administration of law (Mashaw 1985; Heydebrand and Seron 1990).

The second prominent aspect of legal procedure is plea bargaining in criminal prosecutions. While the civil law practice of out-of-court settlements provokes few problems, such informal disposition of roughly 95 percent of felony convictions has sparked sharp debate. Plea bargaining has, in addition, a special sociological significance because it exemplifies the emergence of informal social organization within bureaucratic organizations. Much of the work of the criminal court is conducted outside the formal categories and rules of the law; defense and prosecution replace crime as defined by statutes with negotiated categories of "normal crimes" (Sudnow 1965). Some attention has also been given to comparative analyses of legal systems whose procedures restrict bargaining (Weigend 1980). In locating plea bargaining's origins and studying its operations, sociologists have expanded our general understanding about the nature of bureaucratic organization (Abel 1979; McIntyre 1987).

Another alternative to formal procedure appears in the recent diffusion of neighborhood justice centers and other forms of alternative dispute resolution. These developments have stimulated both descriptive and explanatory studies (Abel 1982). The dispute resolution literature has itself played a role in stimulating this movement. Similarly, research on the other two aspects of procedural variations has had substantial impact in Supreme Court decisions on the death penalty and the legislative construction of sentencing guidelines.

GENERAL THEORY IN THE SOCIOLOGY OF LAW

Ironically, the study of law, which had been a central focus of the founders of sociological theory, is today long on empirical observation and short on general theory that can guide research (for a broad survey of recent investigations, consult Tomasic 1985). The need for such theory becomes apparent, to give but one example, in those comparisons of Japanese and U.S. legal systems that "explain away Japan by attributing every finding to 'Japanese uniqueness' [rather than] treat Japan as a point on a universal continuum" (Miyazawa 1987, p. 239). Black (1976) offers a schematic form of a general theory of law conceived as "government control" cast in terms of such propositions as "the relationship between law and social differentiation is curvilinear." While this work offers a glimpse of the future state of theory, at present much of the general theory utilized by researchers in the sociology of law follows one or a combination of the core classical sociological theories (see, e.g., Beirne and Quinney 1982). The accumulation of such work not only illuminates what we know about the law as an institution but also contributes to our more basic knowledge of social organization.

(SEE ALSO: *Court Systems of the United States; Criminology; International Law; Law and Legal Systems; Law and Society*)

REFERENCES

Abel, Richard (ed.) 1979 Special issue of *Law and Society Review* 13:189–687.

———— 1981 "A Critique of American Tort Law." *British Journal of Law and Society* 8:199–231.

———— (ed.) 1982 *The Politics of Informal Justice.* New York: Academic Press.

————, and Philip S. C. Lewis 1988 *Lawyers in Society: The Civil Law World.* Berkeley: University of California Press.

Baldus, David, and James L. Cole 1980 *Statistical Proof of Discrimination.* New York: Shepards-McGraw.

Beirne, Piers, and Richard Quinney (eds.) 1982 *Marxism and Law.* New York: Wiley.

Black, Donald J. 1976 *The Behavior of Law.* New York: Academic Press.

Burstein, Paul 1985 *Discrimination, Jobs, and Politics: The Struggle for Equal Employment Opportunity in the U.S. since the New Deal.* Chicago: University of Chicago Press.

Dibble, Vernon 1973 "What Is and What Ought to Be: A Comparison of Certain Characteristics of Legal and Ideological Styles of Thought." *American Journal of Sociology* 79:511–549.

Friedman, Lawrence M. 1989 "Litigation and Society." In *Annual Review of Sociology*, vol. 15. Palo Alto, Calif.: Annual Reviews.

Galanter, Marc 1974 "Why the 'Haves' Come Out Ahead: Speculations on the Limits of Legal Change." *Law and Society Review* 9:95–160.

Heydebrand, Wolf, and Carroll Seron 1990 *Rationalizing Justice: The Political Economy of Federal District Courts.* Albany: State University of New York Press.

Horowitz, Donald L. 1977 *The Courts and Social Policy.* Washington, D.C.: Brookings Institution.

Hunt, Alan 1978 *The Sociological Movement in Law.* Philadelphia: Temple University Press.

Jones, Kelvin 1982 *Law and Economy: The Legal Regulation of Corporate Behavior.* New York: Academic Press.

Katz, Leo 1987 *Bad Acts and Guilty Minds: Conundrums of the Criminal Law.* Chicago: University of Chicago Press.

Klare, Karl E. 1978 "Judicial Deradicalization of the Wagner Act and the Origins of Modern Legal Consciousness, 1937–1941." *Minnesota Law Review* 62:265–339.

Kronman, Anthony T. 1983 *Max Weber.* Stanford, Calif.: Stanford University Press.

McIntyre, Lisa J. 1987 *The Public Defender.* Chicago: University of Chicago Press.

Mashaw, Jerry L. 1985 *Due Process in the Administrative State*. New Haven: Yale University Press.

Miyazawa, Setsuo 1987 "Taking Kawashima Seriously: A Review of Japanese Research on Japanese Legal Consciousness and Disputing Behavior." *Law and Society Review* 21:219–241.

Pavalko, Eliza K. 1989 "State Timing of Policy Adoption: Workmen's Compensation in the United States, 1901–1929." *American Journal of Sociology* 95:592–615.

Ratner, Ronnie Steinberg 1980 "The Social Meaning of Industrialization in the U.S.: Determinants of the Scope of Coverage under Wages and Hours Standards Legislation, 1900–1970." *Social Problems* 27:448–466.

Sudnow, David 1965 "Normal Crimes: Sociological Features of the Penal Code in a Public Defender's Office." *Social Problems* 12:255–276.

Therborn, Goeran 1977 "The Rule of Capital and the Rise of Democracy." *New Left Review* 103:3–41.

Tomasic, Roman 1985 "The Sociology of Law." *Current Sociology* 33:1–275.

Trubek, David M. 1984 "Where the Action Is: Critical Legal Studies and Empiricism." *Stanford Law Review* 36:575–622.

Wallace, Michael, Beth A. Rubin, and Brian T. Smith 1988 "American Labor Law: Its Impact on Working-Class Militancy, 1901–1980." *Social Science History* 12:1–29.

Weigend, Thomas 1980 "Continental Cures for American Ailments: European Criminal Procedure as a Model for Law Reform." *Crime and Justice: An Annual Review of Research* 2:381–428.

JAMES INVERARITY

SOCIOLOGY OF RELIGION

Two closely related theses have dominated the sociology of religion since the founding of the field. The first is the secularization thesis, which heralds the rise of secular societies cleansed of all forms of religious beliefs and institutions. This development has been regarded as the inevitable result of the spread of modern, scientific perspectives. The second thesis imputes irrationality, ignorance, and even mental illness to those who believe in invisible, supernatural beings and forces and who are willing to make sacrifices on behalf of their faith.

For well over a century, these theses seemed self-evident to the overwhelming majority of social scientists. Nevertheless, since the early 1980s both theses have come crashing down under the accumulated weight of contrary evidence. Not only does religion show no signs of going away, it displays renewed vigor in many parts of the world. Moreover, decades of research efforts to uncover psychopathological roots of religious commitment have not only failed, but the results suggest that religious people tend to enjoy better mental health than do the irreligious. In similar fashion, the "false consciousness" and "opiate" explanations of religiousness are not supported by research. Finally, the willingness of people to make sacrifices on behalf of their religion turns out to be entirely compatible with rational choice economic theories.

THE SECULARIZATION THESIS RECONSIDERED

Since the mid-nineteenth century, and perhaps earlier, social scientists have awaited the death of religion as eagerly as any dispensationalist Christian sect has awaited the Second Coming. In fact, it would not be an exaggeration to suggest that social scientists invented secular humanism. Consider that in the 1830s when Comte coined the word *sociology*, he expected this new science soon to replace religion as the basis for moral judgments. Moreover, the fact that most of the famous founders of the social sciences devoted much attention to religion is best understood in terms of their antagonism toward faith.

During the early twentieth century, support for the secularization thesis hardened, and perhaps no other social science proposition has been so widely accepted. The distinguished Anthony F. C. Wallace undoubtedly spoke for nearly all of his colleagues when he pronounced the impending doom of the world's religions:

The evolutionary future of religion is extinction. Belief in supernatural beings and supernatural forces that affect nature without obeying nature's laws will erode and become only an interesting historical memory. . . . Belief in supernatural pow-

ers is doomed to die out, all over the world, as a result of the increasing adequacy and diffusion of scientific knowledge. (Wallace 1966, p. 265)

Although Wallace and everyone else "knew" secular societies were just around the corner, the topic continued to inspire endless discussion—brilliant careers were made by sociologists who wrote on virtually no other topic. Closer inspection shows that, rather than simply belaboring the obvious, most of this writing about secularization reflects an unending and unrelenting need to explain away the contrary facts.

One very troublesome problem facing secularization scholarship has been to discover why the United States remains a deviant case. Not only have religious belief and practice failed to decline in what otherwise might appear to be the nation most likely to undergo secularization, but it is the most traditional, otherworldly, and fundamentalist groups that are the most vigorous, while faiths that have made the greatest effort to accommodate their doctrines to "modernity" are rapidly losing ground. For sheer mental gymnastics, some of the efforts to account for the "American exception" surpass medieval scholasticism. Thus, Wilson (1966) used the decline in membership and attendance in Britain as evidence of the march toward secularization, and then he claimed that *high* rates of membership and attendance in the United States *also* were proof of secularization! According to Wilson, both can be true because "the long recognized lack of depth of religious manifestations in the United States suggest[s] that religion is in decline in both countries" (1966, p. 126). In the end, even this kind of reasoning could not save the secularization thesis from a mountain of obstinate facts.

First, not only has religion failed to decline in the United States, it is clear that American religious activity and involvement have increased very substantially over the past several centuries. The proportion of Americans who are active church members has doubled since 1860. In 1931 there was one church for every 763 residents of Muncie, Indiana (sociology's famous Middletown), but by 1970 there was one church for every 473. If

religion is doomed, why has it been on the rise for several centuries in the nation where the public's exposure to science has been the greatest?

A second set of very uncomfortable facts involves the discovery that many claims about the progress of secularization, especially in modern Europe, rest on utterly false perceptions of the widespread piety of these same societies in earlier times. For example, levels of religious participation among the populace seem to have been very low in medieval Europe. Indeed, as Paul Johnson noted, the Church typically made little or no effort to reach the peasantry, at a time when nearly everyone was a peasant:

The truth is that the Church tended to be hostile to the peasants. There were very few peasant saints. Medieval clerical writers emphasize the bestiality, violence and avarice of the peasant. We get few glimpses of peasant life in the documents. . . . [The church] was increasingly an urban phenomenon. . . . It was rare to see a priest in the country districts. (Johnson 1976, pp. 228–229)

In their study of popular religion during the Middle Ages, Brooke and Brooke (1984) note that an extensive survey of surviving parish churches revealed them to be "a small box with a tiny chancel, the whole being no larger than a moderately large living room in a modern house." While the Brookes chose to emphasize the intimacy this made possible between priest and parishioners during mass, tiny churches are indicative of widespread indifference. Given that medieval parishes usually covered a substantial area, it would have been impossible to cram more than a small fraction of the population into such quarters.

Just as no one points to medieval Europe as a secularized society, everyone regards colonial New England as a world of devotion. Nevertheless, as anyone who has toured churches in New England well knows, tiny churches serving relatively large areas were typical in colonial New England too. Moreover, there is solid evidence that fewer than 20 percent of the inhabitants of the colonial Commonwealth of Massachusetts belonged to or attended a church—about the same rate as in the other colonies.

What about Ireland? Who would classify pious and Catholic Ireland in 1840 as a secular society? Nevertheless, religious indifference was rife. Larkin reported that

If, for example, all the priests in Ireland celebrated the two masses they were allowed on a given Sunday in 1840 there would have been 4,300 masses for 6,500,000 people, or one mass for every 1,500 people in attendance, and there were no chapels and very few churches in pre-famine Ireland that would accommodate a thousand worshipers. (1972, p. 636)

In fact, there is quite solid evidence that only about one-third of the Irish attended mass in 1840 (Larkin 1972) and that attendance was never higher than this as far back as anyone can tell. The celebrated Irish piety arose only in the latter part of the nineteenth century, at a time when such fervor was already supposed to be rapidly on its way out.

Of course, even with these low rates of religious participation, it seems reasonable to regard these three societies as essentially religious because it seems likely that the average person in each of these settings was in some general sense religious —that most possessed some semblance of religious beliefs, even if these were somewhat vague and not highly salient except in times of crisis. Doubtlessly, that raises a third major disconfirmation of secularization theory: This same qualification also applies to those nations that are today classified as the most "secularized."

In Iceland, for example, religion has been thought to be so weak that some sociologists have identified this tiny island nation as the first society to fulfill the secularization thesis. Nevertheless, Swatos (1984) reported high levels of in-the-home religion in Iceland today, rising rates of baptism, that nearly all weddings now occur in church, and that "affirmations of personal immortality are typical" (p. 36) in newspaper obituaries, which usually are written by a close friend of the deceased rather than by a newswriter. Is Iceland a secularized society? If so, then why would medieval Europe, colonial Massachusetts, and prefamine Ireland not qualify too? In similar fashion,

poll data suggest that the great majority of the inhabitants even of northern European nations express belief in the existence of God although church attendance rates are below 10 percent.

A fourth major problem for secularizationists involves the recognition of defects in the widely used definition of secularization as "that process by which religious institutions, actions, and consciousness, lose their social significance" (Wilson 1966, p. 14). That is, many writers have noted declines in the social significance of a particular religious institution and inferred from this that religion was in retreat all across the board. Recently it has become clear that such changes need not, and probably do not, occur in concert.

At issue here is the massive loss of power and prestige by "monopoly" faiths when the state no longer was willing to use coercion on their behalf. There can be no doubt that Lutheran and Catholic establishments lost power, wealth, and cultural influence in much of Europe and Latin America. But it is not at all clear that this institutional shift betokens diminished levels of individual piety—or what secularizationists have identified as religious actions and consciousness. For one thing, it now is known that societies with monopoly churches only appear to be universally pious. For example, Catholic religious practice is very strongly, negatively correlated with the percentage of the population that is nominally Catholic; nowhere is Catholic practice as low as in "Catholic" societies, and nowhere is Catholocism more vigorous than where Catholics make up but a small minority. In part, this occurs because monopoly religious firms tend to be lazy, as Adam Smith was careful to note. In part, too, it occurs because no single religious firm can meet the diversity of tastes always present among potential consumers. Thus, religious participation is highest where a proportionately greater number of religious firms compete (Finke and Stark 1988).

In this regard, Latin America offers a most instructive example. So long as the nations of Latin America used coercion against non-Catholic religions, they gave the impression of universal piety, but in reality most people were at best but nominal Catholics. However, as the state abandoned its support of the church in many Latin American nations and anti-Catholic persecution declined, a number of Protestant denominations managed to take root. As a result, in recent years while secularizationists have hailed the decline of Roman Catholic influence, Latin America rapidly has been turning Protestant. Today, evangelical Protestant denominations (most of them of the Pentecostal variety) claim the active participation of in excess of 20 percent of the population in many nations of Latin America (Martin 1990; Stoll 1990). Given the low levels of Catholic practice in these nations, this means that on Sunday the majority of those in church are Protestants. Moreover, while Protestantism is growing extremely rapidly in most of the continent—straight line projections put the Protestant proportion above 50 percent in many nations twenty years hence—the fastest growth is in the most, rather than the least, modernized nations. Such a massive turn toward highly supernatural faiths that impose strict behavioral standards is about the last thing that secularization scholars anticipated.

Events elsewhere in the world have been equally contrary. The recent history of the Moslem world, for example, does not encourage us to expect the imminent decline and extinction of that religion. Of course, the most brutal blow of all has been delivered by Marxist societies. By 1989 it was clear that decades of official exertions to induce secularization by heroic means, to abolish religion and replace it with "scientific atheism," stood revealed as a dismal failure. As the decades passed, especially in Eastern Europe, it was faith in Marxism that decayed, while faith in religion remained vigorous. Indeed, as repression has eased, massive revivalism has erupted in most of the nations of Eastern Europe, and including the Soviet Union.

RELIGIOUS ECONOMIES

The collapse of the secularization thesis has caused sociologists of religion also to discard the unidimensional model of social processes on which it was based. Instead, the field is turning toward a model of interactive processes. Three definitions are essential to this model. First, *religion* is defined as any system of beliefs and practices concerned with ultimate meanings and assuming the existence of the supernatural. Second, *religious firms* refers to social enterprises whose primary purpose is to create, maintain, and supply religion to some set of individuals. Third, *religious economy* refers to all the religious activities going on in any society. Religious economies are like commercial economies in that they consist of a market of current and potential customers, a set of firms seeking to serve that market, and the religious "product lines" offered by the various firms.

Use of an explicitly economic language facilitates application of theories of the market to religious phenomena. Many new propositions have been derived from this enterprise. For example, as with commercial economies, the major factor affecting religious economies is their degree of regulation. Some religious economies are restricted by state-imposed monopolies, others are virtually unregulated. In can be deduced from the general model that to the degree that a religious economy is unregulated, pluralism will thrive. That is, the "natural state" of a religious economy is one in which a variety of firms successfully cater to the special interests of specific market segments. It also follows that overall levels of religious commitment and participation will be lower, to the degree that an economy is monopolized. Conversely, levels of religiousness will be higher to the degree that an economy is pluralistic. These deductions explain the high levels of religious activity in the United States as well as the low levels found in societies where one true faith embraces "everyone."

By analyzing religious economies rather than individual religiousness, sociologists are encouraged to recognize variations in religious activity across societies as a consequence of variations in the vigor of suppliers (religious firms) rather than as rooted in variations in demand. That is, the secularization thesis posits that low levels of religious activity in Scandinavia, for example, reflect a decline in demand—that Scandinavians no longer feel the need for supernatural beliefs. In contrast, sociologists using the notion of religious economies will note that Scandinavians are confronted only by lazy, established churches offering a tepid product. Thus, this new line of theorizing suggests that Scandinavians would respond like their American cousins if they too were confronted by a crowded religious marketplace filled with highly motivated and specialized suppliers. Similarly, the immense changes going on in Latin American religion, as new Protestant firms attract millions of previously indifferent customers, are to be understood on the basis of a radical expansion in the number of energetic suppliers operating in the marketplace.

Finally, the model of religious economies posits religious changes that are constant and substantial but do not disrupt an underlying equilibrium. That is, the overall level of religious activity within a society can fluctuate, particular firms can slump into history to be replaced by their more vigorous competitors, new religious products can gain acceptance, the state can abandon a monopoly faith to face market forces, but through it all religion persists.

TRADITIONAL MODELS OF RELIGIOUS BELIEF AND SACRIFICE

Underlying the secularization thesis is a question that has dominated microsociological thinking about religion from the very beginning: How can people possibly believe in supernatural beings and forces, and whatever drives people to make irrational sacrifices in the name of faith? Posed this way, social scientists virtually have been forced to frame answers that postulate personal flaws in those who believe and sacrifice. Many have offered elaborate psychopathological explanations of religious commitment. For others, the explanation of preference has been ignorance, usually defined in terms of cultural backwardness or false consciousness.

Like the secularization thesis, this whole line of thought has come to an ignominious dead end and rapidly is being replaced by models of individual religiousness based on the assumption that people

typically choose to be, and to remain, religious for entirely rational reasons.

The psychopathological theory of piety appeared in many forms, all of them bristling with antagonism and contempt. Consider Freud, who managed to characterize religion as a "neurosis," an "illusion," a "poison," an "intoxicant," and "childishness to be overcome," all on one page of his famous book on the subject ([1927] 1961, p. 88). Nevertheless, here too the empirical evidence failed to cooperate. In a survey of all published empirical studies Bergin (1983) found that most reported a positive, rather than a negative, relationship between religiosity and mental health and that most of the studies that did report an association between religion and psychopathology were tautological, having included religious items in their measures of psychopathology.

The "false consciousness" explanation has fared equally badly. After conducting a comprehensive survey of the research literature, Wuthnow (1973, p. 121) reported that religious commitment is, "contrary to expectations, either unrelated or negatively related to [political] conservatism." Here too the recent history of Eastern Europe is instructive, since the churches have played a leading role in the democratic transformation of nation after socialist nation. Indeed, while religion may well have been an "opiate" of the people in some times and places (especially when monopoly religious organizations had irrevocably committed their fate into the hands of the ruling elite), in other instances it might be equally apt to describe religion as the amphetamines of the people.

Religiousness cannot merely be dismissed as backwardness and ignorance. There tends to be a positive association between religious involvement and social class. Among American college students, those who say they have been "born again" are slightly more likely than other students to enroll in the sciences. Data on faculty members reveal that it is the engineers, physicists, chemists, mathematicians, and biologists who are most likely to belong to a church and to express religious commitment. Finally, it is the sons and daughters of secular humanists who are most likely to convert to a cult or sect movement (Stark and Bainbridge 1985).

RATIONAL MODELS OF RELIGIOUS BELIEF AND SACRIFICE

In the wake of these many disappointments, sociologists have begun a new approach to explaining personal piety. This line of analysis leads to the conclusion that the more they sacrifice on behalf of their religion, the more benefits individuals receive in return, and hence religious behavior may be fully justified in terms of rational choice theories of behavior (Iannaccone 1987, 1990, n.d.).

Like all rational choice theories, this approach to religion begins with the assumption that individuals will evaluate religious commodities in essentially the same way that they evaluate all other objects of choice. They will evaluate their costs and benefits (including the "opportunity costs" that arise when one action can be undertaken only by forgoing others) and will "consume" those religious commodities that, together with their other actions, maximize net benefits. In particular, individuals will weigh the promise of tremendous rewards (for which the supernatural is the only possible source) against both the costs of qualifying for these rewards and the risk that the rewards will not eventuate.

The second step in the rational choice theory of religious commitment is the postulate that religion is a "collectively produced" commodity. This is true for several reasons. First of all, many of the emotional and psychic rewards of religion are greater to the degree that they are generated and experienced as social events. One can, of course, enjoy singing hymns alone. But that experience falls far short of singing along with hundreds of others to the accompaniment of a pipe organ. A second reason that religion is a collective good is a bit more subtle. Because many results promised by religions can occur only elsewhere and far in the future, religion is inherently risky business. For this reason, only through exchanges with others can an individual have a basis for estimating

whether the value of religious rewards outweighs the risks that they will not be forthcoming as well as the risks of losing the costs of qualifying for these rewards.

The next step in this line of analysis postulates that because religion involves collective action, religious groups always are potentially subject to exploitation by free riders. Free-rider problems are the Achilles heel of collective activities. Hechter (1987, p. 27) summarizes the free-rider problem as follows: "Truly rational actors will (not) join a group to pursue common ends when, without participating, they can reap the benefit of other people's activity in obtaining them. If every member of the relevant group can share in the benefits . . . then the rational thing is to free ride . . . rather than to help attain the corporate interest." The consequence is, of course, that too few collective goods are created because too few contribute and thus everyone suffers—but those who gave their fair share suffer the most.

One need not look far to find examples of anemic congregations plagued by free-rider problems—a visit to the nearest "liberal" congregation usually will suffice to discover "members" who draw upon the group for weddings, funerals, and holiday celebrations but who give little or nothing in return. Indeed, even if they do contribute money, they weaken the group's ability to create collective religious goods in that their inactivity devalues both the direct and the promised religious rewards by reducing the "average" level of commitment. There can be little less inspiring than attending services in a nearly empty church.

Thus, it would seem that religions are caught in the jaws of a dilemma. On the one hand, a congregational structure that relies on the collective action of numerous volunteers is needed to make the religion credible and potent. On the other hand, that same congregational structure threatens to undermine the level of commitment and contributions needed to make a religion viable. However, costly demands offer a solution to the dilemma. That is, the levels of stigma and sacrifice demanded by religious groups will be positively correlated with levels of member participation. Thus do high costs mitigate the free rider problems faced by religious groups.

Religious stigmas consist of all aspects of social deviance that attach to membership in the group. That is, a group may prohibit some activities deemed normal in the external society (dancing, for example) and require other activities deemed abnormal by the world (speaking in tongues, for example). By meeting these expectations of the group, members deviate from the norms of the surrounding society. In the extreme case, when the state attempts to sustain a religious monopoly, membership per se in a dissenting group can be an immense stigma.

Sacrifices consist of investments (material and human) required to gain and retain membership in the group. Clearly, the requirements of some religious groups involve stigma and sacrifice simultaneously in that stigmatized persons often must forgo rewards such as career opportunities.

On the surface it would seem that increased costs must always make a religion less attractive. And indeed, the economists' law of demand predicts just that, other things remaining equal. But it turns out that other things do not remain equal when religions impose these sorts of costs on their members. To the contrary, costly demands strengthen a religious group by mitigating free rider problems that otherwise lead to low levels of member commitment and participation. They do so for two reasons. First, they create a barrier to group entry. No longer is it possible just to drop in and reap the benefits of attendance or membership. To take part at all you must qualify by accepting the stigmas and sacrifices demanded from everyone. Thus, high costs tend to screen out free riders—those potential members whose commitment and participation would otherwise be low. The costs act as nonrefundable registration fees, which, as in secular markets, measure seriousness of interest in the product. Only those willing to pay the price qualify.

Simultaneously, high costs tend to increase participation among those who do join. Group members find that the temptation to free ride is weaker, not because their human nature has somehow been transformed, but rather because the opportunities to free ride have been reduced and the flow of rewards for displaying high levels of commitment have been substantially increased. For example, social stigmas serve to increase participation in a religious group simply by making it more costly (or even impossible) to engage in activities outside the group. Looked at another way, prohibiting an activity effectively increases its price, since the full cost now includes the costs of discovery and, often, the price of concealment. Moreoever, as the increased price of the prohibited activity reduces demand for it, the demand for substitutes rises. If we may not attend dances or movies, play cards, go to taverns, or join fraternal organizations, we will probably look forward rather eagerly to church socials.

Finally, it must be noted that the higher the costs of membership, the greater the material and social, as well as religious, benefits of membership.

At first glance it seems paradoxical that when the cost of membership increases the net gains of membership increase too. However, this is necessarily the case when the commodity involved is collectively produced and when increased costs result in increased levels of participation in collective action, for this results in a greater supply of collective goods. Some examples may help. As noted, an individual's positive experience of a worship service increases to the degree that the church is full, the members enthusiastically participate (everyone sings and recites prayers, for example), and others express their positive evaluations of what is going on. Thus, as each individual member pays the costs of high levels of commitment, each benefits from the higher average level of participation thereby generated by the group. In similar fashion, our earlier discussion of the otherworldly rewards of religion noted that people will value them more highly to the extent that those around them do so. Thus, the higher the level of stigma and sacrifice required to be a member of a group, the higher the value of its commodities as communicated to group members by others. Or, to leave the realm of the immaterial, because Mormons are asked not only to contribute 10 percent of their income but 10 percent of their time to the church, they are enabled to lavish social services upon one another. Thus are the rewards of Mormon membership made tangible.

The point is that membership in strict religions is, for many people, a "good bargain" in terms of a conventional cost-benefit analysis. Hence, efficient religious firms with perfectly rational members may *choose* to embrace stigma, self-sacrifice, and bizarre behavioral standards to increase their capacity to reward members.

CONCLUSION

It must not be supposed that these new approaches to the sociology of religion have solved the major issues that define and animate the field. To paraphrase Winston Churchill, however, it seems plausible that these developments at least mark the end of the beginning. For it now seems that the field finally can proceed from assumptions that are compatible with the phenomena in question rather than on the basis of blatant moral and political agendas.

In any event, a number of interesting "open questions" arise in response to these new approaches. Among them are these. What are the costs, both direct and indirect, associated with different religions and different religious behaviors? How do religious consumers and producers respond to social and technological changes that alter the perceived costs and benefits associated with religious behaviors? How do successful producers shape the attributes of their products, their costs, benefits, and risks, to make them more desirable than those of their (religious and secular) competitors? How do consumers deal with the risk associated with religious promises? Why do religious professionals seem to enjoy greater credibility to the degree that they receive low levels of material reward? How do the nature of religious rewards, the demands of consumers, and the structure of religious markets shape the firms that provide religion? And what kind of outcomes—what costs and benefits, what range of religious firms, and what levels of religious activity—are consistent with "equilibrium" in a religious econ-

omy? That is, how religious or irreligious can societies be?

(SEE ALSO: *Cults; Religion, Politics, and War; Religious Fundamentalism; Religious Movements; Religious Organizations; Religious Orientations*)

REFERENCES

Bergin, Allen E. 1983 "Religiosity and Mental Health: A Critical Reevaluation and Meta-Analysis." *Professional Psychology* 14:170–184.

Brooke, Rosalind, and Christopher Brooke 1984 *Popular Religion in the Middle Ages*. London: Thames and Hudson.

Finke, Roger, and Rodney Stark 1988 "Religious Economies and Sacred Canopies: Religious Mobilization in American Cities, 1906." *American Sociological Review* 28:27–44.

Freud, Sigmund (1927) 1961 *The Future of an Illusion*. New York: Doubleday.

Hechter, Michael 1987 *Principles of Group Solidarity*. Berkeley: University of California Press.

Iannaccone, Laurence R. 1987 "Sacrifice and Stigma: Reducing Free-Riding in Cults, Communes, and Other Collectives." Paper read at the annual meeting of the Western Economics Association, City, dates.

—— 1990 "Religious Practice: A Human Capital Approach." *Journal for the Scientific Study of Religion* 29:297–314.

—— N.d. "The Consequences of Religious Market Regulation: Adam Smith and the Economics of Religion." *Rationality and Society* (forthcoming).

Johnson, Paul 1976 *A History of Christianity*. New York: Atheneum.

Larkin, Emmett 1972 "The Devotional Revolution in Ireland, 1850–1875." *American Historical Review* 77:625–652.

Martin, David 1990 *Tongues of Fire: The Explosion of Protestantism in Latin America*. Oxford: Basil Blackwell.

Stark, Rodney, and William Sims Bainbridge 1985 *The Future of Religion: Secularization, Revival, and Cult Formation*. Berkeley: University of California Press.

Stoll, David 1990 *Is Latin America Turning Protestant: The Politics of Evangelical Growth*. Berkeley: University of California Press.

Swatos, William H., Jr. 1984 "The Relevance of Religion: Iceland and Secularization Theory." *Journal for the Scientific Study of Religion* 23:32–43.

Wallace, Anthony F. C. 1966 *Religion: An Anthropological View*. New York: Random House.

Wilson, Bryan R. 1966 *Religion in Secular Society*. London: Watts and Co.

Wuthnow, Robert 1973 "Religious Commitment and Conservatism: In Search of an Elusive Relationship." In Charles Y. Glock, ed., *Religion in Sociological Perspective*. Belmont, Calif.: Wadsworth.

RODNEY STARK
LAURENCE R. IANNACCONE

SOCIOMETRY *See* Social Network Theory.

SOUTHEAST ASIA STUDIES Southeast Asia consists of the ten countries that lie between the Indian subcontinent and China. On the mainland of Southeast Asia are Myanmar (Burma), Thailand, Laos, Cambodia, and Vietnam. Insular Southeast Asia includes Indonesia, the Philippines, Brunei, Malaysia, and Singapore. While most of Malaysia (Peninsular Malaysia) is on the mainland, it is usually considered part of insular Southeast Asia because the Malay population (the majority ethnic population of Malaysia) shares a common language and religion with much of the Indonesian population. The city-state of Singapore (on an island connected by a mile-long causeway to Peninsular Malaysia) was historically part of Malaysia, but because of its unique ethnic composition (three-quarters of the population is of Chinese origin), it is more similar to East Asia than to Southeast Asia.

While there are some common geographical and cultural features, diversity is the hallmark of the region. Incredible indigenous cultural variation has been overlaid with centuries of contact, trade, migration, and cultural exchange from within the region, from other parts of Asia, and for the past 500 years from Europe (for general overviews of the region, see Osborne 1985 and Wertheim 1968). The common characteristic of mainland Southeast Asia is Buddhism, although

there are very significant variations across and within countries. Islam is the majority religion in Indonesia, Brunei, and Malaysia, while Christianity is the major religion of the Philippines. The lowlands of both mainland and insular Southeast Asia tend to be densely settled, and wet (irrigated) rice agriculture is the predominant feature of the countryside. Rural areas are knitted together with small- and medium-sized market towns. The major metropolitan areas of the region (Jakarta, Bangkok, Singapore, Manila, Rangoon, Kuala Lumpur, Ho Chi Minh City) are typically port cities or located along major rivers. Many of these towns and cities have significant Chinese minorities (often intermarried with the local population) that play an important role in commerce. Every country has remote highland and mountainous regions that are often populated by ethnic minorities.

In terms of land area, population size, and cultural and linguistic diversity, Southeast Asia is comparable to Europe (excluding the Soviet Union). By the year 2000 the population of Southeast Asia will exceed 500 million—about 8 percent of the world's total. Indonesia is the fifth-most populous country in the world, while the oil-rich sultanate of Brunei (located on the island of Borneo) is one of the smallest. The other large countries of the region, Thailand, Vietnam, and the Philippines, are more populous than all European countries, except for the Soviet Union and Germany. The sea (South China Sea, the Indian and Pacific Oceans) surrounds much of the region, especially the immense Indonesian and Filipino archipelagos. While the sea can be a barrier, the ocean and the rivers of the region are avenues that have fostered local and long-distance trade throughout history. Moreover, the ease of movement throughout the region seems to have shaped cultures that easily absorbed new ideas, immigrants, and a tolerance for diversity.

HISTORY

The contemporary political divisions of the region are largely a product of European imperialism, especially of the nineteenth century. Prior to European intervention, there were great regional civilizations—both agrarian states and maritime empires that waxed and waned over the millennium. The remains of temple complexes of Angkor (in Cambodia) and Pagan (in Burma) rival the architectural achievements of any premodern world civilization. Early Western observers of the city of Melaka (a fifteenth-century maritime empire centered on the west coast of the Malayan peninsula) described it as more magnificent than any contemporary European city. These early polities were founded on intensive rice cultivation with complex irrigation systems, the dominance of regional and long-distance trade, or both. The region has also been deeply influenced by contacts with the great civilizations of India and China. The cultural influences from outside have invariably been transformed into distinctive local forms in different Southeast Asian contexts. Because relatively few written records have survived the tropical environment of Southeast Asia, historical research relies heavily on archeological investigations, epigraphs, and records from other world regions, especially Chinese sources.

European influence began in the sixteenth century with the appearance of Portuguese and Spanish naval forces, followed by the arrival of the Dutch in the seventeenth century, and then by the British and French. In the early centuries of contact, European powers were able to dominate the seas and thereby limit the expansion of Southeast Asian polities, but they rarely penetrated very far inland from their coastal trading cities. All of Southeast Asia was transformed, however, in the nineteenth century, as the Industrial Revolution in the West stimulated demand for mineral and agricultural products around the globe. New economic organizations of plantations, mines, and markets led to large-scale migration of people and capital to frontier areas and to the cities of Southeast Asia. There was an accompanying flurry of imperialist wars to grab land, people, and potential resources. In a series of expansions, the British conquered the area of present-day Myanmar (Burma) and Malaysia, the Dutch completed their conquest of the East Indies (now Indonesia), and the French took the areas that formed their Indochina empire (present-day Vietnam, Cambo-

dia, and Laos). At the turn of the twentieth century, the United States defeated nationalist forces to take control of the Philippines just as the Spanish empire was crumbling. Siam (Thailand) was the only indigenous Southeast Asian state to escape the grip of colonialism.

The political history of the region has not been stable. As Western countries moved toward more democratic social and political institutions over the first decades of the twentieth century, the colonists (British, Dutch, American, and French) constructed authoritarian dependencies in the tropics that were based on export economies and racial ideologies. Although there were stirrings of nationalist sentiment during the first half of the twentieth century, it was only after World War II that the nationalist forces were strong enough and the international environment favorable enough to bring political independence to the region. The critical turning point was the Japanese conquest and occupation of Southeast Asia from 1942 to 1945, which permanently shattered the myth of European superiority. The colonial powers returned after World War II, but they encountered popular nationalist movements that demanded the end of colonialism.

Independence was negotiated peacefully by the Americans in the Philippines and the British in Burma and Malaya, but nationalist forces had to wage wars of independence against the Dutch in Indonesia (1945–50) and against the French in Vietnam (1945–54). The interplay of nationalist struggles, class conflicts, and the East–West cold war rivalry had a marked influence on political developments in the region. In almost every country there were radical and Communist movements that held the allegiance of significant sectors of the population. In several cases, Communist parties were part of the nationalist movement but left (or were driven out of) the political arena as domestic and international tensions escalated. Vietnam was unique in that the nationalist movement was led by Communists. After the French were defeated in 1954 and agreed to grant independence to Vietnam, the United States intervened to set up a non-Communist Vietnamese state in the southern region of the country. After another twenty years of war and one million casualties, Vietnam was finally united as an independent state in 1975. Since 1975, however, political tension between the socialist states of Vietnam, Cambodia, and Laos and the other countries has been the dominant feature of international relations in the region.

Domestic political developments within individual countries of the region have been no less dramatic. Governments have oscillated between authoritarian and democratic forms, with no linear trend. Behind the headlines of military coups, regional wars for autonomy, and "managed" elections have been the complex political struggles among various contending groups defined by class, region, ethnicity, and kinship. These struggles have ranged from civil war to fairly open elections. Large-scale violence is not the norm, but massacres in Indonesia, Cambodia, and East Timor have been among the worst of such episodes in modern times. Popular civil protests against ruling elites in the Philippines and Burma have had significant domestic and international reverberations. Neither academic scholarship nor political reporting has offered generalizations or convincing interpretations of the postwar political change in Southeast Asia.

Many of the countries of Southeast Asia have experienced remarkable socioeconomic modernization in the postindependence era. This is most evident for the ASEAN (Association of Southeast Asian Nations) countries of Thailand, Malaysia, Singapore, Indonesia, the Philippines, and Brunei. All indicators of socioeconomic development (GNP, educational levels, occupational structure, infant mortality) suggest that Southeast Asia has successfully narrowed the gap with the first world, while other regions of the third world have fallen further behind. The reasons for the success of some countries and the economic stagnation in other countries is a matter of dispute. The East Asian model of state-sponsored export industrialization is widely discussed in policy and academic circles, but the parallels between East Asian and Southeast Asian economic development strategies are still a matter of considerable uncertainty. There are few scholarly studies that have exam-

ined the causes and consequences of economic modernization of Southeast Asia.

THE STATUS OF WOMEN

Several theoretical concepts and empirical generalizations have arisen from studies of Southeast Asian societies that have relevance far beyond the region. Empirically, the most common cultural characteristic across the region is the relatively high status of women in Southeast Asian societies, especially when compared to East Asia and South Asia. While women still face many social and cultural obstacles in Southeast Asia, the situation appears much different from that in the patriarchal societies of other Asian societies and the traditional female domesticity of many Western societies. While there are a few matrilineal societies in the region, Southeast Asian kinship systems are typically bilateral, with equal importance attached to the husband's and wife's families. The patrilocal custom of an obligatory residence of a newly married couple with or near the groom's family is largely absent in Southeast Asia. The residence of young couples after marriage seems to be largely a matter of choice or dependent on relative economic opportunities. There is no strong sex preference for children in Southeast Asia, with both girl and boy children seen as desirable.

The relatively positive status of women is also evident in earlier times. Reid (1988, pp. 146–172) reports that early European observers were struck by the active role of women in economic and political affairs in Southeast Asia. Traditional folklore also suggests that women play an active role in courtship and that female sexual expectations were as important as men's. Perhaps most unusual was the custom (reported in the fifteenth and sixteenth centuries) of inserting spurs or balls in male genitals to enhance the sexual pleasure of women (Reid 1988, pp. 148–151).

At present, women seem to be well represented in schools, universities, and employment in all modern sectors of the economy in almost every country of Southeast Asia. There is only a modest scholarly literature on the higher status of women in Southeast Asia (Van Esterik 1982), and few efforts have been made to explain the links between traditional roles of women as productive workers in the rural rice economy and their relative ease of entry into the modern sector. Demographic research has revealed very rapid declines in fertility in several Southeast Asian countries, particularly in Singapore, Thailand, Malaysia, and Indonesia. If the current pace of decline continues, replacement-level fertility (two children per woman) should be reached in the near future (Hirschman and Guest 1990).

AGRICULTURAL INVOLUTION

Scholarship on Southeast Asia has often reached beyond the boundaries of the region to influence the debates over social science concepts, theory, and models. Perhaps most influential have been the books and articles on Indonesia by anthropologist Clifford Geertz. His evocative concepts of the "theatre state," "thick description," and "agricultural involution" have stimulated debate and research in several social-science disciplines including sociology. His model of agricultural involution (Geertz 1968) has been one of the most provocative developments in scholarship on Indonesia over the last generation.

A strikingly bold thesis, agricultural involution is an attempt to explain how Java became one of the most densely settled populations in the world within a traditional agricultural economy. To address this question, Geertz presents an ecological interpretation of the evolution (involution) of Javanese social structure in the face of rapid population growth and Dutch colonialism within the constraints (and possibilities) of a wet rice economy. The colonial system prevented industrialization and the development of an indigenous entrepreneurial class. The traditional rice economy, however, could absorb a larger population because additional labor inputs in the maintenance of irrigation facilities, water control, weeding, and harvesting yielded marginal increments in rice production. Over the decades, this refinement of traditional production technology (involution) led to an increasing rigidification of

traditional Javanese culture, thus discouraging innovation and any efforts at social change, and reinforcing the structural limits of the colonial system. Even after independence, when structural limits were lifted, the legacy of the past, as reflected in Javanese culture, remained.

Geertz's thesis remains highly controversial, and many of the components of his thesis have been confronted with negative evidence (for a review of the debate, see White 1983 and Geertz 1984). For example, Geertz deemphasized social class divisions with his interpretation of "shared poverty" as the traditional social strategy. Most research has shown significant inequality of landholding and other socioeconomic dimensions in Javanese villages, although it is not clear if inequality is permanently perpetuated between families across generations. Even accepting many of the criticisms, agricultural involution is a seminal sociological model that should serve to generate empirical research on the historical development of Asian societies.

THE MORAL ECONOMY

A classic question in social science is the causes of revolution or rebellion. Neither Marxian theory, which emphasizes exploitation, nor relative deprivation theory seem to be satisfactory models to explain the occurrence of revolutions or rebellions. The most sophisticated sociological theory of peasant rebellion is based on historical materials from Burma and Vietnam by political scientist James Scott (1973) in his book *The Moral Economy of the Peasant: Subsistence and Rebellion in Southeast Asia*. Scott argues that peasants rebel only when their normative expectations of a minimum subsistence level are not met. These conditions are more likely to occur when capitalist market relations and colonial states erode traditional societies and the reciprocal obligations of peasants and their patrons.

Scott's thesis has been criticized and hotly debated (Popkin 1979; Keyes 1983). One criticism is that Scott believes that peasants prefer traditional societies and are not responsive to economic opportunity. Scott acknowledges that peasants can be quite innovative and individualistic as long as their minimum subsistence is not at risk. This debate, however, does not really address the central theoretical contribution of Scott's thesis about the specification of the causes of peasant rebellion.

In a more recent study based on field work in a rural Malaysian village, Scott (1985) examines how class antagonisms are displayed in everyday life. Given that rebellion is a very rare event in most societies, Scott calls attention to political, social, and linguistic behaviors (in Weapons of the Weak) that reveal the depth of descensus and potential social conflict but do not risk violent reaction from the state and powerful elites. In these two books and related publications, Scott has provided original interpretations of peasant political behavior in Southeast Asia and set a research agenda for scholars of other world regions and, more generally, the development of social theory.

CONCLUSION

Scholarship on Southeast Asia, whether in sociology or other disciplines, has tended to focus on individual countries rather than on the region. Different languages (colonial and indigenous) as well as variations in religious traditions and political and economic systems have reinforced the image of a heterogenous collection of countries that is labeled a region largely by default. There is tremendous political, economic, and sociocultural diversity in the region; many of these differences, however, are a product of the colonial era and its legacy. The similarity of family systems and the status of women throughout Southeast Asia suggest some common historical and cultural roots for the region. There may well be other social and cultural parallels across Southeast Asia that will be revealed as more comparative research is undertaken (Wolters 1982).

Many indicators of development in Southeast Asia, including very low levels of mortality and almost universal secondary schooling, are approaching the prevailing standards of developed countries. Assuming that current socioeconomic trends continue, several countries in the region will probably follow Japan, Korea, and Taiwan along the path of development in the early decades of the twenty-first century. The study of these processes of modernization and the accompanying changes in politics, family structure, ethnic relations, and other social spheres should make Southeast Asia an extraordinarily interesting sociological laboratory.

REFERENCES

Geertz, Clifford 1968 *Agricultural Involution: The Processes of Ecological Change in Indonesia.* Berkeley: University of California Press.

———— 1984 "Culture and Social Change." *Man* 19:511–532.

Hirschman, Charles, and Philip Guest 1990 "The Emerging Demographic Transitions of Southeast Asia." *Population and Development Review* 16:121–152.

Keyes, Charles F. (ed.) 1983 "Peasant Strategies in Asian Societies: Moral or Rational Economic Approaches—A Symposium." *Journal of Asian Studies* 42:753–868.

Osborne, Milton 1985 *Southeast Asia: An Illustrated Introductory History.* Sydney: Allen and Unwin.

Popkin, Samuel L. 1979 *The Rational Peasant.* Berkeley: University of California Press.

Reid, Anthony 1988 *Southeast Asia in the Age of Commerce, 1450–1680,* vol. 1, *The Lands below the Winds.* New Haven: Yale University Press.

Scott, James C. 1976 *The Moral Economy of the Peasant: Subsistence and Rebellion in Southeast Asia.* New Haven: Yale University Press.

———— 1985 *Weapons of the Weak: Everyday Forms of Peasant Resistance.* New Haven: Yale University Press.

Van Esterik, Penny 1982 *Women of Southeast Asia.* Dekalb: Center for Southeast Asian Studies, Northern Illinois University.

Wertheim, W. F. 1968 "Southeast Asia." In David Sills, ed., *International Encyclopedia of the Social Sciences.* New York: Macmillan and Free Press.

White, Benjamin 1983 "Agricultural Involution and Its Critics: Twenty Years After." *Bulletin of Concerned Asian Scholars* 15:18–41.

Wolters, O. W. 1982 *History, Culture, and Region in Southeast Asian Perspectives.* Singapore: Institute of Southeast Asian Studies.

CHARLES HIRSCHMAN

SOVIET SOCIOLOGY In prerevolutionary Russia, sociology was in a marginal position. The state universities offered no instruction in sociology, but there was already a solid intellectual tradition of historical and theoretical sociology (Maxim Kovalevsky, Evgeny de Roberty) and sociology of law (Leon Petrajizky, Pitirim Sorokin) and of social problems (crime, prostitution, etc.). There was also a well-developed literary genre of sociological journalism.

The Bolshevik Revolution gave a mighty stimulus to sociological reflection and empirical social research. In the *Sovnarkom* (Soviet government) decree "About the socialist Academy of the social sciences," drafted in May 1918, Lenin (1962, p. 372) stressed the need "to organize a series of social researches" and called it "one of the most urgent tasks of the day." But the Bolsheviks tolerated only research from Marxist and procommunist positions. In the first postrevolutionary years, censorship was relatively weak or inefficient. For example, Sorokin not only established the first sociological laboratory in Petrograd University but also succeeded in publishing (illegally) his two volumes *System of Sociology* (Sorokin 1920), for which he was awarded his Ph.D. degree in April 1922. He conducted some important empirical investigations on the mass starvation in the famine districts of Samara and Saratov and examined its influence on the various aspects of social life and human behavior (Sorokin 1975).

But this liberalism or, rather, negligence on the part of the authorities was short-lived. In the autumn of 1922, a group of leading Russian intellectuals, including Sorokin and some other prominent social philosophers, was expelled from the country, and that was the end of a non-Marxist sociology in Soviet Russia.

The tightening ideological control proved detrimental to socialist and Marxist social research as well. Nevertheless, the 1920s were fruitful both in empirical research and in theoretico-methodological reflection. The most important theoretical contributions of that period were in the field of economic sociology (A. V. Chajanov, N. D. Kondratjev). There were also interesting studies on the social organization of labor, the budgeting of time

in work and leisure activities (S. G. Strumilin), population dynamics, rural and urban ways of life (A. I. Todorsky, V. E. Kabo), marriage and sexual behavior, social psychology (V. M. Bekhterev), social medicine, and other topics. All this research was finished in the early 1930s.

The Stalinist totalitarian system was absolutely incompatible with any kind of social criticism or problem-oriented thinking or empirical research. Most creative original thinkers were liquidated and their books burned or prohibited. Sociology was declared "bourgeois pseudo-science." Official social statistics was either made secret or completely falsified. Empirical research that relied on questionnaires, participant observation, and similar methods was forbidden. All social theory was reduced to the official dogmatic version of historical materialism, which had very little in common with genuine Marxist dialectics. Practically no first-hand information about Western sociology was available.

The revival of sociology in the Soviet Union began during Khrushchev's era, in the late 1950s. It was initiated from below, by a small group of young philosophers and economists of liberal political orientations. The beginning of economic reforms and partial ideological de-Stalinization stimulated the need for less dogmatic social philosophy and objective information about current social processes. This intellectual initiative also had some support from the reformist and technocratically-oriented elements inside party and state leadership. The first organizational step in this direction was the establishment in 1958 of the Soviet Sociological Association (SSA). The primary aim of this move was simply to facilitate participation in international sociological congresses by the Soviet ideological bureaucracy in administrative academic positions. But gradually, thanks to personal efforts of Gennady Ossipov, among others, SSA became a sort of organizational center for the emerging new discipline.

In order to avoid conflicts with the dominant ideology, it was unanimously agreed that the only acceptable "scientific" sociological theory, methodology, and general sociology was Marxist historical materialism, but that it should be supplemented by "concrete social research" and, eventually, some middle-range theories. In 1960 Ossipov organized, in the Institute of Philosophy of the USSR Academy of Sciences in Moscow, a small unit for research on the new forms of work and daily life. This unit later was transformed into the Department of Concrete Social Research. At about the same time, Vladimir Iadov organized, within the philosophical faculty of Leningrad State University, the Laboratory of Concrete Social Research, dedicated to the study of job orientations and workers' personalities. At the Novosibirsk Institute of Industrial Economics and Organization, Vladimir Shubkin developed a unit for studies of youth issues including high school children's professional orientations and social mobility. Sociology research units appeared, under various names, at the universities of Sverdlovsk and Tartu (Estonia). In 1968 the independent Institute of Concrete Social Research of the USSR Academy of Sciences was established in Moscow, headed by the eminent economist and vice-president of the USSR Academy of Sciences A. M. Rumiantsev.

According to Shlapentokh (1987), 1965 to 1972 were the golden years of Soviet sociology. Important original research was done on workers' job attitudes and on the interrelationship of work and personality (Iadov, Rozhin, and Zdravomyslov 1967), professional orientations of youth (Shubkin 1970), rural sociology and population migrations (Zaslavskaia 1970; Zaslavskaia and Ryvkina 1980; Arutiunian 1971), public opinion and mass media (Grushin 1967; Shlapentokh 1970), industrial sociology (Shkaratan 1978) marriage and the family (Kharchev 1964), personality (Kon 1967), leisure (Gordon and Klopov 1972), political institutions (Fjodor Burlatskiy, Alexandr Galkin), and other topics. At the same time, research on the history of sociology had begun, and a dialogue with Western theoretical ideas (instead of a blunt ideological denunciation of everything "non-Marxist") was initiated (Andreeva 1965; Kon 1967; Zamoshkin 1966). In theoretical terms, of particular interest to Soviet sociologists were structural functionalism, symbolic interactionism, and C. Wright Mills's "new sociology." The Amer-

ican Sociological Association aided these developments by arranging to send professional books and journals to the USSR.

But the social and intellectual situation of the fledgling Soviet sociology was very uncertain. It was completely dependent on the official ideology and goodwill of the Party authorities. Sociology was born on the wave of Khrushchev's reforms not as an independent academic discipline but as an auxiliary means for the implementation of the Party's reform policies. Because of a general conservatism in the Soviet system and strong resistance of the old-style ideologists in the academy itself, the institutionalization of sociology was delayed until 1968. By this time, however, the Party was no longer interested in any social reforms or innovations, so even limited empirical sociology became superfluous and, worse, subversive. Even the smallest hint of social criticism was deemed to be dangerous and could be published only if formulated in the Esopus language. The Institute of Concrete Social Research was under constant attack and pressure. Especially devastating and venomous was an attack on Levada's (1969) "Lectures on Sociology"; soon after the attack, he was dismissed from Moscow University and deprived of a professorial title. In 1972, the liberal head of the institute of Concrete Social Research, A. M. Rumiantsev, was replaced by reactionary Mikhail Rutkevich, who had initiated an ideological campaign against "Western influences" and for the restoration of a neo-Stalinist orthodoxy. As a result of his policies, the most prominent and qualified scholars were forced to leave the institute and take refuge elsewhere.

Until 1986 Soviet sociology was in bad shape. The process of its institutionalization was not discontinued. In 1972 the Institute of Concrete Social Research was renamed the Institute for Sociological Research. In 1974 the first professional journal, *Sotsiologicheskie Issledovania (Sociological Research)*, was inaugurated. SSA membership was continuously growing. In the late 1980s, it had about 8,500 individual and 300 collective members and twenty-one regional branches. The technical and statistical level of sociological research in the 1970s and 1980s also improved considerably. Some new sociological subdisciplines emerged (SSA now has thirty-eight specialized sections, including twelve research committees, directly connected with the respective ISA committees). The geography of sociological research centers has also expanded. But the general intellectual and theoretical level of Soviet sociology, with few exceptions, was inadequate.

Because of general ideological stagnation and strict censorship, tending to deny the existence of problems in Soviet society, open discussion and research on the most important and burning social issues was impossible. Relatively free theoretical reflection was limited to the marginal fields of social psychology, anthropology, and history. Most sociological research was done on the micro level and involved separate industrial plants, without any attempt at broad theoretical generalization. And the publications of a more general character were mostly apologetic for the so-called real socialism. The place of sociological theory was occupied by dogmatic ideological scholasticism—"the theory of scientific communism." Attempts to narrow the gap between sociological statements and social realities were ruthlessly punished by the authorities, and such punishment was greeted by subservient silence or even approval from the sociological community (the case of Andrey Alekseev, Leningrad sociologist, is typical in this respect). The Leningrad sociological school, perhaps the best in the country, was decimated by the local party leadership in the mid-1980s. Tatiana Zaslavskaia was in serious trouble when her report, highly critical of the prospects of the economic reforms without parallel political changes, was published in the West. Even public perception of sociology had changed dramatically. In the 1960s it was a very positive, idealized image, a mixture of a discipline that offered social criticism and technocratic efficiency, opening new possibilities for economic revival. In the 1970s, the industrial sociologist was pictured in several popular plays and movies as a negative figure, a sly manipulator helping plant management to play down the workers' discontent.

Perestroika and glasnost have drastically changed the place of sociology in Soviet society. On the one hand, Gorbachev and his team need an objective social science for information and advice. On the other hand, the majority of Soviet sociologists were, from the very beginning, strong supporters of reform. In 1986, Zaslavskaia was elected president of the SSA. In 1987, a special resolution of the Communist Party Central Committee acknowledged that sociology was an important scientific discipline in its own right. In 1988, the Institute of Sociological Research was transformed into the Institute of Sociology and Iadov appointed its director. Sociologists take an active part in political life not only as advisers to the government but also as deputies of central and local Soviets. There are no longer any official restrictions on the topics suitable for sociological research, and the publication of its results is much easier. Some newspapers now carry regular sociological columns. The subject matter of sociological research is different but concentrated mostly on the problems and trends of perestroika.

The largest and leading Soviet research center is the Institute of Sociology of the USSR Academy of Sciences, with a branch in Leningrad and divisions in Gorki and Krasnodar. Among its main lines of research are the history and theory of sociology; economic reform and its social aspects; social processes in the fields of labor, industry, and industrial relations; social structure and interregional relations; sociopolitical processes, ideology, mass consciousness, and public opinion; sociodemographic processes; everyday life, personality, and family relationships; the sociology of deviance; and the sociology of science, culture, and education. The institute is also coordinating several interdisciplinary and interinstitutional research programs on social processes and personality development under perestroika.

The All-Union Public Opinion Research Center, sponsored by trade unions, is a leading center for public opinion polls. Public opinion surveys are being done also by the Institute of Sociology, the Academy of the Social Sciences, the Communist Party Central Committee, and the Independent Public Opinion Research Service—VP or Vox Populi, founded by Boris Grushin.

Fundamental research on interethnic relationships and economic and regional sociology and comparative studies of family and socialization are concentrated in the research-oriented Institute of Ethnology and Ethnic Anthropology of the USSR Academy of Sciences; population and gender studies at the Institute for Socio-Economic Studies of Population of the USSR Academy of Sciences; and sociology of youth at the new Institute of Youth, sponsored by the Komsomol Central Committee and by the State Committee on Labor, and at the Institute of the International Labor Movement. Important research is going on in Novosibirsk (rural and regional sociology), Kiev (mathematical methods, personality, life course), Tallinn (youth, environmental studies), and many other cities and republics.

The main problem confronting Soviet sociology today is the shortage of money and professional personnel. Until 1989 in the USSR there was practically no general (undergraduate) sociological education; only small courses in applied (mainly industrial) sociology were offered. Now sociological departments and schools are established in Moscow, Leningrad, and Novosibirsk state universities; several more departments, chairs, or sections are beginning to be organized in Kiev, Kharkov, and other Soviet cities. Unfortunately, there is not enough qualified personnel to fill all available teaching positions. In order to close this gap, advanced sociology courses have been organized at the Institute of Youth and the State Committee on Education. Graduate sociology students are studying at the research institutions of the USSR Academy of Sciences.

A fundamental philosophical issue facing Soviet sociology is to come to grips with Marxism-Leninism. Before perestroika, allegiance to this "teaching" was compulsory; elements of other social theories were incorporated only on the basis of their compatibility with and subordination to Marxism. Soviet sociology was by definition "Marxist sociology." But nobody knows the exact meaning of this. Because of its close association with the official dogmatic ideology, Marxism had long ago lost any emotional or intellectual appeal for most Soviet students. They are much more

interested in structuralism, functionalism, interactionism, phenomenology, or psychoanalysis. Already in the 1960s and 1970s, Marxist-Leninist phrases and quotations were often used as mere lip-service to ideological conformity. But these issues were never openly discussed, thus making the philosophical and theoretical premises of Soviet sociology unclear, eclectic, and internally contradictory. Now it is a very difficult theoretical and—for members of the older generation—moral issue. Some scholars want to restore "genuine" Marxist social philosophy, including first of all the theory of alienation. Others prefer completely different theoretical orientations. However, this discussion is only beginning, and its outcome depends not only on the ideological positions of the authors but also on the level of their historico-sociological culture. Few Soviet sociologists have the benefits of the first-hand knowledge of Western sociological classics and contemporary authors. Only now are the many volumes of sociological classics and modern monographs and textbooks being translated and published, though this undertaking is limited by a shortage of paper and printing facilities.

Soviet sociology is now ideologically and organizationally open and very much interested in international contacts and exchanges on all levels. There are many joint research projects with American, German, French, Finnish, Japanese, and other scholars. Most of these projects are related to current political attitudes and value orientations (war, peace, and nuclear disarmament, how East and West see each other, how the United States and the Soviet Union perceive each other, how Soviet and U.S. children feel about nuclear war, etc.). Some of these projects are the results of academic interinstitutional cooperation, while others are initiated and financed by the different charity funds and voluntary associations. Longer and more theory-oriented international projects are under consideration. The exchange of graduate students in sociology between Soviet and American and West European universities is growing rapidly. Prominent Western sociologists are invited regularly for lectures and seminars at the Soviet universities and vice versa.

The prospects for the development of Soviet sociology depend on the fate of perestroika. The gigantic social experiment unfolding in the country needs creative support from the social sciences. It is a powerful stimulus for sociological imagination and theory construction. Today, Soviet sociologists are overburdened with the need to search for immediate practical solutions to too many urgent political and economic issues and have no time for quiet theoretical reflection. The most important sociological contributions to perestroika now are the public opinion polls and information about current social processes. The next step seems to be the emergence of a sociology of social problems interpreted not only in the specific context of contemporary Soviet society but in that of the global problems of civilization as well. This, in turn, may lead to the revival of historical and comparative macrosociology and produce new theoretical insights. All this is feasible, however, only as the result of an intensive international and interdisciplinary intellectual cooperation.

REFERENCES

Andreeva, G. M. 1965 *Sovremennaia Bourzhuaznaia Empiricheskaia Sotsiologia.* Moscow: Mysl'.

Arutiunian, I. V. 1971 *Structura Sel'skogo Naselenia SSSR.* Moscow: Mysl'.

Gabiani, A., and M. Manuilski 1987 "Drug Addiction: Bitter Fruits of Sweet Life." *Sotsiologicheskie Issledovania* 1:48–53.

Gordon, L. A., and E. V. Klopov 1972 *Chelovek Posle Raboty.* Moscow: Nauka.

Grushin, B. A. 1967 *Mnenia o Mire i Mir Mnenij.* Moscow: Politizdat.

Iadov, V. A. (ed.) 1979 *Samoregulatsia i Prognozirovanie Sotsial'nogo Povedehia Lichnosti.* Leningrad: Nauka.

———, V. Rozhin, and A. Zdravomyslov (eds.) 1970 *Man and His Work.* White Plains, N.Y.: International Arts and Sciences Press.

Kon, I. S. 1967 *Sotsiologia Lichnosti.* Moscow: Politizdat.

Lenin, V. I. 1962 *O Sotsialisticheskoi Akademii Obshchestvennykh Nauk.* Vol. 36 of *Polnoe Sobranie Sochinenij.* Moscow: Politizdat.

Levada, I. A. 1969 *Lektsii po Sotsiologii,* Vols. 1 and 2. Moscow: IKSI AN SSSSR.

Shalin, D. 1978 "The Development of Soviet Sociology, 1956–1976." *Annual Review of Sociology* 4:171–192.

——— 1990 "Sociology for the Glasnost Era: Institutional and Substantive Changes in Recent Soviet Sociology." *Social Forces* 68:1019–1039.

Shlapentokh, V. 1987 *The Politics of Sociology in the Soviet Union.* Boulder and London: Westview Press.

Sorokin, P. A. 1920 *Sistema Sotsiologii.* Petrograd.

——— 1975 *Hunger as a Factor in Human Affairs.* Elena Sorokin, ed. Gainesville, Fla.: University Presses of Florida.

Yanowitch, Murray (ed.) 1973 *Social Stratification and Mobility in the USSR.* Armonk, N.Y.: M. E. Sharpe.

——— 1979 *Soviet Work Attitudes: The Issue of Participation in Management.* Armonk, N.Y.: M. E. Sharpe.

——— 1986 *Social Structure of the USSR: Recent Soviet Studies.* Armonk, N.Y.: M. E. Sharpe.

——— 1989a *New Directions in Soviet Social Thought.* Armonk, N.Y.: M. E. Sharpe.

——— 1989b *A Voice of Reform: Essays by Tat'iana I. Zaslavskaia.* Armonk, N.Y.: M. E. Sharpe.

Zamoshkin, Iu. A. 1966 *Krizis Burzhuaznogo Individualizma i Lichnost'.* Moskva: Mysl'.

Zaslavskaia, T. (ed.) 1970 *Migratsia Sel'skogo Naseleniia.* Voskva: Mysl'.

———, and R. Ryvkina (eds.) 1980 *Metodologia i Metodika Sistemnogo Izucheniia Derevni.* Novosibirsk: Nauka.

Zdravomyslov, A. G. (ed.) 1986 *Developments in Marxist Sociological Theory.* New York and London: Sage Publications.

IGOR S. KON

SPORTS The emergence of sports as a major social institution is inextricably linked to general trends of modernization. The twentieth century especially has seen a progressive shift from informal, participant-oriented amateur sports to highly organized, spectator-oriented professional sports. The accompanying shifts from local or regional events to national and international events and from individual to team activities are part of the evolution of sports as big business.

Sporting institutions cannot be understood in isolation from the prevailing social structure. They are inseparable from historical context, technological development, and shifting ideologies. An essential ingredient for the emergence of big-time sports was the development of mass leisure. Although play and games have been a part of every known society (Huizinga 1955), the growth of leisure institutions as a segregated part of life available to the masses required several changes, including the move from rural to urban life, the separation of the workplace from the home, and shorter work schedules. A supportive value system was also essential. For example, not until the mid-nineteenth century did old Puritanical prohibitions on sports and other amusements begin to break down in North America. Expanding railroad networks and local transit systems played an indispensable role in popularizing spectator sports and in the creation of national leagues (Betts 1980).

A system of mass communications was also required for sporting events to become part of mass culture. In the second half of the nineteenth century, fans in Europe and the United States could get instantaneous reports on some events, particularly boxing and horse racing, through the expanding telegraph network, and they could read journalistic accounts in proliferating magazines and newspapers (Betts 1980). By the beginning of the twentieth century the newspaper sports page had arrived, some two decades later came radio, and by mid-century, television. The expansion of cable television in the latter part of the century brought its viewers 24-hour sports coverage. Satellites permit live transmission of televised sports events that reach audiences around the world. Comparative data on audiences for satellite-televised events show that major international sporting contests draw together more spectators than anything else (Lever 1983).

Sports promote connections, from the momentary bonding of two strangers at a game to the creation of a global village. Organized sports parallel the weave of government agencies in their structure: Small towns, even rural areas, are linked to each other and to the big cities for state and regional championships; major cities are knit together into national leagues; and nations that play the same sports are drawn into relationships with one another through continental and worldwide

federations that stage international contests. Nationalistic feelings get fanned while, simultaneously, people are united into a global folk culture. The paradox of sport is that it bonds even as it divides. The same event can serve as an occasion for patriotic display while easing diplomatic relations (Lever 1983).

International sports have succeeded as a basis for global community by providing a common frame of reference and rules that transcend cultural, political, and language barriers. Yet the same sport can be played differently in different places. For example, in Japan baseball games can end in a tie and the emphasis is on team rather than individual achievement. Sports mirror each society as they reflect, while reinforcing, social and cultural values. For this reason sports are ideal for both comparative and historical study.

Across time and place, sports promoters—whether communist or capitalist, private or public management, or mass media executives—have told fans that they can properly assume a victory as their own. Disseminating propaganda, building solidarity, and making profits by selling tickets, media rights, and advertising space are the primary rewards for the promoters. Identification of fans with athletes—whether in terms of a common school, city, nation, race, or religion—and the concomitant sense of collective identity and pride are the primary rewards for the spectators (Roberts 1976). As objects of conversation, publicity, and mass media coverage, organized sports have served to involve people jointly and focus community social life everywhere (Luschen and Sage 1981).

SPORTS AND SOCIAL STRUCTURE

Whether one sees the consequences of sports as beneficial or harmful to society depends on which of two competing theoretical approaches—functionalist or conflict—is adopted (Coakley 1984). The functionalist perspective leads social scientists to examine the ways in which sports contribute to the smooth operation of society as a whole. The benefits of sports are seen to include the promotion of values such as the importance of rules, hard work, organization, and a defined authority structure; the legitimation of the goals of success and achievement; the social integration or reaffirmation of linkages of collectivities represented; and the development of physical skills and the promotion of physical well-being among people who lead otherwise sedentary lives in industrial and postindustrial cities.

Conflict theorists do not disagree that widespread interest in commercialized sports leads to such consequences; rather, their perspective leads them to view those consequences as harmful. Critics of the status quo recognize the role of sports in socializing the young to fit into a regimented, bureaucratic mold. Organized sports as mass entertainment spectacles are viewed as a "mass narcotic" that provides escape and excitement, thus making participation in political or revolutionary organizations less likely (Hoch 1972).

Furthermore, conflict theorists argue that commercialized sports reduce players to material commodities exploited by others for the sake of profit, and the pressure to perform takes its toll on athletes' bodies through injury or the inducement to take harmful drugs (Shaw 1972). The highly visible rewards given to athletes in turn publicize an ideology of upward mobility. Conflict theorists point out that athletes' fame creates illusions about individualism by presenting a model in which success depends on hard work and perseverance, thus distracting attention from organizational bases for blocked mobility (Hoch 1972; Lipsyte 1975). Sports also separate the sexes and idealize an exaggerated notion of masculinity. Finally, fans' identification with athletes is used to sell a host of consumer goods, and the proliferation of participant sports has spawned a huge leisure industry in capitalist societies.

Functionalist theorists have been criticized for ignoring the possibility that sports may benefit some members of society more than others and for failing to note the exploitation found in organized sports. Conflict theorists have been criticized for overemphasizing the influence of capitalism when in fact contemporary sports function much the same way in socialist and commu-

nist societies. Perceptive analysts have noted that theorists tend to apply the functionalist model to social systems they support and the conflict model to those they criticize (Coakley 1984).

The contours of sports specific to a culture shed light on its other institutions, values, myths, and inequalities. In the United States, for example, racial integration in team sports awaited the breakdown of societal segregation, then hastened its demise by virtue of the attendant publicity (Koppett 1981). Yet blacks remain largely absent from elite sports and are excluded from many leadership and management positions in team sports. Media attention to female athletes remains minimal despite women's increased participation in sports.

SPORTS AND AGGRESSION

A different type of controversy surrounds one function of sports presumed to hold true across time and place, namely, that sports serve as a societal safety valve. Sporting rituals have long been thought to be cathartic. Roman elites believed that a diet of "bread and circuses" would keep workers from revolt. Neo-Freudians view the buildup of tension and frustration as inevitable and see violent sports as a healthy channel for expression and control of aggression for participant and spectator alike.

Contemporary empiricists (Goldstein 1983) raise two questions about these assumptions. First, they point out that games and sports are consistent with broader cultural patterns. Cooperative societies encourage noncompetitive sports; societies that stress individual achievement and success encourage competitive sports. Violent societies endorse violent sports. In U.S. football, for example, most of the violence is within the rules, or normative, and even violence outside the rules is often rewarded by coaches, communities, and the media. More than a reflection of societal values, sports as an instrument of socialization also reinforce aggression because they condone it.

Second, it is clear that not all expressions of aggression by fans are harmless; rather, collective violence at sporting events has emerged as a major social problem for many nations. Do aggressive sports attract violence-prone fans, or do they create in them an inclination toward the display of violence? A decade of empirical research suggests that combative sports, as a mirror of cultural norms, teach and stimulate violence. It is not competition per se that increases hostility but rather the aggressive nature of that competition. Those who participate in combative sports show more aggression in response to anger and frustration than those who participate in noncontact sports. Of course, it is also likely that more aggressive people show a preference for combative over noncontact sports. In any case, athletes in combative sports are more likely than others to suffer from hypertension, a finding that further undermines the notion of sports as catharsis (Goldstein 1983).

Whether releasing or promoting aggression is a consequence, what is certain is that sports provide an emotional outlet with few equals in the world of entertainment. Contests offer excitement and drama because the outcome is uncertain, and both luck and injury can intervene. The action is live, not scripted. Each contest is unique, unrehearsed, and finite with a clear-cut beginning, middle, and end. Sport is special because it stands apart from routine reality. The demonstration of the exuberance not only shows the audience's appreciation of effort and skill but is rooted in the fan's personal involvement in the team's or athlete's fate (Lever 1983).

THE SOCIOLOGICAL STUDY OF SPORT

People devote more time and affect in playing, watching, and discussing sport than in any other organized activity in public life. Millions of children are enrolled in sports leagues, high school and collegiate sports share the business orientation of the professional teams, and millions of adults organize their leisure time around playing amateur sports and watching professional athletes. Sports are a major factor in modern nations' economies insofar as billions of dollars are paid for admission tickets, telecast and advertising rights, recreational equipment, and both legal and illegal gambling. Sports so permeate culture that everyday language incorporates game images and metaphors that shape—some would say distort—the way people think about social reality (Koppett 1981).

Given the tremendous emotional and monetary investment in sports, one could rightfully expect it to be a major focus for sociological research, especially in the United States, where interest in sports ranks very high by any measure. However, the study of sport emerged only in the early 1950s in Western Europe and not until the late 1960s in the United States. To date, the subdiscipline is still underdeveloped and unfashionable in the United States, as measured by the relative handful of sociologists who declare the field as their specialty and by the few courses on the subject offered at the graduate level in major universities (Loy, Kenyon, and McPherson 1987).

Sports are largely taken for granted. Intellectuals, viewing play and games as trivial and inconsequential, feel little need for scientific scrutiny of the frivolous side of life. Journalists and philosophers have contributed interesting speculations more often than social scientists have provided empirical data (Weiss 1969). The careful examination of the role of sports in society remains minimal despite growing recognition that leisure pursuits, like occupations, are salient bases for identification in modern life.

REFERENCES

Betts, John R. 1980 "The Technological Revolution and the Rise of Sport, 1850–1900." In George H. Sage, ed., *Sport and American Society*. 3rd ed. Reading, Mass.: Addison-Wesley.

Coakley, Jay J. 1984 "Sport in Society: An Inspiration or an Opiate?" In D. Stanley Eitzen, ed., *Sport in Contemporary Society*. 2nd ed., New York: St. Martin's.

Goldstein, Jeffrey H. (ed.) 1983 *Sports Violence*. New York: Springer-Verlag.

Hoch, Paul 1972 *Rip Off the Big Game: The Exploitation of Sports by the Power Elite*. New York: Doubleday.

Huizinga, Johan 1955 *Homo Ludens: A Study of the Play Element in Culture*. Boston: Beacon Press.

Koppett, Leonard 1981 *Sports Illusion, Sports Reality.* Boston: Houghton Mifflin.

Lever, Janet 1983 *Soccer Madness.* Chicago: University of Chicago Press.

Lipsyte, Robert 1975 *Sportsworld: An American Dreamland.* New York: Quadrangle.

Loy, J., G. Kenyon, and B. McPherson 1987 "The Emergence and Development of the Sociology of Sport as an Academic Specialty." In A. Yiannakis, T. McIntyre, M. Melnick, and D. Hart, eds., *Sport Sociology.* 3d ed. Dubuque, Iowa: Kendall/Hunt.

Luschen, G., and G. H. Sage 1981 *Handbook of Social Science of Sport.* Champaign, Ill.: Stipes.

Roberts, Michael 1976 *Fans! How We Go Crazy over Sports.* Washington, D.C.: New Republic Books.

Shaw, Gary 1972 *Meat on the Hoof.* New York: Dell.

Weiss, Paul 1969 *Sport: A Philosophic Inquiry.* Carbondale, Ill.: Southern Illinois University Press.

JANET LEVER

STANDARDIZATION In many areas of sociology it is desirable to compare the frequency of some event of interest in one or more populations. For example, one may wish to compare the levels of mortality in two countries or the levels of crime in various cities. The technique of standardization provides a way of adjusting crude rates to eliminate the influence of distorting factors and, thus, render the rates more directly comparable, while retaining a single summary index. Standardized rates are simple to calculate, and they require only marginally more data than crude rates. Before a description of the technique of standardization, it is helpful to consider the drawbacks of using either counts of events or crude rates for comparative purposes.

Comparison of counts of events should be avoided, since the total numbers of events in a population reflects the size of that population. Suppose, for example, one wished to compare the levels of mortality in the United States and Guatemala. The number of deaths in the United States in 1985, 2,086,440 (U.S. Bureau of the Census 1989), far exceeded the number in Guatemala in the same year, 69,455 (United Nations 1988). However, it would be erroneous to conclude on

the basis of these figures that mortality is higher in the United States than in Guatemala, since the U.S. population is thirty times that of Guatemala, 240 million compared with 8 million (United Nations 1988; U.S. Bureau of the Census 1989). To ensure that counts of events are related to the population at risk of experiencing those events, the frequency of events is typically reported as a rate per thousand of the population. Crude rates are calculated according to the following formula:

$$CR = \frac{E}{P} \cdot 1000, \qquad (1)$$

where E refers to the number of events of interest in the population during the specified time period, and P refers to the total population during the period.

Thus, in 1985 the crude death rate in both the United States and Guatemala was approximately 8.7 deaths per thousand, implying that the two countries have very similar levels of mortality. However, this conclusion seems implausible when one considers that the residents of the United States enjoy far higher living standards and greater access to health care than do the residents of Guatemala.

Close inspection of the crude rate reveals that, although it offers a better basis for comparison than the absolute number, it is a flawed measure that could yield misleading results. Crude rates do not provide directly comparable indicators of the frequency of an event because they depend partly on the population composition. Specifically, if the occurrence of an event of interest varies according to some factor, the rate will reflect not just the frequency of the event but also the distribution of the factor in the population. The crude rate is simply the weighted average of a set of factor-specific rates, where the weights are the distribution of the factor in the population:

$$CR = \sum \frac{e_a}{p_a} \cdot \frac{p_a}{P}, \qquad (2)$$

where p_a is the population in group a; e_a is the number of events occurring to the population in group a; and P is the total population.

Thus, variations in populations' rates reflect

compositional differences, as well as differences in the frequency of the event of interest. For example, mortality is highly concentrated among older persons, so that the crude death rate reflects not only the level of mortality in a population but also the proportion of a population who are elderly. Therefore, populations with a high proportion of elderly people tend to have higher crude death rates than populations with a low proportion of elderly people. In 1985 in the United States 12 percent of the population was over sixty-five years of age (United States Bureau of the Census 1989), compared with just 3 percent of the population of Guatemala (United Nations 1988). It is this difference in the age structures of the two populations that results in similar crude death rates, even though the actual mortality conditions in the two countries differ widely.

One way to eliminate the distorting effects of extraneous factors is to work with the set of factor-specific rates. For example, the mortality rates of the United States and Guatemala could be compared by examining the two schedules of age-specific mortality rates. The disadvantage of this approach is that the researcher no longer has a single summary measure to use in making comparisons. This is not a trivial point, since a distorting factor may have many levels, leading to a large number of factor-specific rates. Age-specific mortality rates are generally calculated for five-year age groups up to age eighty, with a single open-ended age group for those eighty and over, resulting in seventeen age groups. If two populations are to be compared, this yields thirty-four rates to be examined. If several populations are to be compared, as for example in the analysis of time trends, the volume of material required to undertake a comparison may be overwhelming. Removing the influence of more than one distorting factor from the rates at a time further increases the number of measures to be compared. It is apparent that a method to adjust crude rates for the possible influence of distorting factors, that yields a single index, is highly desirable. Standardization fulfills both objectives.

Two methods of standardization are in common use: direct and indirect. Both rely on the fact that crude rates can be expressed as the weighted average of a set of factor-specific rates. Direct standardization shows what rates would obtain in two or more populations if they all had the same composition. Indirect standardization shows what rates would obtain in two or more populations if they all had the same set of factor-specific rates. It is important to note that neither directly nor indirectly standardized rates have any intrinsic meaning; they are meaningful only in comparison with other similarly standardized rates. The appropriate measures to use for comparisons are differences, percent differences, and ratios of similarly adjusted rates.

Direct standardization is the preferred method of standardization. A single standard population is used to derive a standardized rate for each of the populations to be compared. The formula for direct standardization is

$$DSR = \sum \frac{e_a^j}{p_a^j} \cdot \frac{p_a^s}{P^s} \qquad (3)$$

where e_a^j is the number of events occurring to individuals in group a in population j; p_a^j is the number of individuals in group a in population j; p_a^s is the number of individuals in group a in the standard population; and P^s is the total size of the standard population. Since e_a^j/p_a^j is the factor-specific rate for individuals in group a, denoted m_a^j, the formula simplifies to

$$DSR = \sum m_a^j \cdot \frac{p_a^s}{P_s}, \qquad (4)$$

m_a^j, the formula simplifies to

To calculate a directly standardized rate, one simply takes the sum of the observed factor-specific rates, multiplied by the number of persons having each level of the factor in the standard population; divides by the total number of persons in the standard population; and multiplies by 1,000. Application of this method to the crude death rates of the United States and Guatemala for 1985, using the age distribution of the United States as the standard, yields directly age-standardized death rates of 8.7 for the United States and 14.7 for Guatemala. (Notice that, where a population's crude rate is standardized on itself, the standardized rate is the same as the crude rate.) When the distorting effects of age composition are removed from the crude rates by direct standardization, it is apparent that mortality is substantially higher in Guatemala than in the United States.

Indirect standardization requires less information concerning the area under study than direct standardization and, therefore, offers a useful alternative method of adjusting crude rates when only incomplete data are available. As noted, direct standardization requires the factor-specific rates for the area under study. In many cases, only the total number of events and the total population of the area under study are known, and factor-specific rates are not available. This is common in the study of mortality in historical populations and in the populations of contemporary, less developed countries, where the number of deaths and the size and age structure of the population are known, but ages of the deceased are rarely collected or are very unreliably reported. As with direct standardization, a single standard population is used to calculate indirectly standardized rates for the populations under study. In this case however, only the total number of events and the total population of the areas under study are required, together with factor-specific rates for the standard populations. The formula for indirect standardization is

$$\text{ISR} = \left(\frac{E^j}{\Sigma m_a^s \cdot p_a^j}\right) \cdot CR^s, \tag{5}$$

where m_a^s is the factor-specific rate for group a in the standard population; p_a^j is the number of people in group a in population j; E^j is the number of events in population j; and CR^s is the crude rate in the standard population.

Indirect standardization applies a standard set of factor-specific rates to an observed population structure, generating the expected number of events that would occur in a population if the standard rates applied. The standard population crude rate is then multiplied by the ratio of observed events to expected events, to yield the indirectly standardized rate. Applying this method

to the mortality data of the United States and Guatemala for 1985, using the age-specific mortality rates of the United States as the standard, gives indirectly standardized death rates of 8.7 for the United States (again the United States rate is standardized on itself and so is identical to the unstandardized rate) and 23.5 for Guatemala. Once again, standardization reveals far higher mortality in Guatemala than in the United States. Notice, too, that indirect standardization suggests a greater differential than direct standardization.

The choice of the standard population is of considerable importance for both direct and indirect standardization, because the difference between the standardized rates of two populations is sensitive to the standard population used. Indeed, it is possible that the choice of the standard population can affect the direction of the difference between the rates of the populations being compared. There are three options for the selection of a standard population: one of the populations being compared, as was used in the earlier mortality examples; the (unweighted) average of the populations being compared; or some external population, either real or simulated. For much of this century the age–sex distribution of the population of England and Wales in 1901 was used for the standardization of mortality and fertility rates, so that the distribution became known as the standard million. However, recognition that the results of standardization are sensitive to the choice of standard led to disuse of the standard million. The most common procedure now is to select a standard as close as possible to the observed population distributions. Obviously it is not always possible to select a standard similar to all the populations being compared, especially since the aim of standardization is to facilitate comparison of disparate populations. Where two very different populations are to be compared, the best strategy is to use the average of the two distributions. Where a time series of standardized rates is of interest, a middle point in the series should be used as the standard, rather than either the first or last point.

In the comparison of mortality in the United

States and Guatemala, the United States was used as the standard for both direct and indirect standardization. When Guatemala is used as the standard, the United States' directly standardized death rate is 3.2 and its indirectly standardized rate is 5.18. These results imply far smaller absolute and relative differences between mortality in the two countries than when the United States was used as the standard. Given the very different age structures of the two populations, the average age distribution of the two is the preferred standard for direct standardization, and the average age-specific mortality rates are preferred for indirect standardization. Using these standards generates directly standardized mortality rates of 8.5 and 14.5 for the United States and Guatemala, respectively, and indirectly standardized rates of 6.5 and 12.7. These results are probably the closest indication of the true magnitude of the mortality differential between the two populations. Finally, as should be apparent from the preceding examples, indirect standardization is more sensitive to the selection of the standard than direct standardization, so that particular care should be given to the selection of the standard against which the indirect method is to be applied.

The principal aim of standardization is to eliminate extraneous sources of variation from a set of data, so that they may be meaningfully compared. This is accomplished by holding constant one or more sources of variation in the data. In the case of mortality rates in the United States and Guatemala, the age structures of the two populations were held constant. In some respects then, standardization is similar to various statistical techniques, such as partial correlation, regression, and analysis of variance, that examine the relationships between variables, holding other variables constant. However, unlike these techniques, standardization has the effect of adjusting a set of data. The adjusted data can then be used to derive other summary measures or, indeed, as input into statistical models. For example, in the analysis of mortality differentials among countries, researchers have often been interested in the relative contributions of health care services and the level of economic development. One possible analytic approach would be to regress the number of deaths in a group of countries on variables measuring the levels of development and the availability and cost of health care services in each country, together with control variables for the population size and the proportion of the population in various age groups. However, this approach may yield unsatisfactory results, because most of the variance in the data can be explained by controls for population size and age structure, rather than by the more substantively interesting variables measuring economic development and availability of health care. An alternative approach to the analysis, which would also control for the effects of population size and age structure, would be to use the age-standardized death rates as the dependent variable, leaving only the variables of substantive interest to be included as independent variables.

Although the examples in the preceding discussion all relate to the age standardization of mortality rates, standardization may be used in a wide range of research areas and to control for the effects of a wide variety of confounding factors. In demographic research, some of the best known examples of indirect standardization are Coale's indices of fertility, used to analyze the historical decline of fertility in Europe (Coale and Tredway 1986). Coale developed four fertility indices, measuring total fertility, marital fertility, nonmartial fertility, and marriage, relative to the fertility and nuptiality of the Hutterites, a North American religious sect with the highest recorded levels of fertility. Aside from demographers, other social scientists routinely standardize rates to eliminate the effects of potential confounding factors; for example, crime rates are commonly age standardized. Although age is the variable most widely controlled in standardization, the effects of other variables can be held constant in this way; for example, education, income, occupation. Furthermore, providing suitably cross-classified data are available, more than one variable may be standardized for at a time.

In conclusion, standardization provides a relatively simple method of adjusting rates to eliminate the effects of one or more confounding factors, and so permit meaningful comparisons to be made. Standardization has applications in many areas of sociology and requires only minimal data and computing. Two points should be borne in mind whenever standardization is used. First, the results are sensitive to the selection of the standard. Second, standardized rates should not be interpreted as referring to any actual population, as they are abstractions of use only for comparative purposes.

(SEE ALSO: *Correlation and Regression Analysis; Demographic Methods*)

REFERENCES

Coale, Ansley J., and Roy Tredway 1986 "A Summary of the Changing Distribution of Overall Fertility, Marital Fertility and the Proportion Married in the Provinces of Europe." In A. J. Coale and S. C. Watkins, eds., *The Decline of Fertility in Europe.* Princeton, N.J.: Princeton University Press.

Shryock, Henry S., and Jacob S. Siegel 1976 *The Methods and Materials of Demography* (condensed ed. Edward G. Stockwell). New York: Academic Press.

United Nations 1988 *Demographic Yearbook 1986.* New York: United Nations.

United States Bureau of the Census 1989 *Statistical Abstract of the United States: 1989,* 109th ed. Washington, D.C.: U.S. Government Printing Office.

DIANE N. LYE

STATE *See* Nationalism

STATISTICAL GRAPHICS Statistical graphs present data and the results of statistical analysis, assist in the analysis of data, and, less frequently, facilitate statistical computation. Presentation graphs include the familiar bar graph, pie chart, line graph, scatterplot, and statistical map. Data analysis employs these graphical forms among others. Computational graphs (or "nomographs") sometimes display data but usually show theoretical quantities such as power curves for determining sample size. This article emphasizes the role of graphs in data analysis, although many of the considerations raised also apply to graphical presentation.

While it is generally recognized that pictorial representation of information is a particularly effective mode of communication, statistical graphs seldom appear in sociological publications. Figure 1, from Cleveland (1984), shows the relative space devoted to graphs in leading scientific publications, including four sociology journals. Sociology, of course, is not a wholly quantitative discipline. Nevertheless, even a cursory examination of publications in the field reveals that sociologists much more frequently report numerical information in tabular than in graphical form. Informal observation also suggests that sociologists usually analyze numerical data without the assistance of statistical graphs.

HISTORY

Broadly construed, graphic communication dates to the cave paintings of human prehistory and to the earliest forms of writing, which were pictorial or semipictorial. The first diagrams to communicate quantitative information—about location and distance—were maps: Egyptian cartographers employed coordinate systems in maps prepared five thousand years ago, and cartography remains a relatively developed area of graphical representation. Musical notation, which charts pitch as a function of time, also has an ancient origin and illustrates the spatial display of essentially nonspatial information. Rectilinear coordinate graphs are so familiar to us that it is easy to lose sight of the radical abstraction required to represent diverse quantities, such as pitch, as distances along an axis.

In the seventeenth century, the French mathematician and philosopher René Descartes established the relationship between algebraic equations and curves in a rectilinear coordinate space.

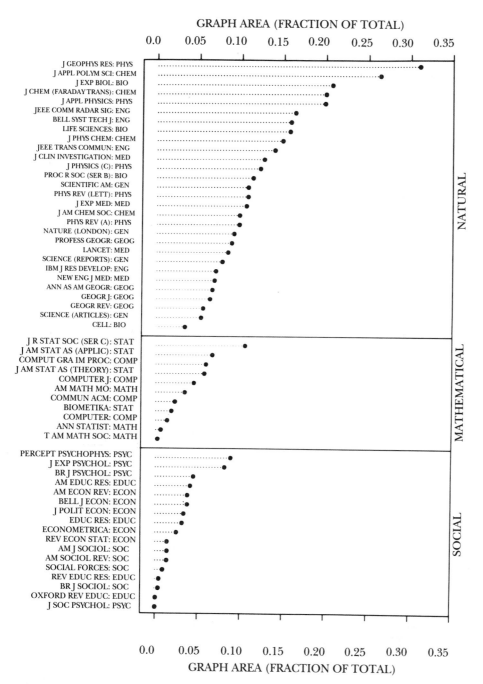

Figure 1

Dot graph showing the fractional area devoted to graphs in fifty-seven journals in the natural, mathematical, and social sciences. Four sociology journals appear near the bottom of the graph. To construct the graph, fifty articles were sampled from each journal during 1980 and 1981. Reprinted from Cleveland (1984) with the permission of the American Statistical Association.

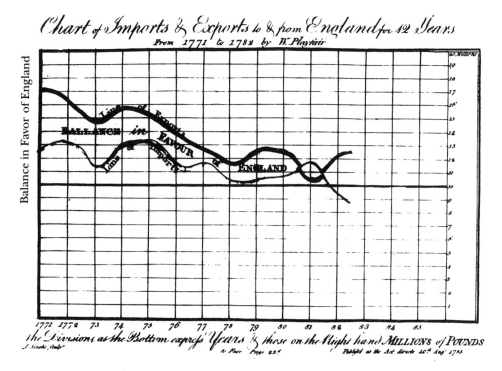

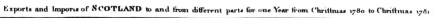

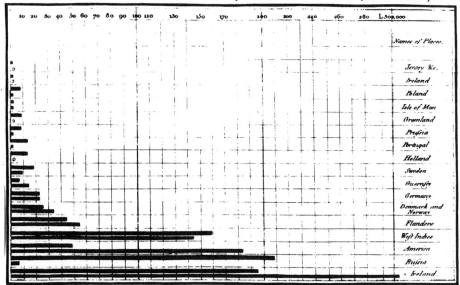

Figure 2

Two graphs from Playfair's 1786 Commercial and Political Atlas: *(a) A
time-series line graph showing imports to and exports from England, 1771 to 1782.
(b) A bar graph showing imports to and exports from Scotland for the year
1780–1781. The originals are in color. Photographs courtesy of the William L.
Clements Library, University of Michigan, Richard W. Ryan, Curator of Books.*

The graphical representation of functions is not logically necessary to the display of empirical data as points in space, and there are isolated examples antedating Descartes of statistical graphs employing abstract coordinate systems. Nevertheless, Descartes's analytic geometry no doubt provided the impetus for the development of statistical graphics, and the most common forms of statistical graphs evolved slowly during the subsequent three-and-a-half centuries.

Among many individuals' contributions to this evolution, the work of William Playfair at the turn of the nineteenth century is of particular importance. First, Playfair either invented or popularized several common graphical forms including the line graph, the bar graph, the pie chart, and the circle chart (in which areas of circles represent quantities). Second, Playfair employed statistical graphs to display social and economic data. Figure 2a, from Playfair's 1786 *Commercial and Political Atlas,* is a time-series line graph of imports to and exports from England during the period 1771 to 1782. In the original, the space between the two curves is colored green when the balance of trade favors England (i.e., when the curve for exports is above that for imports) and red when the balance favors England's trading partners. Of the forty-two graphs in Playfair's atlas, all but one depict time series. The sole exception is a bar graph of imports to and exports from Scotland (Figure 2b), data for which were available only for the year 1780–1781, precluding the construction of time-series plots. Playfair's 1801 *Statistical Breviary* included a wider variety of graphical forms.

The first half of the nineteenth century was a period of innovation and dissemination of statistical graphics, particularly in England and France. The ogive (cumulative frequency curve), the histogram, the contour map, and graphs employing logarithmic and polar coordinates all appeared before 1850. Later in the century, the British scientist Sir Francis Galton exploited an analogy to contour maps in his determination of the bivariate–normal correlation surface, illustrating the role of graphs in discovery.

The nineteenth-century enthusiasm for graphical representation of data produced many memorable and high-quality statistical graphs such as those of Playfair, E. J. Marey, and Charles Joseph Minard (several of which are reproduced in Tufte 1983). The same enthusiasm produced early abuses, however, including the graph from M. G. Mulhall's 1892 *Dictionary of Statistics* in Figure 3: The heights of the triangles indicate the accumulated wealth of each country, but their areas are wildly disproportionate to the quantities represented, conveying a misleading impression of the data. Likewise, the horizontal arrangement of the countries bears no relationship to the purpose of the graph and is apparently simply for artistic effect: It would be more natural to order the countries by wealth. Many modern graphs suffer from similar problems, a situation that has motivated a substantial literature of graphical critique (such as the works by Calvin F. Schmidt and Tufte discussed below).

The evolution of statistical graphics paralleled the general growth of statistical science well into the twentieth century. This relationship changed radically in the 1930s as statisticians such as R. A. Fisher emphasized the development of procedures for statistical inference. Fisher's influential *Statistical Methods for Research Workers,* first published in 1925, includes a brief chapter on "diagrams"; this chapter incorporates line graphs, scatterplots, and a histogram, the latter with a superimposed normal-density curve. The remainder of the book, however, contains many numerical tables but just five additional figures, none of which presents empirical information. Likewise, Fisher's 1935 classic, *The Design of Experiments,* includes just three graphs, all of which are theoretical.

The rebirth of interest in statistical graphics may be traced substantially to John W. Tukey's work on exploratory data analysis, beginning in the 1960s and culminating in the publication of his text on this subject in 1977. Tukey's coworkers and students, most important the group at Bell Laboratories associated with William S. Cleveland, continue to contribute centrally to the modern development of statistical graphics. (See, in partic-

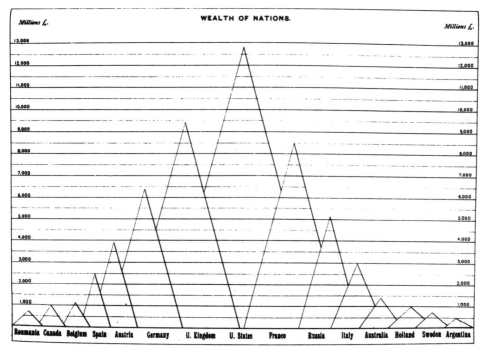

Figure 3

A modified bar graph from Mulhall's 1892 Dictionary of Statistics, *substituting triangles with unequal bases for equal-width rectangular bars. The height of each triangle represents accumulated national wealth in 1888. The original is in color. Photograph by University of Michigan Photographic Services.*

ular, J. M. Chambers et al. 1983; Cleveland 1985.) Further information on the history of statistical graphics may be found in H. Gray Funkhouser (1937), Tufte (1983), and James R. Beninger and Dorothy L. Robyn (1978), the last of which contains a useful chronology and bibliography.

GRAPHICAL STANDARDS

After several abortive efforts, the International Statistical Congresses held in Europe during the nineteenth century abandoned the attempt to formulate graphical standards. Since that time, many authors have proposed standards and principles for the construction of statistical graphs, but consensus on these matters remains elusive. Schmidt (1983, p. 17), for example, suggests that grid lines should always appear on rectilinear line graphs, while Tufte (1983, p. 112) maintains that

grids "should usually be muted or completely suppressed"—an instance of his more general principle that good graphs maximize the "data–ink ratio" (the amount of ink devoted to display of data as a proportion of all ink used to draw the graph) and eliminate "chartjunk" (extraneous graphical elements).

Disagreements such as this are due partly to the lack of systematic data on graphical perception (a situation that is rapidly improving, however), partly to differences in style and taste, and partly to the absence of adequate general theories of graph construction and perception (although there have been attempts, such as Bertin 1973). As well, good graphical display depends upon the purposes for which the graph is drawn and upon particular characteristics of the data, factors that are difficult to specify in advance and in a general manner.

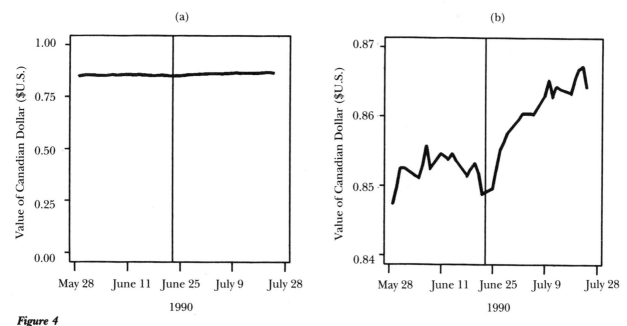

Figure 4

The relative value of the Canadian and U.S. dollars in an eight-week period in 1990 surrounding the failure of the Meech Lake amendment to the Canadian constitution. (a) Beginning the vertical axis at zero. Note that the upper end point of one is arbitrary since the Canadian dollar can trade above par with the U.S. dollar. (b) Scaling the vertical axis to accommodate the range of the data. The vertical line in each graph is drawn at the June 23 deadline for ratifying the Meech Lake accord. Source of data: daily foreign exchange quotations in The New York Times.

Huff (1954, chap. 5), for example, argues that scales displaying ratio quantities should always start at zero so as not to exaggerate the magnitude of differences between data values. This principle, however, often disguises patterns in data clearly revealed by graphical magnification. Consider Figures 4a and 4b, which show the relative value of the Canadian and U.S. dollars for the eight weeks surrounding the June 23, 1990, deadline for the ratification of the ill-fated "Meech Lake" amendment to the constitution of Canada. This period was widely interpreted, both domestically and abroad, as one of constitutional crisis and uncertainty for Canada. Because in the short term the Canadian dollar traditionally trades in a narrow range against the U.S. dollar, Figure 4a is essentially uninformative, while Figure 4b reveals that the Canadian dollar fell slightly as the Meech deadline approached and rose thereafter.

RESEARCH ON GRAPHICAL PERCEPTION

The earliest psychophysical research on perception of graphs, conducted during the 1920s, focused on the relative merits of pie and bar charts for displaying percentage data and proved inconclusive. Recently, statisticians and psychologists have undertaken systematic experimentation on graphical perception. Spence and Lewandowsky (1990) review the burgeoning literature in this area.

Cleveland and McGill (1984), for example, conducted a series of experiments meant to ascertain the relative accuracy of ten elementary perceptual tasks that extract quantitative information from graphs, represented schematically in Figure 5. Ranked in order of decreasing average accuracy, these tasks involve judgment of position along

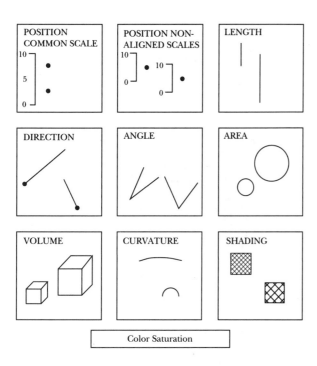

Figure 5

Ten elementary perceptual tasks for decoding quantitative information from statistical graphs. Reprinted from Cleveland and McGill (1984) with the permission of the American Statistical Association.

a common scale; position along nonaligned scales; length, direction, or angle; area; volume or curvature; and shading or color saturation.

Likewise, Spence (reported in Spence and Lewandowsky 1990) has shown in an experiment that categorical information differentiating points on a scatterplot is encoded most effectively by colors and least effectively by confusable letters (e.g., E, F, H); other coding devices, such as different shapes (circles, squares, triangles), degrees of fill, and discriminable letters (H, Q, X) were intermediate in effectiveness.

Cleveland and his colleagues have designed new graphical forms that apply these and similar findings by encoding important information using accurately judged graphical elements. One such form is the dot graph shown in Figure 1. Similarly, Cleveland and McGill (1984) suggest the replacement of quantitative statistical maps that use shading or hue (e.g., Figure 6a) with maps employing framed rectangles (Figure 6b), which exploit the more accurate judgment of position along nonaligned scales.

The effectiveness of statistical graphs is rooted in the remarkable ability of human beings to apprehend, process, and remember pictorial in-

formation. The human visual system, however, is subject to distortion and illusion, processes that can affect the perception of graphs. Good graphical design works to minimize and counteract the limitations of human vision. In Figure 7, for example, it appears that the difference between the hypothetical import and export series is changing when this difference is constant (cf. Playfair's time-series graph in figure 2a). The source of the illusion is our tendency to attend to the least distance between the two curves rather than to the vertical distance. Thus, an alternative is to graph the difference between the two curves —the balance of trade—directly (cf. Figures 10b and 10c below), exploiting the relatively accurate judgment of position along a common scale, or to show vertical lines between the import and export curves, employing the somewhat less accurate judgment of position along nonaligned scales.

GRAPHS IN DATA ANALYSIS

Statistical graphs should play a central role in the analysis of data, a prescription most often honored in the breach. Graphs, unlike numerical summaries of data, facilitate the perception of

Murder Rates, 1978

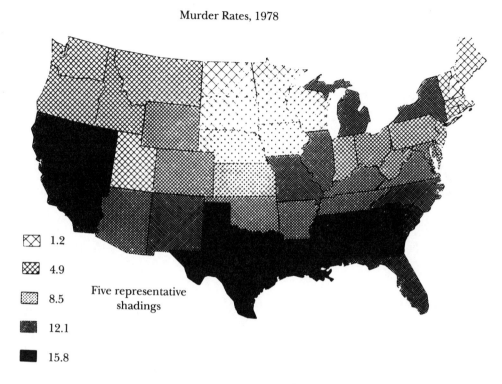

1.2
4.9
8.5 Five representative
        shadings
12.1
15.8

Rates per 100.000 population

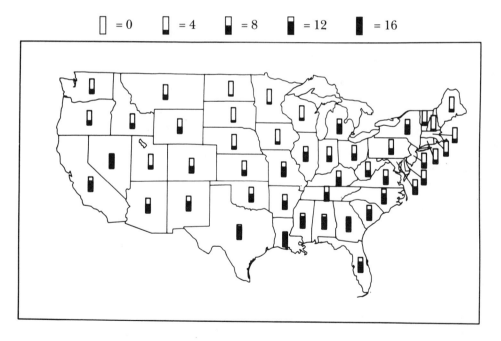

= 0   = 4   = 8   = 12   = 16

MURDER RATES PER 100,000 POPULATION, 1978

Figure 6
*Statistical maps of state murder rates in 1978 employing (a) shading and (b) framed
rectangles. Reprinted from Cleveland and McGill (1984) with the permission of the
American Statistical Association.*

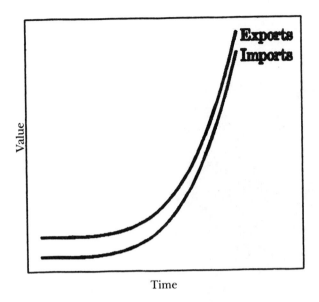

Time

Figure 7
The vertical separation between the exports and imports curves is constant, but the curves appear to converge. The data are contrived.

general patterns and often reveal unusual, anomalous, or unexpected features of the data—characteristics that might well compromise a numerical summary.

The four simple data sets in Figure 8, due to Anscombe (1973) and dubbed "Anscombe's quartet" by Tufte (1983), illustrate this point well. All four data sets yield the same linear least-squares outputs when regression lines are fit to the data, including the regression intercept and slope, coefficient standard errors, the standard error (root mean-square error) of the regression, and the correlation, but—significantly—not residuals. Although the data are contrived, the four graphs tell very different imaginary stories: The least-squares regression line accurately summarizes the tendency of y to increase with x in Figure 8a. In contrast, the data in Figure 8b clearly indicate a curvilinear relationship between y and x, a relationship the linear regression does not capture. In Figure 8c, one point is out of line with the rest and distorts the regression. Perhaps the outlying point represents an error in recording the data or a y-value that is influenced by factors other than x. In Figure 8d, the ability to fit a line, and the line's specific location, depend upon the presence of a single point.

There is a diversity of graphical forms adapted to different purposes in data analysis. Many im-

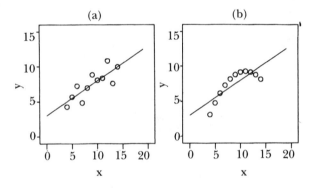

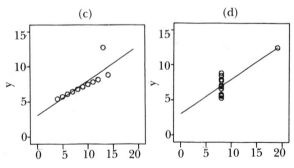

Figure 8
The four data sets have the same linear least-squares regression, including the regression coefficients, their standard errors, the correlation between the variables, and the standard error of the regression. Redrawn from Anscombe (1973) with the permission of the American Statistical Association.

portant applications appear in figures below, roughly in order of increasing complexity, includng graphs for displaying univariate distributions, bivariate relationships, diagnostic quantities in regression analysis, and multivariate data.

Particularly useful for graphically screening data are methods for displaying the distributions of quantitative variables. Several univariate displays of the distribution of infant mortality rates for 101 countries are shown in Figure 9, with data compiled by Leinhardt and Wasserman (1979).

Figure 9a is a traditional histogram for the infant mortality data, a frequency bar graph formed by dissecting the range of infant mortality into class intervals or "bins" and then counting the number of observations in each bin. Figure 9b shows an alternative histogram differing from Figure 9a only in the origin of the bin system (the bars are shifted five units to the right). These graphs demonstrate that the impression conveyed by a histogram partly depends upon the arbitrary location of the bins. Figure 9c is a stem-and-leaf display, a type of histogram (due to Tukey) that records the data values directly in the bars of the graph, thus permitting the recovery of the original data. Here, for example, the values given as 1 | 2 represent infant mortality rates of 120 per 1,000 (rounded to the nearest ten). Note that three outlying observations (the values for Libya, Algeria, and Saudi Arabia) are shown separately on a special "high" stem.

Figure 9d is a kernel density estimate, or smoothed histogram, a display that corrects both the roughness of the traditional histogram and its dependence on the arbitrary choice of bin location. For any value x of infant mortality, the height of the kernel estimate is

$$\hat{f}(x) = \frac{1}{nh} \sum_{i=1}^{n} K\left[\frac{x - x_i}{h}\right] \qquad (1)$$

where n is the number of observations (here, 101); the observations themselves are $x_1, x_2, \ldots, x_n$; h is the "window" half-width for the kernel estimate, analogous to bin width for a histogram; and K is some probability–density function, such as the unit-normal density, ensuring that the total area

under the kernel estimate is one. A univariate scatterplot—another form of distributional display giving the location of each observation—is shown at the bottom of Figure 9d.

Figure 9e, a "boxplot" of the infant mortality data (a graphical form also due to Tukey), summarizes a variety of important distributional information. The box is drawn between the first and third quartiles and therefore encloses the central half of the data. A line within the box marks the position of the median. The whiskers extend either to the most extreme data value (as on the left) or to the most extreme nonoutlying data value (as on the right). The three outlying data values are represented individually. The compactness of the boxplot suggests its use as a component of more complex displays; boxplots may be drawn in the margins of a scatterplot to show the distribution of each variable, for example.

Figure 9f shows a normal quantile comparison plot for the infant mortality data. As the name implies, this graph compares the ordered data with corresponding quantiles of the unit-normal distribution. By convention, the ith largest infant mortality rate, denoted $x_{(i)}$, has $P_i = (i - 1/2)/n$ proportion of the data below it. The corresponding normal quantile is z_i, located so that $\Pr(Z \leq z_i) = P_i$, where Z follows the unit-normal distribution. If X is normally distributed with mean μ and standard deviation σ, then within the bounds of sampling error, $x_{(i)} \simeq \mu + \sigma z_i$. Departure from a linear pattern therefore indicates nonnormality. The line shown in Figure 9f was fit by estimating μ robustly as the median of the x's and σ as the interquartile range of the x's divided by 1.349 (which is the interquartile range of the unit-normal distribution). The positive skew of the infant mortality rates is reflected in the tendency of the plotted points to lie above the fitted line.

While the skewness of the infant mortality data is apparent in all of the displays, the bimodal grouping of the data is clearest in the kernel density estimate. The normal quantile comparison plot, in contrast, retains greatest resolution in the tails of the distribution, where data are sparse, and which are the regions that often prove problematic for numerical summaries of data

(a)

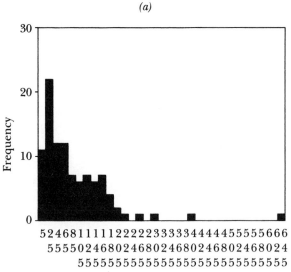

Infant mortality rate per 1,000

(b)

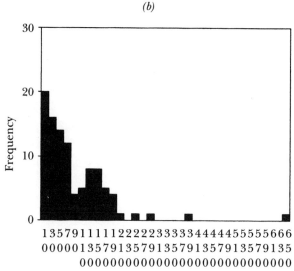

Infant mortality rate per 1,000

(c)

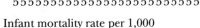

0	11111111111111111111
0	22222222222223333
0	4444445555555
0	6666666677777
0	888
1	000011
1	222222333
1	445555
1	66677
1	8889
2	001
2	
2	5
high	300, 400, 650

leaf unit = 10

$1 \mid 2 = 120$

(d)

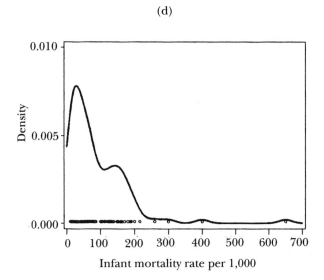

Infant mortality rate per 1,000

such as means or regression surfaces. See Fox (1990) for more information on univariate displays.

Many useful graphs display relationships between variables, including several forms that appeared earlier in this article: bar graphs (Figure 2b) and dot graphs (Figure 1); line graphs such as time-series plots (Figures 2a, 4, and 7); and statistical maps (Figure 6). Parallel boxplots are often informative for comparing the distribution of a quantitative variable across several categories. Scatterplots (as in Figure 8) are invaluable for examining the relationship between two quantitative variables. Other data-analytic graphs adapt these forms.

In graphing quantitative data it is sometimes advantageous to transform variables. Logarithms, the most common transformation, often clarify

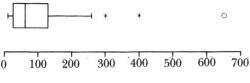

Infant mortality rate per 1,000

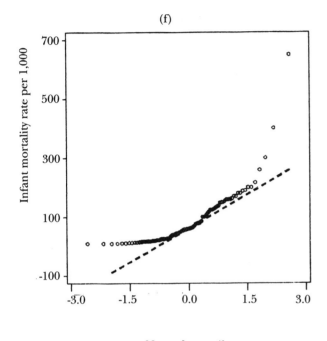

(f)

Normal quantiles

Figure 9

Six univariate displays of the distribution of infant mortality rates in 101 nations around 1970. The histograms (a) and (b) both have bins of width twenty, but the bars of (a) are five units to the left of those of (b). A stem-and-leaf display is shown in (c); a kernel density estimate in (d); a boxplot in (e); and a normal quantile comparison plot in (f). Source of data: Leinhardt and Wasserman (1979).

data that extend over two or more orders of magnitude and are natural for problems in which ratios of data values, rather than their differences, are of central interest.

Consider Figure 10, which shows the size of the Canadian and U.S. populations for census years between 1790 and 1980 in the United States and between 1851 and 1981 in Canada. The data are graphed on the original scale in Figure 10a and the log scale (base ten) in Figure 10b. Because the Canadian population is much smaller than that of the United States, it is difficult to discern the Canadian data in Figure 10a. Moreover, Figure 10b shows more clearly departures from a constant rate of population growth, represented by linear increase on the log scale, and permits a direct comparison of the growth rates in the two

countries. These rates were quite similar, with the U.S. population roughly ten times as large as the Canadian population throughout the past century and a half. Figure 10c, however, which graphs the difference between the two curves in Figure 10b (i.e., the log population ratio), reveals that the United States was growing more rapidly than Canada prior to 1900 and more slowly thereafter.

Graphs also can assist in statistical modeling. Least-squares regression analysis, for example, which fits the model,

$$y_i = \beta_0 + \beta_1 x_{1i} + \beta_2 x_{2i} + \cdots + \beta_k x_{ki} + \epsilon_i \qquad (2)$$

makes strong assumptions about the structure of the data, including assumptions of linearity, equal error variance, normality of errors, and independence. Here y_i is the dependent variable score for

(a)

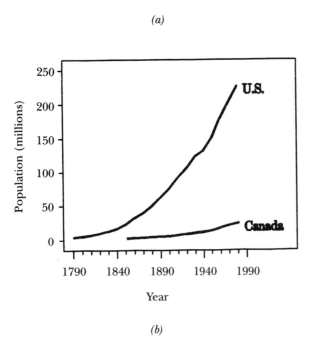

(c)

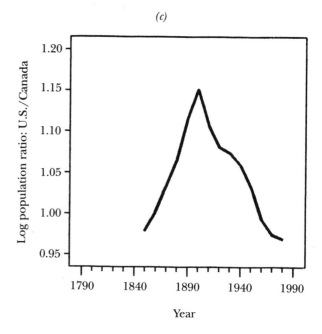

(b)

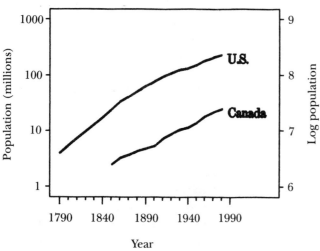

Figure 10
Canadian and U.S. population growth. The population figures are plotted directly in (a) and on a log scale in (b). The difference between the two log series is shown in (c). Sources of data: Canada Year Book 1990 *and* Statistical Abstract of the U.S. 1990.

the ith of n observations; x_{1i}, x_{2i}, . . . , x_{ki} are independent variables; ϵ_i is an unobserved error, assumed to be normally distributed with zero expectation and constant variance σ^2, independent of the x's and of the other errors; and the β's are regression parameters to be estimated along with the error variance from the data.

Graphs of quantities derived from the fitted regression model often prove crucial in determining the adequacy of the model. Figure 11, for

example, plots a measure of leverage in the regression (the "hat values" h_i) against a measure of discrepancy (the "studentized residuals" t_i). Leverage represents the degree to which individual observations can affect the fitted regression, while discrepancy represents the degree to which each observation departs from the pattern suggested by the rest of the data. Actual influence on the estimated regression coefficients is a product of leverage and discrepancy and is displayed on the

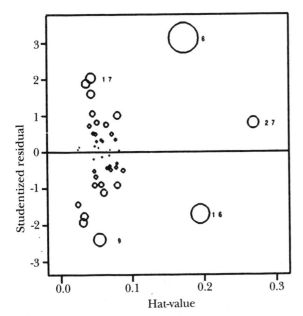

Figure 11
Influence plot for Duncan's regression of the rated prestige of forty-five occupations on their income and educational levels. The hat values measure the leverage of the observations in the regression, while the studentized residuals measure their discrepancy. The plotted circles have area proportional to Cook's D, a measure of influence on the regression coefficients. Observations that have relatively large studentized residuals or hat values are labeled by number. Source of data: Duncan (1961).

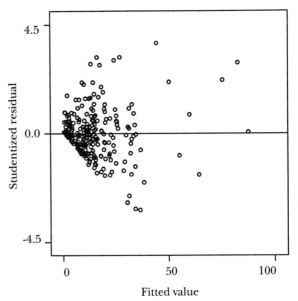

Figure 12
Plot of studentized residuals by fitted values (ŷ) for Ornstein's regression of interlocks maintained by 248 dominant Canadian firms on characteristics of the firms. The manner in which the points line up diagonally at the lower left of the figure is due to the lower limit of zero for the dependent variable (see Fox, forthcoming, for further discussion of these data). Source of data: personal communication from M. Ornstein.

graph by R. Dennis Cook's *D*, represented by the areas of the plotted circles. The data for this graph are drawn from Duncan's (1961) regression of the measured prestige of forty-five occupations on the educational and income levels of the occupations. The plot suggests that two of the data points (observations six and sixteen) may unduly affect the fitted regression.

Figure 12 is a scatterplot of studentized residuals against fitted *y*-values,

$$\hat{y}_i = b_0 + b_1 x_{1i} + b_2 x_{2i} + \cdots + b_k x_{ki} \tag{3}$$

where the *b*'s are sample estimates of the corresponding β's. If the error variance is constant as assumed, then the variation of the studentized residuals should not change systematically with the fitted values. The data for Figure 12 are drawn from work by Ornstein (1976) relating the number of interlocking directorate and executive posi-

tions maintained by 248 dominant Canadian corporations to characteristics of the firms. The plot reveals that the variation of the residuals appears to increase with the level of *y*, casting doubt upon the assumption of constant error variance.

Figure 13 shows a partial residual plot for the relationship between occupational prestige and income, a diagnostic useful for detecting nonlinearity in regression. The plot is for a regression of the directly assessed prestige of 102 Canadian occupations on the gender composition and income and educational levels of the occupations (see Fox and Suschnigg 1989). The partial residuals are formed as $e_{Ii} = b_I x_{Ii} + e_i$, where b_I is the fitted income coefficient in the linear regression; x_{Ii} is the average income of incumbents of occupation *i*; and $e_i = y_i - \hat{y}_i$ is the regression residual. The nonlinear pattern of the data, apparent in the graph, suggests modification of the regression

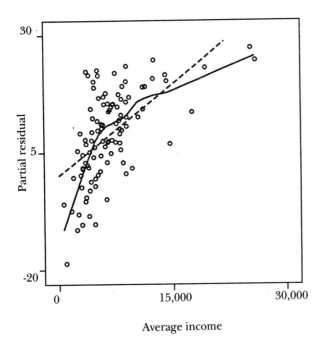

Figure 13

Partial residual plot for income in the regression of occupational prestige on the gender composition and income and educational levels of 102 Canadian occupations in 1971. The broken line gives the least-squares fit, while the solid line shows the lowess fit to the data. Source of data: Fox and Suschnigg (1989).

model. Further information on the role of graphics in regression diagnostics may be found in Atkinson (1985) and Fox (forthcoming).

Scatterplots are sometimes difficult to interpret because of visual noise, uneven distribution of the data, or discreteness of the data values. Visually ambiguous plots may often be enhanced by smoothing the relationship between the variables, as in Figure 13. The curve drawn through this plot was determined by a procedure due to Cleveland (1985) called locally weighted scatterplot smoothing (or "lowess"). Lowess fits n robust regression lines to the data, the ith such line emphasizing observations whose x-values are closest to x_i. The lowess fitted value for the ith observation, $\hat{y}_i$, comes from the ith such regression. Here x and y simply denote the horizontal and vertical variables in the plot. The curve plotted on Figure 13 connects the points $(x_i, \hat{y}_i)$.

Scatterplots for discrete data may be enhanced by (paradoxically) adding a small amount of random noise to the data so as to separate the points in the plot. Cleveland (1985) calls this process "jittering." An example is shown in Figure 14a, which plots scores on a vocabulary test against

years of education; the corresponding jittered plot, in Figure 14b, makes the relationship much clearer and also reveals other characteristics of the data, such as the concentration of points at twelve years of education.

Because graphs are commonly drawn on two-dimensional media such as paper, the display of multivariate data is intrinsically more difficult than of univariate or bivariate data. One solution to the problems posed by multivariate graphical representation is to record additional information on a two-dimensional plot. Symbols such as letters, shapes, degrees of fill, and color may be used to encode categorical information on a scatterplot, for example. Likewise, there are many schemes for representing additional quantitative information, as in Figures 6 and 11.

A scatterplot matrix (also called a "casement plot") is the direct graphic analog of a correlation matrix, displaying the bivariate relationship between each pair of a set of quantitative variables and thus providing a quick overview of the data. In contrast to a correlation matrix, however, a scatterplot matrix can reveal nonlinear relationships, outlying data, and so on. The scatterplot

(a)

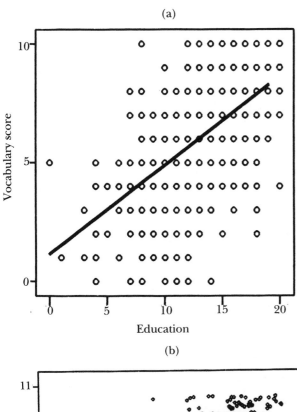

(b)

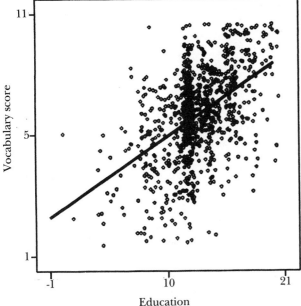

Figure 14
Jittering a scatterplot to clarify discrete data. The original
plot, in (a), shows the relationship between score on a
ten-item vocabulary test and education in years. The same
data are graphed in (b) with a small random quantity
added to each horizontal and vertical coordinate. Both
graphs show the least-squares regression line for the data.
Note that the axes in plot (b) have end points beyond the
range of the original data to accommodate the random
component at each end of the scales. Source of data: 1989
General Social Survey, National Opinion Research Center.

matrix in Figure 15 is for rates of seven different categories of crime in sixteen U.S. cities, as reported by Hartigan (1975). The regression curve shown in each scatterplot was determined by the lowess procedure described above.

A limitation of the scatterplot matrix is that it displays only the marginal relationships between the variables, while conditional relationships are more often the focus of multivariate statistical analysis. This limitation can sometimes be over-

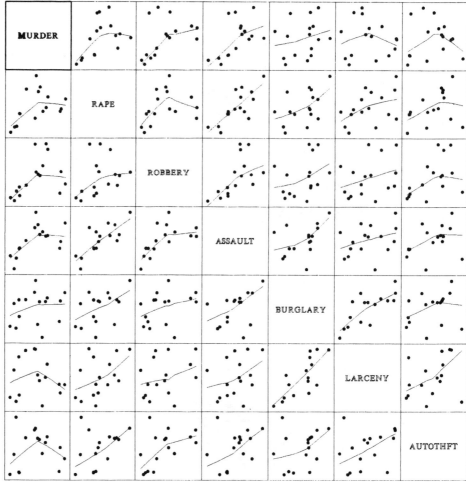

Figure 15
Scatterplot matrix for rates of seven categories of crime in sixteen U.S. cities in 1970. The rate labeled "Murder" represents both murder and manslaughter. The line shown in each plot is a lowess scatterplot smooth. Source of data: Hartigan (1975).

come, however, by labeling individual observations, or groups of observations, and following them across the several plots (see, e.g., the discussion of "brushing" in Cleveland 1985). Such methods are most effective when implemented as part of an interactive computer system for graphical data analysis.

Many of the most useful graphical techniques for multivariate data rely upon two-dimensional projections of the multivariate scatterplot of the data. A statistical model fit to the data often determines these projections. An example of a display employing projection of higher dimension-

al data is the partial residual plot shown in Figure 13. Another common application of this principle is the similarly named, but distinct, partial regression plot. Here, the dependent variable (y) and one independent variable in a multiple regression model (say, x_1) are each regressed on the other independent variables in the model (i.e., $x_2, \ldots, x_k$), producing two sets of residuals (which may be denoted $y^{(1)}$ and $x^{(1)}$). A scatterplot of the residuals (that is, $y^{(1)}$ versus $x^{(1)}$) is frequently useful in revealing high-leverage and influential observations. Implementation on high-performance graphics workstations, which can exploit color, shading, perspective, motion, and interactivity, permits the effective extension of projections to three dimensions (see Monette 1990).

When there are relatively few observations, and each is of separate interest, it is possible to display the data by constructing parallel geometric figures for the individual observations. Some feature of the figure represents the value of each variable. One such display, called a "star plot," is shown in Figure 16 for Hartigan's crime rate data. The cities are arranged in order of roughly increasing general crime rates.

Other common and essentially similar schemes include "trees" (the branches of which represent the variables), faces (whose features encode the variables), and small bar graphs (in which each bar displays a variable). None of these graphs is particularly easy to read, but judicious ordering of observations and encoding of variables can sometimes suggest natural clusterings of the data or similarities between observations. Note in Figure 16, for example, that Denver and Los Angeles have roughly similar "patterns" of crime, even though the rates for Los Angeles are generally larger. If similarities among the observations are of central interest, however, then it is perhaps better to address the issue directly by clustering or ordination; see, e.g., Hartigan (1975) and Kruskal and Wish (1978).

THE PRESENT AND FUTURE OF STATISTICAL GRAPHICS

Computers are revolutionizing the practice of statistical graphics much as they earlier revolutionized numerical statistics. Computers relieve the data analyst of the tedium of drawing graphs by hand and make possible displays, such as lowess scatterplot smoothing and kernel density estimation, that were previously unthinkable. All of the graphs appearing in this article—with the exception of several from other sources—were pre-

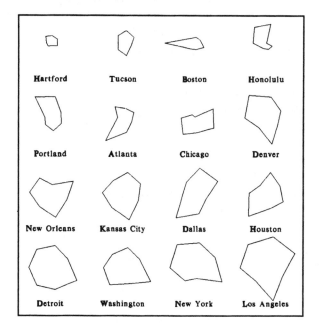

Figure 16

Star plot of rates of seven categories of crime in sixteen U.S. cities. The plot employs polar coordinates to represent each observation: Angles (the "points" of the star) encode variables, while distance from the origin (the center of the star) encodes the value of each variable. The crime rates were each standardized prior to construction of the graph. A key to the points of the star is shown at the bottom of the graph; "Murder" represents both murder and manslaughter. Source of data: Hartigan (1975).

pared with widely available statistical software. Virtually all general statistical computer programs provide facilities for drawing standard graphical forms, and many provide specialized forms as well.

At present, two-dimensional static plots may readily be drawn on relatively inexpensive personal computers. Some programs available for these machines also provide more advanced capabilities such as three-dimensional displays, motion, dynamic labeling of points, and various forms of interactivity. The most advanced software for statistical graphics, previously available only on expensive high-performance workstations, is currently appearing on more modest hardware. Indeed, moderately priced computers are rapidly acquiring the capabilities of graphics workstations.

Although the development of graphical software and hardware is truly impressive, the issue of what to plot in particular data-analytic contexts remains more salient than the technical ability to draw graphs. As many of the simple graphs in this article illustrate, the careful data analyst with minimal computing facilities can make effective use of such basic graphical forms as scatterplots and line graphs.

(SEE ALSO: *Computer Applications to Social Research; Descriptive Statistics; Statistical Methods*)

REFERENCES

Anscombe, Frank J. 1973 "Graphs in Statistical Analysis." *The American Statistician* 27:17–22.

Atkinson, A. C. 1985 *Plots, Transformations, and Regression: An Introduction to Graphical Methods of Diagnostic Regression Analysis.* Oxford: Clarendon Press.

Beninger, James R., and Dorothy L. Robyn 1978 "Quantitative Graphics in Statistics: A Brief History." *The American Statistician* 32:1–11.

Bertin, Jacques 1973 *Semiologie graphique,* 2nd ed. Paris: Mouton.

Chambers, J. M., William S. Cleveland, Beat Kleiner, and Paul A. Tukey 1983 *Graphical Methods for Data Analysis.* Belmont, Calif.: Wadsworth.

Cleveland, William S. 1984 "Graphs in Scientific Publications." *The American Statistician* 38:261–269.

———1985 *The Elements of Graphing Data.* Monterey, Calif.: Wadsworth.

Cleveland, William S., and Robert McGill 1984 "Graphical Perception: Theory, Experimentation, and Application to the Development of Graphical Methods." *Journal of the American Statistical Association* 79:531–554.

Duncan, Otis Dudley 1961 "A Socioeconomic Index for All Occupations." In Albert J. Reiss, Jr., Otis Dudley Duncan, Paul K. Hatt, and Cecil C. North, eds. *Occupations and Social Status.* New York: Free Press.

Fox, John 1990 "Describing Univariate Distributions." In John Fox and J. Scott Long, eds., *Modern Methods of Data Analysis.* Newbury Park, Calif.: Sage.

———forthcoming *Regression Diagnostics.* Newbury Park, Calif.: Sage.

———, and Carole Suschnigg 1989 "A Note on Gender and the Prestige of Occupations." *The Canadian Journal of Sociology* 14:353–360.

Funkhouser, H. Gray 1937 "Historical Development of the Graphical Representation of Statistical Data." *Osiris* 3:267–404.

Hartigan, John A. 1975 *Clustering Algorithms.* New York: Wiley.

Huff, Darrell 1954 *How to Lie with Statistics.* New York: W. W. Norton.

Kruskal, Joseph B., and Myron Wish 1978 *Multidimensional Scaling.* Beverly Hills, Calif.: Sage.

Leinhardt, Samuel, and Stanley S. Wasserman 1979 "Exploratory Data Analysis: An Introduction to Selected Methods." In Karl F. Schuessler, ed., *Sociological Methodology 1979.* San Francisco: Jossey-Bass.

Monette, Georges 1990 "Geometry of Multiple Regression and Interactive 3–D Graphics." In John Fox and J. Scott Long, eds., *Modern Methods of Data Analysis.* Newbury Park, Calif.: Sage.

Ornstein, Michael D. 1976 "The Boards and Executives of the Largest Canadian Corporations: Size, Composition, and Interlocks." *The Canadian Journal of Sociology* 1:411–437.

Schmidt, Calvin F. 1983 *Graphics: Design Principles and Practices.* New York: Wiley.

Spence, Ian, and Stephan Lewandowsky 1990 "Graphical Perception." In John Fox and J. Scott Long, eds., *Modern Methods of Data Analysis.* Newbury Park, Calif.: Sage.

Tufte, Edward R. 1983 *The Visual Display of Quantitative Information.* Cheshire, Conn.: Graphics Press.

Tukey, John W. 1977 *Exploratory Data Analysis.* Reading, Mass.: Addison-Wesley.

JOHN FOX

STATISTICAL INFERENCE

An inference involves drawing a general conclusion from specific observations. People do this every day. Arising in the morning, one observes the sun is shining and infers that the day will be nice. The news reports the arrest of a military veteran for child abuse, and a listener infers that veterans have special adjustment problems. Statistical inference is a way of formalizing the process of drawing general conclusions from limited information. It is a way of stating the degree of confidence one has in an inference using probability theory.

Suppose a sociologist interviews two husbands. Josh, whose wife is employed, does 50 percent of the household chores; Frank, whose wife is not employed, does 10 percent. Should the sociologist infer that husbands do more housework when their wives are employed? No. This difference could happen by chance with only two cases. On the other hand, what if 500 randomly selected husbands with employed wives average 50 percent of the chores and 500 randomly selected husbands with nonemployed wives average 10 percent? Since this difference is not likely to occur by chance, the sociologist infers that husbands do more housework when their wives are employed.

Researchers perform statistical inference in three different ways. Assume that 60 percent of the respondents to a survey say they will vote for Marie Chavez. The *traditional hypothesis testing* approach infers that Chavez will win the election if chance processes would account for the result with less than some a priori specified statistical significance level, for example, if chance could account for the result fewer than five times in a hundred. Statistical significance levels are called the *alpha* (e.g., $\alpha = 0.05$ for the 5 percent level). If Chavez would get 60 percent in a sample of the size selected less than 5 percent of the time by chance, one infers that she will win. The researcher picked the 5 percent level of significance before doing the survey. (The test, including the α level, must be planned *before* looking at the findings.) If one gets this result 6 percent of the time by chance, there is no inference. Note that not making the inference means just that: One does not infer that the opponent will win.

A second strategy involves stating the *likelihood of the results occurring by chance* without an a priori level of significance. This strategy reports the result (60 percent of the sample supported Chavez) and the probability of getting this result by chance, say .042. This gives readers the freedom to make their own inference using whatever level of significance they wish. One person, using the .01 level ($\alpha = .01$) within the traditional approach, would see that the results do not meet this criterion and would not conclude that Chavez will win; another, using the .05 level, would conclude that Chavez will win.

The third strategy places a *confidence interval around a result.* For example, a researcher might be 95 percent confident that Chavez will get between 55 percent and 65 percent of the votes. Since the entire interval, 55 percent to 65 percent, is enough for a victory, that is, greater than 50 percent, one infers that Chavez will win.

Each approach has an element of risk attached to the inference. The risk is the probability of getting the result by chance alone. Sociologists tend to pick low probabilities (e.g., .05, .01, even .001) because they do not want to make a conclusion based on results that are at all likely to have occurred by chance.

TRADITIONAL TESTS OF SIGNIFICANCE

Traditional tests of significance involve six steps. Three examples will be used to illustrate: (1) a candidate will win an election; (2) mothers with at least one daughter will have different views on abortion than mothers with only sons; and (3) the greater a person's internal political efficacy, the more likely the person is to vote.

Step 1: State a hypothesis (*H*) in terms of statistical parameters (characteristics like means, correlations, proportions) of a population:

H1: **P**(vote for the candidate) > .50. [Read: The probability of voting for the candidate is greater than .50.]

H2: μ mothers with daughters $\neq$ μ mothers with sons. [Read: The mean for mothers with daughters is not equal to the mean for mothers with sons.]

H3: $\rho > 0$. [Read: The population correlation, rho, between internal political efficacy and voting is greater than zero.]

H2 says the means are different but does not specify the direction of the difference. This is a two-tail hypothesis, meaning that it can be significant in either direction. In contrast, *H1* and *H3* signify the direction of the difference and are called one-tail hypotheses.

These three hypotheses are not directly testable, because each involves a range of values. *Step 2* states a null hypothesis (which the researcher usually wishes to reject) with a specific value. The null hypotheses are:

H1_0: **P**(vote for the candidate) = .50.

H2_0: μ mothers with daughters = μ mothers with sons.

H3_0: $\rho = 0$.

An important difference between one-tail and two-tail tests may have crossed the reader's mind. Consider $H1_0$. If 40 percent of the sample supported the candidate, one fails to reject $H1_0$ because the result was in the opposite direction of the one-tail hypothesis. In contrast, whether the mothers with daughters have a higher or lower mean attitude toward abortion than mothers with sons, one proceeds to test $H2_0$ because a difference in either direction could be significant.

Step 3 states the a priori level of significance. Sociologists usually use the .05 level. With large samples, they sometimes use the .01 or .001 level. This paper uses the .05 level ($\alpha = .05$). If the result would occur in fewer than 5 percent (corresponding to the .05 level) of the samples if the null hypothesis were true in the population, then the

null hypothesis is rejected in favor of the main hypothesis.

Suppose the sample correlation between internal political efficacy and voting is .56, and this would occur in fewer than 5 percent of the samples this size if the population correlation were 0 (as specified in $H3_0$). One rejects the null hypothesis, $H3_0$, and accepts the main hypothesis, *H3*, that the variables are correlated in the population. What if the sample correlation were .13 and a correlation this large would occur in 25 percent of the samples from a population in which the true correlation were 0? Because 25 percent exceeds the a priori significance level of 5 percent, the null hypothesis is not rejected. One cannot infer that the variables are correlated in the population. Simultaneously, the results do not prove that the population correlation is 0, simply that it could be.

Step 4 selects a test statistic and its critical value. Common test statistics include *z*, *t*, *F*, and χ^2 (chi-square). The *critical value* is the value the test statistic must exceed to be significant at the level specified in step 3. For example, using a one-tail hypothesis, a *z* must exceed 1.645 to be significant at the .05 level. Using a two-tail hypothesis, a *z* must exceed 1.96 to be significant at the .05 level. For *t*, *F*, and χ^2, determining the critical value is more complicated because one needs to know the degrees of freedom. A formal understanding of degrees of freedom is beyond the scope of this paper. An example will give an intuitive idea. If the mean of five cases is 4 and four of the cases have values of 1, 4, 5, and 2, then the last case must have a value of 8 (it is the only value for the fifth case that will give a mean of 4, since $1 + 4 + 5 + 2 + x = 20$ only if $x = 8$, and $20/5 = 4$). Thus, there are $N-1$ degrees of freedom. Most test statistics have different distributions for each number of degrees of freedom.

Figure 1 illustrates a *z* distribution. Under the *z* distribution, an absolute value greater than 1.96 will occur only 5 percent of the time by chance. By chance, a $z > 1.96$ occurs 2.5 percent of the time and a $z < -1.96$ occurs 2.5 percent of the time. Thus, 1.96 is the critical *z*-score for a two-tail .05-level test.

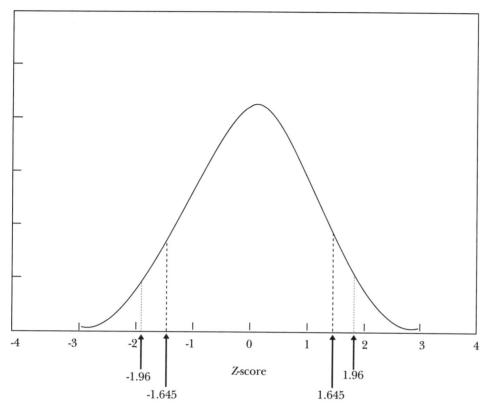

Figure 1
Normal deviate (z) distribution.

Step 5 computes the test statistic. An example appears below.

Step 6 decides whether to reject or fail to reject the null hypothesis. If the computed test statistic exceeds the critical value, then one rejects the null hypothesis and makes the inference to accept the main hypothesis. If the computed test statistic does not exceed the critical value, then one fails to reject the null hypothesis and makes no inference.

Example of Six Steps Applied to *H1*. A random sample of 200 voters finds 60 percent of them supporting the candidate. Having stated the main hypothesis (step 1) and the null hypothesis (step 2), step 3 selects an a priori significance level at $\alpha = .05$, since it is the conventional level. Step 4 selects the test statistic and its critical level. To test a single percentage, a z test is used (standard textbooks on social statistics discuss how to select the appropriate test statistics; see Blalock 1979),

and since the hypothesis is one-tail, the critical value is 1.645 (see Figure 1).

The fifth step computes the formula for the test statistic, here:

$$z = (P_s - P)/\sqrt{(PQ/N)},$$

where P_s is the proportion in the sample,

P is the proportion in the population under H_o,

Q is $1 - P$, and

N is the number of people in the sample.

$$z = (.6 - .5) / \sqrt{[(.5 \times .5)/200]}$$

$$z = 2.828$$

The sixth step makes the decision to reject the null hypothesis, since the difference is in the predicted direction and $2.828 > 1.645$. The statistical inference is that the candidate will win the election.

REPORTING THE PROBABILITY LEVEL

Many sociological researchers do not use the traditional null-hypothesis model. Instead, they report the probability of the result. This way, a reader knows the probability (say, .042 or .058) rather than the significant–not significant dichotomy. Reporting the probability level removes the "magic of the level of significance." A result that is significant at the .058 level is not categorically different from one that is significant at the .042 level. Where the traditional null-hypothesis approach says the first of these results is not significant and the second is, reporting the probability tells the reader that there is only a small difference in degree of confidence attached to the two results. Critics of this strategy argue that the reader may adjust the significance level post hoc, that is, raise or lower the level of significance after seeing the results. It is also argued that it is the researcher, not the reader, who is the person testing the hypothesis; therefore, the researcher is responsible for selecting an a priori level of significance.

The strategy of reporting the probability is illustrated for *H1*. Using tabled values, the one-tail probability of a $z = 2.828$ is .002. The researcher reports that the candidate had 60 percent of the vote in the sample and the probability of getting this much support by chance is .002. This gives us more information than simply saying it is significant at the .05 level. Results that could happen only twice in 1,000 times by chance (.002) are more compelling than results that could happen five times in 100 (.05).

Since journal editors want to keep papers short and many studies include many tests of significance, reporting probabilities is far more efficient than going through the six-step process outlined above. The research must go through these steps, but the paper merely reports the probability for each test and places an asterisk along those that are significant at the .05 level. Some researchers place one asterisk for those significant at the .05 level, two for those significant at the .01 level, and three for those significant at the .001 level.

CONFIDENCE INTERVALS

Rather than reporting the significance of a result, this approach puts a confidence interval around the result. This provides additional information in terms of the width of the confidence interval.

Using a confidence interval, the researcher constructs a range of values such that he or she is 95 percent confident (some use 99 percent confidence intervals) that the range contains the population parameter. The confidence interval uses a two-tail approach, on the assumption that the population value can be either above or below the sample value.

For the election example, *H1,* the confidence interval is:

$$P_s \pm z_{\alpha/2} \sqrt{(PQ/N)}$$
$$= .6 \pm 1.96 \sqrt{[(.5 \times .5)/200]}$$
$$= .6 \pm 1.96 \times .03535$$
$$= .6 \pm .0693$$

The upper and lower limits are expressed as:

upper limit .669
lower limit .531

The researcher is 95 percent confident that the interval, .531 to .669, contains the true population proportion. The focus is on the confidence level (.95) for a result rather than the low likelihood of the null hypothesis (.05) used in the traditional null-hypothesis testing approach.

The confidence interval has more information value than the first two approaches. Since the value specified in the null hypothesis (H_0: $\mathbf{P} = .50$) is not in the confidence interval, the result is statistically significant at the .05 level. Note that a 95 percent confidence level corresponds to a .05 significance level and a 99 percent confidence interval corresponds to a .01 level of significance. Whenever the value specified by the null hypothesis is not in the confidence interval, the result is statistically significant. More important, the confidence interval gives an estimate of the range of possible values for the population. With a sample of 200 cases and results of 60 percent support, there is confidence the candidate will win, but it might be a close election (with the lower limit indicating 53.1 percent of the vote), or a landslide (with the upper limit indicating 66.9 percent of the vote). If the sample were four times as large ($N = 800$), the confidence interval would be half as wide (.565–.635) and give a better fix on the outcome.

COMPUTATION OF TESTS AND CONFIDENCE INTERVALS.

Table 1 presents formulas for some common tests of significance and their corresponding confidence intervals, where appropriate. These are only a sample of the tests that are commonly used, but do cover means, differences of means, proportions, differences of proportions, contingency tables, and correlations. Not included are a variety of multivariate tests for analysis of variance, regression, path analysis, and structural equations. The formulas shown in Table 1 are elaborated in most standard statistics textbooks (Blalock 1979; Bohrnstedt and Knoke 1988; Hays 1988; Tukey 1977).

LOGIC OF STATISTICAL INFERENCE

A formal treatment of the logic behind statistical inference is beyond the scope of this paper; the following is a simplified understanding. Suppose one wants to know whether a telephone survey can be thought of as a random sample. From current census information, suppose the mean (μ) income of the community is $30,100 and the standard deviation (σ) is $10,600. A graph of the complete census enumeration appears in Panel A of Figure 2. The fact that there are only a few people who are quite wealthy skews the distribution.

A telephone survey included interviews with 1,000 households. If random, its sample mean and standard deviations should be close to the population parameters, μ and σ, respectively. Assume the sample has a mean of $31,800 and a standard deviation of $12,000. To distinguish these sample statistics from the population parameters, call them $\overline{X}$ and s. The sample distribution

appears in Panel B in Figure 2. Notice it is similar to the population distribution but not as smooth. The sample has a higher concentration of people making between $50,000 and $100,000, and nobody making over $200,000.

One cannot decide whether the sample could be random by looking at Panels A and B. They are different, but this difference might have occurred by chance. Statistical inference is accomplished by introducing two theoretical distributions. These are the sampling distribution of the mean and the z distribution of the normal deviate. A theoretical distribution is different from either the population or sample distributions in that a theoretical distribution is mathematically derived. A theoretical distribution is not observed directly.

Sampling Distribution of the Mean. Suppose instead of taking a single random sample of 1,000 people, one took two such samples and determined the mean of each. With 1,000 cases it is likely that the two samples would have means that were close together but not the same. For instance, the mean of the second sample might be $30,200. These means, $31,800 and $30,200, are pretty close together. For a sample to have a mean of, say $11,000, it would have to get a greatly disproportionate share of poor families—not likely by chance with a random sample $N = 1,000$. For a sample to have a mean of, say, $115,000 would require getting a greatly disproportionate share of rich families. In contrast, with a sample of just two individuals, one would not be surprised if the first person had an income of $11,000 and the second an income of $115,000.

The larger the samples, the more stable the mean from one sample to the next. With only 20 people in the first and second samples the means may vary a lot, but with 100,000 people in both samples the means should be almost the same. Mathematically, it is possible to derive a distribution of the mean of all possible samples, even though only a single sample is observed. It can be shown that the mean of the sampling distribution of the mean is the population mean, and standard deviation of the sampling distribution of the mean is the population standard deviation divided by the square root of the sample size. The standard deviation of the mean is called the *standard error of the mean*:

standard error of the mean (S.E.M.) $= \sigma_{\bar{x}} = \sigma/\sqrt{N}$

This is an important derivation in statistical theory. Panel C shows the sampling distribution of the mean where the sample size is $N = 1,000$. It also shows the sampling distribution of the mean for $N = 100$. A remarkable property of the sampling distribution of the mean is that it will be normally distributed even though the population and sample distributions are skewed.

TABLE 1. Common Tests of Significance Formulas

What Is Being Tested	H_1	H_0	Test Statistic	Large-Sample Confidence Interval
Single mean against value specified as x in H_0	1-tail: $\mu > x$ 2-tail: $\mu \neq x$	$\mu = x$	t with $N - 1$ degrees of freedom: $t = (\bar{X} - x)/(s/\sqrt{N})$	$\bar{X} \pm t_{\alpha/2}\, \sigma/\sqrt{N}$
Single proportion against value specified as x in H_0	1-tail: $P > x$ 2-tail: $P \neq x$	$P = x$	$z = (P_s - x)/\sqrt{(PQ/N)}$	$P_s \pm z_{\alpha/2}\sqrt{(PQ/N)}$
Difference between two means	1-tail: $\mu_1 > \mu_2$ 2-tail: $\mu_1 \neq \mu_2$	$\mu_1 = \mu_2$	t with $N_1 + N_2 - 2$ degrees of freedom; $t = \dfrac{(\bar{X}_1 - \bar{X}_2)}{\sqrt{s^2(1/N_1 + 1/N_2)}}$, where $s^2 = \dfrac{(N_1-1)s_1^2 + (N_2-1)s_2^2}{N_1 + N_2 - 2}$	$\bar{X}_1 - \bar{X}_2 \pm t_{\alpha/2}\sigma_{\bar{X}_1 - \bar{X}_2}$ where $\sigma_{\bar{X}_1 - \bar{X}_2}$ is defined as the numerator of t-test in the cell to the immediate left
Difference between two proportions	1-tail: $P_1 > P_2$ 2-tail: $P_1 \neq P_2$	$P_1 = P_2$	$z = \dfrac{Ps_1 - Ps_2}{\sqrt{PQ}\sqrt{[(N_1 + N_2)/N_1 N_2]}}$	$Ps_1 - Ps_2 \pm z_{\alpha/2}\sigma_{Ps_1 - Ps_2}$ where $\sigma_{Ps_1 - Ps_2}$ is defined as the numerator of z-test in cell to the immediate left
Significance of contingency table	The level on one variable depends on the level on the second variable	No dependency between variables	$\chi^2 = \Sigma(Fo - Fe)^2/Fe$	Not applicable
Single correlation against value specified as x in H_0, (x is usually zero)	1-tail: $\rho > 0$ 2-tail: $\rho \neq 0$	$\rho = 0$	F with 1 and $N - 2$ degrees of freedom: $F = [r^2(N - 2)]/(1 - r^2)$	Complex, since it is not symmetrical

Definitions of symbols in Table 1:

$\mu, \bar{X}$ population mean, sample mean

σ, s population standard deviation, sample standard deviation

P, Ps, Q population proportion, sample proportion, $1 - P$

ρ, r population correlation, sample correlation

X^2 chi-square

N size of sample

Fo, Fe frequency observed in a table cell, frequency expected in cell computed as $R(C)/N$, where R is total for the row the cell is in, C is total for the column the cell is in, and N is total for entire table

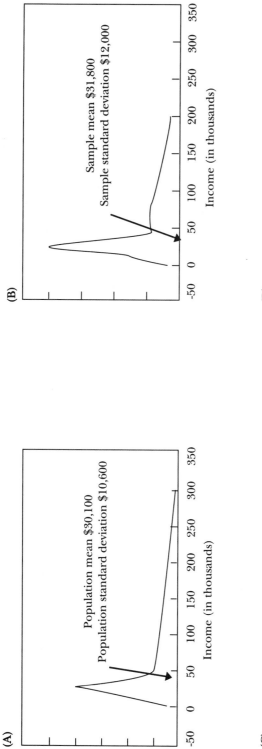

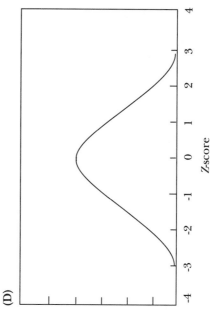

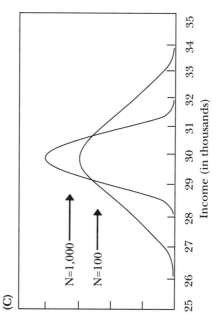

Figure 2.
Four distributions used in making a statistical inference: (A) population distribution; (B) sample distribution; (C) sampling distribution of the mean for N = 100 and N = 1,000; (D) normal deviate (z) distribution.

One gets a general idea of how the sample did by seeing where the sample mean falls along the sampling distribution of the mean. Using Panel C for $N = 1,000$, the sample $\bar{X} = \$31,800$ is a long way from the population mean. Very few samples with $N = 1,000$ would have means this far from the population mean. Thus, one infers that the sample mean is not likely random. Using the distribution in Panel C for $N = 100$, the sample $\bar{X} = \$31,800$ is not so unusual. With 100 cases one should not be surprised to get a sample mean this far from the population mean.

Being able to compare the sample mean with the population mean using the sampling distribution is remarkable, but statistical theory allows more precision. One can transform the values in the sampling distribution of the mean to a distribution of a test statistic. The appropriate test statistic is the distribution of the normal deviate, or z distribution. It can be shown that

$$z = (\bar{X} - \mu)/(\sigma/\sqrt{N})$$

If the z value were computed for the mean of all possible samples taken at random from the population, it would be distributed as shown in Panel D of Figure 2. It would be normal, have a mean of 0, and a variance of 1.

Where is $\bar{X} = \$31,800$ under the distribution of the normal deviate? Its z-score using the above formula is:

$$z = (31,800 - 30,100)/(10,500/\sqrt{1,000})$$

$$z = 5.072$$

Using tabled values for the normal deviate, the probability of a random sample of 1,000 cases from a population with a mean of $30,100 having a sample mean of $31,800 is less than .001. Thus, it is extremely unlikely that the sample is purely random.

With the same sample mean, but with a sample of only 100 people,

$$z^* = (31,800 - 30,100)/(10,500/\sqrt{100})$$

$$z^* = 1.619$$

Using tabled values for a two-tail test, the probability of getting the sample mean this far from the population mean with a sample of 100 people is .105. One should not infer that the sample is not random if the results could happen 10.5 percent of the time by chance.

The four distributions can be described for any sample statistic one wants to test (means, differences of means, proportions, differences of proportions, correlations, etc.). While many of them will be more complex, their logic is identical.

POWER AND TYPE I AND TYPE II ERRORS

To this point only one type of probability has been considered. Sociologists use statistical inference to minimize the chance of accepting a main hypothesis that is false. They reject the null hypothesis only if the chances of it being true in the population are very small, say $\alpha = .05$. Still, by minimizing the chances of this error, sociologists increase the chance of failing to reject the null hypothesis when it should be rejected. Table 2 illustrates these two types of error.

Type I or α error is the probability of rejecting H_0 falsely—that is, the error of deciding H_1 (the main hypothesis) is right when H_0 is true in the population. If one were testing whether a new program reduced drug abuse among pregnant women, the H_1 would be that the program did this and the H_0 would be that the program was no better than the existing one. Type I error should be minimized, because it would be wrong to change programs when the new program is no better than the existing one. Type I error has been described as "the chances of discovering things that aren't so" (Cohen 1990, p. 1304). The focus on Type I error reflects a conservative view among scientists.

Type II or β error is the probability of failing to reject H_0 when H_1 is true in the population. If one fails to reject the null hypothesis that the new program was no better (H_0) when the new program was truly better (H_1), one would put newborn children at needless risk.

Power is $1 - \beta$. It measures the chances of rejecting the null hypothesis when the alternative hypothesis is true. Thus, if there is a real effect in

TABLE 2. Type I (α) and Type II (β) Errors

Decision Made by the Researcher	True Situation in the Population	
	H_0, the null hypothesis, is true	H_1, the main hypothesis, is true
H_0, the null hypothesis, is true	$1 - \alpha$	β
H_1, the main hypothesis, is true	α	$1 - \beta$

the population, a study that has a power of .80 can reject the null hypothesis with a likelihood of .80. Power can be increased. First, get a larger sample. The larger the sample, the more power to find results that exist in the population. Second, increase the α level. Rather than using the .01 level of significance, a researcher can pick the .05, or even the .10. The larger α, the more powerful the test in its ability to reject the null hypothesis when the alternative is true.

There are problems with both approaches. Increasing sample size makes the study more costly. If there are risks to subjects who participate, then adding cases exposes additional people to this risk. An example of this would be a study that exposed subjects to a new drug-treatment program that might create more problems than it solves.

Since Type 1 and Type 2 errors are inversely related, raising α reduces β, thereby increasing the power of the test. However, sociologists are hesitant to raise α, since doing so increases the chance of deciding something is important when it is not. With a small sample, using a small α level such as .001 means there is a great risk of a β error. Many small-scale studies have a Type II error of over .50. This is common in research areas that rely on small samples. For example, a review of one volume of the *Journal of Abnormal Psychology* (a journal that includes many small-sample studies) found that studies had an average Type II error of .56 (Cohen 1990). This means the psychologists had inadequate power to reject the

null hypothesis when H_1 was true. When H_1 was true, the chance of rejecting H_0 (i.e., power) was worse than flipping a coin.

When small samples are necessary because of the cost of gathering data or to minimize the potential risk to subjects, researchers must plan their sample size to balance α, power, sample size, and the minimum size of effect that is theoretically important. For example, if a correlation of .1 is substantively significant, a power of .80 is important, and an $\alpha = .01$ is desired, then a very large sample is required. If a correlation is substantively and theoretically important only if it is over .5, then a much smaller sample is adequate. Procedures for doing a power analysis are available in a book by Cohen (1988).

Power analysis is less important for many sociological studies that have large samples. With a large sample it is possible to use a conservative α error rate and still have sufficient power to reject the null hypothesis when H_1 is true. As a result, sociologists pay less attention to β error and power than researchers in other fields, such as medicine and psychology. When a sociologist has a sample of 10,000 cases, the power is over .90 that he or she will detect a very small effect as statistically significant. When tests are extremely powerful to detect small effects, researchers must focus on the substantive significance of the effects. A correlation of .07 may be significant at the .05 level with 10,000 cases, but a power analysis can show that the correlation is also substantively trivial.

MULTIPLE TESTS OF SIGNIFICANCE

The logic of statistical inference applies to testing a single hypothesis. Since most studies include multiple tests, interpreting results can become extremely complex. If a researcher conducts 100 tests, 5 of them should yield results that are statistically significant at the .05 level by chance. Thus, a study that includes many tests may find some "interesting" results that appear statistically significant as an artifact of the number of tests conducted.

Sociologists pay less attention to "adjusting the error rate" than researchers in most other scientific fields. One conservative approach is to divide the Type 1 error by the number of tests conducted. This is known as the Dunn multiple comparison test, based on the Bonferroni inequality. For example, instead of nine tests being done at the .05 level, each test is done at the $.05/9 = .006$ level. To be viewed as statistically significant at the .05 level, each specific test must be significant at the .006 level.

There are many specialized multiple-comparison procedures, depending on whether the tests are planned before the study starts or after the results are known. Brown and Melamed (1990) provide a useful introduction to these procedures.

NONRANDOM SAMPLES AND STATISTICAL INFERENCE

Very few researchers use true random samples. Sometimes researchers use convenience sampling, for example, a social psychologist who has every student in a class participate in an experiment. Students in this class are not a random sample of the general population or even of students in the university. Should statistical inference be used here? Other researchers may use the entire population. If one wants to know whether male faculty are paid more than female faculty at a particular university, one may check the payroll for every faculty member. There is no sample—one has the entire population. What about statistical inference in this instance?

Many researchers would use a test of significance in both examples, even though the formal logic is violated. They are taking a "what if" approach. If the results they find could have occurred in a random process, then they are less confident in their results than if the results would have been statistically significant. Economists and demographers often report statistical-inference results when they have the entire population. For example, if one examines the unemployment rate of blacks and whites over a ten-year period, one may find that the black rate is about twice that of the white rate. If one does a test of significance, it is unclear what the population is to which one wants to generalize. A ten-year period is not a random selection of all years. The rationale for doing statistical inference with population data and nonprobability samples is to see whether the results could have been attributed to a chance process.

STATISTICAL AND SUBSTANTIVE SIGNIFICANCE

Some researchers and many readers confuse statistical significance with substantive significance. Statistical inference does not ensure the substantive significance, that is, importance, of a result. A correlation of .1 shows a weak relationship between two variables. With a sample of 100 cases this correlation will not be statistically significant; with 10,000 cases it will be. The smaller sample shows a weak relationship that might be a zero relationship in the population. The larger sample shows a weak relationship that is almost certainly also a weak relationship in the population. In this case the statistical significance allows one to be confident that the relationship in the population is weak.

Whenever one reads that a result is statistically significant, he or she is confident that there is some relationship. The next step is to decide whether it is substantively significant or substantively weak.

(SEE ALSO: *Correlation and Regression Analysis; Descriptive Statistics; Nonparametric Statistics; Probability Theory; Scientific Explanation; Statistical Methods*)

REFERENCES

Blalock, Hubert M., Jr. 1979 *Social Statistics.* New York: McGraw-Hill.

Bohrnstedt, George W., and David Knoke 1988 *Statistics for Social Data Analysis,* 2nd ed. Itasca, Ill.: F. E. Peacock.

Brown, Steven R., and Lawrence E. Melamed 1990 *Experimental Design and Analysis.* Newbury Park, Calif.: Sage.

Cohen, Jacob 1988 *Statistical Power Analysis for the Behavioral Sciences,* 2nd ed. Hillsdale, N.J.: Erlbaum.

———1990 "Things I Have Learned (So Far)." *American Psychologist* 45:1304–1312.

Hays, William L. 1988 *Statistics,* 4th ed. New York: Holt, Rinehart, and Winston.

Tukey, John W. 1977 *Exploratory Data Analysis.* Reading, Mass.: Addison-Wesley.

ALAN C. ACOCK

STATISTICAL METHODS During the 1960s quantitative sociological research was transformed by the introduction, acceptance, and application of a variety of multivariate statistical methods. Regression methods from biometrics and economics; factor analysis from psychology; stochastic modeling from engineering, biometrics, and statistics; and methods for contingency table analysis from sociology and statistics were developed and combined to provide the rich variety of statistical methods available today. Along with the introduction of these techniques came the institutionalization of quantitative methods. In 1961 the American Sociological Association (ASA) approved a section on methodology as the result of efforts organized by Robert McGinnis and Albert Reiss. The ASA's yearbook *Sociological Methodology* first appeared in 1969 under the editorship of Edgar F. Borgatta and George W. Bohrnstedt. Borgatta and Bohrnstedt went on to establish the quarterly journal *Sociological Methods and Research* in 1972. During this period the National Institute of Mental Health began funding training programs that included rigorous training in quantitative methods.

This article traces the development of statistical methods in sociology from 1960 to the present.

Regression, factor analysis, stochastic modeling, and contingency table analysis are discussed as the most important methods that were available or introduced by the early 1960s. The development of additional methods through the enhancement and combination of these methods is then considered. Our discussion emphasizes statistical methods for causal modeling. Consequently, methods for data reduction (e.g., cluster analysis, smallest-space analysis, and multidimensional scaling), formal modeling, simulation, and network analysis are excluded from consideration.

THE BROADER CONTEXT

By the end of the 1950s the central ideas of mathematical statistics that emerged from the work of R. A. Fisher and Karl Pearson were firmly established. Works such as Fisher's *Statistical Methods for Research Workers* and *The Design of Experiments* (1925, 1935), Maurice G. Kendall's *Advanced Theory of Statistics* (1943, 1946), Harold Cramér's *Mathematical Methods of Statistics* (1946), S. S. Wilks's *Mathematical Statistics* (1944), E. L. Lehman's *Testing Statistical Hypotheses* (1959), H. Scheffé's *The Analysis of Variance* (1959), and J. L. Doob's *Stochastic Processes* (1953) systematized key results of mathematical statistics and provided the foundations for developments in applied statistics for decades to come. By the start of the 1960s multivariate methods were applied routinely in psychology, economics, and the biological sciences. Applied treatments were available in such works as George W. Snedecor's *Statistical Methods* (1937), Hermon Wold's *Demand Analysis* (Wold and Juréen 1953), T. W. Anderson's *An Introduction to Multivariate Statistical Analysis* (1958), Herbert Simon's *Models of Man* (1957), L. L. Thurstone's *Multiple-Factor Analysis* (1947), and D. J. Finney's *Probit Analysis* (1952).

These types of statistical analyses are computationally intensive. Their routine application depended on developments in computer hardware and software. BMD (for Biomedical Computing Programs) was perhaps the first widely available statistical package, appearing in 1961 (Dixon et al. 1981). SPSS (for Statistical Package for the Social

Sciences) appeared in 1970 as the result of efforts by a group of political scientists at Stanford to develop a general statistical package specifically for social scientists (Nie et al. 1975). In addition to these general-purpose programs, specialized programs appeared that were essential for the methods discussed below. At the same time, dramatic advances in computer hardware decreased the cost and increased the availability of computing by orders of magnitude. These advances in hardware and software were essential for the development, acceptance, and application of the methods described below.

DEVELOPMENTS IN SOCIOLOGY

It is within the context of developments in mathematical statistics, sophisticated applications in other fields, and rapid advances in computing that major changes occurred in quantitative sociological research. Four major methods serve as the cornerstones for later developments: regression analysis, factor analysis, stochastic processes, and contingency table analysis.

Regression Analysis and Structural Equation Models. Regression analysis estimates the effects of a set of independent variables on one or more dependent variables. It is arguably the most commonly applied statistical method in the social sciences. Prior to 1960 the method was relatively unknown to sociologists. It was not treated in standard texts, and was rarely if ever seen in the leading sociological journals. The key notions of multiple regression were introduced to sociologists in Herbert M. Blalock, Jr.'s highly influential *Social Statistics* (1960). Applications of regression, facilitated by computational advances, began appearing regularly. The generalization of regression to systems of equations and the accompanying notion of causal analysis occurred with Blalock's landmark *Causal Inferences in Nonexperimental Research* (1964) and Otis Dudley Duncan's "Path Analysis: Sociological Examples" (1966). Blalock's work was heavily influenced by economist Herbert Simon's work on correlation and causality (Simon 1957) and economist Hermon

Wold's work on simultaneous equation systems (Wold and Juréen 1953). Duncan's work added the influence of geneticist Sewall Wright's work in path analysis (Wright 1934). The acceptance of these methods by sociologists required a substantive application that demonstrated how regression could contribute to our understanding of fundamental sociological questions. In this case, the question was the determination of occupational standing, and the specific work was the substantively and methodologically influential *The American Occupational Structure* by Peter M. Blau and Otis Dudley Duncan (1967), a work that remains unsurpassed in its integration of method and substance. Numerous applications of regression and path analysis soon followed. The diversity of influences, problems, and approaches that resulted from Blalock and Duncan's work is shown in Blalock's reader *Causal Models in the Social Sciences* (1971), which became the methodological handbook of the 1970s.

The regression model has been extended in many ways. Developments involving systems of equations have been reviewed by Bielby and Hauser (1977). Regression methods for time series analysis and forecasting (often called Box-Jenkins models) were given their classic treatment in George E. P. Box and Gwilym M. Jenkins's *Time Series Analysis* (1970). Regression diagnostics have provided tools for exploring characteristics of the data set to be analyzed. Methods for identifying outlying and influential observations have been developed (Belsley et al. 1980). Major advances have been made to deal with classic problems such as heteroscedasticity (White 1980) and specification (Hausman 1978). Developments in theory and computation have made nonlinear, computationally intensive models possible (Gallant 1987). All of these extensions are gradually finding their way into sociological practice.

Factor Analysis. Factor analysis, a technique developed by psychometricians, provides the second major influence on quantitative sociological methods. Factor analysis is based on the idea that the covariation among a larger set of observed variables can be reduced to covariation among a smaller set of unobserved or latent variables. Rather than modeling a causal process, factor analysis reduces the data from a larger number of observed variables to a smaller number of unobserved variables. By 1960 this method was well known, and applications were found in most major journals. Statistical and computational advances made in applying maximum likelihood estimation to the factor model (Jöreskog 1969) were extremely important for the development of the covariance structure model discussed below.

Stochastic Processes. Stochastic processes are the third influence affecting the development of quantitative sociological methods. Stochastic processes model the change in a variable over time, where the change is governed by some chance process. Examples of stochastic processes include change in occupational status over the career (Blumen et al. 1955), friendship patterns, preference for job locations (Coleman 1964), and the distribution of racial disturbances (Spilerman 1971). Although the mathematical and statistical details for many stochastic models had been worked out by 1960, they were relatively unknown to sociologists until the publication of James S. Coleman's *Introduction to Mathematical Sociology* (1964) and D. J. Bartholomew's *Stochastic Models for Social Processes* (1967). Both books presented a large number of models that were customized for dealing with specific social phenomena. While these models had great potential for application, substantive applications were rare. In large part this was due to the greater mathematical sophistication required to apply the models, and the lack of general-purpose software for estimating the models. Nonetheless, the influence of these methods on the development of other techniques was great. For example, Markov chain models for social mobility had important influences on the development of loglinear models.

Contingency Table Analysis and Loglinear Models. Methods for categorical data represent the fourth influence on quantitative methods. The analysis of contingency tables has a long tradition in sociology. Paul F. Lazarsfeld's work on elaboration analysis and panel analysis had a major influ-

ence on the way research was done at the start of the 1960s (Lazarsfeld and Rosenberg 1955). While these methods provided useful tools for analyzing categorical data, and especially survey data, they were nonstatistical in the sense that issues of estimation and hypothesis testing were largely ignored. Important statistical advances for measures of association in two-way tables were made in a series of papers by Leo A. Goodman and William H. Kruskal that appeared during the 1950s and 1960s (Goodman and Kruskal 1979). During the 1960s nonstatistical methods for analyzing contingency tables were replaced by the loglinear model. This model made the statistical analysis of multiway tables possible. Early developments are found in papers by M. W. Birch (1963) and Leo A. Goodman (1964). The development of the general model was largely completed through the efforts of Frederick Mosteller, Stephen E. Fienberg, Yvonne M. M. Bishop, Shelby Haberman, and Leo A. Goodman summarized in Bishop, Fienberg, and Holland's landmark *Discrete Multivariate Analysis* (1975). Applications in sociology appeared shortly after Goodman's (1972) didactic presentation and the availability of ECTA (Fay and Goodman 1974), a program for loglinear analysis. Since then the model has been extended in various ways to reflect both specific types of variables (e.g., ordinal), more complex structures (e.g., association models), and particular substantive problems (e.g., networks). See Agresti (1990) for a thorough treatment of recent developments.

As with regression models, many early applications appeared in the area of stratification research. Indeed, many developments in loglinear analysis were motivated by substantive problems encountered in sociology and related fields.

ADDITIONAL METHODS

From these roots in regression, factor analysis, stochastic processes, and contingency table analysis, a wide variety of methods emerged that are now commonly applied by sociologists. Notions from the various areas were combined and extended to produce new methods. The remainder of this article considers the major methods that resulted.

Covariance Structure Models. The covariance structure model is a combination of the factor and regression models. Its development was motivated by the types of models that sociologists began developing in the 1960s. While the factor model allowed imperfect, multiple indicators to be used to extract a more accurately measured latent variable, it did not allow the modeling of causal relations among the factors. The regression model, conversely, did not allow imperfect measurement and multiple indicators. The covariance structure model resulted from the merger of the structural or causal component of the regression model with the measurement component of the factor model. With this model it is possible to specify that each latent variable has one or more imperfectly measured observed indicators and that a causal relationship exists among these factors. Applications of such a model became practical with computational breakthroughs by Karl G. Jöreskog, who published LISREL (for *li*near *s*tructural *rel*ations) in 1972 (Jöreskog and van Thillo 1972). The importance of this program is reflected in the use of the phrase "LISREL models" to refer to this area. Since 1973 the covariance structure model has been extended in many ways to deal with multiple groups, noninterval observed variables, and estimation with less restrictive assumptions. See Bollen (1989) for a complete discussion of these and other extensions.

Event History Analysis. Many sociological problems deal with the occurrence of an event. For example, does a divorce occur? Or when is one job given up for another? In such problems the variable to be explained is the time that the event occurred. While it is possible to analyze such data with regression, regression is flawed in two basic respects. First, event data can be censored—that is, for some members of the sample the event being predicted may not have occurred, and consequently a specific time for the event is missing. If we assume that the censored time is a large number to reflect that the event has not occurred, this will misrepresent those cases in which the event occurred shortly after the end of the study. If we assign a number equal to the time when the data collection ends or exclude those for whom the event has not occurred, the time of the event will be underestimated. Standard regression does not adequately deal with censoring problems. Second, the regression model often assumes that the errors in predicting the outcome are normally distributed around the prediction. In many cases a normal distribution is unrealistic for event data. Statistical methods for dealing with these problems began appearing in the 1950s and were introduced to sociologists in substantive papers examining social mobility (Spilerman 1972; Sorensen 1975; Tuma 1976). Applications of these methods were encouraged by the publication in 1976 of Nancy Tuma's program RATE for event history analysis (Tuma and Crockford, 1976). Since then, event history analysis has become a major form of analysis and an area in which sociologists have made substantial contributions to the statistical literature and have motivated developments in such fields as econometrics and statistics. For a review of this area see Tuma and Hannan 1984.

Limited and Qualitative Dependent Variables. If the dependent variable is nominal, ordinal, or censored, the usual assumptions of the regression model are violated and estimates are biased. Some of these cases are handled by the methods discussed above. Event history analysis deals with certain types of censored variables; loglinear analysis deals with nominal and ordinal variables. Many other cases require additional methods. These methods are called quantal response models, or models for limited or qualitative dependent variables. Since the types of dependent variables analyzed by these methods occur frequently in the social sciences, they receive a great deal of attention by econometricians and sociologists. See Maddala (1983) for an extensive review of these models.

Perhaps the simplest of these methods is logit analysis, in which the dependent variable is nominal with a combination of interval and nominal independent variables. Logit analysis was introduced to sociologists by H. Theil (1970) and is now routinely applied in substantive work. Probit analysis is a related technique and is based on slightly different assumptions. Extensions to the case where the dependent variable is ordinal were made by McKelvey and Zavonia (1975); extensions for multiple equation systems are reviewed by Winship and Mare (1983). A particularly important type of limited-dependent variable occurs when the sample is nonrandomly selected. For example, in panel studies cases that do not respond to each wave may be dropped from the analysis. If those who do not respond to each wave differ nonrandomly from those who do respond (e.g., those who are lost due to moving may differ from those who do not move), the resulting sample will not be representative. Or, to use an example from a review article by Berk (1983), in cases of domestic violence police may write a report only if the violence exceeds some minimum level. The resulting sample is biased to exclude cases with lower levels of violence. Regression estimates based on this sample will be biased. The development of the sample selection model has been stimulated by an influential paper by Heckman (1979) and has been introduced to sociologists by Berk (1983; Berk and Ray 1982). These and many other models for limited dependent variables are extremely well suited to sociological problems. As software becomes more readily available, their use should become increasingly common.

Latent Structure Analysis. The objective of latent structure analysis is the same as that of factor analysis—to explain covariation among a larger number of observed variables in terms of a smaller number of latent variables. The difference is that factor analysis applies to interval level observed and latent variables, whereas latent structure analysis applies to observed data that is nominal. As part of the American soldier study, Paul F. Lazarsfeld, Sam Stouffer, Louis Guttman, and others began developing techniques for "factor analyzing" nominal data. Although many methods were developed, latent structure analysis has emerged as the most popular. Lazarsfeld coined the term *latent structure analysis* to refer to techniques for extracting latent variables from observed variables obtained from survey research. The specific techniques depend on the characteristics of the observed and latent variables. If both are continuous, the method is called factor analysis, discussed above. If both are discrete, the method is called latent class analysis. If the factors are continuous but the observed data are discrete, we have latent trait analysis. If the factors are discrete but the data are continuous, the method is latent profile analysis. The classic presentation of these methods is found in Lazarsfeld and Henry's *Latent Structure Analysis* (1968). As important as these developments were, and as clearly sociological in their methodological concerns, the ideas saw few applications during the next twenty years. While the programs ECTA, RATE, and LISREL stimulated applications of the loglinear, event history, and covariance structure models, the lack of software for latent structure analysis inhibited its use. This changed as a result of work by Goodman (1974) on algorithms for estimation and Clogg's (1977) MLLSA program for estimating the models. Substantive applications began appearing in the 1980s, and the entire area of latent structure analysis has become a major focus of statistical work.

Other Developments. The methods discussed above represent the major developments in statistical methods in sociology since the 1960s. With the rapid development of mathematical statistics and advances in computing, new methods are constantly appearing. Major advances are being made in the treatment of missing data (Little and Rubin 1987). Developments in statistical graphics (Cleveland 1985) are reflected in the increasing number of graphics appearing in sociological journals. Methods that require less restrictive distributional assumptions and that are less sensitive to errors in the data being analyzed are now computationally feasible. Robust methods are being developed that are insensitive to small departures from the underlying assumptions (Rousseeuw and Leroy 1987). Resampling methods (e.g., bootstrap methods) allow estimation of standard errors and confidence intervals when the underlying distributional assumptions (e.g., normality) are unrealistic or the formulas for computing standard errors are intractable by letting the observed data assume the role of the underlying population (Stine 1990). Recent work by Bengt Muthén and others combines the structural components of the regression model, latent variables from both the factor and latent structure models, and characteristics of limited variables into a single model. Application of this promising set of models is dependent on the software to estimate it. Consequently these models are sometimes called the LISCOMP model (for *li*near *s*tructural relations with a *comp*rehensive measurement model), after the software developed by Muthén (1988). Additional methods, too numerous to describe here, are appearing with each issue of the journals in this area.

CONCLUSIONS

There has been an explosive development of quantitative methods for the analysis of sociological data. The introduction of structural equation models in the 1960s changed the way sociologists viewed their data and how they viewed the social world. Statistical developments in areas such as econometrics, biometrics, and psychometrics were directly imported into sociology. At the same time, other methods were developed by sociologists to deal with substantive problems of traditional concern to sociology. A necessary condition for these changes was the steady decline in the cost of computing, the development of efficient numerical algorithms, and the availability of specialized software. Without developments in computing, these methods would be of little use to substantive researchers.

Acceptance of these methods has neither been universal nor without costs. Critiques of the application of quantitative methods have been written by both sympathetic (Lieberson 1985; Duncan 1984) and unsympathetic (Coser 1975) sociologists, as well as by statisticians (Freedman 1987) and econometricians (Leamer 1983). While these critiques have made practitioners rethink their approaches, the developments in quantitative methods that took shape in the 1960s will contin-

ue to influence sociological practice for decades to come.

(SEE ALSO: *Analysis of Variance and Covariance; Correlation and Regression Analysis; Event History Analysis; Factor Analysis; General Linear Model; Mathematical Sociology; Multiple Indicator Models; Statistical Inference; Tabular Analysis; Time Series Analysis*)

REFERENCES

Agresti, Alan 1990 *Categorical Data Analysis.* New York: Wiley.

Anderson, T. W. 1958 *An Introduction to Multivariate Statistical Analysis.* New York: Wiley.

Bartholomew, D. J. 1967 *Stochastic Models for Social Processes.* New York: Wiley.

Belsley, David A., Edwin Kuh, and Roy E. Welsch 1980 *Regression Diagnostics: Identifying Influential Data and Sources of Collinearity.* New York: Wiley.

Berk, R. A. 1983 "An Introduction to Sample Selection Bias in Sociological Data." *American Sociological Review* 48:386–398.

———, and Subhash C. Ray 1982 "Selection Biases in Sociological Data." *Social Science Research* 11:352–398.

Bielby, William T., and Robert M. Hauser 1977 "Structural Equation Models." *Annual Review of Sociology* 3:137–161.

Birch, M. W. 1963 "Maximum Likelihood in Three-way Contingency Tables." *Journal of the Royal Statistical Society Series B* 27:220–233.

Bishop, Yvonne M. M., Stephen E. Fienberg, and P. W. Holland 1975 *Discrete Multivariate Analysis: Theory and Practice.* Cambridge: MIT Press.

Blalock, Herbert M., Jr. 1964 *Causal Inferences in Nonexperimental Research.* Chapel Hill: University of North Carolina Press.

——— (ed.) 1971 *Causal Models in the Social Sciences.* Chicago: Aldine.

Blau, Peter M., and Otis Dudley Duncan 1967 *The American Occupational Structure.* New York: Wiley.

Blumen, I., M. Kogan, and P. J. McCarthy 1955 *Industrial Mobility of Labor as a Probability Process. Cornell Studies of Industrial and Labor Relations,* Vol. 6. Ithaca, N.Y.: Cornell University Press.

Bollen, Kenneth A. 1989 *Structural Equations with Latent Variables.* New York: Wiley.

Borgatta, Edgar F., and George W. Bohrnstedt (eds.) 1969 *Sociological Methodology.* San Francisco: Jossey-Bass.

———1972 *Sociological Methods and Research.* Beverly Hills, Calif.: Sage.

Box, George E. P., and Gwilym M. Jenkins 1970 *Time Series Analysis.* San Francisco: Holden-Day.

Cleveland, William S. 1985 *The Elements of Graphing Data.* Monterey, Calif.: Wadsworth.

Clogg, Clifford C. 1977 *MLLSA: Maximum Likelihood Latent Structure Analysis.* State College, Pa.: Pennsylvania State University Press.

Coleman, James S. 1964 *Introduction to Mathematical Sociology.* Glencoe, Ill.: The Free Press.

Coser, Lewis F. 1975 "Presidential Address: Two Methods in Search of Substance." *American Sociological Review* 40:691–700.

Cramér, Harald 1946 *Mathematical Methods of Statistics.* Princeton, N.J.: Princeton University Press.

Dixon, W. J., chief ed. 1981 *BMDP Statistical Software: 1981.* Berkeley: University of California Press.

Doob, J. L. 1953 *Stochastic Processes.* New York: Wiley.

Duncan, Otis Dudley 1966 "Path Analysis: Sociological Examples." *American Journal of Sociology* 72:1–16.

———1984 *Notes on Social Measurement: Historical and Critical.* New York: Russell Sage Foundation.

Fay, Robert, and Leo A. Goodman 1974 *ECTA: Everyman's Contingency Table Analysis.* Chicago: Dept of Statistics, University of Chicago.

Finney, D. J. 1952 *Probit Analysis,* 2nd ed. Cambridge: Cambridge University Press.

Fisher, R. A. 1925 *Statistical Methods for Research Workers,* 1st ed. Edinburgh: Oliver and Boyd.

———1935 *The Design of Experiments.* Edinburgh: Oliver and Boyd.

Freedman, David A. 1987 "As Others See Us: A Case Study in Path Analysis." *Journal of Educational Statistics* 12:101–128.

Gallant, A. Ronald 1987 *Nonlinear Statistical Models.* New York: Wiley.

Goodman, Leo A. 1964 "Simple Methods of Analyzing Three-Factor Interaction in Contingency Tables." *Journal of the American Statistical Association* 58: 319–352.

———1972 "A Modified Multiple Regression Approach to the Analysis of Dichotomous Variables." *American Sociological Review* 37:28–46.

———1974 "The Analysis of Systems of Qualitative Variables When Some of the Variables Are Un-observable. Part I: A Modified Latent Structure Approach." *American Journal of Sociology* 79: 1179–1259.

Goodman, Leo A., and William H. Kruskal 1979 *Measures of Association for Cross Classification.* New York: Springer-Verlag.

Hausman, J. A. 1978 "Specification Tests in Econometrics." *Econometrica* 46:1251–1272.

Heckman, James J. 1979 "Sample Selection Bias as a Specification Error." *Econometrica* 47:153–161.

Jöreskog, Karl G. 1969 "A General Approach to Confirmatory Maximum Likelihood Factor Analysis." *Psychometrika* 34:183–202.

———, and Marielle van Thillo 1972 *LISREL: A General Computer Program for Estimating a Linear Structural Equation System Involving Multiple Indicators of Unmeasured Variables.* Princeton, N.J.: Educational Testing Service.

Kendall, Maurice G. 1943 *Advanced Theory of Statistics,* Vol. 1. London: Griffin.

———1946 *Advanced Theory of Statistics,* Vol. 2. London: Griffin.

Lazarsfeld, Paul F., and Neil W. Henry 1968 *Latent Structure Analysis.* Boston: Houghton Mifflin.

Larzarsfeld, Paul F., and Morris Rosenberg, eds. 1955 *The Language of Social Research.* New York: The Free Press.

Leamer, Edward E. 1983 "Let's Take the Con Out of Econometrics." *American Economic Review* 73: 31–43.

Lehmann, E. L. 1959 *Testing Statistical Hypotheses.* New York: Wiley.

Lieberson, Stanley 1985 *Making It Count: The Improvement of Social Research and Theory.* Berkeley: University of California Press.

Little, Roderick J. A., and Donald B. Rubin 1987 *Statistical Analysis with Missing Data.* New York: John Wiley & Sons.

McKelvey, Richard D., and William Zavonia 1975 "A Statistical Model for the Analysis of Ordinal Level Dependent Variables." *Journal of Mathematical Sociology* 4:103–120.

Maddala, G. S. 1983 *Limited-Dependent and Qualitative Variables in Econometrics.* Cambridge: Cambridge University Press.

Muthén, Bengt O. 1988 *LISCOMP: Analysis of Linear Structural Equations with a Comprehensive Measurement Model.* Mooresville, Ind.: Scientific Software.

Nie, Norman H., C. Hadlai Hull, Jean G. Jenkins, Karin Steinbrenner, and Dale H. Bent 1975 *Statistical*

Package for the Social Sciences, 2nd ed. New York: McGraw-Hill.

Rousseeuw, Peter J., and Annick M. Leroy 1987 *Robust Regression and Outlier Detection.* New York: Wiley.

Scheffé, H. 1959 *The Analysis of Variance.* New York: Wiley.

Simon, Herbert 1957 *Models of Man.* New York: Wiley.

Snedecor, George W. 1937 *Statistical Methods,* 1st ed. Ames, Iowa: Iowa State University Press.

Sorensen, Aage 1975 "The Structure of Intragenerational Mobility." *American Sociological Review* 40:456–471.

Spilerman, Seymour 1971 "The Causes of Racial Disturbances: Tests of an Explanation." *American Sociological Review* 36:427–442.

———1972 "The Analysis of Mobility Processes by the Introduction of Independent Variables into a Markov Chain." *American Sociological Review* 37:277–294.

Stine, Robert 1990 "An Introduction to Bootstrap Methods." John Fox and J. Scott Long, eds., *Modern Methods of Data Analysis.* Newbury Park, Calif.: Sage.

Theil, H. 1970 "On the Estimation of Relationships Involving Qualitative Variables." *American Journal of Sociology* 76:103–154.

Thurstone, L. L. 1947 *Multiple-Factor Analysis.* Chicago: University of Chicago Press.

Tuma, Nancy B. 1976 "Rewards, Resources, and the Rate of Mobility." *American Sociological Review* 41:338–360.

———, and D. Crockford 1976 "Invoking RATE." Center for the Study of Welfare Policy. Menlo Park, Calif.: Stanford Research Institute.

———, and Michael T. Hannan 1984 *Social Dynamics: Models and Methods.* New York: Academic Press.

White, Halbert 1980 "A Heteroskedasticity-Consistent Covariance Matrix and a Direct Test for Heteroskedasticity." *Econometrica* 48:817–838.

Wilks, S. S. 1944 *Mathematical Statistics.* Princeton, N.J.: Princeton University Press.

Winship, Christopher, and Robert D. Mare 1983 "Structural Equations and Path Analysis for Discrete Data." *American Journal of Sociology* 89:54–110.

Wold, Herman, and Lars Juréen 1953 *Demand Analysis.* New York: Wiley.

Wright, Sewall 1934 "The Method of Path Coefficients." *Annals of Mathematical Statistics* 5:161–215.

J. SCOTT LONG

STATUS ATTAINMENT Status attainment is the process by which individuals attain positions in the system of social stratification in a society. If we think of social stratification as referring to the rewards society has to offer and the resources individuals use to obtain such rewards, education, occupation, and income are the key factors. The amount and kind of education people attain determines the kinds of jobs they are able to get. The kind of work people do is the main determinant of their income. Moreover, the education, occupation, and income of parents largely determine the kinds of advantages (or disadvantages) they create for their children. Sociologists usually think of education, occupation, and income as the main aspects of socioeconomic status, and the study of status attainment is therefore the study of how these attributes of people are related, both within and across generations.

ESTABLISHMENT OF THE FIELD

Status-attainment research, as a distinctive area of research, had its origins in the work of Otis Dudley Duncan in the 1960s. Duncan reconceptualized the study of intergenerational occupational mobility—which is concerned with the degree and pattern of association between the kind of work done by parents and offspring (in practice, fathers and sons)—as the study of the factors affecting who gets what sort of job, with father's occupation only one of several determining factors. Other researchers extended Duncan's interest to take account of the factors that determine how much schooling people get and how much money they make.

Duncan's conceptual reformulation was accompanied by two important technical innovations. First was the creation of a socioeconomic status scale for occupations. Unlike education and income, occupation has no intrinsic metric: No natural ordering of occupations exists in terms of relative status. For many kinds of research, however, including in particular the study of status attainment, it is desirable to arrange occupations into some sort of status hierarchy—that is, hierarchy of the relative socioeconomic advantage enjoyed by incumbents of different occupations. Duncan created such an ordering of occupations for the categories of the 1950 U.S. Census classification by taking the weighted average of the education and income of typical incumbents, with the weights chosen to maximize the association between the resulting socioeconomic status scale and the relative prestige of occupations as measured by popular evaluations. The reason he was able to do this is that prestige and socioeconomic status are very highly correlated: Occupations that have high socioeconomic status (that is, that require a great deal of education and pay well) also tend to have high prestige, and jobs that require little education and pay poorly tend to have low prestige.

Second, Duncan introduced path analysis into sociology. Path analysis is a way of statistically representing the relative strength of different relationships between variables, both direct and indirect. For example, it is known that educated people tend to earn more than uneducated people, but it is not clear whether this is simply because they have jobs of higher status or whether, among those who have jobs of similar status, the better educated earn more than the less well educated. Path analysis provides a way of answering this question; the answer is that even among people doing the same sort of work, the better educated tend to earn more.

SUBSTANTIVE ISSUES

Four central issues have dominated research on status attainment. The first issue is the extent of "social reproduction," the tendency for class and socioeconomic status position to be perpetuated, or "reproduced" from generation to generation. There is a value assumption underlying this question. "Open" societies, that is, societies with low rates of social reproduction or, to put it differently, high rates of intergenerational social mobility, are regarded as desirable since such societies are presumed to have relatively high equality of opportunity and to emphasize "achievement" rather

than "ascription" as the basis for socioeconomic success.

The second issue is what factors other than the status of parents affect the attainment of education, occupation, and income. Of course, some factors may be correlated with the status of parents and may also have an independent effect. For example, there is a modest negative correlation between socioeconomic status and fertility—high status people tend to have fewer children—and there is also a tendency for people from large families not to go as far in school as people from small families. So part of the reason the children of high status people go further in school is that such people have smaller families. But it is also true that at any given level of parental status (e.g., for families where both parents are college-educated professionals), people from smaller families go further in school. So the number of siblings has an *independent* effect on educational attainment, apart from its correlation with parental status. Sorting out such effects is facilitated by the application of path analysis.

The third issue is the extent to which there are sex and race (or ethnic) differences in patterns of status attainment. With respect to gender, the questions are: Do men and women from similar social origins go equally far in school? Do equally qualified men and women get jobs of equal status? Are women paid as well as men doing similar work? The same set of questions is also asked with respect to differences between racial and ethnic groups.

The fourth issue is whether the process of status attainment operates the same way in different countries or in any one country at different historical periods. What follows is a summary of what is known about each of these four issues with respect to educational attainment, occupational attainment, and income attainment.

EDUCATION

Reproduction. Regarding the extent of educational reproduction, the evidence regarding the United States in the late twentieth century is quite clear: Ours is an "open" society. Educational attainment (how far people go in school) is only weakly dependent upon parental status. Only about 20 percent of the variability in years of school completed can be attributed to the level of education attained by one's father or mother. And when several different family background characteristics are taken into account, the connection is not much stronger; at most, about one-third of the variability in educational attainment can be attributed to the status of the family one comes from. The rest is due to factors unrelated to social origins.

Other Factors. Apart from the social status of parents, the main factors affecting educational attainment are intelligence, the number of siblings (as noted above, all else being equal, people from large families get less schooling), family stability (those from nonintact families, people whose parents have divorced or have died—one or both—go less far in school), the influence of "significant others" (family, friends, and teachers), and academic performance (not surprisingly, the better people do in school the longer they continue to go to school).

The question naturally arises as to why and how origin status and these other factors affect educational attainment. In a country such as the United States, where education up to the college level is free, parental wealth has relatively little effect on whether people stay in school. This claim is further supported by the observation that the effect of social origins on educational attainment declines with each successive educational transition. That is, social origins have a stronger influence on whether people graduate from high school or not than on whether high school graduates go on to college and a still weaker influence on the graduation chances of those who begin college. So, if parental wealth is not important, what is?

There are two underlying factors: "human capital" (sometimes called "cultural capital") is the most important, but "social capital" is involved as well. Human capital refers to the knowledge, skills, and motivations of individuals. The basic argument is that growing up in a high status family enhances one's human capital and that those with high human capital do better in school and therefore gain more education—which, of course, further enhances their human capital. The idea is that children who grow up in well-educated families, or professional families, learn the kinds of skills and acquire the kinds of motivations that enable them to do well in school. There are many books in such houses, and there are often computers. So school work is familiar because it is the same sort of thing they find at home.

Social capital refers to the social connections that people have with others. Here the idea is that people are strongly influenced by the company they keep. So young people whose friends are dropping out of high school are more likely to drop out of high school themselves than are others whose friends have a social background and academic performance level that encourage educational attainment. Similarly, those whose friends are going to college are more likely to go themselves than are others whose friends are going to work after high school; and those whose teachers encourage them to continue their education are more likely to do so than others whose records are just as good. Since people from high status origins tend to live in neighborhoods with others of similar origins, they will tend to have greater social capital than will those from low status origins.

Sex and Race Differences. In the United States, there is little difference in the average amount of education attained by men and women, but more men than women tend to be very well educated or very poorly educated—that is, more men than women graduate from college, but also more men than women drop out of high school. However, the effect of social origins and other factors on educational attainment is very similar for men and women. Race and ethnicity is a different story. Blacks are substantially less well educated than are whites or others. In part, this is because the parents of blacks are poorly educated themselves. But blacks are also less able to convert whatever advantage they do have into corresponding advantage for their children. In particular, blacks do not go as far in school as would be predicted from their parents' status. The sharp difference between blacks and other groups is a continuing legacy of slavery. While there are differences in the educational attainment levels of various other ethnic groups, these are largely the result of differences among these groups in the average status of parents.

Cross-Cultural and Cross-Temporal Variations. Differences between countries in the educational attainment process are due both to general factors, such as the level of industrialization, and to specific differences in the way education is organized. In general, where the level of educational inequality in the parents' generation is high, educational attainment is more dependent upon social origins than in countries where the level of educational inequality in the parents' generation is low. This is a consequence of the effect of human capital acquired at home. In a country such as the United States, where janitors have about ten years of school and high school teachers have about sixteen years of school, the son of a janitor will be able to compete in school much more effectively with the son of a high school teacher than in a society such as India where high school teachers also have about sixteen years of schooling but janitors have no schooling at all and are illiterate. Second, in highly industrialized countries schooling is less dependent on social origins than in less industrialized countries, in part because schooling tends to be free in industrialized countries. Third, where the state provides not only free education but financial subsidies to students, as has been done in Eastern Europe and in some Western European countries as well, education tends to be less dependent on social origins than in countries without such subsidies.

There is a worldwide trend for educational attainment to become less "ascriptive" over time. That is, in almost all countries educational attainment has been less and less dependent on social origins throughout most of the twentieth century. The reason for this is quite straightforward. As mentioned above, the effect of social origins on the probability that people move from one level of education to the next declines with each higher level of education. Therefore, since the average

level of educational attainment has been steadily increasing in most countries, it follows that more and more people are in the educational categories where social origins matter relatively little.

OCCUPATIONAL STATUS

Reproduction. Like educational status, occupational status is only weakly related to social origins. But it is somewhat harder to pin this down than is true for education since, unlike education, which is completed by most people early in life, occupational status may vary over the life course as people change jobs. The convention of most research on occupational attainment is, therefore, to restrict the analysis to men (since women not only change jobs but move in and out of the labor force for marriage or childbearing) and to compare the occupations held by men at the time they are interviewed with the occupations of the fathers when the interviewed men were teenagers, usually age sixteen. The relationship between fathers' and sons' occupational status turns out to be even weaker than the relationship between parents' and offspring's educational attainment. So, with respect to occupational status as well as educational attainment, ours is an open society.

Other Factors. In the analysis of occupational attainment, an important issue has been to assess the relative importance of social origins (measured by father's occupational status) and education as determinants of men's occupational status. The ratio of these two effects has been taken as an indicator of the degree of societal openness. In the United States and most industrial societies, education is by far the most important determinant of occupational status, while the direct effect of a father's occupational status is very limited. While in the past many people directly inherited their occupational position from their parents (for example, the sons of farmers were likely to take over their fathers' farms, the sons of shopkeepers to take over their fathers' shops, and so on), in modern societies such as the United States, where people tend to work in large organizations, most jobs cannot be inherited directly. Rather, occupational status in-heritage, insofar as it occurs at all, results mainly from the children of high status people going further in school and those going further in school attaining better jobs. But since, as we have seen above, education is largely independent of social origins, the result is that education serves mainly as a vehicle of social mobility rather than as a mechanism of social reproduction or status inheritance.

Sex and Race Differences. The most striking difference between men and women is that most men work most of the time once they complete their schooling, whereas the work lives of many women are interrupted for childbearing and child rearing. However, labor force participation rates of women and men are converging in the United States as more and more women remain in the labor force even when their children are very young. In general, men and women work at jobs of equal status, although the specific jobs held by men and women are very different. Most managers, skilled and unskilled manual workers, and farm workers are men. Most clerical and service workers are women. And professional, sales, and semiskilled manual jobs tend to be performed by both men and women. The sex segregation of the labor force has important implications for income differences between men and women, discussed below.

Blacks tend to work at lower status occupations than do whites and others. In part this is due to their lower levels of educational attainment, but in part it is due to the fact that blacks are not able to obtain jobs as good as those that can be obtained by equally well-educated members of other groups. Again, as in the case of education, differences in occupational status among nonblack ethnic groups are largely attributable to differences in their educational attainment.

Cross-Cultural and Cross-Temporal Variations. In highly industrialized societies, and in relatively egalitarian societies, there is little direct transmission of occupational status from one generation to the next; in such societies, occupational transmission is largely indirect, through education. In less industrialized and less egalitarian societies, the importance of the father's occupation as a determinant of occupational status increases and the importance of education decreases, although education always remains more important than the father's occupation, even in the least-developed societies.

As with education, the extent of reproduction of occupational status has been systematically decreasing over time in almost all societies. The reasons for this are not yet clear. There may be a worldwide shift toward an emphasis on achievement as opposed to ascription—although the likelihood that a shift in value orientations could have such a large and systematic effect does not seem great. More likely, the systematic increase in the average level of education in almost all countries is responsible since it is known that the association between fathers' and sons' occupational status decreases for those who have obtained higher levels of education.

INCOME

Reproduction. Little is known about the extent of income reproduction. The reason for this is that it is very difficult to measure income in the parents' generation. Most data used in intergenerational analyses are obtained by asking people to report on their parents' characteristics. While people tend to know how much schooling their parents have had, and what sort of work their fathers were doing when the respondents were teenagers, few people have a very good idea of what their parents' incomes were. There is, however, one major study that has obtained such information, a study of the graduating class of 1957 from Wisconsin high schools, conducted by William Sewell and Robert Hauser. This cohort of graduates has been followed up in a number of surveys over the years, so that information has become available about their occupations and incomes at various stages after completing school. In addition, with careful arrangements to guard confidentiality, the researchers were able to obtain information from the Wisconsin Department of Taxation and the Social Security Administration regarding the incomes of the parents at the time the students were in high school. These data suggest that the intergenerational transmission of income is even weaker than is true for education or occupation. Other ways of indirectly estimating this relationship yield similar results.

One possible reason for this is that income (measured in real dollars—that is, adjusted for inflation) is highly variable over the life cycle and, for some workers—particularly those who are self-employed or whose jobs are dependent on the weather—even from year to year. Moreover, age differences in earnings vary systematically for different occupational groups. The earnings of professionals tend to increase steadily over the course of their careers, while, at the other extreme, the earnings of unskilled laborers do not change at all. Thus, when they first start working, unskilled laborers earn as much as or more than professionals just beginning their careers. But by the time they near retirement, professionals earn several times as much as laborers of the same age. Incomes are also highly variable from place to place, reflecting differences in the cost of living; and even within cities, different firms pay different wages or salaries for the same job. All of these factors make the individual variations in income rather unpredictable.

Other Factors. Unlike parental education and occupational status, which affect educational attainment but have little direct effect on occupational attainment or income, parental income directly affects the income of offspring even when education and occupational attainment are taken into account. In fact, parental income is nearly as important as occupational status in determining income and more important than education. Apparently, there is a propensity to earn money, and this propensity is transmitted from generation to generation. Whether this reflects differences in values that are transmitted from parents to their children—some people choosing jobs on the basis of how well they pay and others choosing jobs on the basis of their intrinsic interest, how secure they are, and so on—or to some other factor is not yet known.

Other factors that affect income even when parental education and the respondent's own education and occupational status are taken into

account include ability, the quality of the college attended, and the kind of work that people do. Doctors earn more than professors, even though the jobs are of similar status, and garbage collectors earn more than ditch diggers. There is an extensive, although inconclusive, literature on differences in earnings across industrial sectors; and there is some evidence that earnings are higher in more strongly unionized occupations and industries.

Sex and Race Differences. Gender is the big story here. In the United States, among full-time year-round workers, women earn about 60 percent of what men earn, and this ratio has remained essentially unchanged since the 1950s. Of the 40 percent gender difference, about 20 percent of earnings can be accounted for by the greater work experience of men, differences in the kind of education received, and similar factors. The other 20 percent difference is due in part to the fact that the jobs performed mainly by women tend to pay less than jobs performed mainly by men, even though many of these jobs are similar with respect to the skill required, the effort involved, and the responsibility entailed—and partly to the fact that women tend to earn less than men in the same occupations. This state of affairs is possible because of the extreme gender segregation of the labor force. Most jobs tend to be performed either mostly by men or mostly by women, with relatively few jobs open to both sexes.

Race differences in income are somewhat smaller than gender differences in income and have been declining steadily for the last half century, as has occupational segregation by race. There is little evidence that the racial composition of jobs affects their pay levels. Rather, racial differences in income are attributable both to the fact that many blacks tend to be less educated and to work at lower status jobs than most whites and others and to the fact that blacks get a lower return on their education and occupational status than do whites and others. Interestingly, there appears to be an across-the-board difference between the earnings of black and other males at any given level of education, occupational status, and so forth. However, the racial difference in the earnings of women is somewhat more complicated. At low levels of education and occupational status, black women earn much less than do other women. But at high levels of education and occupational status there is little or no difference in earnings among women of all races.

Cross-Cultural and Cross-Temporal Variations. This is a relatively understudied topic, due largely to difficulties in equating income data across countries. There is some suggestion that income inequality in general, and the gender gap in income in particular, tend to be smaller in countries with national wage policies—that is, where wages are centrally determined or centrally negotiated, as occurs, for example, in Germany, where many wages are set by a joint union–management wage board. This, however, is an area in which much research remains yet to be done.

CONCLUSION

Although there are still many institutional barriers to complete equality of opportunity for members of different racial or ethnic groups, sexes, and social classes, it is nonetheless fair to characterize U.S. society in the late twentieth century (and other industrialized societies as well) as places where—with one notable exception, the continuing disadvantages experienced by black Americans—status attainment is more a matter of what individuals make of their lives rather than of who their parents are. Some people get a bit of a head start, but it is a long race with many opportunities to get ahead and many reversals of fortune. Fortunately, we do not live in a society where people are destined to poverty or affluence by the economic status or occupation of their parents.

(SEE ALSO: *Education and Mobility; Occupational and Career Mobility; Occupational Prestige; Social Inequality; Social Mobility; Social Stratification*)

REFERENCES

Blau, Peter, and Otis Dudley Duncan 1967 *The American Occupational Structure.* New York: Wiley.

Duncan, Otis Dudley 1961 "A Socioeconomic Index for All Occupations." In Albert J. Reiss, Jr., ed., *Occupations and Social Structure.* New York: Free Press.

———1966 "Path Analysis: Sociological Examples." *American Journal of Sociology* 72:1–16.

———, David L. Featherman, and Beverly Duncan 1972 *Socioeconomic Background and Achievement.* New York: Seminar Press.

Featherman, David L., and Robert M. Hauser 1978 *Opportunity and Change.* New York: Academic Press.

Jencks, Christopher, et al. 1979 *Who Gets Ahead? The Determinants of Economic Success in America.* New York: Basic Books.

———1972 *Inequality: A Reassessment of the Effect of Family and Schooling in America.* New York: Basic Books.

Roos, Patricia A. 1985 *Gender and Work: A Comparative Analysis of Industrial Societies.* Albany: State University of New York Press.

Sewell, William H., and Robert M. Hauser 1975 *Education, Occupation, and Earnings: Achievement in the Early Career.* New York: Academic Press.

Treiman, Donald J. 1977 *Occupational Prestige in Comparative Perspective.* New York: Academic Press.

———, and Kam-Bor Yip 1989 "Educational and Occupational Attainment in 21 Countries." In Melvin L. Kohn, ed., *Cross-National Research in Sociology.* Newbury Park, Calif.: Sage.

DONALD J. TREIMAN

STEREOTYPES. *See* Attitudes.

STRESS The theoretical interest in social epidemiology, the study of effects of social conditions on the diffusion of distress and diseases in the population, can be traced to Durkheim's study of suicide in 1897 (1951). Since then, theory and research have elaborated on the associations among the various forms of social integration and psychiatric disorder. Among the classic works are Faris and Dunham's study of the ecology of mental disorders in urban areas (1939), Hollingshead and Redlick's research on social class and mental illness in New Haven (1958), the midtown Manhattan studies (Srole et al. 1962; Langner and Michael 1962; Srole 1975), the Sterling County studies by the Leightons and their colleagues (A. H. Leighton 1959; C. C. Hughes et al. 1960; D. Leighton et al. 1963) and the British studies by Brown and his associates (Brown and Harris, 1978). Each study illuminates the linkage between social conditions and distress and advances theories, hypotheses and empirical evidence in the specification of the relationships.

A parallel theoretical development has also taken place, over the past thirty-five years, in the formulation of the life stress paradigm in social psychiatry. The birth of this paradigm can be dated to the work of Hans Selye (1956) whose study of the undifferentiated response (physiological and psychological) that is generated by diverse external stimuli (stressors) linked sociological constructs to the internal individualistic responses made by individuals to their environment. This stress-distress model provided impetus for a convergence between the earlier sociological concerns with consequences of social integration and the physiological modeling of internal responses to the external environment.

The stress research enterprise gained further momentum when Holmes and Rahe, and subsequently other researchers, developed measures of life experiences that require social adjustments, known as inventories of life events (Holmes and Rahe 1967; Dohrenwend and Dohrenwend 1974, 1981; Myers and Pepper 1972). The life events schedules provide a convenient instrument that can be applied to a wide range of populations and administered with ease. The instrument has shown a high degree of validity and reliability relative to many measures of distress across populations and time lags.

In general, the research shows that life stressors, as measured by the life events schedules, exert a significant but moderate influence on mental and physical well-being. In a simple zero-order correlation, the relationship between life stressors and well-being (e.g., depressive symptoms) ranges between .25 and .40 (Rabkin and Struening 1976). This figure is somewhat less for physical health (House 1981; Wallston et al. 1987; Ensel 1986). The magnitude of this relationship seems to hold up when other factors are taken into account (e.g., general socioeconomic status measures; age; gender; psychological resources such as self-esteem, personal competence, and locus of control; physical health; and prior mental state).

MODIFICATIONS AND EXTENSIONS—THE MEDIATION PROCESSES

Modifications of the stressors-distress paradigm have taken several directions. In one direction, the conceptualization of stress as undifferentiated response has been modified so that the nature of stressors entails further specification. For example, in the analysis of life events, desirability, controllability, and importance are identified as dimensions exerting differential effects on distress (Thoits 1981; Tausig 1986). Research has shown that when only self-perceived undesirable life events are considered, the effect of the stressor instrument on distress increases marginally but significantly. It has also been shown that when items pertaining to psychological states (sleeping and eating problems) or illnesses are deleted, the magnitude of its effect is only marginally reduced (Ensel and Tausig 1982; Tausig 1982, 1986).

Conceptualization and operationalization of stressors have also been extended to include role strains (Pearlin and Schooler 1978) and daily hassles (Lazarus and Folkman 1984). Generally speaking, these stressors have demonstrated consistent but moderate effects on mental health, with zero-order correlations with various measures of mental health ranging from .15 to .35.

Another direction focuses attention on factors mediating or buffering the stressors-distress relationship. Researchers have identified three major components involved in the stress process: stressors, mediating factors, and outcome variables. Pearlin et al. (1981) viewed these constructs as multifaceted. Mediators consist of both external coping resources (i.e., social support) and internal coping resources (i.e., mastery and self-esteem). Outcome factors consist of psychological and physical symptomatology.

Social support, for example, has been considered a major candidate variable, and the cumulative evidence is that it exerts both direct and indirect effects on mental health (Cobb 1976; Cassel 1974, 1976; Nuckolls, Cassel, and Kaplan 1972; Dean and Lin 1977; Lin et al 1979; Turner 1981; Barrera and Ainlay 1983; Aneshensel and Huba 1984; Sarason and Sarason 1985; Kessler and McLeod 1985; Lin, Dean, and Ensel 1986; Berkman 1985; Cohen and Wills 1985; House, Umberson, and Landis 1988). Coping has also received substantial research attention and been found to be an effective mediator (Pearlin et al, 1981; Wheaton 1983, 1989; Lazarus and Folkman 1984). This type of research has served as the prototype for the sociopsychological study of stress in the 1980s (Pearlin, 1989). Emphasis has been placed on the mechanisms by which social resources, provided or called upon in the presence of a stressor, operate to alter the effect of the stressor (House, Umberson, and Landis 1988; Kessler, Price, and Wortman 1985; Thoits 1985).

DEVELOPMENT OF INTEGRATIVE AND TIME-LAGGED MODELS

While conceptual analysis and research attention have been given to life stress, resources (social support and coping), and psychological stress for their potential effects on health and mental health, only recently have specific proposals emerged in integrating these elements into a coherent theoretical framework. Dohrenwend and Dohrenwend (1981) summarized various formulations of life stress processes involving stressors (life events) and the psychological and social contexts in which they occurred. These formulations were synthesized into six hypotheses, each of which was shown to provide viable conceptual linkages between stressors (life events) and health outcomes and to have received some empirical support. The hypotheses in these models share two common features: (1) The ultimate dependent variable is adverse health or adverse health change rather than mental health problems or disorders, and (2) each hypothesis delineates and explains the possible empirical association between life events and health. Some of the hypotheses affirm

the primary role of life events as causing health problems, while others incorporate mediating factors to explain health problems. The Dohrenwends (1974) proposed that these hypotheses should be examined together for their relative merits. Golden and Dohrenwend (1981) outlined the analytic requirements for testing these causal hypotheses.

Further elaboration of these hypotheses formed the basis of an integrative life stress paradigm in which stressors and resources in three environments—social, psychological, and physiological—are considered as the factors impinging on well-being (Lin and Ensel 1989). This model specifies the enhancing (resources) and detrimental (stressing) forces in each environment. These stressors and resources in the three environments interact in affecting one's physical and mental health. Empirical evidence suggests that social resources tend to mediate the stress process involving mental health, whereas psychological resources are more prominent in mediating the process involving physical health.

Another integrative attempt incorporates multidisciplinary and multilevel variables in the study of life stress. For example, Lazarus and Folkman (1984) and Trumbull and Appley (1986) have conceptualized cognitive mechanisms involved in the stress process. Lazarus and Folkman proposed a model in which three levels of analysis (social, psychological, and physiological) are conducted to understand the antecedent, mediating, and immediate as well as long-term effects on distress. Trumbull and Appley (1986) proposed the simultaneous assessment of the physiological system, psychological system, and social system functioning. These functionings have both intrasystem and intersystem reciprocal relationships and exert joint effects on distress. In the later paradigms, emphasis has been placed on personality factors and coping skills. Additionally, the importance of linking social, psychological, and physical factors in the study of the stress process has been noted. Causal antecedents of both depressive and physical symptomatology are viewed as coming from social, psychological, and physiological sources and are hypothesized to be mediated by a variety of coping factors and perceived social support.

Pearlin and Aneshensel have proposed a synthesized paradigm (Pearlin 1989; Pearlin and Aneshensel 1986) in which health behaviors and illness behaviors have been incorporated into the basic stress process and in which equal attention has been given to the potential mediating and moderating roles of social and psychological resources. Thus, in addition to mediating the effect of stressors on illness outcomes, coping and social support are viewed as having the potential to mediate health and illness behaviors. An important element of this synthesizing paradigm is the recognition that physical illness creates life problems that are reflected in an increase in undesirable life events—that is, in addition to stressors affecting physical illnesses, physical illness also has the potential to bring about the occurrence of stressors. In such a synthesized paradigm, stressors embedded in social structure (e.g., role strains and problems) interact with illness behavior and illnesses. These interactions are mediated by coping and social support.

Finally, growing attention has been given to the need for studying the stress process over time (Wheaton 1989). Not only have there been concerns with causal interpretations of cross-sectional data, but more importantly, a call for longer lags in the panel design to capture the stress process in the life course more realistically (Thoits 1982). Some of the earlier panel studies, such as the midtown Manhattan study (Srole and Fischer 1978), the Kansas City study (Pearlin et al. 1981), the New Haven study (Myers, Lindenthal, and Pepper 1975), and the Cleveland GAO study (Haug and Folmar 1986) have all made significant contributions to understanding the stress process in urban communities. More current efforts, incorporating prevailing models and variables, would substantially add to the knowledge about stress in the life course. Current panel studies, such as those mounted by Aneshensel in Southern California; House and his associates on a national sample; Berkman in New Haven; Murrell in Kentucky; and Lin, Dean, and Ensel in upstate New York have the potential to expand research programs into investigations of the life-course process of stress.

(SEE ALSO: *Mental Illness and Mental Disorders; Personality Theories*)

REFERENCES

Aneshensel, C. S., and G. J. Huba 1984 "An Integrative Causal Model of the Antecedents and Consequences of Depression over One Year." In James R. Greenley, ed., *Research in Community and Mental Health.* Greenwich, Conn.: JAI Press.

Barrera, M., and S. L. Ainlay 1983 "The Structure of Social Support: A Conceptual and Empirical Analysis." *Journal of Community Psychology* 11:133–143.

Berkman 1985 "The Relationship of Social Networks and Social Support to Morbidity and Mortality." In S. Cohen and S. L. Syme, eds., *Social Support and Health.* New York: Academic Press.

Brown, G. W., and T. Harris 1978 *Social Origins of Depression: A Study of Psychiatric Disorder in Women.* New York: The Free Press.

Cassel, J. 1974 "An Epidemiological Perspective of Psychosocial Factors in Disease Etiology." *American Journal of Public Health* 64:1040–1043.

———1976 "The Contribution of the Social Environment to Host Resistance." *American Journal of Epidemiology* 104:107–123.

Cobb, S. 1976 "Social Support as a Moderator of Life Stress." *Psychosomatic Medicine* 38:300–314.

Cohen, S., and T. A. Wills 1985 "Stress, Social Support, and the Buffering Hypothesis." *Psychological Bulletin* 98(2):310–357.

Dean, Alfred, and Nan Lin 1977 "The Stress Buffering Role of Social Support." *Journal of Nervous and Mental Disease* 165(2):403–13.

Dohrenwend, B. S., and B. P. Dohrenwend 1974 *Stressful Life Events: Their Nature and Effect.* New York: Wiley.

———1981 "Life Stress and Illness: Formulation of the Issues." In B. S. Dohrenwend and B. P. Dohrenwend, eds., *Stressful Life Events: Their Nature and Effects.* New York: Prodist.

Durkheim, Emile 1951 *Suicide.* Glencoe, Ill.: The Free Press.

Ensel, Walter M. 1986 "Measuring Depression: The CES-D scale." In Nan Lin, Alfred Dean, and Walter

M. Ensel, eds., *Social Support, Life Events, and Depression*. Orlando, Fla.: Academic Press.

———, and Mark Tausig 1982 "The Social Context of Undesirable Life Events." Presented October 11–12 at the National Conference on Social Stress, Durham, N.H.

Faris, Robert E. K., and H. Warren Dunham 1939 *Mental Disorders in Urban Areas*. Chicago: University of Chicago Press.

Golden, R. R., and B. S. Dohrenwend 1981 "Testing Hypotheses about the Life Stress Process: A Path Analytic Method for Testing Causal Hypotheses." In B. S. Dohrenwend and B. P. Dohrenwend, eds., *Stressful Life Events: Their Nature and Effects*. NY: Prodist.

Haug, M. R., and S. J. Folmar 1986 "Longevity, Gender, and Life Quality." *Journal of Health and Social Behavior* 27:332–346.

Hollingshead, August, and Fredrick Redlick 1958 *Social Class and Mental Illness*. New York: Wiley.

Holmes, T., and R. Rahe 1967 "The Social Readjustment Rating Scale." *Journal of Psychosomatic Research* 11:213–218.

House, James S. 1981 *Work Stress and Social Support*. Reading, Mass.: Addison-Wesley.

———, Karl R. Landis, and Debra Umberson 1988 "Social Relationships and Health." *Science* 241 (July 29):540–545.

———1988 "Structures and Processes of Social Support." *Annual Review of Sociology* 14:293–318.

Hughes, C. C., M. A. Tremblay, et al. 1960 *People of Cove and Woodlot*, vol. 2 of the Sterling County Study. New York: Basic Books.

Kessler, R. C., and J. McLeod 1985 "Sex Differences in Vulnerability to Undesirable Life Events." *American Sociological Review* 49 (5):620–631.

Kessler, R. C., R. H. Price, and C. B. Wortman 1985 "Social Factors in Psychopathology: Stress, Social Support, and Coping Processes." *Annual Review of Psychology* 36:531–572.

Langner, T. S., and S. T. Michael 1962 *Life Stress and Mental Health*. New York: The Free Press.

Lazarus, R. S., and S. Folkman 1984 *Stress, Appraisal, and Coping*. New York: Springer.

Leighton, A. H. 1959 *My Name Is Legion*. New York: Basic Books.

Leighton, D. C., et al. 1963 *The Character of Danger*. New York: Basic Books.

Lin, Nan, Alfred Dean, and Walter M. Ensel 1986 *Social Support, Life Events, and Depression*. Orlando, Fla.: Academic Press.

Lin, Nan, and Walter M. Ensel 1989 "Life Stress and Health: Stressors and Resources." *American Sociological Review* 54:382–399.

Lin, Nan, Ronald Simeone, Walter M. Ensel, and Wen Kuo 1979 "Social Support, Stressful Life Events, and Illness: A Model and an Empirical Test." *Journal of Health and Social Behavior* 20 (1):108–119.

Myers, J. K., and M. P. Pepper 1972 "Life Events and Mental Status: A Longitudinal Study." *Journal of Health and Social Behavior* 13:398–406.

Myers, J. K., J. J. Lindenthal, and M. P. Pepper 1975 "Life Events, Social Integration, and Psychiatric Symptomatology." *Journal of Health and Social Behavior* 16:421–429.

Nuckolls, C. G., J. Cassel, and B. H. Kaplan 1972 "Psychosocial Assets, Life Crises, and the Prognosis of Pregnancy." *American Journal of Epidemiology* 95:431–441.

Pearlin, L. I. 1989 "The Sociological Study of Stress." *Journal of Health and Social Behavior* 30:241–256.

———, and C. Aneshensel 1986 "Coping and Social Supports: Their Function and Applications." In L. Aiken and D. Mechanic, eds., *Applications of Social Science in Clinical Medicine and Health*. New Brunswick, N.J.: Rutgers University Press.

———, M. A. Lieberman, E. G. Menaghan, and J. T. Mullan 1981 "The Stress Process." *Journal of Health and Social Behavior* 22:337–356.

———, and C. Schooler 1978 "The Structure of Coping." *Journal of Health and Social Behavior* 19 (1):2–21.

Rabkin, J. G., and E. L. Struening 1976 "Life Events, Stress, and Illness." *Science* 194:1013–1020.

Sarason, I. G., and B. R. Sarason 1985 *Social Support: Theory, Research, and Application*. The Hague: Martinus-Nijhoff.

Seyle, Hans 1956 *The Stress of Life*. New York: McGraw-Hill.

Srole, L. 1975 "Measurements and Classification in Sociopsychiatric Epidemiology: Midtown Manhattan Study I (1954) and Midtown Manhattan Restudy II (1974)." *Journal of Health and Social Behavior* 16:347–364.

———, T. S. Langner, S. T. Michael, et al. 1962 *The Midtown Manhattan Study*. New York: McGraw-Hill.

Tausig, Mark 1982 "Measuring Life Events." *Journal of Health and Social Behavior* 23 (March):52–64.

———1986 "Measuring Life Events." In Nan Lin, Alfred Dean, and Walter M. Ensel, eds., *Social Support, Life Events, and Depression*. Orlando, Fla.: Academic Press.

Thoits, P. A. 1981 "Undesirable Life Events and Psychophysiological Distress: A Problem of Operational Confounding." *American Sociological Review* 46 (1):97–109.

———1982 "Conceptual, Methodological, and Theoretical Problems in Studying Social Support as a Buffer Against Life Stress." *Journal of Health and Social Behavior* 24:145–159.

———1985 "Social Support Processes and Psychological Well-being: Theoretical Possibilities." In I. G. Sarason and B. R. Sarason, eds., *Social Support: Theory, Research, and Application*. The Hague: Martinus-Nijhoff.

Trumbull, R., and M. H. Appley 1986 "A Conceptual Model for the Examination of Stress Dynamics." In M. H. Appley and R. Trumbull, eds., *Dynamics of Stress: Physiological, Psychological, and Social Perspectives*. New York: Plenum.

Turner, R. J. 1981 "Social Support as a Contingency in Psychological Well-being." *Journal of Health and Social Behavior* 22:357–367.

Uhlenhuth, E. H., et al. 1982 "Symptom Checklist Syndromes in the General Population: Correlations with Psychotherapeutic Drug Use." *Archives of General Psychiatry* 40:1167–1173.

Wallston, B. S., et al. 1987 "Social Support and Physical Health." *Health Psychology* 2 (4):367–391.

Wheaton, B. 1983 "Stress, Personal Coping Resources, and Psychiatric Symptoms: An Investigation of Interactive Models." *Journal of Health and Social Behavior* 24:208–229.

———1989 "Life Transitions, Role Histories, and Mental Health." *American Sociological Review* 2:209–223.

NAN LIN

STRUCTURAL EQUATIONS *See* Causal Inference Models; Multiple Indicator Models.

STUDENT MOVEMENTS

Student movements are generally college student movements. Such young adult movements have a long history and have been evident in widely differing societies (Altbach and Lomotey, 1990; Feuer 1969; Lipset 1971). Some have been related to direct student redress of situational grievances such as the seventeenth-century sacking of their own English Jesuit College of La Fleche to protest a rigid, strained regimen and the student protests led by African-Americans on over one hundred campuses in the 1980s to protest cutbacks in governmental aid and scholarships for lower income students. Other student protest movements have been related to larger social movements such as the nineteenth-century Russian revolutionary student movement, the American civil rights and antiwar student movements of the 1930s and 1960s, and the ill-fated Chinese Tianenmen Square democratic movement in the 1980s.

Other examples could be noted extending back a millennium or more in other societies. What is different about contemporary student movements is a combination of their frequency and their social change consequences on society. This is a reflection of the central role that an extended formal education has on economic and social stability and development globally in both advanced technological societies and developing societies (Gordon 1988, pp. 97–98; Meyer et al. 1977).

The massive growth of higher education is evident from the change in the proportion of young adults in their late teens and early twenties attending college. Prior to World War II, even in the advanced industrial nations of Japan, the United States, and Canada, as well as in Great Britain and Western Europe, less than 10 percent of the young adult age cohort attended college. The figure was less than 1 percent in what is now generally referred to as emerging, often former colonial, developing nations. In contrast, by the late twentieth-century, close to half of young adults were in college in advanced technological societies, and the fastest growing student body in developing countries was collegiate (Meyer et al. 1977). Overall, instead of a few thousand students, major state universities in the United States now generally range between 20,000 and 40,000 or more students, with long-established private universities typically having over 10,000 students. Similarly, large national universities like those in Mexico City, Moscow, and Beijing have student bodies larger than the largest U.S. state universities.

The growth of public education generally and, in particular, collegiate education has placed young adult students in a strategic position respecting protest movement potential for inducing social change. It is not only that college students represent a high proportion of future economic, political, and social influentials. The growth of colleges since the mid-twentieth century is also an international reflection of the general publics' and the democratic or authoritarian regimes' recognition that students represent a key element in the effective future of their various societies.

Strategic positioning aside, there has been extensive research on what motivates consequential proportions of students to periodically engage in protest movements. College students represent a relatively privileged and prospectively influential group in society. These characteristics are generally associated with support for the established social order. Yet students are often in the activist forefront of protest movements.

This dilemma has been addressed in intergenerational conflict terms since at least Socrates and Plato. In sociology, Karl Mannheim (1952) addressed specific attention to this phenomenon as part of his sociology of knowledge concerns. Building upon Mannheim's analyses, Feuer (1969) holds that the need for the emerging young to replace the older adults in societies generates inherent intergenerational conflict that crystallizes in the increasingly influential collegiate settings.

In this context, it is held that students act out their traditional intergenerational conflicts in a setting that is particularly conducive to challenging the older generation. Colleges, and to a lesser extent primary and secondary schools, remove students from familial and kinship settings. While faculty present an adult schooling influence, within the increasingly large school settings, students are placed in a peer-related situation removed from both direct familial influences and the later pressures of occupational positions.

The relatively separated, student peer-influenced, life pattern is evident in the precipitating protest actions of many student movements. Most sociological research attention has been on stu-

dent participation in major protest movements involving civil rights, environmental protection, war, and other momentous public issues. Yet a review of the student movement literature demonstrates that often the early motivation for student protestors against university administrators and more general societal authorities has been related to specific student-experienced grievances over such American situational concerns as poor dormitory food in the 1950s and Italian and Chinese student concerns in the 1960s and 1980s, respectively, that growing numbers of college graduates were either unemployed or receiving less pay than undegreed manual laborers (Altbach and Peterson 1971; Borgatta 1990; Lipset 1971).

Such immediate student self-interest can often be seen in respect to student participation in larger social movements also. This has been evident in respect to direct student concerns about conscription and being forced into combat situations. The 1860s Harvard University student anti-conscription protests during the Civil War helped precipitate the congressional and state legislative acts to enable those with several hundred dollars to commute their draft status to the next young person called up, which in turn was a central factor in the Irish Catholic, New York City, conscription riots of 1863 that left several hundred dead (Catton 1960, p. 485).

Similar immediate self-interest was a part of the American Student Union antiwar movement in the 1930s, as well as of the anti-Vietnam War movement led by the Students for a Democratic Society (SDS) in the 1960s. These student protests partially reflected general public divisiveness over war support, but the most common thread was that of immediate student interest. A particularly clear case of student self-interest was the high involvement of African-American students in the civil rights student movements of the 1960s, working for more openings and support for African-Americans who had long been excluded from equal higher educational opportunity (Edwards 1970).

Yet immediate self-interest does not explain student movements in support of disadvantaged minority and low-income groups, such as extensive involvement in the Student Non-Violent Co-ordinating Committee and other American civil rights organizations in the 1960s or the 1989 student effort to establish democracy in China. In this respect, students tend to activate ideals and values that are perceived to be falling too short in their implementation (Davies 1969). What has become evident in the extensive empirical research on student movement participants since the 1960s is that the conflict of generations thesis advanced by Mannheim, Feuer, and others is less a conflict of generations than an active attempt among the student generation to realize the values they have been socialized to by the parental generation.

Rather than challenging the values of the parental generation, student activists generally support those values and act to see them actualized (DeMartini 1985). A polar case in point is the background characteristics of students who were active in the liberal, politically left SDS, which was strongly against the Vietnam War, and those in the conservative, politically right Young Americans for Freedom (YAF), which was strongly supportive of the Vietnam War. As Lipset (1968) reports, SDS students were largely from high-status, Protestant backgrounds and homes where secular, liberal values prevailed. In contrast, but in intergenerational concurrence, YAF student activists were generally drawn from strongly religious and conservative homes in lower middle-class and working-class settings. Another example of this intergenerational confluence is Bell's (1968) documentation that the largest proportion of white student activists in the Congress of Racial Equality (CORE) were Jewish and actively expressing their home-based familial values in support of minority rights.

Student movement concerns with actualizing ideals have been a dynamic aspect of such movements. The national student Free Speech Movement in 1964 was precipitated by University of California at Berkeley students who protested a specific ban on allowing a CORE civil-rights-information table on the campus in an open mall area. While a relatively small number of students were actively involved with the CORE table, a large majority of students, first at Berkeley and then nationally, supported the right of open expression and led to the larger Free Speech Movement (Altbach and Peterson 1971; Lipset 1968, 1971).

Protest movements are time delimited generally. Given the relatively short age cohort dimensions of student status, student movements tend to have even shorter time constraints. Even with time and leadership delimitations, student movements are sufficiently frequent and consequential that more systematic research is needed on not only who the student protestors are but also where they go after a student activist movement ends.

It is clear that most student activists enter into business and professional, high socioeconomic status positions. What is not clear is to what extent they continue to adhere to the values and related issues that motivated them to engage in one or more student movements. Research in this area of student movement concern may demonstrate additional social change consequences on society long after specific student movements have ended.

(SEE ALSO: *Protest Movements; Social Movements*)

REFERENCES

Altbach, Philip G., and Kofi Lomotey (eds.) 1990 *The Racial Crisis in Higher Education.* Buffalo: State University of New York Press.

Altbach, Philip G., and Patti Peterson 1971 "Before Berkeley: Historical Perspectives on American Student Activism." *Annals of the American Academy of Political and Social Science* 395:1–14.

Bell, Inge Powell 1968 *CORE and the Strategy of Non-Violence.* New York: Random House.

Borgatta, Edgar F. January 3, 1990 Correspondence with author on Student Movements.

Catton, Bruce 1960 *The Civil War.* New York: American Heritage.

Davies, James C. 1969 "The J-Curve of Rising Expectations and Declining Satisfactions as a Cause of Some Great Revolutions and Contained Rebellions." In H. Graham and T. Gurr, eds., *Violence in America.* New York: Bantam.

DeMartini, Joseph R. 1985 "Change Agents and Generational Relationships: A Reevaluation of Mannheim's Problem of Generations." *Social Forces* 64:1–16.

Edwards, Harry 1970 *Black Students.* New York: Macmillan.

Feuer, Lewis S. 1969 *The Conflict of Generations: The Character and Significance of Student Movements.* New York: Basic Books.

Gordon, Leonard 1988 "The Sociology of Education." In E. Borgatta and K. Cook, eds., *The Future of Sociology.* Beverly Hills, Calif.: Sage.

Lipset, Seymour M. 1968 "The Activists: A Profile." *Public Interest* 13:46–50.

—— 1971 *Rebellion in the University.* Boston: Little, Brown.

Mannheim, Karl 1952 *Essays on the Sociology of Knowledge,* pp. 276–322. New York: Oxford University Press.

Meyer, John W., Francisco O. Ramirez, Richard Rubinson, and John Boli 1977 "The World Educational Revolution: 1950–1970." *Sociology of Education* 50:242–258.

LEONARD GORDON

SUBURBANIZATION Suburbanization is one aspect of the more general process of the expansion and spatial reorganization of metropolitan settlements. Settled areas beyond the historical boundaries of what have been considered cities, but still clearly functionally linked to the cities, may be considered suburban, or they may not. What is suburban is a matter of social definition. For example, when small cities are enveloped by the expansion of larger cities, at what point shall they be considered suburbs, if at all? As some cities extend their boundaries outward, will newly settled areas not be considered suburban if they are within the new boundaries?

Many researchers in the United States have chosen to adopt conventions established by the Bureau of the Census. Suburban is the portion of a metropolitan area that is not central city. This definition, then, depends on what is defined as metropolitan and central city, and these definitions change over the years. Such changes are not simply technical adjustments; they respond (among other criteria) to presumptions about what cities and suburbs are. For example, as many

U.S. "suburbs" have become employment centers in the last two decades, altering traditional patterns of commuting to work, Bureau scientists have adjusted the definition of "central city" to include some of these peripheral areas.

For many purposes, it may be preferable to avoid these categories altogether. "Suburban" may be intended to reflect distance from the city center, recency of development, residential density, or commuting patterns—all of which can be measured directly. The main substantive rationale for accepting definitions tied to the juridical boundaries of cities is to emphasize the differences between cities and suburbs (and among suburbs) that are due to municipal governance. An important class of issues revolves around disparities in public resources: In what parts of the metropolis are taxes higher, where are better schools available, where is police protection greater? What are the effects of these differences on opportunities available to people who live in different parts of the metropolis? Another dimension concerns local politics: How do localities establish land use and budget policies, and what are their effects on growth?

Because many suburban residents have traditionally worked in central cities while paying taxes in the suburbs, John Kasarda has described the city–suburb relationship in terms of "exploitation." Political scientists in particular have studied this issue in terms of arguments for the reform of metropolitan governance structures. The normative implications of their arguments have explicit ideological underpinnings. Some, like Dennis Judd, emphasize the values of equality of life chances and interpret differences between cities and suburbs as disparities; others (public choice theorists such as Elinor Ostrom) emphasize freedom of choice and interpret differences as opportunities for the exercise of choice.

Sociologists on the whole have been less willing to be proponents of metropolitan solutions, and they have shown more interest in the causes than in the consequences of suburbanization. Nevertheless, there are differences in theoretical perspective that closely parallel those in political science, and they hinge in part on the importance of political boundaries and the political process. The main lines of explanation reflect two broader currents in sociological theory: structural functionalism is found in the guise of human ecology and neoclassical economics, and variants of Marxian and Weberian theory have been described as the "new" urban theory.

Ecologists and many urban economists conceptualize suburbanization as a process of decentralization, as reflected in Burgess's (1967) concentric zone model of the metropolis. Burgess accepted the postulate of central place theory that the point of highest interaction and most valued land is naturally at the core of the central business district. The central point is most accessible to all other locations in the metropolis, a feature that is especially valuable for commercial firms. At the fringes of the business district, where land is being held for future commercial development, low-income and immigrant households can compete successfully for space, though only at high residential densities. Peripheral areas, by contrast, are most valued by more affluent households, particularly those with children and preferences for more spacious surroundings.

The key to this approach is its acceptance of a competitive land market as the principal mechanism through which locational decisions are reached. More specific hypotheses are drawn from theories about people's preferences and willingness (and ability) to pay for particular locations, or about structural changes (e.g., elevators, transportation technology, or space needs of manufacturers) that affect the value of central location. Many researchers have focused particularly on gradients linking distance from the center to various compositional characteristics of neighborhoods: their population density (Treadway 1969), household composition (Guest 1972), and socioeconomic status (Choldin and Hanson 1982). Comparatively little research has been conducted on the preferences of residents or the factors that lead them to select one location or another.

Other sociologists have argued that growth patterns result from conscious policies and specific institutional interventions in the land and housing markets. Representative of this view is Checko-

way (1980), who emphasizes the role of federal housing programs and institutional support for large-scale residential builders in the suburbanization of the 1950s. The move to suburbs, he argues, was contingent on the alternatives offered to consumers. The redlining of inner city neighborhoods by the Federal Housing Administration, its preference for large new subdivisions, and its explicit discrimination against minority homebuyers are among the major forces structuring these alternatives.

There have been few studies of the housing market from an institutional perspective, although the restructuring of real estate financing and the emergence of new linkages between large-scale developers and finance capital have begun to attract attention. More consideration has been given to the explicitly political aspects of land development (Logan and Molotch 1987). Following Hunter (1953), who believed that growth questions were the "big issue" in local politics, recent studies find that the most powerful voices in local politics are the proponents of growth and urban redevelopment and, in this sense, that the city is a growth machine.

Applying this model to suburbs, most observers portray suburban municipalities as "exclusionary." Suburban municipalities have long used zoning to influence the location and composition of land development. Since environmentalism emerged as a formidable political movement in the early 1970s, it has become commonplace to hear of localities that exercise their powers to preserve open space and historic sites, that impose restraints or even moratoria on new development. The "no-growth movement" is a direct extension of earlier exclusionary zoning policies.

SOCIOECONOMIC DIFFERENCES BETWEEN CITIES AND SUBURBS

These two theoretical perspectives can be illustrated through their application to research on socioeconomic differences between cities and suburbs. It is well known that central cities in most metropolitan regions have a less affluent residential population than their surrounding suburbs.

There is much debate, however, whether this class segregation between cities and their suburbs is a natural sorting out of social classes through the private market or whether its causes are political and institutional. Similar debate surrounds the phenomenon of differentiation *within* suburbia, where there is great variation in economic function, class and racial composition, and other characteristics of suburbs.

Research from an ecological perspective has stressed a comparison between the older, larger, denser cities of the North and the more recently growing cities of the South and West. The principal consistent findings have been that (1) the pattern of low central city relative to suburban social status is more pronounced in older metropolitan regions, but, (2) controlling for metropolitan age, there appears to be a universal generalization of this pattern over time (Guest and Nelson 1978). These sociologists propose that suburbs have natural advantages over central cities. For example, their housing stock is newer, suburban land is less expensive, and suburbs are more accessible to freeways and airports. The socioeconomic differences between cities and suburbs reflect those advantages.

Others argue that disparities are generated primarily by political structures that allocate zoning control and responsibility for public services to local governments and require these governments to finance services from such local sources as the tax on real property. They propose that the typical fragmentation of metropolitan government creates the incentive and opportunity for suburbs to pursue exclusionary growth policies (Danielson 1976).

Seeking to test these theories, Logan and Schneider (1982) found greater disparities in metropolitan areas where central cities were less able to grow through annexation (thus, where suburban municipal governments were more autonomous) and where localities were more reliant on local property taxes (hence, had greater incentive to pursue exclusionary policies). They also found a significant racial dimension: Greater disparities were evident in both 1960 and 1970 in metropoli-

tan areas in the North with a larger proportion of black residents. (The same did not hold for the South and West, however.) This is due both to the concentration of lower income blacks in central cities and to a greater propensity of higher status whites to live in suburbs in these metropolitan areas. This finding is reinforced by William Frey (see Frey and Speare 1988), who reported that the central city proportion of black residents is a significant predictor of white flight, independent of other causes.

If suburbs follow exclusionary growth policies, it seems counterintuitive that suburbs have experienced much more rapid growth than did cities in the postwar decades. The findings on city–suburb disparities, of course, indicate that exclusion has selective effects. Nevertheless, it is surprising that Baldassare and Protash (1982), in a study of northern California cities, found that communities with more restrictive planning controls actually had higher rates of population growth during the 1970s. Similarly, Logan and Zhou (1989) found that suburban growth controls had little if any impact on development patterns (population growth, socioeconomic status, or racial composition). In their view, the exclusionary policies of suburbs may be more apparent than real. The more visible actions, like growth moratoria, are often intended to blunt criticisms by residents concerned with problems arising from rapid-development. Unfortunately, few studies have looked in depth at the political process within suburbs; there is as little direct evidence on the role of local politics as there is on the operation of the land market. Most research from both the ecological and political-institutional perspectives has inferred the *processes* for controlling growth from evidence about the *outcomes*.

SUBURBANIZATION OF EMPLOYMENT

A central problem for early studies of suburban communities was to identify the patterns of functional specialization among them. It was recognized that older industrial satellites coexisted with dormitory towns in the fringe areas around central cities. Both were suburban in the sense that they were integrated into a metropolitan economy dominated by the central city. Their own economic role and the nature of the populations that they housed were quite distinct, however. The greatest population gains in the 1950s were made by residential suburbs, communities that were wealthier, younger, newer, and less densely settled than those towns on the fringes of the region that had higher concentrations of employment. Leo Schnore (see Schnore and Winsborough 1972) distinguished "suburbs" from "satellites" to acknowledge these different origins.

The metaphors of suburbs and satellites reflected the reality of early postwar suburbanization, a period when established towns and small cities were surrounded by successive waves of new subdivisions. The metaphors are no longer appropriate. Since the late 1950s, the bulk of new manufacturing and trade employment in the metropolis is located in small- and middle-sized cities in the suburban ring (Berry and Kasarda 1977, Chapter 13). Downtown department stores compete with new suburban shopping malls. The highly developed expressway network around central cities frees manufacturing plants to take advantage of the lower land prices and taxes and the superior access to the skilled workforce offered by the suburbs. For the period of 1963 to 1977, in the largest twenty-five metropolitan areas, total manufacturing employment in central cities declined by about 700,000 (19 percent), while their suburbs gained 1.1 million (36 percent). At the same time, total central city retail and wholesale employment was stagnant (dropping by 100,000). Trade employment in the suburbs increased by 1.8 million (or 110 percent) in this period. Thus, total employment growth in the suburbs outpaced the growth of population (Logan and Golden 1986).

How has suburbanization of employment affected suburban communities? According to microeconomic and ecological models, locational choices by employers reflect the balance of costs and benefits of competing sites. New employment maintains old patterns because the cost-benefit equation is typically stable, including such important considerations as location relative to workforce, suppliers, markets, and the local infrastructure. In the terms commonly used by urban sociologists, this means that communities find their "ecological niche." Stahura's (1982) findings of marked persistence in manufacturing and trade employment among suburbs from 1960 to 1972 supports this expectation. Once "crystallized," the functional specialization of communities changes only under conditions of major shifts in the needs of firms.

To the extent that changes occur, in this view, they follow a natural life cycle (Hoover and Vernon 1962). Residential suburbs in the inner ring, near the central city, tend over time to undergo two related transformations: first, to higher population density and a conversion to nonresidential development, and second, to a lower socioeconomic status. Thus, inner suburbs that gain employment are—like older satellites—less affluent than residential suburbs.

By contrast, those who emphasize the politics of land development suggest very different conclusions. A growing number of suburbs perceive business and industry as a significant local resource. Once shunned by the higher status suburbs, they now contribute to both property values and the local tax base. Prestigious communities such as Greenwich, Connecticut, and Palo Alto, California, house industrial parks and corporate headquarters. The "good climate for business" that they offer includes public financing of new investments, extensive infrastructure (roads, utilities, parking, police and fire protection), and moderate taxes (Logan and Molotch 1987).

Competition among suburbs introduces a new factor that has the potential to reshape suburban regions. Schneider (1989) reports that location of manufacturing firms is affected by the strength of the local tax base, suggesting that wealthy suburbs are advantaged in this competition. Logan and Golden (1986) find that newly developing suburban employment centers have higher socioeconomic status, as well as stronger fiscal resources, than other suburbs; this is a reversal of the pattern of the 1950s.

MINORITY SUBURBANIZATION

The suburbanization process also increasingly involves minorities and immigrants, and the incorporation of these groups into suburban areas has become an important topic for research on race and ethnic relations. As Massey and Denton (1987) document, the rate of growth of nonwhites and Hispanics in metropolitan areas is far outstripping the rate of growth of non-Hispanic whites. Much of this growth is occurring in suburbs. During the 1970s, for example, the number of blacks in the non–central-city parts of metropolitan areas increased by 70 percent, compared to just 16 percent in central cities; and the number of other nonwhites in them shot up by 150 percent, compared to approximately 70 percent in central cities. One reason for the rapidly increasing racial and ethnic diversity of suburbs may be that some new immigrant groups are bypassing central cities and settling directly in suburbs. Equally important is the increasing suburbanization of older racial and ethnic minorities, such as blacks (Frey and Speare 1988).

This phenomenon has encouraged researchers to study suburbanization as a mirror on the social mobility of minorities. Consistent with classical ecological theory, suburbanization has often been portrayed broadly as a step toward assimilation into the mainstream society and as a sign of the erosion of social boundaries. For European immigrant groups after the turn of the century, residential decentralization appears to have been part of the general process of assimilation (Guest 1980).

Past studies have found that suburbanization of Hispanics and Asians in a metropolitan area is in fact strongly associated with each group's average income level (Massey and Denton 1987, pp. 819–820; see also Frey and Speare 1988, pp. 311–315). Further, again for Hispanics and Asians, Massey and Denton demonstrate that suburban residence is typically associated with lower levels of segregation and, accordingly, higher probabilities

of contact with the Anglo majority. But these and other authors report very different results for blacks. Black suburbanization is unrelated to the average income level of blacks in the metropolitan area, and suburbanization does not result in higher intergroup contact for blacks. The suburbanization process for blacks appears largely to be one of continued ghettoization (Farley 1970), as indicated by high and in some regions increasing levels of segregation and by the concentration of suburban blacks in communities with a high incidence of social problems (e.g., high crime rates), high taxes, and underfunded social services (Logan and Schneider 1984).

These findings regarding black suburbanization have been interpreted in terms of processes that impede the free mobility of racial minorities: steering by realtors, unequal access to mortgage credit, exclusionary zoning, and neighbor hostility (Foley 1973). Home ownership indeed may be one of the gatekeepers for suburban living. Stearns and Logan (1986) report that blacks were less likely to live in suburban areas where higher proportions of the housing stock were owner-occupied.

Further evidence is offered by Alba and Logan (1991), who based their article on an analysis of individual-level data from the 1980 census. They find that suburban residence is more likely among homeowners and persons of higher socioeconomic status. There are stronger effects of family status (marriage and the presence of children in the household) and measures of cultural assimilation (English language use, nativity, and period of immigration). Assimilation is evidently a major part of the suburbanization process for most groups, especially those arising out of immigration.

At the same time, however, they report important differences among ethnic groups. The first is the unusually small effect of family status among blacks, Mexicans, and Puerto Ricans (all three groups rank near the bottom in terms of overall likelihood of suburbanization). In these groups, married couples with young children are more likely than others to be found in suburbs. But the difference made by family type tends to be small, indicating that families with children are comparatively disadvantaged in achieving suburban residence. A second difference is in the magnitude of the socioeconomic gradient in suburbanization. For members of the non-Hispanic white majority, household income has only a small effect (and education has no effect at all). But socioeconomic status is strongly related to suburbanization for some minorities, for example, the Chinese and Puerto Ricans. This gradient appears to indicate that suburban residence does, in fact, "cost" some minorities more than it does members of the majority. A final difference is in the effects of metropolitan characteristics. Some groups face a substantial disadvantage in metropolitan areas where home ownership is a requirement for suburban entry or where the income differential between suburb and city is large (thus indicating that the suburban ring has generally higher status than the central city). Although these factors have little impact on the suburbanization of whites, they have a sizable negative influence on suburbanization for blacks and the Hispanic groups. This suggests that some minorities face obstacles to suburban residence in precisely those metropolitan areas where suburban locations are most desirable.

Parallel results are found for the racial and ethnic sorting process within a suburban region (the New York–New Jersey suburban region, as reported by Logan and Alba 1991). Two sorts of analyses were conducted. First, members of different racial and ethnic groups were compared on the average characteristics of suburbs in which they reside. Second, regression models were estimated for members of each major racial or ethnic group to predict several of these indicators of place advantages or community resources.

There are important differences between whites, blacks, Hispanics, and Asians in the kinds of suburbs that they live in. As some researchers have suspected, suburban Asians have achieved access to relatively advantaged communities, similar in most respects to those of suburban non-Hispanic whites. Hispanics in the New York region have not. Suburban Hispanics, by and large, live in communities that are about the same as black

suburbs: communities with low average income levels and low rates of home ownership.

Is the disadvantage of blacks and Hispanics attributable to individual qualities of group members, or do these groups face collective disadvantages? Analysis of individual characteristics that may predict the quality of suburb that one resides in shows that the same location process does not apply equally to all minorities. The pattern for whites, who are relatively advantaged in access to community resources, lends clear support to assimilation theory. Human capital and indicators of cultural assimilation are strongly associated with access to higher status suburbs. The same can be said of Asians (who are relatively advantaged overall), with the exception that cultural assimilation variables seem not to be important for Asians.

Results for blacks strongly call attention to processes of racial stratification. Even controlling for many other individual characteristics, blacks live in suburbs with lower ownership and income levels than do non-Hispanic whites. Further, most human capital and assimilation variables have a smaller payoff for blacks than for whites. The findings for Hispanics are supportive of the assimilation model in several respects. Hispanics gain more strongly than whites from most human capital characteristics; therefore, at higher levels of socioeconomic achievement and cultural assimilation, Hispanics come progressively closer to matching the community resources of whites. It should be noted, however, that Hispanics begin from a lower starting point and that black Hispanics face a double disadvantage that is inconsistent with an assimilation perspective.

LOOKING TO THE FUTURE

Suburbanization continues to be a key aspect of metropolitan growth. The political boundaries among cities and suburbs accentuate interest in substantive issues of metropolitan inequalities. They also create special opportunities for theories of urbanization to go beyond economic models and to incorporate an understanding of the political process. Research on suburbanization has been most successful in describing patterns of decentralization and spatial differentiation. The movements of people and employment, and the segregation among suburbs by social class, race, ethnicity, and family composition, have been well documented. But these patterns are broadly consistent with a variety of interpretations, ranging from those that assume a competitive land market (human ecology) to those that stress the institutional and political structuring of that market.

The principal gaps in knowledge concern the key processes that are central to these alternative interpretations. Few sociologists have directly studied the housing market from the perspective of either demand (how do people learn about the alternatives, and how do they select among them?) or supply (how does the real estate sector operate, how is racial and ethnic segmentation of the market achieved, how is the complex of construction industries, developers, and financial institutions tied to the rest of the economy?). Rarely have sociologists investigated government decisions (at any level) that impinge on development, from the point of view neither of their effects nor of the political process that led to them. Of course, these observations are not specific to research on suburbanization. It is important to bear in mind that neither the theoretical issues nor the research strategies in this field distinguish suburbanization from other aspects of the urban process.

(SEE ALSO: *Cities; Community; Urbanization*)

REFERENCES

Alba, Richard D., and John R. Logan 1991 "Variations on Two Themes: Racial and Ethnic Patterns in the Attainment of Suburban Residence." *Demography,* forthcoming.

Baldassare, Mark, and William Protash 1982 "Growth Controls, Population Growth, and Community Satisfaction." *American Sociological Review* 47:339–346.

Berry, Brian, and John Kasarda 1977 *Contemporary Urban Ecology.* New York: Macmillan.

Burgess, Ernest W. 1967 "The Growth of the City." In R. E. Park, E. W. Burgess, and R. D. McKenzie, eds., *The City.* Chicago: University of Chicago Press.

Checkoway, Barry 1980 "Large Builders, Federal Housing Programmes, and Postwar Suburbanization." *International Journal of Urban and Regional Research* 4:21–44.

Choldin, Harvey M., and Claudine Hanson 1982 "Status Shifts Within the City." *American Sociological Review* 47:129–141.

Danielson, Michael 1976 *The Politics of Exclusion.* New York: Columbia University Press.

Farley, Reynolds 1970 "The Changing Distribution of Negroes Within Metropolitan Areas: The Emergence of Black Suburbs." *American Journal of Sociology* 75:512–529.

Foley, Donald 1973 "Institutional and Contextual Factors Affecting the Housing Choices of Minority Residents." In Amos Hawley and Vincent Rock, eds., *Segregation in Residential Areas.* Washington, D.C.: National Academy of Sciences.

Frey, William, and Alden Speare 1988 *Regional and Metropolitan Growth and Decline in the United States.* New York: Russell Sage Foundation.

Guest, Avery M. 1972 "Patterns of Family Location." *Demography* 9:159–171.

———1980 "The Suburbanization of Ethnic Groups." *Sociology and Social Research* 64:497–513.

———, and G. Nelson 1978 "Central City/Suburban Status Differences: Fifty Years of Change." *Sociological Quarterly* 19:7–23.

Hoover, Edgar, and Raymond Vernon 1962 *Anatomy of a Metropolis.* Garden City, N.Y.: Doubleday.

Hunter, Floyd 1953 *Community Power Structure.* Chapel Hill: University of North Carolina Press.

Logan, John R., and Richard Alba 1991 "Locational Returns to Human Capital: Minority Access to Suburban Community Resources." Paper presented at the annual meeting of the American Sociological Association, Cincinnati, August 23–27.

Logan, John R., and Reid Golden 1986 "Suburbs and Satellites: Two Decades of Change." *American Sociological Review* 51:430–437.

Logan, John R., and Harvey L. Molotch 1987 *Urban Fortunes: The Political Economy of Place.* Berkeley: University of California Press.

Logan, John R., and Mark Schneider 1982 "Governmental Organization and City–Suburb Income Inequality, 1960–1970." *Urban Affairs Quarterly* 17: 303–318.

———1984 "Racial Segregation and Racial Change in American Suburbs: 1970–1980." *American Journal of Sociology* 89:874–888.

Logan, John R., and Min Zhou 1989 "Do Growth

Controls Control Growth?" *American Sociological Review* 54:461–471.

Massey, Douglas, and Nancy Denton 1987 "Trends in the Residential Segregation of Blacks, Hispanics, and Asians: 1970–1980." *American Sociological Review* 52:802–825.

Schneider, Mark 1989 *The Competitive City: The Political Economy of Suburbia.* Pittsburgh: University of Pittsburgh Press.

Schnore, Leo, and Hal Winsborough 1972 "Functional Classification and the Residential Location of Social Classes." In Brian Berry, ed., *City Classification Handbook: Methods and Application.* New York: Wiley.

Stahura, John 1982 "Determinants of Suburban Job Change in Retailing, Wholesaling, Service, and Manufacturing Industries: 1960–1972." *Sociological Focus* 15:347–357.

Stearns, Linda, and John Logan 1986 "The Racial Structuring of the Housing Market and Segregation in Suburban Areas." *Social Forces* 65:28–42.

Treadway, Roy C. 1969 "Social Components of Metropolitan Population Densities." *Demography* 6:55–74.

JOHN R. LOGAN

SUICIDE To many, suicide, or intentional self-killing, seems like the ultimate asocial act of an individual. Yet sociology itself grew out of Emile Durkheim's argument that suicide rates are social facts and reflect variation in social regulation and social interaction (Durkheim [1897] 1951). The concept of suicide derives from the Latin *sui* ("of oneself") and *cide* ("a killing"). Edwin Shneidman defines suicide as "currently in the Western world a conscious act of self-induced annihilation best understood as a multidimensional malaise in a needful individual who defines an issue for which suicide is perceived as the best solution" (1985, p. 203). Several conceptual implications follow from this definition.

Although suicidal types vary, there probably are some common traits that most suicides share (Shneidman 1985). People who choose suicide tend to

- seek a solution to their life problems by dying;
- want to cease consciousness;

- try to reduce intolerable psychological pain;
- have frustrated psychological needs;
- feel helpless and hopeless;
- be ambivalent about dying;
- be perceptually constricted and rigid thinkers;
- manifest escape, egression, or fugue behaviors;
- communicate their intent to commit suicide or die;
- have lifelong self-destructive coping responses (sometimes called "suicidal careers").

Completed suicides need to be differentiated from nonfatal suicide attempts, suicide ideation, and suicide talk or gestures. Sometimes one speaks of self-injury, self-mutilation, accident proneness, failure to take needed medications, and the like—where suicide intent cannot be demonstrated—as "parasuicide." The most common of all self-destructive behaviors are indirect, for example, alcoholism, obesity, risky sports, gambling, and so forth. There are also mass suicides (Jonestown, Guyana, 1978, and Masada in Roman-ruled Palestine, 73 A.D.) and murder-suicides. Individual and social growth probably require some partial self-destruction.

Although most suicides have much in common, suicide is emphatically not one type of behavior. Suicidology will never be an exact science until it carefully specifies its dependent variable. The predictors or causes of suicide vary immensely with the specific type of suicidal outcome. Suicidologists tend to recognize three to six basic types of suicide, each with two or three of their own subtypes (Maris et al. 1991, chap. 4). For example, Durkheim ([1897] 1951) thought all suicides were basically anomic, egoistic, altruistic, or fatalistic. Freud ([1917] 1953) and Menninger (1938) argued that psychoanalytically all suicides were based on hate or revenge (a "wish to kill"); on depression, melancholia, or hopelessness (a "wish to die"); or on guilt or shame (a "wish to be killed"). Finally, Baechler (1979) added "oblative" (i.e., sacrifice or transfiguration) and "ludic" (i.e., engaging in ordeals or risks and games) suicidal types.

TABLE 1
Ten Leading Causes of Death in the United States, 1987

Rank	Cause of death	Rate*	No. of deaths†
1	Disease of the heart	312.4	760,353
2	Malignant neoplasms	195.9	476,927
3	Cerebrovascular disease	61.6	149,835
4	Accidents	39.0	95,020
5	Chronic obstructive pulmonary disease	32.2	78,380
6	Pneumonia and influenza	28.4	69,225
7	Diabetes mellitus	15.8	38,532
8	Suicide	12.7	30,796
9	Chronic liver disease	10.8	26,201
10	Atherosclerosis	9.2	22,474

*Per 100,000 population.
†Total number of deaths (all causes) in 1987: 2,123,323.

SOURCE: Data from National Center for Health Statistics, 1989.

EPIDEMIOLOGY, RATES, AND PREDICTORS

Suicide is a relatively rare event, one to three in 10,000 in the general U.S. population per year. In 1987 there were 30,796 suicides (about 1.5 percent of all deaths). This number amounts to an overall suicide rate of 12.7 suicides per 100,000 population. Suicide is now the eighth leading cause of death, ranking just ahead of cirrhosis and other liver disease deaths and just behind diabetes deaths. Suicide has been moving up the ladder of the leading causes of death in this century.

Suicide rates in the United States vary considerably by sex, age, and race. The highest rates are observed consistently among white males, who constitute roughly 70 percent of all suicides. White females make up about 20 percent of all suicides. American blacks (especially females) rarely commit suicide (except for some young urban males). Some scholars have argued that black suicides tend to be disguised as homicides or accidents. In general, male suicides outnumber female suicides three or four to one. Suicide rates also increase gradually with age and then drop off some at the very oldest ages. Female suicide rates

TABLE 2
Rates of Completed U.S. Suicide by Race and Gender for 1987*

Race-gender group	Number of suicides	Percent of suicides	Rate per 100,000
White males	22,188	72.0	22.1
White females	6,029	19.6	5.7
Black males	1,635	5.3	11.6
Black females	328	1.1	2.1
Other males*	449	1.5	11.6
Other females*	167	0.5	2.5
Totals	30,796	100.0	12.7

*Includes American Indian, Chinese, Hawaiian, Japanese, Filipino, Other Asian or Pacific Islander, and Other.

SOURCE: Data from National Center for Health Statistics, 1990.

TABLE 3
Rates of Completed U.S. Suicide per 100,000 population by Year and Age

Age*	Year			
	1957	1967	1977	1987
5–14	0.2	0.3	0.5	0.7
15–24	4.0	7.0	13.6	12.9
25–34	8.6	12.4	17.7	15.4
35–44	12.8	16.6	16.8	15.0
45–54	18.0	19.5	18.9	15.9
55–64	22.4	22.4	19.4	16.6
65–74	25.0	19.8	20.1	19.4
75–84	26.8	21.0	21.5	25.8
85 and over	26.3	22.7	17.3	22.1
Total	9.8	10.8	13.3	12.7

*No suicide reported for individuals under five years of age.
SOURCE: Data from National Center for Health Statistics, 1990.

tend to peak earlier than those of males. Note (in Table 3) that from about 1967 to 1977 there was a significant increase in the suicide rate of fifteen- to twenty-four-year-olds and that elderly suicide rates seem to be climbing again.

Typically, marrying and having children protect one against suicide. Usually suicide rates are highest for the widowed, followed by those of the divorced and the never-married or single. Studies of suicide rates by social class have been equivocal. Within each broad census occupational category there are job types with both high and low suicide rates. For example, psychiatrists have high suicide rates, but pediatricians and surgeons have low suicide rates. Operatives usually have low rates, but policemen typically have high suicide rates.

The predominant method of suicide for both males and females in 1987 was firearms. The second most common method among males is hanging and among females is drug and medicine overdoses. Females use a somewhat greater variety of methods than males do. Suicide rates tend to be higher on Mondays and in the springtime (Gabennesch 1988).

Prediction of suicide is a complicated process (Maris et al. 1991). As with other rare events, suicide prediction generates many false positives (i.e., identifying some deaths as suicides when they are in fact not suicides). Correctly identifying true suicides is referred to as "sensitivity," and correctly identifying true nonsuicides is called "specificity." In one celebrated study using common predictors (see Table 5) Porkorny (1983) correctly predicted fifteen of sixty-seven suicides among 4,800 psychiatric patients, but he also got 279 false positives.

Table 5 lists fifteen major predictors of suicide. Single predictor variables seldom if ever correctly identify suicides. Most suicides have "comorbidity" (i.e., several key predictors are involved), and specific predictors vary with the type of suicide and other factors. Depressive disorders and alcoholism are two of the major predictors of suicide. Robins (1981) found that about 72 percent of all completed suicides were either depressed or alcoholic. Roughly 15 percent of all those with depressive illness and 18 percent of all alcoholics will eventually commit suicide. Repeated depressive illness that leads to hopelessness is especially suicidogenic.

Nonfatal suicide attempts, talk about suicide or dying, and explicit plans or preparations for dying or suicide all increased suicide risk. However, for the paradigmatic suicide (older white males) 85 to 90 percent of them make only one fatal suicide attempt and seldom explicitly communicate their suicidal intent or show up at hospitals and clinics.

TABLE 4
Percent of Completed U.S. Suicides (1987) by Method and Gender

	Gender	
	Male	*Female*
Method	*%*	*%*
Firearms (E955.0–955.4)	64.0	39.8
Drugs/Medications (E950.0–950.5)	5.2	25.0
Hanging (E953.0)	13.5	9.4
Carbon monoxide (E952.0–952.1)	9.6	12.6
Jumping from a high place (E957)	1.8	3.0
Drowning (E954)	1.1	2.8
Suffocation by plastic bag (E953.1)	0.4	1.8
Cutting/Piercing instruments (E956)	1.3	1.4
Poisons (E950.6–950.9)	0.6	1.0
Other*	2.5	3.2
TOTALS	100.0	100.0

*Includes gases in domestic use (E951), other specified and unspecified gases and vapors (E952.8–952.9), explosives (E955.5), unspecified firearms and explosives (E955.9), and other specified or unspecified means of hanging, strangulation, or suffocation (E953.8–953.9).

SOURCE: Data from National Center for Health Statistics, 1990.

Social isolation (having no close friends, living alone, being unemployed, unmarried, etc.) and lack of social support is more common among suicides than among controls. Suicide tends to run in families, which suggests both modeling and genetic influences. There are some important biological and sociobiological predictors of suicide emerging, especially low central spinal fluid serotonin in the form of 5-HIAA (Maris et al. 1991).

TABLE 5
Common Single Predictors of Suicide

1. Depressive illness, mental disorder
2. Alcoholism, drug abuse
3. Suicide ideation, talk, preparation, religion
4. Prior suicide attempts
5. Lethal methods
6. Isolation, living alone, loss of support
7. Hopelessness, cognitive rigidity
8. Older white males
9. Modeling, suicide in the family, genetics
10. Work problems, economics, occupation
11. Marital problems, family pathology
12. Stress, life events
13. Anger, aggression, irritability, 5-HIAA
14. Physical illness
15. Repetition and comorbidity of factors 1–14, suicidal careers

SOURCE: Maris et al., 1991, chap. 1.

HISTORY, COMPARATIVE STUDIES, AND SOCIAL SUICIDOLOGISTS

The incidence and study of suicide has a long history and was fundamental to the foundation of sociology. The earliest known visual reference to suicide is Ajax falling on his sword (c. 540 B.C.). Of course, we know that Socrates (about 399 B.C.) drank the hemlock. In the Judeo-Christian scriptures there were eleven men (and no women) who died by suicide (most notably Samson, Judas, and Saul). Common biblical motives for suicide were revenge, shame, or defeat in battle. Other famous suicides in art history include paintings of Lucretia stabbing herself (after a rape), Dido, and work by Edvard Munch and Andy Warhol.

Suicide varies with culture and ethnicity. Most cultures have at least some suicides. However, suicide is rare or absent among the Tiv of Nigeria, Andaman islanders, and Australian aborigenes and relatively infrequent among rural American blacks and Irish Roman Catholics. The highest suicide rates in the world are found in Hungary, the Federal Republic of Germany, Austria, Scandinavia, and Japan (see Table 6). The lowest rates are found in several South American, Pacific Island, and predominantly Roman Catholic countries (including Antigua, Jamaica, New Guinea, the Philippines, Mexico, Italy, and Ireland).

The sociological study of suicide, of course, started with Durkheim ([1897] 1951) and has continued to the present day, primarily by the following sociologists: Henry and Short (1954); Gibbs and Martin (1964); Gibbs (1988); Douglas (1967); Maris (1969; 1981); Phillips (1974; 1991); Stack (1982); Wasserman (1989); and Pescosolido and Georgianna (1989). It is impossible in an encyclopedia to do justice to the full account of the sociological study of suicide. For a more complete review, see Maris (1989). What follows is only a sketch.

Durkheim claimed that the suicide rate varied inversely with social integration and that suicide types were primarily ego-anomic. However, Durkheim did not operationally define "social integration." Gibbs and Martin (1964) created the concept of "status integration" to correct this deficiency in Durkheim. They hypothesized that the less frequently occupied status sets would lead to lower status integration and higher suicide rates. Putting it differently, they expected status integration and suicide rates to be negatively associated. In a large series of tests from 1964 to 1988 Gibbs found his primary hypothesis to be confirmed only for occupational statuses (which Durkheim also had said were of central importance).

Henry and Short (1954) expanded Durkheim's concept of external and constraining social factors to include interaction with social-psychological factors of "internal constraint" (such as strict superego restraint) and frustration-aggression theory. Henry and Short reasoned that suicide rates would be highest when external restraint was low and internal restraint was high (and that

homicide rates would be high when internal restraint was low and external restraint was high).

A vastly different sociological perspective on suicide originated with the work of ethnomethodologist Jack Douglas. Douglas (in the tradition of Max Weber's subjective meanings) argued that Durkheim's reliance on official statistics (like death certificates) as the data base for studying suicide was fundamentally mistaken (Douglas 1967). What Douglas said we need to do is to observe the accounts or situated meanings of actual individuals who are known to be suicidal, not some third-party official like a coroner or medical examiner who is not a suicide and who may use ad hoc criteria to classify a death as a suicide. There are probably just about as many official statistics as there are officials.

Maris (1981) extended Durkheim's empirical survey of suicidal behaviors, but not just by measuring macrosocial and demographic or structural variables. Instead Maris focused on actual interviews ("psychological autopsies") of the intimate survivors of suicides (usually their spouses) and compared these cases with control or comparison groups of natural deaths and nonfatal suicide attempters. Maris claimed that individuals who committed suicide had long "suicidal careers" involving complex mixes of biological, social, and psychological factors.

Phillips (1974) differed with Durkheim's contention that suicides are not suggestable or contagious. In a pioneering and stage-setting paper in the *American Sociological Review* in 1974, Phillips demonstrated that front-page newspaper coverage of celebrity suicides was associated with a statistically significant rise in the national suicide rate seven to ten days after the publicized suicide. The rise in the suicide rate was greater the longer the front-page coverage, greater in the region where the news account ran, and higher if the stimulus suicide and the person supposedly copying the suicide were similar. In a long series of similar studies Phillips and others expanded and documented the suggestion effect for other types of behavior and for other groups. For example, the contagion effect appears to be especially powerful among teenagers. Nevertheless, contagion ac-

TABLE 6
Suicide Rates (per 100,000 of Population) in 62 Countries: 1980–1986

Country	Rate
1. Hungary	45.3
2. Federal Republic of Germany	43.1
3. Sri Lanka	29.0
4. Austria	28.3
5. Denmark	27.8
6. Finland	26.6
7. Belgium	23.8
8. Switzerland	22.8
9. France	22.7
10. Suriname	21.6
11. Japan	21.2
12. German Democratic Republic	19.0
13. Czechoslovakia	18.9
14. Sweden	18.5
15. Cuba	17.7
16. Bulgaria	16.3
17. Yugoslavia	16.1
18. Norway	14.1
19. Luxembourg	13.9
20. Iceland	13.3
21. Poland	13.0
22. Canada	12.9
23. Singapore	12.7
24. United States	12.3
25. Hong Kong	12.2
26. Australia	11.6
27. Scotland	11.6
28. The Netherlands	11.0
29. El Salvador	10.8
30. New Zealand	10.3

(continued)

counts for only a 1 to 6 percent increase over normal expected suicide rates in a population.

Phillips's ideas about contagion have dominated the sociological study of suicide in the 1980s. Work by Stack (1982), Wasserman (1989), Kessler and Stripp (1984), and others have produced equivocal support for the role of suggestion in suicide (Diekstra et al. 1989). Wasserman feels the business cycle and unemployment rates must be controlled for. Some have claimed that imitative effects are statistical artifacts. Most problematic is that the theory of imitation in suicide is underdeveloped.

The most recent sociologist to study suicide is medical sociologist Bernice Pescosolido. She has claimed, contrary to Douglas, that the official statistics of suicide are acceptably reliable and (as Gibbs said earlier) that they are the best basis available for the foundation of a science of suicide. Her latest paper (Pescosolido and Georgianna 1989) examined Durkheim's claim that religious involvement protects against suicide. Pescosolido finds that Roman Catholicism and evangelical Protestantism do protect one against suicide (institutional Protestantism does not) and that Judaism has a small, inconsistent protective effect. Pescosolido concludes that with disintegrating network ties, individuals who were denied both integrative and regulative supports commit suicide more often.

TABLE 6 (con't)

31. Puerto Rico	9.8
32. Uruguay	9.6
33. Northern Ireland	9.3
34. Portugal	9.2
35. England and Wales	8.9
36. Trinidad and Tobago	8.6
37. Guadeloupe	7.9
38. Ireland	7.8
39. Italy	7.6
40. Thailand	6.6
41. Argentina	6.3
42. Chile	6.2
43. Spain	4.9
44. Venezuela	4.8
45. Costa Rica	4.5
46. Ecuador	4.3
47. Greece	4.1
48. Martinique	3.7
49. Colombia	2.9
50. Mauritius	2.8
51. Dominican Republic	2.4
52. Mexico	1.6
53. Panama	1.4
54. Peru	1.4
55. The Philippines	0.5
56. Guatemala	0.5
57. Malta	0.3
58. Nicaragua	0.2
59. Papua New Guinea	0.2
60. Jamaica	0.1
61. Egypt	0.1
62. Antigua and Barbuda	—

SOURCE: Diekstra 1990.

ISSUES AND FUTURE DIRECTIONS

Much of current sociological research on suicide appears myopic and sterile, compared to early work by Durkheim ([1897] 1951), Douglas (1967), and Garfinkel (1967). Not only is the scope of current research limited, there is very little theory and few book-length publications. Almost no research monographs on the sociology of suicide were written in the 1980s. Highly focused scientific journal articles on imitation have predominated. However, none of these papers has been able to establish if suicides ever in fact were exposed to the original media stimulus! Since suicide does not just concern social rela-

tions, the study of suicide needs more interdisciplinary syntheses. The dependent variable (suicide) needs to include comparisons with other types of death and violence, as well as more nonsocial predictor variables (Holinger 1987).

A second issue concerns methods for studying suicide (Lann, Mościcki, and Maris 1989). There has never been a truly national sample survey of suicidal behaviors in the United States. Also, most suicide research is retrospective and based on questionable vital statistics. More prospective or longitudinal research designs are needed, of course, with adequate sample sizes and comparison or control groups. Models of suicidal careers should be analyzed with specific and more appropriate statistical techniques (like logistic regression, log-linear procedures, and event or hazard analysis). It should be noted that federal funds to do any major research on suicide are in short supply and that this is probably the single major obstacle to the contemporary scientific study of suicide.

Third, most studies of suicide are cross-sectional and static. Future research will, it is hoped, include more social developmental designs (Blumenthal and Kupfer 1990). We still have very little solid knowledge about the social dynamics or "suicidal careers" of eventual suicides (Maris 1990). For example, it is well known that completed suicides tend to be socially isolated at the time of death, but how they came to be that way is less well understood. Fourth, in passing it must be noted that even after almost a hundred years of research the relationship of suicide to social class, occupation, and socioeconomic status is still not clear.

Finally, a major issue in the study of suicide is rational suicide, active euthanasia, the right to die, and appropriate death. With a rapidly aging and more secular population and the spread of the AIDS virus, the American public is demanding more information about and legal rights for voluntary assisted death (see the case of Nico Speijer in the Netherlands, Diekstra 1986). The right to die and assisted suicide have been the focus of a few recent legal cases (Humphry and Wickett 1986; Battin and Maris 1983). Rosewell Gilbert, an elderly man who was sentenced to life imprisonment in Florida for the mercy killing of his sick wife, was pardoned in 1990 by the governor of Florida. However, in 1990 the U.S. Supreme Court (*Cruzon v. the State of Missouri*) ruled that hospitals have the right to continue to force-feed even brain-dead patients. The Hemlock Society was founded by Derek Humphry to assist those who wish to end their own lives, make living wills, or pass living-will legislation in their states (however, see the *New York Times*, February 8, 1990, A18). Of course, the state must be cautious that the right to die does not become the obligation to die (e.g., for the aged). These issues are further complicated by strong religious and moral persuasions.

(SEE ALSO: *Death and Dying; Deviance Theories; Mental Illness and Mental Disorders; Stress*)

REFERENCES

Alcohol, Drug Abuse, and Mental Health Administration 1989 *Report of the Secretary's Task Force on Youth Suicide*, Vols. 1–4. Washington, D.C.: U.S. Government Printing Office.

Baechler, Jean 1979 *Suicides*. New York: Basic Books.

Battin, Margaret P., and Ronald W. Maris (eds.) 1983 *Suicide and Ethics*. New York: Human Sciences Press.

Blumenthal, Susan J., and David J. Kupfer (eds.) 1990 *Suicide over the Life Cycle: Risk Factors, Assessment, and Treatment of Suicidal Patients*. Washington, D.C.: American Psychiatric Press.

————Diekstra, René F. W., 1986 "The Significance of Nico Speijer's Suicide: How and When Should Suicide Be Prevented?" *Suicide and Life-Threatening Behavior* 16 (1):13–15.

———— 1990 "An International Perspective on the Epidemiology and Prevention of Suicide." In Susan J. Blumenthal and David J. Kupfer, eds., *Suicide of the Life-cycle*. Washington, D.C.: American Psychiatric Press.

————, Ronald W. Maris, Stephen Platt, Armin Schmidtke, and Gernot Sonneck (eds.) 1989 *Suicide and Its Prevention: The Role of Attitude and Imitation*. Leiden: E. J. Brill.

Douglas, Jack D. 1967 *The Social Meanings of Suicide*. Princeton, N.J.: Princeton University Press.

Dunne, Edward J., John L. McIntosh, and Karen Dunne-Maxim (eds.) 1987 *Suicide and Its Aftermath*. New York: W. W. Norton.

Durkheim, Emile (1897) 1951 *Suicide*. New York: Free Press.

Evans, Glen, and Norman L. Farberow (eds.) 1988 *The Encyclopedia of Suicide*. New York: Facts On File.

Freud, Sigmund (1917) 1953 "Mourning and Melancholia." In James Strachey, ed., *Standard Edition of the Complete Works of Sigmund Freud*. London: Hogarth Press.

Gabennesch, Howard 1988 "When Promises Fail: A Theory of Temporal Fluctuations in Suicide." *Social Forces* 67:129–145.

Garfinkel, Harold 1967 *Studies in Ethnomethodology.* Englewood Cliffs, N.J.: Prentice-Hall.

Gibbs, Jack, and Mark C. Stafford 1988 "Change in the Relation Between Marital Integration and Suicide Rates." *Social Forces* 66:1060–1079.

Gibbs, Jack P., and W. T. Martin 1964 *Status Integration and Suicide.* Eugene: University of Oregon Press.

Gibbs, Jewelle Taylor (ed.) 1988 *Young, Black, and Male in America: An Endangered Species.* Dover, Mass.: Auburn House.

Henry, Andrew F., and James F. Short 1954 *Suicide and Homicide.* New York: Free Press.

Holinger, Paul C. 1987 *Violent Deaths in the United States: An Epidemiological Study of Suicide, Homicide, and Accidents.* New York: Guilford.

Humphry, Derek, and Ann Wickett 1986 *The Right to Die: Understanding Euthanasia.* New York: Harper and Row.

Jacobs, Douglas, and Herbert N. Brown (eds.) 1989 *Suicide, Understanding, and Responding: Harvard Medical School Perspectives.* Madison, Conn.: International Universities Press.

Kessler, Ronald C., and H. Stripp 1984 "The Impact of Fictional Television Stories on U.S. Fatalities: A Replication." *American Journal of Sociology* 90:151–167.

Lann, Irma S., Eve K. Mościcki, and Ronald W. Maris (eds.) 1989 *Strategies for Studying Suicide and Suicidal Behavior.* New York: Guilford.

Maris, Ronald W. 1969 *Social Forces in Urban Suicide.* Chicago: Dorsey Press.

——— 1981 *Pathways to Suicide: A Survey of Self-Destructive Behaviors.* Baltimore: Johns Hopkins University Press.

——— 1986 *Biology of Suicide.* New York: Guilford.

——— 1989 "The Social Relations of Suicide." In Douglas Jacobs and Herbert N. Brown, eds., *Suicide, Understanding, and Responding: Harvard Medical School Perspectives.* Madison, Conn.: International Universities Press.

——— 1990 "The Developmental Perspective of Suicide." In Antoon Leenaars, ed., *Life Span Perspectives of Suicide.* New York: Plenum.

———, Alan L. Berman, John T. Maltsberger, and Robert I. Yufit, eds. 1991 *Assessment and Prediction of Suicide.* New York: Guilford.

Menninger, Karl 1938 *Man Against Himself.* New York: Harcourt, Brace.

Pescosolido, Bernice A., and Sharon Georgianna 1989 "Durkheim, Suicide, and Religion: Toward a Net-work Theory of Suicide." *American Sociological Review* 54:33–48.

Pfeffer, Cynthia R., ed. 1989 *Suicide Among Youth: Perspectives on Risk and Prevention.* Washington, D.C.: American Psychiatric Press.

Phillips, David P. 1974 "The Influence of Suggestion on Suicide." *American Sociological Review* 39:340–354.

———, Katherine Lesyna, and Daniel J. Paight 1991 "Suicide and the Media." In Ronald W. Maris et al., eds., *Assessment and Prediction of Suicide.* New York: Guilford.

Porkorny, Alex D. 1983 "Prediction of Suicide in Psychiatric Patients." *Archives of General Psychiatry* 40:249–257.

Robins, Eli 1981 *The Final Months.* New York: Oxford University Press.

Shneidman, Edwin S. 1985 *Definition of Suicide.* New York: Wiley-Interscience.

Stack, Stephen 1982 "Suicide: A Decade Review of the Sociological Literature." *Deviant Behavior* 4:41–66.

Stafford, Mark C., and Jack P. Gibbs 1988 "Change in the Relation between Marital Integration and Suicide Rates." *Social Forces* 66:1060–1079.

Wasserman, Ira M. 1989 "The Effects of War and Alcohol Consumption Patterns on Suicide: United States, 1910–1933." *Social Forces* 67:129–145.

RONALD W. MARIS

SUPERNATURALISM   *See* Religious Orientations.

SURVEY RESEARCH   Survey research is the method most frequently used by sociologists in their study of American and other large societies. Surveys allow sociologists to move from a relatively small sample of individuals, who are accessible as carriers of information about themselves and their society, to the broad contours of a large population—for example, its class structure or its dominant values. Moreover, surveys conform to major requirements of scientific method by allowing a considerable (though by no means perfect) degree of objectivity in approach and by allowing tests for the reliability and validity of the information obtained.

Like many other important inventions, a survey is composed of several more or less independent parts—sampling, questioning, and analysis of data—and it was their successful combination early in the twentieth century that gave birth to the method as we know it today. (See Converse 1987 for a history of the modern survey.)

SAMPLING

The survey component that laypersons usually find most mysterious is the assumption that a small sample of people (or other units, for example, families or firms) can be used to generalize about the much larger population from which the sample is drawn. Thus, a sample of 1,500 adults might be drawn to represent the population of 185 million Americans over the age of eighteen. Moreover, the sample itself is then used to estimate the extent to which values calculated from it (for example, the percentage of the sample saying "married" to a question about marital status) are likely to deviate from values that would have been obtained if the entire population over eighteen had been surveyed. Such an estimate, referred to as "sampling error" (because it is due to having questioned only a sample and not the full population), is even stranger from the standpoint of common sense, much like pulling oneself up by one's own bootstraps.

It should be emphasized that the estimates discussed here depend on the use of what is called "probability sampling," which implies that at crucial stages the respondents are selected by means of a random procedure. Nonprobability sampling approaches, such as the proverbial person-in-the-street interviews, lack justification for generalizing to a larger population or for estimating sampling error. Consumers of survey information need to be aware of the vast differences in the quality of sampling that occur among organizations claiming to do surveys: It is definitely not the case in this, or in other aspects of survey research, that all published results deserve equal confidence. Unfortunately, media presentations of findings from

surveys seldom provide the information necessary for evaluating the method actually used in gathering the data.

The theory of sampling is a part of mathematics, not of sociology, but it is heavily relied on by sociologists and its implementation with real populations of people involves many nonmathematical problems that sociologists must try to solve. For example, it is one thing to select a sample of people according to the canons of mathematical theory, and quite another to locate those people and persuade them to cooperate in a social survey. To the extent that intended respondents are missed, which is referred to as the problem of nonresponse, the scientific character of the survey is jeopardized. The degree of jeopardy (technically termed "bias") is a function of both the amount of nonresponse and the extent to which the nonrespondents differ from those who do respond. If, for example, young black males are more likely to be missed in survey samples than are other groups in the population, as indeed often happens, the results of the survey do not adequately represent the entire population. Serious survey investigators spend a great deal of time and money attempting to reduce nonresponse to a minimum, and one measure of the scientific adequacy of a survey report is the information provided about nonresponse. (For an introduction to sampling in social surveys, see Kalton 1983, and for a more extensive treatment, Kish 1965.)

QUESTIONING

Unlike sampling, the role of questions as a component of surveys is often regarded as simply a matter of common sense. Asking questions is a part of all human interaction, and it is widely assumed that no special skill or experience is needed to design a survey questionnaire. This is true in the sense that questioning in surveys is seldom very different from questioning in ordinary life but incorrect in the sense that many precautions are needed in developing a questionnaire for a general population. Moreover, the issues that arise in interpreting answers from surveys are extremely difficult ones. We will consider both the precautions needed and the issues of interpretation further below.

ANALYSIS

Although asking *questions* of *samples* of individuals may seem to capture the entire nature of the survey, there is one further component that is vital to sociologists: the logical and statistical analysis of the resulting data. The responses that people give to survey questions do not speak for themselves. Answers take on clear meaning primarily when they are involved in comparisons across time (for example, responses of a sample this year with responses of a sample from the same population five years ago), across social categories like age or education, or across other types of classifications meaningful for the problem being studied. Moreover, since any such comparison may produce a difference that is really due to chance factors because only a sample was drawn, rather than to a true difference between time points or social categories, statistical testing is essential to create confidence that the difference would be found if the entire population could be surveyed. In addition, individual questions are sometimes combined into a larger index in order to decrease idiosyncratic effects due to any single item, and the construction of such an index requires other preliminary types of statistical analysis.

As an example of survey analysis, sociologists often find important age differences in answers to survey questions, but since age and education are negatively associated in most countries—that is, older people tend to have less education than younger people—it is necessary to disentangle the two factors in order to judge whether age itself is a direct cause of responses or only a proxy for education. Moreover, age differences in responses to a question can represent either changes due to the aging process (which in turn may reflect physiological, social, or other developmental factors), or it can reflect experiences and influences from a particular historical point ("cohort effects"). Steps must be taken to distinguish these various explanations from one another. At the same time the survey analyst must bear in mind

and test the possibility that a particular pattern of answers is due to "chance," because of the existence of sampling error.

Thus, the analysis of survey data can become quite complex, well beyond, though not unrelated to, the kinds of tables common to newspaper and magazine presentations of poll data. (The terms *poll* and *survey* are increasingly interchangeable, with the main difference being academic and government preference for "survey" and media preference for "poll.") Such thorough analysis is important, however, if genuine insights into the meaning of answers are to be gained and misinterpretations to be avoided. (A comprehensive but relatively nontechnical presentation of the logic of survey analysis is provided by Rosenberg 1968; among relevant statistical texts are Blalock 1979 and, at a more advanced level, Hanushek and Jackson 1977.)

THE SEQUENCE OF A SURVEY

Surveys should begin with one or more research problems that determine both the content of the questionnaire and the design of the sample. The two types of decisions must go hand in hand since each affects the other. A questionnaire that is intended to focus on the attitudes of different ethnic and racial groups makes sense only if the population sampled and the design of the sample will yield enough members of each group to provide sufficient data for adequate analysis. In addition, decisions must be made early with regard to the mode of administration of the survey —whether it will be conducted through self-administration or interviewing and, if the latter, whether in person or by telephone—since these decisions also influence what can be asked. Each decision has its trade-offs in terms of quality, cost, and other important features of the research.

The development of the questionnaire and the field period follow, after which the data are normally entered in numerical form (e.g., 1 = Yes, 2 = No, 3 = Don't Know) into a computer file for analysis. If open-ended questions—questions that do not present fixed alternatives—are used and respondent answers have been recorded in detail, an intermediate step is needed to code the answers into categories—for example, a question that asks respondents to name the most important problems facing the country today might yield categories for "foreign affairs," "inflation," "racial problems," and so forth, though the words used by respondents would ordinarily have been more concrete. Finally, the data are analyzed in the form of tables and statistical measures that can form the basis for a final report.

QUESTIONS AND QUESTIONNAIRES

Questionnaires can range, on the one hand, from brief attempts to determine factual information (for example, the number of rooms in a sample of dwelling units) or attitudes (the leaning of the electorate toward one or another political candidate) to, on the other hand, extensive explorations of respondents' values and world views. Assuming that the questions have been framed with some serious purpose in mind—an assumption not always warranted because surveys are sometimes initiated with little clear purpose other than a desire to ask some "interesting questions" —there are two important principles to bear in mind, one about the development of the questions and the other about the interpretation of the answers. The first principle is the importance of carrying out as much pilot work and pretesting of the questions as possible, because no one, not even an experienced survey researcher, can foresee all the difficulties and ambiguities a set of questions holds for respondents, especially when administered to a heterogeneous population like that of the United States. For example, a frequently used question about whether "the lot of the average man is getting worse" turned out on close examination to confuse respondents about the meaning of "lot"—some taking it to refer to housing lots. Of course, it is still useful to draw on expert consultation where possible and also to become familiar with discussions of questionnaire design in texts, especially the engaging classic treatment by Payne (1951) and more recent expositions such as that by Sudman and Bradburn (1987).

Pilot work can be done in a number of ways, for example, by having a sample of respondents think aloud while answering, or by listening carefully to the reactions of experienced interviewers who have administered the questionnaire in pretest form, or perhaps best of all by investigators themselves doing a number of practice interviews. The distinction between "pilot" and "pretest" questionnaires is simply that the former refers to the earlier stages of questionnaire development and may involve relatively unstructured interviewing, while the latter is closer to "dress rehearsals" prior to the final survey.

The main principle with regard to interpreting answers is to be extremely skeptical of simple distributions of results, often expressed in percentage form, for example, 65 percent "Yes," 30 percent "No," 5 percent "Don't Know," to a particular question. For several reasons, such absolute percentages suggest a meaningfulness that can be seriously misleading. First, almost any important issue is really a cluster of subissues, each of which can be asked about and each of which may yield a different distribution of responses. For example, responses about the issue of "gun control" will vary dramatically in the United States depending on the type of gun referred to, the amount and method of control, and so forth. No single percentage distribution, or even two or three such distributions, can capture all of this variation. Nor are such problems confined to questions about attitudes: Even a seemingly simple inquiry about the number of rooms in a house necessarily involves somewhat arbitrary definitions of what is and is not to be counted as a room, and more than one question may need to be asked to obtain the information that the investigator is seeking. By the same token, care must be taken not to overgeneralize the results from a single question, since different conclusions might well be drawn if a differently framed question were the focus. Indeed, many apparent disagreements between two or more surveys disappear once one realizes that somewhat different questions had been asked by each, even though the general topic (e.g., gun control) at first looks the same.

Second, even where the substantive issue is kept

constant, seemingly minor differences in the order and wording of questions can change percentage distributions noticeably. Thus, a classic experiment from the 1940s showed a large difference in response to a particular question depending on whether a certain behavior was said to be "forbidden" rather than "not allowed": To the question "Do you think the United States should forbid public speeches against democracy?" 54 percent said Yes, forbid. But to the question "Do you think the United States should allow public speeches against democracy?" 75 percent said No, do not allow. This is a distinction in wording that would not make a practical difference in real life, since not allowing a speech would have the same consequence as forbidding it, yet the variation in wording has a substantial effect on answers. Experiments of this type, called "split-ballot experiments," are frequently carried out by dividing a national sample of respondents in half and asking one wording of the question to each half on a random basis.

The proportion of people who answer "Don't Know" to a survey question can also vary substantially—by 25 percent or more—depending on the extent to which such an answer is explicitly legitimized for respondents by mentioning it along with other alternatives ("Yes," "No," "Don't Know") or omitting it. In other instances simply the location of a question in a series of questions has been shown to affect answers, even though the wording of the question itself is not changed. For example, a widely used question about allowing legalized abortion in the case of a married woman not wanting any more children produces different answers depending entirely on its position before or after another question about abortion in the case of a defective fetus. Thus, the context in which a question is asked can influence the answers that people give. These and a large number of other experiments on the form, wording, and context of survey questions are reported by Schuman and Presser (1981). (See also Turner and Martin 1984 for several treatments of survey questioning.)

A third reason to be cautious about distributions of percentages to a single question is that the interpretation of any distribution almost always involves explicit or implicit comparison with some other distribution, real or ideal. To report that 65 percent of a sample is satisfied with the actions of a particular leader may be grounds for either cheering or booing: It depends on the level of satisfaction typical for the same leader at other points in time or for other persons in comparable leadership positions. Thus, reports of survey data should include such types of comparisons whenever possible, which is why for sociologists the collection of a set of answers to questions is really the beginning and not the end of a research analysis.

MODE OF ADMINISTRATION

Although sampling, questioning, and analysis are the most fundamental components of a survey, decisions about the mode of administering the survey are also very important. A basic distinction can be made between self-administered surveys and those in which interviewers are used. Self-administration, if it is to be based on probability sampling of some sort, is usually carried out by mailing questionnaires to respondents who have been selected through some random procedure. For example, a sample of sociologists might be chosen by taking every twentieth name from an alphabetical listing of all regular members belonging to the American Sociological Association, though with the recognition that any such listing will be incomplete (e.g., not everyone with an advanced degree in sociology belongs to the American Sociological Association).

The major advantage of mail surveys is their relatively low cost, which is limited to payments to clerical employees, stamps, and perhaps an incentive to respondents. One disadvantage of mail surveys is that they have traditionally been seen to produce quite low response rates; many obtain only 25 percent or even less of their target sample. However, Dillman (1978) has argued that designing mail surveys in line with principles of exchange theory can yield response rates at or close to those of other modes of administration. Whether or not this is true for a sample of the U.S. population remains in doubt for the reason given below, but it is clear from numerous experiments that the use of two specific factors, monetary incentives (not necessarily large) and follow-up "reminders," can virtually always improve mail questionnaire response rates appreciably. However, another important disadvantage of mail surveys in the United States is the absence of any available centralized national listing of households for drawing a sample, and indeed because of this it is difficult to say what response rate could be obtained from a national mail sample in this country. For the most part, mail surveys are used where there is a prior list available, as with an organization's membership, which also may add the benefit of loyalty to the organization as a motive for respondent cooperation. Other disadvantages of mail surveys are lack of control over exactly who answers the questions (it may or may not be the target respondent, assuming there is a single target), in what order the questionnaire is filled out, and of course the unavailability of an interviewer for respondents who cannot read well or do not understand the questions. One compensating factor is the greater privacy afforded respondents, which may lead to more candor, although evidence on this issue is thin. (Sometimes similar privacy is attempted within an interview survey by giving a portion of the questionnaire to respondents to fill out themselves, perhaps even providing a separate sealed envelope for the respondent to mail back to the survey headquarters, thus guaranteeing that the interviewer will not read the answers.)

Because of the difficulties described, most surveys aimed at the general population make use of interviewers to locate respondents and administer the questionnaire. Traditionally this has been done on a face-to-face (sometimes called "personal") basis, with interviewers going to households, usually after a letter of introduction has been mailed describing the survey. The sample is ordinarily drawn by means of "area" methods: As a simple example, large units such as counties might be drawn first on a random basis, then from the selected counties smaller units such as blocks drawn, then finally addresses on these blocks are listed by interviewers and a random

sample of the addresses designated for the actual sample, with introductory letters sent. In actual practice, more than two levels would be used, and other steps involving stratification and clustering would be included to improve the efficiency of the sampling and data collection.

A major advantage of face-to-face interviewing is the ability of the interviewer to find the target respondent and persuade her or him to take part in the interview. Face-to-face interviewing has other advantages: Graphic aids can easily be used as part of the questionnaire; interviewers can make observations of the respondent's ability to understand the questions and of other behavior or characteristics of the respondent; unclear answers can be probed and clarified. The major disadvantage of face-to-face interviewing is its cost, since much of the time of interviewers is spent simply locating respondents (many are not at home on a first or second visit). For every actual hour spent interviewing, five to ten hours may be needed for travel and related effort. Furthermore, face-to-face surveys require a great deal of total field time, and when results are needed quickly this is difficult to accomplish and may add still more expense. One other disadvantage of face-to-face interviewing is the need for an extensive supervisory staff spread around the country, and yet another is that survey administrators must place considerable reliance on the competence and integrity of interviewers, who are almost always on their own and unsupervised during actual interviews. This makes standardization of interviewing difficult.

Since the early 1970s, and especially during the 1980s, face-to-face interviewing has been increasingly replaced by telephone interviewing, usually from a centralized location. Telephone surveys are considerably less expensive than face-to-face surveys, though the exact ratio is hard to estimate because they are also normally shorter, usually under forty-five minutes in length; the expense of locating people for face-to-face interviews leads to hour-long or even much lengthier interviews, these being tolerated more readily by respondents when interviewed in person than over the phone. Telephone surveys can also be completed more rapidly than face-to-face surveys, and they have the additional advantage of allowing more direct supervision and monitoring of interviewers. The incorporation of the computer directly into interviewing—known as CATI or computer-assisted telephone interviewing—facilitates questionnaire formatting and postinterview coding, which increases flexibility and shortens total survey time. Still another advantage of telephone surveys is the relative ease of probability sampling: essentially random combinations of digits, ten at a time, can be created by computer to sample any telephone number in the United States (three-digit area code, plus seven-digit number). There are a variety of practical problems to be overcome (e.g., many of the resulting numbers are nonworking), but techniques have been developed that make such sampling easily available and inexpensive in a way that was never true of the area sampling required for face-to-face interviewing.

Because speaking on the telephone seems so different from speaking face-to-face, survey specialists initially thought that results from the two types of survey administration might also be very different. A number of experimental comparisons, however, have failed to find important differences, and indeed those that do occur may have more to do with different constraints on sampling (telephone surveys obviously miss the approximately 8 percent of the American households without telephones, and they also produce somewhat higher levels of refusal by intended respondents). Thus, the remaining reasons for continuing face-to-face surveys have to do with the need for longer interviews or for special additions such as graphic demonstrations or response scales. (Groves 1989 discusses evidence on telephone versus face-to-face survey differences, and Groves et al. 1988 presents detailed accounts of methodological issues involving telephone surveys.)

Face-to-face and telephone surveys share one important feature, namely, the involvement of an interviewer between the questionnaire and the respondent. Although this has many advantages, as already noted, there is always the possibility that some behavior or some characteristic of the interviewer will affect responses. For example, as

shown by Hyman (1954) in one of the classic efforts to study the interview process itself, a visible interviewer characteristic such as racial appearance can have dramatic effects on answers. Although this is probably the largest of all effects discovered, no doubt because of the salience and tension that racial identification produces in America, the possibility of effects from the interview process itself—and from the respondent's assumption about the sponsorship or aim of the survey—must always be borne in mind. This is even more true when surveys are attempted in societies where the assumption of professional neutrality is less common than in the United States, and some recent failures by surveys to predict elections are probably due to bias of this type.

MODIFICATIONS AND EXTENSIONS OF THE SURVEY METHOD

Our discussion has been largely in terms of the single cross-section or one-shot survey, but more informative designs are increasingly possible. The most obvious step, now that surveys of the national population have been carried out for some fifty years, is to study change over time by repeating the same questions at useful intervals. The General Social Survey (known as the GSS) has replicated many attitude and factual questions on an almost annual basis since 1972, and the National Election Study (NES) has done the same in the political area on a biennial basis since the 1950s. From these repeated surveys we have learned about substantial changes in some American attitudes, while in other areas there has been virtually no change at all (see Niemi, Mueller, and Smith 1989 for examples of both change and stability). An important variant on such longitudinal research is the panel study, in which the same respondents are interviewed at two or more points in time. This has certain advantages; for example, even where there is no change for the total sample in the distribution of responses, there may be counterbalancing shifts that can be best studied in this way.

Surveys are also increasingly being carried out

on a cross-national basis, allowing comparisons across societies, though usually with the additional obstacle of translation to be overcome. Even within the framework of a single survey in one country, comparisons across quite different types of samples can be made, as for example in an early study by Stouffer (1955) that administered the same questionnaire to the general public and to a special sample of "community leaders" in order to compare their respective attitudes toward civil liberties. Finally, it is important to recognize that although the survey method is often seen as entirely distinct from, and even opposite to, the experimental method, the two have been usefully wedded in a number of ways. Much of what we know about variations in survey responses due to question form, wording, and context has been obtained by means of split-ballot experiments, while attempts to study the effects of policy changes have involved embedding surveys of attitudes and behaviors within larger experimental designs.

ETHICAL AND OTHER PROBLEMS

As with other social science approaches to the empirical study of human beings, surveys raise important issues of an ethical nature. The success of survey sampling requires persuading individuals to donate their time to being interviewed, usually without compensation, and to trust that their answers will be treated confidentially and used for purposes they would consider worthwhile. A related issue is the extent to which respondents should be told in advance and in detail about the content and aims of a questionnaire (the issue of "informed consent"), especially when this might discourage their willingness to answer questions or affect the kind of answers they might give. In all these instances, the purely professional or scientific goal of completing the survey can conflict with the responsibility of survey investigators to those people who make surveys possible, namely, respondents. These are difficult issues, and there is probably no overall solution. There is a need in each instance to take seriously

wider ethical norms, as well as professional or scientific goals.

From within sociology, reliance on surveys has been criticized on several grounds. Sociologists committed to more qualitative approaches to studying social interaction often view the survey as sacrificing richness of description and depth of understanding in order to obtain data amenable to quantitative analysis. Sociologists concerned with larger social structures sometimes regard the survey approach as focusing too much on the individual level, neglecting the network of relations and institutions of societies. Finally, some see the dependence of surveys on self-report as a limitation because of the presumed difference between what people say in interviews and how they behave outside the interview situation (Schuman and Johnson 1976). Although there are partial answers to each of these criticisms, each has some genuine merit, and those doing survey research need to maintain a self-critical stance toward their own approach. Yet it must also be said that the survey is the best-developed and most systematic method sociologists now have to gather data. Equally valuable methods appropriate to other goals have yet to be evolved.

(SEE ALSO: *Measurement; Measurement Instruments; Sampling Procedures; Secondary Data Analysis and Data Archives; Social Indicators*)

REFERENCES

Blalock, Hubert M., Jr. 1979 *Social Statistics,* 2nd rev. ed. New York: McGraw-Hill.

Bradburn, Norman M., Seymour Sudman, and Associates 1979 *Improving Interview Method and Questionnaire Design.* San Francisco: Jossey-Bass.

Converse, Jean M. 1987 *Survey Research in the United States: Roots and Emergence, 1890–1960.* Berkeley: University of California Press.

Dillman, Don A. 1978 *Mail and Telephone Surveys: The Total Design Method.* New York: Wiley.

Groves, Robert M. 1989 *Survey Errors and Survey Costs.* New York: Wiley.

———, Paul P. Biemer, Lars E. Lyberg, James T. Massey, William L. Nicholls II, and Joseph Waksberg

1988 *Telephone Survey Methodology*. New York: Wiley.

Hanushek, Eric A., and John E. Jackson 1977 *Statistical Methods for Social Scientists*. New York: Academic Press.

Hyman, Herbert H. 1954 *Interviewing in Social Research*. Chicago: University of Chicago Press.

Kalton, Graham 1983 *Introduction to Survey Sampling*. Beverly Hills, Calif.: Sage.

Kish, Leslie 1965 *Survey Sampling*. New York: Wiley.

National Opinion Research Center 1990 *General Social Surveys, 1972–1990: Cumulative Codebook*. Chicago: University of Chicago, National Opinion Research Center.

Niemi, Richard, John Mueller, and Tom W. Smith 1989 *Trends in Public Opinion: A Compendium of Survey Data*. Westport, Conn.: Greenwood Press.

Payne, Stanley L. 1951 *The Art of Asking Questions*. Princeton, N.J.: Princeton University Press.

Rosenberg, Morris 1968 *The Logic of Survey Analysis*. New York: Basic Books.

Schuman, Howard, and Michael P. Johnson 1976 "Attitudes and Behavior." In A. Inkeles, ed., *Annual Review of Sociology*, vol. 2. Palo Alto, Calif.: Annual Reviews.

Schuman, Howard, and Stanley Presser 1981 *Questions and Answers in Attitude Surveys: Experiments on Question Form, Wording, and Context*. New York: Academic Press.

Stouffer, Samuel A. 1955 *Communism, Conformity, and Civil Liberties*. Garden City, N.Y.: Doubleday.

Sudman, Seymour, and Norman M. Bradburn 1987 *Asking Questions: A Practical Guide to Question Design*. San Francisco: Jossey-Bass.

Turner, Charles, and Elizabeth Martin (eds.) 1984 *Surveying Subjective Phenomena*, 2 vols. New York: Russell Sage Foundation.

HOWARD SCHUMAN

SYMBOLIC INTERACTION THEORY

Symbolic interactionism is a term invented by Herbert Blumer (1937) for sociological and social psychological ideas he presented as emanating directly from George Herbert Mead, especially but not exclusively as represented in *Mind, Self and Society* (1934). *Symbolic interaction theory* is a term redolent of those ideas, not necessarily in the specific form presented by Blumer or, for that matter, Mead.

The fundamental character of symbolic-interactionist ideas is suggested by a theoretical proposition, that the self reflects society and organizes behavior, and by a related imagery addressing the nature of society and the human being, the nature of human action and interaction, and the relationship between society and person. The imagery begins with a vision of society as a web of communication: Society *is* interaction, the reciprocal influence of persons who, as they relate, take into account each others' characteristics and actions; and interaction is communication. Interaction is "symbolic," conducted in terms of meanings persons develop in the course of their interdependent conduct. The environment of human action and interaction is symbolically defined: It is the environment as it is interpreted that is context, shaper, and object of action and interaction. Persons act with reference to one another in terms of symbols developed through interaction, and they act via the communication of these symbols. Society is a label aggregating and summarizing such interaction. Society does not "exist"; it is created and continuously recreated as persons interact. Social reality is a flow of events joining two or more persons. More than simply implicated in the social process, society and person derive from that process: They take on their meanings as these meanings emerge in and through social interaction.

Neither society nor individual is ontologically prior to the other in this imagery; persons through their interaction create society, but it is society, a web of communication and interaction, that creates persons as social beings. Society and individual presuppose each other in that neither exists except in relation to the other. This conception of society implicitly incorporates a view of the human being as "minded" and this "mindedness" as potentially reflexive. That is, human beings can and sometimes do take themselves as the object of their own reflection, thus creating selves, doing so from the standpoint of others with whom they interact. Selves are inherently social products, although they involve more than reflected appraisals of others in the immediate situation of interaction; in particular, selves involve persons as subjects responding to themselves as objects. Thinking takes place as internal conversation that uses symbols that develop in the social process. Mind arises in both evolutionary and individual senses in response to problems (interruptions in the flow of activities) and involves formulating and selecting from symbolically defined alternative courses of action to resolve the problems. Choice is an omnipresent reality of the human condition, and the content of choices is contained in the subjective experience of persons as that experience develops in and through the social process.

Following from the imagery thus far presented is a view of human beings, both collectively and individually, as active and creative rather than simply responsive to the environmental stimuli impinging on them. Given that the environment of human action and interaction is symbolic; given that the symbols attaching to persons (including oneself), things, and ideas are the product of interaction and reflexivity and can be altered and manipulated in the course of that interaction; given that thought can be used to anticipate the effectiveness of alternative courses of action in the resolution of problems; and given that choice among alternatives is an integral feature of social conduct, we arrive at an image of social interaction as literally constructed, albeit not necessarily anew in each instance, in the course of interaction itself. We also arrive at an image insistent upon a degree of indeterminacy in human behavior, in the sense that the course and outcome of social interaction cannot as a matter of principle (and not uncertain knowledge) be completely predicted from conditions and factors existing prior to that interaction.

Labeling the ideas of symbolic interactionism, as contained in the imagery presented, a "theory" is misleading. Drawing a distinction between, on the one hand, a systematic set of interrelated propositions about how some segment of the world is organized and functions and, on the other hand, assumptions about and conceptualizations defining the parts of that segment of the world, symbolic interactionism has more the char-

acter of the latter than the former. That is, it is more a theoretical framework rather than a theory per se. While features of the framework appear to militate against attempts to formulate systematic theory using it as a base, and various proponents deny the possibility, a few sociologists in recent years have employed the framework in their efforts to elaborate specific theories (e.g., Heise 1979; Stryker 1980; Stryker and Serpe 1982; Rosenberg 1984; Thoits 1983). It will not be possible to review such specific theories here; nor will it be possible to review or even characterize the research that derives from the framework (for extensive references to classic literature and research literature before 1985, see Stryker and Statham 1985 or one of the texts written from a symbolic interactionist perspective, e.g., Lindesmith, Strauss, and Denzin 1988; for leads into more recent research, see successive volumes of *Symbolic Interaction,* a journal sponsored by the Society for the Study of Symbolic Interaction and devoted to work emanating from the framework).

In the hands of some (e.g., Blumer 1969), symbolic interaction "theory" is intended as a general sociological frame; that is, it is applicable to the intellectual problems of sociology as a discipline from the most micro to the most macro levels. In the hands of others (e.g. Stryker 1980), it is a frame largely restricted in its utility to issues of a social psychology. The first position does not seem defensible, because any framework of necessity brings into special focus particular variables and leaves unattended—at least in a relative way—other variables and because the symbolic interaction frame highlights interaction, social actors related through interaction, and subjective variables "internal" to those actors. It thus neglects features of the sociological landscape relating to large-scale social systems—the state, the economy, the "world system," demographic variables and so forth—and does not easily pose sociological questions having to do with interrelationships among those features of large-scale social systems. It is this neglect that underwrites criticism of the symbolic-interactionist frame as lacking social structural concepts necessary to the analysis of power and consequently as ideological apologia for the status quo (see compendia of criticisms of the framework in Meltzer, Petras, and Reynolds 1975; Stryker 1980; Reynolds 1990). Although many (e.g., Maines 1977) are at pains to deny the validity of the criticism, pointing to work by Hall (1972) and others, the criticisms may be justified if the claim is that symbolic interactionism is a general sociological framework; they are not well taken if the more restricted claim for its utility is made. There remains even then a reasonable concern with the adequacy of the framework for problems of a distinctively *sociological* social psychology, whose domain centers on issues of the reciprocal relationships of social units and social persons. There also remains a concern with the question of whether the framework admits of and provides readily for the articulation of sociological concepts and those of a social psychology. These concerns arise from the ways social structural concepts enter, or fail to enter, the symbolic-interactionist frame. Whatever the intended coverage—from all of sociology to a limited social psychology—the framework has traditionally been conceived as knowing no cultural boundaries; that view, however, may require reconsideration in light of recent analyses (Hewitt 1990).

Implicated in the description of symbolic-interactionist imagery provided above are many of the central concepts of the framework. The meaning of "meaning" is fundamental. Social acts, by definition, involve at least two persons taking each other into account in satisfying impulses or resolving problems. Since social acts occur over time, *gestures*—any parts of an act that come to be indications of parts of the act still to come—can appear. Vocal sounds, physical movements, bodily expressions, clothing, and so forth can serve as gestures. When they do, they have meaning: Their meaning is the behavior following their appearance. Gestures that have the same meaning (implying the same future behavior) to those who emit them and to those who perceive them are *significant symbols*.

Things, ideas, and relationships among things and ideas can all be symbolized and enter the experience of human beings as objects; objects whose meanings are anchored in and emerge from

social interaction constitute social reality. While meanings are unlikely to be identical among participants, communication and social interaction presuppose significant symbols in which meanings are "sufficiently" shared. Because significant symbols anticipate future behavior, they entail plans of action: They organize behavior with reference to what they symbolize. In the context of the ongoing social process, meanings must be at least tentatively assigned to features of the interactive situations in which persons find themselves; without the assignment of meanings, behavior in those situations is likely to be disorganized or random. The situation must be symbolized, as must its constituent parts; the situation must be defined or interpreted, and the products of this symbolization process are *definitions of the situation*. Definitions of the situation focus attention on what is pertinent (to satisfying impulses or resolving problems) in an interactive setting and permit a preliminary organization of actions appropriate to the setting. Tentative definitions are tested and possibly reformulated through ongoing experience.

The most important aspects of a situation requiring definition are, from the point of view of the actors involved, who or what they are in the situation and who or what others with whom they interact are. Defining the others in the situation is typically accomplished by locating those others as members of some socially recognized category of actors—one (or more) of the kinds of persons it is possible to be in a society (e.g., male or female, young or old, employed or unemployed, etc.); doing so provides cues to or predictors of their behavior and permits organization of one's own behavior with reference to those others. When others are recognized as instantiations of a social category, behaviors are expected of them and actions that are premised on these expectations can be organized and directed toward them. While some interactionists disdain the term, expectations attached to social categories—again, the kinds of persons it is possible to be within a society—are *roles*. Situations frequently admit to locating others in multiple categories and open the possibility of conflicting expectations coming into play; under this circumstance, no clear means of organizing responses may be available. Defining oneself in a situation also involves locating oneself in socially recognized categories; to respond reflexively to oneself by classifying, naming, and defining who and what one is to have a *self*. Self, so conceived, involves viewing oneself as an object. The meaning of self, like that of any object, derives from interaction: To have a self is to view oneself from the standpoint of others with whom one interacts. Self, like any significant symbol, provides a plan of action. That plan, by definition, implicates the expected responses of others.

We learn, at least provisionally, what we can expect from others through *role taking,* a process of anticipating responses of others with whom one interacts. One, in effect, puts oneself in the place of those others to see the world as they do, using prior experience with those others, knowledge of the social categories in which those others are located, and symbolic cues available in interaction. On such bases, tentative definitions of others' attitudes are formulated, then validated or reshaped in interaction. Role taking permits one to anticipate the consequences of one's own and others' plans of actions, to monitor the results of those plans as they are carried out behaviorally, and to sustain or redirect one's behavior on the basis of the monitoring. Because roles often lack consistency and concreteness, but actors must organize their behavior as if roles were unequivocal, interaction is also a matter of *role making,* creating and modifying roles through devising performances in response to imputed roles to others (Turner 1962).

Many social acts take place within organized systems of action; consequently, both role taking and role making can occur with reference to a *generalized other,* that is, a differentiated yet interrelated set of others (Mead's example with respect to this concept involves baseball players anticipating the responses of other members of their team and their opponents). Not all others' perspectives are equally relevant to an actor; the concept of *significant other* recognizes that some persons rather than others can be expected to be given greater weight when perspectives differ or are incompatible. Implied here, as elsewhere in this discussion,

is that meanings are not likely to be universally shared or shared in detail; if they are not, accuracy in role taking and difficulty in role making will also vary. Implied as well is that smooth and cooperative interpersonal relations do not necessarily follow from accurate role taking: Conflict may result from such accuracy as well as sharpen it.

The symbolic-interactionist ideas reviewed have, of course, a history. Many issue directly from Mead. Mead's thinking is part of a tradition of philosophical thought with clear roots in the Scottish moral philosophers—Adam Smith, David Hume, Adam Ferguson, Francis Hutcheson —and, more proximately, in the American pragmatists Charles Peirce, William James, and John Dewey. It contains important admixtures of evolutionary and dialectic premises. Mead's thought overlaps considerably with that of a number of sociologists writing at the same time he did, in the first decades of this century, in particular Charles Horton Cooley and William Isaac Thomas; Cooley's axiom, asserting that society and person are two sides of the same coin (the coin, he added, is communication), and that of Thomas, asserting that if humans define situations as real, the situations are real in their consequences, capture much of the essence of symbolic interactionism. A host of sociologists connect that past with the present; leaving a great many unnamed, Burgess, Blumer, Waller, Sutherland, Hughes, Shibutani, Kuhn, Cottrell, Hill, Lemert, Lindesmith, Mills, Miyamoto, and Stone link to a somewhat more contemporary set of persons including Goffman, Lofland, Becker, Lopata, Strauss, Geer, Weinstein, Farberman, Couch, Denzin, Bart, Maines, Reynolds, Turner, Daniels, Scheff, Wiseman, Heise, Stryker, Burke, Heiss, Fine, Hochschild, Weigert, McCall, Snow, and Hewitt. (For reviews of the history and literature of symbolic interactionism, see Stryker and Statham 1985; Meltzer, Petras, and Reynolds 1975; Reynolds 1990; Lewis and Smith 1980.) Presenting these names in a common listing does not argue their complete adherence to a common credo; indeed, there may be as much conceptual difference as similarity.

As this suggests, no single version of symbolic

interaction theory satisfies all who find its core ideas appealing and useful in conducting research and analyses. There appear to be three fundamental premises of a symbolic-interactionist perspective, all of which are shared by those who are self-conscious about their intellectual roots in this tradition of sociological thought (Stryker 1988). The first holds that an adequate account of human social behavior must incorporate the perspective of participants in interaction and cannot rest entirely on the perspective of the observer. The second is that self, that is, persons' reflexive responses to themselves, links larger social organization or structure to the social interaction of those persons. The third asserts that processes of social interaction are prior to both self and social organization, both of which derive and emerge from social interaction.

At the same time, each of these premises leaves open issues of considerable importance with respect to the content, methods, and objectives of interactionist analyses on which symbolic interactionists can and do differ. Some of the sociologists for whom the three core symbolic-interactionist premises serve as starting point believe that social life is so fluid that it can be reasonably described only in process terms, that concepts purportedly describing social structures or social organization belie the reality of social life. Relatedly, some believe that actors' definitions, theoretically central and powerful as generators of lines of action, are continuously reformulated in immediate situations of interaction, making it impossible effectively to use preexistent concepts in the analysis of social life (Blumer 1969). Others accept the "reality" of social structural phenomena. They view social structure as relatively stable patterning of social interaction which then operate as significant constraints on actors' definitions. Social structure is thought to make for sufficient continuity in definitions to allow the use of concepts derived from past analyses of social interaction in the analysis of present and future interaction (Stryker 1980). The first premise hides, in the term *accounts,* the important difference between those who seem to believe that, given the constructed character of social behavior, only "after

the fact" understanding of already past events is possible (Weigert 1981) and those who believe that sociology can build testable predictive explanations of social behavior (Kuhn 1964). Not unrelatedly, there are some who argue that the perspective of the sociologist observer of human social behavior is more than likely to distort accounts of that behavior and so must be essentially abjured in seeking to capture the perspectives of those living the behavior that is observed (Denzin 1970); and there are others who argue, directly or by implication, that the requirement that accounts should incorporate the perspective of the actors whose behavior is observed dictates only that actors' definitions be included in developed explanations and not that they constitute such explanations (Burke forthcoming). The former tend to argue that the best if not the only "legitimate" methods are naturalistic, primarily observational (Becker and Geer 1957); the latter tend to be catholic with respect to methods, refusing to rule out categorically any of the full range of possible social science methods and techniques (Heise 1979). With respect to the second premise, interactionists will differ in the degree to which they assign an independent "causal" role to self as the link between social organization or structure and social behavior. For many, self can and does serve as a (more rather than less) independent source of that behavior (McCall and Simmons 1978). For others, social organization or structure (as the residue of prior interaction) builds selves in its image, thus making self essentially a conduit through which these structures shape behavior and not an independent source of that behavior in its own right (Goffman 1959). Again relatedly, there is variation among symbolic interactionists in the degree to which self is seen as the source of creativity and novelty in social life, in the degree to which creativity and novelty in social life are seen as probable as opposed to simply possible (occurring only under a specific and limited set of social circumstances), and in the degree to which social life is in fact constructed anew rather than "merely" reconstructed in the image of prior patterns (Turner 1962; Hewitt 1988; Stryker and Statham 1985).

The third premise is taken by some to deny that social organization and selves have sufficient constancy to permit generalized conceptualization or the development of useful a priori theory on the basis of any given investigation(s) that can carry over reasonably to any new investigation (Glaser and Strauss 1967). In the view of others, this premise patently does not deny that there is in social life a reasonable constancy that implies a sufficient constancy in both selves and social organization to permit the elaboration of useful theories employing general concepts potentially applicable to wide instances of social behaviors (Heise 1986). Some emphasize the behavioristic elements in their intellectual heritage from Mead, concentrating their attention on how concerted lines of social action are constructed (Couch, Saxon, and Katovich 1986; McPhail and Wohlstein 1986), while others adopt a stance that attends primarily to the phenomenological worlds of the actors (or interactors) whom they study (Denzin 1984).

Clearly, these possibilities for important variations within symbolic-interactionist thought are not independent of one another: Those who subscribe to a view emphasizing the fluidity of social life and the moment-to-moment, situated character of definitions are also likely to emphasize the degree to which social order continuously emerges from fluid process, self organizes social behavior in an unconstrained fashion, and creativity and novelty characterize human behavior. They also tend to insist that the point of view of the observer only contaminates reasonable accounts of social interaction, that there is little utility for an analysis in conceptualizations and theory emanating from earlier analyses, and that understanding and not explanation is the point of sociological effort.

The set of views presented in the preceding paragraph has served to identify symbolic interactionism for many of its most passionate adherents as well as for perhaps a majority of its most vociferous critics. Not surprisingly, those approaching their work from symbolic interactionism so defined tended to present what they did in both conceptual and methodological opposition to available alternatives in sociology. Thus, for example, Blumer (1969) devoted much of his career to polemics championing direct and participant observation aimed at accessing the interpretations of those whose ongoing interaction sociologists sought to understand against both statistical and structural analyses, whose categories, data, and mathematical manipulations seemed to him devoid of actors' meanings. Nor can it surprise that critics of symbolic interactionism scored it and its adherents for being nonscientific and asociological. It bears repeating that to circumscribe symbolic interactionism in the manner of these passionate adherents and vociferous critics belies the diversity in views on relevant key issues represented in the work of those using the framework.

Interest in the symbolic-interactionist framework within sociology has fluctuated through the years. That interest was great from 1920 to 1950, reflecting in part the dominance of the University of Chicago in producing sociologists as well as the institutional structure of sociology. Subsequently, through the 1950s and into the 1970s, interest waned, first as the structural functionalism of Parsons and Merton gained ascendance intellectually and Harvard and Columbia became institutionally dominant, and later as various forms of Marxist and structuralist emphases on macro social processes swept the field. Symbolic interactionism, when not decried as reactionary or asociological, became, in the words of Mullins (1973), the loyal opposition. Indeed, Mullins predicted that it would disappear as a viable sociological framework.

More recent events belie that prediction: Symbolic interactionism has had a remarkable revitalization in the past two decades (Stryker 1987) and there has been a corresponding resurgence of interest in the framework. The revitalization and resurgent interest reflect various sources. One important source is an emerging realization among sociologists with a structural orientation that their theories could benefit from the sociologically sophisticated theory of the social actor and action that symbolic interactionism can provide and the related increasing interest in linking micro to macro social processes. A second is in a series of invigorating changing emphases in the work of contemporary symbolic interactionists. It is certainly true that much recent work from a symbolic-interactionist frame reflects traditional conceptual, theoretical, and methodological themes. However, on the conceptual level, newer work tends to a "multiple selves" perspective, drawing on William James (Stryker 1989; McCall and Simmons 1978), rather than viewing self as singular or unitary. Theoretically, there is greater attention to emotion, to affective dimensions of social life (Hochschild 1979; Thoits 1989), correcting for a "cognitive bias" in the framework; there is also greater appreciation for structural facilitators of and constraints on interaction and on self processes. While not yet prominent in the thinking of contemporary interactionists, the groundwork has been laid (e.g., in Stryker and Statham 1985) for the reintroduction of the concept of habit, central in the writings of John Dewey and other forerunners of interactionism, in recognition that social life is not invariably reflexive and minded. Current symbolic interactionism is methodologically eclectic; and it tends to be more rigorous than in the past, whether the methods be ethnographic (Corsaro 1985) or involve structural equation modeling (Serpe 1987). Also contributing to the revitalization of symbolic interactionism is the attention to its ideas, often unacknowledged but sometimes recognized, paid by a psychological social psychology that is predominately cognitive in its orientation. For cognitive social psychology, concepts are mental or subjective structures formed through experience, and these structures affect recognizing, attending, storage, recall, and utilization of information impinging on the person; of prime significance among concepts functioning in these ways are self-concepts. The link thus forged between cognitive social psychology and symbolic interactionism is mutually advantageous; the latter benefits from the "legitimacy" implicit in attention given its ideas and from the expanded pool of researchers focusing on those ideas; the former benefits (or

can benefit) from understanding that cognitions are rooted in social structures and processes.

(SEE ALSO: *Identity Theory; Role Theory; Self-Concept; Social Psychology*)

REFERENCES

Becker, Howard S., and Blanche Geer 1957 "Participant Observation and Interviewing: A Comparison." *Human Organization* 16:28–32.

Blumer, Herbert 1937 "Social Psychology." In Emerson P. Schmidt, ed., *Man and Society.* New York: Prentice-Hall.

―――― 1969 *Symbolic Interactionism: Perspective and Method.* Englewood Cliffs, N.J.: Prentice-Hall.

Burke, Peter J. Forthcoming "Attitudes, Behavior, and the Self." In Judy Howard and Peter Callero, eds., *The Self–Society Dynamic: Affect, Action, and Social Cognition.* New York: Cambridge University Press.

Corsaro, William A. 1985 *Friendship and Peer Culture in the Early Years.* Norwood, N.J.: Ablex.

Couch, Carl J., Stanley L. Saxon, and Michael A. Katovich 1986 *Studies in Symbolic Interaction: The Iowa School,* 2 vols. Greenwich, Conn.: JAI Press.

Denzin, Norman K. 1970 *The Research Act.* New York: McGraw-Hill.

―――― 1984 "Toward a Phenomenology of Domestic Family Violence." *American Journal of Sociology* 3:483–513.

Glaser, Barney G., and Anselm L. Strauss 1967 *The Discovery of Grounded Theory.* Chicago: Aldine.

Goffman, Erving 1959 *The Presentation of Self in Everyday Life.* Garden City, N.Y.: Doubleday.

Hall, Peter M. 1972 "A Symbolic Interactionist Analysis of Politics." *Sociological Inquiry* 42:35–75.

Heise, David R. 1979 *Understanding Events.* New York: Cambridge University Press.

―――― 1986 "Modeling Symbolic Interaction." In Siegwart Lindenberg, James S. Coleman, and Stefan Nowak, eds., *Approaches to Social Theory.* New York: Russell Sage Foundation.

Hewitt, John P. 1988 *Self and Society: A Symbolic Interactionist Social Psychology,* 4th ed. Boston: Allyn and Bacon.

―――― 1990 *Dilemmas of the American Self.* Philadelphia: Temple University Press.

Hochschild, Arlie R. 1979 "Emotion Work, Feeling

Rules, and Social Structure." *American Journal of Sociology* 85:551–575.

Kuhn, Manfred H. 1964 "Major Trends in Symbolic Interaction Theory in the Past Twenty-Five Years." *Sociological Quarterly* 5:61–84.

Lewis, J. David, and Richard J. Smith 1980 *American Sociology and Pragmatism: Mead, Chicago Sociology, and Symbolic Interaction.* Chicago: University of Chicago Press.

Lindesmith, Alfred R., Anselm L. Strauss, and Norman K. Denzin 1988 *Social Psychology.* Englewood Cliffs, N.J.: Prentice-Hall.

McCall, George J., and J. L. Simmons 1978 *Identities and Interaction,* rev. ed. New York: Free Press.

McPhail, Clark, and Ronald T. Wohlstein 1986 "Collective Locomotion as Collective Behavior. *American Sociological Review* 51:447–464.

Maines, David 1977 "Social Organization and Social Structure in Symbolic Interactionist Thought." *Annual Review of Sociology* 3:235–259.

Mead, George H. 1934 *Mind, Self, and Society.* Chicago: University of Chicago Press.

Meltzer, Bernard N., John W. Petras, and Larry T. Reynolds 1975 *Symbolic Interactionism: Genesis, Varieties, and Criticism.* London: Routledge and Kegan Paul.

Mullins, Nicholas 1973 *Theories and Theory Groups in Contemporary American Sociology.* New York: Harper and Row.

Reynolds, Larry T. 1990 *Interactionism: Exposition and Critique,* 2nd ed. Dix Hills, N.Y.: General Hall.

Rosenberg, Morris 1984 "A Symbolic Interactionist View of Psychosis." *Journal of Health and Social Behavior* 25:289–302.

Serpe, Richard T. 1987 "Stability and Change in Self: A Structural Symbolic Interactionist Explanation." *Social Psychology Quarterly* 50:44–55.

Stryker, Sheldon 1980 *Symbolic Interactionism: A Social Structural Version.* Menlo Park, Calif.: Benjamin/Cummings.

——— 1987 "The Vitalization of Symbolic Interactionism." *Social Psychology Quarterly* 50:83–94.

——— 1988 "Substance and Style: An Appraisal of the Sociological Legacy of Herbert Blumer." *Symbolic Interaction* 11:33–42.

——— 1989 "Further Developments in Identity Theory: Singularity versus Multiplicity of Self." In Joseph Berger, Morris Zelditch, Jr., and Bo Anderson, eds., *Sociological Theories in Progress: New Formulations.* Newbury Park, Calif.: Sage.

———, and Richard T. Serpe 1982 "Commitment,

Identity Salience, and Role Behavior." In William Ickes and Eric Knowles, eds., *Personality, Roles, and Social Behavior.* New York: Springer-Verlage.

Stryker, Sheldon, and Anne Statham 1985 "Symbolic Interactionism and Role Theory." In Gardner Lindzey and Elliot Aronsen, eds., *The Handbook of Social Psychology,* 3rd ed. New York: Random House.

Thoits, Peggy A. 1983 "Multiple Identities and Psychological Well-Being: A Reformulation and Test of the Social Isolation Hypothesis." *American Sociological Review* 48:174–187.

——— 1989 "The Sociology of Emotions." *Annual Review of Sociology* 15:317–342.

Turner, Ralph H. 1962 "Role-Taking: Process versus Conformity." In Arnold M. Rose, ed., *Human Behavior and Social Process.* Boston: Houghton-Mifflin.

Weigert, Andrew J. 1981 *Sociology of Everyday Life.* New York: Longman.

SHELDON STRYKER

SYSTEMS THEORY Systems theory is much more (or perhaps much less) than a label for a set of constructs or research methods. The term *systems* is used in many different ways (Boguslaw 1965; 1981, pp. 29–46). Inevitably this creates considerable confusion. For some it is a "way" of looking at problems in science, technology, philosophy, and many other things; for others it is a specific mode of decision making. In the late twentieth-century Western world it has also become a means of referring to skills of various kinds and defining professional elites. Newspaper "want ads" reflect a widespread demand for persons with a variety of "system" skills, for experts in "systems engineering," "systems analysis," "management systems," "urban systems," "welfare systems," and "educational systems."

As a way of looking at things, the "systems approach" in the first place means examining objects or processes, not as isolated phenomena, but as interrelated components or parts of a complex. An automobile may be seen as a system; a car battery is a component of this system. The automobile, however, may also be seen as a component of a community or a national transportation system. Indeed, most systems can be viewed as subsystems of more encompassing systems.

Second, beyond the idea of interrelatedness, systems imply the idea of control. This always includes some more or less explicit set of values. In some systems, the values involved may be as simple as maintaining a given temperature range. The idea of control was implicit in Walter B. Cannon's original formulation of the concept of homeostasis. Cannon suggested (Cannon 1939, p. 22) that the methods used by animals to control their body temperatures within well-established ranges might be adapted for use in connection with other structures including social and industrial organizations. He referred to the body's ability to maintain its temperature equilibrium as *homeostasis*.

A third idea involved in the system way of looking at things is Ludwig von Bertalannfy's search for a "general systems theory" (von Bertalannfy 1968; Boguslaw 1982, pp. 8–13). This is essentially a call for what many would see as an interdisciplinary approach. Von Bertalannfy noted the tendency toward increased specialization in the modern world and saw entire disciplines—physics, biology, psychology, sociology, and so on—encapsulated in their private universes of discourse, with little communication between any of them. He failed to note, however, that new interdisciplinary disciplines often quickly tend to build their own insulated languages and conceptual cocoons.

A fourth idea in the systems approach to phenomena is in some ways the most pervasive of all. It focuses on the discrepancy between objectives set for a component and those required for the system. In organizations this is illustrated by the difference between goals of individual departments and those of an entire organization. For example, the sales department wants to maximize sales, but the organization finds it more profitable to limit production, for a variety of reasons. If an entire community is viewed as a system, a factory component of this system may decide that short-term profitability is more desirable as an objective than investment in pollution-control devices to

protect the health of its workers and community residents. Countless examples of this sort can be found. They all seem to document the idea that system objectives are more important than those of its subsystems. This is a readily understandable notion with respect to exclusively physical systems. When human beings are involved on any level, things become much more complicated.

Physical components or subsystems are not expected to be innovative. Their existence is ideal when it proceeds in a "normal" routine. If they wear out they can be replaced relatively cheaply, and if they are damaged they can be either repaired or discarded. They have no sense of risk and can be required to work in highly dangerous environments twenty-four hours a day, seven days a week, if necessary. They do not join unions, never ask for increases in pay, and are completely obedient. They have no requirements for leisure time, cultural activities, or diversions of any kind. They are completely expendable if the system demands sacrifices. They thrive on authoritarian or totalitarian controls and cannot deal with the notion of democracy.

As a specific mode of decision making, it is this top-down authoritarianism that seems to characterize systems theory when it is predicated on a physical systems prototype. Computerization of functions previously performed by human beings ostensibly simplifies the process of converting this aspect of the theory into action. Computer hardware is presumably completely obedient to commands received from the top; software prepared by computer programers is presumably similarly responsive to system objectives. Almost imperceptibly, this has led to a condition in which systems increasingly become seen and treated as identical to the machine in large-scale "man-machine systems." (The language continues to reflect deeply embedded traditions of male chauvinism.)

These systems characteristically have a sizable computerized information-processing subsystem that keeps assuming increasing importance. For example the U.S. Internal Revenue Service (IRS) obviously has enormous quantities of information to process. Periodically, IRS officials feel the necessity to increase computer capacity. To accomplish this, the practice has been to obtain bids from computer manufacturers. One bid, accepted years ago at virtually the highest levels of government, proposed a revised system costing between 750 million and one billion dollars.

Examination of the proposal by the congressional Office of Technology Assessment uncovered a range of difficulties. Central to these was the fact that the computer subsystem had been treated as the total system (perhaps understandably since the contractor was a computer corporation). The existing body of IRS procedures, internal regulations, information requirements, and law (all part of the larger system) was accepted as an immutable given. No effort had been made to consider changes in the larger system that could conceivably eliminate a significant portion of the massive computer installation (Office of Technology Assessment 1972).

Almost two decades after attention had been called to these difficulties, system problems at the IRS continued to exist. A proposed Tax System Modernization was formulated to solve them. The General Accounting Office raised questions about whether this proposal, estimated to cost several billion dollars, was in fact "a new way of doing business" or simply intended to lower costs and increase efficiency of current operations. Moreover, the Accounting Office suggested that the lack of a master plan made it difficult to know how or whether the different component subsystems would fit together. Specifically, for example, it asked whether the proposal included a telecommunications subsystem and, if so, why such an item had not been included among the budgeted items (Rhile 1990).

To exclude the larger system from consideration and assume it is equivalent to a subsystem is to engage in a form of fragmentation that has long been criticized in related areas by perceptive sociologists (see Braverman 1974; Kraft 1977). Historically, fragmentation has led to *deskilling* of workers, that is, replacing craft tasks with large numbers of relatively simpler tasks requiring only semiskilled or unskilled labor. This shields the larger system from scrutiny and facilitates centralization of control and power. It also facilitates

computerization of work processes and even more control.

In the contemporary industrial and political worlds, power is justified largely on the basis of "efficiency." It is exercised largely through monopolization of information. Various forms of social organization and social structure can be used for the exercise of this power. Systems theory focuses not on alternative structures but, rather, on *objectives,* a subset of what sociologists think of as *values.* To hold power is to facilitate rapid implementation of the holder's values.

Fragmentation, in the final analysis, is an effort to divide the world of relevant systems into tightly enclosed cubbyholes of thought and practice controlled from the top. This compartmentalization is found in both government and private enterprises. The compartments are filled with those devoid of genuine power and reflect the limitation of decisions available to their occupants. Those at the summit of power pyramids are exempt from these constraints and, accordingly, enjoy considerably more "freedom" (Pelton, Sackmann, and Boguslaw 1990).

An increasingly significant form of fragmentation is found in connection with the operation of many large-scale technological systems. Sociologist Charles Perrow has, in a path-breaking study, examined an enormous variety of such systems. He has reviewed operations in nuclear power, petrochemical, aircraft, marine, and a variety of other systems including those involving dams, mines, space, weapons, and even deoxyribonucleic acid (DNA). He developed a rough scale of the potential for catastrophe, assessing the risk of loss of life and property against expected benefits. He concluded that people would be better off learning to live without some, or with greatly modified, complex technological systems (Perrow 1984). A central problem he found involved "externalities," the social costs of an activity *not* shown in its price, such as pollution, injuries, and anxieties. He notes that these social costs are often borne by those who do not even benefit from the activity or are unaware of the externalities.

This, of course, is another corollary to the fragmentation problem. To consider the technological system in isolation from the larger social system within which it is embedded is to invite enormous difficulties for the larger system while providing spurious profits for those controlling the subsystem.

Another interesting manifestation of the fragmentation problem arises in connection with two relatively new disciplines that address many problems formerly the exclusive province of sociology: operations research and management science. Each of these has its own professional organization and journal.

Operations research traces its ancestry to 1937 in Great Britain when a group of scientists, mathematicians, and engineers was organized to study some military problems. How do you use chaff as a radar countermeasure? What are the most effective bombing patterns? How can destroyers best be deployed if you want to protect a convoy?

The efforts to solve these and related problems gave rise to a body of knowledge initially referred to as Operations Analysis and subsequently referred to as Operations Research. A more or less official definition of the field tells us Operations Research is concerned with scientifically deciding how to best design and operate man-machine systems usually under conditions requiring the allocation of scarce resources. In practice, the work of operations research involved the construction of models of operational activities, initially in the military, subsequently in organizations of all kinds. *Management science,* a term perhaps more congenial to the American industrial and business ear, emerged officially as a discipline in 1953 with the establishment of the Institute of Management Sciences.

In both cases, the declared impetus of the discipline was to focus on the entire system, rather than on components. One text points out that subdivisions of organizations began to solve problems in ways that were not necessarily in the best interests of the overall organizations. Operations research tries to help management solve problems involving the interactions of objectives. It tries to find the "best" decisions for "as large a portion of the *total system* as possible" (Whitehouse and Wechsler 1976).

Another text, using the terms *management science* and *operations research,* interchangeably defines them (or it) as the "application of scientific procedures, techniques, and tools to operating, strategic, and policy problems in order to develop and help evaluate solutions" (Davis, McKeown, and Rakes 1986, p. 4).

The basic procedure used in operations research/management science work involves defining a problem, constructing a model, and, ultimately, finding a solution. An enormous variety of mathematical, statistical, and simulation models have been developed with more or less predictable consequences. "Many management science specialists were accused of being more interested in manipulating problems to fit techniques than . . . (working) to develop suitable solutions" (Davis, McKeown, and Rakes 1986, p. 5). The entire field often evokes the tale of the fabled inebriate who persisted in looking for his lost key under the lamppost, although he had lost it elsewhere, because "it is light here."

Under the sponsorship of the Systems Theory and Operations Research program of the National Science Foundation, a Committee on the Next Decade in Operations Research (CONDOR) held a workshop in 1987. A report later appeared in the journal *Operations Research.* The journal subsequently asked operation researchers to comment on the report (Wagner et al. 1989). One of the commentators expressed what appears to be a growing sentiment in the field by pointing out the limitations of conventional modeling techniques for professional work. Criticizing the CONDOR report for appearing to accept the methodological status quo, he emphasized the character of models as "at best abstractions of selected aspects of reality" (Wagner et al. 1989). He quoted approvingly from another publication, "thus while exploiting their strengths, a prudent analyst recognizes realistically the limitations of quantitative methods" (Quade 1988).

This, however, is an unfortunate repetition of an inaccurate statement of the difficulty. It is not the limitations of quantitative methods that is in question but rather the recognition of the character of the situations to which they are applied.

Sociologists distinguish between *established* situations, those whose parameters can be defined precisely and for which valid analytic means exist to describe meaningful relationship within them and *emergent* situations, whose parameters are known incompletely and for which satisfactory analytic techniques are not available within the time constraints of necessary action (Boguslaw [1965] 1981). In established situations mathematical or statistical models are quite satisfactory, along with other forms of rational analysis. In emergent situations, however, they can yield horrendous distortions. Fifty top U.S. corporation executives, when interviewed, recognized and acted upon this distinction more or less intuitively, although the situations presented to them were referred to as Type 1 and Type 2, respectively (Pelton, Sackmann, and Boguslaw 1990).

Individual persons, organizations, or enterprises may be viewed, on the one hand, as self-contained systems. On the other, they may be viewed as subsystems of larger social systems. Unfortunately, efforts are continually made to gloss over this dichotomy through a form of fragmentation, by treating a subsystem or collection of subsystems as equivalent to a larger system. It is this relationship between system and subsystem that constitutes the core of the dilemma continuing to confront systems theory.

Achieving a satisfactory resolution of the discrepancy between individual needs and objectives of the systems within which individuals find themselves embedded or by which they are affected remains an unsolved problem as the twentieth century draws to a close.

(SEE ALSO: *Decision-Making Theory and Research; Social Dynamics; Social Structure*)

REFERENCES

Boguslaw, Robert (1965) 1981 *The New Utopians: A Study of Systems Design and Social Change.* Englewood Cliffs, N.J.: Prentice-Hall.

———— 1982 *Systems Analysis and Social Planning: Human Problems of Post-Industrial Society.* New York: Irvington.

Braverman, Harry 1974 *Labor and Monopoly Capital: The Degradation of Work in the Twentieth Century.* New York: Monthly Review Press.

Cannon, Walter B. 1939 *The Wisdom of the Body,* rev. ed. New York: Norton.

Davis, K. Roscoe, Patrick G. McKeown, and Terry R. Rakes 1986 *Management Science.* Boston, Mass.: Kent.

Kraft, Philip 1977 *Programmers and Managers: The Routinization of Computer Programming in the United States.* New York: Springer-Verlag.

Office of Technology Assessment 1977 *A Preliminary Assessment of the IRS Tax Administration System.* Washington, D.C.: Office of Technology Assessment.

Pelton, Warren, Sonja Sackmann, and Robert Boguslaw 1990 *Tough Choices: Decision-Making Styles of America's Top 50 CEO's.* Homewood, Ill.: Dow Jones-Irwin.

Perrow, Charles 1984 *Normal Accidents: Living with High-Risk Technologies.* New York: Basic Books.

Quade, E. S. 1988 "Quantitative Methods: Uses and Limitations" In H. J. Miser and E. S. Quade, eds., *Handbook of Systems Analysis: Overview of Uses, Procedures, Applications and Practice,* pp. 283–324. New York: North-Holland.

Rhile, Howard G. (March 22) 1990 "Progress in Meeting the Challenge of Modernizing IRS' Tax Processing System." Testimony before the Subcommittee on Oversight, Committee on Ways and Means, House of Representatives. Washington, D.C.: General Accounting Office.

von Bertalannfy, Ludwig 1968 *General Systems Theory: Foundations, Development, Applications.* New York: George Braziller.

Wagner, Harvey M., Michael H. Rothkopf, Clayton J. Thomas, and Hugh J. Miser 1989 "The Next Decade in Operations Research: Comments on the CONDOR Report," *Operations Research* 37:664–672.

Whitehouse, Gary E., and Ben L. Wechsler 1976 *Applied Operations Research.* New York: Wiley.

ROBERT BOGUSLAW

T

TABULAR ANALYSIS Tabular analysis, in its most general form, may encompass any analysis that uses tables. That ought to include almost any quantitative analysis. In this article, however, it means only the analysis of categorical variables (both nominal and ordered) when that analysis relies on cross-classified tables, whether in the form of frequencies, probabilities, or conditional probabilities (percentages). In general, the use of such cross-tabulated data is practical only with variables having a limited number of categories. Therefore, this article deals with some of the *analytic* problems of *categorical data analysis*. Although it is sometimes difficult to separate analysis from methods of data presentation, the emphasis in this article is decidedly on analysis (see Davis and Jacobs 1968).

Tabular analysis can take many different forms, but there are two methods that deserve special attention. The first method is known as *subgroup analysis*. The underlying logic of this analysis was codified under the name "elaboration paradigm" by Lazarsfeld and his colleagues (Kendall and Lazarsfeld 1950; Lazarsfeld 1955; Hyman 1955; Rosenberg 1968; Zeisel 1985). Because of the simplicity of the method and the ease with which it can facilitate communication with others, subgroup analysis has been the mainstay of research reports dealing with categorical data.

The second method is based on the use of *log-linear* and related models and has become increasingly popular (Bishop, Fienberg, and Holland 1975; Goodman 1978; Haberman 1978, 1979; Fienberg 1980; Agresti 1984). This method is flexible, can handle more complex data (with many variables), and is more readily amenable to statistical modeling and testing (Clogg, Shockey, and Eliason 1990). For this reason the log-linear method is rapidly emerging as the standard method of analyzing multivariate categorical data. Its results, however, are not easily accessible because the resulting tabular data are expressed as multiplicative functions of the parameters (i.e., log-linear rather than linear), and the parameters of these models tend to obscure descriptive information that is often needed for making intelligent comparisons (Davis 1984; Kaufman and Schervish 1986; Alba 1988; Clogg, Shockey, and Eliason 1990).

These two methods, however, share a set of common analytic strategies and problems, and are complementary in their strengths and weaknesses. In order to understand both the promises and the problems of tabular analysis, it is important to understand the logic of analysis and the problems that the tabular analyses share with the simpler statistical analysis of linear systems. As a multivariate analysis tool, tabular analysis must face the same problems that other well-developed linear statistical models face in analyzing data that are collected under less than ideal experimental conditions. It is important, therefore, to have a full understanding of this foundation, and the best way to do that is to examine the simplest linear system.

STATISTICAL CONTROLS, CAUSAL ORDERING, AND IMPROPER SPECIFICATIONS

Consider the simplest linear multivariate system:

$$Y = Xb_{yx \cdot z} + Zb_{yz \cdot x} + e, \qquad (1)$$

where all the variables, including the error term, are assumed to be measured from their respective means. When we use this equation merely to describe the relationship between a dependent variable Y and two other variables, X and Z, the issue of misspecification—in other words, whether the coefficients accurately reflect an intended relationship—does not arise. The coefficients are well-known partial regression coefficients. But when the linear model depicted in (1) is considered as a representation of some underlying theory, these coefficients receive meaning under that theory. Then the issue of whether these coefficients really capture the intended relationship becomes important. Causal relationships are not necessarily the only important relationships. But even so, it is informative to examine this equation with reference to such relationships, considering that this is the implicitly implied type of system.

Many different conceptions of causality exist in the literature (Blalock 1964, 1985a, 1985b; Duncan 1966, 1975; Simon 1954, 1979; Heise 1975; Mosteller and Tukey 1977; Bunge 1979; Singer and Marini 1987). But the one undisputed criterion of causality seems to be the existence of a relationship between manipulated changes in one variable (X) and attendant changes in another variable (Y) in an ideal experiment. That is, a causal connection exists between X and Y if changes in X, and X *alone*, produce changes in Y. It is a very restrictive criterion, and may not be general enough to cover all important cases, but it is good enough as a point of reference. This definition is consistent with the way effects are measured in controlled experiments. In general, even in an ideal experiment, it is often impossible to eliminate or control all the variations in other variables, but their effects are made random by design. A simple linear causal system, describing a relationship produced in an ideal experiment, will then take the following familiar form:

$$Y = Xd_{yx} + e, \qquad (2)$$

where e stands for all the effects of other variables that are randomized. The randomization makes the expected correlation between X and e zero. (Without loss of generality, it is assumed that all the variables [X, Y, and e] are measured as deviations from their respective means.) For the sake of simplicity, we assume for now that Y does not affect X. (For an examination of causal models dealing with reciprocal causation, and with more complex systems in general, see Alwin and Hauser 1975; Blalock 1985a, 1985b; Fisher 1966; Goldberger and Duncan 1973; Duncan 1975.)

The coefficient d_{yx} measures the expected change in Y given a unit change in X. It does not matter whether changes in X affect other variables, and whether some of these variables, in turn, affect Y. As long as all the changes in Y are ultimately produced by the manipulated initial changes in X and X alone, X receives total credit for them. Therefore, d_{yx} is a coefficient of *total causal effect* (referred to as *effect coefficient*, for short).

The customary symbol for a simple regression coefficient, b_{yx}, is not used in equation (2) because b_{yx} is equivalent to d_{yx} only under these very special conditions. If one uses a simple regression equation in the form similar to equation (2) above, and assumes that b_{yx} is equivalent to d_{yx}, the model is misspecified as long as the data do not meet all the assumptions made about the ideal experiment. Such errors in model specification yield biased estimates in general. Implications of some specification errors may be trivial, but they can also be serious, when one is analyzing nonexperimental data. (See Arminger and Bohrnstedt 1987; Kish 1959; Campbell and Stanley 1966; Leamer 1978; Cook and Campbell 1979; Lieberson 1985.)

There are many underlying causal systems that are compatible with the three-variable linear equation shown above. For the purpose at hand, it is enough to examine some simple causal systems, shown in Figure 1. These causal systems imply critical assumptions about the error term and the causal ordering. If these assumptions are right, then there is a definite connection between the underlying causal parameters and the regression coefficients in equation (1). On the other hand, if some of these assumptions are wrong, then equation (1) is a misrepresentation of the assumed causal model. (For fuller description of other possible systems, see Duncan 1975.)

The notation for causal hierarchy ($\geq$) means

that the preceding variable may affect the variables after it, but variables after ($\geq$) may not affect the preceding variables. A connecting arrow between two variables indicates both existence and direction of effects; lack of a connecting arrow indicates no known effects. (For convenience, these diagrams do not show random errors, but their presence is assumed.)

For each causal system in Figure 1, the key relationships among simple regression coefficients, partial regression coefficients, and effect coefficients are listed below each causal diagram. Look at the simple causal chain (or a cascading system) shown in A1, for instance. The introduction of Z as a control variable has no effect on the observed relationship between X and Y. Note also that the simple regression coefficient is equivalent to the effect coefficient ($b_{yx} = b_{yx\cdot z} = d_{yx}$); likewise,

A. $Z \geq X \geq Y$:

1) $Z \longrightarrow X \longrightarrow Y$

$$b_{yx} = b_{yx\cdot z} = d_{yx}$$
$$b_{yz} = b_{xz}\cdot b_{yx\cdot z} = d_{yz}$$
$$\neq b_{yz\cdot x} = 0$$

2) $Z \Longrightarrow X \searrow Y$

$$b_{yx} \neq b_{yx\cdot z} = d_{yx}$$
$$b_{yz} = b_{xz}\cdot b_{yx\cdot z} + b_{yz\cdot x} = d_{yz}$$
$$\neq b_{yz\cdot x}$$

3) $Z \Longrightarrow X \searrow Y$

$$b_{yx} = b_{yx\cdot z} = 0 = d_{yx}$$
$$b_{yz} = b_{yz\cdot x} = d_{yz}$$

B. $(Z,X) \geq Y$:

1)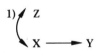

$$b_{yx} = b_{yx\cdot z}$$
$$= d_{yx}$$

2) $Z \longrightarrow Y$, X

$$b_{yx} \neq b_{yx\cdot z} = d_{yx}$$
$$b_{yz} \neq b_{yz\cdot x} = d_{yz}$$

3) $Z \longrightarrow Y$, X

$$b_{yx} \neq b_{yx\cdot z} = 0 = d_{yx}$$
$$b_{yz} \neq b_{yz\cdot x} = d_{yz}$$

C. $X \geq Z \geq Y$:

1) $X \longrightarrow Z \longrightarrow Y$

$$b_{yx} \neq 0 = b_{yx\cdot z}$$
$$b_{yz} = b_{yz\cdot x} = d_{yz}$$

2) $X \Longrightarrow Z \searrow Y$

$$b_{yx} \neq b_{yx\cdot z}$$
$$b_{yz} \neq b_{yz\cdot x}$$

3) $X \Longrightarrow Z \searrow Y$

$$b_{yx} = b_{yx\cdot z}$$
$$b_{yz} \neq b_{yz\cdot x} = 0$$

FIGURE 1
Some Simplified Linear Causal Systems

the simple b_{yz} is equivalent to d_{yz}, but the partial $b_{yz\cdot x}$ becomes zero. (If one were to control Y, the X-Z relationship should not change; but such control is superfluous, given the assumptions about the causal ordering.) In fact, one could argue that these two conditions, given the assumptions about the causal hierarchy, uniquely define a simple causal chain. If the control variable Z enters the X-Y causal system only through X (or effects of a set of variables are mediated completely through [an]other variable[s] in the system), there is no need to introduce Z (or a set of such variables) as a control in order to correctly specify the X-Y relationship.

In A2 the two partials ($b_{yx\cdot z}$ and $b_{yz\cdot x}$) are different from respective bivariate coefficients (b_{yx} and b_{yz}). The key point is that the partial $b_{yx\cdot z}$ is equivalent to d_{yx}, while the partial between Z and Y ($b_{yz\cdot x}$) simply reflects the portion of the causal effect from Z to Y that is not mediated by X.

In A3 there is no direct connection between X and Y once the effect of Z is controlled: the observed bivariate relation between X and Y is spurious. Or, more accurately, the observed association between X and Y is explained by the existence of a common cause. In this case the introduction of Z, and controlling its effects on both X and Y, is critical in ascertaining the true causal parameter of the system (d_{yx}), which happens to be zero.

All the causal systems shown in B share similar patterns with A—the pattern of relationship between the bivariate coefficients and the partials remains the same. For this reason, the X-Y relationship in particular is examined in the same way by introducing Z as a control variable, regardless of the specification of causal hierarchy between X and Z. Note, in particular, that introducing Z as a control variable in B1 and B3 is a misspecification of the model, but such misspecifications (including an irrelevant variable in the equation) do not lead to biased estimation. (For a related discussion, see Arminger and Bohrnstedt 1987.)

The systems shown in C do not need additional comments. Except for the changes in the order of the two variables, X and Z, they are exact replicas of systems in A. The resulting statistics show the

same patterns observed in A. Nevertheless, the attendant interpretation of the results is radically different. For instance, when the partial $b_{yx\cdot z}$ disappears, one does not consider that there is no causal relationship between X and Y; rather, our conviction about the causal relationship is reinforced by the fact that an intervening causal agent is found.

In summary, the assumptions about the causal ordering play a critical role in the interpretation of the coefficients of the linear model shown in equation (1). And the assumptions about the order must come from outside knowledge.

There is one more type to note. All the systems examined so far are linear and additive. The partial coefficients reflect the expected change in the dependent variable given a unit change in a given independent variable while keeping other independent variables constant. If two or more independent variables interact, then such simplicity does not exist. A simple example of such system is given below:

$$Y = X_1 \cdot b_1 + X_2 \cdot b_2 + (X_1 \cdot X_2) \cdot b_3 + e, \qquad (3)$$

which is the same as equation (1), except for the simplification of labels for the variables and coefficients, and for the addition of a multiplicative term ($X_1 \cdot X_2$).

The partial for X_1 *in such a system, for example, no longer properly represents the expected change in Y* for a unit change in X_1, even if the assumptions about the causal order are correct. A partial differentiation of the equation with respect to X_1, for instance, gives $b_1 + X_2 \cdot b_3$, which implies that the rate of change introduced by a change in X_1 is also dependent on the values of the other causal variable (X_2) and the associated coefficient (b_3). One therefore cannot interpret the individual coefficients as measuring something independently of others. This point is important for a fuller understanding of the log-linear models introduced later, because a bivariate relationship is represented by interaction terms. The notion of control often invoked with *ceteris paribus* (other things being unchanged) also becomes ambiguous.

The logic of causal analysis for the additive

systems can easily be extended to a system with more variables. If the assumptions about the causal order, the form of the relationship, and the random errors are right, then we can identify the causal parameters, such as d_{yx}, and decompose the linear connection between any set of variables into spurious (noncausal) and genuine (causal) components, d_{yx}, and the latter (d_{yx}) into indirect (mediated) and direct (residual) components.

To identify d_{yx}, one must control all the potentially relevant variables that precede X in causal ordering, but not the variables that might intervene between X and Y. Under this assumption, then, the partial $b_{yx} \cdot (z \cdots)$, where the variables in parentheses represent all such "antecedent" variables, is equivalent to d_{yx}. In identifying this component, one must not control the variables that X may affect; these variables may work as mediating causal agents and transmit part of the effect of X to Y.

The partial of a linear system in which both antecedent variables (Zs) and intervening variables (Ws) are included ($b_{yx} \cdot [x \cdots w \cdots]$) will represent the residual causal connection between X and Y that is not mediated by any of the variables included in the model. As more Ws are included, this residual component may change. But the linear representation of a causal system without these additional intervening variables is not misspecified. On the other hand, if introduction of additional Zs would change the X-Y partial, an omission of such variables from the equation means a misspecification of the causal system—because some of the spurious components will be confounded with the genuine causal components.

For nonexperimental data the problems of misspecification and misinterpretation are serious. There are many factors that may confound the relationships under consideration (Campbell and Stanley 1966; Cook and Campbell 1979; Lieberson 1985; Arminger and Bohrnstedt 1987; Singer and Marini 1987). There is no guarantee that a set of variables one is considering constitutes a closed system, but neither is the situation totally hopeless. The important point is that one should not ignore these issues and assume away potentially serious problems. Selection biases, contagion effects, limited variations in the data, threshold effects, and so on can be modeled if they are faced seriously (Rubin 1977; Leamer 1978; Hausman 1978; Heckman 1979; Berk 1983, 1986; Heckman and Robb 1986; Arminger and Bohrnstedt 1987; Xie 1989). Furthermore, it does not mean that one has to control (introduce) every conceivable variable. Once a few key variables are controlled, additional variables usually do not affect the remaining variables too much. (This observation is a corollary to the well-known fact that social scientists often have great difficulty finding any variable that can substantially improve R^2 in regression analysis.)

FREQUENCY TABLES, CONDITIONAL PROBABILITIES, AND ODDS RATIOS

In order to fix the ideas and to make the following discussions concrete, it is useful to introduce basic notations and to define two indicators of association for a bivariate table. Consider the simplest contingency table, given by the cross-classification of two dichotomous variables. Let f_{ij} denote the observed frequencies; then the observed frequency distribution will have the following form:

		Observed Frequencies		
	Variable X			
		1	2	total
Variable Y	1	f_{11}	f_{12}	$f_{1\cdot}$
	2	f_{21}	f_{22}	$f_{2\cdot}$
	total	$f_{\cdot 1}$	$f_{\cdot 2}$	N

Note the form of marginal frequencies. Now let p_{ij} denote the corresponding observed probabilities: $p_{ij} = f_{ij}/N$. And let the upper case letters, F_{ij} and P_{ij}, denote the corresponding expected frequencies and probabilities under some model or hypothesis.

If X and Y are statistically independent,

$$\frac{P_{ij}}{P_{\cdot j}} = \frac{P_{i\cdot}P_{j\cdot}}{P_{\cdot j}} = P_{i\cdot}$$

That is, the conditional probability of Y_i, given X_j, is the same as the marginal probability of Y_i. Thus a convenient descriptive indicator of statistical independence is that $b_{yx} = p_{11}/p_{.1} - p_{12}/p_{.2} = 0$. The percentage difference is simply 100 times b_{yx}. The symbol b_{yx} is quite appropriate in this particular case, for it is equivalent to the regression coefficient. That $b_{yx} \neq 0$ implies a lack of statistical independence between X and Y.

Another equally good measure is the odds ratio or cross-product ratio:

$$\text{Odds ratio (t)} = \frac{F_{11}/F_{12}}{F_{21}/F_{22}}$$

$$= \frac{F_{11}/F_{21}}{F_{12}/F_{22}}$$

$$= \frac{F_{11}/F_{22}}{F_{12}/F_{21}}$$

The first line shows that the odds ratio is a ratio of ratios. The second line shows that it is immaterial whether we start with odds (ratio) in one direction or in the opposite direction. And the final line indicates that the odds ratio is equivalent to the cross-product ratio. In general, if all the odds ratios in a given table for two variables are 1, then the two variables are statistically independent; the converse is also true. That t equals 1 implies that X is independent of Y. Therefore, both the odds ratio (t) and the percent difference (b_{yx}) can serve equally well as descriptive indicators of association between variables. (For other measures of association, see Measures of Association.)

Given that observed frequencies are unstable owing to sampling variability, it is useful to test the null hypothesis that $t=b_{yx}=0$ in the population. Such a hypothesis is evaluated using either the conventional chi-square statistic or the $-2*$(likelihood ratio):

$$X^2 = \Sigma\Sigma(f_{ij}-F_{ij})^2/F_{ij}$$

$$L^2 = -2\Sigma\Sigma(f_{ij} \log(F_{ij}/f_{ij}))$$

$$= 2\Sigma\Sigma(f_{ij} \log(f_{ij}/F_{ij})).$$

These values are evaluated against the theoretical distribution with appropriate degrees of freedom. These two tests are equivalent for large samples.

ELABORATION AND SUBGROUP ANALYSIS

The logic of linear systems presented earlier was introduced to the social science audience through the elaboration paradigm and through informal demonstration of certain patterns of relationship among variables (Kendall and Lazarsfeld 1950; Lazarsfeld 1955). Statistical control is achieved by examining relationships within each subgroup that is formed by the relevant categories of the control variable. The typical strategy is to start the analysis with an examination of the association between two variables of interest, say X and Y. If there is an association of some sort between X and Y, the following two questions become relevant: (1) Is the observed relationship spurious or genuine? (2) If some part of the relationship is genuine, which variables mediate the relationship between the two? (The question of sampling variability is handled rather informally, relying on the magnitude of the percentage differences as a simple guide. Moreover, two variables seemingly unrelated at the bivariate level may show stronger association after suppressor variables are controlled. Therefore, in some situations, applying such a test may be premature and uncalled for.)

To answer these questions adequately, one must have a fairly good knowledge of the variables under consideration and the implications of different causal systems. It is clear from earlier examination of the linear causal systems that in order to answer the first question, one must examine the X-Y relationship while controlling for the factors that are antecedent to X (assuming $X \geq Y$). In order to answer the second question, one must in addition control factors that X may affect and that in turn may affect Y. Controlling for many variables is possible in theory but is impractical for two quite different reasons: (a) one runs out of cases very quickly as the number of subgroups increases, and (b) as the number of subgroups increases, so does the number of partial tables to examine and evaluate. Nevertheless, it is quite possible that one might find a strategically critical variable which might help explain the observed relationship either by proving that the observed relationship is spurious or by confirming a causal connection between the two variables.

To make the discussion more concrete, consider the hypothetical bivariate percentage table between involvement in car accidents (Y) and sex of the driver (X).

The percentage difference (10% = 30% − 20%) indicates that men are more likely to be involved in car accidents while driving than are women. Because there are only two categories in (Y), this percentage difference (b_{yx}) captures all the relationship in the table. Given the large sample size and the magnitude of the percentage difference, it is safe to assume that it is not an artifact of sampling variability.

Suppose that a third variable (Z = amount of driving) is suspected to be related to both sex (X) and involvement in accidents (Y). It is therefore prudent to examine whether the X-Y relationship remains the same after the amount of driving is controlled or eliminated. Whether such conjecture is reasonable can be checked before examining the three-variable subgroup analysis: there has to be some relationship between X and Z and between X and Y. Table 1b shows the bivariate relationship between sex (X) and driving (Z). Note

TABLE 1
Hypothetical Bivariate Tables

a) Car Accidents (Y) by Sex (X)	Men	Women
Had at least one accident while driving	30%	20%
Never had an accident while driving	70%	80%
Total	100%	100%
(Number of cases)	(3,000)	(3,000)

b) Amount of Driving (Z) by Sex (X)		
More than 10,000 miles	67.7%	33.3%
Less than 10,000 miles	33.3%	67.7%
Total	100%	100%
(Number of cases)	(3,000)	(3,000)

SOURCE: Adapted from Ziesel (1985; p. 146)

that there is a very strong association—b_{yz}=.333 (33.3%) difference between the sexes.

The conditional tables may show one of the following four patterns: (1) the observed relationship between X and Y disappears within each subgroup—$b_{yx \cdot z} = 0$; (2) the relationship remains the same—$b_{yx \cdot z} = b_{yx}$; (3) the relationships change in magnitude but remain the same across the groups—$b_{yx \cdot z(1)} = b_{yx \cdot z(2)} \neq b_{yx}$; (4) the X-Y relationship in one group is different from the relationship in the other group—$b_{yx \cdot z(1)} \neq b_{yx \cdot z(2)}$. These examples are shown in Table 2. Compare these patterns with the corresponding causal systems shown in Figure 1.

Whether Z should be considered as antecedent or intervening depends on the theory one is entertaining. One's first interpretation might be that the original relationship has sexist implications—that it may mean men are either more aggressive or less careful. Against such a hypothesis, the amount of driving is an extraneous variable. On the other hand, one may entertain a social role theory—that in this society men's roles require more driving, and that more driving leads to more accidents. Then Z can be considered an intervening variable.

Pattern (1) will help to undermine the psychological or biological hypothesis, and pattern (2) will enhance that hypothesis. Pattern (1) will also lend weight to the social role hypothesis. These patterns are simplest to deal with but are rarely encountered in real life. (See Lazarsfeld 1955; Rosenberg 1968; Zeisel 1985, for interesting examples.) If one were lucky enough to come across such a pattern, the results would be considered important findings. Note that there are three causal systems in Figure 1 which share the same statistical pattern (the relationship between partials and original coefficients) with each of these two. Of course, the choice must be dictated by the theory and assumptions about the causal ordering that one is willing to entertain.

Patterns (3) and (4) are more likely outcomes in real life. In (3) the magnitude of the X-Y relationship within each subgroup is reduced. (Sometimes the X-Y relationship may turn out to be even

TABLE 2
Percent Ever Had Accident (Y) by Sex (X) by Amount of Driving (Z)

a) Original X-Y Relationship Disappears
   (Compatible with Causal Systems A3, B3, and C1)

Sex (X)	Amount of Driving (Z)		
	> 10,000 miles	< 10,000 miles	
Men	40% (2,000)	10% (1,000)	$b_{yx \cdot z} = 0$
Women	40% (1,000)	10% (2,000)	$b_{yz \cdot x} = .30$

b) Original X-Y Relationship Unchanged
   (Compatible with Causal Systems A1, B1, and C3)

Sex (X)	> 10,000 miles	< 10,000 miles	
Men	30% (2,000)	30% (1,000)	$b_{yx \cdot z} = .10$
Women	20% (1,000)	20% (2,000)	$b_{yz \cdot x} = 0$

c) Original X-Y Relationship Diminishes
   (Compatible with Causal Systems A2, B2, and C2)

Sex (X)	> 10,000 miles	< 10,000 miles	
Men	34% (2,000)	24% (1,000)	$b_{yx \cdot z} = .06$
Women	28% (1,000)	18% (2,000)	$b_{yz \cdot x} = .10$

d) X-Y Relationship Varies

Sex (X)	> 10,000 miles	< 10,000 miles	
Men	40% (2,000)	20% (1,000)	$b_{yx \cdot z(1)} = .20$
Women	20% (1,000)	20% (2,000)	$b_{yx \cdot z(2)} = 0$
			$b_{yz \cdot x(1)} = .20$
			$b_{yz \cdot x(2)} = 0$

Notes: Number of cases for the percentage base are in parentheses.
Throughout these tables $b_{xz} = .40$ and $b_{yx} = .10$ remain constant.
Compare percent across the categories of that variable.

stronger.) This pattern is compatible with three causal systems, A2, B2, and C2, in Figure 1. Let us assume that we take the causal order indicated in C, that is, we take the gender role theory to account for the observed relationship. Part of the original relationship (.04 out of .10) is mediated by the amount of driving, but a greater part (.06) remains unexplained. If one believes that all the difference in the accident rate has nothing to do with psychological or biological differences between the sexes, one has several other potential role-related connections to consider: men may drive more during the rush hours than women; men may drive during worse weather conditions than women; and so on. One could introduce these variables as additional controls. On the other hand, if one believes in the validity of the psychological explanation, one could collect data on the aggressiveness of each individual and introduce aggressiveness as a control variable.

The final table, 2d, illustrates a pattern in which the effects of the two explanatory variables interact: X's effect on Y varies across the categories of Z, and Z's effect on Y varies across the categories of X. A corresponding example in linear systems was given by equation (3). One must consider both variables at the same time because the effect of one variable depends on the other.

In general, empirical data may exhibit patterns that are mixtures of 2c and 2d. With cross-tabulations of variables with more than two categories, it is often not easy, purely on the basis of eyeballing, to discern the underlying pattern. At this point we need more refined and systematic tools. Moreover, in some instances an application of a log-linear model may indicate patterns that are different from what a linear model (such as using percentage tables) might indicate.

Before ending this section, it should be mentioned that there are some examples in the literature that use the subgroup analysis as a full-fledged multivariate analysis tool. For instance, Davis (1984) shows how the logic of elaboration can be combined with the standardization technique to derive, among other things, the following decomposition of the relationship between father's and son's occupational statuses: where Zs represent father's education and mother's education, and W represents son's education.

a. Total observed relationship—b_{yx} = .256

b. Spurious connection due to
   environmental variables (Zs)   (a-c)   .052

c. Total causal effect—$b_{yx \cdot z \cdots}$ .204

   c1. Unmediated causal effect—$b_{yx \cdot z \cdots w}$ = .138

   c2. Effect mediated by education
        $(b_{yx \cdot z \cdots} - b_{yx \cdot z \cdots w})$ = .066

The power of subgroup analysis comes mainly from the close analogy between the percentage differences and the coefficients of the linear system illustrated in Figure 1. But its uses need not be confined to the analysis of causal systems. There are various applications of this logic to survey data (Hyman 1955; Rosenberg 1968; Zeisel 1985). These accounts remain one of the best sources for learning the method as well as the art of pursuing research ideas through percentage tables.

ODDS RATIOS AND LOG-LINEAR MODELS

A more formal approach to categorical data analysis is provided by the log-linear and related models (Bishop, Fienberg, and Holland 1975; Goodman 1978; Haberman 1978, 1979; Fienberg 1980; Agresti 1984). Some of these models are not even log-linear (Goodman 1984; Clogg 1982a, 1982b). We will examine only the log-linear models.

By an ingenious device the log-linear model describes the relationships among categorical variables in a linear form. The trick is to treat the logarithms of the cell frequencies as the (titular) dependent variable and to treat design vectors as independent variables. The design vectors represent relevant features of the contingency table and hypotheses about them.

Once again consider a concrete example: the simplest bivariate table, in which each variable has only two categories. Such a table contains four frequencies. Logarithms of these frequencies (log-frequencies, for short) can be expressed as an exact function of the following linear equation:

$$Y = b_0 + X_1 \cdot b_1 + X_2 \cdot b_2 + (X_1 \cdot X_2)b_3 \qquad (4)$$

Y in this equation stands for the log-frequencies $(\log(F_{ij}))$. X_1 is a design vector for the first (row) variable, and X_2 a design vector for the second (column) variable. The last vector $(X_1 \cdot X_2)$ is a design vector for interaction between X_1 and X_2, and it is produced literally by multiplying the respective components of X_1 and X_2. It is important to note that the model is linear only in parameters and that there is an interaction term. As is the case with linear models containing interaction terms, one must be careful in interpreting the coefficients for the variables involved in the interaction term.

This type of model in which the observed frequencies are reproduced exactly is also known as a saturated model. (The model is saturated because all the available degrees of freedom are used up. For instance, there are only four data points, but this model requires as many parameters.) Of course, if we can reproduce the exact log-frequencies, we also can reproduce the actual frequencies by taking the exponential of Y—$F_{ij} = \exp(Y_{ij})$. Note also the similarities between equations (3) and (4); both contain a multiplicative term as a variable. (For more general models, a maximum likelihood estimation requires an iterative solution. But that is a technical detail for which readers should consult standard texts, such as Agresti 1984; Fleiss 1981; Goodman 1978, 1984; Haberman 1978, 1979; Plackett 1974. Many computer packages routinely provide solutions to these types of equations. Therefore, what is important is the logic underlying such analysis, not the actual calculation needed.)

It is no exaggeration to say that in more advanced uses of the model, what distinguishes a good and creative analysis from the mundane is how well one can translate one's substantive research ideas into appropriate design vectors. So it is worthwhile to examine these design vectors more carefully. Constructing a design matrix (collection of vectors mentioned above) for a saturated model is easy, because one is not pursuing any specific hypothesis or special pattern that might exist in the relationship. Categories of each variable have to be represented, and there are many equivalent ways of doing it. We will examine only the two most often used ones: effect coding and dummy coding. These design matrices for a 2×2 table are shown in Table 3.

The first column (X_0) in each coding represents a design vector for the constant term (b_0); X_1 is for the row categories, and X_2 is for the column categories. The last column (X_3) is the product of the preceding two, needed to represent interaction between X_1 and X_2. Note the pattern of these design vectors. In the effect coding, except for the constant vector, each vector or column sums to zero. Moreover, the interaction vector sums to zero for each column and row of the original bivariate table. This pattern assures that each effect is measured as a deviation from its respective mean.

In dummy coding the category effect is expressed as a deviation from one reference category—in this case the category that is represented by zero. Whatever codings are used to repre-

sent the categories of each variable, the interaction design vector is produced by multiplying the design vector for the column variable and the design vector for the row variable. Normally, one needs as many design vectors for a given variable as there are categories, minus one—(R-1) for the row variable and (C-1) for the column variable. In that case, there will be (C-1)(R-1) interaction design vectors for the saturated model. These interaction vectors are created by cross-multiplying the vectors in one set with those of the other set. There is only one vector for each of the three independent variables in equation (4) because both variables are dichotomous.

The names for these codings come from the fact that the first coding is customarily used as a convenient way of expressing factor effects in an analysis of variance (ANOVA), while the second coding is often used in regression with dummy variables. As a result of coding differences in the representation of each variable, the constant term in each coding has a different meaning: in effect coding it measures the unweighted grand mean, while in dummy coding it measures the value of the category with all zeros (in this particular case, Y_{22}). (For other coding schemes, see Haberman 1979; Agresti 1984; Long 1984.) Some parameter estimates are invariant under different coding and some are not (Long 1984); therefore it is important to understand fully the implications of a particular design matrix for a proper interpretation of the analysis results.

Panel (b) of Table 3 expresses each cell as a product of the design matrix and corresponding parameters. Since the particular vectors used contain either 1, -1, or 0, the vectors do not seem to appear in these cell representations. But when design vectors contain other numbers (as will be shown later), they will be reflected in the cell representation. Panel (c) is obtained by exponentiation of respective cell entries in (b), the individual t-parameter also being the corresponding exponential of the log-linear parameter in panel (b).

Panel (d) isolates parameters associated with the interaction design vector. Panel (e) contains corresponding antilogs or multiplicative coeffi-

TABLE 3
Design Vectors Used in Log-linear Model for 2×2 Table

a) Design Matrices for Saturated Model:

		Effect Coding				Dummy Coding		
Frequency	X_0	X_1	X_2	X_3	X_0	X_1	X_2	X_3
Y11	1	1	1	1	1	1	1	1
Y12	1	1	-1	-1	1	1	0	0
Y21	1	-1	1	-1	1	0	1	0
Y22	1	-1	-1	1	1	0	0	0

b) Representation of Log-Frequencies in terms of Parameter

$$b_0+b_1+b_2+b_3 \qquad b_0+b_1-b_2-b_3 \qquad b_0+b_1+b_2-b_3 \qquad b_0+b_1$$
$$b_0-b_1+b_2-b_3 \qquad b_0-b_1-b_2+b_3 \qquad b_0+b_2 \qquad b_0$$

c) Representation of Frequencies in terms of Multiplicative Parameters, where $t_i = \exp(b_i)$.

$$t_0*t_1*t_2*t_3 \qquad t_0*t_1/(t_2*t_3) \qquad t_0*t_1*t_2*t_3 \qquad t_0*t_1$$
$$t_0*t_2/(t_1*t_3) \qquad t_0*t_3/(t_1*t_2) \qquad t_0*t_2 \qquad t_0$$

d) Parameters for Interaction in Log-linear Model

$$b_3 \qquad -b_3 \qquad\qquad b_3 \qquad 0$$
$$-b_3 \qquad b_3 \qquad\qquad 0 \qquad 0$$

Log (odds-ratio)
$$4*b_3 \qquad\qquad\qquad b_3$$

e) Multiplicative Parameter for Interaction ($t_3 = \exp(b_3)$)

$$t_3 \qquad 1/t_3 \qquad\qquad t_3 \qquad 1$$
$$1/t_3 \qquad t_3 \qquad\qquad 1 \qquad 1$$

Odds ratio
$$t_3*t_3*t_3*t_3=t_3^4 \qquad\qquad t_3$$

cients. These parameters play a critical role in representing the degree and nature of association between the row and the column variables. If all the odds ratios are 1, then one variable is statistically independent from the other; in other words, information about the association between variables is totally contained in the pattern of odds ratios. Panels (d) and (e) show that the odds ratio, in turn, is completely specified by the parameter(s) of the interaction vector(s). In forming the odds ratio, all the other parameters cancel out (in logarithms, multiplication becomes addition and division becomes subtraction).

In short, we have found an indirect way by which to describe a pattern of association in a bivariate table. Unfortunately, to do so requires a titular dependent variable and multiplicative terms as independent variables. Also, in effect coding the log-odds ratio is given by $4 \times b_3$, but in the dummy coding it is given by b_3. This is a clear indication that one cannot assume there is only one way of describing the parameters of a log-linear model. These facts make the interpretation of these parameters tricky, but the trouble is worth it for two reasons.

First, the advantage of this method for analyzing a 2 × 2 table is trivial, but the model can be generalized and then applied to more complex contingency tables. Because of the ANOVA-like structure, it is easy to deal with higher-level interaction effects. Second, the parameters of the log-linear models (obtained through likelihood procedure) have very nice sampling properties for large samples. Therefore, better tools for statistical testing and estimating are available. Without this second advantage the fact that the approach allows construction of ANOVA-like models may not be of much value, for the log-linear models only indirectly and by analogy reflect the relationship between variables.

Consider the bivariate tables in Table 4. In all these tables the frequencies are such that they add up to 100 in each column. Thus we can take these frequencies as percentages as well. The first table shows a 20 percent difference and an odds ratio of 2.25. The second table shows only half of the percentage difference of the first but the same odds ratio. The last table shows the same percentage difference as the second one, but its odd ratio is greater, 6.68. These descriptive measures indicate that there is some association between the two variables in each table.

Whether this observed association is statistically significant can be tested by applying a model in which the coefficient for the interaction design vector is constrained to be zero. (Here we are utilizing the properties of the log-linear model asserted earlier.) Constraining the interaction pa-

TABLE 4
Odds Ratios (t) and Percentage Differences

FREQUENCIES				MULTIPLICATIVE PARAMETERS			
				Effect Coding		*Dummy Coding*	
a)		X_1	X_2				
	Y_1	60	40	1.225	.816	2.25	1
	Y_2	40	60	.816	1.225	1	1
		$\overline{100}$	$\overline{100}$				
	$b_{yx} = .20$		$t = 2.25$				
	$L^2 = 8.05$		$p = .005$				
b)		X_1	X_2				
	Y_1	20	10	1.225	.816	2.25	1
	Y_2	80	90	.816	1.225	1	1
		$\overline{100}$	$\overline{100}$				
	$b_{yx} = .10$		$t = 2.25$				
	$L^2 = 3.99$		$p = .046$				
c)		X_1	X_2				
	Y_1	12	2	1.608	.622	6.68	1
	Y_2	88	98	.622	1.608	1	1
		$\overline{100}$	$\overline{100}$				
	$b_{yx} = .10$		$t = 6.68$				
	$L^2 = 8.46$		$p = .004$				

rameter to zero is the same as deleting the interaction design vector from the model. Such a design matrix imposes the model of statistical independence (*independence* model, for short) on the data. If such a log-linear model does not fit the data (on the basis of some predetermined criteria), then the observed association is accepted as significant. For large samples both the conventional chi-square test and the likelihood ratio (L^2) test can be used for this purpose. The results of such tests are included in each table, and they indicate that all three associations are statistically significant, at the conventional α level of .05.

Thus, in order to describe fully the underlying pattern of the association in Table 4, one needs to introduce the interaction parameter—which in these cases is the same as using the saturated model. The righthand tables show the multiplicative parameters (*t*-parameters) for the interaction term. (Here only the results of applying effect coding are included.) First, examine the patterns of these parameters. In each of the three tables, the *t*-parameters indicate that the main diagonal cells have higher rates than the off-diagonal cells. This tendency is slightly higher in the last table than in the first two. This interpretation follows from the fact that to reproduce the observed frequency in each cell, the respective *t*-parameter must be multiplied to whatever value might be implied by other parameters in the model. In the first and second tables, the frequencies in the main diagonal are about 22 percent higher (1.22 times) than they would be without the interaction effect. The frequencies in the off-diagonal cells are about 18 percent less than they otherwise would be. If one were to examine only the statistics generated by log-linear models, however, it would be easy to overlook the fact that the percentage of the first cell in the last table is only 12 percent. (See Kaufman and Schervish 1986 for a more extended discussion.) This is one of the reasons why it is advisable to examine the percentage tables even if one is using the log-linear model almost exclusively.

There are other reasons, too. By the linear standard (percent difference), the first table shows a greater degree of association than the second or the third. By the standard of a log-linear model or odds ratio, the last table shows the greatest degree of association. In most cases, where the percentages remain within the range of 20 percent to 80 percent, these two standards are roughly comparable, and the linear and log-linear models may produce similar results (see Goodman 1981). More important, in examining three-way interactions, if two subtables have the patterns shown in 4a and 4b, the log-linear models will indicate no three-factor interaction, while linear models will indicate it. There are models in which a particular standard is explicitly justified by the phenomenon under consideration, but one should not adopt a standard merely because a particular statistical model does so. It is important to understand the differences in the implicit standards that are used by different methods.

SOME MODELS OF ASSOCIATION

The flexibility of log-linear models is not so obvious until one deals with several variables. But even in a bivariate table, if there is some underlying order in the categories of variables involved and in the pattern of association, the model allows some flexibility for exploring this pattern. Consider the hypothetical table shown in Table 5a. The marginal totals are such that each column may be read as percentages. There is a definite pattern in the direction of the relationship, although the tendency is fairly weak. If one were to apply a test of independence, such a null hypothesis would not be rejected. ($L^2 = 6.56$ with 4 degrees of freedom has a probability of .161.) Against an unspecified alternative hypothesis, the null hypothesis cannot be rejected at the conventional level of α.

Knowing that almost every society values these two variables in the same order, one may expect that the underlying pattern of association reflects the advantages of upper class over lower class in obtaining valued objects. Both the pattern of percentage differences and the odds ratios seem to indicate such an ordering in the pattern: the advantage the upper class enjoys over the lower class is greater than that over the middle class. Furthermore, they do better in relation to educa-

TABLE 5
A Hypothetical Table: Level of Educational Attainment (Y) by Social Class (X)

a) Observed Table

Level of Education	Social Class		
	High	Middle	Low
College	17	12	8
High School	41	38	34
Less than High	42	50	58
Total	100	100	100

b) Expected Frequencies Under Assumption of Independence

12.33	12.33	12.33	L^2 = 6.56
37.67	37.67	37.67	df_1 = 4
50.00	50.00	50.00	p = .161

c) Expected Frequencies Under the Assumption of Uniform Association

16.90	11.90	8.20	L^2 = .0082
41.30	38.00	33.80	df_2 = 3
41.80	50.10	58.10	p = .161

d) Log-Linear and Multiplicative Parameters

.264	0	−.264	1.303	1	.768
0	0	0	1	1	1
−.264	0	.264	.768	1	1.303

$L_1^2 - L_1^2 = 6.48;$ $df_1 - df_2 = 1;$ p = 0.0109

tional levels that are farther apart (the odds ratio involving the corner cells is 2.87).

Such a conjecture or hypothesis can be translated into a design vector. Assign any consecutive numbers to the categories of each variable; but to be consistent with the effect coding, express them as deviations from the mean. One such scaling is to use $(R+1)/2-i$ for the row variable and $(C+1)/2-j$ for the column variable. (The mean and category values can be reversed, but this scheme assigns a higher value to a higher class and a higher educational level, to be consistent with everyday language.) Recalling once again that only the interaction terms are relevant for the description of association, one needs to create such an interaction term by multiplying these two vectors, component by component. An example is shown in Table 6.

The log-linear model, then, will include design vectors for the constant term, two vectors for the row, and two vectors for the column, and one vector for the "linear by linear" interaction. This type of model is known as a *uniform association* model. (For a fuller discussion of this and related models, see Anderson 1984; Clogg 1982a, 1982b; Goodman 1984, 1990; Haberman 1979; McCullagh 1978.) The results of applying such a model to Table 5a are presented in 5b and 5c. First, this model fits the data extremely well. Moreover, the reduction of the L^2 statistic (6.557 − .008 =

TABLE 6
Design Matrices for Row-Column Association Models for 3x3 Table

T	A		B		C	D	E	F		G		H		I			J			
							C*D	A*~D		B*~D		F+G		(F~G)*			A*~B			
1	1	0	1	0	1	1	1	1	0	1	0	2	0	1	0	0	1	0	0	0
1	1	0	0	1	1	0	0	0	0	0	1	0	1	0	0	1	0	0	1	0
1	1	0	-1	-1	1	-1	-1	-1	0	-1	-1	-2	-1	-1	0	-1	-1	0	-1	0
1	0	1	1	0	0	1	0	0	1	0	0	0	1	0	1	0	0	1	0	0
1	0	1	0	1	0	0	0	0	0	0	0	0	0	0	0	0	0	0	0	1
1	0	1	-1	-1	0	-1	0	0	-1	0	0	0	-1	0	-1	0	0	-1	0	-1
1	-1	-1	1	0	-1	1	-1	-1	-1	-1	0	-2	-1	-1	-1	0	-1	-1	0	0
1	-1	-1	0	1	-1	0	0	0	0	0	-1	0	-1	0	0	-1	0	0	-1	-1
1	-1	-1	-1	-1	-1	-1	1	1	1	1	1	2	2	1	1	1	1	1	1	1

T: Design vector for the constant term.

A: Effect coding for row variable.

B: Effect coding for column variable.

C: Linear contrasts for row variable—$(R+1)/2-i$; any consecutive numbering will do; for variables with three categories, this is the same as the first code for the row variable.

D: Linear contrasts for column variable—$(C+1)/2-j$.

E: Design for the linear-by-linear interaction or uniform association, obtained by multiplying the linear contrast vector for the row and the same for the column.

F: Design vectors for the row effects model, obtained by multiplying the design vectors for the row categories and the linear contrast vector for the column.

G: Design vectors for column effects model, obtained by multiplying design vectors for the column variable and the linear contrast for the row variable.

H: Homogeneous row-column effects model, obtained by adding each vector in the matrix for the row and the corresponding vector in the matrix for the column.

I: Row and column effects model—concatenation of F and G, minus the redundant linear-by-linear interaction vector.

J: Interaction vectors for saturated model, obtained by multiplying each vector in A with each vector in B.

Design matrix for each type of model is obtained by concatenating relevant vectors from above, and the degrees of freedom by the number of cells in the table − number of columns in the design matrix.

	Vectors	df
Independence model	T~A~B	4
Uniform association	T~A~B~E	3
Row effects model	T~A~B~F	2
Column effects model	T~A~B~G	2
Hom. row-column	T~A~B~H	2
Row and col. effects	T~A~B~I	1
Saturated model	T~A~B~J	0

6.549) with one degree of freedom is statistically significant. Therefore the null hypothesis cannot be accepted against this specific alternative hypothesis. (See Agresti 1984 for a fuller discussion of hypothesis testing of this type.)

Note the pattern of the expected frequencies and the interaction parameters. Both indicate that the odds ratio for every consecutive four cells is uniform. Moreover, the other odds ratios are exact functions of this basic odds ratio and the distances involved. For instance, the odds ratio for the four corner cells is $2.87 = 1.303^{2*2}$, each exponent indicating the number of steps between respective categories in each variable. We have achieved some degree of parsimony in describing the pattern of association, and have gained some statistical power in proposing a more definite alternative hypothesis than the general one that stipulates any lack of statistical independence (hence uses up four degrees of freedom).

The introduction of different design matrices allows one to explore different patterns very easily. We will examine just two. Consider the hypothetical tables shown in Table 7. In the first table the odds ratios remain the same across the columns but vary across the rows, perhaps indicating that order inherent in the row categories is not uniform, while that in the column category is. Or, differently stated, the *distance* between two consecutive row categories varies while it remains constant for the column categories. Such an association pattern is known as the *row-effects association* model, not because the column variable does not have any effect but because an equal-interval scale

works well for it. In this case one needs two design vectors to accommodate the unequal distances in the row categories. In general, the most we need is the number of categories in the row minus one. As shown in Table 6, these design vectors are obtained by cross-multiplying the linear distance vector of the column and the two vectors that we have already used to represent the row categories. (It works just as well to use the dummy coding.) The *column-effects* model is obtained if we reverse the role of these variables.

Table 7b is an example of the simplest possible *homogeneous row-column effects* model. The odds ratios change across the row and across the column, but the corresponding pair of categories in the row and in the column share the same odds ratio. In this particular example, there is a greater distance between the first two categories than

TABLE 7
Hypothetical Tables Illustrating Some Association Models

a) Row-Effects Association Model

	Frequency X			Odds Ratio	
	400	400	50	4	4
Y	200	800	400	2	2
	100	800	800		

Log Parameters			Multiplicative Parameters		
1.155	0	−1.555	3.175	1	.315
−.231	0	.231	.794	1	1.260
−.924	0	.924	.397	1	2.520

b) Homogeneous Row-Column Effects Model

	Frequency X			Odds Ratio	
	400	100	100	4	2
Y	100	100	200	2	1
	100	200	400		

Log Parameters			Multiplicative Parameters		
.924	−.231	−.693	2.520	.794	.500
−.231	0	.231	.794	1.00	1.260
−.693	.231	.462	.500	1.260	1.587

between the second two. In general, a homogeneous row-column effects model can accommodate different intervals in each variable, as long as the corresponding intervals are homogeneous across the variables. The design matrix for such a pattern is easily obtained by adding the row-effects model vectors and the column-effects model vectors. This is also how two variables are constrained to have equal coefficients in any linear model. Such a design matrix for a 3×3 table is also contained in Table 6. The examples shown in Table 6 should be sufficient to indicate strategies for generalizing to a larger table.

There are many other possibilities in formulating specific hypotheses. These relatively simple models are introduced not only for their intrinsic values but also as a reminder that one can incorporate a variety of specialized hypotheses into the log-linear model. (For other possibilities, see Goodman 1984; Clogg 1982a, 1982b; Agresti 1983, 1984.) Before ending this section, it should be noted that when design vectors such as the ones for the homogeneous row-column effects model are used, the connection between the parameters for linear models indicated in this article and the usual ANOVA notation used in the literature is not obvious. Those parameters pertaining to each cell, denoted by t_{ij}, are equivalent to the product of the relevant part of the design matrix and corresponding coefficients.

SOME EXTENSIONS

There are several ways in which one can extend the basic features of the log-linear models examined so far. Among these the following three seem important: (1) to utilize the ANOVA-like structure of the log-linear model and the well-developed sampling theory to explore interaction patterns of multivariate categorical data, (2) to manipulate the design matrices to examine more specific hypotheses and models, and (3) to combine the strategic features of subgroup analysis and the flexibility and power of the log-linear models in order to produce more readily accessible analysis results. These three extensions are briefly discussed below.

General Extension of Log-Linear Models.

The most straightforward and most widely used application of the log-linear model is to explore the interaction pattern of multivariate data by exploiting the ANOVA-like structure of the model. Given several variables to examine, especially when each variable contains more than two categories, it is almost impossible to examine the data structure in detail. The ANOVA-like structure allows us to develop a convenient strategy to explore the existence of multiway relationships among the variables.

This strategy requires that one start with a design matrix for each variable (containing $k-1$ vectors, where k is the number of categories in the variable). It does not matter whether one uses a dummy coding or an effect coding. In order to examine all the possible interrelationships in the data, one needs design matrices corresponding to each two-way interaction to k-way interaction. To construct a design matrix for a two-way interaction between variable A and variable B, simply cross-multiply the design vectors for A with those for B. (This method is illustrated in Table 6.) This general approach to design matrices is extended to k-way. For example, a three-way interaction is handled by cross-multiplying each two-way vector with the basic design vectors for a third variable, and so on.

If one includes in the model all the vectors covering up to k-way interactions, then the resulting model is saturated, and each frequency in the multiway table is completely described. In general, one wants to explore and, if possible, to find some parsimonious way of describing the data structure. One general strategy, perhaps overused, is to examine systematically the hierarchical pattern inherent in the design constraints and serially examine a nested set of models. To illustrate, consider that there are three variables and that the basic design vectors for each variable are represented by A, B, and C, respectively. Let T stand for the constant vector. Then an example of a nested set of models is illustrated below. The commas indicate concatenation, and two or more letters together mean cross-multiplication of basic design vectors for each variable.

H_1:	T	Equiprobability
H_2:	T,A,B,C	Total independence
H_{3a}:	T,A,B,C,AB	One two-way interaction
H_{3b}:	T,A,B,C,AB,AC	Two two-way interactions
H_{3c}:	T,A,B,C,AB,AC,BC	No three-way interaction
H_4:	T,A,B,C,AB,AC,BC,ABC	Saturated model

Each hypothesis is tested, using the appropriate degrees of freedom, which is given by the number of the cells in the frequency table minus the number of vectors contained in the design matrix, and X^2 or L^2 statistics associated with each model. The sequence from hypotheses in set (3) is arbitrary; one may choose any nested set, or directly examine 3c. One would usually accept the simplest hypothesis that is compatible with the data.

If variables contain many categories, even the simplest two-way interactions will use up many degrees of freedom. This type of generic testing does not incorporate into the design matrix any special relationships that might exist between variables. Models of this type are routinely available in standard computer packages and therefore quite accessible. For that reason they are overused. Moreover, the sequential nature of the testing violates some of the assumptions of classical hypothesis testing. Nevertheless, in the hands of an experienced researcher they become a flexible tool for exploring the multivariate data structure.

The Uses of Constrained Models. The flexibility and power of the log-linear models are fully realized only when one incorporates a specific hypothesis about the data into the design matrices. There are virtually endless varieties one can consider. Some of the simple but strategic models of association were introduced in the preceding section.

Incorporating such models into a multivariate analysis is not difficult if one views the task in the context of design matrices. For instance, suppose one suspects that a certain pattern of relationship exists between X and Y (for instance, the social class of origin and destination in intergenerational

mobility). Furthermore, one may have an additional hypothesis that these relationships vary systematically across different political systems (or across societies with different levels of economic development). If one can translate these ideas into appropriate design matrices, then using such a model will provide a much more powerful test than using the generic statistical models described in the previous section. Many social mobility studies incorporate such design matrices as a way of incorporating a special pattern of social mobility in the overall design. (For some good examples, see Duncan 1979; Hout 1984; Yamaguchi 1987.)

In general there are two problems in using such design matrices. The first—which depends in part on the researcher's creative ability—is the problem of translating theoretically relevant models into appropriate design matrices. The second is how to obtain a good statistical solution for the model—but this is no longer much of a problem, due to the wide availability of computer programs that allow the incorporation of design matrices. (See Breen 1984 for a discussion of preparing design matrices for a computer program that handles generalized linear systems.)

One of the general problems has been that researchers often do not make the underlying design matrices explicit, and as a result sometimes misinterpret the results. An antidote for such a problem is to think explicitly in terms of the design matrices, not in analogy to a generic (presumed) ANOVA model.

Use of Percentage Tables in Log-Linear Modeling. Multivariate analysis is in general complex. Categorical analysis is especially so, because one conceptual variable has to be treated as if it were $(k-1)$ variables, k being the number of categories in the variable. Therefore, even with a limited number of variables, if each variable contains more than two categories, examining the multivariate pattern becomes extremely difficult. So the tendency is to rely on the general hypothesis testing discussed earlier.

It is useful to borrow two of the strategies of subgroup analysis: focusing on a bivariate relationship and using percentage distributions. After an acceptable log-linear model is identified, one may therefore display the relationship between two key variables while the effects of other variables are controlled or purged (Clogg and Eliason 1988a; Clogg et al. 1990; Kaufman and Schervish 1986). Furthermore, a percentage distribution for the bivariate distribution may be compared with the corresponding percentage distributions when different sets of variables are so controlled. Fortunately, the log-linear modeling can provide a very attractive way in which the confounding effects of many variables can be purged from the relationship that is under special scrutiny (Kaufman and Schervish 1986; Clogg and Eliason 1988a; Clogg et al. 1990). Clogg et al. (1990) show a general framework under which almost all the known variations in adjustments can be considered a special case. Furthermore, they also describe statistical testing procedures for variety of statistics associated with such adjustments.

(SEE ALSO: *Analysis of Variance and Covariance; Causal Inference Models; Measures of Association; Nonparametric Statistics; Statistical Methods*)

REFERENCES

Agresti, Alan 1983 "A Survey of Strategies for Modeling Cross-Classifications Having Ordinal Variables." *Journal of the American Statistical Association* 78:184–198.

———1984 *Analysis of Ordinal Categorical Data.* New York: Wiley.

Alba, Richard D. 1988 "Interpreting the Parameters of Log-Linear Models." In J. Scott Long, ed., *Common Problems/Proper Solutions.* Beverly Hills, Calif.: Sage.

Alwin, Dwane F., and Robert M. Hauser 1975 "The Decomposition of Effects in Path Analysis." *American Sociological Review* 40:37–47.

Anderson, J. A. 1984 "Regression and Ordered Categorical Variables." *Journal of the Royal Statistical Society* B46:1–30.

Arminger, G., and G. W. Bohrnstedt 1987 "Making It Count Even More: A Review and Critique of Stanley Lieberson's *Making It Count: The Improvement of Social Theory and Research.*" *Sociological Methodology* 17:347–362.

Berk, R. A. 1983 "An Introduction to Sample Selection Bias in Sociological Data." *American Sociological Review* 48:386–398.

———1986 "Review of *Making It Count: The Improve-*

ment of Social Research and Theory." *American Journal of Sociology* 92:462–465.

Bishop, Yvonne M. M., Stephen E. Fienberg, and Paul W. Holland 1975 *Discrete Multivariate Analysis: Theory and Practice.* Cambridge, Mass.: MIT Press.

Blalock, Hubert M., Jr. 1964 *Causal Inferences in Nonexperimental Research.* Chapel Hill: University of North Carolina Press.

———(ed.) 1985a *Causal Models in the Social Sciences,* 2nd ed. New York: Aldine.

———(ed.) 1985b *Causal Models in Panel and Experimental Designs.* New York: Aldine.

Bollen, K. A. 1989 *Structural Equations with Latent Variables.* New York: Wiley.

Breen, Richard 1984 "Fitting Non-Hierarchical and Association Models Using GLIM." *Sociological Methods and Research* 13:77–107.

Bunge, Mario 1979 *Causality and Modern Science,* 3rd rev. ed. New York: Dover.

Campbell, D. T., and J. C. Stanley 1966 *Experimental and Quasi-Experimental Designs for Research.* Boston: Houghton Mifflin.

Clogg, Clifford C. 1982a "Using Association Models in Sociological Research: Some Examples." *American Journal of Sociology* 88:114–134.

———1982b "Some Models for the Analysis of Association in Multiway Cross-Classifications Having Ordered Categories." *Journal of the American Statistical Association* 77:803–815.

———, and Scott R. Eliason 1988a "A Flexible Procedure for Adjusting Rates and Proportions, Including Statistical Methods for Group Comparisons." *American Sociological Review* 53:267–283.

———1988b "Some Common Problems in Log-Linear Analysis." In J. Scott Long, ed., *Common Problems/Proper Solutions.* Beverly Hills, Calif.: Sage.

———, James W. Shockey, and Scott R. Eliason 1990 "A General Statistical Framework for Adjustment of Rates." *Sociological Methods and Research* 19:156–195.

Cook, Thomas D., and Donald T. Campbell 1979 *Quasi-Experimentation: Design and Analysis Issues for Field Settings.* Chicago: Rand McNally.

Davis, James A. 1984 "Extending Rosenberg's Technique for Standardizing Percentage Tables." *Social Forces* 62:679–708.

———, and Ann M. Jacobs 1968 "Tabular Presentations." In David L. Sills, ed., *The International Encyclopedia of the Social Sciences,* vol. 15. New York: Macmillan and Free Press.

Deming, W. E., and F. F. Stephan 1940 "On a Least

Squares Adjustment of a Sampled Frequency Table When the Expected Marginal Totals Are Known." *Annual of Mathematical Statistics* 11:427–444.

Duncan, Otis Dudley 1966 "Path Analysis: Sociological Examples." *American Journal of Sociology* 72:1–16.

——1975 *Introduction to Structural Equation Models.* New York: Academic Press.

——1979 "How Destination Depends on Origin in the Occupational Mobility Table." *American Journal of Sociology* 84:793–803.

Fienberg, Stephen E. 1980 *The Analysis of Cross-Classified Data,* 2nd ed. Cambridge, Mass.: MIT Press.

Fisher, F. M. 1966 *The Identification Problem in Econometrics.* New York: McGraw-Hill.

Fleiss, J. L. 1981 *Statistical Methods for Rates and Proportions,* 2nd ed. New York: Wiley/Interscience.

Goldberger, Arthur S., and Otis Dudley Duncan (eds.) 1973 *Structural Equation Models in the Social Sciences.* New York and London: Seminar Press.

Goodman, Leo A. 1978 *Analyzing Qualitative/Categorical Data: Log-Linear Analysis and Latent Structure Analysis.* Cambridge, Mass.: Abt.

——1981 "Three Elementary Views of Loglinear Models for the Analysis of Cross-Classifications Having Ordered Categories." In Karl F. Schuessler, ed., *Sociological Methodology.* San Francisco: Jossey-Bass.

——1984 *The Analysis of Cross-Classified Categorical Data Having Ordered Categories.* Cambridge, Mass.: Harvard University Press.

——1985 "The Analysis of Cross-Classified Data Having Ordered and/or Unordered Categories: Association Models, Correlation Models, and Asymmetry Models for Contingency Tables with or Without Missing Entries." *Annals of Statistics* 13:10–69.

——1987 "The Analysis of a Set of Multidimensional Contingency Tables Using Log-Linear Models, Latent Class Models, and Correlation Models: The Solomon Data Revisited." In A. E. Gelfand, ed., *Contributions to the Theory and Applications of Statistics: A Volume in Honor of Herbert Solomon.* New York: Academic Press.

——1990 "Total-Score Models and Rasch-Type Models for the Analysis of a Multidimensional Contingency Table, or a Set of Multidimensional Contingency Tables, with Specified and/or Unspecified Order for Response Categories." In Karl F. Schuessler, ed., *Sociological Methodology.* San Francisco: Jossey-Bass.

Haberman, Shelby J. 1978 *Analysis of Qualitative Data,* vol. 1, *Introductory Topics.* New York: Academic Press.

——1979 *Analysis of Qualitative Data,* vol. 2, *New Developments.* New York: Academic Press.

Hausman, J. A. 1978 "Specification Tests in Econometrics." *Econometrica* 46:1251–1272.

Heckman, J. J. 1979 "Sample Selection Bias as a Specification Error." *Econometrica* 47:153–161.

——, and R. Robb 1986 "Alternative Methods for Solving the Problem of Selection Bias in Evaluating the Impact of Treatments on Outcomes." In H. Wainer, ed., *Drawing Inferences from Self-Selected Samples.* New York: Springer-Verlag.

Heise, David R. 1975 *Causal Analysis.* New York: Wiley.

Hout, Michael 1984 "Status, Autonomy, Training in Occupational Mobility." *American Journal of Sociology* 89:1379–1409.

Hyman, Herbert 1955 *Survey Design and Analysis: Principles, Cases and Procedures.* Glencoe, Ill.: Free Press.

Kaufman, Robert L., and Paul G. Schervish 1986 "Using Adjusted Crosstabulations to Interpret Loglinear Relationships." *American Sociological Review* 51:717–733.

Kendall, Patricia L., and Paul Lazarsfeld 1950 "Problems of Survey Analysis." In Robert K. Merton and Paul F. Lazarsfeld, eds., *Continuities in Social Research: Studies in the Scope and Method of The American Soldier.* Glencoe, Ill.: Free Press.

Kish, Leslie 1959 "Some Statistical Problems in Research Design." *American Sociological Review* 24: 328–338.

Lazarsfeld, Paul F. 1955 "Interpretation of Statistical Relations as a Research Operation." In Paul F. Lazarsfeld and Morris Rosenberg, eds., *The Language of Social Research.* Glencoe, Ill.: Free Press.

——, Ann K. Pasanella, and Morris Rosenberg (eds.) 1972 *Continuities in the Language of Social Research.* New York: Free Press.

Leamer, E. E. 1978 *Specification Searches: Ad Hoc Inference with Nonexperimental Data.* New York: Wiley/ Interscience.

Lieberson, Stanley 1985 *Making It Count: The Improvement of Social Research and Theory.* Berkeley and Los Angeles: University of California Press.

Long, J. Scott 1984 "Estimable Functions in Loglinear Models." *Sociological Methods and Research* 12:399–432.

——(ed.) 1988 *Common Problems/Proper Solutions: Avoiding Error in Quantitative Research.* Beverly Hills, Calif.: Sage.

Mare, Robert D., and Christopher Winship 1988 "Endogenous Switching Regression Models for the

Causes and Effects of Discrete Variables." In J. Scott Long, ed., *Common Problems/Proper Solutions.* Beverly Hills, Calif.: Sage.

McCullagh, P. 1978 "A Class of Parametric Models for the Analysis of Square Contingency Tables with Ordered Categories." *Biometrika* 65:413–418.

————, and J. Nelder 1983 *Generalized Linear Models.* London: Chapman and Hall.

Mosteller, F. 1968 "Association and Estimation in Contingency Tables." *Journal of the American Statistical Association* 63:1–28.

————, and John W. Tukey 1977 *Data Analysis and Regression.* Reading, Mass.: Addison-Wesley.

Nelder, J. A., and R. W. M. Wedderburn 1972 "Generalized Linear Models." *Journal of the Royal Statistical Society* A135:370–384.

Plackett, R. L. 1974 *The Analysis of Categorical Data.* London: Griffin.

Press, S. L., and S. Wilson 1978 "Choosing Between Logistic Regression and Discriminant Analysis." *Journal of the American Statistical Association* 73:699–705.

Rosenberg, Morris 1968 *The Logic of Survey Analysis.* New York: Basic Books.

Rubin, D. B. 1977 "Assignment to Treatment Group on the Basis of a Covariance." *Journal of Educational Statistics* 2:1–26.

Simon, Herbert A. 1954 "Spurious Correlation: A Causal Interpretation." *Journal of the American Statistical Association* 49:467–479.

————1979 "The Meaning of Causal Ordering." In Robert K. Merton, James S. Coleman, and Peter H. Rossi, eds., *Qualitative and Quantitative Social Research: Papers in Honor of Paul F. Lazarsfeld.* New York: Free Press.

Singer, Burton, and Margaret Mooney Marini 1987 "Advancing Social Research: An Essay Based on Stanley Lieberson's *Making It Count.*" In Clifford C. Clogg, ed., *Sociological Methodology.* Washington, D.C.: American Sociological Association.

Thiel, Henri 1971 *Principles of Econometrics.* New York: Wiley.

Williams, D. A. 1976 "Improved Likelihood Ratio Tests for Complete Contingency Tables." *Biometrika* 63: 33–37.

Xie, Yu 1989 "An Alternative Purging Method: Controlling the Composition-Dependent Interaction in an Analysis of Rates." *Demography* 26:711–716.

Yamaguchi, Kazuo 1987 "Models for Comparing Mo-
bility Tables: Toward Parsimony and Substance." *American Sociological Review* 52:482–494.

Zeisel, Hans 1985 *Say It with Figures,* 6th ed. New York: Harper and Row.

JAE-ON KIM

TECHNOLOGICAL RISKS AND SOCIETY

Sociologists have long been interested in phenomena that harm people and what they value. Until recently, most such work concentrated on harm from natural events such as earthquakes, floods, and tornadoes. While we have learned much from that research, there is another class of threats that sociologists are now according more attention—"technical or technological risks." Within this class sociologists study a large number of topics, ranging from how individuals think about risks to how nation-states develop strategies to mitigate threats from failures of advanced technology. Some are even interested in risks that might be faced by societies far into the future. Toxic threats have drawn particularly close scrutiny from scholars, and indeed there are important sociological studies of Love Canal, Three Mile Island, Chernobyl, Bhopal, nuclear waste, and nuclear weapons. (It is a somewhat depressing area of study.) One reason toxic risks are so interesting is that they invert the way natural disasters do their damage. Rather than assaulting people from the outside, as do natural calamities, toxic hazards assault bodies from within. Toxic injuries also have no definable end, so victims can never know when they are safe from further damage. The meaning of toxic risks, it seems, is fundamentally different from that of natural disasters (Couch and Kroll-Smith 1985; Erikson 1990).

In general, the sociology of risk is concerned with researching and explaining how interactions between technology and modes of social organization create hazards, or the potential for hazards (Short 1984). "Hazards" can mean actual threats to people's lives (toxic chemical contamination, for example) or the *perception* that there is a threat. Indeed, many researchers focus their intellectual attention on risk perception—what people think is dangerous, and why they think what they do (Freudenburg 1988). The word *technology* in my definition means the social and mechanical tools people use to accomplish something—the design of a nuclear power plant, or even vocabularies used by experts when they talk of effectively evacuating an urban area after a major radiation release from a nuclear power plant (Perrow 1984). "Modes of social organization" refers to both social structure (e.g., the hierarchy of power found in an organization) and culture (e.g., the degree of legitimacy we grant experts). As we move into the twenty-first century, society will continue its seemingly inexorable march toward social and technical complexity, a complexity driven, at least in substantial part, by a distinctly modern capacity to create machines and institutional arrangements that are at once grand and terrifying. With these developments, it seems, the public is increasingly aware of the potentially devastating consequences of modern risks, even as it enjoys the cornucopia engendered by modern social organization and modern technology.

As is true of much sociology, research on risk can be classified into micro and macro studies. Both micro and macro studies have made significant contributions to understanding the connections between risk, technology, and society. Micro-level research, generally speaking, is concerned with personal, political, and social dilemmas, posed by technology and activities, that threaten the quality of people's lives. Macro-level work on risk does not by any means deny the importance of micro-oriented research, but asks different questions, and seeks answers to those questions at an institutional level of analysis.

As some of the examples below illustrate, much macro work emphasizes the importance of the institutional context within which decisions about risk are made. Sociologists of risk are keen to distinguish between public and private decisions. Put differently, some people make choices that affect mainly themselves, while those who are in positions of authority make choices that have significant implications for others. This is only one

among many ways in which the sociology of risk is crucially concerned with issues of power and the distribution of hazards and benefits.

Since the theories, methods, and findings in the sociology of risk cannot possibly be reviewed here, some examples will be used to illustrate the kinds of things sociologists of risk try to understand. It should be noted that this subfield is still very much in its formative stages, so it has no clearly delimited intellectual history to serve as an organizing device for an encyclopedia article. A couple of examples from the micro level of analysis follow.

A substantial body of work has demonstrated that the public overestimates threats that are dramatic (e.g., from airplane accidents), particularly violent (e.g., handguns), and potentially catastrophic (e.g., from nuclear power plants). Similarly, people tend to underestimate more prosaic, chronic threats, such as those from botulism or asthma. Why is this so? Several explanations have been proposed, but the one that is most convincing focuses on the mechanisms through which information about risks is channeled to people (Kahneman, Slovic, and Tversky 1982; Heimer 1988). Specifically, the media—especially newspapers and television—are more likely to feature dramatic, violent, or catastrophic calamities compared with less sensational threats. Pushing the analysis further, we see that one reason the media find such risks more interesting is that they are easier to cover, and hence more easily fit into tight deadlines. Covering prosaic risks is also more time-consuming than covering short, dramatic accidents. What all this adds up to is that there are several fairly good structural reasons why the media pay more attention to high-drama risks and neglect low-drama risks. Thus, sociologists are able to explain why the public holds biased estimates of risk by focusing on the structural connections between people and media, and more specifically on the constraints that lead the media to be biased about certain types of information.

Another example at the micro level of analysis is in the fascinating work of Carol A. Heimer (forthcoming), who has been studying how information is used and transmitted in intensive care units for infants. Heimer's study is cast at a fairly micro level of analysis in the sense that one of her concerns is with how parents think about information regarding terribly sick babies. But like all good sociological studies, Heimer's connects what parents think with the social contexts in which they find themselves. For example, one of Heimer's findings is that when hospital personnel transmit information to parents about their infants, that process is structured to protect the hospital from lawsuits, and only secondarily to apprise parents of the precise condition of their children. Hence, Heimer tells us how parents think, much as a psychologist might, but also demonstrates that how they think is contingent on the organizational needs of hospitals.

Macro-level work on risk includes research on how professionals influence the behavior of regulatory agencies, how organizations blunder and break down, how social movements arise to push certain issues into public debate, even how national cultures shape which risks are considered acceptable (Douglas 1985). Many macro theorists are deeply concerned with how the institutional structure of society makes some risks rather than others more likely to gain political and intellectual attention (Clarke 1988). Consider, for instance, motor vehicle risks. Nearly 50,000 people are killed on U.S. highways every year, which most would agree is an appalling mortality rate. Now, although it is a commonplace that half of those deaths are alcohol-related, the truth of the matter is that we don't really know how much of the carnage is, in fact, due to alcohol (Gusfield 1981). Nevertheless, we can probably reasonably assume that some serious proportion is caused by drunken drivers (even 10 percent would be 5,000 deaths). Most people would agree that 5,000 deaths per year is grounds for concern. Yet we also know that high rates of fatal traffic accidents are associated with speeding, wrong turns, and improper passing. Objectively, there is no difference between a death caused by someone making a wrong turn and one caused by a drunken driver. And yet most nations' cultures say the two deaths are in fact very different indeed. In the United

States there is even a small social movement galvanized around the issue of drunken drivers, one example of which is the organization called Mothers Against Drunk Drivers. But why is there no organization called Mothers Against Improper Passers? A sociological answer is that most cultures frown on using drugs to alter one's degree of self-control, and one who does so is defined as morally decadent and lacking social responsibility. Therefore, the ardent opprobrium unleashed on drunken drivers has less to do with the objective magnitude of the problem than the apparent danger such drivers represent to the cultural value of self-control. This type of analysis tells much about the conditions under which phenomena become socially constructed as social problems.

Another example of macro work on risk, this time concerning organizations, is the massive oil spill from the *Exxon-Valdez* tanker in March 1989. At the time, the spill was the worst ever to occur in U.S. waters, leaking at least 11 million gallons of oil into Prince William Sound and the Gulf of Alaska. The accident caused massive loss of wildlife, and although no people died, it did cause massive disruptions in social relationships, created a political crisis, and reoriented debates about the safety of oil transportation systems in the United States. From a sociological point of view, one of the most interesting things about the Exxon spill has to do with how corporations and regulatory agencies plan for large oil spills. Sound research shows there really isn't much that can be done about large amounts of spilled oil (Clarke 1990). And yet, organizations continue to create elaborate plans for what they will do to contain large spills, and for how they will clean the oil from beaches and shorelines. They do this even though there has never been a case of successful containment or recovery on the open seas. Organizations create plans that will never work because such plans are master metaphors for taming the wild, subjugating uncertainty, and proclaiming expertise. We live in a world in which expert knowledge and rational organization are of paramount importance, and we now seem to have an institutionalized incapacity to admit that some things may be beyond our control.

Yet another example is the 1984 tragedy in Bhopal, India. At least 2,600 people died when a very complex accident in a Union Carbide plant released toxic chemicals into the environment. At the time, Bhopal was the worst single industrial accident in history (the nuclear meltdown at Chernobyl in 1986 will eventually be responsible for more deaths). The Bhopal tragedy was certainly an organizational failure, as a number of studies have documented (Shrivastava 1987). For our purposes here, however, what was interesting about the Bhopal accident was that the risk created by the Union Carbide chemical plant had become institutionalized to the point where very few if any of the key players were worried about potential catastrophe. The poor people who lived next to the plant seemed to have accepted official assurances that they were safe (and in any case had little choice in the matter). Government officials —the ones assuring those who lived near the plant of safety—seemed to have accepted the catastrophic potential of the plant as part of the price of having a large corporation in their country. For their part, corporate officials and experts seem to have given insufficient thought to the possibility of killing several thousand Indians. One reason the Bhopal disaster is sociologically interesting is the degree to which individuals, groups, and organizations come to accept risk as part of their everyday lives. The same observation might be made of automobile driving, nuclear power plants, and lead-contaminated water pipes (even brass pipes have about 7 percent lead in them).

We shall consider one final example of a macro analysis of risk. Every year our natural environment seems more polluted than the preceding year. Why? A common-sense explanation might claim that people just don't care enough about the environment, perhaps attributing callous attitudes or personal greed to politicians and corporations. Such an explanation would focus on the motives of individual managers and politicians, but from a sociological point of view would miss the all-important institutions in which such decision mak-

ers are embedded. Sociologists know that those who occupy top positions in government and corporate organizations are not without intelligence and good sense. Such decision makers may even be individually quite concerned about environmental degradation. But because of their structural locations, they are subject to pressures that may be at odds with environmental health and welfare. These pressures originate in specific social structures that create institutional interests that may be contrary to individual preferences (Clarke 1988; 1989). The corporate executive seeks (and *must* seek) to remain in business, if necessary at the expense of others' well-being or the environment. A similar explanation accounts for why Ford president Lee Iacocca marketed Pintos in the 1970s that had an extraordinary propensity to explode and burn. In other words, market institutions are arranged so that it is sensible for any individual, or individual organization, to force negative externalities on society. For its part, one of the key functions of government is to maintain a political and economic environment that is favorable to business. Thus, an explanation that centers on the institutional constraints and incentives that shape decisions about pollution is better able to account for the behavior of organizations, experts, and officials than an explanation that focuses on their personal characteristics (Vaughan 1990).

Future developments in the sociology of risk will likely revolve around issues of social conflict —its bases, its meaning, its role in spurring social change. Society, and sociology, will be confronted with some fundamental dilemmas in the next century. Modernity, as Max Weber foresaw, brings both fruits and poisons. The fruits include convenience, longer lives, and high standards of living. Yet, many of our most frightening threats—nuclear meltdowns near large cities, toxic leachate in water tables, ozone destruction, explosions of liquefied natural gas from supertankers, failure to contain nuclear waste—almost seem to be beyond our ability to control them. It may well be the case that before we can better control political and technological systems, we must admit that some aspects of the technical world are not within our control. Such an admission would be anathema to cultures dedicated to the notion of personal, social, and environmental mastery.

(SEE ALSO: *Environmental Impact Assessment; Human Ecology and the Environment*)

REFERENCES

Clarke, Lee 1988 "Explaining Choices Among Technological Risks." *Social Problems* 35 (1):501–514.

———1989. *Acceptable Risk? Making Decisions in a Toxic Environment*, Berkeley: University of California Press.

———1990 "Oil Spill Fantasies." *Atlantic Monthly* (Nov.):65–77.

Couch, Stephen R., and J. Stephen Kroll-Smith 1985 "The Chronic Technical Disaster." *Social Science Quarterly* 66 (3):564–575.

Douglas, Mary 1985 *Risk Acceptability According to the Social Sciences*. New York: Russell Sage Foundation.

Erikson, Kai 1990 "Toxic Reckoning: Business Faces a New Kind of Fear." *Harvard Business Review* 90 (1):118–126.

Freudenburg, William R. 1988 "Perceived Risk, Real Risk: Social Science and the Art of Probabilistic Risk Assessment." *Science* 242. (October 7):44–49.

Gusfield, Joseph 1981 *The Culture of Public Problems: Drinking-Driving and the Symbolic Order*. Chicago: University of Chicago Press.

Heimer, Carol A. 1988 "Social Structure, Psychology, and the Estimation of Risk." *Annual Review of Sociology* 14:491–519.

———Forthcoming "Your Baby's Fine, Just Fine: Certification Procedures, Meetings, and the Supply of Information in Neonatal Intensive Care Units." In James F. Short, Jr., and Lee Clarke, eds., *Risky Decision Making: Complexity and Context*.

Kahneman, Daniel, Paul Slovic, and Amos Tversky 1982 *Judgment under Uncertainty: Heuristics and Biases*. Cambridge: Cambridge University Press.

Perrow, Charles 1984 *Normal Accidents: Living with High Risk Technologies*. New York: Basic Books.

Short, James F., Jr. 1984 "Toward the Social Transformation of Risk Analysis." *American Sociological Review* 49 (6):711–755.

Shrivastava, Paul 1987 *Bhopal: Anatomy of a Crisis*. Cambridge: Ballinger.

Vaughan, Diane 1990 "Autonomy, Interdependence, and Social Control: NASA and the Space Shuttle Challenger." *Administrative Science Quarterly* 35 (2):225–257.

LEE CLARKE

TECHNOLOGY AND SOCIETY

Popularization of the word *technology* in the early nineteenth century indicated that an organized body of knowledge was developing about how to produce various useful material objects. The word came to be employed in a way that suggested an awareness that technological change could be directed to specific ends and that the conscious control of technology could be a means of shaping the future direction of society. Thus was inaugurated the explicit relationship between technology and society, a relationship that had previously been implicit.

The technology of a society encompasses the tools its members use and the procedures involved in inventing, producing, maintaining, and using them. Some observers define the term more broadly to include all practices employed in a rational way to achieve specific ends, even if material tools are not directly involved. Popular discussions of technology focus largely on recent and anticipated advances in, and problems related to, weaponry, medicine, computing, communication, transportation, spaceflight, and agricultural and industrial production. However, old and simple tools such as toothpicks, flyswatters, hammers, and baskets are also part of technology, and they do not necessarily disappear as newer and more complicated forms of technology arise.

A major technological item requires an infrastructure, or supporting system. Thus, the automobile as a major element in a society's transportation calls for paved roads, service and repair stations, spare parts, trained drivers, automobile mechanics, traffic laws and authorities to enforce them, and arrangements for manufacturing or importing autos. An inadequate supporting system may inhibit adoption of certain technologies. On the other hand, when the drive to adopt a particular technological item is strong enough, social pressures may be generated to develop the necessary supporting system, which, in turn, may involve major social changes.

Technological determinism, illustrated by the works of Leslie White (1949) and Jacques Ellul (1964), conceives of the technology–society relationship as primarily unidirectional, with technology developing autonomously and shaping the course of development of society, but without having its own developmental direction strongly shaped by society in turn.

In support of technological determinism one might cite numerous instances in which a seemingly minor technological development has had drastic social consequences. Adoption of the stirrup, which enabled warriors on horseback to brace themselves while charging, helped to make possible the fighting style characteristic of medieval knights and the feudal social system centering on knighthood (White 1946). A transition from dry rice cultivation (on hillside land that had to be abandoned after a few years because the soil became depleted) to wet rice cultivation (on lowlying land that could be cultivated year after year without interruption) caused the Tanala tribe of Madagascar to abandon a nomadic life-style and adopt a settled way of life, with consequent changes in diverse institutions (Linton 1957). More recently, the elevator has made possible a life-style centering on skyscrapers, and air conditioning has enormously increased the potential attractiveness of geographical locations with hot climates (making possible, for example, the explosive growth of Phoenix, Arizona).

Evidence against technological determinism includes the fact that the consequences of a technological innovation sometimes vary from one social setting to another. Thus, gunpowder, printing, and the compass had effects in Western Europe very different from their effects when introduced earlier in China. Printing, for example, facilitated standardization of official government documents in China, while in Western Europe printing facilitated an explosive diversification of published literature (Needham 1969). Similarly, computers may have either centralizing or decentralizing

effects, depending on the social context. This casts doubt on the variant of technological determinism that sees modern technologies as increasingly requiring economies of scale that reinforce tendencies toward bureaucratic centralization in modern society (Etzkowitz 1991).

Also opposed to technological determinism and favoring a conception of technological dependence on society is the idea, emphasized by Mumford (1967) and others, that society can choose among alternative technologies. Once a particular technology is chosen (often because it fits in better with established social arrangements than the rejected alternatives would), these alternatives are often largely forgotten, and the commitment to the chosen technology is reinforced by further investment in it and in the social patterns associated with it. What was chosen then appears in retrospect to have been inevitable, even though it actually was not. Examples include the post–World War II American commitment to nuclear power that fit in with the bureaucratic structure of established power companies and the concomitant neglect of a solar-energy alternative that might have bypassed these companies in favor of more decentralized arrangements (Etzkowitz 1984); the selection of the internal-combustion engine for automobiles, with electric and steam-driven models disappearing from public awareness (see Flink 1975); and the American commitment to the automobile while urban public transit systems deteriorated.

Regardless of the causal relationships between technology and society, there are striking structural similarities between some machines that modern technology has given us and some organizational arrangements prevailing in technologically advanced societies. The standardization of machine components that permits their routine replacement with "spare parts" parallels the bureaucratic expectation that performances by certain organizational personnel be standardized. The process of automatic adjustment to changing circumstances as illustrated by the thermostat is also illustrated by arrangements that provide for automatic cost-of-living salary adjustments to inflation and for automatic reapportionment of legislative bodies when new census data are obtained (Richter 1982).

The technologies of the simplest human societies involve few if any *secondary tools* (tools used to make other tools), entail relatively little specialization of human activity, rely primarily on human muscles and on natural rather than artificially produced substances, and focus on adaptation to natural environments rather than on efforts to transform these environments (e.g., on adapting to forest life rather than on wiping out the forest).

The major civilizations of the ancient world, technologically advanced far beyond the level of the simplest societies, produced great engineering feats that are still admired today: impressive buildings, irrigation systems, fortifications, and highways. Ancient technology nevertheless developed very slowly by modern standards, as illustrated by the several thousand years that elapsed between the earliest domestication of horses and the widespread adoption of the stirrup. In recent times the pace of technological change has drastically accelerated, exponentially according to some observers. The Industrial Revolution, developing over several centuries, reaching a climax in late eighteenth- and early nineteenth-century England, and centering around steam power and coal, led to a second great technological transformation centering around electricity and chemistry and to still another transformation now taking place centering on information technology (Bell 1989). Technological innovation has manifestly transformed human life, yet new technology sometimes has conservative, stabilizing implications. Thus, the shift from wood to coal as a fuel in eighteenth-century England helped preserve an established way of life that was threatened by a growing wood shortage (Richter 1980, pp. 69–79).

A major technological task in ancient times was to figure out ways in which the muscles of numerous individual people (or, in some cases, domestic animals) could be effectively combined, e.g., how the muscles of hundreds of oarsmen could be coordinated to propel a large oared ship. Modern technology, in contrast, commonly tends to displace human labor, although movement in this direction is inhibited where labor costs are low

relative to other costs. Thus, where farm labor is cheap and abundant while good farmland is scarce and expensive, agricultural technology seeks to maximize production per acre rather than production per farm worker. Modern businesses also sometimes transfer work from their employees to their customers, rather than transferring it from employees to labor-saving machinery. Thus, in an American supermarket customers (rather than employees or machinery) typically move down the aisles to collect items to be purchased and transport these items to the checkout counter.

Modern technology and modern science powerfully reinforce one another. For example, nuclear science has provided the foundation for nuclear technologies (weapons and power plants), while computer technology has opened up numerous new possibilities for scientific research. However, technology in relatively simple forms developed slowly over many millennia before science came into existence. To understand prescientific technologies we must realize that, even without the systematically controlled observation and experimentation of science, ordinary trial-and-error methods can produce substantial practical knowledge if continued over a long time and also that effective technologies can sometimes develop even without much comprehension of how or why they work (e.g., traditional folk medicine, which is sometimes surprisingly effective even though its practitioners have no adequate theoretical conception of the mechanisms through which their results are obtained).

Even after the rise of modern science in the seventeenth century, technological progress in many areas continued for a long time to occur primarily through craft traditions quite separate from science. Thus, eighteenth-century productive enterprises such as brickmaking and glassblowing were based on the accumulated knowledge and experiences of craftsmen, which were passed on to apprentices through observation and practice under the guidance of a master. Occasionally in the course of making a product, an anomaly would occur that was found to produce an improvement. This improvement might then be incorporated into future production, without necessarily being fully understood or put into writing.

In medieval Europe, and in some other preindustrial civilizations as well, craft traditions and scholarly traditions tended to be sharply separated (Mason 1962). The coming together of these traditions in the sixteenth and seventeenth centuries facilitated the rise of modern science. Engineering disciplines, in turn, emerged in the nineteenth century from a mixture of modern science with craft traditions. These disciplines utilized mathematical and experimental techniques derived from science to organize and expand the knowledge of craft practitioners, who passed on this knowledge to students through schools and written formulations rather than through apprenticeships. Today, much new technology comes from engineers, but some comes from scientists directly, and some still comes from craftspeople, as in the distant past.

In the twentieth century, research and development (R & D) has come to constitute a distinctive and separate activity within industrial corporations, and companies devoted exclusively or primarily to R & D have emerged. The management of technology has become a distinctive occupational specialty, and research managers directing groups of engineers and scientists have become a driving force in technological advance. In the United States these developments have taken place primarily within the private sector. In Japan and Europe governments have come to play a greater direct role in coordinating the relationship between technological change and the economy.

Technological developments have produced diverse, and often negative, reactions. Innovations ranging from streetlights to anesthesia were initially opposed by some on the ground that they interfered with God's plans. The Luddites were English workers in 1811–1816 who smashed machines that they blamed for unemployment and low wages. Many more recent workers have also opposed technological innovations that threaten their jobs. Some business corporations have tried to discourage new technologies that might destroy the market for their existing products. One way they have done this is by obtaining patent rights to products that they then decline to produce and also prevent other corporations from producing (see Stern 1959). Military organizations have often resisted new technologies. Reactions against big technology and a preference for locally controlled, small-scale, technological arrangements have been expressed in an "Appropriate Technology" movement (see Schumacher 1973). There is also considerable concern today about technology-induced damage to the environment and to human health and about dangerous implications of modern technologies of war.

In addition, new technological capacities impose new decision-making burdens on the political system. Technological knowledge must be taken into account in making decisions about weapons procurement, pollution control, funding of medical care, and innumerable other governmental matters. And new technology makes citizens' preferences about various matters relevant to the political process in new ways. If we ever learn to control the weather, our political system will have to cope with the fact that different people have different weather preferences, a fact that has always existed but that will become politically relevant only if and when significant weather-controlling capacities arise.

Despite problems associated with modern technology, we have become fundamentally dependent upon it. For example, without modern technologies of agriculture and transportation we could not feed our population that has grown far beyond the premodern level. Furthermore, we depend on further technological progress to help us overcome problems associated with the technology we already have. Thus, we need new energy sources to enable us to avoid the polluting effects of fuels we use today. Pressure for still further technological innovation arises from unsatisfied needs, from profit-making motives, and from challenges posed by technologically advancing competitors.

The sociological importance of technology is reflected in the fact that technological criteria are often used by sociologists to distinguish among types of societies. Thus we have *hunting and gathering, horticultural, agrarian* and *industrial* societies distinguished on the basis of their levels of technological achievement (see Lenski and Lenski 1982). The importance of technology has also led to numerous attempts to distinguish between good and bad technologies, but such a distinction is complicated not only by the absence of agreement as to what is good or bad but also by the fact that a given technological item may have highly diverse uses and implications. Thus, the same biological knowledge may be used for curing illness and for biological warfare. And the importance of technology has inspired innumerable attempts to predict its future development and implications, often with results that can provide amusement for subsequent generations, such as a wildly overpessimistic prediction in 1903 (a few months before the Wright brothers' first flight) that heavier-than-air machines would never fly, and an overoptimistic prediction by the sociologist William Fielding Ogburn (1946) that numerous Americans would soon acquire private airplanes that would be "roadable" (i.e., convertible to automobiles for ground travel).

Paradoxically, the importance of technology in society has not caused the "sociology of technology" to become an especially prominent sociological specialty. Instead, studies of different kinds of technology have become recognized as belonging to different sociological specializations. Thus, the sociological study of weaponry is part of *military sociology*, while the sociological study of medical technology is part of *medical sociology*. However, this situation now appears to be changing, as a coherent body of sociological knowledge concerning the general relationship between technology and society has been emerging (see Bijker, Hughes, and Pinch 1987; Mackenzie and Wajcman 1985; Richter 1982; Shrum 1985; Westrum 1991).

(SEE ALSO: *Diffusion Theories; Inventions; Science; Technological Risks and Society*)

REFERENCES

Bell, Daniel 1989 "The Third Technological Revolution." *Dissent* (Spring); 164–176.

Bijker, Wiebe E., Thomas P. Hughes, and Trevor J. Pinch, eds. 1987 *The Social Construction of Technological Systems.* Cambridge, Mass.: MIT Press.

Ellul, Jacques 1964 *The Technological Society*, trans. John Wilkinson. New York: Knopf.

Etzkowitz, Henry 1984 "Nuclear vs. Solar Energy: Autonomous or Dependent Technology?" *Social Problems* 31:417–434

———1991 "Technology and Social Change." In Henry Etzkowitz and Ronald Glassman, eds., *The Renascence of Sociological Theory.* Itasca, Ill.: F. E. Peacock.

Flink, James J. 1975 *The Car Culture.* Cambridge, Mass.: MIT Press.

Lenski, Gerhard, and Jean Lenski 1982 *Human Societies: An Introduction to Macrosociology.* New York: McGraw-Hill.

Linton, Ralph 1957 *The Tanala: A Hill Tribe of Madagascar.* Chicago: Field Museum of Natural History.

Mackenzie, Donald A., and Judy Wajcman, eds. 1985 *The Social Shaping of Technology: How the Refrigerator Got Its Hum.* New York: Taylor and Francis.

Mason, Stephen F. 1962 *A History of the Sciences.* New York: Collier.

Mumford, Lewis 1967 *Technics and Human Development.* New York: Harcourt, Brace, and World.

Needham, Joseph 1969 *The Grand Titration: Science and Society in East and West.* Toronto: University of Toronto Press.

Ogburn, William Fielding 1946 *The Social Effects of Aviation.* Boston: Houghton Mifflin.

Richter, Maurice N., Jr. 1980 *Society: A Macroscopic View.* Cambridge, Mass.: Schenkman.

———1982. *Technology and Social Complexity.* Albany, N. Y.: State University of New York Press.

Schumacher, E. F. 1973 *Small Is Beautiful: Economics As If People Mattered.* New York: Harper and Row.

Shrum, Wesley 1985 *Organized Technology: Networks and Innovation in Technical Systems.* West Lafayette, Ind.: Purdue University Press.

Stern, Bernhard J. 1959 "Restraints upon the Utilization of Inventions." In *Historical Sociology.* New York: Citadel Press.

Westrum, Ron 1991 *Technologies and Society: The Shaping of People and Things.* Belmont, Calif.: Wadsworth.

White, Leslie A. 1949 *The Science of Culture.* New York: Farrar, Straus, and Cudahy.

White, Lynn 1946 *Medieval Technology and Social Change.* Oxford: Clarendon Press.

HENRY ETZKOWITZ
MAURICE N. RICHTER, JR.

TERRORISM Terrorism became an issue of worldwide concern during the last third of the twentieth century. Terrorist tactics themselves were not new—they had been used for centuries before being defined as terrorism. The word *terror* entered the political lexicon during the French Revolution's "reign of terror." In the late nineteenth century, the beginning of the twentieth, and again in the 1920s and 1930s—significantly, all periods between major wars on the European continent—terrorism became a technique of revolutionary struggle. Stalin's regime in the 1930s and 1940s was called a reign of terror, but from the late 1940s to the 1960s the word was associated primarily with the armed struggles for independence waged in Palestine and Algeria, from which later generations of terrorists took their inspiration and instruction. Following World War II, "terror" emerged as a component of nuclear strategy; the fear of mutual destruction that would deter nuclear war between the United States and the Soviet Union was referred to as a "balance of terror."

Here was a concept on the move. By the 1970s, *terrorism* became a fad word, promiscuously applied to a wide spectrum of conditions and actions. Bombs in public places were one form of terrorism, but some people asserted that poverty and hunger were also a form of terrorism. Some governments labeled as terrorism all violent acts committed by their opponents, while antigovernment extremists claimed to be, and often were, the victims of government terror.

In an effort to get a firm hold on a slippery subject, those wishing to study the phenomenon of terrorism were obliged to define it more precisely. Terrorism could be described simply as the use or threat of violence, calculated to create an atmosphere of fear and alarm and thereby to bring about some political result. But making this definition operative in political debate, rules of war, or criminal codes was anything but easy. Is all politically motivated violence terrorism? How does terrorism differ from ordinary crime? Should terrorism be considered a crime at all, or should it be seen as simply another form of armed conflict, no less legitimate than any other form of war? Is the term properly reserved for those trying to overthrow governments, or can governments also be terrorists?

Definition was crucial because it ultimately determined the way in which terrorism has been studied. A major problem was that terrorism almost always has a pejorative connotation and thus falls in the same category of words as *tyranny* and *genocide,* unlike such relatively neutral terms as *war* and *revolution.* One can aspire to objective and dispassionate research, but one cannot be neutral about terrorism any more than one can be neutral about torture. Thus, defining terrorism became an effort not only to delineate a subject area but also to maintain its illegitimacy. Even the most clinical inquiry was laden with values and, therefore, political issues. The very study of terrorism implied to some a political decision.

Terrorism can be defined objectively by the quality of the act, not by the identity of the perpetrators or the nature of their cause. All terrorist acts are crimes, and many would also be war crimes or "grave breaches" of the rules of war if one accepted the terrorists' assertion that they wage war. All terrorist acts involve violence or the threat of violence, sometimes coupled with explicit demands. The violence is directed against noncombatants. The purposes are political. The actions are often carried out in a way that will achieve maximum publicity, and the perpetrators are usually members of an organized group.

Terrorist organizations are by necessity clandestine, but, unlike other criminals, terrorists often claim credit for their acts. And finally—the hallmark of terrorism—the acts are intended to produce psychological damage. This introduces a distinction between the actual victims of terrorist violence and the target audience. The connection between the victim and the target of terrorism can be remote. The identity of the victims may be secondary or even irrelevant to the terrorist cause. "Pure terrorism" is entirely indiscriminate violence.

Terrorism differs from ordinary crime in its political purpose and in its primary objective. But not all politically motivated violence is terrorism, nor is terrorism synonymous with guerrilla war or any other kind of war.

Terrorist techniques can be used by governments or those fighting against governments; however, scholars generally use the term *terror* when discussing fear-producing tactics employed by governments and *terrorism* when referring to tactics used by those fighting against governments. The distinction is primarily semantic. Both groups may use threats, assassinations, or abductions, but government terror may also include arbitrary imprisonment, concentration camps, torture, mind-affecting techniques, and the use of drugs for political purposes. Antigovernment terrorists generally lack the infrastructure for such tactics. Government terror produces more victims than terrorism does. Terrorists tend to seek more publicity than do governments.

The term *international terrorism* refers to terrorist attacks on foreign targets or the crossing of national frontiers to carry out terrorist attacks. It was the dramatic rise in international terrorism—especially in the form of attacks on diplomats and commercial aviation in the late 1960s—that caused mounting alarm on the part of governments not directly involved in these local conflicts.

The 1980s recognized a new form of international terrorism—state-sponsored terrorism. Some governments began to use terrorist tactics themselves or to employ terrorist tactics as a mode of surrogate warfare. Unlike government-directed terror, which is primarily domestic, state-sponsored terrorism is directed against foreign governments or domestic foes abroad.

Despite great differences in political perspectives and outlook toward armed conflict, the international community gradually came to accept at least a partial definition of terrorism and prohibited certain tactics and attacks on certain targets. This approach reflected that of the academic community, focusing on the terrorist act and rejecting judgment based on the political objective or cause behind the act. Thus, by 1985, the United Nations General Assembly unanimously condemned international terrorism, including but not limited to those acts covered by previous treaties against airline hijacking and sabotage of aircraft, attacks in any form against internationally protected persons (i.e., diplomats), and the taking of hostages.

This covered roughly half of all incidents of international terrorism but omitted primarily bombings of targets other than airlines or diplomatic facilities. One difficulty in delineating this type of terrorist act is the problem of distinguishing between terrorist bombings and aerial bombardment, which is considered a legitimate form of war. The rules of war prohibit indiscriminate bombing, thus providing at least a theoretical distinction between war and terrorism, although, even with modern precision-guided munitions, collateral civilian casualties from aerial bombing in populated areas vastly exceed casualties caused by the deliberate, indiscriminate bombs of terrorists.

Research has focused narrowly on the phenomenon of terrorism. In part, this reflects the desire of researchers to avoid the murky, politically loaded area of underlying causes, where any discussion might be seen as condemnation or the rationalization of terrorist violence. Nonetheless, there have been some excellent case studies of individual groups and their tactics.

Defining terrorism in terms of the act has enabled researchers to maintain a theoretically objective approach and conduct at least some primitive quantitative analysis. Event-based analysis has enabled them to discern broad patterns and trends and to chart the growth of terrorism and its diffusion around the globe. They have been able to demonstrate statistically that as terrorism has increased in volume it has also become bloodier. Researchers have been able to illustrate a clear trend toward incidents of large-scale indiscriminate violence in the 1980s and to infer that terrorists tend to be more imitative than innovative in their tactics. Event-based analysis has also permitted researchers to distinguish the operational profiles of specific terrorist groups, and these profiles have been useful in identifying changes in a group's *modus operandi*.

At the same time, event-based analysis has led the analysts into some methodological traps. An exclusive focus on terrorist actions, for example, resulted in terrorists being viewed first as if they were all part of a single entity and second as if they were almost extraterrestrial. While there are connections and alliances among some terrorist groups, the only thing the terrorists of the world have in common is a propensity for violence and certain tactics. Moreover, each group is rooted in its own social, political, and cultural soil, and cross-national comparisons are difficult. This has led to the question of whether there are terrorist-prone societies.

Researchers' attempts to discern deeper causes or conditions that lead to high levels of terrorism in certain societies have produced meager results. Terrorism is not demonstrably a response to poverty or political oppression. The liberal democracies of Western Europe have suffered high levels of terrorist violence, while totalitarian states are virtually free of terrorism. Overall, countries with perceived terrorist problems tend to be comparatively advanced politically and economically. They are more highly urbanized, have higher per capita incomes, larger middle classes, more university students, and higher rates of literacy. One may ask whether political and economic advance simply brings a more modern form of political violence.

An obstacle to linking high levels of terrorism with environmental factors is the problem of measuring terrorism. For the most part, this has consisted of counting terrorist incidents. But international terrorism, as we have seen, was narrowly and, more important, artificially defined to include only those incidents that cause international concern, a distinction that has meant very little to the terrorists. Counting *all* terrorist incidents, both local and international, is better but still inadequate. Terrorist tactics, narrowly defined, represent most of what some groups, particularly those in Western Europe, do; but for other groups, terrorism represents only one facet of a broader armed conflict. And what about the extensive uncounted political and communal violence in the rural backlands of numerous third world countries? Broad statements about terrorist-prone or violence-prone societies simply cannot be made on the basis of measuring only a thin terrorist crust of that violence.

If terrorism cannot be explained by environmental factors, then we must look into the mind of the individual terrorist for an explanation. Are there individuals who are prone to becoming terrorists—a preterrorist personality? Encouraged by superficial similarities in the demographic profiles of the terrorists—many of them have been urban middle and upper class (not economically deprived) males, in their early twenties, with university or at least secondary school educations—researchers searched for common psychological features.

Behavioral analysts painted an unappealing portrait: The composite terrorist appeared to be a person who was narcissistic, emotionally flat, easily disillusioned, incapable of enjoyment, rigid, and a true believer who was action-oriented and risk-seeking. Psychiatrists could label terrorists as neurotic, possibly sociopathic, but they found that most of them were not clinically insane. Some behavioral analysts looked for deeper connections between the terrorists' attitude toward parents and their attitudes toward authority. A few went further in claiming a physiological explanation for terrorism based upon inner ear disorders, but these assertions were not given wide credence in the scientific community. The growing number of terrorists apprehended and imprisoned in the 1980s permitted more thorough studies, but while these occasionally unearthed tantalizing similarities, they also showed terrorists to be a diverse if dangerous lot.

Much of the research on terrorism has been government-sponsored and therefore oriented toward the practical goal of understanding terrorism in order to defeat it. While social scientists looked for environmental or behavioral explanations for terrorism, other researchers attempted to identify terrorist vulnerabilities and successful countermeasures. They achieved a measure of success in several areas. Studies of the human dynamics of hostage situations led to the development of psychological tactics that increased the hostages' chances of survival and a better understanding (and therefore more effective treatment) of those who had been held hostage. In some cases, specific psychological vulnerabilities were identified and exploited. With somewhat less success, researchers also examined the effects of broader policies, such as not making concessions to terrorists holding hostages or military retaliation. The conclusions in this area were less clear-cut.

A final area of research concerned the effects of terrorism on society. Here, researchers viewed terrorism as comprising not only the sum of terrorist actions but also the fear and alarm produced by those actions. Public opinion polls, along with measurable decisions like not flying or avoiding certain countries, provided the measure of effect.

Over the years, research on terrorism has become more sophisticated, but in the end, terrorism confronts us with fundamental philosophical questions: Do ends justify means? How far does one go on behalf of a cause? What is the value of an individual human life? What obligations do governments have toward their own citizens, if, for example, they are held hostage? Should governments or corporations ever bargain for human life? What limits can be imposed on individual liberties to ensure public safety? Is the use of military force, as a matter of choice, ever appropriate? Can assassination ever be justified? These are not matters of research. They are issues that have been debated through the ages.

(SEE ALSO: *International Law; Revolutions; Social Control; Violent Crime; War*)

REFERENCES

Kurz, Anat (ed.) 1987 *Contemporary Trends in World Terrorism.* Tel Aviv, Israel: The Jaffee Center for Strategic Studies.

Laqueur, Walter 1976 *Guerrilla—A Historical and Critical Study.* Boston: Little, Brown.

———1977 *Terrorism.* Boston: Little, Brown.

O'Sullivan, Noel (ed.) 1986 *Terrorism, Ideology and Revolution.* Boulder, Colo.: Westview Press.

Schmid, Alex P., and Albert J. Jongman 1988 *Political Terrorism.* Amsterdam/Oxford/New York: North Holland.

Thackrah, John Richard 1987 *Terrorism and Political Violence.* London: Routledge & Kegan Paul.

Wilkinson, Paul, and Alasdair M. Stewart (eds.) 1987 *Contemporary Research on Terrorism.* Aberdeen, Scotland: Aberdeen University Press.

BRIAN MICHAEL JENKINS

THEOCRACY *See* Religion, Politics, and War; Religious Organizations.

TIME SERIES ANALYSIS Longitudinal data are common in sociology, and over the years sociologists have imported a wide variety of statistical procedures from other disciplines by which such data may be analyzed. Examples include survival analysis (Cox and Oakes 1984), dynamic modeling (Harvey 1981, Chapters 7 and 8), and techniques for pooled cross-sectional and time series data (Hsiao 1986). Typically, such procedures are used to represent the causal mechanisms by which one or more outcomes are produced; a stochastic model is provided that is presumed to extract the essential means by which changes in some variables bring about the changes of other variables (Berk 1988).

The cluster of techniques called *time series analysis* have somewhat different intellectual roots. Rather than try to represent explicit causal mechanisms, the goal within classical time series analysis is "simply" to describe in summary form some longitudinal stochastic processes. To be sure, that description may be used to inform existing theory or inductively to extract new theoretical notions, but classical time series analysis does not begin with a fully articulated causal model.

Yet, more recent developments in time series analysis, and in the analysis of longitudinal data more generally, have produced a growing convergence in which the descriptive power of time series analysis has been incorporated into causal modeling, and the capacity to represent certain kinds of causal mechanisms has been introduced into time series analysis (see, for example, Harvey 1981). It may now be fair to say that differences between time series analysis and the causal modeling of longitudinal data are matters of degree.

CLASSICAL TIME SERIES ANALYSIS

Classical time series analysis was developed to describe variability over time for a single unit of observation (Box and Jenkins 1976, Chapter 3 and 4). The single unit could be a person, a household, a city, a business, a market, or some other entity. A popular example in sociology is the crime rate over time for a particular jurisdiction (e.g., Loftin and McDowall 1982; Chamlin 1988). Other examples include longitudinal data on public opinion, unemployment rates, or infant mortality.

Formal Foundations. The mathematical foundations of classical time series analysis are found in difference equations. An equation "relating the values of a function y and one or more of its differences $\Delta y, \Delta^2 y, \ldots$ for each x-value of some set of numbers S (for which each of these functions is defined) is called a difference equation over the set S" ($\Delta y = y_t - y_{t-1}$, $\Delta^2 = \Delta(y_t - y_{t-1}) = y_t - 2y_{t-1} - y_{t-2}$, and so on; Goldberg 1958, p. 50). The x-values specify the numbers for which the relationship holds (i.e., the domain). That is, the relationships may be true for only some values of x. In practice, the x-values are taken to be a set of successive integers, which in effect indicate *when* a measure is taken. Then, requiring that all difference operations Δ be taken with an interval equal to 1 (Goldberg 1958, p. 52), one gets the following kinds of results (with t replacing x): $\Delta^2 y_t + k y_t = 2k + 7$, which can be rewritten as $y_t - 2y_{t-1} + (1-k)y_{t-2} = 2k + 7$.

Difference equations are deterministic. In practice, the social world is taken to be stochastic. Therefore, in order to use difference equations in time series analysis, a disturbance term is added, much as in conventional regression models.

ARIMA Models. Getting from stochastic difference equations to time series analysis requires that an observed time series be conceptualized as a product of some underlying substantive process. In particular, an observed time series is conceptualized as a "realization" of an underlying process assumed to be reasonably well described by an unknown stochastic difference equation. In other words, the realization is treated as if it were a simple random sample from the distribution of all possible realizations that the underlying process might produce. This is a very weighty *substantive* assumption that cannot be made casually or as a matter of convenience. For example, if the time series is the number of lynchings by year in some southern state between 1880 and 1930, how much sense does it make to talk about observed data as a representative realization of an underlying historical process that could have produced a very large number of such realizations? Many time series are alternatively conceptualized as a population; what you see is all there is (e.g., Freedman and Lane 1983). Then, the relevance of time series analysis becomes unclear.

If one can live with the underlying world assumed, then the statistical tools that time series analysis provides can be used to make inferences about which stochastic difference equation is most consistent with the data and what the values of the coefficients are likely to be. This is, of course, not much different from what is done in conventional regression analysis.

For the tools to work properly, however, one must at least assume "weak stationarity." Drawing from Gottman's very useful didactic discussion (1981, pp. 60–66), imagine that a very large number of realizations were actually observed and then displayed in a large two-way table with one time period in each column and one realization in each row. Weak stationarity requires that if one computed the mean for each time period (i.e., for each column), these means would be effectively the same (and identical asymptotically). Likewise, if one computed the variance for each time period (i.e., by column), these variances would be effectively the same (and identical asymptotically). That is, the process is characterized in part by a finite mean and variance that do not change over time.

Weak stationarity also requires that the covariance of the process between periods be independent of time as well. That is, for any given lag in time (e.g., one period, two periods, or three periods), if one computed all possible covariances between columns in the table, these covariances would be effectively the same (and identical asymptotically). For example, at a lag of 2, one would compute covariances between column 1 and column 3, column 2 and column 4, column 3 and column 5, and so on. These covariances would all be effectively the same. In summary, weak stationarity requires that the variance–covariance matrix across realizations be invariant with respect to the displacement of time. Strong stationarity implies that the joint distribution (more generally) is invariant with respect to the displacement of time. When each time period's observations are normally distributed, weak and strong stationarity are the same. In either case, history is effectively assumed to repeat itself.

There are many statistical models, consistent with weak stationarity, that have been used to analyze time series data. Probably the most widely applied (and the model on which we will focus) is associated with the work of Box and Jenkins (1976). Their most basic ARIMA (autoregressive-integrated moving-average) model has three parts: 1) an autoregressive component; 2) a moving average component; and 3) a differencing component.

Consider first the autoregressive component and y_t as the variable of interest. An autoregressive component of order p can be written as $y_t - \Phi_1 y_{t-1} - \cdots - \Phi_p y_{t-p}$.

Alternatively, the autoregressive component of order p (AR[p]) can be written in the form $\Phi(B) y_t$, where B is the backward shift operator—that is, $(B)y_t = y_{t-1}$, $(B^2)y_t = y_{t-2}$, and so on—and $\phi(B) = 1 - \phi_1 B - \cdots - \phi_p B^p$. For example, an autoregressive model of order 2 is $y_t - \phi_1 y_{t-1} - \phi_2 y_{t-2}$.

A moving average component of order q, in contrast, can be written as $\epsilon_t - \theta_1 \epsilon_{t-1} - \cdots - \theta_q \epsilon_{t-q}$. The variable ϵ_t is taken to be "white noise," sometimes called the "innovations process,"

which is much like the disturbance term in regression models. It is assumed that ϵ_t is uncorrelated with itself and has a mean (expected value) of zero and a constant variance. It is sometimes assumed, as well, to be Gaussian.

The moving average component of order q (MA[q]) can also be written in the form $\Theta(B)\epsilon_t$, where B is a backward shift operator and $\Theta(B) = 1 - \Theta_1 B - \cdots - \Theta_q B^q$. For example, a moving average model of order 2 is $\epsilon_t - \theta_1 \epsilon_{t-1} - \theta_2 \epsilon_{t-2}$.

Finally, the differencing component can be written as $\Delta^d y_t$, where the d is the number differences taken (or the degree of differencing). Differencing (see "Formal Foundations") is a method to remove nonstationarity in a time series mean so that weak stationarity is achieved. It is common to see ARIMA models written in general form as $\Phi(B)\Delta^d y_t = \Theta(B)\epsilon_t$.

A seasonal set of components can also be included. The set is structured in exactly the same way but uses a seasonal time reference. That is, instead of time intervals of one time period, seasonal models use time intervals such as quarters. The seasonal component is usually included multiplicatively (Box and Jenkins 1976, Chapter 9; Granger and Newbold 1986, pp. 101–114), but a discussion here is precluded by space limitations.

ARIMA Models in Practice. In practice, one rarely knows which ARIMA model is appropriate for the data on hand. That is, one does not know what orders the autoregressive and moving-average components should be or what degree of differencing is required to achieve stationarity. The values of the coefficients for these models are typically unknown as well. At least three diagnostic procedures are commonly used: time series plots, the autocorrelation function, and the partial autocorrelation function.

A time series plot is simply a graph of the variable to be analyzed arrayed over time. It is always important to study time series plots carefully to get an initial sense of the data: time trends, cyclical patterns, dramatic irregularities, and outliers.

The autocorrelation function and partial autocorrelation function of the time series are used to

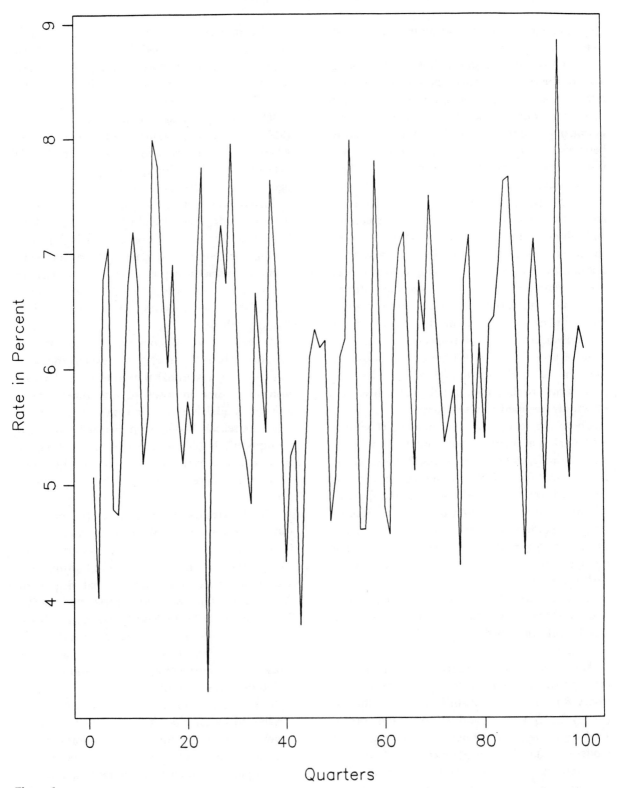

Figure 1
Unemployment Rate by Quarter

help specify which ARIMA model should be applied to the data. The rules of thumb typically employed will be summarized after a brief illustration.

Figure 1 shows a time series plot of the simulated unemployment rate for a small city. The vertical axis is the unemployment rate, and the horizontal axis is time in quarters. There appear to be rather dramatic cycles in the data, but, on closer inspection, they do not fit neatly into any simple story. For example, the cycles are not two or four periods in length (which would correspond to six-month or twelve-month cycles).

Figure 2 shows a plot of the autocorrelation function (ACF) of the simulated data with horizontal bands for the 95-percent confidence interval. Basically, the autocorrelation function produces a series of serial Pearson correlations for the given time series at different lags: 0, 1, 2, 3, and so on (Box and Jenkins 1976, pp. 23–36). If the series is stationary with respect to the mean, the autocorrelations should decline rather rapidly. If they do not, one may difference the series one or more times until the autocorrelations do decline rapidly.

For some kinds of mean nonstationarity, differencing will not solve the problem (e.g., if the nonstationarity has an exponential form). It is also important to note that mean nonstationarity may be seen in the data as differences in level for different parts of the time series or differences in slope for different parts of the data, or even some other pattern.

In figure 2, the autocorrelation for lag 0 is 1.0, as it should be (correlating something with itself). Then, there are three spikes outside of the 95-percent confidence interval at lags 1, 2, and 3. Clearly, the correlations decline gradually but rather rapidly, so that one may reasonably conclude that the series is already mean stationary. The gradual decline is also usually taken as a sign that there are autoregressive processes operating, perhaps in combination with moving-average processes, perhaps not. There also seems to be a cyclical pattern, which is consistent with the patterns in figure 1, and is usually taken as a sign that

the autoregressive process has an order of more than one.

Figure 3 shows the partial autocorrelation function. The partial autocorrelation is similar to the usual partial correlation, except that what is being held constant is values of the times series at shorter lags than the lag of interest. For example, the partial autocorrelation at a lag of 4 holds constant the time series values at lags of 1, 2, and 3.

From figure 3, it is clear that there are large spikes at lags of 1 and 2. This is usually taken to mean that the p for the autoregressive component is equal to 2. That is, an AR[2] component is necessary. In addition, the abrupt decline (rather than a rapid but gradual decline) after a lag of 2 (in this case) is usually interpreted as a sign that there is no moving-average component.

The parameters for an AR[2] model were estimated using maximum likelihood procedures. The first AR parameter estimate was 0.33 and the second was estimate −0.35. Both had t-values well in excess of convention levels. These results are consistent with the cyclical patterns seen in figure 1; a positive value for the first AR parameter and a negative value for the second produced the apparent cyclical patterns.

How well does the model fit? Figures 4 and 5 show respectively the autocorrelation function and partial autocorrelation function for the residuals of the original time series (much like residuals in conventional regression analysis). There are no spikes outside of the 95-percent confidence interval, which indicates that the residuals are probably white noise. That is, the temporal dependence in the data has been removed. One can conclude, therefore, that the data are consistent with an underlying autoregressive process of order 2, with coefficients of 0.33 and −0.35. The relevance of this information will be addressed shortly.

To summarize, the diagnostics have suggested that our ARIMA model need not include any differences or a moving-average component but should include an autoregressive component of order 2. More generally, the following diagnostic

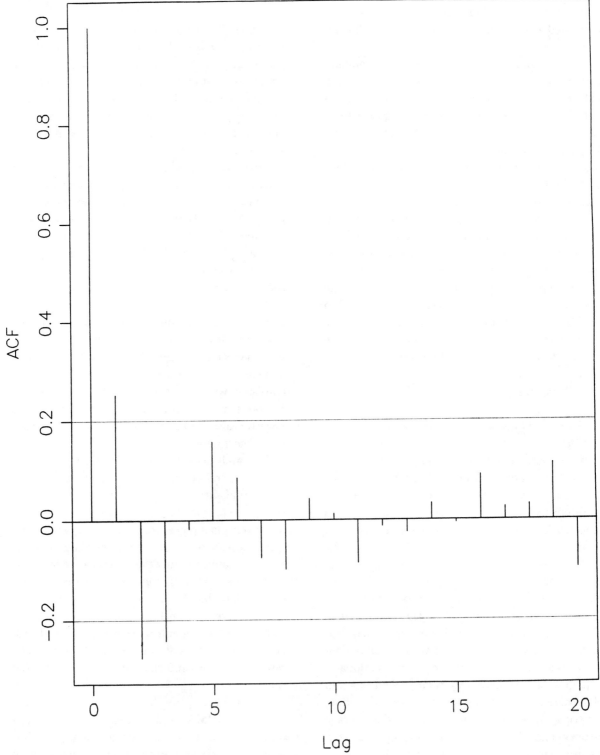

Figure 2
Unemployment Series: Autocorrelation Function

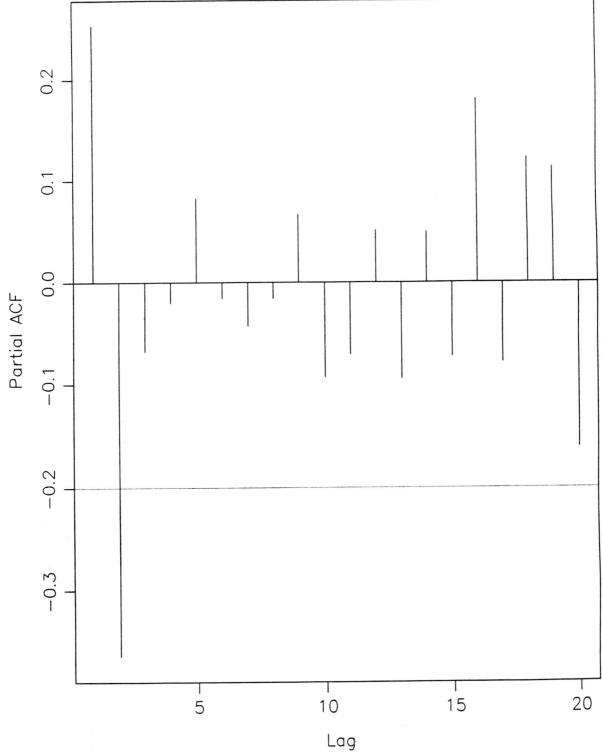

Figure 3
Unemployment Series: Partial Autocorrelation Function

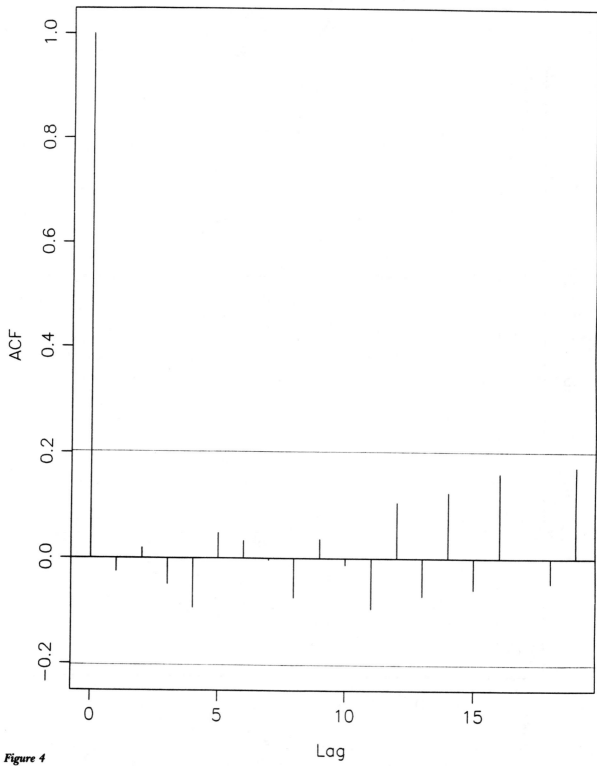

Figure 4
Residuals Series: Autocorrelation Function

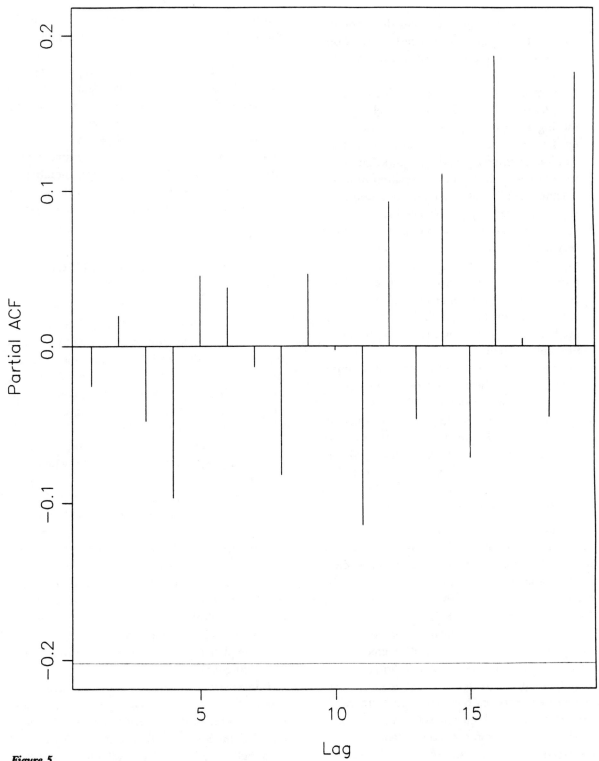

Figure 5
Residuals Series: Partial Autocorrelation Functions

rules of thumb are usually employed, often in the order shown.

1. If the autocorrelation function does not decline rather rapidly, difference the series one or more times (perhaps up to three) until it does.
2. If either before or after differencing the autocorrelation function declines very abruptly, a moving-average component is probably needed. The lag of the last large spike outside of the confidence interval provides a good guess for the value of q. If the autocorrelation function declines rapidly but gradually, an autoregressive component is probably needed.
3. If the partial autocorrelation function declines very abruptly, an autoregressive component is probably needed. The lag of the last large spike outside of the confidence interval provides a good guess for the value of p. If the partial autocorrelation function declines rapidly but gradually, a moving-average component is probably needed.
4. Estimate the model's coefficients and compute the residuals of the model. Use the rules above to examine the residuals. If there are no systematic patterns in the residuals, conclude that the model is consistent with the data. If there are systematic patterns in the residuals, respecify the model and try again. Repeat until the residuals are consistent with a white noise process (i.e., no temporal dependence).

There are several additional diagnostic procedures that are available, but because of space limitations they cannot be discussed even briefly. For an elementary discussion see Gottman (1981), and for a more advanced discussion see Granger and Newbold (1986).

It should be clear that the diagnostic process is heavily dependent on a number of judgment calls about which researchers could well disagree. Fortunately, such disagreements rarely matter. First, the disagreements may revolve around differences between models without any substantive import. There may be, for instance, no substantive consequences from reporting an MA[2] compared with an MA[3]. Second, ARIMA models are often used

primarily to remove "nuisance" patterns in time series data (discussed below), in which case the particular model used is unimportant; it is the result that matters. Finally and more technically, if certain assumptions are met, it is often possible to represent a low-order moving-average model as a high-order autoregressive model and a low-order autoregressive model as a high-order moving-average model. Then, model specification depends solely on the criteria of parsimony. That is, models with a smaller number of parameters are preferred to models with a larger number of parameters. However, this is an aesthetic yardstick that may have nothing to with the substantive story of interest.

USES OF ARIMA MODELS IN SOCIOLOGY

It should be clear that ARIMA models are not especially rich from a substantive point of view. They are essentially univariate descriptive devices that do not readily lend themselves to sociological problems. But ARIMA models are rarely used merely as descriptive devices (see, however, Gottman 1981). In other social science disciplines, especially economics, ARIMA models are often used for forecasting (Granger and Newbold 1986). Klepinger and Weiss (1985) provide a rare sociological example.

More relevant for sociology is that ARIMA models are sometimes used to remove "nuisance" temporal dependence that may be obstructing proper study of "important" temporal dependence. In the simplest case, ARIMA models can be appended to regression models to adjust for serially correlated residuals (Judge et al. 1985, Chapter 8). Probably more interesting is the extension of ARIMA models to include one or more binary explanatory variables or one or more additional time series.

Intervention Analysis. When the goal is to explore how a time series changes after the occurrence of some discrete event, the research design is called an interrupted time series (Cook and Campbell 1979). The relevant statistical procedures are called "intervention analysis"

(Box and Tiao 1975). Basically, one adds a discrete "transfer function" to the ARIMA model to capture how the discrete event (or events) affects the time series. Transfer functions take the general form shown in equation 1.

$$(1 - \delta_1 B - \cdots - \delta_r B^r) y_t = (\omega_0 - \omega_1 B - \cdots - \omega_s B^s) x_{t-b} \quad (1)$$

If both sides of equation 1 are divided by the left-hand side polynomial, the ratio of the two polynomials in B on the right-hand side is called a transfer function. In the form shown in equation 1, r is the order of the polynomial for the "dependent variable" (y_t), s is the order of the polynomial for the discrete "independent variable" (x_t), and b is the lag between when the independent "switches" from 0 to 1 and when its impact is observed. For example, if r equals 1, s equals 0, and b equals 0, the transfer function becomes $\omega_0 / 1 - \delta_1$. Transfer functions can represent a large number of effects depending on the orders of the two polynomials and whether the discrete event is coded as an impulse or step. (In the impulse form, the independent variable is coded over time as 0,0, . . . 0,1,0,0, . . . ,0. In the step form, the independent variable is coded over time as 0,0, . . . 1,1, . . . 1. The zeros represent the absence of the intervention while the ones represent the presence of the intervention. That is, there is a switch from 0 to 1 when the intervention is turned on and a switch from 1 to 0 when the intervention is turned off.) A selection of effects represented by transfer functions is shown in figure 6.

In practice, one may proceed by using the time series data prior to the intervention to determine the model specification for the ARIMA component, much as discussed above. The specification for the transfer function in the discrete case is more ad hoc. Theory certainly helps, but one approach is to regress the time series on the binary intervention variable at a moderate number of lags (e.g., simultaneously for lags of 0 periods to 10 periods). The regression coefficients associated with each of the lagged values of the intervention will roughly trace out the shape of the time path of the response. From this, a very small number of plausible transfer functions can be selected for testing.

As for a sociological example, Loftin, Heumann, and McDowall (1983) estimated the impact of Michigan's Felony Firearm Statute on violent crime. The law imposed a two-year mandatory add-on sentence for defendants convicted of possession of a firearm in the commission of a felony. Several different crime time series (e.g., the number of homicides per month) were explored under the hypothesis that the crime rates for offenses involving guns would drop after the law was implemented. ARIMA models were employed coupled with a variety of transfer functions. Overall, the intervention apparently had no impact.

Multiple Time Series. ARIMA models may also be extended to more than one time series. Just as the goal for the univariate case was to find a model that transformed the single time series into white noise, the goal for the multivariate case is to find a model that will transform a *vector* of time series into a white noise vector. In effect, each series is simultaneously regressed not only on lagged functions of itself and the disturbance term but on functions of all other time series and their disturbance terms. This sometimes reduces, in practice, to building transfer function models that include a single response time series and several input time series, much as in multiple regression. For example, Berk et al. (1980) explored how water consumption varied over time with the marginal price of water, weather, and a number of water conservation programs.

The mathematical generalization from the univariate case is rather straightforward. The generalization of model specification techniques and estimation procedures is not. Moreover, multivariate time series models have not made any significant inroads into sociological work and are, therefore, beyond the scope of this chapter. Interested readers are urged to consult Granger and Newbold's fine text (1986).

CONCLUSIONS

Time series analysis is an active enterprise in economics, statistics, and operations research. Examples of both technical developments and applications can be found routinely in a large

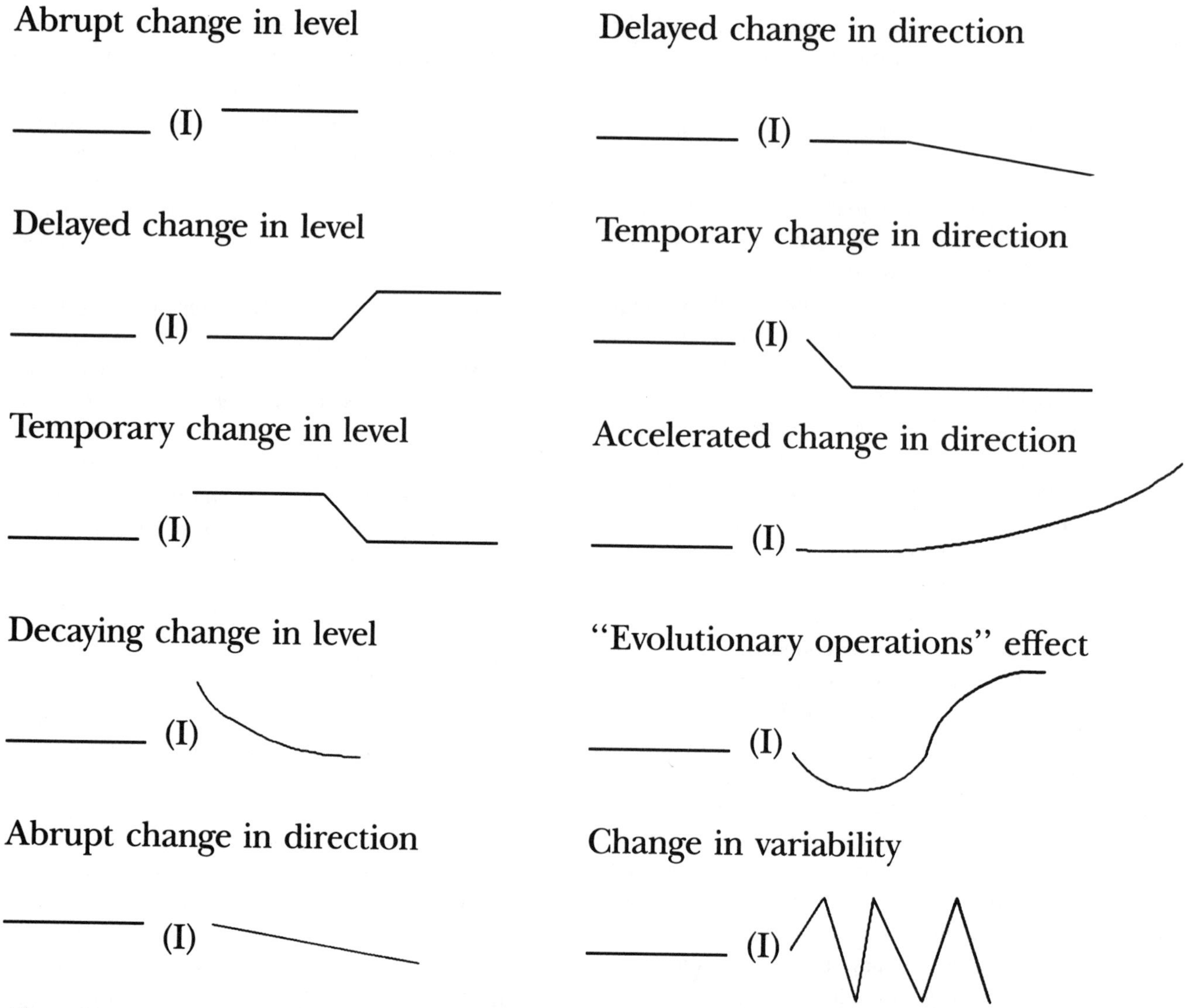

Abrupt change in level

——— (I) ———

Delayed change in direction

——— (I) ———

Delayed change in level

——— (I) ———

Temporary change in direction

——— (I) ———

Temporary change in level

——— (I) ———

Accelerated change in direction

——— (I) ———

Decaying change in level

——— (I) ———

"Evolutionary operations" effect

——— (I) ———

Abrupt change in direction

——— (I) ———

Change in variability

——— (I) ∧∧∧

Figure 6
A Sampler of Intervention Effects. I=Intervention

number of journals (e.g., *Journal of the American Statistical Association, Journal of Business and Economic Statistics, Journal of Forecasting*). Yet time series analysis has not been especially visible in sociology. Part of the explanation is the relative scarcity of true time series for sociological variables, collected over a sufficiently long period. Another part of the explanation is that time series analysis is unabashedly inductive, often making little use of substantive theory; time series analysis

may look to some a lot like "mindless empiricism." Yet, in many sociological fields, true time series data are becoming increasingly available. And, under the banner of "data analysis" and "exploratory research," induction is becoming more legitimate. Time series analysis may well have some future in sociology.

(SEE ALSO: *Longitudinal Research; Statistical Methods*)

REFERENCES

Berk, R. A. 1988 "Causal Inference for Sociological Data." In N. Smelser, ed., *The Handbook of Sociology*. Newbury Park, Calif.: Sage Publications.

———, and Thomas F. Cooley 1987 "Errors in Forecasting Social Phenomena." *Climatic Change* 11:247–265.

———, T. F. Cooley, C. J. LaCivita, S. Parker, K. Sredl, and M. Brewer 1980 "Reducing Consumption in Periods of Acute Scarcity: The Case of Water." *Social Science Research* 9:99–120.

Box, G. E. P., and G. M. Jenkins 1976 *Time Series Analysis: Forecasting and Control*. San Francisco: Holden-Day.

Box, G. E. P., and G. C. Tiao 1975 "Intervention Analysis with Applications to Economic and Environmental Problems." *Journal of the American Statistical Association* 70:70–79.

Chamlin, Mitchel B. 1988 "Crime and Arrests: An Autoregressive Integrated Moving Average (ARIMA) Approach." *Journal of Quantitative Criminology* 4(3):247–258.

Cook, T. D., and D. T. Campbell 1979 *Quasiexperimentation*. Chicago: Rand McNally.

Cox, D. R., and D. Oakes 1984 *Analysis of Survival Data*. London: Chapman and Hall.

Freedman, D. A., and David Lane 1983 "Significance Testing in a Nonstochastic Setting." In P. J. Bickel, K. A. Doksum, and J. L. Hodges, Jr., eds., *A Festschrift for Erich L. Lehman*. Belmont, CA: Wadsworth International Group.

Goldberg, Samuel 1958 *Introduction to Difference Equations*. New York: Wiley.

Gottman, J. M. 1981 *Time-Series Analysis*. Cambridge: Cambridge University Press.

Granger, C. W. J., and P. Newbold 1986 *Forecasting Economic Time Series*. Orlando, Fla.: Academic Press.

Harvey, A. C. 1981 *The Econometric Analysis of Time Series*. New York: Wiley.

Hsiao, Cheng 1986 *Analysis of Panel Data*. Cambridge: Cambridge University Press.

Judge, D. G., W. E. Griffiths, R. C. Hill, H. Lutkepohl, and T.-C. Lee 1985 *The Theory and Practice of Econometrics*. New York: Wiley.

Klepinger, J. D. H., and J. G. Weis 1985 "Projecting Crime Rates: An Age, Period, and Cohort Model Using ARIMA Techniques." *Journal of Quantitative Criminology* 1:387–416.

Loftin, C., M. Heumann, and D. McDowall 1983 "Mandatory Sentencing and Firearms Violence: Evaluating and Alternative to Gun Control." *Law and Society Review* 17(2):287–318.

Loftin, C., and D. McDowall 1982 "The Police, Crime, and Economic Theory." *American Sociological Review* 47:393–401.

RICHARD A. BERK

TRANSNATIONAL CORPORATIONS

A transnational corporation (TNC) is "any enterprise that undertakes foreign direct investment, owns or controls income-gathering assets in more than one country, produces goods or services outside its country of origin, or engages in international production" (Biersteker 1978, p. xii). Variously termed *multinational corporations* (MNCs) or *multinational enterprises* (MNEs), transnational corporations are formal business organizations that have spatially dispersed operations in at least two countries. For example, IBM, the fifth largest publicly held industrial corporation in the world measured by sales, has its headquarters in the United States but has subsidiaries in forty-five other countries (*Fortune* 1989b, p. 282; Moody's 1990, p. 398). More than half of its 1989 sales (62.7 billion) were generated outside the United States (*Business Week* 1990, p. 103).

Although TNCs were in existence prior to the twentieth century (colonial trading companies such as the East India Company, the Hudson's Bay Company, and the Virginia Company of London were precursors of the modern TNC), it is only since the 1960s that they have become a major force on the world scene (World Bank 1987, p. 45). Technological innovations in transportation, communication, and information processing have virtually eliminated the constraints of space and time that made international business operations unwieldy and cumbersome in the past. Now it is as feasible to manage an organization with branches and subsidiaries located throughout the world, and have as much up-to-the-minute information, as it is to run an equal-sized organization at just one site.

Table 1 reveals how popular the transnational option has become. It lists manufacturing companies with a minimum of three billion dollars in

TABLE 1
Leading Transnational Corporations

Company	Home Country	1989 Sales (billions)	Sales Outside Home Country	Assets Outside Home Country
NESTLE	Switzerland	32.9*	98%	95%*
SANDOZ	Switzerland	8.6*	96	94
SKF	Sweden	4.1	96	90
HOFFMANN-LA ROCHE	Switzerland	6.7*	96	60
PHILIPS	Netherlands	30.0	94	85*
SMITHKLINE BEECHAM	Britain	7.0	89	75
ABB	Sweden	20.6	85*	NA
ELECTROLUX	Sweden	13.8	83	80
VOLVO	Sweden	14.8	80	30
ICI	Britain	22.1	78	50
MICHELIN	France	9.4	78	NA
HOECHST	W. Germany	27.3	77	NA
UNILEVER	Brit./Neth.	35.3	75*	70*
AIR LIQUIDE	France	5.0	70	66
CANON	Japan	9.4	69	32
NORTHERN TELECOM	Canada	6.1	67	71
SONY	Japan	16.3	66	NA
BAYER	W. Germany	25.8	65	NA
BASF	W. Germany	13.3	65	NA
GILLETTE	U.S.	3.8	65	63
COLGATE	U.S.	5.0	64	47
HONDA	Japan	26.4	63	36
DAIMLER BENZ	W. Germany	45.5	61	NA
IBM	U.S.	62.7	59	NA
NCR	U.S.	6.0	59	41
CPC INTERNAT'L	U.S.	5.1	56	62
COCA-COLA	U.S.	9.0	54	45
DIGITAL	U.S.	12.7	54	44
DOW CHEMICAL	U.S.	17.6	54	45
SAINT-GOBAIN	France	11.6	54	50
XEROX	U.S.	12.4	54	52
CATERPILLAR	U.S.	11.1	53	NA
HEWLETT-PACKARD	U.S.	11.9	53	39
SIEMENS	W. Germany	36.3	51	NA
CORNING	U.S.	3.1*	50*	45*
JOHNSON & JOHNSON	U.S.	9.8	50	48
UNITED TECHNOLOGIES	U.S.	19.8	50	27

NA = not available.
* = *Business Week* estimates.
SOURCE: *Business Week* 1990, p. 103

annual sales, ranked by the percentage of total sales outside the home country. Although considerably more than half of the TNCs listed are not American in origin, it should not be surprising that most are well-known names. It is the nature of transnational enterprise to create such a degree of familiarity. All of the companies in Table 1 generate at least half their sales outside their home country.

A perusal of these companies reveals their economic might. In the 1980s the two hundred largest TNCs in the world produced an astounding 30 percent of total world output, substantially improving upon the impressive 19 percent share in 1970 (Clairmonte and Cavanagh 1984, p. 52). From these figures it is clear that the transnationalization process is far from complete. When the internationalization of finance and the growing role of transnational banks (TNBs) in the integrated global economy is considered, their combined power is truly awesome. Increasingly, TNBs have become active participants in transnational mergers and takeovers. By encouraging their already huge corporate clients to acquire additional corporations, they have made vast profits through the immense loans extended, as well as ending up with even larger clients to service financially. In this way TNBs have played a direct part in the growing concentration and power of TNCs.

The principal location of both TNCs and TNBs is in the developed market economies. Not only are they headquartered there, they also conduct most of their foreign business in these countries. American TNCs, whether measured by foreign-investment stock, sales, or numbers of companies, account for approximately half of all transnational activity; European TNCs make up a little over one-third; and TNCs from Japan comprise about one-tenth (Buckley 1985, p. 200; Clairmonte and Cavanagh 1984, p. 52). With regard to TNBs, the Japanese financial institutions dominate. Of the fifty largest banks, almost half are Japanese, including the nine largest. Together they account for nearly 60 percent of 8.2 trillion in assets. European banks number twenty, and the United States has four banks in the top fifty (*Fortune* 1989a, p. 286).

The move toward integrated transnational investment may be seen as a logical and rational extension on the part of business enterprises to adapt to their environment. Historically, there have been several distinct strategies: (1) expansion in the size of operations to achieve economies of scale; (2) horizontal integration, or the merging of similar firms to increase market share; (3) vertical integration, or the acquiring of firms that either supply raw materials (backward integration) or handle output (forward integration) to attain greater control; (4) spatial dispersion or regional relocation to expand markets; and (5) product diversification to develop new markets (see Chandler 1962, 1990). Establishing an integrated transnational corporation simply represents a new strategy in this evolutionary chain. Furthermore, depending upon how the corporation is set up, and given recent innovations in communications and information-processing technology, it can incorporate all of the other strategies in such a way that the newly structured enterprise has far greater control and a much less restricted market than it had previously.

Table 2 presents a list of reasons why it may be profitable for an organization to become transnational. First, direct cost factors as they pertain to raw materials, labor, and transportation, as well as indirect cost considerations such as tariff barriers and trade restrictions, local tax structures, and various government inducements, obviously loom large when deciding to establish operations overseas. Second, market factors may be equally important in the decision to become transnational. Direct and easy access to local markets unfettered by foreign trade quotas and other legislative restraints can give TNCs an edge over their non-transnational competitors. Finally, the decision to become transnational may hinge on factors related to organizational control. Control over raw materials (backward integration) and markets (forward integration), and achieving sufficient (regional and product) diversification to withstand temporary downturns of the economy, are other reasons that prompt transnational relocation.

Transnational corporations, aided by information and communications technology, conduct

TABLE 2
Reasons for Corporations Becoming Transnational

1. *Cost-related Reasons*
    a. To take advantage of differences in techno-logical development, labor potential, productivity and mentality, captial market and local taxes
    b. Reduction of transport costs
    c. Avoidance of high tariff barriers
    d. To take advantage of local talents when establishing R&D overseas

2. *Sales Volume Reasons*
    a. Foreign middlemen unable to meet financial demands of expanded marketing
    b. For quicker adaptation to local market changes and better adaptation to local conditions
    c. Following important customers abroad
    d. Keeping up with competitors
    e. Persuasion and coercion of foreign governments
    f. To obtain a better international division of labor, larger production runs, and better utilization of available economies of scale
    g. To avoid home country regulations, e.g., fiscal and antitrust legislation

2. *Reasons Related to Risk Factors*
    a. To avoid exclusion from customers' and suppliers' markets promoting forward and backward integration
    b. To counter inflexibility and avoid country-specific recessions
    c. To reduce risks of social and political disruption by establishing operations in a number of host countries

SOURCE: Taylor and Thrift 1982, p. 21.

their business in an innovative and novel fashion. In large part they can avoid or circumvent national laws and regulations. Through various technological and organizational tactics, they have been able to establish themselves in a twilight zone between national boundaries, and thus beyond the law. As Gill and Law (1988, pp. 364–365) conclude, there is a "growing lack of congruence between the 'world economy,' with its tendencies to promote ever-greater levels of economic integration, and an 'international political system' composed of many rival states."

Never before have we confronted a situation in which foreign organizations have been granted license almost as a matter of course to operate freely within the legally defined boundaries of a sovereign state. This, together with the fact that transnational corporations and nation-states are different organizational forms, established for different purposes, administered by different principles, and loyal to different constituencies, means that structural problems are virtually bound to arise. And to the extent that the headquarters of TNCs are located in powerful nation-states while subsidiary branches are located in less developed countries, there develops a parallelism whose symbolism cannot be ignored.

Although it is estimated that only one-fifth to one-quarter of all foreign direct investment takes place in less developed countries (Buckley 1985, pp. 204–205), nevertheless, because of the immense power of many TNCs, great concern has been raised about the impact of TNCs in these countries. It has even been asserted that the TNC as an emergent organizational form represents a distinct threat to the nation-state, and consequently to the very basis upon which the peoples of the world are presently organized (see Evans 1981, p. 199).

It is certainly clear that the emergence of the TNC into the global economy has resulted in a redistribution of the balance of world power. By almost any indicator—gross sales, assets, numbers employed, control over leading-edge technology, ability to influence the world economy— TNCs represent a viable challenge to many nation-states, particularly in the Third World. For example, the annual sales of General Motors, the largest industrial corporation in the world, far surpass the combined annual gross domestic products of Pakistan, Nigeria, Singapore, Chile, Ecuador, and the Sudan (*Fortune* 1989b, pp. 282–283; World Bank 1989, pp. 168–169). Comparisons such as this, plus the fact that TNCs have been seen to interfere in the previously sacrosanct affairs of the nation-state, have resulted in a voluminous literature and debate dealing with the costs and benefits of TNCs in world development.

The fact that the goals of transnational capitalist enterprise and indigenous national government are fundamentally different constitutes the basis of the debate on whether TNCs are an aid or a hindrance to national development in the Third World. According to Biersteker (1978), the major points of contention in this debate are the degree to which TNCs (1) are responsible for a net outflow of capital from less developed countries; (2) displace indigenous production; (3) engage in technology transfer; (4) introduce "inappropriate" (capital-intensive, labor-displacing) technologies; (5) encourage "inappropriate" (elite-oriented) patterns of consumption; (6) produce divisiveness within the local social structure, owing to competing loyalties to TNC and nation-state; and (7) exacerbate the existing unequal distribution of income.

Critical theorists, employing dependency, colonialist, nationalist, and/or Marxist perspectives, basically argue that transnational corporate investment works to the detriment of less developed countries on each of the above seven points. "Although not always explicitly stated, critical writers assume that there are feasible alternatives to the multinational corporation, in the form of state corporations, an indigenous private sector, or some combination of both" (Biersteker 1978, p. 2). On the other hand, conventional and neoconventional theorists assert that foreign direct investment introduces essential, but missing, ingredients of Third World development in the form of capital, technology, managerial skills, and organizational expertise. They conclude that the net effect of TNCs on host countries is positive.

Whether one adopts a critical or a conventional perspective, it is certain that the introduction of immensely powerful transnational organizations into less developed countries does cause great social upheaval. Furthermore, the impact of these corporate giants not only is great in its initial magnitude, it is prolonged in terms of its effects. In the view of the U.S. Tariff Commission, "It is beyond dispute that the spread of multinational business ranks with the development of the steam engine, electric power, and the automobile as one of the major events of economic history" (cited in Lall and Streeton 1977, p. 15).

(SEE ALSO: *Corporate Organizations; Global Systems Analysis; Industrialization in Less Developed Countries*)

REFERENCES

Biersteker, Thomas J. 1978 *Distortion or Development? Contending Perspectives on the Multinational Corporation.* Cambridge, Mass.: MIT Press.

Buckley, Peter J. 1985 "Testing Theories of the Multinational Enterprise." In Peter J. Buckley and Mark Casson, *The Economic Theory of the Multinational Enterprise.* London: Macmillan.

Business Week 1990 "The Stateless Corporation." May 14:98–105.

Chandler, Alfred D., Jr. 1962 *Strategy and Structure: Chapters in the History of Industrial Enterprise.* Cambridge, Mass.: MIT Press.

———1990 *Scale and Scope: The Dynamics of Industrial Capitalism.* Cambridge, Mass.: Belknap Press of Harvard University Press.

Clairmonte, Frederick F., and John H. Cavanagh 1984 "Transnational Corporations and Global Markets: Changing Power Relations." In Pradip K. Ghosh, ed., *Multinational Corporations and Third World Development.* Westport, Conn.: Greenwood Press.

Evans, Peter B. 1981 "Recent Research of Multinational Corporations." *Annual Review of Sociology* 7:199–223.

Fortune 1989a "The World's Biggest Commerical Banks." 120(3):286.

———1989b "The World's Biggest Industrial Corporations." 120(3):280–283.

Gill, Stephen, and David Law 1988 *The Global Political Economy.* Baltimore: Johns Hopkins University Press.

Lall, Sanjaya, and P. Streeten 1977 *Foreign Investment, Transnationals, and Developing Countries.* London: Macmillan.

Moody's 1990 "International Business Machines Corporation." In *Moody's Industrial Manual,* vol. 1. New York: Moody's Investors Service.

Taylor, M. J., and N. J. Thrift 1982 "Models of Corporate Development and the Multinational Corporation." In Michael Taylor and Nigel Thrift, eds., *The Geography of Multinationals: Studies in the Spatial Development and Economic Consequences of Multinational Corporations.* London: Croom Helm.

World Bank 1987 *World Development Report 1987*. New York: Oxford University Press.

——1989 *World Development Report 1989*. New York: Oxford University Press.

R. ALAN HEDLEY

TRANSSEXUALISM *See* Sexual Orientation.

TRANSVESTISM *See* Sexual Orientation.

TYPOLOGIES A typology is a multidimensional classification. The study of typological procedures is impeded by the plethora of terms, some of which are used interchangeably. *Classification* can be defined as the grouping of entities on the basis of similarity. For example, humans can be classified into female and male. A related term is *taxonomy*. According to Simpson (1961, p. 11), "taxonomy . . . is the theoretical study of classification, including its bases, principles, procedures, and rules." Interestingly, the term *classification* has two meanings: One can speak both of the process of classification and its end product, which is a classification. The terms *classification, typology,* and *taxonomy* are all used widely and somewhat interchangeably in sociology.

Any classification must be mutually exclusive and exhaustive. This requires that there should be one cell (but only one) for each case. For example, if humans are being classified by sex, this requires that every case should be placed in a cell (either male or female) but that *no* case can be placed in more than one cell (and no intermediate cases are allowed). It is further assumed that the bases or dimensions for classification (such as sex) are clear and important (see Tiryakian 1968).

A type is one cell of a full typology. In sociology, emphasis has often been placed upon one or a few types rather than on the full typology. The study of types developed largely as a verbal tradition in sociology and lately has become merged with a more recently developed quantitative approach.

In the verbal tradition, types were often defined as mental constructs or concepts, as contrasted with empirically derived entities. Stinchcombe (1968, p. 43, original emphasis) says, "a *type concept* in scientific discourse is a concept which is constructed out of a *combination of the values of several variables.*" Lazarsfeld (1937, p. 120) says that "one is safe in saying that the concept of type is always used in referring to special compounds of attributes." The variables that combine to form a type must be correlated or "connected to each other" (Stinchcombe 1968, pp. 44–45).

One important function of a type is to serve as a criterion point (for comparative purposes) for the study of other types or empirical phenomena. In this case only a single type is formulated. The most famous single-type formulation is Weber's ideal type:

An ideal type is formed by the one-sided accentuation *of one or more points of view. . . . In its conceptual purity, this mental construct* (Gedankenbild) *cannot be found empirically anywhere in reality. It is a utopia. Historical research faces the task of determining in each individual case the extent to which this ideal-construct approximates to or diverges from reality, to what extent for example, the economic structure of a certain city is to be classified as a "city economy."* (Weber 1947, p. 90, original emphasis)

This strategy has been criticized. Martindale is startled by the suggestion that "we compare actual individuals with the (admittedly imaginary) ideal typical individuals to see how much they deviate from them. This is nothing but a form of intellectual acrobatics, for actual individuals ought to deviate from the ideal type just as much as one made them deviate in the first place" (Martindale 1960, p. 382).

Seizing upon Weber's statement that the pure ideal type "cannot be found empirically anywhere in reality," critics view the ideal type as hypothetical and thus without a fixed position, rendering it useless as a criterion point. A more realistic interpretation is that the ideal type represents a type that *could* be found empirically—it is simply that the purest case is the one most useful as a criterion, and this purest case is unlikely to be found empirically. As an example, a proof specimen of a coin is the best criterion for classifying or grading other coins, but it is not found empirically in the sense of being in circulation. If it were circulated, its features would soon be worn to the extent that its value for comparison with other coins would be greatly diminished.

The strategy of the ideal type is a sound one. Its logic is rather simple, and the confusion surrounding it is unfortunate, perhaps in part due to the translation of Weber's work. The genius of the ideal type is its parsimony. Instead of using a large full typology (say of 144 cells, many of which may turn out to be empirically null or empty), a researcher can utilize instead a single ideal type. Then, instead of dealing needlessly with many null cells, the researcher need only fill in cells for which there are actual empirical cases and only as these cases are encountered. The ideal type is an accentuated or magnified version (or purest form) of the type. Although rarely found empirically in this pure form, the ideal type is a good comparison point. It usually represents the highest value on each of the intercorrelated variables or the end point of the continuum. While one could use the middle of the continuum as a referent (just as one uses the mean or median), it is convenient and perhaps clearer to use the end point (just as one measures from the end of a ruler rather than from its middle or some other intermediate point).

Another single type that is used as a criterion is the constructed type. McKinney (1966, p. 3, original emphasis) defines the constructed type as "a *purposive, planned selection, abstraction, combination, and (sometimes) accentuation of a set of criteria with empirical referents that serves as a basis for comparison of empirical cases.*" The constructed type is simply a more general form of the ideal type.

In addition to formulations using a single type, there are also formulations using two or more types. One strategy is the use of two "polar" types (as in the North and South poles). These serve as two bracketing criteria for the comparison of cases. One famous set of types is Tönnies's (1957) *Gemeinschaft* and *Gesellschaft* ("community" and "society"). Another is introvert and extrovert. Still others are primary and secondary groups and localistic and cosmopolitan communities (see McKinney 1966, p. 101, for these and other examples).

One problem with the common practice of using only a single type or a few types is that the underlying correlated dimensions upon which they are based may not be clear. In some cases it is possible to make these dimensions clear and to extend them all to form a property space or attribute space. This is a set of axes representing the full range of values on each dimension. Then, the existence of other potential related types, which were not originally formulated, can be discerned. This process of extending the full property space and the resulting full typology from a single type or a few types is called *substruction* and was developed by Lazarsfeld (1937; Barton 1955). As an example, Barton (1955, pp. 51–52) performed a substruction in which the attributes underlying the four types of folkways, mores, law, and custom were extended to form a full property space. Barton found three underlying dimensions of the four types ("how originated," "how enforced," and "strength of group feeling") and combined these to form the property space.

The opposite of substruction is *reduction*. Reduction is used where one has a full typology that is unmanageable because of its size. The three basic forms of reduction presented by Lazarsfeld (1937, p. 127) are functional, arbitrary numerical, and pragmatic. Lazarsfeld's functional reduction consists of discarding from the typology all empirically null and thus unnecessary cells.

The second form of reduction is arbitrary numerical. Lazarsfeld (1937, p. 128) provides an example. He says that in constructing an index of housing conditions, one might weight plumbing without central heat or a refrigerator equal to the other two without plumbing. Coding existence of an attribute by 1 and lack of it by 0, and taking variables in this order (plumbing, central heat, refrigerator), Lazarsfeld is saying that $(1, 0, 0) = (0, 1, 1)$. Thus, two previously different three-dimensional cells are equated and so reduced to one.

Lazarsfeld's third form of reduction is pragmatic reduction. It consists of collapsing contiguous cells together to make one larger (but generally more heterogeneous) cell. As Lazarsfeld (1937, p. 128) says, "in the case of pragmatic reduction, certain groups of combinations are contracted to one class in view of the research purpose." For examples of these three forms of reduction, see Bailey (1973).

With the rigor of Lazarsfeld's work as a notable exception, it can be said that most work in the typological tradition has been generally qualitative. Blalock, commenting on McKinney's (1966) constructive typology, says:

> He [McKinney] also claims that there is nothing inherently anti-quantitative in the use of typologies. He notes that historically, however, researchers skilled in the use of typologies have not been statistically or mathematically inclined, and vice-versa. This may be one of the reasons for the existing gap between sociological theory and research. (Blalock, 1969, p. 33)

One persistent problem in the qualitative typological tradition has been the confusion over the status of the type as either a heuristic device, a mental construct, or an empirical entity. Winch (1947) distinguished between heuristic and empirical types. He said that heuristic types are conceptually derived and may not have empirical examples. Empirical types, on the other hand, result solely from data analysis, without prior conceptualization. A persistent problem with the conceptual types, such as the ideal type, has been the problem of inappropriate reification. If a type is a construct, concept, or model, it may not be found empirically but is rather designed merely to be heuristically used in developing theory. However, there is often a tendency over time to reify the type or act as though it is actually found empirically. Figure 1 shows that the qualitative tradition has both heuristic and empirical types, while the quantitative tradition (discussed below) has primarily empirical types, as its types are derived through data analysis.

	Qualitative	Quantitative
Heuristic	Ideal type	Probably null
Empirical	Ethnographic types	Types derived from cluster analysis or numerical taxonomy

Figure 1
A Typology of Typologies

In other cases within the qualitative typological tradition, types are meant as empirical phenomena rather than as heuristic devices. This is particularly true in the area of social ethnography or field research, where researchers eschew statistical analysis but analyze data resulting from field studies by developing typologies based on observations recorded in their field notes (see Spradley and McCurdy 1972). Typologies in this case take the form of tables with names or labels in the cells rather than frequencies of occurrence as in statistical tables. Here, the labels or types are generally inductively or empirically derived through intense study of groups in the field. However, even here there may be a distinction between types as derived by the researcher and those types actually used by the people being studied. For example, the types that tramps identify among themselves (mission stiff, bindle stiff) may be different from the types identified by researchers or the lay public (bums, winos, homeless persons). For a discussion of taxonomies in ethnographic research, as well as a number of examples of actual taxonomies (including the tramp example), see Spradley and McCurdy (1972).

Computerization has brought a whole new era of quantitative typology construction, which now coexists with the older qualitative typological tradition. This new approach is often called numerical taxonomy, cluster analysis, or pattern recognition (see Sneath and Sokal 1973; Bailey 1974). In contrast to the earlier verbal approach, which largely dealt with concepts and mental constructs, this newer quantitative approach is largely empirical and inductive. It begins with a data set and derives empirical types from the data through a variety of quantitative procedures, many of them computerized.

This newer statistical approach to classification can be elucidated through the monothetic–polythetic distinction. A typology is monothetic if possession of a unique set of features is both necessary and sufficient for identifying a specimen as belonging to a particular cell of the typology. That is, each feature is necessary and the set is sufficient. Thus, no specimen can be assigned to a particular type unless it possesses all features (and no others) required of that type. This means that all specimens in a given type are identical in every way (at least in all features specified).

In contrast, a polythetic typology is constructed by grouping together those individuals within a sample that have the greatest number of shared features. No single feature is either necessary or sufficient (Sokal and Sneath 1963, p. 14). The objects or specimens are grouped so as to maximize overall similarity within each group. In a polythetic type, each individual possesses a large number of the classifying properties, and each property is possessed by a large number of individuals. In the case where *no* single property is possessed by every individual in the group, the type is said to be fully polythetic.

While a verbal type (such as the ideal type) may be purely homogeneous (i.e., monothetic), it is unlikely that an empirically constructed type will be monothetic (except for some divisively derived types), especially if it involves a large number of cases grouped on a large number of variables. Thus, most empirically constructed types are polythetic, and some may be fully polythetic, without even a single feature being common to all members of the group.

A basic distinction for all empirical classification techniques is whether one groups objects or variables. The former is known as Q-analysis and the latter as R-analysis (Sokal and Sneath 1963, p. 124). In R-analysis, one computes coefficients (either similarity or distance coefficients) down the columns of the basic score matrix, which includes objects and variables (see Table 1 in Bailey 1972). In Q-analysis, one correlates rows. The interior data cells are the same in any case, and one form is the simple matrix transposition of the other. The difference is that Q-analysis correlates the objects (e.g., persons), while R-analysis correlates the variables (e.g., age). While Q-analysis is the most common form in biology (see Sneath and Sokal 1973), it is rarely used in sociology (for an example, see Butler and Adams 1966). One problem is that Q-analysis requires a small sample of cases measured on a large number of variables, while R-analysis requires a large sample of cases with a smaller number of variables. Biology has the former sort of data; sociology the latter.

Further, most sociologists have simply had little experience with Q-analysis. Most statistical analysis in sociology is concerned with studying relationships between two or more variables, with few studies making inferences concerning individuals rather than variables. Thus, the very notion of correlating individuals is undoubtedly alien to many sociologists.

Once the researcher has decided whether to pursue Q-analysis or R-analysis, the next step is to decide which measure of similarity to use. A researcher can measure similarity either directly, with a correlation coefficient, or indirectly, with a distance coefficient. While similarity coefficients show how close together two objects or variables are in the property space, distance coefficients show how far apart they are in the property space. For discussion of these measures, see Bailey (1974).

The next task of empirical typology construction is to parsimoniously group the cases into homogeneous types. There are two chief ways to proceed. One can envision all *N* cases as forming a single type. This is maximally parsimonious but also maximizes within-group or internal variance. Grouping proceeds "from above" by dividing the cases into smaller groups that are more homogeneous. This is called the *divisive strategy*. Divisive classification generally proceeds by dividing the group on the basis of similarity on one or more variables, either simultaneously or sequentially. According to Sokal and Sneath (1963, p. 16), divisive classification is "inevitably largely monothetic."

The alternative strategy (the *agglomerative strategy*) is to envision the *N* cases as forming *N* separate groups of one case each. Then, each group is homogeneous (including only a single case), but parsimony is minimal. The strategy here is "classification from below" by agglomerating or grouping the most similar cases together, yielding some loss of internal homogeneity but gaining parsimony (as *N* groups are generally too un-

wieldy). Unlike divisively formed types, agglomeratively formed types are generally polythetic and often fully polythetic.

The basic typological strategy is very straightforward and logically simple for divisive methods. All that one must do is to partition the set of cases in all possible ways and choose that grouping that maximizes internal homogeneity in a sufficiently small number of clusters. The problem is that the computation is prohibitive, even for a modest number of cases measured on a modest number of variables.

A basic problem with empirically derived typologies is that they are generally static. This is simply because the measures of similarity or distance that are used are synchronic rather than diachronic. While a problem, it should be noted that this is not a problem unique to classification but rather is shared by most all of sociological analysis. Further, it is possible to deal with this by using diachronic data such as change coefficients or time series data.

Despite procedural differences, there are clear congruences between the qualitative and quantitative typological approaches. The ideal type is essentially monothetic, as are some types produced by quantitative divisive procedures. Quantitative procedures produce types that are polythetic, even fully polythetic. The results of quantitative procedures are generally not full typologies but reduced forms comprising fewer than the potential maximum number of types. Such polythetic types can be seen as analogous to the result of subjecting full monothetic typologies to reduction (either pragmatic or arbitrary numerical). Thus, contemporary typologists meet the need for reduction by using quantitative methods. Any correlational method of typology construction is by definition a method of functional reduction.

Further, the method will usually perform pragmatic reduction along with the functional. Remember that pragmatic reduction collapses monothetic cells. The correlation coefficients utilized in typological methods are never perfect. The lower the correlations, the more diverse are the individuals in a group. Placing diverse individuals in one group is tantamount to collapsing monothetic cells via pragmatic reduction. Thus, there are two basic avenues for constructing reduced types: Begin with monothetic types (such as ideal types) and subject them to the various forms of reduction to yield polythetic types, or construct polythetic types directly through quantitative methods. Thus, the qualitative and quantitative procedures can produce similar results.

Given the breadth and diversity of sociological typologies (for example, from quantitative to qualitative procedures and from heuristic to empirical types), it is not surprising that there have been a number of criticisms of typologies. Some alleged problems are that typologies: are not mutually exclusive and exhaustive; are treated as ends in themselves rather than as means to an end; are not parsimonious; are based upon arbitrary and ad hoc criteria; are essentially static; rely upon dichotomized variables rather than internally measured variables; yield types that are subject to reification; and are basically descriptive rather than explanatory or predictive. All of these can be problems but are also generally relatively easy for a knowledgeable typologist to avoid. The ones that cannot be easily avoided (such as the problem of cross-sectional data) are often seen to be general problems for sociology as a whole and are not specific to typology construction.

Even if pitfalls remain, the merits of carefully constructed typologies are well worth the effort. One of the chief merits of a typology is parsimony. The researcher who is overwhelmed by thousands or even millions of individual cases can work comfortably with them when they are grouped into a few main types. A related merit is the emphasis on bringing simplicity and order out of complexity and chaos. Focus on the relative homogeneity of types provides an emphasis on order, as contrasted with the emphasis on diversity and complexity that is paramount in untyped phenomena. A third chief merit of a full typology is its sheer comprehensiveness. There is no other tool available that can show not only all relevant dimensions but the relationships between them, and the categories created by the intersections. Such a typology shows the entire range of every variable and all of their confluences. A fourth merit (as noted) is a typology's use of a type or types for comparative purposes. A fifth merit is a typology's use as a heuristic tool to highlight the relevant theoretical dimensions of a type. A sixth merit is a typology's ability to show which cells have empirical examples and which are empirically null. This can aid in hypothesis testing, especially when a large number of variables have a small number of values that actually occur (Stinchcombe 1968, p. 47). A seventh merit is a typology's ability to combine two or more variables in such a way that interaction effects can be analyzed (Stinchcombe 1968, pp. 46–47).

A well-constructed typology can work miracles in bringing order out of chaos. It can transform the overwhelming complexity of an apparent eclectic congeries of numerous apparently diverse cases into a well-ordered set of a few rather homogeneous types clearly situated in a property space of a few important dimensions. A sound typology forms a firm foundation and provides direction for both theorizing and empirical research. No other tool has such power to simplify life for the sociologist. Ironically, due to its breadth and complexity, the field of typology construction itself, ranging as it does from qualitative to quantitative and from heuristic to empirical, begs for consolidation and simplification.

Fortunately, the key to integrating the field is at hand. It lies in the recognition of the basic congruence between the qualitative and quantitative approaches to typology construction. That is, types derived qualitatively by first constructing a full monothetic typology and then reducing it (via pragmatic or arbitrary numerical reduction) to a set of polythetic types are *equivalent* in form to the empirical polythetic types that are directly constructed from data sets via quantitative procedures of cluster analysis or numerical taxonomy. This basic equivalence turns an apparently broad and complex field into a rather narrow one.

The task for the future is the further study and elaboration of this crucial nexus between the qualitative and statistical approaches. This requires effort from sociologists having both theoretical and statistical talents. McKinney (1966, p.

49) recognizes the "complementary relationship of quantitative and typological procedures" and advocates "the emergence of a number of social scientists who are procedurally competent in both typology and statistical techniques." Costner (1972, p. xi) also recognizes the basic unity of the qualitative and quantitative approaches to typology construction.

For further information on typologies, see Capecchi (1966), Sokal and Sneath (1963), Sneath and Sokal (1973), Bailey (1973; 1974; 1983; 1989), Hudson and Associates (1982), Aldenderfer and Blashfield (1984), and Kreps (1989).

(SEE ALSO: *Levels of Analysis; Tabular Analysis*)

REFERENCES

Aldenderfer, Mark S., and Roger K. Blashfield 1984 *Cluster Analysis.* Beverly Hills, Calif.: Sage.

Bailey, Kenneth D. 1972 "Polythetic Reduction of Monothetic Property Space." In Herbert L. Costner, ed., *Sociological Methodology 1972.* San Francisco: Jossey-Bass.

———1973 "Monothetic and Polythetic Typologies and Their Relationship to Conceptualization, Measurement, and Scaling." *American Sociological Review* 38:18–33.

———1974 "Cluster Analysis." In David R. Heise, ed., *Sociological Methodology 1975.* San Francisco: Jossey-Bass.

———1983 "Sociological Classification and Cluster Analysis." *Quality and Quantity* 17:251–268.

———1989 "Taxonomy and Disaster: Prospects and Problems." *International Journal of Mass Emergencies and Disasters* 7:419–431.

Barton, Allen H. 1955 "The Concept of Property Space in Social Research." In Paul F. Lazarsfeld and Morris Rosenberg, eds., *The Language of Social Research.* New York: Free Press.

Blalock, Herbert M. 1969 *Theory Construction: From Verbal to Mathematical Formulations.* Englewood Cliffs, N.J.: Prentice-Hall.

Butler, Edgar W., and Stuart N. Adams 1966 "Typologies of Delinquent Girls: Some Alternative Approaches." *Social Forces* 44:401–407.

Capecchi, Vittorio 1966 "Typologies in Relation to Mathematical Models." *Ikon* Suppl. No. 58:1–62.

Costner, Herbert L. 1972 "Prologue." In Herbert L. Costner, ed., *Sociological Methodology 1972.* San Francisco: Jossey-Bass.

Hudson, Herschel C., and Associates, eds. 1982 *Classifying Social Data.* San Francisco: Jossey-Bass.

Kreps, Gary A., ed. 1989 "The Boundaries of Disaster Research: Taxonomy and Comparative Research" (Special Issue). *International Journal of Mass Emergencies and Disasters* 7:213–431.

Lazarsfeld, Paul F. 1937 "Some Remarks on the Typological Procedures in Social Research." *Zeitschrift für Sozialforschung* 6:119–139.

Martindale, Don 1960 *The Nature and Types of Sociological Theory.* Boston: Houghton Mifflin.

McKinney, John C. 1966 *Constructive Typology and Social Theory.* New York: Appleton, Century, Crofts.

Simpson, George G. 1961 *Principles of Animal Taxonomy.* New York: Columbia University Press.

Sneath, Peter H. A., and Robert R. Sokal 1973 *Numerical Taxonomy: The Principles and Practice of Numerical Classification.* San Francisco: Freeman.

Sokal, Robert R., and Peter H. A. Sneath 1963 *Principles of Numerical Taxonomy.* San Francisco: Freeman.

Spradley, James P., and David W. McCurdy 1972 *The Cultural Experience: Ethnography in Complex Society.* Chicago: Science Research Associates.

Stinchcombe, Arthur L. 1968 *Constructing Social Theories.* New York: Harcourt, Brace, and World.

Tiryakian, Edward A. 1968 "Typologies." In David L. Sills, ed., *International Encyclopedia of the Social Sciences.* New York: Macmillan and Free Press.

Tönnies, Ferdinand 1957 *Gemeinschaft und Gesellschaft,* trans. and ed. C. P. Loomis. East Lansing: Michigan State University Press.

Weber, Max 1947 *Theory of Social and Economic Organization.* A. R. Henderson and Talcott Parsons, trans., and Talcott Parsons, ed. New York: Free Press.

Winch, Robert F. 1947 "Heuristic and Empirical Typologies: A Job for Factor Analysis." *American Sociological Review* 12:68–75.

KENNETH D. BAILEY

U

UNIONS *See* Labor Unions and Movements.

URBAN ECONOMIC TRANSITIONS

Urban economic transitions have local, regional, and global dimensions. For each of these dimensions, the type and number of transitions that might be considered vary markedly, predicated on one's substantive interest, conceptual framework, and the degree of detail desired. Emphasis here will be on the economic restructuring of cities within an ecological framework (Hawley 1981; Frisbie and Kasarda 1988; Micklin and Choldin 1984) that has dominated much of the social science literature since the 1960s. Competing perspectives and challenges to this more-mainstream framework are considered as well.

URBAN TRANSITIONS IN THE UNITED STATES

The evolution of economic functions of the oldest and largest cities of the United States well illustrates the urban transition process. These cities (e.g., Boston, New York, Philadelphia) were at the forefront of the development and restructuring of the nation's economy. They spawned America's Industrial Revolution, generating massive numbers of manufacturing and other blue-collar jobs that served to attract and economically upgrade millions of migrants. These cities were later instrumental in transforming the U.S. economy from one centered on producing goods to one centered on providing basic consumer services; most recently, they have likewise played a role in the shift from a basic service economy to one of information processing and multinational corporate control.

The initial economic role of these cities may be traced to their colonial past. They originated as mercantile centers, funneling raw materials from their immediate hinterlands to the nascent metropolitan economy of eighteenth-century Europe. As America entered the nineteenth century, regional and national markets were constrained by limited transport systems, and most urban-goods production was of a cottage industry and handicraft form.

Railroad, highway, and canal systems that developed during the first fifty years of the nineteenth century substantially broadened urban access to the country's inland resources. At the same time, steam-powered machinery and mass-production technologies were introduced that, together with entrepreneurial innovations in credit, banking, and finance capitalism, gave rise to large corporate business organizations and their primary units of production—factories. With high domestic fertility rates and increased immigration from abroad providing both an expanded domestic market for manufactured goods and abundant cheap labor to staff the factories, all the requisites for the rise of America's industrial cities were in place.

Industrial cities developed around the terminal points of rail- and waterways, where coal and raw materials were received and finished products shipped. Given the primitive state of intraurban transportation technologies, complementary units that serviced factories or that used their by-products were located as close to the factories as possible, as were storage warehouses and wholesalers. Workers employed by the factories, service shops, and warehouses clustered tightly within walking distance of their place of employment. As late as 1899, the average commuting distance of workers in New York City from their home to their work site was roughly two blocks (Palen 1975, p. 53).

During the first half of the twentieth century, a number of innovations in transportation, communication, and production technologies markedly reduced the locational advantages the older, compactly structured cities had previously held for manufacturing and distributing activities. Manufacturers and wholesalers soon found that older, urban street patterns were not conducive to automobile and truck movement, and adequate land was not available within the city for newer assembly-line factories and automated freight-transfer systems. At the same time, development of suburban highway systems, widespread automobile ownership, and increased dependence by manufacturers and wholesalers on trucking for receiving and shipping made uncongested suburban sites become attractive. By 1960, further advances in transportation and communication technologies and growing cost competition from outlying areas made the larger, older cities almost obsolete as locations for large-scale manufacturing and warehousing facilities. An exodus of blue-collar jobs from the cities began and has continued ever since.

The urban exodus of many goods-producing blue-collar service jobs was matched with a massive movement of middle-income city residents to the suburbs. Retail and consumer-service establishments followed their suburbanizing clientele. Despite such pervasive deconcentration, a number of economic countertrends occurred in major cities. Advertising agencies, brokerage houses, management-consulting firms, financial institutions, and legal, accounting, communication, and other businesses engaged in coordination and control replaced many downtown department stores and other more traditional urban establishments. The central business districts also experienced a remarkable growth of high-rise administrative office buildings. Even with advances in telecommunications technologies, many headquarters office functions still require a complement of legal, financial, public relations, and other specialized business services that are most accessible at the city's core. Moreover, unlike manufacturing, wholesale trade, and retail activities, which typically have large space-per-employee requirements and whose products cannot be moved efficiently in a vertical direction, most managerial, clerical, professional, and business-service functions are highly space compact and their basic product (information) can be transferred as efficiently vertically as it can horizontally. Thus, people who process information can be stacked, layer after layer, in downtown office towers, with resulting proximity actually increasing the productivity of those whose activities require an extensive amount of nonroutine, face-to-face interaction.

ALTERNATIVE EXPLANATIONS

While there is little disagreement among scholars of urbanization, concerning the types of economic transitions that have occurred in cities, the same cannot be said for interpretation of their causes. Critical theorists (e.g., Castells 1977; Gordon 1984; Gottdiener 1985; Harvey 1975) contend that urban ecology as well as mainstream economics and geography have: (1) ignored the powerful role of the state (allied with business interests) in urban transitions; (2) premised their analyses on a form of technological reductionism; and (3) taken a too-benign view of urban development. Specifically, mainstream theory is criticized for focusing on changing transportation and production technologies as causes of urban industrial deconcentration, rather than capitalists' efforts to control labor unrest, as well as mortgage and highway subsidies provided by the state (Gordon 1977; Gottdiener 1985). In addition, demand forces are heavily discounted as explanations of the explosion of suburban development, in favor of supply-side forces created by developers and real estate interests aided and abetted by government (Feagin 1983).

Similarly, the growth of corporate administrative activities in central cities are viewed not as the result of advantages of centralization and proximity for certain higher-order service functions, but rather of the willingness of the state to accede to the goal of real estate interests to profit from the turnover of land and/or to ameliorate a deteriorating situation when speculation in land creates a crisis of overinvestment and urban blight (Gottdiener 1985). Somewhat analogous perceptions of an alliance between government and capitalists in generating urban economic transitions, often at the expense of the working class and poor, are found in the writings of other critical theorists (e.g., Domhoff 1983; Feagin 1983, 1985; Logan and Molotch 1987).

COMPARATIVE AND HISTORICAL STAGES

Friedrichs (1982, 1988) has shown that transitions like those described for U.S. cities have occurred in major Western and Eastern European cities, with a ten- to twenty-year lag behind the United States. Corresponding patterns have also been documented for Cairo, Mexico City, São Paulo, and Tokyo (Dogan and Kasarda 1988a; 1988b).

Though important and often unique differences can be observed in cross-national and historical comparisons of urban economic transitions, a general sequence of stages does appear to fit many cases. This sequential process moves from: (1) a handicraft and lower-order service structure; to (2) a more formal commercial-industrial based structure; to (3) an information-processing, higher-order service structure. In the first (preindustrial) stage, small-scale, family-owned enterprises utilizing labor-intensive technologies predominate along with traditional sectors such as artisans, petty trade, food vending, and other lower-order services.

In the second stage (where many major cities of the Third World are now), economic activities are partially transformed from family enterprises to corporate production units, capital grows in importance relative to labor, and wage and salary employment expands. In this stage, cities specializing in manufacturing activities grow rapidly. The manufacturing sector, as a powerful export-based industry, has multiplier effects, creating new job opportunities and attracting waves of rural migrants seeking employment.

As the national economy matures and transportation networks expand, competition from lower-cost outlying and offshore sites reduces urban manufacturing employment. During this third stage, large-scale production units move to peripheral areas or abroad and are replaced by knowledge-intensive firms in the core employing well-educated, skilled persons. Higher-order, knowledge-based services are exported nationally and internationally as the functions of major cities gradually transform from goods-processing and lower-order consumer services to information-processing and higher-order producer services.

Again, while general agreement may exist on the descriptive nature of these stages, controversy on their causes and consequences continues among mainstream and critical theorists (see Armstrong and McGee 1985; Kasarda and Crenshaw 1991; Portes and Walton 1981).

(SEE ALSO: *Cities; Suburbanization; Urbanization; Urban Sociology)*

REFERENCES

Armstrong, Warwick, and T. G. McGee 1985 *Theaters of Accumulation: Studies in Asian and Latin American Urbanization*. London: Methuen.

Castells, Manuel 1977 *The Urban Question: A Marxist Approach.* Cambridge: MIT Press.

Dogan, Mattei, and John D. Kasarda (eds.) 1988a *The Metropolis Era.* Vol. I, *A World of Giant Cities.* Beverly Hills, Calif.: Sage.

———— (eds.) 1988b *The Metropolis Era.* Vol. II, *Mega-Cities.* Beverly Hills, Calif.: Sage.

Domhoff, William G. 1983 *Who Rules America Now?* Englewood Cliffs, N.J.: Prentice-Hall.

Feagin, Joe R. 1983 *The Urban Real Estate Game.* Englewood Cliffs, N.J.: Prentice-Hall.

———— 1985 "The Global Context of Metropolitan Growth: Houston and the Oil Industry." *American Journal of Sociology* 90:1204–1230.

Friedrichs, Jurgen 1982 *Spatial Disparities and Social Behavior.* Hamburg, Germany: Christians Verlag.

———— 1988 "Large Cities in Eastern Europe." In Mattei Dogan and John Kasarda, eds., *The Metropolis Era.* Vol. I, *A World of Giant Cities.* Beverly Hills, Calif.: Sage.

Frisbie, W. Parker, and John D. Kasarda 1988 "Spatial Processes." In Neil J. Smelser, ed., *Handbook of Modern Sociology.* Beverly Hills, Calif.: Sage.

Gordon, David 1977 "Class Struggle and the Stages of Urban Development." In D. Perry and A. Watkins, eds., *The Rise of the Sunbelt Cities.* Beverly Hills, Calif.: Sage.

———— 1984 "Capitalist Development and the History of American Cities." In William K. Tabb and Larry Sawets, eds., *Marxism and the Metropolis.* New York: Oxford University Press.

Gottdiener, M. 1983 "Understanding Metropolitan Deconcentration: A Class of Paradigms." *Social Science Quarterly* 64:227–246.

———— 1985 *The Social Production of Urban Space.* Austin: University of Texas Press.

Harvey, David 1975 "The Political Economy of Urbanization in Advanced Capitalist Societies." In G. Gappert and H. Rose, eds., *The Social Economy of Cities.* Beverly Hills, Calif.: Sage.

Hawley, Amos H. 1981 *Urban Society: An Ecological Approach.* New York: Wiley.

Kasarda, John D., and Edward Crenshaw 1991 "Third World Urbanization: Dimensions, Theories, Determinants." *Annual Review of Sociology* 17:467–501.

Logan, John R., and Harvey L. Molotch 1987 *Urban Fortunes: The Political Economy of Place.* Berkeley: University of California Press.

Micklin, Michael, and Harvey Choldin (eds.) 1984 *Modern Sociological Human Ecology.* Boulder Colo.: Westview Press.

Palen, J. John 1975 *The Urban World.* New York: McGraw-Hill.

Portes, Alejandro, and John Walton 1981 *Labor, Class and the International System.* New York: Academic.

JOHN D. KASARDA

URBANIZATION Urbanization is the process of expansion in the entire system of interrelationships by which a population maintains itself in its habitat (Hawley 1981, p. 12). The most evident consequences of the process, and the most common measures of it, are an increase in the number of people at points of population concentration, an increase in the number of points at which population is concentrated, or both (Tisdale 1942). Theories of urbanization attempt to explain how human settlement patterns change as technology expands the scale of social systems.

Because technological regimes, population growth mechanisms, and environmental contingencies change over time and differ in different regions of the world, variations in the pattern of distribution of human settlements can generally be understood by attending to these related processes. In the literature on urbanization, interest in organizational forms of systems of cities is complemented by interest in how growth is accommodated within cities themselves through changes in density gradients, in the location of socially meaningful population subgroups, and in patterns of urban activity. Although the expansion of cities has been the historical focus for describing the urbanization process, revolutionary developments in transportation, communication, and information technology since 1950 have expanded the scale of urban systems and focused attention on the broader system of organization within which cities emerge and grow.

Much of the research on the urbanization process is descriptive in nature, emphasizing the identification and measurement of patterns of change in demographic and social organization within a territorial frame of reference. Territorially circumscribed environments employed as units of analysis include administrative units (villages, cities, counties, states, nations), population concentrations (places, agglomerations, urbanized areas), and networks of interdependency (neighborhoods, metropolitan areas, daily urban systems, city systems, earth).

A *city* is an administratively defined unit of territory containing "a relatively large, dense and permanent settlement of socially heterogeneous individuals" (Wirth 1938, p. 1). *Urban* refers to a set of specialized, nonagricultural activities that are characteristic of, but not exclusive to, city dwellers. A ruling class with a capacity for taxation and capital accumulation and writing and its application to predictive sciences, artistic expression, and trade for vital materials are the kinds of specialized activities necessary to the definition of the emergence of a truly urban place (Childe 1950). Specialized activities such as administration, commerce, and manufacturing have historically been centered in cities, but the scale of the system of interdependence and exchange involved in such activity can range from the immediate hinterland of the earliest known cities to the entire world of today. Urban activities and associated outlooks of people engaged in them are no longer found only in the city.

The extent to which dispersed population is involved in urban systems is quite variable. An estimated 90 percent of the American population now lives within a Daily Urban System (DUS). These units are constructed from counties that are allocated to economic centers on the basis of commuting patterns and economic interdependence. Residents of the DUS are closely tied together by efficient transportation and communication technology. Each DUS has a minimum population of 200,000 within its labor shed and constitutes "a multinode, multiconnective system (which) has replaced the core dominated metropolis as the basic urban unit" (Berry and Kasarda 1977, p. 304). Less than 4 percent of the American labor force is engaged in agricultural occupations. Residents even of remote rural areas are mostly urban in their activities and outlook.

In contrast, many residents inhabiting uncontrolled developments on the fringes of emerging mega-cities in less developed countries are practically isolated from the urban center and carry on much as they have done for generations. Over one-third of the population of the largest cities in India was born elsewhere, and maintainance of rural ways of life in the cities is common due to lack of urban employment, maintainance of village kinship ties, and seasonal circulatory migration to rural areas. And, although India has three of the ten largest cities in the world, it remains decidedly rural, with 75 percent of the population residing in agriculturally oriented villages (Nagpaul 1988).

Measurement of the rate at which urbanization takes place is confounded by the fact that concentrations of population do not correspond to administrative definitions of a city. Although data on population change for cities is widely reported and quite useful for administrative purposes, relatively fixed boundaries of political units make them less useful for examining change. The concept of an *urbanized area* (UA) is based upon a density criterion. In the United States a UA refers to a city of 50,000 or more inhabitants and all of the adjacent area built up to densities of 1,000 or more people per square mile. The UA was developed to be more consistent with the notion of population concentration, and it corresponds roughly with the pattern of lights that can be seen at night from an aircraft. Its boundaries change to reflect changes in concentration of numbers. A *metropolitan statistical area* (MSA) is based on a high degree of social and economic interdependence between a large population nucleus and adjacent communities that, together, are considered part of an integrated urban system. An MSA consists of a politically incorporated *central city* (CC) of 50,000 or more inhabitants (or twin cities meeting similar criteria), the county it is in, and all adjacent counties economically tied to the central city. The area outside the political boundaries of the central city, but within the MSA, is referred to as the *ring* and contains suburban population. When MSAs expand to the borders of adjacent MSAs such as in the New York and Los Angeles areas, these agglomerations of MSAs are referred to as *consolidated metropolitan statistical areas*

(CMSA) and their component parts are called *primary metropolitan statistical areas* (PMSA) (U.S. Bureau of the Census 1989).

As of 1987, there were 282 MSAs and CMSAs containing just over three-quarters of the population of the United States. The remaining 25 percent of Americans resided in counties not economically tied to a city of 50,000 or more and were classified as nonmetropolitan. In 1950, just over half of all Americans (56 percent) lived in the 169 metropolitan areas in existence at that time. In 1980, the largest population agglomeration in the United States was the New York–Northeastern New Jersey CMSA, with 17,539,000 residents, 15,584,000 of whom resided in the densely built-up UA. The New York PMSA had 8,275,000 residents, and New York City proper numbered only 7,072,000 (U.S. Bureau of Census 1989).

Units for analysis must be carefully chosen to best represent research interests. Much of what is known about the direction and pace of change in the internal structure of American cities is derived from dicennial census reports for city blocks and census tracts within MSAs. A census tract is a small geographic subarea containing from one to ten thousand people for which detailed socioeconomic characteristics are reported.

The American urban system is suburbanizing and deconcentrating. One measure of suburbanization is the ratio of the rate of growth in the ring to the rate of growth in the central city over a decade (Schnore 1959). While some MSAs began suburbanizing in the late 1800s, the greatest rates for the majority of places occurred in the decades of the 1950s and 1960s. Widespread use of the automobile, inexpensive energy, efficient production of materials for residential infrastructure, and federal housing policy allowed metropolitan growth to be absorbed by sprawl rather than by increased congestion at the center.

As the scale of territorial organization increased, so did the physical distances between black and white, rich and poor, young and old, and other meaningful population subgroups. The Index of Dissimilarity measures the degree of segregation between two groups by computing the percentage of one group that would have to reside on a different city block in order for it to have the same proportional distribution across urban space as the group to which it is being compared (Taeuber and Taeuber 1965). While there was some decline in indices of dissimilarity between African-Americans and white Americans in the 1960s and 1970s, owing in part to increasing Africa-American suburbanization, the 1980 mean index for central cities of the large MSAs was slightly above 80, meaning that 80 percent of the African-Americans would have to live on different city blocks to have the same distribution in space as whites. A very high degree of residential segregation remains (Taeuber 1983). Although there is great diversity in social status within central cities, and increasing diversity within suburban rings, disadvantaged and minority populations are over-represented in central cities, while the better educated and more affluent are overrepresented in suburban rings.

A related process, deconcentration, involves a shedding of urban activities at the center and is indicated by greater growth in employment and office space in the ring than in the central city. This process was well under way by the mid-1970s and continued unabated through the 1980s. A surprising turn of events in the late 1970s was mounting evidence that nonmetropolitan counties were, for the first time since the depression of the 1930s, growing more rapidly than metropolitan counties (Lichter and Fuguitt 1982). This process has been referred to as *deurbanization* and as *the nonmetropolitan turnaround*. It is unclear whether this trend represents an enlargement of the scale of metropolitan organization to encompass more remote counties or whether new growth nodes are developing in nonmetropolitan areas.

The American urban system is undergoing major changes as a result of shifts from a manufacturing to a service economy, the aging of the population, and the expansion of organizational scale from regional and national to global decision-making contingencies. Older industrial cities in the Northeast and the Midwest lost population as the locus of economic activity shifted from heavy manufacturing to information and residentiary services. Cities in Florida, Arizona, California, and the Northwest have been the recipients of growing numbers of retirees seeking environmental, recreational, and medical amenities not tied to economic production. Investment decisions regarding the location of office complexes, the factories of the future, are made more on the basis of availability of an educated labor pool, favorable tax treatment, and availability of amenities than upon the access to raw materials that underpinned the urbanization process through the mid-twentieth century.

These same shifts are reflected in the internal reorganization of American cities. The scale of local communities expanded from the central-business-district-oriented city to the multinodal metropolis. Daily commuting patterns have been shifting from radial trips between bedroom suburbs and workplaces in the central city to lateral trips among highly differentiated subareas throughout urban regions. Urban villages of affluent residences, high-end retail minimalls, and office complexes are emerging in nonmetropolitan counties beyond the reach of metropolitan political constraints, creating even greater segregation between the most and least affluent Americans.

While suburbanization and deconcentration were general phenomena for most metropolitan areas throughout the 1960s and 1970s, shifts in the economy, in household composition, and in contingencies influencing corporate-development decision making produced quite different growth patterns in different cities across the country in the 1980s. Many older central cities tied to the heavy manufacturing economy of the past have continued to decline while suburbanization and deconcentration continue. Other cities such as San Francisco, Seattle, and Denver, which offer amenities of climate or natural beauty, have witnessed massive investment in their downtown central business districts. Corporate and government office buildings that provide administrative and control functions for national and global organizations have mushroomed as new forms of private–public partnerships have been created to take advantage of existing infrastructure for traffic and other urban services and to protect exist-

ing investments in land and real estate in the central business district.

Deteriorating residential and warehousing districts adjacent to new downtown office complexes are being rehabilitated for residential use by childless professionals, or "gentry." The process of *gentrification,* or the invasion of lower-status, deteriorating neighborhoods of absentee-owned rental housing by middle- to upper-status home or condominium owners is driven by the desire for accessibility to nearby white-collar jobs and cultural amenities, as well as by the relatively higher costs of suburban housing pushed up by competing demand in these rapidly growing metropolitan areas. Although the number of people involved in gentrification is too small to have reversed the overall decline of central cities, the return of affluent middle-class residents has reduced segregation to some extent. Gentrification is positive in that it reclaims deteriorated neighborhoods, but a negative side is the displacement of the poor who have no place else to live at rents they can afford (Feagin and Parker 1990).

The pace and direction of the urbanization process are closely tied to technological advance. As industrialization proceeded in Western Europe and the United States over a 300-year period, an urban system emerged that reflected the interplay between the development of city-centered heavy industry and requirements for energy and raw materials from regional hinterlands. The form of city systems that emerged has been described as *rank-size.* Cities in such a system form a hierarchy of places from large to small such that the number of places of a given size decreases proportionally to the size of the place. Larger places are fewer in number, are more widely spaced, and offer more specialized goods and services than smaller places (Christaller 1933).

City systems that emerged in less industrialized nations are *primate* in character. In a primate system, the largest cities absorb far more than their share of societal population growth. Sharp breaks exist in the size hierarchy of places, with one or two very large, several medium-sized, and many very small places. Rapid declines in mortality beginning in the 1950s, coupled with traditionally high fertility, created unprecedented rates of natural increase. Primate city systems developed with an orientation more toward export of raw materials to the industrialized world than toward manufacturing and development of local markets. As economic development proceeds, it occurs primarily in the large primate cities with very low rates of economic growth in rural areas. Consequently, nearly all the excess of births over deaths in the nation is absorbed by the large cities, which are more integrated into the emerging global urban system (Dogan and Kasarda 1988).

In 1800 only two urbanized areas, London and Beijing, exceeded one million. By 1990, 298 had reached that size, with 408 expected by the year 2000. Between 1960 and 1990, the urbanized area of Mexico City grew from 4.9 to 19.4 million. Sao Paulo increased from 4.7 to 18.4 million. Tokyo-Yokohama doubled to 20.5 million, while New York grew from 14.2 to only 15.7 million over the same period. As of 1990, these were the four largest population agglomerations on the planet. In 1960 only four urbanized areas exceeded 10 million (Tokoyo, New York, Shanghai, and London). Twenty-five cities are expected to be over 10 million by the year 2000, eighteen of them in the less-developed world (U.S. Bureau of the Census 1989, pp. 818–819).

Mega-cities of over 10 million are a very recent phenomenon, and their number is increasing rapidly. Their emergence can be understood only within the context of a globally interdependent system of relationships. The territorial bounds of the relevant environment to which a population collectively adapts have expanded from the immediate hinterland to the entire world in the short span of only half a century.

Convergence theory suggests that cities throughout the world will come to exhibit organizational forms increasingly similar to one another, converging on the North American pattern, as technology becomes more accessible throughout the global system (Young and Young 1962). Divergence theory suggests that increasingly divergent forms of urban organization are likely to emerge due to differences in the timing and pace of the urbanization process, differences in the position of cities within the global system, and increasing effectiveness of deliberate planning of the urbanization process by centralized governments holding differing values and, therefore, pursuing a variety of goals for the future (Berry 1981).

The importance of understanding this process is suggested by Amos H. Hawley (1981, p. 13).

Urbanization is a transformation of society, the effects of which penetrate every sphere of personal and collective life. It affects the status of the individual and his opportunities for advancement, it alters the types of social units in which people group themselves, and it sorts people into new and shifting patterns of stratification. The distribution of power is altered, normal social process are reconstituted, and the rules and norms by which behavior is guided are redesigned.

(SEE ALSO: *Cities; Suburbanization; Urban Economic Transitions; Urban Sociology; Urban Underclass*)

REFERENCES

Berry, Brian J. L. 1981 *Comparative Urbanization: Divergent Paths in the Twentieth Century.* New York: St. Martin's Press.

———, and John D. Kasarda 1977 *Contemporary Urban Ecology.* New York: Macmillan.

Childe, V. Gordon 1950 "The Urban Revolution." *Town Planning Review* 21:4–7.

Christaller, W. 1933 *Central Places in Southern Germany,* trans. C. W. Baskin. Englewood Cliffs, N.J.: Prentice-Hall.

Dogan, Mattei, and John D. Kasarda 1988 "Introduction: How Giant Cities Will Multiply and Grow." In Mattei Dogan and John D. Kasarda, eds., *The Metropolis Era: A World of Giant Cities,* vol. 1. Newbury Park, Calif.: Sage.

Feagin, Joe R., and Robert Parker 1990 *Building American Cities: The Urban Real Estate Game,* 2nd ed. Englewood Cliffs, N.J.: Prentice-Hall.

Hawley, Amos H. 1981 *Urban Society: An Ecological Approach.* New York: Wiley.

Lichter, Daniel T., and Glenn V. Fuguitt 1982 "The Transition to Nonmetropolitan Population Deconcentration." *Demography* 19:211–221.

Nagpaul, Hans 1988 "India's Giant Cities." In Mattei Dogan and John D. Kasarda, eds., *The Metropolis Era: A World of Giant Cities,* vol. 1. Newbury Park, Calif.: Sage.

Schnore, Leo F. 1959 "The Timing of Metropolitan Decentralization." *Journal of the American Institute of Planners* 25:200–206.

Taeuber, Karl E. 1983 *Racial Residential Segregation, 28 Cities, 1970–1980* (working paper 83–12). Madison: University of Wisconsin, Center for Demography and Ecology.

——, and Alma F. Taeuber 1965 *Negroes in Cities: Residential Segregation and Neighborhood Change.* Chicago: Aldine.

Tisdale, Hope 1942 "The Process of Urbanization." *Social Forces* 20:311–316.

U.S. Department of Commerce, Bureau of the Census 1989 *Statistical Abstract of the United States: 1989,* 109th ed. Washington, D.C.: U.S. Government Printing Office.

Wirth, Louis 1938 "Urbanism as a Way of Life." *American Journal of Sociology* 44:1–24.

Young, Frank, and Ruth Young 1962 "The Sequence and Direction of Community Growth: A Cross-Cultural Generalization." *Rural Sociology* 27:374–386.

LEE J. HAGGERTY

URBAN SOCIOLOGY Urban sociology approaches the study of human groups in a territorial frame of reference. Social organization is the major focus of inquiry, with emphasis on the interplay between social and spatial organization and on how changes in spatial organization impinge on social and psychological well-being. A wide variety of interests are tied together by a common curiosity about the changing dynamics, determinants, and consequences of urban society's most characteristic form—the city.

Scholars recognized early that urbanization was accompanied by dramatic structural, cognitive, and behavioral changes. Classic sociologists (Durkheim, Weber, Tönnies, Marx) focused on delineating the differences in institutional forms that seemed to accompany the dual processes of urbanization and industrialization as rural-agrarian societies were transformed into urban-industrial societies (see Table 1).

Guiding contemporary research are several key questions derived from this tradition. How are human communities organized? What are the forces that produce revolutionary transformations in human settlement patterns? What are the organizational forms that accompany these transformations? What difference does urban living make and why do these differences exist? What consequences do increasing sizes of human concentrations have for human beings, their social worlds, and their environment?

Students of the urban scene have long been interested in the emergence of cities (Childe 1950), in how cities grow and change (Weber

TABLE 1
Classic Contrasts Between Urban and Rural Societies

Institution	Urban-Industrial	Rural-Agrarian
Agreements	Contractual	Personal
Authority	Bureaucratic	Paternalistic
Communication	Secondary	Primary
Intergrative mechanism	Specialization	Common experience
Normative standards	Universalistic	Particularistic
Normative structure	Anomic	Integrated
Problem solution	Rational	Traditional
Production	Manufacturing	Agriculture
Social control	Restitutive	Repressive
Social relations	Segmentalized	All encompassing
Socialization	Formal	Informal
Stratification	Achieved status	Ascribed status
Values	Money and power	Family
World views	Secular	Sacred

1899), and in unique ways of life associated with city living (Wirth 1938). These general treatments have historical value for understanding the nature of pre-twentieth-century cities, their determinants, and their human consequences, but comparative analysis of contemporary urbanization processes leads Brian J. L. Berry (1981, p. xv) to conclude that, "what is apparent is an accelerating change in the nature of change itself, speedily rendering not-yet-conventional wisdom inappropriate at best."

Urban sociologists use several different approaches to the notion of "community" to try to capture changes that occur in how individuals are tied together into meaningful social groups and how these groups are tied to other social groups within the broader territory they occupy. An *interactional community* is indicated by networks of routine, face-to-face, primary interaction among members of a group. It is most evident among close friends, family, tribe, and close-knit locality groups. An *ecological community* is delimited by routine patterns of activity in which members engage to meet the basic requirements of daily life. It corresponds with the territory over which the group ranges in performing such necessary activities as work, sleep, shopping, education, and recreation. *Compositional communities* are clusters of people who share common social characteristics. People of similar race, social status, or family characteristics, for example, form a compositional community. A *symbolic community* is defined by a communality of beliefs and attitudes among its members. Members view themselves as belonging to the group and are committed to it.

Research on the general issue of how these forms of organization change as cities grow has spawned a voluminous literature. An ecological and a sociocultural perspective guide two major research traditions. Ecological studies focus on the role of economic competition in shaping the urban environment. Ecological and compositional communities are analyzed with a view toward describing and generalizing about urban forms and processes of urban growth (Hawley 1981).

Sociocultural studies emphasize the importance of cultural, psychological, and other social dimensions of urban life and focus on interactional and symbolic communities that characterize the urban setting (Wellman and Leighton 1979; Suttles 1972).

Early theoretical work suggested that the most evident consequence of increasing size, density, and heterogeneity of human settlements was a breakdown of social ties, a decline in the family, alienation, an erosion of moral codes, and social disorganization (Wirth 1938). Empirical research in subsequent decades has clearly shown that, in general, urbanites are integrated into meaningful social groups (Fischer 1984).

The sociocultural tradition suggests that cultural values derive from socialization into a variety of subcultures and are relatively undisturbed by changes in ecological processes. Different subcultures select, are forced, or unwittingly drift into different areas which come to exhibit the characteristics of that subculture (Gans 1962). Claude Fischer (1975) combines the ecological and subcultural perspectives by suggesting that size, density, and heterogeneity are important but that they produce integrated subcultures rather than fostering alienation and community disorganization. Size provides the critical masses necessary for viable unconventional subcultures to form. With increased variability in subcultural mix in urban areas, subcultures become more intensified as they defend their ways of life against the broad array of others in the environment. The more subcultures, the more diffusion of cultural elements, and the greater the likelihood of new subcultures emerging—creating an ever-changing mosaic of unconventional subcultures that most distinguishes large places from small ones.

Empirical approaches to urban organization vary according to what the unit of analysis is and what is being observed. Patterns of activity (e.g., commuting, retail sales, crime) and characteristics of people (e.g., age, race, income, household composition) are most commonly derived from government reports for units of analysis as small as city blocks and as large as metropolitan areas. This kind of data is used to develop general principles of organization and change in urban systems. General questions range from how certain activities and characteristics come to be organized in particular ways in space to why certain locales exhibit the characteristics and activities found there. Territorial frameworks for the analysis of urban systems include neighborhoods, community areas, cities, urban areas, metropolitan regions, nations, and the world.

Observations of networks of interaction (e.g., visiting patterns, helping networks) and symbolic meanings of people (e.g., alienation, values, world views) are less systematically available because social surveys are more appropriate for obtaining this kind of information. Consequently, less is known about these dimensions of community than is desirable.

What is clear is that territoriality has waned as an integrative force and new forms of extra-local community have emerged. High mobility, expanded scale of organization, and increased range and volume of communication flow coalesce to alter the forms of social groups and their organization in space (Greer 1962). With modern communication and transportation technology, as in the United States today, space becomes less of an organizing principle and new forms of territorial organization are emerging that reflect the power of large-scale corporate organization and the federal government in shaping urban social and spatial organization (Gottdiener 1985).

Amos Hawley's (1950; 1981) ecological approach to the study of urban communities serves as the major paradigm in contemporary research. This approach views social organization as developing in response to basic problems of existence that all populations face in adapting to the environments they occupy. The urban community is conceptualized as the complex system of interdependence that develops as a population collectively adapts to an environment using whatever technology is available. Population, environment, technology, and social organization interact to produce various forms of human communities at different times and in different places (see Table 2). Population is conceptualized as an organized group of humans that function routinely as a unit; the environment is everything that is external to the population, including other organized social groups. Technological advance allows humans to expand and redefine the nature of the relevant environment and therefore influences the forms of community organization that populations develop (Duncan 1973).

Mathematical modeling and high speed computers are customary tools that human ecologists employ using large-scale data bases to investigate complex urban structures and processes. Social area analysis and factorial ecology are two approaches used to isolate general dimensions of spatial organization within the metropolis (Anderson and Bean 1961) and within city systems (Hadden and Borgatta 1964). Regression models serve to disentangle complex effects of density on the human condition (Galle, Gove, and McPherson 1972) and to investigate causal processes such as patterns of family location (Guest 1972). Monitoring and projecting change in the global urban system (Dogan and Kasarda 1988) also relies on these tools.

In the last half of the twentieth century there have been revolutionary transformations in the size and nature of human settlements and in the nature of interrelationships among them. Urban sociology attempts to understand the determinants and the consequences of this transformation.

The global population "explosion," created by unprecedented rapid decline in human mortality in less developed regions of the world since 1950, provided the additional people necessary for a population "implosion"—a rapid increase in the size and number of human agglomerations of unprecedented size in these regions of the world. Expansion in the scale of social organization, created by rapid increases in the volume and range of systematic information, intergroup communication, and bureaucratic administration, provided the infrastructure necessary for the emergence of a highly diversified, global adaptation to pressures of demographic growth. Timing, pace, and direction of urbanization in specific

Table 2
Comparative Urban Features of Major World Regions

Basic feature	19th-century North America	20th-century North America	Third World	Postwar Europe
Summary	Concentrated	Spread out	Constrained	Planned
Size	1–2 million	14 million	19 million	8 million
Density	High	Low	Medium	High
Timing	250 years long period	Emergent no pressure	Very rapid since 1950s	Very slow stationary
Scale	Regional and local	Inter-metro and global	Global and local	National and local
City System	Rank size regional	Daily urban national	Primate national	Rank size national
Occupations	Secondary manufacture	Tertiary services	Family and corporate	Diverse mixture
Spatial mix	Zone-sector core focus	Multinodal mosaic	Reverse zonal	Overlayed mixed use
Rural–Urban				
Differences	Great in all areas	Narrow and declining	Meduim and growing	Narrow except work
Status mix	Diverse hierarchical	High overall poor pockets	Bifurcated high % poor	Medium compacted
Migration	Heavy rural–urban and foreign	Inter-metro and foreign	Heavy rural–urban circulation	Foreign skilled
Planning	Laissez-faire capitalism	Decentral., ineffective	Centralized, ineffective	Decentral., effective

SOURCE: Abstracted from Berry 1981.

TABLE 3
Population of World's Largest Metropolises (in millions), 1950–2000, and Percent Change, 1950–2000

Metropolis	1950	2000	% Change
Mexico City, Mexico	3.1	26.3	748
Sao Paulo, Brazil	2.8	24.0	757
Tokyo/Yokohama, Japan	6.7	17.1	155
Calcutta, India	4.4	16.6	277
Greater Bombay, India	2.9	16.0	452
New York/Northeastern N.J., U.S.A.	12.4	15.5	25
Seoul, Republic of Korea	1.1	13.5	113
Shanghai, China	10.3	13.5	31
Rio De Janeiro, Brazil	3.5	13.3	280
Delhi, India	1.4	13.2	843
Greater Buenos Aires, Argentina	5.3	13.2	149
Cairo/Giza/Imbaba, Egypt	2.5	13.2	428
Jakarta, Indonesia	1.8	12.8	611
Baghdad, Iraq	0.6	12.8	2,033
Teheran, Iran	0.9	12.7	1,311
Karachi, Pakistan	1.0	12.1	1,110
Istanbul, Turkey	1.0	11.9	1,090
Los Angeles/Long Beach, Calif. U.S.A.	4.1	11.2	173
Dacca, Bangladesh	0.4	11.2	2,700
Manila, Philippines	1.6	11.1	594
Beijing (Peking), China	6.7	10.8	61
Moscow, USSR	4.8	10.1	110
Total world population	2500	6300	152

SOURCE: Adapted from Dogan and Kasarda (1988; Table 1.2)

regions are tied to the position of the region within a global system of interdependence and exchange (see Table 3).

The extent to which urban systems differ from one another at different times and in different regions suggests to Berry (1981) that social planners and urban sociologists alike must recognize that modernization has not led to a convergence in urban forms along lines of the North American model. The forms of community and the processes of change that characterize this new urban revolution, and its consequences for individual humans, offer a continuing challenge to urban sociologists for more accurate description and more adequate understanding.

(SEE ALSO: *Cities; Desegregation Indices; Population; Segregation and Desegregation; Suburbanization; Urban Economic Transitions; Urbanization; Urban Underclass*)

REFERENCES

Anderson, Theodore R., and L. Bean 1961 "The Shevky-Bell Social Areas: Confirmation of Results and a Reinterpretation." *Social Forces* 40:119–124.

Berry, Brian J. L. 1981 *Comparative Urbanization: Divergent Paths in the Twentieth Century.* New York: St. Martin's.

Childe, V. Gordon 1950 "The Urban Revolution." *Town Planning Review* 21:4–7.

Dogan, Mattei, and John D. Kasarda 1988 *The Metropolis Era: A World of Giant Cities,* Vol. 1. Newbury Park, Calif.: Sage.

Duncan, Otis Dudley 1973 "From Social System to Ecosystem." In Michael Micklin, ed., *Population, Environment, and Social Organization: Current Issues in Human Ecology.* Hinsdale, Ill.: Dryden.

Fischer, Claude S. 1975 "Toward a Subcultural Theory of Urbanism." *American Journal of Sociology.* 80:1319–1341.

——— 1984 *The Urban Experience.* San Diego, Calif.: Harcourt Brace Jovanovich.

Galle, Omer R., Walter R. Gove, and J. H. McPherson 1972 "Population Density and Pathology: What Are the Relations for Man?" *Science* 176:23–30.

Gans, Herbert J. 1962 "Urbanism and Suburbanism as Ways of Life: A Reevaluation of Definitions." In A. M. Rose, ed., *Human Behavior and Social Processes.* Boston: Houghton Mifflin.

Gottdiener, Mark 1985 *The Social Production of Urban Space.* Austin: University of Texas Press.

Greer, Scott 1962 *The Emerging City.* New York: Free Press.

Guest, Avery M. 1972 "Patterns of Family Location." *Demography* 9:151–172.

Hadden, Jeffory K., and Edgar F. Borgatta 1964 *American Cities: Their Social Characteristics.* Chicago: Rand McNally.

Hawley, Amos H. 1950 *Human Ecology: A Theory of Community Structure.* New York: Ronald.

——— 1981 *Urban Society: An Ecological Approach.* New York: Wiley.

Suttles, Gerald 1972 *The Social Construction of Communities.* Chicago: University of Chicago Press.

Weber, Adna F. 1899 *The Growth of Cities in the Nineteenth Century.* New York: Columbia University Press.

Wellman, B., and B. Leighton 1979 "Networks, Neighborhoods and Communities: Approaches to the Study of the Community Question." *Urban Affairs Quarterly.* 15:369–393.

Wirth, Louis 1938 "Urbanism as a Way of Life." *American Journal of Sociology* 44:1–24.

LEE J. HAGGERTY

URBAN UNDERCLASS Perhaps no social science concept has generated more discussion and controversy in recent years than that of the urban underclass. Some argue that it is little more than new wine in old bottles—a pithy and stigmatizing term for poor or lower-class persons who have always existed in stratified societies (Gans 1990; Jencks 1989; Katz 1989; McGahey 1982). Others contend that the underclass is a distinct and recent phenomenon, which reflects extreme marginalization from mainstream economic institutions, and its aberrant behavior (drug abuse, violent crime, out-of-wedlock births), reached catastrophic proportions in the inner cities by the mid-1970s (Glasgow 1980; Auletta 1982; Reischauer 1987; Nathan 1987;

Wilson 1987). Despite the multifaceted, subjective, and often ambiguous definitions of the urban underclass, common to almost all are the notions of weak labor-force attachment and persistent low income (Jencks and Peterson 1991; Sjoquist 1990). Indeed, the first scholar to introduce the term *underclass* to the literature labeled its members as an emergent substratum of permanently unemployed, unemployables, and underemployed (Myrdal 1962).

Widely differing interpretations of the causes of the underclass have been offered, ranging from Marxist to social Darwinist. The most influential contemporary analysis of the urban underclass is William Julius Wilson's (1987) *The Truly Disadvantaged.* In this treatise, Wilson links the origins and growth of the urban underclass to the structure of opportunities and constraints in American society. Its roots are hypothesized to lie in historical discrimination and the mass migration of blacks to Northern cities during the first half of this century. Its more recent growth and experiences are posited to rest with industrial and geographic changes occurring in Northern metropolitan economies since 1970, in particular the economic transition in central cities, where goods-processing industries have been replaced by information-processing industries and where blue-collar jobs have dispersed and relocated in the suburbs. These changes led to dramatic increases in joblessness among inner-city minorities who neither had the skills to participate in new urban growth industries nor the logistical or financial means to commute or relocate to the suburbs. Rapidly rising joblessness among inner-city blacks, in turn, triggered high concentrations of poverty and related social problems that characterize its definitions (see also Kasarda 1985, 1988; Wilson 1991).

Alternative views on the causes of the underclass can be found in the works of Murray (1984) and Mead (1988). These conservative scholars look at underclass behaviors as rational adaptations to the perverse incentives found in government welfare programs plus a lack of individual responsibility for actions harmful to themselves and to others. Abetted by well-intentioned but misguided social programs, joblessness and persistent poverty are seen more as consequences of the deviant behaviors frequently noted in underclass definitions, rather than as causes of these behaviors.

Measurement of the size of the underclass varies as much as definitions of it. A number of researchers have focused on individual-level indicators of persistent poverty, defined as those who are poor for spells from n to $n + x$ years (Levy 1977; Duncan, Coe, and Hill 1984; Bane and Ellwood 1986) or long-term AFDC recipients (Gottschalk and Danziger 1987). For example, Levy (1977), using the Panel Study of Income Dynamics for years 1967 to 1973, estimated that approximately eleven million Americans were persistently poor for at least five years. When the underclass is defined as being persistently poor for eight or more years, six million people were found to be members of the underclass (Duncan, Coe, and Hill 1984). This represents approximately one-fifth of the thirty-two million Americans living in poor households in 1988 (Mincy, Sawhill, and Wolf 1990).

Another measurement strategy focuses on the geographic concentration of the poor in urban areas. Using Bureau of the Census tract-level definitions of local poverty areas, Reischauer (1987) reports that, of the nation's population living in such poverty areas, central cities housed over half in 1985, up from just one-third in 1972. Jargowsky and Bane (1990) documented that the number of poor people living in extreme poverty tracts in cities (i.e., census tracts where more than 40 percent of the residents fall below the poverty line) expanded by 66 percent between 1970 and 1980, from 975,000 to 1,615,000. Moreover, just four Northern cities (New York, Chicago, Philadelphia, and Detroit) accounted for two-thirds of this increase.

Mincy (1988) further documented that concentrated poverty is predominantly a minority problem. His analysis of extreme poverty tracts in the 100 largest central cities in 1980 showed that of the approximately 1.8 million poor people residing in these tracts, fewer than 10 percent were non-Hispanic white (175,178), while nearly 70 percent were black (1,248,151). Nearly all of the remainder were Hispanic.

As noted above, the concept of underclass is typically considered to entail more than poverty. It is also posited to incorporate certain behavioral characteristics conflicting with mainstream values: joblessness, out-of-wedlock births, welfare dependency, school dropout, and illicit activities.

While considerable debate continues to surround definitions (or even the existence) of the underclass, attempts have been made to measure its size by using multiple "behavioral" indicators derived from census data. Ricketts and Sawhill (1988) measured the underclass as people living in neighborhoods whose residents in 1980 simultaneously exhibited disproportionately high rates of school dropout, joblessness, female-headed families, and welfare dependency. Using a composite definition where tracts must fall at least one standard deviation above the national mean on *all* four characteristics, they found that approximately 2.5 million people lived in such tracts in 1980 and that these tracts were disproportionately located in major cities in the Northeast and Midwest. They reported that in underclass tracts, on average, 63 percent of the resident adults had less than a high school education, that 60 percent of the families with children were headed by women, that 56 percent of the adult men were not regularly employed, and that 34 percent of the households were receiving public assistance. Their research also revealed that, although the total poverty population grew by only 8 percent between 1970 and 1980, the number of people living in the underclass areas grew by 230 percent, from 752,000 to 2,484,000.

Such location-based aggregate measures have been criticized on the grounds that, aside from race, most urban census tracts are quite heterogeneous along economic and social dimensions. Jencks (1989; Jencks and Peterson 1991), for example, observes that, with the exception of tracts made up of public-housing projects, there is considerable diversity in resident income and education levels, joblessness, and public assistance recipiency within urban neighborhoods. According to his calculations, even in extreme poverty tracts only about 50 percent of all families had incomes in 1980 below the poverty line, and some reported incomes up to four times the poverty level. He further notes Ricketts and Sawhill's findings that within the worst urban neighborhoods (those they define as underclass areas) more than 50 percent of the working age adults held steady jobs and only 33 percent of the households received public assistance. Conversely, considerable numbers of urban residents who are poor, jobless, and dependent on public assistance live in census tracts where fewer than 20 percent of the families fall below the poverty line.

Nevertheless, while most scholars concur that behaviors linked to underclass definitions and measurement are found throughout society, it is the concentration of these behaviors in economically declining inner city areas that is said to distinguish the underclass from previously impoverished urban subgroups. Geographic concentration, it is argued, magnifies social problems and accelerates their spread to nearby households through social contagion, peer pressure, and imitative behavior (Wilson 1987). Economically stable households seeking to avoid these problems selectively flee the neighborhood. Left behind in increasingly isolated concentrations are those with the least to offer in terms of marketable skills, role models, and familial stability. The result is a spiral of negative social and economic outcomes for the neighborhoods and the households that remain.

Incorporating the efforts of neighborhoods and social-transmission processes means that the future research agenda on the urban underclass will be qualitative as well as quantative in approach. Ethnographic studies of underclass neighborhoods, family systems, and individual development will complement growing numbers of surveys and sophisticated statistical analyses on the persistence and intergenerational transfer of urban poverty. In fact, some cynics have suggested that a profitable academic industry may well emerge from studying the ghetto poor.

(SEE ALSO: *Cities; Community; Poverty; Segregation and Desegregation; Urbanization; Urban Sociology*)

REFERENCES

Auletta, Ken 1982 *The Underclass.* New York: Random House.

Bane, Mary Jo, and David Ellwood 1986 "Slipping Into and Out of Poverty: The Dynamics of Spells." *Journal of Human Resources* 21:1–23.

Duncan, G. J., R. D. Coe, M. S. Hill 1984 In *Years of Poverty, Years of Plenty.* Ann Arbor: Institute of Social Research, University of Michigan.

Gans, Herbert J. 1990 "Deconstructing the Underclass: The Term's Danger as a Planning Concept." *Journal of the American Planning Association,* pp. 271–277.

Glasgow, Douglas G. 1980 *The Black Underclass: Poverty, Unemployment, and Entrapment of Ghetto Youth.* San Francisco: Jossey-Bass.

Gottschalk, P. and S. Danziger 1987 Testimony on Poverty, Hunger, and the Welfare System, 5 August 1986, *Hearing Before the Select Committee on Hunger, House of Representatives,* 99th Cong., 2nd Sess., ser. no. 23. Washington, D.C.: U.S. Government Printing Office.

Jargowsky, Paul A., and Mary Jo Bane 1990 *Neighborhood Poverty: Basic Questions.* Discussion Paper Series, #H-90-3. Cambridge, Mass.: Malcolm Wiener Center for Social Policy, John F. Kennedy School of Government, Harvard University.

Jencks, Christopher 1989 "What Is the Underclass—And Is It Growing?" *Focus* 12:14–31.

———, and Paul Peterson (eds.) 1991 *The Urban Underclass.* Washington, D.C.: The Brookings Institution.

Kasarda, John D. 1985 "Urban Change and Minority Opportunities." In P. Peterson, ed., *The New Urban Reality.* Washington D.C.: Brookings Institution.

——— 1988 "Economic Restructuring and America's Urban Dilemma." In M. Dogan and J. D. Kasarda, eds., *The Metropolis Era: A World of Giant Cities.* Newbury Park, Calif.: Sage.

Katz, Michael 1989 *The Undeserving Poor: From the War on Poverty to the War on Welfare.* New York: Pantheon Books.

Levy, Frank 1977 "How Big Is the American Underclass?" Washington, D.C.: Urban Institute.

McGahey, R. 1982 "Poverty's Voguish Stigma," *The New York Times,* March 12.

Mincy, Ronald B. 1988 "Industrial Restructuring, Dynamic Events, and the Racial Composition of Concentrated Poverty." Paper prepared for Planning Meeting of Social Science Research Council on

Industrial Restructuring, Local Political Economies, and Communities and Neighborhoods. New York, September 21–23, 1988.

————, Isabel V. Sawhill, Douglas A. Wolf 1990 "The Underclass: Definition and Measurement." *Science* 248:450–53.

Myrdal, Gunner 1962 *Challenge to Affluence*. New York: Pantheon.

Nathan, Richard P. 1987 "Will the Underclass Always Be with Us?" *Society* 24:57–62.

Reischauer, Robert D. 1987 *The Geographic Concentration of Poverty: What Do We Know?* Washington, D.C.: The Brookings Institution.

Ricketts, Erol, and Isabel Sawhill 1988 "Defining and Measuring the Underclass." *Journal of Policy Analysis and Management* 7:316–325.

Sjoquist, David "Concepts, Measurements, and Analysis of the Underclass: A Review of the Literature." Georgia State University. Typescript.

Wilson, William Julius 1987 *The Truly Disadvantaged: The Inner City, the Underclass, and Public Policy*. Chicago: University of Chicago Press.

———— 1991 "Studying Inner-City Social Dislocations." *American Sociological Review* 56:1–14.

JOHN D. KASARDA

UTILITY THEORY   *See* Decision-Making Theory and Research; Rational Choice Theory.

UTOPIAN ANALYSIS AND DESIGN

"From the time of its first discovery, the island of King Utopus has been shrouded in ambiguity, and no latter-day scholars should presume to dispel the fog, polluting utopia's natural environment with an excess of clarity and definition" (Manuel and Manuel 1979, p. 5).

But this ambiguity extends well beyond simple obscurity or murkiness; it reaches to unqualified contradiction. Many utopian visionaries have been denounced for their meticulous delineation of details as they constructed models of social worlds bearing no resemblance to existing, potential, or possible reality. Utopias, it would seem, suffer from the twin infirmities of ambiguity and excessive efforts to achieve clarity and definition. Our

dictionaries tell us they are, on the one hand, ideally perfect places but, on the other hand, are simply impractical thought or theory. Utopians are customarily viewed as zealous but quixotic reformers. The books in which they describe their societies may be praised as fascinating, fanciful literature but not as scientific tomes.

It is quite possible as well as reasonable to view utopians as model builders. Models are quite different objects from what is being modeled and have properties not shared by their counterparts. "The aim of a model is precisely not to reproduce reality in all its complexity. It is, rather, to capture in a vivid, often formal way what is essential to understanding some aspect of its structure or behavior" (Weizenbaum 1976, pp. 149–150).

One occupational disability of model builders everywhere is a sort of pathological obsession with a single element, or at most a strictly circumscribed set of elements, of reality, along with an unwavering refusal to examine the larger milieu in which they are found.

In Sir Thomas More's *Utopia* (1965), a central value or societal goal is the concept of economic equality; but this does not include the notion of social equality. There exists in Utopia a large underclass of slaves who are assigned the more distasteful but necessary tasks of the society. This class is composed of war prisoners (More's society is not free of war), persons born into slavery (it is not free of slavery), condemned criminals from other countries who are purchased from foreign slave markets (crime has not been eliminated), and working-class foreigners (class distinctions persist) who volunteer for slavery in Utopia rather than suffer the unpleasant conditions in their home countries (ethnic and immigration difficulties continue to exist). All able-bodied persons in Utopia become part of its work force—slaves, male nonslaves, and even women! This is seen as an enormous augmentation of the work force. Within each household, however, male dominance prevails. Households are under the authority of the oldest free male. Women are specifically designated as "subordinate" to their husbands, as children are to their parents and younger people generally are to their elders. In Utopia, the applicability of equality is severely restricted.

In discussing utopias it is important to distinguish between analytic and design models. Analytic models purport to be summaries of existing empirical reality; design models are summaries or sketches of future, past, or alternative societies, social structures, or worlds.

Characteristically, utopian literature contains a critique of existing society along with a model of a different one. Frequently the design model incorporates a more or less indirect critique of an existing state of affairs. Plato's *Republic* (1941), the work that seems to have been the prototype of More's *Utopia,* was greatly influenced by the social conditions observed and experienced by Plato. He saw the Athens in which he lived as a very corrupt democracy and felt that in such a system politicians inevitably pandered to mobs. If the mob insisted upon venal demands, politicians found it necessary to agree with them or lose their own positions. Reform, he felt, was not possible in a corrupt society. In the *Republic* Socrates, voicing Plato's sentiments, concludes that "the multitude can never be philosophical. Accordingly, it is bound to disapprove of all who pursue wisdom; and so also, of course, are those individuals who associate with the mob and set their hearts on pleasing it" (1941, p. 201).

Interestingly, it has been suggested that Plato's hostility to democracy was, at least to some extent, shaped by his economic and social background. Members of his family were large landholders who, along with others in a similar position, saw the rise of commerce as a threat to their economic positions. Democratic government undermined their political preeminence, as did militant foreign policies. They had a great deal to lose through war because they were subject to heavy war taxes. Moreover, some had had their lands ravaged by Spartans during the Peloponnesian War; others had retreated behind the walls of Athens. These conservative elements were not above attempting to subvert the democratic system (Klosko 1986, p. 10).

In any event, Plato's utopia is clearly elitist in nature. For a variety of reasons most utopian schemes seem to be controlled by elites of some sort. As one writer explains it:

They begin with the proposition that things are bad; things must become better, perhaps perfect here on earth; things will not improve by themselves; a plan must be developed and carried out; this implies the existence of an enlightened individual, or a few, who will think and act in a way that many by themselves cannot think and act. (Brinton 1965, p. 50)

For Plato, the elites were what he called philosophers. In a sense these were the theoreticians or model makers. The problem he saw was converting their models—their ideal worlds—into reality. Plato was very realistic about this matter of convertibility. He has Socrates ask, "Is it not in the nature of things that action should come less close to truth than thought?" (1941, p. 178). He is, however, concerned about trying to come as close as possible to having the real world correspond to the ideal one. The solution? To have philosophers become rulers or to have rulers become philosophers. In either case enormous, if not complete, power is to be held by a caste of elites.

In effect, social inequality is found even in the work of the triumvirate usually referred to as the "utopian socialists": Claude Henri de Rouvroy de Saint Simon (1760–1825), Charles Fourier (1772–1837), and Robert Owen (1771–1858).

In his early work Saint Simon's elites were scientists, but later he tended to subordinate them or at least to keep them on a par with industrial chiefs. He evaded the problem of social equality by saying that each member of society would be paid in accordance with his or her "investment." This referred to the contribution each made to the productive process. Since different people had different talents, these contributions would differ. Some people's contributions would be more important than others', and accordingly those people would be paid more. But although the rewards of different people would differ, there would not be wide discrepancies between the rewards of the lowest- and highest-paid workers (Manuel and Manuel 1979, pp. 590–614).

Unlike Saint Simon, who never wrote a detailed description of a utopian society, Charles Fourier wrote thousands of pages of detailed descriptions of his "Phalanx," including architectural specifications, work schedules and countless other details. The Phalanx was to be organized essentially as a shareholding corporation. Members were free to buy as many shares as they wished or could afford. Fourier stressed the fact that in his utopia there would be three social classes: the rich, the poor, and the middle. The condition of the poor would be enormously better than their condition in existing society, but the rich or upper class would be entitled to more lavish living quarters, more sumptuous food, and, in general, a more luxurious life-style than the others. During the last fifteen years or so of his life, most of Fourier's efforts were devoted to the search for a wealthy person to subsidize a trial of his Phalanx (Beecher 1986).

Robert Owen insisted on what he regarded to be complete equality. Conceding that people were born with differing abilities, he contended that these abilities were provided by God and should not be the basis for differential rewards. Nevertheless, as a self-made man who became extremely successful and managed the most important cotton-spinning factory in Britain, he never seemed to lose the self-assurance that he knew best how to manage a community and that all members would understand the wisdom of his decisions. He has been characterized as a benevolent autocrat who acted somewhat like a military commander who has little direct contact with his troops (Cole 1969; Manuel and Manuel 1979, pp. 676–693).

In the United States, the most widely read utopian novel based on the assumption of absolute economic equality is undoubtedly Edward Bellamy's Looking Backward (1887). Bellamy (1850–1898), influenced by the development of the large economic trusts in the United States, postulated that by the year 2000 only one enormous trust would remain: the United States government. He went to great pains to make it clear that his utopia was devoid of Marxist or other European influences. The principle of income or reward on which it was based was neither "From each according to his investment or product" nor the classic "From each according to his ability, to each according to his need," although it was much closer to the latter than to the former.

In Bellamy's vision of the United States in the year 2000, each person received an equal share of the total national product. In effect, every inhabitant received a credit card showing his or her share of the product. The share could be spent in any manner. If too many individuals decided to buy a particular product, the price of that product would be raised. The point, however, is that people were entitled to a share of the national product *not* on the basis of their individual productivity but simply because they existed as human beings. In some telling passages Bellamy's characters observe that members of families do not deny food or other needs to other family members because they have been unproductive. In effect, the entire country (and, presumably, ultimately the entire world) would resemble our more primitive notion of one family.

Bellamy's work received widespread attention throughout the world. In England, William Morris (1834–1896) objected strenuously to the centralized control and bureaucratic form of organization in Looking Backward. Morris wrote his own utopian novel, News from Nowhere (1866). Unlike Bellamy's utopia, which came into being through a process of evolution, a violent revolution has occurred in Nowhere. London has become a series of relatively small villages separated by flowers and wooded areas. There is no centralized government—no government at all—as we normally understand it. With the end of private property and domestic arrangements in which women are essentially the property of men, the underlying reasons for criminal behavior have been eliminated. Random acts of violence are regarded as transitory diseases and are dealt with by nurses and doctors rather than by jailers.

It has been argued that Morris was essentially an anarchist theorist, although Morris himself vigorously objected to such characterization of his work. It has been suggested that anarchism has two major forms: collectivist and individualist. Morris is seen as essentially a collectivist anarchist, although not an anarchosyndicalist—the form that stresses trade-union activity. He ridiculed conventional forms of individualism. Anarchism itself is defined as a social theory that advocates a community-centered life with great amounts of personal liberty. It opposes coercion of its population (Sargent 1990, pp. 61–64).

Other commentators see *News from Nowhere* as an effort by Morris to present his arguments against anarchism (Holzman 1990, p. 99). It seems clear that his work does not fit neatly into any prefabricated ideological cubbyhole. Morris cherished aesthetic over intellectual values (he was an architect, artist, poet, designer, and craftsman). When one of his characters in *News from Nowhere* is asked how labor is rewarded, the reply is quite predictable: it is *not* rewarded. Work has become a pleasure—not a hardship. Each person does what he or she can do best; the quandary of extrinsic motivation has substantially disappeared.

Motivation, however, is the central concern in B. F. Skinner's *Walden Two* (1948). Burrhus Frederic Skinner (1904–1990) was a professional psychologist whose utopia was a product of his interest in behavioral engineering. His ideal community has been described as one of means rather than of ends—one in which technique has been elevated to utopian status (Kumar 1987, p. 349).

This is not completely accurate. It does capture the essence of how Skinner himself saw his utopia, but it omits direct consideration of the implicit values held by its designer.

Skinner himself was unquestionably a well-motivated, humanistic scientist, but he neglected his customary penetrating analysis when approaching the area of values held by the boss scientist. At one point in *Walden Two*, however, he does seem to have some insight into this difficulty. Frazier, the founder of the community, voices the unspoken criticism of one of the other characters by pointing to his own insensitivity to the effect he has on others, except when the effect is calculated; his lack of the personal warmth responsible in part for the success of the community; the ulterior and devious nature of his own motives. He then cries out, "But God *damn* it Burris . . . can't you see?

I'm—not—a—product—of—Walden—Two!" (Skinner 1948, p. 233).

Economic and basic social equality exist in this community, but effective control is exercised through the built-in reinforcement techniques of its designer. When Frazier is challenged on this by one of the characters who observes that Frazier, looking at the world from the middle of the twentieth century, assumes he knows the best course for humanity forever, Frazier essentially agrees. His defense is that the techniques of behavioral engineering currently exist (and presumably will continue to be used), but they are in the wrong hands—those of charlatans, salespeople, ward heelers, bullies, cheats, educators, priests, and others. Ultimately, Skinner's designer insists, human beings are never free—their behavior is determined by prior conditioning in the society in which they were raised. The belief in their own freedom is what allows human beings unwittingly to become conditioned by reinforcers in their existing environments.

Thus, in effect, *Walden Two* achieves its effects by changing the psychological characteristics of its inhabitants through environmental modification. Its final form is presumably an experimental question. The queries are simple enough and are stated explicitly at one point: What is the best behavior for the individual as far as the group is concerned? How can an individual be induced to behave in that way? The answer presumably can change over time, on the basis of experimental experience. The entire edifice would seem to depend upon the continuing moral superiority of the reinforcement designers over the charlatans they replace.

Quite a different sort of utopia has been proposed by the philosopher Robert Nozick, who outlines what he calls the framework for a utopia. In a word (or two), this framework is equivalent to what Nozick calls the minimal state (Nozick 1974, pp. 297–334). This is a state "limited to the narrow functions of protection against force, theft, fraud, enforcement of contracts, and so on . . . any more extensive state will violate persons' rights not to be forced to do certain things and is unjustified . . ." (Nozick 1974, p. ix).

Nozick is not concerned with modifying behavior or specifying social structures beyond this minimum state. He begins with the assumption that individual persons have certain rights that may never be violated by any other person or the state. These include the right *not* to be killed or attacked if you are not doing any harm; *not* to be coerced or imprisoned; *not* to be limited in the use of your property if that use does not violate the rights of others.

In arguing for a minimal state, Nozick, on the one hand, is arguing against anarchism (in which there is no state at all). On the other hand, he argues against all forms of the welfare state (in which some people with excessive wealth may be required to surrender some of their property to help others who are less fortunate) (Paul 1981).

As Nozick sees it, rights define a moral boundary around individual persons. The sanctity of this boundary takes priority over all other possible goals. Thus, it becomes readily understandable why he feels that nonvoluntary redistribution of income is morally indefensible:

It is an extraordinary but apparent consequence of this view that for a government to tax each of its able-bodied citizens five dollars a year to support cripples and orphans would violate the rights of the able-bodied and would be morally impermissible, whereas to refrain from taxation even if it meant allowing the cripples and orphans to starve to death would be the morally required governmental policy. (Scheffler 1981, p. 151)

Here again we see the clash of values that lie at the heart of utopian schemes and their critics. A serious and widely discussed effort to resolve these clashes was made late in the twentieth century by another social philosopher, John Rawls. *A Theory of Justice* (Rawls 1971) was not a utopian novel but a meticulously argued tome that has been compared with John Locke's *Second Treatise of Civil Government* and John Stuart Mill's *On Liberty*. The central question confronting his work has been expressed thus: "Is it possible to satisfy the legitimate 'leftist', 'socialist' critics of Western capitalism within a broadly liberal, capitalist and democratic framework?" (Goldman 1980, p. 431).

Unfortunately, Rawls has found himself increasingly caught between attacks from both the left and the right. The left feels he has not gone far enough in constraining property rights; the right feels he places too great an emphasis upon the value of equality, especially at the expense of the right to property (Goldman 1980, pp. 431–432).

A central point argued by Rawls is that there is no injustice if greater benefits are earned by a few, provided the situation of people not so fortunate is thereby improved (Rawls 1971, pp. 14–15).

As one commentator expressed it, for Rawls equality comes first. Goods are to be distributed equally unless it can be shown that an unequal distribution is to the advantage of the least advantaged. This would be a "just" distribution (Schaar 1980). One might add, parenthetically, that this justice would depend substantially upon the nature of the existing social and economic arrangements under which this inequality occurs. Would a different set of arrangements allow greater equality? For example, is capital available only through private sources? Would public sources serve similar ends with less inequality?

The central issue for utopian analysts from Plato through twentieth-century philosophers is how one constructs a "just" society. But there is no single definition of "just"; it all depends on what you consider to be important. Are you concerned exclusively with yourself? your immediate family? others in your community? in your country? in the world?

And so it is that utopian analysis and design ultimately begin with an implicit, if not explicit, value orientation. One school of thought begins with an overwhelming belief that elites of one sort or another must be favored in the new society. Elite status may be gained through existing wealth, birth, talent, skill, intelligence, or physical strength. Another school begins with what is, broadly speaking, the concept of equality. Here the implicit notion is not unlike Western ideas of the family: to each equally, irrespective of either productivity or need. Between these two polar positions lie a range of intermediate proposals that may provide greater amounts of compensation based upon some definition of need or elite status. In turn, compensation may or may not be linked directly to political or other forms of power.

Issues relating to the nation-state (its form, its powers, and even its very existence), ethnicity, and inequality became acute in the final decade of the twentieth century. Ethnic groups throughout the world grew militant in their demands for their own national entities. Many saw this as a path to a solution for their own problems of inequality. With the apparent easing, if not the elimination, of Cold War tensions between the Soviet Union and the United States, widespread controversies began relative to the shape of a "new world order." This posed unprecedented challenges to utopian thought. To deal with these challenges, social scientists, as well as imaginative novelists and others, were confronted with the task of integrating value configurations, social structures, and psychological sets on levels that may well make all previous efforts at utopian analysis and design resemble the stumbling steps of a child just learning to walk.

(SEE ALSO: *Equity Theory; Social Philosophy*)

REFERENCES

Beecher, Jonathan 1986 *Charles Fourier: The Visionary and His World.* Berkeley: University of California Press.

Brinton, Crane 1965 "Utopia and Democracy." In Frank E. Manuel, ed., *Utopias and Utopian Thought.* Boston: Beacon Press.

Cole, Margaret 1969 *Robert Owen of New Lanark 1771–1858.* New York: August M. Kelley.

Goldman, Alan H. 1980 "Responses to Rawls from the Political Right." In H. Gene Blocker and Elizabeth H. Smith, eds., *John Rawls' Theory of Social Justice.* Athens: Ohio University Press.

Holzman, Michael 1990 "The Encouragement and Warning of History: William Morris's *A Dream of John Ball.*" In Florence S. Boos and Carole G. Silver, eds., *Socialism and the Literary Artistry of William Morris.* Columbia: University of Missouri Press.

Klosko, George 1986 *The Development of Plato's Political Theory.* New York: Methuen.

Kumar, Krishan 1987 *Utopia and Anti-Utopia in Modern Times.* New York: Basil Blackwell.

Manuel, Frank E., and Fritzie P. Manuel 1979 *Utopian Thought in the Western World.* Cambridge, Mass.: Harvard University Press.

More, Sir Thomas (1516) 1965 *Utopia.* Paul Turner, trans. London: Penguin.

Morris, William 1966 *News from Nowhere.* In *The Collected Works of William Morris,* vol. 16, pp. 3–211. New York: Russell and Russell.

Nozick, Robert 1974 *Anarchy, State and Utopia.* New York: Basic Books.

Paul, Jeffrey (ed.) 1981 *Reading Nozick.* Totowa, N.J.: Rowan and Littlefield.

Plato 1941 *The Republic of Plato,* Francis MacDonald Cornford, trans. and ed. New York and London: Oxford University Press.

Rawls, John 1971 *A Theory of Justice.* Cambridge, Mass.: Harvard University Press.

Sargent, Lyman Tower 1990 "William Morris and the Anarchist Tradition." In F. S. Boos and C. G. Silver, eds., *Socialism and the Literary Artistry of William Morris.* Columbia: University of Missouri Press.

Schaar, John H. 1980 "Equality of Opportunity and the Just Society." In H. G. Blocker and E. H. Smith, eds., *John Rawls' Theory of Social Justice.* Athens: Ohio University Press.

Scheffler, Samuel 1981 "Natural Rights, Equality and the Minimal State." In Jeffrey Paul, ed., *Reading Nozick.* Totowa, N.J.: Rowan and Littlefield.

Skinner, B. F. 1948 *Walden Two.* New York: Macmillan.

ROBERT BOGUSLAW

VALIDITY In its most simple sense, a measure is said to be valid to the degree it measures that which it is hypothesized to measure (Nunnally 1967, p. 75). More precisely, validity has been defined as the degree to which a score derived from a measurement procedure reflects a point on the underlying construct it is hypothesized to reflect (Bohrnstedt 1983). The most recent *Standards for Educational and Psychological Testing* (American Psychological Association 1985) states that validity "refers to the appropriateness, meaningfulness, and usefulness of the specific inferences made from . . . scores." Note the emphasis; validity refers to the degree to which evidence supports *inferences* drawn from a score rather than to the scores or to the instruments that produce the scores. Inferences drawn from a given measure with one population may be valid, but may not be valid for others. As will be seen below, evidence for inferences about validity can be accumulated in a variety of ways. In spite of this variety, validity *is* a unitary concept. The types of inferential evidence relate to the validity of a particular measure under investigation.

Several important points related to validity need to be noted, however briefly:

1. Validity is a matter of degree rather than an all-or-none matter (Nunnally 1967, p. 75; Messick 1989).

2. Since the constructs of interest in sociology (e.g., normlessness, religiosity, economic conservatism, etc.) generally are not amenable to direct observation, validity can be ascertained only indirectly.

3. Validation is a dynamic process; the evidence for or against the validity of inferences that can be drawn from a measure may change with accumulating evidence. Validity in this sense is always a continuing and evolving matter rather than something that is fixed for once and for all (Messick 1989).

4. Validity is the sine qua non of measurement—without it, measurement is meaningless.

The *Standards* produced jointly by the American Psychological Association, the American Educational Research Association, and the National Council on Measurement in Education distinguish between and among three types of evidence related to validity—*criterion-related, content,* and *construct evidence* (American Psychological Association 1985).

CRITERION-RELATED EVIDENCE FOR VALIDITY

Criterion-related evidence for validity is assessed by the correlation between a measure and some criterion variable of interest. The criterion will vary depending upon the purpose of the researcher and/or the client for the research. Thus, in a study to determine the effect of early childhood education, one criterion of interest might be how well children perform on a standardized reading test at the end of the third grade. In a study for an industrial client, it might be the number of years it takes to reach a certain job level. The question that is always asked when accumulating evidence for criterion-related validity is "How accurately can the criterion be predicted from the scores on a measure?" (American Psychological Association 1985).

Since the criterion variable might be one that exists in the present or one that one might want to predict in the future, evidence for criterion-related validity is broken into two major types: predictive and concurrent.

Evidence for *predictive validity* is assessed by examining future standing on a criterion variable as predicted from present standing on a measure of interest. For example, if one constructs a measure of work orientation, evidence of its predictive validity for job performance might be ascertained by administering the measure to a group of new hires and correlating it with some criterion of success (e.g., supervisors' ratings, regular advances within the organization, etc.) at some later point in time. Importantly, the evidence for the validity of a measure is not limited to a single criterion. There are as many validities as there are criterion variables to be predicted from that measure. The preceding example makes this point clear. In addition, the example makes it clear that the evidence for the validity of a measure will vary depending upon the time at which the criterion is assessed. Generally, the closer in time the measure and the criterion are assessed, the higher the validity, but by no means is this always true.

Evidence for *concurrent validity* is assessed by correlating a measure and a criterion of interest at the *same* point in time. One measure of the concurrent validity of a measure of religious belief, for example, is its correlation with concurrent attendance at religious services. Just as with predictive validity, there are as many concurrent validities as there are criteria to be explained; there is no single concurrent validity for a given measure.

Concurrent validation can also be evaluated by correlating a measure of *X* with extant measures of *X*, for instance, one measure of self-esteem with a second. It is assumed that the two measures reflect the same underlying construct. Two measures might both be labeled *self-esteem,* but if one contains items that deal with one's social competence and the other with how one feels and evaluates self, it would be unsurprising to find no more than a modest correlation between the two.

Evidence for validity based on concurrent studies may not square with evidence for validity based on predictive studies. For example, a measure of an attitude toward a given political issue may correlate highly in August as to which political party one *believes* he or she will vote for in November, but may correlate rather poorly with the *actual* vote in November.

Many of the constructs of interest to sociologists do not have criteria against which the validity of a measure can be easily ascertained. When they do have them, the criteria may themselves be so poorly measured that the validity coefficients are badly attenuated due to measurement error. For these reasons sociological researchers have rarely computed criterion-related validities.

CONTENT VALIDITY

One can imagine a *domain of meaning* that a particular construct is intended to measure. *Content validity* provides evidence for the degree that one has representatively sampled from that domain of meaning (Bohrnstedt 1983). One can think of a given domain as having various facets (Guttman 1959), and just as one can use stratification to obtain a sample of persons, so one can use stratification principles to improve the evidence for content validity.

While content validity has received close attention in the construction of achievement and proficiency measures within the fields of psychology and educational psychology, it has usually been ignored by sociologists. Many sociological researchers have instead been satisfied to construct a few items on an ad hoc, one-shot basis in the apparent belief that they are measuring what they intended to measure. In fact, the construction of good measures is a tedious, arduous, and time-consuming task.

Although it may sound like a good idea to sample the facets of a domain of meaning for a given construct, the fact that the domain cannot be enumerated in the same way that a population of persons or objects might be makes the task less rigorous than one would like. While the educational psychologist can sample four-, five-, or six-letter words in constructing a spelling test, no such clear criteria exist for the sociologist who wanders into the muddy waters of social measurement. But some guidelines can be provided. First, the researcher should search the literature carefully to determine how various authors have used the concept that is to be measured. Sociologists have several excellent handbooks that summarize social measures in use, including Robinson and Shaver's *Measures of Social Psychological Attitudes* (1973); Robinson, Rusk, and Head's *Measures of Political Attitudes* (1968); Robinson, Athanasiou, and Head's *Measures of Occupational Attitudes and Occupational Characteristics* (1969); Shaw and Wright's *Scales for the Measurement of Attitudes* (1967); and Miller's *Handbook of Research Design and Social Measurement* (1977). These volumes not only contain lists of the measures but also provide data on the reliability and validity of the measures. But since these books are out of date as soon as they go to press, researchers developing their own methods must do additional literature searches. Second, sociological researchers should rely on their own observations and insights, and ask whether they yield additional facets to the construct under consideration.

Using these two approaches, one develops *sets* of items, one to capture each of the various facets or strata within the domain of meaning. There is no simple criterion by which one can judge whether a particular domain of meaning has been properly sampled. However, there are several precautions that can be taken to help ensure the representation of the various facets within the domain.

First, the domain can be stratified into its major facets. One first notes the most central meanings of the construct, making certain that the stratification is exhaustive, that is, all major meaning facets are represented. If a particular facet appears to involve a complex of meanings, it should be subdivided further into substrata. *The more one refines the strata and substrata, the easier it is to construct the items later, and the more complete the coverage of meanings associated with the construct.* Second, one should write several items to reflect the meanings associated with each stratum and substratum. Third, after developing the items, one should pretest them on a sample of persons similar to those with whom one intends to use multivariate tools such as multiple regression (Bohrnstedt and Knoke 1988) or structural equation techniques (Bollen 1989).

It is the judgment of this author that what the *Standards* calls content validity is not a separate method for assessing validity. Instead, it is a set of procedures for sampling content domains that, if it is followed, can help provide evidence for construct validity. Messick (1989), in a similar stance, states that so-called content validity does not meet the definition of validity given above because it does not deal directly with scores or their interpretation.

CONSTRUCT VALIDITY

The 1974 *Standards* states: "A construct is . . . a theoretical idea developed to explain and to organize some aspects of existing knowledge. . . . It is a dimension understood or inferred from its network of interrelationships" (American Psychological Association 1974, p. 29). The *Standards* further indicate that in developing evidence for construct validity,

The investigator begins by formulating hypotheses about the characteristics of those who have high scores on the [measure] in contrast to those who have

low scores. Taken together, such hypotheses form at least a tentative theory about the nature of the construct the [measure] is believed to be measuring.

Such hypotheses or theoretical formulations lead to certain predictions about how people . . . will behave . . . in certain defined situations. If the investigator's theory . . . is correct, most predictions should be confirmed. (p. 30)

The notion of a construct implies hypotheses of two types. First, it implies that items from one stratum within the domain of meaning correlate because they all reflect the same underlying construct or "true" score. Second, whereas items from one domain may correlate with items from another domain, the implication is that they do so only because the constructs themselves are correlated. Furthermore, it is assumed that there are *hypotheses* about how measures of different domains correlate with one another. To repeat, construct validation involves two types of evidence. The first is evidence for *theoretical validity* (Lord and Novick 1968)—an assessment of the relationship between items and an underlying, latent, unobserved construct. The second involves evidence that the latent variables themselves correlate as hypothesized. If either or both sets of hypotheses fail, then evidence for construct validation is absent. If one can show evidence for theoretical validity but evidence about the interrelations among the constructs is missing, it suggests that one is not measuring the intended construct, or that the theory is wrong or inadequate. The more unconfirmed hypotheses one has involving the constructs, the more one is likely to assume the former rather than the latter.

Campbell (1953, 1956) uses what he calls the *multitrait-multimethod matrix* to assess the construct validity of a set of measures collected using differing methods. Thus, for example, one might collect data using multiple indicators of three constructs, say prejudice, alienation, and anomie, using three different data collection methods—a face-to-face interview, a telephone interview, and a questionnaire. To the degree that different methods yield the same or very similar results, the construct demonstrates what Campbell (1954) calls *convergent validity*. Campbell argues that in

addition the constructs must not correlate too highly with each other, that is, to use Campbell and Fiske's (1959) term, they must also exhibit *discriminant validity*. Measures that meet both criteria provide evidence for its construct validity.

VALIDITY GENERALIZATION

An important issue for work in educational and industrial settings is the degree to which the criterion-related evidence for validity obtained in one setting generalizes to other settings (American Psychological Association 1985). The point is, of course, that evidence for the validity of an instrument in one setting in no way guarantees its validity in any other setting. On the other hand, the more evidence there is of consistency of findings across settings that are maximally different, the stronger the evidence for *validity generalization*.

Evidence for validity generalization is commonly garnered in one of two ways. The usual way is simply to do a nonquantitative review of the relevant literature and, on the basis of that review, make a conclusion about the generalizability of the measure across a variety of settings. More recently, however, meta-analytic techniques (Hedges and Olkin 1985) have been employed to provide quantitative evidence for validity generalization.

Variables that may affect validity generalization include the particular criterion measure used, the sample to whom the instrument is administered, the time period during which the instrument is used, and the setting in which the assessment is done.

DIFFERENTIAL PREDICTION

When using a measure in different demographic groups, groups that differ in experience or that have received different treatments (e.g., different instructional programs), the possibility exists that the relationship between the criterion measure and the predictor may vary across groups. To the degree that this is true, a measure is said to display *differential prediction*.

Closely related is the notion of *predictive bias*.

While there is some dispute about the best definition, the most commonly accepted definition states that predictive bias exists if different regression equations are needed for different groups, and if predictions result in decisions for those groups that are different from the decisions which would be made on the basis of a pooled groups regression analysis (American Psychological Association 1985). Perhaps the best example to differentiate the two concepts is drawn from examining the relationship between education and income. It has been shown that the relationship between education and income is stronger for whites than for blacks—that is, education differentially predicts income. If education were then used as a basis for selection into jobs at a given income level, education would be said to have a predictive bias against blacks because they would have to have a greater number of years of education to be selected for a given job level, compared with whites.

Differential prediction should not be confused with *differential validity,* a term used in the context of job placement and classification. Differential validity refers to the ability of a measure, or more commonly a battery of measures, to differentially predict success (or failure) in one job compared with another. The armed services use the battery of subtests in the Armed Services Vocational Aptitude Battery (U.S. Government Printing Office 1989; McLaughlin et al. 1984) in making the initial assignment of enlistees to military occupational specialties.

MORE RECENT FORMULATIONS OF VALIDITY

More recent definitions of validity have been even broader than that used in the 1985 *Standards.* Messick (1989) defines validity as an evaluative judgment about the degree to which "empirical and theoretical rationales support the *adequacy* and *appropriateness* of *inferences* and *actions* based on . . . scores or other modes of assessment" (p. 13). For Messick, validity is more than a statement of the existing empirical evidence linking a score to a latent construct; it is also a statement about the evidence for the appropriateness of using and

interpreting the scores. While most measurement specialists separate the use of scores from their interpretation, Messick argues that the value implications and social consequences of testing are inextricably bound to the issue of validity:

> A social consequence of testing, such as adverse impact against females in the use of a quantitative test, either stems from a source of test invalidity or a valid property of the construct assessed, or both. In the former case, this adverse consequence bears on the meaning of the test scores and, in the latter case, on the meaning of the construct. In both cases, therefore, construct validity binds social consequences to the evidential basis of test interpretation and use. (1989, p. 21)

Whether the interpretation and social consequences of the uses of measures become widely adopted (i.e., are adopted in the next edition of the *Standards*) remains to be seen. Messick's definition does reinforce, however, that although there are many facets to and methods for garnering evidence regarding inferences about validity, it remains a unitary concept—evidence bears on inferences about a single measure or instrument.

(SEE ALSO: *Epistemology; Metatheory; Scientific Explanation*)

REFERENCES

American Psychological Association 1974 *Standards for Educational and Psychological Testing.* Washington, D.C.: American Psychological Association.

———1985 *Standards for Educational and Psychological Testing.* Washington, D.C.: American Psychological Association.

Bohrnstedt, G. W. 1983 *Handbook of Survey Research.* New York: Academic Press.

———, and D. Knoke 1988 *Statistics for Social Data Analysis.* Itasca, Ill.: F. E. Peacock.

Bollen, K. A. 1989 *Structural Equations with Latent Variables.* New York: Wiley.

Campbell, D. T. 1953 *A Study of Leadership Among Submarine Officers.* Columbus: Ohio State University Research Foundation.

———1954 "Operational Delineation of 'What is Learned' via the Transportation Experiment." *Psychological Review* 61:167–174.

———1956 *Leadership and Its Effects upon the Group.*

Monograph no. 83. Columbus: Ohio State University Bureau of Business Research.

———and D. W. Fiske 1959 "Convergent and Discriminant Validation by the Multitrait-Multimethod Matrix." *Psychological Bulletin* 56:81–105.

Hedges, L. V., and I. Olkin 1985 *Statistical Methods for Meta-Analysis.* Orlando, Fla.: Academic Press.

Guttman, L. 1959 "A Structural Theory for Intergroup Beliefs and Action." *American Sociological Review* 24:318–328.

Lord, F. M., and M. R. Novick 1968 *Statistical Theories of Mental Test Scores.* Reading, Mass.: Addison-Wesley.

McLaughlin, D. H., et al. 1984 *Validation of Current and Alternative Armed Services Vocational Aptitude Battery (ASVAB) Area Composites.* Washington, D.C.: U.S. Army Research Institute for the Behavioral and Social Sciences.

Messick, S. 1989 "Validity." In L. Linn, ed., *Educational Measurement,* 3rd ed. New York: Macmillan.

Miller, D. 1977 *Handbook of Research Design and Social Measurement,* 3rd ed. New York: David McKay.

Nunnally, J. C. 1967 *Psychometric Theory.* New York: McGraw-Hill.

Robinson, J. P., J. G. Rusk, and K. B. Head 1968 *Measures of Political Attitudes.* Ann Arbor, Mich.: Institute for Social Research.

Robinson, J. P., R. Athanasiou, and K. B. Head 1969 *Measures of Occupational Attitudes and Occupational Characteristics.* Ann Arbor, Mich.: Institute for Social Research.

Robinson, J. P., and P. R. Shaver 1973 *Measures of Social Psychological Attitudes.* Ann Arbor, Mich.: Institute for Social Research.

Shaw, M., and J. Wright 1967 *Scales for the Measurement of Attitudes.* New York: McGraw-Hill.

U.S. Government Printing Office 1989 *A Brief Guide: ASVAB for Counselors and Educators.* Washington, D.C.: U.S. Government Printing Office.

GEORGE W. BOHRNSTEDT

VALUE-FREE ANALYSIS. *See* Epistemology; Scientific Explanation.

VALUE THEORY AND RESEARCH

Values are cognitive representations of human needs (Rokeach 1973; Ball-Rokeach, Rokeach, and Grube 1984). Values indicate preferences people share for certain types of outcomes in their lives and for certain types of conduct. These outcomes and conduct are valued, or preferred, because they lead to the greatest general satisfaction of individual, group, and societal needs or goals. The sociological and social psychological study of human values has been approached from several theoretical positions. Key issues that differentiate value conceptualizations and measurement include: (1) whether values should be conceived as arbitrary preferences or as systems of relative importance; (2) the causal or developmental roots of values; and (3) the role values play in a person's overall psychological structure.

The approach to value as an arbitrary preference is generally associated with economics and with behavioral psychology (Homans 1961). Spates (1983) described the role this conception played in early sociological theories of values. The economic conception of value is a calculation of the worth of an object in use or exchange. Value then is an attribute of an object, not a person. The behavioral psychologist asserts that the role of values in human behavior is that stimuli possess more or less value, and a person's response to any given stimulus is in part determined by the value held by the stimulus. Behavior and values are thus linked arbitrarily; the link depends on encounters between people and stimuli for values to exercise any effect at all.

The clear contrast to the conception of value as an attribute of an object is the conception of a value as a belief. It is in this cognitive conception that the study of values has been most productive from the standpoint of sociology. The cognitive nature of values has undergone significant theoretical examination and empirical test. The theoretical development of the concept of values was advanced significantly by Talcott Parsons and the functionalist theorists he inspired in the late 1940s and early 1950s (Spates 1983). Ultimately, values were held by the functionalists to be the counter to behaviorism; values served to organize behavior according to internal, cognitive preferences rather than according strictly to the characteristics of the stimuli in the world. In turn, values served as a concept that united the individual's needs with the broader needs of society. Societies developed values as a means of balancing members' needs against the needs of the society to maintain and enhance itself (Parsons and Shils 1951).

In addition to the functionalist developments, there was a concept of values, developed by Florence Kluckhohn (1950), that included the important proposition that values are arranged hierarchically in relation to one another. This concept allows a single person to hold a number of distinct values, but to hold them in relation to one another in what Rokeach would call "a continuum of relative importance" (Rokeach 1973, p. 7). People and the societies they live in could be compared and contrasted according to the similarities in their value continua.

Each separate attempt to define and explore values led to slightly different theoretical assumptions regarding the precise ways in which values interacted. In 1951 Parsons, Edward Shils, and Clyde Kluckhohn had introduced the idea of "value orientations" (Parsons and Shils 1951; Kluckhohn 1951). Value orientations were systems of values that could be recognized as distinctly typical of a given society. American society in the 1950s, for instance, was said to be typified by an instrumental activist value orientation. Ralph K. White (1951) offered a "value catalogue," organized along lines similar to the concepts of Parsons, Shils, and Kluckhohn.

F. Kluckhohn and Fred Strodtbeck (1961) argued that the underlying structure of values was built around beliefs that served to answer existential questions about the nature of the universe (e.g., what is human nature?). The answers to these questions would serve to structure all subsequent sense-making and consequent behavior. Charles Morris (1956) developed thirteen different "ways of living" that were distinguished by particular arrangements and emphases of values. Way 4, for instance, begins, "Life is something to be . . . sensuously enjoyed, enjoyed with relish and abandonment" (Morris 1956, p. 16). Morris then surveyed residents of several cultures to examine the ways preferred by members of each. While respondents were offered the opportunity

to construct their own way and add it to the list, few were able to enhance the list of thirteen Morris had settled on by the late 1940s. Each of these research projects developed key aspects of the concept of values. They, however, lacked clear conceptions of specific values and produced ad hoc lists, generated by subjects in each study, that hampered generalization (Kohn 1969).

Progress was made toward greater specialization in the work of Robin Williams. Williams (1968, 1979), who also rejected the economic, arbitrary value conception, proposed "values-as-criteria" for judging objects or cognitions. Williams's concept separates values from other beliefs and recognizes that values have both affective and cognitive components, as well as the essential element of preference, or "directionality." Melvin Kohn (1969) employed these ideas in his study of the values of parents. Kohn developed a stable set of values that, he proposed, virtually exhausted the set of values that parents might hold regarding their children. Kohn was especially interested in the differences in value systems between classes and across cultures. He was able to demonstrate similarities between working-class values in Italy and the United States, and differences between the middle class and working class in each country. Kohn did not, however, articulate a clear theory of the interaction between values, such as the "value orientations" of Parsons, Shils, and Kluckhohn, or Morris's ways of living.

A productive branch of research that sprang from the diverse roots heretofore mentioned was begun by Milton Rokeach and summarized in *The Nature of Human Values* (1973). Rokeach offered the following definitions:

> *A value is an enduring belief that a specific mode of conduct or end-state of existence is personally or socially preferable to an opposite or converse mode of conduct or end-state of existence. A value system is an enduring organization of beliefs concerning desirable modes of conduct or end-states of existence along a continuum of relative importance* (Rokeach 1973, p. 5).

Rokeach observed that his definitions of values and value systems were "wholly compatible" with those offered by C. Kluckhohn (1951). The theoretical contribution of Rokeach's definitions include (1) their incorporation of the notion of *ipsativity,* and (2) their distinction between values concerned with modes of conduct (*instrumental* values) and values concerned with end-states of existence (*terminal* values).

Ipsativity is choice-based cognition wherein values must be weighed against one another. For example, while people may be counted on to believe that honesty is preferable to its converse, in life people must balance their preference for honesty against their preference for politeness. Some people, and some cultures, will encourage one over the other, while different people will encourage other systems of priorities. It is the overall complex of priorities that makes up the value system. Rokeach's conceptualization, in this respect, recalled F. Kluckhohn's (1950) proposition regarding the interplay of values. Rokeach advanced and systematized these relations in a reliable fashion.

Recognizing a distinction between terminal and instrumental values, Rokeach echoed many of the earlier functional theorists. Rokeach developed a theory of the role of values in the human psychology that advanced the state of value theory beyond earlier functionalist propositions. He identified the need to maintain and enhance self-esteem as the primary psychological motivation (Ball-Rokeach, Rokeach, and Grube 1984). Values served this need by providing people with standards for evaluation of their own and others' morality and competence.

While the definition offered by Rokeach serves to distinguish values as cognitions from other cognitions, such as attitudes and interests, it also provides for methodological insight as to the measurement and analysis of values. As did earlier theorists, Rokeach (1973) contended that values were few in number, and that the universe of values—particularly terminal values—was knowable. Reviewing the literature, and conducting tests on several populations, he identified eighteen terminal values and eighteen instrumental values that, while not exhaustive, were sufficiently representative to serve in measurement and comparison.

F. Kluckhohn, Morris, and Kohn had each, independently, developed methods of value measurement that relied implicitly on the notion that each value had a role in the belief system. Rokeach made this notion explicit by abandoning the usual *rating* of values in favor of a *ranking* system. Morris (1956) and Kohn (1969) had subjects rate each value independently of each other value. They then organized the values in orders of preference based on the highest rated, next-highest, and so on.

Rokeach (1973), however, asserted the importance of correspondence between the measurement tool and the concept (Ball-Rokeach and Loges 1990). Since *each* value was, by definition, a universal belief, then each value must be presumed to be held simultaneously with each other value. They are then not independent of one another, but in fact related to one another. One cannot elevate a value in importance without at least marginally reducing another in importance.

These assumptions establish the conceptual logic of the Rokeach Value Survey (RVS) (1967, 1982). The measurement characteristic of particular importance is that both the question and the response formats of the RVS place the respondent in a phenomenological situation of *choice;* respondent behavior is choice behavior (Rokeach and Ball-Rokeach 1989; Ball-Rokeach and Loges 1991). The instructions ask the respondents to rank eighteen terminal and, then, eighteen instrumental values in order of importance to them as guiding principles in their personal life. They choose between positives, or what Rokeach would call "different kinds of sunshine" (Ball-Rokeach and Loges 1991, p. 2). A threat to validity due to social desirability is thus removed. There is every indication that respondents from widely varying educational and age levels are able to understand, and reliably perform, in this choice situation (Ball-Rokeach, Rokeach, and Grube 1984, chap. 3). Ties are not allowed. While some respondents indicate that they would like to be able to employ ties, they nonetheless break ties and do so reliably.

The introduction of the RVS offered a tool for the measurement of values that allowed for replication and for comparative research. With a reliable instrument, it became possible to explore relationships between values and other beliefs, and between values and behavior, more systematically than had been possible in the past. In the course of testing the face and predictive validity of the RVS, Rokeach and his colleagues studied populations varying from college students to national samples of Americans. These studies demonstrated theoretically informative links between values and attitudes and values and behavior. Many subsequent studies undertaken by other scholars, Norman Feather (1975) being notable among them, have provided compatible or supportive findings (Cochrane 1971; Conroy, Katkin, and Barnette 1973; Hopkins 1973; Vidmar and Rokeach 1974; Greenstein 1976; Grube 1979; Sanders and Atwood 1979; Araji and Ball-Rokeach 1984; Tetlock 1986).

Value priorities have been shown to be logically related to a now-extensive array of attitudinal and behavioral patterns exhibited by individuals, groups, organizations, and social institutions, including indicators of racism, sexism, life-style, life cycle, religiosity, environmentalism, media dependency relations, addiction, socioeconomic status, occupational choice and success, political orientation, and organizational and institutional priorities (see Rokeach 1973, 1979; Feather 1975; Ball-Rokeach, Rokeach, and Grube 1984; Rokeach and Ball-Rokeach 1989). More challenging has been a program of research begun by Rokeach in 1967 to develop and demonstrate the validity of a theory of value change and stability. These efforts initially entailed experimental research designed to enduringly change values that were known to underlie racist attitudes and behaviors.

Self-confrontation is the method Rokeach developed to effect value change. The method works through first raising the salience of value priorities (by completing the RVS), then providing information that gives respondents a means of interpreting their value priorities privately, that is, their surveys are not interpreted by the research-

er, but interpreted by the respondents themselves. The general strategy was first to identify distinctive values associated with certain behaviors or attitudes. Second, a message to provoke self-confrontation was designed; that is, a Socratic message meant to instigate a process of specific self-evaluation as to one's morality or competence in light of newly acquired knowledge of one's value priorities and their implications for logically related behaviors or attitudes. Those satisfied that there is no contradiction between their self-conceptions as moral and competent and their value priorities, attitudes, and behavior are likely to exhibit stabilization of their belief–behavior patterns. Given the opportunity to do so, those self-dissatisfied, owing to contradictions between their self-conceptions and their value priorities, attitudes, or behaviors—specific contradictions not known or salient prior to the experience of self-confrontation—are most likely to change the specific values, attitudes, or behaviors that produce self-dissatisfaction, and thereby restore self-esteem.

The successful application of this belief and behavior change and stabilization method in more than twenty-five studies of widely varying populations and social contexts is reviewed in Ball-Rokeach, Rokeach, and Grube (1984, chap. 3). Perhaps the most ambitious of these studies brings together the logic of media system dependency (Ball-Rokeach et al., 1990) and belief system theories; the intention to study, in a natural media exposure field experiment, the long-term effects of a television program created by the researchers and their professional consultants, "The Great American Values Test." The research aims were to bring about value stabilization and change that led to changes in real-life environmental and political attitudes and behaviors some three months postviewing. These aims were achieved, most importantly with respect to behavior. Life-cycle changes and critical event cohort effects are bound to provoke naturally the sort of self-confrontation that Rokeach and his colleagues developed in laboratory and field settings.

The chain of effects that has been suggested

from values to behavior has been examined by Ann Swidler (1986). Swidler suggests that the concept of culture, which Parsons and Shils (1951) and C. Kluckhohn (1952) had seemed to argue was functionally equivalent to values, is actually a combination of values and practices—beliefs and behaviors—neither of which by itself provides a reliable predictor of action. Swidler does, however, suggest that when a person's life is "settled," that is, when a distinct pattern of behaviors has emerged and stabilized, values may play a larger role in affecting behavior than when one's life is undergoing constant change.

Ronald Inglehart (1981) has examined values data from Europe, Japan, and the United States collected in the 1970s to see if the trend toward "postmaterialist values" noted in the early 1970s was maintained throughout the decade. Drawing on Maslow's (1954) hierarchy of needs, Inglehart suggests that change from materialist to postmaterialist values takes place when there is a lessening of scarcity in the socioeconomic environment. People tend to place "the greatest subjective value on those things that are in relatively short supply" (Inglehart 1981, p. 881), whether they be material or nonmaterial states. A "substantial time lag" may be involved, however, owing to the tendency of people's values to "reflect the conditions that prevailed during one's preadult years" (Inglehart 1981, p. 881). A child raised during the Depression, for example, may maintain "depression values" even in the more affluent post-World War II era. Inglehart has employed Rokeach's terminal values to operationalize materialist and postmaterialist goals (e.g., a comfortable life and a sense of accomplishment, respectively). The presence of values, he writes, "can be inferred from a consistent pattern of emphasis on given types of goals" (Inglehart 1981, p. 884).

Inglehart's (1985) longitudinal analysis of data collected between 1968 and 1981 on the terminal values of American adults demonstrated both remarkable stability and some interesting changes in priorities (cf. Rokeach and Ball-Rokeach 1989). On the basis of these findings he challenged Converse's (1964) thesis that "mass publics" have only randomly developed attitudes. Inglehart

(1985) also notes, however, that while at the aggregate level the priorities are stable, certain individual level changes can be observed in what he calls "the level of analysis paradox." The related question of synchronous stability and change of belief systems was explored by Rokeach (1985) in his Kurt Lewin Memorial Address. Whatever the level of analysis, the challenge is to develop theory that brings together the social and personal dynamics of belief stability and change.

The RVS provided the essential starting point for the work of Shalom Schwartz and Wolfgang Bilsky (1987, 1990). Schwartz and Bilsky have attempted to refine the thirty-six instrumental and terminal values Rokeach used to compile his survey. A value for *power* is proposed, and the usefulness of a conceptual distinction between terminal and instrumental values is challenged (Schwartz and Bilsky 1990). Additionally, Schwartz and Bilsky (1990) suggest that values can be said to comprise seven "domains" that may present a more parsimonious theory than Rokeach offers. The contributions to value theory and research of this ambitious research program await completion.

In a world of chaotic contradiction where national borders give way to regionalism at the same time that ethnic subcultures rise up from failed attempts to impose nationhood, classical sociological issues of culture and structure abound. These are, as they have long been conceived to be, issues of values and value systems. Fundamental dilemmas of identity, personal, social, and cultural, are both represented and experienced in value terms. Definitions of development and the good life, again both personal and social, are blurred by a phenomenological vice of value conflict. Such conditions of pervasive and focused ambiguities of structure and cognition (Ball-Rokeach 1973) afford fertile ground for the continuation of value theory and research en route to building understandings of political economy and culture. Freed from the idea that values are too abstract for theoretical and methodological articulation of social, cultural, and personal phenomena in productive terms, equipped with a systematic literature of value theory and research on which to build, and set in a world that demands essential understandings of change and stability, value theory and research will most likely be at the forefront of a much-needed renaissance of social thought.

(SEE ALSO: *Attitudes; Mass Media Research; Public Opinion*)

REFERENCES

Araji, S. K., and Sandra J. Ball-Rokeach 1984 "College Students' Living Arrangements and Attitudes Toward Family Roles: Demographic and Value Correlates." *Alternative Life Styles* 6:284–298.

Ball-Rokeach, Sandra J. 1973 "From Pervasive Ambiguity to a Definition of the Situation." *Sociometry* 36:378–389.

———, and William E. Loges 1990 "The Measurement of Belief: Phenomenological Correspondence between Method and Concept in Values and Attitude Research." Paper to be presented at the Annual Meeting of the American Sociological Association, Cincinnati, Ohio, 1991.

———, Gerard J. Power, Kendall K. Guthrie, and Ross W. Waring 1990 "Value-Framing Abortion in the United States: An Application of Media System Dependency Theory." *International Journal of Public Opinion Research* 2:249–273.

———, Milton Rokeach, and Joel W. Grube 1984 *The Great American Values Test: Influencing Behavior and Belief Through Television.* New York: Free Press.

Cochrane, R. 1971 "The Structure of Value Systems in Male and Female Prisoners." *British Journal of Criminology* 11:73–79.

Conroy, W. J., E. S. Katkin, and W. L. Barnette 1973 "Modification of Smoking Behavior by Rokeach's Self-Confrontation Technique." Paper presented to the 81st Meeting of the Southeastern Psychological Association, New Orleans, La., April 7, 1973.

Converse, Phillip E. 1964 "The Nature of Belief Systems Among Mass Publics." In David Apter, ed., *Ideology and Discontent.* New York: Free Press.

Feather, Norman T. 1975 *Values in Education and Society.* New York: Free Press.

Greenstein, T. 1976 "Behavior Change Through Value Self-Confrontation: A Field Experiment." *Journal of Personality and Social Psychology* 34:254–262.

Grube, Joel W. 1979 "Inconsistencies Among Values, Attitudes, and Behaviors as Determinants of Self-

dissatisfaction and Change." Ph.D. diss., Washington State University.

Homans, George C. 1961 *Social Behavior: Its Elementary Forms.* New York: Harcourt, Brace and World.

Hopkins, S. W., Jr. 1973 "Behavioral and Attitude Changes Produced from Dissonance Created Between Interpersonal Values and Attitudes." Ph.D. diss., University of Texas at Austin.

Inglehart, Ronald 1981 "Post-Materialism in an Environment of Insecurity." *American Political Science Review* 75:880–900.

———1985 "Aggregate Stability and Individual-Level Flux in Mass Belief Systems: The Level of Analysis Paradox." *American Political Science Review* 79:97–116.

Kluckhohn, Clyde 1951 "Values and Value Orientation in the Theory of Action." In Talcott Parsons and Edward A. Shils, eds., *Toward a General Theory of Action.* New York: Harper and Row.

Kluckhohn, Florence 1950 "Dominant and Substitute Profiles of Cultural Orientations." *Social Forces* 28:376–393.

———, and Fred L. Strodtbeck 1961 *Variations in Value Orientations.* Bloomington, Ind.: Row, Peterson.

Kohn, Melvin L. 1969 *Class and Conformity: A Study in Values.* Homewood, Ill.: Dorsey Press.

Maslow, A. H. 1954 *Motivation and Personality.* New York: Harper and Row.

Morris, Charles 1956 *Varieties of Human Value.* Chicago: University of Chicago Press.

Parsons, Talcott, and Edward A. Shils 1951 "Values, Motives, and Systems of Action." In Talcott Parsons and Edward A. Shils, eds., *Toward a General Theory of Action.* New York: Harper and Row.

Rokeach, Milton 1967, 1982 *Value Survey.* Palo Alto, Calif.: Consulting Psychologists Press.

———1973 *The Nature of Human Values.* New York: Free Press.

———(ed.) 1979 *Understanding Human Values: Individual and Societal.* New York: Free Press.

———1985 "Inducing Change and Stability in Belief Systems and Personality Structures." *Journal of Social Issues* 41:153–171.

———, and Sandra J. Ball-Rokeach 1989 "Stability and Change in American Value Priorities 1968–1981." *American Psychologist* 44:775–784.

Sanders, K. R., and L. E. Atwood 1979 "Value Change Initiated by the Mass Media." In M. Rokeach, ed., *Understanding Human Values: Individual and Societal.* New York: Free Press.

Schwartz, Shalom H., and Wolfgang Bilsky 1987 "Toward a Psychological Structure of Human Values." *Journal of Personality and Social Psychology* 53:550–562.

————1990 "Toward a Theory of the Universal Content and Structure of Values: Extensions and Cross-cultural Replications." *Journal of Personality and Social Psychology* 58:878–891.

Spates, James L. 1983 "The Sociology of Values." *Annual Review of Sociology* 9:27–49.

Swidler, Ann 1986 "Culture in Action: Symbols and Strategies." *American Sociological Review* 51:273–286.

Tetlock, P. E. 1986 "A Value Pluralism Model of Ideological Reasoning." *Journal of Personality and Social Psychology* 50:819–827.

Vidmar, Neil, and Milton Rokeach 1974 "Archie Bunker's Bigotry: A Study in Selective Perception and Exposure." *Journal of Communication* 24:36–47.

White, R. K. 1951 *Value Analysis.* New York: Society for the Psychological Study of Social Issues.

Williams, Robin M. 1968 "Values." In David L. Sills, ed., *International Encyclopedia of the Social Sciences.* New York: Macmillan.

————1979 "Change and Stability in Values and Value Systems: A Sociological Perspective." In Milton Rokeach, ed., *Understanding Human Values.* New York: Free Press.

Sandra J. Ball-Rokeach
William E. Loges

VIOLENT CRIME Violent crime is commonly defined as occurring when one person illegally and intentionally physically injures, or threatens to physically injure, another. Assault, robbery, rape, and murder are the classic examples of serious violent crime. This definition is beguilingly simple, however, and one of the first lessons learned in studying violent crime is how much disagreement is possible over its definition and, thus, over its measurement, description, and explanation (Nettler 1982). There are problems in defining intent, in documenting physical injuries, and in determining how threat is perceived. Measuring and comparing both amounts and public conceptions of violent crime in different times and places are problematic for these and other reasons.

Most research on violent crime accepts the legal definitions germane to the jurisdiction under study and relies on official crime reports based on these legal definitions. (Most developed nations compile annual reports on the incidence of crime. For example, in Canada, the Canadian Centre for Justice Statistics publishes Canadian Crime Statistics; in the United States, the Federal Bureau of Investigation publishes the Uniform Crime Reports.) There are two principal difficulties with this approach to measuring crime. While legal definitions and official statistics provide a reliable guide to what is designated as crime *within* a given society, they may not in themselves accurately indicate differences *among* societies in similar types of behavior. This is because the definition of even the most serious violent crimes, including murder, can vary. Abortion, infanticide, and some deaths caused by drivers of motor vehicles have been considered criminal homicide in some societies and not in others. The acceptance of legal definitions as given neglects the issue of why certain acts are defined as crime in some places or eras and not others.

The second difficulty with using legal definitions and official statistics to define the field of study is more serious. Official statistics simply do not accurately measure levels of violent crime even within a single society. Using legal definitions typically directs researchers to official agencies such as the police, the courts, and the coroner for data, but characteristics of these agencies inevitably influence how these acts are interpreted and reported. Furthermore, some acts that appear to fit the legal definitions may only infrequently be subject to criminal enforcement, such as forms of white collar or corporate crime. Since the public is the primary means by which officials learn about violent crime, popular views on both crime and the agencies that deal with it also determine which acts are reported. Less than half of all rapes and assaults are reported to the police in most Western nations. As a result, official statistics on violent crime reflect both more and less than its true incidence (O'Brien 1985). Moreover, reliance on only official statistics neglects the issue of why laws are enforced against certain acts or persons and not others.

Some researchers have attempted to avoid these problems by using victimization surveys and self-report studies, in which people are asked about their experiences as either victims or perpetrators of certain acts. These provide higher estimates of the incidence of violent crime than do official statistics, and they describe the types of acts and actors that are less likely to appear in official statistics. Both have been criticized, however, for their reliance on the honesty and comprehension of respondents and for sometimes including trivial acts that should not be considered "real crime" (O'Brien 1985).

DIFFERENCES IN VIOLENT CRIME OVER TIME, PLACE, AND PERSONS

To describe trends over time or differences among societies in violent crime, researchers presently must rely on official statistics, since self-report and victimization studies are not extensive enough. In so doing, the problems with comparing data from various official sources need to be kept in mind. The most reliable information is for the most serious crimes, especially murder and robbery. This information suggests that rates of violent crime declined over the last several centuries in Western societies, reached a low point in the first half of the twentieth century, and then increased sharply, beginning in the late 1960s. Shorter term crime waves during the early stages of urbanization and industrialization, and after wars, disrupted the general downward trend (Gurr 1989). At present, rates of violent crime are highest in several Latin American and Caribbean countries and lowest in northern and western Europe. The United States is anomalous among developed nations for its level of violent crime: Its rate of homicide is as much as ten times greater than European rates, and its robbery rate is at least thirty times that of Japan's (Archer and Gartner 1984).

Violent crime is unevenly distributed not only *among* but also *within* societies. Large regional differences are common in many countries. For example, rates of violent crime are higher in southern Italy, the southwestern and southern United States, and the western provinces of Canada. Violent crime also tends to be concentrated in urban areas, especially within developed countries. For the most serious of these crimes, offenders are predominantly young adult males, and members of disadvantaged racial and ethnic minority groups tend to be overrepresented among offenders. The majority of violent offenders have a criminal record, but few specialize in a particular type of crime (Miller, Dinitz, and Conrad 1982). Most violent crimes involve little planning, skill, or attention to their consequences.

Victims of violent crime, with the exception of rape victims, generally share many of the characteristics of their victimizers, most being young, economically disadvantaged males. Females make up a larger proportion of victims than they do offenders, the majority victimized by a male they are related to or acquainted with. A substantial number of violent crimes occur among family members, though this proportion is smaller in the United States than other nations and has declined in recent years. In contrast, over one-third of violent crimes in the United States are committed against strangers, a much higher proportion than in most developed nations.

EXPLAINING VIOLENT CRIME

There are three levels of analysis that frame sociological explanations of violent crime: the individual, the situational, and the structural-cultural. Individual-level analyses typically look for characteristics of offenders that either predispose them to violence or fail to discourage them from it. Many individual-level theories focus on how violence is learned, or how restraint is not learned, from family, peers, the media, or the broader culture (Wilson and Herrnstein 1985). The intergenerational transmission of violence and the effects of the mass media on violent behavior are two issues recently addressed by learning theories (Straus and Gelles 1990; Phillips 1983). While learning theories have garnered much support, more systematic evidence of the link between exposure to "lessons" in violence and a person's violent behavior is needed to substantiate them.

Situational approaches focus on the more immediate factors and processes surrounding violent crime (Luckenbill 1984). The interaction of participants, the nature of the conflict, the presence of alcohol, drugs, or weapons, all are examined to understand how conflicts escalate to violence. Situational analyses also emphasize the subjective, symbolic aspects of violent crime. Saving face by responding to insults or resistance with violence and creating a stance of moral superiority in relation to the victim are common themes in accounts of murder, robbery, and rape (Katz 1988).

Structural-cultural approaches tend to emphasize broader social forces, processes, and value systems that affect the motivations, controls, or opportunities for violent crime. Both structural and cultural analyses attempt to explain variations in rates of violent crime among population aggregates: cities, states, regions, and nations. These two approaches differ, however, in the importance placed on individual cognitions and propensities toward violence. Cultural accounts typically see these as crucial for explaining the distribution of violent crime among different groups, whereas structural accounts do not. Instead, structural analyses examine how social conditions either promote violence or distribute opportunities for victimization in a population. Structural analyses have found that the potential for violent conflicts and, hence, rates of violent crime are greater where the distribution of economic resources is more unequal, ethnic or racial heterogeneity and inequality are greater, and divorce rates are higher (Blau and Blau 1982; Gartner 1990). The routine-activity perspective is a structural approach that focuses on the distribution of opportunities for violent crime in social space (Cohen and Felson 1979). According to this perspective,

major social changes since World War II, especially the movement of women into the labor force and the dispersion of daily activities away from the home, have increased the opportunities for victimization.

The best-known example of a cultural approach to explaining violent crime begins with the observation that certain groups in a population (e.g., African-Americans in the United States, aborigines in Canada), certain geographic regions of nations (e.g., Sardinia in Italy, southern states in the United States), or certain nations (e.g., Colombia, Mexico) have especially high rates of violent crime. According to this subcultural perspective, norms and values supporting the use of force in interpersonal and group relations are transmitted by group members through social learning (Wolfgang and Ferracuti 1967). A quite different sort of cultural approach, which integrates structural themes, attributes differences in violent crime between Canada and the United States to differences in political ideologies grounded in historical contingencies (Hagan and Leon 1977).

CONTROLLING VIOLENT CRIME

Each type of explanation has implications for crime-control policies. Incapacitation through long prison sentences or capital punishment, deterrence through increased certainty and severity of punishment, and rehabilitation through individually designed treatment programs are individual-level approaches to controlling violent crime. On the whole, such programs have not been found to be very effective (Martinson 1974). Stricter limits on access to guns, alcohol, and drugs are often proposed as a means to decrease the likelihood that conflictual situations will escalate to serious violence. Here, too, there is much debate and little evidence that such policies could reduce violent crime more than marginally (see, for example, Wright, Rossi, and Daly 1984). Policies designed to reduce economic and racial discrimination, or increase legitimate opportunities, assume that crime prevention requires major structural change. Such policies have been under attack in recent years from those who claim any gains are outweighed by their costs (Wilson 1983).

Pessimism over our ability to control violent crime has not discouraged researchers from posing new approaches and investigating neglected areas. Important advances have been made in research on family violence (Straus and Gelles 1990), violence against women (Gordon and Riger 1988), careers of violent offenders (Miller, Dinitz, and Conrad 1982), and terrorism (Gibbs 1989). Concepts from other disciplines are being integrated to create innovative new frameworks for future analyses (Cohen and Machalek 1988). Together these efforts demonstrate the continued vitality of the sociological study of criminal violence.

(SEE ALSO: *Family Violence; Sexual Violence and Abuse; Terrorism*)

REFERENCES

Archer, Dane, and Rosemary Gartner 1984 *Violence and Crime in Cross-National Perspective.* New Haven, Conn.: Yale University Press.

Blau, Judith R., and Peter Blau 1982 "The Cost of Inequality: Metropolitan Structure and Urban Crime." *American Sociological Review* 48:34–45.

Cohen, Lawrence E., and Marcus Felson 1979 "Social Change and Crime Rate Trends: A Routine Activities Approach." *American Sociological Review* 44:558–607.

Cohen, Lawrence E., and Richard Machalek 1988 "A General Theory of Expropriative Crime: An Evolutionary Ecological Approach." *American Journal of Sociology* 94:465–501.

Gartner, Rosemary 1990 "The Victims of Homicide: A Temporal and Cross-National Comparison." *American Sociological Review* 55:92–106.

Gibbs, Jack P. 1989 "Conceptualization of Terrorism." *American Sociological Review* 54:329–340.

Gordon, Margaret T., and Stephanie Riger 1988 *The Female Fear.* New York: Free Press.

Gurr, Ted Robert 1989 "Historical Trends in Violent Crime: Europe and the United States." Pp. 21–54 in *Violence in America,* vol. 1. Newbury Park, Calif.: Sage.

Hagan, John, and Jeffrey Leon 1977 "Philosophy and Sociology of Crime Control." *Sociological Inquiry* 47:181–208.

Katz, Jack 1988 *Seductions of Crime: Moral and Sensual Attractions of Doing Evil.* New York: Basic Books.

Luckenbill, David F. 1984 "Murder and Assault." In Robert F. Meier, ed., *Major Forms of Crime.* Beverly Hills, Calif.: Sage.

Martinson, Robert 1974 "What Works? Questions and Answers about Prison Reform." *Public Interest* 35: 22–54.

Miller, Stuart J., Simon Dinitz, and John P. Conrad 1982 *Careers of the Violent.* Lexington Mass.: Lexington Books.

Nettler, Gwynn 1982 *Killing One Another.* Cincinnati, Ohio: Anderson.

O'Brien, Robert M. 1985 *Crime and Victimization Data.* Beverly Hills, Calif.: Sage.

Phillips, David 1983 "The Impact of Mass Media Violence on U.S. Homicides." *American Sociological Review* 48:560–568.

Straus, Murray A., and Richard J. Gelles 1990 *Physical Violence in American Families.* New Brunswick, N.J.: Transaction.

Wilson, James Q. 1983 *Thinking about Crime,* rev. ed. New York: Basic Books.

———, and Richard J. Herrnstein 1985 *Crime and Human Nature.* New York: Simon & Schuster.

Wolfgang, Marvin E., and Franco Ferracuti 1967 *The Subculture of Violence: Towards an Integrated Theory in Criminology.* London: Tavistock.

Wright, James, Peter Rossi, and Kathleen Daly 1984 *Under the Gun: Weapons, Crime, and Violence in America.* New York: Aldine.

ROSEMARY GARTNER

VOLUNTARY ASSOCIATIONS Within four years after Mikhail Gorbachev came to power as head of the USSR in 1985, people in the Soviet Union were forming what they called "informal groups," which have the characteristics of voluntary associations as we know them in the West. That is, these groups were independent of control from sources outside themselves, people were free to join or leave, and members established their own objectives and goals and the means to achieve them.

One of the major manifestations of the movement toward political change in Eastern Europe since 1988 has been the emergence of voluntary associations, especially political parties. These have brought with them personal and social freedoms long suppressed.

On the other hand, these voluntary associations emerged because the people valued them and were ready to organize. At the same time, President Gorbachev allowed them to emerge, even encouraged their existence.

In his commentary on American society, Alexis de Tocqueville (1956) took particular note of the degree to which Americans formed groups to serve personal interests and to solve problems, from the most mundane to the most profound. Perhaps New England small-town government acted in important ways as a type of voluntary association, with "town meetings" designed to solve its own problems, from building schools to constructing roads to caring for the poor. Indeed, American nostalgia for local control may owe much to this early form of voluntary association. Certainly the autonomous religious congregations coupled with local governments gave impetus to the growth of voluntary associations in the nineteenth and twentieth centuries. Today these associations are a ubiquitous part of American society.

CHARACTERISTICS AND OBJECTIVES OF VOLUNTARY ASSOCIATIONS

In 1967, Arnold Rose estimated that there were over 100,000 such organizations in the United States (Rose 1967). While no recent census is known to have been taken, it is widely believed that the number may now be close to 200,000. These voluntary associations are diverse in character and have a variety of sizes, structures, and objectives. Some groups, such as neighborhood improvement associations and local bowling leagues, are loosely structured, have relatively few members, and may be short-lived, while organizations such as the American Sociological Association, the American Civil Liberties Union, and the Ku Klux Klan have thousands of members and persist over long periods of time. Furthermore, the structure of voluntary associations can range from highly bureaucratic to very informal. There can be high fees to join some organizations such as a yacht club, or there can be little or no fees to join an organization such as a bowling club.

Voluntary associations also exist for differing reasons and with varying objectives. While some (such as a lobbying organization or a community service group) exist to attain specific external goals, there are others (such as biking clubs or prayer groups) whose goals are more internal. The latter exist as ends in themselves, with objectives that may be religious, social, or recreational. Voluntary associations have also been identified as instrumental or expressive. Of course, some organizations have the characteristics of both types, in which case they would be labeled as expressive–instrumental or instrumental–expressive, depending on the primacy of focus (Gordon and Babchuk 1959). The Rotary and the Elks clubs are two examples of such associations. Furthermore, it is possible that an association, in addition to its expressed objectives and actual functions, may also fulfill certain latent functions for the members, for society, or both. For example, a neighborhood association whose expressed objective is to increase the quality of life of its residents (manifest function) may also provide members with opportunities to gain leadership and organizational skills (latent function) that may later lead them into politics at the local, state, or even national level.

Voluntary associations may serve a number of personal as well as societal functions. For example, researchers have found that membership in voluntary associations provides individuals with the opportunity to learn social norms, acquire information, and develop organizational and leadership skills. In addition, it has been hypothesized that membership serves to combat loneliness, increase self-esteem, and decrease members' sense of powerlessness (Sills 1968). Support groups, as varied as the American Legion and Alcoholics Anonymous, are good examples of organizations that serve the latter set of functions.

At the societal level, voluntary associations have many functions. Clearly, they serve an important governing role at the local, regional, and national level and perform tasks as varied as community decision making, emergency relief, fund-raising, public information campaigns, and professional licensing (Sills 1968). Voluntary associations also provide arenas for social change, the integration of subgroups, and power distribution (Sills 1968). For example, members of minority groups have formed voluntary associations such as the National Association for the Advancement of Colored People (NAACP) and the Mexican-American Legal Defense Education Fund (MALDEF) to increase political power and ensure equal rights. Political parties are the quintessential voluntary associations of Western democracies.

MEMBERSHIP IN VOLUNTARY ASSOCIATIONS

Researchers studying voluntary associations have found varying support for Tocqueville's assessment of the United States as a nation of "joiners." Hyman and Wright (1971) reported that in 1962 57 percent of the adult population did *not* belong to a voluntary association. At about the same time, local and regional studies found higher participation rates. For example, Babchuk and Booth's Nebraska study (1969) found that 80 percent of the adult population belonged to at least one voluntary association. More recently, Knoke observed that "perhaps a third of U.S. adults belong to no formal voluntary organization, and only a third hold membership in more than one (not including churches)" (Knoke 1986, pg. 3). It is not clear from the research whether the differences are a function of different or better samples or of a growth in the number and attraction of voluntary associations.

One of the most consistent findings of voluntary association participation is that individuals with a higher socioeconomic status (SES) are more

likely to participate in voluntary associations (Cutler 1976). Age, race, and gender (while influenced strongly by SES) are also identified as being important factors in membership, with middle-aged persons, whites, and males more likely to be members.

Gender differences in voluntary association membership have been studied in terms of rates of participation as well as differences in the types of organizations to which each sex belongs. Historically, women's participation rates in voluntary associations have been lower than men's. Furthermore, the groups to which women belonged tended to be smaller, single-sex, and expressive (rather than instrumental). There is some evidence that the gender gap in participation rates is lessening (Knoke 1986). That is, more and more women are participating in voluntary associations. Due in part to the increased participation of women in the labor force, it is hypothesized that women's participation in less segregated, more instrumental associations would increase (i.e., membership in professional organizations; Knoke 1986). In a study of voluntary associations in Nebraska, Mc-Pherson and Smith-Lovin (1986) found, however, that the organizations to which women belonged continued to be predominantly female (one-half of the groups were exclusively female, while one-fifth of them were all male). They also found that instrumental groups were more likely than expressive groups to be sex heterogeneous.

Studies of the effect of race on voluntary association membership provide inconsistent findings. For example, Hyman and Wright (1971) documented a sharp increase in membership among blacks between 1955 and 1962 (sharper than that among whites); however, blacks continued to be less likely to belong to a voluntary association. By contrast, a 1973 Texas study found that black participation rates in voluntary associations were higher than both whites and Mexican-Americans (Williams, Babchuk, and Johnson 1973). Knoke summarized more recent research with the statement that "researchers generally found that blacks' participation rates fell below whites' but disagreed on whether the gap could be traced to black SES disadvantages" (Knoke 1986, p. 4).

In addition to studying differences in voluntary association membership due to SES, race, gender, and age, many researchers have examined the relationship between political participation and voluntary association membership. Researchers studying voting behavior and political participation have found that those individuals who are members of organizations are more likely to vote and participate in politics (see, e.g., Wolfinger and Rosenstone 1980; Milbrath and Goel 1977; Sigelman et al. 1985; Rogers, Bultena, and Barb 1975).

Some organizations like the American Medical Association, labor unions, and churches that are hierarchic in structure or practice infant baptism may have some of the characteristics of voluntary associations, but they are not seen as such in the definition adopted here.

In sum, voluntary associations are generally seen as central ingredients of the pluralist, democratic society. Whatever their number in Western societies, their ability to claim legitimacy for themselves and to have the claim accepted by political authorities constitutes a social fact of the free society (D'Antonio and Form 1965).

(SEE ALSO: *Community; Social Support*)

REFERENCES

Babchuk, Nicholas, and Alan Booth 1969 "Voluntary Association Membership: A Longitudinal Analysis." *American Sociological Review* 34:31–45.

Cook, Terence E., and Patrick M. Morgan 1971 *Participatory Democracy.* San Francisco: Canfield Press.

Cutler, Stephen J. 1976 "Age Differences in Voluntary Association Membership." *Social Forces* 55:43–58.

D'Antonio, William V., and William H. Form 1965 *Influentials in Two Border Cities.* South Bend, Ind.: University of Notre Dame Press.

Gordon, C. Wayne, and Nicholas Babchuk 1959 "A Typology of Voluntary Associations." *American Sociological Review* 24:22–29.

Hyman, Herbert H., and Charles R. Wright 1971 "Trends in Voluntary Association Memberships of American Adults: Replication Based on Secondary Analyses of National Sample Surveys." *American Sociological Review* 36:191–206.

Knoke, David 1986 "Associations and Interest Groups." *Annual Review of Sociology* 12:1–21.

McPherson, J. Miller, and Lynn Smith-Lovin 1986 "Sex Segregation in Voluntary Associations." *American Sociological Review* 51:61–79.

Milbrath, Lester W., and M. L. Goel 1977 *Political Participation.* Chicago: Rand McNally.

Rogers, David L., Gordon L. Bultena, and Ken H. Barb 1975 "Voluntary Association Membership and Political Participation: An Exploration of the Mobilization Hypothesis." *The Sociological Quarterly* 16:305–318.

Rose, Arnold M. 1967 *The Power Structure.* New York: Oxford University Press.

Sigelman, Lee, Philip W. Roeder, Malcolm E. Jewell, and Michael A. Baer 1985 "Voting and Nonvoting: A Multi-Election Perspective." *American Journal of Political Science* 29:749–765.

Sills, David L. 1968 "Voluntary Associations: Sociological Aspects." In David L. Sills, ed., *International Encyclopedia of the Social Sciences,* Vol. 16. New York: Macmillan and Free Press.

Smith, Constance, and Ann Freedman 1972 *Voluntary Associations: Perspectives on the Literature.* Cambridge, Mass.: Harvard University Press.

Tocqueville, Alexis de 1956 *Democracy in America,* ed. and abridged Richard D. Heffner. New York: Mentor.

Williams, J. Allen, Jr., Nicholas Babchuk, and David R. Johnson 1973 "Voluntary Associations and Minority Status: A Comparative Analysis of Anglo, Black, and Mexican Americans." *American Sociological Review* 38:637–646.

Wolfinger, Raymond E., and Steven J. Rosenstone 1980 *Who Votes?* New Haven, Conn.: Yale University Press.

MARIA KRYSAN
WILLIAM D'ANTONIO

VOTING BEHAVIOR In addition to sociologists, scholars from many different fields such as history, political science, psychology, and geography have studied elections and voting behavior. In current American sociology, however, these topics are largely neglected. Major advances have been made in neighboring disciplines. Yet, as one of the pioneers, sociologist Stuart Rice (1928, p. vii), succinctly stated: "The phenomena of politics are functions of group life. The study of group life per se is a task of sociology." In general terms, notwithstanding shifts in emphasis between different approaches, the sociological study of voting behavior, then, is concerned with the way individuals obtain, select, and process information related to the political arena, the various forces shaping this process, the relevance individuals attribute to the political sphere, and how individuals decide upon or refrain from specific political action. Elections provide a convenient focus, a point where the often elusive and latent processing of political information renders manifest behavioral correlates: voting or abstaining, supporting one candidate or the other. Forecasting election returns, however, is not a primary goal of the sociological study of voting behavior, while the general public, parties, and politicians are mostly interested in this aspect. Much (applied) research has served these immediate needs and interests, in the past and to this very day. In the field of voting behavior, pure (academic) and applied research peacefully coexist; cross-fertilization rather than mutual irreverence characterizes their relationship.

The study of voting behavior began as early as the late eighteenth century (Jensen 1969), though most of the very early work does not meet strict scholarly standards. In the course of its development as an academic discipline, two different strands—still discernible today—have emerged. The first strand, *aggregate data analysis*, is characterized by the use of actual election returns compiled for geopolitical units like wards, districts, counties, and so forth. These returns are compared with census data, rendering a socio-demographic profile of the same areal units. Starting with the late nineteenth century, there developed a school of quantitative historiography that made extensive use of maps representing voting and census information by different shades and colors (Frederick Jackson Turner in the United States, André Siegfried in France). The mere visual inspection and somewhat subjective interpretation of these maps by the Turner school was later supplemented and replaced by more vigorous statistical techniques, in particular correlation analysis, inspired by sociologist Franklin Giddins

at Columbia. One of Giddins's students, Stuart Rice (1928), persuasively demonstrated the utility of quantitative methods in politics. At the University of Chicago, interdisciplinary cooperation in the social sciences produced some of the most outstanding work at the time (e.g., Gosnell 1930). The advent of modern survey research in the 1930s and 1940s, however, then obscured the aggregate approach for quite some time.

The second strand in the study of voting behavior, the *analysis of survey data,* had some early forerunners as well. Polling individuals about their vote intentions ("straw polls") or about past voting decisions started in the late nineteenth century. In one of the most extensive efforts, more than one-quarter million returns from twelve midwestern states were tabulated by a Chicago newspaper for the 1896 presidential contest between McKinley and Bryant. In the 1920s, straw polls conducted by newspapers and other periodicals were quite common and enjoyed great popularity. Their reputation was ruined, though, by the giant failure of the *Literary Digest* poll to foresee the landslide victory of Franklin D. Roosevelt in the 1936 elections (predicting a victory by Alf Landon instead). At this time, however, pioneers of public opinion research like George Gallup, Archibald Crossley, and Elmo Roper had started to use more rigorous sampling methods as well as trained interviewers to ensure a proper representation of all strata of the electorate (Gallup [1944] 1948).

Interest in voting and political behavior and concern with mass communication, marketing strategies, and the public's attitude toward World War II stimulated the rapid development of modern survey research from about the mid-1930s through the 1940s and led to the establishment of survey research centers in both the academic and the commercial sector (Converse 1986). These include the Survey Research Center/Institute for Social Research (ISR) at the University of Michigan and the National Opinion Research Center (NORC) at the University of Chicago on the academic side, and Gallup's American Institute of Public Opinion on the commercial side—to name a few early organizations still prevalent today.

Modern voting research based on the survey

method typically uses rather small but randomly selected samples of about 1,000 (rarely more than 2,000) eligible voters. Information is collected by use of standardized questionnaires administered by trained interviewers in person or over the phone. "Standardized" means that the question wording is predetermined by the researcher and that the interviewer is supposed to read the questions exactly as stated and in the prearranged order. For the most part, the response alternatives are also predetermined ("closed questions"); sometimes—and for select questions—verbatim answers are recorded ("open questions") and later sorted into a categorical scheme. In contrast to aggregate level analysis and the use of official election returns, survey-based research on voting behavior, then, relies on self-reports by individual citizens. Thus, it is subject to bias and distortion due to insensitive questions, dishonest answers, memory failure, and last-minute mood changes— even if the sample is properly drawn. Its major advantage, though, is the unequivocal linkage of individual traits (such as age, sex, ethnicity, and social class) and political attitudes and behavior.

AGGREGATE DATA ANALYSIS

The use of aggregate data in studying voting behavior poses formidable methodological problems, yet it is the only approach open for the study of voting behavior prior to the mid-1930s. For example, the Germans voted Hitler into power by genuinely democratic elections in the late 1920s and early 1930s. Explaining the voting behavior of the Germans in the Weimar Republic has been subject to much debate and controversy in political sociology. The earlier consensus, that Hitler's support came predominantly from the lower middle classes, has been challenged by more recent studies (e.g., Childers 1983; Falter 1991) contending that this support had a much wider base cutting across all social groups.

Findings based on aggregate data analysis often depend heavily on seemingly technical details of preparing the data base and the choice of specific statistical techniques. As a rule, findings are more reliable if the geopolitical units are small. Still,

even if the greatest care is exercised, there is always the danger of an "ecological fallacy." To use a contemporary example, if the vote for a white candidate increases with a rising percentage of white voters across voting districts, it is plausible to assume that people voted along racial lines. Yet this need not be the case. It may be that ethnic minorities in predominantly white districts are more likely than minorities elsewhere to vote for a white candidate. So they—and not the additional white voters—may be responsible for the increased share of the white candidate.

In spite of all its shortcomings, aggregate data analysis is an indispensable tool for tracing patterns of voting behavior over time (e.g., Silbey, Bogue, and Flanigan 1978) in a sociohistorical analysis or to analyze contemporary voting behavior in the absence of sufficiently detailed and reliable survey data. Particularly for local or regional studies, there may not be sufficient funds to conduct appropriate surveys, or the research interest develops only after the elections have taken place.

SURVEY-BASED VOTING RESEARCH

The Columbia School. Four landmark studies connected with the presidential elections of 1940, 1948, 1952, and 1956 mark the establishment of scholarly survey-based research on voting behavior (Rossi 1959). In essence, these studies still provide the core of the concepts and models used in contemporary voting research. Reviewing these studies, then, provides an introduction to present-day theories of voting behavior in presidential elections, as far as the United States are concerned. Congressional elections here typically follow a very simple pattern: Incumbents are rarely defeated.

The first two studies were conducted by Paul F. Lazarsfeld and his associates at Columbia University. Their main intention was to analyze the developing process, "to relate preceding attitudes, expectations, personal contacts, group affiliations and similar data to the final decision" (Berelson, Lazarsfeld, and McPhee 1954, p. viii) and to trace changes of opinion over the course of the campaign. Emphasizing the particular set of political and social conditions, and its importance for this process, the Columbia group restricted each of their studies to one particular community (Erie County, Ohio, in 1940 and Elmira, New York, in 1948), and they interviewed the same respondents repeatedly—up to seven times in 1940, four times in 1948. Repeated interviews—or the "panel design"—became a standard feature of more sophisticated voting studies, while the major studies to come abandoned the focus on one community in favor of nationwide representation.

Several major findings emerged from the Erie County study (Lazarsfeld, Berelson, and Gaudet [1944] 1968). First, people tend to vote as they always have, in fact as their families had. In the Michigan school of voting behavior (see below), this attitude stability was then conceptualized as "party identification," a stable inclination toward a particular party largely developed during adolescence and early adulthood.

Second, attitudes are formed and reinforced by individuals' membership in social groups such as their social class, their ethnic group, their religious group, and the associations they belong to. More concretely, the research team found that people of lower social status, people in urban areas, and Catholics tended to be Democrats, while people of higher social class, people in rural areas, and Protestants were more likely to be Republicans. Subsequently, the alliance of particular segments of the population with specific parties has been amply documented, some modifications of its particular form notwithstanding. More so than in the United States, voting behavior in the major European democracies (most notably Britain and West Germany) can be explained largely by the links between social groups and particular parties (Lipset and Rokkan 1967).

Third, change does occur and people under cross-pressures are most likely to change. A cross-pressure occurs when the set of different group memberships provides conflicting stimuli. For example, in 1940, Protestant blue-collar workers experienced a pull toward the Republicans because of their religious affiliation and at the same time a pull toward the Democrats due to their class position. In the United States today, the impact of religious affiliation is more complicated, but the general notion of cross-pressure remains important.

Fourth, Lazarsfeld and colleagues developed the concept of a "two-step flow of information." According to this concept, most people are not directly persuaded by mass media, even if they are susceptible to change. Rather, they tend to follow opinion leaders. These are informal leaders in the various social networks (family, friends, associates at the work place) in which individuals are involved. These leaders pay close attention to the media; they redisseminate and validate media messages. Given the ever-increasing impact of mass media (television) over the last fifty years, this last result of the 1940 study may not accurately reflect the situation today. However, with respect to media effects the empirical evidence is still shaky. Several studies suggest a more direct and stronger impact of media (e.g., Iyengar and Kinder 1987), but a generally accepted model of this process has not emerged.

The 1948 Elmira study was designed to test further and—if necessary—modify the findings of the earlier study and to integrate the results into the body of existing knowledge (see Berelson, Lazarsfeld, and McPhee 1954, pp. 327–347 for a comparative synopsis of several major studies). In fact, its main contribution lies in the refinement of several aspects insufficiently covered in the Erie County study. However, the Elmira study still failed to show systematically the links between the efforts of the various institutions in the community and the decisions of the voters themselves. And the focus on these links was the key rationale for limiting these studies to one particular community, at the same time inviting doubt whether the findings can be generalized to American voting behavior in general.

The Michigan School. The sociological approach of the Columbia school was subsequently overshadowed by the social psychological model of the Michigan school, which came to dominate survey-based voting research for many years. After a smaller study in 1948 (Campbell and Kahn 1952), the Michigan team, led by Angus Campbell, conducted two major studies in 1952 and 1956 (Campbell, Gurin, and Miller 1954; Campbell et al. 1960). In contrast to Lazarsfeld and associates, the studies used national samples—expanding geographical coverage—but only two interviews, shortly before and shortly after the elections. In addition, the Michigan group introduced far-reaching changes in the conceptualization of the voting process. On the basis of their national study of 1948, they felt that social group memberships had little direct impact on the voting decision. Instead, they focused on "the psychological variables which intervene between the external events of the voter's world and his ultimate behavior" (Campbell, Gurin, and Miller 1954, pp. 85–86). In particular, they considered three concepts labeled "party identification," "issue orientation," and "candidate orientation." *Party identification* refers to a sense of personal attachment an individual feels toward a party, irrespective of formal membership or direct involvement in the party's activities. It is thought of as a stable attitude developed early in life. In contrast, both issue and candidate orientations depend on the context of a particular election. *Issue orientation* refers to the individuals' involvement in issues they perceive as being affected by the outcome of an election. For example, if individuals are concerned with the economy and feel that it makes a difference whether the country has a Democratic or a Republican president, then this will have an impact on their voting decision. Similarly, *candidate orientation* refers to the individuals' interest in the personality of the candidates and to a possible preference based on the personal traits of the candidates. For example, Ronald Reagan portrayed himself as a firm and determined leader but also as a caring and understanding father. In this way he was able to attract many voters otherwise attached to the Democrats.

The Michigan model posits a "funnel of causality." The social factors emphasized in the Columbia school are not dismissed outright, but they are viewed as at the mouth of this funnel, having an indirect effect only via the three central psychological variables, particularly party identification. Party identification, in turn, affects issue and candidate orientations besides exercising a direct effect on the voting decision. The simplicity of this model is both its strength and its weakness. It clearly marks the shift of emphasis to psychological processes of individual perception and evaluation, but it does not explicitly address the social and political context. However, in *The American Voter* (Campbell et al. 1960) the Michigan group presents a much more comprehensive analysis after the 1956 elections. There they address topics like the role of group membership, social class, and the political system—without, however, explicitly elaborating the basic model.

Additional concepts that have been used widely in further research include the concept of a *normal vote* and the typology of elections as *maintaining, deviating,* or *realigning* (Campbell et al. 1966) and an assessment of mass belief systems (Converse 1964). The normal vote concept follows directly from the basic model: If all voters follow their long-standing inclinations (i.e., vote according to their party identification), they produce a normal vote. Comparing actual election returns with the (hypothetical) normal vote allows one to assess the impact of contemporaneous, mostly short-term factors. In a maintaining election the party with the larger number of partisans wins, but its vote share may be somewhat different from its normal share because of short-term factors. If short-term factors lead to the defeat of this party, the election is considered as deviating. Realigning elections, finally, mark a major shift in basic allegiances. Such shifts are rare and are not typically accomplished in a single election. During the 1930s, the American electorate shifted toward the Democrats as a consequence of economic depression and Roosevelt's New Deal, which promised a way out. However, given their long-term nature, processes of dealignment and realignment are difficult to determine in strict empirical terms (Dalton, Flanagan, and Beck 1984).

With respect to the nature of mass belief systems, Converse's (1964) article triggered a long-lasting debate, which was never finally settled. Converse asserted that the vast majority of the American public has little interest in politics, that their opinions on issues lack consistency and stability over time, and that these opinions are mostly "non-attitudes." Consequently, a large portion of the electorate does not vote at all; and if they do, their vote is based mostly on partisanship or candidate personality but not on an independent and careful evaluation of the issues at stake.

Critique of *The American Voter*. Like other landmark empirical studies, *The American Voter* was not safe from sometimes radical critique, which can be categorized as follows: First, challenges of the allegedly derogatory image of the American electorate and its implications for the democratic process; second, assertions that the findings are valid for the specific period of the 1950s only; and third, methodological critique of operationalization, measurement, and model specification. Most of the methodological critique, however, is too technical to be discussed here (but see, e.g., Asher 1983).

One of the earliest and most vocal critics was V. O. Key (1966). Based on a reanalysis of Gallup data from 1936 to 1960, he developed a typology of "standpatters," "switchers," and "new voters" and asserted that the global outcome of the elections followed a rational pattern based on an appraisal of past government performance. Hence, as a whole, the electorate acts responsibly —notwithstanding "that many individual voters act in odd ways indeed" (Key 1966, p. 7).

The most comprehensive effort to review American voting behavior over time, a critique of the second kind, was presented by Nie, Verba, and Petrocik (1976) and was based on the series of Michigan election studies from 1952 to 1972. Still working within the framework of the Michigan model, they found significant changes in the relative importance of its three central factors: a steady decrease in the level of party identification —particularly among young age groups—and a much stronger relative weight of issue and candidate orientations. In a turbulent period of internal strife and social change (civil rights, the Vietnam war, Watergate), the electorate became more aware of issues and much more critical of parties and the established political process. Nie, Verba,

and Petrocik found a decomposition of the traditional support bases for both Democrats and Republicans, all adding up to an " 'individuation' of American political life" (1976, p. 347).

More Recent Studies and Approaches. Still largely following the path led by the Michigan school, much research in the 1980s was directed toward issue voting that reflected a continued decline of stable party attachments via political socialization or group memberships. In particular, the impact of economic conditions on electoral outcome was investigated both in the United States and in other major Western democracies (Eulau and Lewis-Beck 1985; Lewis-Beck 1988; Norpoth, Lewis-Beck, and Lafay 1991). The findings were diverse, contingent upon specification of the research question and national context. Yet one general pattern clearly emerged: Perceived competence of political actors in economic matters is strongly related to the individual voting decision.

As a distinct break with the Michigan tradition, rational choice models of voting behavior were developed (e.g., Page 1978; Enelow and Hinich 1984; Himmelweit, Humphreys, and Jaeger 1985). Following economic theory, these models see the voter as carefully evaluating pros and cons of each party or candidate, assessing their utility (consumer models) or their proximity (spatial models) to the voter's own position, and then voting for the closest or most useful party or candidate. Rational choice models have become increasingly popular in the explanation of a wide range of social behavior, not just voting behavior. However, in the basic form described here, these models are hardly adequate to portray the process of the voting decision—except for a small segment of the electorate: the highly informed and highly motivated citizens. Conceptually, most of the existing theories can be integrated into a rational choice framework (Bennett and Salisbury 1987). Then, however, an empirical test becomes very difficult, if not impossible.

Fiorina (1981) has presented an attempt to combine the basics of the Michigan model with a rational choice approach. His concept of *retrospective voting* posits that both party identification and issue orientation are largely dependent on the evaluation of past government performance. Party identification thus represents a sort of running tally of past experience. It is still a long-term influence, but it is subject to gradual change, and it is much more based on cognition than on affection compared with its original conceptualization.

Two other strands that have expanded and elaborated the Michigan model have emerged in recent years. In one, the formation and change of political evaluations and orientations are subjected to further scrutiny by employing concepts developed in cognitive psychology (e.g., Lau and Sears 1986). In the other, an attempt is made to assess the impact of the local context on the decision making of the individual. Context information is gathered either by using block level census data or by tracing and interviewing members of the social network of the primary respondents (Huckfeldt 1986; Huckfeldt and Sprague 1987).

Voting Behavior in Other National Contexts. The Michigan school of voting behavior has had a major impact on survey-based voting research in other Western democracies (see, e.g., Beyme and Kaase 1978; Butler and Stokes 1976; Heath, Jowell, and Curtice 1985; Kaase and Klingemann 1990; Rose 1974). A strict replication of the basic model, however, has not been feasible because of considerable differences in political systems, party organization, and electoral rules. In Europe, fairly homogeneous political parties rather than presidential candidates dominate the political contest, and social cleavages relating to class, religion, or both are powerful determinants of voting behavior—though their impact is slowly declining. But various concepts of the Michigan school have been adopted to supplement the dominant explanation based on social group membership (Lipset and Rokkan 1967). Attempts to operationalize the key concept of party identification, though, have produced mixed results at best (e.g., Budge, Crewe, and Fairlie 1976).

Much of current European debate is focused on the evolving changes in the electorate. The once-stable alliances between parties and certain segments in the electorate along social cleavages have begun to deteriorate; the voters have become more volatile; and electoral change is imminent (Crewe and Denver 1985; Franklin, Mackie, and Valen 1991; Miller et al. 1990). Recently, Rose and McAllister (1990) have proposed a *lifetime learning model,* which seeks to integrate various factors in a time-hierarchical model starting with family loyalties in step 1 and gradually proceeding to evaluations of the current government in step 5. Though they explicitly abandon the concept of party identification, their model can be seen as a modification and expansion of the Michigan model.

Another major democracy, Japan, displays even more marked systemic differences from the United States than do the European democracies. In Japan, personal social networks and intraparty competition are important components in the process of forming a voting decision. Still, the Michigan model has guided much research on Japanese voting behavior as well (Flanagan et al. 1991).

OUTLOOK

The widespread but eclectic use of the Michigan model does not compensate for the lack of genuinely comparative cross-national research on voting behavior. Some progress may be made by recent projects, for example, a study in the twelve member states of the European Community on the occasion of the concurrent elections to the European Parliament in 1989 (Schmitt and Mannheimer 1991). However, the theory of voting behavior is still fragmented, and the predominant use of the survey method and of national samples has led to stagnation. It is time to bring sociology back in and to develop more imaginative research designs that mix qualitative and quantitative approaches and use data from various sources. The design of the early Columbia studies still awaits full realization.

(SEE ALSO: *Democracy; Political Organizations; Political Party Systems*)

REFERENCES

Asher, Herbert B. 1983 "Voting Behavior Research in the 1980s." In Ada W. Finifter, ed., *Political Science*. Washington, D.C.: American Political Science Association.

Bennett, W. Lance, and Bart R. Salisbury 1987 "Rational Choice: The Emerging Paradigm in Election Studies." In Samuel Long, ed., *Research in Micropolitics*. Greenwich, Conn.: JAI Press.

Berelson, Bernard, Paul F. Lazarsfeld, and William N. McPhee 1954 *Voting: A Study of Opinion Formation in a Presidential Campaign*. Chicago: University of Chicago Press.

Beyme, Klaus von, and Max Kaase (eds.) 1978 *Elections and Parties*. London: Sage.

Budge, Ian, Ivor Crewe, and Dennis Fairlie (eds.) 1976 *Party Identification and Beyond*. London: Wiley.

Butler, David, and Donald Stokes 1976 *Political Change in Britain*. 2nd ed. New York: St. Martin's Press.

Campbell, Angus, and Robert L. Kahn 1952 *The People Elect a President*. Ann Arbor: University of Michigan, Institute for Social Research.

Campbell, Angus, Gerald Gurin, and Warren E. Miller 1954 *The Voter Decides*. Evanston, Ill.: Row, Peterson and Co.

Campbell, Angus, Philip E. Converse, Warren E. Miller, and Donald E. Stokes 1960 *The American Voter*. New York: Wiley.

———1966 *Elections and the Political Order*. New York: Wiley.

Childers, Thomas 1983 *The Nazi Voter*. Chapel Hill: University of North Carolina Press.

Converse, Jean M. 1986 *Survey Research in the United States: Roots and Emergence*. Berkeley: University of California Press.

Converse, Philip 1964 "The Nature of Belief Systems in Mass Publics." In David Apter, ed., *Ideology and Discontent*. New York: Free Press.

Crewe, Ivor, and David Denver (eds.) 1985 *Electoral Change in Western Democracies: Patterns and Sources of Electoral Volatility*. New York: St. Martin's Press.

Dalton, Russell J., Scott C. Flanagan, and Paul Allen Beck (eds.) 1984 *Electoral Change in Advanced Industrial Democracies: Realignment or Dealignment?* Princeton: Princeton University Press.

Enelow, James M., and Melvin J. Hinich 1984 *The Spatial Theory of Voting*. New York: Cambridge University Press.

Eulau, Heinz, and Michael Lewis-Beck (eds.) 1985 *Economic Conditions and Electoral Outcomes: The United States and Western Europe*. New York: Agathon Press.

Falter, Jürgen W. 1991 *Hitler's Wähler*. Munich: Beck.

Fiorina, Morris P. 1981 *Retrospective Voting in American National Elections*. New Haven: Yale University Press.

Flanagan, Scott C., Shinsaku Kohei, Ichiro Miyake, Bradley M. Richardson, and Joji Watanuki 1991 *The Japanese Voter*. New Haven: Yale University Press.

Franklin, Mark, Tom Mackie, and Henry Valen, eds. 1991 *Electoral Change: Responses to Evolving Social and Attitudinal Structures in Seventeen Democracies*. Cambridge: Cambridge University Press.

Gallup, George (1944) 1948 *A Guide to Public Opinion Polls*. Princeton: Princeton University Press.

Gosnell, Harold 1930 *Why Europe Votes*. Chicago: University of Chicago Press.

Heath, Anthony, Roger Jowell, and John Curtice 1985 *How Britain Votes*. New York: Pergamon Press.

Himmelweit, Hilde, Patrick Humphreys, and Marianne Jaeger 1985 *How Voters Decide*. Milton Keynes, England: Open University Press.

Huckfeldt, Robert 1986 *Politics in Context: Assimilation and Conflict in Urban Neighborhoods*. New York: Agathon Press.

———, and John Sprague 1987 "Networks in Context: The Social Flow of Political Information." *American Political Science Review* 81:1,197–1,216.

Iyengar, Shanto, and Donald Kinder 1987 *News That Matters*. Chicago: University of Chicago Press.

Jensen, Richard 1969 "American Election Analysis: A Case History of Methodological Innovation and Diffusion." In Seymour M. Lipset, ed., *Politics and the Social Sciences*. New York: Oxford University Press.

Kaase, Max, and Hans-Dieter Klingemann (eds.) 1990 *Wahlen and Wähler*. Opladen, Germany: Westdeutscher Verlag.

Key, Valdimer Orlando, Jr. 1966 *The Responsible Electorate*. Cambridge, Mass.: Belknap Press, Harvard University Press.

Lau, Richard, and David Sears 1986 *Political Cognition*. Hillsdale, N.J.: Erlbaum.

Lazarsfeld, Paul F., Bernard Berelson, and Hazel Gaudet (1944) 1968 *The People's Choice*. 3rd ed. New York: Columbia University Press.

Lewis-Beck, Michael 1988 *Economics and Elections: The Major Western Democracies*. Ann Arbor: University of Michigan Press.

Lipset, Seymour Martin, and Stein Rokkan (eds) 1967

Party Systems and Voter Alignments. New York: Free Press.

Miller, William L., Harold D. Clarke, Lawrence Leduc, and Paul Whiteley 1990 *How Voters Change*. New York: Oxford University Press.

Nie, Norman H, Sidney Verba, and John R. Petrocik 1976 *The Changing American Voter*. Cambridge, Mass.: Harvard University Press.

Norpoth, Helmut, Michael Lewis-Beck, and Jean-Dominique Lafay (eds.) 1991 *Making Governments Pay*. Ann Arbor: University of Michigan Press.

Page, Benjamin 1978 *Choices and Echoes in Presidential Elections*. Chicago: University of Chicago Press.

Rice, Stuart A. 1928 *Quantitative Methods in Politics*. New York: Alfred A. Knopf.

Rose, Richard (ed.) 1974 *Electoral Behavior: A Comparative Handbook*. New York: Free Press.

Rose, Richard, and Ian McAllister 1990 *The Loyalties of Voters: A Lifetime Learning Model*. London: Sage.

Rossi, Peter A. 1959 "Four Landmarks in Voting Research." In Eugene Burdick and Arthur Brodbeck, eds., *American Voting Behavior*. Glencoe, Ill.: Free Press.

Schmitt, Hermann, and Renato Mannheimer (eds.) 1991 *The European Elections of 1989* (special issue). *European Journal of Political Research* 19(1).

Silbey, Joel H., Allan G. Bogue, and William H. Flanigan (eds.) 1978 *The History of American Electoral Behavior*. Princeton: Princeton University Press.

MANFRED KUECHLER

WAR The ubiquity and importance of war have made analyses of its causes a central concern of scholars for over two millennia. Although many of the fundamental questions about the causes of war were raised first by Thucydides (fifth century B.C.), the vast amount of work on the topic since has produced ongoing debates instead of generally accepted answers. Some debates focus on characteristics of the interstate system that are thought to increase or decrease war. Are wars more likely during periods of economic prosperity or economic contraction? Which is more likely to maintain peace, a balance of power in the international system or a situation in which one state is hegemonic? Social scientists also disagree about the effects of political and economic factors within states on war. Do capitalist economies make states more or less likely to initiate wars? Do democratic states start wars less often than autocracies? There is also no consensus on which model of individual decision making is most appropriate for the study of war. Is the decision to go to war based on a rational calculation of economic costs and benefits, or is it an irrational outcome of distortions in decision making in small groups and bureaucracies?

Studies of war can be divided into three broad categories (reviews of the literature using similar frameworks are provided by Waltz 1959; Bueno de Mesquita 1980; and Levy 1989). The first type takes the system as whole as the unit of analysis and focuses on how characteristics of the interstate system affect the frequency of war. States are the unit of analysis in the second type, which explores the relationships among political, economic, and cultural features of particular states and their propensity to initiate wars. The third type analyzes war as an outcome of choices made by individual leaders, using models of individual and small-group decision making.

THE INTERSTATE SYSTEM AND WAR

Most studies of war that take the interstate system as the unit of analysis begin with assumptions from the "realist" paradigm. States are seen as unitary actors in realist theories, and their actions are explained in terms of structural characteristics of the system. The most important feature of the interstate system is that it is anarchic. Unlike politics within states, relations between states take place in a Hobbesian state of nature. Since an anarchic system is one in which all states constantly face actual or potential threats, their main goal is security. Security can only be achieved in such a system by maintaining power. In realist theories, the distribution of power in the interstate system is the main determinant of the frequency of war.

Although all realist theories agree on the importance of power distributions in determining war, they disagree about which types of power distributions make war more likely. Balance-of-power theories (Morgenthau 1967) suggest that an equal distribution of power in the system facilitates peace and that unequal power distributions lead to war. They argue that parity deters all states from aggression and that an unequal power distribution will generally result in the strong using force against the weak. When one state begins to gain a preponderance of power in the system, a coalition of weaker states will form to maintain their security by blocking the further expansion of the powerful state. The coalitions that formed against Louis XIV, Napoleon, and Hitler seem to fit this pattern.

Hegemonic stability theory (Gilpin 1981) suggests exactly the opposite, that unequal power in the system produces peace and that parity results in war. When one state has hegemony in the world system, it has both the incentive and the means to maintain order in the system. It is not necessary for the most powerful state to fight wars, since their objectives can be achieved in less costly ways, and it is not rational for other states to challenge a state with overwhelming power. Gilpin notes that the periods of British and U.S. hegemony were relatively peaceful and that World Wars I and II occurred during intervening periods in which power was more equally distributed. Since balance-of-power and hegemonic stability theories each seem to explain some but not all of the cases, what is needed is a theory specifying the conditions under which either parity or hegemony lead to war.

Balance-of-power and hegemonic stability arguments are not applicable to all wars, only those between great powers. A third attempt to explain great-power war is power transition theory (Organski 1968). Power transition theory suggests that differential rates of economic growth create situations in which rising states rapidly catch up with the hegemonic state in the system, and that

this change in relative power leads to war. Organski argues that the rising state will initiate a war to displace the hegemonic state. This final part of the argument is questionable, since it seems at least as plausible that the hegemonic state would initiate the war against the rising challenger in an attempt to keep the small and fleeting advantage it still has (Levy 1989, p. 253).

Another ongoing debate about systemic causes of war concerns the effects of long cycles of economic expansion and contraction. Some scholars argue that economic contraction will increase war, since the increased scarcity of resources will lead to more conflict. Others have suggested the opposite: Major wars will be more frequent during periods of economic expansion because only then will states have the resources necessary to fight. Goldstein's (1988) research suggests that economic expansion tends to increase the severity of great-power wars but that economic cycles have no effect on the frequency of war.

Theoretical debates about the systemic causes of war have not been resolved, in part because the results of empirical research have been inconclusive. To take just one example, equality of power in the interstate system decreased war in the nineteenth century and increased war in the twentieth century. Each theory can point to specific cases that seem to fit its predictions, but each must also admit to many cases that it cannot explain. At least part of the problem is that systemic theories have not incorporated causal factors at lower levels of analysis, such as internal economic and political characteristics of states. Since the effects of system-level factors on war are not direct but are always mediated by the internal political economy of states and the decisions made by individual leaders, complete theories of the causes of war must include these factors as well.

CAPITALISM, DEMOCRACY, AND WAR

One of the longest and most heated debates about the causes of war concerns the effects of capitalism. Beginning with Adam Smith, liberal economists have argued that capitalism promotes peace. Marxists, on the other hand, suggest that capitalism leads to frequent imperialist wars.

Liberal economic theories point to the wealth generated by laissez-faire capitalist economies, the interdependence produced by trade, and the death and destruction of assets caused by war. Since capitalism has both increased the benefits of peace (by increasing productivity and trade) and the costs of war (by producing new and better instruments of destruction), it is no longer rational for states to wage war. The long period of relative peace that followed the triumph of capitalism in the nineteenth century and the two world wars that came after the rise of protectionist barriers to free trade are often cited in support of liberal economic theories, but the same facts can be explained by hegemonic stability theory as a consequence of the rise and decline of British hegemony.

In contrast to the sanguine views of capitalism presented by liberal economic theories, Marxists argue that economic problems inherent in advanced capitalist economies create strong incentives for war. First, the high productivity of industrial capitalism coupled with a limited home market due to the poverty of the working class result in a chronic problem of "underconsumption" (Hobson [1902] 1954). Capitalists will thus seek imperial expansion to control new markets for their goods. Second, Lenin ([1919] 1939) argued that capitalists will fight imperialist wars to gain access to more raw materials and to find more profitable outlets for their capital. These pressures will lead first to wars between powerful capitalist states and weaker peripheral states, and next to wars between great powers over which of them will get to exploit the periphery.

In contrast to the stress on the political causes (power and security) of war in most theories, the Marxist theory of imperialism has the virtue of drawing attention to economic causes. However, there are several important problems with the economic causes posited in theories of imperialism. Like most Marxist arguments about politics, theories of imperialism assume that states are controlled (directly or indirectly) by dominant economic classes and thus that state policies will reflect dominant class interests. Since states are often autonomous from dominant class control, and since many groups other than capitalists often influence state policies, it is much too simplistic to view war as a reflection of the interests of capitalists. Moreover, in light of the arguments made by liberal economists, it is far from clear that capitalists will prefer war to other means of expanding markets and increasing profits.

The form of government in a country may also determine how often that country initiates wars. Kant ([1795] 1949) argued that democratic states (with constitutions and separation of powers) will initiate wars less often than autocratic states. This conclusion follows from a simple analysis of who pays the costs of war and who gets the benefits. Since citizens are required to pay for war with high taxes and their lives, they will rarely support war initiation. Rulers of states, on the other hand, have much to gain from war and can pass on most of the costs to their subjects. Therefore, when decisions about war are made only by rulers (in autocracies), war will be frequent, and when citizens have more control of the decision (in democracies), peace will generally be the result.

Empirical research indicates that democratic states are less likely than nondemocratic states to initiate wars, but the relationship is not strong (Levy 1989, p. 270). Perhaps one reason for the weakness of the relationship is that the assumption that citizens will oppose war initiation is not always correct. Many historical examples indicate that in at least some conditions citizens will support war even though it is not in their economic interests to do so. Nationalism, religion, and other cultural factors are often cited as important causes of particular wars in journalistic and historical accounts, but we still have no general theory of the conditions under which these factors will modify or even override economic interests. This raises the general issue of the factors affecting the choices individuals make about war initiation: Can these be modeled as rational maximization of interests, or is the process more complex?

DECISION MAKING AND WAR

Although they may be only implicit or undeveloped, all theories of war must contain some assumptions about individual decision making. However, few theories of war focus on the individual level of analysis. One notable exception is the rational-choice theory of war developed and tested by Bueno de Mesquita (1981).

Bueno de Mesquita begins by assuming the decision to initiate war is made by a single dominant ruler who is a rational expected-utility maximizer. Utilities are defined in terms of state policies. Rulers fight wars to affect the policies of other states, essentially to make other states' policies more similar to their interests. Rulers calculate the costs and benefits of initiating war, and the probability of victory. War will be initiated only when rulers expect a net gain from them.

This parsimonious set of assumptions has been used to generate several counterintuitive propositions. For example, common sense might suggest that states would fight their enemies and not their allies, but Bueno de Mesquita argues that war will be more common between allies than between enemies. Wars between allies are caused by actual or anticipated policy changes that threaten the existing relationship. The interventions of the United States in Latin America and of the USSR in Eastern Europe since World War II illustrate the process. Other counterintuitive propositions suggest that under some conditions a state may rationally choose to attack the stronger of two allied states instead of the weaker, and under some conditions it is rational for a state with no allies to initiate war against a stronger state with allies. Although these propositions and others derived from the theory have received strong empirical support, many have argued that the basic rational choice assumptions of the theory are unrealistic, and have rejected Bueno de Mesquita's work on those grounds.

Other analyses of the decision to initiate war focus on how the social features of the decision-making process lead to deviations from rational choice. Allison (1971) notes that all political decisions are made within organizations and that this setting often influences the content of the decisions. He argues that standard operating procedures and repertoires tend to limit the flexibility of decisions and make it difficult to respond adequately to novel situations. Janis (1972) focuses on the small groups within political organizations (such as executives and their cabinet advisers) that actually make decisions about war. He suggests that the cohesiveness of these small groups often leads to a striving for unanimity that prevents a full debate about options and produces a premature consensus. Other scholars have discussed common misperceptions that distort decisions about war, such as the tendencies to underestimate the capabilities of enemies and to overestimate one's own. In spite of these promising studies, work on the deviations from rational choice is just beginning, and we are still far short of a general theoretical model of the decision to initiate war.

CONCLUSION

The failure to develop a convincing general theory of the causes of war has convinced some scholars that no such theory is possible, that all we can do is describe the causes of particular wars. This pessimistic conclusion is premature. The existing literature on the causes of war provides several fragments of a general theory, many of which have some empirical support. The difficult goal of theory and research on war in the future will be to combine aspects of arguments at all three levels of analysis to create a general theory of the causes of war.

(SEE ALSO: *Global Systems Analysis; Peace; Revolutions; Terrorism*)

REFERENCES

Allison, Graham 1971 *Essence of Decision.* Boston: Little, Brown.

Bueno de Mesquita, Bruce 1980 "Theories of International Conflict: An Analysis and Appraisal." In Ted Robert Gurr, ed., *Handbook of Political Conflict.* New York: Free Press.

———1981 *The War Trap*. New Haven, Conn.: Yale University Press.

Gilpin, Robert 1981 *War and Change in World Politics*. Cambridge: Cambridge University Press.

Golstein, Joshua 1988 *Long Cycles*. New Haven, Conn.: Yale University Press.

Hobson, J. A. (1902) 1954 *Imperialism*. London: Allen and Unwin.

Janis, Irving 1972 *Victims of Groupthink*. Boston: Houghton Mifflin.

Kant, Immanuel (1795) 1949 "Eternal Peace." In C. J. Friedrich, ed., *The Philosophy of Kant*. New York: Modern Library.

Lenin, V. I. (1917) 1939 *Imperialism*. New York: International.

Levy, Jack S. 1989 "The Causes of War: A Review of Theories and Evidence." In Philip E. Tetlock, Robert Jervis, Paul Stern, and Charles Tilly, eds., *Behavior, Society, and Nuclear War*. Oxford: Oxford University Press.

Morgenthau, Hans 1967 *Politics Among Nations*. New York: Alfred A. Knopf.

Organski, J. F. K. 1968 *World Politics*. New York: Alfred A. Knopf.

Waltz, Kenneth 1959 *Man, the State, and War*. New York: Columbia University Press.

EDGAR KISER

WELFARE *See* Poverty; Public Policy Analysis; Social Security Systems.

WELL-BEING *See* Quality of Life.

WHITE-COLLAR CRIME Edwin Sutherland, the originator of the concept, defined white-collar crime as "a crime committed by a person of respectability and high social status in the course of his occupation" (Sutherland 1961). Sutherland listed the following as white-collar crimes: violations of antitrust laws; misrepresentation in advertising; infringements of patents, trademarks, and copyrights; violations of labor laws; and breaches of trust of various types. A businessperson who committed a murder or rape, whether in a business office or out of it, would not have committed a white-collar crime, nor would a lawyer who committed an aggravated assault upon another person, even though the act occurred in the lawyer's office or in the courtroom.

When Sutherland introduced the concept, he was primarily interested in formulating an overall theory of criminal behavior. He rejected the conventional explanations of criminality because he felt they were based on statistics that indicated a concentration of crime in the lower socioeconomic class of our society. The statistics, he believed, were distorted by two factors: Upperclass persons who commit crimes are frequently able to escape arrest and conviction because their money and social position make them more powerful politically; and laws that apply exclusively to business and the professions, and that therefore involve only upper-class people, are seldom dealt with by criminal courts.

Herbert Edelhertz, a former chief of the fraud section of the Criminal Division of the U.S. Department of Justice, found Sutherland's definition too restrictive, in that it limited the concept to crimes committed in the course of one's occupation. Edelhertz included as white-collar crime filing false income tax returns, making fraudulent claims for social security benefits, concealing assets in personal bankruptcy, and buying on credit with no intention or capability of ever paying for the purchases. He also included the criminal manipulations of "con" games operated in a business milieu. His definition of white-collar crime was that it was an illegal act or series of illegal acts committed by nonphysical means and by concealment of guile to obtain money or property, to avoid the payment or loss of money or property, or to obtain business or personal advantage, including all of the above-described activities. The common elements that Edelhertz saw as basic to all white-collar crimes were (1) intent to commit a wrongful act or to achieve a purpose inconsistent with law or public policy; (2) disguise of purpose or intent; (3) reliance by perpetrator on ignorance or carelessness of victim; (4) acquiescence by victim in what she or he believes to be the true nature and content of the transaction; (5) concealment of crime by preventing the victim from realizing there has been victimization, or relying on the fact that only a small percentage of victims react to what has happened, by making provisions for restitution to, or other handling of, the disgruntled victim; or paper, organizational, or transactional facade to disguise the true nature of what has occurred (Edelhertz 1970).

A study conducted in 1985 by sociologist Amitai Etzioni found that two-thirds of the nation's five hundred largest industrial corporations were convicted of such serious crimes as bribery, falsification of records, tax law violations, and gross violations of workplace safety rules. The findings might not surprise many Americans. A poll, conducted in 1988 by the Roper Organization, concluded that 62 percent of American adults thought that white-collar crime was a "serious and growing problem that shows a real decline in business ethical behavior."

Hardly a week goes by without a newspaper account of charges filed by the government against some large corporation alleging the fixing of prices, the rigging of bids, the forming of illegal combinations in restraint of trade, the making of false claims in its advertising, or the undertaking of some other business activity in violation of the law. Business executives and the corporations with which they are associated are occasionally convicted of such violations. The punishment imposed is usually in the form of a fine. When executives are sentenced to jail, the terms are short, seldom in excess of thirty days.

In the over one-hundred-year history of the Sherman Antitrust Act, businesspeople have been sent to jail on very few occasions. A question raised is, How can jurors send that well-dressed, white, wealthy father of three to jail with unkempt, nonwhite, poor, uneducated criminals? For example, in one recent case of white-collar crime, the executives of seven electrical manufacturing corporations convicted of a price conspiracy involving over $1 billion were sentenced to thirty days in jail each. In the judicial process, severer sentences are meted out to poor people convicted of more petty crimes.

This condition of unequal sentencing was revealed in a 1987 United States Justice Department research report. The researcher revealed that the incarceration rate was only 40 percent of convicted white-collar criminals in 1985, compared with 54 percent of the non-white-collar criminals. The study concluded that financial losses caused by white-collar crime dwarf the amounts lost through other types of crime.

There are many forms of white-collar crime. Following are a number of prototypical cases revealing the dynamics and complexity of white-collar crimes.

CORPORATE TAX FRAUD

According to a recent commissioner of the Internal Revenue Service, corporate tax avoidance schemes have reached shocking proportions. Known losses from corporate tax avoidance have increased enormously. He states, "It is unbelievable that large, publicly held corporations engage in such schemes. Yet, they do. This is flouting the law—deliberate, willful attempts to avoid and evade taxes."

DEFENSE CONTRACT FRAUD

In 1988, a Pentagon procurement scandal was brought to light. Defense contractors used lobbyists and others to illegally acquire data from the Pentagon that would give these companies an edge in the competition for billions of dollars' worth of defense contracts.

STOCK MARKET WHITE-COLLAR CRIME

Previous white-collar crimes involving stock manipulations have been dwarfed by recent criminal capers. American white-collar crimes appear to increase with time. The ingenious white-collar crimes of Ivan Boesky, Michael Milken, and many other tycoons who operated like them in the late 1980s, shook the foundation of Wall Street and the world financial market.

Boesky's criminal activities in the stock market were revealed in 1986. Essentially, those activities involved trading on insider information not known to the general public. His illicit profits came from taking unfair advantage of price movements in a broad range of stocks.

On November 14, 1986, the Securities and Exchange Commission announced that Boesky, forty-nine, one of America's most eminent and successful stock market speculators, had been caught in an ongoing probe of insider trading. Boesky agreed to pay $100 million in penalties, to return profits, and to cease to trade stock professionally for the rest of his life. In December 1986 Boesky was sentenced to a three-year term in prison.

Shortly after the Boesky incident, the public learned of even more astounding crimes in the Wall Street investment firm of Drexel Burnham Lambert, and the alleged illegal activity of its California branch's high-yield bond investment chief executive, Michael Milken. On April 14, 1988, after months of negotiations, Drexel Burnham Lambert and the Securities and Exchange Commission reached a settlement on civil charges involving securities law violations, with the influential Wall Street firm agreeing to sweeping changes in how it does business and how it will be regulated in the future by the government.

The settlement ended a two-and-a-half-year investigation into Drexel's trading practices at its junk bond unit in Beverly Hills, California. *Junk bonds,* risky high-yield bond issues, were developed by Milken and used as part of the financial packages in flamboyant corporate takeovers in the 1980s. Drexel agreed to plead guilty to criminal charges and to pay $650 million in fines and other penalties. Also, as part of its settlement with government prosecutors, Drexel was required to dismiss Milken. Milken was later indicted and convicted on criminal charges including racketeering, securities fraud, and mail fraud.

FRAUD IN BANKS AND SAVINGS AND LOAN COMPANIES

Two hundred ten savings and loan companies failed in the United States between 1984 and 1988. Regulators have found serious abuse, fraud, and misconduct in half, according to the Federal Savings and Loan Insurance Corporation, which regulates the industry. In California, the rate is as high as 77 percent. The thirty-one savings and loans in California seized or closed by regulators between 1984 and 1988 cost the Federal Savings and Loan Insurance Company an estimated $5.6 billion. That is more than half the $10.8 billion Congress appropriated in 1988 to rescue the insolvent deposit insurance fund.

It takes much more time and experience for law enforcement officials to unravel the sophisticated plots of savings and loan insiders than, say, the plots of ordinary bank robbers. And, as indicated, sentences for white-collar criminals, when they are caught and convicted, can be light in comparison with those for robbers who make off with a fraction of the cash.

Most white-collar crime simply involves the theft of considerable money from citizen victims who are usually unaware they are being robbed. The money finds its way into corporate coffers, and the top executives in these companies personally benefit through lucrative stock splits, high salaries, and bonuses. In some cases, however, white-collar crime can result in bodily harm and death. The violence may be indirect and hard to trace, but the results are, nevertheless, assaults on people.

Criminal behavior involves either the commission of an act or the omission, in which someone neglects to do something prescribed by law. Notable in this latter context are neglect in cleaning up pollution-producing industrial wastes, oil spills, and proper health and safety measures for employees. Such white-collar crimes and others that lead to bodily harm, to violence to citizens, are committed to maximize the profits of corporations placing the value of the dollar above the value of the human.

This pattern of white-collar crime is illustrated by the marketing and/or use of substances whose toxic effects are not known, and in some cases cannot be known, until people become ill or die. For example, asbestos fibers, the synthetic hormone diethylstilbestrol (DES), and the defoliant Agent Orange are among the substances that have led to litigation related to white-collar crimes, a notable case being the Lockheed litigation.

In 1988, a number of Lockheed Aircraft employees who were working on the stealth bomber in a hangar full of chemicals instituted a lawsuit because they had a variety of illnesses. The paradox in their case was that, because of security issues, they could not reveal the type of work they performed in the hangar. Among the problems in such cases are the fact that the victim may not discover the injury or harm until years after exposure to the substance and the difficulty of showing a direct link between the substance and the injury. These tend to work to the benefit of the corporate white-collar criminal and to point out the degree to which current laws pertaining to violent, corporate, white-collar crime are outmoded.

The success of white-collar criminals tends to make them models for some people in lower social strata, many of whom decide that these deviant values are worth imitating. The behavior patterns of the con artist, the professional thief with the highest status, closely resemble those of the businessperson engaged in white-collar crime. Despite the sharp increase in the unethical practices and criminal activities that characterize white-collar crime, the great majority of people working in corporate America are ethical, law-abiding citizens.

(SEE ALSO: *Crime Theories; Criminology; Organized Crime; Political Crime*)

REFERENCES

Edelhertz, Herbert 1970 *Nature, Impact, and Prosecution of White-Collar Crime.* Washington, D.C.: U.S. Government Printing Office.

Sutherland, Edwin H. 1961 *White Collar Crime.* New York: Holt, Rinehart and Winston.

Yablonsky, Lewis 1990 *Criminology.* New York: Harper and Row.

LEWIS YABLONSKY

WIDOWHOOD   Marriages that do not end in divorce eventually dissolve through the death of a spouse. Much of the stress of bereavement derives from the disorganization caused by the loss of the deceased from the social support system of the survivor. The difficult and sometimes devastating transition to widowhood (or widowerhood) necessitates a reintegration of roles suitable to this new status. If children are present, parental death precipitates a reorganization of the family as a social system. Roles and status positions must be shifted, values reoriented, and personal and family time restructured. The potential for role strains and interpersonal conflicts becomes evident as relationships are lost, added, or redefined (Pitcher and Larson 1989). Loneliness emerges as a major problem. In many modern societies this adaptive process typically proceeds with few or no guidelines because the role of the widowed person tends to be "roleless," lacking clear norms or prescriptions for behavior (Hiltz 1979).

While the survivors face some common problems and role strains both within and outside the immediate family, it is difficult to specify a normative course of adjustment. This is because the widowed are a heterogeneous group characterized by wide differences in social and psychological characteristics. It is also due to the fact that spousal loss evokes a panorama of emotional and behavioral responses from survivors, depending on such factors as the timing and the circumstances under which death occurred. For example, a wife whose husband was killed in military battle will respond differently than if he had committed suicide or suffered a long terminal illness. Many other antecedent conditions, such as the quality of the marital relationship, affect the bereavement reactions and coping strategies employed by survivors.

THE DEMOGRAPHICS OF WIDOWHOOD

Census data for the United States show that at the end of the 1980s there were more than 13.5 million widowed persons, 85 percent of whom were women. However, people in the widowed category may exit it through remarriage. Hence, the number of people having ever experienced spousal loss is much greater than is indicated by the census.

For some decades the widowed female has outnumbered her male counterpart by an ever-widening margin. Three factors largely account for this: (1) mortality among females is lower than among males and, therefore, greater numbers of women survive to advanced years; (2) wives are typically younger than their husbands and, consequently, have a greater probability of outliving them; and (3) among the widowed, remarriage rates are significantly lower for women than for men. Other factors that contribute to the buildup of widows are war, depressions, and disease pandemics.

For various reasons widowhood has become largely a problem of the aged woman. Advances in medical technology and pervasive health programs have greatly extended life expectancy. The probabilities of mortality prior to middle age have decreased, and widowhood has for the most part been postponed to the latter stages of the life cycle. The gains in longevity have been more rapid for women than for men. Thus, the growing proportion of elderly females accents their more dramatic rates of widowhood. About one-fourth of all married women will become widows by age 65, and one-half of the remaining women will be widowed by age 75. During the same age span, only one-fifth of the men will lose their wives. It is projected that the ratio of widows to widowers will increase dramatically, from five to one currently to ten to one in twenty-five years.

RESEARCH FINDINGS ON WIDOWHOOD

In making the transition from married to widowed status, the bereaved are often confronted with a variety of personal and familial problems. They are not always successful in adapting to these circumstances. This is reflected in the findings that, as compared with married persons, the widowed rather consistently show higher rates of mortality, mental disorders, and suicide (Balkwell 1981). While there is a general consensus that bereavement is stressful, research on its effects on physical health has yielded inconsistent results. The evidence does show that the widowed experience poorer health than the married, but the reasons for this difference remain unclear.

Because widowhood is most likely to occur in the elderly, research has focused on that population. However, there is some evidence that the transition to widowhood varies by developmental stages. Older widows adapt more readily because losing a spouse at advanced ages is more the norm, thus making acceptance of the loss easier than for those who are young and widowed. Grieving over the death of a husband or wife at older ages can be exacerbated if additional significant others also die, requiring multiple grieving. This can cause *bereavement overload*, which makes it difficult for the survivor to complete the grief work and bring closure to the bereavement process (D. Berardo 1988). There is general consensus that the distress associated with conjugal bereavement diminishes over time. Grief becomes less intense as years pass, but this is not a simple, linear process. The emotional and psychological traumas of grief and mourning may recur sporadically long after the spouse has died.

The issue of gender differences in adaptation to widowhood has been widely debated. The evidence suggests a somewhat greater vulnerability for widowers (Stroebe and Stroebe 1983). Men are less likely to have same-sex widowed friends, more likely to be older and less healthy, have fewer family and social ties, and experience greater difficulty in becoming proficient in domestic roles (F. Berardo 1968, 1970). Higher mortality and suicide rates also suggest somewhat greater distress among widowers.

Continuous widowhood has been associated with loss of income and increased risk of poverty. Two-fifths of widows fall into poverty at some time during the five years following the death of their husbands. There is some evidence that widowers also suffer a decline in economic well-being, albeit to a lesser degree than their female counterparts (Zick and Smith 1988). Poor adjustment to widowhood may be related to lack of adequate finances. Elderly individuals often have below-average incomes prior to the death of their spouse. They may be unwilling or unable to seek employment and are likely to face discrimination in the labor market (Morgan 1989). The younger widowed are more likely to have lost a spouse suddenly and may be, therefore, unprepared to cope with lowered financial status.

Widowhood often leads to changes in living arrangements. Reduced income may force surviving spouses to seek more affordable housing. They may also choose to relocate for other reasons such as future financial and health concerns, desire to divest of possessions, or desire to be near kin or friends (Hartwigsen 1987). Most often, the people living alone are women—usually elderly widows. Isolation and lack of social support can lead to deterioration in their physical and mental well-being. Compared with elderly couples, they are much more likely to live in poverty and are less likely to receive medical care when needed (Kasper 1988).

The probability for remarriage is significantly less for widows than for widowers, especially at the older ages. Widows may feel they are committing *psychological bigamy* and therefore reject remarriage as an option (DiGiulio 1989). There is also a tendency to idealize the former partner, a process known as *sanctification* (Lopata 1979). This makes it difficult for widows to find a new partner who can compare favorably with the idealized image of the deceased (D. Berardo 1982). Widows remarry less frequently than widowers also because of the lack of eligible men and because of the existence of cultural norms that degrade the sexuality of older women and discourage them from selecting younger mates. Many women manage to develop and value a new and independent identity beyond widowhood, leading them to be less interested in reentering the marriage market.

There are other barriers to remarriage for the widowed. Dependent children limit the opportunities of their widowed parents to meet potential mates or to develop relationships with them. Older children may oppose remarriage out of concern for their inheritance. Widowed persons who cared for a dependent spouse through a lengthy terminal illness may be unwilling to risk this burden again.

WIDOWHOOD AND MORTALITY

The increased risk of mortality for widowed persons has been widely reported. Men are at a greater risk than women following bereavement. The causes of these differences are unknown. Marital selection theory posits that healthy widowers remarry quickly, leaving a less healthy subset, which experiences premature mortality. Other factors, such as common infection, shared environment, and lack of adequate daily care may also influence the higher mortality rates of the widowed.

TIMING AND MODE OF DEATH

Studies of whether *anticipatory grief,* or forewarning of the pending death of a spouse, contributes to bereavement adjustment have yielded conflicting results (Roach and Kitson 1989). Some suggest that anticipation is important because it allows the survivor to begin the process of role redefinition prior to the death, whereas unanticipated death will produce more severe grief reactions. Survivors who experienced unexpected deaths of their spouses report more somatic problems and longer adjustment periods than those who anticipated the loss. Anticipatory role rehearsal does not consistently produce smoother or more positive adjustment among the bereaved. It appears that the coping strategies employed by survivors vary with the timing and mode of death, which in turn influence the bereavement outcome.

SOCIAL SUPPORT AND REINTEGRATION

It has been suggested that social support plays an important role in bereavement outcome and acts as a buffer for stressful life events, but the research is inconclusive. Nevertheless, there is evidence that the extent to which members of the social network provide various types of support to the bereaved is important to the pattern of recovery and adaptation. Available confidants and access to self-help groups to assist with emotional management can help counter loneliness and promote the survivor's reintegration into society. The social resources of finances and education have been found to be particularly influential in countering the stresses associated with the death of a husband or wife. Community programs that provide education, counseling, and financial services can facilitate the efforts of the widowed and their families to restructure their lives.

(SEE ALSO: *Death and Dying; Filial Responsibility; Remarriage; Social Gerontology*)

REFERENCES

Balkwell, Carolyn 1981 "Transition to Widowhood: A Review of the Literature." *Family Relations* 30:117–127.

Berardo, Donna H. 1982 "Divorce and Remarriage at Middle-Age and Beyond." *Annals of the American Academy of Political and Social Science.* 464:132–139.

———1988 "Bereavement and Mourning." In Hannelore Wass, Felix M. Berardo, and Robert A. Neimeyer, eds., *Dying: Facing the Facts.* 2nd ed. New York: Hemisphere Pub. Co.

Berardo, Felix M. 1968 "Widowhood Status in the United States: A Neglected Aspect of the Family Life-Cycle." *Family Coordinator* 17:191–203.

———1970 "Survivorship and Social Isolation: The Case of the Aged Widower." *Family Coordinator* 19:11–25.

Clark, Philip G., Robert W. Siviski, and Ruth Weiner 1986 "Coping Strategies of Widowers in the First Year." *Family Relations* 35:425–430.

DiGiulio, R. C. 1989 *Beyond Widowhood.* New York: Free Press.

Dimond, Margaret, Dale A. Lund, and Michael S. Caserta 1987 "The Role of Social Support in the First Two Years of Bereavement in an Elderly Sample." *Gerontologist* 27:599–604.

Hartwigsen, G. 1987 "Older Widows and the Transference of Home." *International Journal of Aging and Human Development* 25:195–207.

Hiltz, Starr R. 1979 "Widowhood: A Roleless Role." In Marvin B. Sussman, ed., *Marriage and Family.* Collected Essay Series. New York: Hayworth Press.

Kasper, Judith D. 1988 *Aging Alone: Profiles and Projections.* Baltimore: Commonwealth Fund.

Lopata, Helen Z. 1973 *Widowhood in an American City.* Cambridge, Mass.: Schenkman.

———1979 *Women as Widows.* New York: Elsevier.

Morgan, Leslie 1989 "Economic Well-Being Following Marital Termination: A Comparison of Widowed and Divorced Women." *Journal of Family Issues* 10:86–101.

Pitcher, Brian L., and Don C. Larson 1989 "Elderly Widowhood." In Stephen J. Bahr and Evan T. Peterson, eds., *Aging and the Family.* Lexington, Mass.: D.C. Heath and Co.

Roach, Mary J., and Gay T. Kitson 1989 "Impact of Forewarning and Adjustment to Widowhood and Divorce." In Dale A. Lund, ed., *Older Bereaved Spouses.* New York: Hemisphere.

Stroebe, Margaret S., and Wolfgang Stroebe 1983 "Who Suffers More: Sex Differences in Health Risks of the Widowed." *Psychological Bulletin* 93:279–299.

Zick, Cathleen D., and Ken R. Smith 1988 "Recent Widowhood, Remarriage, and Changes in Economic Well-Being." *Journal of Marriage and the Family* 50:233–244.

FELIX M. BERARDO

WORK AND OCCUPATIONS

In modern society, work is a defining force in people's lives. It shapes people's identity, places them in the stratification system by influencing their social and economic positions, and affects their physical and emotional well-being. People's jobs determine the conditions under which they spend many of their waking hours and influence the quality of their lives. Although the term *work* is popularly used to denote the exertion of effort toward some end (e.g., we speak of "working" on one's backstroke), in an economic sense, work refers to activities oriented to producing goods and services for one's own use or for pay. Unpaid work includes that done in the home (indeed, in 1990 more people were employed at homemaking than any other occupation).

HISTORICAL EVOLUTION OF WORK

Although contemporary work differs dramatically from the work of our forebears, the evolution of the organization of production and people's attitudes toward work have important legacies for today's workers. For much of human history, work and home lives were integrated: Most work was done at or near the home, and people consumed the products of their labor.

The predecessors of the modern labor force were nonagricultural workers including skilled artisans who, under the control of guilds, made and sold products. The development of *industrial work* supplemented human effort with machines, introduced a division of labor that assigned specialized tasks to different workers, and ushered in a wage economy. In Europe, industrial work began as cottage industry in which middlemen brought unfinished goods to cottagers, often women and children, who manufactured products. However, the exploitation of new energy sources that could run large machines, the growing number of displaced peasants forced to sell their labor, and the expansion of markets for industrial goods made it economical to shift industrial work from cottages to factories. The resulting industrial revolution sounded the death knell for artisanal work, while laying the foundation for modern work. It also created the labor force.

THE LABOR FORCE

From a tiny fraction of the population of medieval societies, the labor force, people employed or seeking paid work, has grown steadily to absorb an increasing share of adults in developed societies. In Western industrialized nations it ranged in the late 1980s from about half of the civilian adults for Italy and the Netherlands to about two-thirds in Sweden, Canada, and the United States. In the United States by 1990 the labor force comprised about 125 million persons. Over time, labor force composition changed. Although women and children were well represented in the earliest labor force, as industrial work replaced agricultural work, the labor force became increasingly male. By the late nineteenth century, five out of six American workers were male, and the first half of the twentieth century witnessed children's exodus from the labor force. The growth of jobs that societies label "women's work" brought women back into the work force in

ever-increasing numbers (Oppenheimer 1970). By 1990 women made up slightly more than 45 percent of the U.S. labor force, compared with less than 15 percent in Muslim North Africa and a high of 47 percent in Central Eastern Europe.

The amount of their time people spend at paid work has changed throughout the centuries. In the early decades of industrialization, adults and children often worked fourteen-hour days, six days a week. Workdays shrank in the West after labor organizations won maximum-hours laws and, through collective bargaining, secured unionized workers' right to overtime pay. After 1973, the average work week declined for European and American workers, largely because more workers, especially married women with children, worked less than full-time, either to make time for unpaid family work or because they could not find full-time jobs. Indeed, employers design some jobs as part-time to avoid paying fringe benefits. However, in the 1980s American women increased their working hours, and by 1990 three-quarters of employed women worked full-time. The incidence of women's part-time employment varied sharply cross-nationally, with 43 percent of Swedish women employed less than full-time in contrast with less than 11 percent of Italian women.

People wanting paid work have usually outnumbered jobs, at least in capitalist societies, leaving some would-be workers unemployed. In advanced industrialized nations in the late 1980s, unemployment varied from 2 percent to 3 percent in Sweden and Japan to over 10 percent in France and the United Kingdom. Official estimates set the U.S. unemployment rate at 5.2 percent in 1990. Critics charge that official statistics underestimate the actual level of unemployment in the United States by disregarding "discouraged workers" who have stopped searching for jobs because they believe none exist for which they qualify. The risk of unemployment for racial/ethnic minorities (10.8 percent for African-Americans and 7.7 for Hispanics) and teenagers (14.5 percent) substantially exceeds that for white Anglo-American adults.

THE WORK PEOPLE DO: JOBS AND OCCUPATIONS

To refer to the work people do, social scientists use the terms *jobs* and *occupations*. A job is a set of work activities that one or more people perform in a specific setting. The 1977 edition of the Department of Labor's *Dictionary of Occupational Titles* listed over 12,000 job titles (Miller et al. 1980). The approximately 120 million employed persons hold about one million different jobs. Occupations, in contrast, refer to related jobs that represent a single economic role and, hence, are transferable across employers and work settings. In 1990 the U.S. Census Bureau distinguished 503 such "detailed" occupations (for example, funeral director, meter reader, janitor, accountant) that it grouped into six broad categories: managerial and professional specialties; technical, sales, and administrative-support occupations; service occupations; precision production, craft, and repair occupations; operation, fabrication, and labor occupations; and farming, forestry, and fishing occupations. A steady growth in the number of occupations since the industrial revolution reflects the increasing division of labor in complex societies.

Occupational Structure. A tabulation of the number of workers in each occupation in a society provides a snapshot of its occupational structure. Comparing societies' occupational—and industrial—structures at different times or across nations reveals a lot about their economic and technological development and the job opportunities available to their members. For example, in 1870 agriculture employed half of all American workers; in 1990 it provided jobs for about 2 percent of workers. The decline of smokestack industries in the United States and the explosion of service jobs illustrates the result of changing occupational and industrial structures: A worker's odds of getting a well-paid craft job have fallen sharply, so groups that have historically lacked access to these jobs (minorities, women) are unlikely to appreciably increase their representation. In contrast, the growing number of management jobs in the United States led to a record number of managerial positions for women and minorities in the 1980s.

PREPARING FOR AND GETTING A JOB

Education and Vocational Training. Workers' education affects the jobs they get for several reasons. Schools teach vocational skills, including literacy and numeracy, inculcate traits that employers value, such as punctuality, deference to authority, and competence in dealing with bureaucracies; and provide credentials that suggest that employers can train prospective workers for skills that jobs require. In Germany, for example, vocational training is a major way that workers acquire job skills. In the United States, in contrast, many workers, especially in traditionally male blue-collar jobs, acquire most skills on the job. However, clerical occupations, the professions, and the "semiprofessions" require workers to acquire relevant skills before employment.

Job Outcomes. People end up in particular jobs because of their personal characteristics, the constraints the occupational structure imposes, and the operation of labor markets, mechanisms that match workers to jobs and set wages. Although people decide whether to accept job offers, a minority of workers can be said to have freely chosen their occupations from the full range of possibilities. Labor markets, along with the educational system, limit people's options by restricting their knowledge of job openings, their qualifications, and their access to particular jobs.

Although thousands of distinct labor markets serve different locales and occupations, to understand the job-allocation process it is useful to distinguish *primary* markets that fill jobs characterized by high wages, pleasant working conditions, the chance to acquire skills, job security, and opportunities to advance from *secondary* markets that serve low-paid, dead-end, low-security jobs. Firms in the primary sector fill non-entry-level jobs through *internal labor markets* that provide employees with "ladders" that connect their jobs to related jobs higher in the organization. The failure of secondary-market jobs to provide job ladders that reward seniority and these jobs' general undesirability encourage high turnover (Gordon 1972). Both statistical discrimination and prejudice disproportionately relegate certain workers—the young, inexperienced, and poorly educated; racial and ethnic minorities; immigrants; and women—to jobs filled in secondary labor markets. As a result, one of the most enduring features of the occupational structure is the concentration of workers of different sexes, races, and ethnicities in different occupations. For example, before World War II, American blacks were segregated into farming, service, and unskilled-labor jobs in the secondary sector of the economy, such as domestic worker, porter, and orderly. War-induced labor shortages opened the door for African-Americans to a wider range of jobs, and antidiscrimination regulations (especially Title VII of the 1964 Civil Rights Act) spurred by the Civil Rights Movement helped to expand African-Americans' opportunities. As a result, race segregation has declined sharply in the United States since 1940, especially among women.

Sex segregation, which exists in every society, has been more resilient. In the United States in 1980, of all gainfully employed women, 28 percent were concentrated in just five occupations: secretary, bookkeeper, manager/administrator, clerk, and registered nurse. Over half of employed women worked in just 19 of the 503 occupations the Census Bureau distinguished. Men, in contrast, were spread more evenly across all occupations: The top five—manager/administrator, production supervisor, truck driver, sales supervisor, and wholesale sales representative—accounted for 19 percent of all employed men (Taeuber and Valdisera 1986). The extent of occupational sex segregation varies sharply across nations. In advanced industrial nations, it tends to be higher when more women are in the labor force (Bakker 1988) and in countries that provide paid maternity leaves (Rosenfeld and Kalleberg 1990).

Given the diversity of jobs within the same occupational titles, *job segregation* is more perva-sive than *occupational segregation*. Data for 393 California firms revealed that only about 10 percent of employees worked side by side in the same job with someone of the other sex (Bielby and Baron 1986). Thus, evidence of declining occupational-level sex segregation masks continued job-level segregation (Reskin and Roos 1990). Many scholars favor enforcing existing antidiscrimination laws and affirmative-action regulations and training workers for nontraditional jobs as the most effective remedies for job segregation.

REWARDS OF EMPLOYMENT

People seek jobs to maximize *extrinsic* rewards—a high income, prestige, a good chance for promotion, and security (Rothman 1987; Jencks, Perman and Rainwater 1988)—as well as *intrinsic* rewards—satisfaction, autonomy, and variety.

Earnings. Earnings are the most important job reward for many workers. Although one's age, race, sex, and education influence one's earnings, their effects are largely mediated through occupation. Economic theory holds that supply and demand determine earnings, but sociologists recognize that both employers and workers influence supply and demand (for example, unions and professional associations restrict competition and construe their work as skilled and, hence, meriting high compensation) and that prejudice prompts some employers to make decisions at odds with market principles (Granovetter 1981). As a result, considerable income inequality exists across individuals and social groups. Substantial race, sex, and ethnic inequality in earnings characterizes all industrial societies. In the United States African-Americans have always earned much less than same-sex whites. In 1963 the Equal Pay Act outlawed wage discrimination by race, national origin, and sex. That law and declining occupational segregation by race have reduced the race gap in earnings among men and almost eliminated it among women. The disparity in earnings between American women and men has proven more robust because segregation continues to relegate most women to low-paying jobs and because jobs in which women predominate pay less. Hence, in 1989 female full-time year-round workers earned 65 percent of men's annual earnings. The wage gap varies across nations (and across occupations and industries within countries). In the 1980s Australia came closest to equal pay (female full-time year-round workers earned 80 percent of what men made), compared with 47 percent in Japan (Kalleberg and Rosenfeld 1990). Factors that can reduce the wage gap among full-time workers include equalizing the sexes' educational attainment and labor-market experience, integrating jobs, and implementing pay schemes that compensate workers for the worth of jobs regardless of their sex composition.

Occupational Prestige. People assign prestige to workers partly on the basis of their occupations. In the past, the distinction between blue-collar and white-collar jobs served as a rough proxy for workers' social status. However, as the occupational structure became increasingly complex, social scientists developed more sophisticated ways to measure occupational prestige. The most commonly used is the Duncan Socioeconomic Index (Duncan 1961), which assigns a score to each occupation on the basis of its incumbents' average educational and income levels. The occupational prestige scores permit scholars to study the distribution, determinants, and stability of occupational prestige. Researchers have found that the occupational-status hierarchy has been remarkably stable over time and across cultures (Treiman 1977) and that the occupational standing of American workers is highly stratified. Most people work in occupations with relatively low socioeconomic scores, and only 5 percent hold occupations with scores above 80 (on a scale from 1 to 100).

Intrinsic Rewards: Job Satisfaction. Contemporary workers see their jobs as places to find personal fulfillment, self-expression, and satisfaction (Kalleberg 1982), and they seek jobs that will provide these and other psychic rewards such as autonomy (Jencks, Perman, and Rainwater 1988). Workers in routine jobs try to imbue them with challenge or meaning, in part by creating a workplace culture. These adaptations contribute to the

high levels of satisfaction Americans report with their jobs. Nonetheless, not all jobs are satisfying, nor are all workers satisfied. Although some assume that dissatisfied workers are less productive, James Lincoln and Arne Kalleberg (1990) found that Japanese and German workers, who showed the lowest levels of satisfaction, were among the world's most productive workers. Nonetheless, some employers in the United States and elsewhere have devised strategies such as workplace democracy, job-enrichment programs, and "quality circles" to enhance workers' involvement in their jobs.

WORK AND FAMILY

In moving paid work out of the home, the Industrial Revolution in the West laid the foundation for the separation of work and family and cemented a division of labor that mandated domestic work for women and market work for men. Although married women increasingly hold paid jobs, doing so has not exempted them from primary responsibility for domestic tasks. The resulting time pressures are stressful for employed women, especially mothers, although those whose husbands share child care and who have no difficulty arranging child care fare better on measures of emotional well-being than nonemployed women (Mirowsky and Ross 1989). Women have adapted by cutting down on domestic work, sacrificing leisure time, renegotiating the domestic division of labor with their families, purchasing more services, and working part-time. The tendency to purchase more services has fueled the growth of service jobs in fast-food chains, day-care centers, and cleaning services and, in turn, the demand for low-wage workers. A growing number of mostly women workers are doing paid work at home in what some see as a return to cottage industry (Boris and Daniels 1989).

As more married women work outside the home (by 1989, 58 percent of American women did so), the "role overload" under which they labor has become a societal problem. European countries have responded with paid parental leave and state-run nurseries. American women are increasingly appealing to employers and policy-makers for similar solutions: flextime, parental leave, and assistance with child care. At the start of the 1990s, a limited number of U.S. firms voluntarily offered these options, but employers' increasing reliance on women and politicians' concern with women's votes should make them more heedful of women's needs.

TRENDS IN WORK AND OCCUPATIONS

Changes in Labor Force Composition. The Bureau of Labor Statistics has projected a slowdown in U.S. labor force growth through the 1990s, with a work force of about 140 million in the year 2000. That labor force will be older, and have more female and minority workers than in the past. African-Americans, Asian-Americans, Hispanics, and other races are expected to make up about 57 percent of the labor force growth between 1986 and 2000. In fact, native white males are expected to make up only 15 percent of the labor force entrants from 1985 to 2000. Thus, in 2000 the U.S. labor force is projected to be 47 percent female and 15.5 percent minority (Johnston and Packer 1987), compared with 45 percent female and 14.2 percent minority in 1990. The shrinking number of young workers in the baby bust generation that followed the baby boom will orient employers to other labor sources, such as immigrants, to fill low-wage, entry-level jobs.

Changes in Technology, the Production Process, and the Occupational Structure. The history of work can be seen as a battle between employers and workers over output, autonomy, and remuneration. Employers, taking advantage of their control over the tools of production, have tried to control the labor process through close supervision, embedding control into work technology, deskilling work, and implementing bureaucratic controls such as regular evaluations and career ladders (Edwards 1979). Workers have resisted through collective action and work cultures that enforced production norms (Simpson 1989).

In their search for greater profits and control,

U.S. employers have increasingly subcontracted work outside the firm and exported jobs to the Pacific Rim, Mexico, and the Caribbean, where labor has been cheap and tractable. Since the late 1960s hundreds of thousands of American jobs have been lost to automation or exportation. In the 1980s, fewer than 6 percent of Americans worked on assembly lines, and by 2000 fewer than 14 percent are expected to hold manufacturing jobs. The United States and other advanced industrial nations have become *postindustrial societies* that specialize in producing services rather than goods (Bell 1973). Thus, service occupations in the United States are projected to add six million jobs by the year 2000 (Johnston and Packer 1987). The export of manufacturing jobs from advanced industrial nations, fueled by the growth of multinational corporations, is fostering an international division of labor in which workers in less developed countries manufacture products under conditions resembling those of early European industrialization.

The other strategy in employers' efforts to control labor and contain costs has been technological innovations that have transformed the production of goods and services. In the 1990s, innovations in microprocessor technology will permit advances in robotics and information processing that will further revolutionize the production process and the workplace. Robots work around the clock, can handle hazardous tasks, and are cheap to operate. Pessimists fear that technical innovations will eliminate or deskill many jobs and subject workers to close technological control. Optimists stress the job-creating and job-enhancing potential of these advances. Randy Hodson and Robert Parker's (1988) review of research on high-technology industries suggests that sophisticated technologies, while increasing productivity, are likely to eliminate more jobs, particularly relatively less-skilled jobs, than they create and to erode skills in mid- to low-skill jobs. Clerical jobs are especially vulnerable. While robots may take over some dangerous jobs, Hodson and Parker conclude that technological advances may make the high-technology workplace more stressful and less healthy.

Expected job shortages can create opportunities for historically disadvantaged groups, especially those with education adequate to exploit job opportunities. However, in postindustrial societies, knowledge and technical expertise have become increasingly important, and a growing number of jobs require at least some college education, so workers without a high school diploma will face difficulties finding jobs that pay well and provide advancement opportunities. Moreover, workers will need different skills from those that traditional work required, so job training and retraining will become increasingly important. In the years ahead, societies will have to grapple with the effects of technological innovations on workers' opportunities and experiences in the workplace.

(SEE ALSO: *Comparable Worth; Labor Force; Occupational and Career Mobility; Occupational Prestige; Professions; Work Orientation*)

REFERENCES

Bakker, Isabella 1988 "Women's Employment in Comparative Perspective." In Jane Jenson, Elisabeth Hagen, and Reddy Ceallaigh, eds., *Feminization of the Labor Force.* New York: Oxford University Press.

Bell, Daniel 1973 *The Coming of Post-Industrial Society.* New York: Basic Books.

Bielby, William T., and James N. Baron 1984 "Men and Women at Work: Sex Segregation and Statistical Discrimination." *American Journal of Sociology* 91:759–799.

Boris, Eileen, and Cynthia R. Daniels, eds. 1989 *Homework: Historical and Contemporary Perspectives on Paid Labor at Home.* Urbana: University of Illinois Press.

Duncan, Otis Dudley 1961 "A Socioeconomic Index for All Occupations." In Albert J. Reiss et al. eds., *Occupations and Social Status.* New York: Free Press.

Edwards, Richard 1979 *Contested Terrain: The Transformation of the Workplace in the Twentieth Century.* New York: Basic Books.

Gordon, David M. 1972 *Theories of Poverty and Unemployment.* Lexington, Mass.: Lexington Books.

Granovetter, Mark 1981 "Toward a Sociological Theory of Income Differences." In Ivar Berg, ed., *Sociological Perspectives on Labor Markets,* New York: Academic Press.

Hodson, Randy, and Robert E. Parker 1988 "Work in High Tech Settings: A Literature Review." In Richard L. Simpson and Ida Harper Simpson, eds., *Research in the Sociology of Work,* vol. 4. Greenwich, Conn.: JAI Press.

Jencks, Christopher, Lauri Perman, and Lee Rainwater 1988 "What Is a Good Job?" *American Journal of Sociology* 93:1322–1357.

Johnston, William B., and Arnold E. Packer 1987 *Workforce 2000: Work and Workers for the Twenty-first Century.* Washington, D.C.: U.S. Government Printing Office.

Kalleberg, Arne L. 1982 "Work: Postwar Trends and Future Prospects." *Business Horizons* July/August, pp. 78–84.

———, and Rachel A. Rosenfeld July, 1990 "Gender Inequality in the Labor Market: A Cross-National Perspective." Presented at the 12th World Congress of Sociology, Madrid.

Lincoln, James R., and Arne L. Kalleberg 1990 *Culture, Control and Commitment: A Study of Work Organization and Work Attitudes in the U.S. and Japan.* New York: Cambridge University Press.

Miller, Ann R., Donald J. Treiman, Pamela S. Cain, and Patricia A. Roos (eds.) 1980 *Work, Jobs, and Occupations: A Critical Review of the Dictionary of Occupational Titles.* Washington, D.C.: National Academy Press.

Mirowsky, John, and Catherine E. Ross 1989 *Social Causes of Psychological Distress.* New York: Aldine.

Oppenheimer, Valerie K. 1970 *The Female Labor Force in the United States: Demographic and Economic Factors Governing Its Growth and Changing Composition.* Westport, Conn.: Greenwood Press.

Reskin, Barbara F., and Patricia A. Roos 1990 *Job Queues, Gender Queues: Explaining Women's Inroads into Male Occupations.* Philadelphia: Temple University Press.

Rosenfeld, Rachel A., and Arne L. Kalleberg 1990 "A Cross-National Comparison of the Gender Gap in Income." *American Journal of Sociology* 96:69–106.

Rothman, Robert A. 1987 *Working: Sociological Perspectives.* Englewood Cliffs, N.J.: Prentice Hall.

Simpson, Ida Harper 1989 "The Sociology of Work: Where Have the Workers Gone?" *Social Forces* 67:945–964.

Taeuber, Cynthia M., and Victor Valdisera 1986 *Women in the American Economy.* Current Population Report P-23, Series P-23, No. 146. Washington, D.C.: U.S. Government Printing Office.

Treiman, Donald J. 1977 *Occupational Prestige in Comparative Perspective*. New York: Academic Press.

BARBARA F. RESKIN

WORK ORIENTATION One indicator of the importance of an area of specialization within a discipline is the availability of textbooks published to represent and convey the body of knowledge associated with that specialty. Based on this crude measure, one would have to conclude that the *sociology of work* only recently emerged in the 1980s as a specialty area. Not only did the American Sociological Association prepare a compendium of course syllabi for the area but also a number of textbooks appeared. In reality, however, the name is new but the general area is not. The sociology of work represents an integration of two long-standing specialties, industrial sociology and occupations/professions. It also includes literature from industrial and organizational psychologists and the recent attempts to integrate the stratification and the organization literatures to better understand what is called the *employment relationship* (e.g., Baron and Bielby 1980).

The study of this employment relationship encompasses a multitude of topics all the way from how the individual is initially matched to a job, through all that happens on the job (being paid, becoming satisfied or dissatisfied, forming cliques, etc.), to turnover (quitting or being dismissed). Considered important to these topics are the orientations employees have toward their work. This is the topic to be addressed here.

Definitions of *work* abound, but most of them include the following features. First, although groups or collectivities may be viewed as actors involved in work (e.g., work groups, task groups, teams, or committees), the unit of analysis is usually the individual. Second, the individual is involved in physical or mental activity. Third, this activity usually involves some form of payment, but it need not involve payment to be considered work. This allows housekeeping activities to be included, as well as family members laboring to support some family enterprise and volunteer helpers. Fourth, the activity involves the production or creation of something. Fifth, this something usually is a good or a service. Sixth, this good or service is valued by the individual or others and, thus, is usually consumed by either or both.

From this list of features, work is defined as the mental or physical activity of an individual directed toward the production of goods or services that are valued by that individual or others.

Orientation to work, unfortunately, is a term that does not convey a very clear or precise meaning. Generally, it is used to refer to two broad areas: motivation to work and responses to work. The first area covers why people work and has occupied the attention of psychologists for some time. Questions about need hierarchies, self-actualization, and intrinsic and extrinsic motivations are addressed. The second area has more often attracted the attention of sociologists. It takes the activity of work as given and addresses the ways individuals react to it. Here, the individual is portrayed as (1) being aware of his or her work situation, (2) assessing it (giving meaning to it), and (3) reacting to it. Job satisfaction and commitment have been given the most attention here.

The bulk of this paper is organized around these two topics of work motivation and responses to work. However, because the concept of alienation has been so dominant in sociological accounts of work, it is considered first.

ALIENATION

Sociologists continue to draw from Marx in referring to an alienated individual as being separated or estranged from certain aspects of work that give meaning and significance to that work and life as a whole. For Marx these aspects of work are control over the product, control over the work process, creative activity, and social relations with others. Clearly, a negative side of work is portrayed when alienation is the concept of interest.

A survey of journals and sociology-of-work texts over the past several decades suggests that sociologists have lost interest in this concept. For example, the indexes for the texts by Arne Kalleberg and Ivar Berg (1987), Richard Rothman (1987), and Curt Tausky (1984) do not include the term *alienation*, nor does the James Price and Charles Mueller (1986b) handbook on the measurement of major organization concepts devote even one of its thirty chapters to alienation.

This should not be interpreted to mean that interest in alienation is dead. Three things have happened. First, interest has shifted to conceptualizing and measuring positively worded concepts, like *job satisfaction*. Second, scholars have gotten away from the picture of capitalist work settings universally producing alienated workers and have moved more to a picture of multidimensional work settings and multimotivated employees who respond to work in varying ways. Third, out of this more pluralistic image of work, several concepts such as work motivation, self-actualization, job satisfaction, and commitment have emerged in an attempt to bring more precision to how individuals are oriented to their work. So, alienation has not been forgotten; it has just been absorbed into several other concepts.

Before considering the two major topics, it is important to mention one line of research that grew directly out of an interest in alienation. This is the work initiated by Robert Blauner (1964). Accepting the Marxian definition of alienation, he examines the possibility that changes in how work is organized (technology) could affect worker alienation. After studying four manufacturing industries at different stages of technological development, he concluded that alienation need not be an omnipresent by-product of capitalism. Instead, it follows an inverted U-shaped curve, with alienation lowest for craft industries, increasing with machine tending and repetitive assembly line technology, but decreasing with continuous process technologies. More recent evidence for this pattern, however, is mixed (Hodson and Sullivan 1990).

WORK MOTIVATION

Historically, sociologists have flirted off and on with psychological concepts like *work motivation* and *work involvement*, and there has always been disagreement as to the relevance of such concepts to the study of social phenomena. For example, of the 1980s sociology-of-work textbooks, only Richard Hall's (1986) gives critical attention to the theoretical and empirical literature on the topic. Any treatment of work orientation must include this material, however, because most current literature is an offshoot of, or a reaction to, these psychological theories.

Work motivation is defined as the force that activates people to perform their jobs (Smither 1988). Two theoretical traditions have been dominant. First, need theories argue that individuals are motivated by internal needs that usually develop early in life and often are not consciously recognized by them. Abraham Maslow (1954) identifies a hierarchy of needs and claims that higher order needs (goals) cannot be met until lower order needs have been met sequentially. This hierarchy begins at the bottom, with basic physiological needs, and ends at the top, with self-actualization. Others (e.g., Alderfer 1972) have modified Maslow's hierarchy to view it as a continuum with fewer levels and also with the idea that lower order needs may reemerge as unmet. Frederick Herzberg (1966) was more interested in job satisfaction and argues that individuals are motivated by two types of factors. *Motivators* are the more intrinsic features of work, like responsibility, advancement, and achievement, whereas *hygiene* factors characterize the workplace and include pay, job security, and working conditions. When the motivators are present, employees are satisfied, but if they are absent, they are not satisfied. When the hygiene factors are present, employees are neither dissatisfied nor satisfied, but when they are absent, they are dissatisfied. David McClelland (1961) argues that certain socialization environments produce a need for achievement and that such individuals strive toward excellence in whatever they undertake. Management scholars were especially interested in this theory because it suggested to them who should be hired or promoted. Finally, Douglas McGregor (1960) argues that assumptions about human nature and motivation have resulted in two approaches to organizational design. Theory *X* is based on the assumption that individuals are basically lazy and motivated primarily by extrinsic rewards like pay. Theory Y assumes humans act responsibly and contribute their skills and talents when their intrinsic needs, like self-actualization, are met. This distinction is not unlike the classic debate between functionalist and Marxian portrayals of society and human nature.

Overall, these need theories have lost favor. The empirical support is weak (Fein 1976), use in applied settings has proven difficult because of problems associated with measuring need levels and with attempting to alter the personality patterns that have developed in childhood, and the significance of the environment has been neglected.

The second dominant perspective, expectancy theory, comes from the organizational and industrial psychologists. It bypasses the issue of needs and stresses cognitive and rational processes. The basic underlying assumption is that motivations to work vary substantially from one individual to the next and that these motivations are mutable across time and space (Vroom 1964; Lawler 1973). Motivations reflect interplay of effort, expectations about outcomes, and importance or value given to outcomes. Put another way, a person's motivation to behave in a particular way is a function of the expected results and how valuable those results are to that individual. Until recently, this theory was dominant in studying work motivation in industrial and organizational psychology (Smither 1988).

Sociologists are generally aware of these motivation theories and, like psychologists, now give less attention to need theories. However, unlike psychologists, they have not been overly interested in the theories per se of work motivation. In fact, it is accurate to say that psychologists have led the way in developing theories of motivation, and sociologists usually are a generation behind in adopting or rejecting these theories. For example, Smither (1988) mentions equity, behavioral, and goal setting theories as now receiving much attention in the psychological work-motivation literature. Although equity theory has been explored for some time experimentally by sociologists,

there is no evidence that sociologists have adopted, in any significant way, any of these "newer" approaches to work motivation.

What sociologists do in practice matches more closely the expectancy model. Hall's (1986) treatment of the individual dimension and Hodson and Sullivan's (1990) discussion of job satisfaction are illustrative of this. The picture is one in which "the fit" of an individual's characteristics and expectations with the actual work conditions determines whether that individual is motivated.

What sociologists have emphasized instead of motivation theory is socialization to work, that is, how individuals learn their work roles. This interest is not surprising, given the long-standing concern of both sociologists and social psychologists in socialization processes. One stream of thought in this area concerns socialization into professional roles. A popular strategy here is to examine career stages (e.g., Feldman 1976, 1981). Another approach to the socialization issue is represented by the work of Melvin Kohn and Carmi Schooler (1973, 1978, 1982), who not only argue for the intergenerational, class-based transmission of work values, but also argue for and demonstrate reciprocal effects: An individual's work orientations (e.g., self-direction) are affected by job conditions, but also these orientations affect the kinds of jobs with which the individual is associated.

RESPONSE TO WORK: JOB SATISFACTION

Although the wording of definitions of job satisfaction has varied dramatically across disciplines and scholars, it is one concept for which there is near consensus. For example, Patricia Smith, Lorne Kendall, and Charles Hullin (1969) succinctly define it as the degree to which individuals like their jobs. Edwin Locke's definition is longer but says essentially the same thing: Job satisfaction is a positive emotional state reflecting an affective response to the job situation (Locke 1976). The common element in the definitions is the idea of the individual positively responding emotionally or affectively to the job.

The major issues in the study of job satisfaction

are the following: (1) What produces job satisfaction? (2) What are the consequences of differing levels of job satisfaction? (3) Is it a global or unitary concept, or should facets (dimensions) be investigated?

There exist two dominant arguments regarding the determinants of job satisfaction (Kalleberg 1977; Loscocco 1989; Mortimer 1979). One is that the individual's job satisfaction is determined by disposition or personality traits that she or he brings to the workplace. In simple terms, individuals vary along a continuum from negative to positive orientation. These dispositions are reflected in the person's responses to work conditions, as well as to other aspects of life like family or, more generally, life. The second argument is considered the more "sociological" of the two and emphasizes the importance of the work conditions the employee experiences. This approach is closer to a Marxian perspective in that it is the structural conditions of the workplace that make work rewarding or not rewarding. Any individual dispositional differences that exist wane in importance in the face of these structural features.

Although sociologists give lip service to the disposition argument, the literature unequivocally documents a stronger interest in identifying the features of work that affect job satisfaction. Within this perspective, however, there is considerable disagreement about what features of work are important. One major debate is over whether extrinsic (e.g., pay and fringe benefits) or intrinsic (e.g., self-actualization and task variety) features of work are the most important. Following a needs framework leads one to argue that the extrinsic features must exist before the intrinsic features become important. In contrast, an expectancy argument would be that any of these can be important, but it is the fit of what the individual expects and values with what is found that is crucial in determining the satisfaction level.

In this limited space it is impossible to review and summarize the thousands of studies conducted on the determinants of job satisfaction. Instead, a list of variables found to have some relationship with job satisfaction is provided (the sign indicates the direction of the relationship with satisfaction): variety (+), pay (+), autonomy (+), instrumental communication (+), role conflict (−), role overload (−), work-group cohesion (+), work involvement (+), distributive justice (+), promotional opportunities (+), supervisory support (+), task significance (+), and external job opportunities (−).

This debate over intrinsic versus extrinsic features of work continues to direct the research of sociologists, but the more interesting question that is reemerging is the disposition versus situation debate. As stated, sociologists eschew the dispositional arguments because they "just aren't sociological." Hence, much effort goes into cataloging and operationalizing employee characteristics and objective structural features of work, and little attention is given to identifying and measuring the dispositional traits. As a consequence, the vast body of evidence marshaled for the features of work is not surprising (see Hall's discussion of these issues, 1986). Recent work in organizational and industrial psychology, however, suggests that this dismissal of dispositional factors is perhaps premature. Evidence continues to mount that individuals exhibit basic dispositional traits (e.g., negative and positive affectivity) that are relatively stable throughout their lives and over different employment situations (Watson and Clark 1984; Watson, Pennebaker, and Folger 1986). There exists some evidence that positive affectivity is positively related to job satisfaction, whereas negative affectivity is negatively related to job satisfaction.

Another issue is the consequences of job satisfaction. Two outcomes have received the most attention, primarily because of their practical significance to any business enterprise. One is productivity and the other is withdrawal behavior, which includes absenteeism and voluntary turnover. The satisfaction–productivity argument is of long-standing interest and, thus, has generated considerable empirical data. The hypothesis is that satisfaction is positively and causally related to productivity. This large volume of research, however, indicates that job satisfaction is not strongly related to productivity (Gray and Starke 1984).

With regard to the satisfaction–withdrawal relationship, the hypothesis is that the most satisfied employees are the least often absent and also the least likely to quit voluntarily (Chadwick-Jones, Nicholson, and Brown 1982; Mowday, Porter, and Steers 1982; Price and Mueller 1986a). The meta-analyses for the satisfaction–absenteeism relationship (Hackett and Guion 1985; Scott and Taylor 1985) suggest that the relationship is weak at best. The findings for the satisfaction–turnover relationship are stronger, but the conclusion is that job satisfaction serves more of a mediating function. That is, the structural features of work and employee characteristics (e.g., education) directly affect job satisfaction, which in turn affects turnover. Once organizational commitment (to be discussed next) is included, however, the satisfaction effect is reduced significantly. One lesson to be learned from this is that use of indirect measures of job satisfaction, for example absenteeism and turnover, is a risky enterprise and not one supported by the data.

The final issue is whether job satisfaction is a unitary concept or is really a complex of many facets or dimensions. Since a fairly large number of work features are known to affect job satisfaction, it is logical to expect that individuals can be satisfied with some of these but not others. The data support this logic. In particular, there is evidence that, for almost any distinct feature of the work situation such as pay, autonomy, variety, work-group cohesion, and feedback, scales can be developed with divisions into distinct, but related, factors along these dimensions. This not only poses a problem theoretically but also affects scale construction. As a simple example, a person may be satisfied with pay but not satisfied with feedback about job performance. Combining scores for these two will show the person to be neither satisfied nor dissatisfied for the composite. In such situations the rule of thumb is that scales developed to measure various satisfaction dimensions should not be aggregated. However, global job-satisfaction scales, those that ask more generally about liking one's job, can be used to represent the person's general affective reaction to the job. Sociologists more often use these global scales and assume that work is experienced and responded to globally.

The facet approach clearly becomes more important in applied research. If an employer wishes to alter the work setting to increase job satisfaction, then a global scale is less helpful. A scale that captures such dimensions as satisfaction with pay, routinization, and communication provides the information necessary to implement specific structural changes. There exist numerous established measures of job satisfaction, both global and facet-based (see Cook et al. 1981; Price and Mueller 1986b).

RESPONSE TO WORK: WORK COMMITMENT

Although some concepts go further back than the 1970s, such as Robert Dubin's (1956) central life interest and Thomas Lodahl and Mathilde Kejner's job involvement (1965), most of the interest in work commitment has emerged fairly recently and, to a large extent, during a time when interest in job satisfaction has been diminishing. If employee commitment is defined as the level of attachment to some component or aspect of work, then the door is opened to a large number of types of commitment. In fact, Paula Morrow (1983) identifies over twenty-five commitment-related concepts and measures. She concludes that there is considerable conceptual redundancy and that there are five major types into which all of these fall: commitment to work, to the career, to the organization, to the job, and to the union. Numerous definitions accompany these concepts, but the idea that seems to dominate is that attachment involves an emotional identification with the particular aspect of work. In fact, this attachment is sometimes referred to as loyalty.

Of these five types of commitment it is organizational commitment that has received the most attention, with two conceptualizations predominating. The first is consistent with the loyalty idea and may be labeled *affective organizational commitment*. Organizational and industrial psychologists (e.g., Mowday, Porter, and Steers 1982) are given credit for initiating interest in this concept. They argue that commitment intervenes between various features of work and individual characteristics and outcomes of absenteeism and voluntary turnover. The evidence generally is consistent with these claims (e.g., Mueller and Price 1990; Price and Mueller 1986a). This first conceptualization is also often referred to as *attitudinal commitment*.

The second conceptualization is sometimes called *behavioral commitment* or *continuance commitment*. In practice it is operationalized as the employee's stated intention to stay (or leave). This form of organizational commitment can be traced back to Howard Becker's (1960) side-bet theory. Individuals are portrayed as making investments (e.g., achieving seniority, participating in a pension fund, developing attachments to coworkers as friends) when employed in a particular organization. These side bets accumulate with tenure and, thus, become costs associated with taking employment elsewhere. The employee discontinues employment only when the rewards associated with another job outweigh the accumulated side bets associated with the current one. Although evidence for the reasoning behind this theory has not been supported, the research has consistently shown a relatively strong negative relationship between intent to stay and voluntary turnover (Steele and Ovalle 1984). Much of the literature identifies this form of commitment as intervening between affective commitment and turnover. Sociologists see the structural conditions of work as the ultimate causes of these forms of commitment. Recently, the importance of legitimacy and autonomy in explaining organizational commitment has been examined (Halaby 1985; Halaby and Weakliem 1989).

Work commitment is generally treated the same way as work motivation and so will not be addressed here. *Job commitment* refers to the individual's attachment to the particular job rather than to work in general or the organization. Career commitment, also referred to as *professional commitment* or *occupational commitment*, and union commitment have been viewed by many as part of a zero-sum game along with organizational commitment (Kalleberg and Berg 1987). The argument is that employees cannot be committed to all aspects of work simultaneously. Although much conceptual and empirical investigation is still needed, the empirical evidence has shown that these forms of commitment are not necessarily incompatible with each other.

ADDITIONAL ISSUES

There are four topics also deserving of some discussion. First, Michael Burawoy (1979) has demonstrated that an individual's response to work may not always be revealed by measuring job satisfaction, commitment, absenteeism, or turnover. He finds, as did Donald Roy (1952, 1959), that employees often adjust to work, not by complaining, being tardy, or leaving, but by making it a game. Similarly, but for a different purpose, Mark Granovetter (1985) argues for the study of the embeddedness of economic behavior (like turnover) in the social relations and structure of the workplace. Findings and arguments such as these serve as constant reminders of the complexities and difficulties associated with the study of work orientation.

Second, some additional responses to work concepts exist in the more recent literature and should at least be mentioned. These are stress and burnout. They currently are of interest outside of sociology but may eventually attract more attention within sociology.

Third, data indicate that, although job-satisfaction levels are fairly high in the United States, there has been a moderate decline in workers' job satisfaction since around 1950 (Hamilton and Wright 1986). An explanation for this will come, not from the study of work orientation at the micro level, but only with macro analyses of societal changes in the occupational structure, the structure of work, the income and wealth distribution, or other societal-level phenomena.

Fourth, the discussion presented has not included what may be called the *correlates of work orientations*. These are usually demographic variables like race, gender, job tenure, and age. The studies on motivation, satisfaction, commitment, absenteeism, and turnover consistently provide data on how these correlates are related to work orientations. Generally, however, these variables are not part of the theory used to initiate this research but are the demographic variables routinely measured. Since they usually are empirically related to the orientations, these correlates are utilized, after the fact, to infer that other unmeasured, but more substantive, variables are operating. This can best be illustrated with one example where this is not the case. Rosabeth Kanter's (1977) work on men and women in organizations is premised on the claim that gender makes a difference in organizational leadership behavior. Rather than just looking at outcomes for men and women and inferring that they are treated differently, however, Kanter identifies the variables, such as access to resources, that are producing these gender differences. Understanding why such correlates are related to these work orientations is an important theoretical task confronting sociologists.

(SEE ALSO: *Comparable Worth; Occupational and Career Mobility; Work and Occupations*)

REFERENCES

Alderfer, Clayton 1972 *Existence, Relatedness, and Growth: Human Needs in Organizational Settings.* New York: Free Press.

Baron, James, and William Bielby 1980 "Bringing the Firms Back in: Stratification, Segmentation and the Organization of Work." *American Sociological Review* 45:737–765.

Becker, Howard 1960 "Notes on the Concept of Commitment." *American Sociological Review* 66:32–40.

Blauner, Robert 1964 *Alienation and Freedom.* Chicago: University of Chicago.

Burawoy, Michael 1979 *Manufacturing Consent.* Chicago: University of Chicago Press.

Chadwick-Jones, J., Nigel Nicholson, and Colin Brown 1982 *The Social Psychology of Absenteeism.* New York: Praeger.

Cook, John, Susan Hepworth, Toby Wall, and Peter Warr 1981 *The Experience of Work.* New York: Academic Press.

Dubin, Robert 1956 "Industrial Workers' Worlds: A Study of the Central Life Interests of Industrial Workers." *Social Problems* 3:131–142.

Fein, Mitchell 1976 "Motivation and Work." In Robert Dubin, ed., *Handbook of Work, Organization and Society,* pp. 465–530. Chicago: Rand McNally.

Feldman, Daniel 1976 "A Contingency Theory of Socialization." *Administrative Science Quarterly* 21:433–452.

———1981 "The Multiple Socialization of Organizational Members." *Academy of Management Review* 6:309–318.

Granovetter, Mark 1985 "Economic Action, Social Structure, and Embeddedness." *American Journal of Sociology* 91:481–510.

Gray, Jerry, and Frederick Starke 1984 *Organizational Behavior: Concepts and Applications,* 3rd ed. Columbus, Ohio: Charles E. Merrill.

Hackett, Rick, and Robert Guion 1985 "A Reevaluation of the Absenteeism-Job Satisfaction Relationship." *Organizational Behavior and Human Decision Processes* 35:340–381.

Halaby, Charles 1985 "Worker Attachment and Workplace Authority." *American Sociological Review* 51:634–649.

———, and David Weakliem 1989 "Worker Control and Attachment." *American Journal of Sociology* 95:549–491.

Hall, Richard 1986 *Dimensions of Work.* Beverly Hills, Calif.: Sage.

Hamilton, Richard, and James Wright 1986 *The State of the Masses.* New York: Aldine.

Herzberg, Frederick 1966 *Work and the Nature of Man.* Cleveland: World.

Hodson, Randy, and Teresa Sullivan 1990 *The Social Organization of Work.* Belmont, Calif.: Wadsworth.

Kalleberg, Arne 1977 "Work Values and Job Rewards: A Theory of Job Satisfaction." *American Sociological Review* 42:124–143.

———, and Ivar Berg 1987 *Work and Industry.* New York: Plenum.

Kanter, Rosabeth 1977 *Men and Women of the Corporation.* New York: Basic Books.

Kohn, Melvin, and Carmi Schooler 1973 "Occupational Experience and Psychological Functioning: An Assessment of Reciprocal Effects." *American Sociological Review* 38:97–118.

———1978 "The Reciprocal Effects of Substantive Complexity: A Longitudinal Assessment." *American Journal of Sociology* 84:24–52.

———1982 "Job Conditions and Personality: A Longitudinal Assessment of Their Reciprocal Effects." *American Journal of Sociology* 87:1257–1286.

Lawler, Edward III 1973 *Motivation in Work Organizations*. Monterey, Calif.: Brooks/Cole.

Locke, Edwin 1976 "The Nature and Causes of Job Satisfaction." In Marvin Dunnetter, ed., *Handbook of Industrial and Organizational Psychology*, pp. 1293–1349. Chicago: Rand McNally.

Lodahl, Thomas, and Mathilde Kejner 1965 "The Definition and Measurement of Job Involvement." *Journal of Applied Psychology* 49:24–33.

Loscocco, Karyn 1989 "The Instrumentally Oriented Factory Worker: Myth or Reality?" *Work and Occupations* 16:3–25.

Maslow, Abraham 1954 *Motivation and Personality*. New York: Van Nostrand Reinhold.

McClelland, David 1961 *The Achieving Society*. New York: Van Nostrand.

McGregor, Douglas 1960 *The Human Side of Enterprise*. New York: McGraw-Hill.

Morrow, Paula 1983 "Concept Redundancy in Organizational Research: The Case of Work Commitment." *Academy of Management Review* 8:486–500.

Mortimer, Jeylan 1979 *Changing Attitudes toward Work: Highlights of the Literature*. Work in American Institute Studies in Productivity. New York: Pergamon Press.

Mowday, Richard, Lyman Porter, and Richard Steers 1982 *Employee-Organization Linkages*. New York: Academic Press.

Mueller, Charles, and James Price 1990 "Economic, Psychological, and Sociological Determinants of Voluntary Turnover." *Journal of Behavioral Economics* 19:321–335.

Price, James, and Charles Mueller 1986a *Absenteeism and Turnover of Hospital Employees*. Greenwich, Conn.: JAI Press.

———1986b *Handbook of Organizational Measurement*. Cambridge, Mass.: Ballinger.

Rothman, Richard 1987 *Working*. Englewood Cliffs, N.J.: Prentice-Hall.

Roy, Donald 1952 "Quota Restriction and Goldbricking in a Machine Shop." *American Sociological Review* 57:427–442.

———1959 "'Banana Time': Job Satisfaction and Informal Interaction." *Human Organization* 18:158–168.

Scott, K. Dow, and G. Stephen Taylor 1985 "An Examination of Conflicting Findings on the Relationship between Job Satisfaction and Absenteeism." *Academy of Management Journal* 28:599–612.

Smith, Patricia, Lorne Kendall, and Charles Hullin 1969 *The Measurement of Satisfaction in Work and Retirement*. Chicago: Rand McNally.

Smither, Robert 1988 *The Psychology of Work and Human Performance*. New York: Harper and Row.

Steele, Robert, and Nestor Ovalle 1984 "A Review and Meta-Analysis of Research on the Relationship between Behavioral Intentions and Employee Turnover." *Journal of Applied Psychology* 69:673–686.

Tausky, Curt 1984 *Work and Society*. Itasca, Ill.: F. E. Peacock.

Vroom, Victor 1964 *Work and Motivation*. New York: Wiley.

Watson, David, and Lee Clark 1984 "Negative Affectivity: The Disposition to Experience Aversive Emotional States." *Psychological Bulletin* 96:465–490.

Watson, David, James Pennebaker, and Robert Folger 1986 "Beyond Negative Affectivity: Measuring Stress and Satisfaction in the Workforce." *Journal of Organizational Behavior Management* 8:141–157.

CHARLES W. MUELLER

WORLD RELIGIONS Religious life throughout the world, regardless of the specific tradition, exhibits both personal/psychological and communal/social aspects. Of course, people within the diverse religious traditions of the world understand the spiritual dimension of their faith to transcend both individual psychological and emotional as well as the corporate and social aspects of their faiths' expressions. Nonetheless, two major academic strands of religious studies over the past century have focused primarily on either the psychological (e.g., James 1961; Freud 1928; or Jung 1938) or the social (e.g., Weber 1963; Durkheim 1965; or Wach 1958) dimensions of religion. An example of an Oglala Lakota's ("Sioux," in Algonquian) vision reveals these two interactive aspects of religion.

The Plains Indians in America were noted for their vision quests and, quite often, periods of fasting and life-cycle rituals were associated with the quests. However, the vision of Black Elk, a Lakota shaman (healer and diviner), occurred spontaneously when he was nine years old and was ill with fever and other physical maladies (Neidardt 1972, pp. 17–39). His vision began with two men dressed in traditional garb but shaped like slanting arrows coming from the sky to get him. As a little cloud descended around him the young Black Elk rose into the sky and disappeared into a large cloudbank. He saw an expansive white plain, across which he was led by a beautiful bay horse. As he looked in the four directions, he saw twelve black horses in the west, twelve white horses in the north, twelve sorrel horses in the east, and twelve buckskin horses in the south. Upon the arrival of Black Elk, the horses formed into lines and formations to lead Black Elk to the "Grandfathers." As this heavenly parade proceeded, horses appeared everywhere, dancing and frolicking and changing into all types of animals, such as buffalo, deer, and wild birds. Ahead lay a large tepee.

As Black Elk entered the rainbow door of the tepee, he saw six old men sitting in a row. As he stood before the six, he was struck that these old men reminded him of the ancient hills and stars. The oldest spoke, saying, "Your grandfathers all over the world are having a council, and they have called you here to teach you." Black Elk later remarked of the speaker, "His voice was very kind but I shook all over with fear now, for I knew that these were not old men but the Powers of the World and the first was the Power of the West; the second, of the North; the third, of the East; the fourth, of the South; the fifth, of the Sky; the sixth, of the Earth."

The spokesman of the elders gave Black Elk six sacred objects. First, he received a wooden cup full of water, symbolizing the water of the sky that has the power to make things green and alive. Second, he was given a bow, which has within it the power to destroy. Third, he was given a sacred name, "Eagle Wing Stretches," which he was to embody in his role as shaman for his tribe. Fourth, he was given an herb of power that would henceforth allow him to cleanse and to heal those who were in sick in body or in spirit. Fifth, he was given the sacred pipe, which had as its purpose a strengthening of the collective might of the Lakota tribe and was intended to heal divisions among the Lakota that would allow them to live in peace and harmony. And finally Black Elk received a bright red stick, which was the "center of the nations circle" or hoop. This stick symbolized a sacred centering of the Lakota nation and linked the Lakota to their ancestors as well as to those who would follow after them.

Black Elk's vision ended with a flight into the foreboding future in which the Lakota would encounter the white-skinned "bluecoats" who would threaten the sacred hoop of the Lakota nation. Many years later, as Black Elk reflected on his vision, he realized that even in the devastating upheaval caused by the wars between his Lakota nation and the "bluecoats," his people had been given the sacred objects and rituals that were necessary to rise above mundane exigencies and to heal the nation and restore the hoop in times of trouble.

The vision of Black Elk makes clear that what sometimes appear to be perfunctory religious rituals, fantastic myths, or arcane ethical injunctions often have their roots in a deep sense of the contact between humans and that which they have experienced as a divine power. While the emphasis in this article will be on social aspects of world religions, it is important to keep in mind that the religious experiences codified in the social institutions of the world's religions are not fully captured by either psychological or sociological explanation. There has been a tendency in the academic study of religion to reduce religious experience and behavior to either their psychological or their social antecedents. For example, Freud (1928) reduces religion to unconscious projections of human needs, which he likens to infantile fantasies that rational humans should grow beyond. On the other hand, a contemporary of Freud, Durkheim (1965, p. 466), has a tendency to reduce religions to their social functions: "If religion has given birth to all that is essential in society, it is because the idea of society is the soul of religion."

While the pioneering work of Weber and Durkheim laid the groundwork for much of contemporary social analysis of religion, comparative sociologists of religion such as Joachim Wach (1958) have tempered earlier tendencies toward sociological reductionism. Wach sought to understand the nature of religion by examining traditions throughout the world and noting the primary elements they shared in common. He identified religious experience as the basic and formative element in the rise of religious traditions around the world, then sought to understand the expression of this experience in thought, action, and community.

Wach said that a symbiotic relationship exists between religion and society. On the one hand, religion influences the form and character of social organizations or relations in the family, clan, or nation and also develops new social institutions, such as the Christian church, the Buddhist *sanga*, or the "Lakota nation." On the other hand, social factors shape religious experience, expression, and institutions. For example, in Black Elk's vision the role of the warrior in Lakota society is expressed through the two men who come to escort Black Elk into the sky and, in his later mystical venture into the future, Black Elk as Lakota shaman (*wichash wakan* is one who converses with and transmits the Lakota's ultimate spiritual powers or wakan) becomes the ultimate warrior who battles a "blue man" (perhaps representing personified evil or the dreaded "bluecoats"). Lakota social conventions that name the natural directions as four (north, south, east, and west) are modified by Black Elk's vision to include Sky and Earth, making six vision directions that influence the number of elders Black Elk encounters in the heavenly tepee and the number of sacred objects he is given. Here the vision modifies social conventions, only to create a social subconvention for other visionaries who name the directions as six. The objects themselves are conventional implements of Black Elk's culture that are empowered to serve symbolically as multivocal conveyors of sacred knowledge and wisdom. Finally, Black Elk's vision can be viewed sociologically as confirming the corporate sacredness (the sacred hoop) of the nation of the Lakota. For example, a Lakota's vision was powerful and meaningful only to the extent that the tribe accepted it. In this sense one can understand why Durkheim would say that religion, in this case the Lakota's, is society write large up on the sky.

However, for Wach, and scholars such as Nin-

ian Smart (1969) who follow his lead, the form and expressions of religious life are best understood as emanating from religious experience. Smart identifies six dimensions that all religions throughout the world share: (1) ritual; (2) mythological; (3) doctrinal; (4) ethical; (5) social; and (6) experiential. This author has provided an interpretative framework for understanding the necessary interdependence of these six elements of religious traditions in his book *Two Sacred Worlds: Experience and Structure in the World's Religions* (1977). These six dimensions of the religious life, therefore, form the structure of this analysis of the social aspect of world religions.

RELIGIOUS EXPERIENCE

Building on the insights of William James (1961) and Rudolph Otto (1946), more contemporary scholars such as Wach, Smart, and Mircea Eliade (1959) seek the origin of religion in the religious experience of a founder or religious community. These scholars assert that genuinely religious experiences include an awareness or an immediate experience of an ultimate reality or sacred power. James suggests that transcendental or mystical experiences are immediate apprehensions of the divine that are marked by their ineffability, noetic quality, transiency, and passivity. From one perspective, ineffability can be understood as the inability of language to relay the emotional and cognitive content of a peak religious experience. Ineffability may also be described as a failure of language to capture the divine subject of such an experience—that is, the ultimate reality itself. Nonetheless, religious experiences are inevitably understood as providing new states of knowledge that cannot be grasped fully by the discursive intellect. This "noetic" dimension of religious experience is often described as the revelation of new knowledge (i.e., illumination) that is provided by religious experiences. In fact, it is precisely an awareness of an encounter with a sacred reality in religious experiences that differentiates these experiences from other peak experiences. It is also the case that religious experiences are usually marked by brevity (i.e., transiency) and the passivity of the one receiving the experience. While aesthetic, political, or erotic peak experiences may be characterized by ineffability, transiency, and passivity, only religious experiences bring with them a consciousness of an encounter with a "holy other" sacred reality.

Whether a founding religious experience is immediate and direct, such as the Buddha's enlightenment experience of Nirvana, or cumulative and indirect, as was the exodus experience of the Hebrews, religious experiences are, in Wach's (1958) terms, "the most powerful, comprehensive, shattering, and profound experience" of which humans are capable (p. 35). Wach concluded that a necessary criterion of genuine religious experience "is that it issues in action. It involves imperative; it is the most powerful source of motivation and action" (p. 36). Consequently, religious experiences may be viewed as the wellspring of religion both in the formation of a new religious tradition as well as in the origin of faith of later generations.

Even accepting the primacy of religious experience, it is important to note that founding religious experiences are deeply immersed in the social and cultural realities of their time and place. For example, whether immediate and dramatic or cumulative and more intuitive, religious experiences are inevitably expressed in the language and concepts of the person and culture in which they arose. Black Elk's vision of Wakan in the form of the six grandfathers clearly reflects the Lakota's social and political structure as well as their idealized notions of nation and nature. The Thunder Beings and Grandfathers who are the personifications of Wakan Tanka ("Great Power") obviously arise from the natural, linguistic, and social environments of the Lakota. So does the conception of Wakan itself as a pervasive power permeating animal and human life as well as that of nature. A contemporary Lakota has said, "All life is *Wakan*. So also is everything which exhibits power whether in action, as in the winds and drifting clouds, or in passive endurance, as the boulder by the wayside."

Religious experiences occur to persons who have previous socialization. The most obvious social tool is the language used to express even the most profound religious experiences. The ineffable nature of religious experiences requires the use of metaphors or extensions of everyday language, as in the case of Black Elk. Nonetheless, to some extent the experience itself is shaped by the language in which it is expressed.

Divine names themselves are usually borrowed from the social and linguistic environment of the founder or the founding community. For example, the exodus experience of the Hebrew people was interpreted by them as a liberating religious experience fostered by the God of Abraham, Isaac, and Jacob. This God, whose name is given in the book of Exodus as "Yahweh" ("I am who I am"), is also called El Elyon (God most high), El Shaddai (God of the mountain), and Elohim (though a plural noun, usually translated "God"). Moses likely borrowed the name Yahweh from the Midianites. El Elyon was the high god of Salem (later called Jerusalem) and was worshiped by King Melchizedek. It is also known that the Canaanite high god of the same period was named El and appears in different cultic sites throughout the ancient Near East. While it is clear that the Hebraic religious texts understand Yahweh and El quite differently from their known local counterparts, it cannot be ignored that the Hebrew high god embraced the local deity nomenclatures while modifying their meanings.

In a similar fashion the divinity of the man Jesus is acknowledged in early Christian texts by references to earlier Jewish apocalyptic language and expectations. In the Jewish apocalyptic literature (e.g., I Enoch) the Son of man appears as a righteous judge who will come on earth to signal the beginning of the heavenly kingdom and God's rule. As an eternal savior, the Son of man will come to save righteous followers of God and destroy all those who ignore him. In such linguistic borrowings, however, significant modifications of the original conceptions are made to adjust the titles and expectations to the man Jesus as perceived by his followers. For example, Jesus comes as the Son of man not primarily as a stern and revengeful judge but rather as a savior who is himself the sacrifice. This linguistic and conceptual transformation reflects the dependence of language on experience as much as it reveals the social dimensions of religious experience.

Similar examples of borrowed—and transformed—god names abound in religious literature and history throughout the world. In Saudi Arabia in the sixth century of this era, Muhammad elevated a local polytheistic Meccan god, Allah, to an international deity. In tenth-century Indian Puranic literature, devotees of the god Vishnu promote his *avatar*, Krishna, to a supreme theistic position as the god above all gods. Although the *Bhagavata Purana* recounts the *lilas* or play of Krishna as though the author were describing a historic figure, it is clear to textual scholars that two essentially distinct and dynamic story traditions arise from the Brahminical Krishna of *Bhagavad Gita* fame and from the indigenous cowherd, Gopala, Krishna associated with the Western Indian Abhira tribes.

Although there is no doubt that devotees either of Allah or of Krishna now perceive their divinity and his name as having been "from the beginning," there is little doubt that the local social and linguistic environments provided both some of the content and context for the names of the sacred in these two traditions. Perhaps the most radical example of theistic amalgam is that of the Indian goddess Kali. Described in medieval Indian texts as being synonymous with literally dozens of local and regional goddess names and traditions, Kali is a latecomer to the Indian theistic scene as one who is given the primary attributes of many gods and goddesses. The mythological tale of the birth of Kali reveals an amalgamation process that gave birth to this great goddess now worshiped by millions in India as the "Supreme Mother."

What should be clear from the above examples is that while religious experience of the sacred may be the initiating point of the world's religious traditions or of an individual's faith, that experience is given shape and substance by the linguistic and social context out of which it arises. It is still the case, however, that such life-altering religious experiences as those described above also shape the language and traditions they borrow. We will see this symbiotic relationship repeated in the other dimensions of religious life that are shared by the world's religions.

MYTH AND RITUAL

Formative religious experiences contain within them impulses to expression (myth) and re-creation (ritual) that later become routinized and, finally, institutionalized. Core myths and rituals, therefore, attempt to convey and re-create the experience of the founder or religious community. Both myths and rituals rely on symbols whose content must be shared in order for them to have meaning for the religious group that uses them. Symbols have not only shared cognitive meanings but also common emotional significance and value—that is, symbols do not simply convey intellectual understanding, they also engender an emotive response. Furthermore, religious symbols are integrative and transforming agents as they attempt to point to realities that have been encountered but are hidden from everyday vision and experience. Ricoeur (1972) says that symbols yield their meaning in enigma and not through literal or direct translation. Therefore, symbols suggest rather than explicate; they provide "opaque glimpses" of reality rather than definitive pictures. Understood in this fashion, the journey from symbol to myth is a short one for Ricoeur, who takes the latter to be a narrative form of the former. Put very simply, myths are narratives or stories of the sacred and human encounters with it.

As stories of sacred powers or beings, myths fall into two basic categories: expressive and reflective. Expressive myths are those sacred narratives that attempt to relate the founding or codifying religious experience or experiences of a religious tradition, while reflective stories are composed subsequently to integrate the sacred experience into everyday life. For example, Black Elk's retelling of his vision experience becomes an expressive myth or sacred narrative for the Oglala Lakota, to which they refer again and again in other reflective stories of the Thunderbeings or the Grandfathers, where the Lakota attempt to extend the lessons of this experience to later problems they encountered. Nearly every extant religious tradition tells and retells its sacred narrative of the founder's or founders' encounter with the sacred reality. Black Elk's vision becomes such a story for the Oglala Lakota.

The story of the exodus of the Hebrews is still recounted for contemporary Jewish people as a symbolic and founding narrative of God's liberation. The stories of the life, death, and resurrection of Jesus from the core myths of Christians when one understands the term to mean sacred narrative rather than "untrue story." Likewise, the arduous meditative journey culminating in attainment of Nirvana by the Buddha serves to inspire religious thought and behavior throughout all Buddhist lands even today. Similarly, Muhammad's auditory experience of Allah on Mount Hira that resulted in his recitations of the Qur'an constitutes the sacred history of millions of Muslims on all continents. And finally, even though scholars have been quite confident in their judgment that the life of Krishna as told in the tenth century *Bhagavata Purana* is really an anthology of stories borrowed from various earlier Krishna traditions, these *lilas* or "playful" episodes in the life of Krishna have inspired religious experiences, poetry, and rituals that still enliven the lives of millions of Hindhus throughout the world. From even this selective set of examples of founding myths, it is clear how deeply they drink from the social, linguistic, and institutional contexts of their time and place.

The generative function of core myths is shared by certain rituals that attempt to re-present in a spatial and physical context the core experience of a religious tradition. From one perspective, core rituals are those that emerge from sacred narratives or myths as their active component. From a second perspective, core rituals represent repetitive, institutionalized behavior and clearly are immersed in the social sphere of religious life. For example, the Christian narrative that relates the "Last Supper" of Jesus as a sacramental event (e.g., Mark 14:12–26) is physically presented in the early Christian love feast that later becomes

the Lord's Supper (Eucharistic ritual or Mass) of the Christian churches. The work of Victor Turner (1969) in a traditional African religious context provides vocabulary for the religious and social transactions that take place in core myths and rituals. He says the three phases in ritual reenactments attempt (1) to separate or detach the participant from everyday consciousness and social position; (2) to provide a moment of *liminality* and *communitas* of shared experience with ritual participants; and then (3) to reintegrate ritual participants back into everyday life with its social roles and structure. *Liminality* is that psychological and social state of transition between one's former consciousness and social roles and the new status that one assumes beyond the ritual. *Communitas* for Turner is a mode of social relationship that is marked by egalitarianism uncommon in the stratified roles and relationships of the everyday world. Consequently, Turner would argue that religious rituals may provide an in-between or "liminal" moment of social and psychological experience that religious devotees often assert includes an encounter with their sacred power or reality.

The Passover narrative in the biblical Book of Exodus provides one good example of a core myth that is later enacted in a Passover meal. In its literal meaning, the Passover myth simply refers to the tenth plague, when the angel of death killed Egyptian firstborn children while sparing the Hebrew children just prior to the exodus journey itself. In its symbolic sense, the Passover story that is represented in the Passover sacrificial meal symbolizes Yahweh's power of liberation. To the extent that the story of the exodus reveals the beginning of Yahweh's covenant relationship to the Hebrew people, the Passover ritual attempts to re-create or revivify that relationship.

Beyond the social embodiment of the community in recounting the sacred story of Israel's encounter with Yahweh in a festive and communal sacrificial ritual of the Passover, the social aspects of both the myth and the ritual are obvious. Sacrifices were the common mode of worship for the pre-Mosaic tribal religions as well as for the contemporary cults in Moses' day. It is very likely that the Passover ritual described in Exodus 12 actually derives from a combination of a nomadic animal sacrifice and an agricultural feast of unleavened cakes, both of which predate the exodus event. While the Hebrews' experience of Yahweh in the exodus journey reshapes both the story and the ritual as a liberation event, both the Hebrew myth and ritual have antecedents in the social and religious world of which they were a part.

In a similar fashion, the baptism and Eucharist rituals in the Christian faith are core rituals that stem from the religious narratives that gave birth to them. Likewise, traditional Theravada forms of Buddhist meditation appear to stem directly from the stories of the Buddha's own spiritual struggle and release, but also draw on Jain and Hindu forms that predate it. Among the Oglala Lakota, the horse dance ritual was taught by Black Elk to his tribe in a fashion that replicated as closely as possible the vision he received. Therefore, the six old grandfathers, the horses representing the four cardinal directions, and the various sacred implements he was given all become central elements of the horse dance ritual.

In Islam, the Hajj is one of the five pillars of faith that are incumbent on all Muslims to perform. The Hajj is a pilgrimage reenacting the spiritual journey of Muhammad with periods of fasting, prayer, and meditation that culminate with ritual circumambulations of the Ka'ba, which is the seat of Allah's throne. In the Hindu devotional traditions, it is common for dramatic presentations, stylized ritual dance forms such as the Bharata Natyam, and temple dramatic readings all to convey episodes of the encounter of devotees with the divine. Consequently, dramatic productions of the *lilas* or playful pastimes of the cowherd god Krishna are enjoyed by villagers throughout India not simply as theatrical events but also as re-presentations of Krishna's delightful divine play. The daily ritual reenactment that occurs before the shrines of Krishna or Kali or other Indian divinities is called *puja* and is a ritual ceremony that likely emanates from the stylized honorific behavior one accords to a royal guest.

Here the social precursors to religious ritual are obvious, even though they are transformed by the religious narrative and ritual context into which they are placed.

Scholars across a variety of disciplines and perspectives have asserted the interconnection of myth, ritual, and the religious community. Perhaps the clearest summary of this relationship is given by Bronislaw Malinowski when he says, "an intimate connection exists between the word, the mythos, the sacred tales of a tribe, on the one hand and their ritual acts, their moral deeds, their social organization, and even their practical activities on the other" (1954, p. 96). Malinowski reminds us that while core myths and rituals may have their origin in founding religious experiences, they also serve as social "warrants" for social beliefs of the society out of which they arise and that they help shape. From this perspective, myths and rituals serve primarily as vehicles that legitimate social institutions. Core myths and rituals appear to be charged with the difficult task of re-presenting and re-creating founding religious experiences. As we have seen, they, too, reflect and embrace their social and cultural contexts. Furthermore, not all myths and rituals serve this primary and essentialist function. As we will see shortly, certain myths, rituals, and religious behavior diverge considerably from the impetus that the core narrative seems to suggest.

ETHICS

Malinowski and Wach make clear that ethics arise partly as a result of religious experience but also participate fully in social processes. While it may be that religious experiences give rise to immediate expression (core myths) and reenactments (core rituals), they also give impetus to new attitudes and intentions that are reflected in norms for behavior. In the Christian context such behavior is claimed to be the mark of a "reborn" person whose conduct represents the tangible effects of an experience of God. On the other hand, the ethical norms and traditions that arise within a religious institution may reflect as much the mores of the surrounding culture and society as they do the experience on which the institution was founded. Social factors (such as language, family roles, and social customs) play a role in the process of the externalization of the religious life in ethical laws. William James says simply that subsequent behavior is the empirical criterion for determining the quality and validity of a religious experience. The distinction he makes between the person who has a religious experience and the one who undergoes religious conversion is the distinction between having a highly charged peak experience and that of living a new life born of that experience.

It appears that all religious traditions evidence an interdependent and necessary relationship of conduct to experience such that what is experienced as ecstatic encounter is expressed as a whole mode of living. The committed ethical life of a devotee, then, is ideally understood as an active extension of religious experience expressed through communal or shared norms. While an immediate religious experience may provide a core religious impulse (e.g., to love in the Christian context, or to fear Allah in the Muslim context), that intentional force or impetus gains objectivity in the concrete situations of social behavior. For example, the enlightenment experience of the Buddha resulted in a sense of detachment from the world that was linked to enduring traditions of *metta* and *karuna* (love and compassion) and resulted in "detached compassion" as the complex ethical norm that the Buddha required of his disciples.

The most obvious intrusion of social norms and processes into the religious life occurs in moral decision making. It is the world and living in it that provide the situations and problems that require an ethical response. Consequently, life in the world poses many situations not anticipated in the religious texts and routinized ethical norms of religious traditions. As a result, ethical systems over time often come to reflect the surrounding secular culture and social norms as much as they do the basic religious impulse from which they are supposed to derive their direction. This problem

is mediated during the life of the founder or founders whose authority and behavior provide a model for action. In subsequent generations, however, it is often social roles and institutions such as that of the pope, the Buddhist *sanga* (community of elders), or the Lakota tribal council that determine the ethical norms of a community. When ethical statements and positions stray too far from their initial impulses, they are in danger of mirroring the society they intend to make sacred. Put simply, while ethical impulses may originate from religious experiences, the ethical laws, norms, and traditions that are constituted in scriptures and institutional pronouncements often distort the imperative by rationalizations that conform to social and not religious expectations.

An example of the difference between ethical impulse and moral law can be found in the Hebrew notion of a covenant relationship with God. The experience of Moses and the exodus tribes was of a compassionate, mighty, jealous, and demanding God. The laws of the early Hebrews, therefore, were viewed not simply as commandments arising from a stern leader or group of legalistic lawmakers but rather as expressions of an appreciative and liberating relationship to God. The Sinai story of the transmission of the Ten Commandments is intended to reveal the Hebrews' ethical relationship to Yahweh. It was on that holy mountain that the covenant between Yahweh and his people was given concrete expression. However, it is also clear that this relationship was marked by infidelity on the part of Yahweh's people. Therefore, for many of them the codes of conduct contained in the Ten Commandments and the Levitical Code were experienced as oppressive laws of a judgmental God.

Jesus summarized the essence of ethical behavior in a twofold commandment of love of God and love of neighbor that was enjoined on all who would count themselves as disciples of God. However, the teachings of Jesus and the commandment of love have led over the centuries to disputes about whether Christians should engage in war, permit abortions, treat homosexuals as equals in the church, or allow divorces. Institutionalized Christian churches in their many forms have decreed what proper ethical conduct is with regard to such issues, and these norms vary and even contradict each other across traditions. This is the difference between the imperative to love God and to love neighbor, and ethical laws that must express such divine love in complex and rapidly changing social contexts and situations. A seemingly universal law such as "Do not kill" means quite different things to a Lakota warrior, who may kill (and sometimes scalp) his enemy (but not a tribesman); to a Muslim, who is encouraged to kill an infidel who defames Allah; and to a Buddhist, who is enjoined not to harm *any* animal or human life.

Even within seemingly similar traditions, such as the Hindu devotional sects, the ethical norms can vary immensely. In the Kali goddess tradition, animal sacrifice is still commonly practiced as a way of returning to the goddess the life-giving force she has bestowed on her creation. Some devotees of Kali have interpreted her mythological destruction of demons to be a model for their own behavior and have followed suit as thieves and murderers in the Indian Thuggi tradition. On the other hand, Kali devotees such as Rahmakrishnan understand Kali to be a transcendent "ocean of bliss" who engenders peacefulness and noninjury in her disciples.

What is true of all the above-mentioned religious traditions around the world is that persons are usually taught what constitutes proper or ethical behavior, and in this context ethics are learned conceptions born of the social process and its experiences. Consequently, ethical norms and their expression often reflect the social environment in which religious traditions arise. A clear expression of this fact is found in the Hindu religious tradition's embracing of the caste system that sacralizes a socially elitist and patriarchal social system that predates Hinduism. The mythical and theological texts of the Hindu tradition that sacralize caste distinctions simply serve as warrants for social roles and norms that undergird not only the Hindu traditions but also those of the Buddhists and Jains in India as well.

THEOLOGY/DOCTRINE

Just as religious experience may result in the formation of a religious movement that tells the founding story of contact with a sacred power (core myth), tries to re-create that experience for the beginning and subsequent communities (core rituals), and impels new believers to act in accordance with this vision or revelation (ethical impulse leading to institutionalized ethics), so it is that even very early in a religious tradition's history questions and criticisms arise that must be answered. Religious reflection takes a variety of forms that touch the total corporate life of a religious community. Sacred scriptures often encompass expressive myths that relate in narrative form the founder's or founders' contact with the sacred; core rituals in outline or in full; ethical njunctions and moral codes; and reflective myths, doctrines, and explications that attempt to answer the believers' questions and the opponents' criticisms. Almost inevitably a religious community is provoked from without and within to explain how the sacred reality is related to the origin of the community and, perhaps, even to the origin of the world. Consequently, reflective myths that represent second-level or posterior reflection are incorporated to explain such beginnings.

Three distinct but interrelated purposes and functions of reflective myths are (1) an explanation of origins; (2) a rationalization of aspects of core beliefs; and (3) an apologetic defense of the faith to disbelieving insiders or outsiders. A good example of reflective theologizing is the development of the biography of the Buddha. The oldest Pali texts essentially begin the life of the Buddha with his disillusionment with the world at age twenty-nine, when he was already a husband and a father. The early texts indicate that his name was Siddhartha and that his father, Suddhodana, ruled a small district in the North Indian republic of the Sakyas. This early story indicates that Siddhartha was married at age sixteen or seventeen, had a son, and then became disillusioned with the human suffering he saw around him and renounced the world to seek spiritual liberation while leaving his family behind.

Approximately five hundred years after the death of the Buddha, two separate "biographies" were written containing accumulated legends not only of the miraculous birth of the Buddha but also of the "great renunciation" itself. The birth story is replete with the descent of the Buddha from the heavens as a white elephant who miraculously enters his mother's side, only to be born nine months later as a fully functioning adultlike child. These biographies describe the Buddha's physical features (captured in religious images and icons) as including the lengthened ears of an aristocrat, a smooth-shaped conical bump on his head indicating his intelligence, and other such marks that foretold his later enlightenment.

Likewise, these latter-day scriptures recount his renunciation from the world in a full-blown theologized story of encounters with an ill man, a decrepit old man, a dead man, and a religious ascetic. What the story of the Buddha's four visions accomplishes is a fuller explication of the reasons for his renunciation. Both the birth story (confirming the Buddha's sacred origins) and the story of the four visions of the Buddha (a rationalization of his renunciation) represent reflective myths that fill in biographical gaps in earlier stories of his life in light of his later enlightenment status.

Parallels to the biographical history of the Buddha can be found in the scriptural stories of the miraculous births of Jesus, Mahavira (founder of the Jains), Krishna, Kali, and Muhammad, among others. A similar genre of reflective myths may be found in the creation stories that often are added dozens of years or even centuries after the founding experience. Good examples of this process are the Hebrew creation stories told in Genesis 1 and Genesis 2. God's creation in seven days is the youngest creation story (the priestly story of the seventh century B.C. and told in Genesis 1:1–2:4a) and is placed at the beginning of the Book of Genesis. It is likely that the Akkadian myth of Tiamat served as a model for

this story of the creation of the world out of a watery chaos.

The older Yahwist creation story found in Genesis 2:4b ff. is set in a desert environment instead of a primeval ocean and stems very likely from the tenth century B.C. A decidedly more anthropomorphic story, the Yahwist Garden of Eden represents a story that was added at least three hundred to four hundred years after the exodus experience itself. Neither the priestly nor Yahwist stories received their present form until the sixth or seventh century B.C., as they were called upon to explicate the creative power of their Hebrew God set against a seasonal set of mythologies from the Canaanites, whom the Hebrews encountered in Palestine. For the Palestine farmer, Canaanite, or Israelite, the question was, "Is it Yahweh or Baal to whom one should offer sacrifices and give allegiance if one's crops are to prosper?" The two Genesis creation stories provide not only the answer of who is responsible for the origin of life on earth but also how one can explain human illness, suffering, and death in the context of the God who led the Hebrews out of Egypt. In Africa and in India, the numerous and sometimes contradictory creation stories one finds within a single religious tradition reveal less about the illogical nature of such reflective myths than they do about the human need to have questions of birth, suffering, social relationships, the founding of a tribe, and the death event placed in the context of a tradition's ultimate reality.

When religious traditions develop full-fledged social institutions, it is quite common for sacred texts or other interpretative theological texts to explain the necessity of such a religious organization and its officials. Whether it is the early church fathers' explanations of the seat of Peter on which the pope sits in the Roman Catholic tradition, or a Lakota visionary myth that explains the role of the shaman in their community, reflective myths and theologies develop as intellectual and institutional rationalizations for the extension of the founding tradition into all aspects of life and society. Religious councils, theological traditions, sectarian disputes, and doctrinal formulas all arise as socialized institutions that attempt to explicate, defend, and provide an apology for a religious faith firmly embedded in the personal and social lives of its people. For example, Islamic theology extends the influence of the Qur'anic faith into the economic, political, and social lives of the Muslim people. Likewise, from birth and family relationships through wars and death, the Lakota's life was incorporated within the sacred hoop.

The kind of extension of religious faith into all aspects of life is justified in scriptures and doctrinal tracts by the reflective process of mythmaking and theologizing. Berger (1969) calls such activity the construction of a *nomos*. A theological *nomos* is essentially a socially constructed worldview that attempts to order all human experience in the context of the sacred. Such reflection is determined to a great extent by the social and human circumstances that give rise to the questions that must be answered as well as the language and social conventions through which the reflections are expressed. However, Wach reminds us that the prophetic function of religious traditions often shapes the social environment to a religious vision and not simply vice versa.

INSTITUTIONS

Religious institutions arise as the fullest and most obvious social expression of a religious faith. They are equally the home for the core myths and rituals to be enacted as well as the loci of the religious community whose individual and collective needs must be met. Religious institutions vary from formal collectivities such as the Christian church, the Muslim mosque, the Hindu temple, or the Buddhist *sangha* to their extended representations in festivals and ceremonial events such as weddings and funerals. It is within the social institution that *communitas* understood as a spiritual leveling of religious adherents exists alongside a religious community where social differentiation and hierarchies usually persist. Religious institutions are usually the most deeply embedded social aspect of religion, since it is their primary task to control the external conduct of their members through rites, rituals, and ethical norms while providing an economic and political power base through which they may compete with other social institutions. Simply put, religious institutions are, to a great extent, socially constructed realities that provide for the habituation and rationalization of religious thought and behavior.

William James viewed the church, synagogue, or religious organization as a "secondhand" extension of the religious life. Abraham Maslow (1970) goes so far as to distinguish a category of "prophets" for those who found the religion, as separate from the "legalists," who regulate, systematize, and organize religious behavior in institutional forms. Even from this brief discussion of the interrelationships of the primary aspects of the religious life, it should be apparent why Michael Novak can say, "Institutions are the normal, natural expression of the human spirit. But that spirit is self-transcending. It is never satisfied with its own finite expressions" (1971, p. 156). Novak says that the basic conflict is between the human spirit and all institutions.

No religious institution has escaped criticisms of its creeds, dogmas, ethics, or authoritative pronouncements from those within the tradition who insist that the essential faith demands revisions of the institutions' expressions of that faith. Such criticisms give rise not only to reform movements but also to schisms and new sects that emerge as a result of the clash between the received faith in its textual and social forms and the religious experiences and impulses of a reformer or critic within that organization. Martin Luther is an example of one reformer whose critique of his received Roman Catholic heritage was both personal and theological. Similarly, the numerous Buddhist sects that arose within the first hundred years after the death of the Buddha gained their impetus from quarrels over doctrine, life-style, or interpretations of the essential nature of the faith. The Sunna and Shi'a branches of Islam have dozens of contemporary expressions that emanate from a fundamental split in the tradition that occurred shortly after the death of Muhammad and that focused on the source of authority for future proclamations in Islam. Typical of other religious traditions, Islam gave early birth to a pietistic mystical tradition, known as Sufism, which has consistently criticized both of the major theological branches of Islam for their legalistic and worldly focus to the detriment of the nourishment of the spiritual life. From one perspective, sectarian and schismatic movements are attempts to recapture the original experience and spirit of a religious tradition. In every case, however, the new movement incorporates the same social dimensions discussed previously as they articulate their message and seek to institutionalize their recommended changes.

CONCLUSION

Clifford Geertz argues that each world religion is essentially "(1) a system of symbols which acts (2) to establish powerful, pervasive, and long-lasting moods and motivation in men by (3) formulating conceptions of a general order of existence and (4) clothing these conceptions with such an aura of factuality that (5) the moods and motivations seem uniquely realistic" (1968, p. 1). This social-anthropological definition of religion embraces in a clear and simple fashion most of the underlying interpretation of relationships that this article has attempted to describe. Religion as a system of symbols simultaneously attempts to express and reveal dimensions of experience beyond that of the everyday, while doing so in socially conditioned language and conceptions. Likewise, the general order of existence (nomos) that is formulated in the myths, rituals, and ethical norms of a religious tradition emerge from the social consciousness, communal norms, and shared conceptions of the community that give rise to them. Finally, what Peter Berger calls "legitimation" and Clifford Geertz calls "factuality" are nothing other than broad-based social acceptance of certain religious beliefs. Consequently, from their inception in religious experience to their full social expression in concrete institutions, religious traditions involve an interplay between personal and social forces. No aspect—experiential, mythical, ritual, ethical, doctrinal, or institutional—of any of the world's religious traditions escapes some social conditioning. Likewise, no culture or society is left unchallenged by its religious expressions and lifestyles.

REFERENCES

Berger, Peter 1969 *The Sacred Canopy: Elements of a Sociological Theory of Religion.* Garden City, N.Y.: Doubleday.

———and Thomas Luckmann 1967 *The Social Construction of Reality.* Garden City, N.Y.: Doubleday.

Durkheim, Emile 1965 *The Elementary Forms of the Religious Life,* trans. Joseph Ward Swain, New York: Free Press.

Eliade, Mircea 1959 *The Sacred and the Profane,* trans. Willard R. Trask. New York: Harper and Brothers.

Freud, Sigmund 1928 *The Future of an Illusion,* trans. W. D. Robson-Scott, Horace Liveright, and the Institute of Psychoanalysis. London: Hogarth Press.

Geertz, Clifford 1968 "Religion as a Cultural System." In Michael Banton, ed., *Anthropological Approaches to the Study of Religion.* London: Tavistock.

James, William 1961 *The Varieties of Religious Experience: A Study in Human Nature.* New York: Collier Books.

Jung, Carl 1938 *Psychology and Religion.* New Haven, Conn.: Yale University Press.

Malinowski, Bronislaw 1954 "Myth in Primitive Psychology." In Malinowski, *Magic, Science and Religion.* Garden City, N.Y.: Doubleday.

Maslow, Abraham H. 1970 *Religions, Values, and Peak Experiences.* New York: Penguin Books.

Neidardt, John G. 1972 *Black Elk Speaks.* New York: Pocket Books (from field notes contained in Raymond J. DaMillie 1984 *The Sixth Grandfather: Black's Teachings given to John Neihardt.* Lincoln: University of Nebraska Press).

Novak, Michael 1971 *Ascent of the Mountain, Flight of the Dove.* New York: Harper and Row.

Otto, Rudolph 1946 *The Idea of the Holy,* trans. J. W. Harvey. London: Oxford University Press.

Ricoeur, Paul 1972 "The Symbol Gives Rise to Thought." In Walter H. Capps, ed., *Ways of Understanding Religion.* New York: Macmillan.

Shinn, Larry D. 1977 *Two Sacred Worlds: Experience and Structure in the World's Religions.* Nashville, Tenn.: Abingdon.

Smart, Ninian 1969 *The Religious Experience of Mankind.* New York: Scribners.

Turner, Victor 1969 *The Ritual Process: Structure and Anti-Structure.* Chicago: Aldine.

Wach, Joachim 1958 *The Comparative Study of Religions.* New York: Columbia University Press.

Weber, Max 1963 *The Sociology of Religion,* trans. Ephraim Fischoff. Boston: Beacon.

LARRY DWIGHT SHINN

WORLD-SYSTEMS THEORY. *See* Global Systems Analysis.

Index

Index

*Numbers in **boldface** refer to the main entry on the subject.*

on juvenile delinquency,
1031–1032
macrosociology, 1171
on modernization theory,
1302–1303
on labeling theory, 474
on rural sociology, 1690
on social control, 1821
on social movement leadership,
1088
on social problems, 1919
on social stratification,
1959–1960
on sports, 2048
on war, 2245
see also Coalitions; Interpersonal
power; Marxist sociology
Conformity. *See* Compliance and
conformity
Congregationalism, 1647
Congress, U.S., and court system, 340
Congressional elections. *See* Voting
behavior
Congress of Racial Equality (CORE),
1562, 1733, 2103
Congruity theory, 225–226
Connor, Walker, on ethnic
nationalism, 1335
Consciousness-raising, participatory
research and, 1427–1428
Conscription, military, 1292–1293
draft riots (1863), 2102
Conservation. *See* Environmental
impact assessment;
Environmental movement
Conservative Judaism, 1647
Conservatives
on affirmative action, 17
fundamental beliefs, 1114–1115,
1116–1117, 1119
and fundamentalism, 1629–1640
intellectuals, 939
views on inheritance, 930, 1114,
1115
see also Liberalism/conservatism
Consistency of measurement. *See*
Reliability
Constant-sum games, 738
Constitution, U.S., on census and
representation, 189
Constitutional personality theories,
1450–1451
Constructed type, 2189
Constructionists. *See* Social problems,
subjectivist paradigm
Constructivism
on collective behavior, 243
on sexual orientation, 1763–1764
Construct validity, 1610, 2219–2220
Contagious behavior theories
collective behavior, 239, 240, 491
suicide, 2115–2116
see also Crowds and riots; Social
imitation
Content analysis, **290–294**, 1577
Content validity, 2218–2219
Contextual properties (variables), 1105
Contingencies of reinforcement. *See*
Reinforcement, contingencies of

Contingency tables. *See* Tabular
analysis
Contingency theory,
interorganizational relations,
966–967
Contraception
family law on, 652, 653
and family planning, 656–660,
662
and fertility determinants, 704
and population trends,
1502–1503, 1504–1505
see also Family size; specific kinds,
e.g., Condoms; Vasectomy
Contract laborers. *See* Migrant workers
Contributions to Indian Sociology
(journal), 898
*Contribution to the Critique of Political
Economy, A* (Marx), 523
Control group. *See* Quasi-experimental
research designs
Control theory. *See* Social control
Convergence theories, **295–301**
collective behavior, 238, 400–401
demographic patterns, 299
education, 299–300
family, 299
forms of, 297
industrial sociology, 297–298
on social change, 1819
and social security systems,
1950–1951
stratification, 298
on urbanization, 2202
welfare state, 300–301
see also Diffusion theories
Convergent validity, 2220
Conversation analysis, **303–309**
case studies, 170
and human nature theory, 868
phenomenology, 1459
qualitative methods and models,
1577, 1580, 1584
sociolinguistics, 2000–2001,
2004–2005
SYMLOG system, 1376–1378
Converse, Philip E.
on polls and voting behavior,
1568, 2238–2239
on social indicators, 1846
Cook, Karen S., on interpersonal
power, 1000
Cook, R. D., statistical graphics, 2067
Cook, Thomas, quasi-experiments,
1573
Cooley, Charles H.
group theory, 1797
influence on industrial sociology,
912
pragmatism, 1532, 1533, 1534,
1535
on socialization, 1864–1865,
1908–1909
symbolic interactionism, 2130
Cooperation. *See* Small groups
Cooperative Extension Service, 1687,
1689
Cooperative games. *See* n-person game
theory

Cooperatives, in capitalism, 166
Copenhagen Sociological Institute,
1701
Coping mechanisms, 1365, 2098,
2099
CORE. *See* Congress of Racial Equality
Cornfield, Daniel B., on labor unions,
1058
Corporate model of health-care
systems. *See* Medical-industrial
complex
Corporate organizations, **310–314**
American society, 83–84
as complex organizations, 273
control over employees, 312–313
culture theory, 1401–1402
distinguishing features, 311
medical-industrial complex, 257,
258, 1247–1252
organizational structure,
1394–1403
social control over, 313–314
technological risks and society,
2162
and urban economic transitions,
2197
white-collar crime, 382,
2248–2249
see also Capitalism; Transnational
corporations
Corrections systems. *See* Criminal
sanctions; Criminology; Prisons
Correlation and regression analysis,
316–327
ARIMA models, 2172–2181
causal inference models, 176–188
general linear model, 754–757
measures of association,
1240–1242
multiple indicator models,
1319–1320
multiple regression, 321–326
nonparametric statistics, 1357
partial correlation, 320–321
probability regression model,
1543–1545
problems in, 327
quasi-experimental research
design, 1599–1600,
1605–1606
sampling variation, 326–327
spurious correlations, 320
standard error, 326–327
standardization, 2050–2054
statistical graphics' regression
diagnosis, 2067, 2068–2069,
2070
structural equation models, 2084
of voting behavior, 2235
Cortese, Charles, segregation indices,
1739
Cosaro, William J., sociolinguistic
study, 2008
Coser, Lewis, on intellectuals, 938
Costa Rica. *See* Latin American studies
Cost-benefit and cost-effectiveness
analysis, 1574
Cost/reward factors. *See* Exchange
theory; Rewards

Frankfurt school, 384–387
German sociology, 769–770
Habermas's contribution to,
   387–389
on leisure, 1100, 1105
on mass culture, 1493
participation research, 1429
on postmodernism, 1522
pragmatism relationship, 1534
on social problems, 1917
on transnational corporations,
   2187
see also Marxist sociology
Critical value, statistical inference,
   2074
Croce, Benedetto, Italian sociology,
   1007
Cronbach, L. J., on reliability, 1631
Crop breeding. *See* Agricultural
   innovation
Cross-classification table. *See* Measures
   of association
Cross-cultural analysis, **390–393**
   affective meaning, 12–13, 16
   comparative health-care systems,
      261
   methodology, 391–393
   moral development, 1316
   occupational prestige rankings,
      1389
   personal relationships, 1439
   rape motivation, 1774
   secondary data analysis and
      archives, 1724, 1725–1726
   societal attributions, 129
   status attainment, 2093, 2094,
      2096
   of suicide, 2114–2115
   value theory, 2223
   violent crime theories,
      2229–2230
   world religions, 2275
   see also Comparative-historical
      analysis
Cross-dressing. *See* Transvestism
Cross-impact matrices, social
   forecasting, 1832
Cross-level inferences, levels of
   analysis, 1109–1111
Cross-modality fallacies, levels of
   analysis, 1109
Cross-national analysis. *See* Global
   systems analysis
Cross-sectional fallacies, level of
   analysis, 1109
Cross-sectional studies
   qualitative analysis, 1583
   secondary data analysis, 1722
Cross-tabulated data, 2137
Crowds and riots, **395–401**
   characteristics of crowds,
      396–398
   collective behavior, 237–243, 491
   collective vs. everyday
      individualized behavior, 396
   conditions of emergence,
      399–400
   crowd behavior coordination,
      400–401

diffusion theories, 491
disaster research, 494
participatory variation, 398
riot definition, 397
social imitation instinctivist
   theories, 1842
social psychology perspective,
   1926, 1929
see also Protest movements;
   Student movements
Crude rates. *See* specific subjects, e.g.,
   Birth and death rates;
   Standardization; Statistical
   methods
CSSA: Center for Social and
   Administrative Studies (Italy),
   1009
Cuba
   health-care system, 257, 260–261
   revolution, 1674
   socialism, 1861
   see also Latin American studies
Cuban-Americans, 831–837
Cults, **402–403**
   pejorative connotations, 403
   as religious movements,
      1644–1645, 1648, 2034
Cultural analysis
   of social problems, 1919
   of violent crime, 2230
Cultural bias
   as criticism of modernization
      theory, 1302–1303
   as criticism of moral development
      theory, 1315–1316
Cultural capital, 2024, 2092
Cultural evolution. *See* Evolution:
   biological, social, cultural
Cultural heritage, Bourdieu on, 727
Cultural pluralism, British sociology
   and, 151
Cultural Reality (Znaniecki), 1472
Cultural relativism, and moral
   development, 1315
Cultural Sciences (Znaniecki), 1472
Culture, **404–410**
   American Indian studies, 78–80
   see also Native Americans
   art and society studies, 107–108
   contemporary debate on,
      409–410
   countercultures, 328–332
   cross-cultural analysis, 390–393
   cults and, 402–403
   definitions of, 404–405, 406–407
   deviance and, 478
   diffusion theories, 38–40,
      487–488
   and drinking behavior, 42
   ethnicity, 575, 581–582
   evolutionary theory, 604–605
   as individual behavior influence,
      138
   and intelligence, 943–945
   intergenerational resource
      transfer of, 959
   literature as reflection of, 1141,
      1142, 1144
   Marxist sociology on, 1203–1205

metatheory and, 1273–1274
music studies, 1327–1330
and peacemaking style, 1433
pluralistic society and, 964, 968
popular culture, 407–409,
   1492–1498
postindustrial society and, 1515
and racial assimilation,
   1617–1618, 1619
socialization as transmission of,
   1863
social movements' impact on,
   1885
social structure debate, 405–407
sociological focus on, 404–405
sports and, 2048
urban sociology, 2204
value theory and, 223, 224
see also Social organization
Culture (Czarnowski), 1472
Culture and Evolution (Chmielewski),
   1473–1474
*Culture and Personality Approach in
   American Anthropology, The*
   (Mach), 1474
Culture circles, 487
Culture of poverty thesis, 1526–1527
   see also Urban underclass
Cumming, Elaine
   disengagement theory, 503, 504
   on retirement, 1666
Cummings, George, on organizational
   goals, 1397–1398
Cumulative scale analysis, 1234–1235
Cumulative social change. *See* Social
   change
Currency. *See* Money
*Current Concepts of Positive Mental
   Health* (Jahoda), 1258
Current Sociology (journal), 150
Cynicism. *See* Alienation
Czarnowski, Stefan, Polish sociology,
   1472
Czyzewski, Marek, Polish sociology,
   1473

Dahrendorf, Ralf
   British sociology, 149
   German sociology, 766–767, 768
   role theory, 1682
Daily Urban System, 2199
Daley, Richard, 1735
Damaska, Mirjan, on legal systems,
   1071–1072
Darley, John M., on altruism, 62, 63
Darrow, Clarence, 1638
Darwin, Charles
   fundamentalist attacks on,
      1637–1638
   natural selection, 604,
      1995–1996, 1998
   race, 1616
Data analysis. *See* Analysis of variance
   and covariance; Event history
   analysis; Field research
   methods; Longitudinal
   research; Secondary data
   analysis and data archives;
   Statistical graphics

propositions of, 567–568
and quality of life evaluation,
1839
religious commitment and,
2034–2036
in small groups, 1932
social comparison and, 1817
social stratification and, 1965
see also Decision-making theory
and research; Equality of
opportunity; Social inequality;
Utopian analysis and design
Equivalence. *See* Structural
equivalence
ERA. *See* Equal Rights Amendment
Erie County, New York, study (1944),
voting behavior, 2237
Erikson, Erik H.
lifespan psychology, 1122
on socialization, 1869
Error. *See* Measurement; Reliability;
Validity
Escarpit, Robert, sociology of
literature, 1143
Essay on Population Growth (Malthus),
446
Esteem. *See* Self-esteem; Social honor
Estes, Richard J.
Index of Social Progress,
917–919
on quality of life measurement,
1589
Ethics
countercultures and, 330
religious, 1653, 2273–2277
vs. moral law, 2274
and white-collar crime,
2248–2250
see also Equity theory; Ethics in
social research; Moral
development; Morality
Ethics in social research, **584–588**,
2126
Ethiopia
slavery, 1793
see also African studies
Ethnic enclave theory, 582–583,
1736–1738
Ethnicity, **575–583**
affirmative action programs,
18–21
alcohol consumption patterns, 44
and American family patterns,
68–71, 73
American Indian studies, 74–80
see also Native Americans
Asian-American studies, 109–114
assimilation, 83, 576–578, 581,
835–836, 1617–1619, 2108,
2109
census, 191
characteristics, 575
criminal sanctions and, 483
divorce rates and, 72
genocide, 757–761
group resources, 576, 581–583
Hispanic-American studies,
831–837
income distribution, 893

and intelligence, 943–945
intergroup relations, 962
intermarriage, 968–973
and labor force composition,
2258
and labor market segmentations,
580, 1794
Latin American countries, 1062
and nationalism, 1033–1034,
1038–1039
and occupational equality of
opportunity, 560–561
and organized crime, 1405–1406
and popular culture, 1495
race vs., 1615
segregation indices, 1738–1743
sociolinguistics, 2009
and stratification, 576, 578–581,
1962–1965
subethnicity concept (pluralism),
1289, 1896
and suburbanization, 2108–2109
urban enclaves, 582–583,
1736–1738
see also Cross-cultural analysis;
Discrimination; International
migration; Prejudice; Race;
specific groups, e.g.,
Japanese-Americans
Ethnocentrism, 578, 581, 962
Ethnography
on incest, 885–886
legal system analysis, 1072
qualitative methods, 1577,
1580–1581, 2191
Ethnomethodology, **588–593**, 1914
background and development,
588–590
case studies, 170, 171
China studies, 193, 194
community studies, 247
contemporary research, 590–591
conversation analysis, 303–309
cross-cultural analysis, 331–393
defined, 588
dramaturgy, 513–515
field research methods, 588–593,
713–714, 716
phenomenology, 1458, 1459
qualitative methods, 1578,
1579–1580
social psychology, 1922
sociolinguistics, 2000–2001
on suicide, 2115
work studies, 592–593
Ethology, sociobiology, 1995–1999
Etzioni, Amitai
conformity theory, 98–99
on consensus formation, 1649
"I-We" paradigm, 1118
on white-collar crime, 2248
EU. *See* Expected utility (EU) mode
Eucharist, 2272, 2273
Europe
international law inception,
980–981
voting behavior research, 2240
see also Eastern Europe; specific
country names

European Economic Community, legal
system, 1073
European Fertility Project, 448, 449
Euthanasia. *See* Right to die
Evaluation, potency, and activity (EPA)
structure, 13, 14, 16
Evaluation research, **594–598**
as applied sociology, 103–106
current status of, 595–596
definition, 594
history of, 594–595
public policy analysis, 1573–1574
scope of, 594
social work, 1979–1983
utilization of evaluations, 598
work of evaluators, 596–598
see also Quasi-experimental
research designs
Evangelicalism, 85, 1639
Evans-Pritchard, E. E., on culture, 405
Event history analysis, **599–602**, 2086
accelerated failure-time models,
600
discrete-time methods, 602
life history, 1122, 1123, 1125,
1127, 1134–1137
longitudinal research, 1155–1156
mathematical sociology
application, 1225
multiple and repeated events,
601–602
proportional hazards models,
600–601
qualitative model, 1583
qualitative research, 1579–1580
on social change, 1809
on terrorism, 2169–2170
Event sequence analysis. *See* Event
history analysis
Evers, Medgar, 1732
Evidence. *See* Measurement; Validity
EV mode. *See* Expected value (EV)
mode
Evocative interaction, and life course,
1128
Evolution: biological, social, cultural,
603–605
behaviorism, 132–133, 137–138
game theory analysis, 743–744
macrosociology, 1171
modernization theory, 1300,
1301
racial theories, 1616
religious fundamentalist attacks
on, 1637–1638
secularization thesis, 2029–2030
social change theory, 1808–1809,
1810
sociobiology, 1995–1999
see also Social Darwinism
Exchange and Power in Social Life
(Blau), 606
Exchange theory, **606–609**
economic determinism, 522
intergenerational resource
transfers, 956
interpersonal attraction and, 991
marital adjustment and, 1179
money, 1305–1306

national service issues,
1293–1294
peace, 1433–1435
race and social equity,
1294–1296
see also War
Milken, Michael, 2249
Mill, John Stuart
British sociology, 149
on comparative worth, 254
epistemology, 552
on gender inequality, 254, 696,
697, 1853
on individual freedom,
1091–1092
influence on Japanese sociology,
1015
liberalism/conservatism, 1116
methods approach, 266–267
Millenarianism, 1637
Miller, Gale, enthnomethodology,
170, 1581
Miller, Neal, social imitation theory,
1843
Miller, S. M., liberalism/conservatism,
1118
Mills, C. Wright, 591, 2043
personality and social structure,
1441
postmodernism, 1522
Minard, Charles Joseph, statistical
graphs, 2057
Mind, Self and Society (Mead), 2127,
2128
Minority groups. *See* Discrimination;
Ethnicity; Gender; Race;
specific groups, e.g.,
Asian-Americans; specific
related subjects, e.g.,
Affirmative action
Minors. *See* Youth
Mintz, Beth, on corporate
organizations, 313
Mirkin, Barry, on retirement, 1670
Miscegenation. *See* Intermarriage
Mississippi, civil rights movement,
1733
Miyamoto, Frank, Japanese-American
study, 112
MLLSA (program), 2087
Mobility, physical. *See* Immigration;
Internal migration;
International migration
Mobility, social. *See* Education and
mobility; Intergenerational
mobility; Occupational and
career mobility; Social
mobility
Mode, definition and computation of,
466
Models, research. *See* Mathematical
sociology; Paradigms and
models; specific subjects
Models, social. *See* Role Models; Social
imitation; Social learning
theory
Models of Man (Simon), 2083
Moderne Kapitalismus, Der (Sombart),
531

Modernization theory, **1299–1303**
convergence theories and,
295–296
critiques of, 1302–1303
early influences on, 1301–1302
global systems analysis and,
771–777, 1302–1303
and industrialization in less
developed countries, 914–920
Italian sociology, 1008–1009
on kinship systems, 1036–1037
Latin American studies,
1063–1064
macrosociology, 1171–1173
and nationalism, 1335
on political party systems,
1486–1487
pragmatism relationship, 1524
on religious fundamentalism,
1641
on social change, 1810–1811
and social philosophy, 1914
sports and, 2046
technological risks and society,
2162
tenets of, 1300
varieties of, 1302
see also Postindustrial society;
Postmodernism
Modern Political Issue (Krzywicki), 1472
Modern societies, characterization,
1300–1301
Modern World System, The (Wallerstein),
839–840
Mokrzycki, Edmund, Polish sociology,
1474
Molecular biology. *See* Sociobiology
Money, **1304–1309**
Simmel on, 532, 1304, 1305
sociological invisibility of, 1304
sociological model of, 1306–1309
symbolic meanings of, 1306, 1307
utilitarian model of, 1304–1306,
1308
Money, Sex, and Power (Harstock), 752
Monogamy. *See* Sexual behavior and
marriage
Montesquieu, Charles Louis de
Secondat, on law, 1068
Montgomery, Alabama, civil rights
movement, 1731, 1733
Monthly Review (journal), 1202
Montreal, Université de, Canadian
sociology, 159
Mood-altering substances. *See* Alcohol;
Drug abuse
Moon, Reverend Sun Myung, 1655
Mooney, James, on American Indian
population, 74–75
Moore, Barrington
macrosociology, 1170
on political party systems, 1486
Moore, Wilbert E.
convergence theories, 296
on social forecasting, 1831
Moral Basis of a Backward Society, The
(Banfield), 1009
Moral behavior and judgment. *See*
Moral development

Moral development, **1310–1317**
altruism and, 62
feminist theory, 701
Kohlberg's stages in, 1312–1313
measurement instruments,
1313–1315
Piaget's stages in, 1311–1312
religion and, 2029, 2274
theoretical criticism, 1315–1317
theoretical foundation,
1310–1311
see also Socialization
*Moral Economy of the Peasant:
Subsistence and Rebellion in
Southeast Asia* (Scott), 2040
Morality
and criminal sanctions, 370–373
defined, 1310
divorce in context of, 506
equity theory, 563–573
legislation of, 1089–1094
moral behavior, judgment, and
development theories,
1310–1317
see also Criminalization of
deviance; Ethics; Ethics in
social research
Moral Majority, 1639, 1882
Moral panics. *See* Legislation of
morality
Moral philosophy, and symbolic
interactionism, 2130
More, Sir Thomas, 2211–2212
More developed countries. *See*
Industrialization; Industrial
sociology
Moreno, Jacob L.
on observation systems, 1377
role theory, 1682
small group theory, 1797, 1799
social network theory, 1888
Morgan, C. Lloyd, on instinctive and
voluntary imitation, 1843
Morgan, Lewis Henry, on incest, 885
Morgenstern, Oskar
on coalitions, 208
decision-making theory, 419
game theory, 737, 741
Morris, Aldon D., on protest
movements, 1564
Morris, Charles
pragmatism, 1532
on ways of living, 2233
Morris, Michael, on historical view of
poor people, 1526
Morris, William, utopia, 2213–2214
Morrow, Paula, on work commitment,
2264
Morselli, Enrico, Italian sociology,
1006
Mortality. *See* Birth and death rates;
Death and dying; Infant and
child mortality; Life
expectancy; Suicide
Mortality effects, and validity of
quasi-experimental research,
1600, 1603, 1604
Mosca, Gaetano, Italian sociology,
1006, 1007

social science projects,
2017–2018, 2019, 2021
sociology research support
program, 2020–2021
Systems Theory and Operations
Research program, 2137
National service, military. *See* Military
sociology, national service
National Youth Survey (NYS), 1023
Nation-state. *See* State
Native American Church, 78–79
Native Americans
affirmative action, 18–21
alcohol abuse, 44
American Indian studies, 74–80
culture, 78–80
demography, 74–75
family pattern variations, 66
political and legal structures,
77–78
religion, 78–80, 2267–2268
social and economic status,
76–77
Natural law, as international law
source, 980–981, 982
Natural selection
behaviorism and, 132–133
as corollary of sexual selection,
1998
evolution theory on, 604
theory, 1995–1996
Nature of Human Values, The
(Rokeach), 2223–2224
Nature of Prejudice, The (Allport),
1536
Nature vs. nurture. *See* Gender;
Hereditary factors; Intelligence;
Socialization
Nazism
and forced labor, 1794
and genocide, 757, 758, 759
and German sociology, 763–764,
765, 766
as protest movement, 1561
use of popular culture, 1493
war crimes trials, 983
NCS. *See* National Crime Survey
Need-based approach
job satisfaction, 2261–2263
quality of life, 1588
Needle-sharing. *See* IV-drug users
Neff, Ronald, on incest, 889
Negative Income Tax, 1528, 1573,
1575
Negro Family, The (Moynihan report),
29–30
Neighborhoods. *See* Community
Nelson, Robert L., on organizational
structure, 1400
Neoconservatism, 1117
Neofunctionalism, 731
Neo-Malthusians. *See* Malthusian
theory
Neo-Marxism. *See* Conflict theory
Neo-Weberians, on social stratification,
1961–1962
NES. *See* National Election Study
Netherlands, and Southeast Asian
independence, 2038

Networking. *See* Social network theory;
Social resources theory; Social
support
Neugarten, Bernice, life course
studies, 1124
Neuman, W. Russell, on public
opinion, 1566
Neutralization theory, juvenile
delinquency theory, 1030
New Australia (Paraguay), utopian
community, 1859
Newburyport, Massachusetts. *See*
Yankee City study
Newcomb, Theodore, role theory,
1682
New Directions in Sociolinguistics
(Gumperz and Hymes), 2000
New Harmony (Indiana), utopian
community, 1859
New International Economic Order,
919
New Left. *See* Student movements
Newly industrializing countries. *See*
Industrialization in less
developed countries
New middle class, 1960, 1961
New religions. *See* Religious
movements
New School for Social Research,
1942
News from Nowhere (Morris),
2213–2214
New structuralism, **1342–1346**
see also Functionalism; Labor
force
Newton, Sir Isaac, materialism,
1217
New York City, urbanization, 2202
NIA. *See* National Institute on Aging
NIBRS. *See* National Incident-Based
Recording System
Nicaragua, revolution, 1674
Niceforo, Alfredo, Italian sociology,
1006
NICHD. *See* National Institute of
Child Health and Human
Development
Nichomachean Ethics (Aristotle), 564,
565
Nieboer-Domar hypothesis, on causes
of slavery, 1787, 1788–1789,
1793, 1795
Niebuhr, H. Richard, on religious
movements, 1644, 1647–1648
Nie, Norman H.
on public policy and public
opinion, 1573
on voting behavior, 2239
Nietzsche, Frederick, 1913, 1914
Nigeria, sexually transmitted diseases,
1782
NIH. *See* National Institutes of Health
NIMH. *See* National Institute of
Mental Health
Nisbet, Robert
on alienation concept, 98
on conservatism, 1115, 1116
Nisei, 111
Nixon, Richard, 19, 517, 1569

NLS. *See* National Longitudinal
Surveys of Labor Market
Experience
NLS Handbook, 1722, 1723
Noelle-Neumann, Elisabeth, on public
opinion, 1569
No-fault divorce, 507, 508, 652
Nominal scales of measurement,
1227–1228, 1233
Nomos (theology), 2277
Noncomformity. *See* Compliance and
conformity; Deviance
Nonconstant-sum games, 738
Noncooperative games. *See* *n*-person
game theory
Nonequivalent group design,
1603–1604, 1605, 1609, 1610
Nonmarital childbearing. *See*
Illegitmacy; Single-parent
families
Nonmarital sex. *See* Adultery;
Cohabitation; Premarital sex;
Sexual orientation
Nonparametric statistics, **1348–1359**
definition, 1348
literature, 1349–1352
measurement, 1229–1230
measures of association,
1240–1242
new developments, 1358–1359
tests and techniques, 1350–1358
on trends and changes, 1358
see also Measures of association;
Statistical inference
Nonprobability sampling, 2120
Nonrandom samples, and statistical
inference, 2082
Nonreductionist materialists, 1215
Nonverbal cues and communication,
515, 1751–1752, 2001
Nonviolent confrontation, 1562–1563
Non–zero sum games, 208, 209
NORC. *See* National Opinion Research
Center
Normative consensus. *See* Social norms
North, Cecil C., on occupational
prestige, 1388
North Africa
sociological studies, 1281
see also specific country names
Northern Ireland, religious
movements, 1643–1644
Northwestern University, military
sociology, 1291
Norway
social security system, 1950
see also Scandinavian sociology
Nostalgia, as utopian socialism theme,
1857
Nouveaux riches, social acceptance of,
1961
Novak, Michael, on religious
institutions, 2277
Novels. *See* Literature
Novosibirsk Institute of Industrial
Economics and Organization
(USSR), 2043
Nowak, Stefan, Polish sociology, 1473,
1474

Schooler, Carmie, personality and social structure model, 1442–1443

Schools and schooling. *See* Educational attainment; Educational organization; Education and mobility; Sociology of education

Schucking, L. L., 1144

Schudson, Michael, on popular culture, 1497

Schumpeter, Joseph
economic sociology, 524, 531
on imperialism, 883–884
on intellectuals, 937–938
political parties definition, 1485

Schutz, Alfred
phenomenology, 170, 589, 1457–1458
social philosophy, 1913–1914

Schütze, Fritz, life histories, 1135

Schwartz, Michael, on corporate organizations, 313

Schwartz, Shalom, values theory, 2226

Schwarz, Frederick C., fundamentalism, 1639

Science, **1705–1710**
applied research and development, 1709–1710
environmental impact assessment and, 546
evolution theory, 605
inventions and, 1002, 1004–1005
Kuhn's paradigm of change, 1413–1415
and materialism, 1217
normative ethos of, 1705–1706, 1852
and postindustrial society, 1514
public support for, 2014–2015, 2016
replication in, 1661
and social philosophy, 1913, 1915
social stratification in, 1706–1707
sociobiology, 1995–1999
sociology of scientific knowledge, 1708–1709
work groups, specialties, and disciplines, 1707–1708
see also Scientific explanation; Scientific method; Technological risks and society; Technology and society

Science Indicators (publication), 1848

Scientific explanation, **1711–1719**
causal inference models, 176–188
critiques of hypothetico-deductive model, 1716–1719
epistemology and, 550–554
levels of analysis, 1107–1112
liberal utilitarianism and, 1116
mathematical analysis, 1221–1226
metatheory, 1271–1275
paradigms and models, 1411–1417
positivism and, 1509–1511
pragmatism and, 1532–1533
reliability, 1626–1631
replication, 1661–1663
social philosophy based on, 1913

validity, 2217–2221
see also Quasi-experimental research designs; Science; Scientific method; Social forecasting; Statistical inference

Scientific management. *See* Organizational effectiveness

Scientific method
epistemological analysis of, 551, 552, 553
evaluation research and, 595–596
replication and, 1661
scientific explanation and, 1712, 1713
survey research and, 2119–2220

Scientology, 1655

SCLC. *See* Southern Christian Leadership Conference

Scopes trial (1925), 1637–1638

Scores. *See* Factor analysis; Measurement

Scoring system. *See* Measurement instruments

Scott, James, Southeast Asia studies, 2040–2041

Scott, W. Richard, on organizational structure, 1395, 1396–1397, 1399, 1400

Scripps Foundation, 456

Scriptures, fundamentalist belief in, 1637

Sd. See Discriminative stimulas

SDS. *See* Students for a Democratic Society

Seal, B. N., Indian sociology, 897–898

Seasonal Variations of the Eskimo: A Study in Social Morphology (Mauss and Beuchat), 732

Seattle–Denver Income Maintenance Experiment. *See* SIME–DIME study

Secessionism, and nationalism, 1338, 1339

Secondary data analysis and data archives, **1720–1728**
data archives, 1721–1724
definition of, 1720
nature of, 1724–1728

Secondary groups. *See* Small groups

Second Sex, The (Beauvoir), 696, 697

Second Vatican Council (1962–1965), 1642

Sect-church theory, 1644, 1647–1648

Sects, differentiated from cults, 402–403

Secular humanism, 2029, 2034

Secularism, and religious ideologies, 1633

Secularization. *See* Sociology of religion

Seeman, Melvin, on prejudice, 963

Segal, David and Mady, military sociology, 1291

Segerstedt, Torgny, Scandinavian sociology, 1701

Segmentation forecasting. *See* Componential forecasting

Segmented labor market theory, 1343–1344, 1382–1383, 1622

Segregation and desegregation, **1728–1738**
African-American housing, 32, 1738–1743
American society, 85
apartheid, 23–24, 100–103
desegregation vs. integration, 1733–1735
educational, 539, 1730, 1734, 1735–1736
gender occupational, 253, 1345, 1400
Hispanic-American studies, 835–836
intermarriage and, 968, 969, 970
labor force, 2256
prejudice, 1537
sports and, 2048
suburban, 2108
urban underclass, 1735–1738, 2208
see also Discrimination; Equality of opportunity; Segregation indices

Segregation indices, **1738–1743**
urbanization, 2200
see also Demographic methods

Seidler, John, on religious organizations, 1648

Seki, Eikichi, Japanese sociology, 1016

Selby, Henry A., on kinship systems, 1039–1040

Selection effects, and validity of quasi-experimental research design, 1600, 1604

Selective fallacies, levels of analysis, 1109

Self-actualization, 1258, 1448

Self-appraisal. *See* Self-concept

Self-concept, **1743–1748**
and adulthood transition experiences, 8–9
and altruism, 63
attitudes reinforcing, 118
biases in, 1908
coercive persuasion and, 213, 214, 216
consequences of, 1747–1748
development of, 1745–1747
deviance theories, 482
dramaturgy, 514–515
femininity/masculinity, 692–693
identity theory, 871–873
mental health and, 1259–1260, 1744
nursing home residents, 1365–1366
parental role, 1421
quality of life and, 1586
reference group theory, 1624–1625
role conflict, 1676–1677
and role theory, 1678–1681
situational, 1744–1745, 1930
social comparison and, 1814–1815, 1928
socialization and formation of, 1864–1865, 1867, 1869, 1870, 1927